D0151303

THE CAMBRIDGE ANCIENT HISTORY

EDITORS

Volumes I–VI	*Volumes* VII, VIII
J. B. BURY, M.A., F.B.A.	S. A. COOK, LITT.D.
S. A. COOK, LITT.D.	F. E. ADCOCK, M.A.
F. E. ADCOCK, M.A.	M. P. CHARLESWORTH, M.A.

VOLUME VIII

THE

CAMBRIDGE

ANCIENT HISTORY

VOLUME VIII

ROME AND THE MEDITERRANEAN

218—133 B.C.

EDITED BY

S. A. COOK, Litt.D.

F. E. ADCOCK, M.A.

M. P. CHARLESWORTH, M.A.

SECOND IMPRESSION

CAMBRIDGE

AT THE UNIVERSITY PRESS

1954

PUBLISHED BY
THE SYNDICS OF THE CAMBRIDGE UNIVERSITY PRESS
London Office: Bentley House, N.W.1
American Branch: New York

Agents for Canada, India, and Pakistan: Macmillan

. *First Edition*   1930
Reprinted with corrections   1954

Printed in Great Britain at the University Press, Cambridge
(*Brooke Crutchley, University Printer*)

PREFACE

VOLUME VII ended at a moment of suspense. East of the Adriatic the three great Hellenistic monarchies, Macedon, Syria and Egypt, had attained the appearance of a balance of power. The lesser states of Greece and the East lay beneath their shadow, though there was independent political vigour in the Greek Leagues, Rhodes, and Pergamum. Meanwhile the old Great Power Carthage and the new Great Power Rome were on the eve of a struggle which finally decided the mastery of the West. Before eighty years had passed no state remained in the Mediterranean world strong enough to cross the will of Rome. The political and military triumph of Rome went far to maim the spiritual, social, and economic life of the Hellenistic world, which for more than a century had been sorely tried by the wars of Macedonia, Syria and Egypt; but here too there is much achievement to record. Rome herself gained much from Hellenism and, later, passed on to the West what she herself had gained.

The victory of the new power cannot, in the last decades of the third century, have seemed as inevitable as it seems to us or as it seemed to Polybius. The successes of Hannibal marked him out as a greater Pyrrhus, and Carthaginian statecraft must have hoped to cramp Roman expansion by a coalition with Macedon and Syracuse. But man-power, a political system based on goodwill, and patient strategy prevailed: the unnatural alliance of Carthaginian and Greek came to little; Scipio Africanus drove victory home; and Carthage became definitely a second-rate power. Her defeat set free the Western Mediterranean for trade, and made possible the rise of a native North African kingdom, that of Numidia, which spread civilization and brought stability except to weakened Carthage. Rome succeeded to the Punic empire in Spain, and, at her leisure, confirmed the security of Italy against the Gauls and Ligurians. The Roman people were weary and exhausted, but the Senate, made nervous by the complications which the Hannibalic War had caused, was induced to fear a new danger in the co-operation of the great monarchies of Syria and Macedon. Serving other interests than her own, but at the same time without clear disinterestedness, Rome defeated Philip V of Macedon and then Antiochus of Syria and his Aetolian allies. At the peace of Apamea Pergamum and Rhodes received ample payment for their example and their exertions in resisting both monarchies.

At this point again Rome might hope for a pause. She had not yielded to the temptation of permanent aggrandizement in Greece. She had nothing to fear from Syria and little from Macedon, but the display of her power made her the arbiter of questions for which she cared little. The Senate, composed of administrators with a taste for legalism and an instinct for order, could not refuse to sit in judgment, and Greek envoys, who hoped always for more than justice, were alike eager for its judgments and readily dissatisfied with them. Perseus, Philip's successor, could not forget that Macedon had enjoyed the primacy among the Hellenistic monarchies, and the Senate, too, could not forget it. The Third Macedonian War eliminated the monarchy, but left Rome faced with the problem of giving republican institutions to a monarchical people. The half-hearted conduct of the war had caused Pergamum and Rhodes to waver, so that the Senate, impatient of what seemed disloyalty, showed Rome's effective displeasure. The weakening of these two powers was to produce a vacuum in Asia Minor into which Rome was perforce drawn. Macedonia was in the end made a province, and the unwillingness of the Achaean League to be at once a free power and the client of Rome brought about a crisis which led to the destruction of the one remaining unit of Hellenic force in Greece. The year that witnessed the fall of Corinth saw the destruction of Carthage. Nothing now remained in the Mediterranean to remind Rome that she had not always been invincible.

This isolation of greatness did not mean an isolation of culture. Hellenism had long had a footing in Italy: Campanian towns such as Pompeii looked Greek; in Rome itself admiration for Hellenic literature was raised to a fashion, although the native vigour of Latin saved it from becoming a language of the uncultivated and leaving all literature to be written in Greek. Roman religion had imported elements from kinsmen, from Etruscans and from Greeks, and now in the second century Greek philosophy, especially in the form of Stoicism which could be best adapted to the better mind of the Romans, made its entry. The progress of Greek ideas at Rome can only here and there be traced, as by reference to the almost motionless figure of the elder Cato, but the effect of the period is clear. Rome entered the charmed circle of Hellenic ideas and the Rome of the second century is interpreted to us better by the Greek Polybius than the Roman Livy. But the interpretation is fragmentary, and for the generation that preceded the Gracchi we are ill-informed. The springs of Roman policy in these years lie beyond our tracing, and we know far less of Rome in the third century B.C. than of Athens in the fifth. Time has given us the comedies of Plautus and Terence—Romanized Hellenism, but not—apart from the *de agri cultura* of Cato and a few rugged passages of Ennius—the writings that would have shown us the native mind and manners of Rome.

Despite the overwhelming political strength of Rome it would be false to see in her the one State of flesh and blood in a world of ghosts. Carthage had perished and the kingdom of Macedonia, but in Syria the tenacity of the Seleucids had not wholly relaxed. Again and again Seleucid princes sought to make good their power and uphold hellenization against nationalistic movements from within and encroachments from without, above all from the new power of Parthia. In Asia Minor the second century witnessed the rise and decline of the model of a Hellenistic monarchy in the compact State of Pergamum.

In the north-east we see, both in Thrace and in the Bosporan Kingdom, states which formed a link between the Mediterranean and the outer world of northern and eastern Europe. In the East there were already signs of the beginning of a great reaction of the East upon the West, a reaction of ideas even more than of political forces. Yet the aspect of the Mediterranean was still predominantly Hellenistic. For two centuries there had flourished an art which from Asia Minor and Egypt to Italy and even beyond was the direct inheritor of the art of classical Greece. Greek States continued to send their envoys to and fro and to assist each other to settle their differences by arbitration. More significant than this diplomatic activity is the life of commerce as attested by Delos and by Rhodes. Despite the occasional dislocation due to the intrusions of Rome, the Mediterranean world was becoming thoroughly international. Rome might misgovern or hinder good government, her influence might help to thwart half-understood movements of social revolt or reform, her inertness might leave the seas to pirates; but during this period there was growing up the idea that the countries of the Mediterranean must find in one State their common protector. Reluctant or not, Rome could not escape the charge little as her domestic instincts and institutions were suited to it. During the next century, indeed, the Republican government of Rome broke down, and the manner of its breaking down conditioned the form of the principate, but it is the history of the period described in this volume which made inevitable a Roman Empire.

In the present volume Mr Glover writes on Polybius (Chapter i),
Mr Hallward on the Second and Third Punic Wars (Chapters ii,
iii, iv and xv); in Chapter xv also Mr Charlesworth reviews in an
epilogue the historical significance of Carthage. In Chapters v,
vi and vii M. Holleaux continues the history of Rome's relations
with Greek powers down to the Peace of Apamea. Mr Benecke
then describes the fall of Macedonia and the later Hellenistic
policy of Rome in the remainder of the period (Chapters viii and
ix). Professor Schulten, who wrote on Carthaginian Spain in
Volume vii, now describes the making of Roman Spain
(Chapter x). There remain Italy and Rome itself. In two Chapters
(xi and xii) Professor Tenney Frank, after describing the securing
of the northern borders of Roman Italy, treats of the political,
economic, and social progress of Italy and Rome. The beginnings
and early period of literature form the subject of Chapter xiii by
Professor Wight Duff; Mr Cyril Bailey in Chapter xiv describes
the religion of the early and middle Republic and the advent at
Rome of Greek philosophy. After the chapter on the fall of
Carthage follows the history of the last active Hellenistic monarchy,
that of Syria, in the period of the Jewish national movement of the
Maccabees. This chapter (xvi) is by Dr Edwyn Bevan. The survey
of the Hellenistic world is completed by a chapter (xvii) on Thrace
by Professor Kazarow and three chapters (xviii, xix and xx) by
Professor Rostovtzeff, who writes on the political and economic
character of the Bosporan Kingdom, Pergamum, Rhodes and
Delos, and reviews Hellenistic commerce in general. These
chapters, which go back beyond the period covered by the
volume, are to be read in connection with those on Macedon,
Ptolemaic Egypt and Syria in Volume vii. Finally, Professor
Ashmole in Chapter xxi treats of the art and architecture of the
Hellenistic Age. The notes at the end of the volume which concern
the Second Punic War are written by Mr Hallward, those on the
Maccabees and the son of Seleucus IV by Dr Bevan. Table I is
prepared by Mr Hallward, and is based upon the tables in the
Storia dei Romani of Professor De Sanctis, who has generously
allowed their use.

The editors are indebted to those scholars whom they have
consulted, not in vain, on points of detail, in particular to
Professor Minns, who has advised them on the spelling of
modern geographical names in Chapter xvii. They further desire
to thank the contributors for their ready co-operation and for
their willingness to adapt the scope of their chapters to the general
plan of the volume. Mr Benecke has permitted the insertion in

the second of his chapters of a few paragraphs which go beyond
the limit of his main theme and for which the editors are
responsible. Mr Hallward has to acknowledge the courtesy of
Mr Scullard in allowing him to see the proofs of *Scipio Africanus*
during the revision of his chapters. M. Holleaux desires to thank
for information and suggestions Professors Hiller von Gaertringen,
Kirchner, Münzer, W. Otto, Stähelin, Mr Tarn and M. F.
Thureau-Dangin. Mr Bailey wishes to acknowledge valuable
criticism and suggestions from Mr H. M. Last, Dr Bevan the
assistance of Sir George Macdonald on the coinage of Antiochus
IV. Professor Rostovtzeff desires to thank M. Holleaux for the
use of unpublished inscriptions from Delphi, and Professor
Hiller von Gaertringen for placing at his disposal his forthcoming
article on *Rhodos* in Pauly-Wissowa. Professor Ashmole desires
to make his grateful acknowledgments to Professor J. D. Beazley,
Dr G. F. Hill, Professor D. S. Robertson and Mr Tarn. Professor
Tenney Frank thanks Messrs Putnam for permission to quote
from the Loeb Library Edition of Polybius a passage on p. 381.

The volume is indebted to contributors for the preparation of
bibliographies to their chapters and for their share in the preparation of maps, to Mr Hallward for Maps 1 to 6, to M. Holleaux
and Mr Benecke for Map 9. Mr Charlesworth is responsible for
Map 12; Professor Adcock for Map 7 in consultation with
Mr Tarn, and for Map 13 with Professor Rostovtzeff, for Map
11 with Professor Schulten and for Map 8 with Dr Bevan. For
the geographical detail of Map 3 (taken from De Sanctis,
Storia dei Romani, III, 2) we are indebted to the publishers, the
Fratelli Bocca of Turin. Map 10 is taken by permission of the
publishers (F. Bruckmann A.-G.) from Professor Schulten's
Numantia, as is also the Sheet of Plans 1. We have to thank Mr
Seltman for his assistance with this as with the remaining plans
and for his co-operation in connection with the illustration of the
volume in the third Volume of Plates, which he has prepared,
and which is published at the same time as this volume. For
Plan III and nos 1, 2 and 5 on Sheet of Plans II acknowledgments
are due to Messrs Walter de Gruyter, for no. 3 to Verlag Carl
Gerold's Sohn, for nos 4 and 6 to Messrs E. de Boccard.

Professor Adcock, in consultation with Professor Rostovtzeff,
has drawn up the Genealogical Table of the Spartocid Dynasty;
the Tables of the Ptolemies, Seleucids and Attalids, taken with
slight modifications from Volume VII, were prepared by Mr
Tarn. We owe the translation of M. Holleaux' chapters to Miss
Harrison and Miss Shaw, and that of Professor Schulten's chapter

on Roman Spain and Professor Kazarow's chapter on Thrace to
Mr W. Montgomery. The General Index and Index of passages
referred to are the work of Mr B. Benham, to whose care we
are once more indebted. Finally, we have to express our gratitude
to the Staff of the University Press for the skill and the ready
helpfulness which they have shown during the preparation of this
volume as of its predecessors.

We have chosen for the cover of the volume, which has for its
main theme the impersonal effectiveness of Republican Rome, the
familiar emblem of the fasces.

S.A.C.
F.E.A.
M.P.C.

September, 1930

TABLE OF CONTENTS

CHAPTER I

POLYBIUS

By T. R. Glover, M.A.
Fellow of St John's College, Cambridge, and University Lecturer
in Ancient History

CHAPTER II

HANNIBAL'S INVASION OF ITALY

By B. L. Hallward, M.A.
Fellow of Peterhouse, Cambridge, and University Lecturer in Classics

CHAPTER III

THE ROMAN DEFENSIVE

By B. L. Hallward

CHAPTER IV

SCIPIO AND VICTORY

By B. L. Hallward

CONTENTS

CHAPTER V

ROME AND MACEDON: PHILIP AGAINST THE ROMANS

By Maurice Holleaux

Membre de l'Institut, Professeur au Collège de France

CHAPTER VI

ROME AND MACEDON: THE ROMANS AGAINST PHILIP

By Maurice Holleaux

CHAPTER VII

ROME AND ANTIOCHUS

By Maurice Holleaux

CONTENTS

CHAPTER VIII

THE FALL OF THE MACEDONIAN MONARCHY

By P. V. M. Benecke, M.A.
Fellow of Magdalen College, Oxford

CHAPTER IX

ROME AND THE HELLENISTIC STATES

By P. V. M. Benecke

CHAPTER X

THE ROMANS IN SPAIN

By A. Schulten, Ph.D.
Professor of Ancient History in the University of Erlangen

CHAPTER XI

ITALY

By TENNEY FRANK, Ph.D.
Professor of Latin in Johns Hopkins University

CHAPTER XII

ROME

By TENNEY FRANK

CHAPTER XIII

THE BEGINNINGS OF LATIN LITERATURE

BY J. WIGHT DUFF, M.A., D.Litt., LL.D., F.B.A.

Professor of Classics, Armstrong College (in the University of Durham),
Newcastle-upon-Tyne

CHAPTER XIV

ROMAN RELIGION AND THE ADVENT OF PHILOSOPHY

By Cyril Bailey, M.A., Hon. D.Litt. (Durham)
Jowett Fellow of Balliol College, Lecturer in Greek and Latin Literature
in the University of Oxford

CHAPTER XV

THE FALL OF CARTHAGE

By B. L. Hallward and M. P. Charlesworth, M.A.[1]
Fellow of St John's College, Cambridge, and University Lecturer in Classics

[1] Sections I–IV are by Mr Hallward; section V is by Mr Charlesworth.

CHAPTER XVI

SYRIA AND THE JEWS

By E. R. BEVAN, Litt.D., LL.D.
Hon. Fellow of New College, Oxford, and Lecturer in Hellenistic History
and Literature at King's College, London

CHAPTER XVII

THRACE

By Gawril I. Kazarow
Professor of Ancient History in the University of Sofia

CHAPTER XVIII

THE BOSPORAN KINGDOM

By M. Rostovtzeff, Hon. D.Litt. (Oxon.), Hon. Litt.D. (Wisconsin),
Professor of Ancient History, Yale University

CHAPTER XIX

PERGAMUM

By M. Rostovtzeff

CHAPTER XX

RHODES, DELOS AND HELLENISTIC COMMERCE

By M. Rostovtzeff

CHAPTER XXI

HELLENISTIC ART

By BERNARD ASHMOLE, M.A., B.Litt.
Yates Professor of Archaeology in the University of London;
Formerly Director of the British School at Rome

CONTENTS

PAGE

LIST OF MAPS, TABLES, PLANS, ETC.:

CHAPTER I

POLYBIUS

I. THE YOUTH AND EDUCATION OF POLYBIUS

THE traveller Pausanias tells us that about A.D. 180 there was in the market-place of Megalopolis a likeness of Polybius son of Lycortas, wrought in relief on a monument; and an elegiac inscription set forth that he wandered over every land and sea, that he was an ally of the Romans, and that he appeased their anger against the Greeks. This Polybius, he continues, wrote a history of Rome; and he adds, with the later story of Greece in his mind, that 'whatever the Romans did by the advice of Polybius turned out well; but it is said that whenever they did not listen to his instruction they went wrong. All the Greek states that belonged to the Achaean League obtained from the Romans leave that Polybius should frame constitutions and draw up laws for them.'

It is a very fair summary of the man's career and his significance. Polybius is a son of the Hellenistic age, bone of its bone, and a child of its mind[1]. Born about 200 B.C., he lived precisely when that Hellenistic world met the Roman, when 'the clouds gathering in the West' broke, and there was need for men who understood both the western and the eastern halves of the Mediterranean, and could interpret East to West and West to East on the basis of real affection and admiration for both. Were the Romans barbarians? Was there still value and life in Greek institutions, in Greek genius? What of the leagues and dynasties, and the upstart kingdoms that replaced the great traditions of Solon and Cyrus? And again was there meaning in the strange quick movement of modern history, in the re-modelling and re-grouping of everything the world had known? Not everybody recognized that the whole aspect of the world was for ever changed: to the very end the democrats and the princes would not believe that the age of Antigonus Gonatas had passed, that the age of Flamininus and the philhellenes was passing only too quickly, and that they must make peace and secure the future while they could. It is one of History's most painful lessons that the minds of practical politicians are but ill-adapted for the discovery of a new situation or of new factors, and seldom move as quickly as the events; and in this

[1] This chapter treats of Polybius in his own age. For the use made of his work by later writers see the notes prefixed to chapters II, V, VI, VIII and XV.

instance they were overtaken by the deluge that swept away all their landmarks and opened a wholly new age. Yet men had to live on, and to do this they had to adjust themselves at once to new conditions, which they found terribly hard to do, and to new outlooks and new conceptions, which is always harder. What did it mean, or did it mean anything, this tidal wave of change? The philosophers and the phrase-mongers were playing with the two ideas of Fate and Chance; neither of them served to explain what had happened; was there reason in it? There was a place for the bridge-builder, who should help men to pass from the old to the new, a man with a gift for reconciliation, who could bring men of different races and outlooks to understand one another, and to understand the appalling movement of history that they had witnessed. Every age is an age of transition, but there are times when the transits are horribly rapid; and Greeks and Romans were happy in having a man of the build of Polybius, Greek in race and training, Roman too in sympathy, with an eye if not for everything that was real in his world at least for most of it, a man who may be described in Lucan's striking phrase as 'capacious of the world' (*mundi capacior*).

In a curious way everything in his career helped to mould him for his task. He was neither by birth nor by adoption, like so many Greek men of letters, an Athenian. If he ever even visited Athens, we have no record of it. His criticism of Demosthenes is significant—'measuring everything by the interests of his own city, thinking that all the Greeks should keep their eyes on Athens, and, if they did not, calling them traitors, he seems to me ignorant and very wide of the truth, especially since what actually befel the Greeks then bears witness that he was not good at foreseeing the future'; and he suggests caustically that Athens owed more to Philip's magnanimity and love of glory than to the policy of Demosthenes (xviii, 14)[1]. This was flouting the great Hellenic past with a vengeance; and contemporary Athens impressed him still less with its renunciation of Greece, its obsequious and indecent adulation of kings. He had himself borne a part in Greek political life, life on a larger scale than Athens offered, and, he would have said, a nobler. Like Herodotus, Thucydides and Xenophon, he had the advantages of exile. Exile, like war in the old phrase, is 'a violent teacher,' but the great historians learn much from its dreadful lessons. Polybius in exile gained the detachment that helped to make his predecessors great; he

---

[1] The references throughout this chapter are to the text of Büttner-Wobst followed by the Loeb edition.

acquired new knowledge of royal statecraft and personality; he made friendships that brought him acquainted with the face of the world and with the men who were shaping its destinies, and gave him a range and freedom unequalled by any Greek save Herodotus.

Arcady is a name of invincibly poetic associations from Theocritus and Virgil. It is strange that its one great writer should have written in prose, and the worst prose perhaps that ever a Greek of anything like his power employed. He can be readable in any language but his own. Yet he was Arcadian and he had the Arcadian training. He implies that he learnt the Arcadian music, by his criticism of the Cynaethans who forwent it; 'it is only in Arcadia that by law from their earliest childhood boys are trained to sing hymns and paeans in which they celebrate after the ancestral fashion the heroes and gods of their native place; later on they learn the airs of Philoxenus and Timotheus and dance every year with great rivalry to the music of pipers in the theatres at the Dionysia, boys in boys' contests, and youths in the men's' (IV, 20). Unlike other Greeks, when they feast, they do not hire musicians but they do their own singing; they march to music and take great pains with national dances. This is not English, but it is still Greek, and Polybius is evidently describing with zest what he had enjoyed. He also alludes to the Arcadian folk belief in the *loup-garou* (VII, 13, 7) which lingered long after his day. It is in the Peloponnese that men are most naturally inclined to 'the quiet and human sort of life.'

Arcadia was a rough harsh land, a land of mountains, of forests of oak and pine, haunted by bear and boar and by great tortoises; and hunting was a national pastime. Polybius loved it; he kept it up in exile; he hunted with prince Demetrius, the Seleucid; he emphasizes his friend Scipio's passion for it; and from time to time he lets fall traces of his close observation of wild life[1], and once he pauses to criticize the painters who paint from the stuffed animal (XII, 25 h). Greece was still devoted to athletics, of which Polybius perhaps did not think so highly, though he had some sympathy with boxing. His hero, Philopoemen, gave up the career of an athlete to serve his country.

Megalopolis was his home; he was the son of Lycortas, a man of good family, of sense, of substance, a friend of Philopoemen, and a contemporary of Lydiades. Lydiades is one of the interesting types of the period; he was somehow tyrant of the city, but he

---

[1] XII, 3, 5; XV, 21; XVI, 24, 5.

made a treaty with his citizens, abdicated, took Megalopolis into the Achaean League and became one of the League's chief figures till his death in 227 B.C. (vol. VII, pp. 746 *sqq*.). It was characteristic of Megalopolis, and of one other city alone, that Cleomenes, the socialist king of Sparta, could never buy a partisan among its citizens. In prosperity and in exile there was a nobility about the men of Megalopolis, which their fellow-citizen is not reluctant to record; for his tale, like that of Herodotus, 'sought digressions,' and not in vain. His pride in his city must not be overlooked if we are to understand the man. Born in it and remembering its story, he could not be an admirer of the new Sparta with its faked legends of Lycurgus, its reckless dealing with property, and its essential betrayal of the Peloponnese. Perhaps the old fear of the Gauls is a reminiscence of childhood (II, 35, 9). Nor is it without influence on his whole work that he grew up a statesman's son and was early initiated into politics in that League, and perhaps that city, where the greatest ideals of ancient Hellas had flowered into a new and vigorous life; that the old watchwords of equality, free speech, and democracy were endeared to him from boyhood; and that he not merely learnt them as Plutarch must have, but that he watched them in their practical application to the conduct of affairs. If he is not, as one of his critics urges, lyric, if he never quite rhapsodizes like some of the later historians, but yet holds fast to great ideals, something perhaps is owed to Lycortas; and, on the other side, perhaps the too political atmosphere cost him the childhood that made Herodotus.

Polybius shared the education of his day, and as he counted it vital for the reader of Philopoemen's life to know his early training and his boyhood's ambitions, we may linger a little over his own; it will reveal the man and the age. We forget, he says, 'the lessons in geometry we learnt as children' and judge cities and camps by their circumferences and their slopes (IX, 26 a). He stresses the value of astronomy; he notices the negative criticism of Strato 'the physicist' (vol. VII, p. 297); he is interested in medicine and questions of diet and surgery, and has a quick glance at the poor class of physician who prefers the initial payment to the final fee and the patient who tires of medical treatment and turns to quacks and charms. It is remarkable how little on the whole he cites the authors who wrote before Alexander, yet now and then echoes may be caught of Thucydides[1], and at least one very striking phrase of Herodotus is three times borrowed or reproduced[2]. His

---

[1] Cf. III, 31, 2 and 12; III, 63, 12, 13; XXIII, 12; XXIX, 5.
[2] ἀρχὴ κακῶν, XVIII, 39, 1; XXII, 18, 1; XXIV, 10, 8.

references to Plato do not suggest great sympathy; but a historian's preference for an actual constitution to a mere ideal may be forgiven; yet he is interested in the theory of the natural transformation of governments. Homer, of course, he studied, though it might be with more thought of geography than most men of letters; yet his excuse surely touches a general principle of some import, 'mere invention carries no conviction and is not Homeric' (xxxiv, 4). He counts it a fine feature in a hero and leader of men that Odysseus can use his knowledge of the stars not only at sea but in land operations. He gibbets Timaeus for a piece of silly criticism to the effect that poets and historians show their own natures in what they linger over: Homer, says Timaeus, must have been a bit of a glutton at that rate. Once he quotes Homer very happily, when he speaks of the many tongues of the Carthaginian mercenaries[1]. Other poets he quotes incidentally— Simonides ('it is hard to be good'), Pindar, Euripides, Epicharmus—and it has been suggested, perhaps not unjustly, that his treatment of them all is on the whole prosaic rather than inspired. He knew something, but thought little, of the schools of rhetoric; but Timaeus surely valued them more highly—'no child in such a school busy with a eulogy of Thersites or a censure of Penelope could eclipse him,' so childish, scholastic and unveracious is he (xii, 26 b, 5). To his studies of the other historians we must return at a later point.

II. POLYBIUS AND THE ART OF WAR

That as an Achaean citizen Polybius must have taken his share in military training and in war, is obvious; that it interested him intensely, is evident from his frequent comments. Greek war had long ceased to be the simple matter that moved the ridicule of Mardonius; it was full of intellectual interest, not least for a man trained on the field and well read in military history. The wars of the Greeks, says Polybius, were generally decided in one battle, or more rarely in two; but campaigns that involved half the Mediterranean had meant great changes in the art of war. The immense variety of scene in which men fought, the diversity of tactics required, the evolution of new types of arm and armour and of new tactics, meant a new strategy, a new attention to a hundred things never thought of in the old days. Iphicrates and Alexander represented epochs; Demetrius the Besieger marks another; and the achievements of Hannibal, and those of Polybius'

[1] xv, 12; *Iliad*, iv, 437.

friend Scipio Aemilianus, which he had himself witnessed, made
the art and the history more absorbing. Not to go outside his
friend's family, Aemilius Paullus said that 'the one amusement
of some people, in their social gatherings and as they strolled, was
to manage the war in Macedonia, while they sat in Rome, sometimes blaming what the commanders did, and sometimes ex-
pounding their omissions' (xxix, 1). History was written in the
same way, Polybius tells us, and he quotes the dreadful confession
of Timaeus—'I lived away from home in Athens for fifty years
without a break, and I have, I confess, no experience of active
service in war or personal knowledge of the localities' (xii, 25 h, 1).
No, a man with no experience of warlike operations cannot
possibly tell us what actually happens in war, and a man must
see the places he describes.

Polybius wrote a work upon Tactics (ix, 20) which is lost, but
his History shows abundantly how much the science of war was
in his mind. He is convinced that the chief asset in an army is
the commander—there is an immense difference between him and
the man in the ranks, and 'what is the use of a general who does
not understand that he must as far as possible keep out of minor
risks, when the fortune of the campaign is not involved? or if he
does not know that many men must be sacrificed before the commander is endangered? As the proverb says, "Chance it with the
Carian"' (x, 32, 9–11; cf. x, 24, 3). A commander must know
that a decisive engagement must not be undertaken on a chance
pretext or without a settled design; he must know when he is
beaten or when he is victorious; he will do well to know the mind
and temper of the commander opposed to him. He should study
military records; he will find astronomy in general useful—witness
the failure of Nicias; he should be careful as to climatic effects
(v, 21) and atmospheric conditions; above all he needs detailed
local knowledge, as to roads, the height of the walls he is to
assault and the length of the ladders he is to use, for, if all this is
methodically studied, things can be done well enough, while otherwise the futile cost in life, at the expense of his best men, may be
heavy. Philopoemen made a point of clean accoutrements; bright
armour inspired dismay in the enemy. There is danger in the
fraternizing of troops besieging and besieged; it is often forgotten
how frequently it has happened.

So much for general principles, and he is always alert for detail
of interest. He discusses the strength and the weakness of the
Macedonian phalanx, unassailable in frontal attack, but very
dependent on level and clear ground, vulnerable in the flank,

helpless if broken. He notes improvements in ballistics and siege engines and dilates on fire-signals, in which department he records devices of his own. One of the most famous (and longest) sections of his History he devotes to the Roman army (VI, 19–42). If it be maintained, as a modern scholar has recently urged[1], that Polybius seems in military matters to compare badly with the fragmentary Hieronymus, the fact remains that military science was definitely one of the many interests that engaged the historian of the Mediterranean; and we can hardly be wrong in believing that his experience lay behind his interest. Whether the office was more definitely military or political, he was elected Hipparch in the Achaean League (XXVIII, 6).

III. POLYBIUS AT ROME

The story of the League and of its downfall is told elsewhere (see vol. VII, chaps. VI, XXIII, and below, chaps. V–VII and IX). It will suffice here to note that Polybius, as became the son of Lycortas, took his part in public affairs. He records his speech on the honours of Eumenes in 169 B.C. (XXVIII, 7), and his attitude next year on the question of assisting the Egyptian kings (p. 301). 'People were alarmed lest they should be thought to fail the Romans in any way,' but Lycortas and his son were for standing by treaty engagements. They were outmanœuvred by a sub-servient politician, who later on incurred an unpopularity very thoroughly manifested. Men insisted on fresh water, if Callicrates had been in the baths, and school children called him traitor on the street. Political spirit was far from dead among the Achaeans. But we need not here deal further with it; it will be enough to have noted that Polybius did not belong to the thorough-going pro-Roman party, but that, on the contrary, he was denounced by them to Rome and sent among the thousand to Italy. This manœuvre, unheard of in Greek or Macedonian annals, is recorded by Pausanias (VII, 10, 7–12); there is a gap in the narrative of Polybius, but a signal chapter records the disgraceful plan adopted by the Senate, who neither wished to pronounce judgment nor to let the men go, and solved the matter (and other problems with it) in the curt sentence, 'We do not think it in the interest either of Rome or of your "communities" (demoi) that these men should return home' (XXX, 32, 9). The plural demoi gave an unmistakeable warning to the League that its days were numbered; for Polybius the short sentence meant sixteen years of exile.

[1] W. W. Tarn, *Hellenistic Civilisation*, Ed. 2, p. 231.

It began with 'utter loss of spirit and paralysis of mind' (xxx, 32, 10), as we can understand; but (one guesses) at a fairly early point came the intimacy with the circle of Scipio (see below, pp. 399; 459 *sq.*). The younger Scipio was the son of Aemilius Paullus, conqueror of Perseus, and the story of the beginnings of his long and intimate friendship with Polybius has been aptly called 'one of the most delightful passages in all ancient literature[1].' The acquaintance began with the loan of books and with conversation about them; and then, when the detained Achaeans were being assigned to Italian or Etrurian townships, the sons of Aemilius urgently begged the praetor to allow Polybius to remain in Rome. Their plea was granted; and the intercourse grew closer. One day Scipio, in a quiet and gentle voice, asked Polybius why he so constantly addressed himself to his brother and ignored him; did Polybius share the common opinion that he was too quiet and indolent a person? That was nonsense, rejoined Polybius; he would be delighted to help him in every way. Scipio caught him by the hand and begged him to join lives with him. It pleased Polybius, naturally, but he was embarrassed, he says, when he reflected on the high position of the family and its wealth (xxxi, 23, 24). But from then onward they were inseparable. Books and hunting and every kind of interest drew them together; and years later Polybius was at Scipio's side at the great moment of his life, when he watched the burning of Carthage and confided to his friend his strange foreboding that another great city might find a similar end[2].

> ἔσσεται ἦμαρ ὅταν ποτ' ὀλώλῃ Ἴλιος ἱρή.
> A day will come when holy Troy shall fall.
>
> (XXXVIII, 21, 22.)

Few stories of the intercourse of Greek and Roman are so pleasant; and few such friendships were ever so profitable for the men themselves or for posterity. For what proved the special function of Polybius in life and in literature—the interpretation of the two races to each other, nothing could have been happier. He had known the best of contemporary Greece; here he came to know, perhaps even more intimately, the best of Rome. He had understood from childhood the movements of Greek politics, republican and monarchical, here he stood in the inner circle of

---

[1] Warde Fowler, *The Religious Experience of the Roman People*, p. 363.
[2] We may recall the reflections of Pausanias (VIII, 33) on the ruins of Megalopolis, the home of Polybius, 'brought to naught by the hand of God.'

Roman government, discreet, helpful and intelligent; and its
character was given to his book.

That he was already writing the book or at least preparing for
it in the years of detention, is an easy guess; they were years, at
any rate, of preparation. Of episode we hear little or nothing,
beyond the story of Scipio's friendship and the strange occasion
when Polybius gave a king to Syria. For a hostage prince,
Demetrius, was like himself held in Italy, though heir by now to
the throne at Antioch. In spite of his earnest address to them for
release, the Senate resolved 'to keep Demetrius in Rome and to
help to establish on the throne the child left (by king Antiochus).
This they did, I think, because they mistrusted the manhood of
Demetrius and judged that the youth and helplessness of the child
on the throne would suit them better' (xxxi, 2). But they reckoned
without Polybius, who urged the young prince to be his own
deliverer, and whose tablets, with some very apt quotations in verse
but no signature, were delivered at the critical moment. It is a
bright story, well told, and one to be weighed in any estimate of
the historian (xxxII, 11–15).

The Achaeans had never forgotten their fellow citizens in Italy
and had repeatedly sent embassies on their behalf. Deliverance
came from an unexpected quarter. For it was Cato who suddenly
intervened, with a sentence of kindlier thought than might seem
to go with the rough phrase and 'horse sense' which the old man
affected. Had the Senate, he asked, nothing better to do than sit
all day disputing whether some old Greek fellows should be
carried to their graves by Roman pall-bearers or Achaean? The
argument was sufficient, and release was voted. But a few days
later, when Polybius was thinking of approaching the Senate again
to plead for the restitution of their former honours at home, and
consulted Cato, Cato smiled and said that Polybius, like another
Odysseus, was wanting to re-enter the cave of the Cyclops, because
he had forgotten his cap and his belt (xxxv, 6). The story suggests
a friendliness, perhaps an intimacy, which we might not have
guessed; and acquaintance with that great character was one way
of knowing Rome.

IV. THE TRAVELS OF POLYBIUS

So, after sixteen years, Polybius was free to leave Italy. Of
course he went back to Greece, but he did not stay there. His
historical principles (III, 59), his friendships, his interest in the

world, called him elsewhere; he was not ambitious to be a Timaeus
and do his research on a sofa. 'To look through old records is of
service for knowledge of the views of the ancients and the impressions they had about conditions, nations, politics and events';
but it is also part of a historian's task himself 'to see the cities,
places, rivers, lakes, and in general the peculiar features of land
and sea and to know the distances' (XII, 25 e). So Polybius
travelled, and with a freedom which must prove the possession of
reasonable wealth; and he half hints as much (XII, 27, 6; 28 a, 4).
The dates of his life are in some cases fixed by the public events
at which he was present—such as the sack of Carthage and the
fall of Corinth, both in 146 B.C., and the siege of Numantia,
134–133 B.C., where again he was with Scipio. Pliny tells us
(*N. H.* v, 9–10) that Scipio, while in charge in Africa, gave
Polybius the historian the commission to explore with a fleet the
Atlantic coast of Africa. This was indeed a chance to put a theory
of his into practice; in old days, the perils of land and sea stood
in the way of real knowledge of the ends of the earth, and many
mistakes were made; but, since the conquests of Alexander and
the Romans, nearly all regions were approachable, and, as war and
politics offer so much less scope to active brains, there ought to
be progress in our knowledge of the world.

He visited Alexandria in the reign of Ptolemy Physcon (145–
116 B.C.) and retained a disgust for the place and its mongrel
people. Ptolemy Philadelphus had adorned the city with many
statues of a girl called Cleino clad only in her *chiton*, he tells us,
a fit Athena Parthenos for a people of 'Egyptian dissoluteness and
indolence.' Those who take on trust the historian's dryness (he
pleads guilty to a 'hint of austerity'), who leave him unread
because Dionysius of Halicarnassus groups him with 'the writers
whom nobody can finish' (*de compositione verborum*, 4), will find
his story of the Alexandrine massacres more vivid than they might
expect. It is no mere digression into idle horror and pathos such
as he reprobates in historians like Phylarchus who affect the
moving accident; it is a living picture of Hellenistic civilization at
its worst, a native savagery breaking through the veneer of Macedonian culture, with hideous outrage to court ladies, 'the squares,
the roofs, the steps, full of people, hubbub and clamour, women
and children jostling with men; for in Carthage and Alexandria
the little children (παιδάρια) play no less part in such tumults
than the men' (xv, 27–30). Let us turn westward.

Into the old controversy of Hannibal's pass it is not necessary
here to enter. It begins always with the inquiries made by

Polybius among men present when Hannibal crossed the Alps, which the historian followed up by crossing himself 'to know and to see'—a Herodotean touch. Roads and distances, as we have seen, always interest him; he notes Roman milestones already in Transalpine Gaul and the sea-going traffic of the Rhone. Strabo (II, 104 *sqq.*) says he is wrong in some of his estimates. Again, like Herodotus, he is apt to reflect upon climate and its effects; to note commodities, mines, and fauna. He lingers to tell us of the prosperity, the flowers, the prices of Lusitania, a fat pig 4 drachmae, a lamb 3 obols, a sheep 2 drachmae, a hare 1 obol; he describes vividly the placer-mining at Aquileia, and the nuggets of gold the size of a bean or lupine, and the effect upon the price of gold elsewhere, the Roman silver-mining near New Carthage with 40,000 labourers and the dreadful human equivalent of the stamp (XXXIV, 9, 8). Africa is not arid and desolate, as Timaeus supposed in Athens; it has in places a rich soil and abounds in animal life; Numidia indeed was counted barren, till the energy of Masinissa showed how fruitful it could be (see below, pp. 472 *sqq.*). He pauses to describe how men catch the swordfish off Sicily. The Ocean 'or Atlantic sea as some call it' he had personally sailed. But perhaps the most memorable and enjoyable of his descriptions of race and region are the pages given to the Celts of North Italy.

Their country's fertility is not easy to describe; its wheat is so abundant as to sell at four obols the Sicilian medimnus (ten gallons), and barley at half that price. The oak forests on the plains of the Po nourish enormous herds of swine, to which he returns at a later point (XII, 4) to describe the swineherd and his horn, and to tell us that one sow may in time produce 1000 young. Food is so cheap that travellers do not haggle over items with inn-keepers but simply ask how much they must pay *per diem*, and generally 'it is half an *as*, that is a quarter-obol.' As for the Celts, 'their numbers, their stature and the beauty of their persons, yes and their spirit in war, you may learn from the very events of their history' (II, 15); and Hannibal was safe in counting on their hatred of Rome. The rest of Italy feared them with reason; they had invaded the Etruscans and about the time of the King's Peace, 387/6 B.C. (see vol. VII, p. 321), they had taken Rome itself and held it seven months. They were natural warriors, 'with a mania for war' (λοιμικήν τινα πολέμου διάθεσιν II, 20, 7), and their habit, long kept by Celts, was to fight naked. 'The fine order of the Celtic host, and the dreadful din of innumerable trumpeters and horn blowers' impressed the enemy; 'very terrifying, too, were the appearance and gestures of the naked warriors, all in the prime of life and finely built men, and all in the leading companies richly adorned with gold chains and armlets' (II, 29). To the Greek generally and to the Roman they seemed savages, a *lusus Naturae* disturbing the order of the universe; for long the Romans never felt safe in their own country with such neighbours. But 'the Gallic shield does not cover the whole body; so that their nakedness was a disadvantage, and the bigger they were, the better chance the missiles had of going home' (II, 30, 3); and their war-swords were only good for a cut not a thrust, and would bend and then had to be straightened with foot and hand. It was a more serious defect, the military critic thought, that, for all their courage, they never planned a campaign properly, nor even a battle, but would fling into both 'more by instinct than calculation.' There is plainly sympathy in his admiration, and the picturesque description halts the reader and makes him realize the effect of these splendid savages upon the civilized mind—and that effect was a serious factor in Mediterranean history, as the story of Pergamum shows. The digressions of a great historian are apt to be centripetal.

The Gauls were not the only uncivilized tribe of the Mediterranean, and from time to time the historian glances at the others. Not all savages who sacrifice a horse on the eve of battle are of Trojan descent, he caustically explains, with Timaeus before him. The Celtiberians of Spain, unlike the Greeks, were never content with one battle or two; they fought 'uninterruptedly,' except that in winter they did less. Even when more or less beaten, the envoys of the Aravacae (of Spain), while taking a proper and subdued attitude before the Senate, made it plain that at heart they scarcely admitted defeat; luck was against them, they owned, but they left the impression that all the same they had fought more brilliantly than the Romans.

So he goes through the world, taking pains to learn and to note the shape and nature of this and that region or town—Sparta, Capua, Sinope, Agrigentum—the currents and the economic advantages of Byzantium—the physical geography of the Black Sea—the country life and general wealth of Elis—the craters of the Liparaean islands. No man could be less like Herodotus, as any page will show; yet he has the same instincts, the same interests, and much (if you except historians) of the same tolerance. He was not infallible; his account of New Carthage is adversely criticized; but a man cannot see everything, and at least his principle was to see as much as he could for himself.

The epitaph already quoted from Pausanias and his comment

tells all we need here of his later years. He turned his friendship with the Romans to account for his fellow countrymen, and earned gratitude. One characteristic episode must be noted. When all was over and the Achaean League wrecked and dissolved for ever, Polybius was offered with Roman tactlessness some of the property of his old adversary Diaeus, but like Virgil under closely parallel circumstances *non sustinuit accipere*[1]. Lucian writing three hundred years later tells us, and it is not inconsistent with a youth of hunting and a middle age of travel, that Polybius died when he was eighty years old, of a fall from his horse.

V. THE THEME OF POLYBIUS

The personal story of Polybius is in itself significant. Like Herodotus, he is a man of his age; in each case the age is reflected in the man, and the personality interprets it; for the life's work is not to be separated from the life; the experience makes the History. We have not the whole of the *pragmateia*—the treatise—of Polybius. Of its forty books, five times the length of Herodotus and of all the work of Thucydides, six are practically complete; for the rest we depend on long selections or the references of critics, geographers, essayists, and makers of compendiums. Where others make our selections, we are dependent on their interests, which may be more misleading than the accidents of quotation and transcription. Perhaps, if we had the forty books intact, Timaeus might have less place in the memory; and that of itself might modify our judgment of Polybius. Much has been conjectured as to how historians from Herodotus and Thucydides to Lord Clarendon wrote the books they did write rather than those they designed, how soon they achieved the ultimate plan and what traces they left of former plans, how much revision was needed and how much given. Polybius has not escaped. What was his first plan, and where does the second become effective? A fresh start seems evident early in book III. Matters, so small as his wavering between the phrases 'according to the proverb' and 'as the saying goes,' have been noted, and he has been supplied (by conjecture) at a certain stage with a volume of proverbs, proved by his preference of the former phrase. Do his various utterances on *Tyche* imply progressive change in his conception of the part played by Fortune in human affairs, and, if so, can you group them into periods and roughly date the passages? It is not wholly idle, for his outlook in his captivity cannot have been that of twenty or

---

[1] XXXIX, 4; Suetonius, *vita Vergili*, 12.

thirty years later, when so much had altered the face of the world, when he himself had seen so much of land and sea, borne his part in great actions and shouldered high responsibilities. There is evidence of changing opinion between the parts of the work. He implies as early as book III that he has achieved his forty books; book XXXIX (in the Loeb text; book XL according to others) ends with the statement that he has reached the end of his *pragmateia*. It may be merely a forecast that some will think his work 'difficult to acquire and difficult to read' because of its length (III, 32). Probably, lingering like other authors, and with the example of Zeno the Rhodian before him who published and could not correct (XVI, 20, 6), he delayed publication and revised his work as new reflections occurred to him; and in a manuscript of such length and complexity it is hardly surprising if he forgot statements or allusions here and there inconsistent with some new change. Perhaps some of his repeated explanations of his design, some of his theories as to History, might have been fused or omitted, some of his references to Timaeus abridged or cancelled, if he had not kept writing and adding and revising till he was eighty. The work thus suffers in three ways: it is fragmentary (apart from the first six books) and dependent on the tribe of smaller men who excerpt and condense; it gives the impression of sorely needing the last hand of the author; and, finally, a book, like a child, may suffer from too prolonged parental care.

Like Herodotus and Thucydides, Polybius begins by explaining how he came to write his History. He had lived through times that must make any man think; he had seen the culmination of a great world-wide march of events, of a great and permanent change in all political relations. That unity of the world, which seems to have inspired Alexander and fitfully stirred his successors, which had meanwhile been altering all the thoughts of men, Polybius had seen turned from dream to reality. In international relations, precisians may distinguish between conquest and control; Macedonia was a Roman province for a century or more, before Egypt saw its last queen die; but the realists are generally more correct than the precisians, and from the day when Popillius Laenas drew with his stick the circle in the sand round the feet of Antiochus Epiphanes, there was no doubt who ruled the Mediterranean. 'Fortune had so directed the matter of Perseus and Macedonia that, when the position of Alexandria and the whole of Egypt was almost desperate, all was again set right simply because the fate of Perseus was decided; for had this not been so and had he not been certain of it, I do not think these orders would have been obeyed by Antiochus' (xxix, 27). The small touch of style that ends the sentence with Antiochus in the nominative is significant. Greek opinion counted the action of Popillius abrupt and rude; but a Seleucid king, and that king Antiochus, stepped out of the circle to go home as he was told.

'The very element of unexpectedness (παράδοξον) in the events I have chosen as my theme is enough to challenge and incite every man, old or young, to the study of my treatise. For who among men is so worthless or spiritless as not to wish to know by what means, and under what kind of polity, the Romans in less than fifty-three years have succeeded in subjecting nearly the whole inhabited world to their sole government—a thing un-exampled in history?' (I, 1, 4, 5). So he puts his theme; and the form of it is in itself challenging. Later in his book he reveals in a quotation whence he drew the suggestion for this form; and the reader will notice at once a parallel and a marked difference. 'For if you consider not boundless time nor many generations, but fifty years only, these fifty years immediately before our own day, you will read in them the cruelty of Fortune (*Tyche*). For fifty years ago do you think that either the Persians or the king of the Persians, either the Macedonians or the king of the Macedonians, if some god had foretold them the future, would ever have believed that to-day the very name of the Persians would have utterly perished—the Persians who were lords of almost the whole earth, and that the Macedonians should be masters of it, whose very name was unknown? Yet this Fortune, who makes no treaty with our life, who will baffle all our reckoning by some novel stroke, who displays her own power by her surprises, even now, as I think, makes it clear to all men, now that she brought the Macedonians into the happiness of the Persians, that she has but lent them all these blessings—until she changes her mind about them' (xxix, 21). Polybius has much to say of *Tyche*, and not all of it is easy to reconcile with the rest; but while he takes a hint from Demetrius of Phalerum here, his moral is not the fickleness of Fortune, but the value and the fascination of the study of real causes. Later on (I, 63, 9) he looks back, noting a confirmation of what he said at the outset, 'that the progress of the Romans was not due to *Tyche*, as some Greeks suppose, nor was it automatic, but it was entirely reasonable (καὶ λίαν εἰκότως) that, after they schooled themselves in affairs of such character and such greatness, they not only struck boldly for universal supremacy of dominion, but achieved their project.' 'To talk of *Tyche*,' he says again elsewhere, 'is not proper; it is vulgar' (II,

38, 5). 'What we all want to know is not what happened, but how it happened' (v, 21, 6). 'What chiefly charms (τὸ ψυχαγωγοῦν) and profits students is the clear view of causes and the consequent power of choosing the better in each contingency as it comes' (vi, 2, 8).

He has thus a real theme, and a real problem, an amazing, a 'paradoxical' story—the values of which, as we shall see, he does not miss—and a genuine piece of investigation. 'Tyche' (here he slips a little nearer to Demetrius) 'having guided almost all the affairs of the world in one direction and having forced them all toward one and the same goal' (Tyche like God evidently 'geometrizes'), 'the historian should bring before his readers under one synoptical view the management by which Tyche has accomplished the whole' (I, 4, 1); and a little lower, though with a touch or two of the Demetrian style again, he pronounces this ascendancy of Rome 'the most beautiful and the most beneficent device (ἐπιτήδευμα) of Tyche' (I, 4, 4). A strange judgment for a Greek, an Achaean, and the victim of a cruel piece of Roman dishonesty—but he means what he says; the Roman supremacy was a blessing to the world (cf. xxxviii, 18, 8) and it was perfectly intelligible. There were indeed Greeks who, like St Cyprian, put down the rise and fall of nations to Chance; but (in the great sentence of Gibbon[1]) 'a wiser Greek, who has composed, in a philosophic spirit, the memorable history of his own times, deprived his countrymen of this vain and delusive comfort, by opening to their view the deep foundations of the greatness of Rome.'

A problem—and without the full range of facts that bear upon it, how can a problem be solved at all? Or if the facts are misrepresented? Or what profit is there for life and statesmanship—for Polybius is always thinking of the practical value of historical enquiry—if the parallel cases are not parallel? Neither for intellectual discipline, nor moral profit, nor political example, can History serve, if any other aim be pursued but that of Truth; and where the destiny of the whole world is concerned, where the keynote of the whole thing is the unity of mankind, the whole Truth about the whole world is imperative. All the arts, he says, are becoming sciences, and very highly methodized; and there too lies a point for the historian; History must be properly written, with the exactitude of a science, if it is to be profitable (x, 47, 12).

---

[1] *Decline and Fall*, ch. xxxviii (observations).

VI. HISTORICAL METHOD

'Under one synopsis' (1, 4, 2), 'the general and comprehensive scheme of events' (1, 4, 3)—these are his watchwords. History had been treated in detail; historians had written of a single nation, Greeks or Persians; 'how the Romans took Syracuse and how they occupied Spain, may possibly be learnt from the particular (κατὰ μέρος) histories, but how they attained to universal empire' must be the theme of a general history (viii, 2, 5). History must have a real unity, an organic unity; it must be like a living body (σωματοειδής, 1, 3, 4), each part sustaining and in a sense explaining the whole, and not really intelligible without the whole. The dissected limbs give you no idea of the living animal in its beauty and movement (1, 4, 7). Since the 140th Olympiad (220–216 B.C.) 'History has been an organic whole and the affairs of Italy and Africa have been interlaced with those of Asia and Greece, all bearing to one end' (1, 3, 4). The war with Antiochus derives its origin from that with Philip; the latter war from the Hannibalic; the war of Hannibal depends on the affairs connected with Sicily; and all the intervening events tend to the same goal; and it is only from a universal history that all this can be recognized and understood (iii, 32). The difficulties are considerable; the historian will be blamed, though not justly, for slurring over events, for omissions and rapid abridgements; he is obliged to survey his subject in detail, to attempt at least a chronological parallelism, yet coherence in treatment of one set of details may mean anticipation of some outcome which might as properly come in another section but, as it stands, seems to anticipate the events that led up to it (xv, 24 a; xxviii, 16, 10); he must of necessity allow himself a digression now and then, or an excursus, to deal, for instance, with the Roman constitution or the fall of Syracuse. Yet the digressions are to be, as we said, centripetal; the great central design of what is nowadays called 'world-history' is to be advanced by every step or glance aside. Broadly speaking—if we allow margin for the criticism of other historians which, with perhaps other matter, might to-day be put in an appendix—we may say that Polybius does achieve his aim. His History, however large or awkward some of the limbs, is the 'organic whole' that he designed.

The 'Father of History' had things very much in his own hands and wrote one of the most delightful books in the world. Thucydides did not like it, and set new precedents of his own—he

composed speeches for situations and he cut all his material
ruthlessly into annual sections. Too many historians followed him
in the first of these points, hardly enough in the second; Polybius
reversed the tradition, he is careful of dates and chary of speeches.
Isocrates devised the character sketch which perhaps began as
panegyric and might always too easily become panegyric; and
Xenophon copied him and eclipsed him. Xenophon made but a
poor sequel to the book of Thucydides; he was a careless annalist;
but the man who wrote the *Anabasis* and inspired Arrian, served
History and made a new pattern well. The dramatists, and the
writers upon politics, and, following Isocrates, the school rhetoricians, all had their influence; all suggested matters for thought
and methods of treatment. Every fresh movement in literature
affected the writing of History. Whether the historian realized it
or not, all the traditions played upon him;—character-drawing,
scene-painting, tragic effects, marvels, self-revelation, general
essay-writing, temptation beset him on every hand. One man
cannot get Hannibal over the Alps without the personal intervention of the gods; Polybius crossed them, as we saw, without
such aid, and evidently trusted Hannibal to do the same. Philinus
wrote of the Carthaginians like a lover; they could do no wrong;
and Fabius was as loyal to the Romans. Theopompus must tell
the silly tale of men without a shadow—in Arcadia, too! (XVI,
12, 7) where it survived to be recorded by Pausanias (VIII, 38, 6).
Phylarchus in an ungentlemanly and womanish way overdoes the
emotional, and seems not to understand that Tragedy and History
are two things. There were 'universal historians' who knocked off
Carthaginian or Roman history in three or four pages.

Polybius aims at Truth, as he says, and his affinities are with
the three great predecessors. He sees a whole world with the
first; he is as exactingly precise as the second; and he reveals
himself even more than the third. Thucydides set his conceptions
of History in a preface; Polybius keeps returning to his views and
developing them. With Truth as his object, exact but in all its
breadth, the historian needs several qualifications. First we may
set, though he rather characteristically sets it third, knowledge of
the sources, with which, following others of his statements, we may
group verbal information. Next may come his first point—seeing
things for yourself; and, after that, political experience, and
military experience. Research in libraries is not enough, though
it helps a man to understand the past, and the movements that
make the present. He offers a most significant caution as to the
share of the enquirer in shaping the information he receives from

the men who actually took part in the battle or the siege as it may be—a suggestion which implies a further stage of psychology than the complaint of Thucydides about the carelessness of enquirers and the partial knowledge of informants. We have already noted his emphasis on seeing for oneself as the avowed purpose of his travels, and he recurs to this, quoting Heracleitus' sentence that 'the eyes are more accurate witnesses than the ears[1].' More significant, more modern in tone, is his emphasis on personal experience (αὐτοπάθεια) as the key to historical intelligence and to life in narrative (XII, 25 h, 4; 25 i, 7). Αὐτοπάθεια is a word of the later Greek sort, polysyllabic and abstract, but it was not yet in antiquity a commonplace that to understand you must first experience. Polybius adapts Plato's epigram that for an ideal society philosophers must be kings or kings philosophers; if men of action would write history, not as they do now as a mere side-issue (παρέργως) but in the conviction that it is 'one of the most needful and noble things' they can do, or if would-be authors would count a training in affairs a pre-requisite, we might hope for real history (XII, 28, 4). Plutarch is still the most charming of biographers, but he never handles a political issue without showing that he has not (in Polybius' phrase, XII, 25 h, 5) 'taken a hand in politics and had experience of what happens on that side of life.' It may be difficult to secure that in everything the historian 'has done the thing himself, as a man of action[2],' but in the chief things it is necessary. Nothing perhaps need be added as to his sense of the value of actual military experience. The realism with which he handles policy, the cool analysis of motive, the rather hard rationalism of his outlooks, surely speak of his experience of politicians, Greek and Roman, and, quite apart from his conclusions, illumine the age.

VII. A HISTORY FOR THE WORLD

The question has been raised whether he wrote primarily for Greeks or for Romans—a question he neither asks nor answers. A man, whose mind is set upon the history of the whole Mediterranean world as a unity, is obviously writing for everybody; and by his day everybody of any consequence read Greek. One Roman historian, Aulus Postumius, thought it necessary to write in Greek, which, in spite of immoderate Greek studies, he felt he could not do very well, and incurred Cato's shrewd criticism—the

[1] XII, 27, 1; cf. XX, 12, 8 ἐξ ἀκοῆς opposed to αὐτόπτης.
[2] XII, 25 h, 6 αὐτουργὸν καὶ δράστην.

Amphictyonic council had not ordered him to write in a language he knew imperfectly. That Polybius wrote in Greek was natural. It may be noted that he makes a long digression to describe Roman institutions[1], and that he is constantly remarking upon Roman character, while, in what is left of his work, we have no such Greek detail, even of the Achaean League. Some things, as we saw, can be omitted in a universal history, especially if they have been done before. But the Greeks have so far hardly taken Rome seriously; they are full of admiration for the great wars of Antigonus and Demetrius, the Persian or the Peloponnesian War, but the first Punic War 'lasted without a break for twenty-four years and is of all wars known to us the longest, the most unintermittent, and the greatest' (I, 63). Yet it was not till 217 B.C. that Greek statesmen thought of 'looking westward' (v, 105, 7), and Agelaus made his famous speech about 'the clouds in the west' and expressed his fear that the truces and wars they were all playing at might be brought to so abrupt an end that they would be praying the gods to give them back the power to fight as they liked (see vol. VII, p. 768).

Writing, then, for all the world Polybius obviously tries to hold the balance true between Greek and Roman. A good man should love his friends and his country and share their loves and hates; but a historian has another duty, he must ignore his feelings and, if need be, speak good of the enemy and give him the highest praise, and be quite unreserved in reproach of his closest friends, if that is just; if History be stripped of Truth what is left is a profitless tale (I, 14, 5, 6). Later on, he concedes that historians may have a leaning (ῥοπὰς διδόναι) for their country but must not make statements at variance with fact. That Polybius had a patriot's passion for the Achaean League, and its heroes Aratus and Philopoemen, is evident enough from his book and from his practical services after the conquest. Yet the blunders of the League are not concealed. He is accused of having damned the Aetolians with posterity; but it is arguable that he does not do them substantial injustice—they first invited Roman interference; yet the manly speech of Agelaus belonged to them. As to the Greeks in general, good Hellene as he is, like the good Hellenes who wrote history before him and were blamed by Plutarch and Dionysius for their revelations, Polybius makes no secret of Greek weaknesses. The Greek world about 200 B.C., he says, was infested with bribery, and he contrasts Roman honesty, though

---

[1] Book VI. For a discussion of these see further below, pp. 357 *sqq*.

even that had fallen away from earlier times. Demagogy ran to outrageous lengths; 'the natural passion for novelty' swept Greeks into all sorts of change; the Cynaethans, though Arcadians, are shocking people with never-ending *stasis*, exiles and murders; treachery was too prevalent; and it would be tedious to try to count the embassies and counter-embassies he records as sent to Rome. He cannot be accused of flattering his countrymen; yet he will write that a thing is 'neither just nor Greek'—happy synonyms!

He has been reproached with becoming Roman in sentiment, which might have been called magnanimity in view of all he bore and all he knew. But he is as unsparing of Roman policy in the second century as of Greek. In Roman character, in its greatness (xxvii, 8, 8) and its meanness (xxxi, 26, 9; with ix, 10, 8), he is deeply interested. Rome had looked for the moment and the pretext to destroy Carthage; she let the Greeks see how she would welcome defections from the Achaean League; was it to find a loophole for intervention that the Roman consul urged the Rhodians to reconcile Antiochus and Ptolemy? The affair of the quarrelling Ptolemies prompts the remark that 'many decisions of the Romans are now of this kind; they avail themselves with profound policy of the mistakes of others to augment and strengthen their own empire, under the guise of granting favours and benefiting those who commit the errors' (xxxi, 10, 7). A change for the worse came over Rome when Macedon fell and universal dominion was secure. Perhaps the account which he gives of Greek comment on the destruction of Carthage and the progress of the false Philip (xxxvi, 9) shows his balance as well as any. Let his judgment on Hannibal, foe of the Romans as the Phoenician had for centuries been of the Greek, serve to show his spirit; and if it be contrasted with the words and the mind of Livy, the greatness of Polybius will be more evident.

'Who could withhold admiration for Hannibal's strategic skill, his courage and ability, who looks to the length of this period, who reflects on the pitched battles, the skirmishes, the sieges, the revolutions and counter-revolutions of states, the vicissitudes of events (καιρῶν), at the whole scope of his design and its execution? For sixteen years he maintained ceaseless war with the Romans throughout Italy without once releasing his army from service in the field but kept those great numbers under his control, like a good pilot, without disaffection to himself or one another, though he had troops in his service not only of different tribes but of different races. He had Libyans, Iberians, Ligurians, Celts,

Phoenicians, Italians, Greeks, who had neither law, nor custom, nor speech, nor anything else in nature common to them. None the less the skill of the commander was such, that differences so manifold and so wide did not disturb obedience to one word of command and one single will. And this he achieved not under simple conditions, but most varied, the gale of fortune blowing now fair, now foul. So one may admire the commander's power in all this, and say with confidence that, if he had begun with other parts of the world and attacked the Romans last, not one of his projects would have eluded him' (xi, 19).

The passage is a noble one; but let any one turn to the Greek of it, and he will realize the feet of iron and clay mixed, beneath the head of gold. The grammar is intricate, though not here so involved as it often is; there are for the classical taste too many abstract nouns, many of which the great Attic writers would neither have wished nor needed to use—περίστασις twice, μετα-βολή, περιοχή, ἐπιβολή, and of course the inevitable τοῦτο τὸ μέρος, which may be found three times on a page. Add the recurrent ὁλοσχερῶς and ὁ προειρημένος, προαίρεσις and πολυπραγμονεῖν, and perhaps the cruel judgment of Dionysius, the professed expert in style, will be understood. Nor will the plea be quite sufficient that he uses the jargon of the politicians and treaty-makers of his day. His sentences straggle and draggle beyond belief; he masses short syllables (γέγονε κατάμονος ὁ πόλεμος, XXI, 2, 6); and then he astonishes the reader by sedulous avoidance of hiatus. There is 'something austere' in his style, as he owns, a uniformity, likely only to please one class of reader (IX, 1). He admits, while he criticizes Zeno for over-niceness (and some vanity) in the matter of elegance of style, that we should indeed bestow care and concern on the proper manner of reporting events, for it contributes much to History; but reasonable people ought not to count it the first and master interest; no, no, there are nobler aspects of History, on which rather a man of practical experience in politics might plume himself (xvi, 17).

And so indeed there are; and for all his lumbering sentences, in spite of the soundness of his morals, his readiness to pause to point a lesson for statesman, soldier or citizen, his conscientious digressions to guard the reader against Timaeus and other sinful men, tragic, stylistic, erroneous—it is impossible to spend months with the great historian of the Hellenistic world and not like and admire him. He did know his world, and he is so large and sane and truthful; where he is our guide the path is so plain and the view so broad and clear to the horizon, that you regret more and more that the ancients did not preserve every page of his History and his Life of Philopoemen too. Dionysius and others have greatly overdone his dullness. In his deliberate way he can give you the great scene, the moving episode. That escape of Demetrius, hinted at above, 'stands out,' says a modern historian[1], 'in ancient literature for its vividness and authenticity'; and it is by no means alone. Recall the miser Alexander and his captivity, the mutiny of the mercenaries at Carthage, Hannibal's oath to his father, the crossing of the Rhone and the elephants with their Indian mahouts, the end of Cleomenes, the wild riots in which Agathocles is killed in Alexandria, the scene of the negotiations between Philip, Flamininus and the rest, and the last awful picture of the confusion and despair of Greece before the conquest brought peace and release; and it will be hard to maintain that this man missed the great moments or failed to give them again to the reader. 'He could draw fine pictures when he chose.'

The great personality did not escape him. The friend of Scipio, the writer of that judgment upon Hannibal, knew a great man when he met him, and he comes strangely near Carlyle's doctrine of the Hero. Syracuse is to be besieged; the Romans have all in readiness, penthouses, missiles, siege material; and in five days, they hope, they are sure, their works will be much more advanced than those of the Syracusans; 'but in this they did not reckon with the power of Archimedes nor foresee that in some cases one soul ($\mu\acute{\iota}\alpha$ $\psi\upsilon\chi\acute{\eta}$) is more effective than many hands' ($\pi\upsilon\lambda\upsilon\chi\epsilon\iota\rho\acute{\iota}\alpha$, VIII, 3, 3). Eight months, and the city is not yet taken—'such a great and marvellous thing may be one man and one soul fittingly framed' (VIII, 7, 7). A similar comment is made on Xanthippus, restorer of the fortunes of Carthage—one man and one man's judgment did it (I, 35, 5). The men are many who stand out as the story advances—the elder Scipio, with his force of character; Cleomenes, socialist, king and general; Attalus, conqueror of the Gauls, no mean enemies, as we have seen; Flamininus, the philhellene with his great proclamation and his laughing diplomacy; Perseus, not great but a character; Antiochus Epiphanes, and—one cannot resist it—the disappointing Philip himself. And yet the historian of Hellenistic civilization may be right when he says that the hero of Polybius is Rome.

Other men have drawn great scenes and given us the characters of great men, and many have done it with greater grace of speech, but we may end as we began. The Hellenistic age grows progressively in interest and significance; it is so modern, so near us,

---

[1] E. R. Bevan, *The House of Seleucus*, vol. II, p. 193.

and it is at the same time so near the great days of Alexander, of 'Leuctra and the most brilliant period of Greek history' (VIII, 11, 3). If it has not the amazing brilliance of the century of Themistocles, it yet is creative. Rome and our modern world are unintelligible without it. Polybius is its great interpreter; and at the same time he is the first true historian of Rome, the writer of a book 'like the sun in the field of Roman history[1].' And on every page you feel that you are dealing with a man who loves truth and sees things in perspective, who understands what he sees, and treats you as an equal.

[1] Mommsen, *Roman History*, vol. IV, p. 247.

CHAPTER II

HANNIBAL'S INVASION OF ITALY

I. THE OUTBREAK OF THE WAR

THE Second Punic War has rightly been regarded by ancient and modern writers alike as the greatest in the history of Rome. The deep insight of Polybius, who lived to see Rome undisputed mistress of the Mediterranean, has noted and recorded how the issue of the struggle inaugurated a new era in Europe. A unity of ancient history begins, with Rome as the focus, which ends only when the Roman Empire split into two halves. The military history of the war down to Cannae and the outstanding personality of Hannibal are illuminated by the concise and orderly account of the Greek historian and by the literary skill of Livy.

Note. For detailed criticism of the sources see the works cited in the Bibliography, B. 1. The narrative of the three chapters on the Second Punic War is based upon the following general view of the sources.

For the events down to Cannae including the causes of the war Polybius, Book III, though not above criticism in detail, is by far the most trustworthy source. He was writing the history of the generation which immediately preceded his own and he was able to converse with contemporaries of the events he described. Further, he used on the Roman side the account of Fabius Pictor, a senator who took an active part during the war and headed a mission to Delphi in 216 B.C.; and he may have used amongst other Roman sources, though he never mentions them, the *Origines* (Books IV and V) of Cato, who fought at Tarentum, at the Metaurus and at Zama. To balance these he had before him the works of (*a*) Sosylus, a Greek who accompanied Hannibal and wrote his life in seven books (Diod. XXV, frag. 6) (one fragment has been discovered describing a sea-battle off Spain, see Wilcken, *Hermes*, XLI, 1900, pp. 103 *sqq.*: it is clear and vivid and one suspects that Polybius' strictures of his account as being merely 'the gossip of the barber's shop' are unfair), (*b*) Chaereas, about whom Polybius is equally contemptuous, III, 20, (*c*) Silenus, another Greek who was with Hannibal on his campaigns; he wrote *Sicelica* and *Historiae*. Cicero, *de div.* I, 24, 49, says of him 'diligentissime res Hannibalis persecutus est.' In what presumably comes from these Greeks, however, no signs of inner knowledge of Carthaginian designs and policy can be traced. Lastly, Polybius had access to Roman archives and the records of private families, and he travelled widely to investigate geography and read inscriptions, *e.g.* at Lacinium.

For events after Cannae we have only fragments of Polybius, *e.g.* VII, 9 the treaty between Philip V and Hannibal; VIII, 3–9, 37 Sardinia and the

It is true that Livy's patriotic bias, moral purpose and rhetorical colour, added to a lack of any real understanding of how wars are waged and battles fought, are immediately perceptible where the crystal stream of Polybius can be used for comparison. Consequently, when Polybius is lacking and Livy becomes almost the only source, extreme caution is needed if we would endeavour to reproduce a narrative of what happened rather than a mirror of the garbled Roman tradition. But Polybius and Livy alike reflect the grandeur of the theme which so captured the imagination of the Romans that even under the Empire 'Should Hannibal have crossed the Alps?' or 'Should Hannibal have marched on Rome after Cannae?' were debated by boys in the schools and by mature rhetoricians. And lastly, apart from the intrinsic military interest of the battles and sieges, apart from the dramatic vividness of the personalities of Hannibal and Scipio Africanus, the war reveals

siege of Syracuse, 26–36 the Siege of Tarentum; IX, 3–7 the siege of Capua and the march on Rome, 22–6 the character of Hannibal (cf. XI, 19); X, 1–20, 34–40 Tarentum and Scipio Africanus in Spain, 32 death of Marcellus; XI, 1–3 Metaurus, 20–33 the conquest of Spain; XIV, 1–10 Scipio in Africa; XV, 1–19 Breach of the Armistice, Zama, Peace.

Livy's narrative of the war is contained in Books XXI–XXX. The problem of his sources is extremely complex. It seems probable to the present writer that to a certain extent he used Polybius direct in Books XXI, XXII, just as there is no question that he used him in the later books of the decade. It is possible that at times he follows Polybius' own sources Fabius, Silenus and Sosylus, though more likely only at second-hand through using Coelius (see below). But the good tradition represented by these sources is frequently contaminated or supplanted by passages from rhetorical and untrustworthy Roman annalists such as Cincius Alimentus, Coelius Antipater, Valerius Antias, Claudius Quadrigarius and others. Of these Coelius (second century B.C.) was the best; he made some attempt to use Fabius, Cato and Silenus, but he was rhetorically minded and no Polybius. In fact, for the war in Italy after Cannae and for much of the narrative of Spain and Africa it is clear that Coelius was Livy's principal source. On the other hand, for Sicily Livy uses Polybius. Lastly, Livy had access to the Roman archives and his lists of legions, generals and prodigies seem to be of unimpeachable authority. See the table of legions and commanders facing p. 104.

Appian's *Iberica, Hannibalica, Libyca*; and the fragments of Dio Cassius with the abridgement of Zonaras are still less trustworthy than Livy. They depend almost entirely upon the tradition represented by the post-Fabian Roman annalists. The fragments of Diodorus XXV–XXVII add very little, though they show some traces of the use of Polybius in addition to the annalists. Plutarch's Lives of Fabius and Marcellus reproduce very nearly the same tradition as Livy, partly through use of Livy himself and partly through the use of Coelius. Almost nothing of value can be found in Cornelius Nepos' *Hannibal*, Florus, Orosius, Eutropius, or the *Bellum Punicum* of Silius Italicus.

the Roman character and the Roman constitution tested in the supreme ordeal by fire.

Though the course of the war testifies to the high qualities of the Romans, its causes and occasions are part of a different picture. The differences extend to the sources: even Polybius was dominated by the Roman literature of justification, and at Carthage a *défaitiste* government towards the close of the war sought not so much to justify the action of Carthage as to shift the responsibility wholly on to the broad shoulders of Hannibal. It is, therefore, no wonder that the meagre and distorted tradition or confusion of traditions about the antecedents of the war has left historians in perplexity about both the events and their true interpretation. The general course of Roman policy in the two decades that followed the close of the First Punic War has been described elsewhere (vol. VII, chap. xxv). It remains to examine more closely the causes of the war, and the manner in which it came about[1].

In 237 B.C. the Romans, with no shadow of right, had forced Carthage to surrender Sardinia and to pay an additional indemnity of 1200 talents. Six years later, when the successes of Hamilcar were extending Punic power in Spain, Roman envoys, probably sent at the instance of Massilia to protest, accepted his assurances that he was seeking the means to pay the indemnity imposed by Rome. Two years later, Hasdrubal succeeded Hamilcar and by diplomacy as much as by arms continued the Carthaginian advance, until, in 226 or 225, the Romans, faced by a war with the Gauls of the Po valley, wished to set some limits to the Carthaginian Empire in Spain. Accordingly, Roman envoys came to an agreement with Hasdrubal which pledged the Carthaginians not to carry their arms north of the Ebro. We may assume that the Ebro instead of the Pyrenees was made the dividing line in order to give protection to the Massiliote colonies of Emporium and Rhode and greater protection to Massilia itself, the ally of Rome. It is to be presumed that Hasdrubal, as Hannibal after him, had with him assessors from the home government[2], and that the agreement was as binding as that made by Hannibal and his assessors later with Philip of Macedon (p. 119), that it was, in fact, a valid treaty[3]. As the Romans were not in a position to impose this limit on Hasdrubal by their simple *fiat*[4], it must be assumed

---

[1] On the paragraphs that follow see the works cited in the Bibliography, especially those of De Sanctis, Ed. Meyer, Täubler, Drachmann and Groag.

[2] Polybius III, 20, 8.

[3] As Polybius describes it, III, 30, 3.

[4] *Ib.* II, 13, 5.

further that they undertook in return not to carry their arms south of the Ebro, or to interfere in the Carthaginian dominion. Saguntum, however, a smallish Iberian town of slight strategical and no great commercial importance a hundred miles south of the river, was already under Roman protection[1], probably brought under it through the agency of Massilia, with which city Saguntum, as her coinage testifies, had close trade relations[2]. It is even possible that Rome had made something like an alliance with Saguntum as early as 231 (vol. VII, p. 809). This alliance was not invalidated by the Ebro treaty, which, however, carried with it the implied obligation on Rome not to use the town as an instrument to hinder Carthaginian expansion within the sphere recognized as open to her.

So long as the war with the Gauls hung in the balance, Rome was careful to respect the treaty and its implications. It is admitted that Carthage in turn had done nothing to injure Saguntum, and, if this was of deliberate policy, it points to the fact that the alliance of the town with Rome was taken account of both after and before the treaty. By 221 B.C. the Romans had proved victorious against the Gauls, and they now intervened at Saguntum to bring into power, not without bloodshed, a party hostile to Carthage and to promote friction with the neighbouring tribe of the Torboletae, who were subjects of the Carthaginians. In fact, after enjoying the benefits of the Ebro treaty, Rome began to use Saguntum as a tool to undermine Punic power south of the river and to loosen the hold of Carthage on the enviable wealth of Spain.

This does not mean that the Senate contemplated bringing about an immediate war. For with the threat of Gallic invasion removed, it probably reckoned on repeating, if need be, in Spain the successful bullying by which Rome had secured Sardinia. And so, late in 220 B.C., envoys were sent to warn Hannibal, who had succeeded Hasdrubal as governor of Carthaginian Spain, not to attack Saguntum, because the town was under the protection of Rome. But neither from Hannibal nor at Carthage, whither

---

[1] Polybius III, 30, 1, says that it was admitted that Saguntum had placed herself under Roman protection πλείοσιν ἔτεσιν ἤδη πρότερον τῶν κατ' Ἀννίβαν καιρῶν, and appears to regard this as definitely earlier than the Roman interference in Saguntine affairs, which (writing of late in 220) he sets μικροῖς ἔμπροσθεν χρόνοις (i.e. about 221). The interval between the two events must at least include the years 225–2, during which Rome could do nothing which might be pleaded as contravening the Ebro treaty, and it would be poor diplomacy to make an alliance with Saguntum at the moment (in 226–5) when Rome was seeking to make the treaty with Hasdrubal.

[2] See A. Schulten in *Phil. Woch.* 1927, col. 1582.

they then went, did they receive the submissive assurances which they probably expected. Finally, in the spring of 219 when Saguntum, relying on Rome, remained intransigent, Hannibal attacked the town, which he took after an eight months' siege. All this time the Romans sent no force to assist the defenders. Both consuls were engaged in Illyria, and the Senate was probably undecided how far their protection of Saguntum should go[1]. When about November 219 news came that the town had fallen, the *patres* took long to decide whether or not to regard it as a *casus belli*. Saguntum was unimportant and distant, and the material interests of Rome, and of Massilia, were protected by the Ebro treaty, which Hannibal showed no sign of violating. Many senators, no doubt, were opposed to embarking on a serious war in the West, particularly at a time when Rome might find herself involved in a conflict with Macedon. On the other hand, Roman prestige was concerned, above all in Spain, and, if Rome took no action, she would find it difficult afterwards to hinder the consolidation of Carthaginian power south of the Ebro.

Finally the plea of prestige, which really meant the claim to interfere effectively in Carthaginian Spain, prevailed, and late in March 218 envoys were sent to Carthage to demand the surrender of Hannibal and of his Carthaginian assessors who had concurred in the attack on Saguntum. The demand was the *rerum repetitio* which, if not complied with, led to formal declaration of war, and the Roman envoys were no doubt authorized to state definitely what would be the result of refusal. The Carthaginian Senate denied—and with justice—that they were under any formal obligation not to attack Saguntum, which was not in the list of Roman allies whom Carthage had pledged herself to respect in the peace of 241 B.C. Since that date Carthage had made no engagement with Rome which could affect her dealings with Saguntum. The purely juridical case was irrefutable. Indeed, Roman apologists were later driven to the expedient of declaring that Saguntum was expressly safeguarded by the Ebro treaty, or even that it lay north of the river. This latter fiction seems to find an echo even in Polybius, and both were served by the assertion that the Carthaginian Senate denied the validity of the Ebro treaty[2]. This assertion is probably the perversion of what may be true, that the Carthaginians limited the discussion to the precise legal point at issue. Carthage then refused the Roman demand, and the Roman envoys

[1] It is not impossible that the argument was used that armed intervention to protect Saguntum would be a breach of the Ebro treaty.
[2] Polybius III, 21.

declared that Carthage was choosing war. Strong as was the legal and indeed moral case for Carthage, because Rome was using Saguntum to undermine her power in Spain, the fact remained that Hannibal had attacked and taken—with the approval of his government—a town which Rome had declared to be under her protection. This is the core of truth in the Roman tradition which sought to convince the legally-minded citizens that the cause of Rome was the cause of justice.

It cannot be said that the war which followed was from the beginning inevitable. The first conflict between Rome and Carthage had not entailed the destruction or subjection of either. The two states could continue to exist side by side in the Western Mediterranean, but only if each was willing to respect the other's sphere of influence. The treaty of 241 B.C. might have formed the basis of some such balance of power as Hellenistic statecraft had reached east of the Adriatic. The foreign policy of Carthage in the previous three centuries is evidence of the paramount importance in her counsels of commercial interests and motives, and it is extremely probable that she would have wished to keep the peace in order to exploit the immense resources of her newly re-acquired and extended province in Spain. Rome, in effective possession of Sicily, might well be content to leave to her the Eldorado of the Spanish mines and Spanish markets. Indeed, had the Roman Senate's policy been sincerely pacific, there is small reason to think that the nobles of the house of Barca, great as was their influence due to the services of Hamilcar in crushing the Mercenaries' revolt and to the political adroitness of Hasdrubal, would have been able to lead her into a war of revenge against Rome. The picture of the Barcids as viceroys in Spain independent of the home government is itself false. Neither Hamilcar, Hasdrubal nor Hannibal was a Wallenstein. They knew themselves to be the generals of a Republic, and their policy had to take account of the views of the Carthaginian ring of aristocrats whose hand was upon the machine of government. Many of these nobles doubtless cared more for their estates in Africa than for the old tradition of commercial and naval supremacy in the Western Mediterranean. In fact, the Carthaginian navy had been allowed to decline, partly, it may be, to avoid the semblance of a challenge to Rome, her successful rival by sea. Yet the home government, which knew well that it was the Spanish mines that had made easy the punctual payment of the indemnity and that opened to Carthage a new hope of commercial prosperity, were not likely to risk Spain for the sake of a war, though they might be ready to risk war for the sake of Spain. Finally, had it been the set purpose of the house of Barca to attack Rome, Hasdrubal would not have made the Ebro treaty, but would have urged Carthage to seize at once an opportunity more favourable than any which was likely to offer itself later[1].

The 'wrath of the house of Barca' and 'the revenge of Hannibal' belong mainly to a Roman tradition which obscures, and was meant to obscure, the extent to which the Roman seizure of Sardinia and her interference in Spain drove Carthage to war. Nor does the tradition sufficiently emphasize the effect of Massiliote diplomacy in urging Rome to challenge the eastward expansion of Carthage in Spain which, it is true, menaced the trade, if not the security, of Massilia. The Roman claim to forbid Hannibal to attack Saguntum showed that the Senate had no intention of binding itself by the implications of the Ebro treaty, and Carthage might well feel that Roman aggression which had advanced by way of Sardinia might pass by way of Saguntum to Nova Carthago and even to Africa itself. The process might be slow. Rome's policy at this time was not consistently imperialistic: it was often vacillating, timid, inert, but her malignity, in which now fear, now jealousy, now arrogant self-confidence, now greed of wealth and power was dominant, must have seemed beyond question. It is true that it was Hannibal's attack on Saguntum, undertaken in full knowledge of the almost inevitable consequences, that precipitated the war, but the historian must decide that, so far as attack and defence have a meaning in the clash between states, the balance of aggression must incline against Rome.

The legend that the war sprang from the ambition or revengefulness of Hannibal is one with the legend that Carthage was not behind him when in 220/19 he refused to be turned aside by the menaces of the Senate. Fabius Pictor declared that none of the substantial citizens of Carthage approved of Hannibal's action at Saguntum[2], but this is contradicted by the whole course of events and must be regarded as the self-deception of a Roman at war, turned to the purposes of propaganda. That at Carthage, despite a just resentment of Rome's actions, there were nobles jealous of the house of Barca, or men who believed that Carthage should seek to placate where she could not perhaps hope to conquer, is doubtless true. But Hannibal had acted with the full knowledge

---

[1] See on these points in particular E. Groag, *Hannibal als Politiker*, pp. 42 *sqq.*

[2] *Ap.* Polybius III, 8, 7.

and approval of the home government, he was the chosen general of the finest army and the governor of the richest province of Carthage, and to disown him and his assessors was to divide the State in the face of an enemy whose forbearance could not be trusted. Hannibal himself could not be lightly surrendered to Roman vengeance, even though the full measure of his greatness in the field had not as yet revealed itself to Carthage, much less to Rome. At the age of twenty-six he had succeeded his kinsman Hasdrubal in Spain (221 B.C.). To the diplomatic skill of his predecessor he added his father Hamilcar's unbending spirit and a double portion of his father's energy and generalship. Schooled in arms from boyhood, he had behind him the fruits of long experience in the handling of the mercenaries and levies that made up the mass of the Carthaginian armies. The siege of Saguntum showed him a worthy namesake of the conqueror of Selinus and Himera, and two lightning campaigns in Central Spain had confirmed his innate consciousness of a genius for command. We may well believe that the Carthaginian government had already recognized that this was the moment and the man. If Carthage was to remain secure and untroubled in the enjoyment of her commerce and of Spain she must defend herself resolutely, and to Hannibal the best defence was attack.

Herein lay the responsibility of Hannibal, not for the fact that the war happened—granted that Rome would one day set before Carthage the choice of war or the steady undermining of its power—but for the moment of its happening. Rome's intrigues from Saguntum could be permitted for a time without serious loss; Hannibal decided to force the issue at once, and this he did on the basis of a military calculation which was probably his alone, for the essence of it was secrecy. It was enough that the Carthaginian Senate should be convinced of the need of an immediate defensive war and assured that its young general could make it not entirely hopeless.

The Roman Senate, in its turn, must have realized that the demands which its envoys took to Carthage in 218 were certain to be refused, and it prepared for the conflict with a leisurely confidence that was the legacy of victory and of the proved superiority of her legionaries in the First Punic War. In the previous year the consuls had disposed of Demetrius of Pharos and so secured the protectorate in Illyria (vol. VII, p. 848), and the Senate might hope that the war with Carthage would be over before Philip V of Macedon, now entangled in war with the Aetolians and Sparta, would be free to translate his unconcealed hostility

into action. In Northern Italy the Gauls had been defeated, and
before midsummer 218[1] two Latin colonies, Placentia and Cremona, were settled to watch the Boii and Insubres (vol. VII, p. 815),
in addition to which there were also garrisoned posts such as
Clastidium and Tannetum. The situation seemed secure, though
in reality Hannibal's agents must already have been at work
among the tribesmen assuring them of an ally and deliverer from
beyond the Alps. And so, when early in 218 the returning envoys
brought information of the existence of Carthaginian intrigues in
North Italy, the Senate saw in that no more than an attempt to
embarrass their plans by a Gallic movement; a single legion was
deemed sufficient to make all safe, while the consuls of the year
opened campaigns in Spain and in Africa.

II. THE RIVAL WAR-PLANS

The consuls for 218 B.C., P. Cornelius Scipio and Ti. Sempronius Longus, were provided with the customary consular
armies of two legions each. Scipio's army was made up of 8000
Roman legionaries and 600 Roman cavalry with 14,000 allied
infantry and 1600 allied cavalry and a fleet of 60 ships. Sempronius' army received an additional 2000 allied infantry and 200
allied cavalry, and to him was allotted the major portion of the
fleet, 160 quinqueremes. From the size and disposition of these
forces it is possible to make a fairly certain estimate of the Senate's
intended plan of campaign against Hannibal. Scipio's army was to
sail to Massilia; from this secure base, ensuring good communication with Italy, the invasion of Spain north of the Ebro must have
seemed to promise good hopes of success. Caution and concerted
but carefully prepared advance are the keynotes of this strategy.
The other army under Sempronius was dispatched to Sicily and
was designed to invade Africa. Records of Agathocles' invasion
(vol. VII, pp. 624 *sqq.*) and the initial success of Regulus (*ib.*
p. 682 *sq.*) would have left the Roman senators with no doubt
about the vulnerability of Carthage in Africa, and the Roman
naval supremacy, which had been maintained by steady building
since the First Punic War, enabled Rome to choose her own time
for the invasion. But an army of two legions was not large enough
to reduce Carthage without the help of allies in Africa and it is
possible that the first year was to see a base secured, and that a
serious invasion with a larger army would follow in 217 B.C. The
Roman prospects seemed very fair indeed and in complacent

[1] Asconius, p. 3. Clark, adopting Madvig's emendation *Kal. Iun.* for
Kal. Ian.

confidence the Roman Republic mobilized only five legions out of the vast resources of man-power latent in Italy.

It remains to be seen how strategy dictated by methodical care and experience fared against the rapidity and daring of a great general. Hannibal's strategy was at once political and military. The past afforded no clear refutation of the hope that the Roman political system in Italy might be broken up by the presence of a victorious enemy in the peninsula. Pyrrhus had won two battles, and then Rome had gone near to making peace with him (vol. VII, p. 648). A Carthaginian might well suppose that it was only Carthaginian promises of help that had prevented the Republic from yielding. Some of Rome's allies at that time had deserted her, and a greater Pyrrhus might succeed where he had failed. In the generations that followed Pyrrhus the Italians had been bled white in Rome's quarrels, so that a Carthaginian might well fail to recognize that Rome had by now proved herself to her allies by leadership and fair dealing and had roused a national Italian spirit in the repulse of the barbarian Gauls. In the First Punic War Carthage had never been able to strike home, for she could not find a secure base in Italy nor feel confidence that her armies would win victory in the field. But if these two conditions were fulfilled, it must have seemed a reasonable calculation that Rome might be brought to make a peace which would undo the effects of the First Punic War. Of the two conditions the first might be fulfilled in the adhesion of the Gauls, who were hostile to Rome but not yet completely crushed. To wait two or three years might allow Rome to be entangled in a war with Macedon, but by then the certainty of Gaulish help might be far smaller. Politically, this was the moment to strike if the second condition, a high probability of victory in the open field, was fulfilled. The military problem was threefold, to concentrate a strong and faithful army, to bring it into Italy, and to discover tactics which would counterbalance the Roman superiority in numbers.

By the spring of 218 the first part of the military problem had been solved. After the fall of Saguntum Hannibal had spent the winter in final preparations at Nova Carthago and by granting special furlough nursed the loyalty of his army. Commanded by Carthaginian nobles, the army which re-assembled in March 218 B.C. was a veteran army and not, like many earlier Carthaginian armies, a haphazard collection of mercenaries engaged at short notice for a particular campaign. The African subjects and allies of Carthage provided the unequalled light Numidian cavalry and also the heavy infantry which bore the brunt of Hannibal's battles. The

Spanish mercenaries and levies were good fighting stock, inured to hardships and peculiarly adapted by character and experience to ruses, ambushes and stratagems. Lastly, the whole army was hardened by the discipline and inspired by the loyalty of long service. Such an instrument had been bequeathed to Hannibal as to Alexander, and it lay ready to his hand to direct against the enemy which, it was evident, was bent on the destruction of his country.

The quality of the army is beyond question; its size it is more difficult to estimate. Rome had the command of the sea and that meant that both Spain and Africa must be held in sufficient strength to prevent any rapid Roman successes in either region. Forces amounting to 20,000 men were detailed for Africa; in Spain Hannibal's brother Hasdrubal was given 12,000 infantry, 3000 cavalry and 21 elephants[1], and later Hanno was stationed with 11,000 men north of the Ebro. Polybius (iii, 35, 1) says that the forces with which Hannibal set out from Nova Carthago amounted to 90,000 infantry and 12,000 cavalry, and that he left Spain itself with 50,000 foot and 9000 horse. Neither of these statements is free from exaggeration[2]. What Hannibal expected the march to Italy to cost him we cannot tell, but he probably reckoned on being stronger in the field than Pyrrhus had been, and on being able to recruit Gauls in Italy to make up losses incurred on the way. On the other hand, he knew he had to face the greatest difficulties of commissariat and it is probable that the army with which he left Spain did not number more than 40,000 men.

The Carthaginian navy of rather more than a hundred sail (of which fifty quinqueremes, two quadriremes and five triremes were left with Hasdrubal) was no match for the Roman; it was needed to help the defence of Spain and Africa and to keep open communications between the two; the battle of the Aegates islands had taught an unforgettable lesson of the danger of transporting

[1] These figures Polybius (iii, 33) derived from the record left by Hannibal at the Lacinian promontory. Detailed items are given, presumably to prove beyond doubt that Hannibal did not sacrifice the defence of Spain and Africa to the invasion of Italy. From the same source is derived the number of troops with which he entered Italy (p. 38).

[2] He is represented as losing 33,000 out of 59,000 between the Pyrenees and Italy: these figures have not apparently the authority of the Lacinian inscription behind them and may be regarded as reached by adding computed losses to the well-attested 26,000 with whom Hannibal entered Italy. The losses and therefore the original numbers of the army are exaggerated by Polybius or his source.

a large army by sea, and there was no safe landing-place in Italy. Military and political reasons combined to compel him to invade Italy by land and to appear among the Gauls whom Rome had made her enemies. Finally, as will be seen, Hannibal, who had no doubt deeply studied the military history of Alexander and his successors, together with the reports of the tactics of the Romans, had devised methods by which his superiority in cavalry and the capacity for manœuvre which his veterans had learned, could be used to make victory in a pitched battle almost certain.

To Polybius, with his statistics of Roman man-power[1], his consciousness of the strength of the Roman political system and most of all, his knowledge of the event, Hannibal's invasion of Italy was a desperate though splendid adventure. But as a political and military calculation on such evidence as Hannibal can well have had, it contained no more hazardous factors than any other course open to him. Nor was its least advantage the fact that it was a wholly effective defence against the Roman plan of attack which he foresaw. As will be seen, the Roman project of a simultaneous invasion of Africa and Spain had to be abandoned; Carthage was given time to raise a coalition against Rome and even though the coalition failed to achieve its ends, final defeat was postponed for sixteen years.

III. HANNIBAL'S MARCH TO ITALY

In the spring of 218, not earlier than the beginning of May, Hannibal set out from Nova Carthago. His start was late, not because he need wait for war to be declared before marching to the Ebro, but probably in order to allow the spring flooding of the Spanish rivers to subside so that he could ford them easily instead of having to bridge them. Once he had moved he must march at speed. It was, however, to take him five months to reach the valley of the Po—a longer time than he presumably expected. The task of forcing the passes of the Eastern Pyrenees and brushing aside the resistance of the Gallic tribes who were allied with Massilia cost him dearly in casualties and deserters, and he did not reach the Rhone until towards the end of August. Here he might have found himself already faced by a Roman army, had not a rising in the spring of the Boii and Insubres in North Italy, which began with the ambush of the legion set to guard the newly founded colonies, caused the Senate to dispatch thither Scipio's two legions under a praetor, leaving Scipio to raise a new

---

[1] II, 24. 700,000 foot and 70,000 horse (Romans and allies) in 225 B.C.

consular army for his expedition to Spain. We may fairly assume that the rising was timed by Hannibal's agents. Even so, the consul reached Massilia while the Carthaginian army was still just west of the Rhone. There seems to be no doubt that Scipio did not realize Hannibal's purpose; possibly he believed that it was to gain allies among the barbarians for an attack on Massilia which, if successful, would rob the Romans of their half-way house to Spain. He, accordingly, remained near the city and merely sent a force of cavalry with some Celtic mercenaries in the service of Massilia to observe the enemy's movements.

Hannibal arrived at the Rhone at a point four days' march from the sea and found the opposite bank of the river soon thronged by large numbers of hostile tribes prepared to oppose his passage. Though well provided with wherries by friendly tribes he yet judged after two days' halt that to force a crossing in view of the numbers of the enemy would be a hazardous undertaking attended by severe losses. Accordingly on the next day he sent Hanno with local guides and a force of cavalry twenty-five miles up stream. Building rough rafts they crossed where the river was divided by an islet and rested. Then on the fifth day they rode down the far bank of the stream. Hannibal meanwhile had completed his preparations and had constructed special rafts to carry over his elephants. When in the afternoon a column of smoke arising in the distance on the far shore announced that his manœuvre was complete he gave orders for the army to cross. The barbarians who lined the river seeing their encampments fired in their rear by a detachment of Hanno's force broke in flight and Hannibal completed the crossing without loss. Immediately after this Scipio's scouting force fell in with a Numidian rearguard. They won a slight success in a skirmish but it was small consolation for the sight of Hannibal's deserted camp and the knowledge that he had safely crossed the Rhone. By a narrow margin Hannibal missed a pitched battle with the Roman army. Scipio marched north to investigate and arrived at Hannibal's camp three days after he had left for the Alps.

Hannibal's crossing of the Alps has stirred the imagination and provoked the discussion of succeeding ages—

I demens et saevas curre per Alpes
ut pueris placeas et declamatio fias.

It is impossible to determine with any approach to certainty which pass he chose[1]. The accounts of Livy and Polybius conflict and

[1] It is generally agreed that the limits within which the pass must lie are the Little St Bernard and the Mt Genèvre.

are vague, making the identification of topographical features impossible. Both contain much rhetorical colouring such as the absurd story of the view of the plains of Italy from the top of the pass[1]. The problem, intriguing as it is, is not to be solved *ambulando*, and even if it were solved, we have not the necessary data to relate Hannibal's choice to his strategy or to estimate its wisdom.

The feat of crossing the Alps was in itself nothing remarkable, as Napoleon noted—'*les éléphants seuls ont pu lui donner de l'embarras*[2].' Indeed, whole tribes of Celts with their women-folk and children had crossed in the summer by the passes farther east into the north of Italy (see vol. VII, pp. 61 *sqq.*). Hannibal's difficulties were in the first place military, owing to the hostility of the Allobroges—difficulties which beset armies marching in column in narrow defiles—but more important was the fact that it was now past the first week of September, and a heavy fall of new snow made the descent on the southern side particularly hazardous for the transport and the elephants. Polybius' picturesque description of the difficulty of crossing hard avalanche snow covered by this new melting layer is vivid, and bears the stamp of painful experience perhaps recorded by Silenus. But it seems certain that a month earlier the pass could have been crossed without these added risks and dangers, and one is left to surmise that Hannibal had been too long delayed by the resistance offered north of the Ebro till August, or was misled by false information about the Alpine passes. His losses in the Alps were such that he arrived in Italy with no more than 20,000 foot and 6000 horse.

IV. THE TICINUS AND TREBIA

About a month had passed since Hannibal crossed the Rhone, and now he marched on the chief town of the Taurini (the modern Turin), who were hostile to the Insubres and so to the Carthaginians. The weak fortifications of a Gallic town in the plains were taken after three days, and the massacre of the fighting men in the garrison conveniently proved Hannibal to be a bad enemy to those who would not accept him as a friend. But more important for the purpose of winning over the Gauls was to defeat the Romans in the field, and Hannibal advanced to seek an opportunity. He probably knew that he had to meet the two legions which the Senate had sent to North Italy, and the Gauls soon informed him that the Roman forces were marching west from

[1] Polybius III, 54; Livy XXI, 35. [2] *Commentaries*, VI, p. 163 (Ed. Paris, 1867).

Placentia. He was, however, surprised to find that Publius Scipio was in command, having travelled nearly 1000 miles by land and sea in little more than a month.

His presence was possible because he had come alone. Faced by the fact that Hannibal's objective was Italy, he had taken the momentous decision to send his army and part of the fleet with his brother Gnaeus to invade Spain, while he himself returned to Italy to take command of the troops which would face Hannibal as he came down from the Alps. His action has been interpreted as being no more than a reasonable carrying out of his instructions from the Senate, combined with the wish to be at the disposal of the State for any service which the changed strategical position demanded. He could not be condemned by the Senate for carrying out their instructions so far as his army was concerned, nor for getting into touch with them for new instructions which could be sent to him in northern Etruria as he traversed it on his way to North Italy. It is no doubt true that the Senate did approve his action, and the desire for the Senate's approval may have been his dominating motive. But the energy of his movements and the strategic skill which he displayed now and later suggest that he returned to guide the Senate's policy rather than to be guided by it, and that the decision to go forward with the expedition to Spain was truly his own and dictated by a far-sighted appreciation of what the interests of Rome demanded.

The decision has been impeached by those who, regarding the Italian front as all-important, urge that he should have brought his army with him in order that he and his colleague might confront the invader with a superior force. If Hannibal were defeated, Spain would fall of itself. The first answer to this criticism is that Scipio might hope to engage Hannibal before his troops were rested and reinforced by Gauls, if he himself did not sacrifice the time needed to move his army from the Rhone to the Po. His calculation was refuted by the speed with which, though at a great cost, Hannibal crossed the Alps, but that fact does not prove that the calculation was not the best possible. The second and more decisive answer was that a Roman army north of the Ebro would weaken Hannibal in Italy by denying to him reinforcements from Spain. There was no fear that Hannibal would be south of the Apennines before the year ended, and neither Scipio nor the Senate had any reason to doubt that in the spring of 217 Rome would have enough troops to deal with any situation in Italy which they could imagine. But a footing in Spain must be secured without delay.

By this time Sempronius had concentrated his 26,400 men at
Lilybaeum with the fleet to cover their crossing. In that region
operations had so far been by sea, for the Carthaginians sought to
take advantage of the slow mobilization of the Roman main force.
While Sempronius was still in Italy they sent 20 ships to raid
Southern Italy, while 35 more were to attempt to surprise Lilybaeum, then held by the praetor Aemilius with a squadron of
perhaps as many ships. Three of the 20 ships were captured off
Messana owing to a storm, the remainder carried out a raid on
Vibo and then escaped home. Warned by their prisoners the
Romans informed Aemilius, who beat off the Carthaginian attack,
capturing seven ships. These minor operations attested the naval
superiority of the Romans and, incidentally, the loyalty of Hiero
the king of Syracuse who though ninety years of age was un-
resting in the support of Rome. Sempronius himself, as a counter-
stroke, sailed to the island of Malta and captured it with its
Carthaginian garrison[1]. As he prepared to set out for Africa
with enough ships to brush aside the remnant of the Carthaginian
navy, he may well have thought that it was simply the First Punic
War again in miniature. But then came from Rome a message of
recall.

News had reached Rome from Scipio that Hannibal had crossed
the Rhone and was marching to the Alps and that the consul's
army was being sent on to Spain. Word was at once sent to
inform Sempronius so that he might transfer his army to North
Italy. The Senate was well aware that the troops already in the
Po valley were no more than enough to make head against the
Gauls alone. The Senate's despatch must have reached Sempronius about the time that Hannibal was entering Italy[2]. The
consul acted forthwith. Aemilius with 50 ships at Lilybaeum was
left to cover Sicily while Sext. Pomponius with 25 protected Vibo
and Southern Italy. The army was moved, perhaps by sea, from
Lilybaeum to the Straits of Messina and thence marched in less
than two months the seven hundred miles to Ariminum[3], whither

[1] Livy xxi, 49–51. These operations are not mentioned by Polybius, but
are not inconsistent with his account, and they seem entirely credible.
[2] Polybius III, 61, 9 states that the Senate's despatch informed Sempronius of the presence of the enemy. There is, however, no good reason
why the Senate should wait till Hannibal had entered Italy. No doubt the
letter ran 'has crossed the Rhone and will by now be in Italy,' as Livy
xxi, 51, 5 *de transitu in Italiam Hannibalis*. See De Sanctis, *Storia dei Romani*,
III, 2, p. 85.
[3] Polybius III, 61, which implies that the army marched in small detachments. Its rapid concentration at Ariminum attests the discipline and stamina

the consul transferred his headquarters. Towards the end of November he was able to march on to join his colleague. The two consuls might then either fight a battle, if victory seemed probable, or hold their hand, knowing that winter would protect Central Italy from immediate invasion.

Scipio, meanwhile, with forces amounting to about 20,000 infantry and 2000 cavalry set himself to his task of limiting as far as possible the enemy's progress. Crossing the Po at Placentia, he advanced along the north bank to the Ticinus across which he threw a bridge of boats. Leaving his legions in a camp made on the west of the river he pushed forward with his cavalry and some light-armed troops to reconnoitre as far, perhaps, as the modern Lomello, but he did not cross the Sesia. Here in the country, still to this day screened by light scrub and trees, a cloud of dust gave the first indication of the enemy's presence. It was the cavalry covering Hannibal's advance. Scipio cannot have wished to commit himself to a conflict against odds, but the superior speed of the enemy's horse forced an engagement in which nightfall alone saved him. Scipio himself was wounded, and he only escaped death or capture through the bravery of his son, who thus dramatically enters the stage of the war[1].

Retreating under cover of night, Scipio moved his army across the bridge, breaking it down after him only just in time, for the Carthaginian cavalry came up at once and captured the detachment left to cover the work of destruction. He had done well to withdraw his army without greater losses, but he realized that he must now escape from the open country north of the Po and wait for his colleague's arrival. Yet he did not wish to leave to Hannibal all the Celts west of Placentia. Accordingly he crossed the Po by the Placentia bridge and pushed forward to the strategic position of the Stradella[2], which gave him security against the enemy's cavalry and covered his communications with Placentia some twenty miles away.

Hannibal, divining his opponent's intention, crossed to the south bank near the modern Tortona after marching two days up

of the Roman troops. Livy (XXI, 51, 6) sends it by sea direct. The account of Polybius, apart from his forty days, is inherently more probable in view of the hazards of the Adriatic in November. The part of the Roman fleet no longer needed, and the transports, were presumably dismissed.

[1] This was, at least, the family tradition of the Scipios (Polybius X, 3). Livy (XXI, 46, 10) cites Coelius for a rival version in which the credit is given to a Ligurian slave.

[2] Its strategic value was noted by Napoleon. This position appears to be the most probable despite περὶ πόλιν Πλακεντίαν in Polybius III, 66, 9.

stream to make sure of an unchallenged or easier crossing. He then turned eastwards again and on reaching Scipio's new position encamped and offered battle. Scipio refused it, and his refusal convinced the Gauls in his army that it was time to abandon the losing side. In the night, after killing their Roman officers, they went over to the Carthaginians. This blow forced Scipio to withdraw behind the Trebia, the stream which joins the Po from the south just west of Placentia. The withdrawal was skilfully conducted, but its success owed something to the avidity with which the Numidian cavalry turned aside to plunder the deserted Roman camp. The Gallic tribes hastened to take the Carthaginian side, and to bring in supplies, which were presently augmented by the betrayal to Hannibal of the Roman store depôt at Clastidium, 26 miles west of Placentia. Scipio's new position on the Trebia was well chosen for defence and here he was able to nurse his wound and restore the morale of his troops. Hannibal meanwhile advanced and encamped on the opposite western bank of the Trebia, and, probably by design, made no attempt to hinder the arrival of Sempronius' army.

Sempronius arrived, and a success in a skirmish emboldened him to accept the battle which his adversary desired. After laying a skilful ambush, Hannibal sent his Numidians across the stream to harry the Roman camp. Contrary to the judgment of his colleague Sempronius led the four legions, some Gallic auxiliaries and about 4000 cavalry, against Hannibal's army, which now numbered about 38,000 of whom some 10,000 were cavalry. On a December morning[1] breakfastless the legionaries waded waist-high across the icy stream to fight with their backs to the river on ground chosen by the enemy. Hannibal's few elephants and cavalry drove back the Roman wings, while his brother and Mago fell upon the rear of the centre from the ambush. All happened as Hannibal had planned, except that the Celts who formed the centre of the Carthaginian line were not strong enough to prevent 10,000 Romans from breaking through and reaching Placentia by recrossing a bridge over the Trebia near the town[2]. The rest of the Roman army was driven into the river.

[1] The election of Flaminius for 217 presumably followed the battle, which therefore cannot be later than December.

[2] Polybius, it is true, makes no mention of this crossing under the walls of Placentia and under cover of its garrison as being perhaps too obvious. Mommsen's account (see Bibliography) is still the best statement of the case. Livy's *recto itinere* (XXI, 56, 3) is only true of his own reversed account of the battle.

It was a disaster, for all that Sempronius described it as a battle in which the weather had robbed the Romans of victory[1]. The combined armies of the two consuls had been defeated with the loss of at least two-thirds of their strength. Hannibal's casualties were almost entirely Gauls, and were more than compensated by the accession of those Celts who had so far followed the fortunes of Rome. At the same time Placentia afforded a safe shelter for the remnants of the Roman army, and it was represented at Rome that the legionaries of the centre had once more proved their superiority by cutting their way through the enemy's line. The Senate rewarded the services of Scipio, to whom no blame attached for the battle of the Trebia, by prolonging his *imperium* and sending him to Spain. Meanwhile winter protected Central Italy from attack.

V. TRASIMENE

The Roman people, though their confidence in the legions was unshaken, had too good an instinct for war to be content with the campaign of 218, and at the consular elections they chose, together with Cn. Servilius Geminus, their favourite, C. Flaminius. Six years before, he had returned victorious over the Insubres, and the people, despite the Senate's opposition, had voted him a triumph, ignoring or refusing to credit hostile rumours that the valour of the legions and the skill of the military tribunes had alone covered his military incompetence (vol. VII, p. 814). Since that day, his reputation and popularity had increased rapidly. His censorship in 220 had been marked by a new census and the beginning of the great road to Ariminum. Further, he had been the only senator to support a Lex Claudia (*c.* 218 B.C.) restricting senators from maritime trade. This action enrolled in his support the increasing body of middle-class merchants. But it was a moment fraught with danger to the Roman state and commoner in Greece than in Rome when, at a crisis, a general was elected by a popular majority on the grounds of his political acumen and devotion to the interests of a class rather than for his proved military experience and ability.

According to the hostile tradition which Livy has preserved, he neglected to observe the customary religious ceremonies. If the account is not falsified, as is certainly the case with the story of his entering on his consulship at Ariminum[2], it is beyond doubt

---

[1] Polybius III, 75, 1.

[2] Livy XXI, 63 (a chapter from annalistic sources hostile to Flaminius) conflicts with Polybius' plain statement in III, 77, 1.

that senatorial opposition was so bitter that even if he had not
acted thus, the *patres* would have used every obstruction derived
from the religious machinery to prevent him from exercising
his command, as they had sought to do in 223 B.C. (vol. VII,
p. 813 *sq.*). Political dissension was accompanied by a severe
outbreak of popular superstition. Livy's list of prodigies copied
from the pontifical records, including a phantom navy seen in
the sky and an ox which climbed to the third storey of a house,
is an interesting document of war fever and an indication of the
crass superstition of the populace.

For the campaign of 217 Rome disposed of eleven legions[1], at
least 100,000 men including the allied contingents. Two of these
legions were in Spain, four were to meet Hannibal in the field,
while two were in reserve at Rome, two in Sicily and one in
Sardinia. The defeated army of the Po strengthened to two legions
was taken over at Ariminum, to which it had retired, by the new
consul Cn. Servilius, while Flaminius with two newly-raised
legions marched to Arretium in Etruria. The Senate had decided
not to meet Hannibal in the plains of the Po, where his cavalry
could move freely and where the Gauls were an added danger[2].
The colonies of Cremona and Placentia were left to their own
resources, since Hannibal had not the siege-train for an assault
or the time for a protracted blockade. The Roman plan of campaign was to defend Central Italy, supported by loyal allies and
with assured supplies. The details of the plan were conditioned
by the mountain barrier which sweeps in a semicircle from
Liguria to the backbone of Central Italy. Hannibal might elect
to choose the normal route into Italy skirting the north side of
this barrier by the Po valley to Ravenna, and then along the

---

[1] See De Sanctis, *op. cit.* III, 2, p. 116 and Kahrstedt, *Gesch. der Karthager*,
III, p. 405. That Flaminius had only two legions follows from the topography
of Trasimene; Polybius III, 86, 3 assigns to Servilius 4000 cavalry, which
suggests four legions rather than two. But other considerations make it
more probable that he had only two (see De Sanctis, *ad loc.*), and we must
assume that Servilius' cavalry was strengthened perhaps from the Cenomani,
who remained faithful, and the Veneti. The error of Polybius may be
attributed to an equivocal use of στρατόπεδον in his Greek source. See
P. Cantalupi in *Studi di Storia Antica*, I, pp. 10, 69.

[2] The operations of the winter described in Livy XXI, 57–9 are to be
regarded as fictitious. See O. Seeck in *Hermes*, VII, pp. 152 *sqq.* His cavalry
battle at Victumulae is an obvious doublet of Ticinus; Hannibal's attempt
to cross the Apennines in mid-winter is fantastic; the drawn battle before
Placentia probably goes back to Sempronius' account of the Trebia which
an annalist may be forgiven for failing to recognize.

Adriatic as far as Ariminum, where first there is an easy break-through by the Furlo pass and the route of the Via Flaminia. It was to guard against this possibility that Servilius was sent to Ariminum.

On the other hand, there were several though more difficult passes direct from the Po valley into Etruria, and Flaminius was sent to Arretium to block the most southerly of these. The Roman division of forces has been severely criticized, and at first sight it is difficult to see why Ariminum should be held, if the Po valley were abandoned. But the Metaurus campaign later will show how suited this area is for crushing an invading army where the mountains come close down to the Adriatic and the lateral valleys have no exits. It was also traditional Roman policy to operate with small armies commanded by independent consuls and the application of this policy had recently proved successful against Gallic armies invading from the north (vol. VII, p. 812 *sq.*). Finally, popular sentiment was too strong to allow any further abandonment of territory. Thus the plan of defence was to block both sides of the Apennines at the risk of leaving the two armies, with no communication and liable to be defeated in detail. But it was possible that, if all went well, Hannibal might end by being caught between the two, as the Gauls had been at Telamon.

Hannibal intended to invade Central Italy once he had raised in revolt the Po valley. In the winter he had moved to Bologna; this left it hard for the Romans to decide whether he would march down the Po valley or cut through the Apennines. So soon as he got news that the passes were clear of snow[1], he crossed the Apennines, probably on the route Bologna-Porretta-Pistoia by the pass of Collina (3040 feet)[2], in order to surprise Flaminius at Arretium. Between Pistoia and Florence very great difficulties were experienced owing to marshes formed by the melting snows and flooded Arno. Polybius (III, 79) describes from a Carthaginian source the horrors of four days and three sleepless nights; Hannibal himself, mounted on the one elephant that had survived the winter, pushed on despite a severe inflammation which destroyed the sight of one of his eyes. But his iron frame and

[1] On the chronology see De Sanctis, *op. cit.* III, 2, pp. 119 *sqq.* Ovid, *Fasti*, VI, 765–8 (reading *quintus*) gives June 21st as the date of Trasimene, which is approximately correct. The news reached Greece in July (vol. VII, p. 854).

[2] For the topography see Kromayer, *Antike Schlachtfelder*, III, pp. 110 *sqq.* De Sanctis, *op. cit.* III, 2, pp. 104 *sqq.* It must be assumed that there were then marshes between Pistoia and Florence.

unyielding spirit enabled him almost at once to take the field.

The campaign which Hannibal now conducted exhibits in the highest degree his audacity of conception and masterly co-ordination of accurate topographical appreciation with insight into his adversary's character. It is probable that he had intelligence that one Roman army had been sent to Ariminum before he crossed the Apennines. Now, when his troops had been rested after the crossing of the marshes he sought to exploit the headstrong nature of Flaminius, his immediate opponent. He first endeavoured to entice him into a battle in the plain by marching past Arretium, exposing his flank and ravaging far and wide the luxuriant Roman allied territory. When this lure failed—a fact which proves that Flaminius was not the utterly incompetent and rash general which Livy's hostile sources make him out to be—Hannibal set a far subtler trap. For from the information of his cavalry scouts and perhaps of Etruscan peasants who knew the district, he must have formed a remarkably accurate estimation of the terrain. He knew that Servilius would be hastening south in response to urgent messages from his colleague. Consequently with consummate audacity he deliberately placed his own army between the two Roman armies, making it almost certain that Flaminius would follow him. Instead of marching on Rome[1], he turned due east, disappearing in front of Flaminius by a narrow defile (Borghetto) along the north shore of Lake Trasimene.

Inside this defile[2] the mountains lie back from the lake leaving a small enclosed plain five miles long until they come down again at Montigeto. Nature never designed a better theatre for a battle, and Hannibal proceeded before nightfall to prepare the stage. He placed his light cavalry and Gallic troops along the foothills back from Borghetto to enclose the Roman column when it had entered. His light-armed Balearic troops were to occupy the steep hill where it approached the lake at the other end of the plain. He himself with his African and Spanish troops held the central hills. Meanwhile Flaminius had halted long enough to lose touch with Hannibal and, without reconnoitring the route, he followed him through the narrow pass of Borghetto into the enclosed plain early in the morning while a heavy mist effectually screened the hills from view. His whole army marched in column into the small plain before Hannibal gave the signal for attack. The sur-

[1] Polybius III, 82, 9 merely illustrates that writer's weak geographical orientation.

[2] See map 3 and note 2, p. 709.

prise was complete, and the battle was decided before a blow was struck. Hannibal had achieved one of the most remarkable coups in the history of warfare.

The valour of the Roman legionaries prolonged the fighting for two or three hours and Flaminius fell, fighting bravely, by the hand of a Gaul. A body of 6000 men in the van cut through the Carthaginian troops near Montigeto and pushed on to the rising ground behind Passignano, but they were later surrounded and forced to surrender. Hannibal's losses were small and fell mainly on the Gauls. Whatever the exact number of the killed and prisoners[1], Hannibal had put out of action a complete Roman army of two legions. The Roman allies were ostentatiously given their freedom, being told that Hannibal's quarrel was with Rome alone. When the news reached Rome it was impossible to deceive the people and concoct a victory, as had been done after Trebia. The praetor assembled the people and announced with Roman bluntness 'we have been defeated in a great battle.'

Meanwhile Hannibal by brilliant reconnaissance was continually informed of the movements of Servilius' army. He learned that Servilius' cavalry 4000 strong had been sent on ahead under C. Centenius. Detaching from his own cavalry a sufficient force under Maharbal, he sent him beyond Perugia perhaps into the valley of the Topino near Assisi. Centenius was surprised, half his force was destroyed, and the remainder surrendered[2].

The route lay open for Hannibal to march on Rome. But he had never deceived himself by hopes of capturing the city. His plan of war was to force the proud city to make peace, by confronting her with a victorious enemy marching at will through her lands, supported by the general revolt of her allies and subject cities. He had good precedents for the success of such strategy in Carthaginian history. He would be a new Agathocles in Italy. Consequently he immediately crossed the Apennines to Picenum and arrived ten days later[3] at the Adriatic coast, where in the rich

[1] Polybius (III, 84, 7 and 85, 2) gives 15,000 killed, 15,000 prisoners. Livy (XXII, 7, 2) 15,000 dead, 10,000 escaped and 6000 taken prisoners (XXII, 6, 8). The Roman army cannot well have numbered more than 25,000 men, of whom few can have escaped death or capture.
[2] Polybius III, 86, Livy XXII, 8 agreeing substantially. Appian, Hann. 9, 11 is a confusion of this battle of C. Centenius with that of M. Centenius in Lucania in 212 B.C. (Livy xxv, 19), L. Pareti, Riv. Fil. XL, p. 413, n. 4. Precisely where the engagement happened must remain pure conjecture.
[3] Polybius III, 86, 8 suggests Silenus as the source. This leaves no time for an attack on Spoletium (Livy XXII, 9, 1) about which Polybius is silent. Pareti, Kromayer and Kahrstedt rightly reject it. To deviate south to

well-watered land his army could plunder at will and rest amid plenty after the strenuous spring campaign. From Picenum he moved south into Apulia traversing all the richest territory on the east of the Apennines. Although he met with no resistance, it is clear that there was no revolt in Hannibal's favour, and walled cities such as Luceria and Arpi closed their gates to him. For the first time Hannibal must have learned the strength of Rome's Italic confederation, and perhaps have doubted his ultimate success.

VI. FABIUS CUNCTATOR

In the crisis following the disaster, the Romans had recourse to the traditional measure of appointing a dictator. No dictator with full *imperium* had been created since A. Atilius Calatinus in 249 B.C. Now one consul was dead and the other cut off from the city by Hannibal's army. The usual constitutional practice of nomination by a consul was thus impossible, and the Senate wisely decided that the election should be by the centuriate assembly. Q. Fabius Maximus was elected dictator, a patrician of tried experience (he had been consul in 233 B.C. and 228 B.C. and dictator *sine imperio* in 221 B.C.)[1]. At the same time, instead of following constitutional practice and allowing the dictator to nominate his *Magister Equitum*, the people elected M. Minucius Rufus, also a man of experience, who had seen service as consul in 221 B.C. (vol. VII, p. 815). This separate election of the second-in-command, due to the hampering distrust of the popular party desirous of having a partisan in power, curtailed in an important way the absolute powers of the dictator. For, instead of being a pure subordinate nominated by the dictator to carry out his wishes, Minucius Rufus held an independent, if inferior, position. It was a compromise between dual and sole command which contained the weaknesses of both.

Fabius enrolled two new legions[2] at Tibur and marching along the Via Flaminia met Servilius near Ocriculum[3] and took over his

Spoletium, where there is no easy road through the mountains to the coast, would be folly, and so soon after Trasimene, a surprise would be out of the question.

[1] F. Münzer in *P.W.*, *s.v.* Fabius, col. 1816.

[2] Livy XXII, 11, 3. But Polybius III, 88, 7 says that Fabius raised four new legions, which conflicts with III, 107; it is unlikely that the Romans after raising two new legions before Trasimene should be able to raise four more new legions for the field army immediately afterwards.

[3] Livy XXII, 11, 5. Polybius III, 88, 8 reading Ναρνίαν for Δαυνίαν. O. Seeck, *Hermes*, XII, p. 509, L. Pareti, *Riv. Fil.* XL, p. 546.

two legions. He then turned south with four legions into Apulia and, finding Hannibal at Vibinum, camped five miles away at Aecae. When the Carthaginians offered battle Fabius refused it; whereupon Hannibal decided to move into Samnium and Campania in order to force a pitched battle or demonstrate to the Allies the weakness of Rome. He crossed the Apennines into Samnium, ravaged the lands of Beneventum, and marched down the Volturnus valley, followed by Fabius. Descending by Allifae, Caiatia[1] and Cales into the heart of Campania, he began to spread destruction in the Ager Falernus and Campus Stellas.

All this he did without energetic interference from the dictator's army, and it is easy to imagine how opposition grew in the army, in the country round, and at Rome, to Fabius' strategy of inaction. It was as though the Roman troops occupying the hills sat in the seats of a vast theatre watching the destruction of the fairest region of Italy, the Phlegraean plains for which even gods had contended in rivalry[2]. Equally it is difficult not to admire the Roman tenacity of Fabius in holding to the strategy which alone, he thought, could save Rome. He earned opprobrious sobriquets such as 'Hannibal's lacquey' and 'Cunctator,' which was only later converted by a poet biased by family ties into a term of praise,

cunctando restituit rem.

Fabius was clearly right in avoiding a battle in the plains with an army very little larger than Hannibal's and fatally weak in cavalry. But the real justification of Fabian tactics would have been to outmarch and outmanœuvre Hannibal so as to force a battle where the Punic cavalry could not operate and the sturdiness of the Roman legionary in close fighting might assert itself. For a policy of pure inaction must be highly damaging to the Roman prestige in her Confederation. However, finally, it seemed as if Fabius' patience was to be rewarded, and Hannibal would be forced to an engagement in one of the passes which provide exits from Campania.

As autumn approached, Hannibal wished to return to Apulia for winter quarters, since he possessed no secured base in Campania, which, furthermore, bristled with hostile walled cities into which corn and provisions could be safely gathered and stored from the countryside. And his army had already collected all the cattle and

---

[1] Reading *Caiatinum* in Livy XXII, 13, 6. The story of the guide (Livy XXII, 13) who led Hannibal to Casilinum instead of Casinum is to be rejected. De Sanctis, *op. cit.* p. 125.

[2] Polybius III, 91.

portable booty from this area which had not been withdrawn into safety. It was too dangerous to cross the Volturnus in the face of the enemy, for Fabius could march on interior lines, and to move this heavy-laden army back to Apulia without being forced to battle in one of the passes of north Campania taxed the genius of Hannibal to produce a strange and brilliant manœuvre. Fabius had sent Minucius to occupy the northernmost pass, that of the Via Latina, and he had placed sufficient troops to bar the very narrow exit of the Volturnus itself, while he himself camped on the foothills to watch the pass between Teanum and Cales by which Hannibal had entered Campania[1]. Hannibal's audacious plan was deliberately to force this pass in face of Fabius by a night march. Two thousand bullocks with lighted faggots tied to their horns were driven by pioneers and light-armed troops as a decoy up towards Fabius' camp on to the higher ground on the north of the pass. In the confusion the Roman pickets on the pass abandoned their positions and made to stem what they supposed to be the attack, while Fabius, ever cautious, disliking a night engagement, kept to his camp. Meanwhile Hannibal led the whole of his army with the booty unopposed direct through the pass by Cales (now Taverna Torricella). Crossing the Apennines, he marched to near Luceria in Apulia and captured the small town of Gerunium, which he made into a supply depôt[2]. Fabius was recalled to Rome on the pretext of holding religious sacrifices; the Senate clearly wished to confer with the dictator in consequence of the rising popular opposition to their policy.

While Fabius went to Rome, Minucius marched after Hannibal into Apulia and encamped on the heights of Calena in the territory of Larinum close enough to Gerunium to be able to harass the Carthaginian foraging parties as they gathered in the harvest. To protect these Hannibal moved his camp forward two miles from Gerunium, occupying a low hill facing the Roman camp, and a small force of 2000 was sent still farther forward by night as an outpost to seize a point of vantage between the two camps. Minucius next day attacked this force and, capturing the hill, occupied it himself. Although the armies were now very close to one another, Hannibal was unwilling to desist from completing his foraging operations for the winter. This gave Minucius an

[1] In topography this account follows Nissen, *Italische Landeskunde*, II, 2, 681, which gives by far the easiest and most natural solution.

[2] Gerunium was 25 miles from Luceria; it must have lain on the right bank of the Fortore; but it may have been anywhere between Castel Dragonara and Castelnuovo Monterotara. See De Sanctis, *op. cit.* p. 129.

opportunity of making an attack which cut off and caused considerable losses to the Carthaginian foragers, whereupon Hannibal retreated to Gerunium. When the news of this slight success arrived at Rome it was magnified into an important Roman victory and the popular dissatisfaction with Fabian tactics and the Senate's direction of operations came to a head.

Fabius' attempt to allay the excitement by having an aged senator M. Atilius Regulus elected consul in place of Flaminius had no effect. The Senate had temporarily lost political control, and the people proceeded to the extraordinary and unconstitutional course of electing Minucius Rufus co-dictator with Fabius with equal powers[1]. In this way the whole value of dictatorship was stultified, and one of the oldest institutions of the Roman constitution, which had saved Rome so often in her struggle for supremacy in Italy, received a blow from which it never recovered (p. 110). Fabius joined Minucius at Calena, and the Roman army was split into two halves and even into two camps a mile and a half apart.

Hannibal, fully informed of the dissension in the Roman army and the over-confidence of Minucius, saw a favourable opportunity to force an engagement. The ground between his camp and that of Minucius was very broken and unsuitable for cavalry, which made him all the more certain that Minucius would risk a battle. During the night Hannibal occupied with light troops a small eminence and disposed considerable bodies of troops in hollows and ravines on the flanks. Minucius expecting to repeat his previous success fell into the trap and attacked the eminence in full force. His legions were at once assailed on three sides and a disaster was only avoided by the prompt appearance of Fabius in support. We may well believe, with the Roman annalists, that Fabius forgave his colleague for having proved him right, and that Minucius drew the correct deductions from his narrow escape. The engagement is interesting since it illustrates again Hannibal's tactical skill in enticing his adversary to fight on ground he has chosen and prepared. But the scales were unevenly balanced when a master of strategy who had commanded armies since he was a stripling found such inexperience pitted against him. The six months *imperium* of Fabius was now at an end, and the two consuls, Servilius and Atilius Regulus, took over the command at Gerunium.

[1] Polybius III, 103, 4 is explicit about Minucius' position, which is probably confirmed by the inscription *Dessau*, 11. As in the account of Minucius' appointment (XXII, 31) so here (XXII, 25) Livy is misled by a juristically-minded annalist.

VII. CANNAE

Although the Senate deliberately delayed the elections—Livy notes the interregnum—they were unable to make headway against the tide of popular feeling, and by the side of L. Aemilius Paullus, a noble who had been brilliantly successful in Illyria three years before (vol. VII, p. 849 *sq.*), was elected C. Terentius Varro, the son of a rich merchant. A hostile tradition represents him as a vulgar braggart. Yet he cannot have gained the consulship in face of aristocratic opposition without real capacity. But the qualities which enabled him, as they had enabled Flaminius, to rise to party leadership were ill suited for the conduct of a campaign against Hannibal. In Polybius' account much has to be discounted, since the bias in favour of Aemilius the grandfather of his friend Scipio is very patent, so that Varro is made responsible for all the decisions which in the campaign led directly to the disaster which ensued. That such an ill-assorted pair of consuls worked harmoniously together is unlikely, and there is no reason to doubt the friction upon which the sources lay great stress, but the blame for the disaster must be apportioned more equally between them or rather must be charged against this Roman system of dual command where neither general held precedence over the other except by the primitive arrangement of '*maius imperium*' on alternate days.

The Roman army of four legions at Gerunium had been commanded through the winter and early spring by Servilius and Regulus. Suddenly they informed the Senate that Hannibal had moved away south towards the coast and had captured a Roman supply depôt, Cannae, on the Aufidus. Hannibal no doubt knew from his spies that the Romans had decided to fight a pitched battle, and he was choosing in the plains by the Adriatic the battlefield he desired for his cavalry. The Senate sent the two new consuls to take over the command at Gerunium, and Regulus was permitted to retire from the active service for which his age unfitted him. Part of the Roman army was composed of veteran troops which had cut through Hannibal's centre at Trebia; the two newer legions had been trained by the summer campaign of 217 B.C. under Fabius and seasoned by the skirmishes at Gerunium. All four legions were augmented to a special strength of perhaps 12,000 each, including allies, by a draft which the consuls brought from Rome[1].

[1] Polybius (III, 107) states that the Roman army at Cannae consisted of eight legions, and the account of the losses in him and in the other

A larger army could without doubt have been put into the field, but tradition dictated the size of a Roman consular army as two legions and no army larger than two consular armies combined had ever operated as a unit. The Senate, composed mainly of men with military experience, may have foreseen in any larger combination than four legions practical difficulties of commissariat and of tactical control which might easily outweigh any advantages to be gained by adding legion to legion. Confidence in the valour and fighting qualities of the Roman legionary was unshaken, since both at Trebia and at Trasimene a Roman force had cut their way through the enemy, and they attributed the defeats to the incompetence of the commanders or to ill-fortune. In a fair fight the Romans were still confident that success was assured, the success of superior heavy-armed troops. For with four legions of this augmented strength, 48,000 men, they would considerably outnumber Hannibal's infantry—35,000, his veteran nucleus now reduced to perhaps 19,000 infantry, the remainder unstable Celts whom the Romans knew well and had begun to despise. Cavalry was the weak spot. Even if the Roman horse amounted to 6000, as Polybius' source asserted, it was definitely inferior in numbers and quality to Hannibal's 10,000. But the Romans had ever believed that battles are won by infantry, and only late in the war did the insight of Scipio Africanus appreciate to the full this defect in the Roman military system.

The Roman army marched from Gerunium along the road through Arpi to Salapia, where supplies had been collected. The flat bare plain surrounding the town suggested to Aemilius Paullus the need of moving next day to a more protected position in the rolling hills of the Aufidus valley between Cannae and Canusium. On the march there was a skirmish and Hannibal's Numidian cavalry was beaten off. The Romans then crossed the river and with secure communications to Canusium made their camp on the right bank about three miles or less above Hannibal's camp which was opposite to Cannae on the left bank[1]. A smaller

authorities agrees with this, though the losses, being reached by subtracting the survivors, are not complementary evidence. The complete encirclement and destruction of an army of 90,000 by the forces at Hannibal's disposal would be little less than a miracle. Livy XXII, 36, 2 refers to a tradition which only added 10,000 men to the existing four legions, and that tradition is here followed for the reasons stated above. Polybius' Greek source may have been misled by Greek nomenclature into doubling the legions (p. 44 n. 1); also the Romans were prone to exaggerate their disasters as a foil to their successes. The greater the defeat of Varro at Cannae, the greater the triumph of Scipio at Zama.   [1] On the topography of these events see note 3, p. 710.

Roman outpost was encamped lower down the river on the left bank to protect the Roman foraging parties and to threaten those of Hannibal. At this Hannibal moved his main camp over to the right bank to forestall any possible attempt upon Cannae. Further by this move he calculated that the Romans would be more likely to be enticed into battle in the plain between Salapia and the Aufidus if they were persuaded that they would not be fighting, as at Trebia, upon ground prepared by him. Both armies were now eager for battle; for Hannibal had brought the Romans to terrain he had himself chosen and the Roman generals had not the skill or confidence to attempt to outmanœuvre him.

At daybreak on a summer morning early in August the main armies both crossed the river and were drawn up for battle. The Roman right flank rested on the river, and here was stationed the small force of Roman citizen cavalry; the major part of the cavalry including all the allies was placed on the left flank which lay exposed in the plain, the infantry were massed in deeper files than usual, since all the Roman hopes centred upon break-through tactics, a victorious Trebia. Hannibal drew up his infantry in a crescent formation with an advanced centre of Gauls stiffened by his Spanish veterans; his African troops were stationed on either side of the centre, but held well back; and the flanks were extended by cavalry, Spanish and Gallic next to the river and Numidians in the plain. Polybius' Greek source describes the effect made by the alternate companies of half-naked Celts and Spaniards, with their short linen tunics bordered with purple stripes, and he notes that the African troops were now entirely armed in Roman fashion from spoils taken in previous battles.

The battle opened with the attack of the Roman infantry upon Hannibal's forward centre. As the Romans had hoped, the weight of the maniples was too much for the Gauls and they were pressed steadily back until the convex line of Hannibal's formation became concave. If it broke, the day was lost, and here in the centre Hannibal had posted himself and his young brother Mago. The result of this movement, which Hannibal had deliberately calculated, was to narrow still further the Roman front as they crowded into the pocket left by his receding Gauls, and at the same time his African infantry came into action with their full weight on the flanks of the Roman infantry. Meanwhile the Spanish and Gallic cavalry annihilated the weak Roman horse between the river and their infantry, and began to encircle the Roman rear, while part was detached to the other flank to assist the Numidians and to put to flight the Roman allied horse. The

double victory of Hannibal's cavalry completed the outflanking
tactics of the infantry battle. Only by breaking through the centre
could the Roman army be partially saved. But this they were not
able to effect, both owing to the diversion caused by the attack
on their flanks and because Hannibal's heavy Spanish and African
infantry displayed magnificent fighting qualities, while his Gauls,
on whom fell the heaviest losses, did not fail their alien commander. The Roman legions were held until encirclement brought
about the inevitable disaster. Aemilius fell, Varro rode away: of
the whole army perhaps 10,000 men escaped. The battle is the
supreme achievement of Hannibal, exhibiting in its perfection of
timing and in its co-ordination of cavalry and infantry tactics an
example of military art unsurpassed in ancient warfare.

The Carthaginians had lost no more than 6700 men, 4000 of
whom were Gauls—a low price for the victory. Hannibal was
urged by his officers headed by Maharbal to march immediately
on Rome or at least to send forward a strong cavalry force: 'in
five days we shall dine in the Capitol.' But his deep strategic
insight recognized at once the futility of such an empty demonstration before the walls of Rome, which would have lessened the
moral effect of his victory and would have abandoned the opportunity of obtaining more important gains. Instead, he made a
leisurely and triumphant progress through Samnium into Campania to raise the Roman allies in revolt, while his brother Mago
was sent with a small force into Lucania and Bruttium.

The Roman confederation in Italy was profoundly shaken and
one tithe of Hannibal's hopes was fulfilled. Arpi, in Apulia,
one of the most important cities of Central Italy, and Salapia came
over to him, and the strongholds of Aecae, Herdonea and Compsa
followed suit with most of the tribes of the Samnite mountain
regions including the Hirpini, Pentri and Caudini. They were
the toughest stock of Italy with strong feelings of independent
nationalism which had resisted vigorously the spread of Roman
power and had never borne with resignation the Roman domination. In Lucania and Bruttium, with the exception of the Greek
cities, the revolt was universal; only Petelia maintained a desperate
defence during eleven months' siege by Mago, and Consentia
submitted after the fall of Petelia. But the most important of all
the successes of Hannibal after Cannae, significant of real danger
of disruption in the Roman confederation, was the revolt of Capua
in the autumn, the second city in Italy.

The causes of revolt were numerous. Capua was the industrial
centre of Italy, far surpassing Rome itself at this time in wealth,

and the Roman market had depended largely on the products of Campanian artisans. The numerous democratic party in the city saw their opportunity to overthrow an aristocracy whose power had been strengthened by intermarriage with the leading families of Rome. The demands of Roman conscription in a century of continual wars had been peculiarly irksome to the luxury-loving burghers. And the measure of self-government which the city enjoyed under its two *meddices* had been seriously curtailed by the jurisdiction of a Roman *praefectus*, in whose election the Campanians had no say. The burden of the *civitas sine suffragio* seemed greater than its privileges, and the desire for immediate and selfish advantages was strong enough to drown the national Italian patriotism which Rome had been so successful in fostering in the Confederation. Hannibal wisely agreed to liberal conditions— no conscription for his army, complete autonomy, and the present of three hundred Roman prisoners to be exchanged against the Capuan cavalry serving with the Romans in Sicily.

The example of Capua was followed by smaller Campanian towns—Atella, Calatia, Nuceria and Acerrae. But there the movement ended. The solid core of Roman strength, Latium, Umbria and Etruria stood firm. In Sicily the aged king Hiero, whose unwavering loyalty to Rome had brought to Syracuse fifty years of unparalleled peace and prosperity, hastened to demonstrate it, as he had done after Trebia and Trasimene. The Roman fleet off Sicily, strengthened to seventy-five quinqueremes, held the seas. And finally, as will be seen later, the Scipios had won a great victory in Spain. The skies were dark, but it was not the hour to despair of the Republic.

CHAPTER III

THE ROMAN DEFENSIVE

I. THE INVASION OF SPAIN 218 B.C.—215 B.C.

THE successful invasion of Hannibal's military base by the two Scipios is of very great importance in the war. Only the barest outline of the events stands clear in the evidence, but the greatness of the achievement of the Roman generals in difficult hostile country is unmistakeable. For the battles fought in Spain were no skirmishes and the forces engaged, if smaller than those of the war in Italy, yet were far from negligible. Livy with unerring artistic and historical insight notes how the Roman successes in Spain formed a balance to the disasters in Italy. Indeed if the real objective of war and particularly Hannibal's objective in this war was 'the subjection of the enemy will,' these successes must be given their full value in accounting for the defeat of Hannibal's strategy. The Roman invasion was accomplished by two legions only of Roman troops, commanded by cautious, efficient, but never brilliant generals. The Carthaginians had larger forces at their command and a vast area from which to recruit, but these advantages were largely offset by the necessity of dividing their forces and of posting them immense distances apart in order to hold the newly conquered lands. It is clear that the defence of Spain was a difficult task, and the Carthaginian generals were not equal to it.

When Publius Scipio decided at the Rhone that the Roman offensive against Spain should be carried out as planned (p. 39), he sent his brother Gnaeus with part of the fleet and two legions to land at Emporium, as it was then called, the chief trade-mart in North Spain of the powerful Roman ally Massilia. Massiliote trade had, no doubt, been seriously damaged by the spread of the Carthaginian empire in Spain to the Ebro, and she could be relied upon for vigorous co-operation in providing money and supplies for the invasion. Consequently, Gnaeus' plan of campaign in September 218 B.C. was to make full use of the fleet, bases, and local knowledge of the Greeks in Northern Spain in order to secure a sure footing before the winter. At once he marched south, and near Cissa a few miles inland from Tarraco (Tarragona) he met Hanno who had collected in this fortress the baggage-train which Hannibal had left behind on his march. Two Roman legions faced the 11,000 troops of Hanno augmented by a few local tribesmen. The Roman victory was complete; Hanno and Andobales, the tribal chief, were captured with all the stores and military equipment. The Carthaginians in Spain had been taken entirely by surprise owing to the rapidity of the Roman action. When Hasdrubal arrived, marching with all speed from Nova Carthago, he was too late to do anything except capture some scattered detachments of sailors on the coast. In less than two months the Carthaginians had been driven out of Spain north of the Ebro, and the Romans were free to create a secure base at Tarraco[1].

In the early summer of the next year (217 B.C.) Hasdrubal, mustering all his forces, decided to carry out a combined attack by sea and land upon the Roman position at Tarraco which the lateness of the season had prevented in the previous year. Crossing the Ebro, he encamped near its mouth with his fleet of forty ships in the excellent bay formed by the river delta. Scipio, although his fleet reinforced by the Massiliote vessels only numbered thirty-five ships, decided to attack the Carthaginian fleet from the sea. This rather surprising decision was perhaps due in part to the urgency of the Greeks, who were eager to protect their Spanish trade by destroying at once the Carthaginian navy. The Romans, too, were anxious to answer the challenge to the naval supremacy which they had won in the First Punic War and Hasdrubal's land forces by now perhaps held sufficient numerical superiority to make Scipio unwilling to hazard an open engagement on land, which if disastrous would mean abandoning Spain.

Gnaeus sailed swiftly to the mouth of the Ebro to attack the Carthaginian sailors who, either surprised, or as Polybius thinks ordered by Hasdrubal to fight close inshore under cover of their infantry, offered little resistance, and the Romans sailing right inshore were able to destroy six and capture twenty-five ships. An interesting fragment of the Greek historian Sosylus[2] ascribes the Roman victory in a large measure to the daring and naval skill of the Massiliote sailors. The naval victory had far-reaching effects upon Carthaginian strategy. It deepened the profound distrust in the Punic marine as a fighting force which all the Punic admirals in the war seem to have shared, and for the rest of the war the operations of Punic fleets are limited to rapid raids of

[1] Cf. Pliny, N.H. III, 21, 'Tarracon Scipionum opus.'
[2] See U. Wilcken in Hermes, XLI, 1906, pp. 103 sqq.; XLII, 1907, pp. 516 sqq.

negligible value owing to the fear of their commanders of being brought to an engagement by a Roman fleet. Later in this same year after the Ebro defeat, Livy narrates a half-hearted attempt made by the Carthaginian government to dispute the Roman command of the seas. A fleet of 70 ships sailed from Carthage to Sardinia and then to Pisa hoping to establish contact with Hannibal, news of whose march through Etruria and victory at Trasimene had just arrived. But when a Roman fleet of 120 sail under Servilius the consul, who had been transferred to naval operations, put to sea, the Carthaginians fled precipitately home. The sole achievement of the raid was the destruction of a Roman convoy bound for Spain, and the seas were left clear for the Romans to send Publius Scipio with twenty more warships, 8000 men and supplies to reinforce his brother in Spain.

Hasdrubal had retreated to Nova Carthago after the naval disaster at the Ebro river, and in the autumn of 217 B.C. the two Roman generals with their combined forces were emboldened to cross the Ebro for the first time and make a military demonstration as far as Saguntum to win over the Spanish tribes. But they were neither strong enough nor daring enough to attempt the capture of the Carthaginian fortresses, and the following year 216 B.C. saw a continuation of Roman penetration without any serious threat to the Carthaginian hold on Spain. On his side, Hasdrubal was engaged in reducing a rebellion of the Turdetani on the Baetis river in the south. Thus the war had come almost to a standstill in Spain, neither side feeling strong enough to attack the other. But the advantages which the Romans had won in the first three campaigns were immense. They had taken and kept the offensive, north-east Spain was securely occupied, and the loyalty to Carthage of many of the Spanish tribes south of the Ebro had been undermined.

In the next year 215 B.C. the Carthaginians decided upon a fresh offensive against the Scipios. The time seemed ripe for an attempt to crush the Roman army in Spain. Hasdrubal received reinforcements, 4000 infantry, and 1000 cavalry, and another army was sent over to Spain under Himilco to safeguard the area of the recent revolts in the south in order that Hasdrubal might be set free to move against the Romans. The Scipios were laying siege to a city on the north bank of the Ebro, Dertosa[1], when in midsummer news of Hasdrubal's advance arrived. The armies were probably fairly equally matched, about 25,000 on each side.

[1] Later refounded as a Roman colony Hibera Iulia Ilercavonia Dertosa. See *P.W. s.v.* Dertosa. Hence Livy XXIII, 28–9, calls it Hibera.

Hasdrubal drew up his army with his Spanish levies in the centre extended in a thin line; on his right wing were the best African troops, the Libyphoenicians, with Numidian horse in front of them, while on the left were posted the rest of the African levies also preceded by a cavalry wing. The Romans adopted the usual close formation of three succeeding waves of infantry with the cavalry on the wings. It is clear that Hasdrubal was attempting the tactics by which Hannibal had destroyed the Roman armies at Trebia and Cannae, using a weak extended centre to enable the wings to outflank and if possible surround the Roman army. But the key to success was the resistance of the centre. At the Trebia 10,000 Romans had cut through. In this battle the Spanish levies were too weak to resist the massed attack of the Roman legionaries and the Carthaginian army was cut in two before the cavalry could perform any encircling movement. The defeat of Hasdrubal was complete, and the losses suffered by his best African troops were very heavy.

The results of the battle were far-reaching. A Roman defeat would have probably meant withdrawal from Spain, and the Carthaginians would then have been free to send one Spanish army to Italy[1]. The Roman victory was a real challenge to the Carthaginian empire in Spain. At Rome it restored the confidence in the citizen troops, and throughout Italy the news coming in the darkest period after Cannae must have done much to strengthen the loyalty of the Roman allies.

II. THE NEW CARTHAGINIAN STRATEGY

When Hannibal's brother Mago announced the victory of Cannae in the Carthaginian Senate before a heap of golden rings taken from Roman *equites* killed in the battle, the Carthaginians realized that the decisive period of the struggle had arrived. Hannibal himself was able by now to gauge the real strength of the Roman confederation, and his despatches can have held out

---

[1] The tradition which Livy follows, XXIII, 27, that Hasdrubal had been ordered to march to Italy at the beginning of 215 B.C. is an anticipation of the later campaign in 208 B.C. and is clearly false. If Hannibal needed reinforcements, there was an army available which was sent to Sardinia in this year. Repulse of the Roman invasion of Spain at this time was a primary object of Carthaginian strategy. If, however, Hasdrubal had destroyed the Roman army in this battle, it may well be that he would have marched to Italy. See De Sanctis, *op. cit.* p. 244 n. 68 following J. Frantz, *Die Kriege der Scipionen in Spanien*, 1883, pp. 25 *sqq.*

no prospects of the immediate collapse of Rome in Italy. The sending of a large army to Italy by sea at the risk of another Aegates Islands disaster was neither requested by Hannibal nor refused by the home government, as later tradition asserted. Ultimate victory would not be assured by doubling in Italy the forces which had won Cannae. These were the calculations of Hannibal. Instead, he conceived a new strategy which held out greater hopes of success. The whole strength of Carthage was to be employed in extending the war to new areas to produce the encirclement of Italy. His own task would be to prosecute vigorously the war in Italy, detaching such cities as he could until the Roman Senate was willing to accept a settlement which reversed the verdict of the First Punic War and left Carthage mistress in Spain. It was the task of the home government to prepare the way for it by pushing the Romans out of Spain, by regaining Sardinia and above all by re-establishing themselves in Sicily. The Gauls of the Po valley mattered less, and it is not impossible that Carthage would let them go in the end. What mattered was to regain control of the Western Mediterranean and force Rome to become once more an Italian power and that alone. To that end they could look across the Adriatic for an ally in the king of Macedon, who had already shown how bitterly he resented the Roman protectorate in Illyria (p. 117 *sq.*). If he could be encouraged to drive out the Romans thence, it would be in his interest to stand by Carthage in maintaining the hoped-for settlement. Finally, with Macedon the ally of Carthage, the Greeks of South Italy and of Sicily would find no new Pyrrhus to help them to real independence. Such, it seems probable, was the Carthaginian strategy—subtle and far-sighted, yet tempting to hesitation and to indecisive action and to opportunism which might lag behind opportunity. In seeking to win the peace, Carthage failed to win the war; but her sacrifices and her achievements are not to be despised. Eleven years were to pass before the over-mastering strength of Rome broke through the meshes that Carthage wove around her.

It was not until the year 215 that the first effects of the Carthaginian strategy were felt. In Italy Hannibal needed some reinforcements to keep his army at full strength and to garrison cities which came over to him and needed such support or control. It was at first proposed to send with Mago 12,000 infantry, 1500 cavalry and 20 elephants, but events in Spain diverted these (p. 70), and, as Italy could wait, the Carthaginians contented themselves with landing what was presumably a small force at Locri, escorted there by the admiral Bomilcar, who succeeded in

evading the Roman fleet off Sicily (summer, 215). In the same
year, while Mago was dispatched to Spain, another fair-sized
army was sent under Hasdrubal the 'Bald' to Sardinia, where the
Romans had only one legion. The Sardinians had already learnt
to loathe the harsh rule of the Republic, the governor Q. Mucius
was sick and the opportunity of supporting a native rising seemed
too good to miss. But the enterprise miscarried. A storm drove
the Carthaginian fleet out of its course to the Balearic islands and
there was considerable delay before it could proceed. Meanwhile,
the Romans had superseded Mucius by T. Manlius Torquatus
who brought another legion. He knew the island and people well,
having campaigned there when consul twenty years before. With
prompt energy he attacked and scattered the insurgents before
the Carthaginian force arrived. Hasdrubal, however, succeeded
in landing and rallied the rebellious Sardinians to his standard.
Torquatus with two legions considerably out-numbered Hasdrubal and forcing him to an engagement won a decisive
victory. Hasdrubal himself and other Carthaginian nobles were
captured. The remains of the Carthaginian expedition as it sailed
home crossed the path of the praetor Otacilius who had been
raiding North Africa. Seven ships were lost, the remainder
scattered in flight. The Sardinians, whose leader Hampsicoras
had taken his own life, were forced to submit and pay for their
daring. Hostages were surrendered and Manlius returned to
Italy with his troops announcing, with reason, that the island was
mastered. In Spain, equally, Carthaginian hopes were disappointed
in consequence of events in Africa, where the Numidian chief
Syphax revolted and compelled the hasty recall to Africa of
Hasdrubal and part of the army of Spain (see below, p. 70).

The diplomatic offensive, on the other hand, was far more
successful. As is described elsewhere, Philip V of Macedon, in the
early summer of 215, decided that the time had come, and sent
envoys to Hannibal (p. 119). Presumably he had grounds for supposing that his envoys would be welcome. An alliance was made,
the text of which has been preserved in Polybius. Macedon was
to make war on Rome, and the Carthaginians pledged themselves
to make Philip's possession of the Illyrian coast, Corcyra and
Pharos, a condition of peace with Rome. In case of need each of the
allies was to reinforce the other[1] in such way as they might agree

---

[1] In the text of Polybius (VII, 9, 11) the pledge of assistance is only
binding upon Philip, but each power was committed to war with the other's
enemies (*ib.* 8–9), and it may further be assumed that Philip exacted a like
pledge from Hannibal before confirming the alliance.

upon. This clause implied a limited liability natural for states which
were seeking each their own ends though both at the expense of
Rome. From the Carthaginian point of view, Philip's activities
would distract the energies of her enemy and so hasten her success.
Of perhaps greater importance were the clauses in which the two
powers pledged themselves to a defensive alliance after the war
was over. Roughly speaking, each power was to make its own
gains and then help the other to retain them. The fact of the
alliance was soon known to the Senate, for Philip's envoys were
caught on their way from Italy and there was delay while a new
set of envoys were sent to complete the negotiations. The extent
of the distraction of Rome proved a disappointment to Carthage
and Philip failed to receive the naval help which, above all, was
what he needed. But for the moment the Roman Senate had to
face a new danger, and the alliance with Carthage of the king of
Macedon had its repercussions in Greek sentiment. It may,
indeed, have assisted the carrying-through of the next part of the
Carthaginian plan, the promotion of an anti-Roman movement
among the Greeks of Sicily.

III. THE WAR IN SICILY

In the early summer of 215 B.C. King Hiero died. There was
not wanting in Syracuse a party which, despite the prosperity
enjoyed for a generation in alliance with Rome, were strongly
in sympathy with Carthage. The news of the Roman disaster
at Cannae and the revolt of Roman allies in Italy no doubt
encouraged them in their belief that the war would end in
Rome's defeat. Furthermore, Hiero's son, Gelo, who till then had
studiously supported his father's policy, now began a secret understanding with them. But death removed him a few months before
his father, a stroke of fortune which was fraught with fatal consequences to the royal dynasty. For the heir to the throne was
Hiero's grandson Hieronymus, a boy of only fifteen years of age,
and Hiero had appointed by his will a regency cabinet of fifteen
members, including his sons-in-law Adranodorus and Zoippus.
The cabinet was short-lived. Adranodorus on the plea that
Hieronymus, who was indeed of presumptuous and head-strong
nature, was already fit to rule, resigned himself and forced the
resignation of the others. After this astute move the regency was
reconstructed in the persons of three men, Adranodorus, Zoippus
and a certain Thraso, who alone had access to the king in the royal
palace. Finally Thraso was falsely implicated in a plot to murder

the young prince and judicially put to death. He had been strong
in his loyalty to Rome, and by his removal the way was clear for
the regency of the sons-in-law to open negotiations with Hannibal.
Hannibal sent at once two sharp-witted agents, Hippocrates and
Epicydes, of mixed Carthaginian and Greek blood, who stayed in
Syracuse and arranged an alliance with their master. When
Roman envoys arrived to renew the old-standing Roman alliance,
they were unceremoniously rebuffed, and a treaty was ratified at
Carthage on the basis of the agreement reached with Hannibal.
It seems that Hieronymus in the first draft demanded as the price
of the alliance one half of Sicily, as far as the river Himeras. Later
he opened his mouth wider and demanded the whole of Sicily,
'since Carthage could have Italy.' Again Carthage acquiesced;
the immediate acquisition of Syracuse was of immense value to her
for the war, whereas the terms of the bargain could not be kept if
Carthage lost, and probably need not be kept if Carthage won.

Thus events had moved very rapidly in Sicily since Hiero's
death. Syracuse was already opening hostilities by sending an
expedition to attempt the capture of various Sicilian cities held
by Roman garrisons, when suddenly in the summer of 214 B.C.
at the dependent city of Leontini Hieronymus was assassinated in
the midst of his army. It was a heaven-sent chance for the Romans
to regain the ground they had lost in Syracuse, for with the city
in the throes of revolution foreign policy might be deflected.
The Roman army of occupation in Sicily at the time consisted of
the two disgraced Cannae legions, whose combined strength was
probably not more than 12,000 men. On the urgent representations of the praetor Appius Claudius the Senate, now more confident in Italy (p. 77), sent in the autumn of 214 B.C. the victorious
consul M. Marcellus with one legion to take charge of Sicily.
Meanwhile the fleet under Appius Claudius was raised to one
hundred ships. The political strife at Syracuse had also for the
moment taken a turn in favour of Rome. The regicides, uniting
in their support those who had hated Hieronymus with those who
favoured Rome, had gained the upper hand and murdered first
Adranodorus and then all the women-folk of the royal house.
Envoys were sent to discuss the renewal of the old treaty with Rome.

This complexion of affairs however endured for a very short
time, and the Romans missed their opportunity for intervention.
The savage murder of the royal house soon produced a revulsion
of feeling. When at the elections the new republic proceeded to
elect its officers, the two Carthaginian agents, Hippocrates and
Epicydes, who had stood aloof from the bloodshed, were un-

expectedly nominated and elected Generals. Appius Claudius made a demonstration with the Roman fleet off Syracuse, but he came too late, and his appearance only served to fan the flames of nationalism, the desire for independence and hostility to Rome. At the same time, the news that a Punic fleet was off Cape Pachynus gave the Carthaginian party in the city confidence. And then there arrived from Leontini envoys asking for armed protection against a feared Roman attack. The Syracusans sent Hippocrates with 4000 men, drawn from those who were most active against the interests of Rome. The Roman and Greek lines were now almost contiguous in front of Leontini, and, as constantly happens in such circumstances when feeling is embittered, a small event precipitated war. Small raids across the border of the Roman province ended in the massacre of an outpost by Hippocrates. Marcellus at once informed the Syracusans that the peace had been broken and demanded that Hippocrates and Epicydes should be sent away from Sicily. Epicydes, seeing that even now he might not be able to win over the Syracusans to open war, escaped to join his brother in Leontini, where they declared the city independent of Syracuse whatever the Syracusans might decide. Upon the refusal of his demands, Marcellus in the spring of 213 B.C. marched on Leontini, ordering Appius Claudius to attack from the opposite side. The legionaries, incensed at the recent massacre of their companions, carried the town at the first assault. The city was sacked with the ferocity which was habitual with the Romans when a city was taken by assault. And, later, 2000 Carthaginian sympathizers were scourged and beheaded.

Meanwhile the Syracusan army, 8000 strong, had marched out to succour Leontini. They were immediately confronted with the news of the fall of the city and with exaggerated tales of Roman severity. Hippocrates and Epicydes, who had cleverly escaped during the assault, appeared opportunely and were received by the soldiers with enthusiasm. With the passions of the army inflamed by the fate of Leontini, it was an easy task for the Carthaginian agents to persuade the troops to return to Syracuse and to satisfy their vengeance by a massacre of the Roman party in the town. All wavering was now at an end. The population was unanimous in its determination to defy the Romans, and elected once again Hippocrates and Epicydes as their Generals to make preparations to defend the city. Thus, finally, the brilliant and indefatigable machinations of these two Carthaginian agents had their reward. Syracuse, the capital of western Hellenism, had abandoned the cause of Rome for Carthage.

The Romans were now as quick to act as they had before been slow to intrigue. Five days were given up to preparations for an assault by land and sea. Appius then brought up his pent-houses and scaling-ladders and attempted the wall at Hexapylon opposite the Trogilus harbour where the cliffs are not steep, while Marcellus with sixty ships, carrying siege-engines, attacked the lowest part of the wall of Achradina where it descends to the shore. However, the assault upon the impregnable walls of Dionysius could only hope to succeed by surprise or through treachery amongst the defenders. But these defenders were desperate men, some of them deserters from the Roman armies, who expected no quarter in defeat; they were ably led and the walls bristled with engines and siege devices designed by the greatest practical mathematician and engineer of the ancient world, Archimedes. Polybius describes how great beams swung out from the battlements and released weights of many hundredweight to destroy the Roman hide-covered scaling-ladders or *sambucae*, which, each mounted on two ships lashed together, were brought into position for mounting the walls. The assault having failed, the Romans settled down to a regular siege, part of their army encamped near the Olympieum with the fleet in the Great Harbour and the other part at Leon on the north-west, thus commanding the main roads from Syracuse along both coasts.

At Carthage the news of the revolt of Syracuse and the repulse of the Roman attack, backed by an urgent despatch from Hannibal, roused the citizens to desperate energy. Nothing could appeal more directly to their merchant patriotism than the vision of Sicily reconquered. An army of 25,000 infantry, 3000 cavalry and 12 elephants under Himilco succeeded in landing at Heraclea Minoa, which fell, closely followed by the second city of the island, Agrigentum. Marcellus, meanwhile, unable to detach any considerable force from the siege of Syracuse, could do little. With one-third of the army he had reduced to Roman servitude the dependent cities of Hiero's ancient kingdom, Helorus, Herbessus and Megara Hyblaea, but he arrived too late to strengthen the garrison in Agrigentum. However, he succeeded on his return march in cutting to pieces at Acrillae near Acrae a considerable Syracusan force under Hippocrates which had slipped out of Syracuse to join Himilco.

This success checked further revolts, but the Romans had been badly surprised by the energy of the Carthaginian home government, and the presence of a large Carthaginian army placed the Roman prospects of recovering Sicily in serious jeopardy.

Reinforcements of another legion were quickly sent from Italy, making the Roman forces in Sicily four legions. Meanwhile Himilco, joined by Hippocrates, had encamped on the Anapus eight miles from Syracuse and hoped to surprise this Roman legion, which had been landed at Panormus, as it came across the centre of the island. But a warning was sent in time so that the legion took the coast route round the north of the island to Syracuse. Thus the summer of 213 B.C. ended in stalemate. The Carthaginian army was not strong enough to assault the entrenched positions of the Romans north and south of Syracuse and could do little to hinder the siege. But a significant incident shows how strong was the hatred of Rome in many of the cities of the interior of the island held by Roman garrisons. At Enna the Roman commander discovered that the city was to be betrayed and his garrison cut to pieces. Repaying treachery with treachery, he launched his troops on the people met unarmed in the market-place and perpetrated a ferocious massacre, which was later approved by Marcellus. By such acts of deliberate terrorism the cities were taught the quality of Roman vengeance. One only, Murgantia, which contained large quantities of Roman stores, betrayed its garrison and was occupied by Himilco and used as winter quarters. Meanwhile the Carthaginian fleet of fifty ships under Bomilcar, finding itself outnumbered two to one, had retired to Carthage, abandoning any attempt this summer to relieve Syracuse.

The next year 212 B.C. was the decisive year in the siege. In the early spring by a brilliant stroke Marcellus got possession of parts of Epipolae. Taking advantage of the drunkenness which accompanied the festival of Artemis in the city he sent in the night a scaling party over a low portion of wall on the north circuit, which succeeded in opening the Hexapylon gate so that the whole of the northern Roman army was introduced before Epicydes was fully awake to the danger. Two important suburbs of the town, Neapolis and Tycha, were plundered by the Roman troops. For a time their position was precarious, since Achradina was strongly held and divided off from Epipolae by a defensive wall, and on the other flank lay Euryalus, the impregnable fort built by Dionysius I. Suddenly, however, the Greek governor of this fort lost his head and surrendered the position to the Romans so that Marcellus was made secure from any attack in the rear. To relieve the position the Syracusans within the city made a sortie from Achradina while Himilco's army attacked the Roman camp on the Great Harbour, but both attacks were unsuccessful. Carthage, also, to encourage the defenders had sent in the spring Bomilcar with a fleet of ninety ships; favoured by a strong wind he sailed into the Great Harbour and anchored at Ortygia before the Romans could put out to oppose him. Equally successfully he slipped back again later, leaving fifty-five ships to help the city[1]. As the summer wore on, the pestilential marshes of the Anapus which had so often saved Syracuse from her enemies now proved fatal to her allies. An epidemic of terrible virulence spread swiftly and swept away the entire Carthaginian army with the generals Himilco and Hippo-crates. The Roman troops did not escape, but on the healthier higher ground and with better discipline and understanding of military sanitation their losses were not fatal.

By this intervention of Apollo the whole situation in Sicily was changed. The plague is the turning point in the Roman recovery of Sicily. While the large Carthaginian army was intact, though the Romans were steadily closing the siege of Syracuse, yet the inconstant fortune of war made a surprise and defeat always possible. But now the reduction of Syracuse and of the rest of Sicily was certain before the overwhelming Roman forces. However in the next spring, 211 B.C., Carthage made a final effort to help the city. Bomilcar with a fleet of 130 ships protecting a large convoy arrived off Cape Pachynus where he was held by contrary winds so that the Roman fleet of 100 ships sailed from Syracuse to meet him. Much might have resulted from a great Carthaginian victory. But the actual issue was prophetic of the dominant race. For the First Punic War had undermined the morale of the Punic navy. Bomilcar suddenly crowded on all sail, ordered his transports to return to Africa and with his fighting ships made off for Tarentum, leaving Syracuse to its fate. Thus the Carthaginian fleet had proved itself singularly ineffective in co-operating with the revolt in Sicily, and at the same time Philip of Macedon looked in vain for the naval assistance which might have altered the complexion of affairs in Greece (see p. 126). Epicydes, who had slipped out from Syracuse to meet Bomilcar, was unable or unwilling to return and retired to Agrigentum to help organize yet another relief army from troops which the Carthaginians had sent over under Hanno, while Hannibal had dispatched from Italy his best cavalry officer Muttines. But mean-while discipline was broken in Syracuse, new generals were elected and assassinated, and a Spanish commander of mercenary

---

[1] A second intervention by Bomilcar (Livy xxv, 25, 13; 27, 2) in the same year (212) is to be rejected as due to a repetition of the incident from another source.

troops was persuaded to open one of the gates on Ortygia. Thus Syracuse fell after a siege of two and a half years. Marcellus, according to the Roman custom, after securing the royal treasure abandoned the city to the plunder and rapine of his troops. Archimedes was killed by a common soldier as he sat absorbed in geometrical problems drawn in the sand. Treasures and works of art collected during three centuries of high culture were mutilated or carried off according to the ignorant caprice of peasant soldiery. Much was transported to Italy as soldiers' loot, to be eagerly sought after in later years as the profound change in Roman taste developed. The dedications of Marcellus in shrines near the Porta Capena became one of the Museums of Rome.

Marcellus was eager to finish the war and hold the triumph he had so well deserved by his masterly conduct of the siege of Syracuse. Moving to the river Himeras he encountered the small Carthaginian army. The Numidian horse mutinied, and the battle was a rout, but Agrigentum received the beaten troops, and the season was too late to begin a siege. Marcellus returned to Rome and held a spectacular *ovatio* adorned by the spoils of Syracuse. In his stead a praetor M. Cornelius Cethegus was sent, who during the winter successfully reduced some small towns of the interior which gave trouble. Then, finally, late in the summer of 210 B.C. one of the consuls, M. Valerius Laevinus, arriving with fresh forces secured the betrayal of Agrigentum by taking advantage of the quarrels between Muttines, the commander of the Numidians, and Hanno. All resistance was speedily stamped out in Sicily. The re-settlement of the island as a Roman province was taken in hand (p. 114).

Nothing shows the vigour of the Senate's direction of the war better than the successful reconquest of Sicily. But it must be said that fortune favoured Rome in many ways in addition to the plague. The revolt of Syracuse hung in the balance for a long time and only came to a head three years after Cannae, when the position in Italy had been retrieved. Nor is the effort of the Carthaginian government in the sending of armies and fleets to be minimized. But the effort was wasted through the death of Himilco, the incompetence of Hanno and the pusillanimity of Bomilcar, so that the spread of revolt was speedily checked and, most important of all, the great sea fortresses in the west, Lilybaeum and Panormus, which had once been Carthaginian, were never in serious danger of attack.

IV. THE ADVANCE AND DEFEAT OF THE SCIPIOS

Success in Sicily was soon counterbalanced by defeat in Spain. After the great victory over Hasdrubal at the Ebro in 215 B.C., the Romans for a time reaped the fruits of their earlier cautious penetration. Many of the Celtiberian tribes changed sides, so that Carthage lost a recruiting area which had provided some of the finest troops in Hannibal's army. To prevent a further landslide the Carthaginians had to dispatch at once to Spain under Mago, a brother of Hannibal, who had shown good leadership at the Trebia and Cannae, another army of 12,000 infantry, 1,500 cavalry and 20 elephants with a fleet of 60 ships which had been expressly recruited for Hannibal and was on the point of sailing to Italy. But at this point Carthage was seriously embarrassed. Syphax, king of the powerful Numidian tribes of the Masaesyli in Africa had thrown off his allegiance to Carthage[1] and Hasdrubal was recalled from Spain with an army to deal with the revolt. Consequently during the next three years (214–212 B.C.) the Scipios were able to carry the Roman arms into the heart of the Carthaginian empire in Spain[2]. Saguntum was recaptured in 212 B.C. and amongst many others the important city of Castulo in the Upper Baetis valley opened its gates to their army[3]. When the exaggerations of the annalist narrative have been discounted it remains clear that by the successes of these campaigns the two Scipios earned a just memory as 'the two thunderbolts of war.' For the greatness of the achievement in planning and executing the victorious offensive in Spain cannot be gainsaid. While valuable parts of Italy and Sicily had been lost to Rome, the Scipios had won from Carthage one-third of her empire in Spain.

By the end of 212 B.C. the war in Africa was over. Syphax had been defeated by Hasdrubal and driven from his kingdom. But aided by forces from a king of the Mauri in Morocco he had re-established himself, and the Carthaginians made peace with him[4] in order to turn their attention to Spain. Three armies were sent over. Hasdrubal returned in the autumn of 212 B.C. from Africa, Mago brought over another army, in which Masinissa a young Numidian chief twenty-six years of age commanded a picked force

[1] In 215 B.C., Appian, *Iber.* 15; cf. Livy xxiv, 48, who wrongly places it shortly before 213 B.C.

[2] See Livy xxiii, 49; xxiv, 41, 42, though the details are entirely untrustworthy and the battles and victories largely fictitious.

[3] Appian, *Iber.* 16; part of the Roman army wintered at Castulo 212/211 B.C.

[4] Appian, *Iber.* 15–17; Livy xxiv, 48, 49.

of Numidian cavalry, and the third army was led by Hasdrubal son of Gisgo. The Scipios meanwhile had steadily augmented their army by very large drafts of Celtiberian troops. Livy (xxv, 32), no doubt exaggerating, says that 20,000 had been enlisted. Relying on these new levies the Roman army had been split into two halves and had very probably operated as two units in the campaign of 212 B.C., for Publius wintered at Castulo in the Upper Baetis valley, and Gnaeus at Urso. The division of forces had made possible greater range of action and ease of commissariat, while Spain was almost denuded of Carthaginian troops; but it was now to prove fatal.

For at the opening of the campaign of 211 B.C.[1] in the Upper Baetis valley[2] the Celtiberian troops with Spanish fickleness deserted *en masse* from the two Roman armies. Cut off from one another between the three Carthaginian armies and greatly outnumbered, the Scipios suffered complete disaster. Publius Scipio, leaving Tiberius Fonteius in his camp with a small force, made a night march to intercept and surprise the native chief Indibilis, who was marching with 7500 Suessitani to join Mago. It was a desperate venture and failed. During the encounter next day the Numidian cavalry arrived and enclosed his wings while still later in the day the Carthaginian heavy infantry came on the scene to block his rear. He fell, and his army was destroyed. The fate of Gnaeus soon afterwards was the same. The swift Numidian horse forced a halt in their attempted retreat, and the three Carthaginian armies stormed an improvised barricade of pack-saddles, lumber, and kit to massacre the defenders. The small force under Fonteius, joined by fugitives from the two battles, made good its retreat away to the Ebro and under the command of a Roman knight, L. Marcius Septimus, elected commander by the soldiery, succeeded in preventing further defections of tribes north of the Ebro. But the disaster lost the Romans all Spain south of the Ebro and left them desperately weak in North Spain. There was real danger that everything which the victorious offensive in Spain had won would be lost.

[1] For the chronology see De Sanctis, *op. cit.* p. 446 n. 4. Livy xxv, 32 *sqq.* wrongly narrates the catastrophe under the year 212 B.C., probably misunderstanding Polybius' use of Olympiad 142, 1, covering 212/11 B.C. July to July. In xxv, 36, 14 'octavo anno' is correct.
[2] For the topography see De Sanctis, *op. cit.* p. 446 n. 3; p. 448 n. 8. Livy xxv, 32, 5, gives no clue except the unknown town Amtorgis. Appian, *Iber.* 16, places the disaster in the Baetis watershed. Pliny, *N.H.* III, 9, confirms this: 'Baetis...Tugiensi exoriens saltu...Ilorci refugit Scipionis rogum.'

V. THE ROMAN RESISTANCE IN ITALY AFTER CANNAE

Thus by the year 211 B.C. the Carthaginian attempts to recover Sardinia and to re-establish their influence in Sicily had failed. During the same period the alliance with Macedon had not involved Rome in any great naval or military effort. As will be seen elsewhere (pp. 122 *sqq.*), Philip had failed to win the Greek seaports of Lower Illyria; a Roman fleet of some fifty quinqueremes and an army which may be set at less than one full legion had assisted the clients of Rome to limit his successes and in 212 B.C. an alliance with the Aetolians enabled the Senate to do even less and at the same time to see Philip kept in check. In Spain on the other hand, after various vicissitudes, the two Scipios had met with disaster and there was a real danger that Hasdrubal would appear in Northern Italy bringing an army to rally to himself the Celts of the Po valley and then to join his brother. To prevent this and to regain the slowly won Roman ascendancy on that front the Senate had to find a new commander and another army besides the troops which were sent in haste to hold the Ebro line. This they were able to do. The failure of the Carthaginians elsewhere and above all the state of things in Italy itself made it possible. In Italy, despite Hannibal's genius, the balance of the war had reached equilibrium or had even begun to incline against the Carthaginians. It remains to describe the slow and laborious process by which this was achieved.

Never does the national character of the Roman people appear finer or stronger than in the months that followed the greatest disaster in her history since the day of the Allia. With just pride Livy records how the Senate assumed control and took measures to allay the terrors of the populace, sending Q. Fabius Pictor on a special mission to the oracle at Delphi. The democratic party abandoned its opposition to the Senate and ceased to support political agitators for the command of armies. The *patres* with wise conciliation, and perhaps with a touch of irony which the later annalists did not appreciate, thanked the returning Varro for not despairing of the Republic and even continued him in command of a legion in Picenum for three years. The two weak legions which he brought back with him from the survivors, having no motive of political exigency to save them, were disgraced and were sent next year to serve in Sicily without winter furlough for the remainder of the war.

The next concern of the Senate was to organize resistance to Hannibal. Two legions were in Spain, one in Sardinia, two in Sicily, two in the valley of the Po, while recruits were training for two *legiones urbanae* at Rome which were not yet ready to take the field. Of these legions none could be simply withdrawn from their several stations without very serious risk. For the following year 215 B.C. the Sicilian legions were recalled to Apulia to be replaced, as has been said, by the legions formed from the survivors of Cannae. The supply of allied troops from Apulia, Samnium, and South Italy was now cut off. Yet the need for more troops was urgent to prevent further revolts to Hannibal, and time must elapse before the reserves could be called up from Umbria, the Sabine country, Picenum and Etruria. In this desperate situation the unprecedented step was taken of purchasing the freedom of slaves ready to volunteer as soldiers to increase the force in Campania and to provide garrisons in the Roman fortresses. A Dictator M. Junius Pera with Ti. Sempronius Gracchus as his *magister equitum* was entrusted with the supervision of these operations.

The calmness of the Senate in the crisis is enhanced by a significant notice which shows the suppressed excitement of the populace, which demanded human sacrifice to appease its superstitions; a Gaulish man and woman and a Greek man and woman were buried alive under the Forum Boarium. Indulgence was the best temporary medicine for such superstition, but for the sake of discipline and the exchequer the severe decision was published that prisoners of war would no longer be ransomed, and Hannibal's offer to exchange his prisoners for a price was curtly refused. Such was the temper of Romans at bay. Then in November, almost before the elections for 215 B.C. were finished, news came of a fresh disaster. L. Postumius[1], the commander of the two legions in Cisalpine Gaul, had hardly been declared consul in his absence before it was known that he had been surprised by the revolted tribesmen and his force cut to pieces. It was not until 214 B.C. that the Senate was able to send fresh legions there.

Yet there is another side to this picture of the desperate plight of Rome. No Latin city had revolted, no city of Umbria, Picenum or Etruria. In the midst of Samnium stood the impregnable

---

[1] Polybius III, 118, places the disaster 'a few days after Cannae,' *i.e.* summer 216 B.C. This is clearly a telescoping of the events. Livy XXIII, 24 makes Postumius 'consul designatus' for 215 B.C. confirmed by his appearance in the Fasti, 'L. Postumius A. f. A. n. Albinus III (215 B.C.) in praetura in Gall. occis. est.' For another view see De Sanctis, *op. cit.* pp. 327 *sqq.*

fortresses of Beneventum and Venusia. Among the Greek cities Rhegium and Tarentum were strongly held. In Apulia, Luceria and Canusium threatened Arpi which had revolted (p. 55); while in Campania a ring of walled cities, Cumae, Neapolis, Nola, Saticula, Cales and Teanum, connected by Roman roads, provided the *points d'appui* for the strategy which was to foil Hannibal in Italy. The war of battles now became a war of sieges. The new Roman strategy of Fabius, which was pursued faithfully to the very end of the war in Italy, avoided all pitched battles, admitting without further challenge the absolute tactical mastery of the Carthaginian general. But small armies using Roman roads and fortresses could operate simultaneously in many different parts of Central and South Italy, besieging and reducing the revolted cities when Hannibal was engaged elsewhere. Embarrassed by the necessity of defending his newly won allies, Hannibal would be constrained to abandon his offensive and conform to the tactics of his opponents. His army would steadily dwindle in size, since the fine fighting stocks of Samnium and Apulia, although many of them had welcomed the opportunity to throw off the yoke of Rome, yet were unwilling to fight for interests which ceased to concern them; meanwhile the Romans, drawing upon the vast reserves of central Italy, steadily increased their strength, until in 212 twenty-five legions or about 200,000 men were in the field. In Italy alone by then there were two legions on the Po, two at Rome, two in Etruria, six in Campania, two in Apulia and two in Lucania.

Once the skill of Hannibal had been discounted, numerical superiority must prove decisive in the end. Yet no time limit could be set for success in such defensive strategy and only the tenacity of the Roman character and the solidity and fidelity of her older allies made it possible. And the cost to Italy was prodigious; the fairest and most fertile regions of the land had to be abandoned according as the caprice of the invader or his requirements for provisioning dictated. Very prophetic indeed was the dream which Hannibal is said to have dreamed at his halt in 218 B.C. on the Ebro river, when he looked back and saw behind him 'the dragon of the destruction of Italy.' Lastly the plan depended upon the Roman command of the seas. To maintain a fleet of between 150 and 200 ships of the line the financial resources of the people were also drained. In 215 B.C. and successive years the tributum or war-tax was doubled, in 214 B.C. a special loan for the fleet was raised in addition, inflation was practised by debasing the currency, and every financial expedient was adopted. It is indeed true that owing to the lesson of the First Punic War and to the maintenance of the Roman armament at full strength, Carthage never challenged this supremacy of Rome at sea in the war. She knew that Rome could and would outbuild her as she had done in the previous war. The Romans, in turn, realized that only by maintaining this dominance would they be able to conquer Spain and to prevent Carthage from sending frequent or considerable reinforcements to Hannibal.

At the elections for 215 B.C. Ti. Sempronius Gracchus gained the consulship, having proved his skill in command of cavalry. And in place of Postumius killed in Gaul M. Claudius Marcellus was nominated. But when the Senate made strenuous opposition to the principle of two plebeian consuls and pointed to the disasters for which plebeian consuls had in the last two years been responsible, Marcellus with patriotic wisdom withdrew, whereupon Q. Fabius Maximus was elected consul to carry out the strategy which he had inaugurated.

Hannibal wintered at Capua. The ridiculous annalistic fable that the luxurious quarters undermined the discipline of his army so that 'Capua was Hannibal's Cannae' comes from the pen of a rhetorician ignorant of military affairs and willing, for the sake of his moral, to ignore the testimony of Polybius that Hannibal was never beaten before Zama. In Campania, Atella and Calatia, two small towns, had joined Hannibal when Capua changed sides. Now, in the spring, Hannibal hoped to gain the rest of Campania. However, despite diplomacy and intrigue, none of the ports, Cumae, Neapolis, or Puteoli, were willing to abandon the Roman confederation. To lay siege to them was futile so long as they could be provisioned from the sea. Nola gave some hopes of success since here as in Capua a democratic party was ready to use any means to gain its ends. Hannibal marched to the gates of the city, but Marcellus had foreseen the danger and had brought a small army to reinforce the pro-Roman government. After a slight skirmish, which appears as a serious battle in the Livian *aristeia* of Marcellus, Hannibal retreated after winning over two more small towns, Acerrae and Nuceria. And at the same time the very important fortress Casilinum[1], which commanded the narrow pass of the Volturnus into Samnium, surrendered to him after a siege lasting through the winter of 216–5.

This was the limit of Hannibal's successes in Campania now that he was opposed by three Roman armies, each of two legions.

[1] The details in Livy XXIII, 17–19 are not to be trusted. The kernel of truth is attested by the monument set up for the defence of Casilinum.

At the south end of the plain Marcellus had chosen a position of immense strength (the modern Cancello) on the foothills above Suessula, almost equidistant from Capua and Nola, which he fortified and called the Castra Claudiana. The Via Latina was defended by Fabius at Teanum and Cales, and Gracchus watched the Via Appia and the coast towns from Sinuessa. Hannibal himself formed an immense fortified camp on the triangular plateau of Mt Tifata behind Casilinum. The strategic position was ideal, threatening Campania yet with secure communications through Samnium into Apulia or southwards to Lucania; and the fertile upland plain provided excellent grass for his cavalry. Checked in Campania, he remained inactive except for raids to Nola and Cumae[1] for the rest of the campaigning season of 215 B.C., since he had depleted his own army to reinforce Hanno strongly in Lucania and Bruttium. In this area great successes were recorded. The reduction of Petelia and Consentia had ended the resistance in the interior, and the inhabitants of the Greek coastal cities whose fortifications had been allowed to decay were not made of the stuff to resist unassisted the Carthaginian forces aided by Bruttians eager for plunder. Croton, Locri and Caulonia submitted, leaving Rhegium alone in the extreme South in Roman hands.

The elections for 214 B.C. reflected the confidence of the people in the Senate's conduct of the war. Fabius was re-elected consul with M. Claudius Marcellus as his colleague. For the coming campaign the number of the legions was raised from fourteen to twenty. Two were sent once again to Gaul to prevent Hannibal from recruiting in that area and two *legiones urbanae* of raw recruits were again enrolled and kept at Rome according to the usual practice which had been interrupted in the difficulties of the previous year. This year too Laevinus was reinforced at Brundisium until the troops with his fleet were counted as a *legio classica*. With these in the summer he crossed the Adriatic to defend the Illyrian coast against Philip (p. 122). A legion was also stationed in Picenum under Terentius Varro.

Hannibal moved from his winter quarters in Apulia to Mt Tifata and decided upon a concentrated effort to break the Roman position in Campania. Hanno was recalled from South Italy to join the main army which again made vain attempts to surprise Puteoli and Nola. While he was traversing the territory of the

---

[1] The narrative of Roman successes in Livy XXIV, 14–20, 36 *sqq.*, 41 *sqq.* is so exceptionally unreliable that any attempt to reconstruct the events is historically valueless.

Hirpini, Tiberius Gracchus, issuing from Beneventum, blocked his route and succeeded in inflicting upon his army, composed largely of Bruttians and Lucanians, a sharp defeat. The reverse made Hannibal suddenly change his plans and attempt by a rapid march to surprise Heraclea and Tarentum. But the Roman fleet from Brundisium was able to reinforce the garrisons and save both towns, whereupon Hannibal again retreated to Apulia for the winter. However, Marcellus in the meantime, taking advantage of the withdrawal of Hannibal from Campania, laid siege to Casilinum, which surrendered at the beginning of the winter. In other regions the Romans were equally successful in 214 B.C.; Compsa the chief city of the Hirpini was recovered after the battle of Beneventum, and Aecae in Apulia early in the season while Hannibal was in Campania. Hannibal in this year had not only been held, but had lost ground.

Consequently for 213 B.C. the people in high hopes elected the son of Q. Fabius consul to accompany his father in command of one army and Ti. Sempronius Gracchus for the second time to command the other. Massing four legions round Arpi, based on the ring of fortresses Salapia, Herdonea, Canusium, Aecae and Luceria, Fabius was able to negotiate with success for the betrayal of Arpi, entering the city by night in sufficient force to overpower the garrison. But this solitary gain was offset by very considerable losses. For Hannibal, perhaps deliberately leaving Arpi as a decoy for the Roman armies, again marched on Tarentum. This time he found the city in an uproar because the Romans had thrown from the Tarpeian rock some Tarentine hostages who had attempted to escape, and traitors were ready to open the gates, so that he entered by night and gained possession of the town[1]. Metapontum, Thurii and Heraclea joined in the revolt which was part of a general alienation from Rome of Greek sentiment in Magna Graecia, following the lead of Syracuse. Carthaginian propaganda and the Greek passion for political freedom had combined to make the cities forgetful of the solid advantages of the *pax Romana*. The negligence both of the garrisons and of the Roman legionary commanders supplied with overwhelming superiority of force in Italy was culpable. The citadel of Tarentum, a rock fortress of great strength, remained in the hands of the Romans and by its position nullified a great part of Hannibal's success. For it commanded the narrow entry to the harbour

---

[1] Livy xxv, 11, 20 places the defection of Tarentum in 212 B.C. but says other authorities put it in 213 B.C. The latter is the correct date as is seen from xxvii, 5 and Appian, *Hann.* 35. See De Sanctis, *op. cit.* pp. 334 *sqq.*

and threatened the town. Hannibal thereupon built a wall and
ditch to defend the town against incursions from the citadel and
freed the ships in the harbour by transporting them on rollers
across the isthmus. However the year 213 B.C. had retarded the
progress of Rome towards winning the war. Laevinus in Illyria
had held Apollonia and Dyrrhachium, but Philip had taken Lissus
and won successes at the expense of Rome's clients in the interior
of the country (p. 123 *sq.*). The revolt of Syracuse in the spring,
followed by Agrigentum and the landing in Sicily of a large
Carthaginian army, caused the greatest anxiety. By the autumn
two legions and Marcellus had been transferred for the siege of
Syracuse. In Italy the removal of the energy and dash of Marcellus
was soon apparent, the commanders accomplished nothing except
the recovery of Arpi, the siege of Capua was not begun, and all
the Greek cities of Italy except Rhegium were now in the hands
of the Carthaginians.

VI. THE TAKING OF CAPUA

The dissatisfaction of the people was seen in the elections for
the year 212 B.C. Neither Fabius, father or son, was continued
in command. There was a cry for new men and greater energy
in the conduct of the war. The two new consuls were Q.
Fulvius Flaccus who had been consul twice before in 237 B.C.
and 224 B.C. and Appius Claudius Pulcher who as praetor and
propraetor had been commanding since 215 B.C. in Sicily. All
the commands in Italy were changed except one; Ti. Sempronius
Gracchus remained in Lucania with his two legions. In Picenum
there were now two legions under a new praetor C. Claudius
Nero, in Apulia Cn. Fulvius Flaccus a brother of the consul took
over the command, and the two consuls commanded in Campania.
The total of legions in this year reached its highest number of
the war, twenty-five. The Romans intended to begin the siege of
Capua, and the inhabitants had been prevented from sowing or
harvesting their crops in the previous year. Hannibal consequently ordered Hanno to march to Campania from Bruttium
collecting on the way convoys of supplies in Samnium. The
campaigning season had not yet opened, but the Roman consuls,
encamped at Bovianum, when they learned of Hanno's approach,
arranged that Q. Fulvius Flaccus should secretly enter Beneventum and that Gracchus should march into Campania[1]. While

[1] The whole narrative of these minor engagements in Livy is so contaminated with inventions and falsifications that only a bare outline of the
events can be tentatively reconstructed. The story of M. Centenius (Livy

Hanno was engaged in a foraging expedition Flaccus surprised the strongly entrenched Carthaginian camp and captured immense supplies. All provisioning of Capua was effectively stopped. The Romans, however, were not able to prevent Hannibal himself from marching into Campania to raise the siege of Capua. But the decisive factor now as in the two previous campaigns was that Hannibal could no longer feed his army for more than a few days in Campania. The plain had been continually scoured by three Roman armies and all provisions withdrawn into the fortresses. Hannibal's presence only depleted the reserves of Capua. Consequently once again he retreated into South Italy, and the Romans completed the fosse and rampart closing the lines round Capua. Meanwhile Ti. Sempronius Gracchus was surprised and killed by Numidian cavalry, some said by treachery in Lucania, others while bathing near Beneventum. He had shown energy and resolution in the darkest days of the war and deserved well of the Republic. His two legions of slaves enrolled after Cannae, the *volones*, now leaderless, were disbanded.

Through the winter and the succeeding year the consuls were continued in command of the siege operations of Capua with C. Claudius Nero. The consuls of 211 B.C. were Cn. Fulvius Centumalus and P. Sulpicius Galba, and the total of twenty-five legions was maintained, the *legiones urbanae* of the preceding year taking the place of the disbanded *volones*, while two fresh legions of recruits were enrolled at Rome. The Sicilian fleet was kept at a hundred, and the fleet under Laevinus in Greek waters reduced to twenty-five. In Italy alone in 211 B.C. Rome had sixteen legions, two on the Po, two in Etruria, two at Rome, four in Apulia and six in Campania. At last the effect of this overwhelming force was beginning to outweigh the strategic genius of Hannibal.

The Romans had recovered most of the revolted cities in Samnium and Apulia, and Capua was reduced to dire straits by the siege. Hannibal saw himself more and more confined to South Italy by a solid central Italy defended by large forces. Yet he determined to make one further effort to relieve Capua and perhaps force an engagement. Leaving behind his baggage train, he marched rapidly with a picked force to Mt Tifata and suddenly descended into Campania and attacked the besieging Roman armies. The Roman entrenchments had been designed for such an event, and without siege-engines and a large force nothing could be accomplished. Having failed in his attempt at surprise,

xxv, 19) is extremely suspicious and may well be a doublet of the defeat of C. Centenius in 217 B.C. See Kahrstedt, *op. cit.* pp. 265 *sqq.*

Hannibal determined upon a bold move to draw off by a feint the Roman armies and entice them to battle. He withdrew from Campania into Samnium as suddenly as he had come, and marching by the upper reaches of the Volturnus to disguise his intentions[1], arrived near Venafrum. Here he changed his direction and joining the Via Latina near Casinum advanced unopposed across the Anio until he encamped within three miles of the walls of Rome. With his cavalry he rode up to the Colline Gate. The boldness of the demonstration—for no foreign enemy had been at the gates of Rome since the battle of the Allia—may have caused some consternation in the city. Polybius records that the superstitious women-folk swept the pavements of the temples with their hair to invoke the assistance of the gods. But the walls of Rome were of immense strength, and there happened to be in the city, in addition to the two legions of newly-enrolled recruits, two of last year's legions, which had not yet been sent to Apulia. Fabius prevented any panic resolution to recall the armies from Campania, and Hannibal, disappointed of his hopes, after a small skirmish with the consul Sulpicius Galba returned to Bruttium, abandoning Capua to its fate. The march of Hannibal on Rome is a dramatic event which left a lasting impression upon the memory of the Romans. Its strategic ineffectiveness is the measure of the vast superiority of defence over attack in ancient warfare.

The Capuans when they knew that Hannibal could not help them surrendered at discretion. As a preliminary to wholesale confiscations of land to the Roman State the surviving senators and thirty notable citizens were executed or allowed a more lingering death in prison. Some few others were sold into slavery, but the remainder of the population retained its liberty, and Capua, deprived of all self-government, was administered as a dependent community by a *praefectus* elected yearly at Rome. The fall of Capua was of immense significance for the war in Italy, signalizing the triumph of the Roman strategy of defence. In the same year the fall of Syracuse had assured the collapse of the revolt in Sicily, so that when the news came of the terrible disaster of the Scipios in Spain (p. 71) the Senate could send a fresh army to Spain without jeopardizing the ultimate success of the campaign against Hannibal.

The rebellion of Sicily was at an end and in the East an advantageous alliance had been concluded with the Aetolian League in the late autumn of 212 B.C. against Philip of Macedon

---

[1] Polybius IX, 5, 8, διὰ τῆς Σαυνίτιδος; Livy XXVI, 8 makes Hannibal follow the Via Latina the whole way.

(p. 124). The two men responsible for these successes were elected consuls for 210 B.C., M. Claudius Marcellus and M. Valerius Laevinus. Laevinus' election seems to have been designed both as a reward for his services and as an opportunity for sending a fresh commander to Greece, the consul Sulpicius Galba. Laevinus had not as yet shown any marked military ability, and his administrative gifts were to be employed for the next four years as governor of Sicily. The recent disaster in Spain caused a division of opinion in the Senate as to the policy to be pursued. Should the Romans content themselves with holding the territory north of the Ebro? None of the experienced commanders came forward eager and confident of succeeding where the Scipios had failed. Consequently a praetor C. Claudius Nero who had commanded an army in the siege of Capua was sent out with two legions to drive the Carthaginians from Spain north of the Ebro. Meanwhile for the first time in the war the forces in the field were reduced after the exhausting effort required for the siege of Capua and the reduction of Sicily. In two vital areas of the war the Romans could now breathe more freely and the twenty-five legions were reduced to twenty-one; the number in Italy alone being reduced from sixteen to a total of eleven, including the two in Etruria and the *legiones urbanae* at Rome. This reduction enabled weak legions to be disbanded and others strengthened so that the almost complete loss of two full legions in Spain could be partly met by two new legions sent there this year and still further met in the following year.

With only four legions between them the consul Marcellus and Cn. Fulvius Centumalus, the consul of the preceding year, contented themselves with a cautious policy, slowly attempting to recover more towns from Hannibal. Salapia, south-east of Arpi, and two small fortresses in the Samnite highlands amongst the Hirpini were taken. But Cn. Fulvius was quite inexperienced in military command and, allowing himself to be trapped by Hannibal into battle near Herdonea[1] in Apulia, was killed himself with many of his officers and several thousand troops. Marcellus acted with more circumspection, and in a skirmish with Hannibal near Venusia held his ground. Meanwhile, the Roman garrison in Tarentum was for a short time reduced to severe straits, since the Tarentine fleet succeeded in sinking a convoy from Sicily despite

---

[1] Livy XXVII, 1; the death of Centumalus, which would not have been invented, shows that this is the event which Livy narrates twice, anticipating it in 212 B.C. XXV, 21, where Cn. Fulvius Flaccus is confused with Cn. Fulvius Centumalus. See De Sanctis, *op. cit.* p. 459 n. 28.

the overwhelming Roman command of the sea. It was a year of minor operations, the vigorous offensive being temporarily abandoned. This slackening of effort had a serious indirect result in the autumn when the new recruits were called for from the allies for the *legiones urbanae*. Twelve out of the thirty Latin colonies refused to send their contingents; they were Ardea, Nepete, Sutrium, Alba, Carsioli, Cora, Suessa, Circeii, Setia, Cales, Narnia and Interamna. Fortunately the disaffection spread no further, but it was a most disquieting indication that the exhaustion produced by the protracted conduct of the war was endangering Rome's vital arteries of man-power.

In the next year, however, 209 B.C., the cautious Roman strategy which seemed to be weakening the loyalty of her allies in the North was rewarded in the South by a success of some moral value. Hannibal opened the campaign by marching into Apulia where his manœuvres were countered by Marcellus. At the same time Q. Fulvius Flaccus, one of the consuls marching from Rome through the Hirpini into Lucania, was able to win back a number of hill tribes and small towns, including Vulci in Lucania, which Hannibal's movement across the Apennines left exposed. But the Romans had in view a more striking enterprise which was entrusted to the other consul Fabius himself. Collecting at Brundisium two legions sent from Sicily, where the pacification was complete, he moved upon Tarentum, capturing Manduria on his march. With the help of thirty quinqueremes sent by Laevinus he was able to press the siege by sea and land. Hannibal had returned to Bruttium to defend his base threatened by this large concentration of Roman forces. He set out to relieve Tarentum, but before he could arrive the treachery of the Bruttian garrison commander had done its work, and Tarentum was once more in the hands of Rome. Embittered and exasperated by the long war Fabius permitted his soldiers to sack the city, although it had not been taken by assault, and sold the 30,000 inhabitants into slavery. Despite this blow to Hannibal's security and prestige, the war in Italy seemed to be reaching a deadlock, and many must have wondered whether the war could be won or whether some approach must be made to a peace with Carthage by mutual concessions. But at this very moment there had arisen the one man of genius on the Roman side, whose brilliant campaigns and leadership were to bring victory, complete, decisive and irrevocable.

CHAPTER IV

SCIPIO AND VICTORY

I. NOVA CARTHAGO

AFTER the terrible disaster of the two Roman armies in 211 B.C. the Romans lost their hold upon Spain south of the Ebro except for the fortified cities of Castulo and Saguntum[1]. The Carthaginians were able to cross the Ebro and succeeded in detaching from the Romans the fickle prince Indibilis, chief of the powerful tribe of the Ilergeti[2]. But an able knight L. Marcius collected a small force from the survivors of the recent battle and the garrison troops of Emporium and Tarraco, and prevented the Carthaginians through the rest of the summer from further exploiting their victory by forming a base north of the Ebro[3]. In the autumn the Romans sent fresh forces to Spain, one full legion and the nucleus of a second to be formed by the addition of the troops of Marcius[4]. The new commander was C. Claudius Nero, who had commanded an army in Italy for two years in Picenum and at the siege of Capua. He had been well schooled in Fabian tactics, and through 210 B.C. he maintained a strict defensive[5]. Nor do we hear that Hasdrubal attempted or achieved any operation of importance against the strong Roman position on the coast, since without the command of the seas the Carthaginians could not hope to reduce Emporium or Tarraco. Yet the Senate must have been aware that the Carthaginians were steadily recruiting fresh troops amongst the Celtiberians and that a purely defensive policy would end by failing to prevent a second Carthaginian army from marching from Spain in 209 or 208 B.C. to invade Italy. The situation, in fact, was one which called for a commander

[1] Livy xxvi, 20, 6 may suggest that both were still in Roman hands, unless Saguntum is a mistake for Segontia (see A. Schulten, *Numantia*, I, p. 320 n. 6). Livy's placing of the Carthaginian armies conflicts with Polybius x, 7, 5, and may be, as Frantz, *op. cit.* p. 64, suggests, really their position in the year before the taking of Nova Carthago.

[2] This may be deduced from Polybius ix, 11, 3.

[3] The exploits in Livy xxv, 37–39 are plainly fictions to offset the defeat of the Scipios.   [4] Appian, *Iber.* 17; Livy xxvi, 17, 1.

[5] The story of the trapping of Hasdrubal (Livy xxvi, 17) is indefensible, even when the geographical setting is removed or emended.

of genius, since none of the experienced commanders in Italy were anxious to attempt the reconquest of Spain. The Senate acted with a boldness and independence which must excite the highest admiration. Recognizing the outstanding personal qualities of the younger P. Scipio, though he was only 25 years of age and had hitherto only held the curule aedileship (213 B.C.), the Senate, waiving constitutional precedent, supported his election to proconsular command in Spain amid scenes of popular enthusiasm. The appointment was the more notable in view of the influence of the Claudian family, which is attested by the commands held by members of that grim house[1]. For Scipio's appointment was a criticism of Claudius Nero. We need not, however, suppose that the Senatorial policy was the plaything of noble cliques, whose very existence is far from proved. M. Junius Silanus was appointed as colleague with *imperium minus*, and a force of 10,000 infantry and 1000 cavalry was allotted to them, so that Scipio would have at his disposal in Spain an army of four weak legions[2].

Scipio landed at Emporium towards the end of 210 B.C.[3] and made preparations for an exploit of no less daring than the capture of the chief Carthaginian fortress in Spain, Nova Carthago. His magnetic personality rapidly raised the morale of the Spanish legions and began to mould them into an invincible army. For, in the first place, his boundless self-confidence was part of a genuinely religious and mystic nature which the rationalism of Polybius has quite failed to understand; long vigils in prayer gave his utterances the true quality of inspired fanaticism; Poseidon himself, he declared, when launching the attack on Nova Carthago, had appeared to him in his sleep and suggested the plan of the assault, so that on every soldier's lips was the battle-cry 'Neptunus dux itineris.' The fervour of the troops was fanned by the burning enthusiasm of their general, an enthusiasm which later the cold scepticism of the hellenized circle of Scipio Aemilianus could only misinterpret as assumed deliberately by his great ancestor. At the same time Polybius is right in pointing out

[1] W. Schur, *Scipio Africanus*, pp. 69 *sqq.*

[2] De Sanctis, *op. cit.* p. 455 n. 21. Livy xxvii, 36, 10 shows that there were four legions in Spain in 207 B.C. and Cantalupi, *op. cit.* p. 19, shows that Livy's total of legions in 209 and 208 must include four in Spain.

[3] On the chronology see De Sanctis, *op. cit.* p. 454 n. 18 and p. 468 n. 38. Livy xxvi, 18 wrongly puts it in 211 B.C., allowing Claudius Nero only two months' command. But in xxvii, 7, 5 he mentions the other view. The origin of the error lies in a false equation of Polybius' Olympian year Ol. 142, 3 (July–July) with the Roman consular year 210–9 for the taking of Nova Carthago.

that the chief factor in the success of this exploit was the carefully
premeditated plan of operations, evidence for which he quotes
from an actual letter of Scipio to Philip of Macedon[1]. For the
strategic conception of the campaign was masterly. The three
Carthaginian armies had taken up winter quarters at great distances from each other; Hasdrubal, the son of Gisgo, near the
mouth of the Tagus, Mago 'the Samnite' near the pillars of
Hercules and Hasdrubal Barca in central Spain amongst the
Carpetani more than ten days' march from Nova Carthago[2]. The
way lay open for a swift descent on the city before the enemy
armies could be recalled to its defence. In addition, accurate topographical information gleaned from fishermen on the coast enabled Scipio to plan a tactical surprise which promised great hopes
of success.

The natural position of Nova Carthago was one of immense
strength. In the middle of a stretch of coastline which faces almost
due south a long bottle-shaped inlet ran northward into the land
from a neck of little more than half a mile wide. The inlet was
divided into two halves by the fortress, which lay at the end of an
isthmus jutting out from the eastern side to form a partition. The
inner half was a shallow lagoon joined to the outer half by a narrow
tidal canal crossed by a bridge. The walls of the city followed the
steep rocky slopes of five distinct hills protected on all sides,
except for the narrow isthmus, by water; the lagoon on the north,
the canal on the west and the gulf on the south. Scipio appeared
suddenly in the early spring of 209 B.C. by forced marches from
Tarraco[3]. He built a fortified camp across the end of the isthmus
and blocked the neck of the gulf with his fleet under his friend
Laelius. Next day, after a sortie had been driven in and severe
losses inflicted, Scipio launched about noon an attack with scaling
ladders from the isthmus. The attack was renewed in the afternoon, and when the defence was fully engaged on this side he sent
picked troops to wade across the shallow water of the lagoon[4]

---

[1] Polybius x, 9.   [2] Polybius x, 7, 5; see above p. 83 n. 1.

[3] Scipio's march to Saguntum from his base (or from the Ebro) must have
been continuous. A preliminary concentration, e.g. at Saguntum, would
have set the Carthaginians moving. The six days (Polybius x, 9, 7; Livy
XXVI, 42), if they are accepted, must be regarded as the last part of his march
and be reckoned from some point such as Saguntum (E. Meyer) or the Sucro
(De Sanctis).

[4] 'There are no tides in Cartagena harbour but with winds from south
to south-west the level rises from one to one and a half feet and north to
north-east winds have a contrary effect' (The Mediterranean Pilot, 1, 6th ed.
p. 69). A land or north wind might be expected to spring up towards sunset.

according to the fishermen's information; and, crossing with
speed and safety, this new force was able to surprise a weaker un-
defended portion of the northern walls. Taken in the rear the
defenders were rapidly swept off the walls, and the isthmus gate
was opened to the main attack. In a moment the key fortress of
the Carthaginian domination in south-eastern Spain and their best
base for communications with Africa was in the hands of the
Romans. Immense quantities of military stores and war treasure
were captured, as well as hostages who had guaranteed to Carthage the loyalty of many of the Spanish tribes. The moral effect
was no less great among the natives than in the Roman army and
at one blow most of the ill effects of the disaster of two years
previously were repaired.

The defences reconstructed and the affairs of Nova Carthago
settled, Scipio dispatched Laelius with the news and the chief
prisoners to Rome and himself returned to Tarraco. The rest of
the summer of 209 B.C. he spent in training his troops in the use
of the *gladius hispaniensis*[1], the finely tempered cut-and-thrust
sword, which in future became the standard equipment of the
legionary, replacing the shorter stabbing sword. At the same time
he endeavoured by diplomacy and the effect of his winning personality to detach from the Carthaginians the warlike Spanish
tribes, a potential reservoir of troops for either side. North of the
Ebro the two kings of the Ilergeti, Mandonius and Indibilis,
once again came over to Rome, and between the Ebro and the
Sucro Edesco king of the Edetani followed suit. Meanwhile the
Carthaginian generals pursued a policy of inaction, too jealous of
each other to combine, and content, while they protected the
mineral and agricultural wealth of the Tagus, Anas, and Baetis
valleys, to abandon the eastern littoral to the Romans. None of
them had shown any constructive or organizing ability in developing the empire which the three great chiefs of the Barcid
family had created. No improvements or benefits compensated
for their unabashed exploiting of the country's resources, and the
tribes of the interior only submitted so long as large armies were
in their vicinity. Except in these three river valleys the Punic
domination of Spain was as flimsy as a house of cards. Finally,
there can be little doubt that Hasdrubal was by now devoting
himself to recruiting the Celtiberians in the central plateau for the
project he had already formed of marching to Italy. But at this
stage of the war, though perhaps he could not realize it, the
defence of Spain was of greater importance to Carthage than the
sending of a new army to Italy.

[1] See P. Couissin, *Les Armes Romaines*, pp. 22 *sqq*.

II. BAECULA, ILIPA, THE CONQUEST OF SPAIN

Scipio's spies must have brought him information which enabled him to guess Hasdrubal's intentions. For in the very early spring of 208 B.C. Scipio marched rapidly south in order to force a decisive battle. From Polybius' account it seems clear that Hasdrubal was surprised in the upper Baetis valley near Castulo and retreated to a very strong position at Baecula[1], where he intended to await the coming of the second army from Gades. Scipio, at first daunted by the strength of Hasdrubal's position, but then spurred on by the danger of the arrival of the other Carthaginian armies, took the initiative. His light-armed troops, supported by some picked legionaries, attacked on a wide front to fix the attention of Hasdrubal while the main force, divided into two, scaled the hill on either flank. Scipio's army cannot have numbered less than 35,000 since the accession of Indibilis and a force of the Ilergeti, whereas Hasdrubal's army perhaps amounted to little more than 25,000. Outnumbered by troops definitely superior in quality to his own, Hasdrubal abandoned his strong position directly he saw the flank attacks succeeding and, aided by the lie of the ground to the north, safely withdrew the main portion of his army with his treasure and baggage[2].

The battle itself was a brilliant tactical success for Scipio, but it was not decisive because Hasdrubal had secured his retreat. Nor could Scipio follow in the wake of the retreating army towards the Tagus valley through hostile territory without grave difficulty of commissariat, the certainty of facing two Carthaginian armies and the possibility of being surrounded by three. Yet the escape of Hasdrubal has been, both in ancient and modern times, the subject of censorious judgments upon Scipio's action. The censure ignores the lesson of all campaigning in Spain. One army might follow another along one of the rich river valleys where provisions were plentiful, but across the two plateaux which separate the three great rivers of south-western Spain this meant privations for the leader and starvation for the follower. From the Tagus[3], with drafts from the other armies, Hasdrubal set forth for Italy, doubtless marching up the Douro valley to the northern tributaries and then slipping through the Pyrenees along

[1] The exact position of the battlefield is uncertain, but it is probable that the village of Bailén represents the ancient Baecula. See W. Brewitz, *Scipio Africanus Major*, p. 60, and Kromayer-Veith, *Schlachten-Atlas*, p. 162 b.

[2] Polybius (x, 40, 1) gives 12,000 prisoners, Livy (xxvii, 18) adds 8000 killed: both figures are beyond doubt too high.

[3] Livy (xxvii, 20) stages a meeting of the three Carthaginian generals.

the Atlantic seaboard[1], thus avoiding the eastern passes which Scipio sought to block by detaching troops from the Roman strongholds north of the Ebro. Hasdrubal's escape from Spain was finely executed, but it had always been a possibility by this route, and it is difficult to see how Scipio could prevent it once he had left the upper Ebro valley to campaign in southern Spain.

One Carthaginian army had left Spain for Italy, and it was certain that the next year 207 B.C. would witness a decisive effort on the part of Scipio to destroy the base of Carthaginian power in Baetica. Fully alive to the danger, the Carthaginian home government sent at the beginning of 207 B.C. a fresh army under Hanno. This army marched into central Spain to join Mago, who was, according to the usual plan, endeavouring to recruit Celtiberians. Scipio detached Silanus with 10,000 foot and 500 horse, and he succeeded in surprising the camp where Hanno was training the native troops, but though he captured Hanno he could not prevent Mago and the main army from getting away to join Hasdrubal Gisgo near Gades. However, the operation was of considerable importance in deciding the loyalty of the wavering tribes of central Spain, and Scipio gave generous praise to his second-in-command for the exploit.

Meanwhile[2] Scipio himself concentrating his forces near Castulo and Baecula[3] marched down the Baetis and encamped opposite Hasdrubal Gisgo and Mago near Ilipa[4]. The Carthaginians had collected all their own troops in the peninsula and their Spanish levies for a decisive battle and may have numbered 50,000 infantry and 4500 cavalry, as Livy says[5]. Scipio's army was probably somewhat smaller, perhaps 40,000, of whom little more than 25,000 were Roman troops. While the Romans were building their usual fortified camp with ditch and palisade, Mago

[1] Appian, *Iber.* 28 supplements Livy xxvii, 19; see C. Jullian, *Hist. de la Gaule*, i, p. 51.

[2] For the chronology see De Sanctis, *op. cit.* p. 496 n. 84. Livy places the battle of Ilipa in 206 B.C. (xxviii, 16, 14), leaving the year 207 B.C. almost devoid of operations and crowding all the events of chapters 12–37 into 206 B.C. Ilipa is to be placed in 207 B.C.

[3] Hence Livy (xxviii, 13) misunderstanding Polybius places the battle 'ad Baeculam urbem.'

[4] Probably identified as Alcala del Rio near Seville. Ed. Meyer, *Kleine Schriften*, ii, pp. 406 *sq.*, has shown that the Latin Silpia in Livy xxviii, 12, 15 is Polybius' Ἰλίπας, a certain correction of the MSS. Ἠλίγγας, Polybius xi, 20, 1.

[5] Livy xxviii, 12, possibly going back to Silenus through using Coelius. Polybius xi, 20, 2 using an inferior source gives 74,000 as the total, presumably *ad maiorem gloriam Scipionis.*

made a cavalry attack upon the lines, but the foresight of Scipio had stationed a body of cavalry in concealment on the flank, and the attack was repulsed with considerable loss. For several days the opposing armies were content to make a demonstration in battle order in the evening when no engagement could follow. Scipio deliberately drew up his own army with his Roman legionaries in the centre opposite the African troops and elephants of Hasdrubal, and his Spaniards on both wings. At last Scipio ordered his troops to take their morning meal before sunrise and, leading them into the plain as the sun rose, drew the army up in a new battle order with the Spaniards in the centre and the legions on either flank. Hasdrubal was surprised by the attacks of the Roman cavalry and light-armed troops on his outposts and was compelled hastily to throw his army into their usual battle formation before they could breakfast. After the outpost action had continued for some time indecisively, Scipio advanced wheeling his flanks outwards and well in front of his thinned centre. The Roman legionaries fell with overwhelming force upon the Spanish levies of Hasdrubal's wings and decided the battle almost before the centres were engaged, for Hasdrubal made no attempt to cut through the weak Roman centre which was held back[1]. Scipio, at the risk of disaster, had successfully adapted Hannibal's battle tactics and won a striking victory, though, without a considerable force of cavalry, he could only outflank and could not surround and annihilate the Carthaginian army. The battle decided the fate of the Carthaginian empire in Spain. The Spaniards in the Punic army, after resisting stoutly despite their hunger and the heat, now broke up in flight and dispersed. Hasdrubal and his African troops attempted to make a stand at his camp, but then retreated, closely pursued, to the sea. He himself and Mago escaped on shipboard, but most of the army was cut off and surrendered. The battle and the close pursuit alike exhibit the brilliance of Scipio's generalship.

After the battle Scipio sent his brother Lucius to capture an important town, Orongis, probably in the mining regions of Castulo, with orders to proceed thence to Rome to announce the tidings of his victorious campaign. No Carthaginian army remained in the field to dispute the Roman advance in Spain but there were many towns with strong defences and desperate defenders. The reduction of these strongholds was the task of the

---

1 Polybius' account of the battle presents unsolved, perhaps insoluble, difficulties, chief among them the apparent inaction of the Carthaginian cavalry.

final year's campaign (206 B.C.). In the Segura valley Ilurgia and
Castax[1] were taken, the latter by treachery, the former after a
prolonged defence punished by a massacre; and farther west
Astapa surrendered, but only after the warriors had immolated
their wives and children and rushing out in a sortie had themselves
been killed to a man. An attempt was immediately made to get
into touch with Roman sympathizers inside the city of Gades and
a Roman fleet under Laelius sailed towards the straits to co-
operate. But while Mago was in command of the garrison the
movement in the city had no success, and Laelius retired to Nova
Carthago. For there was serious news from the Roman base.
North of the Ebro the two powerful chieftains Indibilis and
Mandonius were once more in revolt, Scipio was reported ill, and
a mutiny had broken out amongst the garrison troops stationed
on the Sucro. Scipio, recovering quickly from his indisposition,
removed the grievance by distributing arrears of pay, and by
astute management and the effect of his sudden appearance in the
Sucro camp, isolated the ringleaders and with exemplary severity
had them executed. A rapid campaign followed north of the Ebro
which ended, for the time being, in the defeat and surrender of
the recalcitrant tribes.

In the meantime the Carthaginians still held one point of vantage
at Gades. But it was clear that the siege of the town by the Romans
was imminent. Consequently, while Scipio was engaged north of
the Ebro, Mago, embarking his best troops on transports, sailed
through the straits to make a sudden landing and surprise attack
on Nova Carthago. It was the last Carthaginian attempt to avert
the inevitable in Spain. The attack, however, was easily repulsed
by the watchful garrison and on his return Mago was shut out
from Gades and sailed off to the Balearic islands, where the
capital of Minorca (Mahon) still bears his name. This was the end
of the Carthaginian domination in Spain. Gades surrendered to
the Romans the more readily because Mago had by an act of
treachery put to death their chief citizens when they went out to
treat with him. In return, the Romans when making their settlement of Spain gave Gades the position of a free city. And Strabo
(III, 168) attests the great prosperity enjoyed by Gaditane
merchants in succeeding centuries. Meanwhile Masinissa, the

---

[1] Appian, *Iber.* 32. Ilurgia = Ilorci, the scene of Cn. Scipio's defeat (see
Meyer, *op. cit.* p. 444 n. 1), but the site is not certain. See also De Sanctis,
op. cit. p. 501 n. 90; Brewitz, *op. cit.* p. 21; H. H. Scullard, *Scipio Africanus
in the Second Punic War*, p. 142 n. 2. Livy XXVIII, 20, not knowing the
names, transforms them into the familiar Iliturgis and Castulo.

Numidian whose genius was to mould the destines of North Africa for the next sixty years, was given an opportunity to meet Scipio. By his accession to the Roman side an ally was gained of supreme importance for the final stage of the war[1].

Thus by the autumn of 206 B.C. the conquest of Spain was complete. In four years of campaigning Scipio had wrested from Carthage her real military base for the war and had won for Rome a region of immense potential wealth. For the remainder of the war the transference from Carthage to Rome of the mineral wealth of Spain was as decisive in the realm of financial resources as the loss of Spanish tribal alliances was fatal to Carthaginian armies. Polybius tells us that in his own day the mines of Nova Carthago produced 1500 talents a year; and there was a tradition about a mine called Baebelo started by Hannibal which produced 1350 talents yearly. The inadequacy of our evidence leaves the military events of these four years veiled in partial obscurity. But though it seems evident that the Carthaginian generalship was much to blame in the loss of Spain, nothing can dim the grandeur of Scipio's achievement. After founding the first Roman colony in Spain, Italica[2], and leaving a garrison army under Marcius and Silanus, he returned to Rome to stand for the consulship of 205 B.C.

III. THE METAURUS

In the previous chapter the narrative of the war in Italy has been carried down to the recapture of Tarentum in 209 B.C. Grave signs of disaffection or at least war-weariness had appeared, when twelve Latin colonies refused their annual contingents. In Etruria particularly there was serious unrest, and the two legions which were stationed there were reinforced by a third. The people clamoured for a more vigorous offensive in order to end the war in Italy. Consequently, Marcellus was once more elected consul for 208, since he at least was not content with sieges and had dared to cross swords with Hannibal. His colleague was T. Quinctius Crispinus, who had served under him at the siege of Syracuse and had lately been commanding in Campania. Crispinus marched south to assist in the siege of Locri which had been recently undertaken; but he soon moved back into Apulia to join Marcellus near Venusia, since Hannibal had encamped close by and was offering battle. It may well be that with the double

---

[1] The diplomatic attempts to win over Syphax are narrated later (p. 99).
[2] North-west of Seville, the modern Santiponce on the right bank of the Guadalquivir, Appian, *Iber.* 38.

consular army of four legions Marcellus thought of risking a
battle, if by manœuvring he could gain an advantageous position.
But while both consuls were reconnoitring with a small force they
were cut off by the Carthaginians, Crispinus was severely
wounded and Marcellus was killed. So ended in a skirmish a
soldier, whose vigour and bravery had played a large part in
leading the Roman resistance after Cannae. Not inappositely did
Posidonius name Marcellus 'the sword' of Rome beside 'her
shield' Fabius. His conduct of the siege of Syracuse was masterly;
only when matched against Hannibal was his genius rebuked.
Indeed, the fact that the annalist historians attributed to him the
majority of their legendary victories against Hannibal in Italy
suggests that he stood far above the average level of Roman
commanders. A strong tradition affirms that Hannibal with the
magnanimity which recognized a courageous adversary buried his
body with full funeral honours. For the rest of the year the renewed fear of Hannibal's invincible skill prevented any further
offensive. Other reverses, too, were suffered. The commander of
the garrison at Tarentum, Q. Claudius, was surprised near
Petelia when marching along the coast with a small army towards
Locri and suffered severe losses in a disorderly retreat. Finally,
after failing to take Salapia, Hannibal himself marched south,
and, surprising the Roman besiegers of Locri, drove them to their
ships and relieved the city. There seemed no hope or prospect of
defeating Hannibal and expelling him from Italy.

The war in Greece, despite the intervention of Attalus of
Pergamum with his fleet, had on the whole gone in favour
of Philip, but the Carthaginians had not been daring enough to
risk their ships to help him, and, though the Aetolians had cause
enough for anxiety, Rome had, for the moment, little to fear in
the East (pp. 126 *sqq.*). From other quarters, however, came
better news. In a raid on Africa M. Valerius Laevinus with 100
quinqueremes met the Punic navy 83 strong and won a victory,
capturing 18 ships (summer 208)[1]. It was the most important
naval engagement in the war, and it enabled the Romans later to
land in Africa unopposed at sea, and keep open their communications with Italy. In Spain the brilliant capture of Nova Carthago
was followed by the victory at Baecula, and once again the
prospects of the conquest of Carthaginian Spain were promising.
But suddenly a new danger threatened Italy. In the autumn

---

[1] Livy XXVII, 29, 7–8 (repeated as in 207 B.C., XXVIII, 4, 5–7). The
historicity of the battle is confirmed by the failure of the Carthaginians to
oppose at sea Scipio's crossing to Africa in 205 B.C. See De Sanctis, *op. cit.*
p. 476 n. 52, pp. 642 *sq.*; Holleaux, *Rome, La Grèce, etc.* p. 244 n. 2.

news came from Massilia that Hasdrubal had left Spain with an army which perhaps numbered 20,000 men and that he was wintering in Gaul.

At Rome the winter of 208–7 B.C. must have been one of great anxiety in anticipation of the invasion of another Carthaginian army. At the elections experienced commanders were chosen as consuls, C. Claudius Nero, who had commanded an army before Capua and in Spain; and M. Livius Salinator, who, though for ten years he had been out of favour, had commanded with Aemilius Paullus in the brilliant Illyrian campaign of 219 B.C. (vol. VII, pp. 848 *sqq.*). His support by the Senate at this critical moment was an act of wise policy, since his ability had been proved and the campaigns of the coming year needed more adventurous handling than either Fabius or Q. Fulvius Flaccus would be likely to show. Once again the number of the legions was raised to twenty-three: outside Italy there were four in Spain, two in Sardinia and two in Sicily; in the south of Italy there was one legion at Capua and two in garrison at Tarentum, two taken over as a field-army by the new consul Claudius Nero and two by Fulvius Flaccus to operate against Hannibal. Meanwhile, the remaining eight legions were assigned to the defence of North Italy against the invading army: besides two *legiones urbanae* at Rome and two watching Etruria under Terentius Varro, the praetor L. Porcius Licinus advanced to Ariminum with two legions, and Livius with his regular consular army took up a position near Narnia, ready to march into Etruria or Picenum according to the route which the invader took. The Roman plan of defence was the same as in the spring of 217 B.C. but improved by this linking army; and the total array of fifteen legions serving in Italy represented the greatest exertions to meet the crisis of the Italian campaign.

Hasdrubal crossed the Alps in the early spring, directly the snows had melted, probably by the same pass which Hannibal had taken eleven years before[1]. His march was attended with no difficulties owing to the Carthaginian alliance with the Celtic tribes on both sides of the Alps[2]. Arrived in the Po valley, he proceeded to recruit Gauls for his army, perhaps raising his total force by a third to 30,000[3], and at the same time he made an

---

[1] Livy XXVII, 39, 7; Appian, *Hann.* 52. But Varro (*ap.* Serv. *Aen.* x, 13) denies this.

[2] Polybius XI, 1; Livy XXVII, 39, 6.

[3] Appian, *Hann.* 52 gives 56,000; Livy XXVII, 49, 6 gives the same figure as the number of killed at the Metaurus. The real number of Hasdrubal's army can only be deduced from his actions; see De Sanctis, *op. cit.* p. 571.

unsuccessful attempt to capture Placentia. Then he pushed on cautiously till he arrived near Fanum at the Apennine exit of the Via Flaminia and brushed against the outposts of the combined armies of the praetor Porcius, and the consul Livius now encamped in front of Sena Gallica. Meanwhile, in South Italy Hannibal moved late from his winter quarters in Bruttium since he knew that Hasdrubal could not be in Italy before April. His intention no doubt was to effect a junction with Hasdrubal in Central Italy, keeping a watch all the time to prevent an attack on his last remaining bases in Bruttium and especially Locri. Near Grumentum he was lightly engaged with the combined armies of Claudius Nero and Q. Fulvius Flaccus, and then, moving again south to Venusia, he fought another small action in which the Romans as usual claimed the victory. Indeed they were operating with vigour and determination and constantly threatened to attack Locri with a force from Tarentum. Consequently Hannibal did not find it possible to move farther from his southern base than Canusium, where he awaited news from Hasdrubal.

The news had overshot the mark. Four Gauls and two Numidians had ridden in safety to the south of Italy, but then as they turned north again on the track of Hannibal they fell into the hands of Q. Claudius. The consul Nero was swiftly informed that Hasdrubal proposed to cross the Apennines and meet his brother in Umbria. Nero made an instant decision of great boldness and strategic insight. The interception of the message gave him the opportunity to move while Hannibal waited still uncertain. With 6000 picked infantry and 1000 cavalry he hastened by forced marches up the Adriatic coast to join Livius and Porcius, at the same time suggesting to the Senate that the legion at Capua should be withdrawn for the garrison at Rome and the *legiones urbanae* sent forward to Narnia. In this way large forces were concentrated in the northern area, and after the arrival of Claudius Nero the army at Sena Gallica numbered 40,000 men.

The position of the Roman army made it impossible for Hasdrubal to march down the coast to join Hannibal without fighting a pitched engagement. Whether or not Hasdrubal was on the point of making this decision, the sudden discovery from the duplicated bugle-calls of the arrival of the second Roman consul caused him to alter his plans. Avoiding battle against a force so superior to his own, he attempted to slip away by the Via Flaminia. It was a very hazardous move, due in part perhaps to defective information about the natural difficulties of the route, and his army fell into the trap prepared by the Roman strategy.

As Hasdrubal moved up the Metaurus valley by night the Roman army started in pursuit, crossing to the left bank where the road lay. Next morning Hasdrubal was compelled, owing to the disorderliness of his Gallic contingent and the attacks of the Roman vanguard of cavalry, to arrest his march and prepare for battle[1]. He chose a position where a steep ridge lying back from the river protected his left, and here he placed the Gauls. He deliberately massed African and Spanish troops into a close formation, hoping to break through the Roman left wing. The battle hung in the balance so long as the whole of the right wing of the Roman army was out of action owing to the steep intervening hill. But Nero succeeded in detaching part of these troops and leading them behind the Roman centre to pass up the river bed on the left flank and so take the Carthaginian phalanx in the rear. The elephants very quickly got out of hand and becoming more dangerous to the Carthaginians than to their adversaries were felled by the mahout's blow of mallet on chisel behind the ear. When Hasdrubal saw his army surrounded he rode into the thick of the battle and as Livy describes it 'fell fighting—a death worthy of Hamilcar's son and Hannibal's brother.'

It was the most decisive victory hitherto won by the Romans in the war. When the news arrived at Rome the relief was accompanied by scenes of extravagant joy, and a three days' thanksgiving was decreed 'because the consuls, M. Livius and C. Claudius, had preserved their own armies in safety and destroyed the army of the enemy and its commander.'

Hannibal learnt the news of the disaster when Nero marched south to rejoin the rest of his own consular army. He retired to Bruttium, his proud spirit for a time daunted by disappointment. For the disaster had ended the last desperate hope of breaking the Roman hold on Italy. Confidence in the qualities of the Roman troops was restored, and the loyalty of Rome's allies henceforward was assured. Four legions were disbanded so that in 206 B.C. the number was reduced to twenty. Even so there were still thirteen legions in Italy, but the new consuls for 206 B.C., L. Veturius Philo and Q. Caecilius Metellus, did not dare either to attack Hannibal in Bruttium or to lay siege to Locri and Croton, so great was the fear which he still inspired. The Romans were content to await the return of the victorious Scipio from Spain to lead them to final victory, and that not against Hannibal in Italy but against Carthage.

[1] The evidence does not permit any reasonably certain identification of the precise site of the battlefield.

IV. SCIPIO'S PREPARATIONS FOR THE INVASION OF AFRICA

The return of the conqueror of Spain happened towards the close of a year in which the war in South Italy had been pursued with a notable lack of energy and success. No attempt had been made to attack the remaining strongholds of Hannibal, Locri and Croton. At the elections for 205 the admiration and gratitude of the people were shown in the unanimous support of Scipio for the consulship, since he had held no office which entitled him to celebrate a triumph for his victories. As his colleague P. Licinius Crassus was chosen, who by reason of his office of Pontifex Maximus could not leave Italy, so as to ensure for Scipio un-hampered sole command. For he made public that he proposed, notwithstanding the presence of Hannibal in Italy, to invade Africa. His ambition and confidence had grown with his victories, and he had learnt the weakness of the Carthaginian armies and imperial system. The enterprise itself was favoured by every chance of success and could alone bring to Rome decisive and complete victory. Furthermore, it was a reversion to the strategy with which Rome had begun the war. The spirits of the people, long mesmerized by the genius of Hannibal, soared in the hopes inspired by this new leader. Yet in the Senate it is clear that there was strenuous opposition to Scipio's policy on the part of Q. Fabius and Q. Fulvius Flaccus, though the tradition which Livy followed has probably exaggerated it in order to glorify Scipio. 'Let there be peace in Italy before there is war in Africa.' But Scipio saw clearly how difficult it might be to persuade the Romans, weary of the unending war, to launch an attack on Africa once Hannibal had been expelled from Italy. In his speeches he took care to rouse a passionate desire for revenge, a desire to inflict upon the citizens of Carthage in Africa a portion of what Italy had suffered from the army of Hannibal.

The result was that the opposition was so far overcome that Scipio was allotted the province of Sicily with leave to cross over to Africa if he saw fit. But he was given no more than the command of the two legions in Sicily and had to augment his armament by volunteers. The Sicilian legions of the survivors of Cannae had already been brought up to full strength by drafts from Marcellus' veteran army. Eager to wipe out their disgrace and inured to long years of iron discipline in Sicily, they were ideal troops to form the backbone of the army of invasion. The cities of Etruria and Umbria were foremost in providing timber and equipment for a fleet of thirty ships to be built, and in forging weapons and accoutrements for the 7000 volunteers who enlisted. Scipio crossed to Sicily to train his new army in the tactics which he had devised in Spain.

During the summer of 205 B.C. Scipio suddenly saw a chance of recovering Locri. A plot had been secretly hatched between exiled Locrian nobles at Rhegium and some Locrian artisans who had been made prisoners by the Romans and had then returned to their city under ransom. One of the two rocky citadels of the town was to be betrayed and Scipio promised to send a force to assist, although it was beyond the limits of his sphere of command in Sicily. The plan was completely successful, and the town now lay between two citadels, one held by the Romans and the other by the Carthaginians. On hearing the news Hannibal moved to the town hoping to catch the Romans off their guard. But instead he found the population hostile and encountered determined resistance from a considerable force which Scipio had just landed from his fleet. The chance of surprise was gone, and the danger of being taken in the rear by the four legions of the Roman army in Bruttium under Metellus and Crassus remained. Unwillingly Hannibal was forced to abandon the town and the Carthaginian citadel quickly surrendered. It was a final indication of the desperate weakness of his position in Italy.

Until the Senate should decide upon the fate of Locri Scipio left as governor the propraetor Q. Pleminius, who had commanded the attack. Scipio was in urgent need of money for his African war-chest and may very well have instigated his lieutenant to fleece these renegade Greeks, for whom he can have felt no pity. He certainly upheld Pleminius in a quarrel which broke out over the partition of booty and condoned the plundering of the treasure of the temple of Persephone, which Hannibal himself had spared. But the oppression of Pleminius was carried to such lengths that a Locrian embassy of suppliants went to Rome. The superstitions of the populace were excited by the story of the desecration of the temple, and Fabius gladly saw an opportunity for attacking Scipio in the Senate. After a heated discussion a commission was appointed of ten senators headed by a praetor with an aedile and two tribunes to investigate the whole matter. The commission made the expiatory sacrifices due to the goddess and condemned Pleminius, but wisely contented themselves with accompanying Scipio in a review of his army. Such seems to be the bare outline of these strange events, but it is extremely improbable that, as our evidence suggests, the Romans took this drastic action from an outraged sense of justice. The utmost severity to revolted allies was such a normal thing with the Romans that one can only guess that political faction was the real cause for which Pleminius seems to have been sacrificed. Scipio's own position, however, remained unassailable by such methods.

In Spain L. Cornelius Lentulus and L. Manlius Acidinus with proconsular power commanded an army of occupation reduced to two legions. They were faced in the summer of 205 B.C. by a renewed rebellion of the tribes north of the Ebro, incompletely subdued the year before owing to Scipio's haste to return to Rome. The rebellion was completely crushed, and Mandonius was put to death. In the same summer Hannibal's brother Mago made a bold descent on Liguria from the Balearic isles with a fleet of thirty warships and an army of 14,000 men. He captured Genoa by surprise and opened communication with the tribes of the Po valley. It was a desperate attempt to prolong the war in Italy and to divert the Romans from the invasion of Africa. The Romans were content, however, with measures for the defence of central Italy. M. Valerius Laevinus commanded two legions at Arretium and M. Livius Salinator added his two legions to two others under a praetor at Ariminum. Meanwhile Mago was reinforced from Carthage by twenty-five ships, 6000 infantry and 800 cavalry and seven elephants and money. But even with this addition to his forces he did not feel strong enough for the next two years to invade Italy, for he was unable to gain any considerable accession of troops from the Gauls, who had not forgotten the terrible losses they had suffered at the Metaurus. Thus the expedition failed to have any effect upon the Roman plans for the invasion of Africa. Equally ineffective was the Carthaginian attempt to send supplies and money to Hannibal in Bruttium whence the smallness of his forces prevented him from moving. For the fleet of one hundred transports was caught in a storm and driven off Sardinia where the Roman praetor Cn. Octavius had no difficulty in capturing sixty and sinking twenty (summer 205)[1]. Finally, as is described elsewhere (pp. 132 *sqq.*), operations in Greece, which the Romans since the winter of 208–7 had found it convenient to neglect, ended in the Peace of Phoenice[2], which at the price of concessions to Macedon freed Rome from this pre-occupation. By timidity at sea Carthage had forfeited whatever chance she had of keeping Philip in the field, and now with no allies outside Africa except a few Gauls she had herself to face a Roman invasion.

[1] Livy XXVIII, 46, 14; Appian, *Hann.* 54.

V. THE INVASION OF AFRICA

By the end of 205 B.C. preparations for the invasion were complete. Laelius had been sent in the summer with a fleet to prepare the way by diplomacy. His report of the tribes of north Africa gave considerable hopes for the coming expedition. The only unfavourable information concerned Syphax, who ruled over a large kingdom of the Masaesyli in Numidia between the Ampsaga and the Muluchat rivers with his capitals at Cirta and Siga. His rising against Carthage in the year after the battle of Cannae had greatly assisted the advance of the Scipios in Spain (p. 70). Tradition, indeed, affirms that a Roman centurion Statorius was sent over from Spain to introduce Roman military discipline into his army. Although defeated by Hasdrubal Gisgo and driven from his kingdom, he had contrived to return with the help of the Mauri, so that in 212 B.C. the Carthaginians were compelled once again to recognize his sovereignty. In the following years Carthaginian and Roman diplomacy competed for his alliance; in fact a story of doubtful value stages a meeting between Hasdrubal and Scipio at his court[1]. The issue was decided by his marriage with Hasdrubal's beautiful daughter Sophonisba, and, when Laelius sent envoys to him in 205 B.C., he declared his intention of opposing the Romans in Africa with all his forces. But Syphax was not the only prince to be reckoned with. Between his borders and the domains of Carthage lay a smaller kingdom of the Massyli, who were perpetually at war with the Masaesyli. This had been weakened by dynastic factions following upon the death of its king Gaias, until at last his younger son, Masinissa, leaving Spain in 206 B.C., had obtained help from Mauretania, defeated the rival faction, and won for himself his father's throne. His reign was short indeed, since in the following year Laelius found him once more on his travels. Yet Masinissa even in exile was a very valuable ally for the Romans. His ancestral kingdom might easily be regained and would then be a sharp thorn in the side of Carthage. His tribesmen would provide the cavalry which hitherto all the Roman armies had lacked. Lastly, the young prince was a fine leader, who had gained experience in Spain, and was ideally fitted for the delicate task of winning the African tribes from their allegiance to Carthage. Laelius showed his farsighted wisdom by making a firm alliance which was destined to have results extending far beyond its immediate scope and aim.

---

[1] Polybius XI, 24 a, 4; Livy XXVIII, 17–18; Appian, *Iber.* 29.

In the spring of 204 B.C. Scipio set sail from Lilybaeum with
a squadron of forty quinqueremes to cover the transports which
carried his army, probably amounting to about 25,000 men.
The Carthaginian naval strength had sunk so low since their
defeat in 208 B.C. that there was little danger of any hindrance to
the Roman invasion or to the army's communications with Sicily.
A landing was effected at Cape Farina near Utica, which was the
first objective of attack[1], and it was easy for Masinissa with a band
of cavalry to join the Romans. Scipio advanced his camp close to
the town on the hills to the south. Meanwhile, Syphax was
marching with a large Numidian army to join forces with Hasdrubal Gisgo near Carthage. However, an advance-guard of cavalry
under Hasdrubal's son Hanno ventured near the Roman army
and was cleverly lured by Masinissa into an ambush and destroyed[2]. After this initial success Scipio at once pressed on the
siege of Utica by land and sea. But the city withstood the Roman
assaults until the approach of Hasdrubal and Syphax compelled
Scipio to give up the siege and retreat to a rocky peninsula
jutting out into the sea some two miles east of the city, where he
formed a fortified 'Castra Cornelia' for the winter.

So ended the first campaign in Africa. Apart from the successful landing it could hardly seem otherwise than a failure. The
position of an army on this sea-girt tongue of land was precarious
enough, dependent as it was upon provisions brought from overseas and unable to move a step inland without confronting the
powerful forces of Hasdrubal and Syphax encamped six miles
away. It was perhaps fortunate that by sending to Rome the
booty captured in the cavalry engagement, accompanied by exaggerated accounts of the success, Scipio was able to disguise
from the Senate the desperate state of affairs. Nor did his
enemies fully realize his plight. During the winter Syphax took
upon himself the rôle of mediator and brought an offer of peace
terms of which no doubt Hasdrubal had approved. They were
that after the evacuation of Italy by Hannibal and Africa by
Scipio both powers should agree to a treaty on the *status quo*. To
Scipio the offer was welcome not as a road to peace without
victory but as a screen for treachery. He deliberately prolonged
the negotiations, gaining accurate and detailed information as to
the dispositions of the enemy camps through the constant interchange of envoys whose function was more truly that of spies.

[1] Livy's rhetorical narrative (XXIX, 25–7, probably from Coelius) of
calms and fogs and good and bad omens is full of obvious falsifications.
Scipio must from the first have intended to land as near Utica as possible.
[2] The engagement in Livy XXIX, 29, 1 is a doublet of that in XXIX, 34.

Officers of experience were sent to accompany them, disguised as
slaves, so that those in command of the units of the Roman army
became thoroughly familiar with the lie of the ground. And this
knowledge the Roman commander did not propose to waste.

At length the spring of 203 B.C. opened and Scipio prepared
his siege-engines and launched his ships as though to force a
quicker agreement by threatening to renew his assault on Utica.
A force was sent to occupy the hills on the east of the town from
which he had attacked in the previous year, while, at the same time,
he encouraged the enemy's false security by suggesting that his
consilium was on the point of agreeing to the conditions. Finally,
according to Polybius (XIV, 2, 11), to absolve himself from the
charge of treachery, he sent word that his *consilium* would not
accept the peace though he himself favoured it. When the
message reached the enemy orders had already been given for a
night attack. Laelius and Masinissa with half the army were sent
to fire the camp of Syphax, whose soldiers' hutments were built
of thatched reed and osiers without the use of earth or solid
timber, while Scipio himself stood ready to attack the Carthaginians. The plan succeeded completely. Those who escaped from
the conflagration were cut down by Masinissa's Numidians;
Syphax himself barely escaped from the destruction of his army.
Heavy losses were also inflicted upon the Carthaginian army in
the panic retreat, and Hasdrubal, after attempting to stand his
ground at the town of Anda, was forced to retreat farther, leaving
Scipio undisputed master of the country round Utica. It was a
great disaster for Carthage which, perhaps, did more than anything else to decide the last stage of the war. Indeed Scipio's
admirers, incurious of *Romana fides* in their allegations against
Punica fides, regarded this victory as his most brilliant exploit.

Not wholly daunted, the Carthaginians took energetic measures
to form a new army to save Utica, which Scipio proceeded to
besiege. Four thousand brave and well-armed Celtiberian mercenaries had landed in Africa and marched direct to join Hasdrubal
and Syphax who were busy reorganizing their shaken forces in
the Great Plains on the Bagradas river seventy-five miles south of
Utica. Scipio realized that he must strike before the effect of their
defeat wore off and before Syphax could be reinforced. Taking
perhaps one legion in light marching order and all his cavalry,
he made a forced march of four days and offered battle. Trusting
to the Spaniards and perhaps fearing the moral effect of further
retreat, Hasdrubal stood his ground. The Carthaginians faced
Laelius and the Italian cavalry, Syphax faced Masinissa, and the

Celtiberian mercenaries were opposed to the Roman legionaries of the centre. The battle was won, for the first time in Roman history, by a victorious charge of cavalry on both wings. It was made more decisive by tactics which reveal the maturity of Scipio's skill. Having a numerical superiority in infantry, he held the Spaniards in play with his *hastati*, while the *principes* and *triarii* were deployed outwards and, as at Ilipa, fell on the exposed flanks of the enemy's foot[1]. The valiant Spaniards fought and died where they stood. Laelius and Masinissa with all the cavalry of the Roman army and some infantry were sent to pursue Syphax and to reconquer Masinissa's ancestral domains, where the Massyli hastened to acclaim him as their ruler. Finally, Syphax was brought to battle on the borders of his kingdom and taken prisoner. The victorious army was able to push on and occupy his eastern capital Cirta. Thus in a single campaign Numidia with its immense resources had been lost to Carthage, and formidable accessions to the strength of the Roman army would be drawn in the future from the kingdom of Masinissa.

The situation of Carthage was indeed desperate. For Scipio had marched unopposed to within fifteen miles of Carthage and captured Tunes. Men hurried to repair the walls of the capital as if the siege were about to begin. At the same time it was decided to recall Hannibal from Italy, and to consider the offer of fresh proposals for peace. However, in the midst of these resolutions of despair one enterprise stands out. A surprise attack was planned by the small Carthaginian fleet upon Scipio's ships which were still engaged in the siege of Utica. But his vigilance detected the fleet leaving the harbour of Carthage and by a forced march he arrived before Utica in time to form a barricade of transports to protect his own warships, which, burdened with the heavy siege-engines, were quite unprepared to fight at sea. These defences saved the fleet from the loss of more than a few transports, so that the Carthaginian ships returned without having broken through the blockade of the town.

In Italy, too, Carthage could record no successes in the campaigns of 204 B.C. and 203 B.C. When in the latter year Mago finally crossed the Apennines from Liguria and invaded the Po valley, the Roman armies abandoned their cautious defence and marched to meet him. No fewer than seven legions were in the field against him. He had been compelled for greater security to move his base to Savona, and the Romans had thrown one legion into Genoa under Sp. Lucretius. Once he had passed the Apennines, two legions under C. Servilius also crossed from

[1] Scullard, *op. cit.* p. 212.

Etruria and prevented the Boii from joining him. Meanwhile, the main army of four legions under M. Cornelius Cethegus and P. Quintilius Varus advanced from Ariminum. Mago could not avoid battle even if he would, but his army which may have numbered 30,000 men contained a formidable nucleus of African and Spanish veteran troops. In the engagement which followed the Roman legionaries worsted his infantry, but the elephants and cavalry routed the Roman wings, so that the whole Carthaginian army was able to retreat in good order to the Ligurian coast. Here Mago found orders to return to Africa and on the voyage he died of a wound which he had received in the battle. So ended the last threat of invasion from the north, which had succeeded only in so far as large Roman forces, which might have been sent to Africa, were kept busy in North Italy for two years.

Against Hannibal himself in the course of these years four legions under the consul P. Sempronius Tuditanus and P. Licinius Crassus recovered Pandosia, Consentia and other small towns in Bruttium. Our record contains the notice of a success in a skirmish with Hannibal near Croton, for which a temple was dedicated in 194 B.C. to Fortuna Primigenia. But it is clear that neither army wished to fight a pitched battle. Since Metaurus Hannibal with dwindling forces had been at bay in South Italy, outnumbered three to one and forced to lose gradually the towns whose inhabitants were alienated from him, as they found neither profit nor safety in the Carthaginian alliance. He must long since have despaired of breaking the Roman power in Italy. Before the loss of Spain, he had still hoped to force Rome to peace through the exhaustion of her efforts. But for the last two years he had maintained a stubborn defence in the heel of Italy, only in the hope of preventing the Romans from sending large forces to Africa and to give his home government an asset in bargaining for peace. Now, at the end of 203 B.C., he received a message of recall to defend Carthage reduced to desperate straits by a small Roman army through the incompetence of her generals. In bitter disappointment at the failure of his magnificent enterprise he had set up a memorial of what he had achieved. The bilingual inscription written in Phoenician and Greek letters on an altar near the temple of Juno on the promontory of Lacinium recorded in detail how he had led an army from Nova Carthago across the Pyrenees and the Alps to Italy. The monument survived the malice of Rome to be read by Polybius: but no monument was needed beyond the simple fact that for fifteen years he had maintained himself in the enemy's country, unbeaten, at the head of his troops—Africans, Spaniards, Gauls—whose loyalty never wavered.

In the autumn of 203 B.C. the Carthaginians had made a fresh attempt to conclude peace. The peace party of merchants had obtained the upper hand, and an armistice was made with Scipio at the price of a donative to his troops. The following terms offered by Scipio were accepted by the Carthaginian Senate[1]. Carthage was to retain her status as an independent power in Africa, keeping intact her own territory. But she was to recognize Masinissa as king of the Massyli, and he would be left free to extend his kingdom westward into Numidia. On the south-east, while keeping her ancient colonies as far as Leptis Magna, Carthage was to respect the autonomy of the native tribes of Libya and Cyrenaica. She was to renounce all interference in Italy, Gaul and Spain, pay a war indemnity of 5000 talents and surrender all her ships except twenty. The terms were severe, for Carthage would cease to be a great power and she had no security from the growing power of Masinissa. A Carthaginian embassy sailed to Rome where the Senate and the people ratified the peace[2].

Hannibal transported his army to Africa while the peace terms were being ratified at Rome, and, landing at Leptis, marched to Hadrumetum. The army may have numbered 15,000 men, but he no longer had any cavalry and the corps of veterans probably did not amount to more than 8000 after fifteen years of war in Italy[3]. But the loyalty of long service made it of far greater worth than numbers alone can express; and a general who had never suffered defeat was not likely to accept tamely such degrading conditions for Carthage. Then, when Mago's army from Italy also arrived in Africa, there was a revulsion of feeling at Carthage; the peace party was overthrown, and it was clear that a final struggle must decide the future of Carthage. The actual breaking of the armistice followed from a chance event. A convoy of 200 Roman ships sailing with provisions from Sicily was driven by a storm into the Gulf of Tunes. The people of Carthage, no doubt already suffering considerable privations due to the presence of the Roman army in Africa, fell upon the ships and appropriated their cargoes. Envoys sent by Scipio to demand redress were rebuffed, and their ship was treacherously attacked on its return journey. And so the war broke out anew.

---

[1] Livy xxx, 16; Appian, *Lib.* 32; Polybius xv, 8, 7.

[2] This is clear from Polybius xv, 4, 8 and 8, 9. Livy's account of the rejection of the embassy (xxx, 21–3) must be annalistic invention. See De Sanctis, *op. cit.* p. 544 n. 154.

[3] See the computation of Groag, *op. cit.* p. 100 n. 3.

VI. ZAMA[1]

Masinissa was meanwhile engaged upon a campaign against Vermina the son of Syphax, conquering the most westerly regions of Numidia, where it borders on Mauretania. Scipio sent urgent messages to him in the spring of 202 B.C. to recall him for the coming campaign against Hannibal. Then he marched up the valley of the Bagradas river ravaging the countryside. Hannibal seems to have waited at Hadrumetum through the early summer hoping for cavalry reinforcements, above all the Numidian horsemen of Vermina. At last another Numidian prince Tychaeus did join him with 2000 cavalry. In the early autumn, when the heat of the African summer had abated, Hannibal suddenly broke camp and moved to Zama, five days' march from Carthage between Scipio and the coast. He was too late to prevent Scipio's junction with Masinissa and his long-awaited Numidian cavalry. For Scipio moved farther inland to Naraggara and there joined Masinissa, who brought 4000 Numidian cavalry and 6000 infantry. Hannibal followed, and the two armies at last faced each other in the battle which was to decide the war.

Each army numbered about 40,000 men, but Hannibal for the first time was greatly inferior in cavalry. His dispositions aimed at the converse of Cannae: for he must win in the centre if at all. First stood the elephants, more than eighty in number, then the front line formed of the experienced mercenaries of Mago's army, troops recruited from Mauretania, Liguria, Gaul and the Balearic isles, with a nucleus of Libyans. The weak Carthaginian citizen troops and Africans, upon whom he could place no reliance, were stationed behind them, and some distance in the rear he held his own veteran army in reserve. This reserve he intended to keep disengaged in the opening stages of the battle ready either to oppose a break-through or to repulse any enveloping of his wings. Scipio disposed the maniples of his legions in three lines, but the third line, the *triarii*, were held back without being deployed as in the battle of the Great Plains, ready to be thrown in on the flanks. At the same time a more open order was adopted for the *hastati* and *principes*, the maniples of the second line being placed behind those of the first and not in échelon, the spaces between being loosely occupied by the *velites*. Thus when the battle started there were lanes through the Roman lines to lessen the damage done by the charge of elephants. Laelius was on the left wing with the Italian cavalry and Masinissa on the right, opposing the Carthaginians and their Numidian cavalry.

[1] Zama, though less accurate than Naraggara, is kept as more familiar.

In the beginning of the battle the elephants rapidly became unmanageable; a few charged through the Roman lines, but most were driven off to the flanks and some of them fell back upon their own wings, frightening the horses and making the task of Laelius and Masinissa all the easier. The Carthaginian and allied cavalry were swept from the field. The struggle of the infantry was more evenly balanced, until, as the mercenaries began to give ground before the legionaries, the second line broke in panic and could not be forced to fight even when the veterans in their rear killed those who tried to fly. The mercenaries believing themselves deserted at last scattered in flight. Scipio's victorious legionaries were suddenly confronted by Hannibal's veteran army in perfect order. With the instinct of sound generalship Scipio, assisted by the fine discipline of the Roman army, halted and re-formed his legions. This act frustrated the last hope of Hannibal that the charge of his reserve might catch the Roman army in disorder and turn defeat into victory. He was soon surrounded by the cavalry of Masinissa and Laelius, and, though he himself escaped to Hadrumetum, his army was entirely destroyed. In the final battle of the war Hannibal had met a general who, if not his equal in tactical skill, yet by experience and cool judgment used his superior resources so wisely that the issue of the battle was never in doubt. Polybius is moved to admiration of the skill of Hannibal in his last battle and concludes that everything which a great general could do he did. It was the end of a struggle in which the greater strength and resources of Rome had at length prevailed. But the duration and equality of the contest had been due to the genius of Hannibal.

To antiquity Hannibal ranked above Scipio Africanus as a general, and there is no reason to reverse a verdict formed after the claims of the Roman had received full weight[1]. The tactical skill of Scipio was in the main derived from the study of Hannibal's tactical triumphs. It is true that Africanus towers above the Roman generals of the day—in boldness surpassing Fabius, in subtlety surpassing Marcellus. His diplomatic address and freedom from the trammels of Roman military tradition deserve the praise of Polybius, who added to the picture features which belong rather to a Hellenistic statecraft than to the nature of a Roman aristocrat. A generous magnanimity did not preclude occasional barbarity or the treachery which made possible his first victory over Syphax and Hasdrubal. Even if he pressed through his pro-

---

[1] The one exception is Lucian, *Dialogus Mortuorum* 12, with its easy criterion of success.

jects of invading Africa in despite of a powerful section of the Senate, he had behind him the overmastering material forces of Rome. His figure is lit up by the dawn of Rome's imperial greatness, but yet more brilliant is the figure of his opponent which by the fire of genius lit the darkness that was settling upon Carthage.

As a general Hannibal raised to a higher power the tactical conceptions of Alexander. He was deeply versed in the history of Hellenistic warfare and had a Hellenistic appreciation of the value of cavalry. To this he added the power of coordinating the action of infantry, and a love of ambushes which well suited an African who had fought in Spain. At Cannae he took the extremest risk to make possible the most decisive victory: at Zama he all but succeeded in thwarting a general who could add the tactics of Cannae to superiority both in foot and horse. Not less notable than his tactical virtuosity was the patient resource with which he delayed for so long the attrition of his army in Italy. Indeed, the great qualities of Hannibal as a consummate strategist and tactician, gifted with a power of leadership which held firm the loyalty of a mercenary army through the years in which victory was dimmed into defeat, are not disputed, and are little diminished by the degree of truth which may attach to the charges of avarice and cruelty which were levelled at him by the Roman tradition. Had perfidy, cruelty and avarice governed his nature, he could not have achieved what he did. That he hated Rome may well be true: what is certain is that his hatred did not rise above his throat. For neither can it be said that he dragged Carthage into a hopeless struggle from study of revenge nor that he was deluded by fantastic hopes. If we are right in crediting him with the wider sweep of policy which followed Cannae, he cannot be denied the title of a statesman, and the years in which he served Carthage after Zama show him to be more than a great general only. Yet it may be doubted whether a Carthaginian victory which forced Rome back on herself could have been lasting, and still more whether even Hannibal desired or could have brought about the union of the chief power of the West with the Hellenistic world in which lay, as by destiny, the future of Mediterranean civilization. In the fictitious interview with Scipio at Ephesus he is made to give the answer that had he overcome at Zama he would have surpassed Alexander, Pyrrhus and all the commanders of the world. The dexterous subtlety reveals only half a truth: what we cannot say is whether he possessed the greatness which would have made him the equal of Alexander as well as the superior of Pyrrhus.

VII. PEACE: THE EFFECTS OF THE WAR ON ROME

After sacking the Carthaginian camp, Scipio marched down to the coast. He found that a new fleet of fifty ships had arrived under P. Cornelius Lentulus with a convoy of provisions. Without delay he ordered the fleet and legions to move to the investment of Carthage. But the Carthaginians were not willing to stand a siege, and Hannibal used all his influence to persuade them to accept the best terms they could obtain. Nothing could be gained by prolonging the war in Africa, since no fresh troops could be raised from the African tribes. News had come that his last ally, Vermina, arriving too late for the battle, had been overwhelmed by Scipio. His hopes were possibly already centred upon the great Hellenistic kingdoms of Syria and Macedon and he saw the prospect of a conflict between Rome and the powers of the eastern Mediterranean. Consequently he voted for the acceptance of any terms, however severe, which would not involve the destruction of Carthage itself.

An armistice was made for three months, while negotiations were pursued on condition that Carthage paid in full at once the value of the damage done to the shipwrecked convoy in the previous winter, and in addition supplied the whole of the Roman army with provisions and probably double pay for the three months. The conditions finally concluded left Carthage in possession of her own territory in Africa. But the Libyan tribes of her protectorate beyond the 'Phoenician Bounds' on the south-east were to become independent in alliance with Rome. On the west she was to restore to Masinissa 'all the cities and territory which he or his ancestors had possessed.' All her elephants and the whole of the fleet except ten ships were to be surrendered. A hundred hostages chosen by the Romans were to be sent to Rome and an indemnity of 10,000 talents paid in fifty years. Finally, she was to be a client state of Rome promising to wage no war outside Africa and only within Africa by the consent of Rome. Herein lay the chief burden added to the terms which Rome was willing to accept before Zama. The peace put an end to the career of Carthage as one of the great powers of the Mediterranean. But worse still, the terms gave her no security for the future against the aggression of her neighbours (see below, p. 473).

The war was won. The struggle for supremacy in the Mediterranean was over, and no rival would henceforward contest on equal terms the victorious progress of Rome to world-wide dominion. Scipio, now Africanus, was the hero of the hour and the Cornelii for nearly two decades were to hold a preponderating influence at Rome. He had dealt the *coup de grâce*, but it was not he that had made victory possible. The conquest of Spain and the successful conclusion of the war in Africa were military feats which Romans would have appreciated at their true value. But Sicily had been recovered and Hannibal checkmated in Italy by the wise direction of the Senate and the tenacity of the Roman people. While the colossal genius of Hannibal seemed almost to personify Carthage in the war and certainly accounted both for the equality and the duration of the struggle, on the Roman side victory had been achieved by the stubborn resistance of Romans and Central Italians fighting shoulder to shoulder with unshaken trust in themselves, in each other and in their political system. And so though Scipio emerged from the war with great glory, an omnipotent Senate held and continued to hold the reins of government.

The temper of the Roman people has been felt in the narrative of the successive stages of the war as an undercurrent of vital force. Polybius pauses after Cannae to note with the natural wonder and admiration of a Greek that the Romans were more dangerous in defeat than in victory, and to Livy the Second Punic War marked the moment when Roman *virtus* reached its peak before the long decline began. It is indeed a spectacle full of grandeur—the triumph of the Roman character in this supreme ordeal, and inevitably the mind turns to contrast with it the tragic picture drawn by Thucydides of the progressive demoralization of the Athenian character in the stress of war and of the utter failure of the Athenian democracy to direct the war which it had provoked. Many considerations may weaken the force of the comparison and invalidate conclusions based upon it, yet one indisputable and decisive superiority the Romans had in the soundness of their constitution for the direction of the wars which imperialism invites. It remains, therefore, to investigate how the Roman constitution was moulded in the war to suit the exigencies of the situation.

In 287 B.C. the Lex Hortensia had asserted, in theory at least, the sovereignty of the people so strongly that the possibility of the development of the Roman constitution into a modified form of democracy cannot have seemed very remote. Progress in this direction was for a time arrested by the war against Pyrrhus and the First Punic War, since wars need instantaneous decisions, which a popular assembly is particularly unfitted to make, and

in the Senate composed of ex-magistrates with military experience
an ideal body was ready at hand to take control. But in the period
between the two Punic Wars Flaminius, a popular leader of great
political ability, had so ably championed the cause of the people
against the Senate and the great families, that in 232 B.C. a redistribution of the Ager Picenus had been made *viritim* to the
poorer citizens in direct opposition to the Senate's will and some
fourteen years later the Lex Claudia forbade senators to engage in
maritime commerce. The carrying through of these measures
re-affirmed the unfettered sovereignty of the people in legislation.

In the first three years of the Second Punic War the popular
movement provided strong opposition to the direction of the war
by the Senate and after the failures at Ticinus and Trebia secured
the election of Flaminius to the consulship of 217 B.C. although
his military record in the Gallic War had been none too good. In
the same year in which Fabius was made dictator his *magister
equitum*, whose appointment according to precedent had been in
the hands of the dictator himself, was elected by popular vote.
The election of Minucius Rufus, like an ephor to watch the
Spartan king, stultified the whole conception of the absolute
powers of temporary dictatorship in a crisis. The co-dictatorship
which followed as a logical result sealed by its absurdity the fate
of this magistracy. The last dictator *cum imperio* belongs to the
months after Cannae. The office continued to be used in the war
sine imperio for special work of a censorial character, but after
202 B.C. the magistracy ceased to exist even in this shadowy
form. An office of such unlimited powers, which had only been
tolerated in times of great danger, had become so repugnant to
the Roman spirit that other methods were found to respond to the
cry for efficiency (see below, p. 360). However, the popular
movement did not end with the co-dictatorship. In the election
of the consuls for 216 B.C. the people pushed forward Terentius
Varro the son of a butcher—*loco non humili solum sed etiam sordido
ortum*. But the disaster which followed shattered the people's
faith in *novi homines*, and for the rest of the war the popular will
expressed at elections is no longer a criticism but a steady support
of the Senate, intervening only to elevate the young Scipio to
command. In the 100 years from 233 B.C. to 133 B.C. out of 200
consulships (omitting supplementary elections) 159 were held by
twenty-six noble families and one half by ten families. Thus the
Roman constitution became an oligarchy based on popular
election and on the immense prestige which the Senate won in

the Second Punic War. The sovereignty of the Roman people both as an electorate and in legislation became in practice subordinated to the will of the Senate.

But most of all war magnifies the executive power. The meetings of popular assemblies were too infrequent and clumsy for the passing of urgent war measures. It was the Senate which had directed the diplomacy of Rome to a point at which the decision of the people to go to war became almost the recognition of a *fait accompli*. In the war the continuity of the Senate as a supreme war council removed the need for legislation by the popular assembly. Apart from the Lex Claudia, we only hear of three new laws: the Lex Minucia of 216 B.C., a financial measure, the Lex Oppia of 215 B.C., a sumptuary enactment, and the Lex Cincia of 204 B.C., a judicial statute forbidding patrons to receive presents from their clients. In military matters armies were decreed, supplies were granted, and commanders allocated to their duties and spheres of action by the Senate. Police regulations such as the restriction of public mourning after Cannae and the delicate but firm treatment of the Roman allies in Italy were left to the *patres*. The *senatus consultum* became a war ordinance which needed no further ratification.

Important changes also occurred in the powers of the executive magistracies. The censorship and the tribunate, impressive or effective offices in a time of peace, suffered eclipse during the war. The praetors were often taken from legal business to command armies. But four praetors (since 227 B.C.) and two consuls were not enough to fill the commands in the many areas of the war. In 212 B.C. there were no less than fifteen Roman commanders. Efficiency also necessitated the continuance of tried generals in their commands. Traditional constitutional practice which enforced intervals between different offices and before re-election to the same office, later formulated in the Lex Villia Annalis (p. 367), was broken down. Q. Fabius Maximus was consul in 215, 214 and 209, M. Claudius Marcellus in 215, 214, 210 and 208. Secondly, the commands of consuls and praetors were continued as proconsuls and propraetors: thus the Scipios, Publius and Gnaeus, commanded continuously from 218 B.C. to 212 B.C.; Marcellus was in Sicily for the four years 214–211 B.C. without a break, and then after a short interval in Italy till his death in 208. P. Scipio Africanus was practically in command for ten years, 210–201. Still more contrary to constitutional practice was the appointment by a popular vote of *privati cum imperio*, although the candidate had previously held no curule magistracy, as was the case when Publius Scipio was sent to Spain in 210 B.C. or when T. Quinctius Flamininus was appointed propraetor *extra ordinem* to command the garrison at Tarentum in 205 and 204 in recognition of distinguished services at the age of twenty as a military tribune under Marcellus in 208 B.C.

In general the effect of the war upon the magistracies was to free them from the hampering control of a colleague's vote. War commands were often in distant provinces where instant decisions had to be taken on the individual responsibility of the magistrate. He was frequently drawn into close personal relations with allies and subject peoples. Scipio in Spain is the forerunner of the great commanders with long tenures of office of the last century of the Republic. But throughout this war the Senate contrived to maintain a strong measure of control over the magistrates even in Spain and presents the spectacle of a supreme war council directing all the operations of the war.

It was not alone in the general direction of strategy that the Senate discharged a heavy responsibility. The war, conducted largely in an Italy which suffered from the active presence of an invader, strained to the breaking point the financial resources of the state. It was the Senate's duty to mobilize these and it was the duty of its members to set an example of self-sacrifice. Final victory in the First Punic War had been achieved by the raising of a loan (vol. VII, p. 691); in this sterner struggle senators took the lead in subscribing to loans and in supplying at their own charges rowers for the fleet. In 215 and succeeding years the property tax (*tributum*) was doubled. To secure a supply of currency, especially at a time when bronze was a munition of war as well as a raw material of coinage, the *as* was reduced by a half to one ounce, while about the same time there was a slight reduction in the standard silver coinage, which involved a certain degree of inflation. The punishment of the twelve colonies which had withheld their contingents in 209 included the imposition of direct taxation, which the Roman allies in general were spared. Despite these signs of financial stress the Senate succeeded in maintaining the credit of the state. In 204 B.C., even before the war was over, one-third of the loan raised six years before was repaid, and a second repayment was made in 200 B.C. by the assignment of public land in the neighbourhood of Rome (p. 159).

To raise money was one task: to convert it into supplies was another. Assistance in kind came from abroad. Sardinia and Sicily had corn to spare to provision the armies; the legions in Spain doubtless were in part supported by the local chiefs and possibly by the wealth of Massilia. The relatively few troops in Illyria cost less than they earned by their ruthless warfare, and could draw upon allies and clients of the Republic. But apart from their pay, the mere equipment and military supplies of the numerous legions must have taxed the productive resources of the state, especially during the years in which the industrial region of Campania was disputed ground. Rome had no great arsenals and, in any event, her military effort far surpassed what could have been provided for in normal times. Of necessity, therefore, the government had to resort to the private enterprise of contractors and with their syndicates or *societates* the Senate had to make the best bargains that it could. After Cannae it succeeded in persuading the *societates* to agree to deferred payment in return for exemptions from military service and for insurance against losses by storms or enemies at sea. The state was well served, for it may reasonably be assumed that the famous scandal caused by frauds perpetrated under the insurance-clause was the exception which proves the rule. Granted the relative simplicity of Roman warfare, the military efforts put forth by Rome could hardly have been possible without good and plentiful supplies, and we may assume that the Senate strove not to bear too hardly on the Allies by requisitions to augment the burden of military service.

The contractors who share with the Senate, the generals and the soldiers, the credit for victory were not themselves senators. Immediately before the war the Lex Claudia had forbidden senators to engage in large commerce; thus the duty of undertaking the contracts fell chiefly on the next social stratum, that of the *equites*. When the depleted ranks of the Senate were filled up after Cannae the choice of the censors fell upon those who had distinguished themselves in fighting, and it is not impossible that wealthy *equites* were left to serve the state in their own way. A proposal to recruit senators from the gentry of the Latin towns was rejected, and the rejection reflected a hardening of Roman state-consciousness as well as Roman self-reliance. But among the local aristocracies there were doubtless men who undertook for the Republic and repaid the confidence which it always placed in them. Even when account is taken of these, it remains true that the war promoted the rise to influence at Rome of a self-conscious group of *equites*, which in later times was to become a political factor and seek to affect the policy of the state which it served. The Senate itself by contrast became more and more aristocratic in tradition, more immersed in the tasks of war and diplomacy and gradually less vigilant about economic problems.

Of common interest to the Senate and the equites were the provinces. Even before the war was ended, the organization of Roman Spain was taken in hand (p. 306), and the re-organization of Sicily had been completed. A new settlement of the island was drawn up by a senatorial commission after the fall of Syracuse. Special privileges were conferred upon certain cities in recognition of their service and loyalty in the war. A pre-eminent status of independence, autonomy and immunity from taxation was accorded to three cities[1] and ratified in permanent *foedera*[1]. To five others a second grade of privilege was allotted and ratified by a *senatus consultum*, which gave them immunity and a certain measure of freedom (*civitates sine foedere liberae et immunes*)[2]. The rest of the island was reduced to a condition which Cicero described later as being *praedia populi Romani*. The area of *ager censorius* available for distribution in the form of estates to Roman citizens was much enlarged by punitive confiscations for disloyalty in the old province and by considerable expropriation in Hiero's newly conquered kingdom. All the rest of the island became *civitates decumanae*, compelled to pay a tax in kind of 10 per cent. of their produce[3]. The tax was the same as had been enforced in Hiero's kingdom and probably less than what the Carthaginians had exacted. In fact, the seeds of oppression did not lie in this 10 per cent. tax but elsewhere in the multiplication of administrative impositions and benevolences and the opportunities for private gain. In these gains senatorial governors and equestrian financiers had their share, but the days of Verres were still distant.

Finally, Livy has preserved from the pontifical records a considerable amount of valuable evidence which throws light upon the effect of the war upon the populace at Rome. The progress of the Roman religion towards stereotyped formalism on the one hand and rationalism on the other was arrested in the violent emotions of hope and fear produced by the war. It is impossible to decide how far the senators and magistrates still believed in the efficacy of the rites which were prescribed, and how far they were content to use any means they could find to allay the increasing fears of the common people. If some of the nobles wavered between rationalism and the old religion, it is clear that the masses —*moti in religionem*—received a powerful impulse towards every kind of religious observance in the desperate desire to

---

[1] Messana, Tauromenium, Neetum: Cicero, *Verr.* III, 6, 13; v, 22, 56, 51, 133.

[2] Segesta, Halicyae, Panormus, Halaesa, Centuripa.

[3] On the taxation of Sicily see above, vol. VII, pp. 792 *sqq.*

obtain that *pax deorum* which the succession of disasters showed had been somehow violated. The streets of the poorer quarters, and particularly the *forum boarium* and *forum olitorium*, were full of tales of prodigies—an ox which climbed to the third storey of a house, wolves which ran away with sentinels' swords, a cock and hen which interchanged sexes—while in one month simultaneous marvels were reported from Praeneste, Arpi, Capena, Caere, Antium, and Falerii. Later, the death of Marcellus was connected with the nibbling by mice of the gilding of an image. The vague sense of terror, of sin and of duties omitted impelled the magistrates to seek new methods of pacifying the gods since the customary rites seemed of none avail. As is described later (chap. xiv), recourse was had to the gods of Greece and, finally, the 'Black stone' from Pessinus which was the symbol of the Asiatic Magna Mater was brought in state to Rome.

At last the long strain was over. Yet the war was to have more significance than the repulse and defeat of a rival on the Western Mediterranean. In Italy the continued active presence of an invader, and the distraction of the peasantry from their farms to the camp, had lasting economic effects (see chap. xi). Carthaginian Spain was too rich a prize for Rome to forgo (chap. x); and its occupation led the Republic to become a power by land beyond the Alps, until finally, to hold the way to Spain, Rome made that Provincia in Southern France whence Caesar was to conquer Gaul and reach the Rhine and the shores of Britain. Finally, as will be seen in the following chapter, the alliance of Carthage and Macedon compelled the Senate for the first time to pay attention to Greece, and, though in itself the war beyond the Adriatic was no more than an accidental episode without lasting political results, none the less, the *patres* could not banish from their minds the fact that a coalition outside Italy had been conjured up against them, so that the caution natural to experience was complicated by recurring fears of the half-known (chap. vi–vii). Rome had been driven to think outside Italy and Sicily: Scipio, who had conquered Carthaginian Spain and invaded Carthaginian Africa, was, ten years later, to lead the legions through Greece and devise victory on the plains of Asia Minor.

CHAPTER V

ROME AND MACEDON: PHILIP AGAINST THE ROMANS

I. PHILIP THE ALLY OF HANNIBAL

THE Hannibalic War raged not only in Italy, Spain, Sicily and Northern Africa: while fighting Carthage and her Italian, Spanish and Sicilian allies, Rome, as has already been shown, had further to defend herself against Philip V of Macedon, who also had made common cause with the Carthaginians. The war, consequently, extended into Lower Illyria and continental and insular Greece, and its repercussions were even felt in part of Asia Minor: it is this side of the great conflict which forms the subject of the present chapter.

It has been told elsewhere how, in order to be free to deal with Rome, Philip, on hearing the result of the battle of Trasimene, patched up a peace with the Aetolians at Naupactus (Sept. 217) (vol. VII, pp. 768, 854). Many have blamed him, but unjustly,

Note. The chief source for the narrative of this chapter is—or rather was—Polybius, for apart from the close of Book V, his account has survived only in very scanty fragments, very unequal in scope and importance, of Books VII–XI. Where Polybius fails us, Livy, who has largely borrowed from him in Books XXVI–XXIX, becomes, for good or ill, our main source. But it must be borne in mind that this part of his narrative very imperfectly reproduces Polybius—being incomplete, marred by mistakes chronological and otherwise, and sometimes 'contaminated' with Roman annalistic material (*e.g.* XXIX, 12). The annalistic parts of Livy which treat of Macedonian and Greek affairs contain several manifest false statements, and must only be used with extreme caution. Hardly anything can be derived from the jejune fragments of Appian (*Maced.* 1–3), from Justin's feeble abstract of Trogus, or from the narrative of Dio Cassius as we have it over-abridged by Zonaras. Appian appears to draw upon a tradition other than the Polybian and seriously falsified; Dio, who too has many errors, seems to follow, not Polybius, but both Coelius Antipater and Livy; Trogus may derive indirectly from Polybius. Plutarch in his Life of Aratus (49–54, following Polybius) and above all in his Life of Philopoemen (mainly derived from Polybius' biography of him) affords some useful information for the history of Achaea. Pausanias (VIII, 49–51, on Philopoemen) is almost negligible. Inscriptions are few and of secondary interest, apart from the second decree of Larissa which contains the second letter of Philip to the city (*Ditt.*³ 543, IV). For further information, see the Bibliography.

for his slowness both in decision and in action after this peace.
Having chastised the Illyrian Scerdilaidas, Philip returned home
fully determined to profit from Hannibal's victorious invasion of
Italy by wresting Lower Illyria from the Romans, and spent the
winter of 217–6 in preparations for carrying out his purpose.

Circumstances were favourable. Wholly occupied with the
Carthaginians, the Senate, forgetful of Illyria, had, strangely
enough, sent no force thither, even after the defeat of Scerdilaidas.
Moreover, Philip saw no cause for uneasiness in the Hellenic
world. In Greece his resounding successes had established his
authority: he was, for the moment, the 'darling' of his Allies,
whom he had just defended so well; and the Aetolians, guided by
the wise Agelaus and schooled by their failures, seemed resigned
to remain quiet. In the East, where the peace of Antioch interrupted the secular duel between Syria and Egypt, Antiochus III,
after his defeat at Raphia, had the hard task of crushing the usurper
Achaeus, and held aloof from western affairs; besides, he had no
conceivable reason for hostility towards Philip. Victory won, the
imbellis Ptolemy Philopator was resuming the indolent life of a
mystic, pleasure-loving dilettante, which was shortly to be disturbed by a first rebellion, already brewing, of the Egyptians who
had been imprudently enlisted (vol. VII, p. 728 *sq.*). His all-
powerful vizier, Sosibius, engrossed in secretly supporting Achaeus,
wished no ill to Macedonia: on the contrary, distrusting Antiochus
even though vanquished, and fearing his possible revenge, he desired to engage the goodwill of Philip, to which he had a strong
claim by the destruction of Cleomenes. The Egyptian mediation
in 217 between Macedon and Aetolia had shown his friendliness.
Amicable relations existed between Alexandria and Pella; in
Boeotia, a country of especially Macedonian sympathies, Philopator and Sosibius made themselves popular by their munificence[1];
in Crete, where Philip's influence was now predominant (vol. VII,
p. 768), Egypt was left in undisturbed possession of Itanus.

Even before the negotiations at Naupactus were ended, Philip
had subdued Zacynthus, a valuable base in the Ionian Sea[2]. He had,
in fact, decided to attack by sea the Illyrian coast towns. To this end,
it is said, he must first create a great navy; but money was lacking,
and the enterprise would have taken time and been noised abroad:
now he desired to act swiftly, unknown to the Romans, whom he
considered almost invincible at sea. And, indeed, it seemed

---

[1] See *Rev. Ét. gr.* x, 1897, pp. 26 *sqq.*, 47 *sqq.*; *O.G.I.S.* 81 (cf. *Rev. Ét.
gr.* VIII, 1895, p. 190 *sq.*); *O.G.I.S.* 80; *I.G.* VII, 3166.
[2] Polybius v, 102, 10.

obvious that with an improvised fleet he had no chance of defeating them; a naval victory off the Ebro had just shown once more their maritime superiority (p. 58). Advised by Demetrius of Pharos, he merely built a hundred of the light *lembi* dear to the Illyrians; if the sea remained clear of Roman ships this flotilla carrying about 6–7000 men, joined by forces sent overland, might well take by surprise, in Illyrian fashion, Apollonia and Dyrrhachium. But we may presume that Philip aimed at higher game. The vision of Italy, we are told, pursued him even in his sleep: Demetrius ever pointed to it as his necessary objective; there, in fact, would be ultimately settled the fate of Illyria. For to conquer it was not enough; the Romans must be prevented from returning, coerced indeed into resigning it definitely: this was only possible after a decisive defeat of Rome by Carthage in which Philip had played a part. This consideration doubtless decided his conduct: once master of those indispensable bases, the Illyrian seaports, he would sail to Southern Italy with his flotilla increased by the *lembi* captured in Illyria with fresh troops on board, then intervene in the Italian war now reaching its critical stage, co-operate with Hannibal, who could not reject his help, and share in his victory. Possibly, too, haunted by the memory of Pyrrhus, he had hopes of overseas conquests, saw himself greeted as deliverer by the Hellenes of Italy who viewed Rome and Carthage with impartial hatred, and securing for himself at least a large part of Magna Graecia.

However that may be, in the early summer of 216 he passed Cape Malea with 100 *lembi*, his Macedonians themselves acting as rowers, and turned northward. At every port of call, at Cephallenia, at Leucas, he inquired anxiously about the Roman fleet lying in Sicilian waters. Hearing that it had not moved from Lilybaeum, he pursued his course towards Apollonia, reached the bay of Aulon, some 14 miles from the mouths of the Aoüs, and anchored there. His goal was in sight. Unfortunately, Scerdilaidas had got wind of his purpose and warned the Romans, hitherto so indifferent. At his appeal, ten quinqueremes left Lilybaeum for Apollonia. Learning suddenly of their approach and not knowing their numbers, the Macedonians and Philip himself thought that the whole Roman fleet was coming to destroy them: there was a panic, excusable enough despite Polybius, and Philip gave the signal for a retreat, a disorderly flight which only ended at Cephallenia. The surprise had failed and could not be repeated; after a halt at Cephallenia, Philip returned to Macedonia (*c.* July 216).

Cephallenia was a dependency of the Aetolians, who heard immediately of Philip's misfortune and, we may be sure, rejoiced over it. The tide was turning in Aetolia, where Agelaus had lost his political ascendancy. The people were tired of a ruinous peace which closed all Greece to the profitable pillaging expeditions in which they delighted, and the anti-Macedonians were gaining ground. Philip could not view this with indifference; Aetolian hostility might seriously interfere with his new projects, and the desire to be forearmed against it partly explains his designs upon Messene of which we shall speak presently.

No sooner had Philip failed at Apollonia than Hannibal triumphed at Cannae. Philip should, it is said, have straightway concluded an alliance with him; but was there still time? Would not Philip make himself ridiculous by flying, too late, to the succour of the conqueror? Was not Rome, acknowledging defeat, about to come to terms? Uncertainty imposed caution. But by the spring of 215 the situation was clearer: Rome, whom everyone had thought broken, fought doggedly on, and, despite his miraculous success, a hard task lay before Hannibal. The moment had come for Philip to offer his assistance.

His envoys, headed by the Athenian Xenophanes, came to Hannibal's camp during the summer. In other circumstances, Hannibal would probably not have welcomed a partner as powerful as the King of Macedon; but, at the moment, faced by unforeseen difficulties, he was bound to take account of the possible advantage to be secured by Philip's aid. The mere existence of this new enemy might at once embarrass Rome by compelling her to divert to the East a part of her forces. A treaty of alliance was concluded of which we know the terms; Polybius has preserved the 'oath' sworn to Xenophanes in the name of Carthage by Hannibal, the Carthaginian 'gerousiasts' who accompanied him and all the Carthaginians serving in his army[1]. The treaty, in its cautious drafting, reflects the situation created by the Punic victories, and recognized the primacy which Hannibal derived from them. Philip, abandoning his dreams of conquest overseas, left him to deal with Italy and confined himself to the rôle of a second; but his services were to be repaid by valuable advantages.

The alliance was to be permanent, offensive while the war lasted, then defensive. Philip was to act with Carthage against Rome until victory was won. He was to reinforce Hannibal's army if Hannibal requested it, according to conditions to be agreed upon in concert. Victory won, Carthage, in treating with

---

[1] The sham alliance fabricated by the annalists and paraphrased by Livy XXIII, 33, 10–12 (cf. Appian, *Maced.* 1, Zonaras, IX, 4, 2) may be disregarded.

Rome, was to include Philip and demand that Rome should undertake never to fight against him, to abandon Corcyra, Pharos and all her possessions on the Illyrian mainland[1], and, moreover, to return to Demetrius his 'households' detained in Italy since 219 (vol. VII, p. 851). The defensive alliance guaranteed the contracting parties generally against all aggression, but was aimed primarily and expressly against Rome: if, breaking the peace, she attacked Carthage or Macedonia, the two allies were to help one another. Thus, at the price of co-operation for apparently a short time—the Romans seeming at least half-defeated—Macedonia would be freed from their hateful proximity and, strong in the permanent support of Carthage, need not fear a *revanche*. Philip and his faithful Demetrius would reign undisturbed along the Adriatic.

Hardly had Philip allied himself with Hannibal than his relations with the Achaeans became strained. He had made the alliance not only in his own name and in the name of the Macedonians, but also in that of his Greek allies; he hoped therefore for help from them, especially from the Achaeans—a legitimate hope after all he had done for them. But the Achaeans, *i.e.* Aratus, were egotism itself. That the Macedonian king, their unfortunately indispensable protector, should spend himself in their service was well: they owed him no return. Despite Agelaus' warnings neither Rome nor Carthage meant anything to them; moreover, they were unwilling to strengthen Philip by contributing to his military successes. The king came into the Peloponnese and found Aratus hostile to his designs.

Then to set them further at variance, occurred the obscure 'affair of Messene.' The class-war was raging there as in so many other cities: called in as arbitrator, Philip is said to have secretly incited the populace, who massacred the magistrates and 200 *optimates*. The victors were willing, it seems, for him to occupy Ithome— ambition apart, a golden opportunity. Aetolia, indeed, as we have seen, caused Philip anxiety. During his possible absence in Italy— for if Hannibal asked him for troops, he naturally had it in mind to command in person—might not the Aetolians invade the Peloponnese and take revenge upon the Achaeans? By occupying Ithome, he would anticipate this danger, hold in check Elis and Sparta, Aetolia's friends, and thereby paralyse Aetolia itself. Meanwhile Aratus and his son had hastened to Messene on the heels of Philip, intending to counter the democratic victory. In

---

[1] Polybius VII, 9, 13 enumerates Corcyra, Apollonia, Epidamnus (Dyrrhachium), Pharos, Dimale, the Parthinians, Atintania. It is not clear why Issa is not mentioned; possibly it is a merely accidental omission.

their eyes the city, always coveted by Achaea, as good as belonged
to her; to see Philip intriguing, playing the demagogue, apparently
seeking to establish himself in Messene, filled them with anger:
he was already too powerful in the Peloponnese. The younger
Aratus overwhelmed him with reproaches. Then came the famous
scene at Ithome. Having gone there to offer sacrifice with Aratus
and Demetrius of Pharos, Philip put to them the momentous
question: was he to keep the fortress? Demetrius encouraged him
by the celebrated metaphor: to possess Ithome, while already
holding Acrocorinth, would be to 'hold the bull—the Peloponnese—by both horns.' Aratus countered with a vehement homily.
Philip yielded, but henceforth the two men hated one another.
Sulky and peevish, Aratus left the king and next year refused
point blank to accompany him into Illyria.

From this moment dates Philip's 'change of heart' (*metabole*)
so branded by Polybius—his transformation from an exemplary,
amiable, beloved prince, into a hateful tyrant. No doubt, irritated
by opposition, Philip gave rein to his temper; the wild, Epirote
side of his nature showed itself—the passionate lack of self-control
which increased with years; and Demetrius, succeeding to Aratus'
lost influence, urged him to violent courses. But to the Achaeans
his unforgivable sin was to be himself, and no longer merely the
champion of their League. The 'modest stripling[1],' whom Aratus
thought he held in leading-strings, dared to show himself king
of Macedonia, with a will and policy of his own: this was his
unpardonable 'change.' However violent and even cruel he might
be, he would still have pleased the Achaeans had he used his
violence and cruelty in their service.

Philip and Hannibal hoped to keep their treaty secret; the
Romans suspected nothing and had even recalled from Apollonia
the ten quinqueremes sent thither from Lilybaeum. But the gods
watched over Rome. Xenophanes, his companions, and the
Carthaginians commissioned to receive Philip's oath were captured as they left Italy. In consequence, Philip had to send a
second embassy to Hannibal, which caused a vexatious delay; and
the Senate, at long last discovering the new danger which
threatened Rome, strove to avert it. The praetor M. Valerius
Laevinus, commanding the army at Tarentum, was ordered to
keep watch upon Philip with some 50 warships carrying troops[2];
if Philip became too threatening, he was to cross to Illyria.

---

[1] μειράκιον σῶφρον, Plutarch, *Aratus*, 51.
[2] The annalistic tradition (Livy XXIV, 11, 3; 44, 5; XXVI, 1, 12) gives
Laevinus one legion (*legio classica*), but neither the number nor the importance
of his operations makes this credible.

Most probably (though direct proof is lacking) the agreement about Macedonian co-operation in Italy, which the treaty had envisaged, was made by the second Macedonian embassy (? winter 215–4): for Hannibal, having for a year been reduced to comparative inactivity, had serious need of reinforcements. The agreement would of necessity fix the number and character of the troops which Philip was to send and, equally of necessity, guarantee him the help of the Carthaginian navy, without which it was from now onwards practically impossible to cross to Italy. But, without waiting for a Punic fleet, Philip, so often accused of indecision, showed in the summer of 214 astonishing enterprise. In his haste to secure the base needed for his overseas expedition, although the Roman quinqueremes were within striking distance, he boldly repeated with 120 *lembi* his venture of 216, reached again the bay of Aulon, seized Oricus, sailed up the Aoüs and prepared to besiege Apollonia—a fortunate beginning which did not last. Laevinus, called on for help, hurried to Illyria, re-took Oricus, blockaded the mouths of the Aoüs, and threw into Apollonia reinforcements which, with the citizens, surprised and sacked the Macedonian camp. The affair was certainly less serious than the Roman annalists make out (Livy XXIV, 40), but Philip's situation was becoming none the less critical; cut off from the sea, not knowing the strength of the Roman forces, threatened by the Illyrian clients of Rome whom Laevinus called to arms against him, he had to retire overland to Macedonia after burning his *lembi*. The worst was that Laevinus established himself permanently in the Illyrian seaports, holding the coast. To dislodge him Philip needed the Punic fleet; till it arrived he could only act vigorously in the interior of Illyria against the Romans and their local allies, and this he did.

II. THE ROMANS IN ALLIANCE WITH AETOLIA

But, first, determined to strengthen his position in the Peloponnese, the king tried to repeat with better success, probably in the autumn of 214, his attempt on Messene. Again he failed. Little is known of this adventure, but two facts are certain. Demetrius of Pharos was sent against the city, repulsed, and killed, and Philip in futile anger ravaged Messenian territory. The consequences of this brutal attack upon an allied state were deplorable; it roused general indignation in Greece, threw into the arms of Aetolia the Messenians who, rich and poor alike, seceded from the Hellenic League, and completed the

rupture between Aratus and his party, and Philip. Shortly afterwards (213) Aratus died, melancholy, consumed with bitterness,
believing that Philip had poisoned him. The real poison which
caused his death was his cruel disillusionment together with the
discovery of the king's intrigue with his daughter-in-law, Poly-
crateia of Argos, who soon followed her lover to Macedon and was
probably the mother of Perseus.

Philip had blundered in the Peloponnese; in Illyria, whither he
returned in 213, he acted with skill and energy. Apollonia and
Dyrrhachium, strongly held by Laevinus and open to relief by
sea, were beyond his reach; but he invaded Roman territory,
subdued the Atintanes and the Parthini, and took Dimale and
other towns: the Romans held no more than the extreme fringe of
Illyria. Farther north he did even better, drove back Scerdilaidas,
wrested from him part of his subjects, finally captured Lissus and
its citadel, reputed impregnable (?autumn 213). By this great
stroke, which dismayed the Illyrians, he regained access to the
sea; henceforth the Carthaginian admirals would know where to
join hands with him.

During the year 212, indeed, Carthage was making a great
naval effort: a powerful fleet, constantly reinforced, was attempting to save Syracuse, hard pressed by the Romans (p. 67 *sq.*).
Whether successful or not, it might, unless defeated by Marcellus'
fleet, reach Lissus, join Philip, help him to wrest Apollonia and
Dyrrhachium from Laevinus, destroy or scatter the Roman
squadron and, finally, bring Philip to Tarentum, which Hannibal
had recently captured (p. 77). Faced by this danger, prudence
urged the Romans to practise the Hellenic, anti-Macedonian
policy, till then wholly neglected, which was the logical consequence of their Illyrian expeditions (vol. VII, p. 841 *sq.*), and
stir up against Philip a war in Greece which would keep him at
home. Laevinus, though somewhat late, came to realize this; in
212 he conferred secretly with some Aetolian leaders, offered
them an offensive alliance against Philip and the help of a Roman
squadron, and found them ready to listen.

Dorimachus and Scopas of Trichonium, authors of the War of
the Allies, dominated the League at the moment; they burned
for revenge on Philip and his allies, and judged the time propitious. The war between Philip and Rome, Aratus' death and
the madness of his son, which left Achaea leaderless, the recent
alliance of Messene and Aetolia, as a result of which the whole
non-Achaean Peloponnese was now on the Aetolian side, all combined to make the opportunity favourable. Moreover, hopeful

news came from Asia. Great things had happened there, Achaeus' revolt was crushed. In 216/5 Antiochus, allied with Attalus of Pergamum, had blockaded the usurper in Sardes; in 214 he had surprised the town, which the Aetolian mercenaries, surreptitiously sent by Sosibius, had been unable to relieve[1]; Achaeus, who had taken refuge in the unscalable acropolis, had been betrayed by a Cretan, an agent of Sosibius, charged to arrange his escape. Antiochus, merciless to rebels, had ordered him to be mutilated, beheaded, and crucified in an ass's skin; shortly afterwards his last companions and his wife, Laodice, surrendered. In 213 Asia Minor was pacified: Antiochus, leaving behind as satrap of Lydia Zeuxis, one of his most trustworthy servants, was about to depart for Armenia (p. 140); so Attalus was free to leave his kingdom and cross into Europe. This meant much to the Aetolians, since for some ten years he had been their friend and even their hoped-for future ally against Philip (vol. VII, p. 758).

After the collapse of his short-lived Asiatic empire (vol. VII, p. 723), Attalus, as anxious as ever to extend his dominions, had, indeed, turned his ambitions westward. He aspired, it seems, to dominate the Aegean, then masterless, and to found a maritime empire stretching along the Islands, including Euboea, to Greece itself. To this end he had created a small but fine navy. But this design would bring him into conflict with Macedonia: hence his understanding with the Aetolians. Even if he had not already concluded a formal alliance with them, they might certainly count on him if they again went to war with Philip. And now, in addition, they would have the help of the Roman navy: they could hesitate no longer. They attributed, and not without some reason, Philip's successes in the previous war to his command of the sea; this time, the sea would belong to the combined Roman and Pergamene fleets. Kept busy repelling their landings, Philip would be forced to leave the Aetolians and their Greek allies a free field on land; his defeat was therefore certain: so reasoned the war party in Aetolia, carried away by an overweening optimism and followed by almost the whole nation.

About the end of September 212[2], Laevinus visited Aetolia with his fleet—the first Roman fleet seen in the harbours of Greece—and in a federal assembly fired Aetolian enthusiasm,

---

[1] On this see the present writer, *Rev. E.A.* XVIII, 1916, pp. 233 *sqq.*

[2] The date of the conclusion of the alliance between Rome and the Aetolians is a vexed question. Several scholars, basing their view on Livy XXVI, 24, 1–2, put it at the end of the summer of 211. See the Bibliography. The present writer has adopted the conclusion of Niese, which appears to him far the most probable.

making abundant promises guaranteed by Dorimachus and Scopas, the latter just elected General. An agreement was drawn up, Greek rather than Roman in form[1], wherein the contracting parties divided the labours and the profits of the war. The Aetolians, who were to take the field immediately, were to operate by land; the Romans at sea with at least 25 quinqueremes. To the former would fall towns and territory conquered in all directions from the Aetolian frontiers, as far north as Corcyra; to the latter the booty, men and goods: they would leave nothing but the bare 'ground, roofs and walls.' In particular the Romans were to aid the Aetolians to conquer Acarnania. Neither party were to make a separate peace with Philip; further, Rome would forbid him ever to attack the Aetolians and their allies, thus taking them under her permanent protection. Elis, Messene, Sparta and Attalus were free to join the alliance on the Aetolian side, Scerdilaidas and his son and co-regent Pleuratus on the Roman.

Such was the first alliance—shameful enough for both parties— which Rome formed with a Greek people. Laevinus was its author and, in arranging it, showed his grasp of the situation. It was, indeed, a very good stroke of business; its effect was not merely to immobilize Philip in Greece but also to allow Rome to recall to Italy half the ships sent to Illyria in 214, and to lay upon her new allies a large share of the burden of war against Macedon, ensuring for herself abundant booty in return for limited naval co-operation. Nevertheless, it is significant that the Senate took two years to ratify it: apparently Roman intervention in Greece was opposed by many senators who disliked the idea of committing Rome to an Eastern policy. But as the agreement came into effect immediately, operations were not thereby delayed. In fact, they were to be directed less against Macedonia itself, which could not easily be attacked, than against her Greek allies: it was indeed at their expense, beginning with the Acarnanians, that Aetolia intended to enlarge her dominions, and they it was whom she cynically exposed to the fierce rapacity of Rome. Thus the *Macedonicum bellum* became a Roman-Greek war: Rome, through her compact with Aetolia, was to treat mercilessly, as enemies, Greeks whom she could charge with no hostile act, and whose only crime was to be allies, and, till then, ineffective allies, of Philip.

To his lasting honour Philip shouldered the heavy task of defending them; he resolved to show that he was protector of Hellas as well as king of Macedon. Foreseeing constant, unavoidable absences from his kingdom, he first strengthened

---

[1] E. Täubler, *Imperium Romanum*, I, pp. 430–2.

himself against the neighbouring barbarians. With the amazing swiftness of movement which he had already shown during the War of the Allies, after making a demonstration against Oricus and Apollonia, he ravaged the Illyrian borders, took Sintia from the Dardanians, thus closing the gateway into Macedonia, and their capital, Iamphorynna, from the Thracian Maedi, who were especially formidable (autumn 212)[1]. Knowing he was far away, Scopas set out against the Acarnanians, who sent their non-combatants, old men, women and children into safety in Epirus, and swore an heroic oath to conquer or die. But, at Philip's approach, the Aetolians retreated hastily. However, Laevinus, before returning to Corcyra, had served their cause; he had taken Oeniadae and Nasus from the Acarnanians, Zacynthus (except the acropolis) from Philip, and he handed these over to Aetolia. At the very outset three things were clear: Philip's zeal in succouring his allies, his superiority on land, his impotence at sea.

III. THE ROMANS IN GREECE

For this impotence there was seemingly an obvious remedy—Carthaginian intervention. Bomilcar's huge fleet, 130 sail strong, having refused Marcellus' challenge off Cape Pachynus (see p. 68) was intact; it might well detach a squadron for Greece. This was Philip's ever-recurring but ever-disappointed hope: disappointed first in 211 and 210. The Carthaginians did not appear in either year; yet they would only have had to deal with the 25 Roman quinqueremes. Indeed, although Attalus, as appears certain, immediately joined the anti-Macedonian coalition and promptly sent to the Aetolians auxiliaries whom they used sometimes to garrison their towns[2], yet, for whatever reasons, he and his fleet tarried in Asia, so that only the Roman commanders operated by sea. But the troops on board their modest squadron were few[3], and they were perhaps disinclined to risk them for love of Aetolia; hence the war at sea was prosecuted with little energy;

[1] The chronology of these events is much debated. As G. De Sanctis (*Storia dei Romani*, III, 2, p. 441) has seen, the word *hibernanti* in Livy XXVI, 25, 1 (*Philippo Aetolorum defectio Pellae hibernanti allata est*) is probably not to be taken literally. It is likely that Philip took the field and ravaged Roman Illyria (25, 2–3) as soon as he got wind of the agreement between the Aetolians and Laevinus and knew that the latter had set out to Aetolia, *i.e.* in September 212. His subsequent operations would thus fall in the first half of the autumn.   [2] See below, p. 594.

[3] The annalistic tradition itself implies that the supposed *legio classica* of Laevinus (see above, p. 121 n. 2) had been recalled in 210 after Laevinus' return to Italy (Livy XXVI, 28, 9, cf. 28, 2). For the smallness of the Roman forces used in Greece see Ed. Meyer, *Kleine Schriften*, II, p. 418.

it presumably consisted mainly in predatory raids on the Greek coasts which profited the Romans alone. Our information is indeed regrettably scanty; Polybius for the most part fails us, and Livy replaces him to a very inadequate degree, but his exceeding brevity as to Roman operations implies that they were not important. The propraetor Laevinus, who had hastened to take Oeniadae in order to arouse among the Aetolians enthusiasm for the war, did not trouble to conquer the rest of Acarnania for them; in all probability the sole conquest of the coalition in 211 was Anticyra in Phocis[1], which Laevinus with the Aetolian General Scopas captured in a few days and handed over to Aetolia after enslaving the inhabitants—a conquest which, seemingly, was soon lost. In the late summer the consul P. Sulpicius Galba succeeded Laevinus[2]; but the naval warfare went little better. In spring 210 it did not prevent Philip from taking the initiative in the land operations and vigorously attacking the Aetolians. Resuming the task begun in 217 with the taking of Thebes, he endeavoured to expel them from Phthiotic Achaea so as to re-open the roads into Central Greece. His chief operation was the excellently conducted siege of Echinus, which the General Dorimachus, Scopas' successor, and Sulpicius attempted to relieve. Sulpicius could not, strange to say, prevent the provisioning of the besiegers by sea; this first expedition of the Roman navy to the Aegean was a pitiful failure. Echinus capitulated; in the same campaign, the Aetolians also lost in Phthiotic Achaea Pteleum and Larissa Cremaste.

The war upon which they had embarked with such high hopes brought them painful disappointment; they considered that the Romans gave them little aid, and they seem to have addressed reproaches to them on this subject[3]. Yet they had in other directions grounds for satisfaction. The coalition was growing. Elis and Messene[4] had joined it at once; Sparta, at first hesitating, followed them in 210 despite the efforts of the Acarnanians who, on Philip's behalf, urged them to remain neutral. A successful soldier whose antecedents are unknown to us, the 'tyrant' Machanidas, supported by a strong body of mercenaries, was then governing Sparta, as guardian of Pelops, son of Lycurgus who

[1] It is generally admitted—and is highly probable—that *in Locride* in Livy XXVI, 26, 2 is a mistake for *in Phocide* (cf. however, 28, 1), but see the explanation proposed by Oldfather in *P.W.* s.v. *Lokris* (1), col. 1226.

[2] According to Livy XXVI, 22, 1.

[3] Such reproaches are perhaps to be found in the fragment of Polybius IX, 40, 2–3. Cf. X, 25, 1–5 (from a speech by a Macedonian envoy).

[4] Delphian inscriptions (*Ditt.*[3] 555–6, cf. *Fouilles de Delphes*, III, 4, nos. 21–4) attest the presence of a Messenian garrison at Delphi during the war. On the date of these inscriptions see G. Klaffenbach, *Klio*, XX, 1926, p. 82.

had died at some prior, but uncertain, date. Naturally it was against the Achaeans, already at war with Elis and Messene, that this dangerous opponent would act; their army was feeble and their generals were incompetent; resistance was impossible. Thus a serious problem faced Philip, who would have the burden of protecting them, yet could not act by sea. Moreover, Attalus' arrival was now certain. Sulpicius, returning from Echinus, had taken Aegina[1] and handed it over to the Aetolians; but as they had no fleet they did not know what to do with the island, so Attalus bought it from them for the trifling sum of 30 talents, thus acquiring in the heart of the Greek waters an incomparable naval base. He obviously added to the 30 talents a promise of immediate maritime co-operation; the Aetolians, with his consent, voted him the honorific title of *strategos autokrator* for the year 209 (end of September 210).

Philip naturally counted upon the Carthaginians to oppose the Pergamene fleet; he also sought help from Prusias of Bithynia[2], the old rival of Attalus, who promised him ships. With the entry of new combatants—Machanidas, Attalus, Prusias—this detestable war which had opened Greece to western barbarians, threatened far-reaching developments. The Hellenic East was widely and deeply stirred. The Romans showed all the inhumanity which the Greeks of Magna Graecia and Sicily already knew so well: the slavery they imposed upon conquered populations, the sack of the illustrious Aegina, where Sulpicius had at first not allowed the citizens to ransom themselves,—all excited indignation. Some neutrals, moved also, truth to say, by self-interest, endeavoured to break the Roman-Aetolian alliance by reconciling Aetolia with Philip: they were (as in 217) Rhodes, whose commerce was disturbed by any war, Chios, accustomed to act in concert with Rhodes, and finally Egypt. For sixty years she had maintained friendly intercourse with Rome, which had lately become still closer since Philopator had authorized the Romans, who were in great straits for supplies, to come to Egypt for corn (? 210); but this by no means restrained Sosibius. He had reasons for furthering Philip's interests: fearing Antiochus more since the destruction of Achaeus, he was planning a Macedonian alliance

[1] In conformity with the current view, the taking of Aegina is here put after Sulpicius' attempt to relieve Echinus. But it may have preceded it, for the order of the fragments in Polybius IX, 42, 1–4 and 5–8 is uncertain.

[2] Polybius (XV, 22, 1) says that Prusias was κηδεστής of Philip. The precise significance of the word here cannot be determined; cf. A. Wilhelm, *Jahreshefte*, XI, 1908, pp. 79 *sqq.*

against him—a bold novelty in Egyptian policy; and he had also another motive for seeking to bring the war in Greece to an end, namely that it prevented the Egyptian government from raising there the mercenaries which it might require either against the natives who were in revolt or against Antiochus. In the spring of 209 Alexandrian, Rhodian and Chian envoys arrived in Greece; for years they were to labour to reconcile Philip and Aetolia, thereby definitely opposing Roman policy. The Athenians, Ptolemy's protégés, peace-loving on principle and by necessity, followed their example. This conduct on the part of Egypt, Rhodes and Athens is deserving of notice, since it is usual wrongly to represent these three states as having been from the earliest times the devoted, if not subservient, friends of Rome.

That spring, Philip received a not unexpected appeal from the Achaeans, whose position, caught between Machanidas and the Aetolians, who were crossing the strait at Rhium in large numbers, was becoming untenable. He hastened to their defence. The Aetolian army, increased by Roman and Pergamene auxiliaries, attempted to bar his way; but after suffering two defeats, it was driven back into Lamia with the loss of 1000 men. At this point a faint hope of peace appeared. Neutral ambassadors came to Philip at Phalara, the port of Lamia[1]; with them was Amynander, king of the Athamanians, whom the Aetolians, discouraged by their double defeat, had deputed to act as peace-maker. An armistice was concluded; negotiations were to be opened at Aegium, where Philip was going to preside over the Achaean assembly. But, meanwhile, Sulpicius, tardily enough, arrived at Naupactus, and, more important still, Attalus, bringing 35 warships, landed at Aegina. The Aetolians took heart again; at Aegium, prompted by Sulpicius, they submitted impossible conditions; Philip had to break off negotiations, calling his allies to witness that the rupture was forced upon him (c. June 209). The peace he desired eluded him. He had another disappointment: a Punic squadron came from Tarentum to Corcyra, but dared advance no farther, and the ships of Bithynia also apparently failed to arrive.

In Achaea, at least, where his presence brought security, Philip scored a political success: having quarrelled with the upper classes he courted and won popular sympathy. At Argos, the legendary cradle of the Macedonian monarchy, after the Nemean Games, at which he had wished to preside, he openly put off his royal trappings, mingling with the crowd as one of themselves. The 'moderate men' detested him the more and thought he was playing

---

[1] See F. Stählin, *Das hellenische Thessalien*, p. 217 *sq.*

the tyrant; they were also, and not without reason, indignant at
the unbridled effrontery of his gallantries which were bringing dishonour upon the noblest families, but he conquered the hearts of
the people. A slight reverse inflicted upon the Romans, who had
landed near Sicyon, an expedition against Elis in conjunction
with the Achaean army, also endeared him to them. Though he
failed to take Elis and nearly met his death being surprised by
the Romans who had disembarked secretly, yet he gathered in
the country round an immense booty which his allies enjoyed,
and this, too, made him beloved. But his destiny condemned him
to perpetual motion; the threat of a Dardanian invasion, rendered
easy by the treachery of the governor of Lychnidus who had
betrayed to a rebel that border stronghold, recalled him to
Macedonia. Leaving troops to defend Achaea, he hurried in ten
marches across Boeotia and Euboea from Dyme to Demetrias.
The Dardanians, emboldened by a false rumour of his death,
were already raiding Orestis.

Sulpicius wintered (209–8) at Aegina to discuss concerted
action with Attalus. Their arrangement about war-gains closely
resembled Laevinus' compact with Aetolia: the Romans took the
booty (in which, however, Attalus might share), the king, the
conquered cities. Since Attalus was planning conquests on the
east coast of Greece and among the Islands, the maritime war,
waged till then by the Romans chiefly in the Ionian Sea and the
Corinthian Gulf, would be transferred to the Aegean.

The junction of the Roman and Pergamene fleets roused the
fighting spirit of all Philip's enemies; the campaign of 208, which
marked the crucial moment of the war, promised badly for him
and his allies. The Aetolians had fortified Thermopylae to prevent
his progress farther south; the Illyrians and the Maedi were preparing, it was said, an invasion of Macedonia, Machanidas an
attack on Argos. In the early summer Attalus and Sulpicius,
having joined forces, sailed east with 60 warships; terror reigned
along the Greek coasts. In this crisis Philip, with high courage,
promised help to his distracted allies, whose envoys hastened to
implore it; sent assistance to those in greatest peril, the Euboeans,
Boeotians, Phocians; concentrated his army in Thessaly whence it
threatened Aetolia, and remained himself at Demetrias, prepared
for anything, while a system of beacons on Mt Tisaeus signalled
the operations of the hostile fleets. They achieved little. After an
unsuccessful attack on Lemnos which Attalus coveted, the Allies
turned and devastated Peparethus (but without taking the town),
then, after conferring with the Aetolians assembled at Heraclea in
Trachis, attacked Euboea. Oreus was betrayed by its governor,

Chalcis held out. They then took Opus in Locris, where Attalus had a narrow escape: he was levying contributions from the wealthy men when Philip appeared, coming from Demetrias at full speed, after forcing the pass of Thermopylae and thrusting aside the Aetolians. Attalus had to flee hurriedly to his ships, and weighed anchor in great confusion. This was his inglorious farewell to Greece: Prusias, no doubt at Philip's instigation, was invading his kingdom; he returned to Asia, abandoning Opus and Oreus (c. June 208). Sulpicius retired to Aegina and stayed there.

Resuming the land offensive, Philip then captured from the Aetolians Thronium in Locris, Tithronium and Drymaea in Phocis, but, as usual, had to break off to succour the Achaeans. He was at Elatea, conferring with neutrals arrived from Aetolia in pursuance of their pacific task, when he was called again to fight Machanidas (July 208)[1]. He returned therefore to the Peloponnese; and Machanidas retreated at his approach. At Aegium, addressing the Achaeans, Philip could truly say that his enemies were as prompt to flee as he to march against them, and that they thus snatched victory from his grasp; his swift arrival, his sanguine spirit, his burning words strengthened his popularity. Yet, fearing the hostility of the ruling class, he promised the Achaeans to cede to them Heraea, bequeathed to him by Doson, and Triphylia and Alipheira conquered by himself in the War of the Allies. After a profitable descent on the Aetolian coast carried out with their co-operation, he proudly regained Demetrias by sea, Sulpicius not attempting to bar his way.

This fourth campaign, which had seemed so full of danger, ended in his favour: he had suffered no serious loss and gained cities from the Aetolians; but it might have ended in a decisive success. The Carthaginians had again cruised in Greek waters, and even touched at Aegium. Attalus' departure presented to them a fine chance of winning a victory over Sulpicius which would probably have decided the Aetolians to treat for peace; but without waiting for Philip, who had appointed a rendezvous at Aegium and even sent some ships, they had almost immediately retreated towards Acarnania. Despairing of Carthaginian help, Philip ordered the construction of 100 warships at Cassandreia— an undertaking which was to be indefinitely postponed owing, no doubt, to lack of money. Then, again as usual, he went to fight the Dardanians.

[1] Livy (XXVIII, 7, 14) writes: *nuntius adfertur Machanidam Olympiorum sollemne ludicrum parantis Eleos adgredi statuisse.* As the Eleans were allies of the Aetolians and, therefore, of the Spartans, probably Livy has made some mistake in adapting Polybius.

IV. THE PEACE OF PHOENICE. CONCLUSION

The Romans, to make up for Attalus' withdrawal, should surely have redoubled their activities, but they did exactly the opposite, and for two years (207–6), Livy admits that 'Greek affairs were neglected.' Still, it may have been in the spring of 207 that Sulpicius seized Dyme, sacked it, and carried off the inhabitants; if so, it was his last exploit. He continued to guard the Illyrian coast with some vessels, but took no further part in the war: apparently, nearly all his soldiers had been recalled to Italy. Hasdrubal's invasion, it is said, made this necessary, but we may doubt whether, even in this emergency, Rome could not spare these few men and, besides, the explanation would not hold good for 206. Much more probably, convinced at last that the Carthaginians would do nothing for Philip, especially since their defeat at sea in 208 (p. 92), the Senate, who had only adopted half-heartedly Laevinus' policy, lost all interest in the fighting in Greece, in spite of their agreement with Aetolia. If Philip succeeded in equipping a fleet, they would take steps to oppose him; in the meantime the Aetolians could be left to deal with him alone. Thus, by Rome's selfish, disloyal, and, moreover, unwise inaction, the war underwent a third transformation: from Roman-Macedonian, then Roman-Hellenic, it became merely Hellenic and Macedonian— a second 'War of the Allies.'

Henceforth Philip might count on victory, especially if he had not to succour the Achaeans. And suddenly Achaea put off her feebleness and stood forth a military power. This miracle was due to one man, Philopoemen, son of Craugis, an eminent citizen of Megalopolis. Born about 253 B.C. he was soon left an orphan, and was first brought up by Cleander, an exile from Mantinea, and then became the pupil of his townsmen, the academic philosophers, Ecdemus and Demophanes (vol. VII, p. 222). Their teaching failed to broaden and elevate his narrowly definite mind or to soften the harshness of his character: he remained over-imperious, quick to anger and brutality, with a pride and egotism which might lead him to sacrifice even his patriotism to his personal hatreds. He may, however, have learnt from these devoted republicans some of that proud spirit of independence, which, added to contempt for gain and simple austerity of life, was his highest quality and steeled him to present an unyielding front, first to Cleomenes (vol. VII, p. 760), and later to the Romans. In all else he was his own teacher: he owed his career to his own burning and steady energy directed to a single purpose and guided by a truly remarkable practical realism. A born soldier, the passion for fame in arms filled his soul. Slightly endowed with the abilities of a statesman, in which he fell short of his model Epaminondas, he set himself to be an accomplished master of warfare and quickly attained his ambition. He brought to the task great physical endurance, trained and developed above all by the chase and rustic labour, a diligent apprenticeship in every branch of the soldier's craft, a precocious experience acquired in border-raids on Sparta, and the study of tactical treatises which he corrected and supplemented by practical observation of field-manœuvres and their setting. In early days, at Sellasia, Antigonus had divined in him the promise of high generalship, but his independent spirit was deaf to the king's offers of employment, and for the next ten years, with untiring zeal, he perfected his military skill as a condottiere in Crete. He returned a famous captain, to be raised by the Achaeans to their chief military posts, and from that moment, resenting the sight of Achaea reduced to beg for Macedonian help against Sparta, he determined to enable his country to defend herself with her own forces. With lightning speed he reformed and improved the federal army, first, as Hipparch, the cavalry (210/09), then, when General (208/7), the infantry in the short space of eight months; he introduced Macedonian tactics and armament, drilled and trained his men, and showed what a real leader could do with them.

After taking Tegea (date unknown), Machanidas was marching to besiege Mantinea. Philopoemen, protected by a wide ditch, waited for him south of the town, where the plain narrowed between the last spurs of Maenalus on the south-east and the lowest slopes of Alesion to the north-west. The two armies were of almost equal strength, the Spartans having some 15,000, the Achaeans 15–20,000 men. Machanidas with his mercenaries broke the mercenaries and light-armed troops on the Achaean left and pursued them to Mantinea, but Philopoemen reformed and extended his line to cut off the tyrant's retreat, and hurled back with his phalanx the Spartan phalanx as it crossed the ditch to attack him. Thus he gained the day or, better still, regained it after all seemed lost, and when Machanidas returned to aid his men, he killed him with his own hand, thus proving himself the worthy pupil of the tyrannicide philosophers. The Spartan army, completely routed, lost 4000 dead and still more prisoners; the Achaeans immediately re-took Tegea and invaded and ravaged Laconia unhindered[1].

[1] The details of the battle of Mantinea are far from being established with certainty. See the Bibliography.

This battle of Mantinea is memorable for several reasons. The historian of military science notes that, at the outset of the action, Machanidas shot down the Achaean phalanx with the catapults destined for the siege of Mantinea: we may call it a first (and the only) employment by the Greeks of field-artillery in a pitched battle on land. Moreover, Mantinea was the last great action in Greek history between Hellenic armies. Finally, while making the fame of Philopoemen, it covered Achaea with a 'paradoxical' glory— she had beaten Sparta. True, this brilliant success was to have no important or lasting consequences; but, for the moment, Achaea could do without Philip.

Philip, therefore, concentrated all his efforts against the Aetolians; fearing renewed Roman intervention, he was anxious to force them to lay down their arms without delay. Yet the hope of further help from Rome prolonged their resistance. The neutrals, now joined by Byzantium and Mitylene, preached peace to them in vain; vainly Thrasycrates of Rhodes, in a moving speech rewritten, not invented by Polybius, reproached them with their disgraceful treaty with the 'Barbarians,' and pointed to Rome as the real enemy that threatened Greece. Trusting in their great ally, they continued the struggle; but Rome did nothing, and they were overwhelmed by disasters. Driven from Thessaly, they saw their own land invaded. Philip, to whom the Romans now left freedom of action even by sea, reconquering Zacynthus, handed it to Amynander in return for free passage through Athamania, thus entered Aetolia from the north and, as in 218, sacked Thermum (summer 207). In 206 the Aetolians, brought to bay, yielded at last to the exhortations of peace-makers and resigned themselves to making a separate treaty[1]—a 'defection' which Rome never forgave though she had made it inevitable.

It was a costly peace for them. Though they retained Oeniadae, they lost Hestiaeotis and Thessaliotis, Dolopia, Epicnemidian Locris, and at least the greater number of their Phocian towns. It seems, indeed, that Philip, foreseeing that the Romans would do their utmost to make them break the treaty and thinking it would be useful to show himself conciliatory, promised (without, however, any intention of keeping his engagement) to return Pharsalus to them, and if not all, at least much of his conquests in

---

[1] The view has been held, based on the Thermum inscription *Ditt.*[3] 554, that Agelaus of Naupactus became once more General of the Aetolians in 207/6, which would imply the preponderance of the peace party at this date. But the 'second' *strategia* of Agelaus, there mentioned, may be that of 217/16. See Beloch, *Griech. Gesch.*[2] IV, 2, p. 417, Pomtow, *ad Ditt.*[3] 554.

Phthiotic Achaea: Echinus, Larissa Cremaste, and even Thebes[1].
But, even so, the Aetolians had to face a serious diminution of
their federal territory. It was a rude awakening after their dream
of establishing with Roman help their supremacy over Greece:
Macedonia was taking a crushing revenge. The peace obviously
included their Peloponnesian allies[2], Elis, Messene and Sparta,
where Nabis, a Eurypontid, now replaced Machanidas as Pelops'
guardian. The Hellenic war was ended.

This peace, for which she was responsible, roused Rome from
her lethargy. Philip, his hands free, could turn against Roman
Illyria and threaten Apollonia and Dyrrhachium. The Senate
considered it necessary to protect them and, by an imposing
display of strength, attempt to put heart into the Aetolians, so
unwisely left in the lurch. In the spring of 205, the proconsul
P. Sempronius Tuditanus, Sulpicius' successor, brought to
Dyrrhachium 35 warships with 10,000 men and 1000 horse;
and while he undertook some operations in Illyria and besieged
Dimale, his lieutenant, Laetorius, sailed to Aetolia with 15 ships
to add force to his arguments, and urged the Aetolians to take up
arms again. But, disgusted with Roman ways, they refused to
listen: Laetorius had to go back empty-handed. As nine years
before, Rome found herself face to face with Philip.

She immediately renounced the prosecution of the war. Not,
indeed, that it was impossible, for Sempronius' forces sufficed for
a defensive until peace with Carthage—which might soon be
expected—should allow a powerful offensive; but the Senate had
no thought of involving Rome in a great war with Philip. To
draw him from Illyria, they would again have willingly set up the
Aetolians against him, giving them, at need, some assistance; but
since Aetolia refused to fight, they were ready to come to terms,
and had given Sempronius instructions to this effect. The proconsul refused Philip's challenge to battle before Apollonia, then,
the Epirote magistrates having offered themselves as mediators, he
parleyed at Phoenice with Philip, who was equally anxious to
extricate himself from the war. An agreement was quickly
reached at the price of mutual concessions (autumn 205): Philip
restored Parthinian territory, Dimale and other places; the

[1] This assumption is required to explain the form taken by the complaints
of the Aetolians in 198 and 196 about Pharsalus, Thebes, Echinus and
Larissa Cremaste (Polybius XVIII, 3, 12; 38, 3). See the Bibliography,
especially the article of F. Stählin there cited.
[2] On this see the present writer, in *Rome, la Grèce et les monarchies
hellénistiques*, etc. pp. 258 *sqq.*, and E. Täubler, *op. cit.* I, pp. 214 *sqq.*

Romans left him Atintania. The peace, being general, included
on the Macedonian side Philip's Greek allies and Prusias; on the
Roman side, Pleuratus—we may assume that Scerdilaidas was
dead—and Attalus, who had remained faithful to the Roman
alliance even after the Aetolian desertion[1]. Attalus kept Aegina,
Philip most of his conquests from Pleuratus; the terms of agreement between Attalus and Prusias are unknown. The Senate and
the Roman people, the latter by a unanimous vote of all the tribes,
ratified the treaty at the end of 205 or the beginning of 204;
Sempronius became consul, a proof of the satisfaction felt in
Rome at the settlement of Macedonian affairs.

So ended the desultory, intermittent, wholly inglorious war,
which first brought the Romans into prolonged contact with
Greece—a war which they had neither wished nor even foreseen,
which was imposed on them by the enemy, and to which they
only made up their minds late, when compelled by the necessity
of defending themselves; a war which was, on the whole, nothing
more than a tiresome by-product of their great contest with
Carthage. The results were scarcely gratifying to them. They
had, indeed, gained a distant and unexpected friend—Attalus,
with whom they had formed ties which became closer immediately
after the peace, when an embassy headed by Laevinus went to
Pergamum to seek the famous 'Black stone' (p. 115); but they
could not foresee the extraordinary importance which this new
friendship was shortly to assume. On the other hand, they had
no longer any hold over Greece; they had lost their allies, who
cursed them for their faithlessness as Philip's allies did for their
atrocities; and in Greece the Hellenic spirit of solidarity, at length
awakened, now rose against them. Finally, Philip came out of the
conflict strengthened, aggrandized at the expense of the Illyrians,
clients or allies of Rome, as well as of the Aetolians.

Certainly, if the Romans, as many have supposed, had intended
to undermine the Macedonian power, and by forming a permanent, friendly Hellenic group opposed to Philip, to stir up
lasting trouble for him in Greece, their disappointment would have
been bitter. But they had no such far-reaching aims; otherwise,
far from treating Aetolia so cavalierly, they would have carefully
cultivated her alliance, which, being perpetual, gave them constant
opportunities of interfering in Hellenic affairs. In fact, they had
as yet no real Hellenic policy; they had entered Greece and sought

[1] The annalists erroneously add the Ilians, Spartans, Eleans, Messenians
and Athenians. See the works cited above, p. 135 n. 2.

allies there, only accidentally, under pressure of circumstances, and solely to avert an imminent danger. The danger had vanished —thanks above all, it is true, to Carthaginian inaction—and they were satisfied.

They were the more content in that they had not to fear a renewal of it. At close quarters Philip had seemed less formidable than they had imagined. His troops, though excellent, were few; his fleet, not yet in being, had not left the shipyards of Cassandreia; his Greek allies were, on the whole, an embarrassment, and his barbarian neighbours constantly threatened him. Without a powerful ally he could not be dangerous, and where could he find one—a second Hannibal? It mattered little, therefore, that he had enlarged his dominions and even retained the valuable district of Atintania: alone, he could attempt nothing against Rome, and she might allow him to remain as the peace of Phoenice had left him. There is no reason to suppose that, in Roman eyes, this peace without victory was merely a truce.

There are those who blame Philip for concluding it, and maintain that, although it was too late for him to help Hannibal in Italy, the prolongation of hostilities in Illyria would have made easier the last resistance of the Carthaginians, to his and their advantage. But Philip could not have harboured the fantastic notion that the maintenance of a legion or so in Illyria would seriously weaken the Roman effort against Carthage and effectively improve the military situation of Hannibal and his country. Besides, as Carthage had done nothing for him, Philip was justified in considering only his own immediate interests. If she made a successful resistance and so secured a settlement by understanding with Rome, it was very doubtful whether, despite the terms of her alliance with Philip, she could include him within its scope. His greatest danger was to be left exposed alone to Roman vengeance: prudence accordingly impelled him to make peace before Carthage, when the Romans offered honourable terms. Doubtless it was hard for him to recognize by treaty their sovereignty over that Illyrian seaboard (even with the exception of Atintania) which he had hoped to wrest from them, and to leave in their hands the all-important bridge-heads of Dyrrhachium and Apollonia: still he had escaped lightly from his dangerous adventure. Moreover, he had new and urgent reasons for freeing himself from the Roman conflict: the East now occupied his thoughts more than the West. Events of great moment had happened; others were about to happen, of which he did not intend to remain a mere spectator—Antiochus claimed his attention.

CHAPTER VI

ROME AND MACEDON: THE ROMANS AGAINST PHILIP

I. THE 'ANABASIS' OF ANTIOCHUS III

UNLIKE the kings of Macedonia and Egypt, Antiochus of Syria had held wholly aloof from the contest between Rome and Carthage and its repercussions in Greece. Some have censured

Note. Our knowledge of the events described in chapters VI and VII is almost wholly derived from the account of Polybius based on excellent documentary, literary or oral sources; but it is in the main derived indirectly. Of the text of Polybius relating to the subject-matter of these chapters there remain only some 100 excerpts, often very brief, very unevenly divided over books VIII–XI (the Asiatic expedition of Antiochus III), XIII–XVI, XVIII, XX–XXI (books XVII and XIX have wholly perished), so that for us Polybius is chiefly represented by secondary historians who, in one way or another, draw upon him. The first to be considered are Diodorus and Livy, for both of whom he is a direct source. Diodorus in books XXVIII–XXIX had given a *résumé* following Polybius of the period 205–188 B.C., and this *résumé*, which, though very curt and sometimes confused, seems to have been laudably faithful, would be very valuable, especially for the years 205–200; but only a few fragments of it survive. Livy (XXXI, 14–XXXVIII, 41) has taken over from Polybius the account of the Second Macedonian War and the War against Antiochus. This translation or rather adaptation of Polybius by Livy—vastly superior to his performance as regards the narrative of the First Macedonian War (see above, p. 116)—is of outstanding importance. Despite its great deficiencies and although it abounds in misstatements, many of which are tendencious, it remains—except, of course, for the actual fragments of Polybius—the main source for the history of Rome's first two great wars in the East. Essentially dependent on Polybius are also Trogus (Justin XXX–XXXII, 1, 1–3), Appian (*Maced.* frags. IV–IX, 5; *Syr.* I–XLIV) and Dio Cassius (frags. of books XVII–XIX; Zonaras IX, 15, 16, 18–21, 4); but, unlike Livy and Diodorus, these three writers give the Polybian tradition at secondhand and 'contaminated' with heterogeneous elements chiefly derived from the Roman annalists (in Appian and Dio traces of a Greek source other than Polybius but deserving of little credence have been discerned). Consequently these writers must be consulted with extreme caution. Indeed Appian alone, second rate as he is and although he derives from Polybius only indirectly through an annalist, supplies information which is a useful complement to Livy. Something may also be gleaned from Plutarch, whose Life of Flamininus is inspired by Polybius but contains some details from various sources, and whose Life of the elder Cato (XII–XIV) may be indebted to Cato's own writings. For Plutarch's Life of Philopoemen and him for this, saying that he ought to have made common cause with Macedon and Carthage, divining the danger which Rome's victory threatened to the Greek world. But this foreknowledge was not vouchsafed to him any more than to the Romans themselves, who, at the moment, were far from realizing the domination which they were destined to achieve. As he had no relations with Rome and could imagine no possible cause of quarrel between himself and the Republic; as he had, moreover, no direct interests in the West, even in Greece, it is no wonder that Antiochus cared little about the great struggle so far away. He considered that he had a task of supreme importance in Asia: it was natural that he should have given himself to it unreservedly; perhaps, too, he was not ill-pleased to see Philip involved in a war which absorbed his whole activity and diverted his energies from the East.

As early as 219/8, the negotiations concerning Southern Syria (vol. VII, p. 729) had shown how tenaciously Antiochus held to his hereditary rights (Polybius v, 67, 8): he had no intention of ruling over a mutilated kingdom. It was his high purpose to re-constitute, to the limit of what was practicable, the Seleucid Empire, and re-assert his authority over all countries, which, though rightfully dependencies of his house, had broken away from their allegiance. Achaeus out of the way, he set to work and began with Armenia.

the parts of Pausanias (VIII, 50–51) concerning him, see above, p. 116. It is to be observed that while Livy has relied on Polybius for the history of the Macedonian and Syrian Wars, he has usually if not always drawn on the annalists for his account of those political and diplomatic events, connected with these wars, which happened at Rome; so that in his narrative are two strands, the one Polybian, the other annalistic, which are neither coherent nor even reconcilable each with the other (as H. Nissen has convincingly shown); and of which the second is generally quite untrustworthy. Parts of his narrative, e.g. of the course of events which led to the Macedonian War (XXXI, 1, 6–5, 9), may even be classed with the worst products of the annalists. This is not surprising since the authority chiefly followed by Livy seems to be Valerius Antias (see vol. VII, p. 317). There are also numerous inscriptions of which some (about a dozen) are of high historical interest.

A very vexed chronological question of capital importance is the relation of the Roman calendar to the reformed (Julian) calendar since the closing years of the third century. On this the writer has not accepted the system which Beloch proposed in 1918 and 1922, but for all essentials has adopted the results of De Sanctis (see the Bibliography). As space does not permit more than a very brief account of military operations, the reader is in general (when no indication to the contrary is given) referred for all details to the *Antike Schlachtfelder*, vol. II, of J. Kromayer and the *Schlachten-Atlas* of J. Kromayer and G. Veith (see the particular references given in the Bibliography).

The local dynasty no longer paid tribute. In 212, Antiochus marched on the capital, Arsamosata, and prepared to lay siege to it; the young king Xerxes (probably son of Arsames, the former ally of Hierax), who had at first fled, submitted almost immediately. Wisely magnanimous, Antiochus only exacted as arrears of tribute 300 talents with 2000 horses and mules, and betrothed Xerxes to his sister Antiochis, thus inaugurating the policy of dynastic marriages which he always favoured[1].

This settled, he turned to the Far East. Since the interrupted campaign of Seleucus II (vol. VII, p. 722) everything had gone wrong there. Arsaces II Tiridates (vol. VII, p. 720) had conquered (after 217) Western Hyrcania[2] and in Eastern Media Comisene and Choarene; the Graeco-Bactrians, under a new king, Euthydemus of Magnesia, who had overthrown the Diodotids (vol. VII, p. 719), now occupied Areia; Antiochus must strike now before secession spread farther. In the winter of 211–0, coming presumably from Antiocheia, he sailed down the Euphrates; late in 210 he was in Media preparing the vast expedition which brought him fame. To finance the war he despoiled the temple of Anaitis at Ecbatana[3], obtaining, we are told, nearly 4000 talents—an easy but dangerous way of raising money to which he had recourse later to his cost (p. 242). Next year, having taken the precaution of proclaiming his eldest son, Antiochus, a boy of eleven, joint-king, he left Ecbatana with a powerful army[4] to fight Arsaces III (or Artabanus I), successor to Tiridates, who had died, c. 210. Like Alexander he naturally followed the great road which led to Hecatompylos (? Sharud) by Rhagae and the Caspian Gates[5]; once through the Gates he was in enemy country and had soon after

---

[1] It is true that the marriage turned out ill, for Antiochis brought about her husband's death (Johannes Antioch. frag. 53; F.H.G. IV, p. 557). According to the confused account given by that writer, Antiochus himself instigated the murder, but we may take leave to be sceptical. In consequence, at an unknown date Antiochus divided Armenia between two native princes, Zariadres and Artaxias, each of whom held the rank of a royal governor (strategos), Strabo XI, 528, 531.

[2] See Kiessling in P.W. s.vv. Hekatompylos (col. 2791), Hyrkania (col. 501).

[3] Some historians are of the opinion that Ecbatana had been conquered by Arsaces II or III; that is not impossible, but the present writer cannot regard it as proved.

[4] The figures, however, given by Justin (XLI, 5, 7)—100,000 foot, 20,000 horse—plainly belong to legend.

[5] For this part of Antiochus' expedition, to his arrival in Bactria, especially for the identification of places, see Kiessling in P.W. s.vv. Hekatompylos (cols. 2795–6), Hyrkania (cols. 501–2).

to cross the salt steppe which separates Simnan from Damghan. Arsaces intended to block the wells of fresh water as he retired, but Antiochus, throwing forward 1000 cavalry, forestalled him and reached Hecatompylos unhindered. Arsaces had fled to Hyrcania, whither Antiochus, still in the footsteps of Alexander, pressed the pursuit. To cross the Elburz mountains held by the brave Tapurians, who, too, had risen against the Seleucids and were presumably allies of Arsaces, was no easy task: starting from Tagae (? Taq near Damghan), he fought his way through in eight days, forced the pass of Labus (Lamavu); then, descending into the plain, occupied the open town of Tambrax, and reduced after a difficult siege the strong Sirynca (? Tarunga), though he could not save its Greek population which was massacred by the barbarians. After these glorious beginnings we lose sight of him, but Arsaces was finally constrained to sue for terms, withdrawing apparently from Comisene and Hyrcania as well as Choarene, and became his subordinate ally (? winter 209–8).

Next came Bactria; Antiochus, coming from Parthyene, marched against it in 208. Euthydemus, resting upon the fortress of Gouriana[1], awaited him behind the river Arius (Here Rud), his western frontier; 10,000 horsemen challenged his crossing. But these withdrew during the night, and Antiochus, with his leading troops, took advantage of their unwariness, and, after a hot action in which he fought gallantly, had a horse killed under him and was wounded, made good his footing on the eastern bank. Euthydemus retired on Zariaspa Bactra, but did not abandon the struggle, which lasted two years, a stubborn war of which the history has perished: all that has come down to us is a vague memory of the siege of Bactra, which remained famous among the Greeks. In 206, weary of fighting, the two kings began negotiations; Euthydemus represented that more fighting would lay open the country to the 'Nomads' who would 'barbarize' it. Antiochus felt the force of this argument: the Bactrian state was the outpost of Hellenic civilization against barbarism. He, there-

---

[1] Kiessling in *P.W.* *s.v. Guriane* identifies τὰ Γουρίανα (Polybius x, 49, 1: adopting Gutschmid's correction of the MSS reading Ταγουριαν) with Ghurian on the Here Rud, west of Herat. But it is unlikely that Antiochus, coming from Parthyene and about to invade Bactria, should have gone so far south; more probably he was following the usual route to Bactra, which crossed the *lower* Arius, and Euthydemus, who was covering his capital, would await him at the crossing. Now Ptolemy (vi, 10, 4) gives a Guriane 'in Margiana' (Gutschmid); this seems to be τὰ Γουρίανα, which should have been on the route to Bactra, some distance east of the Arius (communicated to the writer by Mr W. W. Tarn).

fore, only exacted the surrender of Euthydemus' elephants in sign of allegiance, but left him his royal title, concluded with him a perpetual alliance, and promised one of his daughters to his son Demetrius.

Reprovisioned by Euthydemus, Antiochus crossed the Hindu-Kush and pushed on to 'India'—which means no more than that he penetrated the Cabul valley. There he renewed with the Hindoo prince called in Greek Sophagasenos—some rajah become independent at the break-up of the Mauryan empire[1]—the 'friendship' formed by Seleucus with Chandragupta, and received from him elephants and treasure.

So ended his 'Anabasis'; he had made Seleucid power felt by peoples who had forgotten it. On the return march he passed through the south of his empire—Arachosia, Drangiana, Carmania, where he wintered (206–5), and Persia where, at Antiocheia (probably Bushire, east of the Persian Gulf), he received the Magnesian envoys requesting him to recognize the festival of Artemis Leucophryene. Coming to the Persian Gulf, more fortunate than Alexander, he embarked for Arabia, paid a peaceful visit to the Gerrhaeans, confirmed their freedom in return for rich presents, and sighted the island of Tylos (Bahrein). It was probably at Seleuceia, which he re-entered in triumph after six years (205/4), bringing 150 elephants and fabulous booty, that he assumed the Achaemenid title of 'Great King' which the Greeks turned into 'Antiochus the Great'—a name deserved by his kingly virtues, his greatness of purpose, untiring energy, martial courage, and generosity towards the vanquished. The tale of his distant exploits, embroidered and magnified by his mercenaries, notably the Aetolians, filled the Hellenic world, until at the end of the third century, Antiochus enjoyed, as no one else, the admiration of the Greeks.

They admired him—and with good grounds—but they did not understand him. They, and after them the Romans, saw in him a second Alexander, a conqueror of inordinate ambitions; and deeming him worthy of world-empire, they believed he aimed at it. The conqueror was, in fact, a prudent statesman, whose head was not turned by success. He had not assayed the dangerous adventure of destroying the Armenian, Parthian, or Bactrian kingdoms, but had been content with including them again in his empire as vassal states. Master of himself, unseduced by fantastic hopes, shrewdly calculating what the moment and his power allowed, he aimed only at the possible.

One thing surely was possible: with the resources of Asia to his hand, he might recover from the Ptolemies the countries they

---

[1] *Cambridge History of India*, i, p. 442.

had stolen from his ancestors. While his reign had raised Syria from weakness to strength, Egypt was declining and, under her sluggish monarch, despite the energetic Sosibius, had fallen on evil days. A son had indeed at length been born to Philopator (9 October 210 or 209), who almost immediately proclaimed him joint-ruler; and thus the future of the dynasty seemed assured. But, about 207/6 (if not before), while Philopator, definitely forsaking the noble Arsinoe, was ruled entirely by an odious trio, his favourite Agathocles, his mistress Agathocleia, Agathocles' sister, and their mother Oenanthe, the native rising became steadily more dangerous (p. 129). At first apparently confined to the Delta, it spread to Upper Egypt, where Thebais seceded; a usurper, Harmachis, presumably a Nubian, founded a kingdom which was to last over twenty years. Meanwhile the Ethiopian prince Ergamenes, formerly Philopator's friend and vassal, seized Philae. The internal calamities of the realm were reflected abroad: Lysimacheia, too difficult to hold against the Thracians, was abandoned; while in most of the towns of Asia Minor dependent upon Ptolemy, his authority had become purely nominal.

Egypt's difficulties were Antiochus' opportunity. He purposed to attack and defeat her, avenge Raphia, and regain what she had usurped in Syria, Asia and Thrace. But could he carry out his purpose unhampered? He could have done so, had the war in Greece continued; but it had ended most inconveniently, at the very moment of his return from the Upper Satrapies. Philip was clear of Rome, and Antiochus now had him to reckon with.

II. BEFORE THE EASTERN CRISIS

Doubtless Philip had been jealously watching eastern events. He and Antiochus were the same age, had ascended their thrones together, and were naturally rivals for power and fame. But while he was making no headway in his contest with Rome, Antiochus now was playing Alexander in Asia—a most painful contrast. And the Seleucid, insatiable, was intending to make the Egyptian empire his prey: this Philip could not allow; Egypt might fall, but not for Antiochus' profit. He had made peace at Phoenice partly to prevent this. Hitherto circumstances had imposed upon him a western policy, not unlike that of Pyrrhus, but now, determined to make up for his failure, he was looking East, returning to the tradition of his great ancestors Demetrius I and Antigonus II.

The Aegean, where only a few islands, such as Andros, were Macedonian and where Ptolemy retained little but Thera, had been for twenty years without a master (vol. VII, pp. 718, 752); the Rhodians alone, who cleared it of pirates, exercised a peaceful control. Thus it was a first natural object for Philip's ambition, who had, moreover, always kept an eye upon it. Like his predecessors, he was a protector of Delos, where, at his accession, the Macedonian League had erected his statue (vol. vii, p. 751); in 216 he had founded the *Philippeia*, then, like Gonatas, built a portico, whose mighty ruins still exist and which hid the portico built by Attalus. In Crete, although his protectorate (vol. vii, p. 768) was no longer recognized everywhere, many towns remained his allies. To dominate the Aegean and the Straits, thus realizing in the reverse direction the daring dream of Attalus, to establish himself on the Asiatic and Thracian shore, such was—for the moment—his new purpose.

To attain this end he was to apply his rare powers and indomitable energy, but also, unfortunately, give rein to his worst instincts. To be sure, his enemies have defamed him; he was not as hateful as the Messenian Alcaeus paints him in his epigrams or the Achaean Polybius in his history. Several of the crimes which are imputed to him are probably imaginary—the attempted assassination of Philopoemen, the poisoning of the Athenian statesmen Eurycleides and Micion. Nevertheless, too many incontrovertible facts prove the increasing savagery of his temper. He had had much to embitter him: the failure of his western project owing to lack of Carthaginian co-operation; the ineradicable enmity of the Aetolians and their unnatural alliance with Rome; the hostility, still less pardonable as it was entirely unprovoked, of the Pergamene princeling; the labours of an exhausting war which he had waged almost alone for nine years; the treason of subordinates[1]; the inertia of most of his allies, active only to implore his help; the ingratitude and hatred which he perceived among the Greek *optimates*, who forgot his services and could pardon neither his imperious control nor his personal policy which had brought the Romans into Greece. By now he despised all men except the Romans, adversaries worthy of him, and openly showed his contempt. Brooking no obstacle to his ambitions, grasping at any means to attain his ends, careless of any scandal he caused, he was to startle the Greek world both by his brutality and his trickery, wantonly provoking fear, anger and distrust.

In Macedonia he rejected Doson's 'constitutional' arrangements (vol. vii, p. 751): the formula 'King Philip and the Macedonians' was replaced by 'Philip King of the Macedonians.' He did not scruple to place his image on his coins[2], as no one of his ancestors had done, except Demetrius I. He became the

---

[1] See, for example, Livy xxvii, 32, 9; xxviii, 6, 1 *sqq.*
[2] See Vol. of Plates iii, 10, *c.*

complete despot who did not shrink from blood; a mere hint
of opposition cost, it is said, five of his counsellors their lives.
Henceforth, indeed, his policy demanded instruments rather than
counsellors. His welcome of Demetrius of Pharos had shown his
taste for adventurers, and his trusted agents were now two
foreigners, a pair of rascals, Dicaearchus, an Aetolian, and a
Tarentine architect, Heracleides, exiled for high treason, who
became his favourite and was to become his admiral. It was soon
seen in 204 for what tasks he employed these men.

Above all he needed a good fleet, since the one he had set out
to build in 208 was still non-existent. The war with Rome had
left him penniless, and so, to restore his finances, he secretly sent
Dicaearchus with 20 ships to scour the Aegean[1]. The time was
opportune, for the Rhodians had their hands full at the moment.
Several Cretan towns, notably Hierapytna, which desired freedom
to carry on piracy at will, were waging with them an annoying
war—the 'Cretan War' of the inscriptions—even entering Asiatic
waters to attack allies or subjects of Rhodes, the islands of Cos,
Calymna and Nisyros. Philip was a friend of Rhodes, whose
interventions during the Roman war deserved his gratitude: his
offerings adorned her sanctuary of Athena Lindia; but he cared
nought for all that. He still had great influence in Crete, and
secretly incited the Cretans to vigorous action against Rhodes,
giving them Dicaearchus' support. He would fain have done
more: seeing in Rhodes the main hindrance to his plans, present
and future, he contemplated burning their fleet, and charged
Heracleides with this honourable mission. That worthy went to
Rhodes and contrived to win the confidence of her magistrates,
revealing, it is said, Philip's intrigues with the Cretans. But, at the
last moment, his design was suspected. He succeeded, however,
in setting fire to 13 triremes before he escaped back to Macedonia.
Lacking any formal proof against Philip, the Rhodians did not
break with him but watched him with the deepest suspicion.

Dicaearchus, while helping the Cretans, plundered navigators
and held to ransom the Cyclades and even the coast towns of the
Troad. The story runs that, wherever he landed, he sacrificed to
his favourite deities, *Asebeia* and *Paranomia*; at all events, his
expedition was profitable. Philip was enabled to build, if not the
100 warships dreamed of in 208, at least some 40 cataphracts[2].

[1] On Dicaearchus' expedition see *Rev. E.G.* xxxiii, 1920, pp. 223 *sqq.*

[2] In 201, at the time of the battle of Chios, the fleet of Philip contained
53 cataphracts (Polybius xvi, 2, 9), but from this total must be subtracted
several ships which came from the Egyptian squadron at Samos, which he

They were mostly quadriremes and quinqueremes, especially equipped for boarding, but also, following Antigonid traditions, some very large ships, a '*dekeres*,' '*ennereis, octereis, heptereis*' and '*hexereis*'; he added to them (and this was a novelty) many *lembi*[1]. During the building of his new fleet, he led a punitive expedition against the Dardanians—a usual precaution when he contemplated leaving his kingdom; in one battle he is said to have slain over 10,000; he certainly struck hard, for the Dardanians remained quiet for four years[2].

Reassured in this direction, Philip felt no uneasiness about the Greeks and treated them cavalierly. Exhausted by war, rent by internal quarrels, Aetolia seemed definitively crippled. Despising her weakness, he broke his engagement to restore to her Pharsalus, Echinus, Larissa Cremaste and Phthiotic Thebes (p. 134). Nor did he give up Heraea, Alipheira and Triphylia, promised in 208 to Achaea (p. 131). The Achaean leaders, elated beyond reason by their victory at Mantinea, affected an independent attitude which exasperated Philip; the antagonism between him and the former party of Aratus, whose present hero was Philopoemen, was now acute. Pursuing his new policy, Philip courted the favour of the masses. He redeemed at his own charges the Dymaeans sold by Sulpicius, a most popular gesture. His treatment of his subject-allies—Thessalians, Euboeans, Phocians, Locrians—while increasingly despotic, displayed demagogic tendencies; he gave orders as master to the cities[3], reduced their autonomy to nothing, imposed his nominees as magistrates[4], but tolerated or encouraged, especially in Thessaly, social disorders, hateful to the well-to-do and agreeable to the mob. In Boeotia, where his influence was dominant, these long-standing disorders were reaching a climax. Thus his popularity increased, and so did the number of his opponents among the propertied classes. He was now the opposite of Doson, who had been the bulwark of the conservatives against social revolution and with whom they reproachfully contrasted him.

But another monarch satisfied more amply the ideals of the 'have-nots'; this was Machanidas' strange and formidable successor in Sparta, which State the Achaeans too readily believed they

had added to his own (p. 153). The unintelligible phrase in Appian, *Maced.* 4, 1, Φίλιππος μὲν τῶν ὑπηκόων τοῖς ἐπὶ θαλάσσης [?] στόλον ἐπαγγείλας, may be disregarded.

[1] See W. W. Tarn, *Hellenistic Civilisation*, Ed. 2, p. 55 *sq.*

[2] In the same period Philip seems to have made an expedition into Thrace, but we have no precise information about it.

[3] See *e.g.* his letter to Chalcis, mentioned in *Ditt.*[3] 561.

[4] Cf., for a later period, Livy xxxiv, 48, 2; xxxix, 27, 8.

had crippled. Of royal blood, descended from the king Dema-
ratus, related through his wife Apia to the late tyrants of Argos,
Nabis, going much further than Cleomenes, was the very type
of a revolutionary prince. Under him the social revolution,
smouldering everywhere, triumphed in Sparta. Having formed
a *Red Guard* of Cretans and mercenaries recruited from among
the adventurers of all Greece, he removed his ward Pelops, seized
the crown, and applied the extremist programme in its entirety—
spoliation, proscription, systematic destruction of the upper
classes, confiscation of private fortunes (ostensibly for the State).
Moreover, he enfranchised many Helots, who were made citizens,
assigned land to these same Helots and to the poor, and distributed among mob-leaders and mercenaries the goods and even
the wives and daughters of the proscribed. At the same time,
being as keen a nationalist as a communist, he strove successfully
to revive Spartan military power, fortified Sparta, increased the
army by enrolling the enfranchised Helots and many Perioeci,
created from the ships of the maritime towns a fleet which, with
the Cretans, harried the seas, restored Gytheum as a great arsenal,
and acquired places of refuge in Crete. A fervent Lacedaemonian, and therefore an uncompromising enemy of Achaea and
especially of Megalopolis, he cherished Cleomenes' designs of
conquest (vol. VII, pp. 752 *sqq.*).

Had he revealed these immediately, Philip would presumably
have been stirred to action: the renewal of Spartan power was a
direct challenge to Doson's successor. But it was not till 201,
when Philip was far away, that Nabis struck hard and surprised
Messene, whence, however, he was driven by Philopoemen, who,
in a private capacity, had hastened to the rescue with his Megalopolitans. Open war then began again between Sparta and
Achaea—a war in which the latter often fared badly, for her one
trust was in Philopoemen, and her army without him relapsed
into its normal incompetence. But in 204 and 203 Nabis confined
himself to border-raids in the territory of Megalopolis, and Philip
was possibly not displeased to see the Megalopolitans, so arrogant
since Mantinea, harassed by a troublesome neighbour.

What also gave him satisfaction was the disappearance of
an old adversary. Aetolia was profoundly disturbed by troubles
between debtors and creditors; Scopas and Dorimachus, scenting
an opportunity to regain power, had themselves elected 'law-
givers' (*nomographoi*) (vol. VII, p. 208), and Scopas, to please the
populace, proposed radical measures, possibly the total cancellation
of debts—a certain method, he thought, of being re-elected
General. But, a leader of the capitalist party, Alexander Isios,

'the richest man in Greece' according to Polybius (he possessed 200 talents), defeated his proposals. Disappointed in his ambitions and deep in debt, Scopas then left Aetolia with a band of followers and went to restore his fortunes by service in Egypt (204).

Scopas was sure of a welcome in Alexandria. To repress the natives and be ready for Antiochus, whose attitude was considered threatening, the Egyptian government, *i.e.* Sosibius, was re-organizing the army regardless of expense. Good officers were badly needed, and Scopas, a famous soldier, was made generalis-simo of the field-army with the enormous daily pay of 10 minae; his companions with lesser commands received a mina each. While thus arming Egypt, Sosibius was busy with diplomatic manœuvres against Antiochus. As has been seen, he had long counted upon using Philip to counter him. He therefore made overtures to the latter regarding an alliance to be sealed later by the betrothal of the young Ptolemy with one of his daughters[1]. This could not but please Philip whose one fear, obviously, was that terror of Antiochus might drive Egypt to purchase peace with Syria at the price of any concessions that the Seleucid king demanded. Already, in proof of friendship, Philip had offered Philopator help against the natives; this offer had, indeed, been refused, since it seemed too dangerous to open Egypt to the Macedonians. But, without bearing Sosibius any grudge for this refusal, Philip welcomed his advances, without, however, con-tracting any immediate engagement.

Sosibius' precautions against Antiochus were soon seen to be justified. He, too, with an impudent assumption of the rôle of friend, had proposed to assist Philopator against the rebels; when this offer was declined, he came, in 203, to Asia Minor and showed himself aggressive. Accompanied by the Lydian governor Zeuxis (p. 124), he stayed in Caria with considerable forces and compelled some towns 'in alliance with Ptolemy,' notably Amyzon, to surrender to him (May-June)[2]. Philip, who also had designs on Caria, must have watched his enterprise ill-content.

Thus ended the year 203 in gathering storm. Antiochus openly threatened Egypt; Philip had not yet declared himself, and was a cause of uneasiness to Antiochus, of hope to the Alexandrians. The two kings were eying one another askance when, about December, they heard the astounding news that Philopator and Arsinoe were dead: the Egyptian empire was vested in a child of six or seven years surrounded by an unworthy camarilla.

---

[1] This follows from Polybius xv, 25, 13 (see below, p. 150), in which passage there is no reason to change ἐπιγαμία into ἐπιμαχία.

[2] See A. Wilhelm, *Wien Anz.* 57, 1920, XVII–XXVII, pp. 51 *sqq.*

III. THE EASTERN CRISIS

The true date of Philopator's death remains a mystery[1]. Incredible as it appears, Sosibius and Agathocles seem to have concealed it for a long time. They made arrangements for seizing the government, had Arsinoe secretly murdered, and forged a will of Philopator appointing them guardians of his son. Then, 28 November 203[2], Agathocles (Sosibius having died in the meantime[3]) summoned the 'hypaspists,' household troops and military leaders, announced the death of the King and Queen, proclaimed the 'child' king, read the forged will, administered to the troops an oath of allegiance, and assumed the regency, which could not have fallen into baser hands. With him ruled Oenanthe and Agathocleia—to whom was entrusted the young Ptolemy—and their creatures, but, universally hated, their rule was precarious; Agathocles was to meet a formidable opponent in the young governor of Pelusium, Tlepolemus, supported by army and people, whom the murder of Arsinoe had enraged.

The regency secured, Agathocles, says Polybius, returned to his debauches. He endeavoured, however, to guard against the danger which threatened Egypt from without. While Scopas, abundantly supplied with funds, was sent to raise mercenaries in Greece, an Egyptian envoy went to invite Antiochus to respect existing treaties; another, Ptolemy of Megalopolis, set out for Rome, obviously to announce the new king's accession and beg for senatorial mediation with Antiochus; but since the Egyptian interference in the Macedonian War must certainly have displeased the Senate, Agathocles hoped little from this proceeding. Indeed, he is said to have sent the Megalopolitan to Rome mainly

---

[1] See the Bibliography. The present writer has not accepted the solution of this problem recently proposed by Ernst Meyer. The Canon of the Kings puts the death of Philopator in the 18th year of his reign, *i.e.* between the 13th Oct. 205 and the 12th Oct. 204 (Egyptian year). But even if the event is put as near as possible to the latter date, more than a year would have elapsed before it was officially made known (28 Nov. 203), and this is highly improbable.

[2] The day and month are given by the so-called Rosetta decree (17 Phaophi = 28 Nov.). The year is to be deduced from the fact that the accession of Ptolemy V is narrated by Polybius in Book XV which covers the year 203/2 B.C. It appears, moreover, that for some reason hitherto unexplained, the first regnal year of Ptolemy V was, at a later period, reckoned as his second year, for the comparison of the Rosetta decree with Polybius XVIII, 53–55 shows that his 9th year corresponded to 196/5.

[3] See Niese, *op. cit.* II, p. 573, n. 2, 3, whose view is here adopted.

with the idea of getting rid of him. The important embassy was that of Sosibius' son Ptolemy, dispatched to Philip to conclude the agreement contracting his daughter to Ptolemy V and request his armed help against Antiochus, no doubt promising in return ample subsidies and, perhaps, even the cession of territory. Agathocles thus continued Sosibius' Macedonian policy, and saw in Philip the chief hope of Egypt.

About the same time, Antiochus also approached the Macedonian king[1]. He desired to profit by Egypt's new internal troubles, but was afraid of Philip. Fearing him as an adversary, he resigned himself to accepting him as a partner, and proposed to divide with him the empire of the Ptolemies. The negotiations were secret, so the exact conditions of the partition compact are unknown. What is certain is that Egypt, which could not well be divided, was excluded from it; and that Antiochus took Southern Syria and left Philip, if not all, at least most, of the Egyptian dependencies along the Aegean coast. It seems obvious, too, that he would take Cyprus and the Cilician and Lycian towns subject to Ptolemy, while Philip received the few Cyclades which still belonged to Egypt, and the Ptolemaic possessions in Thrace as Maronea, Aenus, and Cypsela; finally, perhaps, Cyrenaica, which it was not easy either to conquer or to hold, might go to Philip.

Clearly, such an arrangement could not be really acceptable to either of the high contracting powers. By opening Asia to Philip, ceding him Asiatic and Thracian districts which he regarded as rightfully belonging to Seleucids, Antiochus was doing violence to his own feelings: he was not sincere, and Philip knew it. On his side, Philip would dread any fresh increase of Seleucid power, which had again become so formidable, and fear that, after Southern Syria, Antiochus would seize Egypt. Rather than make a bargain with him and risk being duped, his interests urged him to join the Alexandrians in protecting the child-king's dominions, so that he might later be their sole master. But he did not intend to involve himself at the moment in war against Antiochus, wishing above all to preserve complete freedom of action. He agreed therefore to the Syrian proposals and accepted the partition treaty, but at the same time welcomed Sosibius' son, who stayed for about a year at his court, most honourably treated. Apparently, playing a double game, Philip promised alliance to both Agathocles

---

[1] The study of the situation at the time makes it clear that Antiochus initiated the negotiations which led to the partition treaty (see A. Wilhelm, *Wien Anz.* 57, 1920, p. 54), although Polybius in his moral reflections on the matter (xv, 20, 2) makes the two kings each invite the other.

and Antiochus, thus assuring himself of freedom during
the struggle between them to make what conquests he might
consider immediately necessary. For the time being he deceived
both parties; but everything leads one to believe that, having
strengthened himself at leisure, he counted on turning against
Antiochus in the end, and revealing himself as the interested
defender of Ptolemy—his future son-in-law.

It was probably late in the winter of 203–2 that Antiochus
and Philip, apparently reviving the time-honoured coalition of
Syria and Macedonia against Egypt, concluded the disgraceful
agreement which roused Polybius' honest indignation—in fact,
a lying compact which neither intended to keep. Then, in the
spring, they got to work, without any pretence of justifying their
aggressions. Antiochus invaded Southern Syria, but his operations are unknown and he seems to have achieved little. Philip,
careless of the provisions of the partition treaty, sought to subdue,
not towns subject to Egypt, but free cities; he wished to establish
himself both on the Straits from the Hellespont to the Bosporus
and in Caria, where he coveted Iasus, an excellent naval base.

He brought against Iasus Olympichus, probably a Carian
dynast (vol. VII, pp. 184, 720), his ally, who began to harry it.
He himself directed operations on the Straits. There Lysimacheia,
formerly Egyptian, in the Chersonese; Chalcedon, on the
Bosporus; Cius, on the Propontis, were—since some unknown
date—dependent allies of the Aetolian League. Philip imposed
his alliance, i.e. his authority, upon Lysimacheia, expelled its
Aetolian governor, and garrisoned it; he also occupied Chalcedon,
and Perinthus, a Byzantine dependency lying between the two;
then, acting as ally of Prusias, who had a quarrel with Cius, he
besieged and took that town, but, before handing it over, sacked
it and sold the population. Its neighbour Myrleia suffered the same
fate. Returning to Macedonia, Philip seized Thasos by treachery,
so it is said, and, perhaps for some reason unknown to us, enslaved part of its inhabitants. It is noteworthy that he respected
the Egyptian dependencies on the coast of Thrace.

This attack launched against inoffensive communities in profound peace raised a storm of indignation: the Greek world was
outraged by the fate of Cius and Thasos. It also, beyond doubt,
annoyed Antiochus, who was irritated by his ally's cool high-
handedness, his co-operation with Prusias, a natural opponent of
the Seleucids, and above all his occupation of Lysimacheia to
which he himself had claims. Moreover, Philip's expedition
naturally embroiled him with Aetolia, already angered by his

non-observance of the treaty of 206, and Byzantium, and, more serious still, it made the Rhodians his declared enemies. His indirect attack upon Iasus, their friend, had moved them to protest, and they believed that his establishment upon the Straits endangered their trade; Philip added the last straw by making mock of them, promising, at their intercession, to spare Cius and then sacking it beneath the eyes of their envoys. Exasperated, and incited to action by an energetic citizen, Theophiliscus, whom they elected *navarch*, the Rhodians, peace-loving though they were, decided to fight Philip, bringing in also their allies, Byzantium, Cyzicus, Chios, Cos and the rest (end of summer 202).

Philip was unwise enough to despise Rhodes, but he feared the Romans, whose victory at Zama, during his maritime campaign, had freed them to intervene in the East. His spies at Rome kept him informed of their intentions; he soon had proof that these were not alarming. The Aetolians, furious but not daring to challenge him unaided, had attempted to renew friendly relations with the Senate and interest it in their cause (probably autumn 202 B.C.[1]); but, harshly reminding their envoys of their 'defection' in 206, the *patres* rejected their appeal. This rebuff implied that Rome had, at the moment, no mind to take action again in Greece against Macedonia; so Philip thought that he could safely pursue his eastern enterprises. He was, however, to meet adversaries whom he had rashly underrated.

In the spring of 201 the two kings resumed operations. Antiochus continued the conquest of Southern Syria, favoured by persistent disorders in Egypt. Agathocles, Agathocleia and their clique had indeed vanished, massacred in a military and popular rising, fomented by Tlepolemus, of which Polybius gives a vivid and pathetic picture (xv, 26 *a sqq.*). But, as soon as he became regent, Tlepolemus, able soldier as he was, proved a feeble administrator, indolent, careless, wasteful of public funds, and by his misgovernment roused a strong opposition. Meanwhile the native revolt still raged from Nubia to the Delta, where Lycopolis was its main centre, and, doubtless, many mercenaries, chiefly

---

[1] Appian (*Maced.* 4, 2) puts the Aetolian embassy to Rome after that of Attalus and the Rhodians, *i.e.* in 201–0 B.C. This clearly reverses the true chronological order. In 201–0 the Senate would have received the Aetolians with open arms. Their *démarche* at Rome must have followed closely on Philip's operations against Lysimacheia, Chalcedon and Cius; on the other hand, it is probable that it did not happen until after Rome's decisive victory over Carthage. Thus the most probable date is the autumn of 202 B.C.

Aetolians, brought from Greece by Scopas, were used in suppressing it. Under these circumstances, Antiochus was able to reach Gaza; but, faithful to its heroic traditions and firmly loyal to Ptolemy, the town defended itself stoutly and enabled Scopas to gather an army to face the invader (autumn 201).

On his side, Philip crossed the Aegean, probably subdued the numerous independent islands (including perhaps Cythnos and Paros), but left Thera to the Egyptians. Coming to Samos, a Ptolemaic dependency where lay an Egyptian squadron, he apparently expected to be received with open arms, but met with a resistance explained by the uneasiness he inspired: possibly the inhabitants feared the fate of Thasos. It seems that, in order to reduce the town, he was forced to blockade it and storm the forts on the surrounding heights[1]. At last the city fell, and Philip incorporated some, though not all, of the Egyptian vessels in his fleet: for the Ptolemaic squadron was not fitted out for war (Polybius XVI, 2, 9), a fact which is sufficient evidence that Philip had not, at this time, acted as the enemy of Egypt. Thus he found himself in possession of 53 cataphracts besides some light ships and 150 *lembi*, and with these he could defy the Rhodians and their allies. But he became involved with a new enemy. The common danger brought together Attalus and Rhodes hitherto unfriendly. In each new progress of the Macedonian eastward, Attalus saw a menace to himself, for Philip had a heavy score to settle with him. Theophiliscus came to Pergamum and persuaded him to abandon his hesitations and to unite his fleet with that of the Rhodians, whereupon Philip found himself threatened by 65 cataphracts and 12 'undecked' vessels.

As before, he proceeded against non-Ptolemaic cities. Leaving Samos, he coasted along Ionia, imposed his protectorate upon Teos[2], and was besieging Chios[3], when Theophiliscus and Attalus, bearing down upon him from the north, caused him to raise the siege and brought him to action in the south of the Chian channel.

---

[1] If, that is, the decree of the Samians recently published by G. Klaffenbach (*Ath. Mitt.* LI, 1926, p. 28) belongs to this time.

[2] Teos was a subject-ally of Attalus in 218 (Polybius V, 77, 5–6) and so possibly in 201, like the two Colophons of which Philip must also have gained control.

[3] On the order of the two battles Chios and Lade see the present writer in *Rev. E.A.* 1920, pp. 244 *sqq.* An additional argument for placing Chios before Lade is that if Philip still had his fleet (of 53 cataphracts) intact at the time of Lade, the Rhodians, who single-handed had at most about 30 cataphracts, would certainly not have risked a battle.

The battle which followed, the last great engagement fought by
the Macedonian navy, was worthy of the great days of Cos and
Andros and, although indecisive, did Philip much credit. His
Macedonians showed, as usual, unequalled valour in boarding;
and his *lembi*, skilfully handled, seriously impeded the movements
of the enemy ships. The Rhodians, by superior seamanship, but
not without hard fighting, defeated the Macedonian left, but on
the right, Philip, attacked by Attalus, proved victorious, drove
Attalus ashore, compelled him to flee by land, captured his royal
flagship, and forced the Pergamenes to break off the action. But
his partial victory, which he emphasized by dedicating his spoils
at Delos, cost him dear. Polybius, copying patriotic Rhodian
historians, must have exaggerated his loss in men—about 12,000
including over 3000 Macedonians—but he lost 28 cataphracts,
among them six of his largest vessels, and 72 *lembi*, while his
opponents suffered only slightly, save for the death of the brave
Theophiliscus, who was mortally wounded. This meant that Philip's
enemies, united, would have in future a crushing superiority at
sea.

For the present they separated. Attalus returned home to put
his kingdom into a state of defence; the Rhodians took up their
station at Lade, covering the Milesian coast. Seizing this opportunity, Philip attacked and defeated them, but without inflicting
on them serious losses, and compelled them to retreat southwards.
He should perhaps have pressed the pursuit and completed their
destruction, but his rage against Attalus turned him aside. After a
triumphal welcome from the Milesians, Ptolemy's nominal allies,
he left his fleet to operate against the Sporades, allies or subjects
of Rhodes, and hurried with some light-armed troops to Pergamum, hoping to surprise it and capture Attalus—which,
it is true, would in all likelihood have finished the war. But
Pergamum was well defended; he could only plunder the sanctuaries outside the city, especially the Nicephorium, and as
Attalus had laid waste the countryside, he traversed it in all
directions without finding provisions for his men[1].

After this abortive raid, Philip returned through Hiera Come
and Maeandrian Magnesia to the district near Latmus, probably
seizing on his way Pedasa and Euromus; then, aided by his fleet,
which had unsuccessfully attacked Cos and Calymna, but taken
Nisyrus from the Rhodians, he invaded Southern Caria. He
failed to capture Cnidus, a free city, but, pushing eastward along

---

[1] From this point onwards the reconstruction of Philip's operations is
bound to be conjectural; see the articles of the present writer (*Rev. E.A.*
1920, 1921, 1923) cited in the Bibliography.

the Triopian Chersonese, he conquered the Rhodian Peraea; then, turning northward, he occupied Panamara where, for reasons of policy, he honoured Zeus Carios, the great deity of the region, and Stratoniceia, perhaps Rhodian, more probably an independent town. Finally, regaining the Aegean coast, and co-operating with his fleet, he reduced Iasus and Bargylia. The conquered districts, where he appointed a general (*strategos*) commanding forces of occupation, and some *epistatai*, were to remain for four years a Macedonian province. So far as we know they included no Ptolemaic dependencies; Philip left the Egyptians Caunus which adjoined Rhodian territory, and apparently made no attempt on Myndus and Halicarnassus; he had seemingly evacuated Samos[1].

When autumn (201) came, Philip was anxious to cross to Macedonia again, but met with an obstacle which he should have foreseen. To besiege Iasus and Bargylia in their remote inlet, he had rashly left free the open sea. Attalus and the Rhodians joined forces; then, barring the entrance to the harbour of Bargylia, blockaded his fleet, which was too weak to risk a battle, and his army, which was almost starving. The dubious ally of Antiochus was now repaid in his own coin. A demonstration against Pergamum by the Lydian governor Zeuxis would have drawn off Attalus, but Zeuxis made no move. He had besides, during the whole campaign, purposely neglected, contrary to the terms of the partition treaty, to re-victual the Macedonians. His master set him an example of bad faith: Antiochus had recently reconciled with Rhodes the Cretan cities friendly to Philip, thereby depriving the latter of valuable auxiliaries[2].

Accordingly the winter of 201–0 found Philip in a critical situation. Forced to lead the 'life of a wolf,' to extort provisions from neighbouring towns by prayers or threats, feeding his troops on figs for lack of corn, he was cut off from his kingdom, although he knew that his presence in Macedonia was indispensable in order to face dangers nearer home.

IV. ATTALUS AND THE RHODIANS APPEAL TO ROME

It was the obvious interest of Philip's enemies to raise up adversaries to him in the West. Attalus, who had remained the ally of the Aetolians after 206, had tried to move them, but in vain; their bad reception by the Senate (p. 152) had daunted them. He also thought not unnaturally of appealing to the

---

[1] Cf. Livy XXXIII, 20, 11–12, where Samos appears among the *civitates sociae Ptolemaei* (in 197 B.C.).

[2] See *Klio*, XIII, 1913, pp. 137 *sqq.* The treaty of alliance between Rhodes and Hierapytna (*Ditt.*[3] 581) may be dated to this time.

Romans. It is true that, formally, he was neither their ally nor perhaps even their 'friend' (*amicus populi Romani*), but they had included him in the peace of Phoenice and his relations with them were extremely cordial. On the other hand, the Rhodians, as we have seen, had been constantly opposed to Rome and were largely responsible for the defection of the Aetolians. But their fear of Philip led them to reverse their policy; it had made them ally themselves with Attalus, and now it decided them to appeal, like him, to Rome for help. In the late summer of 201 Pergamene and Rhodian envoys appeared before the Senate.

Careful of their dignity, the *patres* deferred giving any promise, but their decision was taken at once. About November Sulpicius Galba was re-elected consul; this meant that he would be commander in a new Macedonian war. 'Macedonia' was indeed one of the consular provinces and fell to him.

This decision of the Senate, on the morrow of the struggle against Carthage, with people and army war-weary and longing for peace, the treasury empty, the state-creditors restive, is most astonishing—the more so since Rome had certainly no grievance against Philip. The force he is said to have sent to Hannibal before Zama, and his aggressions against certain unnamed 'Greek allies of Rome,' are merely clumsy fabrications of later times[1], invented to justify the hostile behaviour of the Roman government. In reality, fearing Rome greatly, Philip kept peace with her most correctly. As for his conflict with Attalus and Rhodes, that obviously could not justify the armed intervention of the Romans. Rhodes had naturally no title to their assistance; Attalus, included in the recent peace, might claim it in principle, but, in fact, he— like the Rhodians—in attacking Philip had been the aggressor. This war, decided upon so quickly, was thus without legitimate cause; it was simply willed by the Senate. A year earlier, they had apparently no thought of it: otherwise they would have forgotten for the moment their grievances against Aetolia (as later

[1] Livy xxx, 26, 2–4; 42, 1–11 (cf. xxxi, 1, 9) following the annalists. The *sociae urbes ex Graecia, socii populi Romani*, mentioned in these passages, are imaginary. They have been placed in Illyria—no other position indeed can be found for them—in reliance on Polybius xviii, 1, 14, but wrongly. In the passage of Polybius the words οἱ κατὰ τὴν Ἰλλυρίδα τόποι...ὧν γέγονε (Φίλιππος) κύριος μετὰ τὰς ἐν Ἠπείρῳ διαλύσεις mean simply the parts of Illyria that had fallen into the power of Philip after, and in virtue of, the peace of Phoenice, and not any territories which Philip may have conquered later in violation of this peace. The alleged sending of Laevinus, in 201, to 'Macedonia' with a squadron (Livy xxxi, 3, 2–6) is only a mistaken reminiscence of the first war with Philip.

in 200), and would have listened to her complaints against Philip.
Thus their conversion to a warlike policy was sudden indeed.

The reason for this change—evidently a strong one—is not
directly known, for the explanations given by our sources are quite
untrustworthy; it can only be inferred from an examination of
the circumstances. The present writer would therefore indicate
what seems to him the most probable.

Attalus, a warm friend of Rome, the Rhodians, serious, sensible,
trusted and esteemed, inspired confidence in the Senate. Knowing
little of eastern affairs, the *patres* must have listened attentively to
their representatives; doubtless their arguments greatly influenced
the Roman decision, and we can conjecture, with some probability, what they were. Apparently the envoys laid little stress on
the grievances of Attalus and Rhodes against Philip, since these
were unlikely to move the Senate, which would care little about
the seizure by Philip of some Hellespontine or Asiatic towns
whose very name was unknown in Rome. Wishing to persuade
them to fight Philip immediately, they must have reviewed the
matter from the standpoint of Roman interests, showing how
dangerous inaction would be to Rome, and how easy it was to
act at once. Rhodes and Attalus had got wind of the compact
between Antiochus and Philip; they had good reasons for
doubting its stability, but their envoys could use it to frighten
the Senate. According to them, Antiochus was a conqueror from
whom anything might be feared; his understanding with Philip
constituted a certain danger for Rome. At the moment, the two
kings aspired to make Egypt their prey, but, once strengthened
by its spoils, what might they not do? Would not Philip, ever
the enemy of Rome, bring in Antiochus against her? She must
break this threatening alliance by crushing the ally within reach.
Antiochus was just then occupied in Syria, Philip, much weakened,
blockaded in Caria—it was a fine opportunity to invade Macedonia.
If Philip succeeded in returning home, his defeat would nevertheless be swiftly achieved. Rome would have with her, besides
the Pergamene and Rhodian fleets, the Aetolians thirsting for vengeance, Amynander who had recently quarrelled with Philip, and,
of course, the barbarian enemies of Macedonia. Moreover, Philip's
Greek allies now hated him; his crimes at Cius and Thasos aroused
their common horror; all Greece, doubtless, would join Rome.

The ambassadors could not fail to move the senators by talking
of Antiochus. Rome had no relations with him, but his resounding
fame had long made them uneasy. Laevinus and Sulpicius had
many times in Greece heard first the Aetolians, then Attalus,

relate his exploits; Laevinus was in Pergamum when Antiochus returned from the Far East; and the Alexandrians had recently asked for protection against him. The Romans were very ready to see an enemy in every monarch, and Antiochus, so powerful, fortunate, and undoubtedly of unbounded ambitions, seemed especially disquieting. They pictured him lord of the fabulous treasures, the unnumbered hosts of Asia; he reminded them at once of Xerxes and of Alexander; above all, he was for them the unknown that is terrible. When they heard that he was secretly in league with Philip, his hostility to them seemed beyond doubt. Conqueror of the East, he would assuredly dispute the West with Rome, thus helping Philip to his revenge.

Therefore it was necessary to take prompt measures to counteract this danger, profit by Antiochus' momentary absence to act against Philip—not to destroy him (a too difficult and lengthy undertaking), but cripple him and, further, drive him from Greece. Greece which had hitherto meant little to the Senate, since they did not fear Philip alone, suddenly assumed peculiar importance: it was the natural point of concentration for the two kings, their common base against Italy. They must, accordingly, be prevented from using it, and it must at the same time be brought under Roman control. Not that there was any question of subjugating it—that would have been to provide Philip and Antiochus with the profitable rôle of 'liberator.' This rôle Rome would assume herself; she would restore Greek freedom, destroyed or restricted by Philip, thereby securing the enthusiastic gratitude of the Greeks, and then constitute herself their permanent protectress. Liberated and shielded by Rome, Greece would be closed to the kings, Rome's enemies, closed to Antiochus if, after Philip's defeat, he should pursue alone the aggressive designs concerted with him.

Such, it seems, were the fears and calculations which gave rise to the warlike policy of the Senate, hitherto so little inclined to entangle itself in Eastern affairs. Apparently aggressive, but really preventive, its object was to checkmate the dangerous purposes attributed to Antiochus and Philip, and, with this aim, make Greece the outwork of Italy's defences to the East. It is, however, quite possible that these leading motives were reinforced by subsidiary considerations of sentiment: the longing to cancel an inglorious peace and punish Philip for his alliance with Carthage, a proud desire in some Romans to conquer the unconquerable Macedonians, and also accomplish something spectacular in extending Roman primacy over the illustrious peoples of Greece. Of an over-romantic ardent sympathy for the Greeks, Philip's

victims, such as is often attributed to the Senate, the present writer
can find no clear evidence. The Roman nobility had steeped itself
in Hellenic culture, but had no tenderness for Greeks, as the late
war had shown plainly enough. Their philhellenism confined itself
to things of the spirit, and was not allowed to be a factor in their
public actions. They were, it is true, going to use against Philip
a 'philhellenic' policy, but only as Hannibal, for instance, had
used a 'philitalian' policy against Rome—because it suited their
purpose, not through love of Greece.

However urgent may have been Attalus and the Rhodians,
Rome could not begin the war before 200 B.C. The Senate had first
to make ready for it. Military preparation was easy: Macedonia
was known to be drained of men, and if Philip returned before
the Romans arrived, he would only dispose of a very limited field-
army[1], the more as he would have to garrison his many strongholds in Greece. It would be enough to pit against him a normal
consular army of two legions, especially as Rome counted upon
numerous allies; and this army would partly be raised by the
enlistment, nominally voluntary, of veterans returning from Africa.
As for the fleet, Pergamene and Rhodian assistance would allow
of its reduction to some 50 warships. Under such conditions the
war would cost little. However, as the treasury was depleted, the
repayment of loans contracted during the Hannibalic War had to
be suspended, and to disarm the opposition of creditors the Senate
decided to indemnify them by large concessions of public land.

There remained the main achievement of statecraft, the political
preparation for the war, that is the creation in peace time of a
clash between Rome and Philip which would inevitably result in
war. This seemed a difficult problem; for, as we have noticed,
Rome had no grievance against Philip, and if the Senate desired
war, it stood alone in desiring it. Philip would do anything to
avoid war if he were allowed to negotiate, and would not shrink
from even considerable concessions provided they were not dis-
honouring. As for the Roman people, upon whose vote everything ultimately depended, its feelings were entirely peaceful. In
this apparently embarrassing situation the Senate, despite what
has often been asserted, experienced no difficulty; supreme in
matters of foreign policy and unhampered by scruples, it

[1] Attalus and the Rhodians of course must have exaggerated Philip's
losses in Asia (see above, p. 154). None the less, the military exhaustion of
Macedon was extreme: Livy XXXIII, 3, 1–3 (following Polybius). W. W.
Tarn, *Antigonos Gonatas*, pp. 424–5, assesses, with great probability, Philip's
forces when the war began at a maximum of 30,000 men.

manœuvred so that Philip and the Roman citizens were driven
into a war which neither desired. It had only to present to Philip,
without previous negotiation, an offensive ultimatum based on an
imaginary *casus belli*, then use his refusal to comply with it to
secure the people's vote for war.

According to the *ius fetiale*, Philip—although, in fact, he had
committed no offence—must be confronted with a 'demand for
satisfaction' (*rerum repetitio*). This demand was drawn up by the
Senate, who contrived to turn it into an intolerable provocation.
It is summarized thus by Polybius: 'Philip was to grant to
Attalus, for injuries caused to him, reparations to be fixed by
arbitrators; if he complied, he might consider himself at peace
with Rome, but if he refused, the consequences would be the
reverse.' It can be seen how insulting was the form of this
demand: without giving him any opportunity of justifying himself, Rome exacted from Philip, under threat of war, immediate
submission. But the substance was even worse; in plain contradiction to the facts, Philip was represented as the aggressor; the
Roman ultimatum really amounted to this: the Pergamene fleet,
together with the Rhodian, had attacked the Macedonian fleet at
Chios, therefore the successor of Alexander must humiliate himself
before the parvenu kinglet of Pergamum.

But the Senate went still further: its *rerum repetitio* was preceded
by the injunction that 'Philip should make war henceforth upon
no Greek state.' This was outrageous from the standpoint of
international law. In the first place, by what right did the Romans
concern themselves with Greek interests? They had now no
Greek allies. Secondly, in 204, they had recognized Philip's
full sovereignty and implicitly admitted his authority over many
Greeks. Now, without urging any reasons, they claimed, contrary
to treaty, to reverse this state of affairs. In denying Philip the
right to make war upon Greeks, they impaired his sovereignty,
and virtually destroyed the authority which he exercised in Greece,
for it became a mere illusion if he might not uphold it by force;
and, finally, by implication they declared unjustified all former
wars waged by himself or his predecessors against Greeks, and
thus denied validity to results of their victories. The destruction
of all that Macedon had achieved in Greece since Philip II was in
fact what the Senate demanded. It demanded the impossible, but
in this it showed its skill, for it drove Philip to extremes and also,
by declaring the Greeks immune from attack, won them over (at
least so it hoped) to the side of Rome, and stated a principle which
it could, at need, apply later to Antiochus.

In the spring of 200 the Senate sent three *legati* to deliver its ultimatum to Philip[1]. They were at the same time to foment in Greece an agitation favourable to Rome, guarantee Roman support to Attalus and Rhodes, and, lastly, visit the Syrian and Egyptian courts. This last proceeding had as pretext Agathocles' request for the Senate's mediation on behalf of Ptolemy V; in reality the Roman government, which was very uneasy about Antiochus, wished to discover his intentions, to find out if he was now inclined to support Philip and, in that case, to try to dissuade him from doing so.

V. ROMAN INTERVENTION IN GREECE AND THE EAST

Blockaded at Bargylia, Philip had against his will wintered in Caria; but, about March-April 200, forcing the blockade by a stratagem, he returned to Macedonia, closely followed by Attalus and the Rhodians, who posted themselves at Aegina. Immediately after his return he entered indirectly into a conflict with Athens. The Athenians, with stupid fanaticism, had put to death two young Acarnanians who, though uninitiated, had rashly found their way into the Eleusinian Mysteries (September 201). As they could not obtain redress, the Acarnanians begged Philip for troops to join their own in invading Attica. Philip granted them the men: the Acarnanians were his staunchest allies; their vengeance was just, the outrage they had suffered moved him; perhaps, too, he had grievances against Athens of which we know nothing. Attica was devastated, and the Athenians, powerless to resist, implored help on every hand, from Attalus and the Rhodians, from Aetolia, perhaps also from Egypt and some Cretan towns, but, despite annalistic tradition, not from Rome; they had as yet no ties with the Republic (vol. VII, p. 842); the Senate received no embassy from them[2]. It was they, on the contrary, who were visited by the senatorial *legati*.

[1] According to the annalists (Livy XXXI, 2, 3–4; cf. 18, 1), the *legati* set out in the summer of 201 B.C. and went only to Egypt, *ut nuntiarent victum Hannibalem Poenosque et gratias agerent regi*, etc. It is to be observed that Hannibal's defeat happened a year before.

[2] The late annalists have imagined, as a deciding cause of the Second Macedonian War, an appeal of the Athenians to the Senate—an appeal provoked by an invasion of Attica or even a siege of Athens directed by Philip in person. The somewhat frigid reception of the Roman envoys by the Athenians, the reserve of these same envoys, and the text of the Roman ultimatum, in which there is no mention of reparations due to the Athenians (Polybius XVI, 25–26; 27, 2), disprove beyond all doubt the reality of any such appeal. See the present writer in *Rev. E.A.* XXII, 1920, pp. 113 *sqq.*

The latter, C. Claudius Nero, victor at the Metaurus, P. Sempronius Tuditanus, author of the peace of Phoenice, and the young M. Aemilius Lepidus, arrived in Greece shortly after Philip's return. They halted at many places—in Epirus, in Athamania at Amynander's court, in Aetolia and Achaea, visiting indiscriminately Macedonia's allies and adversaries, publishing the ultimatum which they bore, dilating upon it, and making it clear that Rome was determined to protect against Philip all Greeks without distinction: these strange ambassadors thus stirred up war wherever they passed, and endeavoured to gain allies for the Republic. But, though welcomed by Amynander, they were coldly received by Epirotes, Aetolians, and Achaeans. The Epirotes were a timid people and feared to commit themselves; the Aetolians could hardly forget their desertion by Rome in 207–6, and the affront to their envoys in 202: they adopted a waiting attitude; as for the Achaeans, who at that time were busy fighting Nabis (against whom Philopoemen, then General, won a brilliant victory near Mt Scotitas in Laconia), they remembered with horror the recent Roman war. The anti-Macedonians, though powerful in Achaea, made no move at first. In the Hellenic League generally the idea of a Roman return to Greece aroused nothing but alarm; and, indeed, how could Philip's allies, still smarting from Roman blows, believe in this sudden transformation of Rome into a champion of Hellenism?

From Achaea the *legati* proceeded to the Piraeus; the anger of the Athenians against Philip, the helper of the Acarnanian invasion, gave them an opportunity; they must add fuel to the flames. At the Piraeus they met Attalus who had hastened from Aegina to join them, informed him, to his great joy, of the Senate's warlike resolutions and, on the morrow, accompanied him to Athens where he was welcomed as a saviour hero. The object of this visit was to bring the Athenians to the point of declaring war upon Philip. They were hesitating, for fear of his vengeance, yet, upon the warm persuasions first of Attalus, who sent them a written message, and then of the Rhodians, the Assembly enthusiastically passed the desired decree (c. May 200). It is noteworthy that the Roman envoys remained in the background; they had authorized Attalus to guarantee publicly to the Athenians the armed assistance of Rome but kept silence themselves; they

That is why Livy, after following the annalistic tradition in his account of the causes of the war (XXXI, 1, 10; 5, 5–9), has purposely omitted all reference to the presence of the *legati* at Athens in his adaptation of Polybius' narrative (XXXI, 14, 12–15, 7).

apparently knew that they had little influence in Athens, hence
their reserved attitude. The Athenians loaded Attalus with almost
divine honours, resolved to create a tribe *Attalis*[1], and conferred
isopoliteia upon the Rhodians, but bestowed no special distinction
upon the Roman people: Rome was still out of favour. But the
legati soon had an opportunity to be of use. Nicanor, the commander of the Macedonian auxiliaries sent to the Acarnanians,
had remained to observe Athens; learning of the decree against
Philip, he ravaged the suburbs up to the Academy; the Romans
then intervened and communicated to him the senatorial ultimatum for transmission to Philip. Nicanor retired; Attica was
freed from the invader. It is characteristic of Roman methods of
action that they forbade Philip 'to make war upon any Greek
people' at the very moment when Athens, instigated at least
indirectly by them, had just declared war upon him.

To have Athens, powerless as she was, on their side was a great
moral success; yet the *beau geste* of the Athenians found no
imitators. The Aetolians remained deaf to Attalus' appeals; the
Achaeans showed their sentiments some months later by electing
as General Cycliadas who was well-disposed to Philip, and by
attempting to reconcile Philip and the Rhodians (autumn 200).

From Athens, on their voyage to Syria and Egypt, the Roman
envoys reached Rhodes, where they made a considerable stay,
devising plans with the Rhodians and watching Philip, whose new
enterprise called for their full attention. Apprised of the Roman
demands by Nicanor, Philip naturally scorned to reply, but
immediately took steps to face the coming war. Obviously too
weak to dispute with the Romans the command of the open sea,
he wished to maintain communications by way of Thrace and
the Hellespont with Asia, where he had left troops to guard his
conquests—at Iasus, Bargylia, Euromus, Pedasa, Stratoniceia and
in the Rhodian Peraea; besides, since Macedonia was especially
vulnerable on the east, he must prevent a possible hostile landing
in Thrace: so, for both reasons, Philip decided to seize the
Thracian coast, which still belonged to Egypt, and also the eastern
shore of the Dardanelles. Answering the Athenian decree by
sending Philocles, governor of Euboea, to ravage Attica, he
marched with 2000 light-armed troops and 200 cavalry against
Maronea, where his fleet awaited him under Heracleides, stormed
the town, took Cypsela, Aenus, which was finally betrayed by its
Egyptian governor, and the Chersonese (where he already held Lysi-

---

[1] In the place of one of the two 'Macedonian' tribes, Antigonis and
Demetrias, which, seemingly, had just been abolished.

macheia); then, crossing the Straits, he besieged the free city of
Abydos, which defended itself desperately. With strange lack of
energy, Attalus and the Rhodians did nothing to hinder him, and
only sent very inadequate assistance to Abydos. Ever intent upon
their maritime interests, the Rhodians had, on their return from
Athens, hastened to bring into alliance with themselves the
Cyclades, except for Cythnos, Andros and Paros which were held
by Macedonian garrisons, but they considered the saving of
Abydos too laborious an undertaking. The siege was nearing its
end, when Philip received, probably late in September, a new
communication from the Senate.

At Rome events had moved quickly. The Senate had learnt
from its envoys of Philocles' invasion of Attica and of Philip's
entry into Thrace: Philip was not only opposing an insulting
silence to their commands, but was showing by his warlike acts
that he cared nothing for them—which was what the *patres* had
anticipated and desired. War thus became inevitable, the honour
of Rome was at stake. The consul Sulpicius presented the *lex de
bello indicendo* to the centuries, on the ground that Philip 'had
attacked the allies of the Roman people,' an allegation which was,
as we know, an audacious lie, since Attalus (besides not being,
strictly speaking, the ally of Rome) had been the aggressor in the
contest with Philip. According to the Roman annalists, the
proposal was at first rejected almost unanimously, which would
be naturally explained by the war-weariness of the people after the
nightmare of the Punic War; but, returning to the charge at the
Senate's orders, Sulpicius secured an affirmative vote (*c.* July[1]),
then prepared at once to cross the sea. It remained, according
to the practice of the *fetiales*, to communicate to the enemy, if
possible to Philip in person, the *indictio belli*. Charged with this
formality, the *legati* sent Aemilius Lepidus, the youngest of them,
from Rhodes to Abydos[2]. As the *indictio belli* usually took the
form of a final *rerum repetitio*, the Senate had taken advantage of
it to increase their demands, a sure method of depriving Philip

[1] Mommsen (*Röm. Geschichte*[7], I, p. 700, Engl. transl. vol. II, p. 419) had
already seen that the voting of the war at Rome happened in 'the summer of
200'; cf. Niese, *Grundriss der röm. Geschichte*[5], p. 131, n. 2, who, however,
wrongly places it after the interview at Abydos. The annalists have mis-
takenly assigned the vote to the beginning of the consular year (A.U.C. 554).

[2] The *démarche* of Aemilius, which coincides in time with the crossing
of Sulpicius to Illyria, *i.e.* with the opening of hostilities, and is therefore
subsequent to the voting of the war, was not, as has often been thought, in
order to convey to Philip the Senate's ultimatum; that had been done by
Nicanor. Its only object must have been to notify the king of the *indictio belli*.

of any possible retreat; they forbade him to touch Egyptian dependencies, and commanded him to make reparations not only to Attalus but to Rhodes. Aemilius notified him of this, and a stormy altercation followed; Philip objected that the Rhodians had attacked him, whereupon Aemilius interrupted him violently. With ironic courtesy, Philip excused him 'because he was young and inexperienced, the handsomest man of his day ('as was indeed true,' says Polybius), and, above all, a Roman.' He added: 'if it please the Romans to violate the treaty between us, we will defend ourselves with the help of the gods,' thus proclaiming the manifest unrighteousness of the war. Upon Aemilius' departure, Philip took Abydos, whose inhabitants killed themselves in a paroxysm of heroic frenzy, garrisoned it, and returned home in haste; he learnt on the way of the Roman arrival in Illyria. Sulpicius, with two legions—about 25,000 men—consisting partly of veterans en- listed as volunteers, was encamped between Apollonia and Dyr- rhachium (*c.* early October).

The *legati* had still to carry out the most delicate part of their mission, visit Antiochus and, if possible, persuade him to declare himself neutral in the contest between Philip and Rome. Extreme prudence was necessary. For the first time the Romans came into contact with the dreaded king of Asia; they must be careful not to estrange a conqueror who had just won fresh laurels. After taking Gaza (p. 153), Antiochus had suffered a momentary reverse; resuming the offensive in the winter of 201/0, Scopas reconquered Palestine up to the sources of the Jordan; but at the battle of Panion, Antiochus avenged Raphia. Decisively defeated, Scopas, with the 10,000 men that remained of his army, was forced to take refuge in Sidon, which Antiochus besieged by land and sea (summer 200). It was a few months later that the *legati* came from Rhodes to visit him. What passed between them is not known directly, but can be inferred from subsequent events. Certainly, the Romans so arrogant towards Philip showed themselves blandness itself towards Antiochus. Their ostensible instructions were to 'reconcile him with Ptolemy'; their real instructions were quite different. Apart from the fact that indiscreet mediation might have irritated Antiochus, his war against Egypt was valuable to Rome: it turned him from Philip. The *legati* assured him of the Senate's goodwill, giving him to understand that, whatever the displeasure of the *patres* at the sight of danger to Ptolemy, a friend of Rome, they would not hamper his conqueror. Antiochus was lavish in demonstrations of friendship: he rejoiced to enter into relations with the Republic, and proposed to send an embassy to Rome. He made much of the Roman envoys, but that was all. In return for their complaisance they hoped for a promise of neutrality; they obtained none. The uneasiness which Antiochus inspired at Rome guaranteed him, better than all their words, full liberty of action in the East, and he was wise enough not to dispel this useful uneasiness. The *legati* left him, mistrustful and uncertain of his intentions, never suspecting his satisfaction at being rid, thanks to Rome, of a dangerous ally. The fear that he might come to Philip's help was left to haunt the Senate.

The Roman embassy, returning from Syria, necessarily touched at Alexandria, where the results of the supposed mediation were anxiously awaited. The *legati* probably got over the difficulty by telling the Egyptians that their efforts had failed before Antiochus' obstinacy; they then returned to Rome. Later, a legend arose in the Aemilian family, which was illustrated by a coin[1], that M. Aemilius had stayed in Alexandria as guardian of the child Ptolemy in the name of the Roman Senate. The truth is that the Romans abandoned Egypt to its fate. They ordered Philip to respect Egyptian possessions, but allowed Antiochus to have his way with them. While the Seleucid king was conquering in the distant East, they hoped to make an end of the Antigonid.

VI. THE FIRST TWO YEARS OF THE MACEDONIAN WAR

No sooner had he landed than Sulpicius made use of the days of fine weather that remained, and sent his lieutenant, L. Apustius, to ravage the Macedonian borders. Apustius took and destroyed, among other towns, the important Antipatreia (vol. VII, p. 836). Meanwhile a squadron dispatched to the Piraeus to protect Athens succeeded in surprising Chalcis, one of Philip's *places d'armes*, where the Romans did enormous damage, though they had not men enough to hold the town. Hastening thither too late, Philip vented his rage upon Athens. He attacked the city twice, but failed to take it, failed also against Eleusis and the Piraeus; but twice he spread havoc through ill-fated Attica which thus within a few months suffered five invasions. It is said that the king was not content with destroying buildings, but had the very stones broken to prevent their reconstruction. This insane violence merely made him more detested.

Between his two attempts on Athens he visited the Achaeans in the hope of securing military aid. But the thought of a war with Rome terrified them, and their own affairs were going badly:

[1] See Vol. of Plates iii, 10, *a*.

since the end of Philopoemen's term as General in October 200, Nabis was again becoming aggressive. Philip's requests were met by evasions, and Achaea remained his ally only in name. He could expect no official help from her or from his 'independent allies' in general; all he got from them was some volunteers, chiefly Acarnanians and Boeotians. His one field-army—he possessed no reserves—amounting to about 20,000 foot and 2000 horse, consisted almost entirely of Macedonians (including Thessalians) reinforced by Thracians, Illyrians, and mercenaries.

His isolation and weakness condemned Philip to a defensive limited by the need to spare his troops as much as possible. Sulpicius, on the other hand, received offers of co-operation from Bato, the Dardanian king, Pleuratus and Amynander. These were useful allies, but barbarians or semi-barbarians, and the Romans, who had proclaimed themselves the defenders of the Greeks, aspired higher. However, apart from Athens, the Greek peoples fought shy of allying themselves with Rome and remained passive. The presence of Sulpicius, whose previous sojourn in Greece had left bitter memories, did not make them any less reluctant. Even the Aetolians played a waiting game, and although Sulpicius sent an envoy and mobilized the eloquence of their friends the Athenians (end of March 199), all was in vain. Before they moved, they wished to see which way the war would go.

Impatient for results, Sulpicius proposed to end the war at once by a combined offensive. He was to invade Macedonia from the west, Pleuratus and Bato from the north, Amynander from the south; the fleets of Rome, Pergamum and Rhodes, amounting together to some 100 sail, were to master Cassandreia and Chalcidice. While his barbarian allies were getting into motion, the consul, following what was to become the *via Egnatia*, boldly advanced into Lyncestis, where he encountered Philip, who from the centre of his kingdom had kept watch on his various opponents, and inflicted a slight reverse upon him at Ottolobus near the middle waters of the Erigon. Here the Roman successes ended. Philip pursued a skilful defensive, harassing and wearing down the enemy without ever risking a pitched battle. After fruitless operations in Lyncestis, Sulpicius at last contrived to force the pass of Banitza, the key to Lower Macedonia. But the season was advanced, he was far from his base and found it hard to feed his army. He, therefore, decided to retire and, after laying waste Eordaea and Elimiotis, he regained Illyria by way of Orestis, where he captured Celetrum. Thus after five months he was back again at his starting point (October). His retreat saved

Philip. To check the Roman advance he had been compelled to recall the troops, under the nominal command of his youthful son Perseus, that held the Axius passes, so that the Dardanians had entered Paeonia unhindered. Moreover, after Ottolobus, the Aetolians had spontaneously taken the field once more, and with the Athamanians were overrunning Thessaly, pushing on as far as Perrhaebia. But, freed from the Romans, Philip made short work of them, and the Dardanians returned home with the Macedonian general Athenagoras at their heels. On land, through lack of concert, the coalition effected nothing. More fortunate by sea, where the Macedonian fleet dared not appear, Apustius and Attalus began by taking Andros and ended by conquering Oreus, but, though helped by the Rhodians, their attack upon Cassandreia was a complete failure; they had to content themselves with the capture and sack of the Chalcidian town of Acanthus.

This campaign, barren though it was of military results, made a deep impression in Greece. Philip had allowed Macedonia to be invaded and had abandoned the sea to the enemy: his defeat seemed probable. This explains the revived ardour of Aetolia and, in Achaea, the election as General, against Philopoemen himself, of Aristaenus (or Aristaenetus) of Dyme, an anti-Macedonian leader (end of September 199). To parry the blow, Philip went beyond his promises of 208, and handed over to the Achaeans all his Peloponnesian possessions. He realized, too, that, if he would regain his prestige, he must modify his defensive strategy, and not shut himself in his kingdom, but stand and fight on his western frontier, and deny the Romans access to Greece. On the sound assumption that, in order to join the Aetolians, they would now advance on Macedonia through Epirus and Thessaly, he took up and fortified a position near Antigoneia commanding the gorges of the Aoüs[1], thus closing both the Drynus valley towards Epirus and the Aoüs valley towards Thessaly (spring 198). Sulpicius' successor, the consul P. Villius Tappulus, after having checked by conciliation a serious mutiny among his so-called volunteers, came to seek him there. But he was almost at once replaced by his own successor, the consul for 198, T. Quinctius Flamininus, a young man not yet thirty (p. 112), who reached Greece earlier in the year than any previous commander, bringing important reinforcements of 8000 foot and 800 horse.

Sulpicius, a grim soldier, could not be the man to carry out the new Hellenic policy of the Senate. But this policy was well suited

[1] See vol. VII, p. 830. Philip's position is certainly that indicated by De Sanctis, *op. cit.* IV, 1, p. 60, n. 117.

to the temper and aims of the new consul. At heart Flamininus
was masterful, and determined to set up firmly a Roman protectorate in Greece. But he was also vanity itself, thirsting for
honour and glory, and above all for the praises of the Greeks which
his fervent admiration for Hellenism caused him to set above
everything. He was haunted by the vision of Greece, freed by his
efforts from the yoke of Macedon, lauding him as her liberator,
accepting Roman protection as a boon bestowed by him, and
abiding in lasting gratitude and loyalty to the Republic—an
achievement to be his and his alone. His first object was to detach
from Philip as many of his allies as he could and bring them
definitely over to the side of Rome. To this end he proposed to
employ a method, natural enough but hitherto too rarely tried,
for which he was peculiarly fitted by his profound and skilfully
paraded Hellenic culture and his un-Roman qualities of suppleness and tact. The method was to give a warm welcome to any
Greeks who approached him, to win their confidence, and persuade them that Rome's one purpose in fighting Philip was to
bring to them freedom. Philhellene or not at heart, he knew well
how to appear so. It was his special gift to display to the Greeks
such a Roman consul as hitherto they had never seen nor hoped
to see: a Roman consul who delighted to speak their language,
who knew their customs, was like them, and—strangest of all—
desired to please them. His graciousness won over a number of
well-to-do Greeks, hostile to Philip, who entered into close
relations with him and became useful helpers. But the triumphs
of his diplomacy have been overrated; they were not substantial
and were due far less to his finesse than to the presence in every
Greek city of a strongly anti-Macedonian upper class, ready or at
least resigned to treat with Philip's enemies, and to an even more
potent factor, the terror inspired by the Roman arms. And in
the end his great design was not achieved: he did not bring to
pass the close and lasting union of the Greeks with Rome of
which he dreamed.

Shortly after his arrival, the Epirote magistrates arranged a
meeting between him and the king on the banks of the Aoüs.
This gave him the opportunity for a resounding declaration. He
proclaimed as an indispensable condition of peace the abandonment by Philip of all his Hellenic dependencies, even those which
he had inherited, beginning with Thessaly. Now the Greeks
knew beyond all doubt what was the Senate's purpose—the expulsion from Greece of the Macedonians. It was to the Greeks,
no less than to Philip, that Flamininus spoke.

Indignant at being treated as vanquished, Philip broke off the conference. His defences, impregnable from the front, could not be stormed, but were turned by 4300 Romans who were furnished with a guide by a prominent Epirote, Charops (probably 24 June 198). Threatened with envelopment, Philip extricated himself with the loss of 2000 men and all his baggage, marched hurriedly up the Aoüs into Thessaly, where he left no region unvisited, wasting the open country but leaving garrisons in the fortresses, and took up position at Tempe. Behind him Thessaly was invaded from three sides: from the south by the Aetolians, who overran Dolopia and the borders of Thessaliotis and Phthiotic Achaea, from the west by Amynander, who crossing the Pindus seized the important town of Gomphi, finally from the north by Flamininus. Coming from Epirus, he descended the Zygos-pass into the valley of the Peneus, but found his advance checked by the Thessalian strongholds, which were stoutly defended by the inhabitants as well as the Macedonian garrisons. Though after great efforts he took Phaloria, Atrax withstood all his attacks. He then turned southward and pushed on towards the Corinthian Gulf, intending to winter at Anticyra where he could regain touch with supplies from Italy, and reduced on his way numerous Phocian towns. While he was besieging Elatea, which had refused to open its gates, the allied fleets, which had just captured Eretria and Carystus in Euboea, arrived at Cenchreae thus threatening Corinth (September).

Their presence had a political purpose. Up till then the Greeks had disappointed Flamininus' hopes; despite his declaration at the Aoüs meeting, none of Philip's allies, not even the Epirotes, whose lands he had purposely spared, had yet come over to the Romans[1]. Flamininus, in secret understanding with Aristaenus, wished to secure the adhesion of Achaea. Accordingly, his brother, L. Quinctius, commanding the Roman fleet, Attalus, and the Rhodian admiral sent envoys to Sicyon to invite the League to joint action, offering in return to help them to recover Corinth. There could be no doubt about the answer. Powerless even against Nabis, perforce unaided by Philip—and abandoned by Philopoemen, who had withdrawn in disgust to be again a condottiere in Crete—the Achaeans had to choose between Rome as ally or as enemy: the knife was at their throat. Refusal meant immediate attack by the three fleets. Yet, despite their peril, despite the lure

---

[1] It follows from Livy xxxii, 14, 5–6 that the formal adhesion of the Epirotes to Flamininus did not follow immediately on the victory at the Aoüs but later, probably in the autumn.

of Corinth, the passionate exhortations of an Athenian envoy, and the pressure exerted by Aristaenus and his party, they only voted the decree of alliance after three days of anguish, amid furious dissensions, and thanks to the tardy transference of one suffrage in the council of *damiourgoi*, perhaps also because many recalcitrants, the Dymaeans, the Megalopolitans, some Argives, were intimidated into withdrawal before the final vote. So strong remained the ties which bound Achaea to Macedon, while stronger still was the popular aversion towards the foreigner.

The sequel was equally significant. In accordance with their promise, L. Quinctius and Attalus, along with the Achaean army, attacked Corinth. The hope that the inhabitants would rise against the Macedonian garrison proved vain. Corinthians and Macedonians fought shoulder to shoulder; help came from Philocles in Chalcis, and the besiegers ended by retreating. Shortly afterwards, Argos, firmly loyal to the Macedonian alliance, welcomed Philocles within its walls and seceded from Achaea. Thus Philip kept Corinth and gained Argos.

Nevertheless, after this second campaign, his case was desperate. His retreat in haste and disorder had looked like flight and the confession of defeat. Western Thessaly was lost, all Euboea but Chalcis, most of Locris and Phocis, including Elatea which had at last fallen to Flamininus. The defection of the Achaeans was a political disaster; the Hellenic League was breaking up from fear of Rome. Besides he was short of men and supplies; he had had to recall several distant garrisons, evacuate in particular Lysimacheia, which was then destroyed by the Thracians. Reason bade him negotiate even at great sacrifice, in the hope of saving what might yet be saved. About November a conference at his request was opened at Nicaea in Locris. Flamininus demanded that he should cede to Rome all his Illyrian possessions, restore the towns taken from Ptolemy[1], and, as before, evacuate Greece. He then let his allies speak[2]. Attalus' representative required reparations for damages committed near Pergamum; Rhodes, the abandonment of all Philip's conquests in Asia and on the Hellespont and

---

[1] Only the Thracian coast cities conquered in 202 are involved; for no Ptolemaic city in Asia was then apparently in Philip's possession (see above, p. 155 and below, p. 181). It is to be observed, moreover, that Flamininus left it to the Rhodians to claim the evacuation of the cities in Asia (Polybius XVIII, 2, 3–4). That would be hardly intelligible if several of these cities had belonged to Ptolemy, since it is Flamininus who defends the interests of Ptolemy at Nicaea.

[2] Apparently by an omission, Polybius does not mention the Athenians.

Bosporus; the Achaeans claimed Corinth and Argos; the Aetolians, the cities wrested from their League, particularly Echinus, Larissa Cremaste, Pharsalus and Phthiotic Thebes, unfairly retained by Philip since 206. All, in addition, joined Flamininus in demanding the complete evacuation of Greece[1]. They demanded the impossible. Philip agreed to renounce, besides what he had already lost, Illyria, the Ptolemaic towns, the Rhodian Peraea, and even, in Greece, Larissa, Pharsalus, Argos, Corinth (the lower town), but naturally intended to keep the rest of his last Hellenic territories, including the three great strongholds, Demetrias, Chalcis and Acrocorinth. Finally, faced by the opposition of the Greeks, he appealed from them to the Senate—this at a secret suggestion by Flamininus, who throughout had studiously endeavoured to win his confidence[2]. Determined to secure the credit for ending the war, Flamininus sought to protract negotiations until the provinces for 197 were allotted; if he was not continued in command, his friends would persuade the Senate to patch up a peace which Philip could accept. But he was made proconsul, and his friends influenced the *patres* against concessions. Called upon to declare if the king would abandon Demetrias, Chalcis and Acrocorinth, Philip's envoys remained silent, and the Senate broke off negotiations. The only outcome was that Philip lost his last Phocian and Locrian fortresses, yielded to Flamininus as the price of the truce during which he had tried to placate the Senate.

Thus condemned to continue a hopeless struggle, Philip had to endure, early in 197, new discomfitures and growing isolation. Abandoned by the Achaeans, he had turned to Nabis and, as an earnest of alliance, betrayed to him Argos which he could not hope to keep for himself. Abandoned by Philocles, the unhappy Argives had to bear the application of Spartan communism. Then, judging Philip's cause lost, Nabis with cool effrontery made overtures to the Romans, which were at once accepted. An agreement was concluded at Mycenae in the presence of Flamininus himself, his brother, Attalus, and Nicostratus, the Achaean General. Nabis broke with Philip, supplied 600 Cretan mercenaries to the Roman army, and granted a truce to the Achaeans, which enabled them to operate against Corinth unhindered. He had—so he hoped—his reward, the tacit guarantee by Rome of his possession of Argos, where his wife and accomplice, the fierce

---

[1] This is at first demanded by the Aetolians (Polybius XVIII, 2, 6), then by all the other delegates (9, 1).

[2] See the present writer in *Rev. E.G.* XXXVI, 1923, pp. 115 *sqq.*

Apia, was set to despoil, with menaces and violence, the noble ladies of Argos who were her compatriots.

The whole Peloponnese was henceforward against Philip. Flamininus, continuing his work of disruption, next detached from him Boeotia, reinforcing his persuasions by even harsher methods of intimidation than the Achaeans had had to face. With Attalus and Aristaenus, he went to Thebes, where the federal archon Antiphilus, a Boeotian Aristaenus, waited for his coming. Two thousand legionaries slipped into the city after him, and in their presence the Boeotians, surprised and terrified, voted adhesion to Rome. What the vote was worth, the future was to show. But, for the moment, the great work of Antigonus Doson was undone —the Hellenic 'Symmachia' was destroyed. Apart from Acarnania, where L. Quinctius was intriguing, Eastern Thessaly with Magnesia and Eastern Phthiotis, Chalcis and Corinth, all the Greek allies of Macedon had either been forced into submission by Rome or won over—at least in appearance—to her cause. Flamininus had good reason to be proud of what he had achieved.

VII. CYNOSCEPHALAE: ANTIOCHUS IN THE WEST

Western events had their repercussion in the East. The Macedonian war had given Antiochus a free field, and he had vigorously turned to account his victory at Panion, defeated an Egyptian army on its way to relieve Sidon, starved Scopas into surrender, allowing him, however, free withdrawal with his troops (spring 199), re-taken Jerusalem, where he had the support of a strong party, and mastered all Palestine as far as the Sinai desert. In 198 he was in a position to invade Egypt. But, besides the fact that it might have proved a difficult undertaking, since Scopas had raised 6500 mercenaries in Aetolia during the summer of 199[1], Antiochus, ever methodical, considered that he had for the present more urgent claims upon his energy. Philip's defeat seemed imminent and, before it set the Romans free to hinder him, Antiochus must regain his hereditary possessions in Asia Minor and Thrace, which had fallen into the hands of Ptolemy or Philip. In the winter of 198 to 197, while his ambassadors carried friendly assurances to Rome, he was at Antioch preparing a great expedition. When spring came, the army under his sons Antiochus and Seleucus, advised by the generals Ardys and Mithridates[2], pro-

---

[1] Livy XXXI, 43, 5–7; cf. the present writer in *Klio*, VIII, 1908, pp. 277 *sqq.*
[2] Mithridates was a nephew of Antiochus. See the present writer in *Hermes*, XLVII, 1912, pp. 481 *sqq.*

ceeded along the coast towards Sardes; he himself commanded
the fleet, which is said to have comprised 100 warships and 200
light vessels. On the Cilician coast the Ptolemaic towns from
Mallus to Selinus submitted immediately. Coracesium resisted;
he was besieging it when he was met by a Rhodian embassy.

Philip's enemies, especially the Romans, were anxiously
watching Antiochus; in their eyes his departure for the West could
only mean that he was coming to Philip's aid. Accordingly the
Rhodians, certainly at Flamininus' instigation, announced, though
with all due courtesy, that they would not allow him to pass the
Chelidonian islands. Antiochus wished to avoid at all costs a
collision with Rhodes, who would doubtless be supported by
the fleets of Rome and Pergamum. The Rhodians, on their side,
having extensive interests in his empire[1], did not wish to go to
war with him. Both anxious to reach an understanding, they were
parleying—Antiochus protesting, in all good faith, that he had
no aggressive designs against Rome or her allies and adducing
the compliments sent to him by his ambassadors as proof of
Roman friendship—when news arrived of Philip's decisive defeat.
The Rhodians judged it unnecessary to bar Antiochus' path any
longer; an agreement, by which the king, in deference to Rhodian
wishes, renounced the intention of annexing certain Ptolemaic
possessions (see below, p. 178), was, it seems, arrived at, and he
pursued his way unhindered.

Early in June, Philip had in fact played his last card, and lost.
By a supreme effort, enlisting even boys of sixteen, he had
collected 23,500 foot (18,000 of them Macedonians) and 2000
horse. While he was training his recruits at Dium, Flamininus
left Elatea (end of March) and passed Thermopylae. He was
present, at Heraclea, at the Assembly of the Aetolians, who
supplied 6000 foot and 400 horse under the General Phaeneas;
Amynander brought him 1200 Athamanians: his forces thus exceeded 26,000 including 2400 cavalry. Having traversed Phthiotic
Achaea, where Thebes in spite of the pro-Roman leaders resisted
him, the proconsul entered Thessaly knowing that he would meet
Philip, who was indeed advancing towards him. Near Pherae there
was some fighting, and then the two armies, seeking better ground,
turned west and, losing touch, marched for two days on parallel
lines, Philip to the north, Flamininus to the south of the range of
hills called Cynoscephalae (Karadagh) till they neared Scotussa[2].

---

[1] Cf. Polybius XXI, 43, 16–17 and v, 89, 8.
[2] For the site of the battle see De Sanctis, *op. cit.* IV, 1, p. 85, n. 166
(against Kromayer); cf. F. Stählin, *Das hellenische Thessalien*, pp. 108 *sqq.*

There, on a hazy morning, covering detachments met unexpectedly upon the hills. As reinforcements arrived, the troops became heavily engaged, and when the Romans gave way despite the Aetolian horse, which boldly charged the Macedonians, Flamininus in support deployed his whole army facing the hills 'and advanced with his left to meet the enemy in imposing style.' At the same time, yielding to the appeals of his men, Philip moved forward to occupy the heights. An unexpected general engagement was thus brought on, almost against Philip's will, on the southern slopes of Karadagh, on broken ground unfavourable to the phalanx, even before the Macedonian left was in position. The battle consisted of two separate and successive actions. On the west, Philip, descending from the hills with the right half of the phalanx, drove back in great disorder the Roman left under Flamininus. At this critical moment the Roman general rode off to his right, which till then had been inactive, and with this force, which was preceded by some elephants, fell upon the left half of the phalanx which, still in marching order, had just occupied the heights, and routed it[1], assisted by the terror inspired by the elephants. The initiative of an unknown tribune, 'who judged on the spur of the moment what ought to be done,' translated this success into triumph: detaching from the Roman right 20 maniples, *i.e.* the *principes* and *triarii* (*c.* 2000 men), he attacked the victorious half of the phalanx from behind, and broke it.

Cynoscephalae was the Jena of Macedon. The descendants of the soldiers of Alexander had given way at the first shock before the 'unknown quantity' of the Roman army. Greece learned with stupefaction that the phalanx had found its master. To be sure, the phalanx of the Antigonids, too heavy and unwieldy and therein inferior to that of Alexander, was a tactical weapon of far less value than the legion; but in the fortuitous and unforeseen battle of Cynoscephalae, the Romans, by no merit of their own, were able to fight under conditions so remarkably disadvantageous to the Macedonians, that the result, whatever Polybius may say, fell short of proving the superiority of their military system. In reality, their victory was mainly due to the good fortune which never deserted them during their first two great wars in the East.

Philip, realizing that all was lost, immediately retired on Tempe, rallied the fugitives, and returned to Macedonia, having

---

[1] Despite the silence of Polybius, the Aetolian infantry, on the Roman right, played a part in this victorious attack: hence the excessive but not wholly unjustified boasts of the Aetolians.

lost over 13,000 men, including 8000 dead. The struggle was over. Disasters were, moreover, overtaking him on every side. The garrison of Corinth, making a sortie, was defeated by the Achaeans —their sole exploit. The Roman fleet attacked Macedonia's last remaining allies, the faithful Acarnanians, who had disowned the agreement secretly concluded between L. Quinctius and certain of their leaders; Leucas stoutly repelled the most terrible assaults until it fell by treachery. In Asia, the Rhodians reinforced by Achaean auxiliaries retook their Peraea from the Macedonians, though they failed to dislodge them from Stratoniceia. Finally, Macedonia itself was threatened by an invasion of the Dardanians whom, however, Philip crushed near Stobi.

Before this, he had sent envoys to Flamininus to make overtures for peace. They were welcomed, for Flamininus, convinced that Antiochus would soon arrive in Europe, feared that Philip would hold out in the Macedonian fortresses until he came. What he most dreaded was that the two kings would join hands, and an immediate peace would rid him of this anxiety and also spare him the chagrin of seeing another consul end the war. So he received the envoys amicably, granted a truce, and consented to meet Philip at Tempe. This decision, taken without reference to them, exasperated the Aetolians who wanted war *à outrance*—a war of which the Romans of course would bear the brunt—and dreamed of dethroning Philip. But now Flamininus deliberately ignored them; the eagerness with which they had monopolized the pillaging of the Macedonian camp, their boastful claim to divide equally with the Romans the credit for the victory, the way in which they filled all Greece with the story of their prowess had made them hateful to him. Flamininus did not pardon wounds to his pride.

Moreover, his relations with his allies[1] could not but suffer a change. Hitherto apparent equality had existed in the coalition between Greeks and Romans. The compact of 212 with the Aetolians had not been renewed, but they believed that it had been tacitly revived, and the Romans had permitted this belief. As in 208, their admirals had let Attalus occupy the towns— Andros, Oreus, probably Eretria—taken by the united fleets. At Nicaea, Flamininus, while secretly negotiating with Philip, had shown the Greeks the utmost deference, inviting them to inform Philip directly of their claims (see p. 171 *sq.*). Now that victory was

---

[1] The word 'allies' is used here in default of a more exact term. It is not to be taken in a juridical sense, for Rome had not at that time a formal alliance with any of the states that had fought on her side.

won, he had to put matters in order and reassert the predominant position of Rome, for, of this victory, *her* victory, the Republic intended to settle the consequences alone. Flamininus summoned his allies to Tempe, but merely as a matter of form. Assuming as settled the main question—whether peace should be made at all—he merely consulted them, and then only in appearance, as to the terms of the treaty. The Aetolians dared to speak against peace[1]; he rebuffed them harshly, then pronounced his decision: 'He and the Romans present had determined, subject to the Senate's approval, to make peace with Philip upon the conditions laid down at Nicaea,' *i.e.* the abandonment of all his extra-Macedonian dependencies. Thus Rome imposed both peace and conditions of peace.

What followed was no less significant. At Tempe, Philip, having come to an understanding with Flamininus, declared his acceptance of the conditions of Nicaea. It seemed, therefore, that the Greeks would recover at once what they had then claimed from him. But when Phaeneas asked Philip if he restored to Aetolia Pharsalus, Echinus, Larissa Cremaste, and Thebes, all of which she had claimed at Nicaea, Flamininus intervened and opposed his veto. He denied the Aetolians any right to Larissa, Echinus, Pharsalus and the Thessalian towns generally, on the ground that they had surrendered to him; all he could grant them, and that only 'as he thought fit' was Phthiotic Thebes, which had resisted the Romans. Phaeneas indignantly pointed out that Aetolia had taken up arms again and fought on the side of Rome solely to recover her lost cities; he recalled also the alliance of 212 by which the captured towns were to go to the Aetolians. Flamininus answered that their defection in 206 had annulled that alliance, the terms of which he moreover contested. As for Phaeneas' first and strongest argument, he wholly ignored it.

This acrid discussion revealed Flamininus' hostility towards Aetolia; but a wider inference might also be drawn from it: their position as belligerents gave the Greeks no real right to Philip's former possessions; the Romans, looking upon themselves as sole victors, considered these possessions their *praemia belli* and reserved the right to dispose of them at will. It was a bitter blow to

---

[1] In order to justify to the Aetolians his refusal to destroy the Macedonian monarchy, Flamininus is said (Polybius xviii, 37, 9) to have urged that Macedon was the indispensable bulwark of Greece against the barbarians. Modern writers have, in general, taken this argument very seriously, but it must be recognized that it lost not a little of its force when it was advanced by the ally of the Illyrians, the Thracians and the Dardanians.

the Aetolians who, having counted upon the immediate restoration of their Thessalian and Phthiotic territories, now saw them withheld; but the application of this new principle laid down by Rome might well cause uneasiness to her other allies, the Achaeans, Amynander and the new Pergamene king, Eumenes II, the eldest son of Attalus, who had had an apoplectic stroke at Thebes (c. February 197) and had died soon afterwards.

When preliminaries were concluded and Philip announced that in regard to details he would submit to the Senate's decision, Flamininus granted him a four months armistice upon payment of 200 talents and delivery of hostages, among them his younger son Demetrius. All parties then sent deputations to Rome, where the Senate would finally settle the question of the peace, which the Aetolians still vainly hoped to hinder.

Flamininus felt Antiochus coming; he was indeed drawing near, spurred on by the news of Cynoscephalae. Philip's *débâcle* delivered over to the Great King his possessions in Asia and Thrace, but the Romans, victorious a little too soon, might put obstacles in his way. To leave them no time for this, Antiochus pressed on. He received in Lycia the submission—sometimes, as at Xanthus, merely nominal—of the cities that were dependencies of Ptolemy, then set about re-establishing his authority over the Greek towns bordering the Aegean. Their political status, as we know, was varied. Leaving out of account those which were included in the Pergamene kingdom, some were still, in fact or theory, vassals of Egypt; a few were subject-allies of Pergamum; others were held by the Macedonians; then came the numerous 'autonomous cities' which, after obtaining extensive privileges from the Seleucids—especially from Antiochus II—had profited by their difficulties to make themselves wholly independent. In this undertaking Antiochus, as usual, joined prudence to energy. Anxious to retain the useful friendship of Rhodes, he allowed her to take under her protection (that is her control) Halicarnassus, Myndus, Samos, former Egyptian dependencies, and redeem Caunus 'from Ptolemy's generals'; he even handed over to her Stratoniceia, which he had recaptured from the Macedonians. With his consent Rhodes gained a preponderant influence over the region south of the Maeander. He was also careful to respect the hereditary dominions of Eumenes, contenting himself with claiming the submission of cities, outside these dominions, which Attalus had made subject-allies and of which several seemingly had seceded from Eumenes. Finally he showed moderation towards the autonomous towns, exacting little but recognition of his suzerainty and giving them hopes of large concessions in return; in case of dispute he consented to accept the Rhodians as arbitrators between himself and the towns. From Caria to the Hellespont his success was rapid. On the Carian seaboard, the Macedonians, driven from Iasus, whose self-government Antiochus left untouched[1], only held Bargylia. Master of Ephesus, the great Ptolemaic city, without striking a blow, he also seized before winter Abydos, which was still in Philip's hands. Intimidated, or won over by his friendliness, most of the autonomous cities did not hesitate to do him homage; two refused, Smyrna in Ionia, Lampsacus in Aeolis. They were formerly free allies of Attalus, and their resistance was certainly prompted by Eumenes, who was alarmed and indignant at seeing his dominions surrounded on all sides by the revived Seleucid power. After vain pourparlers, Antiochus sent troops against the refractory towns. On Eumenes' advice they then took a step of the utmost importance: although hitherto without any relations with Rome, they appealed to her for protection. The Lampsacenes conveniently discovered that, as inhabitants of Troas, they had blood-ties with Rome and, as colonists from Phocaea, were brothers of the Massiliotes, Rome's model allies; their envoys, whose journey is described in an inscription (*Ditt.*[3] 591), went to Massilia to find sponsors to recommend them to the Senate. Despite these elements of comedy, the action of Lampsacus and Smyrna was a momentous new departure. After defending against Philip the freedom of the Greeks of Europe, the Romans were now invited to defend against Antiochus the freedom of the Greeks of Asia.

VIII. THE ISTHMIAN GAMES

Like Flamininus, the Senate was anxious to end the Macedonian war. The struggle going on in Cisalpine Gaul and the great insurrection in Spain made this desirable (pp. 312, 329); but first and foremost, the *patres*, like Flamininus, wished to anticipate Antiochus' crossing into Europe, now judged imminent. So they ratified, after revision, the preliminaries of Tempe, and, in spite of the opposition of the consul M. Claudius Marcellus who hoped for the command in Greece, the people unanimously voted the peace (winter 197–6). They then fixed by decree, without consulting the Greeks, the main clauses of the final treaty, and nominated ten Commissioners, who, with

---

[1] *O.G.I.S.* 237. Later a Syrian garrison is found at Iasus (Livy xxxvii, 17, 3–7).

Flamininus, whose command was again prolonged, were to 'settle Hellenic affairs' on the spot. This decision showed that Rome's task in Greece was not ended with the establishment of peace.

At the same time, they turned their minds to thwarting Antiochus and, to this end, judged it expedient to raise up difficulties for him in the East. Ptolemy V, whom they had neglected for three years, now again became worthy of their care. They determined to resume in his favour the mediation abandoned in 200: a *legatus*, L. Cornelius (Lentulus), especially sent to Antiochus, was to defend Egyptian interests. It was expedient also to profit by his opportune quarrel with Lampsacus and Smyrna, and espouse the cause of the 'autonomous cities'; were not, indeed, Greeks everywhere equally deserving of protection? Envoys from Smyrna and Lampsacus were received with open arms and warmly recommended to Flamininus and the Ten. So the Senate extended to Asia, in order to counter Antiochus, its 'philhellenic' policy, hitherto confined to Greece proper.

Their feeling towards the Seleucid king was reflected in the decree which regulated the peace with Philip—a memorable document summarized as follows by Polybius (XVIII, 44, 2–7):

All the rest of the Greeks in Asia and Europe were to be free and governed by their own laws; as for the Greeks subject to Philip and the cities garrisoned by him, he was to surrender them to the Romans before the Isthmian festival; [however,] he was to leave free, withdrawing his garrisons from them, Euromus, Pedasa, Bargylia, Iasus, Abydos, [Sestos], Thasos, Myrina [and Hephaestia in Lemnos], Perinthus[1]. Flamininus, in accordance with the Senate's decree, was to write to Prusias about restoring the freedom of Cius. Philip was to restore to the Romans, before the same date, all prisoners and deserters, to surrender all his warships except five and his 'hekkaidekeres,' and to pay 1000 talents, half at once, and the other half by instalments extending over ten years.

It is clear that the Senate, though going beyond the terms of the preliminaries, yet treated Philip without excessive harshness. The war indemnity was bearable; he lost his navy (a precaution justified by his former Adriatic enterprises), but his military power, despite some annalists, suffered no limitation. Doubtless the *patres* considered it wise not to drive Philip to extremes, but their comparative moderation had, as soon appeared, another cause—they planned to use him, at need, against Antiochus.

Their decree contained, moreover, two provisions of capital importance. The first showed that Rome aimed at more than

[1] Polybius' enumeration (XVIII, 44, 4) is obviously incomplete. Hephaestia in Lemnos and Sestos must be added (Polybius XVIII, 48, 2; cf. 2, 4).

merely peace with Philip; it affected all the Greeks then independent and never subject to the king. By pronouncing that they
were to remain 'free and autonomous,' she guaranteed their
independence and forced Philip to do the same, thus con-
stituting herself the permanent protectress of Hellenic freedom
wherever it existed. This was the logical outcome of her whole
policy and was already implied in her command to Philip, in 200,
to abstain from hostilities against any Greek people; but—and
this is significant—the Greeks of Asia, *i.e.* the inhabitants of the
autonomous towns, were now expressly mentioned together with
the Greeks of Europe: Antiochus was consequently barred from
any enterprise against these towns. A second provision related
to the cities and populations still subject to Philip. The fact that
the Senate pronounced upon them all signified that all were by
right of conquest at the exclusive disposal of Rome. This principle
once formulated, a distinction was made between the cities in
Greece proper and those outside it. Philip was to evacuate the
latter, *i.e.* those in Asia, the Islands, and Thrace, expressly
mentioned[1], and 'leave them free': so Rome, after emphasizing
her rights over them, granted them liberty forthwith—a liberty
which, of course, all had to respect. Rome's eagerness to do this
is easily explained: Philip's eastern possessions were directly
threatened by Antiochus, who already occupied almost all those
in Asia[2]; Rome hastened to let him know that they were not to
be touched and that his annexations consequently could not be
recognized as legitimate. The Senate carried its zeal for the
Asiatic Greeks, Philip's victims, to the point of requiring Prusias
to liberate Cius—another warning to Antiochus. As for the last
remaining Macedonian dependencies in Greece, the *patres*, for
the moment, only insisted that Philip should surrender them to

---

[1] Polybius' *résumé* makes no mention of the 'cities of Thrace' properly
so-called, viz. Aenus, Maronea and the neighbouring towns which, before
202, were Egyptian possessions, because he has passed over in silence the
clause of the *senatus consultum* which referred to retrocessions to be made
by Philip to Ptolemy, just as he omits the clauses which governed Philip's
abandonment of his Illyrian territories and the reparations to be made by him
to Attalus. From this may be deduced (see also above, p. 171 n. 1) that
Euromus, Pedasa, Bargylia, Iasus, Abydos, [Sestos] and Thasos, which
Polybius cites from the *senatus consultum*, did not belong to Ptolemy before
their occupation by Philip. Besides, it is clear that had these cities been
'Ptolemaic' the Senate would not simply have ordered Philip to leave them
free but would have required him to restore them to Ptolemy (cf. Polybius
XVIII, 1, 14).

[2] Apparently Bargylia alone still belonged to Macedonia (see p. 179).

Rome; the decree said nothing about their ultimate fate, which was apparently a matter for the Ten Commissioners.

These left for Greece in the spring of 196, bearing with them the senatorial decree; Flamininus awaited them at Elatea, where he had wintered. He was disappointed to find that Philip's defeat had not brought tranquillity to Greece. The Aetolians, thinking themselves duped, were everywhere loud in complaint and recrimination, even accusing him of taking bribes from Philip. Moreover, incidents, serious above all as symptoms, had occurred in Boeotia. Flamininus, at the request of the Boeotian government, had authorized the return of the volunteers who had served in Philip's army, with their leader Brachyllas, a hereditary client of the Antigonids. Perceiving the hostility of the Boeotians and 'foreseeing Antiochus' arrival,' says Polybius, he wished to conciliate them. Now, upon the volunteers' return, the Boeotians publicly thanked not Flamininus, but Philip, elected Brachyllas Boeotarch and heaped honours upon the other Macedonian sympathizers. This alarmed the few partisans of the Roman alliance, and they resolved to kill Brachyllas: Flamininus, when consulted, let them proceed and even advised them to go to the Aetolian General Alexamenus, who actually procured them six picked bravoes. Even after Cynoscephalae, it was by such means that Roman interests in Boeotia had to be upheld. The assassination of Brachyllas, intended to intimidate the masses, roused them to fury. While the pro-Roman instigators of the crime were executed or forced to flee, any legionaries who ventured into Boeotia were murdered, until the victims reached five hundred. Flamininus, being denied both the punishment of the guilty and payment of the 500 talents imposed as fine, was driven to invade the country; but at the prayers of Athenians and Achaeans he soon pardoned Boeotia, reducing the fine to 30 talents: too great harshness would probably have been impolitic.

Amid these troubled circumstances the Commissioners arrived (c. May 196), and immediately published the senatorial decree. It made a mixed impression. The distinction between Philip's different possessions roused disquietude. While his eastern possessions regained their freedom, what was to become of the great strongholds—the 'fetters of Greece'—Demetrias, Chalcis, Acrocorinth, which Philip had duly handed over to Rome, and the districts already lost by him and now in Roman occupation? The silence of the Senate on this point, the determination of the Romans to figure as sole victors, the mystery with which Flamininus and the Ten surrounded their deliberations at Corinth, gave grounds for this uneasiness. The Aetolians, naturally, asserted that 'Greece was merely changing masters, the Romans replacing Philip, as the only result of the war.' Flamininus was pained to find these statements widely repeated and believed; it was important to reassure the Greeks, to convince them, without delay, of Roman disinterestedness. They were reassured by the striking manifesto at the Isthmian Games—a *coup de théâtre* arranged by Flamininus to impress their imagination and provoke their applause.

At the Isthmian festival (June–July 196), before the opening of the Games, the herald, advancing into the stadium, proclaimed: 'The Roman Senate and the consul Titus Quinctius, having overcome king Philip and the Macedonians, leave free, without garrisons or tribute, and governed by their ancestral laws, the Corinthians, Phocians, [Eastern] Locrians, Euboeans, Phthiotic Achaeans, Magnesians, Thessalians and Perrhaebians.' This proclamation, which the herald had to repeat, evoked frenzied enthusiasm, the more ardent as the anxiety had been so intense. The crowd nearly suffocated Flamininus in their outburst of joy. He had—for a time—his heart's desire: he was the idol of the Greeks, the Aetolians and probably the Boeotians alone excepted. In fact, in accordance with his promises, the Romans kept nothing in Greece; the Corinthian declaration splendidly completed what had been begun by the decree about the peace: in this decree Rome had guaranteed liberty to all Greeks who then enjoyed it and had restored it to Philip's former eastern subjects; she now restored liberty to his former subject-allies in Greece.

This was true. Yet the 'liberated' Greeks in Corinth did not obtain complete *eleutheria*. Rome, reviving the time-honoured formula of Antigonus (vol. vi, p. 485) and renouncing the oppressive rights of victors, imposed upon them neither tribute, garrisons, nor foreign laws, but she retained authority over them. This appeared when, after the Isthmian Games, the Commissioners, presided over by Flamininus, proceeded to the 'settlement of Hellenic affairs.' They settled the political status of the freed peoples as absolutely as that of the Illyrians wrested from Philip, who were allotted generally to Pleuratus. Certain of these peoples were used to recompense the Greeks who had sided with Rome: thus they restored Phocis and Eastern Locris to Aetolia[1];

---

[1] The Aetolians kept, besides, the cities of Dolopia, Thessaliotis and Phthiotic Achaea which they had conquered in 198 (p. 170). The Romans probably confirmed their possession, as they did for Amynander. It is to be

and re-incorporated Corinth, according to Flamininus' engagement, in Achaea (p. 170). They also authorized Amynander to retain the towns of Hestiaeotis taken by him in 198—Gomphi and the surrounding country. It is noteworthy that when Eumenes, heir to the claims of Attalus, asked for Oreus and Eretria, the Ten, interpreting rather strangely the Corinthian declaration, were prepared to let him have them; but Flamininus protested: it would have made the 'freedom' of these Euboeans a mere illusion. The Senate, when consulted, supported him. On the other hand, Flamininus and the Ten decided that Perrhaebia, Dolopia[1] (not mentioned at Corinth), Magnesia, Thessaly proper, and Euboea should form separate states, while they placed under the suzerainty of Thessaly Phthiotic Achaea, including Echinus and Larissa Cremaste vainly claimed by Aetolia, who only received Phthiotic Thebes. Finally, although Corinthians, Magnesians and Euboeans were declared 'ungarrisoned,' Roman troops held—temporarily, it is true—Acrocorinth, Demetrias, Chalcis, Oreus and Eretria; Flamininus, ever anxious to spare the susceptibilities of the Greeks and to convince them of the purity of Rome's intentions, had difficulty in obtaining from the Ten exemption for Corinth.

These temporary occupations were a precaution against Antiochus which the Commissioners, in conformity with the uneasiness felt by the Senate, considered to be indispensable. He had just, as had been feared, landed in Europe (early summer 196). From Abydos his army had crossed the Hellespont; he himself had moved his fleet thither from Ephesus; then, with united land and sea forces, had reduced Madytus and Sestos, and mastered the whole Chersonese. Finding Lysimacheia deserted, burnt by the Thracians, he undertook to rebuild it and sought everywhere for the dispersed inhabitants while with half his army he waged war on the barbarians. This meant that he intended to establish his authority permanently on the Thracian coast. To him this was his last conquest, the recovery of the last piece of his heritage; but, in the eyes of the Romans, Thrace could only be the first stage of an invasion planned to drive them from Greece.

observed, on the other hand, that the south-east corner of Hypocnemidian Locris (the district of Larymna and Halae) was left by them to Boeotia; see G. Klaffenbach, *Klio*, xx, 1926, p. 83.

[1] By Dolopia is here meant that part of it not conquered by the Aetolians in 198; on its later union with Aetolia, see below, p. 195.

IX. THE FIRST CLASH BETWEEN ROME
AND ANTIOCHUS

The Senate therefore hastened to open its diplomatic offensive against Antiochus. A preliminary skirmish occurred at Corinth after the Isthmian Games. Eager to conciliate the Romans and remove their suspicions, Antiochus had sent an embassy to greet Flamininus and the Ten. The envoys, one of whom was the historian and poet Hegesianax of Alexandria in the Troad, were coldly received. Philip's defeat had enabled the Romans, hitherto so guarded towards the Great King, to change their tone. The Commissioners declared that the 'autonomous' cities of Asia must not be touched, protested against the occupation of towns belonging to Ptolemy or Philip and, above all, against Antiochus' crossing into Europe[1]. What business had he there? 'No Greek was henceforth to be attacked or subjugated by anyone'—a notable announcement: Greek freedom, restored and guaranteed by Rome, was thus held before Antiochus as an insuperable barrier. The Commissioners ended by announcing that some of them would shortly come to confer with the king.

Meanwhile, in diverse places, they tried to hinder him. They were haunted by the fear that he would win over Philip and the Aetolians. The result was the twofold mission of the Commissioner Cn. Cornelius. He invited Philip, who obviously had already been sounded, to conclude an immediate alliance with Rome. Philip had reason to complain of the Ten who had just declared free— and this after the peace—the Orestae, who had seceded from his rule. Nevertheless, indignant at seeing Antiochus take his Asiatic spoils, he forthwith accepted Cornelius' proposal. Thus Rome turned Antiochus' former ally against him, a master-stroke should Philip remain faithful. Cornelius then went on to Aetolia (Sept. 196), where he had a peculiarly hard task. The Aetolians seemed determined to break with Rome; this must be at least delayed. They had now two grounds of quarrel. They were furious at having failed to obtain Echinus and Larissa Cremaste; nothing could be done about this, the matter was *res iudicata*. They were also clamouring for Pharsalus, and, in virtue of the treaty of 212, for Leucas, which the Romans had conquered; and because of these claims the Ten had deferred pronouncing on these towns. After heated altercations, Cornelius, playing for time, prevailed

---

[1] According to Polybius (XVIII, 47, 2) the Ten 'forbade Antiochus to cross over into Europe,' but his crossing into Thrace had already happened and the Ten must have known it. Possibly they affected ignorance.

upon the Aetolians to refer their claim to the Senate, 'where they would obtain full justice.' At the same time two Commissioners went in person, one to Bargylia, the other to Thasos, Hephaestia and Myrina (Lemnos), and 'the towns on the Thracian coast[1],' to free them from their Macedonian garrisons. Thus Rome showed her interest in the safety of these places menaced by Antiochus, and, to some extent, took them under her protection.

All this was but a prelude. L. Cornelius Lentulus, sent from Rome as mediator between Antiochus and Ptolemy, having landed in Thrace, three Commissioners joined him, and all four proceeded to Lysimacheia for a determined assault upon the king (c. October 196). Antiochus welcomed them courteously, but once discussions began, 'affairs assumed another aspect.' Lentulus elaborated with vigour the communication previously made at Corinth. He first raised the question of the Ptolemaic cities and called on Antiochus to evacuate them. Then came a similar injunction regarding the towns taken by Philip: 'it would indeed be ridiculous that the Romans, after conquering Philip, should see their prizes swept away at the last moment by Antiochus.' As for the autonomous cities, they must be respected. Lastly, he made no secret of the Senate's uneasiness: the presence of Antiochus in Europe with such a display of naval and military force was disquieting; how could the Romans not feel menaced? The inference, unexpressed but obvious, was that he must withdraw into Asia. Antiochus' reply was firm. He could not understand this discussion about the Asiatic towns: what had the affairs of Asia to do with Rome? was he meddling with those of Italy? It was not to Roman intervention but solely to his own generosity that the autonomous cities could look for freedom. He had come into Europe to recover the Chersonese and the coast towns of Thrace, a region which indeed had fallen to Seleucus Nicator as had all Lysimachus' kingdom. First the Ptolemies, then Philip had seized it, but unrightfully; he was but reclaiming his own. How could the re-building of Lysimacheia endanger the Romans? He merely wished to provide a royal residence there for his second son Seleucus. As for his differences with Ptolemy, they were about to be settled amicably and the two royal houses were to be allied in marriage.

[1] Clearly Maronea, Aenus, etc., which had been Egyptian dependencies. The Romans ought to have waited for Ptolemy to resume possession of them (cf. Polybius XVIII, 1, 14): they had no strict title to intervene. But they 'liberated' them in haste for fear Antiochus should lay hold of them.

Antiochus had kept this for the end, and he now hurled the unwelcome news at the astounded Romans. And the news was true. Expecting no more from Rome, the Acarnanian Aristomenes, who was now prudently filling the office of Regent at Alexandria in succession to Tlepolemus, had resigned himself to making terms with the enemy. Egypt was exhausted and needed peace, which was about to be concluded, the price being the renunciation of all her Syrian, Asiatic and Thracian dependencies, and the betrothal of Ptolemy V to Antiochus' daughter Cleopatra. Fortune had again rewarded Antiochus at Philip's expense, for the Macedonian had once counted on having Ptolemy as son-in-law. By revealing to the Romans that they were warmly defending a protégé who had dispensed with their protection, Antiochus made them look extremely foolish. Lentulus, to retrieve his position, returned to the subject of the autonomous cities; he called in the delegates from Lampsacus and Smyrna, who spoke out boldly. Antiochus silenced them; in this matter he would admit Rhodian but not Roman arbitration. It is noteworthy that the Romans dared not insist.

A rumour of Ptolemy's death interrupted the conference, but indeed there was nothing more to say. For a moment Antiochus hoped to mount the vacant Egyptian throne. Leaving Seleucus in Thrace, he sailed at all speed for Alexandria, but in Lycia he learnt that the dead man was alive. He was preparing, it is said, to seize Cyprus when a storm wrecked part of his fleet off the Cilician coast and forced him to return to Seleuceia. He wintered in Antioch (196–5) where he married his eldest son and co-regent, the 'king' Antiochus, to his daughter Laodice.

The false report of Ptolemy's death had its origin in an abortive insurrection of Scopas and his Aetolians. Apparently they were discontented at the prospective peace with Antiochus, which would lead to their dismissal. To prevent it Scopas prepared a *coup d'État*, but was forestalled by Aristomenes and executed together with his household and his accomplices, amongst whom was the sea-robber Dicaearchus, while many Aetolians were dismissed. Calm was thus restored in Alexandria. Thebais, where the usurper Anchmachis had succeeded to Harmachis (? 200), was still in revolt, but the recent capture of Lycopolis (197), followed by amnesties, seemed to have pacified Lower Egypt. The trusty Aristomenes, supported by the loyal governor of Cyprus, Polycrates of Argos, thought it an opportune moment to proclaim that the king's minority was over though he was but 13 or 14 years old. Ptolemy 'Epiphanes Eucharistos' was therefore consecrated at Memphis in Egyptian fashion—a concession to the natives—most probably on 28 November 196, the anniversary of his accession. In honour of this was passed, on 28 March 195, the so-called 'Rosetta decree[1]' in which the priests delighted to enumerate the privileges with which the government, from prudence or necessity, overwhelmed them. Thanks to this conciliatory policy, Epiphanes might hope to end troubles in his own realm, but his empire had collapsed under the blows of the Syrian king.

Thus at the very moment that Rome had wished to paralyse Antiochus by reviving the 'Egyptian question' it had ceased to exist: Antiochus had settled it to his own profit. Moreover, it was becoming certain that he would give way to the Romans neither on the question of Philip's Asiatic conquests, nor on that of the autonomous cities; he was not disposed to bow before this 'Greek freedom' of which Rome made herself the interested champion. The Senate's diplomatic offensive was a complete fiasco. No wonder the Romans were embittered, but had they been less prejudiced, they would have realized that the fears which had led to this failure were probably ill-founded. Antiochus' attitude was unyielding but not provocative; his explanation of his crossing into Europe was reasonable: his work, considered as a whole, had its natural crowning point in Thrace. Nothing indicated that he wished to push on farther or that Greece attracted him. He had neither sent his fleet into the Aegean, nor disputed the Roman right to settle Hellenic affairs; nor had he, though for long on friendly terms with them[2], sent envoys to the Aetolians; and his dealings with Philip made an understanding with him almost impossible. In fact, he was sincere when he declared that he cherished no designs against Rome. Unfortunately, the Romans did not then or ever afterwards believe in his sincerity.

X. THE WAR WITH NABIS. THE ROMAN EVACUATION OF GREECE

In the early summer of 195 Antiochus showed what was to be his attitude towards Rome. He returned to Thrace in greater force; determined to forgo none of his rights, he ignored the rulings of the Senate; but, at the same time, he sent envoys to Flamininus to negotiate a treaty of friendship with Rome, thus affirming his intention of undertaking nothing against her. It was in vain. Resenting the idea that Antiochus should aspire to a

[1] See vol. 1, pp. 117 sqq.   [2] O.G.I.S. 234.

treaty which would allow him to remain in Europe and confirm
Rome's diplomatic defeat at Lysimacheia, Flamininus evaded
answering. The Commissioners had left Greece (late 196); he
declared he had no powers to settle anything; the embassy must
go to Rome. Antiochus did not send it; if the Romans sulked, he
would dispense with their friendship. While he consolidated his
position in Thrace, Flamininus remained in Greece watching him.
Opportunely enough, the need to chastise Nabis, whose impunity
was an outrage, could be advanced as a reason for not returning
home with his army.

Formerly, when at war with Philip, Flamininus had not hesitated to associate himself with Nabis, whom he then called 'King
of Sparta,' which was indeed his true title[1]; but, now that Philip
was crushed, his sentiments had changed. No longer needed,
Nabis again became the 'tyrant,' odious to the liberators of Greece,
the communist abhorred by all Greek rich men, who looked to
Rome to punish him, the pirate, accomplice of the Cretans,
dreaded even by the Roman transports, the oppressor from whom
Argos must be delivered, for apart from the Achaeans' just claim
to it, an enslaved Argos was a blot on a liberated Greece.

Having been given a free hand by the Senate, Flamininus
summoned to Corinth representatives of all the Greek peoples
(c. May 195)—a symbolic event: like Alexander, the Roman
commander presided over the assembled Hellenes. Doubly clever,
he asked them but one question: 'Was Argos to be liberated?'
and flattered them by declaring that he awaited their decision: it
was a purely Greek affair and for them to settle. The Aetolians
replied only with furious recriminations; the Senate, having
received their request about Pharsalus and Leucas, had sent them
back to Flamininus who had just rebuffed them—*inde irae*. But
the other delegates voted unanimously in favour of the liberation
of Argos. This then became the declared object of the war; as
to what was to become of Nabis, Flamininus evaded the problem.
Here indeed opinions differed: the Greek representatives wished
to destroy him together with his contagious revolutionary innovations; the Achaeans desired besides to become masters of
Sparta; Flamininus thought it enough simply to render Nabis
harmless. To overthrow him would raise the inextricable question
of the recall and the re-establishment of the exiles—an embarrass-

---

[1] Some at least of the Greek states showed no unwillingness to give him
the title, as is shown by the decree of Delos in his honour (*Ditt.*[3] 584). On
the disputed date of this decree, see F. Durrbach, *Choix*, no. 58, p. 74. The
title also appeared on his coins. See Vol. of Plates iii, 10, *d*.

ment he intended to avoid. He was also loth to favour the ambition of the Achaeans, which would only cause other difficulties: would the Spartans consent to be annexed by Achaea; would it not lead to interminable conflict? Flamininus had, finally, two motives for wishing to shorten the war and avoid the long and arduous siege of Sparta: he dreaded what Antiochus might do, and he feared that, if hostilities were protracted, his successor would have the honour of bringing them to a victorious close.

An imposing force assembled against Nabis. All Greece, except Aetolia, sent contingents to serve with Flamininus. Aristaenus, again General, brought 11,000 Achaeans; Philip, fulfilling his new duties as ally, sent 1500 Macedonians; the banished Lacedaemonians with King Agesipolis, exiled in childhood by Lycurgus, crowded in. At sea, 18 Rhodian and 10 Pergamene warships joined the Roman fleet of 40 sail which L. Quinctius brought from Leucas. Rhodes could not forgive the piracies of Nabis, while Eumenes, having need of Rome against Antiochus, served her as zealously as did Attalus, and with hopes of a better reward.

Nabis faced the storm boldly, and entrusted the defence of Argos to his son-in-law and step-brother, the Argive noble Pythagoras, while with 15,000 combatants—Cretans, mercenaries, Helots and poorer Spartiates—he stood at bay in Sparta, where terrorism secured his safety. War was chiefly at sea. While the allied army after failing both to surprise Argos, where the hoped-for risings were abortive, and to lure Nabis out of Sparta, simply laid waste Laconia, L. Quinctius reduced the maritime towns. Gytheum, the tyrant's arsenal and basis of his naval power, was attacked by the Romans, Rhodians and Eumenes, and surrendered last of all after a gallant resistance. Hereupon, although Pythagoras had come with 3000 men to reinforce him, Nabis lost his nerve and approached Flamininus. Deaf to the advances of Aristaenus, who would have promised him anything had he followed the example of Lydiades and Aristomachus and abdicated in favour of Achaea, he offered to the proconsul to abandon Argos—that is, he asked for terms. Consent would mean an implicit undertaking to leave Sparta to him, and there was a sharp controversy between the Greek leaders and Flamininus, the former determined to ruin, the latter to spare Nabis. At last Flamininus got his way and proceeded as with Philip: the war had been in common, but the peace must be Roman: he alone settled the terms. Nabis considered them too hard, and the mob that followed his fortunes, above all his bandit mercenaries, furiously rejected them. The war began anew. Resolved not to lay regular siege to Sparta,

Flamininus attempted to storm it. The combined army, increased by the disembarked crews, numbered 50,000; a general assault was made, and Sparta would have fallen had not Pythagoras started fires which drove out the assailants. Daunted at last, Nabis accepted the terms, and at the same time, about August, Argos expelled its Lacedaemonian garrison.

Flamininus dictated the treaty, in which the Romans alone were recognized as victors. Nabis surrendered to them Argos, Argolis, and the places he held in Crete, gave up the Laconian coast towns, ceded his fleet to these cities, renounced the right to make any alliance especially in Crete, to wage war, to build any fortress; he was to pay the Romans 500 talents, 100 at once, the rest in eight annual instalments, and to send to Flamininus five chosen hostages, including his son Armenas. The war thus finished, Flamininus came to Argos to preside at the Nemean festival (c. September), where the scene at Corinth was repeated in miniature, the herald proclaiming that Rome granted freedom to Argos. The town was returned to the Achaeans and immediately entered their League. As for the Laconian coastal cities, Flamininus ingeniously arranged that they should be entrusted to the Achaean League without becoming members of it.

The Senate ratified the peace in the following winter. Nabis' fate was thus settled by the sovereign will of the Romans, who assumed the rôle of protecting the Greeks from him. Shut off from the sea, and almost encircled by the Achaeans, he seemed powerless for the future. But his revolutionary despotism, his anti-social reforms, survived intact and even received a kind of sanction from the Roman treaty; his victims obtained no redress; the banished, including Agesipolis, remained in exile. The Aetolians loudly proclaimed that the Romans were behaving as the tyrant's satellites.

As the war against Nabis was drawing to a close, a momentous event turned Rome's attention once more to Antiochus. Hannibal, Sufete in 196, had by his rigorous financial administration made many enemies in Carthage who accused him to Rome of intriguing with Antiochus against her. When three Roman Commissioners arrived, Hannibal felt himself in danger; he slipped away by night, embarked for Syria, reached Tyre and then Antioch (c. July–August 195). Antiochus had left in the spring for Ephesus and Thrace; Hannibal awaited him at Ephesus where the king, on his return, welcomed him. There is no hint of any previous understanding between them; Hannibal in seeking his only possible refuge from Roman vengeance, and Antiochus in har-

bouring him, were each doing only what was natural. But once
he became the host of the terrible Carthaginian, Antiochus was
bound to be both more formidable and more suspected. Advised,
perhaps directed, by Hannibal, what might he not do? How
would a war go if Hannibal, as the Great King's general, turned
the resources of Asia against Rome? Scipio Africanus, recalled
to the consulate, is said to have voiced the common anxiety by
asking that, as a precaution, Greece should remain one of the
consular provinces. But to continue to occupy Greece, now completely pacified by Nabis' submission, would put the Aetolians in
the right when they declared that the Romans, in spite of their
promises, would never withdraw. Also it would bitterly disappoint
the Greeks in general and raise their anger, anger which would
clearly profit Antiochus. True to his policy of trust, Flamininus
wished Rome to keep faith and deserve the confidence of the
Greeks, the best way he judged to have them on the Roman side
against the Great King. Perhaps, besides, when he saw Rome so
careful of Greek liberty, Antiochus would realize how dangerous
it was for him to assail it. The Senate followed Flamininus' advice
and decreed the recall of the army.

Flamininus passed a fourth winter in Elatea (195–4), establishing order in the countries abandoned by Philip. It was
probably at this time that he gave back to various communities,
e.g. to the Chyretians, the properties confiscated by the Romans;
to the last he wished to show his goodwill towards the Greeks.
In the spring he had the joy of presiding over a second panhellenic congress at Corinth; he bade a pathetic farewell to the
Greeks, announced the coming departure of his troops and the
freeing of the great fortresses within ten days: they would see
who spoke the truth, Aetolians or Romans. These undertakings
were punctually fulfilled. Acrocorinth was immediately evacuated
and handed over to Achaea. Having returned to Elatea, Flamininus sent off the army to embark at Oricus, then, going on to
Euboea, he withdrew the garrisons from Chalcis, Eretria and
Oreus, and presided over the Euboeans, whose League he had
reconstituted. Last came the turn of Demetrias, which was
evacuated. After this he stayed awhile in Thessaly and gave a
constitution to the Thessalian towns. Finally, in the late summer
of 194, he set sail from Oricus to Brundisium, leaving behind him
not a single Roman.

Greece was full of his renown, and his munificence was
perpetuated by his splendid offerings to her gods. Statues of
him rose everywhere, staters of gold were struck with his

image[1], the people of Gytheum and doubtless of other cities worshipped him as their preserver. He had received from Greek cities 114 crowns of gold, and he took back to Italy a more precious gift, some two thousand Romans and Italians, sold into slavery by Hannibal, who, at his request, had been bought back to freedom at the public charge. Laden with these signs of gratitude and flown with pride, he could not doubt that his achievement in Greece was solid and lasting, but in truth it was neither.

XI. THE ROMAN PROTECTORATE IN GREECE

One cloud on the horizon of Roman policy was the hostility of the Aetolians. To speak truth, this was inevitable. Flamininus' conduct towards them had been overbearing and plainly less than loyal, and, perhaps unwisely, he had persisted in denying to them a few towns which would not have greatly increased their power: this was the immediate occasion of their hostility; but its underlying cause was that, on the defeat of Macedon, they had for the second time reckoned on assuming, with Roman help, her place in Greece. Deceived of their hope, their quarrel with Rome was foreordained, and the Republic was bound to reckon with it. But the violence of their propaganda, the efforts which they would certainly make to win Antiochus to advance their interests, and their warlike spirit, made them dangerous as well as hostile.

To hold them in check Flamininus and the Senate counted on the fidelity of the Greeks who had been delivered from the burdensome hegemony or the tyrannical rule of the King of Macedon. Not wholly without justice, for, however interested their motives, the action of the Romans in not keeping a foothold in Greece, in not leaving there a single soldier or agent, had displayed an unexampled generosity, unknown to the many self-styled 'liberators of Hellas' who had preceded them. They might legitimately hope that the Greeks would not forget, but, in their delight at regaining their freedom and their solicitude to preserve it, would be bound by gratitude and self-interest to the state that declared itself the champion of the liberty which it had restored to them. But the sentiments of the Greeks went beyond this simple formula.

First of all, they found in the Romans one blot which not all the efforts of Flamininus could efface: they were barbarians, the first whose continued presence Greece had endured since the Persian wars. And everything about these barbarians wounded Hellenic pride. Their victory was in fact as much over Hellenism as over

[1] See Volume of Plates iii, 10, b.

Macedon; their crushing strength set in relief the weakness of the
Greek peoples; their parade of magnanimity was a constant humiliation, and, finally, they never—not even Flamininus—ceased
to repeat that, without their help, Greece would have remained
enslaved. Moreover, their boasted benefits were dearly bought.
They declared that they had come to Greece only to bring it freedom, and they had in fact brought also, and for the second time,
war of the brutal Roman sort. Oreus, in 199 as in 208, had seen
its people enslaved; the 'liberator' Flamininus had spread cruel
havoc throughout Thessaly, Phocis, Euboea, Acarnania and,
later, Laconia; besides, three years of occupation with its train of
requisitions and exactions, and the great mobilization against
Nabis, had produced widespread exhaustion. Flamininus had, it
is true, restored their property to the Chyretians, but he had
freighted his ships deep not only with heaps of coin but also with
works of art carried off from many cities which, like Andros and
Eretria, had obeyed Philip against their will. The price of Greek
'freedom' was that Greece lay bruised, ruined and despoiled.

But was Greece free?—that was the question. The Aetolians,
and not they alone, denied it. The Romans had gone, but their
'protectorate,' as we may call it, remained. We must, then,
consider what this meant to Greece.

Of the old allies of Philip, the 'free' or so-called 'free' allies—
the Achaeans, Epirotes, Boeotians, Acarnanians (these last,
although conquered, Rome treated with especial benevolence)—
were theoretically entirely free, but they were bound to Rome by
alliances[1] which, of necessity, fettered their foreign policy. As for
the 'subject-allies' of Philip, Rome, as we have seen, counted
them her *praemia belli*, and retained over them, even after the
declaration at the Isthmus, indefeasible rights. In virtue of these,
Flamininus and the Ten had disposed of them as they saw fit,
assigning some to third parties, making others self-governing
states which naturally remained under Roman control. These
states Flamininus had afterwards organized, reviving or creating
the Leagues of Thessaly, Euboea, Magnesia and Perrhaebia, and
even settling the governments of the Thessalian cities. On the
other hand, after Nabis was crushed, he had dismembered the
state of Sparta. It went without saying that all these territorial
and political arrangements might neither be challenged nor
changed—what Rome had set up, Rome alone could modify.
This meant that the main lines of the map of Greece were thence-

---

[1] It is not, however, certain that a formal treaty of alliance had been
concluded between the Boeotians and Rome, cf. Livy XLII, 12, 5.

forward fixed, and that, consequently, lasting peace should reign, as indeed already followed from the principle that all the Greeks were to be 'free and autonomous.' So far from cherishing a 'machiavellian' desire (as many have unwisely declared) to perpetuate Greek disputes, Flamininus and the Senate, who well understood what chances these disputes gave to Antiochus and the Aetolians, would have wished to end them by creating an immutable order of things.

Thus the 'liberated' Greece of 194 was a Greece in which most of the states, in varying degrees, were dependent upon Rome, which the authority of Rome had reconstituted, ordered and pacified, and which remained in the shadow of that authority. Its liberty was certainly of a special stamp.

None the less, the Aetolians had small right to assert that the Greeks 'now bore on their necks the chains in which Philip had shackled their feet,' for there was no sign that Rome wished to turn its authority into oppression. Every act of Flamininus argued the opposite. He had abstained from interference in the domestic affairs of the Roman allies: for instance, the party of Brachyllas remained dominant in Boeotia. If he did use his right as conqueror to reorganize radically the old dependencies of Macedon, he did no more than must be done. The brutal rule of Philip's agents had reduced these countries, especially Thessaly, to chaos; he had to restore order and, at the eleventh hour—a fact which suggests that this was not his first intention—to 'give laws to the Thessalians.' The territorial adjustments over which he presided do not deserve the reproach of being arbitrary and 'machiavellian.' Historical precedents justified the restoration of Phocis and Locris to Aetolia, and the future was to show how wise Flamininus was in curbing the Achaean greed to annex Sparta. He has been credited with the perfidious purpose of fostering Greek disunion, because he did not create a greater Thessaly, but left on the Thessalian border three 'perioecic' districts—Magnesia, Perrhaebia, and Dolopia. But these regions had never been integral parts of Thessaly and had long been separated from it. Moreover, he gave proof that his guiding principle was not *divide ut imperes*: he attached Phthiotic Achaea to Thessaly, authorized, seemingly, the adhesion of Dolopia to Aetolia, and, far from imposing isolation upon the several cities in the newly constituted states, he restored or founded among the Thessalians, Euboeans, Magnesians and Perrhaebians federal institutions, which at that time were what the Greeks preferred. His constant care was indeed to leave behind him a contented Greece; in that his own glory and the interests of Rome found their reward. Once satisfied, the Greeks would, he thought, remain quiet, loyal to the Republic, impervious to the intrigues of Rome's enemies. Rome asked no more; she was ready to leave them to live their lives undisturbed, without hampering them by her interference or making them feel the weight of her tutelage.

Unfortunately there were many Greeks who already found it too burdensome. The fact that Rome arrogated to herself the sole right of regulating the destiny of Greece, and also the manner in which she exercised the right aroused resentment. The general peace set up to be permanent in Greece—a peace imposed by a foreigner and only too reminiscent of the 'King's Peace[1]'— was doubtless a blessing: but its denial of all change in the future cut across the hopes of expansion cherished by ambitious States. The alliances between Rome and the old 'free allies' of Philip were in theory concluded as between equals, but the reality refuted this fiction. The Achaeans, for instance, had had to pledge themselves to call a special meeting of their federal assembly whenever the Senate sent a message to them. No one could fail to see the painful truth, that Rome was the predominant partner, and vastly predominant. The subject-allies of Philip which became new states were on no treaty footing with her, and felt themselves in the hollow of her hand. Their freedom was a gift, which depended on Rome's good pleasure: this meant both humiliation and insecurity, for Rome's good pleasure might change. The recent territorial readjustments provoked, as they were bound to do, recriminations: those who had benefited by them were, of course, far from satisfied: of the Aetolians we need not speak; nothing could console the Achaeans for having made no gains in Laconia. The peoples assigned without their consent to this state or that could hardly be pleased with their cavalier treatment. It is likely enough that many among the Locrians and Phocians protested against their forced inclusion in Aetolia, which, moreover, seemed to contradict the declaration of Corinth: for, once incorporated in the Aetolian League, their autonomy was endangered. Flamininus' political innovations in Thessaly raised a like objection: the 'laws' imposed by his decrees, though possibly admirable, were not the 'ancestral laws' of the Thessalians. Finally, in striking contradiction to her professed policy, Rome had not denied Amynander and Eumenes their reward. The former kept his Thessalian conquests; Eumenes had not been spoilt—unjustly enough he had been refused Oreus and Eretria: however, he retained Andros and

[1] See vol. VI, p. 54 *sq.*

naturally, despite the anger of the Aeginetans and Achaeans, succeeded to the possession of Aegina. Thus Rome, which excluded Philip from Greece, lent her authority to the subjection of Greeks to two other monarchs simply because they were her friends.

Set to the ungrateful task of satisfying opposing interests and of reconciling Greek liberty with Roman supremacy—*res dissociabiles*—Flamininus and the Senate, despite their honest efforts, had everywhere sown ill-feeling against the Republic.

There was, none the less, one class of people that might, at first sight, pass for Roman sympathizers, and on whom indeed Flamininus did rely, the *optimates*, the well-to-do, whose position entitled them to be the governing class, men who hated revolutionary socialism and royal despotism alike and whose hostility Philip had brought upon himself[1]. As we have seen, many of them had joined Rome against him, and Flamininus, who saw in them the natural champions of order, had done his best to secure their preponderant influence. For example, the institutions granted by him to the Thessalian cities were timocratic, and gave them control of the 'senates' and the courts of justice. But, despite their debt to Rome, these 'conservatives,' for the most part, were in no way devoted to her, and it is an exaggeration to call them the 'Roman party.' Indeed, apart from a handful of men, who from base personal motives courted the Romans, there did not exist then in Greece any such thing as a 'Roman party.' Necessity and politic calculation had ranged the *optimates* with Rome in their hatred of Philip, but they viewed their association with her as at best a necessary evil. Dreaming of the unattainable, they would have wished to enjoy the benefits of Roman support without sacrificing anything of their independence, their republican pride, their patriotic ambition; they had loathed the rule of Macedon, they submitted with reluctance to the ascendancy of Rome. The Republic was soon to realize, in the course of long-drawn debate with the Achaeans, the cross-grained temper of the Greek notables. In 194 B.C. they bore Flamininus a bitter grudge for having settled the Spartan question without them and having spared Nabis; and Flamininus himself, realizing their irritation, had felt bound to defend himself before them, on the eve of his departure. He had, however, no need to fear that they would lean to Antiochus; but with the masses, whose real feelings he had not divined, it was far different.

Steeped in Roman ideas, Flamininus and the Senate convinced

---

[1] There were, however, among them exceptions, clients, protégés, and partisans of Macedon, *e.g.* Brachyllas in Boeotia, and, in Achaea, Cycliadas.

themselves that all Greeks cherished a deep-rooted hatred of kings, so that, when they ceased to obey Philip, their cup of blessings was full. This was a grave mistake. Reduced to misery, the multitudes in the Greek cities cared for nothing save the relief of the misery—their problem was social far more than political. They had no horror of kings, among whom they had found benefactors like Cleomenes or Nabis; and Philip had shown himself indulgent to them. The domination that they did abominate was that of their creditors, the rich, and deliverance from these was all that mattered. Rome had done nothing to bring them this deliverance; she had rather done the opposite. The poor never saw Flamininus show any interest in their evil case; what they saw was his alliance with the hated capitalists, in concert with whom, and in order to secure whose power, he had crippled Nabis, the avenging champion of the have-nots. Accordingly, they saw with loathing the victory of Rome, which, so far from bringing them benefits, made strong their oppressors, and they turned their eyes to Antiochus. That distant and somewhat fabulous monarch was credited with boundless wealth and regal generosity, and that was enough to fire the popular imagination. In the cities of Asia debtors counted on Antiochus cancelling debts; the masses in Greece, who desired 'the overthrow of the existing order' and saw clearly that no beneficent change would come out of Rome, set their hopes on him. *Multitudo avida novandi res tota Antiochi erat*, writes Livy, translating Polybius.

Flamininus had reckoned that 'liberated' Greece would hasten to close her borders and her heart against the King of Syria if he sought to enter, but the proletariate in Greece understood their interests in a way which he did not. They rejected this 'freedom' which he had created, which meant, to all seeming, merely that the rich were to be free to tread down the poor, and they were ready, hardly delivered from one monarch, to throw themselves into the arms of another.

CHAPTER VII

ROME AND ANTIOCHUS

I. THE BREACH BETWEEN ANTIOCHUS AND ROME

SINCE the early summer of 195 all relations between Syria and Rome had ceased. Antiochus had turned his thoughts elsewhere, and, without provoking Rome in any way, had strengthened his position on all sides. With Egypt he had concluded (? early in 195) the triumphal peace, announced at Lysimacheia, which was further to be cemented in the winter of 194 to 193 B.C. by the marriage to Ptolemy V of the princess Cleopatra; perhaps as a concession to his son-in-law, Antiochus gave as dowry to Cleopatra the revenues of Coele-Syria[1]; in any event, he retained the sovereignty of the country, and hoped, through his daughter, to bring Egypt under Seleucid influence. In Asia, where he was already allied with Ariarathes IV of Cappadocia, husband of his daughter Antiochis, arrangements made with the Galatian kings enabled him to raise mercenaries in their dominions. He had returned to Thrace in 194 and, besides restoring Lysimacheia, had pushed his annexations westward by occupying the former Egyptian possessions of Aenus and Maronea, won over the Greeks, especially of Byzantium, by protecting them against the barbarians, and made advantageous arrangements with the neighbouring Gauls. Finally, Hannibal was at his court.

Amid so many successes, one source of irritation remained. Lampsacus and Smyrna, the two towns which had asked Roman protection, still refused allegiance to him; they were incited to this by Eumenes, who, openly hostile, had repelled his advances, refused the hand of one of his daughters and was obviously seeking to revive the quarrel dormant since Lysimacheia. Antiochus wished to end both this quarrel and the resistance of the rebellious cities, and to this end he decided to take action at Rome. This might well seem a risky proceeding, but for two years the Romans had made no move; from this he concluded that they lacked courage or energy to maintain their opposition, and would settle

---

[1] On this very controversial question see the works cited in the Bibliography. The present writer is unable to accept the arrangement recently proposed by E. Cuq in *Syria*, VIII, 1927, pp. 143 *sqq.*

old differences to his satisfaction. But it would have been far better to have left matters alone.

In the winter of 194 to 193, resuming the negotiations which had miscarried in 195 (see above, pp. 188 *sq.*), Antiochus again proposed to the Senate a treaty of friendship, implying naturally— his ambassadors, Menippus and Hegesianax, insisted upon this— recognition of his unrestricted sovereignty over Asia and Thrace. But he had not taken into account the suspicious and stubborn temper of the *patres*. They had reluctantly, for the time being, endured his presence in Thrace because war with him and Hannibal seemed hazardous, and Rome had her hands full in Spain and Cisalpine Gaul (pp. 312, 327); but they were by no means resigned to this, and persisted in fearing Antiochus as the probable enemy whom they must drive from Europe; moreover, their pride would not let him have the last word. Regarding his overtures as a challenge, they hastened to re-open the old quarrel. Less imperious than at Lysimacheia they did, indeed, lay before the Syrian envoys two alternatives: as a preliminary to the treaty they called upon Antiochus to renounce not Thrace *and* the autonomous cities of Asia, but one *or* the other—this, however, was an unreal choice, for the first alternative, the abandonment of Thrace, was their only concern. But, even in this reduced form, their demands were still intolerable. Considering his rights in Thrace and Asia as equally beyond question, why should Antiochus give up one in order to secure the other, or indeed sacrifice either to please the Romans? They made it clear themselves that their interference in favour of the Asiatic towns was a mere diplomatic manœuvre. Flamininus, president of the senatorial commission charged to treat with the Syrian envoys, is said to have told the delegates from these towns, then in Rome, that the Roman people would uphold their claims to the end 'unless Antiochus withdraw from Europe[1].' This ingenuous confession showed that all their zeal for the Greeks of Asia was no more than a means of forcing the hand of Antiochus, and after justifiable protests his representatives could only retire.

In leaving they asked the Senate to do nothing hastily, thus showing the peaceful intentions of their master. Nor were the *patres* themselves inclined to hasty action; uneasy at the thought of an armed conflict with the Great King and wishing to avert it by diplomatic pressure, they also desired further information about affairs in Asia. Three *legati*, P. Sulpicius at their head,

---

[1] Livy xxxiv, 59, 4–5; Diodorus xxviii, 15, 4 (both following Polybius).

proceeded thither to continue the negotiations[1]. Delayed by a visit to Pergamum, where Eumenes preached against conciliation, and by the absence of Antiochus, who was campaigning against the Pisidians, interrupted by the unexpected death of his eldest son and co-regent, transferred from Apamea to Ephesus, these negotiations dragged on and, as both parties refused to abandon their positions, remained fruitless. The season for discussions was ended. The *legati* left Asia, though without delivering an ultimatum—it was a definite breach, but so far it was no more (late summer 193)[2]. But it was attended by circumstances particularly irritating for Antiochus. The conferences at Ephesus had culminated in a disgraceful incident—a repetition of the incident at Lysimacheia (p. 187); delegates from the autonomous cities, introduced by the Romans and prompted by Eumenes, had spoken in violent terms. This was going too far. Could Antiochus bear any longer to see his rebellious subjects encouraged in their boldness? When could he again be master in his own house?

To accomplish this one way remained which was in the minds of all—war. His councillors urged him to it, but he himself hung back. War with Rome had never been part of his plans; apart from its uncertainty, it would seriously upset them. He was now fifty, his ambitions were satisfied, his great task of restoration had reached fulfilment, and he now sought to devote the remainder of his reign to the strengthening of his authority in the west of his dominions. Troubles which had broken out in Lydia and Phrygia during his expedition to the Upper Satrapies and the constant insurrections of the Pisidian tribes showed that the need was urgent; a great war would distract him from this, and, if it were prolonged or if the issue seemed doubtful, might have dangerous repercussions in his vast empire.

At all events, Antiochus put aside entirely the idea of carrying the war into the enemy's country, as Hannibal is said to have urged. Let the king place at his disposal 10,000 foot, 1000 cavalry,

---

[1] On the much disputed question of Scipio Africanus' presence in this embassy see the works cited in the Bibliography. Whatever view is adopted, the supposed interview of Scipio and Hannibal at Ephesus is to be regarded as a legend.

[2] For the chronology, which does not admit of doubt, see finally O. Leuze, *Hermes*, LVIII, 1923, pp. 242 *sq.*, 246 *sq.* The younger Antiochus is still mentioned as co-regent in a contract at Erech (Warka) dated January 192 (O. Schroeder, *Kontrakte der Seleukidenzeit aus Warka*, p. 42, no. 32; cf. E. Cavaignac, *Rev. d'Assyriologie*, XIX, 1922, p. 161), but this mention is certainly anachronistic. He died in the summer of 193, probably not earlier than August.

and 100 warships (*i.e.* the entire Syrian fleet); with these he would make for Carthage, raise it against Rome, then land in Southern Italy. To raise Carthage might have been advisable; the plan, so far, appears to have received Antiochus' consent; and he probably countenanced the fruitless attempt of the Tyrian Ariston, Hannibal's emissary, to foment a revolution there in 193. But he could not well have approved the fantastic scheme of invasion attributed to his guest. Even commanded by Hannibal, a body of 11,000 men landing in Italy would have been foredoomed, and Antiochus would not have risked his fleet in such a venture. Indeed it is doubtful if Hannibal entertained the strange project imputed to him; but if, as is quite possible, he incited Antiochus to fight the Romans in Italy, the king, despite what has been often asserted, had excellent reasons for refusing to listen. Tradition ascribes to Antiochus feelings of jealousy and distrust towards Hannibal which were sedulously fomented by his courtiers; these seem improbable or at least greatly exaggerated; but the truth is that the aims of the two men were irreconcilable.

An invasion of Italy, carried out so far from his Asiatic base, would not only have entailed enormous difficulties, but Antiochus judged it useless. Not having, like Hannibal, a passionate hatred of Rome he did not contemplate her ruin but merely wished to force her to cease thwarting him. To achieve this there was no need to go to Italy, for he had near at hand a hold upon the Romans. Hitherto he had done nothing to hinder their control of Greece, now he might well harass them. The irritation of the Aetolians, the discontent caused by the Roman protectorate, the desire shared by so many Greeks for deliverance from their 'deliverers,' lastly his own popularity in Greece were all known to him. As things were, he might oppose Rome in Europe as she sought to oppose him in Asia; she interfered in his quarrel with the autonomous cities, he might interfere in hers with the Aetolians and, playing her game, offer himself to Aetolia as the champion of her interests, to all Greece as the restorer of her freedom. By destroying the Romans' authority there he would inflict on them a crushing political defeat. Should they, in reply, attack him, strong as he would be in Greece, with the resources of Asia at his back, and with the support of the Aetolians and the general adhesion of the Greeks, he could presumably maintain the struggle with success. And—as he secretly hoped—these considerations, rightly weighed, might dissuade the Romans from forcing matters to extremes; threatened with the loss of Greece they would yield and let him rule undisturbed over Thrace and Asia.

Such were, we may assume, Antiochus' thoughts after the ambassadors' departure. Indeed he cherished no warlike feelings against Rome; the enterprise he was contemplating would have chiefly the character of a political offensive, seconded, however, by a powerful military demonstration—a species of armed mediation. It would rest with the Romans whether war resulted from it. He had no thirst for victories, still less for conquests; but since Rome imposed conditions upon him he must be ready to impose them in his turn upon her. Greece was a surety which he would do well to secure in order to make them renounce their insulting demands.

At the moment when a rightful care for his dignity and independence was thus leading Antiochus to intervene in Aetolian and Greek affairs, the Aetolian government was looking to him for revenge.

II. THE AETOLIAN MOVEMENT

Flamininus had left the Aetolians all indignant with Rome, all burning to claim their disregarded rights. Their leaders, however, were divided: some, such as Phaeneas, who had seen too much of the Romans in the field to envisage their defeat, were for diplomatic methods; others, such as Thoas of Trichonium, Damocritus, and Nicander, were for war. The masses were on the side of the latter, so Thoas became General (end of September 194). The destruction by force of what Rome had achieved in Greece and the substitution of Aetolian supremacy was his party's programme; to secure the first, Thoas and his friends counted upon Antiochus' all-powerful aid. They exulted over the failure of the conferences in Asia, and pictured the Great King now ready to fly to arms; possibly, too, Philip and Nabis might be brought to the same mind. The League sent delegates to the three kings, hoping to combine them against Rome; but its diplomacy met with some disappointments (late summer 193). Dicaearchus, Thoas' brother, sent to Asia to offer Antiochus the military aid of Aetolia and her full support if he came to Greece, was certainly well received, but Antiochus was not the man for hasty resolutions and he needed time for reflection; Philip remained unmoved by the persuasions of Nicander: co-operation with Antiochus and Aetolia did not tempt him, especially as he was left in ignorance how his help would be rewarded. On the other hand, prompted by Damocritus, Nabis was quickly persuaded to break his treaty with Rome—too quickly: he would have been wiser to wait till Antiochus moved.

But he resented keenly the loss of his seaports, the riches of

his kingdom, which Flamininus had placed in the keeping of the
Achaeans (p. 191); urged by the Aetolians, he stirred up rebellions
in them and so regained all except Gytheum, into which an
Achaean garrison was thrown. This town he besieged. The
Achaeans denounced him to Rome and prepared to fight; they
had in Philopoemen, now returned from Crete and elected General
(end of September 193), the very man for the occasion. Rome was
roused: one short year after the departure of the legions Roman
authority in Greece was seriously challenged, and the evil, spread
by the Aetolians, might extend farther, to Antiochus' great
advantage. Military measures were decreed; the praetor A. Atilius
Serranus was to operate against Nabis in the spring of 192 with
25 quinqueremes; two legions were to be assembled in Bruttium
ready for emergencies. But, in order to limit the conflagration in
the Peloponnese, counter the manœuvres of the Aetolians,
and forearm the Greeks against the prestige of Antiochus, Flamininus thought that his presence and his words would count for
more than all else; he proceeded to Greece with three other *legati*
(winter 193–2). Eumenes soon joined them[1]; zealous through
self-interest, he put at their disposal some ships, some men, but
above all himself and his influence.

Flamininus, fearing the encroaching temper of the Achaeans,
would have liked to suppress Nabis with as little help as possible
from them, and accordingly to have deferred battle until Atilius'
arrival: but hostilities were opened by Philopoemen, eager to
relieve Gytheum and its Achaean garrison, and wishing *fare da se*
and enlarge Achaea at the expense of Sparta. Ignominiously
defeated at sea by the flotilla which the tyrant had re-formed, he
retrieved his fortunes on land; though he failed to save Gytheum,
he defeated Nabis at Mt Barbosthenes, almost destroyed his army,
blockaded him in Sparta and for long ravaged Laconia. Atilius,
probably aided by Eumenes, then re-took Gytheum and the other
coast towns[2]; whereupon Flamininus, unwilling to see his work
undone, imposed upon Nabis and Achaea a truce and re-established the *status quo* in the Peloponnese. Aetolians and Achaeans
were equally disappointed: the former because the tyrant's insurrection had failed, the latter because they gained nothing by
his defeat (spring 192).

[1] *Ditt.*³ 605 A attests the participation of Eumenes in the second Roman
war with Nabis but the history of it remains obscure. See the Bibliography.

[2] The time of Atilius' arrival in Greece is in dispute, for the passage in
Livy xxxv, 37, 3 is variously interpreted, but it seems impossible to put it
as late as the summer, as some have proposed to do.

Meanwhile the Roman envoys had journeyed through Greece—except Aetolia and Boeotia where their efforts would have been useless—striving to impose calm, overawe the turbulent and ensure the preponderance of 'right-thinking' men, lovers of order and peace, hence anti-Aetolian, republicans and enemies of kings, and so hostile to Antiochus. They seemed successful on the whole: the fear of Rome went with them. They noted, nevertheless, disquieting signs: in Achaea, the effervescence of local patriotism, elated by Philopoemen's victories (which the populace ostentatiously set above those of Flamininus), irritated also at their unfruitfulness, and restive under foreign interference; in Athens, a dangerous demagogic agitation; at Chalcis, the existence of a powerful anti-Roman party, whose chiefs had to be exiled; everywhere smouldering hostility of the masses towards Rome, their desire for changes, social and political, their instinctive sympathy with Antiochus. At Demetrias, where his tour ended, Flamininus had some difficult moments; there, indeed, the situation was peculiarly delicate, for the anti-Macedonian *optimates* in power since 196 and led by Eurylochus[1], 'General' of the Magnetes, considered themselves betrayed by the Romans. The latter, indeed, with the brusque and slightly cynical opportunism which characterized their policy, had now, from fear of Antiochus, turned to Philip and made much of him. A well-founded rumour declared that to ensure his fidelity the Senate, which had already promised to release his son Demetrius, who was a hostage, and to remit the unpaid instalments of his war-indemnity, was disposed also to make in his favour some sacrifice of Hellenic liberty, and to restore to him Demetrias. Incensed at the idea of falling again under the Macedonian yoke, Eurylochus and his party leaned towards the Aetolians. Flamininus reproached them with this, but did not contradict the rumour which alarmed them; Eurylochus replied hotly and, although disowned by other *principes* he had to flee and was declared an exile; he had dared to say openly that 'under a show of freedom, all things happened at Rome's will and pleasure.' Flamininus had seen that in Greece many thought thus.

Still the envoys' activity made the Aetolian leaders uneasy. Thoas, who had visited Antiochus in the winter (193–2), urged him not to leave the Romans a free field in Greece nor allow their authority there to be strengthened. The king thought it was time to act. Until then he had held back and sent no official deputation

[1] Possibly to be identified with Eurylochus of Magnesia who commanded the *agema* in Egypt under Philopator (Polybius v, 63, 12; 65, 2).

to Aetolia; he now commissioned Menippus, formerly ambassador
to Rome, to return with Thoas and announce his intentions. In
private interviews Menippus led the Aetolians to expect Antiochus' speedy arrival, insisting on his formidable military power
and, to stir up popular feeling, on his inexhaustible riches; then,
at the spring Assembly (end of March 192), he declared that
Antiochus was willing to join the Aetolians in restoring true
Greek freedom, 'standing by its own strength, independent of the
caprice of others.' This evoked widespread enthusiasm; despite
the Athenian delegates, come at Flamininus' request, who adjured
the Aetolians to reflect; despite Flamininus himself who, admitted
under protest into the assembly with his colleagues, preached
prudence, Thoas caused to be passed, in the presence of the
legati, a decree in terms of which Antiochus had undoubtedly
approved. In it the Aetolians invited him to deliver Greece and
settle the quarrel between themselves and the Romans; the General
Damocritus added, it is said, insults to Flamininus and to Rome.

Antiochus' position was thus made perfectly clear; turning
against the Romans their own weapon, he was now pursuing, like
them, a Hellenic policy. To bring pressure upon him, they upheld
the cause of the Hellenes of Asia; to bring pressure upon them,
he was taking up the cause of the Hellenes of Europe, especially
the Aetolians, letting it be understood that, at need, he would
defend it by arms. But with his usual prudence he had avoided in
Menippus' declaration and in the Aetolian decree the actual word
'war'; he would only make war if forced by the Romans. Moreover, although bound to the Aetolians, he showed no haste to
join them and was even guilty of neglecting to prepare for his
expedition. He spent the summer of 192 in Thrace, probably
unwilling to leave his kingdom before the fall of the rebellious
towns which were being besieged, Smyrna and Lampsacus, to
which was now added Alexandria Troas; possibly, too, he had
only wished to warn the Romans, in the hope that his new attitude
would make them more conciliatory. But if he reckoned so, he
was mistaken. His new attitude seemed to justify all their fears:
it seemed to them to herald the aggression which they had long
expected, and to threaten Italy by way of Greece. Attalus,
Eumenes' brother, came to Rome and alarmed them still further.
A rumour was current that Antiochus, on his arrival in Aetolia,
would immediately attack Sicily and the neighbouring coasts of
Italy; so defence and counter-offensive were energetically prepared,
70 quinqueremes were equipped or built, 20 protected Sicily, on
whose eastern seaboard troops were stationed, while 50 formed

a reserve; the army in Bruttium was sent to Tarentum and Brundisium, ready to embark. Meanwhile a new army of about 30,000 men was concentrated in Bruttium, and considerable reserves were set on foot. Antiochus might now be convinced that the Senate was in no mood for negotiation; consequently, he owed it to himself to advance into Greece.

The Aetolians awaited him all the more impatiently as their decree exposed them to the Roman anger; to hasten his coming the *apokletoi*[1] resolved upon three great strokes. Diocles, the Hipparch, Thoas, and Alexamenus, the contriver of the murder of Brachyllas (p. 182), received secret instructions to surprise Demetrias, Chalcis, and Sparta; in Sparta Alexamenus was to remove Nabis, an ineffective ally, whose treasure would be invaluable to the Aetolians. Success was only partial. Thoas failed completely at Chalcis, which the new magistrates set up by Flamininus had put into a state of defence with the help of the Eretrians and Carystians. At Sparta Alexamenus brought up some troops as if to succour Nabis and was thus able by base treachery to compass his assassination, and become for a moment master of the town; but he and his men were soon massacred by the people, who were furious at their pillaging. Profiting by the ensuing disorder, Philopoemen then occupied Sparta and incorporated it by treaty into the Achaean League; Flamininus closed his eyes to this, and so the Aetolian attempt turned to the advantage of their enemies. At Demetrias, all went well. Diocles brought back Eurylochus, then ensured his triumph by introducing into the town Aetolian cavalry who killed his chief opponents. In vain the Roman *legatus* Villius made a last attempt to conciliate the Magnetes: thus the principal fortress and port of Northern Greece was brought under Aetolian control, and they offered to Antiochus this splendid base of operations.

Thoas hastened to inform him of this; but taken unawares, Antiochus hesitated to move. Various reasons held him back: the obstinate resistance of Smyrna, Lampsacus and Alexandria Troas —when he had gone the revolt might spread—, the late season, unfavourable for operations by sea, his inadequate preparations. But if he postponed his departure, Aetolian ardour might cool and the useful impression produced by events at Demetrias be effaced in Greece, where Flamininus would redouble his intrigues. His expeditionary army could join him as soon as winter was past; it was unlikely that the Romans would attack him before

[1] On the *apokletoi* as executive committee of the Aetolian League, see vol. VII, p. 209.

then; at all events, their absence at the moment (he did not count Atilius' insignificant squadron) made it possible for him to establish himself firmly in Greece. This decided him. He had planned, it appears, to send Hannibal to Carthage with a flying squadron; the necessity of collecting in haste all available troops and vessels caused him to postpone this diversion. He embarked 10,000 foot, 500 horse, 6 elephants in a fleet consisting of 40 'decked' ships, 60 'open,' 200 transports, and sailed from the Hellespont, Hannibal accompanying him. He landed unhindered at Pteleum in Phthiotic Achaea, whither the Magnesian magistrates came to welcome him, disembarked at Demetrias and encamped his army outside the walls. Then, at the invitation of the Aetolians, he went to them at Lamia (probably late October 192).

III. ANTIOCHUS IN GREECE

The 10,500 men brought by Antiochus were only an advance force; he expressly stated this to the Aetolians assembled at Lamia, and it was obvious. Nevertheless the contrast between this tiny army and what was expected from the Great King, made disappointment inevitable. In spite of the acclamations with which they greeted him, the Aetolians felt this disappointment keenly and little relished Antiochus' request that they should revictual his troops who were short of provisions. At Lamia, after his departure, the peace-lovers made their voices heard; Phaeneas, who had been re-elected General at the end of September, proposed, in accordance with the previous decree of the League, to employ Antiochus as arbitrator between Aetolia and Rome, without conferring upon him any command. Only Thoas' vehement intervention secured his appointment as *strategos autokrator* (the same honour which had formerly been conferred upon Attalus) with thirty *apokletoi* attached to his person. But the federal forces were not called up, the new generalissimo had a staff but no army, and he was to experience the stubborn ill-will of Phaeneas and most of the Aetolians who, in their hearts, had counted upon Antiochus fighting their battles. Nor did he receive the hoped-for welcome of the other Greek peoples. Thoas had promised that he should see their embassies flocking in—not one appeared: Antiochus, too, was disappointed.

Yet, although Greece kept silence, she was deeply moved: Antiochus' arrival 'made her waver,' says Plutarch. By bold action he might probably—at least for a time—have drawn her over to his side. The masses, whose hope he was, were heartily

with him; at his coming disturbances broke out spontaneously
in several towns. At Patrae, Aegium, Corinth, and Athens,
M. Porcius Cato, sent from Rome as *legatus*, had to interpose;
Flamininus had a troublesome agitator, Apollodorus, banished
from Athens. Now was the moment for Antiochus to distribute
to the 'have-nots' the expected largesse and give them a glimpse
of an end to their wretchedness; to emulate the Aetolians and strike
vigorous blows with his 10,000 men and his fleet, seizing some
strong points, notably the Piraeus and Athens; to arouse national
sentiment by proclaiming a crusade against Rome. Had he done
this, he might have unloosed an irresistible popular movement
which would have swept away the governments of the propertied
classes which leaned on Roman support. But he had no taste for
playing the demagogue; moreover, presenting himself to the
Greeks as a liberator, he was loth to apply force—he was utterly
unlike the Aetolians; lastly, at heart nearer to Phaeneas than to
Thoas, still desiring to settle matters peaceably, he wished to
intimidate Rome, not provoke her by an openly aggressive
attitude. As the Greeks did not come to him, he went to them,
not to threaten but to persuade, parleying, inviting them—comic
as it seems—to let themselves be 'freed' by him, protesting his
peaceful intentions, disclaiming even the wish to detach them
violently from Rome. Such moderation, construed as weakness,
inevitably injured him: his opponents, encouraged by the Roman
envoys, gained ground, his partisans lost faith in him; everywhere—in Euboea, Achaea, Boeotia—his efforts failed.

In Achaea, indeed, despite sporadic manifestations of popular
sympathy, he had small chance of success. It was true that
Flamininus' Peloponnesian policy, his repeated patience with
Sparta, his personal animosity to Philopoemen, whose military glory
and independent spirit were an offence to him, had embittered
the patriotic Achaeans. Antiochus counted on this, and, moreover,
only asked the Achaeans to remain neutral. But he was to them
the champion of Aetolia, hence their natural enemy: his victory,
assuring the triumph of their foes, would have been fatal to them;
on the other hand, his defeat, which must entail that of Aetolia,
and thereby of Elis and Messene, might bring great gains to
Achaea. Already masters of Sparta, the Achaeans would make
this an opportunity for dominating the whole Peloponnese—an
opportunity which the Romans would probably let them seize if
they served them faithfully: the hope of satisfying their age-long
ambition bound them to Rome. So Philopoemen and Flamininus
acted in accord; it was Flamininus whom the Achaeans com-

missioned to reply to the Aetolo-Syrian embassy; whereupon they unanimously voted war against Antiochus and Aetolia, and forthwith supplied Flamininus with 1000 soldiers, half of whom he sent to Chalcis and half to the Piraeus (November).

More mortifying because more unforeseen was the attitude of the Chalcidians and Boeotians. At Chalcis, the same magistrates who had previously repulsed Thoas refused Antiochus entrance to the town: 'Free, thanks to Rome, Chalcis had,' they said, 'no need of a liberator.' Boeotia, in spite of its deep-seated hatred of Rome, returned only a temporizing answer to a Syrian envoy: if Antiochus came to them the Boeotians would see what they would do. His campaign of negotiations brought him but a single ally, the unstable Amynander who, ever ready to change sides, forsook the Romans for the absurd reason that the Aetolians affected to encourage the ambitions of his brother-in-law, one Philip of Megalopolis, the self-styled descendant of Alexander and fantastic claimant to the Macedonian throne.

These repeated rebuffs compelled Antiochus to change his methods; he was destined like almost all 'liberators' of Greece, to have to force liberty upon her—liberty of a Seleucid pattern to replace liberty of a Roman pattern. He needed Chalcis as a port of disembarkation for the army from Asia, and Eumenes and the Achaeans, at Flamininus' command, were hurrying troops into it. From Demetrias Antiochus marched in strength against the town, which now capitulated, despite its rulers, who had to leave it. The Achaean and Pergamene soldiers defending the fort of Salganeus (on the left bank of the Euripus) surrendered. Shortly before, 500 Romans sent by Atilius had been surprised in the sacred precinct of Delium and, notwithstanding the sanctity of the place, all but annihilated by Menippus—an easy victory which the king probably regretted since, contrary to his policy, it made him the aggressor in the quarrel with Rome. Flamininus, then at Corinth, forthwith called gods and men to witness that the responsibility for the first bloodshed rested on Antiochus. The seizure of Chalcis produced immediate and valuable effects. All Euboea submitted; the Epirotes, too near the Romans to dare more, at least assured Antiochus of their goodwill; the Boeotians, whom he visited, confessed their real sentiments and enthusiastically declared for him. But his new friends supplied not a single soldier, while he had to lend the Eleans 1000 men to resist Achaea.

Thessaly did not move. Antiochus invaded it, seemingly against the advice of Hannibal who must have persisted in his plans for the invasion of Italy, but such plans could obviously not be attempted with the insufficient forces at the king's disposal. Having proceeded to Pherae, Antiochus was joined before it by Amynander and the Aetolians, the latter only 3000 strong and without their General. Reverting to his earlier methods, he made some advances to the Thessalians, which were rejected with contempt. The upper classes put into power by Flamininus, and still in touch with him[1], showed themselves resolute; they had suffered too much from Philip willingly to try another king. The federal authorities, resident at Larissa, invited Antiochus to withdraw his troops, and attempted to relieve Pherae which still held out. Antiochus had to reduce it by force, and this brought about the surrender or fall of Scotussa, Crannon, Cierium and Metropolis; but, ever generous, finding in Scotussa 500 Thessalian soldiers sent from Larissa to Pherae, he allowed them to depart unharmed. Meanwhile Amynander, greedy for new conquests beyond Pindus, was aggrandizing himself in Hestiaeotis, notably occupying Pelinna and Limnaeum; the Aetolians, under Menippus, were invading Perrhaebia, taking numerous towns, among others Malloea and Chyretiae, and ravaging Tripolis. After about a fortnight the south, west and north of Thessaly seemed subdued; there remained the eastern region with Larissa, the federal capital. Antiochus, with his allies, was preparing for the siege, after receiving the capitulation of Pharsalus, when the glow of many camp-fires augured the presence at Gonni of a Roman-Macedonian army. To besiege Larissa now seemed dangerous; besides, it was January (191) and the troops were weary, so operations were suspended. Antiochus had scattered garrisons through Thessaly—thereby weakening himself—but small, isolated, and formed of troops whose loyalty was none too sure, their power to hold out might well be doubted.

As the king soon learnt, the hostile force at Gonni was, not an army, but only a Roman detachment, sent through Macedonia to the succour of Larissa, the many camp-fires being the device of its commander Appius Claudius Pulcher. Its arrival, however, was significant both of the entrance of the Romans into the war, and of their understanding with Philip. Antiochus had hoped that Rome would hesitate to attack him, and that Philip would remain neutral—two illusions now lost.

Antiochus' landing in late autumn probably caused surprise at Rome; but, in any event, his crossing to Greece, the prologue, it was thought, of an attack upon Italy, was expected. Rome was on her guard. Nevertheless she did not hasten to dispatch large

---

[1] Livy xxxv, 39, 4.

forces to Greece. About early November the praetor M. Baebius
Tamphilus crossed to Illyria with only a few troops, chiefly to watch
Philip's conduct, which caused much uneasiness. He was soon
reassured; Philip warned him of Antiochus' entrance into Thessaly,
came to see him, and promised his aid; hence the free passage
granted to the Romans who had now arrived at Gonni.

Philip's decision vexes historians. They would gladly have seen
the Antigonid and the Seleucid make common cause against
Rome, as desired by Hannibal, but this desire was impossible of
realization. The interests of the Aetolians were directly opposed to
those of Philip, Antiochus was the ally of the Aetolians; how then
could he be Philip's ally or reward his services? Indeed he does
not seem to have thought of asking for them[1], thinking also that it
was impossible that Philip would join Rome. But everything that
Antiochus did exasperated Philip: he saw him ever profiting by
his misfortunes, formerly in Asia, Thrace and Egypt, now in
Greece. This rôle of protector of the Greeks, which Antiochus
dared to appropriate, belonged to the Macedonian monarchy; he
was once more usurping its right; even his claim to stand up to
the Romans irritated the king whom they had beaten. His allies,
Aetolians, Magnesians, Athamanians (not to speak of the ridiculous Megalopolitan adventurer), were all enemies of Philip. The
invasion of Thessaly, which he burned to recover, was the final
insult which decided him; we may add also Antiochus' unwitting
affront in directing Philip of Megalopolis to bury the bones of
Macedonians fallen at Cynoscephalae. The Romans, fearing his
intentions, promised him, with Demetrias, whatever towns he
should take from the common enemies[2]: self-interest would be
the guarantee of their sincerity. Thinking he had an unique
opportunity of retrieving his defeat, Philip decided for Rome, and
so—risking bitter disappointment for himself—dealt Antiochus
a fatal blow.

In the three months since his landing Antiochus had displayed
untiring activity. On his return from Thessaly he spent the
month of February (191) in Chalcis, now his headquarters, and
there married the daughter of a private citizen. This marriage,
which perhaps had a political object—he called his wife Euboea,
and we know how he favoured a matrimonial policy—and which
increased his popularity, would scarcely deserve mention, had it

[1] The supposed offers of Antiochus to Philip related in Livy xxxix,
28, 6 may be disregarded.
[2] On the difficulties caused later by the Roman promises to Philip, see
below, p. 247 *sq.*

not given rise to the foolish story which represents him as spending the winter in wedding festivities[1]. In March, taking the field again, he marched on Acarnania, the only state in Central Greece that had remained beyond his reach. It would have been wiser to watch Thessaly, but in Acarnania a powerful party was working for him, and this drew him thither. Unfortunately, the presence at Cephallenia, then at Leucas, of vessels detailed from Atilius' fleet, hindered the efforts of his friends, who could hand over only Medeon, and Thyrrheum closed its gates to him. Thereupon alarming tidings from Thessaly made him retrace his steps. This abortive expedition was his last offensive enterprise; despite his repeated summons, his great army had not appeared, and now it was the turn of Rome.

IV. THERMOPYLAE

As Antiochus had profited by the absence of the Romans to enter Greece, so they were to profit by his momentary weakness to drive him out again. They acted, however, as has been seen, somewhat slowly, and for about four months they had only the inadequate force of Baebius east of the Adriatic. It is true that war was voted at Rome immediately on the entry of the new consuls into office (Nov. 192); but it was not till late in February that 20,000 foot, 2000 horse and 15 elephants were disembarked at Apollonia by the consul M'. Acilius Glabrio, Scipio's friend, who then marched towards Thessaly. Baebius and Philip, who worked together, were already fighting there: thus the Romans joined with the Macedonian king to reconquer the land whence they had expelled him six years earlier. The apparent successes of Antiochus and his allies were now seen to be highly precarious. Though the Aetolians, who lost among other towns Chyretiae and Malloea, contrived to retain a few points in Perrhaebia, the Athamanians were easily driven from the greater part of Hestiaeotis, including Gomphi and the neighbouring towns conquered by them since 198 B.C. With the arrival of the consul in March all resistance ceased. Pelinna, where Philip of Megalopolis was in command, and Limnaeum, till then besieged by Baebius and Philip, capitulated, and Cierium and Metropolis opened their gates. Philip unopposed invaded Athamania, whence Amynander had fled to Ambracia, while Acilius, as he came south from Larissa, received the surrender of all the towns held for

[1] J. Kromayer (*Ant. Schlachtfelder*, II, pp. 135, 221), anticipated by E. A. Heyden (see the Bibliography), has disposed of this legend.

Antiochus, which were glad enough to place in his hands their alien garrisons. He thereupon broke into Phthiotic Achaea, took Thaumaci, and the next day reached the Spercheus and threatened Hypata. Thessaly was lost to Antiochus, his garrisons—over 3000 men—captured, his Athamanian allies put out of action, their land overrun, the Othrys barrier forced, Aetolia in danger: all this was the work of three weeks (March–April).

Despite this collapse, Antiochus marched stoutly to meet the enemy, pushing on from Chalcis to Lamia. The scanty reinforcements that had dribbled in from Asia only gave him his original strength of 10,000 foot and 500 horse in the field; so the Aetolians were his last hope; he summoned them to muster in full force. But uneasy perhaps at Philip's presence in Athamania, above all anxious not to face the Romans openly, and played upon by the discouragements of Phaeneas, they only offered him 4000 men. He was therefore forced to fall back on the Oeta-Thermopylae line; so long as he could hold the enemy here, he would command the entrance to Central Greece, remain in contact with Aetolia, and cover his base at Chalcis. Fearing to be turned on his left, he entrusted the Asopus gorge and the mountain tracks west of Thermopylae to the Aetolians, who left 2000 men at Heraclea in Trachis and with the remaining 2000 held the three forts of Callidromus, Rhoduntia and Teichius which guard these routes. He himself took the eastern 'Gate' of the famous Pass, which he carefully fortified. Acilius attacked the position about the end of April, and was warmly received. Nearly overwhelmed by the rain of missiles from slingers, archers and javelin-men whom Antiochus had massed on the heights on his left, the Romans made two assaults before they pierced the first Syrian line, composed of light-armed troops, only to fling themselves vainly on the phalanx in its strong earthworks. Things were going badly, especially as the Aetolians from Heraclea threatened to strike in behind them and storm their camp, when suddenly a body of soldiers dashed down the mountain on to the Syrian rear; it was a force of 2000 Romans, led by Cato, which had contrived to find its way by night round Anopaea, and surprised the Aetolians posted on the *col* of Callidromus, thus repeating the historic manœuvre of Hydarnes which Antiochus had feared (vol. IV, pp. 293 *sqq.*). Panic-stricken, the Syrians crushed one another to death in the pass or fled to Scarpheia with the Romans on their heels. Swept away in the rout, Antiochus rode straight to Elatea where he rallied 500 men, the wreckage of his army. Retiring on Chalcis, he took the only reasonable course, now that resistance was impossible, and set sail for Ephesus, which he reached unhindered. Atilius, who had come from the Piraeus, was not strong enough to cut off his retreat, and only managed to capture a convoy from Asia off Andros. Ancient and modern writers, who are all set against Antiochus, observe with malice that he took his young bride with him—but, when all is said, why should he have abandoned her?

Thus a single battle ended his rash Greek enterprise. Imprudent for the first time, Antiochus by undertaking it made two capital mistakes. He erred in believing, not that the Romans feared him, but that they would yield to this fear instead of conjuring it by crushing the man who had caused it: he little knew the Roman spirit. Moreover, he deceived himself in assuming that Philip would remain quiescent between Rome and Syria: he failed to see that, unable to have him as an ally, he would have him as an enemy, and that this meant his certain ruin. But, apart from this, two particular misfortunes hastened on the disaster, the Aetolians' inertia and his ministers' failure to procure him a good army within six months. He might, perhaps, have realized how unwieldy was the military machinery of his empire; but no one could have foreseen the ineffectiveness of the Aetolians.

These two misfortunes of the Great King were for the Romans the greatest of good luck. But, granted that they could not be foreseen, the Romans could not have counted upon them. They, too, began with a mistake in not sending a strong army to Greece so soon as they knew of Antiochus' landing. Had he acted more boldly, he could, as has been seen, have produced, even with no more than his advanced forces, a violent anti-Roman movement. More important still, the delay of the Romans exposed them to the risk of having to meet Antiochus at the head both of all his own forces and those of the Aetolians ranged at last under his banner. In that event, their victory would presumably have been less rapid, even with Philip's help. This piece of imprudence, as we shall see, was not the only one they committed in this war, but, unlike the errors of Antiochus, it went unpunished. Fortune, the ruling goddess of these days, was on the side of Rome. From the very beginning of the war, Rome's adversary was beset with a coincidence of difficulties so hampering as to render useless all the genius of Hannibal. Herein lay the ill luck of Antiochus and the good luck of Rome.

V. THE WAR IN AETOLIA. CORYCUS

At Rome, the news of Thermopylae, brought with astonishing speed by Cato, put an end to public alarm; but for the Senate, now swayed by Scipio's energetic counsels, this victory was in no wise final. What did the loss of 10,000 men mean to the Great King? His forces remained intact, and, to prevent a renewal of the Seleucid menace in Europe, he must be defeated in Asia. Antiochus was now clear-sighted enough and realized his peril; but, after all, his fleet commanded the sea which the Romans must master in order to reach him; and possibly, too, Aetolia would refuse to submit, and so keep them in Greece. When two Aetolian envoys, Thoas and Nicander, came to Ephesus to beg him not to forget his allies, he spared neither money nor promises of help, and, to give the Aetolians confidence, he kept Thoas at his court.

This time Antiochus' trust in the Aetolians was not misplaced. They had served him badly, but, when the Romans turned against their towns, their fierce spirit blazed out once more. Acilius, after receiving the trembling submission of the Phocians, Boeotians and Chalcidians, vainly summoned Heraclea to surrender; for nearly a month the city, attacked on four sides, resisted with heroic courage (June). When it fell, Phaeneas, judging further struggle hopeless, sought to make terms. But Acilius was a brutal soldier with none of Flamininus' clemency. His implacable insistence on unconditional surrender, his threats to the envoys, guilty only of not understanding the significance of the expression 'entrust themselves to the faith of the Roman people' (the formula of the *deditio*), the violence, real or assumed, by which he meant to terrify the Aetolians, only incensed them. The Assembly at Hypata refused even to hear his demands discussed, and Nicander's return with comfortable words and money from Ephesus strengthened the League in its obstinacy. So, Heraclea taken, Acilius, after crossing with great trouble the dangerous passes of Oeta, had to besiege Naupactus; at the end of two months it still held out (August–September). When would the Romans be done with Aetolia and this long-drawn war which paralysed them and diverted them from their true objective—Antiochus? Besides, it served Philip's ends too well. During his parleys with Phaeneas, Acilius, pleading presumably the suspension of hostilities, had prevented Philip from taking Lamia which the king was besieging while the Romans were assailing Heraclea—treatment which long rankled in Philip's mind (see p. 245). Afterwards, however, forced to show him consideration, Acilius had given him a free hand, and while he himself lay before Naupactus, Philip had quickly re-taken Demetrias, Magnesia, Antron, Pteleum and Larissa Cremaste, and wrested from the Aetolians their remaining Perrhaebian towns, Dolopia, and Aperantia. An ironical situation thus arose: the Romans by persisting in their attacks on the Aetolian strongholds were serving Philip's aims and allowing him to regain his power in Northern Greece.

This roused the anger of Flamininus, who saw his great edifice of 'Free Greece' crumbling away. He was now engaged in curbing the greed of other allies, the Achaeans, who, without having effectively assisted to achieve the defeat of Antiochus, were profiting by it to realize their inordinate ambitions in the Peloponnese. They had to be reminded that 'it was not to serve them alone that the Romans had fought and won at Thermopylae.' He had prevented them from conquering by arms Messene, which had made surrender to him, allowing them, however, to annex it peacefully on terms which he dictated; he had also just taken back Zacynthus, a possession of Amynander, which they had, with no shadow of right, bought from its governor. This affair settled, he went to Acilius, showed him that it was better to spare Aetolia than to enrich Philip with her spoils, and obtained for the Aetolians, henceforth resigned to any endurable peace, permission to appeal to the Senate. So ended hostilities in Greece, and Flamininus hoped it was indeed the end.

This bad news was made worse for Antiochus by a naval defeat. Master of the sea since Thermopylae, he had, while encouraging the Aetolians, fortified the Chersonese, where Lysimacheia became his chief stronghold, and both shores of the Hellespont, thus indirectly and directly impeding the Roman invasion of Asia. It was to cut him off from the Aetolians and prepare for this invasion that the praetor C. Livius Salinator left Ostia about April and, in August, bringing 50 Roman and 6 Punic warships, some 25 light vessels, and the 25 quinqueremes of Atilius, crossed the Aegean. Enemies and friends awaited him. The royal fleet, consisting of 70 'decked' and seemingly over 100 'open' ships[1], was concentrated at Ephesus under the admiral Polyxenidas, an exiled Rhodian; troops assembled at Magnesia ad Sipylum were to prevent any disembarkation. As for Rome's friends, Livius could count on their immediate co-operation. There was Eumenes of course; and there were also the Rhodians. Till then they had behaved as neutrals and they had no complaint against Antiochus,

[1] The number is disputed. The writer follows Kromayer, *op. cit.* II, p. 157 n. 4.

indeed the contrary (see above, p. 178), but now, foreseeing his ruin, jealous of the advantages which Eumenes would gain from it, and incited by ambition to enlarge their dominions on the mainland, they claimed their part of the spoils. They needed no justification for fighting in Asia alongside the Romans as they had formerly done in Europe: had not Rome come to continue her defence of Greek freedom?

As Livius' first care must be to join his allies, who would pilot him in these unknown waters and reinforce him with some 50 warships, Polyxenidas had to try to defeat him before this junction. He therefore left Ephesus, but failed to prevent the Romans from reaching Phocaea and making contact with Eumenes, who brought from Elaea 24 ships of the line and about 30 light craft. Though now outnumbered by 35 warships, he bravely determined to risk an action before the imminent arrival of the Rhodians. But when battle was joined off Cape Corycus, south of the Ionian peninsula, the Roman use of grappling-irons gave the advantage to Livius; Polyxenidas, having lost 23 large ships, returned to Ephesus. Reinforced by the Rhodian contingent of 27 cataphracts which arrived next day, the combined fleet of 130 warships a second time offered battle, which was of course declined, and they separated to winter, Eumenes and the Rhodians at home, Livius at Canae in Pergamene territory. Once victorious, the Romans received the adhesion of several Greek towns; they also had at their disposal along the coast and in the islands numerous cities which were allies or friends of Rhodes—an inestimable advantage. Chios became their centre of supplies, but in default of supplies from Italy, the crews and marines of Livius were usually to re-provision at the cost of the Greeks (late September 191).

At Thermopylae the Romans had re-won Greece from Antiochus; at Corycus they seemed to have won the sea also. But Antiochus meant to dispute this further; and in winter good news reached him. In its anger against the Aetolians the Senate had made brutally severe demands. The envoys were offered the choice between unconditional surrender (already demanded by Acilius) and the immediate payment of 1000 talents—impossible for a ruined people—coupled with the obligation to have 'the same enemies and friends as Rome,' that is, the renunciation of all independent foreign policy. The embassy had left without settling anything. In spring, therefore, war would break out again in Greece; the Romans were not yet able to turn all their efforts towards Asia.

VI. THE STRUGGLE FOR THE HELLESPONT

Such, however, was their firm intention. The Senate had decided that the consul invested in 190 with the 'province of Greece' would be free to lead his army into Asia, and popular desire pointed to the leader of the expedition: whom should Rome oppose to Antiochus and Hannibal in alliance but the conqueror of Hannibal, Scipio Africanus? Consul in 194, Scipio could not be re-elected so soon, but his friend C. Laelius and his brother Lucius were chosen and entered office on November 18, 191. 'Greece,' renounced by Laelius, fell to Lucius Scipio. His incompetence was notorious and immediately, according to arrangement, Publius was associated with him[1], though seemingly without any official duty[2]; he thus indirectly obtained supreme command.

Arriving in Aetolia late in April 190, the Scipios found that Acilius, pending their coming, had returned to his tedious siege-warfare; he had taken Lamia, and was laboriously pushing on the reduction of Amphissa. This did not suit the great Scipio: his real enemy was Antiochus, Asia drew him as Africa had done. Consequently, the Aetolians, longing for peace, were treated almost as in the preceding year. An Athenian embassy interceded for them; prompted by Publius Scipio, the Athenians persuaded them to return to Rome and beg the Senate to grant easier terms. Lucius authorized this, the siege of Amphissa was raised, and a six months' armistice was concluded. This was doubly advantageous to the Romans, for it set free their army and checked the progress of Philip, who had just conquered Amphilochia. The Scipios at once proceeded to lead to Asia the troops of Acilius and the reinforcements brought by themselves from Italy— 13,000 foot and 500 horse. As the sea-crossing seemed too hazardous, and as, besides, the Roman fleet was too engaged elsewhere to provide transport, they set out about May through Thessaly and Macedonia, where Philip was to welcome them, for the Hellespont.

The control of the Hellespont was the key to Asia, and the prize of victory in the war at sea. So, during the winter, while gathering an army in Phrygia, Antiochus had been preparing to checkmate

---

[1] The explanation of F. Münzer in *P.W.* *s.v.* C. Laelius (2) is here accepted.

[2] In the Scipios' letters to Heraclea-by-Latmus and Colophon Publius is given no title but simply described as the brother of the consul Lucius. In Polybius XXI, 10, 11 it is necessary to adopt Reiske's correction of ἀνθύπατον to ὕπατον, a title which naturally describes L. Scipio.

the Allied fleets, both by bringing against them a greatly increased navy, and by making diversions to force them to separate. Strengthening Polyxenidas' fleet to 90 warships and directing Hannibal to raise a second fleet in Phoenicia to join the first, he concentrated in Aeolis under Seleucus a force to operate against the Pergamene kingdom and take from the enemy the support of the coastal towns, and stationed in Lycia, notably at Patara, other troops who, with the Lycians, would harry the Rhodians and raid their mainland possessions. Meanwhile cruisers and privateers, dispatched to the Aegean, would intercept the convoys bringing supplies from Italy. All this was sound strategy.

Begun late in March, the naval campaign was for a long time indecisive. While Livius, seconded by Eumenes, strove to open the Dardanelles to the Scipios by reducing Sestos and besieging Abydos, Polyxenidas, by an adroit stroke of trickery, surprised and almost annihilated the Rhodian fleet stationed at Samos; and to this misfortune, which forced Livius to withdraw, must be added the loss of Phocaea (where a popular rising against the Romans had broken out), Cyme and several neighbouring towns recaptured by Seleucus. Livius and Eumenes, joined by a fresh Rhodian squadron, then established themselves in Samos, shutting up Polyxenidas in Ephesus; but their attempts at a landing failed, and while this blockade kept them immobile, there was no one to oppose Hannibal's fleet when it should appear from the east. When the praetor L. Aemilius Regillus came about April to succeed Livius, he found the Allies dispirited and bewildered, and matters did not improve under his command. Two expeditions against Patara—the second with all three fleets—undertaken to relieve the Rhodians, who were seriously threatened in the Peraea, came to nothing; and, in Eumenes' absence, Seleucus and Antiochus invaded his kingdom. He hastened to the relief of Pergamum, where he, too, found himself blockaded, and his allies, neglecting all else, had to hurry to his aid. At this point, informed by the Aetolians that he must no longer count on them, Antiochus attempted to negotiate (c. May–June); it is significant that Rhodes raised no objection and, but for Eumenes, Regillus would perhaps have assented: indeed the Allies had so far known nothing but failure.

Auxiliaries recalled by Eumenes from Achaea relieved Pergamum, but the combined fleets failed to re-take Phocaea, and as Seleucus remained in Aeolis, Eumenes dared not leave his kingdom; meanwhile news was brought that Hannibal would soon arrive. Regillus must stay at Samos to keep watch on

Polyxenidas; the Rhodians, willing to sacrifice themselves, went alone with 36 ships under the admiral Eudamus to face Hannibal. Antiochus' plan to divide his three opponents had succeeded.

They were in grave danger. The advent of Hannibal's fleet marked the crisis of the war at sea; Regillus might be defeated by Polyxenidas, while Hannibal had 11 more ships and far more powerful ships than the Rhodians. But, for whatever reason, Polyxenidas did not attack, and the seamanship of the Rhodians, who went in search of Hannibal beyond the mouth of the Eurymedon, was more than a match for the fleet improvised in Phoenicia. Near Side, it was so roughly handled—20 vessels disabled, one *hepteres* captured—that Hannibal retreated with no hope of taking action again for a long time (August); hence the situation became extremely critical for Antiochus, reduced to his fleet at Ephesus. Yet, occupied in watching Hannibal and containing the enemy at Patara, the Rhodians kept most of their forces in Lycia, and sent back but few ships with Eudamus to Regillus; Eumenes remained in Troas to guard his dominions and prepare for the Scipios' crossing. Polyxenidas thus found himself with eighty-nine ships to Regillus' eighty, and Antiochus resolved to risk a decisive action. Indeed, he could do no other. To keep his one fleet stationary in port was to surrender to the enemy the command of the sea and leave the Hellespont and Asia open; and he had nothing to gain by delay: Eumenes and the whole Rhodian fleet might rejoin Regillus at any moment. Polyxenidas was ordered to sail from Ephesus. A demonstration against Notium, friendly to Rome, drew Regillus from Samos; Polyxenidas went near to trapping him in the northern harbour of Teos, but the projected surprise miscarried. Finally, the two fleets met between Myonnesus and Corycus, near the scene of the Syrian defeat in the previous year. This time the Syrians met with even greater disaster. This was mainly due to the Rhodian Eudamus, who while foiling their attempt to surround the Roman right, threw their left into disorder by the skilful use of fire, until the Romans, who had broken through the centre of the Syrian line, took it in reverse and crushed it. Polyxenidas, after losing 42 ships, retired to Ephesus with the ships of his right wing which had hardly been engaged (September). Reduced to little more than half its strength the royal fleet could no longer dispute the command of the sea. The way was open for the Scipios.

VII. MAGNESIA

They came, having with Philip's loyal assistance easily passed through Macedonia and Thrace, where 2000 volunteers joined them. The news of Myonnesus found them beyond the Hebrus, just reaching the Chersonese where Lysimacheia opened its gates. Antiochus had withdrawn the garrison and with wisdom; for the great fortress could not arrest an enemy in command of the sea; but his officers did less wisely in failing to destroy the vast stores collected there. The Romans rested, and re-provisioned, then peacefully crossed the Hellespont in the Pergamene and Rhodian fleets and a detachment of their own (the rest, under Regillus, was recapturing Phocaea). They next made a long halt, while P. Scipio remained on the European shore—as Salian priest he might not move for a month[1]. When he crossed a royal envoy, who was awaiting his coming, asked for an audience. Troubled by the Roman arrival, realizing the doubtful solidity of his empire, with no ally but Ariarathes—for Prusias, counselled by the Scipios, had just refused his aid—Antiochus, practical and deliberate as usual, desired peace even at a heavy cost; he offered to pay half the Roman war-expenses, to abandon his European dependencies, as well as Lampsacus, Smyrna and Alexandria Troas, and even such other Ionian and Aeolian cities as had sided with Rome; in short, he conceded more than Rome had claimed in 196, the time of her greatest demands. But this was now too little: Rome meant this time to make an end; she intended to have nothing to fear in future from the Seleucid monarchs, but to drive them back eastward. Advised by his brother, L. Scipio declared that, as the price of peace, Antiochus must retire from all Asia Minor 'on this side Taurus' (*i.e.* to the north and west of that range) and pay the whole cost of the war. A private interview at which the ambassador confided to Publius that the king was prepared to return, without ransom, his son taken prisoner in Greece, and hinted, it is said, at offers of money, was naturally without effect. The situation of Antiochus after these vain parleyings recalled that of Philip before Cynoscephalae; like Philip, he estimated that defeat would probably cost no more and would save his honour.

The preparations actively carried on since his return from Greece had procured him an army of over 70,000 men, more than twice as large as that of the Scipios, which numbered about

---

[1] It is probable that the month in question was March, corresponding at that time to Oct.–Nov. (25 Oct.–22 Nov.) or Nov.–Dec. (16/17 Nov.–14/15 Dec.) 190. See De Sanctis, *op. cit.* IV, 1, p. 393.

30,000, including 6–7000 auxiliaries, 2800 of which were furnished by Eumenes. In advancing to confront the huge and hitherto redoubtable royal army with such modest forces, Africanus displayed his wonted boldness. But in fact, as probably he knew from Eumenes, the Syrian array was composed, eastern fashion, of heterogeneous elements with little cohesion, of widely different value and mostly lacking in training. Besides the regular troops which consisted of the military settlers Macedonian or Greek in origin, the Greek and Galatian mercenaries, and the Cappadocians sent by Ariarathes, most of the peoples of the Empire were represented, from Dahae horse-archers of the Caspian to Arabs mounted on dromedaries. It was strong in cavalry—at least 12,000 horse—light or 'cataphract' (vol. VII, p. 170), in light-armed infantry—more than 20,000—archers, slingers and javelin-men; it included, besides 54 elephants, that engine of war dear to the Ancient East, the dreaded scythed-chariots. To deploy his cavalry and light infantry upon which he counted to outflank the enemy, Antiochus needed open ground; after going from Sardes to Thyatira, he finally gained the *Campus Hyrcanius*, east of Magnesia ad Sipylum, and there awaited the Romans.

The latter, on leaving the Hellespont, followed the coast and gained Elaea, where they joined Eumenes and where Publius Scipio was left ill; then they marched inland through the allied Pergamene kingdom, seeking the enemy. To the last Antiochus had hoped to conciliate Africanus. Learning of his illness, with calculating magnanimity, he had sent his son to him from Thyatira without ransom. But Scipio is said to have given him in exchange merely the enigmatic advice not to fight a battle until his return to headquarters[1]. Disappointed in his hopes and seeing the Romans marching against him, Antiochus, twice refusing battle, manoeuvred them on to the ground he had chosen, a wide, flat plain behind the confluence of the Phrygius (Kum) and the Hermus, where he had carefully fortified a camp.

There the two armies joined battle on a rainy winter morning (probably January 189). Impetuous as at Raphia, though over fifty, Antiochus, leading the cavalry on his right wing, broke the Roman left which rested on the Phrygius, and threatened their camp; but, meanwhile, his own left and centre had met with disaster. Fearing the outflanking of their right, which was much shorter than the enemy's left, the Romans, contrary to custom,

[1] The Roman tradition (Livy XXXVII, 37, 9) wrongly attributes to Scipio's advice the 'retreat' of Antiochus from Thyatira to the east of Magnesia; it was a movement dictated solely by strategic considerations.

had massed there, as a striking force, almost all their cavalry, 2800 horse. Eumenes, who commanded on this wing, first dispersed with the light-armed troops the scythed-chariots, hurling them back upon the Syrian line, which they threw into confusion; then, charging suddenly with all his squadrons, he drove back the 3000 'cataphract' horsemen facing him, and so broke up and put to flight the whole royal left. The massive phalanx, 16,000 strong and 32 ranks deep, which formed the enemy's centre, was thus uncovered on the left; Eumenes assailed it in flank, while the legionaries, led by the consular Cn. Domitius Ahenobarbus, who in Publius' absence was the effective commander, delivered a frontal attack and showered darts and *pila* upon it. Half enveloped, wilting beneath the rain of missiles, the phalanx had to fall back towards the camp; the 22 elephants which were posted between its ten sections went wild and in their fury broke its ordered ranks, and the legionaries attacking at close quarters with the sword cut it to pieces. The victory, the chief honour for which was due to Eumenes, was completed by the capture of the stoutly defended Syrian camp and the pursuit of the fugitives. Antiochus lost, it is said, over 50,000 men; in fact, he was now a king without an army; the victors' losses were insignificant. In Asia Minor as in Greece, a single battle decided the issue.

Antiochus fled to Sardes, then to Apamea, where he rejoined Seleucus. Behind him, Sardes, despite his governor and the Lydian satrap, welcomed the Romans, as did all the towns of the region, Thyatira, Tralles, the two Magnesias, finally Ephesus, whence Polyxenidas had contrived to withdraw what remained of the fleet to Patara. Asia 'this side Taurus' was offering itself to the victors; the Romans had declared that this was all they sought; as there was no hope of regaining it, it was useless to attempt to resist longer: and Antiochus, acquiescing in the inevitable, laid down his arms[1].

It must be observed that this prompt decision of Antiochus was of great advantage to the Romans. Had he, without further fighting, retreated far to the east, they would certainly not have followed him, but they would have been under the unwelcome necessity of occupying Western Asia Minor for an indefinite period. This embarrassment they were spared—a piece of good luck crowning many others. Indeed, throughout all the second phase of the war, even more than the first, Fortune was their constant friend. Not only did they find in Eumenes and the Rhodians

---

[1] For the ultimate effects of the battle of Magnesia on the history of the Seleucid Empire, see below, chap. XVI.

zealous and indefatigable helpers to whom they owed at least half
their military success, but at two critical moments they enjoyed
strokes of luck almost beyond hope. First, the Senate's grave
blunder of refusing to grant acceptable terms to the Aetolians
and of persisting in fighting Aetolia and Antiochus with a
single army brought no evil consequences: indeed, the Aetolians
who, had they continued the struggle, would have kept the
Scipios in Greece and so helped to strengthen Antiochus' position,
were blind enough to confer upon Africanus the inestimable
benefit of concluding the armistice which was for him indispensable. Second, the Romans had the yet greater good fortune
of beholding a happy issue to the dangerous adventure on which
they had embarked in 190, when they staked the game on what
was apparently a highly hazardous card—Philip's loyalty and his
hatred of Antiochus, a hatred assuredly mitigated by Antiochus'
failure in Greece. It is clear that Philip held in his hands the
fate of the Roman army as it threaded the dangerous defiles of
Macedon and Thrace on its march to the Hellespont. In all probability he could have involved it in a disaster which would have
had incalculable consequences, for he could then have rallied the
Aetolians to his cause[1], made himself master of Greece and joined
hands with Antiochus. It is not easy to view without astonishment
the fact that a monarch, whose most conspicuous virtue was not
loyalty, and who had already seen his alliance with Rome ill-
requited, did not yield to so alluring a temptation. However, the
Romans were so fortunate that Philip, who in his courteous dealings with Africanus probably came under the spell of his prestige
and personality, did not yield to it, and ministered to the need of
their army as the most faithful of allies. Within ten years the
gods in their kindness granted to Rome this double boon, that
Antiochus did nothing to prevent her from crushing Philip, and
that Philip did his best to help her to crush Antiochus.

VIII. PEACE IN ASIA AND GREECE

Shortly after the battle, the king's plenipotentiaries sued for
peace from the Scipios, now arrived at Sardes, and, except for
some aggravations of detail, obtained it upon the terms already
stated. Antiochus renounced his possessions in Europe and
'Cistauric Asia'; agreed to pay a war indemnity of 15,000 Euboic
talents (500 at once, 2500 upon the ratification at Rome of the
preliminaries, the remainder in twelve annual instalments), to

---

[1] On Philip's tendency towards a *rapprochement* with the Aetolians see
Polybius xx, 11, 5–8 (the king's reception of Nicander).

pay to Eumenes an old debt contracted with Attalus (400 talents together with a certain quantity of corn), surrender Hannibal, Thoas and other enemies of Rome, and give twenty selected hostages, among them the royal prince Antiochus, the future Antiochus Epiphanes. Upon the handing-over of the hostages an armistice was concluded during which the king had to re-provision the Roman army. Antiochus saw to it that Hannibal escaped.

As in 197 B.C. the Romans considered themselves the sole victors and alone dictated the peace; the districts yielded up by Antiochus were thus their prize and became their property. It was expected indeed that, true to their practice, they would retain none of them, but they would dispose of them as they wished; therefore Eumenes, envoys from Rhodes and from innumerable Greek cities of Asia sailed to Rome in the early summer of 189—'the hopes of all,' says Polybius, 'rested upon the Senate.'

Rome had settled with Antiochus; it remained to settle with Aetolia. The unhappy Aetolians had been deceived once more in their journey to plead with the Senate, and the comedy of 191 was repeated in 190. Their envoys, come to Rome at the Scipios' suggestion, found the *patres* inexorable; the war would begin afresh for the second time in the spring of 189. War between Aetolia and Macedon actually began the winter before. Tired of obeying Philip, the Athamanians came to regret Amynander, who had taken refuge in Ambracia; a rising concerted with him broke out in Athamania. The Aetolians first helped him to recover his kingdom, drive out the Macedonian garrisons, and repel Philip, who had come himself to the rescue; they then reconquered for themselves Amphilochia, Aperantia and Dolopia. Their hopes were rising when the news of Magnesia dashed them to the ground. In despair, they were sending another embassy to Rome, when the consul M. Fulvius Nobilior landed at Apollonia with the troops which, since 192, were in reserve in Bruttium; Rome, hitherto so sparing of her men that she waged two wars with a single army, was now mobilizing a second to crush Aetolia.

Counselled and aided by the Epirotes, who were anxious to atone for having shown goodwill to Antiochus, Fulvius in the early summer of 189 besieged Ambracia (into which the Aetolians threw 1000 men), for Pyrrhus' former capital promised rich spoils. Meanwhile Perseus, Philip's son, reconquered Dolopia and invaded Amphilochia, and the Achaeans joining the Illyrians ravaged the seaboard of Aetolia. Too busy elsewhere, the federal army, despite the promises of the General Nicander, could not, or dared not, relieve the besieged; but their resistance, heroically prolonged, facilitated Aetolia's negotiations with the consul. Pressed by Athenian and Rhodian envoys, by Amynander, now restored to Roman favour, and by C. Valerius Laevinus, his half-brother, the son of the author of the treaty of 212, Fulvius, at first implacable, relented. When the Ambraciotes, on Amynander's advice, made full surrender, he treated them with comparative moderation (not omitting, however, to extort from them a present of 150 talents and to despoil their city of its artistic treasures), and let the Aetolian garrison go free; then, he consented to reduce by a half the fine to be exacted from the Aetolians, and ceased to demand their unconditional surrender, imposing only territorial sacrifices. A provisional agreement was concluded, which the Senate at last ratified at the instance, it is said, of the Athenians (autumn 189). The treaty granted to the Aetolians was, however, a *foedus iniquum* which made them subordinate to Rome, for they engaged to respect 'the empire and the majesty of the Roman people,' and to fight their enemies as their own. They had further to pay 500 Euboic talents, 200 immediately, the remaining 300 in six yearly instalments, to hand over 40 hostages for six years, to abandon all the districts and cities, formerly belonging to Aetolia, which since 192 had been conquered by the Romans or had become the 'friends' of Rome, to restore Oeniadae to Acarnania, and to abandon Cephallenia which was expressly excluded from the treaty.

They thus lost—besides Oeniadae, Cephallenia, and Dolopia recovered by Philip—Ambracia, their last Thessalian and Phthiotic towns, Malis and Phocis; Delphi, declared *libera et immunis*, first, in 191, by Acilius, who recognized its control of the sanctuary and heaped benefits upon it, then in 189 by the Senate, escaped from their rule, together with Amphictyonia from which they were formally though not actually excluded. But they kept Aenis, Oetaea at least in part, East and West Locris, and even, despite Philip's justifiable protests, Aperantia and Amphilochia[1]: it is noteworthy that in this Rome favoured her defeated enemy at the expense of her great ally. Aetolia's fate was indeed strange: after being the first of the Greek peoples to make an alliance with Rome, she was also the first to fall to the humiliation of being a Roman

---

[1] According to Polybius xxi, 31, 4, Philip had laid claim to Athamania and Dolopia (Livy xxxviii, 10, 3 adds *Amphilochos*) unjustly taken from him by the Aetolians. But there seems here to be some confusion, for Dolopia was apparently reconquered by Perseus (Livy xxxviii, 5, 10) and Athamania was now in the possession, not of the Aetolians, but of Amynander. Probably it was Aperantia and Amphilochia which Philip claimed in vain from the Aetolians.

client, but although politically dead, she remained the largest state in Central Greece.

The Romans had excluded the Cephallenians from the treaty for two reasons: they desired to chastise the pirates who had often harried their convoys and, already controlling Corcyra and Zacynthus, they wished to master Cephallenia, thus securing a third valuable base in the Ionian sea. Fulvius came thither from Ambracia; Same, alone of the four island cities, dared to resist him and was taken by assault after a four months' siege late in January 188[1]. It was the epilogue of the Aetolian War.

The war in Asia, too, did not lack its epilogue. In the spring of 189 the consul Cn. Manlius Volso and the praetor Q. Fabius Labeo had succeeded L. Scipio and Regillus; for Africanus' political opponents, after allowing him to eliminate Antiochus, ungenerously prevented him from settling the consequences of his victory. Labeo found occupation for the fleet by demonstrating with small success against Crete, in order to secure the freedom of the many Romans and Italians held captive in the island. Manlius led his army against the Galatians. Their supplying of mercenaries to Antiochus and, still more, the fact that they were a perpetual menace to the Hellenic towns and the kings of Pergamum justified the undertaking; the Romans had to leave behind them a pacified Asia and impose upon the barbarians respect for the new order of things. But the consul contrived to make the expedition a profitable venture. Wishing, and with reason, to impress the unruly populations of Pisidia and Phrygia by a display of Roman might, Manlius, with Attalus and Athenaeus, brothers of Eumenes, at the head of a Pergamene contingent, arrived in Galatia by a long *détour*. Starting from Ephesus, he crossed Caria and Pisidia obliquely, reached Pamphylia, where the town of Isinda invited his help against the Termessians, and entered into relations with the Pamphylian towns, notably Aspendus. He then turned north through Pisidia and Phrygia, and penetrated from the south-west the country of the Tolistoagii, where he was welcomed by the priests of Pessinus, and occupied without meeting resistance the important trading centre of Gordium. The regions thus traversed underwent methodical extortion: every town on the line of march had to submit under threat of sack and pillage, but it was only by paying money that it obtained 'Roman friendship.' Manlius indulged in disgraceful bargaining with Moagetes, dynast of Cibyra. Large sums, sometimes amounting to 200 talents, were

[1] The chronology of the siege proposed by Beloch (*Klio*, XXII, 1929, pp. 464–6) is not here accepted. See the present writer in *B.C.H.* LIV, 1930.

extorted in this way from numerous cities, besides requisitions of food; those deserted by their terrified inhabitants were systematically plundered.

Of the three Galatian peoples, the Tolistoagii and the Tectosages had retired and entrenched themselves, the former on Mt Olympus, the latter on Mt Magaba near Ancyra, thinking to hold out till winter repelled the invader. The Trocmi joined forces with the Tectosages as did Cappadocians sent by Ariarathes and Paphlagonians furnished by Morzius dynast of Gangra. Manlius attacked the barbarians in their mountain strongholds, which he stormed; he owed his double victory, at Olympus and Magaba, to his *velites* and the light-armed troops supplied by Eumenes, as the Gauls were defenceless against missiles. Their losses were enormous: 40,000 Tolistoagii, men, women and children, are said to have been captured and sold; the taking of the two camps, containing the plunder of nearly a century's raiding, yielded immense booty. On his return to Ephesus Manlius received the fervent thanks of the Greek and native communities, 'for,' writes Polybius (xxi, 41, 2), 'all those who dwelt on this side Taurus did not rejoice so much at the defeat of Antiochus...as at their release from the terror of the barbarians' (autumn 189).

While the Aetolians were being worsted and the Galatians receiving punishment, the Senate at Rome was ratifying the preliminaries of Sardes, but inserting clauses which were so many precautions against Antiochus. He was forbidden to engage in war in Europe or the Aegean; he might, indeed, repel attacks from the West, but take no territory from the aggressors nor attach them to himself as friends, Rome reserving for herself the right of arbitration in such conflicts; he had to give up his elephants, which he might not replace, and his fleet except for 10 'cataphract' ships, which, as was expressly stated, should never go farther along the Cilician coast than Cape Sarpedonium, though this coast, which remained his, stretched westward far beyond that point. Moreover, the Senate defined, undoubtedly on information furnished by Eumenes and the Rhodians, the exact meaning of the term 'Cistauric Asia' (ἡ ἐπὶ τάδε τοῦ Ταύρου Ἀσία), which was to include the area bounded on the east by the Halys, the traditional boundary of Asia Minor, then by a line running from north to south, coinciding roughly with the western frontier of Cappadocia and joining the middle Halys at Taurus, and on the south by that part of the Taurus range which runs westward of the point of junction[1]. Within this region Antiochus

---

[1] The view here adopted is that of Viereck, Cardinali, Täubler and De Sanctis (see the Bibliography). In Livy xxxviii, 38, 4 the correction of

retained nothing; he might carry nothing away but the arms borne by his soldiers, nor might he henceforward hire mercenaries there. His envoys did not resist these additional demands, and the preliminaries, voted by the people, were solemnly confirmed by oaths.

It remained to reduce the treaty to writing, ensure its execution, and settle the fate of the conquered countries; as in 196, the Senate entrusted this threefold task to ten Commissioners who with Manlius were to regulate on the spot 'the affairs of Asia'; and, with regard to Antiochus' former possessions, laid down general instructions for them to follow. While emphasizing formally her right over these possessions (called in the treaty ἡ ὑπὸ Ῥωμαίους ταττομένη) Rome abandoned them purely as an act of grace: to Eumenes were to be 'given,' with the Thracian Chersonese and the surrounding country, almost all the Seleucid territory—Lycaonia, Greater Phrygia and Pisidia, Hellespontine Phrygia, Mysia, Lydia, Carian districts north of the Maeander, Milyas and lastly, in Lycia, Telmessus; Rhodes was to receive Caria south of the Maeander and Lycia, except Telmessus. Needless to say, as Rhodes later discovered, these 'gifts' were revocable (p. 289).

A thorny question, which had been debated before the Senate from opposite standpoints by Eumenes and the Rhodians soon after their arrival at Rome, was that of the Greek towns of the Aegean seaboard taken from Antiochus: were they to obtain the liberty that they claimed? There was a conflict of two rival policies. Eumenes, formerly an ardent champion of the 'autonomous cities,' now opposed the wholesale liberation of the 'Hellenes of Asia,' because he desired to annex many towns which had belonged to Antiochus—in particular Ephesus—because he claimed especially to re-establish his sovereignty over those which had been once subject to Attalus, and because the freedom of the Asiatic Hellenes, if decreed by the Senate, might lead to the rebellion of the Greek towns included in his hereditary dominions. On the other hand, the Rhodians upheld the cause of the Hellenes from attachment to their liberal traditions, in order to curb the power of Eumenes, and because they hoped to extend their protectorate over the towns thus freed. As for the Romans, their whole previous conduct, as the Rhodians strongly pointed out,

---

ea or *a valle* to *ab Halye* proposed to the present writer by Prof. Ph. Fabia seems particularly attractive. According to the present writer, the discussion over Pamphylia (see below, p. 233) renders unacceptable the view of Kahrstedt, Ernst Meyer and Ruge (see the Bibliography).

seemed to oblige them to grant independence to the conquered cities; and, in fact, the Scipios had actually promised it to those towns which surrendered to them[1]. But, as we have seen, the Senate had only embraced the cause of the Asiatic Hellenes in order to thwart Antiochus; at heart it cared little for them—what mattered was to satisfy Eumenes, the useful friend of Rome. The result was a compromise: the towns formerly subject to Antiochus were to be free, except those which had once been subject to Attalus and those which, during the war, had resisted or seceded from Rome[2]; these two classes were to pay to Eumenes the tribute once paid to Antiochus or Attalus.

Thus Greek freedom was largely sacrificed by the Romans. Egypt, once the object of their care, was sacrificed too; they had no thought of restoring to her the 'Ptolemaic' Greek towns which, in 196, they had attempted to save from Antiochus. What, after all, could be more legitimate? Ptolemy, treating with the Seleucid, without Rome's knowledge, had renounced his Asiatic dependencies; Rome had no reason to be more Egyptian than the king of Egypt.

IX. THE TREATY OF APAMEA

Having arrived in Asia with Eumenes in the spring of 188, the ten Commissioners sat at Apamea, presided over by Manlius, just as the Commissioners formerly sent to Greece had sat at Corinth under Flamininus. The definitive treaty was then drawn up; Manlius swore to it and dispatched a Commissioner and his own brother Lucius to Syria to receive the oath of Antiochus, who scrupulously observed all his engagements. Manlius had already received the 2500 talents payable after the ratification of the preliminaries; the Syrian ships were delivered to Labeo at Patara and burnt; the elephants were brought to the proconsul who bestowed them on Eumenes. The Seleucid king was disarmed; and, according to the treaty, became the 'friend' of Rome. His allies also obtained peace; Ariarathes, with whose daughter, Stratonice, Eumenes made a marriage of policy, paid an indemnity finally reduced to 300 talents, and entered by treaty into the Roman friendship; the Galatians, with whom Manlius treated

[1] See the letter of the Scipios (not of *Manlius*) to Heraclea-by-Latmus (*Ditt.*[3] 618 and the Bibliography).

[2] This last decision is generally attributed to the ten Commissioners, but it is more probable that it derives from the Senate. Cf. in Polybius xxi, 19, 12; 21, 10–11, the allusions made by Eumenes before the Senate to the cities hostile to Rome.

shortly afterwards, had to give Eumenes pledges to cease their incursions and confine themselves to their own territory.

The chief task of Manlius and the Ten was to make a settlement of 'Cistauric Asia' according to senatorial instructions. They first considered the Greek cities of the Aegean seaboard. Naturally all who enjoyed independence before the war saw their freedom confirmed; those which, formerly subject to Antiochus, had never paid tribute to Attalus and had faithfully served Rome through the war, were declared *liberae et immunes*, thus receiving the precarious liberty; the others became tributary to Eumenes. However, as exceptions, Colophon nova and Cyme, once tributary to Attalus, became free. Several especially favoured towns, such as Ilium, Chios, Smyrna, Clazomenae, Erythrae and Miletus, gained territory besides their freedom; Phocaea was pardoned, recovered her land and self-government, but had to obey Eumenes; Mylasa, so far, it seems, independent, was, we know not why, expressly declared free.

Then came the repartition of the lands formerly Seleucid. The attribution to Rhodes of Caria south of the Maeander, and of Lycia, quadrupled her continental dominions. But, as the commission neglected to specify the new political position of the Lycians, they thought they were becoming the *allies* of Rhodes, while she treated them as *subjects*: hence arose a disagreement which was to lead to a long and bloody conflict (see below, p. 287). Eumenes found his kingdom vastly enlarged. In Europe it embraced the Thracian Chersonese with Lysimacheia, and the Propontis coast including Bisanthe; Aenus and Maronea, whose Syrian garrisons had been driven out by Labeo, were excluded, but Eumenes looked with longing upon them[1]. In Asia the Pergamene kingdom became the largest in the Anatolian peninsula; in truth, several semi-barbarous districts—Isauria, nearly all Pisidia, Cibyratis under its dynasts—escaped its sway, yet officially it stretched from Bithynia to Lycia, from Ephesus to Cappadocia[2]. Nevertheless something was lacking: the liberated Greek towns shut it off too much from the Aegean. Eumenes therefore ardently desired to possess access to the sea on the

[1] On the later occupation of these cities by Philip and the ensuing complications, see below, pp. 247 *sqq.*

[2] Mysia Olympene and the north-east part of Great Phrygia (hereafter called Phrygia *epiktetos*), although 'given' to Eumenes by the Senate since 189, do not seem to have been conquered by him from Prusias till 184/3. See Ernst Meyer, *Die Grenzen der hellenist. Staaten in Kleinasien*, pp. 148–51, but the matter is highly obscure.

south. The Senate had given him Telmessus, an enclave in Rhodian territory; after the treaty was confirmed by oath he claimed Pamphylia, alleging, in spite of the Syrian representatives, that it was 'on this side Taurus.' In point of fact, the hastily drafted treaty left this point somewhat uncertain: it made the western section of the Taurus range the new north-western limit of Seleucid territory (p. 229) without determining the point on the coast at which, on the west, this limit began. Since the western chain of the Taurus ends in spurs that approach the sea, some on the east others on the west of the Pamphylian plain, that plain could be regarded as being either on this or that side Taurus[1]. The Senate, on being called in to decide, adopted in favour of Eumenes the former interpretation. But he got only Western Pamphylia; Aspendus and Side, which had treated with Manlius, remained independent.

Towards autumn, as soon as the Ten had finished their task— a task of which they clearly made short work in four or five months—Manlius evacuated Asia; the Romans had no desire to prolong their occupation. Labeo, whose fortune it was to receive a singularly undeserved triumph *de rege Antiocho*[2], had already taken home the fleet; the army crossed the Hellespont on the Pergamene vessels and returned the way it had come. In Thrace it had difficult moments; before and after crossing the Hebrus the immense convoys of gold and booty were attacked by the barbarians; the first engagement was serious, a Commissioner was killed, and much of the baggage plundered. Having crossed Macedonia and Thessaly Manlius wintered at Apollonia and reached Italy in the spring of 187.

It seems clear enough that in Asia the Romans did simply what their security appeared to demand. They had no thought of greatly weakening the Seleucid monarchy; they left it the valuable maritime provinces, Western Cilicia and Southern Syria, which Antiochus had wrested from Ptolemy; bereft of its Cistauric dominions, it remained very powerful, but, losing all contact with Europe, became purely Asiatic. To keep it penned up into the East, the opportunist Roman Senate forgot its hostility to kings in Greece, and almost revived the Empire of Lysimachus in favour of Eumenes, sacrificing to him, in order to strengthen him, much of the Greek liberty that they had defended against Antiochus. Raised to great sovereignty by Rome, Eumenes was like an eastern Masinissa opposed to the Seleucids—and also to the Antigonids.

[1] This point is well explained by E. Täubler, *op. cit.* i, p. 75 *sq.*
[2] A. M. Colini, *Bull. della Comm. arch. com.* LV, 1927, pp. 272 *sqq.*

At once Asiatic and European, bestriding the Hellespont, his kingdom served to isolate both Syria and Macedon; and Eumenes hoped, as Rome well knew, to isolate them still more by extending his power into Thrace to Philip's detriment. Thus the bulwark that was to protect Italy from a possible coalition of enemy kings was pushed farther east; the rôle that a 'free Greece' was to have played passed to the Attalid monarchy.

This defensive end attained, the Romans were satisfied. They gave no sign of imperialistic ambitions. The regions this side Taurus pacified and re-organized; 'friendships' concluded with Cappadocia and some Greek cities; the Galatians taught to be peaceful; differences settled (at their own request) between several Hellenic communities—Manlius had to arbitrate in the eternal Samian-Prienean dispute—to this minimum they limited their action in the East. Content with Prusias' neutrality, they abstained from binding him with a treaty; they seemingly left in peace the Paphlagonian dynast Morzius although he had supported the Galatians. The liberated Greek cities were so far masters of their own actions as to fight each other on occasion[1]. Rome rewarded Rhodes without seeking to impose upon her a formal alliance that might gall her independent spirit, and let her lead in her own way a powerful group of cities in Asia and, in the Aegean, the reconstituted Island League. Eumenes, the Romans' protégé, was in no way their vassal: they respected his sovereignty and he kept a free hand in foreign affairs.

Obviously Rome intended to save herself the cares of an Asiatic policy. She succeeded for a while; then, as will be seen below, she found it gradually forced upon her. A protector has duties towards his protégé; the appeals of Eumenes, threatened by his neighbours of Bithynia and Pontus, evoked her intervention. This, however, was reserved for the future; at the moment, it was Greece which began to give trouble again.

X. ACHAEA AND SPARTA

The war with Antiochus had opened the eyes of Rome to the feelings of the great mass of the Greeks; she could not conceal from herself the failure of her 'philhellenic' policy: had he won at Thermopylae, Antiochus would have had Greece at his feet. But, though convinced of their 'ingratitude,' the Romans did not trouble to treat the Greeks with severity. Acilius, harsh as he was, had shown unexpected leniency towards the states guilty

[1] See the treaty between Heraclea-by-Latmus and Miletus, A. Rehm, *Milet*, I, 3, no. 150 (= *Ditt.*[3] 633), and the commentary on it.

of open defection: the Boeotians had set up a statue to Antiochus, they escaped with a brief raid on the territory of Coronea, and the anti-Roman party remained in power; Chalcis was spared at the request of Flamininus, whom she worshipped as her 'Saviour.' It occurred to no Roman statesman to make the régime of 196 more oppressive after Magnesia, and, apart from Aetolia, Greece remained 'free.' In 188 B.C. or perhaps 187 Fulvius withdrew as Flamininus had done, and not a single Roman remained behind in Greece. This forbearance certainly cloaked an indifference born of disdain; once Antiochus was vanquished Rome took little interest in petty Greek affairs: all she asked was that the Greeks should remain quiet and spare her the need to trouble about them. But this was not to be. Rome's allies, Philip and the Achaeans, had worked for their own ends during the Syrian War, and the territorial and political changes that resulted from it eventually led to new complications.

The Romans, as has already been seen, had laboured to limit Philip's gains; nevertheless in 188 he still held on one hand Magnesia with Demetrias, and on the Phthiotic coast, Pteleum, Antron, Larissa and Alope; on the other, several Perrhaebian towns including Malloea; in Hestiaeotis, Gomphi, Tricca, Phaloria, Eurymenae; two border fortresses in Athamania, and Dolopia. He had well earned this reward; but Philip once more in Greece, reigning anew over Greeks, meant, if not a real danger, at least the denial of all Rome's achievements after the Macedonian War: the declarations of the Senate and Flamininus and the treaty of 196 were thereby nullified. The past compelled Rome to appear ungrateful and to dispute the conquests of her loyal ally the moment the Greeks once more under his yoke claimed their deliverance. The unavoidable clash was not long delayed; partially dispossessed, Philip was to emerge from it the implacable enemy of Rome (pp. 244 *sqq.*).

The difficulties born of Achaean ambition were still swifter to appear. In the summer of 191 the Achaeans had continued hastily to exploit the Roman victory to the full, showing the Republic less consideration than she had the right to expect. Thus to their annexation of Messene (p. 217) they had added, with the somewhat reluctant consent of Flamininus and Acilius, that of Elis which had surrendered to them. Their great dream was realized: the League embraced the whole Peloponnese, but with their triumph began their perplexities, and these first became visible at Sparta.

Here the pro-Achaean party with whom Philopoemen had treated in 192 (p. 207) was powerless. Spartan patriotism and pride were revolted by attachment to Achaea; besides, all those who had benefited by the tyrants' reforms dreaded the recall of the exiles and the ensuing redistribution of property which, though provisionally postponed by Philopoemen, was inevitable under the new régime. As early as 191 there had been an outbreak; Philopoemen, acting in an unofficial capacity, quelled it without allowing either the General Diophanes or Flamininus to intervene. In the late summer of 189 the situation again became critical; the return of Nabis' hostages from Italy may have contributed to this. The coast towns, entrusted to Achaea by Flamininus, were crowded with exiles; their proximity and their intrigues exasperated the Spartans, already irritated at their exclusion from the sea; they tried, although without success, to storm Las near Gytheum and a few exiles were killed. Obviously the affair, as a breach of the Spartan-Roman treaty of 195 put into force again in 192, concerned Rome even more than Achaea; but Philopoemen, then General, made the quarrel his own. Without even notifying the consul Fulvius, then at Cephallenia, he demanded under threat of war the surrender of the authors of the attack. In an outburst of anger thirty pro-Achaeans were murdered at Sparta, and the Spartans voted secession from Achaea and an embassy to Fulvius to make formal surrender to Rome (autumn 189).

Disregarding this, the Achaeans, *i.e.* Philopoemen, who had been re-elected General[1], decided on immediate war with Sparta, which was only delayed by winter. Forced to intervene, but much embarrassed, Fulvius, who had gone to the Peloponnese after the fall of Same, referred both parties to the Senate, forbidding provisionally further fighting. The Senate, equally embarrassed—especially as the Achaean envoys, Lycortas and Diophanes, one the friend, the other the adversary of Philopoemen, were in disagreement—would have liked to satisfy Achaea without sacrificing Sparta; its answer was ambiguous. Philopoemen hastened to take full advantage of this; he led the Achaean army unopposed into Laconia, accompanied by crowds of exiles, and had the supporters of the secession delivered to him for judgment. On arriving at the Achaean camp in Compasium, 80 of them (others say 350) were massacred by the exiles and Achaeans in violation of their pledged word or were executed after the farce of a trial (spring 188).

Nor did this content Philopoemen, who laid a heavy hand on Sparta which was powerless to resist: her walls were dismantled;

---

[1] The present writer, with most scholars, admits two successive *strategiai* of Philopoemen (190/89 and 189/8): for the opposite view see A. Aymard, cited in the Bibliography.

all mercenaries and enfranchised Helots were doomed to expulsion; the institutions of Lycurgus were changed to those of the Achaeans. A federal decree, passed later at Tegea, ordained the return of the exiles *en masse*, the seizure and sale of the Helots and mercenaries (3000 in all) who refused to leave Laconia, the restitution of Belbinatis (vol. VII, p. 753) to Megalopolis. The anti-Achaean leaders were exiled save a few who were executed; Sparta, against her will and despite her appeal to Rome, was bound to Achaea by a new treaty. Thus Philopoemen, the instrument of ancient Achaean or even Megalopolitan rancour and of the capitalists' new-born hatred, hoped by violence to end the Spartan question. What he did was to open it afresh. His brutality was to compel Rome, as guardian of the common peace, to intervene. A tiresome endless quarrel resulted which will be described below (chap. ix). Rome till then had met with opposition from the masses; she was henceforward to know the opposition, now plaintive, now arrogant, of the Achaean ruling class, and, like Macedon, to learn that, to keep their friendship, she must satisfy their interests without reserve. This quarrel, in which, however, there were wrongs on each side, was destined to lead to a breach which marked the complete breakdown of the Senate's Greek policy.

Assuredly the *patres*, as will be seen better by what follows, had underrated the difficulty of imposing upon the Greeks Rome's benevolent protection. In this, despite the insight which is attributed to them, they were mistaken. And moreover, if we have rightly interpreted their purposes and their actions since 200 B.C., it appears manifest that, in general, the Senate's boasted perspicacity was to seek, and that all its eastern achievements, whatever the glory and profit which Rome gained from them, had as their starting point a failure to understand the foreign situation, an error of judgment.

XI. CONCLUSION

According to a generally accepted opinion, the decisive struggle in which Rome engaged, first against Macedonia, then against Syria, was, in essence, not indeed a struggle for territorial aggrandizement, but a struggle for wealth and even more for power, initiated by the imperialistic ambition of the Senate. And the results of the Macedonian and Syrian Wars would, at first sight, seem to justify this opinion. That the Romans, in waging these wars, did not yield to a desire for territorial expansion, is unquestionably true. Beyond the Adriatic they limited themselves to the recovery of Lower Illyria[1], of which they had become masters in 228, adding to it only the two island dependencies of Zacynthus and Cephallenia—modest acquisitions indeed: in Greece, Macedonia, Asia, where they might have seized land at their pleasure, they took nothing; this is conclusive. On the other hand, these wars were highly lucrative. The indemnities and booty of their defeated enemies caused vast wealth to pour into Rome. In ten years alone (197 to 187) the minted and unminted gold and silver paid into the treasury exceeded 90 million *denarii*[2], and to this must be added the multitude of works of art and precious objects of incalculable value, which lent such unexampled brilliance to the triumphs of Flamininus, L. Scipio 'Asiagenus', Manlius and Fulvius. And above all, these wars had political consequences infinitely more important than any pecuniary benefits. Following upon the defeat of Carthage, they brought about the supreme control of the Roman people over the civilized world. The supremacy of Rome by land and sea

$$\gamma\hat{\eta}s \ \kappa\alpha\grave{\iota} \ \theta\alpha\lambda\acute{\alpha}\sigma\sigma\eta s \ \sigma\kappa\hat{\eta}\pi\tau\rho\alpha \ \kappa\alpha\grave{\iota} \ \mu\text{o}\nu\alpha\rho\chi\acute{\iota}\alpha\nu$$

already sung by the poet Lycophron on the morrow of Cynoscephalae was an established fact after Magnesia.

The Romans were certainly not indifferent to money (as is proved by the example of Manlius and Fulvius) or to power: their victory over Antiochus, the thought that they had no longer a rival, filled them with pride[3]. Yet it does not follow nor does it seem probable to the present writer that it was greed of wealth and empire which determined their course of action. Indeed it is most noteworthy that they never thought of turning their victories to economic advantage: the treaties which they made contained no commercial stipulation in their own favour (though the treaty of Apamea contained one in favour of Rhodes[4]), and they did not impose tribute on any of the peoples whom they conquered—a sufficiently clear proof that in deciding on their policy they were little if at all obsessed by thoughts of gain[5]. And, as we have seen, not one of their political acts from 200 to 188 bears the clear stamp of imperialism or cannot be explained except by a passion for domination. The attribution to the Senate of 'Eastern plans' or of a 'Mediterranean programme' which it was only waiting for

[1] The territory under the protectorate of Rome was, however, appreciably enlarged towards the east.

[2] Equivalent to over three and a half million pounds sterling in gold values.

[3] See Appian, *Syr.* 37.   [4] Polybius XXI, 43, 17.

[5] The immunity from *portoria* exacted from the Ambraciotes in 187 (p. 348) is apparently exceptional and is unimportant.

a favourable opportunity to carry out, is no more than arbitrary conjecture, unsupported by the facts. There is nothing to show that in 200 the *patres* were more attracted than before to Greek lands or that their eastern policy, hitherto entirely dictated by the needs of the moment, changed its character at that date. Everything leads us to believe that then, as before, their intervention was merely the result of external circumstances which seemed to impose action upon them. As in 229 they would not have crossed the Adriatic but for the provocation offered them by Teuta, and in 214 would not have gone into Greece but for the necessity of countering the alliance of Philip with Hannibal, so, in all likelihood, they would not have turned eastward again but for their discovery of the alliance between Philip and Antiochus and the threat which they saw in it.

The truth is that they imagined themselves to be threatened when they were not. The insincere alliance of the two kings was in no way aimed at them; and, moreover, when they did allow it to alarm them, it was already breaking down. If their intervention had been less prompt, they would probably have seen the erstwhile allies open enemies: a war would have broken out between them, which would have freed Rome from all anxiety from that quarter. In any event, as is shown by his prompt seizure of Lysimacheia, Philip would have prevented Antiochus from setting foot in Europe, and so would have vanished even the phantom of that 'Seleucid peril' which, from the first, was the constant preoccupation of the Romans. Indeed it was their act, when they crippled Philip thinking thereby to weaken Antiochus, that allowed the latter a free road westwards and enabled him to cross the Hellespont. But, even then, there was, as we have seen, no real Seleucid peril. If it ever existed, it was in 192, when the Great King marched down into Greece with Hannibal in his train, and it was again the Romans who created it by their errors of policy, the fruit of their vain alarms. To guard against an imaginary threat of aggression they were unconscionably persistent in urging Antiochus to withdraw from Europe and their offensive insistence only succeeded in exhausting his patience. By an ironic paradox, the two enterprises which brought them so much glory and laid the foundation of their world-supremacy had their origin in a groundless fear. Had they been more keen-sighted and less easily alarmed, they would not have come to dominate the Hellenic world. More probably they would have concentrated their efforts in the neighbouring barbarian countries west of Italy—and that with more reason and more advantage to themselves.

If they were thus misled by unfounded fears it was due partly to the suspicious temper of the Senate which inclined them to detect only too readily dangerous neighbours plotting the ruin of Rome, partly to their profound ignorance of eastern affairs. The *patres* had omitted to inform themselves about these matters, and strangely neglected for a long time to do so—one is surprised to find, for example, that in 196 they had not got wind of the treaty about to be concluded between Antiochus and Egypt. Lacking the knowledge necessary for forming an opinion of their own, they believed what they were told and were curiously swayed by foreign influences. This was no new thing: it has been maintained, and with much probability, that the quarrel between Rome and Carthage over Spain was largely due to the reports and intrigues of the Massiliotes in Rome[1]. It is even more certain that the real authors of the Second Macedonian War were Attalus and Rhodes, and that the war against Antiochus was mainly the work of Eumenes—the same Eumenes who was to have so large a hand in bringing about the war against Perseus (see below, p. 256). So far as the East is concerned, the Senate, so jealous of its authority and reputed so clear-sighted, only saw through the eyes of others and only acted upon the impulse of others—of others who had an interest in impelling it to act. After 200 B.C. in their eastern policy the Romans, little as they knew it, followed where others led: while they thought they were only providing for the safety of Rome, they were, in reality, serving the cause and furthering the interests of Pergamum and Rhodes[2].

[1] Vol. VII, p. 809 *sq.* Cf. T. Frank, *Roman Imperialism*, pp. 121 *sqq.* See also above, pp. 27 *sqq.*

[2] Cf. A. Piganiol, *Rev. E.A.* XXVI, 1924, pp. 181 *sqq.*

CHAPTER VIII

THE FALL OF THE MACEDONIAN MONARCHY

I. THE SETTLEMENT AFTER MAGNESIA

THE Romans hoped that the settlement of 188 B.C. would procure them some respite from distant wars on a large scale. They had plenty of troubles nearer home, and, whatever advantage individual generals may have expected to gain from their conduct of campaigns, any wise Roman statesman must have aimed at reducing the drain on Roman resources which great wars involved. The Senate felt bound to fight against Philip immediately after the long struggle with Hannibal. The war against Philip had been succeeded by a period of anxiety culminating in the war against Antiochus; and now at last it seemed possible that an arrangement might be made which, while securing sufficiently the prestige and influence of Rome over all that part of the civilized world in which she was interested, would at the same time set her free for the solution of her own special problems.

So far as Asia is concerned the Romans may well have regarded the settlement as satisfactory. The kingdom of Antiochus had been regarded as the source of danger, and it was now reduced to a less important position. Both Armenia and Sophene, which had been provinces of Antiochus, became independent. Bithynia, Pontus and Cappadocia grew in importance. Antiochus himself, who had contributed much by his personality to the successes gained by his kingdom during the earlier part of his reign, did not long survive his defeat. In 187 he met his death at the hands of the

Note. All reliable information (apart from a very few inscriptions) for the period covered by this chapter and the next comes ultimately from Polybius. Only fragments of the relevant books (XXII–XL) have reached us. We possess Livy's complete story (XXXVIII–XLV), except for some serious gaps, as far as 167 B.C.; thenceforward he is only represented by epitomes, and in later writers who borrowed from him. Livy, Diodorus, Plutarch and others help us to reconstruct part of the missing narrative of Polybius, but they also contain a good deal of unreliable matter. See the note to chapter VI above. See also Map 9 facing p. 304.

people of Elymaïs as he sought to seize the treasures of one of their temples[1].

Something had been done to reward Rhodes (pp. 230 *sqq.*): from the Roman point of view this reward could be justified both on the ground of valuable services rendered by Rhodes and of general agreement between the policies which commended themselves to Rhodes and to Rome. Though the Romans had not set free all the Greek cities in Asia, they might claim to have shown preference for this treatment, and they might hope for some moral advantage from the fact that nothing in Asia was to be subject to Rome. Of the newer kingdoms, Pergamum had gained a very large extension of territory (p. 232); the consciousness that this was due to the support of Rome should suffice to cause its king to maintain a pro-Roman attitude. The attitude of the other kings might be more doubtful, but the Roman campaign against the Galatians had been useful to all of them, and fear of his neighbours ought to prove enough to prevent any one of them from becoming pronouncedly anti-Roman. Egypt could be expected to remain friendly, if only on the ground that Syria would not be too friendly; circumstances might arise in which the quarrels between them or the differences within Egypt itself would make Roman intervention necessary; but nothing could be done to prevent those contingencies, and the reduced strength of the Syrian kingdom would at any rate postpone one of these dangers for a time. Indeed, it was twenty years before the traditional struggle between Syria and Egypt became a serious source of anxiety to Rome (p. 283 *sq.*).

It is possible to criticize certain points in this settlement, and to say, in the light of later events, that causes of friction should have been foreseen and prevented. But it is not at all likely that the Romans wished to promote friction or to provide themselves with frequent opportunities for interference: they had quite enough to occupy their attention without having to fight in the East. Diplomatic missions had to be sent frequently: the object was generally to prevent the incipient quarrels from growing so serious as to make it necessary for Rome to intervene by force, and, in so far as such means produced the end for which they were designed, the Romans could be satisfied with the results of their policy.

In Europe the problems were harder and the attempts to solve them were less successful. The Aetolians probably expected to be treated more severely than they actually were: the treaty made their foreign policy dependent on that of Rome, but any soreness

[1] E. R. Bevan, *House of Seleucus*, II, p. 120 n. 1.

which the war left was not increased by an unnecessarily harsh settlement. The Peloponnese presented greater difficulties. The Achaean League claimed now to include the whole Peloponnese, but in view of the circumstances under which Elis and Sparta had become members (p. 235), either or both of these might cause trouble in the future. Further, the rival tendencies to strengthen the central authority and to maintain the independence of each several part, and the lack of sympathy between Flamininus, who was over-ready with advice, and Philopoemen, who was reluctant to take it, made any decision far from easy.

It was only to be expected that the guarantee of the freedom of Greek cities would be followed by a number of appeals to Rome on the part of those who felt, whether justly or not, that their cause could be supported by reference to that principle. What were the Romans to do? They could not refuse to take any further interest in Greek questions: it did not require philhellenic enthusiasm to convince Rome that, as matters were, she could not regard these things as entirely outside the sphere of her interests. Still less could she be expected to undertake direct responsibility for the affairs of Greece. Even if she had the power, such a course would have satisfied neither those Romans who preferred to be free from the entanglements of Greek quarrels, nor those who believed in the Greeks and whose creed accordingly included the article that it must be for the Greeks themselves to solve their own difficulties. The Romans may have shown hesitation in dealing with the questions raised by the Achaean League, even hesitation to act upon Roman decisions; but, in so far as they encouraged the Greeks to settle their own difficulties, discouraged violence, and endeavoured to show that they wished to be the friends of all parties, their behaviour was as correct as circumstances allowed it to be. Their character inclined them to settle things on what seemed likely to be a permanent basis; if this could not be done without undue interference with the concerns of their friends, the process of time and the influence of conciliatory advice might effect a gradual improvement. They had already discovered that it was difficult to find out the truth from the involved or contradictory explanations of Greek spokesmen, and they may have anticipated that there would be more trouble of the same kind in the future: but those who were interested in Greek questions as such and those whose outlook was more definitely Roman could agree in holding that careful consideration of each question as it presented itself, conducted with patience and an endeavour to understand the principles involved, was the only available course.

The attitude both of the Achaean and of the Aetolian League towards Rome was bound to be affected by the possibility that Philip of Macedon might one day re-assert his claims in Greece. The king's earlier life had shown strange changes of fortune; he had recovered from difficult positions by that energy which his enemies never denied to him. What attitude should Rome have adopted towards him? The treaty at the close of the Second Macedonian War had not professed to alter his position as a free monarch: its provisions had dealt only with the withdrawal of his claims outside his own dominions and with details arising out of the war. He was encouraged at the same time to apply to the Roman Senate for recognition as a friend and ally of Rome: probably some form of this favour was granted him. He was suspected of doubting at one time whether it would be better for him to support Rome or Antiochus, but it would be unsafe to build anything on the existence of such suspicions. At any rate, the Romans had no cause to complain of the facilities provided for their army on its march to the Hellespont: their envoy was duly impressed with the admirable nature of the arrangements, and this sense of Philip's power in that neighbourhood may have had something to do with the further suspicion that he was in part responsible for the severe losses of Manlius Vulso on his return through Thrace (p. 233). Philip had not been asked to contribute troops for the campaign in Asia; in Greece he had helped considerably, and the only fear seems to have been whether he was not doing too much. He may have hoped to be left in possession of some of those districts which he had overrun in the course of aiding Rome against the Aetolians (p. 235). But he had certainly sent messengers to Rome, whose congratulations were accepted as sufficient, not only to justify a polite answer, but to allow of the return of the king's son Demetrius who had been a hostage.

It is sometimes contended that the services of Philip deserved more generous recognition, and that such recognition by Rome would have maintained the integrity of the Macedonian kingdom, or, if its end was bound to come, would have caused that end to come in a peaceful way. Generosity to a former opponent is often good policy, but generosity should not be shown at the expense of others. The return of the hostage and the remission of part of the remaining instalments of tribute are eminently proper actions on the part of Rome. But the rewarding of Philip's co-operation by the reduction of certain districts to a lower status than that to which Roman principles entitled them, would not have been easy to defend.

It is probable that Philip, who presumably attached little importance to the principle of liberty, was dissatisfied with the return for his assistance. Though the grievances which Livy mentions (xxxix, 23, 5 *sq.*) can hardly be more than guesses, since the king is not likely to have announced them publicly in this form, they may well reflect his real feelings. He hoped that the Romans would not trouble to prevent him from punishing any Macedonians who may have deserted him during his war against Rome; he was justly annoyed at the lack of tact which ordered him to desist from the siege of Lamia under circumstances that showed too obviously how little he was trusted; and, if he was to be consoled for losing the honour of receiving the surrender of Lamia by receiving permission to attack certain Thessalian towns, he probably expected that his kingdom would be increased as the result of his efforts (p. 216 *sq.*). The consul Acilius Glabrio promised that, when any towns or districts had sided with the Aetolians of their own accord and were subsequently reduced by Philip, the king might retain them, but stipulated that those which had taken the anti-Roman side under compulsion should become free[1]. This distinction is in accordance with what the Romans had decided in Asia about Eumenes, and the Senate, if we may judge from the attitude of the Roman commissioners at a later date, were prepared to agree with it: but, unless the particulars of each case were investigated carefully at once, it would be difficult to act upon it fairly, and, even if such an investigation were made, there would be room for difference of opinion.

The Romans may have been mistaken in insisting too strongly on the principle of liberty. This principle had caused trouble enough to the Greeks, and perhaps the Greeks themselves were trying to find their way to something which, while preserving all the advantages of full local autonomy, should allow for more permanent unions than had been possible in the past. But here again it is hard to criticize the Roman attitude; it is evident that Polybius thought it generous[2], though his Greek political experience would have been quite sufficient to show him any disadvantages to which the rigid application of the principle might lead. If the Greeks were looking for some more practicable formula, we have no reason for supposing that they had found it; and the Romans can hardly be blamed for not taking that step in Greek political philosophy which the Greeks had been powerless

---

[1] Livy xxxix, 25, 5; 26, 14; see above, pp. 212 *sqq.*
[2] See, *e.g.* Polybius xviii, 46, 14, 15.

to take. The Romans believed themselves to be asserting what the best Greeks believed: at any rate a Greek city was better off in independence or isolation than under the unsatisfactory control of most of the kings of the time. From Philip's point of view the Romans were a distant people who had accepted a rather unpractical principle of action: their practical nature might cause them not to apply it too strictly. From the Roman point of view Philip, even if he were not actuated by any definitely-conceived purpose of revenge for the humiliation of his defeat, was a powerful king whose past history showed that he was not to be trusted blindly; yet his power was a safeguard against the anarchy which might easily follow on its destruction. The relations between the two in 188 were probably as satisfactory as it was possible to make them: tact on both sides would be necessary to maintain them in that condition, and, as tact was not the most conspicuous virtue of the Romans, there might well be trouble between them: but it is easier to see this than to say what should have been done to improve the position.

II. THE CLOSING YEARS OF PHILIP'S REIGN

Polybius (xxii, 18) formed the opinion that Philip had decided on a fresh war against Rome so soon as circumstances were favourable, that his preparations were ready by the time of his death, and that his successor Perseus only carried into execution the plans which his father had formed. It may seem rash to question the authority of Polybius on such a matter. But, though the actions of Philip during the last years of his life, so far as we know them, are not inconsistent with this view, they do not necessarily amount to more than attempts to strengthen the position of his kingdom, and, in the absence of direct evidence, it is not certain what use he intended to make of his increased strength. Philip may have wondered whether Rome would stand the strain to which she had been subjected, or may have speculated on the chance that she might ultimately decide to concentrate on the west of Europe. It could do no harm to consolidate his kingdom, provided he could do this without arousing Roman suspicions. No doubt he had jealous neighbours ready to represent each of his actions as directed against Rome, but their representations were not necessarily any more disinterested than the actions of Philip himself. We cannot be sure that a ruler, who had lived through such surprising changes of fortune and whose character had been marked by such inconsistencies even in his best days, had formed definite intentions for the future; we can only consider what he did, so far as the fragmentary accounts allow us to do so, and leave Perseus to bear his own share of praise or blame for the results which he attained from the materials provided by his father.

Philip certainly strengthened his economic resources. He increased the taxes on agricultural products and import duties, resumed the working of disused mines and started many new ones. He took measures to add to the population, and imported a large number of Thracians into Macedonia. All these steps may have been intended to provide in peace time for a future war[1]: but improved resources can be devoted to other purposes than war, and, though it is only too probable that the interchange of inhabitants between Thrace and Macedonia was attended by that suffering which often accompanied such proceedings in antiquity, its object need not have been entirely military. The signs of increasing strength in Macedonia led to envoys being sent to Rome in the winter of 186–5[2] to point out that Philip was not observing the conditions of the peace. Thessalians, Perrhaebians and Athamanians came with complaints: the points which they raised were detailed and puzzling, and the Senate felt that, though these might be unimportant, the questions asked by the envoys from Eumenes, about Thrace and especially about Aenus and Maronea which Philip had occupied, could not be disregarded. They adopted the only possible course, of sending three Commissioners to investigate matters on the spot.

The Commissioners went to Tempe and gave audience to a large number of representatives. Those who spoke first were polite in their references to Philip, but, as matters proceeded, an increasingly bitter tone showed itself. Even if these questions could have been discussed without heat, a decision would not have been easy. Acilius Glabrio had promised Philip that he might retain any places which had joined the Aetolians voluntarily (p. 245). The Aetolians had confused the issue by extending their influence widely during the war, thus making it hard to determine whether this condition had been fulfilled. Questions accordingly arose in regard to Philippopolis, Tricca, Phaloria and Eurymenae in Thessaly, and Gonnocondylum (Olympias), Malloea and Ericinium in Perrhaebia; the Athamanians said that the liberty of their country was in process of being lost and they also

---

[1] Polybius XXIII, 10; Livy XXXIX, 24.

[2] In support of this date see Niese, *Gesch. der griech. und maked. Staaten,* III, p. 22 n. I.

claimed the border forts of Athenaeum and Poetneum[1]. It was complained that Philip had despoiled some of these places or removed prominent citizens in the expectation of having to restore the cities, that he had unfairly pressed the commercial interests of Demetrias against those of Phthiotic Thebes and that he had prevented free access to the Romans by waylaying envoys.

Philip was able to give a confident reply to these last charges: he could not prevent sailors from choosing whither they would sail; vague allegations of interference with one set only of the many envoys who had been sent to injure his cause, were valueless. As regards the places whose status was called in question he made a counterclaim to the Menelaïs and the Paracheloïs in Dolopia, and to Petra in Pieria, all of which he asserted should really be his. Probably he hoped for a decision which would leave the existing position unchanged by showing that there were claims on both sides which could be left to balance each other. Perhaps that was why he adduced Xyniae, a town which had been taken by the Aetolians after its inhabitants had deserted it, and had been allowed to remain in Philip's possession, though on the strict application of the Roman principle it was entitled to be free. But his impatience at the charges caused him to make injudicious remarks: he spoke lightly of the value of freedom as used by those with no experience of it, and compared some of his accusers with recently emancipated slaves who did not know that liberty involved responsibility. He added the menacing phrase 'that his sun had not altogether set' (*nondum omnium dierum solem occidisse*)[2]. Such an attitude was unfortunate in the presence of the Roman Commissioners, who would be only too likely to think of it as directed not only against the Thessalians but also against Rome. He did not make matters better by adding that he was well aware that he would have to yield what had been given to him, whether his cause were just or not[3].

The Commissioners decided that the Macedonian garrisons should be withdrawn from all the places about which doubts had been raised and that legal machinery was to be devised for settling any further questions that might arise between the Macedonians and their neighbours. They added an opinion that the boundaries of the Macedonian kingdom should be the ancient ones. Probably they meant no more by this than that Rome would not countenance

---

[1] Livy xxxix, 25. Not much reliance can be put on the names in the text of this passage, several of which present considerable difficulties.
[2] Livy xxxix, 26, 9.   [3] *Ib.* xxxix, 28, 1.

any aggression; but the boundaries had varied so much at different times that it is difficult to see whither this principle might lead, and the grave offence which Livy tells us that the king took at the result may be connected as much with doubts on this point as with any disappointment which he felt about particular places. He may have thought that, in what they said about his hereditary dominions, as in the value which they set upon liberty, the Romans were enunciating a principle which sounded well but admitted of diverse applications, and that, having stated the principle without due consideration, they would be obliged to defend any deductions that might be drawn from it. In so far as the Commissioners did not secure general agreement with their decisions, they failed; but it is easier to see reasons why Philip should have been dissatisfied with them than to find much positive ground for criticizing their procedure. They desired that, so far as his relation with other Greek states was concerned, he should neither be better nor worse off for having helped Rome. We need not attribute sentimental views, either to Romans in general or to these particular Commissioners, of whose opinions we know little, to feel that this was the reasonable attitude for Rome to adopt.

The Commissioners then moved to Thessalonica, to consider the questions about Aenus and Maronea, which were regarded at Rome as more serious. The representatives of Eumenes said that they had no comment to offer on the Roman wish (if it were the Roman wish) that these cities should be free, except to express a hope that their freedom would be a reality. If, however, the cities were to be regarded as a prize of war captured from Antiochus, Eumenes claimed to be a more proper recipient than Philip. The ten Commissioners had assigned the Chersonese and Lysimacheia to Eumenes; did not the possession of Aenus and Maronea follow as a matter of course? Philip pointed out that this was a doubtful argument: if the Commissioners expressly named the Chersonese and Lysimacheia, and made no mention of these cities, it was as legitimate to argue that they were meant to be excluded. But the contention that Eumenes had rendered greater assistance to the Romans than Philip drove him to say, truly or not (p. 212 n. 1), that favourable offers of alliance had been made to him by Antiochus and that, in spite of them, he had rendered to Rome the services for which he was asked, while Eumenes could not have retained his kingdom at all if Antiochus had been victorious. The fact that claims could be made now which had not been put forward before the ten Commissioners showed in itself that he must not expect equitable treatment from the Romans. He repeated his old grievances: he had been forbidden the favour, unimportant in itself but of some value to his prestige, of reasserting his authority over the subjects who had deserted him during a period of truce; the recent decision had taken from him the advantage which was to compensate him for his rebuff about Lamia (p. 248). After all, he was a friend and an ally to Rome; why should he be treated as an enemy?

The Commissioners, impressed by the substance of this complaint, were reluctant to pronounce further decisions against Philip. But the inhabitants of Maronea were not satisfied with the existing state of things. They complained that they had to endure several garrisons, not one only, that the place was full of Macedonians, that there was no freedom of speech, and that opponents of the Macedonians had to suffer loss of rights or exile. They contended that a recent construction of a new road had enabled Philip to pretend that the city and the portion of the sea-coast had been recognized as part of his sphere of influence, whereas it had definitely been intended to exclude him from them. It appeared therefore that matters had reached a state which went outside the competence of the three Commissioners: their function was one of interpretation, and, if new questions of policy were to be raised, it was for the Senate to decide them. If the ten Commissioners had given the cities to Eumenes, they were his, and the three Commissioners introduced no alteration; but it seemed very doubtful whether they could be assigned to Eumenes on this ground. If Philip had been able to assert that he had captured the cities in war, they might be his on that ground; but this, too, was doubtful. If the question could not be decided on either of these grounds, the Senate must investigate the matter further. Meanwhile, however, the garrisons must be removed pending the decision: and, as the garrisons were Macedonian, Philip would feel that it was he again who lost by the arrangement; for, if garrisons were once removed from a place where they were evidently unpopular, it was not likely that they would ever return.

It was plain to the Senate, as soon as the Commissioners delivered their report, that a further commission must be sent to Greece. The three had not been received at a meeting of the Achaean League: at this they had taken offence, and, in regard to that part of their duties, they were said—not unfairly—to have left matters more uncertain than they had been before. More investigation was therefore necessary, and a fresh mission under Appius Claudius was sent. In regard to the points left open by the three Commissioners, the Senate decided that Aenus and Maronea should be free: apparently they took the view that Philip's boundary was fixed by the old royal road, which went inland and did not touch that part of the coast, and there would have been even less justification for assigning these cities to Eumenes. So Claudius and his colleagues were to see whether Philip had withdrawn his garrisons and whether he had done what he had been told to do in relation to Thessaly and Perrhaebia.

The intimation that he was not to retain Aenus or Maronea seems to have inspired Philip to one of those acts of miscalculated cruelty of which he was always capable. He was determined that in any event his opponents in Maronea should not gain. He ordered Onomastus, his officer commanding the coast district, to arrange through Casander, an agent who had lived long in Maronea, for the introduction at night of a band of Thracians who perpetrated a massacre. Philip, who believed in the effect of terrorism, thought that the truth would not be discovered; it proved otherwise, and Appius Claudius demanded that Onomastus and Casander should be sent to Rome to be examined there. No doubt he took the ground that, if these men were innocent, they had nothing to fear; but the attitude of Philip increased the suspicion against him. He declared that he had duly removed his garrison and that the massacre was due to the dissensions of the citizens and not to Macedonian soldiers[1]: but that plea would be vain if the facts were truly stated. He tried to excuse Onomastus on the ground that he was not in the neighbourhood at the time. He was very reluctant to allow Casander to go: and, when he at last consented, Casander died on the journey. Philip may have been maligned in being accused of poisoning Casander[2], but the story told us is not so inconsistent with Philip's character as to justify us in saying that it is impossible (cf. p. 144).

It must have been plain to Philip that the Romans distrusted him: he was not ready for war with Rome, even if he looked forward to it, and, unless he took some action, there might be a risk of his being asked to comply with fresh conditions which he would regard as humiliating. He accordingly sent Demetrius, his son, to Rome, in the hope that the young man, who had created a favourable impression as a hostage, would be able to serve his father's interests. The task was not an easy one. Rumours had arisen that the Romans were ready to receive and credit accusations against Philip, and it was certainly the duty of the Romans to see

[1] Polybius XXII, 13.
[2] Polybius XXII, 14; Livy XXXIX, 34, 10, 'veneno creditur sublatus.'

that the judicial methods which they had prescribed for boundary disputes should be acted upon. Accordingly in 184 B.C. a bewildering number of representatives came to Rome, from individuals, cities, or tribes, alleging grievances of all kinds, connected with land, slaves or cattle, with Philip's refusal to act upon arbitral decisions or with his corrupt methods for securing decisions in his favour. Philip was never popular with his neighbours and Polybius (XXIII, 1) describes these representatives as including all who lived near the frontier of Macedonia. Athenaeus, brother of Eumenes, was there also, complaining of aid given by Philip to Prusias of Bithynia in his quarrel with Pergamum (p. 282) and raising again the old question of the Thracian cities.

After statements which had occupied three days, the Senate did not know what to do, and Demetrius was asked whether he was the bearer of written instructions from his father. He had a paper with him, and produced it, though probably Philip never contemplated that it should be read aloud as it stood. It stated that Philip had done all that was required of him, or that, if in any case he had not done so, it was the fault of others; it also made it plain, as would be natural enough in notes prepared solely for his son's use, that Philip did not admit the justice of all the decisions. The Senate returned a general answer which indicated that they were willing to put the most favourable construction on all that Philip had done or would do, in view of his having sent so acceptable a messenger as Demetrius. Further envoys would satisfy themselves as to the position of the several controverted matters and would explain personally to the king how much the Romans appreciated the friendly feelings of his son.

Polybius (XXIII, 3) tells us that this visit by Demetrius, though it served to check for a time a growing feeling of misunderstanding between Rome and Macedonia, tended in the long run to accentuate the difficulties. The Romans may have intended no more than to show kindness towards Demetrius: they can hardly be supposed to have known intimately his exact personal relation to his father, or, if they had reason for guessing that those relations were not all that they should have been, to have wished to make them worse. The reports of confidential conversations with Flamininus, in which Roman support was promised to Demetrius as his father's successor, cannot be accepted without question even on the authority of Polybius: popularity in Rome might easily be misinterpreted in Macedonia, and stories of what a man may have said in an interview are often retailed without inquiry, on the basis of reports from those who are or claim to be his friends. Probably things were not made better by the fact that Philocles, who had been sent by the king to represent him specially on the subject of Prusias, received scant attention, and that the answer to this part of the enquiry was, if we may trust the report, rudely curt. Philocles was one of those with whom the king had discussed the mission of Demetrius, and he presumably belonged to the king's intimate advisers; he would not have been likely to carry back a favourable account of the visit; for its results, so far as Philip could regard them as satisfactory, were attributed exclusively to the favourable impression produced by Demetrius. Perhaps the Romans indulged in language of excessive courtliness, without enough experience to enable them to make it innocuous; and it is safer to attribute to them dangerous experiments of that kind than to suppose that they wished to produce dissensions in the royal house of Macedonia which were at least as likely to cause trouble to the friends of Rome as to her enemies.

On his return, Demetrius found himself regarded in Macedonia as having saved the situation. His relation to Rome suggested that he might in time become king through Roman influence, and Macedonian time-servers would naturally try to gain favour with him. He may not have been careful enough in a difficult situation, and his elder brother, about whose parentage there was some doubt, might well feel jealous. Their father obeyed the commands of Rome; but his reluctance was obvious to the Roman envoy Q. Marcius Philippus, who reported on his return that Philip would continue to be obedient no longer than he was obliged. It is not surprising that the next message from Rome, while giving the king some praise for his conformity to Roman wishes, added a warning for the future.

Philip's active nature demanded that he should do something further to strengthen his position. Henceforward he neglected places on the coast, where Rome had curbed Macedonian expansion, and undertook expeditions in the opposite direction. An attack on the centre of Thrace reached Philippopolis and established a garrison, which could not however maintain itself there for very long: a new town in the Paeonian north of Macedonia, not far from Stobi, was called Perseïs in honour of his elder son; large shiftings of population were effected, under circumstances that caused much suffering, with the object of providing reliable supporters of the king in the most important districts. His suspicions continually increased, and he issued orders for the arrest of the children of those whom he had previously executed.

In 181 B.C. he undertook an expedition into the Balkans: the object is said to have been the investigation of a rumour that the Black Sea, the Adriatic, the Danube and the Alps could all be seen from one place, and those who interpreted every action of the king as directed against Rome added that a plan for the invasion of Italy was to be devised from this point[1]. Whatever its object, the expedition was a failure, and it was accompanied by such privations that a friendly tribe were nearly ruined by the hungry soldiers in their retreat. A further ambitious scheme was to destroy the Dardani, who were always regarded as dangerous to the Macedonians, by means of Bastarnae brought across the Danube; this plan also is represented as directed ultimately against Rome.

But Philip's life was drawing near its end. The elder son, Perseus, nervous as to the succession, and afraid lest Demetrius should succeed his father through Roman influence, managed to lead Philip to believe that Demetrius was too dangerous to be allowed to live. The story, which ends with the poisoning and suffocation of Demetrius[2], has reached us in a form that suggests, as do also certain other features of the later life of Philip and of the reign of Perseus, that some author or authors wrote tragedies or historical novels dealing with the ruin of the Macedonian royal house. But the general outline of the incidents is so like other family quarrels that we have no sufficient ground for doubting its substantial truth. The death of Demetrius was followed by a period of acute remorse in the mind of Philip, when he found that the evidence on which he had acted was largely unreliable, and that a letter from Flamininus, in which the writer made charges against Demetrius while pretending to excuse him, was a forgery. The king endeavoured to secure that Perseus should not gain by the deceit; but most of those in attendance on Philip were so completely won over to Perseus' interest as to enable him to succeed without opposition on his father's death (179 B.C.).

If the substance of these stories is true, it is easy to believe that the death of Philip in his fifty-ninth year was due to agony of mind rather than of body: for, though there is much in his career which cannot be commended or excused, he was capable of generous instincts. One may well believe that he only gave the fatal orders reluctantly, that he was convinced at the time of the truth of the accusation against his son, and that he afterwards

[1] Livy XL, 21, 2; cf. Polybius XXIV, 4.
[2] Livy XL, 24.

came to see that it was, at least in part, contrary to the facts. Demetrius was popular at Rome; but Philip is not likely to have regarded such popularity as an offence in itself, apart from evidence as to the use to be made of it, and the discovery that the friends of Perseus were relying on forged evidence would be enough to show him that disloyalty to the Macedonian cause could not be proved against Demetrius without false witness.

III. THE EARLY REIGN OF PERSEUS

We shall probably never know what degree of blame should attach to Perseus for his brother's death. But, after all doubtful details of the story have been removed, there remains the fact that ugly rumours to the discredit of Perseus were bound to arise and to be believed by many in Rome. The attitude of Perseus on succeeding to his father's throne was quite correct: he asked at once for a renewal of the alliance on the existing terms. But, though this was granted, little would be known about him except that he was not on good terms with the young Macedonian who had been popular in Rome, that this very popularity had come to be regarded as the ground of the dissension between them, and that Perseus rather than Demetrius had been associated with his father in those schemes for strengthening his kingdom which nervous Romans persisted in considering as directed against the Republic. If Perseus intended to maintain peaceful relations with Rome while at the same time safeguarding the dignity and independence of Macedonia, if, in fact, he wished to attempt what could under no circumstances have been an easy task, he began under a severe handicap.

It is plain that he possessed certain good qualities. His appearance and manner were kingly, he avoided some of his father's faults and the measures with which his reign commenced showed generosity and broad-mindedness. He released state prisoners, recalled exiles, restored them their property, and adopted a more conciliatory attitude than his father to the Greeks outside Macedonia. He showed vigour in repelling the attack made by Abrupolis, the ruler of the Thracian Sapaei, on the mines of Pangaeus, and he can hardly be criticized for going on to expel Abrupolis from his kingdom, though this action was treated some years later as an offence against an ally of Rome, and made into the primary cause of the Third Macedonian War. Perseus, as was natural, sought to magnify the importance and dignity of his rule. He married Laodice, daughter of Seleucus IV of Syria, who was escorted by the Rhodians with a great parade of naval strength, and gave his sister to Prusias king of Bithynia; subjugated Dolopia, and paid a somewhat ostentatious visit to Delphi (174 B.C.).

All these acts might have been accepted as harmless efforts at consolidating his position in relation to his own subjects and his neighbours, had he not begun with the reputation of being an enemy to Rome, and had not his enemies, Eumenes in particular, seen to it that this reputation was not forgotten. At last the conviction grew strong on both sides that a third war between Rome and Macedonia was inevitable, and wars that seem bound to come sooner or later are not easily averted or even delayed. That Perseus wished to make war at once is improbable, whatever confidence he may have had in the military establishment bequeathed him by his father. The Romans sent embassies in bewildering succession, and these missions show at least that Rome had no wish to proceed to extremes so long as an explanation was possible. But each group of envoys were more convinced than their predecessors that Perseus was not prepared for a satisfactory agreement: they complained that he avoided seeing them, and they gained increasing evidence of the strength of the king's resources.

Finally in 172 B.C. came the visit of Eumenes to Rome which did most to drive Rome into war. We are not obliged to suppose that the Romans took seriously all the charges brought by Eumenes. He dwelt on Perseus' long experience in distant wars; but, even if his presence in Pelagonia as early as 199 B.C. and in Dolopia in 189 (p. 226) are only specimens of the duties with which his father had entrusted him, the Romans could hardly have been offended at the successor to the throne being trained in this way. Strength of body and suppleness of mind were made into accusations against him. It must have been clear to the Roman senators, in spite of the disclaimer of Eumenes, that this and much else was inspired by personal dislike and jealousy.

But no doubt many of his points were based upon fact. It was true that Perseus had expelled Abrupolis, though the Romans had not at the time complained of this treatment of one whom it now suited them to call a friend and ally. The Illyrian chieftain Artetaurus had been murdered and the murderers had taken refuge in the kingdom of Perseus: the king denied all knowledge of the crime and added that he had expelled the murderers from his country when he learned that their presence was unacceptable to the Romans, but it would be easy to suggest that the murderers

of one who had also now come to be described as a friend and
ally had good reasons for going to Perseus rather than elsewhere.
The quarrels between the Dardani and the Bastarnae had ended
unfavourably for the Bastarnae (p. 254). Perseus had denied any
complicity in their invasion, but the fact that the destruction of
the Dardani would have freed his hands had caused anxiety in
Rome, which this failure had probably not entirely removed.
There were mysterious rumours about an intrigue with Carthage,
where messengers were alleged to have been received at night
and answers returned to Macedonia: Romans, who had been in
Africa recently, reported that Masinissa was ready to tell them
all about it, though of the Carthaginians themselves it could only
be said that they were not sufficiently emphatic in denying it
(p. 471). Perseus assisted the people of Byzantium against their
Thracian enemies, and this action may have been, as Eumenes said
it was, contrary to the terms of his treaty, even though the Romans
had accepted the excuses made for it. He had attained greater
success than his father in securing influence in Greece. He had
come near securing from the Achaean League the withdrawal of
their refusal to allow any Macedonian in their territory, and it
had been openly argued on that occasion by a supporter of Rome
that war was certain to come before long. Some Thebans of
Roman sympathies had perished on their way to Rome, and, though
it was asserted that this was due to shipwreck, suspicion could be
cast on Perseus of being concerned in their fate, just as easily as
though they had died suddenly and he had been accused of
poisoning them. Troubles in Aetolia, Thessaly and Perrhaebia
could be represented as stirred up by him so as to give him excuse
for meddling: inscriptions at Delphi and Delos could be cited as
evidence of his far-reaching designs[1].

Probably it was as difficult for Perseus as for the Romans to
avoid interference in Greece. The Roman influence was thrown
on the side of order, and that frequently meant the predominance
of the aristocratic party (p. 197). It was not to be expected that
all the citizens of Greek states would be content with this: the
democrats, always active in a time of social difficulty and unrest,
looked for help where they might hope to get it, and the first
actions of Perseus, involving the relief of debtors, must have
marked him at once as the friend of the poor, though he may have
been inspired only by the wish to secure popularity in his

[1] Several of these charges and others are set forth in the formal accusation
of Perseus before the Delphic Amphictiony which has been found at Delphi
(*Ditt.*[3] 643).

own kingdom. The proceedings of Perseus, taken all together, amounted, even after all allowance had been made for exaggeration, to a formidable list: many may have been capable of explanation, but some, even though not harmful in themselves, may have been against the letter of his agreement: he had attained a position in which he might easily have been represented as the head of an anti-Roman faction, and Rome apparently decided henceforth that she must regard him in that light.

The Romans had discovered for themselves that Eumenes was not popular in Greece; and, as they professed to be convinced of his excellent qualities, they could hardly fail to draw the inference that his notorious friendship for them had made for his unpopularity. It was not thought proper to give the other representatives the opportunity of being confronted with Eumenes, but the speeches which they afterwards delivered in the Senate were calculated, by their hostility to Eumenes, to add to the effect which he had produced. The Rhodians, in particular, accused him of stirring up trouble for them by inciting the Lycians against Rhodes and of being a greater danger in Asia than Antiochus had been. The Romans took this as further evidence of the designs of Perseus and conferred additional honours on Eumenes.

But, if the visit of Eumenes to Rome had done much to harden the Roman temper towards Perseus, an incident near Delphi, which occurred on his return home, did more. As he was on his way to perform a sacrifice to Apollo, he was struck down by a rock, rolled down the hillside and for some time lay between life and death. Indeed he was long believed, even in Asia, to be dead, and his brother Attalus took measures to secure himself in the succession, including the project of a marriage with the queen Stratonice, which would have been inconceivable if he had had any idea that his brother might still be alive. However, Eumenes recovered and the responsibility for the attack was inevitably thrown upon Perseus. Of his guilt Polybius expresses no doubt (xxii, 18, xxvii, 6; cp. Livy xlii, 15). The evidence consisted, partly of the testimony of a woman with whom Eumenes' assailants are said to have lodged, partly of the allegation that a Cretan named Evander was subsequently put to death by Perseus for fear of what he might reveal. Though Polybius is no friend to Perseus, that does not prove the accusation false. If Perseus was guilty, his behaviour was not only criminal but foolish. He must have known that Eumenes had brothers well able to maintain the power of Pergamum, and that there were moderate men, including statesmen responsible for the guidance of their communities, who would be reluctant to condone political assassination or to be associated with the authors of such crimes. It is clear that Perseus was trying to gain the advantages of being considered moderate and popular, and it is not clear why he should have wished to sacrifice any of those advantages by a useless murder. Perhaps the crime was engineered by enthusiasts with a private grudge against the king of Pergamum, who was not universally beloved. But certainly Perseus was believed to have arranged it, and the incident is deemed by Polybius, though he refuses to call it a cause, to be a real 'beginning' of the war between Perseus and Rome.

IV. THE OUTBREAK OF WAR: THE FIRST CAMPAIGNS

By this time the Romans were prepared to believe anything against Perseus. Their envoy C. Valerius, who reported that he had found abundant confirmation in Greece of all that Eumenes had said, brought with him one Rammius[1] of Brundisium. His residence at the port, through which most of the envoys passed, had brought him into relations with Perseus; he seems to have become involved in Macedonian secrets further than was quite comfortable, and finally reported to the Romans that the king had endeavoured to persuade him to poison various senators and that he had been obliged to promise to do so for fear of being poisoned himself. The story may not be impossible, but it sounds wildly improbable, and perhaps Rammius thought that his best way out of a dangerous situation was to give information which the Romans would be ready to accept at a moment when their minds were made up against the king.

The actual declaration of war did not come immediately. In 172 B.C. the praetor Cn. Sicinius was instructed to cross to Apollonia and secure the coast for the future transport of troops. But much diplomatic work had to be done first, to counteract the popularity of Perseus in Greece. Of the kings, Ariarathes of Cappadocia selected this moment to send his son to be educated in Rome; Antiochus of Syria and Ptolemy of Egypt, though engaged in struggles with each other, professed to be equally loyal to the Republic; Prusias of Bithynia, though as a brother-in-law of Perseus he expressed a wish to be neutral, was evidently not likely to oppose Rome actively. The attitude of Genthius, the Illyrian chief who reigned in Scodra, was the most doubtful. In the republics the lower classes tended to dislike Rome: the well-to-do were more favourable, but there was a strong feeling, even

---

[1] Or Rennius. See F. Münzer in *P.W.* VIII, 1, col. 662, *s.v.* Herennius I.

among those who, if the choice were forced upon them, preferred Rome to Macedonia, that the exclusive predominance of any one power was dangerous for them. This feeling had made Perseus popular in certain quarters, but it did not follow that it would gain him active support against Rome.

The Roman mission met with considerable success. The Achaeans showed signs of discontent that a body which had supported Rome against Philip and Antiochus should be treated in the same way as those who had formerly taken the other side and were now unwilling members of the League, and perhaps they hoped that their ready adhesion would be met by some recognition of the permanence of their League as such; but there was no doubt on which side they stood. The Boeotian League could not arrive at any general policy owing to internal differences; while Coronea, Haliartus and Thisbe[1] took the Macedonian side, the majority of the cities, some with hesitation, agreed to support Rome, and the Boeotian League broke up. The Rhodians adopted a correct attitude which satisfied the Roman envoys, Claudius and Postumius. While there was no doubt that Cotys, king of the Odrysae, was a firm ally of Perseus, some of the Thracian rulers promised support to Rome which might be useful.

After the return of the envoys, who reported that Perseus had repudiated his renewal of the treaty made with Philip and had proposed to substitute another after due consideration of the terms, Q. Marcius Philippus, who had been a friend of Philip and, with other envoys, had been sent to Greece, accepted an invitation to a final interview with Perseus, that took place on the Peneus. Marcius expressed himself as anxious that no chance of peace should be omitted, and advised the king to send a further embassy to Rome, though his last envoys had received no answer. No change was effected in the attitude of Rome, and Marcius is said to have boasted on his return that he had secured six months' delay by inducing the king not to begin hostilities at once, to the great advantage of the Romans, whose preparations were far behind those of the Macedonians. We are told that some of the senators denounced as un-Roman this method of outwitting an opponent but that the majority agreed to profit by it, and Marcius was sent back to Greece. Polybius, who had a private quarrel with

---

[1] The text of Polybius (xxvII, 5) gives *Thebes*, but the context makes it plain that this cannot be right. Livy (xLII, 46, 7: cf. 63, 12) apparently read *Thebes* in Polybius and tried to make sense of the passage. The decrees about *Thisbe* (*Ditt.*[3], 646) show that this is what Polybius wrote. See Mommsen in *Eph. Epigr.* I, p. 290.

Marcius, may have accepted too readily an ill-natured story of his boasting. But, if Perseus was not deceived, he had helped his enemies by deceiving himself.

Rome had at last decided to declare war, and it is evident that the war was regarded at Rome as serious. There was no difficulty in enlisting volunteers from among those who had served in previous wars in Greece and Asia Minor and found them profitable, while the anxiety of both the consuls to secure the command[1] shows that it was a duty which would be gladly undertaken. But special provisions were adopted for allowing soldiers of experience to serve up to fifty years of age, for choosing the military tribunes otherwise than by lot, and for investing the departure of the consul with all due solemnity. Yet the number of troops sent out was smaller than might have been expected, if one supposes the Romans to be making a real effort. The consul, P. Licinius, to whom Macedonia was assigned, received the usual consular force of two legions; and, though Livy[2] tells us that these legions had 6000 men each, the testimony of Polybius[3] as to the largest size of the legions known to him renders this doubtful.

The Macedonians had 43,000 men available (39,000 infantry, 4000 cavalry) and their opponents (with a total of 37,600)[4] were in a position of considerable inferiority. The Italian part of the Roman forces consisted largely of recruits, and it would require time before the miscellaneous allies would act effectively with them. Perseus, who could move earlier, began by a rapid march which, besides securing his position in northern Thessaly, had the moral advantage of a surprise, and he was able to secure control of the pass of Tempe without difficulty. After showing by a series of movements over a wide area that it was open to him to take the offensive, he approached the Roman force, which had rested for a time at Gomphi after a tiring advance over the mountains from Apollonia and was now about three miles from Larissa. The first attempts to draw out the Romans failed to do more than induce a small number of cavalry and light-armed troops to take part in an indecisive skirmish; but finally Perseus drew nearer and brought on an engagement near the hill Callicinus in which the whole of the cavalry and light-armed on both sides took part. The battle,

[1] Livy XLII, 32.
[2] XLII, 31, 2.
[3] III, 107, 11; VI, 20, 8.
[4] For details of the forces, see Kromayer, *Antike Schlachtfelder*, II, pp. 335, 340 *sqq.*

with some 12,000 men engaged on each side, is described for us in the account which Livy drew from Polybius[1], and it has been noted that, though the heavy-armed troops were not in action, each side used the manœuvres which they adopted when the heavy-armed troops were also taking part. The shock tactics of the massed Macedonian cavalry produced an instant effect which might have been overwhelming had it not been for the reserves on the Roman side. The neglect of the king to make use of his phalanx, which had advanced of its own accord so as not to miss a chance of joining in, may have robbed him of a decisive victory.

Perhaps he felt satisfied with the moral effect produced by a very considerable success: for the Romans withdrew at once across the river Peneus into a place of greater safety, and it was now clear that the king, by using his proved superiority in cavalry and light-armed troops, could compel his enemy to fight. Alternatively he could try to use his advantage as an opportunity for gaining a favourable peace. He sent messengers offering to pay an indemnity and withdraw from such places as his father had agreed to abandon. The object of this strictly moderate proposal was no doubt to show that one who was in a position to do damage to the Romans was ready to sacrifice much for the chance of being their friend and ally. But the Romans could not accept such suggestions immediately after a defeat: they declined to consider any terms except unconditional surrender.

Perseus, in spite of the indignation which this answer produced among his followers, made renewed attempts at negotiation and suggested a still ampler indemnity. The failure of all his efforts may have affected his nerve, at least for the time. He remained generally at a considerable distance from the Romans, and no further engagement took place this year on a large scale except one near Phalanna, which arose accidentally and was probably not of great importance, though some Roman annalists, whose testimony Livy (XLII, 66, 9) evidently doubts, claimed a great Roman victory. At the end of the year the king withdrew from Thessaly, leaving only such garrisons as might help to make possible an easy re-entry. Evidently he had done little to satisfy those of his advisers who wished for a total overthrow of the Roman forces; we must suppose him to have been anxious, with whatever justification, to try the effect of a protracted series of campaigns, which might possibly induce the Romans to think at last that it was not worth while to continue them.

---

[1] Livy XLII, 58 sq.; see Kromayer, op. cit. p. 241.

The Roman consul, who ended by marching into Boeotia and taking Coronea[1], cannot fairly be blamed for not achieving more: the forces at his command did not enable him to compel the enemy to accept battle except under conditions of their own choosing. It is harder to understand why the Roman fleet did so little. The Romans themselves had provided at least 45 quinqueremes, the Rhodians 5 triremes, Eumenes enough ships to convey 6000 infantry and 1000 cavalry, and the states in the west of Greece 76 smaller vessels. The Roman admiral, the praetor C. Lucretius Gallus, found no one opposing him at sea, and sent home from Chalcis some of the allied naval contingents. If the Macedonian fleet was negligible, as at this time it seems to have been, why was nothing done to make it more difficult for the king to maintain his connection with Thessaly, otherwise than by the mountainous western routes? Instead, Lucretius operated by land in Boeotia, capturing Haliartus after a stout resistance and receiving the surrender of Thisbe. He has none too good a reputation: he is declared to have treated his allies as though they were enemies, and there must have been some substance in these charges, as he was subsequently condemned and fined. It is therefore not unnatural that he has been accused of sacrificing Roman interests by preferring to win booty in Boeotia rather than to cruise along the shore of Thessaly.

It is possible, however, that the Senate were not averse from a plan of action in which the fleet played a secondary part. The strength of Rome was in her army, and, although a fleet was required for a campaign against Macedonia, Roman interests demanded that the decision should be reached on land. A strategy which depended largely on naval operations might suggest that the co-operation of Pergamum or Rhodes was of primary value to Rome. It is not necessary to suppose that the Romans had at this time any definite grievance against Pergamum or Rhodes, in order to understand why Roman plans were constructed in such a way as not to make the allies too prominent.

The Romans, judged on what may be supposed to have been their own principles, deserve more criticism for not supplying in this first year of war a sufficiently large force on land, than for conniving at the inaction of the fleet. That, in spite of previous experience, ignorance of geography contributed something to their underestimate of the problem may perhaps be inferred from the action of the other consul of 171 B.C., C. Cassius, who, being

---

[1] This seems to follow from Livy XLIII, 4, 11.

disappointed at receiving Cisalpine Gaul for his charge, proposed to leave his province and march his army through Illyria into Macedonia, without consulting the Senate and with no further preparations than the collection of guides and of corn for thirty days at Aquileia.

The campaign of the following year was uneventful, so far as we are able to judge from the few details about it which are known. The consul, A. Hostilius Mancinus, tried once and perhaps twice to invade Macedonia from Thessaly by passing to the west of the great belt of mountains which separated the two. Probably it was legitimate to make such an attempt, but he was severely repulsed, and Perseus once more occupied northern Thessaly, the Romans retiring from Larissa to Pharsalus. The consul did not claim any military success, but it is reported of him that he restored discipline to the army and protected the allies from injuries, a commendation which reflects little credit on his predecessor. The praetor, L. Hortensius, who commanded the fleet, does not receive similar commendation: in conjunction with Eumenes and a Pergamene squadron[1], he captured Abdera, and this may have had more military value than anything done by Lucretius in the preceding year, but he is accused of cruelty and avarice by allies as well as by enemies. Perseus availed himself of the inaction of the Romans to undertake expeditions to the west. One was against the Dardani, in another he captured and held Uscana in the Drin valley with a garrison which a Roman commander vainly tried to dislodge. He supported the Molossians who had declared for him, leaving in their territory a commander with troops that might be useful for interfering with the usual Roman route from Apollonia; and finally he went as far south as Stratus. His last march did not attain its full object, the winning over of the Aetolian League, but this series of movements served to show that the difficulties of the Romans were not getting less, and might add to his hopes that his offers of peace would ultimately be accepted.

The consul of 169 B.C., Q. Marcius Philippus, who arrived with a fresh supply of men and began by summoning the commander of the fleet to discuss concerted measures of attack, was a man of vigour who started to move his forces within ten days of his arrival. He may have turned his previous knowledge of the country to good use: he certainly succeeded in reaching the Macedonian coast after a difficult march in the course of which he

---

[1] Livy XLIII, 4, 8; Diodorus XXX, 6; see Niese, *op. cit.* III, p. 129 n. 7.

is said to have admitted that his army might have been destroyed by a small opposing force. The details of this march can only be reconstructed conjecturally: perhaps he deceived the commander of the hill garrison, whom he had vainly tried to force from his position, by feigning retreat, leaving a covering force to fight a defensive action, and then moving towards the coast by a difficult route through thick woods, which caused the enemy commander to have no idea that he was not still retreating along the way by which he had come[1]. The king, when news arrived that the coast had been reached, supposed that his mountain force had been overpowered and that the situation was desperate. He withdrew his garrisons, not only from Dium but also from Tempe, and thereby relieved the Roman general from what would have been a very critical situation owing to the absence of provisions and the non-arrival of his transports.

The commanders on both sides have been severely blamed by critics from Polybius downwards, and with the greater confidence that Polybius was himself present with the Roman force on a mission from the Achaean League, and must therefore have known the military situation. But, great as were the difficulties of the Roman march, it is not easy to see how they were to be avoided if Macedonia was ever to be entered at all, and, if supplies failed to arrive, that can hardly have been the consul's fault. Nor can the king be blamed for more than having failed to make a brilliant guess as to what had actually happened, and, had the facts been such as he may legitimately have supposed them to be, the withdrawal of his garrisons and the concentration of his troops was his proper course.

So far as the Roman consul is concerned, his successor was able to start from a very different position from that which had hitherto faced the Romans. It is true that, if Perseus had been really willing, as Polybius tells us was at this time expected, to come down again into Thessaly, and decide the war by a general engagement, the Romans would have been saved the necessity of crossing the mountains: but, though Perseus had begun the campaign of 171 by a march into Thessaly and had offered battle in the early part of the year, his later actions had shown that he was not to be hurried and that he was not likely to offer battle except on his own terms. If the Romans wished to force an engagement, they had much more chance of doing this successfully near the coast than in northern Thessaly. The scheme formed by Philippus only

[1] This is the probable suggestion of Kromayer, *op. cit.* ii, p. 282.

partly succeeded: the co-operation with the fleet on which it depended was very imperfectly carried out, and the absence of the provision ships forced him to retire and to allow the king to return to a position on the Elpeus which could be so strongly defended that the consul thought it hopeless to attack during this year. He had enough to do to secure his own position, and in particular to capture the fortress of Heracleum which threatened his communications. In this operation also he recognized the value of the fleet's help.

Another charge has been brought against Philippus, that of not remembering the importance of the western theatre of war where Roman influence was endangered by Perseus' operations in the previous year (p. 264). The commander in that district, Appius Claudius Cento, asked the Achaeans to send him 5000 men: Philippus advised Polybius that this demand was unreasonable and sent him home with the recommendation that it should not be granted. Polybius made use of the Senate's order that no requisitions from Roman commanders should be carried out unless they were accompanied by decrees from the Senate; the assistance was not sent, and, if it had been sent, it might have been useful. But it is not necessary to suppose that Philippus was actuated either by an underestimate of what had to be done on the west side of Greece or by jealousy of the success which another commander might possibly win. He may well have thought that the charges against Rome of showing lack of consideration for her allies were having serious effects, that scrupulous accuracy ought to be observed in carrying out the orders of the Senate in this matter, and that it was better to let military operations be deferred than to run a risk of imposing an unnecessary burden on the Achaeans. At a time when the lack of progress made by Rome in the main campaign was causing the anti-Roman party in Rhodes to become prominent, Prusias to hint apologetically at the possibility of peace, Eumenes to be spoken of as engaged in mysterious negotiations with Perseus, it was worth while to sacrifice something for the sake of showing that the allies of Rome were to be spared as much as possible. Even if the lack of help sent by the Achaeans might cause Genthius definitely to ally himself with Perseus, it was better for Rome to make an additional effort, as she did next year, than to alienate her friends.

The consul was well aware that much remained to be done. He asked for clothing to be sent from Rome for his troops and for horses to be supplied: he also asked that payment should be made for the wheat and barley which he had drawn from Epirus.

It could easily be seen that he regarded the war as likely to continue, and the consul of 168 B.C., L. Aemilius Paullus, as soon as it was decided that Macedonia was to be his province, caused three commissioners to be sent to investigate on the spot the actual position of affairs, and declined to have any discussion of the campaign in the Senate until their report had been received. Many amateur strategists in Rome were ready with suggestions how to conduct the war, and the consuls of the last three years may have been bewildered by ill-considered suggestions, and handicapped by not knowing for what they ought to ask, until they had themselves arrived at the front and found that the available resources were not adequate.

When the report arrived, it was not encouraging. The king, whose army, estimated at 30,000, was only separated from the Romans by the river Elpeus, occupied an unassailable position and would not give battle. It was even represented as doubtful whether any advantage had been gained by the dangerous march of Philippus. Appius Claudius to the west, so far from doing anything to relieve the pressure, would require to be heavily reinforced himself if he was to hold his ground. Genthius had thrown in his lot with Macedon in the autumn of 169, and the next spring was certain to see a new Illyrian War. The fleet was suffering from disease, from deficiency of clothing and irregularity of pay. The attitude of Eumenes was uncertain, though no doubts were thrown on the loyalty of his brother Attalus.

This report produced the requisite effect. It was decided to bring the legions up to strength by replacing men who were unfit, to select as military tribunes for the year only soldiers of experience, and to put a considerable force at the disposal of L. Anicius, the praetor who was to succeed Claudius in Illyria. The consul, having caused the Latin festival to be fixed for an early date to avoid unnecessary delay, did not hesitate to start as soon as his preparations were made. On the fifth day after leaving Brundisium he sacrificed at Delphi: four days later he was with the army and at work.

V. THE CAMPAIGN OF PYDNA

Perseus had not been idle in trying to win allies. Envoys were sent to Rhodes, to Antiochus IV, and to Eumenes. The Macedonian fleet, of which little has been heard hitherto, began to display signs of activity and raided the coast of Asia Minor; this may have been due, not only to a suspicion that the Roman ships and crews were not in a good state, but also to a hope of co-operation from those powers that had navies and to a desire of showing them that the Macedonians were worth supporting. But we are told that Perseus forfeited through avarice the assistance of large forces of Celtic horse and foot from beyond the Danube, and deceived his Illyrian ally Genthius by paying him enough to make him commit himself irrevocably in the sight of the Romans and then withholding the rest of what had been promised.

This habit of avarice, with which Perseus is so often charged, is also said to have lost him a real chance of gaining over Eumenes. Polybius refers to the intrigue between Perseus and Eumenes as a contest between the most avaricious and the most unscrupulous of kings. The story is hard to accept as he tells it; for, though it is true that Roman progress in the war had been slow, Eumenes can hardly have meant to endanger his whole position by giving active assistance to Perseus. There could not be reliable evidence of these uncompleted negotiations, either at the time or later. If they were believed to have occurred, something in the characters of both kings must have made them seem plausible, but beyond that it is unsafe to go (p. 286).

Paullus was not content to rely on the report brought to him in Rome by the commissioners: it was clearly necessary for him to test it on the spot. He examined the Macedonian position carefully, and found it so strong as to be impregnable to a frontal attack. Accordingly he rejected this method which commended itself to some of his council of war, particularly to the younger men, and he rejected also the suggestion that a movement of the fleet northward would be enough to induce the king to retire. But it might be possible to induce the Macedonians to believe that the Romans were trusting to this manoeuvre. Accordingly the fleet was called to Heracleum and provisioned, while a force of 8200 selected infantry and 120 horsemen, commanded by Scipio Nasica, was ordered to the same place, giving the impression that it was to be embarked. Instructions were, however, given to this force to proceed farther south, and then, by a series of night marches, to make a circuit of the mountains to the west and arrive at a point well to the north of the Roman position. The plan succeeded: the one force encountered on the way was surprised, and failed to interrupt the march by its resistance; the king, whose attention had been divided by a series of attacks and who may have been alarmed by threatening movements of the fleet, being anxious to retain the right of giving battle under his own conditions, even at the cost of sacrificing a stronger for a weaker position, withdrew northwards. A letter in which Scipio Nasica gave an account of his march was quoted by one of Plutarch's authorities for his life of Aemilius Paullus (c. 15). It gives useful information, but, as it is only concerned with what seems to have been a part of a combined operation, we are left in some doubt as to what actually happened. The plan may have been a rash one which might have resulted in disaster: but, as it was successful and we are not fully informed about it, criticism of it would be unsafe.

Paullus was able to effect a junction with Scipio without difficulty, but the king's new position, protected by the two rivers, Aeson and Leucus (Pelicas and Mavroneri), was strong. The consul resisted the wishes of his army that an attack should be made at once, and even on the next day he was evidently reluctant to take the offensive, assigning as the official reason that his camp must first be fully secured. The king was equally unwilling to attack unless he could do so in a position which seemed to give him an advantage. Neither he nor his advisers could have forgotten Cynoscephalae, and they were well aware that the phalanx could only be successful against an efficient Roman force under certain conditions. Livy tells us that neither commander wished for an engagement that day and that the encounter took place as the result of an accident, which only concerned a very small number of men in the first instance. This may be in some sense true, but it is disappointing that so much doubt should remain. Polybius, who was not himself present, must have made careful enquiries about this important event; we possess small fragments in his own words, we have clear evidence of the use of his work by later writers, and we know that Plutarch consulted other sources, including a biography of Perseus by a certain Posidonius who described the fight from the Macedonian side. Unfortunately the text of Livy contains a great lacuna, and it is only possible to guess in part what may have stood there. Modern critics have endeavoured to reconstruct in detail what happened, but no one seems to have succeeded yet in providing a reconstruction which escapes all the difficulties.

We learn that an eclipse of the moon took place on the night before the battle: if this evidence is accepted—and there is no sufficient reason for rejecting it—the eclipse must be identified with that of the night 21–22 June 168, and the battle of Pydna thus occurred on 22 June. If we may judge from a monument erected in honour of Paullus, it appears that an incident connected with the escape of a horse across the river which separated the armies was considered to have a good deal to do with the actual beginning of the fight. Later tradition made this into a ruse on the part of the Roman commander, and, even if that may seem absurd, it is not likely that the incident should be mentioned prominently unless it had really serious consequences. Another feature of the story is the heroism shown by some Roman allied cohorts who met the first shock of the Macedonian advance and, by their self-sacrifice, gave to the Romans the time they needed.

But the course of the battle, in which a decision was reached in about an hour, is very hard to understand. It is stated that the Macedonians lost 20,000 killed[1], while the killed on the Roman side did not exceed 100, of whom the greater part were the Paelignians who had had to face the first attack. The accounts do not suggest that the Roman general succeeded in effecting a surprise: he was ready, no doubt, and on the watch, as a general in such close contact with the enemy ought to be, and his measures were taken calmly and without hesitation. But he had to send Scipio Nasica to report to him on the order in which the enemy were advancing, he admitted himself that he had never seen anything more terrifying than the Macedonian phalanx as it came on, and the first of the enemy did actually advance so far that some of the dead were within a quarter of a mile of the Roman camp.

It would seem, then, that it was the Macedonians who brought on the battle; for, whatever allowance be made for an accidental encounter by the river, a general engagement could not have resulted from an incident that could easily have been localized, if neither side had desired to fight. It must remain difficult to understand why a leader, who had shown so plainly that he wished to avoid an engagement on a large scale so long as it could be avoided, should have decided to risk everything, otherwise than under conditions exceptionally favourable, and how it can have been possible to make such a miscalculation as to lose so heavily in such a short time under conditions of his own choosing. It is not surprising that the suggestion should have been made that Perseus lost his head, that his men, who had previously shown a wish to fight when they were not permitted to do so, forced his hand and that he allowed events to take their course. Paullus earned justly the reputation of being a great general, and posterity has

---

[1] Livy XLIV, 42, 7, gives 20,000 killed, Plutarch, *Aemilius Paullus*, c. 21, more than 25,000; Livy gives 6000 captured in Pydna and 5000 taken prisoner in the flight.

not reversed the judgment of his contemporaries; the recovery of the full story of Polybius might perhaps reveal to us some exceptionally brilliant piece of generalship on his part. As the narrative stands, the question how the Macedonians should have come to repeat the error of Cynoscephalae in a far worse form remains unsolved. The Macedonian cavalry were roughly handled by their countrymen for not having taken part in the battle and having escaped from it; whether this charge is justified or not, no similar accusation was brought against the Macedonian infantry, most of whom fought bravely to the last.

The personal conduct of the king is variously reported: the story of Polybius (xxix, 17), that he made the need of sacrificing to Heracles an excuse for being among the first to flee, sounds like an ill-natured jest, and the story of Posidonius[1], that he insisted on fighting in spite of an accident on the previous day and suffered wounds in the battle itself, is suspiciously like an official apology. But he must have seen at once that the battle was decisive. He fled to Pella, thence to Amphipolis, and finally to Samothrace. He found everywhere a desire to be rid of him, his attempts to secure from the Romans a recognition of some part of his position were met by demands for unconditional surrender, and it may have been a relief to him when his attempts to escape failed through treachery and he had to give himself up to Paullus, who in the first instance treated him with personal courtesy. Subsequently he was obliged to figure in the consul's triumph and was confined at Alba under degrading conditions; though Paullus is said to have tried to secure him better treatment, ugly stories are told of what happened to him during the remainder of his life, which apparently lasted for some two years. His elder son is said to have died two years later, and the younger to have followed the profession of a magistrate's clerk in Italy.

The battle of Pydna ended the war. The Macedonian fleet decided without hesitation that it would be unable to maintain itself. So long as the position on land had appeared to remain stationary and the attitude of Rhodes[2], perhaps of Pergamum too, could be looked on as doubtful, Macedonian ships might perform useful service, but the complete defeat of the Macedonian army would have the immediate result of bringing the supporters of Rome to the front at Rhodes and of removing any doubt about Pergamum; the Roman fleet was also taking itself more seriously

---

[1] Plutarch, *Aemilius Paullus*, c. 19.
[2] See below, p. 288.

than before, and the Macedonian admiral, Antenor, recognized the situation at once. The Macedonian towns, despairing of a king who himself despaired, surrendered in rapid succession, and Paullus was able to refer to his campaign as one of fifteen days. Some places had to be punished for having gone back on their earlier professions of supporting Rome or for conspicuous actions on the Macedonian side, but these punishments appear to have been few.

The fighting in Illyria had come to an end before the decisive action at Pydna. Genthius had probably relied on not being taken too seriously, and the proceedings of the Romans in the preceding years may have done something to justify this expectation. When an effective army was brought into operation against him, he appears to have made things easy for the Romans by his rashness. In the spring of 168 he had concentrated near Lissus a fleet of 80 *lembi* and an army of 15,000 men. Appius had already called up the levies of the Roman allies in Illyria, Apollonia and Dyrrhachium, and his successor the praetor Anicius, who arrived with a full consular army of two legions, had some 30,000 men under his command. The Romans took the offensive, and in less than 30 days Scodra had fallen, the king was captured with his family and his leading chieftains, and the first reports of this campaign which reached Rome announced its ending. Anicius had time to march through Epirus and back again before he was called upon to deal with Illyria. He met with little serious opposition in Epirus; but it is evident that strong sympathy had been shown there with Perseus, and perhaps the Romans thought it wise to use the presence of a Roman army to impress places like those in the Molossian territory, which would regard themselves as sufficiently inaccessible at ordinary times to be able to do what they pleased.

This expedition by Anicius is easy to understand, but it is not easy to justify or even to explain the treatment of Epirus by Paullus in the following year. Polybius (xxx, 15) tells us the bare fact that Paullus took 70 cities in Epirus and enslaved 150,000 men. The account in Livy (xLv, 34) explains how this was done without loss, the plan being that all the places should be attacked on one day. Both Livy and Plutarch describe Paullus as carrying out the orders of the Senate. It is unfortunate that our information only gives the general purport of the senatorial decree and does not tell us on what ground it was officially justified; for even the version which describes it as a punishment for deserting to Perseus is unintelligible, unless we suppose that the Romans regarded these Epirotes as guilty of some treachery which the extant accounts do not record. The soldiers of Paullus are said to have been dissatisfied with the amount of the booty, large as it was, while the soldiers of Anicius may well have been annoyed for not being allowed any part of it, since they had done the fighting. It is, however, possible that the expedition of Anicius to Epirus, though useful from a military point of view, was not carried out in accordance with definite instructions either from the Senate or from the consul, and did not therefore fall, strictly speaking, within his sphere of duty.

The affairs of Macedonia and Illyria had to be settled, in accordance with the usual Roman custom, by Senatorial Commissioners acting in concert with the officer on the spot, and subject to any definite instructions which might be given by the Senate. The Commissioners were instructed that all Macedonians and Illyrians were to be free, that Macedonia was to be divided into four and Illyria into three divisions, that the tribute payable to Rome was to be half the amount payable to the kings, that special precautions were to be taken in dealing with the Macedonian mines which had produced such a large revenue, and that measures must be devised to prevent the newly-found liberty from degenerating into licence.

Paullus was continued in office on the spot until the Commissioners came, and he spent part of the interval in undertaking an extensive journey through Greece, during which he went to the Peloponnese as well as to Athens, Delphi, and the other famous cities. No doubt he was inspired by a natural wish to see the places which were well known for their importance in Greek history, as he and his sons had a genuine love of art and culture. It is, however, possible that the journey was not without political significance and that it was meant to present a contrast to the visit of Perseus to Delphi some years back about which much had been said (p. 256). Perseus was able to pride himself on the orderly conduct of his troops; but their good behaviour did not rob his journey of the air of a military demonstration. The conqueror of Perseus went with only a few attendants, abstaining from asking any questions about the attitude of particular cities during the late war, and showing himself as an example of that orderly and peaceful liberty which the Romans professed themselves anxious to encourage.

On his return Paullus met the Commissioners, and at Amphipolis the settlement was announced. The gift of liberty had apparently not been anticipated and, as in 196 b.c., it was well received at first. Liberty meant that the Romans had no intention of annexing the country themselves, and this was so far well.

The divisions, though we may not be able to trace their boundaries in detail, corresponded to the natural physical features of the country[1]. The first, mainly between the Nestus and the Strymon, included also Heraclea Sintica and Bisaltica: it possessed valuable estates and mines. The second stretched from the Strymon to the Axius: eastern Paeonia, and the whole of Chalcidice, with its agricultural and mercantile advantages, were in it. The third, from the Axius to the Peneus, contained Edessa, Beroea and western Paeonia: the large number of Gauls and Illyrians who were among its inhabitants gave it a good supply of workers. Finally, there was the fourth division, west of Mount Bora and bordering on Illyria and Epirus, comprising the wilder parts of the country. The capitals were Amphipolis, Thessalonica, Pella, and Pelagonia[2]. Only one of the four divisions, the third, had no barbarians on its boundaries: the remaining three were accordingly allowed to retain armed forces near their frontiers, the rest of the country being disarmed.

Many of the other arrangements were also reasonable. The tribute was reduced, the gold and silver mines were closed as being likely to prove a source of oppression to the natives, the iron and copper mines were allowed to be worked on payment of half the previous rent, and the enactment that no timber was to be cut for naval purposes was probably a relief from a burden. Whatever the exact object of a mysterious provision forbidding the use of imported salt, there does not seem to be any reason to suppose that it was meant to help Roman traders; and the refusal to allow the Dardani, who had suffered from their friendship for Rome, to regain the part of Paeonia which they asserted had formerly been theirs, showed that the Romans meant to adhere to their gift of liberty. The proposed constitutional arrangements were theoretically good and each of the divisions could have maintained successfully its economic independence.

If in spite of all this the division did not work successfully, the reason seems to be that the Macedonians, for all their differences of tribe and occupation, felt themselves as one people and resented the destruction of that unity on which the importance of Macedonia had depended since the days of Philip, son of Amyntas.

[1] Livy XLV, 29, 30.
[2] Usually identified with Heraclea Lyncestis.

However true it may have been that they had made good their claim to be considered Greeks rather than barbarians, it is unlikely that a people whose only experience of government was to be ruled by kings, can have felt strongly, as most Greeks did, the essential superiority of republicanism. They had very little enthusiasm for liberty but a very strong feeling for their country. The Roman system of division was intended to meet the fact that Macedonia, so long as it remained a single state, was too large to make one among a number of Greek states; while smaller sections, kept rigidly apart by the rule that no intermarriage was to be allowed and that no citizen of one section might own real property in another, were less likely to create trouble. The Romans no doubt thought that the Macedonians ought to be grateful for the consideration which gave each division its own character and, as compared with the territorial extent of most Greek states, a very substantial size. They may have been disappointed, and rather surprised, that the Macedonians did not value the gift of liberty at the price of division: probably if the Macedonians wished to be considered as Greeks, they should have thought liberty the more important. But it is hard to alter national sentiment artificially, even if that sentiment be regarded as unreasonable: considering the past history of Macedonia, it is perhaps strange that Rome should have thought the experiment worth a trial.

VI. MACEDONIA AND ILLYRIA AFTER PYDNA

The introduction of the new institutions was probably accompanied by the removal of most of those who had been prominent in political life, owing to the fear that they would prove to be a centre of intrigues in favour of restoring the monarchy; but to remove politicians of monarchical views was not the same thing as to supply statesmen who were anxious to make republicanism into a success. At any rate, it was not long before the Romans heard that the Macedonians, unused to democracy, were splitting up into factions whose quarrels might prove dangerous; and the three Commissioners who were sent to Syria after the death of Antiochus Epiphanes in 164 B.C. received instructions to inspect the state of things in Macedonia. Two years later we hear incidentally of one Damasippus, as having murdered the members of the council at Phacus near Pella and then having fled with his family from Macedonia. Whether the re-opening of the mines in 158 B.C. was intended to provide employment as an antidote to discontent it is impossible to say. But it is significant that Scipio Aemilianus, when he volunteered to go to Spain in 152 B.C., had to relinquish for that purpose an invitation which he had received to go to Macedonia and settle disputes that had arisen there. Perhaps this request, which had been addressed to him personally, was due to favourable memories of his father Aemilius Paullus, and, as Scipio referred to this expedition as less hazardous than the journey to Spain, it may be assumed that there was at any rate a hope that his advice might be received respectfully; but the Macedonians would not have asked for a Roman arbitrator unless their troubles had been too serious to be settled without such help.

This proposed mission by Scipio may have been connected with the first appearance of Andriscus, a man who claimed to be a son of King Perseus, possibly also of his wife Laodice, but is said to have been actually born in Adramyttium of low origin. His first attempts in Macedonia met with little success, and he is next found in Syria, where he was seized by Demetrius, and sent to Rome. Perhaps the imposture was regarded as too obvious to be serious; at any rate he was allowed to escape, and, when he was again taken in Miletus, he was released. One of Perseus' wives, who had married an inhabitant of Pergamum, claimed to recognize him; so also did a Thracian chieftain Teres, a son-in-law of the Philip whom Andriscus personated, though it was well known that Philip had died in Italy some two years after his father. He now gained a considerable following; he won a victory to the east of the Strymon and three or four months later in 149 B.C. another on the west of that river. These successes made him master of all Macedonia and alarmed the Thessalians, who sent urgent messages to the Achaeans asking for assistance. Apparently the reports from Macedonia were received with incredulity both in Greece and in Rome: the Romans do not seem to have realized how rapidly enthusiasm may gather round a popular claimant to monarchical authority in a country with a strong monarchical tradition. They thought that the matter might be settled by a peaceful mission under Scipio Nasica; but things had gone too far, and Juventius Thalna had to be sent with a legion, which was defeated and its commander killed. Rumours were now heard of attempts at an alliance between Macedonia and Carthage; success may have turned the head of Andriscus, and it is said to have led him into various acts of tyranny. But he could hardly in any case have maintained himself against Q. Caecilius Metellus, who was sent with a considerable army in 148 B.C. Andriscus lost a large number of men in a battle, and, after he had fled into Thrace and tried to re-establish himself from there, he was defeated again and finally captured to adorn Metellus' triumph and then be put to death. His power therefore was short-lived: but two or more other pretenders arose in the course of the next few years, showing that anyone who could put forward a claim to belong to the royal house could still count on some support.

The Romans now decided that Macedonia should be made the province of a Roman magistrate, and, though this method of government was not intended to supersede the local communities in Macedonia any more than elsewhere, it would necessarily mean, in a country which had shown itself so unused to self-government, that the Roman magistrate would have to be responsible for whatever was done. The four divisions had been a reality, as is shown by their coinage[1], but they were given up when the country could once more be safely treated as a whole; the Roman governor undertook the administration of all Macedon, and of Illyria and Epirus as well. So far as we can tell, Macedonia now enjoyed comparative peace, in spite of occasional pretenders to the throne. There is some evidence of the survival of the local dialects, and local institutions were left unaltered. A statue was erected at Olympia by a Macedonian to Metellus for his services to Macedonia: this shows at any rate that some persons were content with the condition of things which Metellus had helped to bring about, and perhaps it is more significant at this date than similar erections half a century later. The construction of the *Via Egnatia* from Epidamnus and Apollonia to Cypsela on the Hebrus, passing by Lychnidus, Edessa, Pella and Thessalonica, may certainly be regarded as a great benefit to the country. Polybius (xxxiv, 12) tells us that it was marked by milestones for its whole length of 535 miles; it was therefore completed within his lifetime, that is, not more than some thirty years from the formation of the province.

The defeat of Genthius and the collapse of his power secured Roman control of the Adriatic coast as far as the Narenta. North of that river the chief tribe was now the Dalmatae, and they began to molest their southern neighbours and the Greek colonists at Epetum and Tragyrium. In 157 B.C. the Romans decided to intervene, partly actuated according to Polybius (xxxii, 13) by the fear that the long-continued peace since Pydna might enervate their citizens. The ostensible *casus belli* was the uncivil treatment of envoys whom the Senate had dispatched to command the Dalmatians to offer redress. The Dalmatians argued that Rome had

---

[1] See Volume of Plates iii, 12, *a*, *b*, *c*.

no concern with their neighbourly quarrels. The Romans proved the contrary by sending the consul C. Marcius Figulus who, after suffering a serious reverse, devastated the country and laid siege to the chief town, Delminium. His successor, P. Scipio Nasica, continued the good work and took Delminium. This ended the war, and Scipio was rewarded with a triumph (155). Meanwhile another Roman army under L. Cornelius Lentulus, the colleague of Marcius, had advanced from Aquileia and may have reached the neighbourhood of Siscia[1]. But this campaign had little success and was not followed up by further action. Thus Rome did not complete her control of the Adriatic coast by linking up Istria with her newly-extended protectorate north of the Narenta. It was not till a generation later that this was achieved.

[1] See G. Zippel, *Die römische Herrschaft in Illyrien*, p. 135, who deduces this from Appian, *Illyr.* 22.

CHAPTER IX

ROME AND THE HELLENISTIC STATES (188–146)

I. THE GENERAL CHARACTER OF ROMAN POLICY

THE preceding chapter has described the Roman settlement with the Macedonian monarchy; it remains to consider Roman policy towards the other states of the Hellenistic world during the period which begins with the Peace of Apamea and ends with the destruction of the Achaean League. For the second half of this period we are very ill-informed. Neither the fragments of Polybius nor the epitomes of those who derived from him give us the means of reconstructing his criticism of the general course of Roman policy. And even where we possess material from Polybius, we have to remember that he has the disadvantages as well as the advantage of being a contemporary. He would have been more than human if he had given us a wholly impartial account of the downfall of the Achaean League, in whose affairs he had borne an honourable part, brought about as it was partly by the agency of leaders of whom he disapproved, partly by a State which had kept him prisoner for sixteen years (p. 301 *sq*.).

The whole of the period under review is filled with the journeys of envoys to Rome from kings or cities or leagues and of Commissioners sent out by the Republic. The victory of Rome over the two Great Powers, Macedon and Syria, had deeply impressed the rulers and states of the Eastern Mediterranean. They could not know enough of Roman doubts and preoccupations to expect anything but that Rome would be ambitious to spread her influence as far as possible. In disputes it was plainly an advantage to be the first to enlist Roman support, and the common answer of the Senate that, if the facts were as stated, the claimant's contention seemed to be well-founded, encouraged envoys to report and believe that they were successful. Even where Roman intervention was not expected, it was natural that each party in a dispute should wish the Senate to know its official version. Thus, whether Rome wished it or not, she was bound to be constantly invited to pronounce on questions of internal or external policy which concerned the states of the Hellenistic world.

The Senate could not but be flattered by these constant embassies, and they might legitimately wish to use their influence and to hold high their prestige. If Rome was to judge between the stories of rival embassies, she could find no better way than to send out Commissioners to discover the true facts, and in order to avoid being drawn into wars not of her making, it was in her interest to reach agreed settlements by compromise or to maintain, so far as possible, the existing state of things. The view that Rome constantly sought to promote rivalries and encourage quarrels can be rejected without supposing that she was only moved by the unselfish desire that right should triumph. Besides seeking to avoid exhausting wars, the Senate might well prefer that their advice and judgment should be regarded as equitable and should enhance rather than undermine the reputation of Rome. There were changing currents in the general course of Roman opinion towards foreign powers, due in part to the influence of individuals or groups in the Senate, and an account of these is reserved for a later chapter (pp. 363 *sqq.*). But each of the Hellenistic powers presented Rome with a separate problem. Little is to be gained by an annalistic treatment of Rome's Greek and Eastern policy as a whole, for we have not the evidence necessary for knowing the precise interrelation of its various parts, and we are bound to remain doubtful whether our judgment on each incident does Rome too great or too little justice.

II. ROME AND THE EASTERN POWERS

Considering first the kingdoms at the greatest distance from Rome, we find that Pontus stands outside the Roman sphere during the earlier part of the period under review[1]. King Pharnaces, it is true, sent ambassadors to Rome to explain away the allegations of his enemy King Eumenes of Pergamum (p. 234). But on at least one occasion the statement is made that he treated a reference to Rome with contempt; and, when in 180 B.C. Roman envoys attempted to put an end to a war in which he was involved, they found that he disputed all their points at such length that they apparently gave up the problem as insoluble. Evidently Rome, though prepared to give advice when it was asked, was not ready to take an active part in quarrels at this distance. But when Mithridates V Euergetes offered assistance, it was welcome, and he did in fact help Rome against Carthage and against the pretender Aristonicus.

[1] A general account of Pontus, Galatia, and Bithynia, culminating in the career of Mithridates Eupator, will be given in vol. IX.

The king of Cappadocia, Ariarathes IV, who had sided with Antiochus, was promised peace by Manlius at the price of 300 talents (p. 231). Thenceforward his kingdom remained loyal to Rome and is found supporting Pergamum, for instance, against Pontus. On the death of this Ariarathes in 163 B.C. there was a dispute as to the succession; for the king of Syria was induced by a gift of 1000 talents to assist Orophernes to supplant the true prince Ariarathes V. The Romans advised that the kingdom should be shared between the two. But they showed a preference for Ariarathes. Thus, when the people of Priene had their territory pillaged by Ariarathes because they insisted on returning 400 talents, which had been deposited with them by Orophernes, to him and not to Ariarathes, who claimed it as part of the property of his kingdom, the Romans do not seem to have taken any steps to check this unjustifiable procedure, though an appeal had been made to them. Perhaps they were influenced by the encouragement given to Ariarathes by their friend Attalus of Pergamum, who had a grudge against Priene. But the Romans interfered as little as possible with Cappadocia, even in the interest of a king whose merits in civilizing his country appear to have been great, and who closed a long reign of friendship to Rome by falling in battle against the Republic's enemies.

The Roman attitude towards the Galatians seems to be defined in a fragment of Polybius (xxx, 28), which tells us that they might preserve their autonomy, provided they remained within their own territory and did not undertake warlike expeditions outside it. It was natural that Manlius, after subjugating them in the expedition that followed the defeat of Antiochus, should have conferred with Eumenes about the terms to be granted them, and should have laid special stress on the need of their keeping peace with Pergamum (p. 231 *sq.*). When, at the time of Pydna, Eumenes fell into disfavour with Rome, the result was felt at once in a Galatian invasion of his kingdom. The Galatians were certain to act in this way, so soon as any sign appeared that the Romans would no longer regard Eumenes as a friend whose interests they must support by force. It is not probable that Rome encouraged the Galatians or would wish Pergamum to suffer serious injury from them, for such a consequence would have run contrary to the Roman wish not to be driven into interference. Instead of this, we find Roman envoys continuing to urge the Galatians to maintain peaceful relations with their neighbours, though it is likely enough that this warning was accompanied in later days by less explicit insistence on its application to Pergamum.

Bithynia was ruled during most of this period by a father and son named Prusias, of whom the son succeeded the father about 180 B.C. Prusias I was the rival and enemy of Eumenes of Pergamum and, though he had remained neutral during the war with Antiochus, he was alarmed at the extension of the Pergamene power which Rome had permitted. In 186 he ventured to challenge the settlement of Apamea, attacked Eumenes, and, what was even more menacing to Rome, took into his service Hannibal, the greatest of Rome's enemies.

The war that ensued went on the whole in favour of Pergamum, though at sea Hannibal won the last of his victories. The Romans thought it necessary to intervene, and Prusias made peace. Flamininus himself was sent to demand the surrender of Hannibal, the king of Bithynia did not dare to refuse, and Hannibal took his own life. Prusias had learnt his lesson, and his successor acquiesced in the prosperity of Pergamum, until after Pydna he sought to turn to his own advantage the declining fortunes of Eumenes. He visited Rome and, according to Polybius, disgraced himself by assuming the dress of a freedman to show his subservience to his Roman patrons. Livy (XLV, 44), though he mentions the account of Polybius and does not explicitly contradict it, indicates that Roman historians gave a less undignified story of his behaviour. Roman writers would hardly have suppressed a tradition so flattering to their pride, and perhaps Polybius accepted a picturesque story which caricatured Prusias' humble attitude.

The death of Eumenes in 160/59 B.C. put an end to the hopes of Prusias, for the Romans showed that Attalus II the new king of Pergamum had their support. Prusias had raised up enemies against Pergamum, especially the Galatians, but Rome opposed him by diplomatic intervention, and, though Prusias at first resisted, a short campaign in which Pergamum had support from Cappadocia, Pontus, Rhodes and Cyzicus, induced him to make peace in the presence of three Roman Commissioners. He was compelled to hand over twenty ships, to pay 100 talents on account of damage done to certain towns and a war indemnity of 500 talents in twenty annual instalments. The territory of Pergamum was not increased, and some have seen in this an indication that the Romans were anxious to prevent Attalus from enjoying the results of his victory. But increase of territory is not a necessary criterion of success in war.

Peace followed, but not friendly relations. Attalus incited the prince Nicomedes against his father and supported him in arms. Prusias' only hope was in Rome, and Rome was slow to move.

Nicomedes had resided at Rome and made powerful friends, but at last three Commissioners were sent to cause Attalus to hold his hand. If we may trust Polybius (xxxvi, 14) one of them, M. Licinius, was lamed with gout, the second, A. Mancinus, had imperfectly recovered from the fall of a tile upon his head, and the third, L. Malleolus, was reported the stupidest man in Rome. The choice of these in a matter which called for speed moved Cato to tell the Senate that 'Before they arrived Prusias would be dead and Nicomedes grown old in his kingdom. For how could a commission make haste, or accomplish anything when it had neither feet, head, nor intelligence?' Their success was what Cato expected. Prusias was killed and Nicomedes reigned in his stead. Rome recognized what it could not or would not hinder, content perhaps to see good relations restored between Bithynia and Pergamum.

In Egypt Ptolemy Epiphanes at the beginning of his reign had received some protection from Rome against Philip, though none against Antiochus (p. 166); but he forfeited all claim to Roman goodwill by his negotiations with Antiochus (p. 186 *sq.*). Accordingly Egypt had gained nothing at the settlement of Apamea (p. 231), and the Ptolemaic monarchy was kept weak by nationalist risings, the last of which was not crushed till 183. In 185 and 183 attempts were made to establish an *entente* with the Achaean League which suggest that the Egyptian court was reviving its traditional policy of posing as a champion of Greek liberty. The death of Epiphanes in 181/0 B.C. ended these projects, and Rome was spared the necessity of making it plain that she alone was the arbiter of Greek freedom.

The new king Ptolemy Philometor was a child, and for some time the true ruler of Egypt was the queen-mother Cleopatra. She was of the house of Seleucus (p. 199) and kept peace with Syria, while doing nothing to give Rome cause of complaint. On Cleopatra's death the proclamation of the king's majority was hastened by the new regents Eulaeus and Lenaeus, whose barbarian and perhaps servile origin could not gain for them respect. Rome, preoccupied with the Third Macedonian War, was content to recognize the new king and did nothing to hinder the renewal of Egyptian ambition to recover Coele-Syria. The result of the war probably disconcerted the Senate, for Antiochus won a great victory and invaded Egypt (169). Ptolemy was ready to accept a Syrian protectorate which would have united in one power the Hellenistic East. But the Alexandrians would have none of it, and proclaimed as king Ptolemy Euergetes, nicknamed

Physcon, the brother of Philometor. The elder Ptolemy chose to share power with his brother rather than to owe the semblance of it to the king of Syria, and Antiochus prepared in the spring of 168 to master Egypt by open force. Rome could hesitate no longer; her envoy, Popillius Laenas, bade Antiochus withdraw from Egypt and the command was obeyed. The Seleucid fleet which, in violation of the treaty of Apamea, had advanced to Cyprus, was forced to withdraw, and the word of Rome had restored the existing balance between the two monarchies.

For the next five years there were two kings in Egypt, but Ptolemy Physcon who, as the creation of a popular movement, was the stronger, worked secretly against his brother. Late in 164 Philometor was forced to fly from Alexandria. The Senate could not evade the responsibility of deciding whether or not to take up the cause of a king whom Rome had once recognized. They proposed that Philometor should rule over Egypt and Cyprus, while his brother received the Cyrenaica. There had been a revulsion of feeling at Alexandria, and Roman Commissioners carried through this arrangement without recourse to military action. But Ptolemy Physcon claimed Cyprus, and the Senate in 162 decided in his favour. The division of Egypt may have been in the best interests of the kingdom, and if the inheritance of the Ptolemies was to be halved, the addition of Cyprus to the Cyrenaica made that share more equivalent to Egypt. But Philometor did not give way, and Rome did not take overt action. In 154 Physcon accused his brother of an attempt on his life; the Senate refused to listen to any answer to the charge and instructed their allies in the East to install him in Cyprus. The allies did little or nothing and Philometor took his brother prisoner but treated him with generosity, leaving him in possession of Cyrenaica. This generosity was politic, and Rome ceased to support Physcon. Philometor had found a powerful advocate in the elder Cato, and had the skill to maintain a correct attitude towards the Republic[1]. The climax of this was the moment when after reconquering Coele-Syria for Egypt he refused to accept the crown of the Seleucids and bring about the union which the Senate had feared in 168 B.C. (p. 507). In general during this period the interests of Rome and of Egypt coincided, and the action and the inaction of the Senate may both have been guided by the realization of this fact. Polybius, in one of his most anti-Roman passages (xxxi, 10, 7), treats Roman policy in regard to Egypt as typical of the method by which Rome availed herself of the mistakes of

---

[1] See *O.G.I.S.* 116 and Holleaux, *Arch. Pap.* VI, 1920, p. 10 *sq.*

others to strengthen her own position. But it is not clear that the criticism is justified.

Roman policy in relation to the Syrian monarchy is harder to defend. The death of Antiochus the Great was doubtless felt as a relief, for he might take some opportunity of repairing his sudden and complete defeat. Seleucus, his successor, was too shrewd to provoke the Republic, though the Achaean League thought it wise to decline a present of ten ships which might suggest that they were intriguing with Syria. More dangerous was Antiochus Epiphanes, but he had spent years at Rome as a hostage, and his open admiration for Roman institutions did something to disarm suspicion. The Roman intervention to protect Egypt marked the limit set to his power; not long afterwards we find a Roman embassy instructed to discover if he was making any preparations for war. His death may have been not unwelcome to the Senate, and Roman Commissioners were instructed to settle matters in Syria in such a way as to relieve Rome of any future anxiety. The new king was only nine years of age; his minister Lysias, who had practical control of the kingdom, bore a bad character, and was expected to acquiesce in anything for a consideration. But the Syrians were not so complaisant, and the Roman Commissioners were ill-advised to neglect the warnings of Ariarathes, king of Cappadocia. Without accepting his assistance, they proceeded to Syria and began to carry out what Polybius (xxxi, 2) describes as the Senate's instructions, by burning ships, killing elephants and generally weakening the resources of the kingdom. The result was an insurrection in which the leading Commissioner Cn. Octavius lost his life (162 B.C.). The Senate neither accepted nor rejected Lysias' assurances of his innocence, and remained equally inactive when Demetrius the son of Seleucus escaped from Rome and recovered his father's kingdom for himself (p. 518).

Demetrius had acquired the reputation in Rome of being fond of enjoyment, and perhaps the Romans underrated his capacity. But they kept a close watch on his activities, and one of the objects of the treaty which the Senate made with the Jews in 161 B.C. may have been to enable it to stir up trouble in Syria (p. 519). More plainly hostile to Demetrius was the moral support given to the pretender Alexander Balas some ten years later. A decree, which, according to Polybius (xxxiii, 18), did not represent the view of all the senators, accepted his claim to be the son of Antiochus Epiphanes and gave him authority to return to the kingdom of his ancestors. It is not probable, however, that this meant more than moral support, and the Romans did not interfere when Alexander, who had made an end of Demetrius in 150, was killed some five years later by a son of Demetrius with help from Egypt, or when that son was expelled in favour of a son of Alexander. Despite the loyalty of the Graeco-Macedonian population to the Seleucid dynasty and the capacity of several of the kings, the disintegration of the Syrian Empire and with it the weakening of Hellenism went steadily on. Rome had less and less cause for active interference, but the paralysing effects of her passive suspicion were more fatal to Greek culture in the East than any senator can well have anticipated or desired.

III. ROMAN POLICY TOWARDS PERGAMUM AND RHODES[1]

The extension of the power of Pergamum after the defeat of Antiochus has already been described (p. 232 *sq.*). Of the capacity of King Eumenes there can be no doubt, and we have already seen how he maintained his extended kingdom against his Galatian and Bithynian neighbours (p. 281 *sq.*). The reviving power of Macedon under Perseus may have seemed to him a menace and he did more than any other man to bring about the Third Macedonian War. He may well have shared the general belief that the king of Macedon instigated the attempt to assassinate him near Delphi (see above, p. 258 *sq.*). If he entered into negotiations with Perseus, offering his neutrality or even his active help, it can only be supposed that he was setting aside his personal feelings and trying to secure his country's position against the possible, though unlikely, event of Perseus proving to be the victor. It is difficult to judge the real meaning of diplomatic proceedings without the account of either negotiator, and perhaps Eumenes deliberately set too high a price on his neutrality or his help. This would prevent the negotiations issuing in action and yet, if Perseus survived the contest, it would serve to show that Eumenes had not been absolutely unwilling to do Macedon a service, in spite of the past. But the suspicion that such negotiations had taken place would be bound to tell heavily against Eumenes at Rome, when, with startling rapidity, the war ended in the utter defeat of Macedon.

Once suspicion was aroused, Eumenes saw all his actions interpreted unfavourably. The visit to Rome of his brother Attalus in

[1] For a general account of Pergamum and Rhodes in the Hellenistic period, see below, chaps. XIX and XX.

167 B.C., to ask for help against the Galatians as well as to offer his congratulations, might easily have had serious consequence for Pergamum. The Romans had nothing against him, and he might have been tempted to try to supplant his brother. But he used his popularity at Rome, both on this and subsequent occasions, solely in the interests of his country. Eumenes was allowed no opportunity of clearing himself and when he proposed to defend himself in the Senate, a resolution was hastily passed that no king should be received in Rome. As the resolution followed closely on the favourable reception of Prusias of Bithynia, it was plain that the Romans regarded Eumenes as one who had received great benefits from Rome and had repaid them by playing false. Eumenes however concealed any resentment that he might have felt, and on his death in 160/59 Attalus with the countenance of Rome was able to maintain his kingdom intact and guard himself against his neighbours.

The kingdom of Pergamum, accordingly, did not lose its position during these years, whatever the personal humiliation to which one of its rulers, Eumenes, was subjected. The republic of Rhodes fared differently. Like Pergamum, she had done Rome good service in the war against Antiochus: indeed, without the Rhodian fleet Rome might have found it very difficult to conduct a campaign in Asia. Her reward was the accession of Caria south of the Maeander and of Lycia, except that the port of Telmessus and perhaps a corridor leading to it were reserved for Eumenes. But the Senate had failed to define the new status of the Lycians, who believed that they were to be *allies* of Rhodes, whereas Rhodes treated them as *subjects* (p. 232). At the outset the Lycians showed themselves very ready to be allies, but soon they made it plain that they would not easily be subjects. Rhodes used force, and in 177 B.C., as a result of appeals, the Senate interpreted their decision as having meant that the Lycians were to be assigned to Rhodes only as friends and allies. This interpretation denied to the Lycians complete independence, but it cannot have satisfied the Rhodians, nor was it likely to settle the question now; for the Lycians had ceased to be friendly to Rhodes and the Rhodians thought that Rome was turning against them in annoyance at their having convoyed the bride of Perseus from Syria and receiving in return a present of Macedonian timber for their shipyards. Rome may indeed have resented the parade of Rhodian naval strength, and was probably secretly displeased when the Rhodians invited her to intervene in favour of Sinope against the king of Pontus (183 B.C.).

Relations were not improving; but when it came to a question of choosing between Rome and Perseus, Rhodes was for the moment under the influence of one Agesilochus, who had been in Rome and was favourable to the Roman side. While, therefore, the envoys sent by Perseus to Rhodes in 171 B.C. were politely received and Rhodes gave a promise to mediate if Perseus were unjustly attacked, this promise was accompanied by a request that Rhodes should not be asked to do anything which might bear the appearance of hostility to Rome. There was, however, a strong party in Rhodes which took the opposite view, and, even if the motives of its leaders, Deinon and Polyaratus, were as unscrupulous as Polybius says[1], it is only in accordance with the usual history of Greek politics that differences of opinion should be strongly expressed and should be widely represented among the population. The Roman requests for naval help were agreed to and even exceeded, but the capture of a Rhodian quadrireme by the Macedonian admiral Diophanes heightened the annoyance of the anti-Roman party (p. 268). Political recriminations increased: each side tried to strengthen its position by securing concessions or promises from the party it supported, and the Romans wisely granted a licence to the Rhodians to import 150,000 bushels of corn from Sicily. Q. Marcius Philippus, when he was in command against Macedonia in 169 B.C., flattered Rhodian envoys by suggesting to them that Rhodes could do good service to Rome as well as to the general cause of peace by inducing the kings of Syria and Egypt to cease fighting.

The long continuance of the war against Perseus had its effect on the prevailing policy of Rhodes, as it may have had also on Eumenes. Till 168 B.C. nothing had been done that could justly offend Rome; but early in that year[2] Perseus induced Rhodes to send an embassy to Rome to urge that the war should cease. The envoys reached Rome at a most unfortunate moment, when the news of Pydna had already been received. They made an attempt to substitute a message of congratulation for what they honestly admitted that they had been sent to say. But they could not hope that this would be well received, for the Senate complained that Perseus had been allowed to do harm in Greece for some two years without remonstrance on the part of Rhodes, and Rhodes had only begun to take action when the position of Perseus was be-

[1] XXVII, 7.
[2] Polybius XXIX, 19. Livy (XLIV, 14), who dates this embassy a year earlier, may be choosing a version which seemed to him more effective rhetorically.

coming desperate. The reply may not have been quite fair, but it is what the Rhodians must have expected under the circumstances. They were, however, much frightened by it, and sent further embassies, including the orator Astymedes, whose advocacy exaggerating the services of Rhodes and minimizing those of her neighbours earned him the contempt of Polybius (xxx, 4). A praetor, Juventius Thalna, even proposed to the people to declare war on Rhodes. This proposal was rejected through the intervention of a tribune and of Cato, who did not scruple to hint that the Romans could not complain if they were more feared than loved. In their relief the Rhodians at once voted a valuable crown to Rome, and decided to depart from the independent policy which they had pursued hitherto by asking for an alliance with Rome. They tried to guard against the humiliation and practical consequences of a refusal by instructing their envoy Theaetetus, who was also navarch, to make the request on his own initiative, a course which the constitution allowed him to adopt without any precedent vote of the people.

The alliance was not conceded at first: the Romans postponed the question at least once, and once gave a negative answer; it was not till some two years later, after several embassies, and after Rhodes had gone through repeated difficulties, that it was granted. The Rhodians had to meet an attack by Mylasa and Alabanda on their possessions; which, indeed, they repelled by a victory won in Caria. Moreover, some of their subjects in the Peraea and in Caunus revolted; the Rhodians put down the revolt without difficulty, but the Romans ordered them to withdraw their garrisons from Caunus and Stratoniceia, and a decree of the Senate declared that all the Carians and Lycians who had been 'given' to Rhodes after the war with Antiochus were free. Even if this decree merely reasserted the principle that these peoples were to be regarded as friends and allies of Rhodes and not as subjects, it assumed fresh importance by coming at a time when any sign of Roman dissatisfaction with Rhodes was watched with keen interest by her friends and enemies. Its practical effect would be that all the efforts made to reduce these peoples to order were wasted, while in 165 B.C. the Rhodians asserted that the loss of Caunus, which they had purchased from Egypt for 200 talents, and of Stratoniceia, which had been given them as a special favour by Antiochus III, meant a loss of revenue amounting to 120 talents a year. A still heavier blow had been inflicted by the transference of Delos to Athens. That Delos was declared a free port may have benefited Italian traders in the Levant; any gain which Rhodian merchants may have shared with others was more than counter-balanced by loss to the Rhodian State, if it is true, as the Rhodians appear to have asserted, that their revenue from harbour dues declined from 1,000,000 to 150,000 drachmae[1].

Rhodes might justly complain of severe treatment if she was suffering all this in spite of having put to death those who were in any way responsible for her short-lived anti-Roman policy. The Senate evidently thought the humiliation enough, for the alliance was concluded in 165 B.C., and hopes may have been held out of further concessions, as we find an embassy some two years later asking not only that the rights of Rhodian citizens who had had property in Lycia or Caria should be recognized, but also that Calynda in Lycia should be assigned to Rhodes. It appears that the Rhodians were now content to play a subordinate part, and they were probably satisfied if their conduct was regarded by Rome as correct. They accepted a present from Eumenes towards the cost of their children's education: Polybius (XXXI, 31) censures this as undignified, and the Rhodians may not have liked doing it, but they could not afford to offend any possible friend. They showed their gratitude and their wisdom by supporting Attalus in the war which he waged against Prusias with the moral support of Rome.

The latest reference to the Rhodians which we have from Polybius (XXXIII, 17) describes the discouragement and despair that were causing them to think of their traditional high position as wholly lost beyond hope of recovery. The opinion was gaining ground that the Romans were well content to see troubles persisting so long as the effect of those troubles was to prevent any other power from attaining importance, and that Rome made little difference in this respect between those who had been her former friends and others. This may not have been just to Rome, for the Romans, unless they were alarmed, desired to interfere as little as possible, and the skill with which a Greek advocate could present a case made it hard to be sure on which side right stood, if indeed either party to a quarrel was wholly right. Nor could Rome readily trust a state which a group of political leaders had caused to change sides during a struggle in which Rome was concerned. Yet sympathy with the past history

---

[1] Polybius XXX, 31, 12, reading εὑρίσκει. The emendation of Van Gelder, which makes the loss 150,000 drachmae, is not here accepted. The loss of so relatively small a sum could not be described as the greatest result of Roman disfavour. On Rhodian trade at this time see further below, pp. 621 *sqq.*

of Rhodes makes us regret that Rome did not find it possible to show whole-hearted friendship to another republic whose ideals were in some respects so similar to her own.

Whatever may have been the justification for Rome's attitude from her own point of view, it was disastrous for the Aegean world. The greatest among the many services which Rhodes had rendered to the cause of civilization was the policing of the seas (p. 627). For two generations the chief scourge to Aegean commerce had been the free-booting of the Cretans. Since the middle of the third century at least, there had existed in Crete a form of federation which had brought neither true unity nor peace to the island. First the influence of Egypt and then that of Macedon had prevailed, but never without opposition, except for the moment of hope for the Greek world in 216, when the Cretan League put itself under the leading of Philip V (vol. VII, p. 768). But the power of Macedon waned, the cities resumed their feuds and settled down to wars and litigation in which they invoked the help or the judgment of Pergamum and Rome. In 189 the praetor Q. Fabius Labeo tried in vain to end a war waged by Cydonia against Cnossus and Gortyn. Four or five years later a settlement was laid down by Roman Commissioners. In 183 B.C. thirty Cretan cities allied themselves with Eumenes II (*Ditt.*[3] 627), but this group did not compose the whole island: Itanus was still a Ptolemaic protectorate, while Cydonia stood aloof and made a separate alliance with Pergamum. In 174 Rome intervened, but failed to make the intervention effective. During the war with Perseus Cretans are found fighting on both sides, and the sending of troops to help Ptolemy Philometor is a sign that the influence of Egypt was not extinct. Crete, in fact, could not find unity in a foreign policy of dependence on a single external power, and within the island federal justice was not allowed to impose peace and order or to end the disputes which, at the best, issued in shortlived arbitration awards rather than open war.

But whereas their internal differences taxed the patience of their neighbours, all Cretans agreed in a form of activity which made them unbearable. That activity was piracy, which, with mercenary service, provided a livelihood for the surplus population of the island. One way of checking this was by agreements with the Cretan towns which were the bases of the free-booters, and that way Rhodes took. But where that failed, it was to the fleet of Rhodes and her island allies to whom the Aegean had to look for peace. Rome was well content to patrol her own waters and to leave all else to others. In the moment of self-confidence in which she had offered to mediate between Rome and Perseus, Rhodes had invited the Cretans to unite in an alliance with her which might perhaps have proscribed piracy, but the news of Pydna ended all that, and the weakening of Rhodes made her less able to impose order by force. In 155 B.C. she found herself faced by Crete united in defence of piracy, and a war followed in which, even with help from Attalus, the Rhodian squadrons could not crush their nimble enemies. Rome neither supported Rhodes by force at sea nor by diplomatic intervention in Crete itself, and the doubt of the Senate's good will towards the Rhodians prevented the Achaean League from helping against the common enemy. Siphnos, the treasure-house of the Aegean, was sacked, and the war dragged on, with what final result we do not know. One thing seems certain, that with it ended the capacity of Rhodes to police the seas. Meanwhile the decline of the Seleucids and the enforced limitation of their naval strength permitted the rise of Cilician piracy. In the end the Senate was to pay a heavy penalty for failure to extend the *pax Romana* to the Eastern Mediterranean.

IV. CENTRAL AND SOUTHERN GREECE: ATHENS AND BOEOTIA

In considering the relations between Rome and the political associations in Central and Southern Greece we have to remember that we only know of a few of the disputes which the Romans were so often called upon to settle, and that the numerous journeys by Roman Commissioners about which we are told represent only a portion of the whole number. Roman envoys were always moving backwards and forwards, endeavouring to restore peace between conflicting parties whose one idea of political liberty was to fight each other. Even though it may be true that there were parts of Greece where politics were conducted without violence, and even if the Greek cities of which we happen to hear nothing all presented exceptions to the general rule, it can be imagined that the feeling must gradually have grown up in Rome that nothing but force would really quiet the Greeks. Further, the wish to do justice between appellants, which the Romans felt during their earlier experiences of such dealings with the Greeks, was seriously prejudiced by the rise of those Greek politicians whose advice at home was to do what the Romans would be likely to approve and who, when in Rome, urged the Senate to assert its will strongly (p. 300). They represented that the Roman approval would be enough in itself to secure what was desired and to render unnecessary that military effort which seemed to be the only effective alternative. Such men as Lyciscus in Aetolia, Mnasippus at Coronea, Chremes in Acarnania, may not all have been of the same type as Charops of Epirus or Callicrates, but the context in which they are mentioned suggests that they had some of the same characteristics[1]. While there is no reason to suppose that this was the support which the Romans would have wished to have in Greece if they had been able to choose, the mere existence of such unscrupulous supporters, who could not easily be repudiated, was bound to intensify the bitterness of their anti-Roman opponents and to make partisanship for or against Rome into the test question of Greek politics, however little the Romans desired it. The envoys of Perseus found it easy to win sympathy in many cities. Sometimes this movement subsided so soon as it appeared that to favour Perseus would mean fighting against Rome; but elsewhere support was actually given to Macedonia, and the revulsion of feeling which followed on the capture of a town or on the conclusion of the war generally gave the pro-Romans an opportunity to injure their personal enemies and to make the Roman cause highly unpopular.

With Athens the Romans did not find it hard to maintain friendly relations. If she had wavered for a moment in the days of Antiochus, she showed no hesitation in siding with Rome throughout the struggle with Perseus. Complaints are indeed made that Athens, in common with other allies, was harshly treated by P. Licinius the consul of 171 B.C. and by the praetor C. Lucretius Gallus, inasmuch as her offers of men and ships were declined and 150,000 bushels of corn were asked for in their place[2]. This was a grievous burden to lay upon a country which could not grow enough corn to feed herself, but the enactment of the Senate which declined to authorize for the future any demands made by Roman officers without a senatorial decree to back them, may have produced an improvement at least so far as Athens was concerned. L. Hortensius, the praetor in charge of the fleet during the next year, received an Attic decree in his honour[3], and the fact that Lucretius was condemned at Rome shows that some at least of his proceedings were recognized as being incapable of defence.

The unquestioned loyalty of Athens, which allowed her to enter

---

[1] Polybius xxx, 13.

[2] The amount seems incredible, but see W. S. Ferguson, *Hellenistic Athens*, p. 313, *n.* 1.　　　[3] *I.G.* ii, 423 = *I.G.*² ii–iii, 907.

into friendly relations with Ariarathes, Pharnaces, Antiochus Epiphanes and other kings, also put her in a position to adopt in 167 B.C. the same rôle as in 190 and 189, and to plead for mercy to a beaten enemy of Rome (p. 219). But whereas Rome had accepted the request that she should not go to extremities against the Aetolians, she was not inclined to restore Haliartus after it had been destroyed by Lucretius in 171. The Athenians accordingly changed their tone and asked that the territory of Haliartus should be given to them, as well as Delos and Lemnos, possibly Imbros and Scyros also. As we should expect, this action is censured by Polybius (xxx, 20), who records with evident satisfaction that the territory of Haliartus brought disgrace and little profit to Athens, while Delos and Lemnos involved her in many troubles. An Athenian cleruchy was sent to Delos, and the former inhabitants, who were ordered to leave but allowed to remove their property, complained that they were not treated fairly, and attempted to retaliate on Athens by becoming citizens of the Achaean League and then laying claims under the commercial treaty between the two countries. The inevitable appeal to Rome produced an answer in which Rome seems not to have entered into the facts of the dispute. As it was a decision on the facts for which both sides must have hoped, if they treated the appeal seriously, this could not settle the quarrel.

The consequences of a dispute between Athens and Oropus were more serious, as it appears to have been somehow responsible for the outbreak of war between Rome and the Achaean League. The Athenians, in the course of collecting tolls and tribute from this city which they claimed as theirs, were asserted by the Oropians to have been guilty of violence and illegality. The Roman Senate appointed the Sicyonians as arbitrators, and the Sicyonians, before whom the Athenians did not appear, condemned them to pay the enormous sum of 500 talents in damages. The Athenians then (in 155 B.C.) sent to Rome the heads of three of the chief philosophical schools, Carneades, Diogenes, and Critolaus, to make a protest. This visit, which had an important effect on the view taken by many Romans of Greek morals and philosophy (pp. 399, 459), was so far successful that the damages were reduced to 100 talents. It looks as though the Romans took substantially the anti-Athenian view, but, as the question to be settled was on this occasion not so much one of principle as of the proper amount of the penalty, substituted a severe but reasonable sum for one which was plainly unreasonable. The Athenians declined to pay the smaller amount, and the quarrel continued until a temporary

arrangement was arrived at, by which the Athenians apparently
established cleruchs in Oropus on an understanding that they
were not to molest the natives, while the Oropians sent hostages
to Athens as security that they would not molest the Athenians[1].
This plan, if such is the correct interpretation of it, could not succeed for long. A further appeal was made by Oropus to the Achaean League against alleged oppression by the Athenian garrison;
the League decided against Athens and employed force to carry
out their decision. At this point the dispute becomes merged in
the obscure quarrels which brought the Achaean League to an
end (p. 302): the leaders of the League were not popular in Rome,
and this may be the reason why Athenian charges of bribery and
corruption, brought against those leaders in connection with their
decision, came to be accepted as true, though the story as told
does not sound convincing. It is natural that Athens should have
suffered less than most other parts of Greece from the changes
which now followed, for her past reputation was quite sufficient
to secure her permanently a position of dignity, and her claim to
intellectual primacy was one which Rome could recognize without difficulty.

The Leagues naturally fared worse. In any Greek League there
was bound to be a contest between those who were zealous for the
independence of the individual cities and those who desired to
strengthen the central authority. Even where attempts had been
made to prevent the central authority from being vested permanently in one city, this was an important difference of principle;
but sometimes, as in Boeotia, the superiority of one city was so
marked that the question became one between that city and the
other members of the League. The Romans may have begun
with a prejudice in favour of a strong central authority which tended on the whole to support orderly government; but, in so far as
a League, thus made stronger, became a larger and more powerful
unit than its neighbours, jealousies, nervousness and quarrels
might easily arise, while the endeavours of one city to force other
members to associate themselves with the central authority would
be repugnant to the Romans, both as being contrary to the principle of liberty, and as never being likely to achieve permanent
results. It is not surprising that the opinion of Rome should come
to be in favour of the individual cities and against the Leagues,
even where the Leagues had few internal troubles.

[1] The account of Pausanias (VII, 11) is to be corrected by reference to
Ditt.[3] 675 and the literature there cited. See also W. S. Ferguson, *op. cit.*
p. 327.

In Boeotia the Romans were hampered by the zeal of their friends. During the war with Perseus the Theban politician Ismenias offered the support of Boeotia as a whole to the Romans; but it was clear to the Roman Commissioners that he was not in a position to carry out his promise, as feelings were divided, and the only practicable alternative was to deal with the cities individually. Ismenias was apparently trying to secure the unity of Boeotia by helping Rome: but, as there were some who did not wish to help Rome, and others whose main concern was with the independence of the single cities, he could hardly hope to succeed in this policy, though it may have been patriotic in intention. Coronea, Thisbe and Haliartus joined Perseus and suffered for it. Thebes did not lose anything then, as the party dominant in that city was pro-Roman. But a period of confusion followed in Boeotia, for Mnasippus of Coronea is one of those named by Polybius among the promoters of disorder whose death some ten years later caused relief and improvement. In the final war against Rome Thebes was less fortunate: for her most influential man at that time, Pytheas, who is described as bold, ambitious, and of bad character, brought Boeotia into the struggle, and the destruction of Thebes followed the defeat of the Achaean League. So far as our knowledge goes, the loss of Boeotian independence gives little cause for regret: Polybius (xx, 7) indeed tells us that the severe punishment which befell Boeotia might almost be regarded as retribution for the exceptional good fortune which had enabled her to escape the consequences of political disorder and misgovernment at an earlier date. The study of Boeotian history at any other period than the first half of the fourth century b.c. leaves us with renewed admiration for the leaders who succeeded in raising Thebes to so great a height at that time.

V. CENTRAL AND SOUTHERN GREECE: THE ACHAEAN LEAGUE

If there is little reason to regret the disappearance of the Boeotian League, and if in regard to Leagues such as those in Phocis, Locris or Euboea, too little is known for us to be able to judge fairly whether their cessation was a loss or not, it is otherwise with the Achaean League. With it were associated some of the greatest names in the history of Greece, it had contributed a considerable part of what is best in Greek politics since the days of Aratus, and there must have been grave faults (not necessarily confined to one side) in the conduct of affairs which brought this valuable association to its end.

The Achaeans had preferred Rome to Macedon in the war with Philip and had declared war on Antiochus. With the crushing of the Aetolian League, which ceased to have any political importance, they became the chief power in Greece. The reward which they expected for their wisdom in taking the side of Rome was that they should be allowed to complete their domination of the Peloponnese by keeping Sparta and the whole of Messenia. The leader in this policy was Philopoemen, who believed that it could be carried through by the assertion of the legal rights of the League, which the Senate would not contest if they were laid before it firmly but unprovocatively. In this policy he had the support of Archon and of Lycortas, the father of Polybius, who is careful to point out[1] that Philopoemen was not opposed to Rome except in the sense that he did not wish to acquiesce in Roman decisions which seemed to him unjustified. The military strength of the League was largely his creation, his personal position was secured by the dominant Arcadian representation on the League, and he knew himself to be the most famous Hellene of the day. He was too experienced a soldier to wish to provoke a conflict with Rome, but he believed that the rights of the Achaeans could be pressed by arms in Greece and defended by words at Rome, and he resented the attitude of Flamininus, who did not reserve his philhellenism for Achaeans and had more than once been in conflict with him. Also he had a rival in Aristaenus who, though reluctant to sacrifice laws or decrees of the League, was willing to do so if it should prove necessary in order to carry out or even to anticipate the wishes of the Romans. Naturally he seemed to Rome betteraffected than Philopoemen, and this fact helped to make the Senate unsympathetic to those ambitions of the League which Philopoemen embodied.

In their policy towards outside powers the Achaeans showed themselves prudently unenterprising. Aristaenus prevented the Assembly from a hasty renewal of alliance with Egypt, and though friendship with Syria was renewed at the accession of Seleucus, the League declined a present of ships of war, and also an offer of Eumenes to present them with 120 talents to form a fund for the payment of members of the League's Council. The acceptance of this gift would have made possible a more democratic representation in the Council of the League; and that may have been one reason why it was unwelcome to those in power. In order to secure its rejection an Aeginetan pointed out that a more acceptable

---

[1] XXIV, 11.

gift would be the restoration of the island of Aegina, which
Attalus I had bought from the Aetolians. Behind these considerations of sentiment there may have been the politic calculation that
it would be wise not to seem to have important allies or patrons
except Rome. On the other hand, the Senate was displeased by
the stiffness with which the League stood on its rights towards
Q. Caecilius Metellus who, as he returned from Macedonia in 185,
lectured the League magistrates on their harshness to Sparta. He
was met by long arguments from Philopoemen, Lycortas and Archon, and thereupon demanded that the League assembly should
be summoned. This was refused as illegal in the absence of a
written demand by the Senate for a meeting to consider a specific
point. No doubt law was on the side of the Achaeans, but their
action brought a sharp admonition from the Senate to treat envoys
with more respect.

The Spartan question continued to be troublesome, and the
Senate made an attempt to reach an agreed settlement by the
deliberations of a committee of three, including Flamininus and
Caecilius. The definite and recognized inclusion of Sparta in the
League was at issue, but also the question of the return of several
groups of Spartan exiles, and the restoration of their property. It
was ruled that Sparta should remain a member of the League but
that the exiles should be restored. The Achaean envoys who were
at Rome decided to accept this decision; but the return of
exiles was always unwelcome to the fierce partisans in Greek
cities, the acceptance of this condition meant setting aside a
decree of the League, and they may have thought that Rome was
giving them nothing that was not already theirs. The settlement
was not carried through with goodwill, and the Senate was even
less sympathetic with the League when in 183 the Messenians
sought to secede. Q. Marcius Philippus, who had just returned
from Greece, advised that, if the Senate showed itself unfriendly,
the movement for secession might spread and drive the League
to welcome Roman protection. The Senate accordingly refused
to take steps to prevent arms and food reaching Messenia from
Italy and warned the League that persistence in conducting a
policy opposed to the views of Rome might cause, not only Sparta,
but Corinth and Argos, to secede.

The Achaeans, led by Philopoemen, were not intimidated and
the Messenians were quickly defeated, though during the war
Philopoemen himself was taken prisoner in a skirmish and put to
death.

Plutarch says that a certain Roman called Philopoemen the

last of the Greeks. It is true that with him ended the line of Hellenic generals who added a touch of genius to their virtuosity in the art of war. In the forty years that followed his first exploit at Sellasia he had not lost a battle by land, and he had made an army out of the Achaean levies. He had matched his cunning against the Cretans, his courage against the Spartans, and he had withstood Flamininus in the day of his success. Yet herein lay the great disservice that he did to Greece. His fame held high the imperialism of the Achaeans, and his spirit forbade him to make it easy for Rome to leave the Greeks really free. He was more of a soldier than a statesman, at a time when Achaea needed a statesman rather than a soldier. The most Roman of the Greeks, yet he had in him the almost unreasoning rancour of a Greek partisan, and his moments of violence robbed of their effect his insistence on treaty rights which the Romans were generally ready to respect. Furthermore, the successes which had given to the League greater power than it had ever before enjoyed had been achieved in a way which outraged panhellenic feeling so far as that existed, and by a reaction against economic movements which were born of deeply-felt economic stress. If the Achaeans were not to be the servants of Rome, neither could they be the leaders of the Greeks. Had we the whole of Polybius' history or still more his life of Philopoemen, we should be better able to discover, beneath the qualities which Polybius admired, the defects of judgment and the narrowness of vision to which Polybius could not have been blind. It may well be doubted if any statesman, whether a Cavour, or a Mazzini, or a Bismarck, could have saved Greece from the power of Rome, and made her a nation, but the high qualities of Philopoemen were spent in rendering the task impossible. He died *felix opportunitate mortis*, and his friend and successor Lycortas was the heir to his policy but not to the influence and capacity which it demanded.

Though compelled to re-enter the League, the Messenians were treated with statesmanlike forbearance. The Senate declared that, after all, they had hindered supplies from reaching Messenia, and the Achaeans were allowed to interpret the return of exiles to Sparta as excluding those who had been definitely hostile to the League. An independent policy had so far proved successful, and only the death of Ptolemy Epiphanes saved the League from the dangerous temptation of an Egyptian alliance. In Sparta the Achaeans had to intervene to put down a demagogue Chaeron who might have become a second Nabis. The Romans were concerned that the restoration of the exiles had not been complete, and the

Achaean leaders were divided about the wisdom of giving way on
the point. Three envoys were sent to Rome, one of whom, Callicrates of Leontium, gave to the Senate the advice which, in the
judgment of Polybius (xxiv, 10), produced a disastrous change of
Roman policy towards Greece. Callicrates pointed out that politicians would always be under a temptation to advocate the strict
observance of laws and decrees, since a reputation for patriotism
and independence was most easily won in this way, and he urged
that the Romans, if they really wished to exert effective influence
in Greece, should take strong measures to make their wishes
known. The speaker described some of the recent actions of the
League, in regard both to Messene and to Sparta, as done without
Roman consent or in defiance of Rome's expressed wishes; and,
though the Senate may have suspected that his argument was inspired by political partisanship, it agreed that there was much
to be said for the policy which he recommended. Hitherto, though
the Romans might have shown occasional impatience, and used
language of serious warning, coming near to threats, they had
not gone outside the limits permissible to candid friends whose
advice had been asked. Henceforward they showed a tendency
to regard a desire to carry out the wishes of Rome as the test of
patriotism. They included in their official answer a wish that all
men in the various states should be like Callicrates; and, in order
that now at any rate there should be no ambiguity as to their
opinion, they insisted on the restoration of all the Spartan exiles,
and, though the question concerned the Achaean League only,
they addressed their rescript not only to the Achaeans but also to
the Aetolians, Epirotes, Athenians, Boeotians and Acarnanians.

On his return Callicrates played upon the fear of hostility to
Rome, and thus secured his election as General, in which capacity
he carried out the restoration of the Spartan and Messenian exiles[1].
Sparta was re-fortified and the constitution of Lycurgus was restored. This seemed to be the end of this thorny question, and for
nearly a decade there was an uneasy peace in Achaean politics.
But once Roman distrust of the Achaean statesmen had been
aroused, there was small prospect of the League being able to
pursue a policy which would preserve both its own self-respect
and the goodwill of Rome. There was no power to whom the
Achaeans could turn, except possibly Macedon, and not only
Callicrates but also his political opponents, Archon and Lycortas,
had no wish to be friends to that power. Perseus wished to be on

---

[1] Polybius xxiv, 10; Ditt.[3] 634.

good terms with the League but his overtures were rejected, and
when at last it came to war between Rome and Macedon, Archon,
no less than Callicrates, favoured active assistance against Perseus, though he may have seen the danger to Achaea of the final
and complete victory of either side. Lycortas was for neutrality,
and in 169 B.C. there was a rumour that the Roman Commissioners
in Greece were thinking of accusing him and his son Polybius
and even Archon himself before the League. It is true that none
of the three reached Callicrates' high standard of pro-Romanism,
but Rome had no just grounds of complaint. Polybius, indeed,
who was Hipparch of the League in this year, was sent to arrange
for the co-operation of the full strength of the League in what
appeared likely to be the decisive campaign in Thessaly.

During this and the next year the Achaean leaders gave to
Rome no reasonable ground for complaint. When Appius
Claudius applied to the League for 5000 men to help him in
Epirus, Polybius was sent by Marcius Philippus to urge the
League to refuse, in the absence of written orders from the Senate
(p. 266). The only other question of policy which arose in the
League at this time was of its attitude towards the war between
Syria and Egypt. Lycortas and Polybius were in favour of giving
help to Egypt, while Callicrates argued that the Achaeans should
reserve their strength to assist Rome and should content themselves with offering mediation. This was no doubt what the Senate
preferred, but it could not well object if the Achaeans wished
to help Egypt, with which they had some kind of treaty engagement and which had so often served the League, if only for its own
purposes. Callicrates succeeded in contriving that ambassadors
and not troops were sent to Egypt, but their good offices were
not needed, for Rome herself intervened.

One thing is certain, that the Romans were not only exasperated
by their long-continued ill-success against Perseus, but suspected
that Achaean statesmen availed themselves of the complicated
machinery of the League constitution to place obstacles in the
way of decisions which they did not like. It was doubtless more
convenient to have in authority persons like Callicrates who only
asked what Rome's wishes were. But this does not make clear why
the Roman Commissioners sent to Achaea behaved as they did.
First they asked that a vote be passed condemning to death certain
persons unnamed who had supported Perseus; next they said that
all the Generals since the beginning of the war were suspect, and
finally, when Xenon, one of these Generals, expressed his readiness to be tried before any court that the Romans might appoint,

they used this opportunity to command a body of 1000 men, from a list supplied by Callicrates, to proceed to Italy as prisoners. Still less intelligible or defensible is the fact that these accused persons, who were quartered in various parts of Italy, were never brought to trial, and that requests that this should be done, or that they should be allowed to return home, received only curt answers. We hear of such requests being received in or about the years 165, 160, 155 and 153 b.c. On one of the occasions the request might have been granted but for the way in which the presiding Roman magistrate put the question; with this exception there is no indication of any division of opinion among the Romans on the subject. It was not till 151 b.c. that those who still survived (rather less than 300) were allowed to go back, on the contemptuous advice of Cato who suggested that they were too old to do much harm.

The Roman policy of removing from Achaean affairs all experienced statesmen except those who would support Rome blindly was for a time successful in preventing complications. In 165 Rome allowed an Achaean court to settle a boundary dispute between Sparta and Megalopolis: the Achaeans decided in favour of Megalopolis, probably with justice or at least in accordance with previous decisions, but the decision was bound to irritate the Lacedaemonians. In 151/0 the Achaean General Menalcidas, perhaps for a bribe, used force to eject the Athenians from Oropus. Then came the return of the *détenus* from Rome, with inevitable disputes about their property. That they played any important part in the crisis which soon followed is not recorded, and some of them, like Polybius, may have seen that Rome was too strong for it to be wise to resent her injustices. The poorer in the Achaean cities found leaders in Diaeus and Critolaus, the former of whom became General in 150 b.c. He sought to suppress the separatist movement in Sparta, and after his term of office expired he set out with Callicrates for Rome to represent the League before the Senate. Callicrates died on the journey, and his death was of some importance, for, whatever his defects, he was not likely to have encouraged a reckless challenge of Rome. Diaeus, on the other hand, took up so aggressive an attitude as to alienate the Senate. For the moment no answer was given but the Romans decided to weaken the League by encouraging a movement of secession in other states beside Sparta.

The Senate had good reason to proceed slowly. Roman armies were engaged in Spain and in Africa, and the rising in Macedonia was still not crushed. But Diaeus used the delay to press on opera-

tions against Sparta, which had formally seceded. A warning
from Metellus the praetor in Macedonia went unheeded. Then
came news that he had defeated Andriscus; a second message led
to an armistice, and, after a further interval of hostilities, Sparta
and the Achaeans came nearer to a settlement (summer, 147 B.C.).
But the faint hope of peace was dispelled by the arrival of the
Roman commission under L. Aurelius Orestes, who announced
to a League assembly at Corinth that the Senate had decided to
detach from the League not only Sparta but also Corinth, Argos,
Orchomenus in Arcadia and a new accession Heraclea. There was
an outburst of anger, in which the Romans could not protect anyone who was suspected of being a Spartan from rough handling
and came near to being treated with violence themselves. Rome
had no desire for war if she could compel obedience otherwise,
but her calmness was misinterpreted; Critolaus was elected
General, the punishment of those responsible for the disorder was
refused, and the Senate pushed on its preparations. Metellus was
to advance from Macedonia, and Attalus was called upon for
contingents.

Early in 146 B.C. it became clear that the Achaeans had
behind them wide-spread sympathy. The Boeotians and Euboeans
took up arms, the masses in the Greek cities were encouraged by
promises of a social revolution, and the new Achaean General
Critolaus did not dare to disappoint them. When Metellus once
more sent envoys to the League Assembly, his well-meant ad-
monitions were in vain: Critolaus declared that the Achaeans
sought in the Romans friends not masters. The Romans wished
to be both; the alternative was war. L. Mummius the consul was
placed in command of an army of nearly 30,000 men and orders
were given to equip a fleet. The task of the Romans was made
easier by the faulty strategy of Critolaus who, instead of concentrating on defence, pressed forward to besiege Heraclea with part
of the Achaean forces. Metellus saw his opportunity and struck
hard, Critolaus was defeated and killed at Scarpheia in Locris as
he tried to disengage his army, and the advancing Achaean reinforcements were cut to pieces. The Boeotians, whose accession
had perhaps helped to lure the Achaeans north of the Isthmus of
Corinth, were at the mercy of Rome.

The courage of the Achaeans rose to face the danger. Diaeus
was made General and a promising attempt to negotiate was
checked. Metellus reached the Isthmus where the Achaean forces
based on Corinth barred his way. The Roman fleet was still in the
dockyard and, till it came to turn their position, the Achaeans might

hope to hold their own. Meanwhile Mummius arrived and took over the command, and his army followed. Diaeus was encouraged by a slight success to offer battle to the superior Roman forces and was utterly defeated. Corinth opened its gates, most of its inhabitants had fled, the remainder suffered the rigour of a Roman sack. The city itself awaited the decision of the Senate.

Thus one short campaign had broken the last military power in Greece. Diaeus killed himself; the Achaean cities did not venture to resist. Individuals who had opposed Rome were visited with death and confiscation, democracies which had encouraged the masses against Rome were overthrown, leagues—Achaean, Boeotian, Euboean, Phocian and Locrian—were dissolved. Thebes and Chalcis were partly destroyed. But for Corinth was reserved a harder fate. The city was burnt and its contents, above all its art treasures, were sold or carried off to Rome. However much truth there is in the anecdotes about Mummius and about his soldiers dicing on masterpieces, the Greeks may have lost less than the Romans gained. Other trading communities, including Italian, doubtless profited by the destruction of a competitor, but there is no direct evidence that commercial ambitions or jealousy influenced the decision of the Senate. To Livy it is a reprisal for disrespect to the Roman Commissioners: it is more intelligible as a lesson to the Greeks that the patience of Rome was exhausted. It was a crime, but like other crimes in history, in part salutary, and Greece did not forget the lesson.

Such is the story, so far as it can be reconstructed from the scanty and not always trustworthy tradition that has come down to us. The ultimate authority is Polybius, who disapproved of the Achaean policy and despised the Achaean leaders; his account has only reached us, apart from a short fragment elsewhere, in a very unsatisfactory narrative given by Pausanias. That Critolaus, Diaeus and their colleagues could not reasonably hope for victory is clear; whether they were so wholly senseless and irresponsible as the account represents them may be doubted, but we have no materials to paint a more favourable picture. It is equally easy to see that the Romans' patience gave out with disastrous suddenness. For them to guide Greece without ruling it demanded infinite patience, and they deserve perhaps more praise than blame, even if their policy was rarely idealistic or unselfish. But at last they tried to take a short cut and to solve political problems by removing the men who alone were capable of endeavouring to solve them intelligently. Whatever excuse may have been given for the unjust removal and detention of the

Achaean leaders, it carried with it consequences which it became impossible to undo, and the end of the Achaean League is an incident for which admirers of Rome can find nothing but regret.

It was not until much later that the Romans regarded Southern Greece as a district in which they were to be separately represented: for the present, the Roman representative in Macedonia, in addition to his other duties, received a general responsibility for Achaea, as that part came to be called. Measures were adopted to divide cities by abolishing common councils and by preventing individuals from holding property in the territory of more than one community. Part at least of Greece was made subject to tribute. Polybius earned the gratitude of his countrymen by counselling moderation to the Roman Commissioners who effected the settlement, by refusing to accept any reward for the help which he or his friends had given to the Romans, and by assisting the cities to accustom themselves to altered conditions and to solve any difficulties which the new position raised. It may be due to his influence that some amelioration was effected very soon: perhaps about 140 B.C., which Pausanias gives as the date of the end of the Achaean War.

CHAPTER X

THE ROMANS IN SPAIN

I. THE PROVINCES IN SPAIN AND THEIR ORGANIZATION

BY the year 206 B.C. Rome already possessed the most important part of Spain: the lower portion of the valley of the Ebro as far as Osca and Saragossa, the east coast and the valley of the Baetis; the extent of her possessions being mainly due to the bold conceptions, the military skill and the political address of Scipio Africanus. With this year the provincial Era begins[1]. In 205 B.C. there appear for the first time governors of the two provinces, Nearer and Further Spain (*Hispania Citerior* and *Hispania Ulterior*). The founding of the Colony of Italica, the first Roman town in Spain, marks the completion of the conquest. The governorships were held in the earlier years by private persons with proconsular power; from 197 onwards by praetors also of proconsular rank[2]. From this year, too, a fixed boundary existed between the two provinces; Nearer Spain included the valley of the Ebro and the east coast, down to just north of Baria (Vera); Further Spain embraced the Baetis region south of the *Saltus Castulonensis* (Sierra Morena) which, north of Baria, approaches the coast, and here forms a well-defined natural boundary. New Carthage belonged to the nearer, Baria to the further province[3]. The establishment of two provinces was due to military necessity, for owing to the narrowness of the coastal strip, communications between the two could easily be cut, so that each province must be independent of the other. Co-operation between the two armies was of course not excluded, and, indeed, frequently occurred, as for instance in 195 and 150 B.C.

Note. The main sources for the narrative of this chapter are to be found in Appian, *Iberica*, 39–99, and scattered through Livy XXXI–XLV and epitomes, XLVI–LIX. For further details and for the relations of the sources, see the Bibliography.

[1] E. Albertini, *Les Divisions administratives de l'Espagne*, p. 11.

[2] Livy XXXI, 20; Mommsen, *Röm. Staatsrecht*, II, 647, 652.

[3] For the demarcation of the provinces in 197 B.C. see Livy XXXII, 28; there is mention of *Hispania Citerior* and *Ulterior* in Livy XXXIII, 27 as early as 199 B.C. That New Carthage belonged to Nearer Spain is attested for 180 B.C. by Livy XL, 41, 10, for 100 B.C. by Artemidorus (Stephanus Byz. *s.v.* Ἰβηρία); that Baria belonged to Further Spain by Pliny, *N.H.* III, 19; Ptol. 2, 4, 8 (see *P.W. s.v.* Baria). The boundary was no doubt the river Almanzora. See Map 11 facing p. 324.

The conquest of the Carthaginian province in Spain had been a necessary step in the war against Hannibal, for Spain was the arsenal of the Carthaginians. In fact, with the capture in 209 B.C. of New Carthage, which was the great mining centre and store-house of supplies (vol. VII, p. 792), the resistance of the Carthaginians began to weaken. It is true that Rome might have contented herself with this acquisition, as Carthage had contented herself with the possession of the south and east. But such a limitation was not in accordance with the character of Rome, whose habit it was to complete what she began. Moreover the highlands, too, were rich in metals and therefore tempting to Roman greed and worth a strenuous effort. The safety of the Roman province was not seriously jeopardized by the occasional forays of the mountain tribes, especially the Lusitanians. Carthage, after all, had lived at peace with them for more than 250 years (500–230 B.C.), for Hannibal had been the first to attack them, and he had done so, not in order to conquer them but to reduce them to quiescence before the outbreak of war with Rome. But Rome was determined to exploit the Spanish provinces (as she had exploited her earlier provinces, Sicily and the islands of Sardinia and Corsica), partly, that is to say, by the imposition of taxes, but also, in view of the notable military qualities of the Iberians, by raising levies of auxiliary troops. They had hitherto been recruited voluntarily, and for pay, but military service was now no doubt made obligatory.

We have no detailed information regarding the conditions under which the Iberian communes entered the Roman confederation, but, generally speaking, the expulsion of the Carthaginians simply meant that they became subjects of Rome. Special treaties would be made only with the larger tribal units, and to some of these the better conditions of the *foedus* would be granted, as was done to Gades and no doubt to the other Phoenician towns. In the internal affairs of the communes Rome intervened only so far as was necessary in her own interests, as, for example, in bringing together the inhabitants of the small and often petty strongholds (*castella, turres*) into towns. In Nearer Spain, out of 293 communes, there were still in the time of Augustus 114 rural communes (*gentilitates*), i.e. communes without an urban centre, especially among the Astures and Cantabri, but there were none in the rest of the peninsula[1]. The coins which Rome caused to be minted name only towns, not kings or tribes. More-

[1] A. Schulten, *Die peregrinen Gaugemeinden des röm. Reiches*, Rhein. Mus. L, 1895, pp. 489 *sqq.*

over larger tribes (*gentes*) such as we find in Gaul scarcely existed
as political entities. The chiefs (*reguli, principes*) were no doubt
mostly done away with. When we find the Turdetanian chief
Culchas in the year 206 ruling over 28 towns, but in 197 only
over 17[1], it would seem that some of his towns had been taken
from him, and that was probably a reason for his defection. In the
same way a small community Lascuta, which had been subject to
Hasta, was taken from it and made independent (*C.I.L.* II, 5041).
The only form of political organization which Rome as a rule recognized in the communes was the Council of Elders, the primeval
form of government among Iberians and Berbers. It is spoken
of as the *senatus* (Livy XXXIV, 17). Any concentration of power
in the hands of chiefs was unwelcome to Rome, while, on the
other hand, the looser form of government by the Elders was
convenient, if only because it was a guarantee of separatism.
Generally speaking, both tribute and auxiliaries would be demanded; and the Iberians no doubt accommodated themselves to
these conditions with characteristic indifference. But it was not
to be expected that the governors would content themselves
merely with the legal imposts either in the interests of the State
or of themselves; they were likely to proceed to further exactions,
and herein they had to reckon upon an obstinate resistance.
Besides, some of the Iberian communities made the Carthaginian
cause their own, and from the first fought with determination for
Carthage, or rather for their own autonomy. This was the case
with two important towns of *Hispania Ulterior*, Ilurci (Lorca) and
Astapa (Estepa); Ilurci was only taken after a desperate resistance,
while the citizens of Astapa ended by flinging themselves into the
flames which were devouring their possessions[2] (206 B.C.).

We have no information about the amount of the tribute imposed on the Iberian communities. It did not consist, as in Sicily
and later in Asia, of a percentage of the harvest, varying according
to the yield (*decuma*), but of a fixed impost (*stipendium*)[3], and, in
accordance with this, the Spanish communes were called 'civitates
stipendiariae' (Pliny, *N.H.* III, 6 *sq.*; IV, 110 *sq.*). We may infer
from the statements about the amounts of the precious metals
brought home by the governors as plunder that it was made up

---

[1] Livy XXVIII, 13; XXXIII, 21.

[2] Ilurci is called by Livy Iliturgi, and is confused with the Iliturgi on
the Baetis and with that in Catalonia. See the present writer in *Hermes*,
LXIII, 1928, pp. 228 *sqq.*

[3] Livy XXIX, 3, 5 referring to the year 205; Cicero, *Verr.* III, 6, 12,
pro Balbo, 18, 41.

of payments in silver and gold, partly in bullion and partly in coined money. A confirmation of this is the identity of design in the various coins bearing Iberian legends, which, coupled with the fact that the Iberians of earlier days had no coinage, shows that these coins were struck at the instance of Rome, her purpose being first the payment of tribute in coin and second the provision of a convenient medium of exchange for commerce within Spain. As the uniform design of the coins can only have been prescribed by Rome, so the monetary standard too is Roman, for the Iberian silver pieces have the weight of the denarius, and the copper coins bear the symbols of the *as* and its parts (*e.g.* two dots for the sextans, four for the triens)[1]. The earlier coins are struck on the uncial standard, the later on the semiuncial. Further evidence for the Roman origin of the coinage is found in the facts that, on coins of *Hispania Citerior* we sometimes meet, alongside of the Iberian, a Latin superscription (on coins of Celsa and Osicerda) or a Roman word is written in Iberian form (as at Meduinum) and all the towns of Baetica, with the exception of the Phoenician towns and a few others, have legends on their coins in Latin letters. About 100 towns of Nearer Spain show Iberian writing and about 40 of Further Spain Latin. Lusitania minted no coins, which is an indication of its poverty and inferior civilization; it had no silver, nor did it need a medium of exchange for its trade.

The minting of Iberian coins begins soon after the first conquests. The earliest coins with Iberian legends seem to be those of Saguntum, Emporium and Ilerda. The design common to all Iberian coins—head on the obverse and a horseman with lance in rest on the reverse—is derived from the coins of Hiero II of Syracuse[2] who died in 215 B.C. The tribute coins are often called *argentum Oscense*, money of Osca. This commune in the Ebro valley must therefore have had an important mint. To it have been attributed the most numerous of all Iberian coins, which bear the inscription *k l s t h n*, although this name has nothing to do with that of Osca. No fewer than 1300 silver coins with this inscription have been found in a hoard near Soria[3]. Although the

---

[1] See Volume of Plates iii, 10, *h*.

[2] This fact is established by Vives in his *La Moneda hispanica*, 5 vols. Madrid, 1926, the most complete collection of material, which supersedes the older works of Delgado and Heiss. See vol. ii for the Iberian coins of Nearer Spain, vol. iii for those of Further Spain. The best treatment of the political significance of the Iberian coins is by Haeberlin in Schulten, *Numantia*, vol. iv, p. 273 *sq.* For the likeness to the coins of Hiero II see Volume of Plates iii, 10, *f, g*.

[3] Hübner, *Monumenta Linguae Ibericae*, p. 213.

subjects of Rome were elsewhere only permitted to strike copper coins, the Iberian towns also minted a great deal of silver. This is to be explained, not by their having enjoyed a specially privileged position, but by the abundance of the silver, and the fact that tribute had to be paid in it.

In addition to precious metals the Iberian communes had also to deliver other natural products, especially corn and perhaps oil. To collect the tribute *praefecti* were sent to the communes, a practice against which the Spaniards petitioned in the year 171 B.C. (Livy XLIII, 2). Apart from the fixed tribute a *vigesima*, or five per cent. tax, was levied on corn (Livy XLIII, 3), in connection with which it was customary for the Roman officials to settle the price, but in 171 the Spaniards protested against this procedure with success.

More burdensome than the high tribute were the extortions of the governors. In the history of provincial administration Spain marks an epoch, since it was the extortions practised there which caused the establishment and development of courts for trying claims for redress (*repetundae*[1]). In the year 171, in consequence of complaints from both provinces, the first such court was set up, and in the year 149, after the outrages perpetrated by Lucullus and Galba, this court was made permanent. Livy (XL, 44) relates the highly significant fact that a governor, who in the stress of war had vowed games and a temple, wrung from the Iberians the means to perform his vow. Equally oppressive was the levying of troops, the scale of which is shown by the credible statement in ancient writers that the small tribes of the Belli and Titti in eastern Celtiberia had to provide 5000 fighting men, and that Scipio before Numantia had some 40,000 auxiliaries[2]. If the Romans were at first welcomed as deliverers from the Carthaginian yoke, the Spaniards soon saw that they had only exchanged one master for another, and that the change was for the worse (Livy XXXIV, 18). A recent historian writes with justice 'What the pages of the history of Rome in Spain down to the year 133 have to tell us, whether explicitly or implicitly, takes its place among the most shameful records in the whole of that history[3].'

The few communities to which Rome had granted a *foedus* were, however, in a slightly better position. The Greek city of

[1] Mommsen, *Strafrecht*, p. 707.

[2] It is to be remembered, however, that numbers given by ancient authorities, especially where they had no certain means of controlling them, cannot be regarded as wholly above suspicion.

[3] K. Götzfried, *Annalen der röm. Provinzen beider Spanien*, Erlangen Diss., 1907, p. 24.

Emporium, which had long had an alliance with Rome, was allowed to continue to strike its own coinage, with Greek legends, upon its own monetary standard, and a similar privilege was granted to the Phoenician towns newly admitted to alliance, like Gades and Ebusus, which continued to use Phoenician legends[1]. The Romans had every reason to treat the inhabitants of Emporium well, for it had constantly served the conquerors as a *point d'appui*. Here the Scipios had landed in 218; here, too, Cato in 195 when the whole of Nearer Spain was as good as lost. The only town with Roman citizenship was the colony of Italica founded by Scipio Africanus. In the year 171 the Latin colony of Carteia, for the sons of soldiers who had taken native wives, was founded, or rather planted in the existing town (Livy XLIII, 3). The colony is further described as *libertinorum*, from which it appears that these people of mixed Roman and Iberian race did not become *peregrini* but freedmen[2]. There was no *conubium* between Romans and Iberians.

In wealth the two provinces were unequal. Nearer Spain possessed great abundance of silver in the neighbourhood of New Carthage, but, apart from that, was the poorer. Further Spain had from ancient times carried on intensive mining operations for copper (Rio Tinto), silver (Sierra Morena), and gold, while the valley of the Baetis was very rich in wheat, olives and wine. As early as 203 B.C. great quantities of corn were exported to Rome (Livy xxx, 26). It is easy to imagine how greedily both magistrates and private persons flew upon these rich spoils—the sixteenth-century Spaniards in Peru and Mexico offer a parallel. The Roman annals tell us of the vast body of silver and gold which the governors brought to Rome. In the years 206–197 alone the quantities of bullion amounted to 130,000 lb. of silver and 4000 lb. of gold.

The figures cited below[3] show that Further Spain provided much richer spoil than the neighbouring province. Livy expressly states that L. Stertinius, the praetor of Further Spain, made no claim to a triumph, so that he must have obtained these masses of gold and silver not as booty in war but by taxation and extor-

---

[1] A. Vives, *op. cit.* vol. I, p. 13 (Emporium), 54 (Gades), 62 (Ebusus). See Volume of Plates iii, 10, *i, j*.   [2] Mommsen, *Staatsrecht*, III, 1, p. xiii.
[3] In the year 206, 14,342 lb. silver (Livy xxviii, 38); in the year 200, 43,000 lb. silver and 2450 lb. gold (*Id.* xxxi, 20); in 199, 1200 lb. silver, 30 lb. gold (*Id.* xxxii, 7); in 198, 20,000 lb. silver from Nearer Spain, 50,000 from Further Spain, and 1515 lb. gold from Nearer Spain (*Id.* xxxiii, 27).

tion[1]. The outbreak in the following year, 197, of a formidable revolt which extended to both provinces needs no further explanation. Nor is it without significance that the revolt broke out among the unwarlike Turdetanians and that the wholly peaceable Phoenician trading towns of Malaca and Sexi took part in it. Indeed the fact that Rome had not spared even these towns, with which it doubtless had an alliance as it had with Gades, is shown by the treatment of Gades itself, which in 199 B.C. had to complain that, contrary to the treaty, a *praefectus* had been placed over it[2].

II. CATO AND TIBERIUS SEMPRONIUS GRACCHUS IN SPAIN

The revolt was begun by two Turdetanian kings, Culchas and Luxinius. The former, as we have seen, ruled over 17 towns, the latter over the Carmo region. In addition to the two Phoenician towns the country district of Baeturia joined in the revolt, so that the whole western part of Further Spain was up in arms. It was perhaps no accident that the revolt coincided with the Gallic and Macedonian Wars (chaps. vi, xi). Fortunately for Rome, however, the latter could be brought to an end promptly, though the struggle with the Italian Gauls had to be continued for some time longer. The revolt soon spread to the other Spanish province, whose warlike inhabitants inflicted on the praetor C. Sempronius Tuditanus a severe defeat. It is true that in the following year, 196, a victory is recorded over two kings of Further Spain, Budares and Besadines, near a town called Turba (for which perhaps we should read Turta, the name by which Cato describes the country of the Turdetani), but in Nearer Spain the outlook was darker, and in 195 B.C. the Romans found themselves obliged to send out a consul, Cato, with a full consular army, bringing their forces in Spain up to about 50,000 men.

Starting from Emporium Cato succeeded in subduing Nearer Spain, and then marched to the assistance of the governor of the further province in his struggle against the Turdetanians, and the Celtiberians, whom they had enlisted in their cause. Though here he gained no great military successes he succeeded in buying over the Celtiberians to his side. On his way back, as during his advance, he passed through the highland country, that is to say through Celtiberian territory. He laid siege, though without success, to the town of Segontia (Siguenza) on its boundary, and was apparently equally unsuccessful in an attack on Numantia,

[1] Livy xxxiii, 27.   [2] *Ib.* xxxii, 2.

which lay on his route from Segontia to the Ebro. The Roman
camp near Aguilar (13 miles east of Segontia), that near Alpan-
seque (16 miles north of Segontia), and the oldest of the five
camps on the Gran Atalaya (4 miles east of Numantia) seem to
date from the time of Cato[1]. It was this campaign which began
the war against the Celtiberians, the finest fighters in all Spain,
and this war, constantly breaking out afresh, like a forest fire,
lasted down to the year 133, when Numantia fell.

After his return Cato had to conduct a campaign against the
tribes who inhabited the mountains of Catalonia. Livy (xxxiv, 21)
expressly states that this resulted in the better exploitation of the
mines of that region. That was the main thing. In the following
years, 194 to 193, the war continued, and spread to the Lusitanians
whose name now appears for the first time among the enemies of
Rome. According to the Roman annals, the Lusitanians were the
aggressors; but Baeturia, which lies on the frontiers of Lusitania,
was in the hands of the Romans as early as 197 B.C., so that the
encroachment on the neighbouring country was probably the act
of Rome. From the further province the Romans now advanced
against the highland country, subjugating the Oretani (round
Castulo) and the Carpetani (round Toledo). In 190 B.C. Aemilius
Paullus, later the conqueror of Perseus, sustained a severe defeat
at the hands of the Lusitanians, which he soon afterwards
retrieved by a victory.

An interesting administrative record from this period has come
down to us, the earliest Roman inscription from Spain (*C.I.L.*
II, 5041 = *Dessau* 15). In it Paullus issues a decree about a small
Iberian stronghold which is called 'Turris Lascutana' but later
becomes known to us as the town of Lascuta and has left behind
coins with an unusual form of writing, which is perhaps Tar-
tessian. This place is to be taken from the people of Hasta, and
the slaves of the town of Hasta who are in Lascuta are to be free,
i.e. to enter the service of Rome.

In 181 B.C. the Romans began to penetrate into the highlands
from the north also and to subdue the tribes in the valley of the
Jalon (a tributary on the south side of the Ebro) and the Jiloca,
the Lusones, Belli and Titti, just as earlier, penetrating it from
the south, they had subjugated the Oretani and Carpetani. The
conquest of the Lusones with their capital of Contrebia was
successfully carried through. In the treaty which Gracchus, the
father of the tribunes, made with them in 179, they bound

---

[1] A. Schulten, *Numantia*, vol. IV, p. 37; 191; 196. See Map 10 below,
facing p. 322.

themselves to pay tribute and provide auxiliaries, while Gracchus in return gave them better land. On the other hand, an expedition of Gracchus against the Celtiberians on the upper Douro, in the neighbourhood of Numantia, achieved no more than the conclusion of a treaty on terms rather favourable to the enemy. It was mainly by these conciliatory treaties, rather than by force of arms, that Gracchus brought to an end the Celtiberian war (181–179), which did not break out again until twenty-five years had elapsed (153 B.C.). The foundation of two towns, Graccuris and Corduba, the former by Gracchus, the latter by M. Claudius Marcellus in 168 or 151 B.C., indicate some attempt at romanization.

Long after the Gracchan treaties had been broken by repeated wars the Iberians still regarded their terms as a political ideal—and when, in the year 137, Mancinus capitulated to them they were unwilling to trust anyone but Tiberius Gracchus, the son of the treaty-maker (p. 320 *sq.*). It is evident from this that more could be effected with the Iberians by clemency than by force. It was the same policy which the elder Scipio and Hasdrubal had applied; but only a few of the Roman generals had the wisdom to use these milder methods, the majority merely piled war on war through senseless deeds of violence. Though Gracchus in his report to the Senate boasted of having subjugated three hundred Iberian towns, these were for the most part, as Posidonius justly remarks, castles of no great size, some of them very small indeed, such as were found all over Spain, often containing only a clan or sept of fifty to a hundred men.

III. THE WARS WITH THE LUSITANIANS: VIRIATHUS

Between 179 and 154 there was respite from war, but as we have seen extortion continued (see above, p. 310). Finally, the Romans had to face new troubles. As on a former occasion, during the Celtiberian revolt of 153 and the following years a parallel revolt was running its course in Lusitania, though it was only occasionally that the military operations came into connection with one another. The Lusitanian War lasted uninterruptedly from 154 to 138, down to the death of Viriathus, the Celtiberian War from 153 to 151 and from 143 to 133. The Lusitanians in 154 B.C. struck the first blow by making a raid into Roman territory merely for plunder, not for freedom. In the course of this year the Lusitanians under their leader Punicus defeated several praetors, induced the neighbouring Vettones to take part in the war, and penetrated into the Roman province. After the death of Punicus the new leader Kaisaros inflicted on Mummius, the future destroyer of Corinth, a defeat in which nine thousand Romans fell. Kaisaros now sent the captured standards to the Celtiberians, by way of rousing them to take part in the struggle. This they did, but only till 152, when, won over by favourable treaties, they withdrew from the war. The Lusitanians next invaded the district of Algarve, the land of the Conii, and even crossed the Straits of Gibraltar and carried their ravages as far as Ocilis (Arzila), until Mummius drove them back. In 152 a new governor, M. Atilius, gained some successes, so that the Lusitanians made peace, but as soon as he had retired into winter quarters they broke out again. His successor Galba suffered a great defeat in 151, with the loss of 7000 men, and fled to Carmona. Lucullus, from Nearer Spain, where peace had reigned since 152, came to his assistance, and won some success. Galba found a more excellent way. He induced the Lusitanians to submit, promising them land. When they had delivered up their weapons and had allowed themselves, ostensibly with a view to the settlement, to be divided into several bands, he surrounded them, unarmed as they were, and put them to the sword. Few escaped; but among them was the future hero Viriathus. We read that Galba retained most of the booty for himself. It was not for nothing that he had to stand his trial, and suffer the onslaughts of the aged Cato.

Gradually some 10,000 Lusitanians collected together again and invaded the province. But the praetor Vetilius surrounded them and they were once more on the point of surrendering, when Viriathus dissuaded them, and became their leader. He succeeded in breaking through, and when the Romans pressed the pursuit, he cut them off in a defile of the Sierra Ronda, slaying four thousand of them along with their general (147 B.C.). Viriathus now marched through the fertile land of the Carpetani (La Mancha, which is still rich in wine and oil), defeated Plautius, killing 4000 men, and established himself on the 'Hill of Venus' (Sierra S. Vincente), and from that fastness laid waste the whole surrounding country (146 B.C.). He even ventured to cross the Guadarrama and advanced as far as Segovia. One praetor after another met with disaster, so that in 145 the Romans had once more to send a consular army of two legions, under the consul Fabius Maximus, the brother of Scipio Aemilianus. In that year and the next Fabius had some successes, but in the years 143 and 142 one Roman defeat followed another, until the Celtiberians also were encouraged to renew the war.

The situation was dangerous indeed. Viriathus had in fact succeeded in rousing the whole of the highland country to revolt. He probably aimed at carrying on a concerted war with a common plan, but the undisciplined anarchy of the two peoples brought his schemes to nought. The Iberians were on a much lower level of intelligence and of civilization than the Gauls whom Vercingetorix induced to make common cause in the struggle for freedom. In the year 141 we again find a consular army in the field, and once more under a relative of Scipio, who since 151 had been the moving spirit of the war against the Iberians. Fabius Maximus Servilianus, the adoptive brother of Fabius Maximus, was however repeatedly defeated, and finally surrounded, with his army. Viriathus might have put the whole army to the sword, and thereby ended the war, for the Romans would never have retrieved such a loss; but the incredible happened. Viriathus permitted the army of Servilianus to withdraw in safety—in return for a treaty, the worthlessness of which he must have known. The blame for this piece of folly rests doubtless wholly upon Viriathus' followers, who had wearied of the war, as happened again and again both with them and with the Celtiberians. Strange to say, the peace was ratified by Rome. But the successor of Servilianus, Servilius Caepio, renewed the war on his own initiative, just as in the same year Pompeius repudiated the peace he had concluded with the Celtiberians.

Caepio was defeated like his predecessors, but found a way to end the war at a single blow. He bribed three friends of Viriathus to murder him (138 B.C.). That ended the Lusitanian War, though the Celtiberian War went on from defeat to defeat. Viriathus was the greatest leader of their own nation whom the Iberians ever possessed—and obeyed. To maintain his leadership for fully eight years (146–138) was an astonishing feat. Almost always victorious, he was overcome at last only by a treacherous assassination, the fate of Sertorius, whom he so greatly resembles. Like him, Viriathus was able to exercise a kind of fascination over his wild tribesmen. Both in strategy and tactics he surpassed his Roman adversaries, and succeeded again and again in defeating them by a feigned flight or by drawing them into ambuscades, practising the time-honoured stratagems of their kinsmen in Africa. But even he, like other leaders, was robbed of success by the inability of the Iberians to prosecute the war with energy. D. Junius Brutus, Caepio's successor (137), marched through Lusitania and made war upon the wild Callaici, their northern neighbours. His vigour and occasional clemency were not without effect and he earned his cognomen of Callaicus, but the establishment of a province of Lusitania was as yet far distant. As late as 49 B.C. it was merely a kind of military annex of Further Spain—much in the same way as under Augustus Germania was an annex of Gallia Belgica.

It has been pointed out earlier (vol. VII, p. 783) that the Iberians of the mountain country were ill-equipped for a war with Rome, for they were split up into a thousand communities of various sizes but all small, and not even those who belonged to the same tribe held together. In addition to this, they lacked that determination which gives staying-power in war, whereas it was just by her tenacity that Rome, in spite of all her defeats, had brought the war with Hannibal to a triumphant close. The highlanders' best defence was the nature of their country with its arid bare waterless deserts, its mountains and ravines which seemed as though created for the laying of ambushes, its extremes of climate, burning heat in summer and bitter cold in winter. To crown all, there was the great distance which separated Spain from Rome, making the conveyance of troops a long, arduous and costly undertaking.

IV. THE CELTIBERIAN WAR

The Celtiberian War is one of the best known episodes in the military history of Rome, for Appian has preserved for us the narrative of Polybius, which is based on the reports of the generals, and, for the years 134–133, on his own first-hand observation (p. 322). Moreover, on the bare surface of the highlands of Castille the Roman camps of that period have been preserved in a remarkable way and supply a continuous commentary on the admirable narrative of Appian. Of the camps of Cato we have already spoken (p. 313). On the mountain of the Gran Atalaya near Renieblas, 4 miles east of Numantia, lies the camp in which Nobilior passed the winter of 153–152; near Almazan, 20 miles south of Numantia, is a summer camp which marks a stage on the Ocilis (Medinaceli)-Numantia road, by which Nobilior in 153 marched against Numantia; on the hill of Castillejo there are the remains of the camp of Marcellus (151) and of Pompeius (141). Round Numantia lie the seven camps of Scipio, belonging to the years 134–133, two of which, the headquarters on Castillejo in the north, and the camp of Peña Redonda in the south, are well preserved[1].

These camps are highly instructive, not only for the history and

[1] See Volume of Plates iii, 48, *b* and Plan 1 facing p. 322.

topography of the Celtiberian Wars, but also for the Roman camps of those days in general, the arrangement of which was previously known to us only from the description of Polybius (vi, 27–32). We see how Nobilior, despite the difficulty of the terrain, was able to maintain the customary arrangement of the camp, with a skill which evokes our admiration, whereas the camps of Scipio, having a primarily defensive purpose, adapt themselves to the terrain and break away from the regular arrangement. We can learn also from these camps many details of the military practices of the time; here can be seen the method of building barracks, the fortification of the camp with a wall 9 to 12 feet thick, the numerous towers for the light and heavy artillery, here too the weapons, especially the *pilum* of which more than twenty examples occur, other details of equipment and utensils, and, not least, contemporary silver and copper coins, which supply a valuable extension of our knowledge of the old Roman coinage, for which (from the exactness with which these camps can be dated) we obtain fixed points such as had hitherto been lacking.

The Celtiberian War broke out in the year 153 B.C. The Belli, a tribe of Nearer Celtiberia which had an alliance with Rome, refused to stop building a great tribal fortress for themselves at Segeda, and the Romans thereupon began hostilities. They now had to face a widespread combination of warlike tribes[1]. How serious the war was may be seen from the fact that from 153 onwards, instead of praetors with smaller armies, consuls with consular armies of two legions were sent to Celtiberia—as had only happened once before, in 195 (p. 312)—and that they remained two years, the second year as proconsuls. This continued until the end of the war in 133. The consul Nobilior, who, in order to have longer time for his campaign, entered office on the 1st of January, began by marching up the Jalon valley to attack Segeda. The inhabitants fled, and sought refuge with the Arevaci, who received them, and thus brought Further Celtiberia also into the war. From Ocilis, where he established his base of supplies, Nobilior marched against Numantia by way of Almazan, but while on the march he was caught in a defile and sustained a crushing defeat. The date was the 23rd of August, the *Vulcanalia*,

---

[1] It is possible that a bronze tablet, found in Luzaga in the territory of the Lusones, which names on the one side the 'Arekratoks,' the commune of Aregrada (now Agreda), and on the other, nine other towns, among them apparently Lutia, which was allied with Numantia, has reference to a treaty between the town of Aregrada and other Celtiberian towns. See the present writer in *Hermes*, L, 1915, p. 247.

so that this day became henceforward a *dies ater*. Of the legionaries alone six thousand, or more than half, fell. As however the Arevaci also had serious losses including Karos their general, they did not take full advantage of their victory, but withdrew into Numantia. It was therefore possible for Nobilior to establish on the mountain Gran Atalaya 4 miles east of Numantia a fortified camp, which is still in existence. In spite of Nobilior's losses, which amounted to a good 40 per cent. of his force, the camp is laid out for two complete legions, for he could reckon on receiving reinforcements, and moreover the Romans generally constructed their camps according to a fixed scheme. From this base Nobilior made an attack upon the Numantines, but was again defeated. Similar ill-success attended an attempt upon Uxama (Osma) on the Douro. Nobilior then went into winter quarters in the camp on the Gran Atalaya, the horrors of which—cold, snow and privation—were described by Polybius, a description preserved in Appian (*Iber.* 47).

In 152 he was succeeded by an experienced general, Marcellus, who had been consul three years before, so that a special dispensation was necessary to enable the consulship to be again conferred upon him. His first task was the subjugation of the Jalon valley, which was successfully accomplished, since he offered favourable conditions. He promised peace, provided the tribes on the further side, the Arevaci, were willing to come to terms. In the event, the tribes of the Douro as well as of the Jalon sent embassies to Rome. But the negotiations fell through, owing to the arrogant language of the Arevaci, and Marcellus received orders to carry on the war. Instead of obeying, he made peace with Numantia in return for a payment of six hundred talents of silver (three million denarii), an amazingly large sum, which was no doubt raised by contributions from all the tribes.

When the new consul, Lucullus, arrived in 151 he found peace already established. The raising of his army had caused hardship; it had been necessary owing to popular pressure to take the soldiers by lot and to reduce the period of service to six years. Scipio Aemilianus offered to accompany the expedition as a volunteer. Henceforward he dominated the Spanish war, which he made his own personal concern and conducted with the same success as his great ancestor. Lucullus, instead of returning home, attacked the Vaccaei and treacherously gained possession of the town of Cauca, where he ordered an indiscriminate massacre[1]; but he failed in attempts on Intercatia and Pallantia,

[1] See Schulten on Cauca in *Deutsche Zeitung für Spanien*, 1927.

and so withdrew into Further Spain. Here he came to the assistance of Galba who had been following his example in carrying on the war by means of treachery and breach of treaty (p. 310). As we have seen, the setting up, in 149, of a permanent court to deal with extortion was a consequence of the shameful actions of Lucullus and Galba.

From 151–143 the war was at a standstill, but then broke out afresh, the Lusitanians again being the aggressors, and lasted ten years. This ten-years war is generally distinguished as the Numantine (*bellum Numantinum*), though Polybius treats the war of 153–151 and the Numantine war together as a twenty-years war. The conduct of the war was again entrusted to a consul, Metellus, who had dealt successfully with the Macedonian revolt (p. 276 *sq.*). He remained in Spain two years, and succeeded in bringing the tribes of the Jalon valley into subjection again; but it took him so long to subjugate the Vaccaei, who had aided the Numantines with supplies of corn, that his period of office came to an end before he could attack Numantia. His successor, Pompeius, was a very poor general. He encamped before Numantia on the hill of Castillejo (p. 317), and made an attempt to take it by storm. The attempt failed, though after the wall which surrounded the upper town had fallen, the city was protected only by hastily constructed palisades and a force of 8000 defenders, whereas Pompeius had at his disposal more than 30,000 men, who had been admirably trained by Metellus. He was equally unsuccessful against Termantia, which lies south of the Douro. Next he attempted to reduce Numantia by surrounding it with siege-works; but that also was a failure. Finally, however, he induced the Numantines to accept terms of peace by which they paid him thirty talents of silver. But when his successor, Popillius Laenas, arrived (139 B.C.), Pompeius declared the treaty to be void, since the Senate had not ratified it. Needless to say, the silver was not returned. This was the third time in twelve years that a Roman general had played the Iberians false and Pompeius took his place beside Lucullus and Galba.

Popillius enjoyed no greater success in his attack upon Numantia (139–138). The crowning disgrace however was reached under his successor Mancinus in 137 B.C. After a succession of defeats he retreated hastily towards the Ebro, but before he could reach it he was surrounded, in the neighbourhood of Nobilior's former camp, and surrendered with 20,000 men. Tiberius Gracchus, the future tribune, made himself responsible for the fulfilment of the terms, since the Numantines were prepared to trust his word for his father's sake. But this treaty, too, the Senate broke, chiefly owing to the influence of Scipio. The capitulation of Mancinus was perhaps the bitterest disgrace in the whole of Roman military history—the surrender of 20,000 men to between 8000 and 4000[1]. The breaking of this treaty and Scipio's part therein gave rise to lasting enmity between him and his brother-in-law Gracchus.

For the Senate to hand over Mancinus, as it did, was sheer mockery, a fine exchange for the army whose fate the Iberians had held in their hand, but whom they had foolishly let go, like Viriathus four years before. The generals who followed did not venture to attack the Numantines at all, contenting themselves with plundering the Vaccaei. At length, in 135, popular insistence secured the sending to Spain of Scipio, the conqueror of Carthage.

V. SCIPIO AND THE SIEGE OF NUMANTIA

When he arrived in Spain, in the middle of the year 134, Scipio's first task was to restore to the thoroughly demoralized army some semblance of efficiency and military spirit; but in this he was only partially successful. With such troops it was useless for Scipio to think of attempting to carry Numantia by assault, and he made up his mind from the first to blockade it and reduce it by starvation. After preparing his army by practice in entrenching operations he marched up the valley of the Ebro, but even so did not immediately attack Numantia; he paused first to deal with the Vaccaei, whose corn he seized in order to cut off from the Numantines this source of supply. Then he marched up the Douro to Numantia, before which he arrived about October 134. By the use of stakes prepared beforehand he was able to effect at once a preliminary encirclement with earthworks and a palisade, under the protection of which the circumvallation proper, the building of a stout wall with towers, was carried out[2]. The circle was commanded by seven camps, the sites of all of which have been brought to light by excavation (p. 317). The chief camp was Castillejo, half-a-mile north of Numantia, where Scipio himself had his headquarters, since this hill commanded the wide plain to the east of Numantia. Altogether Scipio had 60,000 men, but about 40,000 of these were Iberian auxiliaries. The camp at Peña Redonda[3], south of Numantia, was under the

---

[1] 8000 at the beginning of the war in 143 (Appian, *Iber.* 76), 4000 at its end in 133 B.C. (Livy, *Epit.* 55).

[2] See Volume of Plates iii, 48, *a*.   [3] See Plan 1 facing p. 322.

command of his brother Fabius Maximus. Each of them had under him a legion, though not at full strength. The other camps were held partly by men of the Italian allies, partly by Iberians. The intervening sectors were no doubt chiefly occupied by Iberians. A system of signals, apparently suggested by Polybius[1], who here, as before Carthage, accompanied Scipio as military adviser, enabled an immediate alarm to be sent out to the whole line the moment an attack was begun. It was in vain that the besieged made attempt after attempt to break through the ring, in vain that the chief, Rectugenos, who succeeded in slipping through, endeavoured to rouse the other towns to send help. In the end hunger did its work. After Scipio had repulsed a last attempt of the Numantines to obtain honourable terms, and the besieged had finally been driven even to cannibalism, a great number of them took their own lives, and the rest laid down their arms. Fifty were chosen to adorn their conqueror's triumph. Thus Numantia, after a heroic resistance, had been overcome, not by the sword but by famine. Without waiting to ask the Senate's permission, Scipio burnt to the ground the valiant town which, with 4000 men, had defied 60,000. In the following year (132 B.C.) he celebrated his triumph for the taking of Numantia, and assumed the cognomen of Numantinus.

So ended the last Celtiberian war, after a duration of ten or— if we reckon, like Polybius, from 153—of twenty years, and the loss of enormous numbers of troops. These great losses did much to give an impulse to the reforms of Tiberius Gracchus, who sought by increasing the numbers of the farming class to increase the number of those qualified to serve in the army. But even apart from this, the war bit deep into the life of the Roman state[2]. In particular it was responsible for exceptional laws, as when the ten years interval between consulships had to be dispensed with, as for Marcellus, or the prohibition to re-election to the consulship waived in favour of Scipio. It led, further, to the beginning of the official year with the first of January instead of the first of March (so that the time at which Europe to-day begins its year may be called a by-product of the Celtiberian War). As we have seen, the establishment of a permanent court to deal with extortion falls within the period of this war and followed the outrages of Lucullus and Galba. The constant ill-success of the ruling oligarchy resulted in an increase of the power of the people who were able to insist on the use of the lot in the raising of levies and the reduction of the period of service to six years. Again, instead of

---

[1] x, 43.   [2] Schulten, *Numantia*, vol. I, p. 270 *sq*.

the assignment of the provinces by lot as was usual, Spain was assigned to Scipio in 135 by the decision of the people, and it was the people who insisted on waiving the existing constitutional safeguards in favour of Marcellus and Scipio. On the other hand the war also prepared the way for the coming of the monarchy. The holding of commands for several years and the maintenance of a standing army were all steps towards it. There was something not a little monarchical about the position of Scipio. From 145 onwards most of the generals in Spain were chosen from his family or friends, he surrounded himself with a body-guard (from which arose the *Cohors Praetoria*), it was to him personally that the rulers of the east sent reinforcements, and he took it upon himself to destroy Numantia without consulting the Senate at all. If he had been bolder or less scrupulous the monarchy might have come from Spain in 133 instead of from Gaul in 49, for, when Scipio returned to Rome as her deliverer, no element was lacking but his own resolve to be monarch.

VI. ROMAN RULE IN SPAIN

After the conclusion of the wars with the Lusitanians and Celtiberians Rome remained in undisturbed possession of the Spanish provinces, and could carry on with still greater thoroughness that exploitation of their resources which had begun earlier. The most valuable accession to the State property was the mines, which passed over from the possession of Carthage to that of Rome. Later, many of the mines were sold, and we have bars of lead dating from as early as the second century B.C. which bear the stamp of private owners[1]. Only the gold mines seem to have been reserved for the State. In the period of the Empire private mines were again taken over by confiscation, and Tiberius, for example, seized the silver mines of a certain Marius, from whom the Sierra Morena takes its name (Mons Marianus). In the silver mines of New Carthage there were, when Polybius visited them, 40,000 slaves at work. These mines occupied an area of 30 square miles, and brought the State a daily yield of 25,000 denarii. Posidonius paints in sombre colours the sufferings of the slaves who worked in them. Whether these slaves were Iberians or foreigners we do not know, but the probability is that they were Iberians, for the wars must have provided a multitude of slaves[2].

[1] *C.I.L.* ii, p. 1001; cf. Strabo iii, 148; Diodorus v, 36, 3.
[2] The chief ancient evidence for the Spanish mines is Strabo iii, 147 *sq.* (from Posidonius and Polybius) and Diodorus v, 36 *sqq.* (from Posidonius); cf. Schulten in *P.W. s.v. Hispania*, cols. 2004 *sqq.*

The collection of the tribute with the extortion which accompanied it was certainly no less cruel than formerly, when it had constantly led to insurrections. And in fact insurrection broke out again in 98 B.C.; and again later, when Sertorius became the hero of the oppressed; and yet again, in the Augustan period. If the State and its officials set themselves to suck the provinces dry, private persons were no whit behind them in rapacity. As everywhere, so in Spain, at least in the towns of the south and east, *negotiatores* must have settled with a view to exploiting the Iberians by usury. It is true that finance was not yet highly developed, but as the communes easily fell into arrears with the taxes, there was an excellent opportunity of making fifty per cent., as happened in Rome's eastern possessions. How far the Romans themselves at this time engaged in trade and industry in Spain we have no means of knowing.

In general the Roman rule in Spain can only be described as brutal. The Iberians were treated little better than cattle. That was a blunder, and cost the Romans much blood and treasure, which a more statesmanlike understanding of the character of the Iberians would have spared them. Gracchus and Scipio effected more by clemency than their colleagues by the sword—just as recently in Morocco we have seen better results obtained by politic lenity than by force. Iberians and Berbers alike could only be won over by showing them the advantage which accrued from the ending of their unceasing feuds and the introduction of order, while in general respecting their racial characteristics. But Republican Rome did not concern herself with the psychology of barbarian races. Augustus was the first to break with the system followed by the oligarchy, and with him begins an era of colonization and prosperity in the Spanish provinces. It is from the Augustan age that our knowledge of the division of the Spanish communes is derived. There were at this time more than 500 of these communes (*civitates*), most of which were single towns; it was only among the highlanders of the north that there were any rural communes. This subdivision into an immense number of small communes is also found in Africa, where, also, there were over five hundred of them (Plin. *N.H.* v, 29), whereas in Gaul we find only sixty-four *civitates*, these *civitates* being tribes. In Gaul therefore the tribe felt itself to be a united whole; in Spain as in Africa, inhabited by the kindred races of Libyans and Berbers, there was no such feeling of unity. Under Augustus, therefore, these communes are found united into *conventus*, districts under one jurisdiction. Whether this organization originated with him we do not know. Within the communes the clans or septs (*gentilitates*) were not interfered with, for they continue to be mentioned in the imperial period, especially in the highland country (*e.g.* 'Aper Accaeicum Mauri filius,' *i.e.* Aper, son of Maurus, of the clan of Acco).

Of the public works which Rome carried out after the fall of Numantia, the great road, which crossed the Pyrenees from Gaul and ran right down to the Straits of Gibraltar, is known to us from Polybius (iii, 39), who gives its length as about 8000 stadia (= 1000 miles), and says that it was marked with milestones, though this applied perhaps at that time only to the northern part. Since it is mentioned by Polybius, this road must have been in existence as early as 120 B.C. It followed the primeval trade route, the 'Way of Hercules', and linked up the two provinces[1]. There was of course constant building in those towns which were the main bases of the Roman domination, Tarraco, Saguntum and Carthago Nova. A 'Porta Popillia' in Cartagena may have been built by the consul of the year 139 B.C. (*C.I.L.* ii, 3426). The great walls which have been found under the buildings of the imperial period on the hill of Saguntum[2] are probably to be assigned to the Romans of the Republic, not to the Carthaginians, for the latter were in possession of the city for a few years only (219–212), and we have evidence for the rebuilding of the destroyed town by the Romans[3]. It may indeed be said that characteristic misrule did not prevent the Republic from conferring on Spain characteristic benefits.

---

[1] O. Cuntz, *Studien zu Polybios*, p. 20.
[2] Simancas in *Mem. de la Junta de Excavaciones* 1923, 1927.
[3] *C.I.L.* ii, 3836; Livy xxviii, 39, 5, where, however, the phrase *oppidum restituerunt* may also be interpreted to mean the giving back of the town.

CHAPTER XI

ITALY

I. THE SUBJUGATION OF CISALPINE GAUL

THE battle of Pydna marked for the time being the end of Rome's startling advance into the old world of the Aegean. Meanwhile Roman armies had again penetrated the Po valley to the natural boundaries of Italy, a work that was far less spectacular but for the future of Rome far more essential. It will be remembered that just before the Second Punic War Rome had compelled the Gauls of the Po valley to acknowledge Rome's suzerainty up to the Alps (vol. VII, pp. 8 1 3 *sqq.*). The approach of Hannibal had set the Insubres and Boii in revolt and the loyalty of some of the Cenomani was shaken during the long war. Hannibal not only enlisted large bands of mercenaries in that region but his recruiting officers stirred the tribes to such a state of revolt that Rome constantly had to keep a strong northern guard stationed at Ariminum and Pisa. Hannibal's diplomatic agent, Hamilcar, was still among the Gauls when Carthage surrendered; and by reminding them that their day of reckoning was near at hand, he was able to induce the Insubres to organize a concerted attack as soon as it was learned that the Romans were about to send their armies to Greece. This was in the year 200. The first blow fell on the old Latin colony of Placentia (Piacenza), which was captured and razed before the praetor Furius could come up from Ariminum. Furius succeeded, however, in relieving Cremona, which was next attacked, and in defeating the Insubrian army. For this he was apparently accorded a triumph in the year 200 although he was only a praetor.

Note. The most important source for this and the following chapter is Livy, who in books XXX–XLV gives brief but numerous references to internal history. However, Livy's own sources for Italian affairs were meagre because the Roman historians of the second century had, before the Gracchan period, confined their brief accounts largely to the foreign wars. The description of the Roman constitution in Polybius, book VI, is invaluable. The rest of Polybius' work provides a few important facts for our purpose. Plutarch's life of Cato and occasional sentences in his lives of Flamininus, Aemilius, and of the Gracchi are of value. Cato's *de agri cultura* is useful for economic history. For the rest one must depend upon incidental references in Cicero's works, in the fragments of Diodorus, Appian and Dio Cassius and in the epitomes of Livy. See further the Bibliography.

Rome had no intention of leaving matters at a loose end in the north, but the war in Greece lagged, and the northern commanders had to content themselves with watchful waiting. The Insubres were not in fact a strong tribe. They possessed only about 1800 square miles of arable land, and it is doubtful whether they numbered over a hundred thousand souls at this time. Their strength in days past had lain in their dominance over their neighbours and in their ability to hire forces of mercenaries (*Gaesati*) from beyond the Alps. Now they would have to fight their own battles. In 197 B.C., when the success of Flamininus in Greece relieved the Senate of undue anxiety, the Romans were ready to settle scores with the barbarians. And the time was ripe, for Hamilcar was organizing a Gallic raid on Rome in the old manner. Cornelius Cethegus marched from Ariminum into the country of the Cenomani and recalled them to their old allegiance; he then met the forces of the Insubres on the Mincio not far from Mantua and defeated them decisively. In the following year M. Claudius Marcellus, the son of the famous hero of Clastidium (vol. VII, p. 814), completed the work by winning a final battle near Lake Como. The Insubres, those who were left, signed a treaty, one clause of which stipulated that no Insubrian should ever be admitted to Roman citizenship. It was not long before Italians began to settle in the neighbourhood of Mediolanium (Milan), and in a century the Insubrian lowlands revealed hardly any traces of Celtic civilization.

The Boii who lived south of the Po, between Placentia and Ariminum, were still in rebellion though by no means dangerous, since they were now hemmed in by Roman alliances. They caused some anxiety in 196 by attacking Claudius on his return from the north, but Rome was then too busy to take decisive action. We hear also of minor engagements in 194, 193 and 192. Finally, in 191 Scipio Nasica, a cousin of Scipio Africanus, invaded in force and won a battle which cost the barbarians heavy losses. What followed is not quite clear. Livy says that Rome deprived the Boii of Bononia (Bologna), their chief town, and of half their land—presumably a half of what remained after the extensive confiscations of 222. Strabo (v, 213 and 216) says that the Boii were completely driven out and retired to Bohemia. In view of the fact that Rome established colonies and *fora* throughout the region and even assigned individual plots of land without formal colonization (Livy XLII, 4), it is likely that most of the Boii left the region in time, even if not compelled to go at once. Brixillum near the Po—where the land must have been subject to floods—

is later found to have a different *tribus* from the rest of the Cispa-
dane towns. Here, if anywhere, we may assume that a group of the
Boii remained until citizenship was granted in 89 B.C.

The Celtic portion of the Po valley was now subdued, but the
dangerous passes of the Carnic and Julian Alps to the rear of the
friendly Veneti were not yet secure and here the mountaineers
were constantly coming down in search of arable land. The
garrisons established here long before had had to be abandoned
during the Hannibalic War, and the warnings repeatedly sent to
the mountaineers usually arrived too late. Finally, Rome determined to place a permanent barrier across the raiding path, and
in 181 Aquileia was founded as a Latin colony. Retired soldiers
were chosen for the post and unusually large allotments given:
50 *iugera* to ordinary citizens, 100 to centurions and 140 to
knights. Apparently it was intended that the colonists should be
well-to-do farmers who could afford to work their land with hired
or slave labour and enjoy leisure for administrative and guard
duty if need be. Needless to say, the Istri were angered at the
erection of this barrier and began a series of annoying raids. In
178 Rome sent a strong punitive expedition against them.
Manlius Vulso led the army into Istria, but was surprised by the
enemy near Trieste and lost most of one legion. He rallied his
forces, however, and routed the enemy. During the next year he
and his successor C. Claudius again defeated the Istrian king in
battle and claimed the Istrian peninsula as far as Pola for Rome.
The poet Ennius, who had accompanied Manlius on this expedition, included an account of it in his annals, from which Livy's
picturesque record derives. It is perhaps more significant of
factional politics at Rome than of military accomplishment that
Claudius and not Manlius was accorded the triumph by the
Senate. By this war the north-eastern frontier of Italy was secured.
The whole of the Po valley east of the Ticinus river was now at
last under Roman control.

II. THE LIGURIANS

Meanwhile Roman generals were also slowly subduing the
Ligurians. These barbaric tribes inhabited the Apennines all the
way from the Arno to Savoy. The strongest tribes were the
Apuani, who lived in the hills above Pisa and Luna (near Spezia),
and the Ingauni who lived north and west of Genoa. Before the
Hannibalic War Rome had come to terms with most of these
people so that the ports of Genoa and Luna were then both at the

disposal of the State. Indeed, Scipio had landed at Genoa in 218 and was able to march through the Apennines from there in order to meet Hannibal on his descent into Italy, but during the war that followed the Carthaginians got possession of the harbour. Luna seems to have remained an open port for the Romans (Cato embarked for Spain at that point in 195), but later the Apuani overran the territory of Luna and the northern township of Pisa. Now that the Po valley was subjugated, the military roads from Genoa to Milan, from Luna to Piacenza and from Florence to Bologna must be made safe. Furthermore, a coast road must be opened from Pisa through Luna to Genoa; and this coast road must, if possible, be extended westward to Spain so that armies might be moved to the new province by land in the winter when navigation was closed.

Skirmishes in the Ligurian region occurred in 197, when a Roman army attempted to march into the Insubrian country from the south-west. Four years later the Apuani were reported raiding the lands of Pisa in the neighbourhood of Luca. Q. Minucius Thermus was then sent to bring the tribesmen to terms, but though he laboured for three years and claimed a triumph he accomplished little against the mountaineers, who had preferred guerilla warfare to open battle. In the Senate Cato derided Thermus—a political enemy—claiming that the general exaggerated the importance of his battles and that he had put several natives to death without sufficient cause.

In 186 B.C., while the Roman army was engaged in building the coast road from Pisa towards Genoa, the consul Marcius Philippus penetrated into the mountains, was caught in a dangerous pass and routed with a heavy loss of men. This led to a more determined attack on the part of Rome, but the mountaineers succeeded in avoiding disastrous battles for several years. Aemilius Paullus, who later won the battle of Pydna, compelled the Ingauni, west of Genoa, to sign a treaty in 181. The Apuani were more obdurate, but in 181/0 B.C. the two consuls, Cornelius and Baebius, rounded up 40,000 of them and removed them far from home, settling them on some public lands in Samnium, north of Beneventum. Nearly three centuries later we have a record of Trajan's commission of public charities making provision for the support of the children of these *Ligures Corneliani et Baebiani* (*C.I.L.* ix, 1455). The forcible removal of these Ligurians released some land which fell to Pisa, and Pisa gave it to Rome for the establishment of a Latin colony. In 180 Luca was accordingly founded; we are not told how many settlers it received—probably not over 2000 or 3000. Three years later 2000 Roman citizens were settled at Luna to act as a safeguard for that very important harbour. This town seems to have been placed not at the point in the bay where Spezia is now, but nearer to the Macra river a few miles farther south where there was more arable land to distribute; thirty-five acres were given to each colonist. The mouth of the Macra river probably provided an adequate harbour for ordinary shipping, and the magnificent bay of Spezia was near enough to provide protection and anchorage for a large fleet.

The Ligurians were by no means pacified as yet. Aemilius Lepidus and Mucius Scaevola were voted triumphs for battles fought in this region in 175. The Fasti record other triumphs in 166, 158 and 155. These may not all have been deserved. The barbarians were not inclined to give up what the Romans chose to call brigandage, and the Roman generals, incensed at the irregular warfare of the elusive tribes and all too eager for the glory of a triumph, seem to have resorted at times to cruelty and dishonesty. In 172 Popillius Laenas for instance was compelled by the Senate to release the captives whom he took during his campaign against the Statielli. The watchful Cato repeatedly attacked generals in the Senate—especially if they were his political opponents—for triumph-hunting among the Ligurians, and in Cicero's day a 'Ligurian triumph' was a proverbial joke. In point of fact the removal of the Apuani in 180 marked the end of serious warfare in this region.

After that date the only campaign of real importance was beyond the confines of what was later considered to be Italy. In 154 Massilia asked for aid against the Oxybian Ligures who lived in the Alps on the common border of the Massiliote and Roman spheres of activity. These Ligurians were disturbing the Massiliote trading ports at Nice and Antibes[1] (Antipolis). The Roman envoys who were sent at the request of Massilia to remonstrate were attacked and driven off. The consul Opimius, accordingly, marched into the mountains from Placentia and in two engagements subdued the enemy. He took much of their land, giving it to Massilia, and compelled the tribesmen to send hostages to that city at stated times. It seems to have been on this occasion that the natives of the French riviera signed a treaty not to raise wine[2], a measure presumably inserted at the request of Massilia, and certainly to her advantage.

While the Romans were engaged in subduing the Ligurians, several tribes of Sardinia and Corsica also revolted, possibly

---

[1] Polybius XXXIII, 7–11.   [2] Cicero, de Re publica, III, 16.

through sympathy with their friends on the mainland. Cato, who
had been governor of Sardinia in 198, had won the esteem of the
islanders by reducing Roman exactions and banishing the money-
lenders—presumably Punic traders, remaining from the former
régime. Thereafter there had been peace on the islands for nearly
two decades. But in 181, when Aemilius Paullus was engaged
in a vigorous campaign against the Ligurians, some tribes of the
islands attacked the pacified coast-towns. The praetor, Pinarius,
speedily repelled the Corsicans but proved too weak for the revolting Sardinians. His successor, T. Aebutius Parus, also failed.
Hence in 177 the consul, Ti. Sempronius Gracchus, the father of
the reformers, was sent with a full consular army to complete the
work. In 177–176 he won a series of victories, and, if we may
believe the fulsome statement which he inscribed in the temple of
Mater Matuta over a painted description of his victory, the slain
and captured Sardinians numbered 80,000. That his work was
thoroughly done we may conclude from the fact that, though he
imposed a double tribute, the Sardinians did not revolt thereafter.
During the next few years we hear time and again of desultory
fighting in Corsica, but this island also was finally pacified—in
163, by Juventius Thalna and by Sempronius, who was now
consul for the second time.

III. COLONIES AND ROADS IN THE NORTH

The organization of the new areas of Northern Italy required
far more time than the conquest. Numerous military roads were
needed and vacated areas had to be settled at a time when there
were relatively few land-seekers. The havoc wrought by the
Hannibalic War in Central and Southern Italy had diminished the
population of Italy and left large areas without inhabitants. Besides, the southern ports needed colonial garrisons fully as much
as Cisalpine Gaul, especially when an invasion by Antiochus was
expected. In the devastated areas of Lucania and Calabria it was
possible for the State to restore production to some extent by
permitting Roman landlords to rent large tracts for grazing and
for plantations to be exploited by slave labour. But the deserted
areas of the Boian country needed trustworthy farmers who might
take an active part in the defence of the country in case of future
Gallic raids. The most pressing need was the resettlement of
Placentia and Cremona, the two great frontier colonies. In 190,
accordingly, 6000 settlers—Latins as well as Romans—were
somehow found for these places. If Polybius and Livy are correct
in their description of the battle of Trebia in 218 the original

colony of Placentia had stood west of the Trebia river[1]. It is not impossible that the new walls of the city were built on a fresh site, the present site east of the river. More good land had now been acquired from the Boii, and since no effort was to be made for the present to conquer the country west of Clastidium the new farmers may have preferred a safer location. In 189, 3000 settlers, again taken from Latins as well as Romans, were sent to Bologna and given large plots—fifty *iugera* to the commons, seventy to knights—and two years later Flaminius brought the highway over the mountains from Arretium to this new colony. In the same year his colleague Aemilius Lepidus built the great Via Aemilia from Ariminum through Bologna to Placentia, a distance of over 150 miles. When these roads had been built the land became more attractive, though much of the plain near the Po was still very marshy and needed draining before it could be cultivated. In 183 Parma and Mutina, on the Aemilian Way, were settled by citizens—2000 in each—and these men were given the small old-time allotments of five to eight *iugera* (vol. VII, p. 538). Settlers were probably less in demand now, since with these two colonies Rome inaugurated a selfish new system of giving inland agrarian assignments only to citizens.

These (besides the colonies of Aquileia, Luca and Luna mentioned above) were the only colonies organized for this region during the early period. But the migration northward did not thereby come to an end. The existence of several *fora*—official market places—along the Aemilian Way would seem to indicate that individual settlers were encouraged to buy and settle plots in this district. And what is more, we have a remark in Livy (XLII, 4) that in 173 a commission was sent out to allot the unoccupied lands of the region to individual applicants in small lots. Ten *iugera* were to be given away to citizen applicants and three to applicants of allied status. It is not unlikely that by the year 173 Italy had so far recovered that the commission received an adequate number of applications. And from this time on we may assume that even the marshy fields were gradually reclaimed by men who were willing to drain them in return for a title to the land.

North of the Po, except for Cremona and Aquileia, we do not hear of colonies during the second century, but the rapid romanization of Transpadane Gaul as well as the slow growth of census statistics in Central Italy would indicate that the migration northward did not stop at the Po. The Romans and Italians were good farmers and could make more of their plots than the Celts. There

---

[1] See *Journal of Roman Studies*, IX, 1919, p. 202, and below, p. 709.

can be little doubt that they gradually bought most of the richer lands from such Insubres, Cenomani and Veneti as were still there. It has been suggested that Polybius exaggerated when he said that the Celts had disappeared from the valley and were to be found only in the foot-hills, but his statement is not unplausible. In our collections of religious inscriptions of the region—which unfortunately are almost all from the Empire—there are exceedingly few traces of Celtic or Celto-Roman cults south of the Alpine foot-hills.

That the process of romanization was not simply a cultural conversion of the natives is indicated by the Veleian tablet found in the mountain region south of Placentia. Here the Ligurian mountaineers had never been disturbed by the Roman State: indeed they were granted Latin rights in 89 B.C. But, even in the rough mountain-country, Roman settlers had bought up the lands to such an extent that most of the plots (which apparently received their names in an Augustan survey) bear Roman names[1]. The Romans and Italians of the Republic were good colonizers of land within reach of home. The same processes went on in the western Po region which was not at first subdued. A few official settlements in colonies and *fora* are recorded during the century south of the Po, but the Taurini and Salassi remained undisturbed where they were and met the unofficial Italian immigration as best they could.

Road building continued of course throughout Cisalpine Gaul. We have mentioned the Aemilian Way of 187, and the Flaminian which was brought from Arretium to Bologna in the same year. Soon after the foundation of Aquileia that colony was connected with Bologna for military purposes by a branch of the Aemilian Way which ran through Hostilia and Padua. This road is usually credited to the second consulship of Aemilius Lepidus (175). In 148 Verona was connected with Aquileia and Cremona, an indication that Roman investors were then interested in the Transpadane. This road, the Via Postumia, then ran on to Placentia and crossed the Apennines to Genoa. Presently Popillius built a road from Ariminum northward along the coast past Ravenna to Hadria and Padua. Some of these roads served also as embankments against flood in the lower valleys and were flanked with ditches so as to aid in the drainage of the marshy ground.

[1] De Pachtère, *La Table Hypothécaire de Veleia*, 1920.

IV. THE DEVASTATED AREAS OF THE SOUTH

The Hannibalic War had utterly changed Italy, indeed it has been argued that parts of Italy are still suffering from the consequences of that war. Most of the Greek and Oscan cities of the south were in ruins. The Romans and Carthaginians had driven each other over the region year after year, pursuer and pursued devastating with equal determination. As the war continued the vengeful spirit of both increased and toward the end cities that fell after a protracted siege met with little mercy from either side. In the sacking of captured towns the inhabitants that escaped the sword were often sold into slavery. Many refugees had crossed the seas to Greece and the Hellenistic empires in order to escape slavery. The country districts had fared no better. The farmers had been compelled to serve in the armies and their fields were laid waste by the foragers of the conquerors or by the rearguard of retreating armies determined to diminish the food supplies of the opponent. In 210 Rome had punished Capua by confiscating all the land except that of the surviving loyalists. In this case the former owners, except along the coast, were left on their lands as tenants of the ground, which was now *ager publicus*, and in time they were again restored to the census rolls in Campania; therefore the change in population was not very great. But in the south the results were far worse. When Tarentum fell in 209 the Roman soldiers sacked the lower town without mercy, 30,000 prisoners were sold into slavery, and much of the land confiscated by the State. The city remained autonomous and in the hands of the loyalists, but it was now a very different city. When finally Hannibal departed from Italy, in order to damage his enemy as much as possible he emptied several cities which he had to evacuate, took many of the inhabitants with him, and finally slew some 20,000 who refused to go (Diodorus xxvii, 9).

When peace was signed Rhegium was practically the only city intact south of Campania. Locri, Thurii, and Tarentum existed as allies of Rome with favourable treaties but they were much reduced in size. In Rome's war with Perseus in 171 these three were the only cities of South Italy which provided triremes (Livy xlii, 48). Vast areas now fell to the government. Much of this was confiscated explicitly by way of punishment for defection. The instances of Tarentum and Capua have been mentioned. At the former the land was finally used for a Gracchan colony; at the latter most of the land remained in the hands of the original owners but as public leaseholds, while some portions on the coast were used for the maritime colonies of Puteoli, Volturnum and Liternum. Other towns, like Thurii and Petelia, which had been stripped of most of their inhabitants by Hannibal, were apparently taken over for recolonization. The Bruttii were severely punished for their allegiance to Hannibal, and Rome occupied at least enough land to found the citizen colonies of Tempsa and Croton, the Latin colony of Vibo Valentia at Hipponium, and later the Gracchan colony of Scylacium.

When Rome confiscated land during the war it was quite out of the question to lay down a permanent policy of resettlement. If old custom were to be followed, the land would presumably be divided, the allies receiving a share by participation in Latin colonies, and citizens a share by viritane assignments. The treasury would benefit to some extent by receiving rental according to the terms of the Licinian-Sextian laws on such lands as were not at once assigned (vol. VII, pp. 538 sqq.). Such at least was the theory still in vogue. A practical application of that theory, however, was for the present very difficult because of the great scarcity of men. Small Latin colonies were soon settled at Thurii (Copia) and Hipponium (Vibo), but the strategic needs of the Gallic frontier were greater and had to receive the first assignments. Tradition held that citizen-colonies should be reserved for the guarding of seaports and it was difficult to find enough citizens to assign 300 men to each of the places where guards were needed. To be sure, Flaminius had long ago set the example of granting individual farms to citizens in the Ager Gallicus, and Tiberius Gracchus later revived this tradition for the settlement of public lands in the south. But the Senate could hardly have proposed that method in 200 B.C. when it would have found but few land-seekers. Land was then to be had in great abundance near home at low prices (Livy XXXI, 13). In the south the market towns had been burned down, the harbours were in ruins, the country deserted, and the climate not favourable to the crops to which Romans were accustomed, and finally the region lay so far from home that settlement there would preclude participation in the privileges of citizenship. Colonial allotments in the south were not desired. Buxentum for instance, which was settled in 194, was quickly deserted. Even in the days of the Gracchi, when the demand for land was strong, the grants in the south proved disappointing and many of the settlers soon demanded the right to sell their lots.

What the Senate did was at the time the only practical course for a State which was too poor to embark on very expensive re-

clamation projects. It simply permitted the censors to rent out
lots on the terms of the old laws to anyone who had the courage,
the necessary capital, and the imagination to see the possibilities
of the region, and permission to rent was granted not only to
citizens but to Latins and allies as well (Appian, *Bell. Civ.* i, 7).
Tarentine wool had long been famous, and there were Romans
who saw that sheep grazing in the south might prove profitable
again. Cattle could be driven to market over distances too great
for the carriage of grain. Horses, too, were in greater demand for
cavalry, for private use and for the games. The combination of
summer pasturage in the high mountains with winter grazing in
the Apulian plain was already well established. The region was
fairly well known to many Romans who, as young officers of the
army, had campaigned there. Numerous leases of 500 *iugera*
were soon given out by the censors, especially to Romans, who
had suffered less from the war than the natives, and stock and
slaves were bought for ranches. The new investments must have
been successful, for within a few years we have reports that the
aediles were busy imposing fines on the ranchers for taking more
than the lawful areas of public land, and by 185 the slave population on the ranches of Apulia was so numerous that there was
fear of a slave revolt. The country regions of the south were
therefore not permitted to lie waste. And the towns also recovered
somewhat. Tarentum became known again for its wool market,
and before long its citizens are found engaged in the wine and oil
trade. Several of the other towns also recovered partially, and we
find their merchants in the Aegean trade during the next hundred
years. But great cities they could never again be so long as the
land behind was given over to herds and slave herders; and as the
forests on the mountains gave way to the grazers the arable lands
of the region began to suffer from want of subsoil moisture. Plans
to reforest these mountains are at last being made by the present
government of Italy.

V. THE SPREAD OF LARGE PLANTATIONS

It was not only in the devastated and confiscated areas that the
long war changed the economic order. Throughout rural Italy the
second century is a period of gradual transformation. When the
State hesitated to pay the second instalment on the loan made
during the war (p. 112) because funds were needed for the Macedonian War, the creditors pressed for payment and claimed that
there was much good land to be had at a low price near Rome. Ap-

parently the depletion of population was felt everywhere. Many landowners had of course fallen on the battlefields, and many had served so long in the army that they had mortgaged and lost their neglected farms. Tenants and farm labourers had also diminished, for in that war conscription was by no means limited to property-holders.

In short, much land was on the market, free labour was scarce, there were few small farmers about with means to buy plots for themselves, and war captives were abundant on the market. It was inevitable that men who could command credit should buy the land and go into capitalistic farming with the use of slave labour. There had been some large plantations before, especially in Etruria, where Etruscan landlords had long exploited serf labour. Through the second century the plantations gradually spread over the more fertile parts of Italy. The senatorial families who, partly by law, partly by rigid social custom, were kept from investing in commerce, industry and money-lending, usually invested their surplus in land, and others who were ambitious to found families and win a respectable social station now welcomed the opportunity to accumulate estates.

We have not the evidence by which we can trace in detail the changes in rural Italy, but we have the fragmentary brochure of Cato, *de agri cultura*, which gives for the middle of the century some valuable information regarding the economics of the new capitalistic farming. To be sure, Cato usually mentions plots of from 100 to 240 *iugera* (60–160 acres) which in our day of machinery are considered of moderate size. The standard homestead in America which, except at harvest time, is usually cared for by two men is in fact 160 acres. But with hand tools a Roman farmer was supposed to have all he could do with from five to eight acres, and in Italy and France to-day a vineyard of four or five acres is normal. Farms that require from fifteen to twenty-five labourers may well rank as large.

In speaking of the profitable rural occupations Cato apparently held that grazing promised the best returns[1]. He probably did not mean that good arable land should be turned into continuous grazing. If we had the complete passage we should doubtless find that he referred to opportunities still offered on the public lands. The quotation seems to imply that the demand for wool was increasing, that many Romans were getting more accustomed to a diet of mutton and beef in place of the standard cereals, and that horses were in demand. In another passage where Cato is

[1] Cf. Cicero, *de off.* ii, 89.

speaking of agriculture without reference to grazing (*de agri cult.* 1, 7) he lists the crops he would choose as most profitable, provided he could in each case select the plot, soil, and climate suited to the crop.

Here vineyards come first. In this passage he is chiefly interested in land near Casinum, which was in good wine and olive country and too rough for grain, and he also has in mind the fact that in proportion to its value the cost of transportation to a distant market is less for wine than for grain. We may assume that if viticulture was very profitable at Casinum, there was probably a growing market for wine at Rome. Perhaps less wine was being imported from Greece, which was through this century declining economically; the vineyards between Capua and Rome must also have profited from the devastation in Lucania and Apulia; and doubtless the city of Rome, growing in size and wealth, was making use of much more wine than in the days before the war.

The next two items mentioned by Cato, the irrigated vegetable garden and the willow rows raised for osiers, need not concern us, because these two crops were necessarily confined to relatively small areas. Gardens may be very profitable when they are near enough to thriving cities, so that quick delivery to market may be depended upon. Since irrigation was not feasible near Rome, Cato apparently had in mind the gardens that supplied the growing industrial towns of Campania. The osiers were used for basket weaving, and the demand for them is an indication that orchard and garden crops were increasing.

The next product—the second of those involving large acreages—is the olive. To this item Cato gives such explicit directions that we may assume a widespread interest in its cultivation. Cato wrote at a time when Greek agriculture and horticulture were on the wane, when the devastated olive groves of Magna Graecia had not yet been brought back to normal production, and when the Romans were using more oil than heretofore both for their new diversified diet and for the lighting of their larger houses. It would seem that the farmers of Campania and Latium would in the future have to supply a large part of Italy's growing needs. Indeed they did not for a long time quite overtake those needs, for Pliny remarks that Italian oil was not exported till Cicero's day. Even then Italy produced but little for the foreign market, for Spain and Africa captured this and throughout the Empire even supplied large quantities to Rome itself.

The economy of Cato's olive farm reveals some primitive elements not found later. For 160 acres of trees already mature he requires a regular staff of thirteen slaves (*de agri cult.* 10 and 11); the foreman and his wife, five common drudges, three men to plough in the orchard and three herdsmen. This apparently does not account for the olive picking and the oil making. He assumes that the standing crop may be sold to a contractor (144, 145), or that fruit-pickers may be hired from the neighbourhood. In that event the children of the adjacent villages apparently were hired for the work, or contractors made up gangs of pickers, slave or free, from the neighbourhood (64). Since olives require relatively little labour except at harvest time, this system of economizing in the staff may well have been customary. Cato sometimes assumes that the oil might be pressed on the plantation, for he gives directions for the construction of a press and also gives the price of one at Suessa—reckoned partly in money, partly in oil. But it is apparent that the farm-press was still not considered essential. It was not till the screw-press was invented, somewhat later, that it proved economical to complete the processes of production at home. On the whole, Cato's account indicates that olive plantations were on the increase, that olive growers were apt to be capitalists using much slave labour, but also that they were still dependent upon the use of some free labour and that in his day the plantation was not always fully equipped.

Continuing his account of profitable crops, Cato next recommends the irrigation of meadow lands. With the growth of cities fodder for saddle horses, draft mules, and dairy animals was an increasing necessity.

Only in the sixth place does Cato mention cereal culture. This position cannot mean that cereals were unimportant or that the importation of wheat was seriously encroaching upon the home-grown supply. A population of at least 5,000,000 inhabitants within Italy south of the Rubicon must have required about 60,000,000 bushels of cereals, and the Sicilian tithe provided only about 1,000,000 bushels or less than 2 per cent. of the requirement. How to account for Cato's low rating of this product we are not told. If his list gives precedence to the most profitable products in the region that supplies the neighbourhood of Rome we may perhaps comprehend it. Land in Latium had long been overcropped in cereals and had for some time been inviting new crops; a part of the Sicilian tithe—what was left after feeding the army of about four legions and 20,000 allied troops—was usually marketed cheaply at Rome. The residue, about half a million bushels, would probably not cover more than a fifth of the city's needs. Furthermore, the new lands of the Po were supplying wheat at very low prices, some of which could be transhipped to Rome[1], and the aediles often spoilt the market by distributing grain free at the games. Finally, the gradual change of diet must have to some extent reduced the demand for cereals. However, these considerations apply chiefly to the immediate vicinity of Rome and must not be applied too generally to the rest of Italy. The agrarian population was certainly still engaged primarily in cereal culture. The large number of small farmers—a group for which Cato was not writing—could not afford to engage in raising the crops that attracted the great landlord, nor did they need instructions from a senator regarding wheat-growing. We have, therefore, no reason to repeat the conjecture that Cato's book justifies the inference that throughout Italy cereal culture was on the wane during the second century. At most we may only infer that a circumscribed area near Rome produced less wheat than before. It is quite likely that before Cato's day vineyards covered the slopes of the Alban hills, olive orchards the lower Sabine hills and that in many places in the Latin plain sheep were already grazing through the winter months, exchanging this pasture for the hills during the dry months. We hear of farms in the Campagna belonging to old heroes like Regulus and Fabius, and later we hear of princely pleasure villas there, but none of these date from the Catonian period. The old senatorial families were at that time transferring their manors to more lucrative regions farther away.

The methods of farming on the great estates, the *latifundia*, did not materially differ from the old. Much of Italy is too rough for the use of agricultural machines, and slave labour was too cheap to invite the invention of labour-saving methods. Besides, olive and vine-raising are essentially hand-work. Hence the extensive plantations simply applied intensive culture over wider areas. The tools were the hoe, spade, mattock and hand-rake, and, where the nature of the ground allowed, an ox-drawn plough, which, however, did not completely turn a furrow. Barnyard manure and wood ashes were the standard fertilizers, and never quite sufficed for the needs of the land. If cereals were grown, leguminous plants were now and then put in to relieve and enrich the soil: indeed the green crop was sometimes ploughed in. Occasionally also the ground stood fallow for a year when the sheep were let in to graze. Much useful knowledge had been accumulated about the various plants and fruits, and especially what kind of soil and climate each preferred. The Romans had farmed Italy for many centuries and they were as expert in this, their favourite occupa-

[1] Polybius II, 15.

tion, as any people of ancient times. It would be misunderstanding conditions to assume that Cato's wisdom had come from
Mago's Carthaginian books (p. 491). They were translated into
Latin, but only after Cato's death, and then doubtless to aid
colonists in Africa to comprehend African climatic requirements,
hardly for the instruction of Italian farmers. Indeed, methods
applicable to Carthaginian lands which required some knowledge
of 'dry farming' would prove quite useless in Italy. Even the
employment of chained labour by Cato need not be explained by
reference to African customs. To be sure, the Romans of old had
not chained their slaves, but new problems bring new solutions.
The bands of war captives that came on the market from Africa,
Spain, Sardinia, Gaul and Macedonia in the early part of the
century were probably intractable unless chained.

VI. ECONOMICS, POPULATION, PROPERTY VALUES

If we may hazard a picture of agrarian conditions in Italy at
the time when Cato wrote his book it would be something like
this. In Apulia, Lucania, and Bruttium there was much ranching
on the public lands, agriculture was slowly recovering, here and
there vineyards and orchards were being planted. In Campania,
from the Liris to Salerno, vineyards, orchards and gardens seem
to have been prosperous. In the central Apennines the native
population, thinned by the Hannibalic War, recovered sufficiently
to provide very strong armies before 90 B.C. Here in the valleys
and on the mountain slopes the old small-farm system must have
continued in vogue since the free population grew without the
rise of large cities. In Latium cereal culture was on the decline
and winter pasturage on the increase. In Etruria, as we learn
from Tiberius Gracchus, Etruscan and Roman landlords had
extended *latifundia* with slave labour over most of the region.
The favourite crop was probably wheat, while pigs were kept in
the oak-forests of the coast lands (Polybius xii, 4). In the Po
valley, most of the land south of the river was held by Roman and
Italian colonists in small plots, whereas immigrant farmers were
buying up the land in the Celtic region north of the river. From
the Alps to the northern slopes of the Apennines farmers were
prospering. A century later Padua had more knights on the
census than any Italian city except Rome. In the foot-hills sheep-
and pig-farming prospered. The chief product of the plain was
apparently wheat, which because of poor communications glutted
the market here and there.

The extension of slavery on the public lands of the south and on the private *latifundia* in Etruria, Latium and Campania was gradually creating a large class of poor free folk who were drifting to the towns in search of work. But the cities were employing more and more slaves to the exclusion of freemen, partly, we are told, because slave labour was not disturbed by the military levies, partly because the offspring of slaves brought added profit to the owner (Appian, *Bell. Civ.* 1, 7). Before Cato's death it was becoming difficult to make up the army levies of allies as well as of citizens who had property enough to qualify. As early as 187 the Latin towns asked Rome to send the Latins back home because emigration to Rome made it difficult to fill the quotas. The shortage of soldiers was particularly apparent in the middle of the century when armies had to be furnished for Spain, Africa, and Greece. The tribunes actually interfered in 151, 140 and 138 because conscription was pressing hardly on the poor.

When we refer to the growth of large plantations we must remember that the adjective has reference to previous conditions, not to later ones. The economic system of this time seemed exceedingly simple to men of Cicero's day. If we attempt a practical calculation of what profits the model estate of Cato would produce, we shall soon bring our fancies down from the clouds. It is usual to accept Columella's reckoning of about 1000 sesterces (£10) per *iugerum* as the price of unimproved land. For Cato's olive orchard of 240 *iugera* the land on this basis would cost £2400. The thirteen slaves at £40 each would come to £520. The farm house and implements mentioned in Cato (*de agricult.* 10, 20–22, 44) could hardly be placed at less than £800. This amounts to £3720, which, at 6 per cent., is £223 a year. What are the returns? An olive farm of 240 *iugera* would contain about 2400 trees, each of which would yield about 100 lb. of olives or about 25 lb. of olive oil, *i.e.* 70,000 Roman lb. of oil in all[1]. Cato's selling-price is 25 sestertii for 50 lb. or 2 asses per lb., which would give £280 for the crop. Even assuming that the olives would bear a fair crop every year (which they do not), that the slaves found their food by gardening, that the cost of the place during the ten first years of immature trees was covered by cereal and vegetable growing, we have but £57 with which to meet the cost of wear and tear and of replacement of aged slaves. And there are no profits left to the owner except the interest on his investment. This calculation is of course based upon very meagre data, but it proves at least that when historians speak of the profitable

---

[1] E. Cavaignac, *Population et Capital*, p. 97.

establishments of the nobility of this period they have forgotten to make use of very simple mathematics. It is likely that land values were less than we have assumed above, but in any case the returns were so low that we can comprehend why the senators were ready to support laws proscribing meals which cost more than five pence.

The rise and fall of the population during the century seems to be connected to some extent with the agrarian conditions discussed above. The census statistics of Rome took account only of male citizens of seventeen years or over (including the propertyless and the freedmen)[1]. For Rome they are as follows for the period which concerns us.

234—270,713[2]	179—258,794	147—322,000
225—291,200	174—269,015	142—327,442
209—137,108	169—312,805	136—317,933
204—214,000	164—337,452	131—318,823
194—143,704	159—328,316	125—394,736
189—258,318	154—324,000	(after much colonization)

Before we discuss the general trend of these items a remark is in place regarding the very low figures for 209 and 194[3]. The decrease of one-half during the Punic War is probably not all due to the war casualties (over 50,000) and the loss of the Capuan citizens (about 50,000), but also to the fact that the legionaries when serving abroad were at times not enrolled (Livy XXIII, 5), and in 209 many were serving in Sicily, Spain and Cisalpine Gaul. The item for 204 is probably correct because in that year the censors sent agents to take a complete roll of all soldiers (Livy XXXIX, 32). The number for 194 is probably to be explained by the failure to enrol the troops stationed in Greece, in Spain, and in Gaul. On the other hand the increase of 189 over 204 is largely due to the renewed enrolment of the Capuans who had been struck off the list in 210. There were probably at this time about 40,000 of these. To get a fair estimate of the citizen population through the second century one ought to add this item of about 40,000—which was later enrolled—to the census of 204, which would make the Romans and Campanians number about 254,000 in that year.

[1] On this disputed point the present writer agrees with Beloch, *Bevölkerung der griechisch-röm. Welt*, pp. 312 *sqq.*
[2] Based on Polybius II, 24.
[3] See *Classical Philology*, XIX, 1924, p. 332.

Since there were no important wars in 179 and most of the soldiers were in that year within reach of the censors, and since the *tributum* was then still levied we may suppose that the census for that year was accurately taken. We then have an increase of about one and a half per cent. in the twenty-five years from 204 to 179, which is of course abnormally low, since Italy to-day expects such an increase annually. This was the very period in which war-captives came in largest numbers from Africa, Sardinia, Spain, Gaul and the East, the period also in which the public lands were being taken up in large leaseholds to be worked by slaves. From 179 to 163, a period of sixteen years, there was a good increase of 5000 per year or nearly two per cent. per year. Through most of these years—up to the return of Paullus in 167 —few prisoners were brought in. It is likely that with the death of the earlier war-captives there set in a season of more normal conditions for the poorer citizens. We may also suppose that the more liberal registration of freedmen in the rural tribes raised the numbers somewhat and that when the *tributum* was discontinued in 167 the immediate effect was a more willing enrolment of citizens. But from 163 onwards there was a steady decline for the next thirty years. The fall from 337,000 in 163 to 317,000 in 135 is 20,000, whereas we should expect an increase of over 90,000 citizens by a normal birthrate and not a few by manumission. This decrease is difficult to explain. It is possible that the unpopular wars of the period resulted in an increased evasion of service, but the most plausible explanation is that since the plantations were increasing through Italy, the younger generation of the rural population was drifting off in large numbers to the Transpadane region to acquire new homes among the Celts. We have in the rapid romanization of that region only indirect evidence of this migration, but the hypothesis would explain the census figures in that such migrants would be likely to avoid enrolling in order to escape army service. Be that as it may, the statistics are a clear indication of unhealthy conditions in Italy when in the century after 234—the century in which Rome conquered Spain, Africa, Cisalpine Gaul, Macedonia, and Asia, and doubled her arable acreage in Italy—her citizens increased less than sixteen per cent. in a hundred years, while during the last thirty years of the period there was a decided decrease.

Population statistics for the non-citizen portions of Italy are unfortunately not available. Only a very rough estimate can be attempted. Dionysius of Halicarnassus, who had access to the Augustan census, adopted the method of multiplying the number of *civium capita* by four to reach the total population, including women, children and slaves. Since the proportion of slaves was lower in the second century than in the Augustan period, we may perhaps estimate the free citizen population of the whole city-state at somewhat over 1,000,000 (a fourth or a third of whom may well have lived at Rome). Before the Punic War Italy contained about three times as many non-Romans as Romans. If this ratio still held during the second century (which is doubtful) Italy south of the Rubicon would have had a free population of about 4,000,000 people in the middle of the second century and a population of slaves that could hardly have reached 1,000,000. The region between the Alps and the Rubicon now supports a population equal to that south of the Rubicon (including Sicily and Sardinia), but that area had then only just begun to be developed and possessed as yet no cities of any consequence. An estimate of its population is not feasible.

A satisfactory estimate of property values cannot be made. However, there is an interesting item which, if reliable, seems to give some indication of taxable values. In 187 Manlius brought back booty in the form of money and precious metals which De Sanctis[1] has estimated as equivalent to about 22,000,000 denarii (or nearly 1,000,000 pounds sterling in gold values). Now this booty was used for the repayment of twenty-five and one-half assessments of the *tributum* that had been collected from citizens and not yet repaid. Accordingly we may estimate that the annual *tributum simplex* during the Punic war was about 880,000 denarii (*c.* £36,000). This sum in fact—considering that the price of the daily rations was deducted from the soldiers' pay —would ordinarily support four regular legions for six months. Now since the *tributum simplex* was a $\frac{1}{1000}$ levy on property, this sum would indicate that near the beginning of the second century the citizens' property was valued on the censors' books at nearly 1,000,000,000 denarii (*c.* £40,000,000) with, of course, a purchasing power of several times as much as that sum would yield to-day. This would mean a property distribution of only £40 per free person or £160 per citizen of the military roll. If, as is supposed from Livy xxiv, 11, the census of the five classes used in military service was now (1) 1,000,000, (2) 300,000, (3) 100,000, (4) 50,000, (5) 6400 asses[2], the average property of citizens subject to military service was slightly above that of the minimum

---

[1] *Storia dei Romani*, iii, 2, p. 627.
[2] After 217 b.c. the silver denarius, weighing about four grammes, was equated with sixteen bronze asses.

census of the fourth class. This estimate, of course, gives property values for taxation during war times when values were at
their lowest because of distress and fear. If we estimate citizen-
property at three times this amount in 150 B.C., that is, c.
£120,000,000, we shall hardly be exaggerating. Since the *ager
Romanus* then comprised about 14,000,000 acres, about 9,000,000
of which were arable, it does not seem unreasonable to assign
about three-fourths of this sum, or £90,000,000, to rural property. Urban property in Rome must in that period have been
far from high-priced when Cato could estimate the personal
property of a normal household at 1500 denarii (c. £60), and could
impose a luxury tax tenfold the normal on any property exceeding
that amount. All of these estimates are hypothetical, but when
we view them all together—the amount of the *tributum simplex*,
the consequent amount of taxable values, the very small amount
of personal property that escaped supertaxes, and the low pro-
perty-qualifications of the five classes of voters—and when we
also consider the other items of daily economy—the returns
yielded by Cato's model farm, the petty bonuses distributed to
soldiers, the prices of food and wages of labour—then the
estimates given above, which certainly point to an undeveloped
economic system, seem to be fairly within reason. These figures,
however, apply only to the part of Italy which constituted the
Roman city-state, that is, to about a third of Italy. For the rest
it is impossible to hazard any conjectures.

VII. THE INDUSTRY AND COMMERCE OF SOUTH ITALY

There was one region in Italy which was fairly prosperous because of its diversified production, that is, the Campanian cities
and gardens between Cales and Nola. The Greeks of Campania
had preserved an un-Roman respect for industry and commerce
and had not only kept their work in their own hands with relatively little use of slaves but had instilled a spirit of industry
into the Oscan population of the vicinity. Cato's list of market
towns and their staple products makes little mention of Rome.
He buys his iron ware—sickles, hoes, axes and ploughshares—
in Minturnae, Cales and Suessa; he buys his olive mills of lava in
Pompeii and Suessa, his copper and bronze ware—bronze
buckets for oil, water and wine, and other bronze utensils—in
Capua and Nola. We learn from Diodorus (v, 13) that the iron
ore mined at Elba was now no longer smelted in Etruria, but was
shipped to Puteoli. Apparently the towns of the neighbourhood,

especially Cales and Minturnae, had forges for making the farm implements so extensively used on the Campanian lands. Since there was an abundance of timber close at hand for the forges, and an excellent harbour at Puteoli, the neighbouring towns developed an industry in iron ware which in time produced enough for export as well as for the domestic trade. Capua's bronze ware eventually became well known everywhere, and Cato's note indicates that the reputation of the place was already established. Its fame as a producer of ointments and perfumes was known even to Plautus. These ointments were made from the olive oil of the region and the essences of roses and herbs grown in the Campanian gardens. There were other products, especially jewellery, silver ware and furniture, which of course did not interest Cato enough to elicit mention, but which come to our notice from later sources. They may safely be assumed for the second century as well. The Campanian region, in fact, was the chief centre of industry in Italy at this period. It is not unlikely that the industrial towns of Campania made use of some of the free labour that was displaced elsewhere by the spread of slave-worked plantations.

The remarkable increase of splendid houses at Pompeii during the second century also indicates a rapid increase in prosperity in Campania. The earlier houses were constructed with a simple atrium and a few small rooms about it, but the so-called houses of the 'Faun' and of 'Pansa,' which were built during the second century, cover a whole block and contain splendid peristyles. The former indeed has given us the Alexander mosaic[1] which surpasses in beauty any mosaic work that pagan Rome has yielded. It is hardly probable that any of the Scipios or Aemilii of Rome lived in palaces as large and elaborate as either of these houses. Whence the wealth came which supported the owners we cannot say. It may have come in part from vineyards, gardens, and olive orchards lying below Vesuvius, but it is more likely that shipping, money-lending, and industry yielded the greater part of it. These rich Pompeians were at any rate not Romans. They were Oscans who profited by the extension of trade and industry which Roman conquest and Roman peace-treaties secured for Rome's allies.

How the Greek and Oscan merchants of South Italy had reaped the harvest of trade that followed Rome's conquests eastward has now become quite clear[2]. The Greeks of Southern Italy as far up as Naples and Cumae had for hundreds of years par-

---

[1] See Volume of Plates ii, 110.
[2] See *Am. Hist. Rev.* 1913, p. 233; J. Hatzfeld, *Les trafiquants italiens*; M. Holleaux, *Rome, La Grèce, et les monarchies hellénistiques*, pp. 85 *sqq.*

ticipated in the active trade of the Aegean, and many Campanians, Lucanians and Apulians had been drawn into this commerce, as well as the Brundisian Latins and allies. Several of the southern cities were now too weak to continue this trade, but Brundisium, Tarentum, Rhegium, Naples and the Campanian towns still shared in it and found their field of operations extending with the advance of the *pax Romana*.

The Roman treaties which have come down to us unfortunately give little light on the subject because the Senate was so immersed in political diplomacy that commercial rights were seldom mentioned in them. The Carthaginian treaty of 201, and the treaties made with the Macedonians in 196 and with Antiochus in 189 do not seem to have stipulated for any commercial rights for Rome. The treaty of 189 with Ambracia required free trade for Romans and Italians[1], which, in view of the scarcity of Romans on the seas, meant that Rome was then ready to aid the trade of South Italy. Perhaps that clause thereafter went into several treaties, since *Italici* from this time on appear in increasing number in eastern ports. Yet Rome was not as yet ready to exert herself with vigour to protect anyone's commerce. The treaties made with Nabis in 197 and with the Cretans in 189 who engaged in piracy prove that the Senate was more concerned with political than with economic matters. When in Cato's day the Istrian pirates attacked the shipping that passed between Italy and Greece it was the merchants of Tarentum and Brundisium, not of Rome, who asked the Senate for protection (Livy XL, 18). And when *c.* 183/2 Eumenes closed the Hellespont the protest came from the Rhodians, not from the Romans (p. 627 *sq.*). Later when Delos was handed over to Athens it was made a free port to all comers. The Roman allies benefited as we may see from Delian inscriptions, but we must add that the Alexandrians and Orientals benefited even more (see below, p. 643 *sq.*). When Carthage was destroyed in 146 and Africa was made a Roman province, the Senate provided no Roman harbour. Probably Utica was asked to admit Romans and Italians free, but we do not yet know this. The evidence from these documents is slight enough. All it proves is that the Senate was still apt to neglect the needs of commerce, but that, when reminded, it was ready to require open ports for all Italian traders[2] entering the harbours of treaty-powers in the Aegean. We may assume, however, that even without specific

[1] On the meaning of *socii (ac) nominis Latini* see Mommsen, *Staatsrecht*, III, 660.
[2] See also the later law concerning piracy, *S.E.G.* III, 378, l. 6.

commercial clauses, the growing prestige of the Roman name secured advantages for Italians who were known to be Rome's allies.

When we turn to the inscriptions of the Greek world we find an occasional mention of Italians, rarely of Romans, who seem to be engaged in foreign commerce. Thus at Delphi[1] between 188 and 178 B.C. we find mentioned three Greeks from Velia, one from Rhegium, one from Ancona, one from Tarentum, several from Sicily, Apulians from Canusium and Arpi, a member of the colony of Brundisium, and two men whose places of residence are not given. An Italian had a contract of some sort with the city of Thisbe in 167, and in 183 the Achaeans protested to the Roman Senate that Italians were carrying grain to the revolting Messenians. On this occasion the Senate after some hesitation forbade the contraband trade. Finally, an important banker of Syracuse lent money at Tenos and Delos (p. 628). Some of these men may have been travellers or visitors consulting oracles, but the larger number— and of course our record gives but a small fraction—seem to have been money-lenders and traders.

After the middle of the century eastern trade began to concentrate at Delos which was now a free port[2]. The destruction of the trading city of Corinth gave new opportunities to the merchants of Alexandria, Syria, Asia and Southern Italy. The island became a commercial centre where wine, oil, grain, slaves, jewellery and especially oriental wares were bought and sold. The market-place must have resembled the great souks of Constantinople. Many of the Italians who resorted there were money-lenders, who profited by the high rates of interest on mercantile loans, but we also find some of them dealing in wine and oil, doubtless bringing the costlier Greek brands to the Roman markets, and possibly some Campanian brands eastward. The Italian firms seem to have had agents in offices at the port, usually freedmen, who could execute the orders to buy, sell and ship. A market-place of their own the Italians required only after the Gracchan period and in this they showed less enterprise than the Syrians and Egyptians, but the inscriptions are proof that they were numerous before that time. For the Campanians and the South Italians in general the period of commercial and financial prosperity was the second half of the second century, the period represented by the splendid houses of the 'Faun' and of 'Pansa' at Pompeii. Later, when the Gracchi had opened Asia to Roman tax-farmers, and had accorded a powerful organization to the

[1] Hatzfeld, op. cit. p. 25.	[2] On Delos, see below, pp. 643 sqq.

Roman knights, the tax-gathering associations entered the eastern field at an advantage over the allies. At first they must have employed the experienced South Italians in large numbers (the 80,000 slain in Asia in 88 were chiefly non-Romans), but in time they built up their own organization at Rome. And this seems to be the chief reason why the Campanian and Greek cities which enjoyed temporary prosperity after Cato's death could not retain their gains later. The Roman success was also only temporary. When at last tax-farming on an extensive scale was abolished by Caesar the Romans also lost their advantage, and the Orientals regained their dominant position on the seas.

VIII. ROME'S GOVERNMENT OF ITALY

The Hannibalic War had reduced the members of the old Roman federation to virtual dependence upon Rome. The allied cities could hardly consider themselves Rome's equals after they had for eighteen years obeyed the consuls' demands for full levies under pain of such punishment as Capua, Tarentum, and Syracuse had suffered, nor could the Latins well consider themselves brothers after the treatment of those who begged in vain for relief from war-service in 209 (p. 82). It cannot be said that Rome had been unnecessarily harsh, except towards Capua, nor had the allies complained unduly. They knew that the war concerned their safety as well as Rome's. Rome had done what any efficient and responsible leader must do; the least inclination to temporize with rebellion would have been disastrous. And the fact that the legions always bore the brunt of the attack in every battle kept the respect of the allies for their leader. Nevertheless, a feeling of equality could not possibly last when commands came in quick succession and obedience must be prompt. The imposition of a double levy and an annual tax on the twelve recusant Latin colonies was a notice to the whole league that the Senate was at critical times ready to assume the rôle of inquisitor, judge and executioner throughout the federation. A sense of common responsibility could have been preserved only if a court provided by the whole league had tried such cases, and no such court existed.

After the war we find in Italy relatively few instances of Roman tyranny, but these are significant and reveal the fact that the word *societas* had gradually acquired connotations not originally intended. The *socii* are distinctly subjects, so much so that when the senators wished to designate allies who had signed treaties *aequo foedere* outside of Italy, they found it necessary to employ a more agreeable term and speak of them as *socii et amici* (see below, p. 361 *sq.*). Rome usually avoided any interference in the internal affairs of Italian cities, and probably did not intervene in local concerns unless requested to do so, or unless—as in one or two instances—the Senate thought, or pretended to think, that Rome's welfare was endangered. The most definite instance of undue interference is in connection with the suppression of what seemed a vicious religious cult, the Bacchic worship, and in this instance the repressive measures were at first taken in Rome and in Roman territory and extended to the allied districts only when it became evident that these measures at home would be ineffective unless the cults were followed to the sources which lay beyond Roman territory.

The circumstances seem to have been as follows. In the last years of the Hannibalic War very many prisoners were taken in the Greek towns of South Italy, where the mystical cults of Dionysus and of Proserpina had long had a great vogue[1]. We are told of 30,000 such captives from Tarentum, and captives as well as refugees had also come from towns like Locri. These slaves were later found in Rome, on the growing plantations of Etruria and Campania and on the new ranches of Apulia, and these are the places where Livy reports that police repression was most vigorously exercised in the years 186–181 B.C. The devotees were organized, as at home, in secret societies, and performed mystical rites which the Romans could not comprehend, rites somewhat like those that are symbolically represented on the walls of the Villa Item at Pompeii (p. 697). Some of these slaves were afterwards liberated and mingled freely with the populace, probably making converts in the lower strata of society. Secret associations were of course prohibited by Roman law, and clubs of slaves and freedmen would, if discovered, be considered particularly obnoxious, since bands of Punic slaves and hostages had, only a few years before, raised a rebellion both in the hill-towns of southern Latium and in Etruria. But in this instance a question of morals seems also to have been raised. We need not believe all that Livy relates—drawn ultimately, it would seem, from a speech of Cato about this *coniuratio*—connecting the cult with murders, thefts, and an ugly promiscuity among the worshippers. Nevertheless it would not be incredible if even respectable Tarentines, who had lived in oppressive slavery for twenty years, far removed from the

[1] See *Classical Quarterly*, xxi, 1927, p. 128. Evidence of a cult at Tusculum during the Republic has recently been found, *C.R. Ac. Inscr.* 1927, 1.

restraining influences of their familiar society and of their own priests, had taken to the less elevated aspects of the orgiastic Bacchic cult. At any rate, charges were made in the Senate that serious crimes were being committed, that the laws of association had been broken, and that a 'conspiracy' detrimental to Rome existed.

The Senate authorized an investigation and, discovering that the devotees were to be found in allied cities as well as on Roman soil, instructed the magistrates to root out the evil wherever it might be found in Italy. Of course, the Senate did not dare take the stand that a worshipper could be kept from paying the vows that he had solemnly made to a god, but worship in groups was forbidden and even for individual worship permission from the Senate after difficult formalities was prescribed. The penalty for infraction was death. This decree, a copy of which has survived on a bronze tablet, was issued in 186 by the Senate and addressed explicitly to Rome's allies (*quei foideratei esent*), imposing upon them the same regulations and penalties that were laid down at Rome.

This is a drastic example of interference in the internal concerns of allies. But the conditions were not quite normal and the decree should not be taken as signifying more than it does. What drove the Senate to adopt severe measures at this moment was a strong reaction among the conservatives, led by Cato, and probably by Aemilius Lepidus and Valerius Flaccus, against the Scipionic group which was mainly responsible for Rome's Eastern policy and the consequent introduction of Greek and Asiatic ways in Rome. This reactionary party gained dominance in the Senate after the armies of Fulvius and Manlius had returned in triumph. The orgies associated with the Bacchic cult had not come directly from the East, but in the eyes of the Romans they represented the Aegean cults. We also need to remember that the 'allied cities' obliged by this decree to submit to the police inquisition were in point of fact towns like Tarentum and Locri that had been in Hannibal's hands and had already been chastised as rebels. They would hardly protest against infractions of treaty rights. Rome's behaviour in this instance does not prove that the Senate would have interfered with the cults of the Marsian or Umbrian allies, for example. And finally it is likely that the Senate excused its extension of authority to Latins and allies by an equivocation of terms, that is, by calling the societies 'conspiracies.' The most serious effect of the incident proved in time to concern the home government since the Senate in this instance tacitly assumed and delegated judicial powers in cases involving citizens, and also, by its instructions to praetors, assumed and delegated executive powers. These were vital extensions of senatorial powers which the Gracchi later declared to be unconstitutional.

The plebiscite of Sempronius, passed at the request of the Senate in 193, is another instance of interference that grew out of Roman conditions. Since Rome's laws on usury were strict, it had become customary for some money-lenders to employ as agents citizens of allied states who were not compelled to adhere to the rates prescribed by Roman law. To stop this practice the plebiscite declared that the Roman laws of usury should in future be applicable to all transactions of this sort in which a Roman citizen was involved. This is the beginning of the extension of Roman law through the federation. It was, of course, at one point a reversal of the liberal practice that had created the tribunal *inter cives et peregrinos* in the forum, but one can hardly question the necessity or justice of the law. It would restrict a liberal practice that had been abused and it could cause no injustice, since for the future money-lenders were adequately warned on what terms they could do business of this kind with Romans. It does, however, disclose a tendency on the part of the Senate to disregard the provisions of old treaties without asking for a revision of them.

The subordinate position of the Italians is also revealed in a number of minor acts. In the distribution of booty to soldiers at the triumph—small sums, to be sure, amounting usually to from five to twenty-five denarii—the allied soldiers had formerly received the same bonus as the legionaries; but beginning with the year 177 the shares of the allies were reduced by one-half. Again, in colonizing land taken by the united armies it had been customary (except at the sea-port settlements) to establish Latin colonies in which all shared. During the first two decades of the century this custom was generally observed: indeed citizens were so scarce that Latins had been accepted in the citizen colonies. However, as we have seen, inland colonies of citizens were placed at Mutina and Parma in 183, and Aquileia and Luca (181–180) proved to be the last of the Latin colonies. In 173, when the unsettled remnants of the Boian lands were given out *viritim*, the citizens were assigned larger lots than the applicants that came from allied towns. These things were significant and began to arouse the hostility which in two generations led to a demand for citizenship under threats of a war of independence.

Concomitant with such acts we find that Roman magistrates

and military officials were beginning to make invidious distinctions that aroused anger among the allies. In their journeys through allied towns Roman magistrates were supposed to impose no burdens upon the people they visited. Tents and supplies were provided by the home treasury unless personal friends in the various cities, by way of exchanging courtesies, chose to lodge the travellers. In a few cases of emergency the Senate had requested towns to supply a post-horse for a day. Postumius, the consul of 173, introduced a new and dangerous custom when he sent a personal letter to Praeneste demanding entertainment on his journey through the city. Livy holds that this was the first instance of the kind and that it was done because of a personal spite. At any rate, it set a precedent which led to many of the grievances later cited by the Gracchi. In the armies also the time had come when officers began to distinguish between citizen and allied troops, for while new laws were being made at Rome to protect citizen soldiers in the armies from summary punishment by their officers, no such concern was shown for the soldiers enrolled in the allied contingents. We have very little evidence that the auxiliaries were unjustly treated, but since citizens were being given unusual consideration it is apparent that here too invidious distinctions were arising that were cited in the days of rebellion.

As will be seen (p. 373), the Senate seems to have been more liberal in the government of Italy during the years when the Scipionic group was still popular than afterwards. In 188 B.C. three old municipalities, Arpinum, Formiae and Fundi, that had long possessed the *civitas sine suffragio*, were given the full citizenship by a plebiscite. This was a reversion to the best traditions of the third century and seemed for the moment to indicate that the Romans still believed in a progressive incorporation of Italians. To our surprise, the deed was done by means of a plebiscite without a preliminary *senatus consultum*, but it could hardly have occurred unless the leading men of the State had approved and indeed sponsored the motion. In the preceding year a *senatus consultum* had decreed that the Capuans, who had been deprived of citizenship in 210 B.C., should be enrolled by the censors— presumably as without voting rights—and in this year they were permitted the right of intermarriage with Romans. Thus they also were placed on probation for full citizenship, despite the interdict of 210.

Many discussions arose with the cities called Latin. These were numerous, comprising several old cities like Praeneste and Tibur, the thirty colonies that existed during the Punic War and several added since. The Latins in fact were probably as numerous now as the Romans. According to an old law, the date of which is not known, Latins had acquired the right to register as Roman citizens upon taking up their residence at Rome, provided they left children behind them in the Latin towns from which they came (Livy xli, 8, 9). It seems that many of the Latin towns were now depleted, and, as we have seen, delegates came from them to Rome stating that their towns had difficulty in filling their military quotas because of the migration to Rome. They informed the Senate that many of the emigrants had evaded the specific requirements of the law, that in fact they had either deceived the censors by a false oath or had hastily adopted some one to leave behind as 'children.' In some cases these adopted 'sons' were in fact merely liberated slaves. The delegates asked that the censors should be more careful in scrutinizing the Latin applicants for citizenship, and that those falsely enrolled should be re-inscribed on the registers of their native towns. The first recorded instance of such complaints belongs to the year 187 B.C. (Livy xxxix, 3), but it is probable that protests had come in even before, since in 194 the consuls of the year summoned the levy of allied troops, not according to the old *formula sociorum*, the list of fixed quotas, but according to the proportion of *juniores* fit for service found in each town (Livy xxxiv, 56). It would seem that this change of custom had been introduced in order to lighten the burden of cities that had lost in population during the war or by emigration, and perhaps also to relieve the twelve recusant Latin towns of the double levy that had been imposed in 204.

In response to the protests made in 187 the Senate delegated a praetor, Q. Terentius Culleo, to examine the evidence of unlawful registration and to order those found guilty to return to their respective towns. Twelve thousand were struck off the citizen register and ordered to enrol in their native colonies. This act has frequently been cited as the first instance of a narrow interpretation of citizen privileges on the part of the Senate. A century later, when Mucius Scaevola passed a law completely forbidding Latins to acquire citizenship by taking up residence in Rome, the accusation had point, for that later law cancelled old treaties against the will of the other signatory. But this was not so in 187, when the Senate merely acceded to the request of the Latins themselves that the provisions of the law be enforced by the censors. It is hardly probable that the magistrates desired to lose good citizen soldiers, or that the business interests cared to have prospective purchasers of property excluded. The praetor,

Terentius Culleo, who was entrusted with the execution of the order, was himself a liberal associated with the Scipionic group, and had two years before this carried a very generous plebiscite which authorized the enrolling of *libertini* in the rural tribes. In a word, the first 'expulsion' of Latins from Rome was made to the disadvantage of the Romans and at the urgent request of the Latins. Ten years later, when the Fulvian group, friendly to Scipionic policies, again succeeded to influential positions in the State, the Latins again appealed for a strict observance of the old laws—which apparently had been disregarded by the Catonian group—and this time a Lex Claudia, approved by a *senatus consultum*, acceded to their wishes (Livy XLI, 8 and 9). The censors of 173, Q. Fulvius and A. Postumius, carefully carried out the provisions of this act (Livy XLII, 10) with the result that many Latins were again struck off the rolls.

In conclusion it must be said that the Roman government drifted without pronounced intentions into the habit of treating the Italian allies as subjects, largely because the allies had been so weakened by the Punic War that they no longer asked for serious consideration as equals. They had of necessity obeyed orders during the war, and when peace came the custom had been established. The Roman government assumed after a time that the *ager publicus* was wholly Rome's, and the Gracchi were able to act on that assumption. When the *tributum* was dropped in 167 B.C. the Senate needed the annual rentals derived from these public lands, and it became a fixed dogma in the Senate that no more should be given away to colonies, Roman or Latin. This dogma crystallized all the more quickly because many senators were profiting from their leaseholds. Vested interests at Rome grew constantly more convinced that Rome was sovereign in Italy and was competent to direct the concerns of the federation. And in this view the Italians seem to have concurred to such an extent that we may doubt whether they would ever have raised the question of equality in a menacing way unless it had been raised in the Senate by the Gracchi. However, when all is said, the senators must on the whole be credited with no little moderation in the treatment of Italy. This was a period when kings like Prusias and Eumenes were visiting Rome and addressing the senators as 'Divinities' and 'Saviours,' when senators spoke to the deified kings of Syria as to messenger boys. Roman officials were receiving a dangerous course of training in such diplomatic encounters. That they forgot the true status of their old Italian allies until reconciliation became impossible is not surprising.

CHAPTER XII

ROME

I. THE SENATE IN CONTROL

IT was by organizing and using all the resources of Italy that Rome had made herself a world-power. The government which had accomplished this had in the process drifted far from the popular constitution of 287 B.C. toward a compact oligarchy, and the city of Rome was now sloughing off the appearance of a rural market-town and gradually assuming the aspects of a large metropolis. We have first to speak of the government that ruled the empire, and then of the city which was the seat of that government. During the first half of the second century B.C., the Roman government was more nearly an oligarchy than at any time after 287, when the theory of popular sovereignty was incorporated into Rome's laws. The famous description of the constitution which Polybius set down in his sixth book was apparently written about 150 B.C. His observations are remarkably keen, for, though a foreigner, he noticed the effects of several powers and functions that were somewhat in abeyance in his day. Nevertheless the description, strongly influenced by a desire to show how closely the Roman form of government resembled the ideal mixed form that Dicaearchus had advocated in his *Tripoliticus* (vol. VI, p. 534), must be read with some caution. A careful consideration of the document will show that while theoretically the executive magistrates, the administrative Senate and the electoral and legislative popular assemblies were evenly balanced and checked each other equably, the Senate was after all the dominant organ in the state.

Polybius notes (VI, 12) that the consuls summon and preside over the Senate and the assembly, and as presiding officers exercise unusual powers in directing the discussion and deciding the issue, that the execution of laws lies in their control, that as commanders-in-chief of the army they often decide the policies of war, control the levies of allies and in part those of citizens, have large powers of rewarding and punishing, and make whatever use they see fit of the war-chest. All of this is of course true, but it is also true that during this period the consuls, who were life-members of the Senate, seldom considered it wise to oppose the wishes and policies of that body. In other words the Senate had come to be far more than an advisory body.

When he proceeds to discuss the functions of the popular assemblies Polybius is aware (vi, 14) that the people are in theory sovereign. They may accept or reject any bill, they determine the form of the constitution, they alone have the right to declare war and ratify treaties of peace, they are the electoral bodies, choosing all executive magistrates and thus indirectly also determining the composition of the Senate. And finally, the assemblies have from of old retained the right to decide every case of capital punishment of citizens as well as the right to summon magistrates to account for their acts while in office. This is entirely correct, but it is also true that at elections the assemblies continued to elect to high office hardly any but representatives of the noble families, that there was no important legislation during the period which had not first been shaped by senatorial discussion to suit the senatorial majority, that the Senate through extra-legal judicial commissions usually controlled the judicial proceedings in capital cases by ordering the preliminary investigations and presenting the charges, and that when impeachments were laid against magistrates it was quite regularly at the instance of some group inside the Senate. And what is most significant, the people of Rome, though considering themselves sovereign, did not during this period assert their right to control taxation or to initiate financial legislation.

In discussing the Senate's functions, Polybius (vi, 13 and 17) notices first the strange fact that the Senate had control of the treasury, regulating all revenues and expenditure. Next he is struck by the fact that the Senate is constantly exerting judicial powers throughout the great federation by the appointment of commissions with final judicial and executive powers. He likewise observes the Senate's remarkable control over foreign policies by its custom of hearing and answering foreign embassies, and sending commissions of investigation and arbitration to foreign countries whenever any dispute arises. Finally, he notices the indirect power it has over individuals by its control of public contracts, and the influence individual senators obtain by reason of the rule that all court juries and all individual *iudices* appointed to hear cases must be drawn from the list of senators.

These were surprisingly numerous and important functions for a body which was not representative, and which in theory met only to give advice to the magistrates. The Senate's control of revenues and expenditure was of course an old function, dating from the time when the censorship split off from the consulship (vol. vii, p. 521), and was not seriously questioned till the Gracchi drew the logical consequences of the Hortensian law and insisted that the people were responsible for the budget. The custom of appointing judicial commissions was more recent, and seems to have grown up gradually as a logical consequence of war-time administration. When, during the Hannibalic war, threats of secession were heard in allied cities and quick action was necessary, the Senate would give to investigating committees judicial and police powers which, strictly speaking, it did not possess. These committees at first reported to the Senate and the Senate pronounced judgment. Thus the Senate tacitly assumed judicial powers within the federation in matters that concerned Rome's safety. And in time the procedure was extended to questions of treason or of crimes endangering the state of peace even among citizens. This practice also the Gracchi attempted to stop, and later, after their failure, their argument against it was accepted by Julius Caesar as one of the most important articles of his programme.

The Senate's administrative powers and control over foreign affairs were by no means overstated by Polybius. The people were too widely scattered, too ill-informed and too busy to discuss every detail that had to be determined quickly during the many wars. They acquiesced gladly in the Senate's assumption of responsibility; and the Senate gained such prestige by its quick and wise decisions that the people gradually grew accustomed to allowing a *senatus consultum* to come into force without ratification until *senatus consulta* were often accepted as though ratified. Even the people's ultimate right to declare war and confirm peace came to be practically ignored. It was only in 200 B.C. that it was for a while insisted upon, when the assembly at first refused to declare war against Philip; but even then the assembly was soon argued into assent (p. 164). The Senate usually conducted the diplomatic preliminaries up to such a point that the people could not reasonably demur when the question was finally put to them. In 196 the tribal assembly, to be sure, insisted that the war in Macedonia should be brought to an end, but it is clear that a strong senatorial party gave its support to this demand. In most of the wars of the period the campaigns were begun and carried out without reference to the people[1]. Manlius' invasion of Galatia was considered a necessary step in the settlement of the dispute with Antiochus, and the extension of the northern war in Italy against the Gauls, Istri and Ligurians required no popular vote, since the Senate assumed that a state of war existed. The Senate decided how far the conquest might go, and the generals in the field employed the

[1] In 167 a praetor asked the assembly to declare war against Rhodes, but the proposal was vetoed by two tribunes; Livy XLV, 21.

opportunities offered in the field to advance. Similarly, the terms of peace were usually drawn up and imposed by the Senate. Formal ratification was necessary when the people had made a formal declaration of war, but peace with Antiochus, for instance, which was ratified by the people[1], was a small matter as compared with the settlements made with Pergamum, Rhodes and the scores of cities and tribes of Asia Minor and Greece in consequence of the peace. As has been seen, the Senate employed *legati*, a commission of ten, to draw up the terms for discussion in the Senate, and ever new commissions to suggest revisions and compromises as difficulties arose from the original agreements. And the assembly acquiesced. In all such matters it was probably felt that the people were in a way represented in the Senate by the tribunes, who could always enter the Senate and follow the discussions. Presumably, if the tribunes acquiesced in the arrangements, they might be considered satisfactory, and tribunician acquiescence came to be regarded in the Senate as equivalent to popular ratification.

There is also noticeable during the period a continuation of the senatorial custom that had grown up during the struggle with Hannibal of dispensing with the practice of sortition and of assigning the consuls and praetors directly to their work in time of important wars. Often this was done indirectly by proroguing the command of a general in the field. The word itself, *prorogatio*, is an indication that the extension of a command beyond the year of office was originally in the hands of the people[2]. But now the Senate had assumed the privilege. When Flamininus succeeded in crossing the mountain pass into Thessaly, the Senate prorogued his command in Greece, thus removing the most important province of the year from the consular allotment. And he was thus kept in Greece for four years. During these years the consuls were allowed to draw lots for the work to be done in Italy. But the lot could also be interfered with in that a special task (to return to Rome and conduct the elections, for instance, or to carry on a special investigation) might be assigned to one of the two consuls, thereby indirectly assigning to the other the command of the army. And finally, in many instances armies and provinces were explicitly assigned by the Senate. That this infringement of power did not become customary seems to indicate that the practice was questioned, though we hear of few objections at the time (cf. Livy xxxi, 50; xxxiii, 25). It is significant, however, that the Gracchi passed

[1] Livy xxxvii, 55. See above, p. 230.
[2] In 202 Scipio's command was prorogued by the people when the Senate referred the question to the assembly, Livy xxx, 27.

a law compelling the Senate to name the two consular provinces before the elections so that favouritism would be prevented. Evidently the Senate had been accused of yielding to personal motives in these assignments.

II. THE SENATE IN FOREIGN AFFAIRS: *SOCII ET AMICI*

The functions of the Senate increased immensely because of the new turn of foreign affairs during the second century. In the olden days Rome's diplomacy had been simple. Alliances had regularly been made within Italy 'for all time.' Under the rules of the *fetiales* (vol. VII, p. 429) it was regularly assumed that Rome went to war only in defence of herself and her allies. These treaties of mutual defence were ratified by the people and were explicit enough regarding the contingents that the *socii* were bound to furnish to the common army in case of war so that disputes seldom arose. Except in Etruria, where temporary alliances were for a while forced upon Rome, the State had been able to impose this uniform type of alliance in building the ever-increasing federation throughout Italy (see vol. VII, chaps. XX, XXI and XXV).

In dealing with outside powers, Greek or other, that came to Rome with requests for friendly relations, Rome was of course compelled to adopt other forms. Massilia and Carthage had long ago asked for and received commercial privileges. After the First Punic War such requests were sure to increase in number. During the Hannibalic War, Rome had even had to enter into a temporary alliance with the Aetolians and other states associated against Philip V (pp. 123 *sqq.*). When that war was over Rome had learned of several forms of alliance in usage in the East which were very far from resembling those of her confederation, but for all that the old statesmen were still accustomed to think in terms of permanent defensive alliances in which Rome was the predominant partner.

It was when Rome entered the Second Macedonian War against Philip that the ancient diplomatic rules of the fetial law received their hardest blow. Here Rome joined a coalition for the defence of states which were *amici*, some of which had been temporary allies in a previous war. But no one could in this instance hold that Rome was bound under fetial practice to enter the war. There were no clauses calling for continued mutual defence in these treaties of friendship. It is apparent that the new phrase *socii et amici* came into use in parliamentary speeches and in apologetic history to slur over a transition in diplomatic practice which circumstances required but which priestly scruples found difficulty in accepting. These new *amici* were not required to aid Rome in war, but since Roman arms were in the East ostensibly in support of the smaller states of Greece, the pressure of public opinion was such as to make neutrality unpopular. And Rome did not hesitate to send delegations with rather pressing invitations to participate. In Rome's war with Antiochus III, the Achaeans and King Philip, who were *amici*, found that neutrality was regarded with suspicion (pp. 209 *sqq.*). The Senate knew well enough the difference in status between the Italian *socius* and the Greek *amicus*, but the diplomatic usage of centuries was not easy to slough off. The Senate had so long accustomed itself to receive aid from its allies and was so convinced of the utility of the old forms that when the *amicus* proved to be of no service or assumed an attitude of critical neutrality, the Senate eventually compelled him to exchange his '*amicitia*' for a '*societas*' which acknowledged Rome's leadership in external affairs. Rhodes, for instance, after trying to preserve neutrality in Rome's war with Perseus found herself so compromised that she decided to ask for a defensive alliance whereby she lost her independence (p. 289). Several minor states silently kept their treaties of friendship, and in order to preserve an appearance of independence and avoid compulsion were quick to send promises of military aid when Rome seemed to be in need of it. After the middle of the century there is *de facto* very little difference between a *socius* and an *amicus*.

What brought the Senate into international politics very directly was the agreement in the year 200 B.C. to enter the war against Philip together with several other powers (pp. 156 *sqq.*). In 198 Philip offered to make peace and the other powers appointed delegates to discuss and arrive at satisfactory terms, whereupon the Senate, which never delegated plenary powers to its Commissioners, virtually compelled the peace conference of the several associated powers to meet at Rome and discuss their proposals in the Senate. This was a critical moment in Rome's diplomatic history. It was a warning to all associates that Rome's constitution was not adapted to her participation in a league of equal states. Indeed, the conference broke down partly because Rome's demands were too severe, but partly, doubtless, because Philip had a good opportunity to observe that the allies were displeased by the Senate's assumption of hegemony and were likely to be less active in the future if the struggle continued. In point of fact, Rome had to complete the war with but little aid from her associates. Rome did not afterwards enter into wars with the aid of friends and allies on equal terms. In the conflicts with Antiochus and Perseus she directed affairs and accepted contingents from the others. When a war was over, the Roman general conducted the preliminary negotiations. At the division of the territory taken the representatives of the allies were invited, not to a plenary conference, but to a meeting with Rome's ten Commissioners to present their suggestions and pleas. They did not participate as equals. The Senate based its decisions on the information and recommendation of the ten commissioners and these decisions were presented to the people for ratification. The allies, if dissatisfied with what they received, had the privilege of going to Rome to present their pleas to the Senate. Rome had in a brief space of thirty years reduced the Greek and Eastern allies, with whom in the past she had been proud to co-operate, virtually to the position of the humbler *socii* of Italy.

This complete change of attitude was not wholly intentional on the part of the Senate. During the Scipionic régime from 200 to 187 it is safest to interpret changes in diplomatic usage as due largely to a generous willingness to experiment with new and more liberal forms of alliance and association with the cultured peoples of Greece. Here and there, the Senate betrayed impatience at the length of Greek speeches delivered at peace conferences, and then undue pressure was exerted to expedite affairs. But on the whole it cannot be said that the Senate during the early period showed a deliberate intention of extending the old subject-federation eastward. It was only when the Scipios had been discredited and Cato, then risen to the influential position of censor, succeeded in directing policies of state for a while that the Senate reverted to the harsher doctrine. Though the Achaean League, disregarding the Roman treaty with Sparta, had annexed Sparta by force in 188 B.C., torn down its walls and banished, enslaved or slain all opponents, the Senate, eager to keep out of Greek affairs, had refused for several years to give ear to the delegations that came from both sides. This policy, however, was reversed in 185 B.C. when the Scipios had lost their prestige. In that year, Caecilius Metellus, on his way from a conference with Philip, asked the League to make restitution to Sparta. When it refused, the Senate sent Appius Claudius (in 184) to warn the Achaeans that they would do well to listen to suggestions from the Senate or they might receive commands. Thus threatened, the League submitted its case for review and the Senate appointed a commission of three to hear both sides and give its decision. The decision as to the allies was adverse to the Achaeans. The League, asserting its independence, entered into a compromise agreement of its own with Sparta. This offended the Senate, which immediately sent envoys to the cities of the League with the grim advice to elect only such delegates to the federal congress as were friendly to Rome (p. 300). Thus by indirection the Senate had its orders to the League obeyed.

It cannot be said that Cato was for any long period the dominant man in the Senate, but he was influential long enough to point the way back to the old theory that Rome should always keep control over her federation, direct its policies, insist upon having her decisions obeyed, and enter into alliances that could and would give her practical support. From that time on the Senate betrayed distrust of liberal politics in foreign affairs.

Needless to say, the direction of foreign affairs in the enlarged federation brought the Senate great prestige at home and abroad. Each year, in the month of February, kings or envoys from kings, republics, and tribes throughout the empire—from Spain to Syria—stood waiting upon its pleasure. The Senate preferred to have requests presented in the senate-house, and if business became too pressing, it delegated the fate of nations to small commissions. When business could not be settled at Rome, envoys, clad in the power of the august body, carried its messages to kings and assemblies, and delivered them with all due display of dignity. The Romans never wearied of telling how Popillius, sent in 168 to order Antiochus Epiphanes to observe a proper regard for Rome's friend in Egypt, drew a circle around the divinity and demanded that he answer the Senate's ultimatum before he left the spot (p. 284). Popillius was no great personage at home, indeed it was generally said that his consular election was due to an accident. It was only by virtue of the Senate's authority that such as he could thus address an Epiphanes. One must admit that when the Senate had grown so powerful in foreign affairs as this, its moderation in home affairs and in the administration of Italy deserves some acknowledgment.

III. THE DOMINANT FAMILIES

There is no evidence of any democratic revolt from senatorial dominance within fifty years after the Hannibalic War. However, it is probable that the nobility exerted itself to retain its position. There was a tendency at work in the Senate, on the one hand, not to let any member become so strong that he might either assume dangerous leadership or vault into autocracy by way of demagogy, and on the other, not to admit into the Senate many outsiders who might elbow out the nobles already recognized. For a while the Scipionic group, for instance, was very strong, resting its authority on the prestige of Africanus. Those who had supported his policies were grateful for the success which had justified their support of him, and the soldiers and commons were deeply devoted to the hero. For a few years his advice must have swayed the counsels of the Senate, and it was probably owing to the influence of the Scipionic group that Flamininus was allowed to complete the Second Macedonian War in 196. In 194 Scipio was re-elected to the consulship; then in 193, two protégés, Q. Minucius Thermus and L. Cornelius Merula; in 192 a brother of Flamininus; in 191 Scipio's cousin, Nasica, with a friend, the *novus homo*, M'. Acilius Glabrio; in 190 L. Cornelius, a brother, and a trusted friend, Laelius, and finally in 189 M. Fulvius and Cn. Manlius, of whom the first showed himself moderate towards the Aetolians and Ambraciotes (p. 227), and the second earned the thanks of the Greeks of Asia Minor by his treatment of the Galatians (p. 229).

However, not even this group held unquestioned dominance. In 196 B.C., when it seemed that the war in the East might be protracted needlessly, L. Furius Purpureo and M. Claudius Marcellus were elected to the highest office, apparently because they were not of the group; and these were followed the next year by Cato and Valerius Flaccus, who were outspoken critics of Scipio. Indeed there was strong enough opposition in the Senate to prevent Scipio from taking Cato's command in Spain in 194, and from remaining to carry through the final settlement of the affairs of Asia, a privilege which the victory of Magnesia might well have won for him and for his brother (p. 228). However grateful Rome was to the victor of Zama, the Valerii, Claudii, Servilii, Furii, Aemilii, Sulpicii, Fabii, Marcii, and Caecilii, whose families were as old as his, were always free to express their opinions independently and had no desire to permit any man to win complete control. And Scipio himself was too sound an aristocrat to desert his class and attempt to retain power by appealing to the devoted populace for support. Scipio's experience is significant. If a quietly exerted pressure could keep so great a hero in his place, respectful of senatorial custom, the prestige of the Senate could hardly be endangered by any one of its members.

For reasons not wholly clear the ranks of the nobility seem not to have been threatened to any extent by parvenus. Between 200 and 146 B.C. there were one hundred and eight consuls elected. Only about eight of these belonged to families that had not been represented in consular office before, and it was consular office that lifted a family to the much coveted *nobilitas*[1]. We have no right to assume that this condition was chiefly due to exertions on the part of the nobles. Indeed, members of the nobility not infrequently aided friends to gain office, as, for instance, when Valerius Flaccus aided Cato, and the Scipios raised the unknown Acilius Glabrio to the consulship. The chief reason for the failure of outsiders to break into the Senate was apparently their inability to place their claims before the voters. Political parties, which promote individual leadership, are slow to form in a state where the people are given the right to vote directly on every measure of importance. Wealth, which was requisite for the holding of unremunerated offices and for the expenses of the annual games, came to but few in an agricultural society where citizens seldom engaged in commerce or industry, and very few fortunes were made except by generals who were, of course, already members of the ruling group. Furthermore, private citizens could not, as at Athens, attract attention to themselves by addressing the assembly, for political meetings were very carefully controlled by the magistrates. The private citizen of unknown family remained unknown, and so long as the Senate ruled satisfactorily, making no serious mistakes that invited a popular uprising, the people were satisfied to continue the old families in positions of dignity.

It has been suggested that the legislation of the period reveals an effort on the part of the nobility to keep their ranks closed, but the proof is not wholly satisfactory. The Baebian law—soon repealed despite the efforts of Cato (in 179)—cut down the praetorships in alternate years from six to four, but this measure was designed not so much to limit the number of magistrates as to grant terms of two years to praetors in the far-off province of Spain because the long journey there and back wasted a valuable part of a year. It has been surmised that the Senate opposed the addition of new provinces between 200 and 146 in order to limit the number of praetorships. However, even if the imperialistic party had been very strong in the Senate, there could hardly have been a question of adding more than two new provinces at most, and these could have been cared for by proroguing the terms of praetors, as was repeatedly done, or by extending the Baebian law to other provinces besides Spain. The absence of an imperialistic sentiment in the Senate at this time can be explained more simply. After going into a war with the explicit programme of 'freeing the Greeks,'

[1] The evidence for this view is set out by M. Gelzer, *Die Nobilität der röm. Republik*, pp. 21 *sqq.*

the claims of disinterestedness could hardly be disregarded for a generation or two. The Lex Villia Annalis[1] of 180, which set an age qualification for the several offices of the *cursus honorum* and required a term of two years between each, whatever its primary purpose, worked chiefly as a check upon the too rapid advancement of well-known nobles, and the complete prohibition of iteration in the consulship by the law of 151 also served as a check upon powerful members of the nobility. We do not find that either law resulted in the increase of *novi homines*, but both of them might at least have proved an aid to parvenus if the demand for new blood had been strong.

Neither can we say that the Senate made any attempt for a long time to suppress tribunician activity in order to protect its ranks from new men who might win prestige by political activity in the plebeian assembly. The Senate employed tribunes as presiding officers for legislative purposes more freely than consuls. The Leges Atinia (197), Marcia Atinia, Licinia (196), Aelia (194), Sempronia (193), Terentia (189), Valeria (188), Villia (180), Voconia (169), Calpurnia (149), and Livia (146) were tribunician measures and were probably all previously discussed and approved by the Senate. About a half of these were passed while the Scipionic group was still very influential. The list is longer than that of the consular laws. It was not till about the middle of the century that a measure was passed that can be said to reveal a distrust of the plebeian assembly. The exact date of this Lex Aelia Fufia is not known, but Cicero, speaking in 55 B.C., apparently assumed that at that time it was about a century old. This strange law, not clearly defined in our sources, seems to have given magistrates the right to dismiss plebeian assemblies by *obnuntiatio*, that is, by announcing unfavourable omens. The *obnuntiatio* was later used with great unfairness, but we are not sure that it was so employed with any frequency in the second century. Perhaps, though we must acknowledge that there is no positive evidence of it, we may infer from this bill that some tribune had attempted to override the wishes of the Senate about the year 150 B.C. On the whole, however, we must conclude that the Senate remained in power because it did its work well and fairly and because it

---

[1] The sources give little information about this law, but since every citizen was liable to ten years of public service before holding the quaestorship, that office could hardly be held before the candidate had reached the age of twenty-eight. One might then become praetor at thirty-one and consul at thirty-four. In the days of Cicero the minimum ages for the three offices were thirty-seven, forty and forty-three, respectively.

retained the confidence of the voters. Not only does Cicero in his conservative days refer to this period as an era of harmony, but Sallust, the democratic historian, calls it a time of concord and good government.

IV. FACTIONS WITHIN THE SENATE: SCIPIO AND CATO

Though there is no real evidence of party divisions segregating the voters at this time, it is clear that now and then the nobles themselves separated temporarily into factions. In the later years of the Second Punic War Fabius Maximus had been very powerful but had lost his influence because in 205 the younger men supported Scipio in a demand for a more aggressive plan of warfare. Then while the final victory lagged, the Servilii gathered enough strength in 203 and 202 to capture the chief offices though not enough to displace Scipio in Africa. In fact C. Servilius so abused his power by holding the dictatorship beyond the lawful term that the Senate would hear no more of dictators, and the Servilii retired into obscurity for many years. The victory at Zama made Cornelius Scipio the most powerful man at Rome. It would seem that any member of his family could then have any office which he desired. Seven Cornelii are recorded as consuls during the ten years after Zama, and also men, like the two Aelii, Minucius Thermus and Acilius Glabrio, who were closely identified with Scipio's policies. Historians who have recently attempted to reconstruct the senatorial parties of this period on the basis of family relationships, neglecting the firm evidence of party programmes, have somewhat underestimated the range of Scipio's influence. A letter written by the Scipios to the Greek city of Heraclea in 190[1] displays the same philhellenic sentiments as the pronouncements of Flamininus in 196. There can be no doubt that it is the powerful Scipio[2], rather than the very young Flamininus, who was responsible for the adoption by the Senate of the policy these pronouncements represent. To insist in the face of such agreement that Flamininus must have been an opponent of Scipio because his wife's sister was the wife of a distant relative of Fabius Maximus is to misunderstand the political-mindedness of Roman nobles. Time and again members of noble

---

[1] *Ditt.*[3] 618, as restored by De Sanctis, *Atti Acc. Torino*, LVII, p. 242. In view of these pronouncements and of the remarkable vogue of the Greek drama at Rome the present writer considers the sentiment of philhellenism one of the motives of Rome's foreign policy during the decade after Zama.

[2] See for example W. Schur, *Scipio Africanus*, pp. 137 *sqq.*, for a different view.

families fall apart on political questions, just as it happened that senators, when personal enemies, would often for reasons of state become reconciled. One has but to recall Livius and Claudius Nero, Fulvius and Lepidus, Scipio and Gracchus, to become convinced that the State frequently meant more to them than family ties. If then we may infer Scipio's position in the state from the success of his foreign policy and the frequent appearance of his friends in the highest offices of state we may conclude that his opinion usually prevailed in the Senate until the return of the Eastern armies in 187. He lost that influence gradually, in part because of a natural reaction among the practical Romans against a policy which seemed to subordinate Roman to Greek interests, in part because several of the men elected to office through his support or ostensibly to carry out his programme—men like Minucius Thermus, Acilius Glabrio, Fulvius Nobilior and Manlius Vulso—offended the conservatives by their incapacity or their reckless behaviour. The attacks upon him and his partisans began about 190 B.C. and continued till Africanus withdrew from the city in disgust some six years later.

The man who usually led in the opposition to Scipio was M. Porcius Cato, a Tusculan farmer of some wealth and no family, who had won the respect of his generals by his courage, of the people by his honesty and his picturesque, incisive speech, and of the Fabian party by his conservatism. He was by no means a democrat. Though a *novus homo* himself he seems not to have aided other 'new men' to office. His speeches and legislative proposals reveal no desire to bring up the subject of popular sovereignty, to weaken the Senate or to strengthen the tribunician power. Like other senators of the period he was willing to make use of the tribunician machinery when it was most convenient, but he probably employed it less than did the Scipionic group. He supported all the laws that proved to be factors in keeping an even balance of power between the old senatorial families and therefore helped to perpetuate senatorial rule. He was deeply interested in agriculture, but can hardly be said to have led an agrarian faction except that in his most influential days citizen colonies seem to have been favoured rather than 'Latin' settlements. If he had a programme it was not so much political and economic as moral and social. He opposed several magistrates on moral and legal issues: for corruption, for inefficiency, for disregarding niceties of law or established custom, and at times because he feared their dominance in the Senate. On the question of foreign policy his moving prejudice seems to have been a very strong nationalism which was particularly excited by the Macedonian

War. He volunteered, to be sure, in order to take part as a subordinate officer in the war against Antiochus, which he apparently
regarded as a necessary defensive war, but he had no sympathy
for the generous sentiments of the Scipios towards the Greeks.
The harsh tone of the senatorial commands to Greek states issued
in the years when Cato was a dominant figure, and the sarcastic
remarks he made to the Senate for wasting valuable time in discussing the fate of mere *Graeculi* (Plutarch, *Cato*, 9), reveal what
his attitude must have been toward the programme of Scipio and
Flamininus. We may not infer that he would have annexed and
exploited new provinces. His speeches on the Macedonian settlement and on the proposal to declare war against Rhodes prove that
he did not favour annexation. He would have preferred simply to
have nothing to do with Greece, and he was a consistent advocate
of non-intervention.

In this his conviction was based not only upon a fear of what
he considered impractical sentiment but upon a deep-seated puri-
tanism that disliked un-Roman ideas and strange customs which
seemed to him vicious. His attacks upon Manlius Vulso and his
officers, corrupted, as he said, by learning new vices in the East,
long provided phrases to the moralists who dated the change of
Roman manners from the return of the Eastern army; his persecution of the Bacchanal worshippers who had come up from Magna
Graecia was carried to great cruelty, and his insults to Greek
ambassadors who gave proof of their skill in Greek dialectic furnished entertainment to the rabble. He favoured every sumptuary
law proposed to check the elegant habits of dressing and dining
that the Romans brought back from Greece. Thus it is that Cato,
though seldom concerned with large policies of state, whether
foreign or domestic, became repeatedly involved in political
battles through his deep puritanic conservatism and his fervent
nationalism. He delivered more than 150 speeches, the majority
of them attacks upon important men, and he was himself haled
into court some fifty times by his political and personal opponents.

The political downfall of Scipio and his group (p. 371) was
mainly caused by Cato. In the year 190 B.C. Cato prevented
Minucius Thermus from securing a triumph for victories in
Liguria, by exposing an act of cruelty committed against ten
Ligurian commissioners. After serving with Acilius Glabrio he
brought charges that Acilius had sequestrated for his own use
some of the booty taken at Thermopylae. In this case he failed,
perhaps because the old customs of Rome permitted generals to
use part of any booty obtained in rewarding their officers and men.

Acilius, however, was so far damaged in reputation that he withdrew his candidacy for the censorship. In 187 Cato attempted to deprive M. Fulvius Nobilior, another friend of the Greeks, of his triumph over the Aetolians, and in this he was strongly supported by Aemilius Lepidus who was a personal enemy of Fulvius. The charge was that Fulvius had distributed war-bounties too liberally to his officers and men, and it was noted with sarcasm that Fulvius had taken the poet Ennius in his train to celebrate his deeds (p. 403). In the same year Cato supported two of the diplomatic *legati* in attacking Manlius for his campaign in Asia Minor.

Despite these attacks both Fulvius and Manlius were accorded triumphs by the Senate. Nevertheless, Cato must have found much support among the *patres*, for he extended his attacks to the Scipios themselves. In 187, two tribunes—at Cato's request, we are told—made a demand in the Senate that Lucius Scipio should give an account of the 500 talents which he had received from Antiochus as a preliminary instalment of the indemnities due after the battle of Magnesia. Cato delivered a speech in support of the demand[1]. Africanus, who knew that the attack was directed against himself, brought the records into the Senate and tore them to shreds. Whether he had a right to do this was perhaps a matter of definition. Generals, according to Polybius, were as yet not compelled to furnish an exact account of their booty, though what was not distributed in bounties was customarily sent to the treasury; but it is questionable whether the 500 talents exacted as part of the war indemnity could be classified as booty. This haughty procedure stopped open debate for a while, but in time it gave support to rumours that the accounts had not been above suspicion. Hence a tribune, apparently M. Naevius, who held that office in 184, the year of Cato's censorship, summoned Lucius Scipio before the plebeian assembly to render his account. Again Africanus repelled the attack, this time by reminding the people that it was by grace of his victories that the Romans were a free people. When the assembly was summoned once more and this time imposed a heavy fine on Lucius, and he was about to be led off to prison for refusal to pay, he was saved from disgrace only by the timely intervention of another tribune, his political opponent Sempronius Gracchus. That Lucius Scipio, the victor of Magnesia, despite the strenuous support of his great brother could thus be led off to prison on a doubtful charge can be explained only on the assumption that the Scipios had lost the

---

[1] The details are uncertain; see e.g. De Sanctis, *Storia dei Romani*, IV, I, pp. 591 *sqq.*

support of most of the nobility. Their prestige was now wholly gone, and Africanus died, apparently the next year, in seclusion on a country estate at Liternum far from Rome.

Meanwhile Cato, the new man who had successfully concentrated aristocratic and popular antagonism against the Scipionic coterie, had been elected to the censorship in 184 B.C. And in that office he was in a position to humiliate other members of the group by removing them from the Senate, to lay down sumptuary restrictions, to impose stricter methods of accounting in public records, and to bring Rome back to old-time customs. In all this he would, of course, not have succeeded unless there had been among the nobles a very strong undercurrent of conservatism and nationalism, not to say of jealousy, directed against the group so long in power. But Cato himself carried out his reforms and his vengeance with scant regard for human sympathies. He was too independent and too rigid to play politics with tact. He made few friends. He never compromised. And, what was more important, the Scipios had opened the channels to Greek culture and to new ideas so widely that Cato could not check the current. He was indeed too old-fashioned to become for long a dominant force in the newer Rome, and was eventually defeated by silent influences fostered by the very men he had himself overthrown.

The Fulvian family, which to some extent represented the policies of the Scipios, came into influential positions after 180, perhaps because of a general feeling that the Scipios had been disgracefully treated. However when, in 173, Q. Fulvius Flaccus was brought to trial for sacrilege, having robbed a temple of Magna Graecia for the embellishment of one which he was building in Rome, the family suffered in prestige, and new groups, among them the Postumii, assumed the leadership. At times it would seem that some of these groups succeeded in gaining office for their members by the mere chance of presiding at the elections. Apparently a presiding officer at elections could exert enough influence in the manner of presenting and commending candidates to win the election for a friend or relative. Such a possibility would hardly be conceivable at times of bitter factional fights. Be that as it may, no strong party trend is noticeable for a long time after the year of Cato's censorship. In 170 B.C., when the new war with Macedonia united all factions there was again a demand for strong and tried men of the oldest families, and Marcius Philippus and after him Aemilius Paullus were elected to the consulship. This sketch has mentioned only a part of the evidence, but it is enough to show that party divisions did not penetrate into the large body of voters, that there were no important party programmes, and that the occasional factional contests of this period, at least before the middle of the century, occurred between cliques within the Senate which were shaped on personal motives rather than on programmes that might create political parties.

V. LEGISLATION

There is little important legislation to record for this period. The public interest was centred chiefly on affairs in Greece, Asia, Cisalpine Gaul, Spain, and Africa which the Senate was very busy in directing. The laws that were passed were probably discussed and drafted in the Senate, and the tribal assembly was usually employed to pass the bills because it could be summoned more quickly and could be brought to action more readily than the cumbersome centuriate assembly. Whether consuls or tribunes should propose laws was also a question of convenience. During the Second Punic War the tribunes had been trained into complete docility and now continued for two generations to treat the Senate with entire respect. Since the consuls were frequently away on long campaigns it was convenient to have friendly tribunes to summon the tribal assembly and to put through necessary bills.

In reviewing the legislation of the years 200–187, when the Scipionic group was predominant, we find many more tribunician than consular measures. This, however, was a period when the consuls were seldom at home. The bills reveal on the whole a spirit of fairness and liberality. The number of praetors was increased to six in 198 in order to provide governors for Spain; the Oppian law, a very strict sumptuary law meant for war conditions, was repealed by a plebiscite in 195 despite the opposition of Cato. In 189 a *senatus consultum* ordered the enrolment of the Campanians in the census, though the law of 210 had declared that they had for ever forfeited citizenship. The *senatus consultum* was not a law, but in this instance its validity was not questioned. In 188 the tribal assembly—doubtless with the tacit approval of the leading senators—granted full citizenship to the people of Arpinum, Fundi and Formiae who had been *cives sine suffragio* (vol. VII, pp. 592, 608). Had this generous policy been continued later, the Social War would have been prevented. In 189 a tribune carried a bill granting full rights of citizenship to sons of ex-slaves, that is, the law permitted them to be enrolled in the rural tribes.

That this was an aristocratic measure appears from the fact that the censor Sempronius, who usually passed as a democrat, modified it in 167 (Livy XLV, 15) because *libertini* were too ready to vote according to the wishes of their patrons.

The disposal of public land acquired in the south because of the devastation caused by the war, and by confiscations in the Po valley, might conceivably have issued in party alignments, but seems not to have done so. In the preceding chapter we have indicated that the Scipionic régime was in this matter more liberal toward the allies than the Catonian group, but the amount of unoccupied land was of course decreasing with time and this may have been the chief determining factor in the change of policy. In discussing Italy we have noticed that the plebiscite of 193, extending over Italy the force of Rome's laws on usury, was a necessity, and that the exclusion of illegally registered Latins in 187 simply acceded to a request of the Latin towns. Neither of these bills can be called party measures. The suppression of the Bacchic cult in 186, on the other hand, must be attributed largely to the narrow nationalism of Cato and his friends, who were willing to infringe the treaty-rights of the allies in their determination to oppose non-Roman cults and customs (p. 352). Cato's penchant for regulation by law may also be seen in the consular law of Baebius which attempted to restrict undue electioneering (181), in the bill of the same consul which in effect gave praetors in Spain two years of governorship (p. 366), in the tribunician sumptuary law of Orchius which limited the number of guests one might entertain at dinner, and in the tribunician Lex Villia Annalis which defined the age-qualifications of candidates for the magistracies.

Colonization in the years of Cato's dominance was, strangely enough, directed by the Senate, and it betrays a reversal of the liberal policy of the Scipios in that citizens were favoured to the disadvantage of Latins and allies in the granting of lots. Potentia and Pisaurum received settlements of citizens in 184. This was quite regular, since these were coast towns. But when in 183 agrarian colonies of citizens were planted at Mutina and Parma we have proof of a narrow policy which was destined to cause antagonism among the allies who had taken part in the conquest of the Gallic country. Latin colonies were later planted at Aquileia (181) and Luca (180), but the proximity of these places to hostile tribes probably made the lots none too desirable. With the return of the Fulvian group a more generous method of distribution came into effect: in 173 a *senatus consultum* ordered the allotment of the remainder of vacant lands in the Po valley to Roman and allied applicants, but the evil precedent of the Catonian methods was followed in that citizens received larger lots than the allies. This was quite in conformity with a custom which had then recently grown up in the army of giving lesser bounties to allied soldiers when the booty and the rewards of valour were distributed.

After the Catonian period there are few laws to record and these few hardly reveal any consistent tendency. In 179 the Baebian law, which had cut down the praetorships to four in alternate years, was repealed. Magistracies were in great demand and Cato's protest went unheeded. In 177 B.C. Latins were again expelled from Rome at the request of Latin towns (see above, p. 356). In 169 the Voconian law was passed disqualifying women from being named as principal heirs (*i.e.* of over fifty per cent.) of large estates. The purpose of the law was apparently to ensure in some measure the preservation of estates of nobles in the hands of those who bore the responsibilities of government. Legal fictions were of course soon invented which made the law practically void. There was another stringent sumptuary law in 161, proposed by the consul Fannius, and the death penalty was imposed for bribery in 159 by a consular law. In 151 Cato, now very old, supported a measure to forbid the holding of the consulship a second time. In this he was of course advocating the policies of the ruling nobility which did not care to have any one member grow unduly powerful. About the same time, as we have seen, the Lex Aelia Fufia was passed. Finally in 149 we reach the excellent tribunician law of Calpurnius Piso which established a special court for the hearing of the complaints of provincials lodged against governors. This was the first of the *quaestiones perpetuae*. Its purpose was to relieve the tribal assembly from having to hear charges which it obviously was unfit to judge, to substitute regular judicial procedure for political harangues and a jury of intelligent senators for an ignorant mob. It may not have been a party measure, since the Senate was at this time as eager as any tribune to keep generals and governors from abusing legitimate office. The legislation that falls after 149 has significance for the Gracchan period.

When we survey the legislation of this period we are struck by the lack of initiative on the part of the tribunes and the people. Whatever factional strife there was can best be referred to temporarily opposing groups within the nobility. The people were so freely called upon to legislate in the tribal assembly that they probably felt they had their due share in the government. The old respect for the noble houses had not been shaken by any serious errors. The question of taxation, which is so vital a part of modern legislation, awakened no comment, and was removed from the field of political discussion in 167 when the provincial revenues were declared sufficient to cover Rome's modest budget. Land distributions had been generous enough to satisfy the slow increase of population for at least three or four decades, so that as yet it had not occurred to any one to demand that the rented plots should be resumed and distributed. And finally trade and industry were making such slow progress in Rome that paternal legislation in favour of groups usually requiring support or protection from modern parliaments had not yet been demanded.

About the middle of the century there are signs that the Senate's control might come to be questioned and that the *patres* were aware of the fact. At no time during the century had the leading men forgotten that the oligarchic régime continued merely by popular consent. There were good jurists who knew precisely what were the constitutional powers accorded each department and organ of State. And the Senate so frequently needed to make use of the tribunician machinery that it kept the people fairly well informed as to the powers and capacity of the popular assembly. When in 188, for instance, several tribunes were ready to veto the plebiscite giving full citizenship to several towns, they were informed, presumably by the senatorial jurists, that the tribal assembly was competent to grant citizenship without being authorized by the Senate. Yet this was a question which lay at the roots of federal administration. In the treatment of powerful individuals we find the Senate equally meticulous. While it apparently feared the rise of outstanding men who might threaten to impose a monarchy, it was exceedingly careful, when giving advice to magistrates, to observe the customary forms. In a few emergencies the Senate resorted to astute devices to shift a consul of special fitness into a position that required particular competence, but it was careful not to claim the right to supersede the lot. The Senate's power in fact grew by acquiescence, not by usurpation. The check upon the individual was obtained not so much by senatorial obstruction as by regular enactment of legislation; first, the requirement of a term of ten years between consular terms, then the Lex Villia Annalis which guaranteed a reasonably mature age before the first term was reached, and finally in 151, after the re-election of Claudius Marcellus proved that the people might disregard their own laws, by a new bill which forbade a second consulship.

It seems to have been the unpopularity of the protracted Spanish

Wars from 154 to 133 (pp. 314 *sqq.*) that finally awakened a readiness to protest against senatorial domination a few years before the Gracchan period. The continued levies revealed the scarcity of free recruits throughout Italy, and the opposition to them inspired tribunes to create machinery of obstruction and to attack returning generals on charges of incapacity, fraud and treason. In 144 very serious riots occurred because of heavy recruiting; a tribune even attempted to prevent the consul from marching to Spain, and in 138 the two consuls were for a while imprisoned by the tribunes. It was doubtless because of such disturbances that the secret ballot was introduced at the elections and in the courts by the Gabinian (139) and Cassian (137) laws. The growing discontent is also shown by the fact that the people could compel the Senate to disregard the Lex Villia Annalis and the law of 152 so that the popular Scipio Aemilianus, natural son and political heir of the moderate Aemilius Paullus, could be elected to the consulship out of turn in 146 and later re-elected[1]. When Tiberius Gracchus became tribune in 133, the Senate was sharply divided into factions, and the tribunate knew how to use its powers to the full. It then needed only a daring leader to apply the lessons of twenty years of discussion.

VI. ROMAN SOCIETY

This period is one of very important changes in Roman society. How simple life had been even in the households of the old nobles we may judge from the anecdotes that tell of the dismay awakened by the first divorce case of Rome—shortly before the Hannibalic War, according to tradition—and of the scandal occasioned by the appearance of the first professional cooks—after the war with Antiochus. Cato was of course very old-fashioned, but it is significant that as consul and censor he could live in farm-houses that were not plastered. As late as 161 the consul Fannius could pass a bill through the Senate and assembly prescribing that ordinary meals should cost no more than ten asses. During the Second Punic War life in Italy had been very strenuous; there had been little time and no means for pleasure, little interest in culture, and a willingness to submit to the severest self-denial. The most exacting sumptuary laws were passed, not so much to enforce the making of sacrifices to the bankrupt state as to reflect the popular disapproval of display at a time of distress and mourning. Women had been forbidden to wear jewellery, the fabrics that could be used in clothing had been carefully defined, expensive gifts had been

[1] Appian, *Lib.* 112.

prohibited at the Saturnalia, lawyers were forbidden to exact fees
for their services to clients, games of chance were outlawed, and
the expenses of the table strictly limited.

After the war, when the severest financial strain was over, money
was more easily made and more freely spent. Soldiers returned
from the wars with savings and some part of the distributed booty,
taxes were lowered, and fields that had been devastated or neglected in the absence of campaigning soldiers were giving better
yields. Slaves were also brought in at low prices, which afforded
leisure from work to those who could invest in slave labour. Many
slaves had been brought up from Tarentum and Locri before the
war ended, and Punic and Spanish captives came with the peace.
Cynoscephalae added Macedonian captives and some precious
metals, and after Magnesia there were Syrian captives and a good
indemnity. The troops of Manlius who had marched through the
towns of Pamphylia and Galatia returned with full purses—as well
as shameless manners. Even the Spanish and Gallic campaigns
brought captives and some booty. Most of the booty flowed to
the treasury, but it relieved taxation and supplied funds for public
works which gave occupation to artisans and a competence to
contractors. In 187 the treasury had a large enough surplus to
repay the war taxes of twenty-five assessments, though not enough
to redeem the mortgaged public land.

However, the change in Roman society came slowly because of
the ingrained conservatism of the old noble families. It must not
be overstated. Cato's exaggerated tirades made an impression on
later writers because they provided the only contemporary comment on this theme, but the phrases that we have from them
betray how primitive was the luxury against which he inveighed.
Modern historians have too often drawn incorrect conclusions
from the plays of Plautus which were written between 210 and
184. These, in point of fact, do not picture Roman street scenes:
the spendthrifts wasting their estates on courtesans, the scheming
parasites, the extravagant *meretrices* with their gorgeous ward-
robes, the purse-proud slave-dealers, the saucy slaves of these plays
—all these are un-Roman. They come from the Greek New Comedy
and picture the characters that walked the streets of Athens in the
days of Demetrius of Phalerum when slaves and luxurious women
and gilded mercenaries had come in from Alexander's raids in the
East (see vol. VII, p. 225). Plautus is careful to say that the scene
is Athenian. He repeatedly lets the actors drop the remark to the
amazed Roman audience that 'such things are possible in Athens,'
and the audience enjoyed the spectacle as wholly exotic, with a

sense of emotional purgation not wholly exempt from a self-righteous satisfaction that they themselves were more respectable. The comedies produced the effect of a modern French farce when played in some provincial English or American town. Before the Menander papyri were found, it was the fashion to say that the coarser scenes depicting cruelty to slaves, the ranting of the *leno*, the low regard for women, belonged to Plautus rather than to his Greek originals. We now know that the New Comedy provided all these things from life. It is of course quite likely that vice is a trifle less attractive in the Plautine versions than it was in the original. Rome had as yet relatively few impudent and spoiled slaves, and Roman society had nothing to compare with the pampered *hetaerae* of Athens. The courtesans of Rome were still kept in the dark and treated as the scum of the earth if they appeared above ground. Hence where Roman colouring shows in the Plautine play, some of the glamour of the original is naturally rubbed off. But this only enforces the main thesis, that Rome was by no means ready to comprehend the sophistication of the Hellenistic New Comedy (see further, pp. 409 *sqq.*).

Roman society was still simple in its tastes, hard-working and puritanic in the virtues that go with a strenuous agrarian military régime. During the first decades of the century there was as yet no dearth of independent small farms from which to draw goodly armies of peasant yeomen—four or more legions of citizens annually, with nearly twice as many Italian allies. Until then slaves had not been numerous, so scarce that in the countryside they were usually treated as members of the household. Yet Cato's treatise on farming—written about 150 B.C.—shows that capitalistic farming with slave labour, supervised by slaves, was fast appearing. The last campaign of the Hannibalic War brought in the first large hordes. Being war-captives scarcely adapted to farm work, they proved unruly, and a few years later we hear of attempts to escape at Signia, in Etruria, and elsewhere. However, the war-captives were soon succeeded by more docile bought slaves and we read no more of such revolts in Italy for a long time. Slave-culture, however, had come to stay; plantations and ranches were growing, especially on the *ager publicus* and in the hilly Etruscan region where the land, as now, was doubtless suffering erosion to such an extent as to make farming precarious. Gracchus in passing through Etruria in 137 was impressed by the number of slaves employed there.

The second century is the period in which the social classes began to be stereotyped into the forms that are usually considered the most typical of the Roman Republic: the agrarian-political nobility, a capitalistic middle class, and a lowly artisan class crushed between the middle class and the slaves. In their economic interests and aims the nobility was perhaps closer to the English landed nobility of a generation ago than to the Junkers of Prussia or to the plantation-owners of the southern states of America of two generations ago. And yet the differences were considerable. The English estates had originated largely in grants and by the use of enclosure and eviction and had been preserved intact through the legal devices of entail and primogeniture. At Rome, on the other hand, the estates were in no small part due to acquisitions in early wars, distribution of *ager publicus*, and investment of war booty as well as to success and diligence in farming. Entail was not encouraged by Roman law, nor did the eldest son have any superior rights; nevertheless estates were preserved with remarkable consistency through many generations. In the first place, since it was the custom in making wills to assign shares in an estate rather than particular objects or properties, landed estates could readily be saved from subdivision. Moreover, the Voconian law prevented the escape of an estate from the family through a female line. When we add that Roman families seldom were large, that religious considerations connected with the *parentalia* insisted on the adoption of a male heir when none existed, that no little care was taken to strengthen estates by insistence upon the dowry, we can comprehend how family properties were possessed intact for centuries. The possession of profitable estates was quite essential to a noble. The property-qualification for senatorial office was not very large, but was insisted on. More burdensome was the requirement that a senator must live at Rome and be constantly available for meetings of the Senate, and since trade and commerce were for him taboo, an income from land was essential. Thus family pride provided a strong spur to use every device possible in keeping estates intact for sons and heirs.

In the inner circle of the thirty or forty families that produced most of the consuls of this century a social life was coming into existence which found its stimulus and interest more and more in arts and letters, in polite conversation, and in lavish entertainment. Something of the sort had appeared in the exclusive regal courts of Antioch and Alexandria before, but now for the first time it made its appearance outside of a royal community, since now for the first time there existed in a democracy a sufficiently large group of families that possessed the necessary wealth and leisure, the prestige and desire, and above all the inherited customs that per-

mitted the matron to have her share in social life on a basis of
equality with men. To reconstruct a picture of that social life at
its beginnings is not easy, since the sources are so fragmentary.
In fact later Roman writers seldom mentioned its details, which
were assumed to be generally known, so that we usually have to
depend upon the observations of Greek authors. Polybius[1] mentions the somewhat elaborate entourage of Aemilia, the wife of
the great Scipio: 'This lady, whose name was Aemilia, having
participated in the fortunes of Scipio when he was at the height
of his prosperity, used to display great magnificence whenever she
took part in the religious ceremonies of the women. For apart
from the richness of her own dress and of the decorations of her
carriage, all the baskets, cups, and other utensils of the sacrifice
were of gold or silver and were borne in her train on such solemn
occasions, while the number of maids and servants in attendance
was correspondingly large.' Such women were not confined to a
gynaeceum. Regarding her daughter, Cornelia, the mother of the
Gracchi, Plutarch chanced to drop a few phrases that reveal a
salon of a very modern type[2]: 'She had many friends, and kept a
good table that she might show hospitality, for she always had
Greeks and other literary men about her, and all the reigning
kings interchanged gifts with her.' Indeed the king of Egypt had
sued for her hand and offered her the crown. It was this society
which encouraged the production of Greek tragedies and comedies
in translation at Rome. And to lend prestige to the performances,
as well as to invite the presence of a suitable audience, Scipio had
the front rows of the orchestra reserved for the senators. This
society it was that encouraged the nationalistic as well as the
exotic poetry of Ennius, the adornment of Rome with many public
buildings, that enlarged the old Roman house with the garden
peristyle and demanded artistic decoration for the houses. But it
must also be remembered that the coterie was as yet relatively
small, and that the conservative, puritanic, anti-foreign group
criticized it severely and succeeded time and again in forcing it
into obscurity. This aristocratic caste, based economically upon
slave-worked land and socially upon political privilege, was
destined to drift into snobbish exclusiveness and intransigent
rigidity.

By its side there was now arising the middle equestrian class
that drew its power from money, the first powerful capitalistic
class known to history. Its rise to influence was very gradual since
its resources were at first confined to moderate state contracts, the

---

[1] xxxi, 26, trans. Loeb. [2] *C. Gracchus*, 19.

more lucrative business being still in the hands of Greeks and Campanians. In Central Italy commerce and industry failed to make progress, largely because of the opening up of more land both for plantations and for small farms. From this source there was no great accumulation of wealth. However, public contracts, beginning with those given out in the course of Rome's conflict with Carthage (p. 113), were increasing, and the companies of the equites which were formed to carry these through were much in evidence during the period. The *publicani* had as yet not entered the lucrative field of provincial tax-collecting. They were apparently excluded from tithe-gathering in Sicily by the Lex Hieronica[1], and the contributions of Spain were gathered by the quaestors of the provincial governors. The mines of Spain, the harbour-dues, the river-dues and the public lands were farmed by these associations. Since returns from all of them were generally well-known amounts, the contracts were readily estimated and the profits not large. The investments required for public works, however, were at times heavy, for this was an era of much building. To what extent the companies shared in the extensive road construction in Cisalpine Gaul is not known. Most of those roads bear consular names, and it is not unlikely that the army engineers laid out the greater number, employing local and military labour for their construction. At Rome, however, many streets were laid out and paved for the first time, three basilicas were built, a harbour, several temples, and a bridge, and most of these works were let out by the censors to the contractors. At times we also hear of public works let out by the censors for various colonies, and it was in the second century that the first efforts were made to drain the Pontine marshes.

These constructions were carefully supervised and the work skilfully executed, to judge from the pavements and foundations still visible. We can hardly assume that great fortunes were accumulated by the contractors who financed them. That the knights who took the contracts at this time did not have much capital at their disposal is apparent not only from the fact that the largest undertaking, the construction of the Marcian aqueduct, which cost the state 180,000,000 sesterces (almost £2,000,000), was undertaken as public work by the praetor Marcius[2], but also by the statement of Polybius (vi, 17), that the contractors needed the aid of many partners, shareholders and guarantors for the work which they financed. However, this period of building was one

[1] See vol. vii, p. 795, and J. Carcopino, *La loi de Hiéron*, p. 92.
[2] Frontinus, *de aquaeductibus*, 7.

in which the knights could perfect a large organization, accustom the people to invest in shares, create a class-consciousness among themselves and a respect for their accomplishments, as the work of useful and faithful civil servants. It is apparent that they had succeeded in all this before the period was over, so that the Gracchi were ready to employ the equites as a distinct group worthy of official recognition and of great trust in the extensive undertakings which they proposed to carry out. It was when they received political power, and the opportunity to exploit provinces far distant from the watchful eye of Roman censors and tribunes that the Roman knights developed the ugly traits that made the epithet 'publicanus' a byword. In general we may conclude that public contracts during this period provided a method for disbursing through the middle and lower classes at Rome much of the wealth that reached the treasury after lucrative wars, and that through these an easier standard of living came to prevail at Rome.

Before the Gracchi the knights had not yet formed a separate social caste of peculiar distinction. That some were wealthy and kept elaborate households in imitation of the senators is probable. They provided well-dowered daughters now and then to save noble families from financial ruin, and after a few such connections had been formed with the influential, a member of an equestrian family occasionally succeeded in gaining enough support to dare to be a candidate for aristocratic office. But during the Republic the road to social distinction was always difficult for the financial group. The Gracchi gave them some political recognition and prestige, but also created a hostility toward them which cost them dearly whenever—as under Sulla—the nobility was secure in the saddle. Rarely has a capitalist class as such suffered the disasters that it did at Rome.

The lower strata of Rome's society were also undergoing very great changes in the second century. We know how the rise of the slave-worked plantation in the North American continent drove free labour to the mountains and coast towns, creating the pitiful and futile 'poor whites,' how the normal towns of the agrarian regions dwindled into listless market-places, and how free industry surrendered to the slave work of the plantation. Conditions must have been similar in Italy all the way from the Arno to the Volturnus, even though we have no description of the process. From the fourth and third centuries, we still have excellent silver and bronze work from Praeneste, good architectural terracotta work and some pleasing artistry in bronze from several Etruscan towns. These few objects are all that have come down to us, since textiles and furniture would naturally disappear. But if these articles are significant of the condition of industry in the towns of the fourth and third centuries, we may conclude from their absence in the second century and thereafter that, where the slave-plantation prospered, free and healthy industry gave way. Campanian towns benefited somewhat, and foreign importation must have profited too. For the cheaper work, household drudges would satisfy all needs. But as for the artisans and peasants who did not emigrate they must have drifted into the towns to become 'poor white trash.' The social evolution of the second century accounts for the first gatherings of that discontented urban rabble, which consisted of free citizens deprived of their usual occupations and of emancipated slaves that wanted none.

VII. THE CITY

Until after the Hannibalic War the city of Rome looked exceedingly tawdry. For three centuries few public or sacred structures of any distinction had been erected. The magnificent Tuscan temples built by the Etruscan princes and by the Romans during the first few years of the Republic had been patched up with new stucco from time to time, but no effort had been made to restore or enlarge them. The Capitoline temple was still a structure of stuccoed tufa with Tuscan columns and timbered architraves decorated with figured terracotta revetments. The old temples of Saturn and of Castor in the Forum, of Ceres and of Diana on the Aventine and of Apollo in the Campus could hardly be distinguished from the decaying fifth- and sixth-century temples of Caere and Falerii. Nothing reveals so completely what vicissitudes the Roman State had passed through in the fifth and fourth centuries as do the remains of these old buildings. Incidentally they provide excellent evidence that the traditional history of early Rome is not wholly unsound. Rome's contact with the Sicilians in the First Punic War had created a desire for a new type of architecture, and the custom had arisen among generals of promising a part of the booty for the building of some temple in case of victory, but all of these buildings had been smaller than those of the sixth and fifth centuries.

The new temples of the second century were not large and costly, and some of them were still being erected in the Tuscan style which held an unusually tenacious place in the affections of conservative Romans. But we also have evidence of a new Hellenistic type of architecture that we can best judge from such build-

ings as the Apollo temple and the basilica at Pompeii, both of
which belong to the 'tufa' period. The Magna Mater temple of
the Palatine at Rome, dedicated in 191 B.C., was a building of some
dignity. The walls were of Etruscan tufa, stuccoed. If we may
judge from fragments included in the rebuilt podium, it had architraves, columns and capitals of the best Alban tufa, neatly stuccoed
in pleasing designs, as were the Pompeian buildings of the same
period. At Rome, as in Campania, the art of designing for architectural decoration in the glistening gypsum stucco was quickly
developed and this type of decoration gave a far more pleasing
effect than the crude marble work of the period that followed.
Three basilicas also arose in the Forum in quick succession, presumably in the same manner—though Cato in his fondness for
terracotta adornment may have demanded the Tuscan style for
his basilica. This Porcian basilica (184), a small enough building
near the senate-house, was apparently the first of its kind at Rome.
The censors, Aemilius and Fulvius, raised a larger one behind the
'new shops' in 179, and of this we have a few foundations still in
view; and presently Sempronius matched this with a third basilica
behind the 'old shops' in 170. None of these, however, had the
space or dimensions of the basilica erected a little later in Pompeii.
Covered walks, porticoes and stoas in the Greek manner were
also erected here and there at Rome. A series of three of these,
apparently contiguous, provided a shaded walk for considerably
over half a mile, from the emporium to Apollo's temple in the
Campus (179 B.C.), and Cn. Octavius constructed in the Campus
a double stoa decorated with bronze capitals from Macedonia
which was used for the housing of captured objects of art
(168 B.C.).

Among the temples that were built, we hear of one to Vediovis
and one to Faunus on the island of the Tiber (194); in the vegetable market Juno Sospita was given a temple (194), of which we
may still see the foundations, and Pietas had one near by (181).
Apollo's temple in the Campus was rebuilt, apparently in the tufa-
stucco style, and near that a new one was erected to Hercules
Musarum (187). The most distinguished temples were those of
Juppiter Stator and Juno Regina erected about 147 in the Campus
by the Greek architect, Hermodorus, for Metellus, the conqueror
of Andriscus. They were constructed of Greek marble, enclosed by
a pleasing portico, and their areas were adorned with the splendid
equestrian statues of the heroes that fell at the battle of Granicus,
made by Lysippus at Alexander's orders. Such was the booty that
conquerors like Metellus were now bringing to Rome. But for

over sixty years these were the only marble structures seen at the capital.

All this building activity led to the discovery of new materials which in time revolutionized building methods at Rome. At first several strong grades of volcanic tufa were found—on the banks of the Anio, on Monte Verde and at Gabii—that would support taller buildings and wider intercolumniations. Then, about the middle of the century, some enterprising builder discovered the well-hidden vein of excellent limestone which is now called travertine, the quality of which was later abundantly proved by the Colosseum and St Peter's. Finally, before the Gracchan period, the architects found that a very durable cement could be made at little expense by mixing lime with the volcanic ash which lay in great abundance everywhere outside the city walls. This cement was soon used for the construction of heavy concrete foundations and massive walls. Its possibilities were not fully realized at once, but it was the material which during the Empire made possible the construction of the magnificent domes so characteristic of Roman architecture. It is, in fact, to the experiments of architects of the second century that later Rome seems to owe its most important structural materials.

During his censorship Cato modernized and extended the drainage system of the city at a cost of 20,000,000 sesterces (184 B.C.), and in 179 the first stone piers were laid for a bridge over the Tiber. The architect did not then have the courage to finish the arches of this bridge, and it was not till 142, when builders had gained experience from raising the great Marcian aqueduct (144), that it was completed. During this period the censors also began systematically to pave the streets of the city with stone instead of with river gravel that had been spread over them before. For this they found an excellent material in the hard lava that extended from the Alban hills to within two miles of the city; but in order to pave the steep streets of the Capitoline and Palatine they brought from the neighbourhood of Falerii, nearly forty miles away, a rougher and more practical variety of lava. These censors may have known little about the beauties of refined architecture, but they insisted on good materials and honest work. By the middle of the century the streets and public buildings had at least attained to the respectability of those of the Campanian towns.

Of domestic architecture and its decoration we know but little from the remains at Rome. As we have noticed, Pompeii flourished remarkably during this second century. Several palatial houses were built at that time over the foundations of complexes of small houses, which proves a rapid increase of wealth. Probably the same process was going on at Rome at about the same time. It would be daring to assume that such palaces as the 'house of Pansa' or the 'house of the Faun'[1] could be matched at Rome before Cato's death, but the type and style of some of the houses there must have been approximately the same. Certainly there must have been many houses at Rome which resembled the Pompeian house of the 'Labyrinth,' the 'Centaur,' the 'Silver Wedding,' of 'Ariadne,' of Sallustius and of Popidius, to mention but a few of the well-known houses of the 'tufa' period. Most of these had the large open central atrium with vestibule, a series of bedrooms at the sides, a tablinum in the rear corner, and several had a peristyle with other rooms about it or at least a garden behind the atrium.

The rooms were decorated with stucco which was moulded in blocks and tinted in various colours to represent a veneer of precious marbles. The roof-beams of the atrium were usually borne by lofty stuccoed columns of the Corinthian or Ionic orders. In the 'house of the Silver Wedding' the tetrastyle atrium measuring more than forty feet square gives a sense of spaciousness and dignity that would well befit a Roman senator. The furniture that has been found in these houses is chiefly of a later period, but it represents fairly well the kind of ware that the wealthier Romans were bringing back from the sale of plunder in the East during the second century B.C. We cannot suppose that any one at Rome then possessed such floor mosaics as have been found in the 'house of the Faun,' for these betray workmanship of the most skilled Alexandrian school, and Romans were not yet importing such decorations to any extent. To be sure, Lucilius' phrases reveal a knowledge of a finer mosaic than the crude black-and-white work that has survived for us from the Republic, and some examples there doubtless were at Rome; but the best technique was apparently allowed to die before the Romans began to demand this kind of pavement in large quantities. In general, we have a right to draw upon the 'tufa' architecture of Pompeii in trying to restore the second-century dwellings of Rome, but we dare not assume that many Romans had acquired a taste for decorative refinements such as are found in the best of the old houses of Pompeii.

[1] See Volume of Plates iii, 50.

CHAPTER XIII

THE BEGINNINGS OF LATIN LITERATURE

I. INTRODUCTION

THE period from which the earliest remains of Latin literature have survived was one of vast significance for Rome and for civilization. In the annals of mankind there is no more wonderful evolution than that of the premier city-state of Italy into the controller of the Mediterranean world. At the opening of the strictly literary period, in 240 B.C., Rome, now mistress of the peninsula south of Cisalpine Gaul, had defeated Carthage, her formidable rival in the West, and had just secured her first province; a century and a half later, her power had spread eastwards at the expense of the Hellenistic monarchies. Herculean tasks of organization remained; but Macedon, Greece and much of Asia Minor lay subject to her as truly as did Spain and southern Gaul. History shows how pervasive were the political and social effects of this aggrandizement, and how alarmed some leading citizens were at novel habits distrusted as over-refined or denounced as pernicious. The literature displays a parallel enhancement in taste and sophistication, though it never loses a Roman tone. Writers faced the new circumstances of the victorious republic, and to meet a Roman need for entertainment, as in drama, or to deal with Roman themes, as in epic, they freely re-handled models from the extensive repertory of Greece.

The study of incipient Roman literature exercises an enlivening fascination in virtue of problems which make it a field of vigorous and at times contentious inquiry. We ask, what traces exist of archaic Latin; how far we can believe in legendary lays in ancient Rome; what legacy of poetic inspiration or what modicum of historical truth such lays transmitted; what was the metrical character of the native Saturnian verse; whether the native *satura* was dramatic; and how records were kept by pontiffs and priestly colleges. Passing into the literary period, we realize the need for assessing Greek influence in relation to Roman individuality— a matter of difficulty where, as in Roman comedy, all Greek originals are lost, and conversely where, as in tragedy, we possess many originals without the copies. An aesthetic estimate of the period is hindered by the paucity of works preserved. In poetry,

no complete remains are available except a score of Plautus's plays
and six by Terence. In prose, Cato's *de agri cultura* is well represented, and portions of speeches survive; but most of the
oratory and history exists only in fragments, often quoted, as much
of the poetry was, by grammarians to illustrate some curiously
obsolete word or expression. Difficulties also arise in the texts,
which suffered from both modernization and false archaizing.

Latin literature, in so far as a literature can begin with a particular year, starts at 240 B.C. In that year, Livius Andronicus, a
Tarentine freedman who came to Rome as far back as 272, was
called upon for plays to be performed at the public games. He
responded with a tragedy and a comedy from the Greek. It was a
time of rejoicing over the victories of the First Punic War, and
henceforward, except for dark intervals during the next war,
literary activity kept pace with national exaltation. The *terminus
a quo* may indeed be set back, nine years earlier than 240, to the
occasion when the Romans, depressed by the duration of hostilities
and by disaster in Sicily, introduced at the bidding of the Sibylline
books a *carmen saeculare* to be chanted at 'Tarentine' games for
the appeasement of two Greek deities, Dis and Proserpina. Long
afterwards, in 207, when threatened by Hannibal and Hasdrubal,
Rome turned to the poet Andronicus for a solemn hymn; and it
is a plausible guess[1] that the same Tarentine author fully forty
years before had been commissioned to compose the *chorus Pro-
serpinae*. To be meticulously nice, one might claim a more remote
date still in prose; for, as the oration by Appius Claudius against
peace with Pyrrhus in 280 was extant in Cicero's day, it must have
been written down. But, whatever the variation in fixing an
initial date, the origins lie deeper. It is reasonable, then, to notice
the language which authors had to use, and certain primitive products of the native Roman and Italian mind—the raw materials
which made possible the quick growth of a literature when Greek
fertilization came to operate fully.

II. PRIMITIVE LATIN

Latin was the dialect spoken by the tribesmen of Latium, the
plain-lands on the left bank of the lower Tiber. An Indo-European
language, it exhibits in roots and inflections marked affinities with
two prehistoric congeners, Greek and Celtic. These resemblances,
due to primeval contact, are independent of words borrowed in
historic times from Celtic and the much larger borrowing from

[1] C. Cichorius, 'Das älteste carmen saeculare,' *Römische Studien*, pp. 1–7.

Greek (vol. VII, p. 696 *sq.*). Among Italic kinds of speech Latin is classed with Faliscan as a 'q' dialect in contradistinction to the Umbro-Sabellian 'p' group, so called because of the labial pronunciation of an Indo-European guttural velar. Thus Latin *quis* corresponds to Oscan and Umbro-Volscian *pis*. But the Latin vocabulary was affected by Oscan and Umbrian importations, such as *rufus* (red) and *scrofa* (a sow), where true Latin would have *b* for *f*, and *popina* (cook-shop) for the Latin *coquina* (vol. IV, p. 450).

The oldest official inscription in Latin is the partially legible one upon an incomplete rectangular stele exhumed in the comitium near the Forum Romanum: among its words is *regei*, perhaps the archaic dative of *rex*, who may here be the *rex sacrorum*. An instructive example from the sixth century is the oldest Latin inscription on metal, that on a gold brooch found at Praeneste (vol. IV, p. 455). The letters, running in retrograde order, are modelled on the Greek alphabet. '*Mánios med fhéfhaked Númasioi*' is the legend, equivalent to '*Manius me fecit Numerio.*' *Numasioi*, with archaic stress-accent on its first syllable, has not yet reduced *a* to *e*, or changed intervocalic *s* into *r*. An unreduplicated and weakened descendant of *fhéfhaked* is *feked* in the Duenos inscription, referred on epigraphical grounds to the fourth century. The diversity of interpretations[1] put upon this inscription illustrates the archaic unintelligibility of the Latin of 400 B.C. and the magnitude of the task awaiting those who shaped the language into a literary instrument. Its accomplishment is one of the triumphs of the period between 240 and 100 B.C. In its earliest examples Latin displays almost barbaric uncouthness. It was weighted with endings in *-orum*, *-arum*, *-bam* and *-bo*, lacking in the fine subtlety of Greek grammar and syntax, clumsy in its compounds, and slow to invent abstract terms for philosophy and science, as was felt by Lucretius in his moan over 'the poverty of the ancestral tongue.' Yet it was destined to become one of the greatest means for the utterance of poetry, pathos and thought. It had, from of old, its merits. It was logical, direct, compact and sonorous, with an ideal capacity for the expression of legal enactment or ritual devotion. A tool for a practical people, Latin was certain in time admirably to serve moralist, orator, and administrator. But, even after literature was well begun, a striking course of development was necessary between the heavy spondaic verse of Ennius (like the

---

[1] E. Goldmann, *Die Duenosinschrift* (Heidelberg, 1926), treats it as a magical formula. He records 36 interpretations since its first publication in 1880. See *Class. Rev.* XLI, 1927, p. 151; *Gnomon*, III, Heft 11–12, Nov., Dec., 1927.

'hexameter minimus' *olli respondit rex Albaï Longaï*) and the
charming lightness of movement and enjambement which marks
Virgil's poetry at his comparatively early stage in the *Eclogues.*
This transformation of a rude tongue was the achievement of will-
power guided by increasing taste; neither Rome nor its language
was built in a day. Authors, however, besides improving it by
literary experiment, studied it theoretically. Ennius, Accius and
Lucilius all took interest in grammatical investigation: it was a
Greek thing thus to pursue scholarly inquiry, and it helps to explain the divergence of literary from spoken Latin.

III. THE GERMS OF LITERATURE

How in early times was this language used as a medium of
expression? Many events in life seem naturally to call for something more rhythmic than ordinary speech: so in Latium lullabies
(*lalla, lalla, lalla: i aut dormi aut lacta*), wedding-songs, *neniae* over
the dead, accompaniments to dancing or to the work of peasants
in the field or of women at the loom, showed the primitive instinct for singing. Old-world wisdom in proverbs and everything
didactic gained from being in some sort of verse. A charm against
illness, like an Anglo-Saxon spell or a medieval exorcism, sounded
more effective if its set form (*carmen*) fell into rhythm, with as-
sonance, it might be, or rhyme added (*terra pestem teneto: salus
hic maneto*, Varro, *R.R.* 1, ii, 27). The essential features of a
carmen were Italic, and can be as well illustrated from the Umbrian
of the Iguvine tables as from Latin (p. 443 *sq.*). Religion and
festivals also fostered rhythmic expression. Formulae proper in
addressing gods, hymns chanted in the hour of peril, plague,
drought or victory, prophecies, oracles, curses, even certain sentences of the law in prose, were alike *carmina*. The fragments of
the Saliar litany, unintelligible by Horace's day to its priestly
singers, and the quaint forms of the Arval hymn beginning *Enos,
Lases, iuvate* ('Help us, O Lares!') bear the imprint of a distant
past. This indigenous sense of rhythm and natural liking for song
should be remembered in connection with Plautus's elaboration
of a lyric element in his comedies.

The existence of heroic lays sung on convivial occasions to
celebrate great lives or deeds cannot reasonably be denied in the
face of clear statements from ancient authors[1]. Cicero (*Brutus,*

---

[1] Cicero, *Brut.* 16, 62; 19, 75; *Tusc. Disp.* 1, 2, 3; IV, 2, 3; *de leg.* II, 24,
62; Varro *ap.* Non. 1, p. 107 *sq.*; Hor. *Od.* IV, 15, 25–32; Val. Max. II,
1, 10; Dion. Hal. *Ant. Rom.* 1, 79; Plutarch, *Numa*, v.

19, 75) wishes that these songs, for whose vogue Cato vouched in his *Origines*, were still available. The Dutch scholar Voorbroek, or 'Perizonius,' first discussed their importance in shaping Roman legends[1]; and Niebuhr based on the evidence his theory of a mass of popular poems—miniature epics about the most interesting figures of regal and early republican times. Hence, he argued, came much of the poetic substance and colour in Livy. Though this romantic hypothesis captivated many, including Macaulay, it suffered destructive criticism from Sir G. C. Lewis and others. Schwegler, laying stress on the cramping limitations of early Roman life, asked in a tone of ironical disdain 'How could these Romans have been expected to develop a saga-poetry?' Taine, while he subjected the theory to a vivacious refutation, was judicial enough to declare that it was a case of truth pushed to the verge of error. One may, then, disbelieve in Niebuhr's complete fabric of plebeian ballads, one may fail to hear the ballads echoing in Livy's sentences, and yet accept both Varro's record that boys once sang to banqueters such lays either with or without musical accompaniment, and Cato's record that banqueters personally took turns in contributing songs, as long afterwards the English etiquette of Caedmon's age required. Since these two accounts vary, it has been contended that one may imply an earlier and the other a later custom; it is, however, fully as reasonable to suppose that the custom itself varied according to place and family. The subsequent non-existence of the lays does not prove them mere figments: their disappearance may be due to the emergence of more artistic poetry which brought neglect upon primitive ruggedness. But the songs themselves must have left their mark on oral legend.

These lays were presumably in Saturnian verse, as afterwards were the sepulchral inscriptions of the Scipios. The name 'Saturnian' marks either ritual associations or primeval character. Caesius Bassus, in the first century A.D., notes a common opinion (*nostri existimaverunt*) that the Saturnian was native to Italy, but declares this erroneous. The error, however, was his own, and not unnatural, because like other ancient metrists he approached all verse from the standpoint of Greek metres. The apparent absence of fixed principle in the verses which he examined and their variation in length, so puzzled Bassus that he owns he could scarcely find lines in Naevius to adduce as normal examples. While, however, he cites other instances, he gives what has become the standard specimen, *Malum dabunt Metelli Naevio poetae.* The typical line consists of five words or word-groups separated into two *cola*

---

[1] *Animadversiones historicae*, ch. VI, Amsterdam, 1685.

by a strong diaeresis; but as to its fundamental nature scholars are divided, and the case cannot be argued here. The old strictly quantitative theory has tended towards a semi-quantitative one. Most French opinion, which usually denies that Latin had a tonic accent, upholds the quantitative view. But a powerful array of authority maintains that the verse is accentual (*málum dábunt*, not *malúm dabúnt*), and has descended from a primitive Indo-European type in which the minstrel's beat was the determining characteristic. A parallel might then be found in such Anglo-Saxon poetry as *Beowulf*. But even on the accentual theory questions arise. Did the word-accent vary in the history of the verse? And can it be said that this primitive verse, at first accentual, did in time fall under rules suggested by Greek metre? If so, there is nothing surprising in the difficulty of finding a form applicable to all Saturnians.

That there was an ingrained Italian aptitude for some kind of drama might have been guessed from traits of character in the people and from analogy with other civilizations. The licence of scurrilous Fescennine verses sung in amoebean fashion[1] to avert the evil eye, at a marriage or a triumph, descended from the primitive banter of the harvest-home or vintage-festival, when rustic mummery gave outlet to improvisation in sharp dialogue and to the *Italum acetum*[2] of mockery. The name is most likely drawn from the Faliscan town of Fescennium. From Atella in Campania came the Oscan farce, *fabula Atellana*, increasingly familiar at Rome in both Oscan and Latin from the fourth century, after the Via Appia secured closer contact with Campania. Its stock characters were male—Pappus, the greybeard; Bucco, the glutton; Dossennus, the hump-back; and Maccus, the clown. To this last person Plautus alludes in a pun on his own gentile name, *Demophilus scripsit, 'Maccus' vortit barbare (Asinaria*, prol. 11). This crude improvisation, in which masks were worn, enjoyed such a vogue that Roman citizens appeared in it without losing caste, like despised *histriones*. The *locus classicus* on the early drama is a vexed chapter of Livy (VII, 2). There we learn that in 364 B.C. Etruscan dancers to flute-music were summoned to Rome when scenic performances were joined to the circus games: Roman youths followed their example, adding sportive amoebean verse: next, Fescennine rudeness was replaced by *saturae* with musical accompaniment, song and gesture. Later, 'Livius' (Andronicus) made a departure by introducing drama with a connected plot, *i.e.* the *fabula palliata* based on Greek models. The separation of singer and actor in Latin plays is set down to the failure of

[1] Hor. *Epist.* II, I, 146. [2] Hor. *Sat.* I, 7, 32.

Andronicus' voice after constant encores, necessitating the arrangement that a youth should sing in front of the musician while the actor concentrated on life-like gesticulations. *Saturae* being thus driven from the stage by more finished performances, young Romans turned as amateurs to acting Atellan plays, which came to be used for light after-pieces (*exodia*). Some modern scholars have impugned this account as a reconstruction by an antiquary desirous of making the history of Roman drama appear to run parallel to the Aristotelian account of Greek comedy. There have also been guesses at an intermediate source, such as Accius or Varro, for Livy's passage. The whole intricate question cannot be argued or even fully stated here; but the traditional position has not lacked defenders against sceptical attacks[1]. If—what cannot be said to be unanimously conceded—there was no such thing as dramatic *satura*, then *satura* in its sense of a critical miscellany begins with Ennius; and whether this typically Latin literary form had a dramatic ancestry or not, it exhibited throughout its course no little share of dramatic quality.

For centuries the Romans, amid struggles for civic privileges and economic fairness, underwent the best imaginable political training, just as outside their city they underwent constant training in war. If there was scant time for the poetic, they learned much concerning the duties of citizenship and the operation of law. Though the moulding of prose for written composition or finished utterance was slow, still, before 240, solid foundations were laid in documents at the outset mostly of an official nature. Priestly *commentarii* and *acta*, the calendar, *fasti* recording consulates or triumphs, the *annales* of the Pontifex Maximus, the Twelve Tables dating from c. 450 B.C., and other legal codifications like the *ius Papirianum* and the *ius Flavianum*, all bear testimony to the development of formal expression. In time the proved value of records was sure to point towards connected history, even though annalistically wooden to begin with. Like religion, law insisted on the *mot juste* and on definite, if at first awkwardly expressed, formulae. The Twelve Tables, learned by rote in schools till Cicero's days, influenced the mode of conveying thought; but, despite their utility in later life, a boy would declare them arid and unimaginative alongside the *Odyssey*, the rival school-book introduced by Andronicus. The jerkiness of the legal text is seen in the following extracts on the justifiable homicide of a burglar

[1] *E.g.* in *A.J.Ph.* XXXIII, 1912, pp. 125–148, Professor Knapp subjected the arguments of Leo and Hendrickson to discriminating criticism: see Bibliography V. G.

si nox furtum faxsit, si im occisit, iure caesus esto, and on the regulations affecting debtors *si in ius vocat, ito: ni it, antestamino: igitur em capito. si calvitur pedemve struit, manum endo iacito: si morbus aevitasve vitium escit, iumentum dato* ('If the debtor is summoned to court, he must go: if he does not, let one get witnesses, then seize him. If he plays false and takes leg bail, lay a hand on him: if illness or age be the default, let him give a beast of burden'). Towards oratory the stimulus came from occasions of domestic bereavement calling for a *laudatio funebris,* which tended to replace the *nenia,* or from national crises. Politics and especially political conflict, as Tacitus reminds us[1], inevitably fostered public speaking.

IV. THE GROWTH OF GREEK INFLUENCE

Most of the verse and prose so far considered may be called raw material—promise rather than fulfilment. It is as useless to speculate whether fine literary art could have sprung from indigenous germs alone as to ask why Etruscans or Oscans never developed a literature. Our present concern is to sketch the operation of Greek influence upon Rome, and to consider what the individual genius of early Latin writers achieved towards fusing the two streams of Hellenic precedent and Roman tradition. The manifold changes between 240 and 100 B.C. could not fail to affect deeply the native genius. The quick elevation into world-power, the accretion of riches and luxury, the decline of agriculture, and the eventual democratic inroad upon the ancient primacy of the Senate brought in their train serious responsibilities which worked as a disturbing ferment in politics and society. The magnitude of the change in external relations, in internal politics, and in social conditions may be grasped from the historical features of the period (chaps. IV, XII). Here it is essential to lay stress on the stimulus given to intellectual and aesthetic advance in Rome by Greece and the Greeks.

Greece, whose literature manifested the superiority of simple, concise, restrained beauty over complicated, verbose, extravagant formlessness, had in a spirit of triumphant adventure travelled for centuries far beyond the experimental stage at which a Latin writer found himself about 240 B.C. Greece had attained to unsurpassed eminence in the main divisions of literature—in epic, lyric, drama both tragic and comic, history and oratory: she had won results of permanent value in philosophy, criticism, science

[1] *Dial. de Or.* 37, 8–10; 40, 2.

and medicine. If in her politics the communal spirit had been too stringently limited to the conceptions of the city-state, she had bequeathed imperishable ideas of constitutional government and of individual liberty. The introduction of Greek writings into Rome implied an extraordinary confluence of currents. The Romans, at an epoch of exhilarating victory, but as yet innocent of elevated artistic creation, were confronted with this splendidly varied literature. Everything might seem to have been already felt, known, expressed in such a galaxy of letters, which in all its phases had long since risen to its zenith, but which even in its decline, whether at Athens or Alexandria, was for the relatively untutored Roman rich in patterns of aesthetic construction and style.

There is nothing in literary history comparable with the opening of Roman eyes to the potentialities of such a vista. Just as the international horizon had widened, there now dawned a revelation of new worlds of thought and of creative artistry, presenting the far-off heroic age, the lyric utterance of reflection or love, the problems in the drama of human life, the record of political clash or momentous wars, as well as philosophical inquiries into the meaning of the universe and into the bases of the State and of morality. The Latin author could and did find models in all periods of this literature from its alpha to its omega. At the outset, Andronicus shows the influence of Homer, of the Attic drama, and of the New Comedy side by side. Indeed, the latest phases of Greek literature, being nearest in time, were likely to make the most direct appeal. Although under the catastrophes of Greece literature had lost the old sureness of touch and sublimity of tone, it had yet in it much to reinforce the expansion of spirit already begun in Rome. The cosmopolitanism and individualism of the New Comedy (vol. VII, pp. 226 *sqq.*) struck fresh notes for a Roman mind. To watch a Plautine play was to get a novel sensation of imaginary contact with social life at Athens, with money-making journeys in the archipelago, or with the Orient, from which soldiers of fortune came home to boast, like the *Miles Gloriosus*, of adventures as campaigner and gallant (see p. 378).

Not in all its spheres, however, did Greek activity capture the Roman with equal immediacy. Greeks had lavished their keen energy of brain on literature, art and philosophy: with a free instinct for beauty, they had been unafraid lest thought might prove a deterrent to action. The Roman never quite renounced a shy suspicion that thinking might impede doing. The insistent call of utility, while it explains why art came slowly up the Roman way, also explains a recurrent distrust of philosophers, as well as explicit warnings that it is judicious 'to dip but not to plunge' into philosophy. Yet, after all, one of the greatest gifts of Hellas to the western world was its faith in ideas which stimulated the use of pure intellect and the enjoyment of beauty—something that for Latin literature ensured an ascent above the level of folk-song, heroic lays, proverbial wisdom, rustic mumming and dry annals into art more aesthetic and universal. So Greece won her immortal revenge for political overthrow when the elegant elasticity of her culture mastered her conquerors. This was the domination of a wider and subtler spirit, inherited from a long past, over a circumscribed and less sophisticated spirit; but it was no enslavement, because the traditional sense and moral dignity of Rome served in turn to mould what was borrowed. It was well that the almost embarrassing wealth of Greek literature, instead of paralyzing effort, actually provoked a vigorous appropriation from originals which at first it lay beyond the power of imitators to rival. The task before a Latin author was to make this heritage vitally expressive for a different civilization and towards this end to shape a comparatively formless language into a finished instrument destined even in the Middle Ages to preserve for a Greekless Western Europe some essentials in the Hellenic legacy. If the Roman ethos excelled in war, administration and engineering, there was also, if not genius, at any rate an infinite capacity for taking pains, underlying the pioneer efforts which fitted to contemporary needs the best that was available from Greece. Appius Claudius' saying that 'every one is the fashioner of his own fortune' can be transferred to a people who with their talent for expansion combined an impressive power of assimilation.

Before examining the reaction of Latin writers to Greek example, we have to look at certain other channels of Hellenism. Commercial, diplomatic and military dealings with Hellenes in Italy, Sicily and Greece itself, caused a prolonged infiltration of foreign things, words and ideas. In 282 B.C. the Roman envoy Postumius was able to address the Tarentines in their own language, and Pyrrhus' emissary, Cineas, needed no interpreter in the Roman Senate two years later. The establishment of the Ludi Apollinares in 212 and of the cult of Cybele in 205 illustrates the operation of what was not merely mythology but religion. Greek opulence came home to the popular mind on occasions like Flamininus' triumph in 194 for victories over Philip V of Macedon, regarding which Plutarch (*Tit. Flam.* 14) quotes Tuditanus' testimony to the gorgeous spoils paraded. Objects of art grew familiar: in 212 Marcellus brought an imposing array of statues and pictures from Syracuse; Capua on its recapture next year was stripped of its art; from Tarentum, ransacked by Q. Fabius in 209, there came the colossal Heracles by Lysippus. Where, as at Syracuse, opportunity offered for seeing masterpieces of sculpture, and of drama in plays by Euripides and Menander, Romans could not but awaken to their backwardness in plastic and literary skill. To those who had eyes to see some aesthetic education was thus inevitably conveyed, though the soldier-consul Mummius in 146 might prove himself so incapable of valuing unique masterpieces in Corinth as to bargain naïvely with his contractors that any damaged in transport to Rome should be made good. This constant stream of beauty was augmented by the royal treasures of Pergamum in 133 B.C.

Other instruments of culture were books. When in 167 Aemilius Paullus brought to Rome the library of Perseus of Macedon, he reinforced the action of Greek erudition on savants and particularly on the circle of Aemilianus, Paullus' son, who had been adopted into the Scipio family. By this time Greeks had taken an active part in many spheres of Roman life for some generations: household slaves, teachers, architects, musicians, ship-captains, and physicians were largely Greek. According to Cassius Hemina[1], the first practising doctor in Rome was Archagathon, a Peloponnesian, whose popularity waned when his ruthless surgery earned him the nickname of 'executioner' (*carnifex*). The intransigent Cato himself could not avoid Hellenic infection: the sentiment, for instance, cited from his *Origines* by Cicero[2], that the employment of leisure by eminent men should be as important as their work, looks quite Roman but is really from Xenophon. Nothing, however, rooted Hellenism more firmly at Rome than education. Greek professors directed the study of the principles of expression through grammar and rhetoric, the study of consummate examples of Greek poetry, history and oratory, and the study of the great systems of Hellenic thought. By 173 B.C. two Epicureans had become sufficiently suspect to be banished, and in 161 an edict went forth against some resident rhetors and philosophers. Yet nothing—neither senatorial decree nor Catonian fulmination—could check the inrush.

A few occurrences within a dozen years may be adduced for their significance. The first happened about the time when the Macedonian library was conveyed to Rome. One thousand Achaean hostages, men of social standing, were deported to Italy and lodged at various centres. Among these influential exiles was

---

[1] Pliny, *N.H.* XXIX, 12. [2] *pro Plancio*, 27, 66.

Polybius, a traveller and a thinker, who expressed admiration for the Roman character in a broad-minded history of the times (see above, chap. 1). His influence in determining the Greek studies of nobles and authors, like Terence and Lucilius, in the younger Scipio's circle, was strengthened by Panaetius, who had been invited from Greece to expound one of the most impressive of ancient philosophies, Stoicism[1]. The Stoic creed, through magnifying virtue, found a response in the semi-puritanical austerity of Roman *gravitas*. Its effect on society was immediate, while its imprint on law, that typical monument of Roman genius, was destined to be ineffaceable. Scipio's own training in Greek records embodying historical experience and political wisdom equipped him to be at once the literary patron of his day and a sagacious discerner of dangers threatening the State from unbridled imperialism, pleasure-hunting, cupidity, celibacy and social weaknesses such as his friend Lucilius satirized. Yet by a strange irony it fell to this lover of cultured moderation to carry through the destruction of Carthage and Numantia. Another event fraught with far-reaching consequences was the visit paid to Rome by Crates as envoy from Attalus of Pergamum (p. 459). He broke his leg in the city, and during his convalescence delivered lectures on 'Grammar' in the broad sense of literature. His treatment was fresh in contrast with the deadly dullness of Alexandrian pedants.

The next suggestive event was the arrival in 155 of three philosophers deputed from Athens to plead for remission of a fine. The trio consisted of Critolaus the Peripatetic, Diogenes the Stoic, and Carneades the Academic. They did more than represent three schools: they illustrated different styles of oratory; for Gellius (*N.A.* VI, 14, 8–10) quotes, on the authority of Rutilius and Polybius, the reports that Critolaus spoke with art and polish (*scita et teretia*), Diogenes with restraint and sobriety (*modesta et sobria*), Carneades with vehemence and force (*violenta et rapida*). We can infer that the visit left its mark on systematic thought and on oratorical composition. Carneades made a particularly interesting figure. A professed Academic, he was an apostle of probability, rather than dogmatism, in the realm of intellect and conduct. His adroit eclecticism might well attract some Romans as sound sense, but his applied scepticism was certain to shock others as subversive of truth and morality. We learn without surprise that Cato clamoured for an unceremonious dismissal of the deputation. But new manners had come to stay at Rome: already for three generations Menandrian laxities had been witnessed on the comic stage.

[1] On Greek philosophy at Rome see further below, chap. XIV.

V. THE EARLIEST LITERARY AUTHORS

LIVIUS ANDRONICUS (c. 284–204 B.C.) has importance out of all proportion to his surviving fragments—not a hundred lines altogether, and no passage over three lines long. Into mistakes about his date made by Jerome and before Jerome, certainly by Accius and possibly by Suetonius, we need not enter. There are well-attested facts[1] to secure his place in Roman epic and education, drama and lyric. Brought a slave-boy to Rome on the capture of Tarentum in 272, this 'half-Greek,' to use Suetonius' term, had nearly all his Latin to learn. Recollections of the gay Tarentine enthusiasm for the theatre may have prompted his study of Athenian dramatists; and he must have utilized such study in teaching the children of his master Livius Salinator. If Andronicus cannot be proved to have been exactly a schoolmaster, he unquestionably exercised a potent influence on schools. We may imagine two questions often crossing his mind—why had Romans no literary text in Latin for school-reading to relieve the drab monotony of the Twelve Tables? and why had they no plays such as his own people enjoyed at Tarentum? He was to supply both wants. A stroke of genius sent him to the *Odyssey*, which he latinized by employing the Saturnian metre and by introducing Roman turns of thought and typical Italian words or forms like *Camena*, *Mercurius* and *Ulixes*. While the *Odyssey* was both romantic and domestic in interest, perhaps the homelier scenes in Ithaca held a Roman as much as the thrilling adventures, and its deities propitious or hostile fitted Roman religious conceptions. But in this pioneer transplanting of Homeric epic no approach to a varied Virgilian colour is to be expected. The translation, sometimes exact, is at other times defective or over-full or erroneous[2]. *Virum mihi, Camena, insece versutum* renders with adequacy the familiar opening Ἄνδρα μοι ἔννεπε, Μοῦσα, πολύτροπον; but *ore*, later, makes a weak substitute for 'the barrier of the teeth' (*Od.* I, 64); and *topper facit homines ut prius fuerunt*, 'quick she (Circe) turns them to men as they were before,' alters the original sense[3]. Scaliger[4] considered that in *affatim edi, bibi, lusi*, the *lusi* was a misunderstanding of the Greek[5]; the four words, however, may be

---

[1] Cic. *Brut.* 18, 71–72; Hor. *Epist.* II, 1, 60–63, 69–72; Livy VII, 2, 8; XXVII, 37; Suet. *Gram.* 1; Gell. *N.A.* XVIII, 9, 5.

[2] The Greek, where identifiable, is given by Morel, *Fragmenta Poetarum Latinorum.*

[3] ἄνδρες δ' ἂψ ἐγένοντο νεώτεροι ἢ πάρος ἦσαν. *Od.* X, 395.

[4] Lejay agrees, *La littérature latine*, pp. 213–214.

[5] τῶν ἔφαγόν τ' ἔπιόν τε καὶ αἰδοίοισιν ἔδωκα. *Od.* XV, 373.

from a comedy. By calling Livius' *Odyssia* an *opus Daedali* Cicero suggests its earliness and strange craftsmanship; for the author's task involved a wrestle with a language not his mother-tongue and a metre never before put to so continuous a test. Horace, though a stickler for polish, refrained from advocating the expulsion of Livius' translation from schools: clearly he credited the rough Saturnians with living force despite a juvenile grudge against them and a critical disdain for their lack of Augustan refinement.

It may have been this provision of a good literary reader that drew upon Andronicus, now a freedman, the notice of the aediles in 240. Here was the man to vary a Roman holiday with tragedy and comedy. Thus his career as dramatic adapter and actor-manager began in the prime of his life. The titles of nine of his tragedies are accepted: three comedies are represented by scraps, and in two cases by uncertain titles. In tragedy Sophoclean models attracted him, and titles such as *Achilles, Aegisthus, Aiax, Equos Troianus,* prove his belief in the Trojan cycle as up-to-date material for the stage. It was but recently in Sicily that the Romans first encountered the pleasant fable that their ancestors had long ago come from Troy (vol. VII, p. 676). The dramatic activity in Rome, particularly the flourishing of comedy, which continued during the grim struggle against Hannibal, may be at first sight surprising. Yet there was method in a governmental policy which sanctioned popular amusement at festival-times to counteract the effect of repeated disasters in war. It was the Senate that voted funds to furnish plays, and, if these exhibited a questionable morality, the more puritanical senators might argue that they were at most permitting the erection of a temporary stage. Archaic in style, Andronicus' plays were dismissed by Cicero as not worth a second reading. But this is not the last word, and does injustice to his great services as an innovator. Increase of metrical skill is evident where he had to use iambic, trochaic and lyric measures. Examples retaining the native alliteration may be quoted:

> *tum autem lascivum Nerei simum pecus*
> *ludens ad cantum classem lustratur* [*choro*]:
> 'Then Nereus' wanton snub-nosed flock in fun
> Frolic to music choir-like round the fleet';

or his rapid septenarius

> *Confluges ubi conventu campum totum inumigant:*
> 'When the waters in their concourse congregate to flood the plain.'

The creation of a literary diction is evident in phrases like *florem Liberi* for 'wine,' or the abstract expression for 'a mother's milk' in *lacteam immulgens opem.* To mark the old poet's lyric ability in composing the *carmen* of 207 B.C. the state decreed the foundation on the Aventine of an Athenaeum for *scribae* and *histriones*, a combined club and academy of letters.

A still more original genius was the Italian-born CN. NAEVIUS (*c.* 270–*c.* 199 B.C.). He was daringly independent in his public criticism; he set the fashion of 'contaminating' two borrowed plots into a new play[1]; the first to handle Roman subjects in tragedy, he began the *fabula praetexta* with his *Alimonia Romuli et Remi* and *Clastidium* (commemorating Marcellus' fight in 222 B.C. against a Gallic chieftain); finally, he chose for epic treatment a national theme—the First Punic War, in which he served. His earliest piece was played in 235. We know of seven tragedies by him from Greek mythology, and about five times as many comedies. Enough is left of his *Lycurgus* to make us wish for more of this drama on the theme of Euripides' *Bacchae*: his forte, however, lay in lighter plays, where the Campanian arrogance assigned to him found vent in satiric ridicule. The *Colax*, a Menandrian comedy, shows that he shares such Greek characters as the swashbuckler (*Gladiolus*) with Andronicus and Plautus: some titles, *e.g.* *Colax* or *Acontizomenos*, are Greek: several, *e.g.* *Carbonaria* or *Nervolaria* (*sc. fabula*), have the Latin ending familiar in *Mostellaria* and other plays by Plautus. The *Hariolus*, to judge by its passage about dainty dishes fit to set before the folk of Praeneste or Lanuvium, looks like a drama of native life (*togata*); and we have missed genuine fun in losing 'The Girl from Tarentum,' *Tarentilla*, from which comes the lively delineation of a flirt with several strings to her bow. A man of irrepressible self-confidence and democratic leanings, Naevius might have taken as motto his line 'at the festival of Bacchus shall our words flow frank and free (*libera lingua loquemur ludis Liberalibus*)'. Frankness of speech, according to a famous story[2], brought him into conflict with the noble Metelli, when his ambiguous senarius *fato Metelli Romae fiunt consules* evoked the Saturnian rejoinder *dabunt malum Metelli Naevio poetae*. Doubt has been thrown on the authenticity of the lines and on the story about Naevius' consequent incarceration; but, though a parallel case of punishment for criticism of political personages in republican times may be hard to find, it is reasonable to suppose that during war some over-zealous praetor of the Scipionic party strained a clause of the Twelve Tables on offensive *carmina* to bring Naevius within its scope[3].

---

[1] Terence, *Andria*, prol. 18 *sqq.*
[2] Ps.-Asconius on Cicero, *Verr. Act.* I, 10, 28.
[3] Tenney Frank, *A.J.P.* XLVIII, 1927, p. 109.

His liberation was followed by exile about 204, and a few years later by his death.

The *Bellum Punicum* was the work of his advanced years. Its earlier portion (the division into seven books is due to Lampadio) relates the legendary origins of Rome; for he does not plunge *in medias res*. Later, when he reaches the Punic War, the fact that he was an eye-witness of certain events gives him historical value[1]. His literary position is intelligible if he is viewed as the last Saturnian poet. Despite experience in naturalizing Greek metres, he selected the native verse for his epic, a choice scarcely imaginable unless it had been already used for narratives of some dimensions. But, while we learn from Macrobius and Servius how much Virgil borrowed from Naevius, the fragments are disappointingly bald. 'Valerius the consul led a portion of his army on an expedition' may be our unique record of a military movement in Sicily; but it is even less poetic than the English lines about that 'noble Duke of York' who had ten thousand men. It is but a rugged force that appears in his alliterative *vicissatim volvi victoriam* on the 'turns of the tide in triumphs,' or in the lines which we owe to Festus' interest in the word *stuprum* with the general sense of 'dishonour.' They describe the gallant disdain felt by the entrapped remnant of Regulus' army for terms of surrender:

> *seseque ei perire mavolunt ibidem*
> *quam cum stupro redire ad suos popularis.*

The tragedies show more poetic feeling: a few memorable sentiments have survived (*e.g. male parta male dilabuntur* and *laudari a laudato viro*). Compounds like *arquitenens, frundiferos, suavisonum*, and *thyrsigerae* mark the divergence from spoken Latin. His contribution to style is one of the claims made in the Saturnian epitaph, which he is credited with having written:

> Were it heaven's will that the immortals weep
> For mortal men, our goddesses of song
> Must weep to lose the poet Naevius.
> When he was ta'en to Orcus' treasury
> Folk lost the power of Latin speech at Rome.

Q. ENNIUS (239–169), born at Rudiae in Calabria, served in the Roman army after his education at Tarentum, and in 204 was brought by Cato to Rome. There he taught Greek and followed the fashion of adapting Attic tragedies (*fabulae crepidatae*). Intimate with the Scipios and the Fulvii, he accompanied Fulvius Nobilior on his Aetolian campaign, and through his son received

---

[1] C. Cichorius, 'Die Fragmente historischen Inhalts aus Naevius Bellum Punicum,' *Römische Studien*, pp. 24 *sqq.*

citizenship (*nos sumu' Romani qui fuimus ante Rudini*). A South-
erner with 'three hearts,' he said, Oscan, Greek and Roman, he
grew enamoured of the greatness of his adoptive city. Although
he modelled quite twenty tragedies on Greek plays, put much
Greek thought into Latin dress, and introduced the hexameter,
it was his epic, 'the tale of the years' (*Annales*), which earned him
for generations the affectionate reverence of Rome. To say without qualification that Ennius hellenized Roman literature is to
overlook his intense absorption of the national spirit. His Latin
reproduction of some of the finest plays of Sophocles and Euripides during the first two decades of the second century, when
Rome was using a Hellenic policy to checkmate Macedon, may
have materially aided the national policy. His *Sabinae*, and
perhaps the *Ambracia*, dramatized episodes in Roman history.
Comedy he attempted slightly, but he wrote a good deal of miscellaneous work. His *saturae* (iambic, trochaic, hexametric and
sotadic) contained anecdotes such as the fable of the lark and her
young, designed to teach the moral:

> This will be a proved conclusion always close at hand for you—
> Never look for friends' assistance in what you yourself can do[1].

Though enthusiastically receptive of Roman traditions, Ennius
was a fresh force in thought as well as in metre. In South Italy,
he had imbibed ideas from Pythagoreanism, Epicureanism and
Euhemerism, while the rationalistic spirit of Euripides led him
back to the sceptical outlook of the Sicilian Epicharmus. The fruit
appeared in his minor works—*Epicharmus*, the beginning of
dream literature in Latin, and *Euhemerus*, on gods as deified men.
Quotations from the latter in Lactantius[2] suggest that there we
have echoes of a prose work by Ennius written in an unpretentious
style with a well-marked rhythm. Morality was preached in the
Protrepticus and gastronomy in the *Hedyphagetica*, a 'Gourmet's
Guide' based on Archestratus of Gela. The quotation *nunquam
poetor nisi si podager* from Ennius and his recorded death from
gout may support Horace's allusion (*Epist.* I, 19, 7) to the inspiration which he found in his cups.

A critical spirit invades his plays. He loves the sententious element
in his originals, knowing that it would make unerring appeal to the
Roman mind. One of his iambic adaptations will illustrate this:

> Kindly to point a wanderer to the way
> Is but to light another's lamp from ours:
> Ours glows no less for setting his aflame.
> (*nilo minus ipsi lucet, cum illi accenderit.*)

---

[1] Gell. *N.A.* II, 29.   [2] *Inst. Div.* I, II, 34; 14, I.

But, with his fondness for Greek speculation, he is not content simply to transplant a safe proverbial wisdom. There is a turn for satiric observation in the trochaics of the *Telamo* jesting at fortune-telling impostors who

> Point the highroad to another, though a path they cannot see.

From the same play comes an Epicurean denial of Providence:

> 'Tis my creed both now and ever—there are gods beyond the skies;
> But I hold they never trouble what we human beings do,
> Else the good would thrive and villains wither—which is far from true!
> (*nam si curent, bene bonis sit, male malis—quod nunc abest.*)

His version of the opening of Euripides' *Medea* possesses a victorious beauty of its own, in the vain sigh over the building of the Argo and over the quest for the Golden Fleece, harmoniously leading up to two lines of wonderful pity for the heroine as a victim of unrequited self-sacrifice—the princess Medea, who is called by a subtly symbolic word-play an *era errans*,

> In her sick heart wounded by ruthless love.
> (*Medea animo aegro amore saevo saucia.*)

A passage from the *Iphigenia* has an effective anapaestic movement, which may be rendered:

> Say, what of the night in the resonant height
> Of the shield of the sky? The Wain is on high,
> Driving star after star from near and from far,
> Along the road sped of the night overhead.

The eighteen books of *Annales* recounted in hexameters (of which 600 survive) the story of Rome. Here was a gallery of valorous heroes and ideal virtue. In this poem, which began with an invocation to the Greek 'Muses whose feet do great Olympus tread', there was much to thrill the patriotic Roman—the coming of Trojan Aeneas, the auspicious dream of his Vestal daughter Ilia, the fortunes of her twin boys, the founding of the city, the mysterious assumption of Romulus, all in the first book, to be followed by regal legends, figures like Numa, Ancus Marcius, the Tarquin, and so on to dangers from Samnite or Epirote. 'Who can unfold the mighty tracts of war?' (*quis potis ingentes oras evolvere belli?*) he asks, conscious of his lofty theme. In dispensing himself from narrating the First Punic War he made an allusion meant for Naevius' Saturnians:

> Others have writ the tale
> In verse which whilome elves and warlocks crooned
> When no man yet had scaled the Muses' scaurs
> Or felt the lure of style.

The eighth and ninth were the Hannibalic books, and the fifteenth had the personal interest of sketching the Aetolian War. The mystic vein of a poet who believed himself Homer reincarnate found freest outlet in the earlier books, where Ilia's dream is a fair example. While, however, he can express feeling as in the farewell to Romulus, and has an eye for colour, it cannot be pretended that there is sustained beauty in the narrative: rough and caesura-less lines with a plethora of spondees and uncouth forms often spoil all musical effect, while there are lapses into the prosaic, such as *septingenti sunt paulo plus aut minus anni*. Yet Roman memories cherished the undeniable dignity of many old-fashioned verses such as those on the masterly inactivity of Fabius Cunctator, *unus homo nobis cunctando restituit rem*; on an invincible general, *quem nemo ferro potuit superare neque auro*; on a nation that never knew defeat, *qui vincit non est victor nisi victu' fatetur*; and on the secret of national strength, *moribus antiquis res stat Romana virisque* ('Rome's pillars are old customs and her men'). The few elegiac verses ascribed to him are of a memorial character—sepulchral tributes to Scipio or to his own position in poetry:

> Let none shed tears—none for my passing grieve:
> I flit upon the lips of men and live.

VI. THE SPECIALISTS IN DRAMA

T. MACCIUS PLAUTUS (*c.* 254–184 B.C.), an Umbrian, is the first Latin writer whose genius can be judged by complete surviving works, and the first who restricted himself to a single *métier*. When after hardships in Rome he found his true vocation, he amused his contemporaries in a succession of plays, all the more natural for his experience in life and his practical acquaintance with the theatre. So strong was his popular appeal that 130 pieces circulated under his name and a notable Plautine revival on the stage took place in Terence's time. Nothing is more likely than that he anticipated his eighteenth-century compatriot Goldoni in comic fertility, and that many of his plays have perished. Scholars like Accius and Aelius Stilo busied themselves with his text, and Varro drew up a canon of twenty-one genuine plays, which correspond with those now extant, except that the *Vidularia* is in fragments and some others have gaps. Only a few can be dated exactly. The *Miles Gloriosus*, which seems to allude to Naevius' imprisonment (211–212), must have been written about 205 B.C.; and the *Cistellaria* preceded the close of the Hannibalic War, as

is plain from its advice given through the god Auxilium to the
Romans (197 *sqq.*):

> Farewell: may victory crown you evermore
> By veriest valour won, as heretofore!
> Bind fast your allies, old or new: secure
> Fresh aid in warfare by your justice pure.
> Lay low your foemen: laud and laurels gain:
> Let conquered Carthage pay the price in pain!
> (*ut vobis victi Poeni poenas sufferant.*)

Most of the surviving plays, however, belong to the first fifteen
years of the second century.

The New Comedy, from which Plautus mainly drew, has been described (vol. VII, pp. 226 *sqq.*). We can name some of his lost originals
by Diphilus, Demophilus, Menander and Philemon, and guess
plausibly at others. But these models were not slavishly followed,
nor does any one formula fit the adaptations or contaminations.
Amid the predominant atmosphere of intrigue considerable variety
in motive and incident is attained, and much is added by the author.
One is unique, the *Amphitruo*, a tragi-comedy with an admixture
of a South Italian type of humour, burlesquing the myth of
Alcmena's betrayal by Jupiter. Mercury, as Jupiter's jackal,
creates farcical merriment by getting himself up as a double of the
slave Sosia. Yet the play has a spice of that serious element which,
often overlooked amidst Plautus' rollicking gaiety, is nevertheless present to elevate his comedy to a higher level than mere jest;
for the dignity of the wronged queen in contrast with the libertine
Jupiter or the flippant Mercury stirs questioning reflection.
Another stands alone, the *Captivi*; without any love element it
turns on the self-effacing devotion of man to master through a
dangerous impersonation. Its *dénoûment*, a 'recognition' of two
lost sons, is contrived differently from the recovery of a lost
daughter in the *Cistellaria*, *Epidicus* and *Rudens*. The mistakes
due to the confusion between twin brothers act as sure provo-
catives of laughter in the *Menaechmi*. Some plays gain from a
psychological interest—the boastful *Miles*, the two faithful young
grasswidows in the *Stichus*, a greedy *meretrix* and a repulsive pro-
fligate in the *Truculentus*. The miserly nervousness of Euclio in
the *Aulularia* is not all caricature; the hardening of Hegio's heart
in the *Captivi* owing to the loss of his son is unpleasantly true to
human weakness; the loyal friendship of old Callicles in the
Trinummus for the absent Charmides and, in the same play, the
concern of Lysiteles for his intemperate comrade, and the fidelity
of the slave Stasimus to the old house are winning traits effectively

presented. But, no doubt, the changes are prevailingly though
ingeniously rung on the smart trickery requisite in a slave (or in
a parasite, *Curculio*) to secure money for a young master's amour.
The intrigue may be combined with a scheme to defeat an
amorous greybeard (*Bacchides, Casina, Mercator*), or the turning-
point may be the outwitting of a rapacious *leno* (*Persa, Poenulus,
Pseudolus, Rudens*). The brazen ingenuity of Chrysalus in the
Bacchides, Tranio in the *Mostellaria*, and Pseudolus in the clever
play of that name compels an enjoyable amazement, although in
the *Epidicus* the plot is so involved that modern taste will scarcely
share Plautus' own liking for it. The slave's rascality and his
familiarity with his master accorded rather with Greek custom.
Nevertheless Rome transmitted this feature to live again in *Les
fourberies de Scapin* and the Danish drama of Holberg. The trickster
is an engaging scamp who views himself as an artist in fraud:

> The poet, taking tablets up, pursues
> What nowhere is on earth, yet finds the same,
> And turns a fib to semblance of the truth.
> So now let me play poet: eighty pounds
> That nowhere are on earth, I yet must find.
> (*Pseudolus*, 401 *sqq.*)

The parasite, though his Gargantuan raptures over a feast contain
Plautine additions, was an imported figure. It was also a foreign
fashion which conceded to a courtesan her prominent rôle. Presumably, therefore, the lost comedies on Roman life (*togatae*) laid
more stress on normal domestic scenes and less on the illicit connections of the Hellenic stage. Certainly in the *palliata* married
life is not made attractive: we meet in Eunomia of the *Aulularia*
a sensible matron whose ironic humility towards the other sex is
amusing, but in general the wives are shrewish. The housewife
in the *Asinaria* keeps, not without reason, a tight hand over her
husband and his money; and in the *Casina*, where an old fellow
has become a perfumed dandy again since he grew infatuated with
a young damsel, it is no wonder if his spouse proves 'a surly Juno
to her Jupiter,' whom she calls 'a worthless grey mosquito.' The
exposure of such slack-principled seniors, who believe in continuing to sow the wild oats of youth, shows that, if political satire
was tabooed, the comedy of manners could indulge in social
criticism. A definitely satiric picture is drawn in trochaics by the
paedagogus Lydus when he shakes his head over the new-fangled
doctrine of self-expression in education (*Bacch.* 438 *sqq.*):

> In the past a youth took office chosen by the people's vote
> Ere he'd ceased his tutor's precepts most obediently to note.

Nowadays, before he's seven, if you give him but a smack,
This young hopeful with his notebook straight his teacher's crown will crack!
When you take the case to father, this is what he tells his son:
'Show the family spirit, sonny, and stand up for number one!'
Next the tutor gets his summons: 'Hey, you worthless dotard there!
Don't you touch the boy for acting with an independent air....'
That's the verdict—case is over! Can a pedagogue retain
On such lines control o'er others, if he first must feel the cane?

The cleavage between the Rome of the day and the Greek social world staged in the *palliata* served to flavour with piquancy a spectator's enjoyment. While the drama transported him to distant surroundings, it enabled him, if Roman *gravitas* ran the risk of being unduly shocked, to look on with complacent superiority at depraved foreigners 'going the whole Greek hog' (*pergraecari*) in extravagance, amours and junketings, while slaves ventured on impudence inconceivable in a Roman household. The audience could remember that the scene was somewhere in the East—at Athens, Ephesus, or Cyrene. Yet a purely alien drama could not have kept hold on Roman playgoers. If society and scene were Hellenic, comedy had to reflect enough of universal human nature to guarantee its successful appeal. Besides, Plautus incorporated plentiful Roman colour. He may logically refer to the Roman law as *barbarica* (*Capt.* 492) or to a Roman artist as 'a porridge-eating barbarian' (*Most.* 828); but he does not trouble uniformly to be so strict. If it suits, an Aetolian town shall have one of the gates of Rome, or the Capitol shall be transported to Epidaurus. Greek slaves are threatened with Roman punishments, *lora, furca* or *crux*, or the place (*Asin.* 33 *sqq.*)

> Where naughty slaves grind barley-meal in tears,
> The Whackland Islands, Ironclanky Isles,
> Where dead ox-leather slashes living men.

Some jests have, it is true, a Greek flavour; a cook after a sound drubbing says 'the old boy treated me like a gymnasium' (*Aul.* 410), or Chrysalus affects a Socratic ignorance about money he means to steal (*Bacch.* 324, *de auro nil scio nisi nescio*). But much of the humour is Plautus' own, drawn from ingenious inroads on the spoken language and from reminiscences of native drama to give the dialogue a natural swing, with an accumulated patter of synonyms and epithets not seldom abusive, with parodies, alliterations and puns. Then there is the typically Plautine fun of a boisterous order; the nerve-shattering pranks of the disguised male bride with an elephantine tread (*Cas.* 845, *institit plantam quasi luca bos*); the cock-a-hoop slave who makes his young master carry him on his back to celebrate their joint triumph in chicanery; the rowdy banging at doors (*Bacch.* 579–586, *fores paene ecfregisti*), a piece of 'comic business' handed on from Greek to modern times; the mutual buffetings of slaves; the itching of fists to be 'tooth-crackers' (*Bacch.* 596, *dentifrangibula*), while the menaced parasite fears for his 'nut-crackers'; and the wild revels which cut short the promising psychology of the *Stichus*.

Nearly all the scheming turns ultimately on sexual passion: as Ovid has it, 'Love comes in gay Menander's every play' (*Trist.* II, 369). It is, then, of interest to note Plautus' attitude to so central a theme. That these attachments, where intentions might or might not be honourable, were usually romantic, no one will pretend: too often the chink of money can be overheard. The comic capital made out of them is obvious; but Plautus has a way of linking, as Menander did, the humorous with the serious: so his treatment of love varies. Half jocularly, half gravely, it is regarded as an incalculably risky adventure. Punning on *amare* and *amarum* a girl asks (*Cist.* 68):

> Is a bit of true love, tell me, but a bit of bitterness?

to be answered

> Heavens! Love is big with honey, honey mixed with gall galore—
> Just a snack of sweets but heaps of bitter till you hold no more.

One friend delivers to another a homily on the dangers of love (*Trin.* 668 *sqq.*):

> Love is like artillery-shooting: nothing has such speed or wings.
> Mad and moody are the manners which this love to mortal brings:
> Urge a lover—will he do it? Urge him not to, and he will!
> When a thing is scarce, it's longed for; when there's plenty, wants are nil.
> Warning-off appears inducement: good advice is shunned like sin.
> 'Tis insanely bad for travellers to put up at Cupid's Inn.

The very friend thus lectured had earlier in the play uttered an unromantic farewell to love, serving on it notice of divorce (*Trin.* 266, *apage te, Amor: tuas res tibi habeto*):

> Begone, O Love, take yours and go!
> Henceforth be never friend to me:
> Some you can hold in pain and woe—
> The victims of your tyranny.

On the other hand, we have an impetuous lover's serenade in cretics to a barred door (*Curc.* 147 *sqq.*):

> Ho, you bolts! Ho, you bolts! to salute you is sweet:
> I'm in love with you, want you, and crave and entreat.
> Will you humour, my pretties, a lover's desire,
> And to help me, please, turn to a wild dancing choir?

Make a leap, I implore you, and bring to my sight
Her who drains the heart's blood of this love-stricken wight....
But just see how the blackguardly bolts won't awake,
And don't trouble to budge for a true lover's sake!

The course of true love never did run smooth, and we find
Philaenium arguing in trochaics (*Asin.* 506 *sqq.*) against her
mother's sordid advice to throw her sweetheart over because he
is short of money:

Daughter. Shall I pay my dues to duty, mother, if I mould my mind
            And, to please you, play precisely every part by you defined?...
Mother.   Is it paying dues to duty not to do what mother says?
Daughter. Mothers who do right are blameless; those who don't I cannot
            praise.
Mother.   What a chattering little baggage!
Daughter.   Mother, there's my capital—
            Wheedling tongue, attractive figure, fancy's lure, the moment's
            call.

Later, when the lovers meet and for the moment dread a final
parting, even under the 'laughing' measure of the iambic
septenarius the notes of feeling are discernible (606 *sqq.*):

She. Where haste you?
He.   Ah, farewell! In Death's realm we'll be meeting;
       For I, as far as in me lies, from life must be retreating.
She. Why, prythee—what I don't deserve—desire that Death should
       seize me?
He. What! *I*? Your *death*? If you had need, no sacrifice could please me
       Like giving up my life for yours or making your life longer.
She. Why, then, against your threats of death the case for life grows stronger;
       For what d'you think that *I* shall do, if *you* do what you mention?
       To treat myself the selfsame way is fully my intention.
He. That's sweet, quite honey-sweet, of you!
She.   Without you life were frightful.
       So kiss me.
He.   Willingly.
She.   Ah, so—the grave would be delightful.

This is not the place to discuss Plautine prosody[1]. The clue to
much of its difficulty, to its shortenings like *domĭ* or *volŭptatem*,
to its slurrings and hiatus, lies ultimately in the stress-accent of
spoken Latin. Plautus was an independent versifier who made
departures from Menander's verse-technique even in the iambic
senarius of his recitative (*diverbium*), while in the *cantica* sung to
musical accompaniment, though their lineage may be traceable to
the *hilarotragoedia* of Sicily and to the Euripidean monody, he
exhibited a genuine originality and a steadily increasing lyrical
skill.

----

[1] See the works cited in the Bibliography V, E.

After Plautus the *palliata* became more hellenized. Caecilius Statius (*c.* 219–166 B.C.), an Insubrian captive and the first Celtic author in Rome, chose Greek titles more often than not for his plays and so marks the transition to Terence. Gellius' examination of his *Plocium* has been mentioned (vol. VII, p. 227). Though Gellius preferred Menander, Caecilius was set highest among the ten Latin comic writers by the critic Sedigitus (*c.* 100 B.C.), and Varro awarded him the palm for plots. He retained stock characters like the slave, parasite and courtesan, and the quotation from his *Heiress* (*Epicleros*) in the *de Amicitia* indicates that the old gentleman of his stage was there traditionally to be cheated:

> To-day, beyond all greybeard fools in comedy,
> You've choused and cozened me most handsomely.

Contemporary composers of *palliatae* were Trabea, commended by Varro for range of feeling; Atilius, who also wrote tragedy; Aquilius, author, it is likely, of a *Boeotia*; Licinius Imbrex; and Luscius Lanuvinus, the 'spiteful old poet' with whom Terence in five of his prologues was at daggers drawn, and whose Menandrian adaptations he criticized for blunders. Though Terence himself was rather a literary than a popular success, the writing of *palliatae* lasted to the end of our period; for Turpilius, who died in 103, composed plays with exclusively Greek titles—*Boethuntes* (*The Rescue*), *Hetaera* (*La Fille de Joie*), *Paraterusa* (*The Woman on the Prowl*). Like Caecilius, he rehandled Menander's *Epicleros*, and his *Lady of Leucas* was a burlesque on the story of Sappho.

We turn to the author who in Latin comedy approached most nearly to Attic grace. P. TERENTIUS AFER (*c.* 195–159 B.C.), brought a slave to Rome, was educated and emancipated by his owner. Possibly his African origin recommended him to Scipio Africanus the younger: in any case, he enjoyed the intimacy of members of the Scipionic circle who, gossip alleged, did far more than make occasional contributions to the young foreigner's dramas. The anecdote about the encouragement he got on reading his first play to Caecilius at dinner deserves to be true, but is no more guaranteed than his birth-year or the exact chronology of his plays. Between 166 and 160, drawing freely from Menander and to a less extent from Apollodorus and Diphilus, he produced under Greek titles *The Girl from Andros*, *The Self-Punisher*, *The Eunuch*, *Phormio*, *The Brothers*, and finally a play twice unsuccessfully tried on the stage, *The Mother-in-Law*. Throughout he had to contend with rival popular attractions and ill-natured strictures. He therefore used his prologues, not as dramatic introductions in Plautus' way, but partly as explanations of his literary method, partly as polemics against unfair criticism. With a disarming modesty he owns his debt to Menander—a double debt, in truth, for those ingeniously contaminated plots at which contemporary critics cavilled. But what should it matter, he argues (*Andr.* 9–21), if he did combine the Menandrian *Andria* and *Perinthia*: 'he that knows the one as good as knows the other'—an acknowledgment of sameness which Menander might have scouted but which anticipates the feeling of some modern readers about Terentian comedy. In reality his deft interweaving of a twofold plot testifies to his originality and independence in craftsmanship. For his language he does not pitch his claim too high in what looks a frank confession of plagiarism (*Eun.* 41), 'naught here is said but has been said before.' A justifiably emended form would run 'what's borrowed here was ne'er so well expressed'; for one of Terence's charms lies in that terse simplicity to which the world owes many quotations expressing familiar thoughts like 'many men, many minds,' 'fortune favours the brave,' and 'while there's life, there's hope.'

His world is Plautus's—with a difference: its characters are more refined, more studied. The very grace of manner and expression in this society makes its lapses more seductive. Young men in amorous difficulties have perhaps a little more initiative than in Plautus—they may seem less dependent on the *callidus servus*: but how unromantic the treatment is! In the *Andria*, though the play turns on Pamphilus' passion for Glycerium and on the question who is to marry Chremes' other daughter, yet the former girl appears only in the background and the latter not at all. Compared with Plautus, there is more dexterous plot-construction, more careful psychology, more finesse in language: there is, however, a falling off in *vis comica* and the gift of song. Terentian comedy awakes not laughter but thought: even smiles are rare. It is a serious and consistent attention to character-drawing which helps towards developing so well-knit a plot as that which in *The Mother-in-Law* leads through a network of cross-purposes to a half-cryptic conclusion. A spectator's psychological interest is at once aroused and the dramatic keynote struck when Menedemus in *The Self-Punisher* is challenged by Chremes to reveal his reason for imposing field-labour on himself. Curiosity regarding a secret in his past is whetted when, by telling the solicitous inquirer to mind his own business, he evokes the most famous retort in Terence:

> *Men.* Chremes, do your affairs leave you alone
>   To mind what's others' business, not your own?
> *Chr.* I'm human: what's a man's affair is mine.

A few simple strokes (*Phorm.* 326 *sqq.*) bring out the airy cynicism
of Phormio's confidence that he can elude detection in impostures
of the sort bequeathed to an English comedy like Vanbrugh's
Confederacy. A clever little scene occurs later in the *Phormio*
(441 *sqq.*) where the dialogue satirizes the futility of friends'
advice by showing that even in a trio of counsellors there is confusion. It is with human sympathy that Terence loves to draw
the easy-going character from several angles. There is a pleasant
irony in the shrewd comment by the freedman Sosia on the
agreeable disposition of young Pamphilus which his father has
been praising (*Andr.* 67–68):

> How wise a start in life—he's up to date.
> Complaisance wins you friends, but frankness hate.

So the bigamist in the *Phormio* has drifted into his predicament
more through weakness than through calculated villainy. Again
in *The Self-Punisher* and *The Brothers* there is a contrast drawn
between strictness and indulgence in handling the young. Inherent kindliness underlies Chremes' character in the *Andria*, and
a similar spirit distinguishes some of Terence's women. Thais, the
meretrix of the *Eunuchus*, with some of the possibilities of *La
Dame aux Camélias*, has sparks of genuine feeling. Notably in
The Mother-in-Law feminine interest predominates; for around
the slighted bride, though she never appears, her bridegroom's
conduct revolves, as well as that of all four parents of the young
couple: the two matrons and Bacchis, once the bridegroom's
mistress, are excellently portrayed.

Caesar's well-known characterization of Terence as 'Menander
halved' is not so much an exact arithmetical valuation as a re-
minder of his adroitness in weaving two dramas into one. His
praise of Terence as 'a lover of pure Latin' (*puri sermonis amator*)
indicates the value attached to sheer literary skill. The dramatist
himself asked for applause on the score of sound idiom: clearly,
then, professors of rhetoric had not taught in vain, when such a
standard could be set up. Fundamentally it is the same quality
which Cicero admired in him:

> O Terence, you alone in choicest style
> Have turned Menander into Latin speech.
> With tones restrained you set him in our midst:
> Much you refined, to all you lent a charm.

Mainly after Terence, and partly because of his literary aloof-
ness, there set in a reaction in favour of *togatae* dramatizing the
everyday life of Italy. Three names stand out here: Titinius,

perhaps slightly senior to Terence; Afranius, an admirer of
Menandrian and Terentian comedy; and Atta, who died in
77 B.C. In this *bourgeois* drama, whose remains are regrettably
scarce, women and family life played a great part, as the titles, no
longer Greek, suggest. Among other plays Titinius composed
A Lady Lawyer, *A Twin Sister*, *A Stepdaughter*; Afranius, from
whom over forty titles survive, wrote *The Girl He Ran Off With*,
Auction, *Divorce*, *A Letter*, and not only *Husbands* but in separate
plays *Sisters* (*Sorores*), *Cousins* (*Consobrini*) and *Aunts* (*Materterae*).
Atta's titles include *The Watering-Place*, *The Mother-in-Law*
(*Socrus*), *Thanksgiving*, and *The Start of the Recruit*. About the end
of the period the Atellan farce was made more literary by Pomponius and Novius. Their adaptations of native drama, however,
could not long hold their own against the coarse and lively mime
imported from Greece through Southern Italy.

In tragedy the Ennian tradition descended through Ennius'
nephew PACUVIUS (*c.* 220–*c.* 130 B.C.), a native of Brundisium, to
Accius (170–*c.* 86 B.C.), who when young submitted his *Atreus* to
Pacuvius for criticism. Neither of the two was so entirely specialist
in tragedy as Plautus and Terence were in comedy; for Pacuvius,
besides his *praetexta* entitled *Paul(l)us*, wrote *saturae*, and Accius,
besides two national dramas, *Brutus* and *Decius*, produced work
(including prose) on literary history and agriculture. But their
strength lay in tragedy, and ancient opinion varied as to which of
the two was the greatest tragic author of Rome. A list of titles,
mainly from Sophocles and Euripides, and fragments amounting
to several hundred lines cannot now give a sufficient basis for a
decision between their merits. Certain qualities, however, stand
out. A cumbrous pomposity in Pacuvius exposed him to Lucilius'
satire; and in imperial days, Persius, solemn young Stoic though
he was, could not refrain from joking at his overstrained compounds or from burlesquing the elephantine legerdemain of his
style in a reference to 'wartful *Antiopa* in tribulation propping her
dolorific heart.' Critics found fair game in a description of dol-
phins as 'Nereus' turn-up-snouted bandy-throated herd' (*Nerei
repandirostrum incurvicervicum pecus*). But there was more in him
than eccentric mannerism. The questioning trend of thought ob-
servable in Ennius is continued by the nephew: and Cicero testifies to his depth of feeling[1]. An elegiac quatrain ascribed to him
has caught the restrained neatness of a Greek epigram and is a
modest epitaph compared with the claims made for Naevius,
Ennius and Plautus:

[1] *de orat.* ii, 46.

> Youth, though thou haste, this stone asks thee to heed
> And look on it, then what is written read:
> 'Here doth Pacuvius the poet lie
> In death. I wished to tell thee this. Good-bye.'

ACCIUS, born on the Celtic fringe of Umbria, wrote over forty tragedies. Like Pacuvius, but with departures from his plot, he treated in an *Armorum Iudicium* the fateful claim of Ajax to the arms of Achilles—a theme burlesqued in one of Pomponius's Atellanes. Accius renders the Sophoclean prayer of Ajax for his son, *virtuti sis par, dispar fortunis patris!* But his most immortal words are those from the *Atreus*—*oderint dum metuant!* At Rome republican sentiment kept such utterances alive. Descriptive power he distinctly possessed. The *Medea* gave a picture of the gigantic Argo, and a choral fragment can still transport one to a shore where the startled seabird circles among the resounding rocks with weirdly sardonic cry:

> simul et circum merga sonantibus
> excita saxis saeva sonando
> crepitu clangente cachinnat.

For some plays, *e.g. Philoctetes*, all three of the great tragic poets of Greece were laid under contribution. He deserved equally with Pacuvius the coveted epithet *doctus*, for he was acquainted with Greek criticism (perhaps both Pergamene and Alexandrian) as well as with Greek drama. Faulty he may have been in chronology and trivial in his absurd contention that Hesiod preceded Homer; but the disappearance of his *Didascalica*, except for a few scraps, left a serious blank in literary history. Among its subjects were epic, drama (Greek and Roman) and theatrical apparatus. Accius is the last great name—and even he but a *magni nominis umbra*—in the chronicle of Latin tragedy. Plays continued to be written and staged in the Augustan age and later; but nothing has survived except Seneca's declamatory dramas, more notable for influence than for intrinsic worth. The question how far Seneca knew or used these early tragic poets of Rome has received various answers[1]. As to *praetextae*, neither Accius's fame nor national interest kept them alive. They tended to degenerate into spectacular pageantry, if we may judge from Horace's disdainful words (*Epist.* II, 1, 189–207) about the ludicrous parade of *captiva Corinthus* on the stage. Tragedy had to be more than a mere show of fallen kings or opulent spoil; and dramatic art could not flourish on a vulgar appeal to the eye. We know, however, of

[1] See J. Wight Duff, *A Literary History of Rome in the Silver Age*, 1927, pp. 252, 256–257.

a few *praetextae* in the first century A.D., but the sole surviving example, the post-Neronian *Octavia*, cannot be expected to recall the notes of the lost republican drama.

VII. SATIRE

Satire was a distinctively Roman invention in the sense of a poem, moderate in length, subjecting to raillery more or less easy-going any theme of public, moral or literary interest. The medley of subjects within its purview and its semi-conversational manner allied satire to prose: scraps of the common speech found an entry into it. LUCILIUS (180–102 B.C.), a native of Suessa Aurunca on the Campanian confines of Latium, called his writings *sermones* ('talks'), and it was he who fixed the type of satire in the main and ultimately its metre, so that from him the other three eminent satirists of Rome, Horace, Persius and Juvenal, drew inspiration. His service under Scipio in 134–133 B.C.[1] negatives his birth in 148, the date got from Jerome. The mistake is best rectified by supposing that Jerome confused the consuls of that year with the similarly named ones of 180[2]. An Italian of good standing, Lucilius was in touch with the Scipionic circle: Scipio's political enemies were his enemies and his butts. Possibly his invectives escaped the attention of the law because lampoons circulating in a friendly coterie did not constitute a public attack as the old Greek comedy did. There is no proof that he ever resided in Greece, though he was well acquainted with Greek manners and thought, and Clitomachus, head of the Academy at Athens, dedicated a work to him. Lucilius' literary activity belonged to his later life, extending from 132 till his death thirty years after. His works were collected in a posthumous edition of thirty books, of which the last five had probably been the first issued in 123; but the whole chronology presents difficulties. Many of his 1400 complete or partial lines (mostly preserved by Nonius) have been patched together with varying plausibility by a series of scholars. Attempts have also been made to infer the themes of different satires in a given book. But while metrical reasons suggest, for instance, that, since Book 28 yields trochaic, iambic and hexametric quotations, it had at least three separate satires, yet transitions of thought are so abrupt in a satiric medley that different subject-matter does not necessarily imply a different satire.

---

[1] Vell. Pat. II, 9, 4.
[2] M. Haupt, *Jahrbücher für klass. Phil.* cvii, 1873, pp. 72, 365. Cichorius, *Untersuchungen zu Lucilius*, prefers 157 or 167 B.C.

Caution is imperative when it is found that in Book 26 one scholar distinguishes three satires, another four, a third seven. Without problematic reconstruction, however, we may illustrate from the fragments of this book the diversity of his topics: it touches on aims in writing, on history, tragedy, marriage, luxury, management of life, literary squabbles. So with the rest: everything in human experience which might attract or offend this intensely critical *ego* went to constitute an astonishing miscellany. His own personality, too, interested the author so much that Horace admired the way in which the old man's life (*vita senis*) stood out in his books as if in a picture. Frank self-disclosure had its counterpart in outspoken strictures on the grievances, abuses, shams and oddities of the Gracchan age. Aggressive personalities, a dramatic ring, and actual Aristophanic echoes link him in spirit with the old Attic comedy, and go towards justifying Horace's too sweeping declaration of his dependence on Eupolis, Cratinus and Aristophanes. His indignant fervour was bequeathed to Persius and Juvenal. But he had a lighter vein. Jests were launched at Albucius' Greek ways and at his style (*lepide* λέξεις *compostae*):

> A smart *compote de phrases* like pavement-cubes
> In wriggly lines inlaid mosaic-wise.

In Book I the amusing debate among the gods (whether Rome should perish or the unjust judge Lupus die) was a Naevian and Ennian device thus handed on to Seneca's *Apocolocyntosis*: as in the imperial skit, Lucilius introduced the deities in senatorial fashion to parody the rhetoric of the day—'how mankind worries, and how vain is all!' (*O curas hominum! O quantum est in rebus inane!*). Book III contained the pattern for Horace's *Journey to Brundisium* (Porphyr. *ad Sat.* I, 5). The extant scraps of Lucilius' *Journey to the Sicilian Straits* relate to muddy roads, the ups and downs of the route, places visited, a Syrian hostess, deficiencies in food—just teasingly enough to make us wish for the full tale. Elsewhere literary epistles handled questions of expression, grammar, orthography or the style of other poets. He allowed himself compounds like *monstrificabile* and *contemnificus*; but he seems to be glancing at Pacuvius in his verbs for a burglar's raid, *depoclassere* ('debeakerize') and *deargentassere* ('desilverplatize'). If those poems were none the better in Horace's eyes for being written by Pompey's grand-uncle, and if they fell short of the Horatian standard of elegance, still as an experiment Lucilius' adaptation of the hexameter was not to be despised. Rambling talk was compatible with skill and vigour, while his final adherence to the hexameter was endorsed by its acceptance throughout Roman literature as the proper medium for satire.

VIII. PROSE—HISTORY AND ORATORY

An era of self-consciousness and reflection tended to produce prose as well as, though more slowly than, poetry. The task of history, the literary re-creation of the past, was even harder than that of oratory. The pattern of the *annales*, an arid string of occurrences, made a deadening weight for experimenters in historical composition. In its earlier phases history was simply annalistic[1] and, as a more critical age felt, nothing could be drier[2]. A long way, then, had to be travelled before prose became either artistic or scientific; but the desire for improvement grew. Quintilian remarks that without advance on models Rome in his day would have had nothing better in history than the pontifical annals[3]. This aim at a higher standard is evident in the distinction drawn by Sempronius Asellio (who served under Scipio in 134) between annals baldly recording events in order and history investigating motives and reasons. Shortly before 200 B.C. the first prose history of Rome from its origins was written. It was composed in Greek by the senator Fabius Pictor (cf. vol. VII, pp. 316 *sqq.*). For material he relied mainly on pontifical records, treaties, laws, family archives and oral tradition. That he used Greek was not entirely due to his recognition of the supremacy of the Greeks as historians: he had also a patriotic wish to produce an account of Rome's wonderful rise which should be read by Greeks and impress the world. His not unnatural Roman bias incurs the censure of Polybius, who, however, acknowledges that veracity which won Fabius respect from Livy and the elder Pliny. The story of Romulus and Remus taken from him by Dionysius (I, 79 *sqq.*) gives an inkling of his straightforward manner in narrative. It was probably a later Fabius who turned his work into Latin. Three other Roman historians used Greek—Cincius Alimentus (a man of military experience and one of Hannibal's war-prisoners), whose *annales* from 729 B.C. were outlived by those of Fabius; Albinus, praetor in 155 (fifty years after Cincius), whose apology for his Greek did not deter Polybius from calling him a babbler; and Acilius (or Aculius) who started from the

---

[1] Cic. *de or.* II, 12, 52, *erat historia nihil aliud nisi annalium confectio.*

[2] *de leg.* I, 2, 6, *annales pontificum maximorum quibus nihil potest esse ieiunius.*

[3] *Inst. Or.* X, 2, 7.

legendary age and was perhaps identical with the interpreter for the Athenian mission of 155. It is noticeable that, while the early poets were mostly strangers and of humble rank, the prose-writers were Romans of old family, themselves makers of history.

A great stimulus towards the development of Latin prose was given by M. PORCIUS CATO (234–149), 'the Censor,' who stands in the forefront of a group of historians using their own language. Old-fashioned even in his own day to the verge of eccentricity, he transmitted to his great-grandson Cato 'of Utica' the traits of honesty, parsimony and intransigence. He did not confine himself to history. Affecting a brusque disdain for culture, he yet showed a rugged versatility in oratory and in encyclopaedic writings on law, medicine, war and agriculture, of which the last is well preserved. He addressed *praecepta* to his son and wrote verse on morals. Nepos tells us the subjects of the books of the lost *Origines*: I, the kings; II, III, the rise of Italian states, whence the title; IV, V, Punic Wars; VI, VII, later wars down to the plundering of Lusitania by Galba, whom Cato impeached in the year of his death, 149. From this speech, given in *Origines* VII, Gellius cites a passage verbatim. In contemporary history Cato neither spared political opponents nor failed to register his own deeds and words. But apart from insertions in the *Origines* which link together his oratorical and historical style, Cato's speeches were published to the number of about 150, and just as they had been listened to for their pith and fire, so were they enjoyed in the reading. His oratory, as we should expect on the analogy of the extant *de agri cultura*, was blunt and forcible: it ignored polish, but made palpable hits with its homely illustrations. The guiding principle lay in his maxim *rem tene, verba sequentur*; and the moral weight was conformable to his definition of an orator as *vir bonus dicendi peritus*. The artless, if not inartistic, effect in the tautological accumulation of words is seen in this exordium: *multa me dehortata sunt huc prodire, anni, aetas, vox, vires, senectus*. His *de agri cultura*, a quaintly interesting social document, was a handbook for the Italian farmer, and based, far from methodically, on personal notes. Its instructions on details of estate-management, on production of crops, live-stock, vines and olives, on the treatment of slaves, and on cures for ailments, constantly echo the ring of ancient Latin formulae of law or religion. The staccato imperative sentences smack of the Twelve Tables.

A group of Latin annalists, including several consuls, followed Cato. They were L. Cassius Hemina; L. Calpurnius Censorius Frugi, an anti-Gracchan, whose pleasant gift of narrative Aulus

Gellius notes (*N.A.* xi, 14); C. Fannius; Vennonius; C. Sempronius Tuditanus, who treated of Italian aborigines and, like his contemporary M. Junius 'Gracchanus,' wrote upon magisterial powers; and Cn. Gellius, whose interest in such inventions as letters, mud-houses, and mineral medicines attracted the elder Pliny. A more eminent historian was Coelius Antipater, to whose special study of the Second Punic War Livy was beholden. Though he reached no high level in style (Cic. *de Or.* ii, 13, 54), even his limited rhetoric marks a revolt against merely annalistic work. The interest in contemporary history is shown by the publication of the *Letters* of Cornelia, mother of the Gracchi, and of memoirs by sundry public men. Other kinds of learning were also advanced, jurisprudence by the Scaevolae and their legal brethren, astronomy by Sulpicius Gallus (consul, 166) and natural history by Trebius Niger.

In oratory, little survives to illustrate a long list of speakers and speeches. For the most part, we must be content with Cicero's skilled criticisms in the *Brutus* and through them discern a development from the rugged oratory of a Cethegus in the Second Punic War towards systematically grounded eloquence. Steady advance in technique was made on Cato, who, though well worth study, had by Cicero's time come to be neglected as antiquated and harsh—too like the stiffness of archaic statuary (*Brut.* 17, 65 *sqq.*). The three periods in pre-Ciceronian oratory were the Catonian; the Scipionic and Gracchan; and that of Antonius and Crassus. In the first, the funeral speeches by Fabius Cunctator on his son and by Q. Caecilius Metellus on his father circulated for a time; oratorical ability was shown by the elder Scipio, by Sempronius, the father of the Gracchi, and by Aemilius Paullus, who delivered a renowned speech on his Macedonian exploits. The increasing influence of Greek rhetoric is seen in the younger Scipio and Laelius, and then in the Gracchi as well as in their supporters or opponents. Scipio's *oratiunculae* were among the studies of Marcus Aurelius: and in a climax like *ex innocentia nascitur dignitas, ex dignitate honor, ex honore imperium, ex imperio libertas* we note the progress towards variety of rhythm. Of the Gracchi, Gaius was more passionate than Tiberius, and, if too rapid for consummate finish, still the master of an intricate and harmonious period beyond the reach of Cato. M. Antonius and L. Crassus were the great orators in the generation before Cicero, and are introduced as chief interlocutors in the *de Oratore*. Perhaps a jealous patriotism led them to understate their debt to Greek theory and practice, but enough is left to prove that Greek models guided them in rhythm and arrangement. Antonius, expert in marshalling material, stressed an orator's need for wide learning less than did Crassus, whose strength lay in style and delivery: on the other hand, the ideal standard of eloquence set up in Antonius' single published treatise won Cicero's approbation (*Or. 5*, 18–19). Different in many ways, both left an impress on oratorical prose and shaped it further for the supreme touch of Cicero.

It may be claimed that unique interest attaches to a period when the foundations of Latin literature were well and truly laid. The Roman power of response to Greek epic, drama and prose, and Alexandrian erudition, has been everywhere manifest. If the imported hexameter eclipsed the native Saturnian, a national ring is unmistakable in the Ennian epic itself and explains its powerful attraction for Virgil. An equally national spirit pervaded Plautine anachronisms, Lucilian invective, serious *praetextae*, light *togatae*, history, law and eloquence. While we may view the period as an indispensable preliminary to the Golden Age, yet its own positive achievement deserves clear recognition. In language, advance was marked. At the outset, aspirants after artistic production had little, except archaic poetry, ritual chants, and legal formulae, to draw upon outside the common tongue. Two vitalizing forces, however, were operative: Greek was a stimulating model, and the fulness of the national life supplied sustenance. The prime material lay, not in a conventional vocabulary weakened through over-use or divorce from reality, but largely in the speech of ordinary folk. We come nearest to this *sermo cotidianus* in the rollicking dialogue of Plautus; but in general it made a memorable contribution to the earliest literary phases before a sublimated diction was evolved. Prose and verse alike owed a great debt to the varied features of colloquial Latin— its forthright strength, its preference for a forcible word over a feebler synonym, its penchant for long compounds (despite a liking for simplicity), its turn for diminutives, now tender, now disdainful, and its readiness to invigorate conversation by expressive novelties. Out of such material a long process of inventive refinement hammered the Latin of literature. In Ennius especially uncouthness is outshone by dignified utterance, sometimes indeed by a strange beauty which seems a harbinger of romance. Finally, as regards literary accomplishment, Roman drama may almost be said to have lived its life during this period; epic and satire took a form which influenced every Roman successor in these fields: in prose, miscellaneous learning, including criticism and philology, began its career alongside of notable development in oratory, history and law.

CHAPTER XIV

ROMAN RELIGION AND THE ADVENT
OF PHILOSOPHY

I. INVESTIGATION AND SOURCES OF INFORMATION

THE constitutional aspect of the religion of Rome organized as a State-cult—the place of the *ius divinum* in the city-community—and its institutional development under the Colleges of the *pontifices* and *augures* have been dealt with in a previous chapter (vol. VII, chap. XIII). Frequent reference too has been made (vol. VII, chaps. XI and XII) to Roman religious customs and cults in so far as they afford evidence for the reconstruction of the early history of the Latins and the Romans. It is the task of the present chapter to trace the 'religious experience' of the Roman people from the time when they were one of the many agricultural settlements of Latium to the period at the end of the second century B.C. when Greek philosophy came to Rome and laid its hold on the educated classes as a substitute for a 'creed outworn.'

Until comparatively recently scholars and historians were content to accept the strange Graeco-Roman compound, which dominates the poets and is criticized and commented on by Roman and Greek writers on antiquities, as the true Roman religion, to believe that Juno, Mars and Venus were indeed the Roman counterparts of Hera, Ares and Aphrodite, as fully anthropomorphic in their conception and as fully endowed with character and history. It has been the task of students of Roman religion for the last half-century to unravel the tangled skein, to clear away Greek and Etruscan accretions, to remove borrowings from other Italic peoples and so to present a picture of the early religion of Rome. As regards the later stages the task presents no great difficulties; it is possible to trace the period and circumstances and in many cases even the dates of the introduction of Greek and Oriental cults; historical records are available. With the growing knowledge of things Etruscan the changes brought about by the Etruscan domination can be recognized with greater certainty. But the genuine religion of the Romans, prehistoric and unrecorded, has to be pieced together by a process of excavation and inference. We have not, as we have in dealing with Greek religion, a wealth of mythology, from which ritual and belief may be inferred, nor of art, which may be taken as a representation of popular conceptions; for an animistic religion, which knows nothing of 'gods,' but only of vague 'spirits' or 'powers' (*numina*), can have neither art nor mythology, and both, when they appear in Rome, must be regarded with suspicion as evidence of Greek influence, coming either directly from Greek sources or through Etruria. Nor again for similar reasons can archaeology help much; it can tell of burial customs and thus by inference something of beliefs as to the condition of the dead, but little of deities who had no sensuous representation or symbols and did not dwell in 'temples made with hands.' Considerable assistance is given by inscriptions, though these are all of a later age and usually contaminated by later ideas; most valuable among them are the Calendars[1], drawn up under pontifical influence, and though these date only from the first century A.D., yet they preserve a true record of the ancient religious year of the 'religion of Numa.' The bulk of the evidence comes of course from literature, but it has to be used with discretion. The explanations of Roman and Greek antiquarians can never be accepted without question, for they had little understanding of the mental attitude of the people among whom the Roman religion grew up. But their records of custom and ritual are invaluable, for if the facts are known, comparative religion and the insight which we now have into the mind of primitive man can make interpretation often probable, sometimes certain. And of such facts, thanks to the intense conservatism of the Roman mind, which jealously preserved ritual long after its meaning was gone, there is happily abundance. They are embedded[2] in the remains of Roman antiquaries such as Cato, Nigidius Figulus, Verrius Flaccus (who is partially preserved in Festus) and Varro, whose *Antiquitates Rerum Romanarum* was the chief source of information to later writers, in the surviving *Antiquitates* of Dionysius of Halicarnassus and the *Roman Questions* of Plutarch; in the theological dialogues of Cicero and the miscellanies of Aulus Gellius and later of Macrobius; in the poets, especially in the *Fasti* of Ovid and the casual references of Plautus, Virgil, and Horace; in the incidental records of the historians, and mainly of Polybius and Livy; in the comments

---

[1] The remains of nearly thirty Calendars have been discovered, the majority ranging in date from about 30 B.C. to the time of the Emperor Claudius. The most interesting are the Fasti Maffeiani, in which the year is almost complete, and the Fasti Praenestini, which contain comments probably coming from Verrius Flaccus; see *C.I.L.* vol. I, pp. 293 *sqq.*; Wissowa, *Religion und Kultus der Römer*, pp. 2, 3; and Warde Fowler, *Roman Festivals*, pp. 11–13.　　　　[2] See vol. VII, pp. 329 *sqq.*

of scholiasts and in particular of Servius on Virgil, and in the fierce attacks of the Christian Fathers, especially of St Augustine, who has preserved for us many of the facts recorded by Varro about the pontifical *indigitamenta*. The task of collecting the information may be said to be almost complete, but much has yet to be done in the way of interpretation, and there are many puzzles for which a solution can hardly be expected. In the following sections an attempt has been made to put together the salient features of the genuine Roman religion and to trace the lines of its modification under alien influences.

II. TRACES OF PRIMITIVE IDEAS AND CUSTOMS

The early religion of Rome, thus disentangled from its later accretions, has been described above as a 'well-developed Animism.' This description is in the main true, but it is rough and insufficiently comprehensive; for in fact the early religion is itself composite. The greater part is undoubtedly due to Indo-European invaders from the north, for ethnology has established that tribes of Indo-European race were in the first millennium B.C. settled all over Italy with the possible exception of Etruria; moreover, the undoubted identity of the Greek and Roman sky-deities, Zeus and Juppiter, associated among both peoples with the sacred oak, and of the hearth-spirits, Hestia and Vesta, are sufficient to show that some elements at least in Roman religion—and those not the least developed—must go back to a period before the two groups of northern invaders descended into the parallel peninsulas. But archaeology has revealed among the early inhabitants of Italy a succession of stages of culture, neolithic, bronze and iron: the first may represent a primitive Mediterranean people, the two latter Indo-European stocks, probably closely related. Which exactly of these ingredients went to the making of the Romans is still doubtful (see vol. VII, pp. 333 *sqq.*), but it is clear that they were a composite stock. Similarly, the religion of the early agricultural settlers in the neighbourhood of what was to be the city of Rome, reveals several strata and modes of thought, some of which go back to a period antecedent to Animism. Occasionally a very primitive practice survives intact and independent, more often it has become embedded in a later animistic cult or has dictated ritual which betrays a primitive attitude of mind[1]. At the other end of the scale some of the vague 'spirits' are already

[1] An interesting account of such survivals will be found in H. J. Rose's *Primitive Culture in Italy*, pp. 63–110.

acquiring names and personality, and functions which extend beyond the restricted sphere of a *numen*.

Among these primitive elements may be reckoned first a certain class of rites concerned with sacred objects and in particular with stones, which, although in a later period they were associated with a deity, were clearly in origin themselves sacred and possessed divine or magic power. Such for instance was the ancient *silex* preserved in the temple of Juppiter Feretrius and used alike by individuals taking the most solemn oaths and by the *fetiales* in the striking of a treaty. The stone was in historical times known as Juppiter Lapis, but 'it is clear enough that the stone is older than Juppiter[1].' Such again was the 'Dripping-stone' (*lapis manalis*) preserved near the Porta Capena and used in the magic rain-making ceremony of the *aquaelicium*. Such, too, may have been the *termini*, the sacred boundary-stones of properties, laid with due rites to be annually renewed by the owners of the marching lands (see below, p. 436).

Whether there are traces of a stage of animal-worship among the Italians is a disputed point and it is safest to say that it is 'not proven.' The theory was once held that when an animal or bird is found in constant association with a god, such as Juppiter's eagle, Juno's peacock or Mars' wolf, the inference is that the animal was itself once a god. But it is more probable that the animal, if not a mere accompaniment, is, like the doves of the Cretan goddesses, a sign of the god's epiphany[2]. A nearer approach might be found in the occasions when worshippers dressed themselves in the skins of animals, as did the *luperci* in the skins of the goat-victims, or the priests of Soracte, who called themselves *hirpi* ('wolves'). In such cases it has been held that the worshippers were attempting to assimilate themselves to an animal-deity; but it is simpler to believe that they were striving to acquire the 'mana' which always attaches to animals. Be this as it may, it is clear that the developed Roman religion knew nothing of animal-worship.

The primitive notion of taboo is manifest again and again in the ritual and custom of early Rome, and though it appears as a rule in connection with some well-developed institution, and may perhaps lie at the root of the Roman idea of *religio* as a 'sense of awe,' yet it is in its nature akin to much more primitive ideas. In many ceremonies, both in the private and public cult, such as the worship of Silvanus *in silva* or of Hercules at the Ara Maxima, women were excluded; they were thought of in this connection as

[1] Rose, *op. cit.* p. 46.
[2] M. P. Nilsson, *The Minoan-Mycenean Religion*, pp. 285 *sqq.*

'infectious[1].' Strangers again and slaves are similarly excluded, and men at the rites of the Bona Dea. An odd instance of exclusive taboo was that which forbade the bringing of a horse into the grove of Diana at Aricia (see vol. VII, p. 344). But far the most conspicuous example of taboo is to be found in the regulations which surrounded the person of the *flamen Dialis*, who might not look upon an army drawn up for battle, might not do or see any kind of secular work, might wear no ring or girdle, and might only cut his hair or nails with a bronze knife (see vol. VII, p. 426). Some have seen evidence in these taboos that the *flamen* was originally a priest-king, but without subscribing to that view, we may safely say that the restrictions go back to a remotely ancient conception of a sacred person.

Most conspicuous of all are the traces in Roman ritual of magic, of ceremonies where no deity is concerned, but either man's acts are supposed to constrain nature or the instruments he uses to contain supernatural efficacy in themselves. Reference has been made already to the *lapis manalis* at the Porta Capena, which in times of drought was carried in procession; what exactly was done with it is not known, but it was certainly some process of 'sympathetic magic' intended to produce rain. Of the same character most probably was the much-disputed[2] ceremony of the Argei on May 15, when wicker figures, popularly known as *senes*, were thrown over the bridge into the Tiber—a symbolical wetting of the corn-spirit to procure the fertility of the crops. As an example of a magical instrument—another primitive idea buried in the strange compound ceremony of the *Lupercalia*—may be taken the *februa*, strips cut from the hide of the victim, with which the running *luperci* struck the bystanding women to procure their fertility—a transference, it would seem, of the *mana* of the sacrificed animal. Outside the range of the regular ceremonies of religion popular magic was rife in the *dirae, carmina,* and *defixiones*, designed to bring harm to one's enemies, of which there is abundant evidence. That magic lay behind Roman religion there can be little doubt, though care was exercised to exclude it from the State-cults. Magic and religion are not intellectually compatible—for magic implies an occult power in man, religion an appeal to a superhuman being—but they are often confused in practice.

[1] Warde Fowler, *The Religious Experience of the Roman People*, p. 29.
[2] *E.g.* Wissowa, *Gesammelte Abhandlungen*, x, pp. 211 *sqq.*, holds that the ceremony was of much later date and commemorated the actual sacrifice of Greeks (Argei) at a time of national stress.

III. ANIMISM

The primitive ideas and customs which have just been noticed rest on two main beliefs, firstly that in the power of the sacred person or thing itself to work good or evil, and secondly that in the power of man by symbolical acts to control the workings of nature.

But the main body of Roman religion was based on a conception which anthropologists regard as a later development of the former of these two, the belief, that is, in the existence of 'spirits' or 'powers,' having their abode in natural objects or localities, or concerned functionally with natural processes or with definite activities. These spirits are regarded as having control in their special spheres, and on their favour or displeasure depends the prosperity or ill-fortune of man. Such 'Animism' may itself have many phases or stages of development varying from the cringing fear of evil spirits, which is characteristic of the more savage peoples—the Greek δεισιδαιμονία, the Latin *superstitio*, which is seen in the demon-haunted religion of the Etruscans—up to a stable and, on the whole, happy relation of the 'spirits' and man, which is achieved by the more settled and civilized peoples, the relation which the Romans designated by *religio*. The religion of the early Roman was by no means free from the element of fear— indeed the word *religio* itself probably denotes primarily a sense of awe or anxiety[1]—but, in the main, he believed that it was possible to establish and maintain a friendly understanding between 'spirits' and men. The object of his cults was the preservation of the *pax deorum*.

The *numina* whom the Romans worshipped were not, any more than the gods of the Greeks (vol. II, pp. 609 *sqq.*), 'personifications of the powers of nature.' There is no trace in the early religion of any worship of sun, moon or stars; the cult of Neptunus suggests no connection with the sea, a connection almost certainly due to his later identification with Poseidon; nor is there any Roman cult of wind-gods or storm-gods. Individual springs and streams and rivers were no doubt to them the abode of spirits, but their functions were strictly limited and local. In two instances alone could a case be made out for 'nature-worship.' Juppiter, the sky-god, was, as has been seen, an Indo-European inheritance and though he early attained a wide development, the Calendar suggests that his functions too were originally limited, for his special festival is the *Vinalia*. Of wider significance was Tellus, the earth,

---

[1] Warde Fowler, *Roman Essays*, pp. 7 *sqq.*

to whom an offering was made at the *Feriae Sementivae* in January to secure the fruitfulness of the sown seed, and pregnant cows sacrificed at the *Fordicidia* in April, a clear survival of a magic fertility rite; but in both of these ceremonies the worshipper is more concerned with his own particular plot of earth and not with any wide conception of the 'Earth-Mother': Tellus is not Demeter.

The 'spirits' are at once more limited and vaguer in conception than nature-powers. The word *numen* appears to denote 'a being with will-power,' and it is as such that the 'spirits' are approached by their worshippers. The older and simpler notion of the *numen* is of the indwelling spirit of a place or object. A grove (*lucus*) may be his abode and it must not be entered save with a sense of awe and due offerings made to secure his goodwill; the ritual of the Arval Brethren enjoined an expiatory offering (*piaculum*) if a tree in their grove, or even the branch of a tree, fell through old age or storm (*vetustate tempestateve*). A spring, a hill-top, or almost any chance locality might similarly be the abode of a *numen*. So in the house the door, the hearth and the store-cupboard are the sacred spots, where the *numina* live; on the farm they dwell in the boundary-stones (*termini*) and in the places where properties marched (*compita*), the seat of the worship of the field-spirits (Lares). And in the wilder land, on the borders of civilization, lived the Fauni and Silvanus, the denizen of the woods. But what marks out the religion of Rome as a 'higher Animism' is the extension of the *numen*-idea from sphere to function, the association of 'spirits' with actions, occasions and activities as well as with places. This is prominent throughout the festivals of the agricultural year, which are recorded in the Calendars. The 'spirits' are not there localized; they may be summoned to help by any farmer, wherever his land may be, provided that he appeals to them on the right occasion. It would be useless to pray to Consus, the spirit of the harvest-home, to assist in the sowing of the crops, or to Pales, the guardian of the flocks and herds, to protect the vine; each 'spirit' has its own function and must be worshipped and propitiated accordingly. The notion of function had ultimately more vitality in Roman religion than the notion of sphere and was immensely elaborated in the priestly *indigitamenta*, which assigned petty *numina* to every stage and action of human life.

The conception of the *numen* was also vague; there is no sense of a well-defined personality, such as that of a Greek god. It is often difficult to discover, as for instance at the *Lupercalia*, to what deity a festival is addressed and the solution may be that in origin the appeal was made 'to all *numina* concerned.' *Sive mas sive femina, sive deus sive dea,* are constantly recurring prayer-formulae. Again, certain 'spirits' are thought of in groups and not as individuals, such as the Lares, the 'spirits' of the field, the Penates, the 'spirits' of the store-cupboard (*penus*), who were only individualized and identified with other existing gods at a much later period, when anthropomorphism had come in. And even when the 'spirits' have names, these are in most instances either the name of the object with which they are associated, such as Fons, Tellus, Ianus ('door-way'), or more often an adjectival formation indicative of locality or function, such as Silvanus, Saturnus, Consus, Portunus, and others obviously of like formation, though we do not know the function which they expressed, such as Neptunus, Volcanus, Volturnus. 'Saturnus suggests no personality, but rather a sphere of operations in which a certain *numen* is helpful[1].'

The attitude of man to the 'spirits' is primarily one of awe; it starts from fear. And in some of the acts of worship fear is still uppermost: the ritual is apotropaic, the 'spirits' concerned are evil and must be banished. This is perhaps most apparent in the ceremonies of the *Lemuria*, the older of the two festivals of the dead; the spirits of the dead are hostile and must be exorcised —*manes exite paterni*—like the κῆρες of the Greek Anthesteria; it is seen, too, in the precautions taken to keep off evil spirits in the ceremonies attendant on birth and death. Normally the 'spirits' are not regarded as essentially hostile, but rather as neutral powers, whose goodwill can be secured, if the appropriate offerings are made to them on the appropriate occasion in the appropriate way. And so man's life among the community of the 'spirits' comes to be looked on as a kind of compact, or when Rome later had developed her city life and her strong sense of law, as an almost legal contract. The worshipper offers the 'spirits' their due, be it the solemn blood-offering of the *suovetaurilia* or the simplest rustic gifts (*farre pio et saliente mica*[2]), and then, if all is rightly performed, the 'spirit' is expected to reply with the gift of prosperity for himself, his household, his cattle or his crops for which he has prayed. And so the most frequent form of prayer is the expression of this anticipation: 'Juppiter, I offer thee this cake and pray my prayer aright, *in order that* thou mayest be kind and propitious to me and my children, to my house and household.' The spirit is not quite constrained, but is expected to do his duty.

[1] Warde Fowler, *Religious Experience*, p. 118.
[2] Horace, *Odes*, III, 23, 20.

It is manifest that this scrupulous care in the performance of
the human part of the cult-contract would result soon enough in
a meticulous formalism. And this is obviously so from the first.
The right deity must be addressed at the right place, the offerings
must be rightly chosen, the 'mola salsa' will not suffice when a
blood-offering is required, nor must male animals be offered to a
female deity. The traditional prayer-formula must be recited without slip or change; if anything is omitted or altered, the whole
must be repeated from the beginning. The Roman was not always
averse to subterfuge in covering lapses in the almost impossible
liturgical rigidity demanded of him. It was common to engage
the services of a *tibicen* to play during the sacrifice in order to
drown by his music any unfavourable speech or profane noise;
by a series of *piacula* the worshipper might atone for various faults
and mistakes committed in the main ceremony; by the offering
of the *porca praecidanea* before the beginning of the harvest atone-
ment was characteristically made beforehand for any error which
might occur. But the exception and its solemnity show more clearly
the binding character of the obligation of exact ritual; it was indeed
a 'burden heavy to bear,' and it made directly for the stereotyping
of religious practice, which later deprived it of its reality.

These general characteristics of the early religion may be illustrated by the quotation of a prayer-formula[1] of the Roman farmer
to be recited when a clearing is made in a wood. 'Be thou god or
goddess, to whom this wood is sacred, as it is right to make
expiation by the offering of a pig because of the clearing of this
sacred wood, for this cause, that all may be rightly done, whether
I have done it or another at my bidding, on this account, as I
sacrifice this pig as expiation, I make pious prayer that thou
wouldest be kind and gracious to me, my home, my household
and my children; for which cause be thou enriched (*macte esto*)
with the sacrifice of this pig for expiation.'

The application of these ideas may be seen first in the cults of
the household and then in the worship of the fields.

IV. CULTS OF THE HOUSEHOLD

The household was the prime religious unit. Though from time
to time the actions of the individual and important occasions in
his life might form the motive of household celebrations, the individual as such had no direct relation to the 'spirits,' but only as
a member of the family group. The group, consisting of all the
living descendants of a living ancestor together with their wives

---

[1] Cato, *de agri cultura*, 139.

and the slaves and dependents, were united under the rule of the *paterfamilias*, who in all religious matters was the family priest.

The household gods were few in number and in character form an interesting illustration of the various phases of Animism which were noted in the last section. Two of them are well-defined local 'spirits' with names and a clear sphere of action. One Ianus[1], 'the door-way' (*ianua* is a by-form), is the natural religious focus of the household in its relation to the outer world; it 'faces both ways,' by it the members of the family 'have their exits and their entrances,' it admits friends and excludes foes. Ianus is therefore in the later period of sensuous representation depicted as two-faced (*bifrons*). Oddly enough we have no record of the domestic cult of Ianus, and it is indeed an inference from the State-cult; but his position at the head of all invocations addressed to many spirits is sufficient indication of his importance. Vesta was, as has been noted, an Indo-European inheritance, and to the end she remains uncontaminated by anthropomorphism, the 'spirit of the hearth-flame,' the internal focus of the family life, the source of warmth and the provider of the family food. Her worship was never neglected, but was usually combined with that of the other household deities. As Ianus begins, so Vesta must close, the roll of deities in prayers. The Penates are a conspicuous example of a nameless 'spirit-group,' the guardians of the store-cupboard, 'whoever they may be.' Later on each household would select its own Penates among the known gods and in Pompeian shrines we find little statuettes set out, recognizable as Venus, Asclepius, and so on. Closely associated with the Penates is the Lar familiaris—the plural Lares does not occur in connection with domestic worship till Augustan times—a 'spirit' whose origin is disputed; he was once believed to be the family ancestor, but it may be taken as almost certain that he was one of the field Lares (see below, p. 436), brought in, as it were, to the house by the *familia* of slaves and adopted by the whole household.

The combined worship of Vesta, Penates and the Lar took place at the hearth (*focus*) and was of a simple character. There is evidence of 'family prayers' at the beginning of the day, but the chief offering was made at the main family meal. On the table, set before the hearth, lay the sacred salt-cake (*mola salsa*), and during the meal a portion of it was placed on the sacrificial dish (*patella*) and thrown into the fire. The meal could not be resumed

---

[1] In a brief sketch it is necessary to be dogmatic and to ignore alternative theories; *e.g.* many scholars would see in Ianus a masculine form corresponding to Diana.

till the announcement had been made '*di propitii*,' and the scrupulousness of ritual is testified by the requirement of a special *piaculum* in case any crumb of the cake fell on the floor (*piaculum cibi prolapsi*). Pompeian drawings show a more elaborate family ritual, the *paterfamilias* standing by an altar with veiled head (*operto capite*, as always at Rome), the sons acting as acolytes (*camilli*) and bringing the victim, the *tibicen* playing in the background.

Rather apart from the other domestic 'spirits' lies the typically Roman conception of the Genius. Roman theory held that every male had his 'genius' and every woman her 'iuno[1],' not quite the 'soul,' which maintained life and departed at death, still less an attendant 'spirit,' like the Greek δαίμων, which acted as a 'guardian-angel,' but rather, consistently with the general run of Roman ideas, the *numen* indwelling in the man or woman. That *genius* means 'the begetter' there can be no doubt, and its constant association with the marriage-bed (*lectus genialis*) bears this out; the idea which the word thus conveys is just the virile powers of the man, which make primarily for the continuance of the family; the woman's 'iuno' may be similarly the powers in her which fit her to be a bride. But this is to some extent theoretical, and the Genius actually worshipped in the household is always that of the *paterfamilias*, the ultimate author of the family's continuity, and the main celebration took place on his birthday. The idea proved capable of almost infinite extension and was one of the elements which paved the way for the worship of the emperor.

Family worship thus implied and maintained the sanctity of family life (*pietas*), and its ideas are those of the developed Animism which is the main basis of Roman religious conceptions. An examination of the ceremonies attendant on the important occasions of family life, birth, puberty, marriage, death—the 'rites de passage'—shows a similar connection with religion, but it is interesting to find that here the underlying ideas are on the whole more primitive. Thus the custom that after the birth of a child three men should strike the threshold with staff, axe and broom in the name of the obviously functional 'spirits' Pilumnus, Intercidona and Deverra is clearly an early apotropaic rite, and though in later times it was said to be directed against the incursion of Silvanus, it is probable that the original enemy was a vaguer host of evil powers. Similarly, the *bulla* which was placed round the child's neck on the ninth day after birth was a magic charm against

[1] It is doubtful whether this idea is as old as that of the Genius; but see Wissowa, *Religion und Kultus der Römer*, p. 182.

evil and probably took the primitive form of the *fascinum*. It was solemnly laid aside when he assumed the *toga virilis* in his seventeenth year. So again in the marriage ceremony the parting of the bride's hair with a spear-point, the obscene jests with which she was greeted on her journey to her new home (*fescennina locutio*), the carrying across the threshold, were all designed to insure good 'luck,' to avert evil influences and sterility and to promote fertility—all charms and symbols of magic power rather than religious acts. In the most solemn form of matrimony, however, the *confarreatio*, blessed by the presence of the *pontifex maximus* and the *flamen Dialis*, we have a higher conception in the partaking of the sacred cake of *far* by bride and bridegroom in communion with one another and with the gods. At death, although there is little ceremonial which is not merely secular, the intention seems to be the cleansing of the house and the survivors from the pollution caused by the presence of the dead body, and precaution against the return of the dead as an unholy visitor.

This interpretation is borne out by what can be gathered of early burial-customs and ideas of the relation of the living to the dead. The usual practice for the disposal of the dead—at any rate in the nobler families—was cremation, but the early Italian cemeteries show the burial-urns huddled together indiscriminately without marks of identification or care for any individual grave; later, no doubt, there were family vaults and tombs, but the special tomb of the particular person belongs to the highly civilized period of the late Republic. In correspondence with this practice the dead are thought of as the undiscriminated mass of the *di manes* ('the kindly gods'), a term which may originally have included the chthonic deities as well as the human dead; the specialization of the *di manes* of an individual, so common in imperial inscriptions, is not met with till the last century of the Republic. There is no information as to any clear conception of the state of the dead; and the terrors of the future life, against which Lucretius argues so passionately, and which we must suppose held the popular mind in his day, were derived from Greek sources. Similarly, the notion of the permission to the dead to return at the opening of the *mundus* on three days round about the time of harvest, may well be a Graeco-Roman[1] accretion (which may be compared with the ceremonies of the *Anthesteria*) on an original agricultural ceremony, the opening of the subterranean storehouse. The two festivals in the Calendar which were undoubtedly connected with the dead, the *Lemuria* in May and the *Parentalia* in February,

[1] Warde Fowler, *Roman Festivals*, p. 211.

reveal, as has often been pointed out, two different attitudes towards the *di manes*. The *Lemuria*, as we know it from Ovid's vivid description, is essentially an apotropaic rite[1]: the dead spirits are thought of as hostile and must be driven from the house by the spitting of black beans, the clashing of brass vessels and the repeated formula *manes exite paterni*; the days are marked in the Calendars as *nefasti*. That something of this primitive *religio* survived in the later festival of the *Parentalia* may be inferred from the typical chthonic offering of the blood of black beasts (*nigras mactant pecudes*, Lucretius III, 52). But in the main the element of fear is gone and the festival is more a kindly recognition of the dead as still in a sense members of the family, who have a claim as such upon the living (*ius sacrum*). The family graves are visited and decorated with flowers and simple offerings of food and drink —water, milk and honey—are made. The day is not 'nefast' and concludes with a family feast, the *Caristia* or *cara cognatio*.

In all this there are two prominent features, firstly, that the dead are thought of collectively, and secondly, that though offerings are made, there is no idea of prayer or invocation. Such acts of prayer and worship to an individual as Aeneas, for instance, conducts at the tomb of Anchises, are derived from Greek customs of hero-worship. In the genuine Roman religion the dead are neither individualized nor worshipped. This conclusion would of course have to be modified, if it could be established that the Lar familiaris was the dead ancestor of the family, but it has been seen already that the evidence points to a quite different account of his origin.

V. WORSHIP IN THE FIELDS

Besides the cult of the 'spirits' in the house the early Roman was concerned as a farmer with many forms of ritual in the fields. These he conducted either for himself and his family on his own land, or with his neighbours as a member of a *pagus*, the community of farmers in a particular district—possibly in origin that occupied by the *gens*—each of whom probably owned his own arable land and had grazing rights in a common pasturage. These field-cults, too, are addressed partly to local, partly to functional 'spirits,' the former for the most part the inhabitants of the individual farm, the latter the deities operating in the seasonal celebrations of the *pagus*.

The natural local focus of the worship of the farm is the boundary of the property and with it are concerned several of the festivals

[1] *Fasti*, v, 419 *sqq.*

of the farmer's year. The festival of the boundary-stones (*Terminalia*) in February must go back to a remote antiquity; for, though in Ovid's account of the ceremonies they are performed in honour of a god Terminus[1], yet the celebration of the rite by the two neighbouring farmers at the boundary-stone itself, which was garlanded and sprinkled with the blood of the victims, points clearly to a time when the stone was not merely the abode of a 'spirit,' but itself endowed with magic power (see above, p. 426). The *Compitalia*, celebrated at the end of the agricultural year in December, was a festival of the Lares regarded as spirits of the fields, which was held at the places where several properties marched (see p. 429). Here was a shrine of the Lares containing altars looking out on the various properties, the owners of which made simultaneous sacrifice. It was an occasion of general hilarity, shared by the slaves as well as the family, and it is notable that the offering might be made by the overseer (*vilicus*), himself a slave. This is a celebration not so much of the boundaries as of the whole adjacent properties, and the Lares are exactly typical of the true animistic deity, limited in sphere and vague in conception. The most interesting and picturesque of the boundary festivals was the *Ambarvalia*, which occurred in May. Three times the farmer and his household traversed the boundaries of his fields driving the solemn offering of the pig, sheep and bull (*suovetaurilia*) which represented the best of his possessions, and at the conclusion of the third round the victims were sacrificed and a prayer made, of which Cato has preserved us a specimen[2]; its petition is for the aversion of evil influences and the granting of prosperity to crops, cattle and household. Here is an unmistakable lustration, a purificatory rite with its usual double character, apotropaic and fertilizing. It does not seem easy to be certain what deity was concerned: Cato tells us it was Mars; from a famous passage in Virgil[3] it would appear that it was Ceres and in the Acts of the Arval Brethren—if it may be assumed that it was they who performed the *Ambarvalia*—the deity addressed is the Dea Dia. Possibly here again the ritual was originally directed to 'all spirits concerned' and the specialization came later and varied at different periods. But once again the rite is very old and the 'spirits' are local.

The second class of field-festivals consists of those celebrated by the farmers united in their *pagus*, the festivals of the agricultural year recorded in the Calendars. The Calendars belong to the

[1] *Fasti*, ii, 639 *sqq.*   [2] *de agri cultura*, 141.
[3] *Georgics*, i, 343 *sqq.*

period when Rome had already become a city-state, and contain some ceremonies which are only appropriate to an urban community, but with a characteristically faithful conservatism they include the old agricultural festivals which were still kept up in the city-state, though they had lost their significance. These can easily be picked out and are seen to represent the normal activities of the farmer's year.

They fall naturally into three main divisions: first the festivals of preparation in March, April and May, in which prayer is made either for the fertility of the crops, as at the *Liberalia* and *Cerealia*, direct celebrations of fertility deities, the *Fordicidia*, a magic offering of pregnant cows to give life to the young crops, and the *Robigalia*, an apotropaic rite for the aversion of mildew, or, as at the shepherds' festival of the *Parilia*, for the increase and preservation of the flocks and herds. The second group is formed by harvest-homes, the *Consualia* on August 21 and the *Opiconsivia* four days later, and the third by the sowing festival of the *Saturnalia* and a renewal of offerings to the harvest deities in December. June and July were months of waiting; September, October and November contain little of an agricultural character; in January and February—the 'blank period' in the old ten-month Calendar —nothing is noted but a second sowing feast, the *Feriae Sementivae*, and the mysterious and complex festival of the *Lupercalia*, in which part of the intention was no doubt lustration, both apotropaic and fertilizing, as at the *Ambarvalia*.

As a typical example of these rustic festivals may be taken Ovid's directions for the *Feriae Sementivae*[1], a movable feast held in January on the completion of the winter sowing. The cattle, he ordains, should be garlanded in their stalls and the yoke hung up upon a pole; both the earth and its tillers must have a rest. A lustral procession must make the round of the boundaries of the *pagus* and the accustomed cakes (*liba*) should be offered on the hearth of the *pagus*. The 'mothers of the crops,' Tellus and Ceres, should be appeased with an offering of corn and the entrails of a pregnant sow, and prayer made to them for the protection of the sown crops from harm and positively for their fertility. Here are combined many of the characteristic features of the agricultural festival, the garlanding of the herds, as at the *Parilia*, the cessation of work, the lustration, the offering representing both crops and cattle, the symbolic magic of the pregnant sow, the prayer at once apotropaic and petitional.

The agricultural festivals thus confirm the picture derived from

[1] *Fasti*, 1, 655 *sqq.*

the study of the household cults. Worship is nowhere individual, but always that of the group, either the smaller unit of the household or the larger unit of the *pagus*. The offerings symbolize the normal life of the worshippers, a share in the family meal, the produce of the earth, animals from the flocks and herds. Their purpose is purely external: protection from harm for the household, crops and cattle, and the promotion of fertility. There is no moral or spiritual intention in the prayers, yet the union of the family in worship and to a less extent the union with their neighbours in the *pagus* created a bond of *pietas* which was not without its effect in practical life. The rites contain certain primitive elements of magic, but are mostly conceived as petition to 'spirits' to whom their due is rendered. The 'spirits' are often still thought of in the manner of earlier Animism as vague and impersonal, sometimes they are gathered together in indefinite groups like the Lares and Penates. But for the most part they have advanced to a later and more definite stage in which they have names. These are sometimes merely descriptive of their function, like Robigus, Consus, Ops, Saturnus, all clearly limited in sphere or function. Among them, however, even at this early date there are some *numina* who seem well on the way to become *dei*, emerging from animism into anthropomorphism. Of two deities in particular this may safely be asserted, and the test is that they have already begun to transcend the limitation of province. Mars is in this early period an agricultural deity and is so prayed to by the farmer at the *Ambarvalia*; but he is also already a god of war. The development of his military character came no doubt in the period of the State-cult, but the series of military ceremonies in March belong to the oldest stratum of the Calendars and, as far back as it is possible to go, his Salii are armed priests. Juppiter appears in the Calendar at the *Vinalia* with his limited province in the care of the vine; but from the first he is the sky-god, with the control of the lightning by day (Juppiter Fulgur) and the lightning by night (Juppiter Summanus), and from a very early period the sky-god was the deity who watched over the sanctity of the oath, and was thus the first to assume a direct connection with morality. Here the confines of animism are passed, though the puzzle is not yet solved how a developed god, inherited from a time before the invasions of Italy, was embedded in a more primitive and animistic religion. When the first evidence of a synoecism on the Roman hills appears, these two emerge above the rest and with them is united Quirinus, the Mars of the Quirinal-Esquiline settlement (vol. VII, p. 365)—a trio of supreme deities, though not yet a triad. The way has been paved for a State-cult and for anthropomorphism.

VI. THE STATE-CULT OF ROME

In course of time the early agricultural settlement became the city of Rome, and the religion of the State was developed and organized. Its institutional character has already been discussed (vol. vii, chap. xiii), and here an attempt must be made to estimate the religious effect of the change in the minds and lives of the Romans.

In the first place a new religious unit had been created. In the agricultural communities there was the family and the *pagus*, and to these must be added the *gens*, though our knowledge of the gentile *sacra* and their effective influence is scanty[1]. The State embraces them all; through its proper officials it performs religious ceremonies on behalf of the whole community, and by its efforts on a grand scale to secure the *pax deorum* it strives to insure the *salus rei publicae*. The State itself is essentially a religious institution. Later theorists (see p. 464) could speak of the gods as a kind of senior citizens; the city of Rome had, according to tradition, been 'inaugurated' by Romulus with the religious ceremonies always afterwards used at the foundation of a new colony, and the *pomoerium* was a religious rather than a civic boundary, within which the admission of a new cult was jealously guarded. Thus a new and wider focus was applied to the religious conceptions of the Roman citizens. Not merely so, but the State-religion took over the responsibility for the performance of the old cults on behalf of the community, provided for the presence of its own religious officials at many of them, and even claimed to be represented in private rites such as the celebration of marriage by *confarreatio*.

The general character of the transition to the State-cult may be described as conservative adaptation. There was little attempt to construct a religion suited to the needs of the State, or to become aware, so to speak, of other *numina* who might provide for the needs of town-dwellers; the introduction of Minerva was an almost solitary exception. The old *numina* of the household and the fields were taken over and worshipped, as best they might be, within the city-boundaries; adjustment and development were almost accidental or were forced by the change of circumstances. Thus

---

[1] See vol. vii, p. 417, and De Marchi, *Il Culto Privato di Roma Antica*, vol. ii, pt. i, where the evidence is well collected and interpreted.

among the household deities Vesta was adopted as the Hearth of the State and established in her 'home' (*domus*) at the end of the Forum, where the eternal fire, rekindled only on March 1, the first day of the State-year, was tended by her priestesses, the Vestal Virgins. Near her hearth was the *penus Vestae*, the receptacle now of sacred emblems and implements. Ianus becomes the doorway of the State, open so long as the State is at war, closed only in time of peace, and by a characteristic metaphorical transition, the spirit of beginnings, of the opening of the day (*matutine pater, seu Iane libentius audis*, Hor. *Sat.* II, vi, 20), of the first day of the month, of the first month of the year (Ianuarius) in the later Calendar. The *di Penates populi Romani Quiritium* are united in a widely inclusive but still vague conception with Juppiter in the oath of the magistrates, and the household Lar gives rise to the *Lares praestites* of the State. Even the Genius has its counterpart in the *Genius populi Romani* or the *Genius urbis Romae*, though the idea did not become really popular till a later period, and the adaptation was felt to be easier when it could attach itself to the person of the Princeps.

More elastic in their transition were the field-cults at the boundaries. The State *Terminalia* was celebrated at the sixth milestone on the Via Laurentina, at one time the boundary of Roman territory (see vol. VII, p. 400); and the god Terminus, represented of course by a stone, has his place in the great temple of Juppiter on the Capitol, having refused to budge, so it was said, when the temple was built—possibly he was in origin just the boundary-stone between the Palatine and Quirinal settlements. The *Compitalia* were now kept at the places in the city where *vici* (streets with houses) met, at shrines built to the Lares Compitales. The festival, which never had a fixed date till late in the Empire, was celebrated at first by the inhabitants of the neighbourhood and afterwards taken over by the State; here the whole process of transition and adaptation can be followed. In much the same way the *Ambarvalia*, the most persistent of the rites of the field, is not only celebrated as such at the fifth milestone on the Via Campana but gives rise to the parallel ceremony of the *Amburbium*, a lustration of the city-boundaries. In all these instances there seems to be a reasonable adaptation to new needs.

On the other hand, the festivals of the agricultural year were preserved with quite uninventive conservatism. The inhabitants of Rome ceased in course of time to till the land, yet the old festivals appear in the State-Calendar and were celebrated by the State-officials. Sometimes they would go out for this purpose beyond the

city; the *Robigalia* was kept in a grove of Robigus at the fifth milestone on the Via Claudia, the festival of Anna Perenna in the Campus
Martius by the riverside, but for the most part sites in Rome were
chosen with apparently little appropriateness. The *Lupercalia*
was a lustration of the Palatine, Consus kept his harvest-home
at an underground altar in the Circus Maximus and Ops hers in
a shrine in the Regia. It is clear that all this made for unreality;
the fiction of agricultural pursuits in the midst of urban life could
not arouse or retain any real religious feeling among the citizens,
and the keeping of the festivals passed unnoticed, except in so far
as they stopped business either because their days were 'nefast'
—or because they were public holidays (*feriae*). Religion was at
once stereotyped and sterilized.

A similar result was brought about by the institutional development of the State-religion and the placing of its performance on
behalf of the State in the hands of priesthoods and priestly Colleges. It was not necessary for the ordinary citizen to take any
part in the rites which were performed for him. The functions of
the various deities became unknown and inexplicable; Varro[1] tells
us that in his day the very name of Furrina 'was hardly known
even to a few,' and Ovid[2] expresses a naïve surprise and pleasure
at meeting the 'white procession' celebrating the *Robigalia*. The
regulation and formalization of cults by the *pontifices* told in the
same direction and their attempts to rouse popular interest by the
elaboration of little functional deities in the *indigitamenta* had no
effect. The State-religion became a matter of antiquarian interest
without vitality. Under the rule of the priestly Colleges Rome
suffered from 'an arrested religious development[3].'

Yet if ceremonial fiction and sacerdotalism made for the stunt-
ing of true religion, it would be untrue to say that the State-
religion was, in its earlier stages at least, entirely without development. If some of the early agricultural *numina* sank into oblivion,
others expanded and grew both in function and personality.
Prominent among these are the two which had already attained
a kind of pre-eminence in the old agricultural days. Mars, shed-
ding now his agricultural character, except perhaps in the stereotyped ritual of the *Ambarvalia*, waxed mighty in his military
capacity, as war became more and more the business of the Roman
citizen. His altar in the Campus Martius—the god of armies was
never admitted inside the *pomoerium* till the time of Augustus—
became, as it were, the radiating point of Rome's military power.

[1] *L.L.* vi, 19.   [2] *Fasti*, iv, 905 *sqq.*
[3] Warde Fowler, *Religious Experience*, p. 287.

Around it would be encamped the armies which the consul was gathering to take with him on campaign, and the victorious legions waiting for their triumph; it too was the scene of the quinquennial *lustratio* of the whole people, marshalled as the *exercitus*. Even more notable was the development of Juppiter to cover almost the whole field of civic life; in war he becomes the stayer of rout (*Stator*) and the giver of victory (*Victor*), in peace the guardian of oaths (*dius Fidius*) and the custodian of justice; enthroned ultimately in his temple on the Capitol as *Optimus Maximus* he was the centre of Roman patriotism. More and more he emerges into a prominence above the other gods with a spiritual personality comparatively untouched by anthropomorphic representation and legend, and thus, as religious thought developed, it is round Juppiter that there gathers the first tendency to syncretism and monotheism.

A lesser demonstration of a capacity for growth lies in the deification of abstract conceptions. It is possible that this arose through the intermediate cult-title, the Dius Fidius, for instance (an offshoot of Juppiter), giving birth to the abstract Fides, and Juppiter Victor similarly to Victoria. But the habit spread wider, Pax, Salus, Concordia, Virtus and others were given their altars and temples. How far these abstractions had a real religious association, how far they promoted the virtues after which they were named is a matter of doubt—the temple of Concord was re-built after the slaughter of the Gracchi—but the frequency of their formation may be taken as evidence of a semi-conscious desire to secure a closer association between religion and morality.

Despite these signs of life and growth, the general effect of the organization of religion in the State-cult was deadening, and the history of Roman religion from about the period of the Etruscan domination becomes a record of attempts to obtain fresh life by importations from without. The real centres of vitality are the household-cults, and outside Rome in Roman Italy some parts of the field-cult—the 'paganism' of later times—remained alive. Nor must it be forgotten that in the common people there was always a strong element of superstition, which found an outlet at first in the belief in omens, and was ready to accept, when they came, the obscurer forms of divination practised in Etruria, and later the astrology of the Orient.

VII. EXTERNAL INFLUENCES

(a) *Other Italian Peoples*

The agricultural settlement on the Palatine hill was only one of many such throughout Italy and at first it was neither very important nor very advanced. If the view now taken of the ultimate kinship of the majority of the Italian peoples and their general similarity in culture be correct, we should expect to find that the religion of other settlements did not differ materially from that of Rome: a special similarity would be natural among the peoples of Latium, Rome's nearest kin, with greater divergence further afield. And this is indeed borne out; the evidence is scanty and is confined for the most part to cities in close contact with Rome, and to cults which Rome adopted, and it refers mostly to a stage when *numina* had become personalized as *dei* and their cult defined. But there is enough to give some notion of the religious life of the early Italian peoples.

By far the most important evidence is supplied by the famous Iguvine Tables, which were discovered at the Umbrian town of Iguvium (Gubbio) in 1444, but have only recently been satisfactorily interpreted. They give a tradition independent of Roman influence, afford a minute insight into ritual, and, though the existing bronze tablets cannot be placed earlier than the first century B.C., they record very ancient ceremonies; moreover, the strikingly close correspondence of ritual and underlying belief to that which is known of early Roman practice, occurring as it does among a non-Latin people, is strong evidence for a general uniformity of religion among the Italian peoples. The Tables are the records of a religious guild, the twelve *Fratres Attiedii*, who may be compared with the *Fratres Arvales* of Rome, and the most important documents contain directions for two ceremonies, the lustration of the *Ocris Fisius*, the sacred hill which rises at the back of the town, and the lustration of the people; these are preserved in a shorter and earlier form recorded in Umbrian characters, and in a later and more elaborate form, still in the Umbrian language but in the Roman alphabet. A full account must be sought elsewhere[1]: here a few significant points may be noted. Both ceremonies are to be opened by the taking of the auspices: the celestial *templum* is marked out with its counterpart drawn as a guide upon the ground, the 'adfertor' (president of the *Fratres*)

---

[1] Bréal, *Les Tables Eugubines*, Bücheler, *Umbrica*: revised text in Conway, *The Italic Dialects*, I, pp. 409 *sqq.*

takes the omens but is told by the official what he is to observe, and he must make no movement. A procession moves round the boundaries and at certain points there is a halt—notably at the gates, which are the weak points in the religious defence of the city—and offerings are made. The offerings are simple, oxen, pigs and lambs for blood-offerings, cakes for bloodless: the direction at one point '*seu vino, seu lacte*' seems to look back to the period when wine was superseding milk as the libation (see vol. VII, p. 343) and the offering of a dog to the apparently chthonic deity Hondus Jovius may be compared with that at the *Robigalia*. The details of ritual are minutely regulated even to the indication of the arrangement of dress—the head of course being veiled—and of the hand in which the sacred vessels are to be held. The prayers are set out in full and almost surpass Roman examples in their meticulous specification and their wearisome repetition: they are made for the safety and preservation of the sacred hill and the State of Iguvium, for their 'name[1],' and for the prosperity of men, herds and crops. Precaution is taken against mistakes in ritual and prayer: the deity is asked to ignore them (*ne velis*) and directions given for *piaculum* and, if necessary, for *instauratio*. Among the deities addressed Juppiter and Mars are recognized at once, Poimonus suggests the Roman Pomona and the epithet Sancius attached both to Juppiter and to Fisovius, the tutelary deity of the hill, recalls the Sabine Sancus: other deities such as Vofionus, Vesuna, Tursa, and Hondus are peculiar to the Tables and have no parallels. The prayers in the first lustration are addressed mainly to Juppiter, Mars and Vofionus, all with the hitherto unexplained cult-title of Grabovius. The deities in the second seem all to be within the sphere of Mars[2] and are known as Cerfus Martius, Praestita Cerfi Martii, and Tursa Cerfia Cerfi Martii; the prefix Cerfus recalls the epithet *kerriios* in the inscription from Agnone and *cerus* in the hymn of the Salii, and is probably connected with the root seen in *Ceres* and *creare*[3]. The points of contact with Roman ritual are both numerous and close and a Roman would

[1] VI, a, 23. Bréal suggests (p. 72) that *nomen* (*nomne*) is here used in the double sense of 'name' and 'race' as in *nomen Latinum*.

[2] Other deities are similarly within the sphere of Juppiter; Tefrus, Trebus and Hondus Jovius, and Tursa Jovia. These epithets must not be taken to express any personal relationship, but are comparable to the Nerio Martis of Roman religion.

[3] It is difficult not to connect it also with *Ceri*, the title of the curious obelisks still carried in procession at Gubbio on May 15: the festival shows many of the features of a lustration and is closely connected with the sacred hill: see H. M. Bower, *The Elevation and Procession of the Ceri at Gubbio*.

have felt himself at home in all the ceremonies at Iguvium, save for a failure to recognize some of the deities concerned.

The only other record comparable to the Iguvine Tables is the bronze tablet in Oscan from Agnone[1], just referred to, which, besides its constant repetition of the epithet *kerriios*, supplies links with Rome in the mention of Juppiter, Hercules, and Flora.

Such documents are unique and our main information is of the prevalence of certain cults in definite localities. In most cities there appear to have been one or more deities in a supreme position above others—not quite πολιοῦχος in the Greek sense, but holding the same place as Juppiter and Mars did in early Rome. Sometimes there is found a deity who is one of the *di indigetes* of Rome, and the antiquity of the cult precludes the explanation of borrowing from Rome and suggests rather a common Italian origin. Juppiter has already been seen at Iguvium and Agnone and his cult, as a common Indo-European inheritance, was spread all over the peninsula. Juno was a special favourite in Latium: in five Latin towns she gave her name to a month in the year and in many she was worshipped with special cult-titles which afterwards found their way to Rome, Juno Regina at Ardea, Juno Sospita at Lanuvium, Juno Curitis at Tibur, and, perhaps more famous than the others, Juno Lucina at Tusculum. Outside Latium her cult was prominent in Southern Etruria: Falerii, originally an Italic town, though within the borders of Etruria, had a famous cult of Juno Curitis, with which was associated an apparently Greek rite resembling the 'sacred marriage'; Veii was the seat of a famous worship of Juno Regina, who is also found at Perusia, and her association in Etruria with Juppiter and Minerva in the State-triad is attested in many towns. In Umbria she is worshipped as Lucina and Regina in Pisaurum, and in Oscan territory she appears as Juno Populonia. Mars also had a wide popularity: he gave his name to a month not only in Latium and at Falerii but in Sabine communities; among the Umbrians he was worshipped at the ancient city of Tuder, and, as has been seen, played a prominent part at Iguvium, but in Etruria there is little evidence of his presence. Other *di indigetes* may similarly be traced in Italian towns; among the more unexpected of these are Flora, whose cult is found among both Oscan and Sabine communities and the Mater Matuta, who was worshipped in many mid-Italian cities including Cales, Cora and Praeneste.

These are all deities of common Italian stock: others would

---

[1] Text in Conway, *Italic Dialects*, I, pp. 191 *sqq.* Agnone is near the site of the ancient Bovianum Vetus in Samnium.

seem to be more local in character. Several such were prominent in Latium, of whom two at least were justly famous both for their worship in their original home and for their subsequent connection with Rome. Diana was worshipped at Aricia, where her sacred grove at the foot of the Alban Mount was associated with the strange ritual of the *rex nemorensis*; there she would appear to have been the religious centre of an early Latin synoecism or federation, like the more famous Latin league which had its focus in the worship of Juppiter Latiaris on the Alban Mount (see vol. VII, p. 348). Antium and still more Praeneste, where she had the strange title of Primigenia, were the seats of the worship of Fortuna, originally an agricultural *numen* of fertility, then of childbirth, then conceived as able to foretell the fate of children, then a prophetic deity in general: her temple at Praeneste, where men's future was told by the drawing of lots, was almost the Italian equivalent of the Delphic oracle. Similarly, Venus, the protectress of gardens and fruit-trees, and later associated with the vine, had her homes in Latium at Ardea and Lavinium. Outside Latium, Minerva, the deity of handicraft, had her special seat at Falerii, while the cults of Feronia, a fertility goddess of the clan of Ceres, and Vortumnus, a deity, like Venus, of gardens and fruits, were common all over Italy. Finally, from the Greek colonies in South Italy and specially perhaps from Cumae, the worship of Greek gods penetrated the Italian towns and in some places attained to a position of supremacy. Thus in Tibur the Greek Heracles became the chief deity, his name Italicized as Hercules and his cult by an Italian specialization associated with commerce. In the same way the worship of the Dioscuri, their names once again Italicized as Castor and Pollux, was established at Capua, Assisi, Ardea and Ostia and in Latium specially at Tusculum.

It looks, then, as if the religious development among the majority of the Italian peoples—Etruria stands apart and must be treated separately—was parallel to that at Rome and this conclusion is borne out by the ease with which Rome assimilated many of their cults, when she came across them. Polytheism, it has often been said, is never exclusive; if you believe in many gods, why not one more? And the Roman was by nature impressible and acquisitive; the manners and customs, particularly the religious customs, of peoples whom he met in commerce or conquered in war interested him, and he was always ready in a spirit of experiment to take them for his own. And so, as far back as the time of the monarchy, new cults were introduced by Rome from her neighbours, and side by side with the original *numina*, the *di indigetes*, there came to be recognized a class of *di novensiles* or *novensides* ('newcomers'). Diana of Aricia was established on the Aventine according to tradition by Servius Tullius in a shrine described as 'commune Latinorum Dianae templum'—an attempt, it may be, to transfer the Diana-league to Rome (see above, vol. vii, p. 351). To Servius too is attributed the introduction of Fortuna of Praeneste, to whom he dedicated many shrines; prominent among them were the *fanum Fortis Fortunae* on the right bank of the Tiber and the *aedes Fortunae in foro boario*, the latter containing a wooden image of the goddess. Venus was similarly brought from Ardea and established both in the grove of Libitina, which led to a subsequent assimilation, and in the Circus Maximus. Feronia was placed in a temple in the Campus Martius and Vortumnus on the Aventine. Hardly different was the habit of re-establishing the *di indigetes* with a new cult-title and new associations learned from an Italian town; Juno Lucina takes her place on the Cispian hill and Juno Regina on the Quirinal. Each of these *novensides* or re-established *indigetes* must have brought some new element into Roman religious thought and practice and widened the horizon, but there are three of the cults to which special attention must be given, because they mark the beginnings of new contacts made by Rome, which were of lasting influence and importance.

The advent of Minerva to Rome seems to indicate the completion of the transition from rustic to city life. She is pre-eminently the goddess of handicraft, and has under her protection the guilds of scribes and actors, fullers and flute-players, doctors and schoolmasters—a wide range, but clearly indicative of the ordered life of an urban community; she was thus introduced not, as it were, by accidental contiguity, but to meet a new need, which could not be covered by any of the *di indigetes*. That she came to Rome from Falerii may be taken as established, and Falerii is within the borders of Etruria. It has therefore been assumed that she was an Etruscan goddess, introduced at the time of the Etruscan domination as a member of the 'Etruscan triad,' Juppiter, Juno, Minerva, which was established in the great Etruscan temple on the Capitol. Of the building of that temple under Etruscan influence there can be no doubt, nor that the goddess was worshipped under the form Menrva in many Etruscan towns[1]; but the name itself is Italic, not Etruscan, and it is highly probable that Minerva came to Rome before the period of Etruscan domination, and indeed that the triad itself had Roman sanction before

[1] See vol. iv, p. 416. Cf. L. Ross Taylor, *Local cults in Etruria*, p. 242.

it was consecrated in the Capitoline temple. But the introduction of Minerva raises for the first time the question of Etruscan influence.

The establishment of the other two cults, those of Hercules and of Castor and Pollux, marks the first—though as yet indirect—contact of Rome with Greece. The worship of Hercules *graeco ritu*, with unveiled head, at the *ara maxima* in the *forum boarium*, within the *pomoerium*, raises many difficult questions, but it may be taken as established that he is the Greek Heracles Latinized at Tibur in a commercial character marked by the offering of the *decumae*, and that he was brought thence to Rome and placed under the special care of the two patrician *gentes* of the Potitii and Pinarii, possibly the 'patrons' of settlers from Tibur in Rome. The cult of Castor and Pollux is even more clearly Greek in origin. Its introduction was traditionally connected with the building of the temple in the Forum as a thankoffering after the battle of Lake Regillus in 499 B.C., but there is no doubt that the cult had come long before that from Tusculum. The connection of the Twins with oaths and their place in the Forum suggests a commercial character, and the association with horses and particularly with the cavalry is probably of later date.

(b) The Etruscans

Archaeology and the study of language have not yet reached any final conclusion as to the origin of the Etruscan people, and there is still strong support for each of the two very divergent views[1] that they were an immigrant people from Asia Minor and that they were of 'Villanovan' descent with an admixture of 'neolithic' stock, to which they owed their language—substantially the two theories advanced in antiquity by Herodotus and Dionysius respectively. This is no place in which to take sides on this debatable question; all that is essential for the understanding of Etruscan influence on Roman religion is the assumption that they were at some period—whether in their Asiatic home or through commercial relations in Italy—subject to a very strong penetration of Greek ideas and Greek modes of religious cult. Further it must be postulated that in the latter part of the regal period there was an epoch of Etruscan domination in Rome, and that apart from this direct impress there was an early and continuous infiltration of ideas from a people separated from Rome only by the Tiber.

[1] For the former view see vol. IV, chap. XII, for the latter vol. VII, pp. 379 *sqq.*

On these points it may safely be said that all parties would agree.

It used to be the custom of historians[1] to attribute a great deal in Roman religion to Etruscan influence—even such essentially Roman conceptions as the Lares and the Genius—and to suppose that when they became masters of Rome, they forced their civilization on a subject people with such success that it revolutionized Roman ideas and left a deep and permanent mark. Though it would be untrue to say that this idea has been abandoned, it has certainly been considerably modified, largely for two reasons. In the first place it is now clear that many elements in Etruscan civilization were in reality assimilated by them from the Italian peoples, so that even if Rome acquired them through the Etruscans, their origin was Italian. Of the great Etruscan 'deity-triad,' for instance, Tinia, Uni and Menrva, Tinia is indeed a genuine Etruscan deity and his relation to Juppiter is one of identification, but Uni (Juno) and Menrva (Minerva) are purely Italian names; Juno was among the *di indigetes* of Rome, while Minerva, as has been seen, probably came to Rome from Falerii independently of Etruscan influence. Or again, the shape of the *templum*, which is so prominent in the foundation of Roman towns and in the formation of their camps, was once thought to have come from the Etruscans as part of the 'Etruscan' system of augury: it is now known that it has its close parallels among the *terremare* people of the Bronze Age (vol. vii, p. 334). And secondly, the more our knowledge of Etruscan custom and religion increases, the clearer it becomes that Rome had a great power of resistance to Etruscan ideas and tended only to assimilate that which was really akin to her own civilization or assisted in developing it. Etruscan tomb-paintings, though late in date and based on Greek ideas, give evidence of demonic terrors associated with the underworld, which must be an expression of their own demon-haunted religious consciousness. No sign of this religion of terror re-appears in Roman literature or art; the fear of punishment after death, against which Lucretius wrote, is a far soberer thing, derived directly from Greek sources. It is significant again that there is not found in the Roman hierarchy a single deity of purely Etruscan origin.

But though caution must thus be observed in finding Etruscan influence in Roman things, yet it is certain that there are elements in the developed religion which Rome owed to her contact with Etruria. In the first place, Rome certainly learned from Etruria the practice of temple-building and probably the introduction of

[1] See *e.g.* Deecke-Müller, *Die Etrusker*, 1877.

the cult-statue. The true Roman *numen* was worshipped on a *locus sacer*, where there was often an altar (*ara*), not of stone, but of piled sods (*caespites*), which might be covered by a loose open roof and so constitute a *sacellum*. Nor was the vague impersonal 'spirit' ever represented in sensuous form; 'for more than 170 years[1],' says Varro, with characteristic Roman exactitude in chronology, 'the Romans worshipped their gods without images (*simulacra*).' To the Etruscans these things would be known from their contact with the Greeks, and it is significant that the first temple in Rome, to which any date can be assigned, is the great temple on the Capitol, which is said to have been begun under the Tarquins and completed and dedicated in the first year of the Republic to the Etruscan triad Juppiter, Juno and Minerva. The temple was built in Etruscan style, its foundations were of Etruscan masonry and in it was a statue of Juppiter. It is of course possible that some of the ancient temples whose building cannot be dated, such as those of Diana and Minerva on the Aventine, were prior to the Capitoline temple, but none the less the inspiration probably came from Etruria. Thus the existing trend from animism to anthropomorphism (see p. 438) received a strong stimulus, and there is much in Varro's[2] comment that 'those who first made images of the gods for the nations, both removed fear from their States and added error.' The Roman lost fear because the visible representation of the deity bred familiarity: he learnt error because he substituted an anthropomorphic image for the idea of the *numen*, which was at least capable of a more spiritual development.

The other sphere in which Roman religious thought was certainly influenced by the Etruscans is that of divination[3]. That the art was itself undoubtedly of genuine Roman origin is sufficiently proved by the Latin words *auspicium* and *augur*[4]; the observation of the flight of birds was a genuine Roman practice. But the Etruscans had greatly elaborated the whole business of divination and the *disciplina Etrusca* had become a very complicated system[5]. From it the Romans probably derived the framework of the State practice of augury, the division of the sky into *templa* and of the *templa* into *regiones*. Much, too, of the practice of divination by lightning was undoubtedly due to Etruscan 'discipline,' though the old cult-titles of Juppiter Fulgur and

---

[1] Augustine, *de civitate Dei*, IV, 31.

[2] Augustine, *loc. cit.*   [3] See vol. VII, pp. 429 *sq.*

[4] The word *augur* is probably not connected with the root *av*, but rather with *aug* (cf. *Augustus*): the augur 'gives the blessing.'

[5] See further, vol. VII, p. 384.

Juppiter Summanus ('Juppiter of the lightning by day and the lightning by night') suggest an early Roman observation of lightning for purposes of augury. At a later period, too, Rome learnt from Etruria the Greek practice of *extispicium*, divination from the examination of the entrails of animals, though it was not carried out by Romans themselves, but by *haruspices* summoned from Etruria for the purpose. The popularity of Etruscan divination was a downward step in the history of Roman religion: it increased superstition and encouraged the political manipulation of religious practices.

The influence of the Etruscans on Roman religion was thus less than has sometimes been supposed, but in these two respects, the encouragement of anthropomorphism through the introduction of temples and temple-statues, and the superstitious elaboration of divination, it had a lasting and deteriorating effect.

(c) Greece

The beginnings of Rome's indirect contact with Greek religious ideas, partly through the Etruscans and partly through the Italian towns to which Greek influence had penetrated, have already been noticed. But about the end of the regal period a more direct connection was established. The cities of Magna Graecia were still too far away to come into close contact with Rome, but much nearer was the Greek colony of Cumae. Now Cumae was a famous seat of the worship of Apollo and the home of one of the Sibyls, those strange sources of prophecy which had sprung up in several Greek cities in the sixth century. When exactly Apollo came to Rome is uncertain, but Wissowa is clearly right in maintaining that he must have been there at least as early as the beginning of the Sibylline period[1]: he was established in an *Apollinar* in the *prata Flaminia* outside the *pomoerium*, where a temple was erected to him in 431 B.C. The famous legend connects the coming of the 'Sibylline books' with the last of the Tarquins, but it is improbable that definite collections of the oracles existed so early, and more likely that the original *duoviri sacris faciundis* went on each occasion to seek their oracles at Cumae[2]. In any case the start of 'Sibylline influence' must be placed before its first intervention in 493 B.C., when the oracle, at a time of corn-famine, ordered the building of a temple to Ceres, Liber and Libera at the foot of the Aventine. Apollo had been established in his own name, and this new triad is only a thin disguise for the introduction of the Greek corn-

[1] *Op. cit.* p. 293.
[2] See Warde Fowler, *Religious Experience*, p. 259.

deities, Demeter, Iacchus and Persephone, with whom they are henceforth identified. From this time onwards the Sibylline oracles, to meet great crises of famine or war, when the old rites of the *ius divinum* were thought to have failed, ordered the introduction of Greek deities, sometimes with their names roughly Latinized like Aesculapius, sometimes identified with an equivalent Latin *numen*, as Hermes was with Mercurius or Poseidon with Neptunus: the series ends with the advent of the Magna Mater from Asia Minor in 205 B.C.

The historical facts and circumstances of these importations have no great religious significance, but it is of importance to note what changes of ritual came with them and to determine the motive of their introduction and the effect on the Roman mind. There can be no doubt that it was the failure of the State-cult, divorced from the life of the people, which led in a spirit of experiment to these innovations. As war or pestilence or famine pressed hard and no orthodox attempt to secure the *pax deorum* availed to stay it, it was felt that an appeal to a god of a new kind, worshipped in a new way, might prove more effective; it may be that even at this early date magistrates and Senate were deliberately using novelties to distract and soothe an agitated populace.

All these Greek divinities were housed outside the *pomoerium* and until the time of the Hannibalic War the distinction between *di indigetes* and *di novensides* is strictly maintained. But the new deities had their cult-statues, and they were worshipped *graeco ritu*, with the head uncovered, nor was it long before new methods of worship were introduced in which the populace had its part to play. In 399 B.C., in a time of pestilence, the Sibylline books ordered a *lectisternium*: for eight days the images of three pairs of deities, all Greek or the Roman equivalents of Greek gods, were exhibited reclining on couches (*pulvinaria*) before tables spread with food and drink; here was at least a strange popular spectacle. Later on was instituted the *supplicatio*, in which men, women and children, wreathed and carrying branches of laurel, like Greek suppliants, went round the temples making prayer for deliverance or giving thanks for benefits received. Sometimes the two were combined and we read of *supplicationes circum omnia pulvinaria*. Here the people takes religious ceremony into its own hands and the outlet provided is strongly emotional.

In the terrible stress and anxiety of the war against Hannibal further developments and experiments were tried, though they look more like the devices of rulers to provide new outlets for popular feeling than spontaneous outbursts. Already in a time of pestilence in 349 B.C. the Sibylline books had ordained the institution of *ludi scenici*; now in the disastrous year of the defeat at Trasimene, 217 B.C., the authorities ordered the addition of special games, *ludi magni*, to the regular *ludi Romani*, and again in 212 B.C., in response to an oracle of the prophet 'Marcius', were instituted the *ludi Apollinares*. Though in effect the *ludi* contained but little of a religious character in them, and were more in the nature of a public amusement, yet their ostensible purpose was religious—the fulfilment of a vow or the offering of a spectacle pleasing to the gods—and once again the idea of the *ludi* came from Greece. The same year, 217, produced other expedients to relieve popular feeling. A *ver sacrum* was prescribed, the revival of an old Italian custom in which all the products of the year (including originally all male children born) were devoted to the gods; more strange and revolting, a Greek man and woman and a Gallic man and woman were buried alive in the *forum boarium, sacro*, as Livy says in narrating it, *minime Romano*, for human sacrifice, if it ever existed in Roman ritual, had long since been abolished. More interesting for the present purpose was the decreeing of a *supplicatio* and a *lectisternium* in which twelve gods, Greek and Roman side by side, were exhibited on the *pulvinaria*; for the first time, as Wissowa notes[1], the distinction between *di indigetes* and *novensides* was broken down and Greek ritual applied to both. It is the turning-point, and henceforth it may be said that the religion of Rome was not Roman but Graeco-Roman.

So far the cults and forms of worship introduced under Sibylline influence had been solely Greek, but the last Sibylline ordinance in 205 B.C. took a further step: it was announced that Hannibal would have to leave Italy, if the Magna Mater of Pessinus were brought to Rome. In April of the following year the black stone which represented the goddess was solemnly received by Scipio and the noblest women of the State, and deposited in the temple of Victory on the Palatine within the *pomoerium*. It may be that the Roman officials were unaware at the time of the orgiastic worship of the mutilated priests, but they soon came to know it and a *senatusconsultum* forbade any Roman citizen to take part in it. But the example of wild emotion had been given, and it is not surprising that twenty years later the Senate had similarly to suppress the *Bacchanalia*, which had come from Etruria or Magna Graecia and had spread with alarming and disastrous effect among the young people (p. 351 *sq.*). These ordinances may have had an immediate effect, but the gates were now open for the novel and

[1] *Op. cit.* p. 422.

exciting cults of the East and Egypt. The flood did not come till the next century, but the religious temper of the common people was set and not even the judicious reaction of Augustus could turn it back.

While the religious practices of Greece were thus pandering to the emotions of the populace, its literature was having a corresponding effect on the newly-established literature of Rome. Legend and anthropomorphic mythology were the essential background at any rate of the epic and drama of the Greeks, and when they came to model their own new poetry on their Greek originals, Roman poets were in the difficulty that, from the very nature of their animistic religion, there were no stories of Roman gods and heroes to work upon. As for legends, though they made some attempts to work on native subjects, they were content for the most part to write Latin plays on Greek hero-stories, but this would not suffice for mythology. The State-religion had led the way by the identification of the Greek gods with the old Latin *numina*, and in literature this process spread apace. The Greek gods were all given their Latin counterparts and took their names; and on to these Latin gods were foisted all the personal features and characteristics, the relationships and the stories—creditable or discreditable—which had attached to their Greek originals. As early as Plautus[1] we find the relationships of Juno, Saturn and Ops (Hera, Cronos and Rhea) a subject of jesting, and the *Amphitruo* is a burlesque of the amours of Juppiter (Zeus) in the manner of the Old Comedy. It is probable that the heavenly machinery and the elaborate mythology had for the poets themselves an aesthetic rather than a religious significance, and that this 'religion of the poets' had little popular effect except to put the seal on anthropomorphism. The educated classes, who had lost belief in the old religion, were to turn for their consolation to yet one more gift from Greece, philosophy.

VIII. THE ADVENT OF PHILOSOPHY

(a) Greek philosophy in the second century B.C.

The striking changes which came over Greek philosophy in the third century, the foundation of the two new schools of Epicureanism and Stoicism and the new turn in the teaching of the Academy under the influence of the scepticism of Pyrrhon, have been described in an earlier chapter (vol. VII, chap. VII, pp. 230 *sqq.*). The

---

[1] *Cistellaria*, 513 *sqq.*

second century saw no such great revolutions and contains no great names. It was rather a period of consolidation and development, in which the new schools took stock of their position and their relations to one another. Doctrine is defined and applied in new spheres; there is polemic and there is assimilation, and the way is prepared for the eclecticism of the next century, but there is little that is really new. The most salient feature is perhaps the emergence of the picture of the 'Wise Man,' viewed no longer in the abstract but in relation to practical life.

Among the Epicureans modification and development would not be expected. It was a cardinal principle of the school that the system set out by the Master, whom they spoke of as 'a god,' must not be added to, diminished or changed: 'the faith once delivered' must be maintained intact. The fragments which survive of the writings of Epicurus' immediate disciples Metrodorus[1] and Colotes[2] are largely occupied with polemic both against the older writings of Plato and against contemporary critics; they show a certain anxious pre-occupation as to the attitude taken up by the Master to culture and education and in particular to the arts of rhetoric and poetry. The names of the successive heads of the school are known, but little or nothing of their opinions; towards the end of the second century Apollodorus—the κηποτύραννος— is said to have been an exceptionally prolific writer, and his successor, Zeno of Sidon, had a high reputation. But it was left to Philodemus in the next century, possibly under the influence of contact with Stoicism, to take a marked step in the widening of the field of Epicureanism.

The Stoic school showed a greater elasticity of development and could claim a larger number of distinguished teachers, of whom the most prominent were Boëthus of Sidon, a contemporary of Chrysippus, Zeno of Tarsus, who wrote little but had many disciples, Diogenes of Seleuceia (*circ.* 238–150 b.c.), Antipater of Tarsus, who was unable to withstand Carneades to the face, but confuted him in many volumes, and in a later generation Apollodorus of Seleuceia, Archedemus of Tarsus and Crates of Mallus. These leaders extended the principles of Stoicism to new fields and demonstrated the comparative freedom of the school by controversies with one another. That Stoics, like Epicureans, found it necessary to define their relation to contemporary culture is shown by the treatises of Diogenes on music and rhetoric, which were afterwards much used by Philodemus, the Epicurean: the

---

[1] See A. Koerte, *Metrodori Epicurei Fragmenta.*
[2] See W. Crönert, *Kolotes und Menedemos.*

study of speech and of the elements of grammar was also promoted
by Diogenes and became the principal interest of Crates: divination, too, and all the metaphysical questions it implies were studied
by Boëthus and Antipater. In the physical theory of Stoicism the
main focus of interest would appear to have been the question of
the periodical conflagration (ἐκπύρωσις) of the world, which was
an essential part of the strict doctrine. Boethus denied it and
maintained that the world was indestructible[1], giving as his reasons
firstly that no causes of destruction, internal or external, could be
adduced, and secondly that in the intervals between the destruction of one world and the creation of its successor, God, whose
function was to look after the world, would be left idle. In this
view he was followed by Panaetius, while Zeno and Diogenes in
the latter part of his life stated that they 'suspended judgment'
on the question: Posidonius returned to the older view. It was
clearly a vexed problem. Of more significance were the modifications and discussions in the moral sphere. Diogenes openly proclaimed that the end of life is 'reasonableness in the choice of
natural ends[2],' a clear move from the heavenly vision of the ideal
σοφός to a practical life on earth: the notion was pushed a step
further by Archedemus who defined the good life as 'the fulfilment
of all practical duties[3].' Apollodorus showed an inclination to
compromise with other schools when he maintained that 'cynicism
was a short cut to virtue[4].' In something of the same spirit these
later Stoics dealt with problems of casuistry and Cicero[5] gives us
an interesting picture of a discussion between Antipater and
Diogenes as to whether a vendor should always expose the defects
of the article he was selling; the former maintained the strictest
morality, Diogenes allowed a certain laxity. We might well ask
'where is the *sapiens* now?'

These movements in Stoicism are not perhaps of great importance, but they are indicative of a real vitality in the school and are
premonitory symptoms of a certain weakening in the base-prin-
ciples and a tendency to adapt a theoretic system to the needs of
ordinary life.

For some eighty years the followers of the New Academy appear
to have been content to repeat the doctrines of Arcesilas, but
towards the middle of the second century the school produced the

---

[1] Philo, *de incorruptione mundi*, 15, 16.
[2] τὸ εὐλογιστεῖν ἐν τῇ τῶν κατὰ φύσιν ἐκλογῇ. Diog. Laert. vii, 88.
[3] πάντα τὰ καθήκοντα ἐπιτελοῦντας ζῆν. Stobaeus, *Ecl.* ii, 75, 11.
[4] εἶναι γὰρ τὸν κυνισμὸν σύντομον ἐπ' ἀρετὴν ὁδόν. Diog. Laert. vii,
121.   [5] *de off.* iii, 51.

most notable philosophical figure of the epoch in Carneades (214–
129 B.C.). He was a brusque uncouth creature, whose teaching
was almost entirely oral; his doctrines were recorded by his pupil
Clitomachus and are known to us chiefly from the accounts of
Sextus Empiricus and their eclectic use in the philosophical and
theological dialogues of Cicero. He shows himself in harmony
with the spirit of his age in that while he reinforced the sceptical
teaching of Arcesilas and applied it in new fields, he also endeavoured on a sceptical basis to provide a foundation for thought
and practice. His chief contribution lay in the sphere of the 'theory
of knowledge.' Attacking with even greater vigour than Arcesilas
the Stoic belief in the 'apprehensive presentation' (*kataleptike
phantasia*, see vol. VII, p. 237), he yet maintained that we accept
as a practical criterion of truth 'that which appears true' and is to
us 'convincing' or 'probable' (πιθανόν). On this basis he built
up a scale of three degrees of 'probability.' The first stage[1] is that
which is probable in itself: this we may have to accept in circumstances which do not permit of further investigation, as, for instance, when we come upon a party of presumable enemies in a
trench and have to flee without further investigation. But we
never receive a single 'presentation' by itself: there is always a
group (συνδρομή) and the second step in probability is when the
'presentation' is both 'convincing' in itself and 'uncontroverted'
(ἀπερίσπαστος) by any of the associated 'presentations.' Lastly
the greatest security may be obtained when a 'presentation' is
both 'convincing' and 'uncontroverted' and 'tested' (περιω-
δευμένη), when we have examined into all its concomitant circumstances and conditions, place, time, size, distance, etc., and
find that they agree. These various grades of probability are
required according to the importance of the decision to be based
upon them. There is always a liability of falsehood in all our
impressions but 'the presentation is usually true and in practice
we regulate our judgments and our actions by what usually
happens[2].' It is perhaps significant of the bias of Carneades' philosophical interest that his examples are always those in which something is to be done and that the 'tested' presentation is said to be
required 'in matters which tend to happiness[3].'
    In the field of theology, Carneades attacked in true sceptical
manner not only the belief in prophecy and divination, but both

[1] The account here given is that of Sex. Emp. *Adv. math.* VII, 173–189:
this is to be preferred to the slightly different account given by him in *Pyrrh.
Hyp.* I, 227 *sq.* See von Arnim in *P. W. s.v.* Karneades, col. 1968 *sqq.*
[2] Sex. Emp. *Adv. math.* VII, 175.   [3] *Ib.* 184.

the popular and the Stoic conceptions of God and even the belief in a divine being at all, and provided 'an armoury of stock arguments' for use in theological dialogues[1]. Yet, Cicero[2] tells us, 'Carneades did not wish to deny the existence of the gods—for what could be less appropriate to a philosopher?—but only to discredit the Stoic arguments': his destructiveness was largely a delight in argument. In a possibly more serious mood he would have none of the Stoic belief in fate ($\epsilon i\mu\alpha\rho\mu\acute{\epsilon}\nu\eta$) and insisted on man's free-will.

In the sphere of politics he argued, largely from the conflicting views persisting in different countries and different ages, that there was no such thing as justice in itself, but that it was a mere convention, approximating here to the teaching of Epicurus. In ethics[3] he made an elaborate analysis of the six possible theories which could be held of the 'highest good,' according as they selected as the object of desire pleasure, the absence of pain or conformity with nature, and looked either to attainment or to the activity directed towards it: four of the six had in practice been recommended by the philosophical schools. To what view he himself inclined is not clear, but probably he believed that man should aim at 'the first things in accordance with nature' ($\tau\grave{\alpha}$ $\pi\rho\hat{\omega}\tau\alpha$ $\kappa\alpha\tau\grave{\alpha}$ $\phi\acute{\upsilon}\sigma\iota\nu$)[4].

Carneades is a strange figure in the history of philosophy, but he finds his place naturally in the general movement of the second century. As the Stoic was tending to lower his gaze from the abstract idealism of Zeno and Chrysippus to a practical standard for the ordinary man, so Carneades wished to extract from the paralysis of a pure scepticism a foundation of 'probable' thought and 'reasonable' action. For all their polemic the schools were approaching one another.

The first penetration of Greek philosophy to Rome may safely be dated from the knowledge of Greek literature acquired during and after the Second Punic War. Cicero indeed, though he rightly rejects on chronological grounds the old legend of the connection of Numa with Pythagoras, yet believes in an early permeation of Pythagorean influence in Italy, and sees evidence of it in a *carmen* of Appius Claudius Caecus[5]. But this is fanciful, and the first real traces occur at the beginning of the second century, though even then they are vague and sporadic. Ennius was caught by the

---

[1] E. R. Bevan, *Stoics and Sceptics*, p. 133.
[2] *de nat. deor.* III, 17, 44.   [3] Cicero, *de fin.* v, 6, 16 to 8, 23.
[4] See von Arnim in *P. W. s.v.* Karneades, col. 1983.
[5] *Tusc. Disp.* IV, 1, 2.

theory of Euhemerus that the gods were great men deified and tried to spread the doctrine in Rome; he, too, in significant lines expresses the Epicurean doctrine of the indifference of the gods to the lives of men[1]. A well-known fragment of Pacuvius[2] reproduces the physical teaching of Anaxagoras, and it is perhaps not unreasonable to attribute some of the moral aphorisms, of which the remains of Roman tragedy are full, to a superficial acquaintance with Greek moral teaching.

The expulsion from Rome of two Epicurean philosophers in 173 B.C.[3] may represent a first failure to establish systematic teaching, but by the middle of the century it was becoming impossible to resist the movement. In 159 the Stoic Crates of Mallus, detained at Rome by an accident, started to lecture, and four years later the heads of three of the great philosophical schools, Critolaus the Peripatetic, Diogenes the Stoic and Carneades the Academic, coming to Rome from Athens on an embassy, made a considerable stay, during which they expounded their views; Carneades[4] in a famous lecture startled Roman respectability by announcing his theory that justice was a convention. Shortly afterwards one C. Amafinius[5] made a sensation by his writings and discussions in Latin on the doctrines of Epicurus.

Among the hearers of the ambassador-philosophers may well have been the band of young 'intellectuals' who were already gathering round the younger Scipio. Of these the most prominent Roman was Scipio's intimate friend, C. Laelius, who figures as his interlocutor in several of Cicero's dialogues; literature was represented by C. Lucilius, the satirist and Terence, the manumitted African slave, and to these were added two distinguished Greeks, Polybius, the historian, and, as the recognized teacher of philosophy in the 'circle,' Panaetius. In the work of Panaetius is seen for the first time a deliberate attempt to transplant Greek philosophy to Roman soil.

(b) Romanized Stoicism—Panaetius

Panaetius was a member of a prominent Rhodian family, born probably between 185 and 180 B.C. He was instructed first by Crates at Pergamum, and then went to Athens, where he attached himself to Diogenes and after his death to his successor Antipater

---

[1] In the *Telamo*: quoted by Cicero, *de div.* I, 58, 132; II, 50, 104.
[2] In the *Chryses*: quoted by Varro, *L.L.* 5, 17.
[3] Athen. XII, 547A.
[4] Lactantius, *Inst. div.* V, 14.   [5] Cicero, *Tusc. Disp.* IV, 3, 6.

of Tarsus, thus definitely giving his allegiance to the Stoic tradition. Somewhere about 144 he was already in the company of Polybius in Scipio's entourage and in 139 went as Scipio's sole companion during a mission of inspection and pacification in the East. For the next ten or twelve years Panaetius lived alternately in Rome and Athens, but after Scipio's death in 129 he came to Rome no more and succeeded Antipater as head of the Stoic school in Athens, where he died in 110 or 109 B.C. Of his personal character there is no information, but his writings were held in high esteem and he is said to have abandoned the traditionally rough and dry manner of the Stoic school, 'but in one branch of writing was more mellow, in another more luminous than they, and always had on his lips Plato, Aristotle, Xenocrates, Theophrastus and Dicaearchus[1]': Posidonius adds that he was in the habit of quoting the poets. This information suggests firstly a literary rather than an intellectual exposition of philosophy and secondly an eclectic choosing of his doctrine from different schools and teachers. Both are characteristic of his teaching and indeed of Roman philosophy as a whole.

The direct information about the doctrines of Panaetius is very scanty, but indirectly much can be known from the philosophical writings of Cicero, in particular from the first two books of the *de Officiis*, the *de Republica* and the *de Legibus*; in the two former treatises he explicitly acknowledges his debt to Panaetius and admits that he was following his lead. Modern research[2] has disentangled the teaching of the master from the amplifications, additions and modifications of his Roman follower and it is possible to speak with confidence of Panaetius' views on ethics and politics.

That Panaetius was a Stoic there can be no possible doubt: he was the disciple of Diogenes and Antipater, the successive heads of the Stoic school, and he himself succeeded them. Like them, he taught the more elastic Stoicism of the second century and was prepared to admire and adopt the theories of other schools. He had a profound admiration for Plato, whom he described as the 'Homer among philosophers' and, in his exposition of the forms of constitution in the State, followed the *Republic* closely. This was not inconsistent with orthodoxy, but elsewhere he is at variance with more fundamental Stoic conceptions. Thus he followed Boethus in the belief that the world, as it is, is eternal and rejected the idea of its periodical destruction by fire (ἐκπύρωσις). Similarly

---

[1] Cicero, *de fin.* IV, 28, 79.
[2] See especially A. Schmekel, *Die Philosophie der mittleren Stoa.*

he expressed doubt as to the validity of divination, which must mean that he did not accept the important Stoic doctrine on which it rested of the 'sympathy' between all parts of the universe. Other divergences may be detected in his astronomy and his psychology. All this is proof of the latitude claimed by the leaders of the Stoic school, and so incidentally of its vitality.

But apart from such divergences the Greek leaders of Stoicism at Rome must have been conscious of the necessity of some adaptation of its tenets to new surroundings. Stoicism (see vol. vii, pp. 238 *sqq*.) had been founded at a period when the Greek city-state was collapsing, when the good man was no longer thought of as necessarily the good citizen, and the focus of attention had passed from the State to the individual. But Rome was still a city-state and was rapidly becoming a world-wide Empire. Political theory was therefore still an essential for any system which was to grip the Roman imagination, and if Stoicism was naturally defective on this side, it must be supplemented, and Plato and Aristotle pressed into the service. Again, the Roman character was profoundly different from that of the Greek and was but little attracted by general and abstract speculation; the Roman was a man of action, and if he reflected at all, he liked to think of the practical business of life and the requirements of his State. Physical theory about the ultimate constitution of the world did not greatly appeal to him—Lucretius was a solitary exception—and so, when it came to ethical discussion, the great abstract propositions so dear to earlier Stoicism that 'the wise man is free' and that 'all sins are equal,' and the like, no longer held the first place; the ideal *sapiens* and his perfect life are relegated by Cicero to a short dialogue which he characteristically entitles the 'Paradoxes of the Stoics.' Attention is concentrated on the ordinary man and his 'duties' and on such practical accord with nature and with reason as he can reach in his daily life as a Roman citizen.

A brief sketch of Panaetius' theories of ethics and politics may serve to bring out this practical side of his Romanized Stoicism. The two subjects are closely united in the root-conception of 'reason,' the perfect possession of the gods, which is present in varying degrees in every man and so binds gods and men together in a great community. This idea rests on the Stoic physics and psychology. The ultimate reality is the 'material spirit' ($\pi\nu\epsilon\hat{\upsilon}\mu\alpha$) which is divine and by condensation forms the grosser elements which it always controls: the Stoic view of the world has been described as a 'monistic dynamic materialism,' or from another point of view as 'Pantheism.' The divine spirit immanent in and controlling the world manifests itself as 'providence' (πρόνοια), not an external fate, but an inner necessity. In plants the 'spirit' appears as the power of growth (φύσις), in beasts soul (ψυχή) is added and manifests itself in the five senses (αἰσθήσεις) and the appetites (ὁρμαί), and in man comes the final gift of reason (λόγος). The moral end of man then is to live in accordance with reason. Such a life in its perfection could only be attained by the perfectly wise man, who is able to perform perfect action (κατόρθωμα, *perfectum officium, rectum*). The ordinary man, in whom Roman Stoicism is interested, can only attain to 'middle' actions, or 'duties' (καθήκοντα, *officia*), and it is with these Cicero deals in the first two books of the *de Officiis*, which are confessedly modelled on Panaetius' περὶ καθηκόντων. The realized end exhibits itself in 'virtue,' and 'virtue' for the ordinary man will vary in its form according to his own nature and his circumstances: for a man's individual character depends on the degree of 'tension' of the 'spirit' in his soul, and his actions must be determined by his station, his profession and mode of life. Still, general principles may be laid down and 'virtue' is subdivided into the traditional Greek cardinal virtues, wisdom, justice, fortitude and temperance. In his description of the virtues it is interesting to note that Panaetius in true Aristotelian manner finds that virtuous action is in each case a mean. Thus wisdom is a mean between careless or hasty judgment and—here the Roman comes out strong—a waste of time on unprofitable studies which bear no relation to practical life; temperance, again, is the mean between the gratification of desires and asceticism, and consists in the control of the appetites by reason, showing itself in a 'propriety' (τὸ πρέπον, *decorum*) both in the greater actions of life and in details of dress, bearing and behaviour. In all this may be recognized the severer Stoicism of the old school mixed with the doctrines of Plato and Aristotle and watered down to suit the respectable characteristics of the Roman gentleman: the old Roman *virtus* and *gravitas* and *pietas* appear under the cloak of a philosophic sanction. Similarly, the second book of the *de Officiis*, again closely modelled on Panaetius, in which Cicero discusses the relation of the expedient (*utile*) to the morally good (*honestum*) and decides that there can be no real distinction between them, reads almost like a philosophic apology for the position of the well-to-do Roman citizen and the respected statesman. Cicero justifies Cicero, we may infer, by Panaetius' justification of Scipio.

The political theory of Panaetius, contained in the first three Books of Cicero's *de Republica* and re-echoed in the first Book of the *de Legibus*[1], rests on the same foundations, shows the same eclectic development and in an almost more marked degree a Roman bias. Men are bound to one another and to the gods by the common possession of the 'reason' which is the basis of personal virtue: it must therefore be also the foundation of the life of the community. The State is a 'commonwealth of the people' (*res populi*) or a 'union' (σύστημα[2]) of men, not an enforced union, as in the Epicurean view of the 'Social Contract,' but 'a combination of a number of men united by common consent to law and by a community of interest[3].' In this community reason expresses itself by some sort of government (*consilium*), but there are various forms of government, the three main types being monarchy, aristocracy and democracy, of which the corrupt forms are tyranny, oligarchy and ochlocracy. Here the influence of Plato is obvious and his account of the 'cycle' in which these constitutions successively follow one another in the history of a State is also adopted with some modifications. Of the three Panaetius apparently selected monarchy as the best, placed aristocracy next and democracy last, but reversed the order in the corrupt forms, choosing ochlocracy as the least bad, oligarchy next and tyranny as the worst. Here Plato is deserted, as he is again most markedly in the conclusion, which since it occurs in Polybius as well as in Cicero, must be attributed to Panaetius, that the ideal constitution is that in which all the three elements are combined, as it was in Lycurgus' constitution of Sparta and is still more conspicuously in that of Rome, where the magistrates represent monarchy, the Senate aristocracy, and the people democracy. In this theory the adaptation of Stoic tradition to its new surroundings is almost flagrant: Greek philosophy is indeed modifying itself to suit the taste of its new disciples.

The introduction of philosophy no doubt gave a new and permanent interest to the educated classes at Rome, but it was never a wholesale foisting of Greek thought on to an alien race. From the first Rome chose what she would study, modified the tradition she received and thought out her ethics and her politics to suit her own circumstances. Panaetius' Stoicism is in this respect typical and prophetic of what was to follow in the next generation and under the Empire. It has been the fashion of late years to ascribe almost the whole of Roman Stoicism to the influence of Panaetius' pupil Posidonius, nor can there be any doubt that he greatly impressed the generation of Cicero; he was in some respects more

---

[1] The parallel exposition in Polybius vi, 3–19 should be compared.
[2] Polybius vi, 4 and 5.   [3] Cicero, *de Rep.* i, 25, 39.

orthodox than his master. But Panaetius was at least as great a figure. To him is due the credit of having planted Stoicism at Rome and of grasping the lines on which it would have to be modified to win Roman approval.

It would be of great interest to know in detail what was Panaetius' attitude to religion (which is after all the main subject of this chapter); unfortunately there are but scattered notices, which do not suffice for a general account. As a Stoic he was bound to base his theory on the root-conception of the immanent divine reason: his philosophic creed must have been the 'materialistic pantheism' which was accepted generally by his school. Consistently with the prevalent Stoic view he was bound to reject the ordinary gods of mythology as the legendary fictions of poets or statesmen[1], and it has been noticed already that he had grave doubts as to divination and definitely rejected astrology. Yet, like most Stoics, he seems to have made some concessions to popular belief. He allowed himself to speak of 'gods' in the plural, though he seems to have tried to reconcile such common parlance with the esoteric belief of the philosopher: 'men obey this celestial ordinance and the divine mind and the almighty god[2].' In the State, too, he allowed that the gods have their place as a kind of senior citizens, though it is clear that he deprecated any lavish expense on their temples or worship[3]. It is as though he again made the distinction between the perfect wisdom of the *sapiens* and the religion attainable by the ordinary man.

Two prominent conclusions may be made from this sporadic information, first that Panaetius rejected the popular religion and its manifestations, and second that he approached the whole question of religion with the eye of the statesman. That this was the attitude of the educated Roman of his time—at any rate of Scipio and his circle—is clear from the occasional comments of Polybius. In a passage[4] where he is comparing the constitution of Rome with that of other peoples, he praises Rome for her attitude to the gods and in particular for the encouragement of superstition (δεισιδαιμονία), not because it is true or rational, but because it holds the State together and is a valuable means of checking the extravagances of the people. And so in practice when he is later commenting on the story of the dream which impelled the elder Scipio to stand for the aedileship, he rejects it altogether

[1] Sextus Empiricus, *Adv. math.* IX, 61–63.
[2] Cicero, *de leg.* I, 7, 23.
[3] Cicero, *de off.* II, 17, 60; cf. *de leg.* II, 18, 45.
[4] VI, 56.

and regards its invention as an instance of Scipio's astute states-manship[1]. This is the attitude of the sceptic, who may indeed have some inner religious conviction of his own, but intends to use the superstition of the mob for political purposes. The history of the next century at Rome shows how strongly this attitude had seized the minds of the educated: the political use of augury and auspices in Cicero's time is but the practical application of the theory of the Scipionic circle.

In the next generation the great jurist Q. Mucius Scaevola[2] said that there were three classes of gods, those of the poets, those of the philosophers and those of the statesmen. This distinction had already begun to be true in the age of Scipio. Greek literature had brought myth and legend, Greek philosophy had brought scepti-cism and taught the politicians to play on the beliefs of the vulgar, but it had also brought the Stoic idea of divine immanence, which was destined to be the seed of educated religion for a long while to come and to find its expression in the Letters of Seneca and the Meditations of Marcus Aurelius. The immanent reason in the universe, which was in fact God, provided a new basis for religion, which was to some extent linked up with the old Roman cult, as the new idea of God was attached more and more to the name of Juppiter; and the reason in man, which bound him close to God, supplied a religious motive for morality, which in the old religion had, except possibly in the household, always been sadly lacking. Stoicism was indeed a nobler creed than Rome had yet known, and might have made a great popular appeal, but that it was too intellectual; 'a real active enthusiasm of humanity was wanting in it[3].'

[1] x, 5.
[2] Augustine, de civitate Dei, IV, 27.
[3] Warde Fowler, Religious Experience, p. 375.

CHAPTER XV

THE FALL OF CARTHAGE

I. HANNIBAL AS SUFETE

AT the close of the Second Punic War the plight of Carthage was gloomy in the extreme. Her older citizens could look back and recollect with bitterness that in less than seventy years their city, from being mistress of the Western Mediterranean, had sunk to the level of some second-rate Hellenistic state. The islands of Sicily, Sardinia and Corsica were lost for ever, the rich treasure-house and recruiting-ground of Spain was now in Roman hands, her fleet was crippled, and she had been ordered to pay what seemed a crushing indemnity: once the rival of Rome she was now to be an obsequious ally. True, her walls and her territory had been left intact, but even on her own territory she could not feel secure; with Masinissa, the spoilt child of Rome, on her

Note. For the condition of Africa between the Second and Third Punic Wars the literary evidence is slight and the archaeological evidence is not abundant. In the extant books Livy only mentions Carthaginian affairs incidentally, except for the five chapters (xxxiii, 45–9) on Hannibal's year of office and his flight. With the Third Punic War the sources become fuller. Polybius was in Africa in the last year of the war and saw the taking of Carthage. His intimate friendship with Scipio Aemilianus gave him also the fullest opportunities of historical enquiry for the period before he arrived. Certain reservations must be made in respect of his inevitable bias in favour of Scipio. Unfortunately only meagre fragments of his books xxxvi and xxxvii have survived. But Appian (*Libyca*, 68–135) and Diodorus have in the main preserved Polybius' account. Diodorus used Polybius directly, but only fragments of his book xxxii have come down to us. Appian's account however is entire. The study of the differences between the fragments of Polybius and Appian seems to show that Appian did not use Polybius directly, but through an intermediary, probably a Roman annalist (see Schwartz in *P.W. s.v.* Appianus and Kahrstedt, *Geschichte der Karthager*, pp. 620 and 624 *sqq.*). The good tradition in Appian derived from Polybius is contaminated with much rhetorical and annalistic dross. There remains the Epitome of Livy xlix, l and li and the short excerpts of Florus, *De Viris Illustribus*, Eutropius, and Orosius which depend directly or indirectly upon Livy. Though the Polybian tradition is at the base of Livy's account, it is clear that he has used to a far greater extent than Appian the secondary annalist sources Valerius Antias, Claudius Quadrigarius and others. Lastly, Zonaras' abbreviation of Dio Cassius, ix, 26–27, 29–30, is so short as to be of only slight use, but it seems that the part played by Scipio in the first year of the siege is here given a smaller importance than in Polybius.

western border, Masinissa, ever ready to increase his 'ancestral' domains at the expense of Carthage and against whose aggressions she could only appeal meekly to Rome, how could the fallen city have any real sense of security? But even though the greater part of her former territory had gone, her harbours and her mercantile marine still remained, and Rome had not apparently demanded the opening of the Punic ports to Italian ships[1]: the Apulian and Campanian ware which had been imported to the Carthaginian possessions during the third century might increase in volume, but it was still carried in Carthaginian ships. Herein lay her best opportunities for revival, but as well it was her obvious policy to keep on friendly terms with the new kingdom of Numidia, to promote trade there and also with the natives of the interior, and to engage in a more intensive cultivation of the large estates in her own territory.

But the most pressing problem was the payment of the indemnity imposed upon the city, and the problem was mishandled from the start. Had the richer classes only been prepared to face the economic situation resolutely, to show some degree of self-sacrifice and apportion the burden equitably, all might have been well; but they were determined to shirk their responsibilities and pay the smallest possible contribution, while a heavy tax was to be imposed on the impoverished lower classes (Livy xxxiii, 46, 9). And the usual corrupt practices continued; in the year 199 B.C. the yearly instalment from Carthage was paid over in such poor silver that the quaestors in Rome refused to accept it (Livy xxxii, 2). It is natural enough that with the loss of the mines in Spain, Carthage should have had difficulty with silver (and it is noticeable that her silver coins of this period show a low percentage of the metal) but such methods were not likely to win favour or sympathy at Rome or enhance the reputation of *Punica fides*. Nor was the revenue properly collected or looked after, and much of it found its way into the hands or hoards of magistrates and high officials (Livy xxxiii, 46, 8). It is not surprising that after three or four years of such misgovernment the populace should have grown restless and discontented, and in their desperation finally called upon the one man who by his own genius and by family tradition might oppose the oligarchs, Hannibal.

During the years immediately subsequent to the signature of

---

[1] See Fenestella (in Peter, *Frag. Rom. Hist.* p. 273), '*nullo commercio inter Italicos et Afros nisi post deletam Carthaginem coepto*,' and cf. T. Frank, *Roman Imperialism*, p. 283. For the archaeological finds see Gsell, *Hist. anc. de l'Afrique du Nord*, vol. iv, pp. 159 *sqq.*

peace, Hannibal had not taken any part in politics; for a time he had remained in command of an army (possibly safeguarding the frontiers against nomad attacks) and had employed his troops in the useful work of re-planting olives and repairing the devastations and ravages caused by the Roman invasion[1]. But in 200 B.C. he had been relieved of his command, possibly in consequence of intrigues between his opponents and Rome, and had retired into private life. But it would have been strange indeed if no appeal had been made by the people to their most famous citizen, and in the year 196 Hannibal duly took office as Sufete[2].

The ruling oligarchs could expect no good from Hannibal's election. But they must have felt themselves immune from danger; they controlled the Senate, and Hannibal's tenure of office would not last beyond the year. And in the Court of the Hundred and Four Judges (see p. 486) they had supporters who could bring to book even a Sufete who had proved intransigent. But their comfortable expectations were rudely shattered: Hannibal had seen what was necessary, knew precisely what he wanted, and how to achieve it; he showed the same insight and energy in opening and developing his political campaign, as he had on the field of battle. He was determined, by securing better payment of the indemnity, to leave Rome no ground for complaint, while at home he meant to weaken the power of the ruling classes and so make for a more equitable government. Over the question of the indemnity he soon came into conflict with one of the financial officials (Livy calls him a *quaestor*, XXXIII, 96) and summoned him before his tribunal. The quaestor, who knew that he would pass next year into the Court of the Hundred and Four and was confident of their support and help, defied Hannibal, but was immediately put under arrest. He appealed for aid to his friends in the Senate; in a dispute such as this, where Sufete and Senate were at variance, an assembly of the people must be summoned, and at last Hannibal had got the opportunity he desired. Before the popular assembly he not only defended his own action, but carried the war into the enemy's camp by inveighing bitterly against the power, wealth, and arrogance of the Hundred and Four. The people were free to express their feelings against their masters, and Hannibal's attack was greeted with such acclamation that he immediately proposed and passed a law decreeing that

[1] Aurelius Victor, *Probus*, XXXVII, 2, 3.
[2] On the much-disputed questions of the date of Hannibal's holding office and of his flight, the view adopted here is that set forth by M. Holleaux in *Rev. E.A.* XV, 1913, pp. 1 *sqq.*

henceforward the Hundred and Four Judges must be elected annually (presumably by the people) and that no Judge should hold office for two years running. It was a reform of tremendous importance; the supreme control over magistrates and officials was now vested in a popularly-elected body, whose personnel was bound to change yearly. At one stroke Hannibal had swept away the oligarchic control exercised by a court of life-members chosen by cliques; even though the old property-qualification for membership may have been still demanded, the people were now to some extent masters in their own house. There can be no doubt that the whole proceeding was no sudden impulse of the moment, but a carefully calculated plan on Hannibal's part; the conflict with the *quaestor* was no accident, but deliberately provoked in order to give Hannibal a chance of addressing the people and promulgating his reform. It was a great achievement, but whether it lasted long, whether it even survived Hannibal's withdrawal is unfortunately unknown.

Secure on this ground Hannibal could now go on to devise measures for the better collection and conservation of the city's revenues; he made careful investigations into the sources of the national income and the amount needed for the proper running of the State, and by checking leakages and corruption he was able to announce to the people that there was sufficient money to pay the yearly indemnity to Rome without having recourse to any special taxation. Of his capable handling of the situation and of the rapid revival of Carthaginian commerce a proof can be seen in the fact that in 191 the city offered to pay the remaining indemnity outright[1]. But though he had the mass of the people with him he had by now offended beyond repair not only the oligarchs, whose influence he had seriously crippled, but also the horde of corrupt officials, profiteers, and hangers-on, who had been living on the robbery of the State. To the Court of the Hundred and Four they could no longer look for help, but there was one quarter where their complaints might still gain a hearing, that was, in Rome itself. The anti-Barcid faction had their friends in Rome, and had previously been in correspondence with them (which may have resulted in Hannibal being relieved of his generalship in 200 B.C.) and now they took up their parable with redoubled vigour; but for some time their efforts were a failure, for Scipio Africanus used all the weight of his authority and prestige against hounding Hannibal down or interfering in the party politics of Carthage. But in the end he was overcome, for

[1] Livy xxxvi, 4, 7. The exact amount still outstanding is not known.

the dread of Hannibal was too strong, and finally in 195 B.C. three *legati*, Cn. Servilius, M. Claudius Marcellus, and Q. Terentius Culleo were dispatched to Africa.

Their real mission was to complain to the Carthaginian Senate that they had information that Hannibal was acting in concert with Antiochus and making preparations for a general war (p. 191). But the anti-Barcid faction, knowing the strength of the hold which Hannibal exercised over the people, advised them to give out at first that they had come to adjust differences between the city and Masinissa, whose depredations on Carthaginian territory had already begun (p. 473), and this announcement was believed. But Hannibal was not deceived, he guessed the real purpose of the delegation, and saw that in flight lay his only refuge. He made his plans with his usual care and skill; during the daytime he appeared as usual in the city, but as soon as night fell, he stole out accompanied by but two attendants, and by using relays of horses rode during that night and the following day 150 miles to a spot on the coast near Thapsus, where a ship was in readiness for him; setting sail he landed at Cercina, and so straight to Tyre and on to Antioch, as has already been narrated. At Carthage the next morning, when his absence was discovered, and while the crowd clamoured that he had been murdered by Roman treachery, the Roman delegation laid before the Senate formal charges of Hannibal's plotting with Antiochus, and demanded his punishment. The Senate meekly replied that it would do whatever Rome thought right.

The commission could now return satisfied to Rome; its object had been achieved; Rome had learnt the usefulness of bullying tactics, and Carthage, by sacrificing her greatest citizen, had demonstrated her complete submission. The only party who emerged with credit from the sorry business was Hannibal himself: in his decision to withdraw from the city that he could no longer help, where indeed his continued presence might have involved her in further humiliation, there is something at once noble and tragic; and the quiet dignity of his withdrawal and subsequent behaviour contrasts strangely with the petulant bitterness of his great antagonist Scipio when he retired to Liternum to execrate the ingratitude of the Roman people (p. 372). And while Hannibal was utterly without that deep sense of injustice which so rankled with the Roman, he had also none of the political levity which had impelled many a Greek to draw a supple living from the winning side; he lived and died in a single-minded devotion to a city that all his genius could not save.

The oligarchs could heave a sigh of relief over the removal of this inconvenient soldier, and could congratulate themselves that all might now go on as before. But by calling in Rome to rid them of a political opponent they had made a fatal error, and revealed the rottenness of their government by intrigue. And worse still, they had been confirmed in their power; there was no longer any hope of reform from within; it is not surprising if some malcontents began to look to another quarter for salvation, and wonder whether a friendly and protecting king of Numidia might not prove a present help in trouble. From now onwards Masinissa begins to play the preponderant rôle in African affairs.

II. MASINISSA

During the fifty years that followed the close of the Second Punic War the rulers of Carthage could boast that they were scrupulously carrying out the obligations imposed upon them by the treaty of peace, and that their submissiveness to Rome never wavered. The greatest and most searching test of their deference had been given when they evinced their readiness to punish Hannibal, but throughout their conduct was correct to a degree. After 201 B.C. a Carthaginian officer raised an independent revolt in Northern Italy (p. 326 *sq.*); he was promptly disavowed and exiled by the home government. In the wars against Philip, Antiochus, or Perseus Carthage furnished naval or military assistance as an ally of Rome, and was even zealous to offer more than the treaty required, an offer which was always coldly refused: the Carthaginian envoy Banno could claim in 149 B.C. 'We have fought with you against three kings.' In 200 B.C., 191 B.C., 171 B.C. and again a few years later Livy[1] records large presents of corn sent to the support of the Roman armies. In fact, it can hardly be doubted that there was no shadow of truth in the allegations of treachery which Masinissa made against Carthage in 174 B.C. and through his son Gulussa in 171 B.C.[2] Charges of secret conspiracy with Perseus and the still vaguer statement that Carthage had decided to build a large fleet were inventions which the Numidian circulated at Rome when the question of his territorial acquisitions at the expense of Carthage was *sub judice*. For true to the terms of the treaty Carthage offered no armed resistance to Masinissa's spoliation for nearly fifty years, patiently submitting her wrongs to Roman arbitration until finally, exasperated into an attempt to defend the last of the Punic empire,

[1] XXXI, 19, 2; XXXVI, 3, 1, 4, 5–6 and 9; XLII, 35; XLIII, 6.
[2] Livy XLII, 23; XLIII, 3.

she provoked her destruction at the hands of Rome. Revenge, hatred and fear had so swayed the Roman Senate that they had deliberately allowed the balance of power between Carthage and Masinissa to be destroyed until the very weakness of Carthage endangered the peace of North Africa and pointed the way to the formation of a Roman province. The final destruction of Carthage had become partly a matter of cold policy and partly the last desire of unsated revenge. But before describing this final act of the drama we must watch the growth of the power of Numidia under its able monarch Masinissa.

Masinissa was thirty-seven years old at the close of the Hannibalic War. Tall and handsome, he was endowed with astonishing and enduring bodily vigour. At the age of ninety he still mounted unaided and rode bare-backed, and four years before this one of his wives presented to him his forty-fourth son. In addition to the physical qualities which exact the admiration of primitive peoples he was gifted with great powers of leadership and insatiable ambition. His Numidian blood gave him inherited mastery of all the arts of cunning and dissimulation which made him an incomparable diplomat. Lastly a youth spent at Carthage had enabled him to absorb and appreciate the benefits of her culture and his marriage with the daughter of Hasdrubal made permanent the lessons of education. He was pre-eminently fitted for the immense task to which he devoted the rest of his long life. For he set himself to make a united nation out of the nomad tribes of Numidia, to wean them from their barbaric predatory habits to a settled life of agriculture and to extend his kingdom until, as he hoped, it should stretch from Morocco to Egypt, embracing Carthage itself.

In the Second Punic War with Roman help Masinissa had conquered the Numidian empire of Syphax from Siga to Cirta, and in the years that followed most of the independent princedoms which surrounded this dominion were reduced to vassaldom. But the chief accessions of territory were at the expense of Carthage. To the peasants whom he could bring under his rule he offered more security and lighter taxation than his burdened and enfeebled rival, and his sway was commended by his dominating personality and a powerful standing army which numbered 50,000 when in 154 B.C. he engaged Carthage in war. But it is as the 'agent of civilization' that his true greatness lies. He established his sons like barons in newly-won areas of nomad tribes and in this way spread the improved knowledge of agriculture from the centres to the most backward parts of his kingdom. Strabo's statement (XVII, 833) that Masinissa 'made nomads into farmers and welded them into a State' sums up a great achievement. With the rise of the Libyans a new and native civilization, based on a capital at Cirta and combining Libyan and Phoenician strains, had appeared in the Mediterranean world.

The treaty made by Scipio after Zama contained certain definite and certain indefinite territorial delimitations between the empire of Carthage and the kingdom of Masinissa (p. 108). The first principle was that Carthage should confine herself strictly within the frontiers of her empire as it existed at the beginning of the Second Punic War. This frontier line was to a considerable extent marked by what were called the 'Phœnician Bounds' comparable to the Roman Imperial *limites*. It was an enclave extending from a point on the coast west of Carthage where the lands of the Massyli adjoined, southward in a semicircle across the Great Plains until it rejoined the coast east of Carthage perhaps near the north of the Little Syrtis. But, in addition to the land within these Bounds, the treaty recognized the Carthaginian colonies and trade-marts westward on the shores of the Mediterranean as far as Morocco and eastward the region of the Syrtis, her richest province, known as the Emporia. Carthage was not to move outside these limits, whereas Masinissa might occupy within these same limits any territory which either during the Second Punic War he or his father at any time had occupied, or his ancestors had held previously. The clause, of course, was deliberately designed to provide a source of friction which would steadily weaken Carthage and strengthen the client protectorate of Masinissa. When it was made, Rome was not yet mistress of the Mediterranean and she saw her imperial interests best served by fostering rather than allaying dissension in Africa.

In the fifty years which followed the treaty Masinissa proceeded to filch from Carthage all her maritime colonies, the Emporia on the Syrtis and equally those westward from Carthage. In addition he occupied a considerable extent of territory in the interior within the 'Phœnician Bounds.' Carthage was forbidden by the treaty to wage even defensive war against her neighbour, and our evidence shows a succession of Roman boundary commissions sent to arbitrate after a *fait accompli* and always deciding in favour of the client king[1]. The exact chronology of these commissions cannot be recovered with certainty, but their cumulative

[1] Zonaras IX, 18. Appian, *Lib.* 67, 68, 69. Polybius XXXI, 21. Livy XXXIII, 47, 8 (195 B.C.), XXXIV, 62 (193 B.C., Gsell, *op. cit.* pp. 315 *sqq.*; cf. Kahrstedt, pp. 592 and 613), XL, 17, 34 (182/1 B.C.), XLI, 22 (174 B.C.), XLII, 23, 24 (172/1 B.C.). Livy, *Epit.* XLVII (153 B.C.), XLVIII (152 B.C.), cf. Zon. IX, 26.

effect is plain. It is sufficient to follow the events which finally exhausted the patience of Carthage and precipitated an open breach with Masinissa.

In the years between 160 B.C. and 155 B.C.[1] a plundering expedition had been made by a Carthaginian officer Carthalo into the territory which Masinissa had usurped. Raid and counter-raid followed until a Roman commission was sent which returned leaving the dispute unsettled. Then Masinissa proceeded to occupy a district in the Great Plains between Souk el Arba and Souk el Kremis called Tusca[2]. Commissioners headed by Cato visited Africa in 153 B.C., and again retired after finding the Carthaginians unwilling to be entirely submissive to Roman dictation. All the old hatred of Roman for Semite seems to have been roused in Cato's breast. He was now eighty-one years old, and on the voyage home this hatred crystallized into an old man's *idée fixe* that Carthage must be destroyed. It was an unreasoning passion which only later clothed itself in arguments of imperial policy and advantage. Cato must have seen how Carthage was bleeding to death, and even if he hated to witness the prosperity which still flourished beneath the shadow of the city, he cannot have believed that Carthage could be a serious economic rival to Rome, still less a political menace to the power that had struck down Macedon and set bounds to the power of Syria. His hatred did not at once sway the Senate, and in the following year (152) Scipio Nasica at the head of another commission forced Masinissa to give up part of the land which he had occupied. But in Carthage itself the last fifty years had taught some men to hope for something from Masinissa and others to hope for nothing from Rome; but to trust to themselves at the last. In the winter of 151–0 the leaders of those who wished to submit to Masinissa were driven into exile and took refuge with the king, who sent his sons, Micipsa and Gulussa, to demand their recall. The more democratic nationalist party refused to admit the envoys to the city and, as they returned, the general Hamilcar the Samnite attacked them and killed part of their retinue. War was declared, and Masinissa laid siege to a town called Oroscopa.

The Carthaginian army of 25,000 foot was entrusted to a Hasdrubal whom Polybius describes as 'vain boastful and without experience in command' though he was to show energy and deter-

[1] Appian, *Lib.* 68 seems to date it 153 B.C., but this is too late; see Gsell, *op. cit.* III, p. 320.

[2] Perhaps to be identified with the Thugga (modern Dougga); see Gsell, *op. cit.* II, p. 110, III, p. 321.

mination later in the siege of Carthage. He advanced and was joined by two sons of the king, Agasis and Soubas, who brought the invaluable help of 6000 Numidian cavalry. Masinissa withdrew slowly into a broad plain flanked by steep rocky hills to force an engagement. Both armies had meanwhile been swelled by fresh levies until each numbered nearly 60,000 men. Scipio Aemilianus arrived from Spain on an embassy to procure elephants the day before the battle, and in later times recounted how like Zeus on Ida or Poseidon on Samothrace he had witnessed the struggle in the plain. The battle lasted till nightfall ending in a slight advantage to Masinissa. The Carthaginians, learning of Scipio's presence, called upon him to effect a settlement, offering to renounce all claim to the country of the Emporia and to pay 1000 talents indemnity. But negotiations broke down when they refused to hand over the Numidians who had deserted to them. Scipio returned to Spain with his elephants and meanwhile Masinissa drew a line of entrenchments round the Punic army and so cut them off from all supplies. Pestilence broke out in their army and, reduced to desperate straits, unable either to bury or to burn the dead and having eaten all their horses and transport animals, they surrendered and promised to pay 5000 talents in fifty years. As the survivors marched out with a single garment apiece, Gulussa took his revenge and fell upon them with his cavalry. Only a very small remnant returned from this disastrous expedition.

As a result of his victory Masinissa was confirmed in the possession of a considerable additional amount of disputed territory. The later Roman province of Africa had the same boundaries marked out by the 'fossa regia' as the realm of Carthage at the commencement of the Third Punic War. The limits have been in part determined by the finding of boundary stones, and for the rest reconstructed from literary and epigraphic evidence[1], and Carthage is seen now reduced to domination of North-east Tunisia and a narrow strip of coast line on the gulfs of Hammamet and Gabès. The Great Plains were in the possession of Masinissa and where the frontier crossed the Medjerda it was little more than ninety miles from Carthage.

III. THE DECLARATION OF WAR

Carthage had broken the Zama treaty by engaging in war without Rome's consent, and she had thus given an argument to her enemies in the Senate. On each occasion that Cato had spoken on a question he used his right to add one more sentiment to his

---

[1] Gsell, *op. cit.* III, pp. 327 *sqq.*

sententia—ceterum censeo delendam esse Carthaginem. This simple formula he once illustrated by holding up before the *patres* a ripe fig, saying, 'This was gathered at Carthage three days ago.' There is no evidence that this act was an appeal for the destruction of a commercial rival—it was the excitement of Roman cupidity and of revengeful envy at the fertility of North Africa. But besides these emotions there were reasons of State that had their force and plausibility. The balance of power in North Africa had broken down. Numidia threatened to absorb Carthage into a strong North African kingdom with an interest in the Mediterranean. A powerful Numidian ruling in Carthage might be a new Hannibal. The danger from Carthage was not that she was too strong, but that she had become too weak, and that her weakness might make Masinissa too strong. The last instalment of the war indemnity after Zama had been duly paid. This was an argument for the correctness of Carthage's behaviour in the past, but it offered no inducement to preserve her in the future. Such subtle considerations of callous self-interest, perhaps only half-avowed, reinforced the more respectable plea of ancient enmity and recent disobedience, and carried the day against the party in the Senate, headed by Nasica, who strove to save Carthage, as Cato himself had once striven to shield Rhodes[1].

When the Romans heard of the outbreak of war between Masinissa and Carthage they mobilized four legions. The Carthaginians realized what this meant, and after the disaster strove to show their penitence and obtain pardon. Hasdrubal and Carthalo with others who had shared the responsibility of the war against Masinissa were condemned to death, but Hasdrubal escaped and later managed to collect a force of 20,000 men from the outer districts of the Carthaginian dominion. Envoys came from Rome and enquired why these men had not been condemned before instead of after the war, and, when asked how Carthage could obtain pardon, they replied deliberately in vague terms that the Carthaginians must give satisfaction to Rome and they knew well what this must be. Rome was purposely obscuring her real in-

---

[1] The narrative in Livy, *Epit.* XLVII, XLVIII, conflicts with Appian, *Lib.* 74 based on Polybius, and seems to derive from the Roman propaganda of self-justification and to possess no historical value (see Kahrstedt, *op. cit.* pp. 621–4). Appian knows the one cause—the breach of the Zama treaty. On the other hand the argument put into the mouth of Scipio (Appian, *Lib.* 69, Diodorus XXXIV–V, 33, 4) that Rome must not lose all her enemies for fear of losing her virility is a rhetorical commonplace, perhaps first suggested by a remark of Hannibal (Appian, *op. cit.* 65).

tentions until her preparations were complete and by diplomacy
Carthage might have been persuaded to render herself defenceless.
Repeated embassies from Carthage to Rome were put off with
the same obscure answers. Then after the consuls for 149 B.C.
had entered office Utica deserted Carthage and sent envoys to
Rome, promising all the help she could give against her ancient
rival. The news was expected at Rome, since Roman agents had
been busy in Utica; the Senate met on the Capitol and declared
war, entrusting the two consuls M'. Manilius and L. Marcius
Censorinus with the conduct of the operations. They crossed to
Sicily and thence to the base thus secured. The armament numbered four legions with 4000 cavalry, and together with a horde
of volunteers who scented easy booty and a profitable campaign,
may have numbered 80,000 men, as Appian says. There were fifty
quinqueremes and one hundred smaller warships. The fleet was
commanded by Censorinus, a man of quiet philosophic tastes,
and the army by the orator Manilius. Scipio Aemilianus, aged
thirty-five, was one of the military tribunes.

Meanwhile the Carthaginians, deserted by Utica and weak
after their recent disaster, saw their one hope in unconditional
submission and they sent five deputies with plenary powers.
Arrived at Rome, they learnt that war had been declared and that
the consuls had set out for Africa. They were informed by a
praetor in the Senate that taking account of their unconditional
surrender it had been decided to grant them 'freedom and the
enjoyment of their laws; and moreover all their territory and the
possession of their other property public and private[1].' These
terms were granted with the reservation that the Carthaginians
should send to Rome 300 noble hostages and should obey such
commands as the consuls should impose upon them. It was
ominous that in these vague terms there was no mention of the
city of Carthage, but the envoys could do no more than return
and procure the sending of the hostages to the consuls who had now
arrived at Utica. Having dispatched the hostages to Sicily these
delivered their next commands, that Carthage should surrender
all her arms and war engines. Even these orders were promptly
complied with, though it was pointed out that the city would be
left at the mercy of the exiled Hasdrubal and his 20,000 troops;
200,000 panoplies and about 2000 catapults were handed over.
When this had been finished, the consuls told the Carthaginians
to send a deputation of thirty of their most important citizens to
hear the final injunctions of the Senate. This body was chosen

[1] Polybius XXXVI, 4.

and sent and at last the consuls informed them of the will of the Roman people which had till then been kept secret. The inhabitants of the city of Carthage must leave their city which would be destroyed and could settle where they liked so long as it was at least ten Roman miles from the sea. At last the Roman intentions were seen in all their nakedness. Carthage had been disarmed, now came her death sentence. Once the fortifications had been pulled down and the superb harbour had been rendered defenceless Carthaginian territory would cease to have any importance if occupied by Masinissa. The inhabitants of a vast city were ordered to live or die without trade and without protection.

One of the Carthaginian envoys, Banno, then rose to make a famous plea for mercy on behalf of his fatherland[1]. But the Romans were obdurate and it was time for the envoys to return to announce the news at Carthage. Some of them, foreseeing the danger, took to flight and left the remainder to bring the ultimatum to Carthage. They entered the city through vast multitudes assembled to hear the tidings. Their gloomy countenances were witness to the character of their message. But refusing to speak they persisted until they came before the senate and there revealed Rome's decree. The people crowded outside guessed their report from the cries of dismay which greeted it in the senate, and bursting into the building stoned to death the envoys and killed many others who had counselled submission to Rome.

The scene in the city was one of utter confusion as men were swayed by despair, hatred, fear or anger. The mothers of the hostages, like the Tragic Furies, maddened them with their taunts. Others took measures for the defence of the city; the gates were closed, the walls manned and slaves were given their freedom. Two new generals were elected of whom one was the banished Hasdrubal and the other a grandson of Masinissa. To gain time a truce of thirty days was demanded for an embassy to go to Rome, but the demand was refused. The whole city became a workshop and the population toiled feverishly day and night to forge new weapons of war, while the hair which made the best strings for catapults was freely offered by the noblest and the poorest of the women. Hasdrubal, meanwhile, master of the Carthaginian domains, was able to send provisions into the city and to ensure the loyalty of the Libyan subject tribes. But the cities on the coast, Hadrumetum, Leptis, Thapsus, Acholla and probably Usilla, with another city, inland in Bizerta, Theudalis, went

---

[1] Appian, *Lib.* 83–85, perhaps preserving much of what was actually spoken through using Polybius. The speech has the true ring of actuality.

over to the Romans. The consuls, however, made no haste to commence hostilities, believing that this opposition would soon collapse and that there could be no difficulty in entering a city which they thought had been disarmed. At the same time the attitude of Masinissa was none too friendly. He saw the hope of the completion of his life-work dashed from him, and when the consuls asked for assistance he put them off with promises of sending troops when they had need of them. Later, it is said, when he offered assistance it was declined—'when we have need we will let you know.' Besides, it was not easy to forget that a grandson of Masinissa was in command of the Carthaginian army. Finally at the beginning of summer the consuls advanced on the city from the Castra Cornelia.

IV. THE SIEGE OF CARTHAGE

Carthage was immensely strong, both by the nature of its situation and by its elaborate defensive fortifications. Into the broad gulf of Tunes there projects eastward a promontary with a narrow neck and a head shaped like a double-axe. Two considerable hills, Tebel el Kravni and Sidi bu Saïd, with steep cliffs descending into the sea crown the head, providing impregnable defences on the north and east from Cape Kamart to Cape Carthago. The ancient city lay between the hills and spread southward using an outlying spur of the second hill as its citadel, the Byrsa. Still farther south, on the lower ground near the sea were the agora and the harbours, and outside the town wall the narrow spit of sandbank, on which now stands the fort of La Goulette, projected to form a bar across the inland lake of Tunes. The city could only be attacked from two directions, the main isthmus neck and the narrow sand bar, now called Kherredine. Excavation has revealed the remains of the colossal triple wall, forty-five feet high and thirty-three broad, which defended the city across the isthmus, and the siege proved how adequate this defence was. The walls protecting the market-place and the harbour were, no doubt, also very strong, but it was only with Scipio's arrival as consul that the siege was pressed in this region to complete the blockade. For the problem of the Romans was complicated by the existence of the considerable army under Hasdrubal in the interior amongst the numerous Libyan tribes still loyal to Carthage, which for two years succeeded effectually in transmitting provisions into the city either through the Roman lines or by sea.

The consuls advanced to besiege Carthage, Censorinus, supported by the fleet, taking up a position close to the city on the lake of Tunes on the south, where the wall was weakest. Manilius camped on the north of the main isthmus to prevent Hasdrubal's army from approaching the city and to cut off supplies. The first necessity was to collect timber for the siege machines. Censorinus found the area close under the walls deforested, and was forced to forage south of the lake of Tunes. Here a Carthaginian cavalry commander, Himilco Phameas, succeeded in surprising the Romans, killing 500 men. At last preparations were completed for a combined assault by both consuls. The first attack on the Byrsa and the strong western wall failed along the outer defences, but from the south a portion of the wall was broken down, leaving an opening into the city. But in the night the Carthaginians succeeded in throwing up a fresh barrier and the Roman storming-parties were beaten off on the following day. The assault had failed, and it was necessary to settle down to a blockade. In the ensuing summer Censorinus' army suffered severely in the unhealthy marshes of the lake, so that he moved to the sea near El Kram. The fleet, too, was transferred to the east side of the La Goulette isthmus, where the defenders were able with a favourable wind to attack it with fire-ships, which did considerable damage. In the autumn Censorinus occupied the island of Aegimurus and then returned to Rome to hold the elections, operations from the south having been brought to a complete standstill. Manilius was left isolated, and the defenders made a night attack on his entrenchments, causing severe losses. The desperate position was only relieved by a brilliant counter-attack led by Scipio himself.

Manilius, in view of this reverse, fortified a stronger position on the coast at Sebka er-Riana for his army, and built a stockade to protect his ships. Himself he marched inland with 12,000 troops to attempt to attack the Carthaginian force in the interior. His march was ill-managed and the force narrowly escaped disaster at the hands of Phameas' cavalry, owing its safety largely to the energy and foresight of Scipio. On its return there were fresh sallies of the defenders upon the lines and Scipio's reputation for skill and bravery grew steadily. Finally, in the winter of 149–8 Manilius attempted another expedition into the interior which came to grips with Hasdrubal near Nepheris, but the Roman commander's military incapacity risked an engagement on very unfavourable ground with a river at his back. Once again only the most signal bravery of Scipio in a rearguard action enabled most of the force to be extricated.

At this point Masinissa died. He had been bitterly disappointed to see the crowning of his life's work prevented by Rome's interference, and through this winter he had met Roman requests for assistance by vague promises. But he had learnt at least to respect and admire Scipio, and in his will he entrusted his sons to the Roman's protection. Scipio headed the commission which was sent to set in order Numidia. The unity and centralization which Masinissa had spent a long life to achieve were now undone. The three legitimate sons, Micipsa, Gulussa and Mastanabal, divided the main portion of Numidia, while the numerous other sons received fiefs in the outlying parts. This partition of Numidia was strictly in accordance with the traditional policy of 'divide ut imperes.' But more important for the immediate success of the war was Scipio's success in compelling Gulussa, the most warlike of Masinissa's sons, who commanded the Numidian army, to bring a picked force to assist in the destruction of Carthage. Then, at the end of the winter, Scipio won a further success, while Manilius conducted once more an expedition inland near Nepheris. He persuaded Phameas, the commander of Hasdrubal's cavalry force, to desert by the offer of a free pardon. But the expedition suffered the severest privations on its return march owing to the failure of proper organization for its commissariat by its commander.

The new consuls for 148 B.C. were Calpurnius Piso to command the land force, and L. Mancinus for the navy. They continued the ineffective strategy of their predecessors, attacking the small towns on the gulf of Carthage and in the interior in order to deprive the capital of its sources of supplies. After an attack on Clupea had failed, a neighbouring Libyan town, whose name the Greeks and Romans pronounced Neapolis, surrendered at discretion. Nevertheless, it was sacked with brutal thoroughness. Consequently, when Hippo Diarrhytus was besieged through the summer and autumn the defence was desperate and Piso had to abandon the siege. Meanwhile the blockade of Carthage made no advance, and part of Gulussa's cavalry changed their allegiance once more to help Carthage. Indeed, the danger to Carthage seemed much greater from her own dissensions than from the Romans. For the commander of the city garrison was killed in the Carthaginian senate in a riot following upon an accusation of treachery. Masinissa's sons were now holding back from sending any further help to the Romans, and the Carthaginians had been able to get into touch with the Mauri, as well as with the pretender Andriscus, who was winning victories against the Romans in Macedonia (p. 276).

Thus the campaigning season of 148 B.C. wore on. Calpurnius

Piso and Mancinus had been as completely unsuccessful as Censorinus and Manilius the year before. Dissatisfaction with the conduct of the war was rife at Rome and Cato voiced the general opinion that Scipio should be put in command, adapting a Homeric line,

$$\text{οἷος πέπνυται, τοὶ δὲ σκιαὶ ἀΐσσουσι}^1.$$

At the elections Scipio was standing for the office of curule aedile, being still too young for the consulship. Nevertheless he was nominated and elected to the consulship in the Comitia. The consul presiding refused to return the illegal vote, but a way out of the deadlock was found, when a tribune proposed with the consent of the Senate a special bill legalizing Scipio's candidature. Even then there was further opposition when his colleague in the consulate, C. Livius Drusus, demanded that the lot should decide which consul should go to Africa. Once again a tribune's bill asserted the will of the people.

Scipio arrived in Africa to find Mancinus in a pretty pass. He had noticed that there was a weak spot in the walls of the suburb Megara close to the cliffs of the sea on the north. But his preparations for an attack with scaling ladders were noticed by the defenders, who sallied out of a gate against it. However, the attacking force of Mancinus managed to beat back the sally and 500 men forced an entrance through the gate. Next day they were surrounded on all sides by Carthaginians, who could roll down rocks upon them. Suddenly, as their fate seemed certain, a fleet was seen approaching the coast. It was Scipio coming in the nick of time. The ships could stand close in shore, and the Carthaginians lost heart and allowed Mancinus' force to be taken off in the Roman galleys.

With Scipio's appearance the siege of the city once more became the central objective, and the Carthaginians realized that the decisive moment of the struggle had arrived. Hasdrubal was recalled from the interior to a fortified post close to the walls near Malga. Scipio spent some months in re-establishing discipline in the Roman army and then in the spring of 147 B.C. launched an attack on Megara. A gate was broken in and 4000 troops penetrated inside. Hasdrubal thought that nothing could now prevent the city being taken, and he hastened to leave his fort and enter the city by another gate. He was determined that resistance should be carried to the bitter end and deliberately had the Roman prisoners mutilated and murdered on the walls in front of the Roman army to prevent the citizens from daring to surrender. Meanwhile Scipio's troops had to fight every inch of

<hr>
[1] Homer, *Odyssey*, x, 495.

ground in the olive groves and vineyards of the suburb. Indeed it was an ideal place for defence and, finally, to avoid heavy losses for small gains Scipio ordered retreat.

But the effort had not been wasted. He was able to demolish the fort which Hasdrubal had abandoned, and the blockade of Carthage was drawn close. An elaborate line of earthworks was drawn right across from the gulf of Tunes to Sebka er-Riana which made it quite impossible for the small force of Libyans in the interior, who were still loyal to Carthage, to send any further supplies. Finally in the autumn Scipio built a mole across the gulf of Kherredine to stop the only remaining gap in the blockade, where with a favourable wind transports could sometimes slip through into the outer harbour. At first the defenders paid little heed, but, as the mole made steady headway, they contrived in secret a last enterprise. A fleet of fifty ships was built inside the inner harbour, unknown to the Romans, and when the harbour boom was opened and the fleet sailed out, the Romans were completely surprised. An immediate attack might have carried the Roman position, but the Carthaginians waited a day to make trial of the sailing qualities of their new vessels. Next day the Roman fleet joined battle. The struggle in the narrow space where manœuvring was impossible continued fiercely through the day, until towards evening the Carthaginian ships gave ground. Many were driven on to Scipio's mole and on the two days following were defended desperately by men swimming out with lighted torches to fire the defence works of the mole. But, in the end, the Carthaginian fleet was destroyed, and the last effort of the defenders was spent in vain. The mole was completed and strongly protected against attack. Carthage was entirely blockaded. Nothing could now prevent hunger and disease bringing about the fall of the city. Consequently, Scipio sent envoys through Gulussa to offer favourable conditions of surrender. But the envoys were prevented by Hasdrubal from even reaching the walls of the city by volleys of missiles (autumn 147).

Winter came on, and Scipio succeeded in rounding up by two flying columns a small force which was still at large in the interior near Nepheris. The Libyan tribes one and all submitted to Rome. With the approach of spring the endurance of the Carthaginians reached the breaking point. In order to narrow the line of defence Hasdrubal ordered the dockyards and magazines round the outer harbour to be burnt. Scipio at once attacked the citadel Byrsa, while Laelius assaulted the wall of the city where it adjoined the inner harbour. Laelius' force overpowered the weakened defenders, and forced its way to the market-place. At last the defences had been pierced. For six days and nights the Romans fought their way from house to house and street to street towards the Byrsa. On the seventh, when the lower part of the town had been burnt, the citadel surrendered. The deserters from the Roman army perished in the flames of the temple of Eşmun; Hasdrubal saved his own life, to be preserved as a proof of Roman clemency. The starving inhabitants poured out, fifty thousand, men, women and children, to be sold into slavery. For them the Romans knew no mercy, and if Scipio wept as he saw Carthage destroyed, it was not mercy that stirred in him, but a strange streak of fatalism as he prophesied that one day a like fate would overtake Rome. Buildings and walls were razed to the ground; the plough passed over the site, and salt was sown in the furrows made. A solemn curse was pronounced that neither house nor crops should ever rise again. By all its legal and religious forms the Senate thus declared the end of the great city, and satisfied alike its hatred of an old enemy and its fear of a new rival.

The few cities which had stood by Carthage were destroyed, whereas those that had deserted her, above all Utica, received freedom and a share in the land that had belonged to the Carthaginians. Allotments were also made to Phameas and his deserting cavalry; while the sons of Masinissa were granted the usufruct of certain lands. The remainder of the territory over which Carthage had ruled when the war began passed into the possession of the Roman people, and the whole, some 5000 square miles, was made a new Roman province, Africa, governed by a praetor stationed at Utica[1].

V. EPILOGUE

For seventeen days the fires of Carthage blazed, and then for long years the salt-sown ground and pitiful heaps of blackened stone alone remained where once had been a great city. But though the Senators by their simple fiat might raze the buildings to the ground they could not destroy the geographical advantages of its incomparable situation, and in a little over a hundred years a Roman was to set up again what his predecessors had overturned. But the day of Punic Carthage was over. Scarcely more than seven centuries had passed since some unnamed Tyrian settlers had landed to make their home there, and now at the end of her story it is natural to ask what effect the civilization of Carthage had produced in the realm over which it once ruled, and what was permanent and lasting in that civilization.

[1] See further vol. IX, chap. II.

To the modern world the very name of Carthage stands, and has long stood, as a symbol for mercantilism, for a State in which money was the first pre-occupation, and art or letters the last. Yet, by some curious chance, Carthage can claim one of the most famous and tragic figures in legend and literature. Greek authors, musing on the history of a city that had been so formidable a foe to Greek and Roman alike, demanded for her origin something more impressive than the silent growth of a trading port: if Rome had been the creation of a band of splendid adventurers fleeing from an unjust ruler, Carthage too must have her saga. And so from the primitive native tradition of Elissa, refashioned by generations of later writers, there slowly grew up the romantic tale of Dido, Princess of Tyre, who had fled from the persecution of King Pygmalion, and with a few faithful followers reached Africa. Here, when she wished to buy land, the natives mockingly offered her as much as a cowhide could cover. To this she replied by cutting a cowhide into thin strips and so enclosed a space large enough to contain her new city; here she welcomed the wandering Trojan hero Aeneas, and here deserted by him stabbed herself to death on her pyre. As history the tale is worthless, a compost of legend, folk-lore, aetiological myth and cult practice, seasoned with the love interest so dear to the Hellenistic heart[1]. In this form it might well have been the subject of an antiquarian chapter in Gellius, but it had the good fortune to be taken over by Virgil, and in his hands the passion and death of Dido was moulded into one of the great stories of the world, and Dido herself has become one of the imperishable names in literature.

But in one detail legend, perhaps unknowingly, hit the mark when it made the history of Carthage begin with a bargain. It was throughout its life a city of merchants and bargainers, and the policy that its rulers followed was that of a mercantile State, cautious and uninspired, demanding a clear return for effort made. Yet against this background of calculating mediocrity there stood out from time to time the figures of nobles or generals, Hamilcar or Mago or Himilco, who sought to lead Carthage along new paths of conquest or adventure, and so occasionally produced the appearance of an aggressive policy. It was the conflict between these great figures and the ruling oligarchy that generated certain institutions and bodies for which the city was celebrated, and which, by acting as a check upon individual ambitions or excessive power, gave to the constitution that stability which

---

[1] On the legend of Dido see De Sanctis, *Storia dei Romani*, III, I, pp. 20 *sqq.*, and the appendix *Didone nella tradizione Greco-Romana*, pp. 89 *sqq.*

Aristotle so admired. They merit some discussion here, for they are quite distinct from the ordinary elements of Sufetes, Senate, and popular assembly; their forms are peculiar to Carthage itself, and typical of the balance, half-democratic, half-oligarchic, which she achieved in her highly organized and complex state.

The first of these institutions was the Court of the Hundred and Four Judges[1]. Most states, in antiquity, had to grapple with the problem of the successful general or influential noble who might make himself monarch and so derail the constitution, and at Carthage the establishment of the Court was expressly designed to check and curtail the influence and ascendancy which the family of Mago had gained. Its members were chosen from men of senatorial rank and though nominally elected yearly actually held office for life. Its function was to demand an account from all public officers of their conduct during their term of office and to approve or punish; it was the Carthaginian form of the Athenian *euthynai*, though it had far more extensive power. But obviously any Court possessed of such far-reaching and quasi-censorial influence—Aristotle compares it with the Ephorate at Sparta,—however useful it may have been at the time of its establishment, was bound imperceptibly to enlarge its competence, and by the second century it had ended by becoming the most dreaded body in the whole State. There was no escape from its all-pervading influence, both magistrates and people were equally under its domination, and the arrogance with which the Judges exercised it made them the more hated; they were, in Livy's strong phrase, 'absolute masters of the city[2].'

True it was an elective body, but the mode of its election is instructive. These Judges were chosen not by popular vote, but selected by a mysterious set of magistracies termed by Aristotle (for we do not know the Punic equivalent) *pentarchiai* or Boards of Five[3]. It is characteristic of the tantalizing scantiness of our knowledge about Carthage that little more is known about the Pentarchies than their name and the fact that they were important, but some other slight pieces of evidence serve to support the conjecture that these Boards of Five were special committees dealing with finance, army and navy, and other executive and administrative matters; and it is not impossible that these Boards themselves may have constituted the famous Small Senate of 30 members (see vol. VII, p. 666) which assumed direction of affairs

[1] Aristotle, *Politics*, II, 1272 *b*, 33 *sqq.*
[2] Livy XXXIII, 46, 1. *Iudicum ordo Carthagine ea tempestate dominabatur.*
[3] For the Pentarchies see Aristotle, *loc. cit.*, especially 1273 *a*, 13 *sqq.*

in times of crisis. Between them, the Hundred and Four Judges and the Pentarchies controlled everything in the city and controlled with complete impunity; a man, after holding office as a Pentarch, could by his own nomination pass into the Court of the Judges, and no one could accuse him or bring him to book. Thus in spite of the elaborate and imposing apparatus of Sufetes, Senate, and assembly of the people, in spite, too, of the freedom of speech allowed in that assembly, the city was really dominated by a small number of men who played into each other's hands, and the result was a venality and corruption which shocked even Greek observers. Aristotle had noted that the highest offices could be bought, and two centuries later Polybius (vi, 56, 4) contrasted the open bribery and corruption prevalent in Carthage with the stricter morality which prevailed in Rome. In fact the typical political institutions of Carthage, the Pentarchies, the Small Senate of 30 members, and the Court of the Hundred and Four Judges, are the products which might be expected of a close mercantile oligarchy determined to preserve its rights jealously against possible claims of the lower orders or the efforts of powerful individuals to assert themselves; and the parallel often drawn with such cities as Venice is not unjust. The populace was bribed into acquiescence by the possibility of money-making in the surrounding cities[1], and so long as the government could pay its way all was well. It must be confessed that, contrasted with the achievements of Greece or Rome, the contribution of Carthage to political thought or theory was not great.

In the realm of commerce and economics Carthage had early created for herself a monopoly in the Western Mediterranean and was determined not to allow other states to tap the rich markets she had found; with the intruding Greeks she waged ceaseless war, and though she could not keep them wholly out of Sicily she was able to reserve Sardinia, Corsica and Spain to herself; even those states with whom she had entered into alliance were not permitted much freedom of commerce, as the early treaty with Rome in 509 B.C. shows (vol. VII, p. 465). She was not, however, a great productive state and certainly not to be compared with Antioch or Alexandria: the industry of Carthage was comparatively small; pottery and lamps of small artistic merit, the making of rugs and tapestries and cushions, such luxury crafts as the working of precious stones, ivory, gold and silver, and some glass-making are

---

[1] This seems to be the meaning of the phrase Aristotle uses, in *Politics*, VI, 1320 *b*, 5 ἀεὶ γάρ τινας ἐκπέμποντες τοῦ δήμου πρὸς τὰς περιοικίδας ποιοῦσιν εὐπόρους.

among the industries that can be enumerated, but there was little
original work, for the craftsmen were mostly content to copy
Greek or Oriental models and never struck out for themselves.
Some raw materials (such as hides or timber) were exported, and
the export of slaves was a considerable source of revenue; the
sending out of finished products, such as pottery, glass and
textiles, added to her income; but she was a carrying rather
than a productive state. It was from this commerce, from the
merchants who brought amber or tin from the North or slaves
and precious stones from the South, and from the minerals that
she gained from Spain that she must have drawn most of her
revenue: like many Hellenistic states of this period she lived on
transit trade (see p. 657). She was, in fact, an entrepôt state,
importing for re-export, like the Low Countries in medieval
times. Her merchants travelled far and wide, to Britain or to
Africa, and have left monuments of their activity in Massilia or
Spain, where they doubtless resided for trade; it is interesting to
find a Carthaginian acting as guarantor for a loan, in the second
century, at Alexandria itself[1]. But Carthage also needed food
for her large population, and for this reason agriculture always
held a very important place in her economic life. Big estates were
owned and farmed by noble or wealthy families, who through
long experience of the conditions of soil and climate had developed
Punic agriculture into a science with a technical literature of its
own; in fact they had industrialized it, and cheap slave-labour
working for large-scale production brought in a handsome profit.
In its own country it was undoubtedly efficient, and after 146 B.C.
the Roman Senate had the thirty-two books of Mago on Agriculture translated into Latin as a guide for intending settlers in
Africa[2] (see p. 341).

With such resources Carthage ranked amongst the wealthiest
of ancient cities: Thucydides (VI, 34, 2) makes a Syracusan speak
of her stores of silver and gold, and Polybius declares (XVIII, 35, 9)
that at the time of her fall she was reputed the wealthiest city in the
world. It has sometimes been taken as a proof of lack of inventive
power that she never adopted coinage until late in her career. Silver
coinage does not appear until the end of the fifth century, and even
then only in Sicily, struck on Greek models, and for use on an island
accustomed to Greek money[3]. The first domestic coinage was one
of gold and bronze in the fourth century[4], and silver money only

[1] U. Wilcken, *Punt-Fahrten in der Ptolemäerzeit, Z.* für Aeg. Sprache
und Altertumskunde, LX, 1925, pp. 86 *sqq.*   [2] Pliny, *N.H.* XVIII, 22.
[3] See Volume of Plates ii, 2, *d.*   [4] *Ib.* iii, 20, *k, l.*

began in Africa when the conquest of Spain poured the wealth of the mines there into the Carthaginian treasury. Yet such a state of things does not imply a backward civilization; Carthage did not need a coinage for her long trading voyages, where commerce with the natives would be carried on by barter, or in her own territory. It is interesting to find that for some time she experimented with a token coinage, consisting of weights wrapped in a covering of leather[1]. But our authorities do not produce any evidence for anything like the developed banking and commercial systems that are found in such cities as Hellenistic Rhodes or Alexandria (pp. 630, 662 *sqq.*).

Of her art numerous examples have been found in the tombs and graves of her citizens and now lie displayed in the Museums of Tunis. But the verdict upon it cannot be favourable; it was assimilative and unoriginal, and instead of improving in the course of years it is noticeable that the technique steadily declines. In the early centuries a strong Egyptian influence can be observed, as for instance in scarabs and amulets and in some of the clay masks. Later comes the importation of Greek vases and Greek articles of luxury, which grows stronger from the fifth century onwards. By the third and second centuries the graves are full of Hellenistic wares, especially from Rhodes, or of their imitations by native artists and craftsmen, who even signed their names in Greek characters, not in Punic. A curious feature is the great quantity of clay masks, grotesque faces with wide grinning mouths: their purpose is unknown, it may have been apotropaic, but they can be scarcely regarded as a contribution to art[2]. The little that is known of Punic building does not suggest that it was original, though under Roman rule a new style developed (the so-called Neo-Punic) that was not merely Roman but owed something to native art and motifs as well. But nothing so far found bears witness to any deep artistic impulse or feeling in the Carthaginian people, and it is not an exaggeration to say that the finer work was either imported from Greek centres or else made in Carthage by resident Greeks[3]. It is obvious that the people had some admiration for Greek art and that the richer nobles imported it for their houses and tables, while the statues and spoils from many a Sicilian city stood in private houses or public places for all to see; but what might have been a real stimulus (as it was in Rome) was here ineffective, and at its best gave rise merely to unintelligent copying. Carthaginian artists were too intent on

---

[1] [Plato], *Eryxias*, 399 E *sqq.* and cf. Meltzer, *Geschichte der Karthager*, II, pp. 106 *sqq.*   [2] See Volume of Plates iii, 194.   [3] *Ib.* 196 *a*, 198.

producing at a cheap rate what was necessary, and never troubled to enquire whether it might be beautiful as well.

In language and literature the story is different. Punic belonged to the North Semitic family of languages and has left some thousands of inscriptions and dedications which enable its structure and general characteristics to be analysed and determined with fair certainty. They are not, however, very informing from the social or historical side[1], consisting as they do mostly of epitaphs, or of dedicatory inscriptions, in which the dedicator thanks Tanit or Ba'al Hammon for granting his appeal and sending aid. The great commemoratory inscriptions, which we know it was the custom to set up, have perished in the ruin that overtook the city, save for one strange exception, an account of an exploratory voyage made by the Admiral Hanno down the Western coast of Africa about the turn of the sixth century B.C. The record of the voyage was inscribed in the temple of Melkart, and a Greek translation of it (possibly made at the instigation of Polybius) has been fortunately preserved[2]: it is a plain straightforward account of places visited and things seen, and carries conviction by its directness and brevity. But the total number of all the inscriptions so far found is not large, and their content somewhat monotonous.

Apart from the inscriptions there remains a certain amount of evidence for the existence of books and writings in the Punic tongue. Books there must have been to fill the libraries, which after the fall of the city were so generously presented by the Senate to various African princes[3], but we have little information about their writers. According to St Augustine (*Epistulae*, xvii, 2), 'in Carthaginian books there were many things wisely handed down to memory,' but detail is lacking. There were apparently Carthaginian histories, such as the writings of a certain Hiempsal, or the *libri Punici* used by Juba, the erudite and voluminous author king of Mauretania, or the *Punica Historia* mentioned by Servius, but they are names and nothing more. Nowhere is there a trace or a suggestion of drama, or of poetry, or of philosophy. It is true that by a curious freak of circumstance a son of Carthage became head of the New Academy: this was Hasdrubal, who migrated to Greece and, changing his name to Clitomachus, became first the pupil and then the successor of Carneades, and wrote over 400 volumes, though he was honest enough to confess

---

[1] The Punic sacrificial tariff-list found at Marseilles in 1845 and similar fragments found elsewhere are not important exceptions to this statement.

[2] *Geog. Graec. Min.* I, pp. 1–14.

[3] Pliny, *N.H.* xviii, 22.

that he had never ascertained the real opinion of his master on any subject[1]. But neither his treatises, which were in Greek and belong to the domain of Greek philosophy, nor those of Mago on Agriculture can be claimed as proving that Carthage possessed a sense of literature, or gave anything of value to the world in that sphere. On the other hand the language itself had struck its roots deeper, and endured (with the alterations and development natural in a living tongue) for a considerable period over the former domain of Carthage: inscriptions (sometimes bi-lingual) show that in towns *sufetes* only slowly gave way to *duoviri*[2], and although Latin was apparently made the official language in the first century A.D., there were plenty of people a hundred years after and even later to whom it was unfamiliar[3].

If we had a greater knowledge of Punic religion, if we knew more than the mere externals of name and cult, it might be possible to draw closer to the heart and character of this isolated people. For there can be no doubt that both people and nobles clung with a splendid and blind devotion to their national religion, that they fought desperately for their traditions and for the honour of the deities whom they regarded as protecting their city and its welfare. Such was the great goddess Tanit[4], the Lady of the Heavens, 'the face of Ba'al,' whose precinct was filled with offerings and dedications, and who long survived the overthrow of the city that had worshipped her; indeed, in Latin dress as *Caelestis*, she is not only found in many parts of Africa under the Roman Empire but actually won her way into Rome itself and had her adorers there. The chief deity of Carthage was a goddess, and as the *daimon* of the Carthaginians she heads the array of Punic gods and goddesses in the impressive oath which bound Hannibal and Philip together. After Tanit in importance came the gods Ba'al Hammon and Melkart ('King of the city'), but there was a host of minor Ba'als and other deities as well. To honour their gods and to win their help the citizens would not shrink from human sacrifice, and from the passing of children

---

[1] Cicero, *Acad.* II, 137.

[2] For the persistence of Punic as a language see Mommsen, *Prov. of the Rom. Empire*, vol. II, pp. 326 *sqq.* For *sufetes* in Sardinia see *C.I.L.* x, 7856 =*C.I.S.* 143 (Cagliari, 2nd century) or *C.I.L.* x. 7813 (Sulci), and *Not. Scavi*, 1913, p. 88. A first-century inscription from Volubilis in Mauretania mentions a Bostar, who was *aedilis sufes IIvir* (*C.R. Ac. Inscr.* 1915, p. 396).

[3] The sister of Septimius Severus, when she visited him in Rome, could only speak Latin very imperfectly (*Hist. Aug.* Severus, 15). Cf. Mommsen, *op. cit.* vol. II, p. 328.   [4] See Volume of Plates iii, 196, *b*.

through the fire, though it would appear that in course of time
the practice was mitigated: but in times of despair the rite would
break out again, as it did in the final siege of the doomed city. If
we are to believe Tertullian[1] the rite still persisted in parts of
Africa down to the first century of the Christian era, and the
credit for its suppression must be given to the emperors of that
time. It is certainly not a mere piece of Christian scandal; in the
burial-ground at Salammbô the calcined bones of the victims have
been discovered, most of them young children[2]. And the tale of
Hamilcar's self-immolation at the battle of Himera (see vol. IV,
p. 381), recounted by Herodotus, shows the same spirit of un-
questioning obedience and sacrifice. Faith may have waned
somewhat with the lapse of time; the cheapness of the later tomb-
furniture may be some indication of this, and it is said that in the
last two centuries the rich were no longer willing to offer up their
own children and procured other victims. But the gods remained,
and the rites remained, untouched by any inroads of the Greek
spirit of enquiry and doubt, unvisited by any searchings after a
deeper spiritual content or a more exalted conception of the divine
nature. The faith of their fathers persisted unaltered, and no
prophets arose in Carthage.

It is unfortunate that throughout for our knowledge of things
Carthaginian we have to rely upon the statements or views of men
who not only had a tradition of national hostility towards Carthage,
but who by race, language, and training were completely sundered
and unsympathetic. It is rare that justice is done to the Jews by
Greeks or Romans, and it is not surprising that Carthage should
receive a like handling. Yet it cannot be denied that, even when
due discount has been made for this bias, both Greek and Roman
agree strikingly in their judgments. In Aristotle's few pages and
occasional references we are conscious of an implied censure of
their love of wealth, and later writers are more explicit and
more damaging in their characterization. Polybius notes how
open bribery and corruption were, and declares nothing was regarded by them as disgraceful if it brought profit: Livy can
attribute to Hannibal *perfidia plus quam Punica*, and Cicero can
assure his hearers that all history proves the Phoenicians to be a
lying race. But the most bitter picture is reserved for Plutarch:
'how different,' he exclaims, 'the nature of the Carthaginian
people, harsh and gloomy, docile to its rulers, hard to its subjects,

[1] *Apologeticus*, 9. The date of suppression may be even later.
[2] See Cagnat, *En pays Romain*, pp. 192 *sqq*. and cf. Pace in *Mon. Linc.* xxx,
col. 155.

running to extremes of cowardice in fear and of savagery in anger:
keeping stubbornly to its decisions, austere and unresponsive to
amusement or the graces of life[1].' It was precisely this dour
outlook, this grimness of life (which manifested itself as efficiency
in business and fanaticism in religion), that seemed to a Greek
or a Roman harsh and repellent, a temper of mind which he was
utterly unable to comprehend. And this spirit lived on for generations and worked still among the Punic population that remained
settled in the Roman province of Africa or scattered in outlying
regions. It appeared in many guises: in mocking or angry riots
against governors[2]; in bitter commercial rivalry, such as caused
the cities of Leptis and Oea actually to go to war against each
other[3]; most of all in fervid religious conviction. Centuries later
Africa was to be the home of one of the great heresies, Donatism,
and such famous controversialists and champions of the Christian
faith as Tertullian, Augustine, or Lactantius all sprang from soil
that had once been Punic.

It may be felt perhaps that this verdict on Carthage is too unfavourable: our knowledge, such as it is, depends upon alien
sources; if more were available, if Carthage could speak for herself,
might we not judge more kindly? This may be: but the historian
is bound to use what materials he finds. The only way in which
he can know and appreciate a past civilization is by close and
intimate association with the writings and monuments belonging
to it which time has spared; where these do not exist and where
there is not a suggestion that they ever did exist, he must reluctantly conclude that the creative spirit was lacking. It is hard to
name anything which mankind can be said to owe to Carthage.
Some slight improvements in shipbuilding, a new type of siege-
artillery[4], some technical advances in agriculture, may possibly be
placed to her credit: in thought, in art, in literature, in language we
can find nothing, except that the word *gorilla* seems to have been
brought first to civilization by the Carthaginian Admiral Hanno.
The truth is that these colonial Semites lived as a race apart; cut
off from their mother-country they proved unable to produce a

---

[1] Plutarch, *de re pub. ger.* 3, 6.
[2] Cf. the amusing outburst against Vespasian. Suetonius, *Vesp.* 4, 3.
[3] Tacitus, *Hist.* IV, 50.
[4] The invention of the *aries*, used in besieging Gades: see Vitruvius
(ed. F. Krohn) x, 13, 1.

living culture of their own. As a consequence Carthage remains in the background of history, a shadowy though formidable figure, never emerging into light save when she comes into conflict with some people of a more robust civilization than her own. To Greeks and Romans alike she was a barbarian State, whose language was uncouth, whose customs smacked of primitive savagery, whose religion was an excessive superstition. With all her power, her wealth, and her material prosperity, she left scarcely a trace behind, and with the fall of Carthage it looked as though the last champion of the Semitic-speaking peoples had gone. But a greater destiny, to make a greater mark on history, was reserved for another people of that stock, the Jews, who were struggling to maintain their national and religious character in the cosmopolitan kingdom of Seleucid Syria.

CHAPTER XVI

SYRIA AND THE JEWS

I. SYRIA UNDER SELEUCUS IV

THE realm to which Seleucus IV Philopator succeeded, as a man of about thirty years old, in 187 B.C. was no longer the great empire over which his father had ruled before the war with Rome. But it covered the whole of Syria and Palestine, with Cilicia still attached to it on the west, Mesopotamia, Babylonia and the nearer regions of Iran on the east. A careful government, re-organizing this smaller dominion, might still make it a formidable power, when the effects of the disastrous war with Rome had been repaired. But for the moment the only sound policy was to abstain from expensive adventures, and so order the finances of the kingdom, that it might bear the crushing indemnity to be paid to Rome. So far as we can see, Seleucus IV dealt with the situation prudently. If the kingdom was to recover power and prestige, such an inglorious period of quiet and recuperation was the necessary first stage. With the resources still remaining to the house of Seleucus, it would not have been too late, even now, to build up a solid power, provided the government could go on without interruption in resolute hands. That proviso was not to be fulfilled. The rule of Seleucus IV himself was to be cut short by assassination. After that set-back able and active kings were still to come—Antiochus Epiphanes, Demetrius I, Antiochus VII Sidetes—but each new work of restoration was to be frustrated by new confusion, and after the untimely death of Antiochus VII there was no salvation for the kingdom any more. The recurring confusion was brought about by quarrels within the kingdom— within the royal house—fomented and sustained by outside powers, Egypt or Pergamum, while in the background stood the sinister figure of Rome, always supporting the elements of disruption.

The chief task of Seleucus IV, as has just been said, was to replenish the treasury of the kingdom against the drain of the Roman indemnity. It was with the passage of the 'exactor' that his subjects in recollection associated his reign (Daniel xi, 20). But

Note. For the Greek, Latin and Jewish sources see the Bibliography. A note on the *Maccabees* and a genealogical table of the Seleucid dynasty will be found at the end of the volume. See Map 8 facing p. 139.

he obviously also kept in careful touch with what was happening in the other states of the Hellenistic east, maintained friendly relations with the Achaean League, gave his daughter in marriage to Perseus of Macedonia (177 B.C.), and at one time, we are told, was even on the point of leading an army across the Taurus, to mix in the wars of Asia Minor, but wisely thought better of it. One significant action on his part was an innovation in the royal nomenclature. He called his son Demetrius. The practice of the dynasty hitherto would have made his eldest son bear the name Antiochus, and his second son that of Seleucus. According to the view taken in this chapter, Demetrius was the elder son of Seleucus IV; it was the younger son who was called Antiochus. The name Demetrius was one of the royal names in the house of Antigonus. It was indeed the name of a possible successor to the Macedonian throne when the son of Seleucus was born in 187/6 B.C. Unquestionably the introduction of this name into the Seleucid dynasty was meant as a declaration that the house of Seleucus had Antigonid blood, and might, in the event of the issue of Philip V failing, claim a right to the Antigonid inheritance. Since Demetrius the son of Philip was killed in 181, and Philip's elder son, Perseus, was begotten of a bourgeois mother, the name may have been given to the little Seleucid prince, instead of some other original name, when Philip was seen to have no fully qualified issue. In any case the child Demetrius had to be sent as a hostage to Rome, in place of the king's brother Antiochus, who had gone as hostage for his father Antiochus III. Just so the Macedonian Demetrius, the Antigonid prince of bluest blood, had been sent to Rome as hostage for his father in 194. When the exchange took place we do not know; it is only certain that when Seleucus was killed in 175, the boy Demetrius was in Rome, and Antiochus, the boy's uncle, was residing in Athens, where the office of hoplite general had been conferred upon him.

There was always the possibility of trouble with Egypt so long as Ptolemy Epiphanes lived, since a party at the Ptolemaic court was in favour of Egypt trying issues again with the Seleucids on the field of battle, for the recovery of Coele-Syria, whenever a favourable occasion offered. But when Ptolemy Epiphanes died at the age of 28 in 181—by poison, it was asserted—the government of Egypt passed into the hands of Seleucus' sister, Cleopatra I, as queen-regent for her infant son, Ptolemy VI Philometor, and the party for maintaining peace with Syria came securely into power in Alexandria, for the rest of Seleucus' reign.

Seleucus Philopator was assassinated in 175 B.C. by his chief minister Heliodorus. This man probably belonged to one of the

XVI, II] END OF SELEUCUS IV

great Graeco-Macedonian families of the Seleucid kingdom, since he was a *syntrophos*[1] of the king's, that is, had been one of the boys brought up at court with the royal children. That he had, as minister, shown special interest in the economic prosperity of the kingdom may be indicated by the memorial of gratitude which a body of merchants belonging to the Syrian Laodicea (Latakieh) put up in his honour at Delos (*O.G.I.S.* 247).

II. ANTIOCHUS EPIPHANES

When Seleucus had been murdered, there were three princes of the royal house who might claim the diadem. There was the legitimate heir, the elder son of Seleucus, the boy Demetrius, detained as a hostage in Rome; there was the younger son, Antiochus, still a baby in Syria; and there was the late king's brother, Antiochus, now probably about forty, living in Athens. The plan of Heliodorus was apparently to proclaim the baby Antiochus as king, and rule himself in the child's name. That would give him the substance of power without such provocation to public sentiment as his formally assuming the diadem would have been. But as soon as the news of Seleucus's death reached Athens, Antiochus, the child's uncle, made ready to seize the inheritance. Without a force at his disposal, it might have been impossible for him to overthrow the usurper in power, had not at this moment the king of Pergamum come forward to conduct him to Syria with a Pergamene army. Eumenes II may have regarded it as a clever move in his political game, when there was a danger of Rome becoming hostile to him, to put as his neighbour on the Seleucid throne a king upon whose goodwill he could count. Or it is possible that a hint may have come to Eumenes from Rome, since Antiochus, after his long residence in Rome as a hostage, had friends amongst the Roman aristocracy, and it may have been believed in Rome that Antiochus as king of Syria would be subservient to their desires. A broken inscription found at Pergamum (*O.G.I.S.* 248) is believed to be the copy of a decree passed by the Athenian people, thanking Eumenes for having set their late general upon the throne of his fathers.

Evidently when Antiochus had once appeared in Syria with a Pergamene force the country soon rallied to him. Heliodorus probably had little support and disappeared. We are not told that Antiochus put him to death. In fact it has been conjectured, on the strength of a passage in Athenaeus, that Heliodorus' latter

[1] It is to be noted, however, that the contemporary Aristonicus is called a *syntrophos* of Ptolemy V, though he was an eunuch, *i.e.* an ex-slave.

years were spent in literary leisure in some Greek city, and that he gave his memoirs to the world[1]. The more formidable opposition which Antiochus had to encounter was probably from those who held that the baby Antiochus, or the boy Demetrius, had a better title to the throne, and were disposed to look upon the uncle as a usurper. The way in which he is spoken of in the book of Daniel—'a contemptible person upon whom had not been conferred royal majesty,' who 'shall come in unawares and seize the kingship by guile' (xi, 21)—is probably not due entirely to the abhorrence excited later on by Antiochus' assault on the Jewish religion, but echoes things already said in Coele-Syria at the beginning of his reign. Possibly in this region the opposition to him was also combined with a movement for bringing back Ptolemaic rule[2]. Our scrappy data indicate that it required a good deal of dexterity and intrigue on the part of Antiochus for him to establish his position in Syria, but that he did get the better of the opposing elements. According to the view taken in this chapter, he did not in the first instance displace his nephew, the baby Antiochus, but assumed by his side the position of king-regent, much as Antigonus Doson had done in Macedonia beside the infant Philip V[3]. The coins which bear the legend 'Of King Antiochus' and show the portrait of a child, seemingly of not more than four or five years, whose resemblance to Seleucus is striking, may be regarded as coins issued in the first years of the new reign[4]. Other coins with the same legend, but with the portrait of Antiochus the uncle, which seem to belong to the time between 175 and 170, may have been issued concurrently with the coins of the baby-king, or the coinage may at first have borne the head of the baby, and the uncle may later on have substituted his own[5]. Cuneiform documents from the first year of Antiochus to the year 169 have in their dating 'Antiochus and Antiochus kings.'

So many attempts have been made to describe the singular character of Antiochus IV from our documentary data that not much need be said here. Energy we can see and ability, possibly some peculiar charm of manner, but a *bonhomie* which often concealed a hostile design, a Bohemian curiosity to experience life in its diverse kinds, an unconventional familiarity which delighted in playing practical jokes upon solemn dignitaries, yet a ready interest in intellectual discussion, which made Antiochus an ardent

[1] See W. Otto in *P.W. s.v.* Heliodorus (6).
[2] See Jerome *In Daniel* xi, 21: cf. Bouché-Leclercq, *Histoire des Séleucides*, I, p. 241.   [3] See note 5 at end of volume.
[4] See Volume of Plates iii, 12, *f*.   [5] *Ib.* 12, *h*.

adherent of the Stoic philosophy at the beginning of his reign, but a promising convert for the Epicurean philosopher Philonides of Laodicea, later on. Above all, the theatrical vein was strongly marked: Antiochus IV loved pageantry and the imposing external of things. It seemed to him capital fun to institute in Antioch an office closely copying the aedileship he had known in Rome, and himself play the part of aedile with all the proper accessories. How far his philhellenic passion was a serious appreciation of what was valuable in Greek culture, how far a delight in its beautiful outside, we cannot know. We can believe that in the vehement following of his caprices, his intolerance of control, he was essentially a tyrant in spite of all his republican freedom of manners. It was his theatrical vein, no doubt, which made him find pleasure in being recognized as a god. His name on his coins in the later years of his reign has a title attached to it—an innovation in Seleucid coinage: he is described as *Epiphanes* or *Theos Epiphanes*, 'God Manifest,' a title which had been given in Egypt to his brother-in-law, Ptolemy V. Yet his policy of unifying the kingdom by promoting a common Hellenistic culture was not without a sane purpose. One may only observe here how a new development of civic life in the cities of the kingdom is shown by the bronze coinage which many of them now begin to issue with the head of the king, and the assumption of a new name, Antioch, or Seleuceia or Epiphaneia[1].

III. THE JEWISH FACTIONS

When Coele-Syria passed in 200 B.C. from the Ptolemies to the Seleucids (p. 173 *sq.*), the little Jewish state on the hills of Judaea acquired, by its geographical position, new importance. It was now close to the frontier between the two realms, just above the coast-road, the main line of communication between Syria and Egypt. For the Seleucid king it was thus both an important point in his defences and also a weak point, should the Jews be drawn, by old memories or by intrigues directed from Egypt, to side with Ptolemy.

To the reign of Seleucus Philopator belongs the first incident we hear of in the conflict between the Jews and the Seleucid

[1] For the general character of Seleucid rule at this time see vol. VII, chap. v. In Cilicia, Adana becomes Antioch, Oeniandus becomes Epiphaneia, Mopsu-Hestia becomes Seleuceia; in Syria, Hamath becomes Epiphaneia, Gadara changes between Antioch and Seleuceia, Ptolemaïs becomes Antioch. Tarsus had already been named Antioch in the third century (*Fouilles de Delphes*, III, 2, no. 208; see Roussel's note to *I.G.* XI, 4, 822).

government, and Heliodorus plays a principal part in it. It was connected with the financial exigencies of the government which marked this reign. Heliodorus visited Jerusalem in person, and made an attempt to enter the Holy of Holies and confiscate some of the treasure stored in the Temple. The attempt was frustrated. Our only account of the incident comes from the Second Book of Maccabees, which declares that Heliodorus was met in the Temple by angels who scourged him severely and drove him out. It is easy to rationalize the story, if it is worth while doing so. Indeed the rationalization began at the time, since the opponents of the High Priest told the government that it was a fraud got up by him, to defeat the government demand.

If the religious and nationalist revolt in Judaea was provoked by the interference of the Seleucid government, that interference was itself brought about by happenings in the Jewish high-priestly state which we can only imperfectly trace. Various kinds of quarrel had been going on there. The High Priest was Ḥonya III, called by the Greeks Onias. 'A certain Simon,' II Maccabees tells us, 'of the tribe of Benjamin, who held the office of *prostates* of the Temple, quarrelled with the High Priest about the control of the city's market.' What functions belonged to the *prostates* of the Temple nobody knows, though scholars conjecture with probability that he had something to do with the Temple treasury. In these quarrels one of the most powerful families in the Jewish community was involved, the house of Tobiah. We hear of a Tobiah at Jerusalem in the fifth century. Nehemiah calls him an 'Ammonite' (iv, 3), yet he is allied with Eliashib the High Priest and has a chamber reserved for his use in the Temple (xiii, 4, 5). In the third and second centuries members of the family are found holding the position of chieftains in the Ammonite country, and one may conjecture that the family already had possessions there in the days of Nehemiah, and that it was this which caused Nehemiah to fix the opprobrious description of 'Ammonite' upon his adversary. Evidently Tobiah was regarded by the Jerusalem aristocracy of the time as an eminent member of the Jewish community, and the name is a distinctly Jewish one ('Yah is good'). It is of course possible that Tobiah had a mixture of Ammonite blood, or was of proselyte origin.

The Zeno papyri have revealed to us a 'Tubias' ruling in the Ammonite country under Ptolemy II a hundred years before the time with which we are now concerned. Galleries and chambers hewn out of the rock are still to be seen in Transjordania, over one of which the name 'Tobiah' is inscribed in

Hebrew characters[1]. They show us a stronghold of chiefs of the house of Tobiah in Hellenistic times: it may be the place indicated in one of the papyri by the name 'Birta of the Ammanitis' (*birta* is the Aramaic for 'fortress'); or it may be the stronghold which Josephus (*Ant.* XII, 230) calls a *baris*, another way apparently of graecizing the same Aramaic word. In the latter part of the third century one of the Tobiad family, called Joseph, had amassed great riches as a farmer of taxes for the Ptolemaic government in Palestine (vol. VII, p. 193). In the days of Seleucus IV the family was itself divided by quarrels; a younger member of it, ambitious and violent, called Hyrcanus, was at daggers drawn with his brothers. Josephus (*Ant.* XII, 239) tells us that the 'sons of Tobias' were partisans of Menelaus (the brother of Simon the *prostates*) and in *Wars*, I, 31, he attributes to them the action which the *Antiquities* and II Maccabees ascribe to Menelaus. This has led some scholars to believe that Simon and Menelaus were themselves of the Tobiad house, though our text is rather against the supposition.

The father of Onias, the preceding High Priest Simon II, is said by Josephus (*Ant.* XII, 229) to have sided with the elder sons of Joseph the Tobiad against Hyrcanus. Hyrcanus withdrew into the Ammonite country and established a power there by raiding the Arabs. He built the cave-fortress which Josephus, as we have seen, calls a *baris*. One would conjecture that he copied, or enlarged, the fortress of his ancestor Tobiah in this region. Yet he deposited large sums of money (II Macc. iii, 11) in the Temple at Jerusalem for safe-keeping, and Onias is found earnestly protecting this deposit from spoliation. The High Priest would therefore seem to be now favourable to Hyrcanus and against the bulk of the Tobiad family. According to Josephus[2], Onias 'drove the sons of Tobiah out of the city.' It was Simon the *prostates*, according to II Maccabees, who instigated the Seleucid government, through his suggestions to Apollonius, the governor of Coele-Syria, to lay hands on the Temple treasure, and brought about the visit of Heliodorus.

At Jerusalem the intervention of the Seleucid government, after Antiochus Epiphanes had occupied the throne, was again brought about by the contentions which divided the Jewish people. Personal strife between the leaders was now complicated by a

---

[1] At Araq el-Amir: see the description given by Butler, Princeton Expedition, Division II, A 1 *sqq.*

[2] *Wars*, I, 31. The statement is perhaps drawn from Nicolaus of Damascus: see Hölscher in *P.W. s.v.* Josephus.

religious struggle between those who wished to introduce Hellenistic culture and those who stood by traditional custom and law.
The initiative in the attempt to hellenize Jerusalem was not
taken by Antiochus; it was taken by a certain section of the Jews
themselves, and the interference of Antiochus was directed to
carry through a process already begun. Probably there was yet
a third kind of quarrel, that between the partisans of the Seleucid
king and the partisans of Ptolemy. There were still those who
regretted the former rule and took their cue from Egypt. How
all these different quarrels worked in together, we cannot precisely say; it looks as if those faithful to the old religion tended
to be drawn into the pro-Egyptian and anti-Tobiad camp, and
regarded the High Priest Onias as their leader.

After the death of Seleucus IV we hear no more of Simon the
prostates. Onias now has another antagonist—his own brother,
Jason, whose Greek name probably represented the Hebrew name
Yeshua (Jesus). Jason had gone over to the hellenizing camp, and
is soon found associated with Menelaus the brother of Simon. By
the promise of a larger tribute he induced the Seleucid government
to establish him as High Priest in the place of his brother. No
doubt Antiochus would be delighted to further the desire of the
Jewish Hellenizers. Jerusalem under Jason was converted into
a Greek city. Its citizens 'were registered as Antiochenes'
(II Macc. iv, 9), which probably does not mean that they were
given the citizenship of Antioch the capital, but that Jerusalem
itself became another of the many Antiochs. The chief horror to
the faithful was the institution of the gymnasium, essential to
every Greek city, where the young men, even priests, exercised
naked and formed bodies of *epheboi* who wore Greek hats. No
doubt, in order to judge the attitude of the faithful fairly, it has
to be remembered that when a tradition, like that of the Jewish
people, combines elements of great spiritual and moral value with
indurated conventions and taboos, it is not easy for contemporaries
to distinguish clearly the valuable elements from the merely conventional ones. The tradition presents itself as a single structure,
and if its authority is repudiated in regard to the conventional
parts there is a real danger of the valuable parts also being
weakened. It is noteworthy that in the modern East, orthodox
Mohammedans have till recently attached great importance to
the traditional head-dress being worn, and European hats have
been regarded with abhorrence. The Turkey of to-day, like the
Jewish Hellenizers of 175 B.C., has thrown over all those parts of
the Islamic tradition which seem useless conventions, discarding

the *fez*: it remains to be seen how far the rest of the Islamic tradition will continue unimpaired. That heathen worships were admitted into Jerusalem, even under Jason, seems improbable; but a sacred embassy of Jews was sent to take part in the penta-eteric festival of Herakles (Melkart) at Tyre.

Antiochus IV had his anxieties soon directed to his southern frontier. Before 172 his sister Cleopatra I, the queen-regent of Egypt, died and the power was seized by two creatures of the palace, Eulaeus and Lenaeus, both of barbarian and servile ante-cedents. Cleopatra's pacific policy was abandoned, and the war-party at Alexandria gained the ascendant, the party which wanted to fight to get back Coele-Syria. Antiochus' envoy, Apollonius, sent to Alexandria to represent him at the enthronement ceremony of the young king Ptolemy VI Philometor, who was now fourteen or fifteen, brought back a report of the designs of the Egyptian court so disquieting that Antiochus moved south with a force as far as Joppa to encounter a possible invasion. From Joppa he paid a visit to Jerusalem and was welcomed by the High Priest Jason with torchlight processions. It did not yet come to actual war between Syria and Egypt, and Antiochus returned north.

At Jerusalem a new rift occurred—personal rivalry within the dominant Hellenistic party. Menelaus, the brother of Simon the *prostates*, intrigued at court and got himself made High Priest by royal decree instead of Jason (170/169 B.C.). Jason took refuge in the Ammonite country, where Hyrcanus the Tobiad no longer ruled. Soon after the accession of Antiochus IV, Hyrcanus had felt his position desperate—the new government would not tolerate an independent aggressive power in Transjordania—and had committed suicide. Menelaus, according to II Maccabees, did not even belong to the tribe of Levi; he was, as we have seen, a Benjamite. His tenure of the High Priesthood was a flagrant violation of the Law. A Greek officer of the king's was installed, probably with a small force, in the citadel (*akropolis*) of Jerusalem to the north of the Temple (II Macc. iv, 28)[1].

In the winter of 170–69 Antiochus was in Cilicia, where trouble had occurred because the cities of Tarsus and Mallus resented being assigned as an appanage to the king's concubine Antiochis. In his absence the government of Syria was in the hands of a certain Andronicus, who had also, no doubt, charge of the boy-king Antiochus, son of Seleucus IV. Andronicus now, apparently, put him out of the way. The crime excited great popular indignation

[1] Not to be identified with the *akra* spoken of later on: see E. Schürer, *Gesch. des Volkes Israel*, vol. I, 4th ed., p. 198.

in Antioch, and the uncle on his return declared that he had had
no part in it. He put Andronicus to death. Whether Antiochus IV
was really innocent we shall never know. It seems certain that
Andronicus would not have committed the crime unless he had
believed that he was doing Antiochus a service which would be
counted in his favour.

In the account given by II Maccabees of the execution of
Andronicus, after Antiochus' return from Cilicia, not a word is
said of the infant king. The crime of Andronicus, for which the
people rise in indignation and Antiochus sheds tears of pity, is
the murder of the High Priest Onias III. There is no reason to
doubt that Andronicus did cause Onias to be assassinated about
the same time that he murdered the infant king; but the Jewish
writer, it is now commonly recognized, attaches to the murder of
Onias the sentiments, or show of sentiments, which were really
called forth in the people and in Antiochus IV by the murder of
the royal child (Diodorus xxx, 7, 2; Johannes Antioch. frag. 58).

The old High Priest had resided in Antioch, probably since he
had been supplanted by Jason. There was evidently a risk of his
being assassinated in Antioch by Jews of the opposite faction, since
he had taken sanctuary in the precinct of Apollo at Daphne. When
Menelaus came to Antioch in the winter of 170/69, during the
absence of the king in Cilicia, in order to explain why the excessive
tribute he had promised was in arrears, he contrived to persuade
Andronicus that Onias should be put out of the way. The High
Priest was induced to come out of sanctuary, and was instantly
killed. To the faithful he was the true Anointed of the Lord, the
'Messiah' who had been cut off (Daniel ix, 26). The business of
the tribute from Jerusalem made trouble. Menelaus in outbidding
Jason had promised more than he could raise without despoiling
the Temple. While he was away in Antioch, his brother Lysimachus,
whom he had left in command, laid hands on some of the Temple's
golden furniture. This provoked rioting in which Lysimachus was
killed. The court was disposed to hold Menelaus responsible for
the disorder, and the insurgent people sent envoys to accuse
Menelaus before the king, when the king was at Tyre. But
Menelaus succeeded in bribing a courtier, Ptolemy, son of Dorymenes, who had the king's ear. Menelaus was re-established in
power by the royal arm.

IV. THE EGYPTIAN WAR AND THE
MACCABAEAN REVOLT

In the summer of 169 it really did come to war between Syria
and Egypt. Under the hare-brained direction of Eulaeus and
Lenaeus an army was mustered to invade Palestine. Then
Antiochus, who had intelligence of what was afoot, struck first. He
had already sent his minister of finance, the unsavoury Heracleides,
to convince the Senate, by argument or bribery, that Egypt was
the aggressor, as indeed it was. Heracleides must have appeared in
Rome in the early summer of 169[1]; Rome for the moment had its
hands full with the Macedonian War; for Antiochus there was
scope for independent military action against Egypt. He met the
Egyptian invading army before they had traversed the desert
which separates Egypt from Syria, and drove it back in headlong
rout. Then Antiochus invaded Egypt. The great marshals of
Alexander, Perdiccas and Antigonus, had failed in the attempt
to get through the frontier defences of Egypt; Antiochus the
Great had been defeated by Ptolemy Philopator on the Syrian
edge of the desert; no army-leader had invaded Egypt from
Syria since Alexander had done so, 163 years before. Antiochus
possessed himself of the frontier fortress, Pelusium, by some ruse
which Polybius (xxviii, 18) considered discreditable. Then he
moved up the Nile to Memphis, the natural road for an invader.
The Alexandrian court was panic-stricken, and the young Ptolemy
tried to escape by sea. Antiochus had the good luck to capture
him. The Alexandrian people showed some spirit in this crisis.
They put the king's younger brother, to be known 24 years later
as Ptolemy Euergetes II, upon the throne and gave him ministers
more efficient than the ex-slaves of the late régime. This afforded
Antiochus the opportunity of posing as the champion of the
legitimate king, whom he held in his hands at Memphis. Jerome,
following Porphyry, tells us that Antiochus had himself crowned
as a Pharaoh by traditional Egyptian rites at Memphis. This would
have been inconsistent with his professed support of the rights
of Ptolemy Philometor. It would also have been a dangerous provocation of Rome, which would hardly consent to see Egypt and
Syria united under a Seleucid. Yet with a man of the character of
Antiochus the temptation to have the ancient and mysterious ritual
of a Pharaonic coronation performed upon him, while he was in
Memphis as a conqueror, may have been too strong for considerations of consistency or fear of Rome to deter him.

[1] W. Kolbe, *Beiträge zur syrischen und jüdischen Geschichte*, p. 34.

From Memphis Antiochus moved down upon Alexandria, and the city manned its defences. Ambassadors from Athens, the Achaean League, and various other Greek states, who happened to be in Alexandria at the time, met Antiochus near Saïs and endeavoured to mediate. Soon the Syrian army cut off Alexandria from Egypt, but its communications by sea remained open. An embassy came from Rhodes, to make a fresh attempt at mediation. In view of the danger to all Hellenic and Hellenistic states from Rome, it was felt desirable that the quarrel between Syria and Egypt should be brought to an end. Antiochus professed himself ready to make peace, so soon as the Alexandrians would readmit the lawful king of Egypt, Ptolemy Philometor. He did not continue to press the siege of Alexandria. Towards the end of 169 he withdrew from Egypt, leaving Ptolemy Philometor king in Memphis and the younger Ptolemy king in Alexandria. The withdrawal, when he seemed to have made himself master of Egypt and when Alexandria was feeling the distress of the siege, is strange. But he certainly hoped that Egypt would remain paralysed by the rivalry of the two brother kings. He kept a garrison in Pelusium.

At Jerusalem, during the time when Antiochus was in Egypt, fresh troubles had occurred. A false rumour ran through Palestine that Antiochus was dead. Immediately Jason returned from Transjordania with a band, broke into Jerusalem and began putting the adherents of Menelaus to the sword. No doubt he had a good proportion of the people on his side, yet Menelaus, helped perhaps by the government troops in the citadel overlooking the Temple, succeeded ultimately in repelling the raid. To Antiochus it naturally meant that the people of Jerusalem, a vital point in his frontier defences, was on the side of Ptolemy. On his return from Egypt, in the latter part of 169, he turned aside to beat down the disaffected people under the High Priest of his appointment. Some blood flowed in the streets, but the outrage which most cut the faithful to the heart was that Antiochus entered into the Holy of Holies, and carried off a quantity of gold and silver vessels from the Temple. No angels appeared to protect the House of the Lord.

In the following winter the plans of Antiochus met with a reverse. The two brothers in Egypt agreed to unite against their uncle. Philometor returned to Alexandria, and it was settled that they should rule Egypt together as joint-kings. This inevitably brought back Antiochus and a Syrian army into Egypt in the spring of 168. The Ptolemaic kingdom was in no condition to offer an effectual resistance. Ptolemy Macron, the governor of

Cyprus, went over to Antiochus and admitted his forces into the island. Envoys from the brother kings had in vain tried to come to an agreement with Antiochus before he crossed the frontier. He had demanded the formal cession of Pelusium and Cyprus to the house of Seleucus. Once more his army marched from the frontier to Memphis; once more from Memphis down upon Alexandria. Then came the celebrated scene when in Eleusis, a suburb of Alexandria, Antiochus was met by Popillius Laenas, the representative of Rome (p. 284). The conquest of Macedonia had at last set Rome's hands free. Antiochus had to evacuate completely both Egypt and Cyprus. The 'ships of Kittim had come against him, and he was grieved and returned' (Daniel xi, 30).

If Antiochus must see Egypt once more an independent power, it was the more urgent that the south of Palestine should be solidly organized as a Seleucid province. It was in 167 that he took the momentous step of trying to suppress the religious peculiarities of the Jews and recast their forms of worship after the Greek type. It probably seemed to him that, if the party amongst the Jews most stubbornly devoted to the Jewish religious eccentricities was also the party which had leanings to the house of Ptolemy, then, surely, to carry the process of hellenization right through would be to establish in control at Jerusalem those loyal to Seleucid rule. Of course he had no conception what the significance of the Hebrew religion really was: he did not know what he was about.

The policy of Antiochus to unify his kingdom on the basis of a common Hellenic culture clashed at Jerusalem with another tradition unlike any other in the world. Already since the days of Jason, Jerusalem had been called Antioch and had adopted many of the characteristics of a Greek town. But the old religious rites had been continued in the Temple, and no other god set up there beside Yahweh. The hellenization up to this point had been carried out voluntarily by a part of the Jewish people: the extension of the process which displaced Yahweh for Zeus Olympios and Dionysus was forced upon the Jews by Antiochus. The first move was that Apollonius, commander of the Mysian mercenaries, appeared with a force before the city, but concealed his hostile intentions till he got a footing within, when he chose the occasion of a Sabbath-day to set his troops upon the multitude. Many of the population were sent off into slavery. A new fortress was constructed to hold Jerusalem in check. The site chosen was that of the old 'city of David' to the south of the Temple hill, in those days still high ground separated from the Temple hill by a depression, though later changes have left no elevation here discernible to-day. Elaborate fortifications were built and a considerable force of Gentile soldiers established as a permanent garrison. It is this fortress which our Greek texts call the *akra*.

Then the hellenization of the public religion was carried through by force. Yahweh was perhaps identified with Dionysus; in any case it was to Zeus Olympios that the Temple was re-dedicated. Similar measures were taken in regard to the Samaritans; the temple of Yahweh on Mount Gerizim was also declared a temple of Zeus Xenios (II Macc. vi, 2) or Zeus Hellenios (Josephus, *Ant.* xii, 263). The Jewish books represent the Samaritans as gladly falling in with the king's policy, and Josephus gives what purports to be a petition from the Samaritans to Antiochus, themselves asking for the conversion of their temple. This may, as has been supposed[1], be a Jewish forgery, but one would imagine a hellenizing party to have existed amongst the Samaritans, as amongst the Jews. If there was also a body of faithful amongst the Samaritans, our Jewish sources do not allow us to hear anything of it. At Jerusalem an image of Zeus Olympios was set up in the Temple, which, there is reason to conjecture, may have displayed the features of Antiochus himself, disguised with a beard[2]. It was explained to the Jews in their own tongue that this was *Baal Shamin*, 'the Lord of Heaven.' The king's ordinance made it penal to carry out the Law, to circumcise children, to possess the books of the Law, or to refuse to eat pig's flesh. On December 25th, 167 B.C., the pagan festival of 'lights' which celebrated the rebirth of the sun, a Greek altar was erected upon the old altar in the Temple court (perhaps the 'abomination of desolation,' Daniel ix, 27). The 'sacrifice and oblation,' which had daily maintained the connection between Yahweh and his people, ceased.

We have therefore now what we have not had hitherto, a definitely religious persecution. In the first phase of the persecution, the faithful endured martyrdom. If the government forces attacked them on the Sabbath-day, they would offer no resistance. The story of the Seven Brethren martyred for their fidelity became later on the model for the martyrologies of the Christian Church. The second phase began when a number of the faithful banded themselves together for a counter-attack and resolved that they would fight in self-defence even on the Sabbath. That phase was initiated by a priest, Mattathiah, of the house of Hashmon, whose family possessions were in the little town of Modiin.

[1] By E. Meyer, *Ursprung und Anfänge des Christentums*, vol. ii, p. 154 n. 3. See vol. vii, p. 191 *sq.*

[2] Antiochus appears thus as Zeus on some of his coins. See Vol. of Plates iii, 12, *i*.

Mattathiah had cut down a renegade Jew who was about to offer sacrifice before the king's officer in Modiin and had slain the officer himself. After that he had fled with his five sons into the wilderness, where they formed the nucleus of a band which eluded capture, made descents upon the country towns and villages and killed hellenizing Jews. The little band grew continually as the 'godly' (the Chasīdim) gathered to them. Mattathiah himself died soon after this new phase began (166/5 B.C.); but his sons, the five brethren of the house of Hashmon (the Hasmonaean family, as it is commonly called), continued to lead the nationalist bands. The third brother, Judah (Judas), was the best soldier and had the military command. His surname Maccabaeus is generally explained as meaning 'hammer' (makkabah), but there are linguistic difficulties about this supposition. It has recently been suggested that the name was an allusion to Isaiah lxii, 2, and meant 'the naming of the Lord[1].'

Encounters between the nationalist bands and local forces of the Seleucid government in Palestine went successfully for the nationalists. They are reflected in the battles fought by Judas against Apollonius and against Seron (I Maccabees iii, 10–25). No doubt the history of the Jewish war of independence shows that whenever the strength of the Seleucid realm was seriously put forth against the Jewish bands these were worsted in the encounter. We must not indeed conceive the Jews of those days as like the Jews of Medieval Europe, an unwarlike people given to sedentary pursuits and the handling of money. It was the policy of the Christian Roman Empire which barred to the Jews the profession of arms, and produced the type commonly regarded in later times as Jewish. The Jews of Palestine in the second century B.C. were not distinguished by any marked aptitude for trade and finance. Even at the end of the first century A.D. Josephus could write, 'We are not a commercial people' (*Contra Apion.* I, 60). In Palestine the main occupation of the Jewish people was agriculture and stock-breeding. Jews were also in demand as good soldiers; we hear of a Jewish garrison in Upper Egypt in the fifth century B.C.: the Ptolemies settled Jewish military allotment-holders in different parts of the country; Antiochus III had done the same in Asia Minor. Ptolemy Philometor and Cleopatra III, later on, had armies commanded by Jewish generals. To picture the bands of Judas Maccabaeus we should not think of the Jews of medieval and modern times, but of people more like the fierce monotheistic *ghazis* of the Indian

---

[1] A. A. Bevan in *Journal of Theol. Studies,* xxx, 1929, pp. 191 *sqq.*

frontier—Afghans and Pathans. Against such desperate fighters, filled with the flame of a religious enthusiasm, it may well be that the government troops, recruited amongst the hellenized Syrians or half-blood Macedonians of the Seleucid realm, were often broken, even when they had a marked superiority of numbers. Yet the government's command of numbers and equipment was such that the Jewish bands could not stand against the king's forces when a really large army was put in the field. 'With heaven it is all one, to save by many or by few,' Judas is represented as saying to his followers (I Macc. iii, 18). Yet, if one had to take victory in battle as the index of Divine favour, one would have to say that in Palestine, in the second century B.C., as so often elsewhere, heaven was on the side of the large and well-equipped battalions.

V. THE BOOK OF DANIEL

It was probably in 166 B.C., when the godly still had to see their religion suppressed by the heathen power, when they were still helpless to rid the Temple of the abominations which polluted it, when the days of darkness and tribulation still continued, even though certain zealots among the people had taken the sword in hand and here and there driven back the persecuting power, that the Book of Daniel was given forth. Copies of it began to pass from hand to hand among the godly. It was the work, they believed, of a prophet who had lived in Babylonia some 370 years before. How was it that no one had heard of the writing till now? The writing itself gave the answer: it had been concealed by Divine command till the critical moment when its message was needed. The earlier part of the book, consisting of a series of stories which showed Daniel and his companions faithful to their religion in the face of the power of heathen kings, had perhaps been in circulation earlier; the stories, at any rate, may have been popular stories before the days of Antiochus; but the latter part, consisting of visions in which the course of the world during recent centuries, so far as it affected Israel, was set forth either in symbolical imagery or in the oracular utterance of angel interpreters, is fixed by its contents to the short period between the beginning of the religious persecution and the recovery of the Temple.

It portrayed the Greek rule as the fourth heathen rule to which the people of God had been subjected since the Babylonian captivity. For some traditional reason, probably, the scheme had to make four kingdoms. Since, as a matter of fact, there had been three only—Babylonian, Persian, Graeco-Macedonian—

the Persian had to be divided into two, a Median and a Persian proper, though in chapter viii the writer shows that he is aware of their practical identity by making both Media and Persia typified by a single emblematic animal, the two-horned ram. The Greek kingdom in its power of crushing and destroying is the most terrible of all, as we can well understand it was from the standpoint of the godly, who saw Hellenism dissolve the old national traditions in a way neither Babylon nor Persia had done. And in the Greek Kingdom, evil had been ultimately concentrated in the Satanic figure of Antiochus Epiphanes, the 'little horn,' who in his claim to deity had exalted himself against the God of gods, had caused the sacrifice and oblation to cease, and had set up in the Temple an image of Baal Shamin, whose name the writer represents by a phrase which for 'Baal' substitutes 'Abomination' and, for Shamin, Shomem 'Desolation.'

But the book is one of consolation in so far as it tells the godly that all that has happened falls within a divine scheme, pre-ordained long ago, a scheme which makes the deliverance near at hand. The tribulation is to last only three years and a half, 'a time, times, and a dividing of time.' In the eleventh chapter a survey is given of recent history, so far as it concerned the Jews, from the days of Alexander to the present moment. The utterance is oracular in that no names are given: the Seleucid kings are indicated by the term 'king of the north' and the Ptolemies by the term 'king of the south,' but the events are described with sufficient particularity to be easily recognizable. Up to the point when the 'king of the north' institutes the worship of a strange god and sets a garrison of heathen in the *akra*, the account follows actual history; then it carries on the story, as the writer imagined that the sequel would be, a forecast which the real course of events did not follow, except in this, that the religious tribulation came to an end in the near future, and the old worship in the temple was restored. Ptolemy, the writer anticipates, will begin a new war of revenge and Antiochus will once more come south with an immense force, military and naval. The Seleucid armies will sweep across Southern Palestine, across Judaea, though the Edomites and people of Transjordania will escape complete destruction. Once more Antiochus will overrun Egypt and possess himself of vast booty. 'But tidings from the East and North will trouble him'—the Parthian peril. He will return to Palestine to meet the new enemy, slaughtering as he goes. 'And he shall plant the tents of his pavilion between the sea and the Holy Mount of Delight,' and there, somewhere in the Philistine plain, north of

Gaza,' he shall come at last to his end, and none to help him.' His end will be a supernatural act of God: 'without hand,' the writer had said earlier in the book (viii, 25), 'shall he be broken.'

The book seems to have been written when the first successes of the Hasmonaean brethren had brought encouragement. The faithful indeed are still falling 'by sword and by flame, by captivity and by despoilment,' but Daniel is represented as predicting that 'they shall be helped with a little help; and many shall join themselves to them in guile' (xi, 34). The last phrase perhaps refers to those who under terror of chastisement by the Hasmonaean bands insincerely professed adherence to the godly.

The book of Daniel is perhaps the earliest document[1] of that extensive 'apocalyptic' literature which continued to be produced throughout the next three centuries by Jews and, at the end of that time, by Christians. The Jewish apocalypses are all pseudonymous: they profess to be the work of some prophet in the remote past, which had been concealed till the actual moment. They differ from the older Hebrew prophecy in giving a formal scheme of world-history: a succession of epochs are distinguished in the fight between good and evil up to the final triumph of good and the coming of the kingdom of God. It is likely that we may see here the influence of Persian Zoroastrianism. The chief importance of this literature in the development of Hebraic religion is that it spread amongst the Jews a new belief in a life after death for the individual—whether that life was held to be a spiritual discarnate existence or a resurrection of the body or a combination of both— and in a Divine cosmic event as the consummation of human history. Rabbinic Judaism, which paid little regard to the apocalyptic literature, retained from that literature a firm belief in personal immortality and in a 'world to come,' while the Christian attitude to the world is essentially marked by hope. We can hardly doubt that it was the martyrdoms of the faithful under the persecution of Antiochus Epiphanes which first made the belief in a future life vivid and important amongst the Jews. In Daniel, whilst there is as yet no announcement of a general resurrection, the belief is expressed that the martyrs who have not received their reward here, and the sinners who have not been duly punished, will be raised again at the last day, for joy or pain. 'Many of them that sleep in the dust of the earth shall awake,

---

[1] R. H. Charles holds that certain parts of the book of Enoch are earlier than Daniel (*Pseudepigrapha*, pp. 170, 171).

some to everlasting life, and some to shame and to everlasting contempt. And they that be wise shall shine as the brightness of the firmament; and they that turn many to righteousness as the stars for ever and ever' (xii, 2, 3). In no earlier writing of the Hebrew scriptures had the belief in a future life been quite so clearly uttered.

VI. ANTIOCHUS IN THE EAST.
THE HASMONAEANS

Antiochus Epiphanes in the spring of 165 had not moved any considerable forces against the Jewish bands. He was preparing to use his military strength in another direction. Since his father had recovered the Eastern provinces forty years before, the Parthian power had grown to menacing proportions[1]. Probably Persia too had already broken away from the Seleucid realm under native rulers. Parthia was ruled at this time by the sixth Arsaces, Mithridates I (171 to 138 B.C.). He had conquered the northern region of Media about Rhagae, though Southern Media with the royal city, Ecbatana, was still held by the Milesian Timarchus as governor for the Seleucid king. We do not hear of any immediate danger of a Parthian attack: Mithridates was busy rather in the East, conquering at the expense of the Greek rulers of Bactria. But it was obvious that the rise of such a power in Iran made it a vital necessity for the Seleucid house to strengthen its position in the frontier provinces of the East. In the spring of 165, accordingly, Antiochus set forth with the main force of his kingdom for the countries beyond the Euphrates and Tigris. He left Judaea in an uneasy condition. Jerusalem itself no doubt seemed secure, and Menelaus probably continued to act as High Priest in the hellenized Temple. But the rebel bands, led by the Hasmonaean brethren, were at large, and adherents of the government in outlying places were liable to be suddenly overrun by wild fighters, charged with religious passion, bursting upon them out of the wilderness.

It is probable that to Antiochus the Jewish trouble seemed a small enough affair compared with the huge Parthian menace in the East. Some modern scholars speak sarcastically of the Jewish books which represent the events in Judaea as the things of central importance in the world and pretend that Antiochus' chief preoccupation was the ill-success of the local government

---

[1] On the Parthian Empire see further vol. IX.

forces in dealing with Jewish bands. No doubt, from the point of view of Antiochus, the Jewish books greatly exaggerate the importance of events in Judaea, just as from the point of view of the Persian King, we may believe, the Greek books greatly exaggerated the importance of the battle of Marathon. In regard to the influence destined to be exerted upon the subsequent history of mankind, the Greek books and the Jewish books were right. Of all that was happening in the kingdom of Antiochus, the events in Judaea were by far the most important in their consequence for the mind of man in ages to come.

Antiochus left his infant son, Antiochus, in Syria, when he departed for the East. A certain Lysias, who had the rank of Kinsman, was to act for the king in Syria during his absence and no doubt have charge of the little prince. Of Antiochus IV's campaigns in the East we have only fragmentary knowledge. His first advance apparently was into Armenia, which under his father had been governed by Artaxias (a man probably of Persian race) as satrap for the Seleucid king (p. 140 n. 1). After Magnesia Artaxias had declared himself independent. Before the Seleucid power Artaxias now once more bowed, and was left, on his submission, to go on governing Armenia. It is conjectured that the giving of the name Epiphaneia to Ecbatana indicates the temporary presence of Antiochus in the Median capital. We hear of him in Babylonia, where an older Greek city, one of the Alexandrias, was restored as another Antioch. It is now perhaps that the satrap Numenius, who governed Mesene (Basra) for the Seleucid, fought a battle with the Persians (Pliny, *N.H.* vi, 152). Then we hear of him in Elymaïs, the hill-country of Khuzistan, where his father had come to grief in an attempt to despoil some native shrine. Antiochus Epiphanes likewise made an attempt to rob a temple of Nanaia in this region (vol. vii, 163 *sq.*). He was repelled by the natives, but, unlike his father, escaped with his life. It was after this that he developed some illness which seems to have affected his mind. Polybius mentions a story that, as a punishment for the outrage he had done the goddess, he became supernaturally deranged. At Gabae in Media (Ispahan) he died in the midst of his plans, in the spring or summer of 163 B.C. Before his death, he had, according to I Maccabees, appointed a man of his entourage, Philip, to be regent during the minority of Antiochus V. If this is true, he must have become dissatisfied with Lysias and intended to replace him.

Whilst Antiochus had been in the East, Lysias had attempted, amongst other things, to suppress the Jewish bands. In the

summer of 165 (?)[1] a more substantial army, commanded by
Nicanor and Gorgias, under the orders of the governor of Coele-
Syria and Phoenicia, who was now Ptolemy son of Dorymenes,
came down the Philistine coast, in order to enter Judaea from the
west. While, however, a detachment under Gorgias made its way
up through the hills, Judas Maccabaeus fell upon its camp at
Emmaus and put both sections of the government army to flight.
Evidently the Jewish bands, under a guerilla leader like Judas,
were a more formidable enemy than the court of Antioch had
supposed. In the following year (summer, 164) Lysias himself
came south with a force in order to ascertain what the situation
required. He moved round to the south of Jerusalem, to Beth-
sur, whence the approach to the city was more open and easy, and
was soon satisfied that a larger army was necessary to clear Judaea
of the bands. His expedition had been probably more a reconnaissance than a regular attack, but its arrest at Beth-sur was
represented in the national memory as another great victory,
'Lysias himself escaped by shameful flight' (II Macc. xi, 12).

The result of the reconnaissance was a signal change of policy
on the part of the court. It seemed possible that the tiresome
labour of annihilating the bands, which the Seleucid king no doubt
could do when he put forth his full power, might be saved, if the
court agreed to a compromise: Menelaus to continue High Priest,
but the faithful to be admitted to live in Jerusalem, side by side
with the Hellenizers, and the Temple to be restored to the worship
of Yahweh according to the traditional Law: no more religious
persecution. Accordingly the Hasmonaean brethren with their
bands were allowed to re-enter the city. The emblems of pagan
worship were cleared out of the Temple; it was purified from the
defilement; a new stone altar was built on the place of the pagan
one. On December 25, 164 B.C., the house of Yahweh was dedicated anew—the same day of the year on which the pagan worship
had been instituted three years before. The date, as has been said,
was that of the pagan festival celebrating the moment when the
daylight begins again to increase; and the Jews have continued
from that time to this day to observe it as a festival, but with a new
memorial meaning—the 'Feast of the Dedication of the House,'
'Chanukkath hab-bayith,' 'Encaenia' (John x, 22). Yet the

[1] In Kolbe's scheme, the summer of 164; but Kolbe eliminates as
fiction the first expedition of Lysias which I Maccabees puts in 164/3, the
'year following' the expedition of Nicanor and Gorgias. If there really was
an expedition of Lysias in the summer of 164, we have to put back the expedition of Nicanor and Gorgias to summer 165.

Greek-speaking Jews also kept up the old name for it, the 'feast of lights' (Josephus, *Ant.* XII, 325) and made an evening illumination by lamps part of its celebration, which originally had typified the increase of daylight after the shortest day.

The prediction of Daniel that the tribulation would last three years and a half was thus singularly verified. The godly had now secured in Jerusalem what they had been fighting for—toleration of their religion. The compromise required that they should on their side give toleration to the Hellenizers in Jerusalem. That they would not do. Besides, they had not yet secured toleration for the scattered colonies of their brethren in the Gentile towns of Idumaea and Transjordania, who were exposed to the hostility of the heathen populations. The Hasmonaean bands were therefore still active in 163, but their task was now to storm the towns in which isolated bodies of Jews were persecuted, massacre the heathen population, and bring the rescued companies of Jews back in triumph to Jerusalem. Psalm lxviii is perhaps the song composed for such a triumphal return of Judas from Transjordania: 'Thou hast ascended on high, thou hast led thy train of captives....The Lord said "I will bring again from Bashan, I will bring them again from the deep of the sea, that thou mayest dip thy foot in blood, that the tongue of thy dogs may be red through the same[1]."'

In Jerusalem there was anything but peace between the two parties. The Hasmonaeans fortified the 'hill of Zion' (*i.e.* the Temple hill with the old citadel to the north of the Temple) with walls and towers as a fortress in opposition to the *akra*, where the government garrison continued to act as a refuge for the Hellenizers[2]. It was not a situation which the Seleucid could allow to continue. Then came the sudden death of Antiochus Epiphanes in 163. This secured a respite for the Jewish nationalists. For it became at once a question whether Lysias could hold his position as regent for the boy-king, Antiochus V Eupator, in opposition to Philip, whom Antiochus had nominated on his deathbed, and who might momently return to Syria at the head of an army. Lysias had for a while to leave the Jews alone. Also the present governor of Coele-Syria, Ptolemy Macron, the man who had governed Cyprus for King Ptolemy in 168, in contrast to the former governor of Coele-Syria, Ptolemy son of Dorymenes,

---

[1] See R. H. Kennett, *Old Testament Essays*, p. 175.

[2] 'Zion' is thus in I Maccabees not to be identified with the 'city of David,' the *akra*. Since it was the 'city of David' to which the name Zion had originally belonged (II Sam. v, 7), confusion may easily arise unless this change in the application of the name is understood.

was friendly to the Jews and advocated a policy of conciliation (II Macc. x, 12 *sqq.*).

But in 162 the garrison of the *akra* was being hard pressed, and the Hellenizers sent a bitter cry to Antioch for deliverance from the intolerance of the godly. Lysias was forced to do something, and he directed a really adequate force against Judaea, complete with elephants, led by himself and the boy-king. The army moved again round Judaea and advanced from the south. The Hasmonaeans had fortified and garrisoned Beth-sur to hold the road. Lysias left it invested and moved on to attack Jerusalem itself. In vain the bands of Judas flung themselves against the royal army: at Beth-zachariah they were decisively beaten back. Beth-sur had to capitulate. It was only the fact that Philip had at last actually reached Syria which saved the nationalists from utter suppression. A new peace of compromise was arranged. The old religion was to continue unmolested, and an amnesty was to be granted the Hasmonaean brethren; but the nationalist fortress on the Temple hill was dismantled; the government garrison continued to hold the *akra*; a new military governor, Hegemonides, was appointed for southern Palestine, and the Temple ritual was to include a burnt-offering for the Seleucid king. Menelaus was removed to be tried in Northern Syria and was there put to death. It was now, probably, that the High Priesthood was conferred upon a man of proper Aaronic descent, Eliakim, who nevertheless belonged to the hellenizing party and had incurred pollution by pagan practices in the days of the persecution. He bore, together with his Hebrew name, the Greek name Alcimus, similar in sound. If he was now appointed, the Hasmonaean chiefs must soon have prevented him from officiating. It may have been now also that the son of Onias III, himself called Onias, who at his father's death had been, according to Josephus (*Ant.* xii, 237), an infant, fled to Egypt, where he was allowed by Ptolemy to build a Temple and institute a cult of Yahweh at Leontopolis, modelled on the Temple and cult of Jerusalem, which continued till A.D. 73.

On Lysias' return to Northern Syria he found Philip with the forces brought back from the East, ready to fight for the chief power in the kingdom. In the conflict Lysias had the better of it, and Philip took refuge with Ptolemy Philometor in Egypt. Lysias, as regent for Antiochus Eupator, had secured his position against the immediate peril; but there were still circumstances to make him uneasy. Many remembered that the legitimate heir to the throne was the young Demetrius, far away in Rome. An aunt of both Demetrius and Antiochus Eupator, Antiochis, was residing in

Antioch at the time with her daughter. She had been the wife of Ariarathes IV, king of Cappadocia, and was the (putative) mother of the reigning king Ariarathes V. Her, too, Lysias for some reason felt to be dangerous to his supremacy, and he had both her and her daughter assassinated. Soon after his return from Judaea to Antioch in 162, the mission sent from Rome to regulate the affairs of the East, headed by Gnaeus Octavius, was in Syria. They had come by way of Cappadocia and had naturally been urged by King Ariarathes to put down the murderer of his mother. As has been narrated elsewhere, Octavius was assassinated in Laodicea by a Syrian Greek in a burst of fanatical patriotism (p. 285).

Lysias did what he could, by giving Octavius funeral honours and by sending ambassadors to Rome, to turn aside the displeasure of the Romans. Rome reserved its judgment. When Demetrius, now a young man of twenty-five, begged the Senate to allow him to return to Syria and assert his claim to the throne, the Senate refused. Then, without the permission of the Senate, helped by his experienced friend, the historian Polybius, Demetrius escaped from Rome and reached Syria by way of Lycia. It seems probable that even if the Senate as a whole had no cognizance of Demetrius' venture, Polybius had reason to know that it was not unwelcome to some of his powerful friends in the Roman aristocracy, though discretion forbade him to divulge this when later on he wrote his account of the affair[1].

VII. DEMETRIUS SOTER

Demetrius landed in the Phoenician Tripolis, probably in the early autumn of 162. The population of Syria quickly rallied to him. The army abandoned the cause of Lysias and Antiochus Eupator, and put the boy-king to death on a hint conveyed from Demetrius, before the new king had met his unfortunate cousin. But beyond the Euphrates Timarchus, the favourite of Antiochus Epiphanes, declared himself independent and assumed the style of Great King in Babylonia and Media[2]. It was important for Demetrius to induce Rome to accept the *fait accompli* and recognize him as king. Simultaneously Timarchus was busy at Rome to gain the support of the Republic for his claims[3]. Rome hesitated

[1] H. Volkmann in *Klio*, xix, 1925, pp. 382 *sqq.*
[2] He also issued coins with his portrait. See Volume of Plates iii, 14, *a*.
[3] Diod. xxxi, 27*a*, says that Timarchus went in person to Rome. E. Meyer thinks this impossible. It certainly seems hard to imagine Timarchus absenting himself from his province at such a crisis for the time required by a journey to Rome and back, especially as he could not have travelled through Syria, where Demetrius ruled, but would presumably have had to go to and fro by Armenia, Cappadocia, and the Pergamene kingdom.

to commit itself. It was not yet prepared to recognize Demetrius, for it preferred to see a weakling on the Syrian throne, and Demetrius was inconveniently able and enterprising: it gave Timarchus verbal recognition, but no material help. But the disapproval of Rome entailed real disadvantages for Demetrius. It led the king of Cappadocia, Ariarathes V, to reject the hand of Demetrius' sister, so that, instead of the two courts standing together for independence, the relations between them became hostile.

Demetrius had soon to deal with the thorny Jewish question. In the spring of 161 a deputation of hellenizing Jews, headed by Alcimus, presented themselves, appealing again for protection against the Hasmonaeans. Alcimus also claimed for himself the High Priesthood which he had held for a moment the year before. The Hasmonaeans on their side saw how the ill-will of Rome towards Demetrius could be turned to account. In 161 they entered for the first time into diplomatic relations with the Western Power. An embassy went from Jerusalem to Rome and concluded with the Senate a treaty, by which they got a qualified promise of Roman help and friendship, in the event of their being attacked by another power[1]. The treaty was one of those concluded by the Senate, without ratification by the people, and therefore less binding. Doubts have been thrown upon its existence on the ground that to recognize the Jewish state as an independent power would have been a *casus belli* between Rome and Demetrius, and that, as a matter of fact, Rome let the Hasmonaeans go down before Demetrius without giving them any help. These objections have no force in view of the fact that Rome behaved in just the same way in regard to the rebel Timarchus. It recognized him as king, but allowed him to fall before Demetrius unassisted. The Senate had indeed no intention of intervening by armed force in Syria: it desired only to embarrass Demetrius, and that it did by giving countenance to his enemies.

Demetrius was not the man to deal slackly. His general Bacchides[2] at the head of an adequate force established Alcimus as High Priest in Jerusalem and left troops in the country to

---

[1] For the date of this treaty see Kolbe, *op. cit.* pp. 36 *sqq.*, and for its contents E. Täubler, *Imperium Romanum*, I, pp. 240 *sqq.*, Michel S. Ginsburg, *Rome et la Judée*, pp. 34 *sqq.*

[2] He is described in I Macc. vii. 8 as κυριεύων ἐν τῷ πέραν τοῦ ποταμοῦ. It is uncertain whether this means that Bacchides was governor of Mesopotamia or of Coele-Syria, which in the Aramaic phraseology of the old Persian Empire formed part of the province 'beyond the River.' There is no evidence that the name was still at this date used of Coele-Syria.

support his authority. Alcimus was at first welcomed by the godly, as a man of the house of Aaron, though opposed, of course, by the Hasmonaean brethren and their partizans. If therefore during the last five years the terms Hasmonaean and Chasīdim ('godly') have coincided in their application, from now onwards a rift between them begins. Yet Alcimus soon forfeited the good-will of the godly by his conduct, and the Hasmonaean bands again overran the country, putting Hellenizers to the sword.

While Bacchides was conducting operations in Judaea, Timarchus was advancing from the East. He obtained the alliance of Artaxias of Armenia, who had once more renounced his allegiance to the Seleucid. In the winter of 161/0, Demetrius went east to close with the rebel. The Greek cities beyond the Euphrates eagerly espoused his cause. Timarchus had made himself hated, and before the lawful king of the old house his power broke up. He was captured and met with a rebel's death. The capital city of Babylonia, Seleuceia on the Tigris, received the victor with acclamations as Demetrius Soter, 'the Saviour.' In the summer of 160 envoys of Demetrius met in Rhodes the Roman commission dispatched to the East under Tiberius Sempronius Gracchus. Gracchus, from old acquaintance in Rome, was friendly to Demetrius and recognized him as king. After this it was hard for the Senate to refuse recognition, so that when, in the autumn of 160, another embassy from Syria appeared in Rome, bringing the assassin of Octavius and a golden crown, formal recognition was at last given.

In the same year (160) a fresh force had been sent to crush the Jewish revolt, under Nicanor, commandant of the elephant corps. Nicanor, however, allowed himself to be surprised by Judas at Adasa, near Beth-horon, on the 13th of Adar (March 160) and fell in the mellay. 'Nicanor's Day' was observed thenceforward by the Jews as an annual day of joy; Nicanor's head was cut off and hung up in the Temple. It was the last victory of Judas.

With Demetrius on the throne such a success was transient. A month later Bacchides was again in Judaea with an army which made resistance hopeless. Judas with a handful of zealots tried the desperate chance of a battle, and he fell fighting (battle of Elasa, April 160). This might have been the end of the Jewish revolt, had the Seleucid government continued to be in firm hands. Things seemed to have gone back to the *status quo*. On the government side the same toleration was given to the Jewish religion that had been given before the unwise attempt of Antiochus IV, but politically the Jewish state had to acquiesce in being subject to the Gentile government. Alcimus continued to be High Priest, which meant toleration also for the Hellenizers. The Gentile garrison still held the *akra*, and the countryside was kept quiet by a system of fortresses. Bacchides, however, failed to capture the three surviving Hasmonaean brethren, who took to the wilderness with a part of their bands. The eldest, John, soon fell into the hands of an Arab tribe, who put him to death: the second brother, Simon, and the youngest, Jonathan, remained.

A year after the battle of Elasa, Alcimus died of a paralytic stroke, and the place of High Priest seems to have been left for a time unfilled. In 157/6 B.C. Bacchides made an attempt to follow up the two Hasmonaean brothers beyond Jordan. When he found the difficulties of the enterprise, he was alienated from the Hellenistic Jews who had urged him to it, and came to the conclusion that it would be better to have a *modus vivendi* with the Hasmonaean brothers which would allow them to reside in Judaea, though not in Jerusalem. Jonathan therefore established himself by government permission in Michmash. This was a relaxation of its grasp on the part of the Seleucid government— the first concession after the drastic measures of 160; and it afforded the Hasmonaean brothers the opportunity for a fresh start after their prostration. From this point the Hasmonaean power grows bit by bit, till Judaea becomes an independent principality under a Hasmonaean High Priest. The relaxation was no doubt due to the increasing difficulties which surrounded Demetrius as his reign continued. During the latter part of it Jonathan, we are told (I Macc. ix, 73), was, from his headquarters in Michmash, 'rooting the ungodly out of Israel'; that is to say, the toleration of Hellenizers in the Jewish country towns had ceased, and the Hasmonaean bands were beginning again, no doubt with the sympathy of the bulk of the population, to dominate Judaea outside Jerusalem.

Demetrius Soter had evidently some of the qualities of a great ruler—energy and high courage. But he seems to have been deficient in the gift of conciliating men. How far it was his fault that by 150 B.C. his three neighbour kings were his enemies— Attalus II of Pergamum, Ariarathes V of Cappadocia and Ptolemy Philometor of Egypt—we cannot be sure. It may be that any really strong king in Syria would have excited the ill-will of each of those three powers, as well as that of Rome. The court of Pergamum had put Antiochus Epiphanes on the throne and probably felt its interests prejudiced when the family of Antiochus Epiphanes was replaced by the representative of the elder line.

It was also sensitive to any attempt of the king of Syria to regain the influence in Asia Minor which his house had lost after Magnesia, and this was precisely what Demetrius might seem to be trying to do when he interfered in the rivalry between Ariarathes V and his brother Orophernes for the Cappadocian throne. Attalus supported Ariarathes and Demetrius Orophernes. Since Demetrius' candidate was worsted in 156 and had to take refuge in Antioch, the king of Cappadocia was Demetrius' enemy. Even Orophernes Demetrius failed to attach to himself personally; he had not long been a refugee in Syria before he tried to create, or use, a popular movement, in order to oust Demetrius from the throne of Syria: he was himself, through his mother, a grandson of Antiochus the Great. Demetrius interned him after that in Seleuceia: he might still be useful for the purpose of intimidating Ariarathes. Ptolemy Philometor had been friends with Demetrius in Rome, but when in 155/4 Demetrius made an attempt to get possession of Cyprus, Ptolemy too became hostile.

Nor was Demetrius more successful in conciliating his own subjects in Syria. He became unpopular with the populace of Antioch. Here again the fault may not have been altogether his. The Greek or hellenized population of Syria was of very degenerate fibre: perhaps Demetrius had good enough reason to despise them, and his contempt will have been more bitter, inasmuch as his schemes for regenerating the kingdom must have required some good quality in the human material, and he saw them fail for want of that. At any rate, he could not conceal his contempt, and his subjects hated him for it. Demetrius withdrew from their contact into the seclusion of a castle he built himself near Antioch. More and more he sought escape from the bitterness of his spirit in wine. But he may still have maintained intellectual interests with chosen associates: the philosopher Philonides of Laodicea, who had converted Antiochus Epiphanes to Epicureanism, continued to receive marked attentions from Demetrius.

The trouble was that all the neighbour powers and Rome desired to see some one contemptible on the Syrian throne. And the king of Pergamum ingeniously produced the contemptible person required—a youth called Balas whom he had discovered in Smyrna, and who showed a remarkable resemblance to Antiochus Epiphanes. Attalus declared that he was in fact a son of the late king. He was given the name of Alexander and already some time between 158 and 153 Attalus placed the young man close to the Syrian frontier in Cilicia, as a threat to Demetrius. Heracleides, the finance minister of Antiochus Epiphanes, now

a refugee in Asia Minor, took Alexander to Rome. Heracleides
had the death of his brother Timarchus to avenge and was experienced in the way to bribe Roman senators. The Senate, as
desirous as Attalus to see a weakling on the Syrian throne, actually
in the winter 153/2 gave Alexander recognition. Before the
summer of 152 was out Alexander had got a footing in Ptolemaïs,
where he had Ptolemy in support close at hand, and could threaten
Demetrius from the troublous region of Palestine.

Demetrius was now really hard beset. It was urgent for him
to get all whom he could on his side. The Hasmonaean brothers
found themselves in a position to secure a great advance in power,
not by any new effort or victory of their own, but by the necessities
of the two rivals for the Seleucid throne, who bid against each
other for their support. Demetrius began by ordering the hostages
given by Jonathan to be restored to him and authorizing Jonathan
to levy troops as an ally of the king. The fortified posts established
by Bacchides over Judaea were abandoned, with the exception of
Beth-sur, which was a place of refuge for hellenizing Jews.
Jonathan took full advantage of this order of the king's, but he
felt no obligation of loyalty if Alexander offered him something
better. This Alexander soon did by conferring on Jonathan the
High Priesthood with the rank of 'Friend.' On the Feast of
Tabernacles in October 152, Jonathan officiated in Jerusalem as
High Priest for the first time—'High Priest,' as Wellhausen
has called him, 'by the grace of Balas.' Then Demetrius sought to
outbid Alexander by larger concessions. The letter however, given
in I Maccabees x, which professes to embody these concessions,
can hardly be the translation of any real document, so that we are
not in a position to say precisely what the new concessions of
Demetrius were. In any case Jonathan thought it good policy
to adhere to Alexander. Though he might be the son of Antiochus
Epiphanes, the Jews would be happier under a worthless creature
of this kind than under Demetrius whose hand they had felt.

The defection of the Jews gave Palestine to Alexander.
Demetrius fought to the end. He sent two of his sons, Demetrius
and Antiochus, to Cnidus to be out of the way of danger. Ptolemy
dispatched a force from Egypt under an Athamanian prince,
Galaestes, to support Alexander. Probably Pergamene and
Cappadocian forces penetrated into Syria from the north. Some
of Demetrius' own generals went over to the enemy. The populace
of Antioch rose against him. In the final battle Demetrius fell,
fighting to his last breath, pierced with many wounds (summer
150). Alexander Balas became king of Syria and Babylonia.

VIII. ALEXANDER BALAS AND EGYPT

It was a sign of the subordination to Egypt which marked the new state of things in Syria that Alexander seems to have resided more in Ptolemaïs than in Antioch. Ptolemy Philometor gave Alexander his daughter Cleopatra to wife. (She is distinguished among the many Cleopatras as Cleopatra Thea.) There was a great wedding at Ptolemaïs (150/49) to which the king of Egypt came in person. Among the honoured guests was the High Priest Jonathan, wearing the purple which the Gentile king had conferred upon him. He was advanced to a higher degree— from the order of 'Friends' to that of 'First Friends.' He was also appointed *strategos* and *meridarches* of Judaea, governor of the country in the service of the king. The hellenizing Jews might raise a bitter cry that they were being thrown over by the government—they who under the king's father had been the party loyal to the court and had suffered persecution from their countrymen. So indeed they were: the house of Hashmon had become for good the dominant power in the Jewish state.

Cleopatra Thea bore Alexander a son who was given the name Antiochus. As a king, Alexander proved hopelessly frivolous and incompetent. The administration of the kingdom was left mainly to his minister Ammonius. At Antioch, in the king's absence, the power was in the hands of two military leaders who had deserted the cause of Demetrius, Diodotus and Hierax. The son of Demetrius who had remained in Syria, Antigonus, they put to death[1]. We get indications how, with the weakening of the royal power in Syria, the Greek cities more and more acted as independent states.

It was probably in the spring of 147 when it became known that the boy Demetrius had set foot in Northern Syria or Cilicia with an army of Cretan mercenaries under the Cretan Lasthenes. Since Demetrius was only 14 at most, Lasthenes must have been the real director of operations. Alexander had to go north to defend Antioch against the legitimate king. In the south of the

---

[1] We are not told whether Antigonus was older or younger than his brothers Demetrius and Antiochus. A reason for conjecturing him to have been older is that it was not the common practice in the Seleucid dynasty for the eldest son to be given the name of his father. It was the second son who usually bore his father's name. One would have expected Demetrius I to give his eldest son the name Seleucus; if he called him Antigonus it was in pursuance of the policy adopted in his own case, of emphasizing the right of the Seleucids to represent the otherwise extinct house of Antigonus as well (see above, p. 496).

kingdom there was fresh confusion. A new governor of Coele-
Syria, Apollonius, established himself on behalf of King Demetrius.
It at once came to fighting between Apollonius, who held the
coast, and the High Priest of Jerusalem. Jonathan took Joppa,
Azotus (Ashdod) and Ascalon. At Azotus he burnt the temple
of Dagon over the heads of the fugitives who had crowded into
it. Alexander, hearing of these exploits, raised Jonathan to the
highest order, that of 'Kinsman,' and assigned him the city of
Ekron as a personal possession.

Ptolemy Philometor thought the moment come to intervene.
He came up from the south with a large army, leaving garrisons
in the coast-cities as he went. Diodorus and Josephus (possibly
drawing from Polybius) say that his original intention was to
support his son-in-law Alexander against Demetrius; I Maccabees
says that he came with the purpose of overthrowing Alexander.
Quite probably he did not disclose his intentions and may even have
left it to future events to determine his line. He will almost certainly
have intended in any case to recover Coele-Syria for his house.
When Ptolemy had the chief coast-cities as far as Seleuceia in his
hands, he declared against Alexander, whom he accused of having
plotted to assassinate him. He offered the hand of Cleopatra (whom
he now had with him) to Demetrius. Alexander fled to Cilicia, and
Ptolemy entered Antioch. Had he followed the wish of the people
of Antioch, he would now have assumed himself the diadem of
Syria, as well as of Egypt; but he was too prudent to offer such
provocation to Rome. He persuaded Antioch to receive the boy
Demetrius as king. Alexander meantime had got together an
army in Cilicia and was once more in Northern Syria. The combined forces of Ptolemy and Demetrius engaged him on the river
Oenoparas. They were completely victorious, but Ptolemy received a wound of which he died a few days later—not however
before he had been shown the severed head of his late son-in-law
(early summer 145).

By the death of Ptolemy the Egyptian occupation came to an
end. Demetrius II reigned as Demetrius Nicator Theos Philadelphus. But the boy was in no position to restore order in the
distracted kingdom. His Cretan soldiery drove the Syrian Greeks
to desperation. Jonathan saw the opportunity for fresh acquisitions. When Demetrius came south, Jonathan presented himself
before him at Ptolemaïs. Demetrius agreed to accept 300 talents
down in discharge of the annual tribute from Judaea, and allowed
the Jews to annex three toparchies on the north which had belonged
to Samaria. Jonathan was put in the order of 'First Friends' of

the new king. There remained indeed the government garrison in the *akra*. Probably it was a condition of the concessions of Demetrius that the Jews should cease to press the siege. For the moment the relations between Demetrius and the Jews were friendly. A Jewish force was sent to form part of the royal guards in Antioch, and helped to massacre the people when they broke out against the Cretan tyranny.

The revolt of the Syrian Greeks against Demetrius II found within a few months of his accession a leader in Diodotus, a man of Apamea, already mentioned as a military leader. Diodotus put forward the infant son of Alexander as king (before October 143) with the style Antiochus Theos Epiphanes Dionysos (Antiochus VI). Diodotus himself assumed the name of Tryphon. With the infant he soon entered Antioch in triumph. The kingdom was now held partly by Tryphon, partly by Demetrius—Tryphon with his headquarters in Antioch, master of the Orontes valley, Demetrius with his headquarters in Seleuceia, master of most of the seaboard and of the provinces beyond the Euphrates. The division gave further opportunity to the Jews. Jonathan transferred his allegiance to Antiochus Dionysos: he was made a 'Kinsman,' and his elder brother Simon was made king's *strategos* for the whole of Coele-Syria without Phoenicia. This enabled the Hasmonaean chief to use government forces for furthering the aggrandizement of his own house. He replaced the government garrison in Beth-sur by a Jewish one, and fortified Adida, which commanded the road from Joppa to the Judaean upland. There is no reason to doubt the statement of I Maccabees that Jonathan about this time sent another Jewish embassy to Rome to renew the friendship which had been contracted under Judas. Experience may have shown him that material help was not to be hoped for, but the friendship of Rome had value by increasing prestige in Syria. Tryphon thought by a surprise stroke to check the growth of the Hasmonaean power. When Jonathan was with him in Ptolemaïs, separated from his main body of troops, Tryphon seized his person. Simon at once assumed command at Jerusalem, and the Jews expelled the Gentile population from Joppa, settling Jewish families in their place. Tryphon had not forces which would enable him to penetrate on to the upland and relieve the garrison in the *akra*, now almost at starvation point. But, keeping Jonathan with him as he moved east of the Jordan, he there put him to death (143/2 ?).

IX. THE NEW JEWISH STATE

In 142 Tryphon took the step of dethroning the boy-king, Antiochus Dionysos, and establishing himself as sovereign, to the exclusion of the house of Seleucus as a whole. He assumed the title *basileus autokrator*, and started a new Era on his coins[1]. His murder of Jonathan had made the Jews his enemies, and Simon now offered Demetrius the support of the Jewish forces. Demetrius was glad enough to purchase that by fresh concessions. He renounced, on behalf of the Seleucid monarchy, all claims to arrears of tribute and all claims to tribute in the future. The Jews were to be allowed to fortify their city. Nothing now remained to make their independence complete except the garrison in the *akra*. And the garrison at last surrendered. In May 141 B.C. the Jewish nationalists entered the *akra* 'with praise and palm-branches, and with harps and with cymbals, and with viols and with hymns and with songs.' 'The yoke of the heathen was taken away from Israel.'

Already in the year before (April 142 to March 141) the Jewish state had started a new Era as independent. Simon reigned as High Priest, but it was felt by the religious that his title lacked that Divine authorization which had belonged to the old line terminated in Onias III. There was no prophet to declare the will of the Lord. It was hardly a substitute that Simon's brother had been instituted by King Alexander Balas. An appointment by the people, gathered in formal assembly at Jerusalem, might seem the next best thing. And this took place in September 140. The High Priesthood was conferred provisionally upon the house of Hashmon—'until there should arise a faithful prophet.' Simon's official title seems to have been 'High Priest and General (Hebrew *sagan*, Greek *strategos*) and Prince of the People of God (Hebrew *sar am El*, Greek *ethnarches*).'

When in 145 B.C. Demetrius had allowed the Jews to annex three toparchies of Samaria, a new movement of expansion had begun. In the days of Judas it had been a question of concentrating the scattered colonies of Jews in Jerusalem: now it was a question of extending the frontiers of the Jewish domain. Simon, as we have just seen, had taken possession of Joppa, and a few months later what had been done in Joppa was done in Gazara (Gezer). Early

[1] For coins of the boy-king Antiochus and Tryphon, see Volume of Plates iii, 14, *b, c*.

in Simon's reign, according to I Maccabees, he sent to Rome the third Jewish embassy of which we know, bearing a shield of gold[1]. Rome still showed itself willing to give the Jews all that its authority in the East, unaccompanied by military help, could do. I Maccabees inserts what purports to be a letter in their favour sent to the principal monarchies and city-states of the Near East[2].

The growth of the Jewish power depended upon events in the surrounding world. In the weakness of the Seleucid government since the last days of Demetrius I the Jewish state had continuously advanced: now once more a strong king was to take up the Seleucid inheritance, and the Jewish state fell back into complete subjection. In Babylonia, as we have seen, Tryphon had been unable to supplant the old royal house: there Demetrius II was recognized as king. But in 141 the province had been wrested from him by a stronger foe—the Parthian. A cuneiform document[3] shows Mithridates I entering in triumph the capital of Babylonia, Seleuceia on the Tigris, in the early days of July, 141. The expedition of Demetrius II to the East, which seems so odd when a good part of Syria was still held by Tryphon, is explained by the necessity of recovering the eastern provinces which were an essential support of the Seleucid power. In 140 Demetrius crossed the Euphrates to engage the Parthian invaders. He seems to have been successful in expelling them from the province. When, however, the following year (139) he pressed the Parthian retreat and advanced on to the Iranian plateau, he was taken prisoner by Mithridates. Although kept in confinement, he was treated as a prince and given a daughter of the Parthian king's to wife. It was convenient for Mithridates to have the legitimate king of Syria in his hands, as a piece to play, should occasion arise.

---

[1] It appears to the writer of this chapter that as regards this embassy Willrich has made out a good case for regarding the details given about it in I Maccabees as belonging to an embassy sent later by John Hyrcanus. This would still leave it probable that Simon also sent an embassy of some kind. In any case there are difficulties about the date, see Schürer, *op. cit.* 1, p. 250: M. S. Ginsburg, *op. cit.* pp. 56 *sqq.* All that can be definitely said is that the letter of the Senate is addressed, amongst others, to Demetrius, *i.e.* it was written, if genuine, before the place of Demetrius in Syria had been taken by Antiochus VII.

[2] The *senatus consultum*, issued on the same occasion as the original document behind I Macc. xv, 16–24, is probably represented by Josephus, *Ant.* xIV, 145–148, though whether this is so has been a matter of voluminous controversy.

[3] F. X. Kugler, *Von Moses bis Paulus*, pp. 338–343. See vol. IX, the chapter on Parthia.

This left Tryphon for a moment sole king in Syria, but on the news of Demetrius' capture, his brother Antiochus set foot quickly in Syria and took up the task of restoring Seleucid authority in the land.

Antiochus VII Euergetes, nicknamed Sidetes, was the last strong representative of the old royal house. At the beginning of his reign (before the spring of 138) he was only about 20. He married, as her third husband, Cleopatra Thea, his captive brother's wife. The power of Tryphon melted away. The boy Antiochus VI, whom he had kept in his hands since his dethronement in 142, he put to death in 138. Within a month or two he was himself captured by Antiochus VII and compelled to commit suicide.

The new king soon had the Jewish question in hand. According to I Maccabees he had written to Simon, before he landed in the kingdom, confirming the concessions already made and granting the new right to coin money[1]. When he was established in Syria he began to regulate the Jewish position. He did not demand again the tribute which had been remitted for the territory which the Jews had occupied by authorization of the Seleucid government—Judaea and the three Samarian toparchies—but he did demand tribute for the places which Simon had taken possession of with a high hand—Joppa and Gazara and the *akra*. This brought about new conflicts between the Seleucid forces and the Jews. A detachment sent by Antiochus in 138 to invade Judaea was defeated by Simon's two sons, John Hyrcanus and Judas. For more than three years after this Antiochus left the Jews unassailed: he had no doubt enough to do elsewhere. Then in the February of 134 Simon was assassinated at a feast by his son-in-law, Ptolemy, while the old High Priest was heavy with wine. Ptolemy had intended to seize the chief power in the Jewish state, but he was forestalled by John Hyrcanus, who swiftly possessed himself of Jerusalem and was installed as High Priest in his father's room.

John had hardly entered upon his office when Antiochus VII dealt the blow which had been impending since 138. It was again seen that when the strength of the Seleucid kingdom was concentrated and resolutely used, the Jewish state was no match for it. The Jewish bands were soon driven from the field. Joppa,

---

[1] Though no Jewish silver coins of this period survive, half- and quarter-shekels of bronze struck under Simon have been identified as the first coinage of the Jews. See G. F. Hill, *B.M. Cat. Coins of Palestine*, p. xciii, and Volume of Plates iii, 14, *d*.

Gazara, and other recent conquests of the Jews, were reoccupied by Seleucid forces. In vain Hyrcanus sent an appeal to Rome, Rome would still give nothing but words. A *senatus consultum* preserved by Josephus (*Ant.* xix, 260 *sqq.*) re-affirms the friendship subsisting between Rome and Jerusalem, and declares that Antiochus is to give back the places occupied and not invade Jewish territory. Antiochus saw that the thunder was without a thunderbolt. He went forward in disregard of Rome. Soon Jerusalem was subjected to a regular siege. The spring and summer of 135 had fallen within a Sabbatic year, so that corn supplies in the spring of 134 were shorter in the city than at ordinary times. After a siege of more than a year, during which Jerusalem suffered the extremities of famine, it had to surrender. Many of the king's councillors now urged him to complete the work of his predecessor, Antiochus Epiphanes, and exterminate the turbulent people. Antiochus VII refused. He did not even re-impose the tribute which had been remitted. He gave back to the Jews, probably in order to conform so far with the expressed will of Rome, the places which the Jews had conquered beyond the frontiers of Judaea—Joppa, Gazara and the rest. But he insisted on the Jews paying tribute for these, and also on their paying a war indemnity of 500 talents. The High Priest had to give hostages—his own brother for one—and the fortifications of Jerusalem were demolished. Antiochus VII was willing to conciliate the Jews by marks of respect to their religion: during the siege he had even sent animals for sacrifice into the city on the Feast of Tabernacles (October 134). But politically the Jews were to be, as before, a people subject to the house of Seleucus. It may well have seemed at that moment that the last few years of independence under a Hasmonaean High Priest had been a transient episode.

Having restored the kingdom in Syria, Antiochus VII set himself to restore it in the eastern provinces. A victorious campaign in 130 seemed to make him master of Babylonia and Media. In the winter or early spring of 129, however, his camp was surprised by the Parthians, and he fell on the field. The last attempt of the house of Seleucus to restore its authority had failed. A cuneiform document of June 130[1], is the last we have from Babylonia, which gives in its dating the name of a Seleucid king.

But in 129 Demetrius II was back in Syria, for the Parthians, when hard pressed, had set him free to create a diversion in his brother's rear. Demetrius was quite incapable of continuing the strong government of his brother. After the death of Antiochus

[1] Reisner, *Sumerisch-babylonische Hymnen*, no. 25 (Kugler, *op. cit.* p. 337).

VII the final disintegration of the kingdom set in. Demetrius quarrelled with Egypt, and his brother-in law, Ptolemy VII, sent into Syria a protégé of his own, who claimed to be Alexander son of Alexander Balas, to fight with Demetrius for the throne. Antioch accepted him, while Demetrius apparently held his own in Phoenicia and Palestine. Cleopatra Thea was established in Ptolemaïs and was little disposed to have her futile second husband back again in exchange for Antiochus VII. After suffering a defeat at Damascus which made his position insecure even in the south, Demetrius attempted to escape by ship from Tyre, but was assassinated when on the point of sailing (126/5).

After this there were almost always rival kings fighting over what remained of the Seleucid inheritance. Alexander II, whom the Antiochenes nicknamed, in Aramaic, Zabinas, 'the Bought One,' was swept away by Antiochus VIII Grypus, a son of Demetrius II and Cleopatra Thea, in 123/2. Then the son of Cleopatra Thea by Antiochus VII, Antiochus IX, nicknamed Cyzicenus, entered the field, and the struggle between princes of the two branches of the royal house was protracted into the next generation. These men who called themselves kings and bore the old dynastic names of the house of Seleucus and the house of Antigonus—Seleucus, Antiochus, Demetrius, Philip—were little better than captains of bands, who dominated now one region, now another, and preyed on the unhappy country. In this break-up of the royal authority, the Greek cities of Syria acted more and more as independent states and went to war, or made alliance, with each other on their own account. Local native chieftains, Syrian or Arab, set up principalities of their own in the less hellenized districts. Two native peoples became considerable powers—the Nabataeans and the Jews.

Up to the death of Antiochus VII his fresh subjugation of the Jews held good. A Jewish contingent, commanded by the High Priest, formed part of the army with which he marched to the East. But when Antiochus fell in Iran, his work in Judaea was all undone. John Hyrcanus once more assumed the position of an independent prince, striking bronze coins which bear in Hebrew the legend 'Jehohanan the High Priest and the Commonwealth of the Jews[1].' Hyrcanus did not yet, as his son Jannai Alexander did, assume the title of 'King' conjointly with that of 'High Priest.' Two processes have to be traced in the Jewish state from the acquisition of independence to the end of the reign of Jannai Alexander—one is the growing alienation between the ruling

[1] See Volume of Plates iii, 14, e.

Hasmonaean house and the party of strict religion, and the other is the process of territorial expansion. Both these processes had begun before the death of Jonathan. Under John Hyrcanus came the definite breach between the Hasmonaean High Priest and the religious sect, who had been called Chasīdim in the days of Judas Maccabaeus, but who now perhaps began to be known by the name 'Pharisees,' 'those who separate themselves.' The occasion of the breach is obscured for us in Rabbinic legend. But it is possible to see in the Jewish apocalyptic literature traces of the abhorrence with which the godly had come to regard the Hasmonaean priesthood.

The other process of territorial expansion, which had begun with the acquisition of the three Samarian toparchies and the seizure of Joppa and Gazara, was continued on a more ambitious scale by John Hyrcanus. He pushed forward the Jewish frontiers east and north and south. Beyond Jordan he conquered Medaba. On the north he subjected the Samaritans. The rival Samaritan temple on Mount Gerizim he destroyed: it was never rebuilt, only the site remained a holy one for the Samaritans and their Passover lambs continued to be killed there. On the south Hyrcanus began the subjugation of the Idumaeans and took possession of Adora and Marissa. In the case of the conquered Idumaeans a step was taken which, so far as we know, was something quite new. The heathen population was not driven out, as it had been at Joppa and Gazara, but compelled to embrace Judaism and undergo circumcision. Henceforward the Idumaeans formed religiously one people with the Jews; their forcible incorporation brought a century later its terrible revenge, when the Jewish people were subjected to the iron despotism of the Idumaean Herod. In the last days of Hyrcanus the Jews laid siege to the Greek city of Samaria. Antiochus IX Cyzicenus, who had some power in the neighbouring region, attempted to relieve the city. He overran the Jewish territory for a time[1], but was defeated by the Jewish

---

[1] Theodore Reinach, *Revue d. études juives*, xxxvii, 1899, p. 161, has made it probable that the *senatus consultum* contained in a decree of the city of Pergamum (Josephus, *Ant.* xiv, 247 *sqq.*) belongs to this moment. In answer to an appeal from Hyrcanus, the Senate declares that king 'Antiochus son of Antiochus' is to retrocede to the Jews the places he has occupied. Schürer supposed that it belonged to the time of Antiochus Sidetes, like the other *senatus consultum* mentioned on page 530 but, apart from the inaccuracy in calling Sidetes 'son of Antiochus,' a decree of the city of Pergamum, as an ally of Rome, with no mention of a king of Pergamum, is not likely before 129 B.C.

forces under two sons of the old High Priest (108). A story which reached Josephus and is reproduced in a distorted form in the Rabbinic books, tells us that while Hyrcanus was ministering in the Temple a supernatural intimation was given him of this victory, before the news of it reached Jerusalem. When Samaria fell the Jews turned the water-courses over its site, so as to obliterate all traces of the hated city. Shortly before this, another important Greek city, Scythopolis (Beth-shan), which commanded the passage of the Jordan south of the Sea of Galilee, had passed by voluntary surrender into the power of the Jews.

Hyrcanus died in 104 B.C. It was under his son Jannai Alexander that the two processes just spoken of reached their final stage; the conquests of Jannai made the new Jewish kingdom roughly co-extensive with the kingdom of David, and the enmity between the Hasmonaean king and the Pharisees reached a pitch of savagery which caused the Pharisees to suffer worse atrocities at the hands of the Jewish High Priest, the great-nephew of Judas Maccabaeus, than the religious had suffered during the great tribulation at the hands of the pagan king, Antiochus Epiphanes.

CHAPTER XVII

THRACE

I. INTRODUCTION: STATE AND SOCIETY

AMONG the peoples who came into immediate contact with the Mediterranean powers the Thracians may claim more attention than is due only to their direct effect on the main course of political history. It is true that scholars have usually adopted a very unfavourable view of their capacity for any high degree of cultural development. Such a judgment, founded chiefly on the evidence of the writers of antiquity, by whom the Thracians are represented as in many respects a primitive people, seems, however, to be too sweeping. Although archaeological exploration of the regions inhabited by the Thracians is still in its infancy, it is already clear that by the middle of the second millennium B.C., the tribes there had developed a flourishing Bronze Age civilization. The political and social life of the people at this period must have corresponded to that of the Achaeans as represented in the *Iliad*. Indeed, we find the South Thracians appearing in the *Iliad* with the same weapons and methods of fighting as the Achaeans. Homer expressly mentions Thracian swords, and it is worthy of note that two swords and a lance-head of Mycenean form and workmanship, as well as a small bronze votive double-axe have been found in the district of Philippopolis in Southern Bulgaria. The well-known tholos-tomb near Kirk-Kilisse (Lozengrad), dating from the fourth century B.C., the gold diadems and other ornaments found in Thracian burial mounds, furnish evidence for the survival of Mycenean influence even down into the Classical period. In view of these facts, and of the circumstance that the Thraco-Phrygians exercised, at any rate in religious matters, a considerable influence upon the Greeks, Thracian civilization must have its place in any account of the development of European culture.

Neither the scanty and often incidental statements about the civilization of the Thracians which have come down to us in Classical authors, nor the archaeological material, as yet incomplete, enable us to trace the historical development of their culture. We are often obliged to combine earlier and later sources in order to obtain at least a general picture. But we ought not to assume that the same conditions obtained among all the Thracian tribes. The southern races, who were early exposed to influences coming from the south and east, stood on a higher cultural level than those of the interior, who even at a comparatively late period were living in primitive conditions recalling those which may be postulated of the undivided Indo-European peoples (vol. II, p. 28 *sq.*).

The greatness and the wide distribution of the Thracian people were well known to the ancients. According to Herodotus (v, 3) it was the largest of all nations after the Indians; if it had found a leader or had been united, it would have been far the strongest. And in point of fact the Thracians were at one time in possession of the whole of the Balkan peninsula from the Euxine to the Adriatic; while northwards, the Dacian peoples extended as far as the middle course of the Oder, the lower reaches of the Vistula and the rapids of the Dnieper.

Information about the total numbers of the Thracian population has naturally not come down to us; it is only regarding the numbers of their army that we have some scattered notices. In 429 B.C. the Odrysian King Sitalces (vol. v, p. 206) is credited with an army of 150,000 men, of whom a third were cavalry and two-thirds infantry. The area of the Odrysian kingdom is estimated at about 50,000 square miles; and 150,000 men capable of bearing arms would imply a population of at least 600,000. This is not in itself impossible, but Sitalces' army was probably magnified by rumour. In 376 B.C. 30,000 Triballi invaded Thrace and laid waste the territory of Abdera. The Getae, north of the Danube, put into the field to oppose Alexander an army of 4000 cavalry and more than 10,000 infantry (vol. vi, p. 355). The Odrysian prince Seuthes III, in the year 323 B.C., could assemble against Lysimachus an army of 20,000 foot soldiers and 8000 horsemen. The Roman general Manlius, in the year 188 B.C., was attacked in the defile between Cypsela and the Hebrus by 10,000 Thracians, drawn from the tribes of the Astii, Caeni, Maduateni and Corpili. According to Strabo, writing under Augustus, Thrace south of the Danube counted 22 races, and was able, though then much exhausted, to raise an army of 15,000 cavalry and 200,000 infantry. These numbers obviously are not reached by a census but by conjecture.

Among the Thracians polygamy and marriage by purchase prevailed. The husband bought his wife from her parents with money or with goods, and thereupon she became his property. Unmarried women were allowed to have intercourse with whatever men they wished, but the married women on the other hand were very strictly guarded. Naturally, only the chiefs and men of wealth could buy a number of wives, the generality had to content themselves with few or one. The social status of the women was low. They had to grind corn, to weave, to draw water, to prepare food, and to perform various services for the men.

Among the Agathyrsi, Herodotus (IV, 104) informs us, community of women prevailed, while in general their manners and customs resembled those of the Thracians. Herodotus received this information—on which doubt has been cast, but without justification—from merchants in the colonies on the north-western shores of the Euxine, who carried on an active trade with the inhabitants of the interior, and were well acquainted with this wealthy tribe. The Agathyrsi were Scythians, who in the course of the migration of this people towards the west had settled in Transylvania and had conquered the indigenous Dacian population. They had abundance of gold ornaments, for they inhabited a rich gold-bearing region, and indeed archaeological finds have proved that from the latest period of the Bronze Age onwards Dacia was rich in articles of gold. As the Agathyrsi had for a long time lived side by side with the numerically much stronger Dacians, they had naturally adopted Thracian customs.

In social life there is plenty of evidence for a division of the Thracian population into nobles and commons. In the Thracian language the nobles were called Zibythides; among the Dacians, Tarabostesei (cap-wearers), because they alone had the right to wear the felt cap (*pileus*); the common people, generally, went bare-headed. Herodotus tells us that the Thracians held agriculture to be an unworthy occupation; the life of the warrior or the robber, on the other hand, was the most honourable. A life of leisure was of course the prerogative of the rich; the mass of the people had to work hard, as is clearly shown by the flourishing condition of agriculture in various parts of ancient Thrace.

As a reaction against the prevalent vices of unchastity and drunkenness there arose 'sects' or ascetic orders who strove after a strict and virtuous way of life. Among the Dacians there were the so-called *Polistai*, whom Josephus compares with the Jewish sect of the Essenes. South of the Danube among the Moesi there was the sect of the *Ktistai*, whose members abstained from all flesh, and confined themselves to a diet of milk, cheese and honey; they also practised community of goods and avoided intercourse with women. They were known as 'the God-fearing' ($\theta\epsilon o\sigma\epsilon\beta\epsilon\hat{\iota}\varsigma$) and the *Kapnobatai* (the latter term being perhaps a Thracian word corrupted by the Greeks).

There was of course a servile population in Thrace as elsewhere, but we have no detailed information about it. The Greeks drew many slaves from that country; according to Herodotus the Thracians even sold their children into slavery, and kidnapping and slave-trading were certainly quite common. At Athens Thracian women often appear as slaves and nurses; in the New Comedy the names Geta and Davus are the most usual names for slaves. In Italy, Thracian slaves appear as early as the period of the Republic; and from them were drawn some of the gladiators.

The Thracian people was divided into many tribes. Herodotus mentions nineteen, Strabo, twenty-two south of the Danube, Stephanus of Byzantium enumerates forty-three, and obviously the number must have varied in the course of centuries. The larger tribes had several subdivisions; in the incessant feuds many of the smaller ones were wiped out or absorbed by the larger.

Throughout the whole course of their history the Thracians never succeeded in combining into one State. The mountain tribes in particular, who lived mainly by hunting, cattle-breeding and brigandage, maintained their independence down to a late period. The first State of any considerable magnitude arose in the Hebrus valley, which was early exposed to cultural influences from the south: along the Hebrus there ran at this period an important trade-route which led northwards from Philippopolis across the Haemus to Moesia. This State was founded shortly after 480 B.C. by the Odrysian king Teres who extended his sovereignty as far as the Euxine and the Hellespont (vol. v, p. 173). His son Sitalces (*ibid.* p. 199) subjugated the tribes of Mt Rhodope, part of the Paeonians, as far as the Strymon, and the Getae north of the Haemus. It is probable that even the Greek towns on the Pontic coast were compelled to acknowledge the overlordship of the Odrysae and to pay them tribute. Thenceforward the king of the Odrysae called himself 'King of the Thracians.'

The annual imposts which were levied in the country itself and from the Greek towns on the coast amounted in the time of Seuthes I to about 400 talents of gold and silver; and an almost equal sum was represented by the presents in gold and silver which were offered to the king, without taking into account the offerings of brightly coloured stuffs, both worked and plain, besides other presents (Thucydides II, 97). These presents were made not only to the king but also to the lesser chiefs and to the other Odrysian nobles; no man could effect anything at court unless he brought a gift with him. It was, however, counted more disgraceful to refuse a request than to have a request refused. This universal Thracian custom is pleasantly illustrated in Xenophon (*Anabasis*, VII, 3, 26 *sq.*). During the banquet given by Seuthes II in honour of Xenophon (vol. VI, p. 17), a Thracian appeared leading a white horse, took up a full horn, drank to Seuthes and presented him with the horse; another brought him a young slave; a third, garments for his queen; a fourth, a silver vessel[1], and so on. From this description the inference has been drawn that there existed among the Thracians a solemn form for the conclusion of treaties: a meal eaten in common by the contracting parties, accompanied by presents, the acceptance of which laid the recipient under obligation to do as much or more in return.

The Odrysian State had a quasi-feudal character, the mass of the people being in economic dependence on the king and his nobles. In this respect it offers analogies to the Bosporan kingdom (chap. XVIII). The royal power was unlimited; after the death of the king his realm was divided among his sons, at any rate when the circumstances were normal. Whether the kings at this time had a fixed royal residence we do not know; in the fourth century Cypsela was the capital. There was as yet no standing army.

Besides the king there were lesser tribal chiefs, usually members of the reigning house, who, under his overlordship, administered the several territories. Under weak sovereigns these vassal rulers (παραδυναστεύοντες) grew so strong that they could even declare their independence. Circumstances of this kind naturally often gave occasion for the outbreak of conflicts between the several chiefs, especially when any king took upon himself the task of suppressing them, as did Cotys I. On the other hand, this state of things made it always possible for the neighbouring powers, Athens, or Macedonia, to keep Thrace permanently disunited by giving support now to one and now to another of the lesser chiefs.

The union of kingship with priestly power, frequently found among primitive peoples, existed in several of the Thracian tribes; thus, among the Cebreni and Scaeboae the holder of the office of priest of Hera was at the same time ruler of the people. Among the Dacians the kingly power had been separated from that of the priests, but the High Priest of Zalmoxis, who was called a god and dwelt in a cave in Mt Cogaeonon, played an important part as the king's counsellor and helper. According to Herodotus (v, 7) the Thracian kings worshipped Hermes above all gods,

[1] Such silver vessels are often found in Thracian graves (see below, p. 557).

swore only by him, and claimed him for their ancestor. This statement, which no doubt applies only to the tribes living in the vicinity of Mt Pangaeus, is confirmed by the silver octadrachms of the Derroni. It is possible that the kings of these tribes belonged to a different race from their subjects. Finally it may be mentioned that among many of the Thracian tribes kingship did not exist.

The kingdoms which sprang up among the Getae after the fall of the Odrysian State did not attain to any great importance, since they were too greatly exposed to the Scythian invasions (vol. vi, p. 251; see below, p. 573 *sq.*). At the beginning of the second century B.C., there arose a Dacian kingdom, which had to wage war with the Bastarnae, but this also was of no long duration. Later, however, the Dacians succeeded in forming a powerful state, which drew upon itself the attention of the Romans; this was the kingdom of Burebista (see vol. ix).

The Thracians lived for the most part in numerous open villages (in Thracian: *para*, in Dacian: *dava*), which were scattered about the plains, hills and mountains. It is probable that originally each tribe had a fortified village or mountain fortress in which the chief resided. They preserved this agricultural and village life down into Classical times; city life, with any considerable trade and industry, did not develop till Roman times. Exchange of goods between the various tribes took place at annual fairs, as is still the case among primitive peoples[1].

The graphic description given by Herodotus (v, 16) of the pile-villages of the Paeonians on the lakes of Cercinitis and Prasias is well known; from it we gather that each wife had a new hut built for her, as is still usual among primitive polygamous races. Herodotus' statement that the horses and draught-oxen were fed on fish is confirmed by parallels from Scandinavia[2]. Among the Dacians also, houses built on piles were usual. Xenophon (*Anabasis*, vii, 1, 13; 4, 5 and 14) mentions villages in the territory of the Thyni, and describes the houses, which lay at a distance from each other and were fenced about with high palisades to keep in the sheep.

The Dacian villages of the La Tène period are better known. They were small (covering not more than five acres), the huts huddled together, surrounded with palisades and deep ditches. The furniture found in them is poor, consisting chiefly of pottery (native, Celtic and Greek) and various objects in iron, bone, stone

[1] M. Rostovtzeff, *Social and Economic History of the Roman Empire*, p. 230.

[2] R. von Lichtenberg, *Haus, Dorf, Stadt*, p. 120.

and glass, and more rarely of bronze and gold. The graves (all cremation burials) lie close to the settlements, or under the houses, and very little has been found in them. As in the neolithic period the houses were really huts with a rectangular ground-plan and a saddle-roof, thatched with straw or reeds. The walls were of wattle, plastered with a mixture of clay and straw. In the mountainous parts they were built of planks and beams, with foundation-walls of stone. The hearth was usually placed in a corner or near a wall, not in the middle of the room. In the Dobrudsha we hear of Troglodytes who lived in underground dwellings, a mode of life which in the Balkan peninsula survived down to recent times. Caves also were used as human habitations.

In the interior of Thrace few towns are mentioned—apart from the colonies founded by Philip II—and it is hard to form any definite conception of them. Among those known are Cypsela, Doriscus, Xantheia (the modern Xanthi) and Bizye (modern Viza), the seat of the latest Odrysian royal house. A poorly fortified town on the left bank of the Danube was taken by Alexander the Great. In south-east Wallachia there was the town of Helis where the Getic King Dromichaetes entertained his prisoner Lysimachus.

Some of the hill-top towns in the territory of the Dacians (*e.g.* Costeşti, Grădiştea Muncelului) have recently been scientifically excavated. They are placed on hill-tops which command plains and roads, and consist of a series of concentric terraces, strengthened on the outer side with palisades on walls. On one of the lower terraces stands the great fortification-wall (2–4 yards thick), with square towers at intervals. Its foundation is of squared limestone blocks bonded together with wooden beams; above that, the wall is built of sun-dried bricks. On the highest terrace stands a square tower, which was the dwelling of the chief. Such fortified towns are especially numerous in Transylvania, date for the most part from the late La Tène period, and were centres of considerable industrial activity.

II. AGRICULTURE AND MINING

From the days of Peisistratus down to Roman times foreign nations repeatedly made attempts to get a foothold in Thrace in order to exploit the natural resources of the country.

Thrace, like Macedon, was well wooded; it was chiefly thence that the Greeks, from the fifth century B.C., drew their supplies of timber for shipbuilding. In the neighbourhood of Dysorus

(Krusha-Planina) lay a town called Xylopolis, the name of which is an index to its trade. The region of the lower Strymon was very rich in timber, and the loss of Amphipolis in 424 B.C. deprived the Athenians of one of their most important sources of shipbuilding material (vol. v, p. 245).

For the cultivation of cereals we have abundant evidence. Thracian wheat had many husks and was late in germinating. The corn of the plain of the Hebrus was heavy, free from bran, and ripened in the second month after sowing. In this neighbourhood lived the tribe of the Pyrogeri (*i.e.* dwellers in the wheat region); Pyrumerulas ('Protector of the Corn') is the name of a Hero worshipped by the Thracians. Thracian corn was as important to the Athenians as the South Russian (see vol. v, p. 173, and below, pp. 574 *sqq.*). Lysimachus sent to Rhodes, when it was being besieged by Demetrius Poliorcetes, 60,000 bushels of barley and the same quantity of wheat. In addition to wheat, barley, millet, olyra (a kind of spelt) and rye (in Thracian: $\beta\rho\acute{\iota}\zeta\alpha$) were cultivated. Corn was also grown by the Getae[1]. Among the Dacians there were even special officials charged with the supervision of the cultivators. Part of the corn which the Greek merchants imported from the Black Sea regions was drawn from the Dobrudsha. For the storage of the products of the soil, underground chambers (in Thracian: *siroi*) were used.

The relatively high standard of agriculture in Thrace is attested by the flourishing cultivation of the vine and of vegetables (especially onions and garlic), and also of fruit trees. Homer (*Iliad*, ix, 71) knows of Thracian wine. During the whole of antiquity the strong aromatic wine of the Ciconian town of Ismarus (in the neighbourhood of Maronea) was famous, and the wine of Biblinos was exported to Greece and Sicily. The country of the Bisaltae, west of the lower Strymon, was very rich in figs, olives and grapes, especially the coast-lands on both sides of the Nestus. According to Pomponius Mela the interior of Thrace was not very favourable to viticulture, and the vine ripened only when it was protected from the cold, a statement that naturally applies only to the higher and colder regions. Even in Dacia vine-growing was not unknown, although Greek wine was imported in large quantities. Nor was wine the only strong drink of this region.

The Thracians, like the Phrygians, knew how to make a kind of barley beer (in Thracian: *bryton*), which, as it had barleycorns

---

[1] That common ownership of land and a yearly exchange of arable lands existed among them, as has been inferred from one of the Odes of Horace (iii, 24), is hardly credible.

floating in it, was sucked up through straws. Hemp was grown in all parts of Thrace, and garments were made of it which could hardly be distinguished from those of linen. In southern Thrace, however, flax was not unknown.

In addition to agriculture, cattle-raising flourished, especially among the mountain tribes of the Haemus, of Rhodope, and of the Carpathians. Homer speaks of Thrace as 'breeder of horses,' and praises the horses of Rhesus. In later times the Thracians worshipped a Hero who was a Protector of Horses (Ἥρως Οὐτάσπιος). A warrior with his horse appears upon the silver coins of the Orrescii, Tynteni and Bisaltae; a rider, or a horse alone, is met with on the coins of many Thracian kings. The Thracian horse was of small size, compact and well-knit, had a long thick tail and a short mane, and carried its head high. The ass, too, was of small size like that of Illyria. For sheep, goats and cattle, Thrace, like the whole northern part of the Balkan peninsula, was an excellent grazing country, and milk, cheese and butter were important elements in the national diet. The breeding of swine, too, was part of the national economy.

As the inland Thracians, with the exception of the Dacians, had no salt, they were obliged to buy it from the Greeks; on the lower Strymon this trade was in the hands of the Athenians. In exchange for salt, the Thracians traded, among other things, slaves. The Greek colonies on the shores of the Aegean and the Euxine used to dry salt from the lagoons, *e.g.* in Mesembria, Anchialus and Aenus, and then take it inland to sell.

We have no information about metal-working in the interior of Thrace previous to Roman times. But in southern Thrace, there were the mines of Dysorus which produced for Alexander I of Macedon a talent of silver daily, and also the great mining region of Mt Pangaeus, the abundant silver and gold of which was exploited in the time of Herodotus by the Odomanti and Satrae. East of Crenides or Datum (vol. vi, p. 208) there were gold mines, as also at Skaptesyle south of Pangaeus, opposite Thasos, which, according to Herodotus (vi, 46), produced 80 talents of gold, presumably annually. It is possible that ancient accounts of the productivity of these mines are exaggerated, but the abundant silver coinage of the Thracian tribes of this region (Derroni, Orrescii, Edoni, Bisaltae, etc.) certainly show that, as early as the sixth century B.C., these mines were being actively worked, and had given rise to a notable degree of skill in metal-working (vol. iv, p. 130). Many of the Thracian rivers, too (*e.g.* Hebrus), brought down alluvial gold, which could be extracted by the use of primitive gold-washing devices. In Transylvania the Dacians exploited the gold mines, and probably also mined the silver from which they produced large numbers of coins and ornaments. The smelting and working of iron was for the most part carried on in works in the neighbourhood of the mountain fortresses which have been mentioned above.

III. COSTUME, PHYSICAL CHARACTERISTICS, SPORT AND WAR

The Thracians loved gaily-coloured and embroidered garments, which were for the most part made out of hempen cloth. On Greek vases they are represented, like the bards Orpheus and Thamyris and the Storm-god Boreas, in native costume, wearing caps of fox-fur with ear-pieces and long woollen cloaks ornamented with geometrical patterns[1]. The high leather boots (*embades*), which, together with the horseman's cloak (*zeira*), found their way into Greece in the fifth century, are all part of the Thracian dress; their fur cap, indeed, was for a time adopted as the fashionable wear of the Athenian knights. Equally Thracian are the breeches which are worn by a horseman on a sepulchral monument from Abdera[2]. A silver plaque from Czóra (in Transylvania) bears a representation of a Dacian wearing a belt, long close-fitting breeches and laced shoes[3]. The typical Dacian dress of both men and women can be seen on Trajan's column. In winter the Getae wore fur cloaks and long loose breeches.

The custom of tattooing and painting the body, which was highly esteemed among the Thracians, is mentioned by Herodotus. It was in special favour with the women, and the more nobly born they were, the richer and brighter coloured were the designs they used. The Agathyrsi painted both their faces and their limbs with indelible designs (distinctive tribal marks), while the nobles also dyed their hair blue. Painting of the body was customary among the Dacians also. It is probable that the tattooing had originally a magical significance, as on Attic vases the Maenads are sometimes represented with the figure of a stag tattooed upon them, *i.e.* with the figure of the sacred animal which in the Dionysiac Mysteries was torn in pieces by the Bacchantes[4]. Men perhaps used for this purpose the mark of the

[1] See Volume of Plates iii, 52, *a*.   [2] *Ib.* 54, *c*.
[3] F. Drexel, *J.D.A.I.* 1915, p. 8, Fig. 4.
[4] See Volume of Plates iii, 52, *b*.

ivy-leaf, which played an important part in the Dionysus-cult.
But later on the custom of tattooing was practised from purely
ornamental motives.

In appearance the Thracians were large, powerfully built men,
with fair or even reddish hair, and a skin white, delicate and cold;
and they had a tendency to put on flesh[1]. They are spoken of as
straight-haired (εὐθύτριχες) and with their hair dressed in a
kind of top-knot (ἀκρόκομοι). The chin-beard of the Thracian
on the Orpheus vase from Gela is characteristic of his race, as
also of the Dacians; the cheeks are shaved, apart from short side-
whiskers[2]. It is likely that the Thracians were not an unmixed
type even at the time of their immigration into the Balkan
peninsula; it is also probable that in their new home they were
superimposed upon an earlier autochthonous population which
was perhaps of a darker complexion.

The favourite occupation of the Thracians was the chase, and
they even represented their principal gods in the guise of hunters.
Besides leopards, foxes, panthers and bears, in earlier times both
the lion and the aurochs were hunted in southern Thrace; and
the huge horns of the latter were exported to Greece. The kings
of the Odrysae, Paeonians and Getae, were accustomed to use
aurochs' horns, sometimes overlaid with gold and silver, as
drinking vessels. The bison (vison), which the Thracians knew
how to capture alive, was found in the mountains of Orbelus and
Messapium (the modern Svigor and Maleshovska-Planina, on
the Strymon). The stag, the boar and the hare were widely
distributed. As we know from Herodotus (v, 16), the lakes and
rivers were full of fish, while the Strymon was particularly rich
in eels. In the navigation of these lakes and rivers small dug-
outs were used. On the lower part of the Danube larger boats
and ships were also known, the use of which had been learnt
by the inhabitants from the Greeks, who came up the river to
trade.

The Thracians, as other Indo-European races, were devoted
to drinking. They intoxicated themselves not only with wine but
also by inhaling the smoke produced by the burning of certain
seeds (perhaps of hemp). Even the women drank wine undiluted.
Among the Thracian Ligyri (?) the soothsayers made themselves
drunk with wine before giving their prophecies; and before the
beginning of a battle the warriors used to prepare themselves for
the fray in a similar fashion.

---

[1] Galen, περὶ κράσεων, ΙΙ, ed. Helmreich.
[2] See Volume of Plates iii, 52, a.

An interesting description of a native banquet is given by Xenophon in a passage cited above (p. 538). The Thracians and their guests sat down in a circle, and before each banqueter was set a three-legged table with meat and leavened bread. The chief, Seuthes II, and the other Thracians, threw bread and meat to the guests, while horns of wine were handed round. When Xenophon drank friendship to Seuthes, the latter rose and drank along with him, and then poured the remainder of the wine from the horn over himself. Then came men who blew a blast upon horns and played a tune upon leather trumpets, whereupon Seuthes sprang up, uttered a war-cry, and made vigorous leaps, as though he were trying to avoid a missile.

The same author describes the sword dance (κολαβρισμός): 'the Thracians danced, with weapons in their hands, to the music of the flute, springing lightly to and fro and brandishing their swords. At last one seemed to strike down the other, and the stricken dancer pretended to fall dead. The other stripped him of his arms and went off singing the Sitalkas. Others then dragged the fallen man away, as though he had been really dead.'

We hear of other sports, which were cruel and often highly dangerous, for example the hanging game described by Seleucus (*ap. Athen.* IV, p. 155 E), in which the feasters drew lots who should put his head in a noose, and cut himself down before it tightened. 'And if he is not quick enough in severing the rope with his scimitar, he is a dead man, and the others laugh and make merry at his death.' So slight was the value set on human life.

The national weapons of the Thracians were the sabre, in the form known as μάχαιρα (yataghan), and especially the sickle-shaped iron sword and knife (ἅρπη, ξιφοδρέπανον)[1]; also the six-foot pike, half of which consisted of a heavy iron double-edged blade (ῥομφαία). The double-axe appears upon the coins of some of the Thracian kings, and also in the hands of the Thracian Maenads; it is possible that the double-axe was a hereditary symbol of authority in the Odrysian royal house[2]. In addition they used javelin (ἀκόντιον) and bow; and it was said that the mounted bowmen of the Getae used to tip their arrows with poison. For defence there was a light, crescent-shaped shield (πέλτη) made of wood, or wicker-work, covered with leather, and

[1] See Volume of Plates iii, 56, c.
[2] A small double-axe of silver was found in the tholos-tomb at Kirk-Kilisse.

sometimes strengthened by a round iron or bronze boss. The various forms of Thracian cap were early converted by the Thracians into helmet shapes, the use of which spread also to Greece[1]. Mention is also found of armoured Thracian cavalry. The Thracians in the army of Perseus bore long shields, greaves and heavy pikes. The Dacians in the late La Tène period fought with bows, heavily-curved sabres and spears, but wore no helmets. They had a special battle-standard in the form of a dragon with open wolf-like jaws.

Warlike temper, courage, and soldierly qualities are generally recognized to have been characteristic of the Thracians, and in the second century B.C. Thrace was an inexhaustible source of fighting men. One motive, indeed, which led foreign powers to contend with one another for the possession of the land was the desire to be able to levy fighting forces there. In these circumstances it is not difficult to explain the large use made of Thracian mercenaries, especially from the time of the Peloponnesian War onwards. In Athens they served also in the corps of mounted and unmounted bowmen. Thracian peltasts and cavalry appear, during the Peloponnesian War, in the armies both of the Athenians and Spartans in the Thracian theatre of war; and, later on, in the army of the Ten Thousand. A very important part was played by the Agrianes and Paeonians in the armies of Alexander the Great; they served as javelin-men, archers and slingers, as light cavalry, mounted scouts and pioneers[2]; and Thracian mercenaries in larger or smaller numbers took part in almost all the great battles in the times of the Diadochi and Epigoni; a considerable number of them were planted as military colonists in the Egyptian *katoikiai* (vol. VII, p. 117); they served also in the armies of the Pergamene kings, of the Achaean League, and of Mithridates Eupator.

Of the art of war as practised by the Thracians we know little. Arrian (*Tactica*, XVI, 6) reports that the northern Thracians had learnt the wedge-shaped battle formation from the Scythians. The Triballi were accustomed to draw up their forces in four ranks: in the first were placed the weaker, in the second the stronger men, behind them the cavalry and, last of all, the women, who, if the men wavered, rallied them with cries and taunts. When Alexander the Great forced the passage of the Haemus the

[1] As examples we may cite two bronze helmets found in Bulgaria. Volume of Plates iii, 56, *a*, *b*.
[2] See vol. VI, p. 358, and J. Kromayer and G. Veith, *Heerwesen und Kriegführung der Griechen und Römer*, p. 101.

Thracians had drawn up large numbers of waggons in front of them, intending to use them in the fight as a kind of wall, and also, as the enemy were mounting the slopes, to roll them down upon them, in order to break up the Macedonian phalanx. Parallel to this is the remarkable device which the Bessi used to defend themselves against the Roman general, M. Lucullus, in 73 B.C.: wheels fastened together by their axles and studded with short spear-points were hurled down upon the enemy as they advanced up a steep slope (Sallust, *Hist.* iii, 36 M). Similar devices though in a more developed form are also found in use among the Dacians; they may therefore be considered to be a Thracian invention. Thucydides describes (vii, 30) how Dian mercenaries from Mt Rhodope made a successful defence against the Theban cavalry in 413 B.C. by first skirmishing in open order and then closing their ranks again. Watchfires were left burning in front of the camp of Seuthes II in order that no one might be able to approach it without being observed by the sentries. Before a battle the Thracians used to rattle their weapons in order to strike terror into the enemy. When in flight they slung their shields upon their backs. According to Livy, the Thracians used to return from a victorious battle singing and bearing on the points of their lances the severed heads of their enemies. Among the Paeonians it was the custom for any man who had slain an enemy to bring his head to the king, and receive in reward a golden cup.

IV. RELIGION AND FUNERAL CUSTOMS

Traces, though not very clear ones, have been found of animal-worship among the Thracians. We may recall the representation of Dionysus in animal form, Artemis Tauropolos, and the religious significance of the fox (*bassara*), which according to many scholars was treated as the totem of the Bessi (vol. iv, p. 533). It is at least clear that the Alopekis (fox skin) and the Nebris (fawn skin) had a religious significance; the votaries clothed themselves in the skins of the animals which they sacrificed and devoured, in order to become like the god. And the Getic Zalmoxis was originally thought of as having the form of a bear.

That the Thracians worshipped the universal Indo-European sky-god *Dios*, is attested by the personal and tribal names in which *dio*, *deo* or *deos* is found as an element. A Thracian secondary name of the god was Sbelsurdos (Zibelsurdos), which appears in dedications of the Roman period. A goddess whom the Greeks identified with Hera was worshipped by the Cebreni and Scaeboae. It is noteworthy that recently in the interior of Thrace a sanctuary of Roman times has been discovered with many votive reliefs which almost without exception have a representation of Hera.

There was also another god worshipped, to whom the Greeks gave the name Helios. Sophocles, for example, speaks of Helios as 'the eldest divinity of the horse-loving Thracians.' The Bithynians, who were of kindred race to the Thracians, held their courts of justice in the open air, facing the sun, that the god might look upon their judgments; here, as often elsewhere, the sun-god has become a god of justice. The Paeonians worshipped Helios in the form of a disc attached to a staff. The coinage, too, of the Thracian populations in Macedonia and Paeonia before the time of the Persian War affords proof that sun-worship was actively practised. The Thracian Helios-cult was taken up into Orphism, in which Helios became identified with Dionysus.

From the wide-spread worship of Apollo in Thrace in the Roman period we may fairly conclude that this divinity had found entrance in early times: there is evidence in an inscription of the third century B.C. for the existence of a Temple of Apollo in the territory of the Bessi (in the neighbourhood of Tatarpazardjik).

Herodotus names Ares, Dionysus and Artemis as native gods of the Thracians. Throughout the whole of antiquity, too, Thrace was recognized as the native home of Dionysus; it was thence that his cult was brought, by Thracian tribes, into Greece. As early as Homer we have mention of his nurses (nymphs = *nysai*), who were attacked by Lycurgus in Nysa. Dionysus (= 'god's son') is a Thracian name like Sabazios; the 'Nysian Fields' are the Land of the Gods, the counterpart of the Hyperborean country, the Thracian land of blessedness which lay high 'Above the Mount' (*Bora*)—the Thracian origin of the Hyperborean belief may be considered certain. There was a sanctuary of Dionysus upon Mt Pangaeus; it was a possession of the Satrae, but the men who served as priests were of the tribe of the Bessi. A woman soothsayer (*promantis*) gave oracles there in the same way as the Pythia at Delphi. A second, more important sanctuary was situated on Mt Rhodope, in the territory of the Bessi; it was visited in 340 B.C. by Alexander the Great.

Dionysus was originally a god of vegetation and fruitfulness. Ivy, the evergreen plant, was held to be one of the forms in which the god appeared; the Thracians even wreathed their weapons with it. In the land of the Bisaltae Dionysus, by a sheet of flame, made known to his votaries, assembled in the sacred grove, when it was his will to grant a fruitful year. Every spring, at the awakening of nature, the god appeared upon the mountains attended by a troop of semi-divine beings. His worshippers, for the most part women, thrown into an ecstasy by the whirling dance and the shrill music of the flute, called aloud upon the god, and professed to recognize him in some beast, ox or goat, which they tore in pieces and devoured raw. Through this sacrament they received the power of the god, felt themselves united with him, and so were called Bacchi (Bacchae), Saboi and Sabazioi. The Orphic Mysteries (vol. iv, p. 532) had their roots in the Dionysus-cult. The story of the sufferings of Zagreus which they embody, was invented to explain the Thracian rite of tearing animals to pieces and devouring them. It has, moreover, been conjectured that the Titans already had a place in the Thracian religion[1]. Finally, it may be remarked that in his native country Dionysus was worshipped early not only as a vegetation god, but also as a great lord of life and of the whole of Nature. As the lord of souls he guaranteed immortality to his votaries.

Along with Dionysus there also came into Greece the Thracian Earth-goddess Semele, who had already in her native home been associated with the sky-god. It can scarcely be doubted that the Indo-European myth of the marriage of the sky-god with the earth and of the child who sprang from this union (Dionysus) was also current among the Thracians.

The goddess whom Herodotus calls Artemis was doubtless the Thracian Bendis (Mendis), to whom the Thracian and Paeonian women presented offerings wrapped in wheat-sheaves. She was a great goddess of fruitfulness and was also a goddess of hunting; as such she bore two lances. She was also identified with Hecate. In the time of Pericles her cult was introduced into Athens, and served as an object of ridicule to the Comic poets. Plato in the *Republic* gives a description of the first celebration of the Bendideia at the Piraeus. The festival consisted of a procession in which the Athenian citizens, and especially the Thracians who had settled at the Piraeus, took part, and in a torch-race on horseback and a night celebration of an orgiastic character. A temple of the goddess was situated in the neighbourhood of the lower Hebrus (Maritza). In Greek bas-reliefs she is represented in Thracian costume[2].

[1] M. Pohlenz, *N.J. kl. Alt.* xxxvii, 1916, p. 549; U. von Wilamowitz-Moellendorff, *Berl. S.B.* 1929, p. 51.
[2] See Volume of Plates iii, **54,** *a.*

Amphipolis was the seat of the worship of Artemis Tauropolos, who was doubtless a Thracian goddess of hunting allied to Bendis. Another goddess identified with Bendis is the Mystery-goddess Hecate (or Aphrodite), who was worshipped in the cave of Zerynthia on the island of Samothrace and on the opposite coast with sacrifices of dogs. She was, as it seems, goddess both of life and death. And the enigmatic cult-names Axiokersos, Axiokersa in the Mysteries of the Cabiri seem also to have been of Thracian origin. In an inscription of a brotherhood (ὀργεῶνες) found at the Piraeus the Thracian god Deloptes is mentioned along with Bendis and he appears also as the Hero Deloptes in a votive tablet from Samos, where he is represented after the fashion of Asclepius, leaning upon a staff. This great Thracian goddess was worshipped also by the Dacians, and in the Roman period is often spoken of under the name Diana Regina. We may note that Diodorus (1, 94) ascribes to the Dacians the worship of Hestia (κοινὴ Ἑστία) also, for, as a matter of fact, there are traits in the nature of Bendis which remind us of Hestia.

Another goddess with close affinities to Bendis is Cotys or Cotyto, the goddess of the Edoni, whose worship, probably following the course of trade, also found its way into Greece. In the orgies of this goddess dances were performed to a musical accompaniment, in which men appeared in women's garments. Mention is also made of a baptism of the mystae with water, which is doubtless to be thought of as rain-making magic. Cotys, too, was a goddess of fruitfulness.

In antiquity Ares was always represented as coming originally from Thrace, and he plays a part in the genealogical legends of the Edoni and Bisaltae. It is doubtless true that the Thracians worshipped a god of war; but a Thracian origin for the Greek Ares cannot be proved. We do not even know what the name of the Thracian war-god was; among the Crestonii he was called Kandaon. Perhaps the Apsinthian Pleistoros (Herod. IX, 119) was a war-god.

A prominent part in the Thracian pantheon was played by the god whom the hellenized Thracians called by the name of 'Heros.' This was the Thracian 'Horseman Hero' who is known to us more widely from monuments of the Roman Empire. He is, above all, a chthonic deity and as such is also a god of vegetation and the bestower of all the gifts of nature. He is, therefore, represented on some second-century B.C. coins of Odessus as bearing a cornucopia though later he appears without it; in inscriptions he is designated by the Thracian name Derzelas.

In other towns on the Black Sea coast also (Tomi, Istros, Callatis) the Greek god of the underworld was identified with the Thracian Hero. The latter was also held to be the bestower of health and the guardian of the house and of the roads against all evil. Sometimes he is represented with three heads. He was also a god of the chase, like the Thracian king Rhesus (*rex*), known to us from the Greek mythology, who lived as a hunter-god upon Mt Rhodope, and upon whose altars the wild beasts offered themselves voluntarily for sacrifice. Rhesus was likewise a chthonic divinity and protected his worshippers from pestilence and other diseases. Traces of his cult are found at Amphipolis, Aenus and Byzantium. The Thracian Hero and Rhesus show a certain affinity with Dionysus, who is sometimes called a Hero, and appears as a hunter-god. They were perhaps hypostases of this many-formed Thraco-Phrygian chief god.

The extraordinary frequency of dedications to Asclepius from the Roman period warrants the conclusion that there was also a special god of healing who was worshipped in Thrace. Finally we may mention the Thraco-Phrygian god of springs and rivers, Bedy; also the goddesses of springs, who correspond to the Greek nymphs.

The strong religious feeling of the Thracians and their lively faith in another life were generally recognized in antiquity. Herodotus (IV, 94) says of the Getae that they held themselves to be immortal; they had only one god, Zalmoxis, to whom they believed they would go after death. The Greeks who lived on the shores of the Hellespont and the Euxine gave the historian a rationalized version of the legend, which brought Zalmoxis into connection with Pythagoras.

The same writer tells us that every four years the Getae sent to Zalmoxis a messenger, chosen by lot, to make known to the god their desires. The messenger was flung into the air and caught upon the points of three spears; if he was pierced by the spears and died, he was held to be acceptable to the god; if not, another messenger was sent in his place. This custom is normally explained as the offering of a human sacrifice to the god. Such sacrifices were, it is true, customary in other tribes, but it may be that it was nothing else than the periodical slaying of the vegetation spirit with the purpose of increasing fruitfulness, and in this case we might conceive of Zalmoxis as a vegetation god. No doubt the slaying would originally take place every year, and the custom would gradually be mitigated later. It is in any case clear from the statements which have come down to us that Zalmoxis was a divinity of the Lower World, who was also thought of as a god who gave oracles and revelations. Whether the epiphany of the god was celebrated in enthusiastic festivals is not clear. Many scholars deny the existence of orgiastic cults among the Getae and conceive of Zalmoxis as a sky-god. In any case it must be assumed that the Getae did worship a sky-god (perhaps Gebeleïzis, which was, according to Herodotus, another name for Zalmoxis), and we may venture on the conjecture that this sky-god had coalesced with an older chthonic divinity and so became a god of the Lower World, as happened also with the Greek Zeus in certain local cults[1]. Another remarkable custom of the Getae is that of shooting arrows against a thunderstorm in order to frighten away the hostile power.

We have mentioned above the Thracian belief in immortality, but this immortality was doubtless conceived of as a corporeal existence. They believed that the soul after death took on a new human or, it might be, animal body. If in the legend Zalmoxis appears as the pupil of Pythagoras, that is only to be explained by the need that was felt to bring Pythagoras into connection with Thrace, because his teaching had become fused with Orphism.

Of the appearance of a Thracian temple at this period we can form no clear idea. A remarkable double ring of squared stones was found on the lowest terrace of the fortress at Grădiştea Muncelului (in Dacia), which recalls the cromlechs of western Europe. Its significance, however, is not yet certain; perhaps we have here an open-air temple like the circular sanctuary of Sabazios on the hill of Zilmissus in Thrace which Macrobius mentions[2].

The funeral ceremonies of the Thracians of high rank are described by Herodotus. For three days the body was exhibited and lamented, then animal sacrifices were offered and a banquet was held. Thereafter the body was either burned or simply buried in the earth; over the grave a mound was raised and contests (obviously funeral games) were held at which the highest prize was awarded for single combat[3]. This statement has been fully confirmed by archaeological discoveries. In the neighbourhood of Bailovo (near Sofia) eleven tumuli of the fifth century B.C. were explored, and nine cremation burials and two graves containing skeletons came to light. The objects found included pottery, iron

[1] S. Wide, *Archiv für Religionswissenschaft*, x, p. 258.
[2] M. Ebert, *Reallex. der Vorgeschichte*, xi, p. 168 (Wilke).
[3] L. Malten, *Röm. Mitt.* 1923–4, p. 331.

and bronze fibulae, swords, lances and remains of sacrifices (bones of oxen). In the Necropolis of Vlashko-Selo (near Vratza in northern Bulgaria) both inhumation and cremation burials were found. In a tumulus dating from the fifth or fourth century B.C. near Ezerovo the sepulchral urn was found with its mouth turned downwards. The bottom, which was bored through, was covered with a perforated earthenware disc. Obviously the soul, conceived as a serpent, was to creep out of this opening in order to taste the offerings of food which were made to it. Cases also occur in which the tumulus has simply been piled up over the burnt body (which was not placed in a special grave). In other tumuli of the fifth to third centuries the bodies were placed in stone cists, and the dead man's horse buried with it or laid in the earth of the tumulus. The furniture of these graves recalls the contemporary Scythian graves in Southern Russia (vol. III, p. 201 *sq.*). The similarity of the method of burial among Thracians and Scythians is probably to be explained by their ethnic relationship and geographical proximity. A funeral chamber which had been plundered at some earlier date, with an ante-chamber built of squared limestone blocks, was found in a tumulus near Staronovo-Selo (near Philippopolis). The walls of the chamber were coated with plaster and showed traces of painting. The tholos-tomb near Kirk-Kilisse has already been mentioned. In the neighbourhood of Apollonia (now Sozopolis) a tholos-tomb was discovered, the construction of which recalls the Kostromskaya Kurgan. In this, as in other Thracian graves, gold wreaths and diadems of the same kind as those in Scythian graves were found.

There survived among the Thracians and Getae the custom, which goes back to remote antiquity, of slaying at the grave the dead man's favourite wife; and it is even related that the wives disputed among themselves which had been the favourite, and that the friends of the dead took much trouble to discover who this was. The low estimation in which human life was held, coupled with the belief in immortality (see p. 551), explains other customs. When a child was born, for instance, the relatives wailed over it, because of the evils which awaited it in life; the dead, on the other hand, were buried amid jubilations because they were now freed from all sufferings, and living in complete blessedness[1]. And the Thracian tendency to suicide, of which we have ample evidence, has its roots in the same belief.

[1] But cf. E. Nestle, *N.J. kl. Alt.* 1921, p. 81.

V. CULTURE. FOREIGN INFLUENCES

With the exception of a short Thracian inscription in Greek letters, which has not yet been interpreted with certainty (vol. ii, p. 32)[1], all we know of the Thracian language—which was still a living language in the sixth century A.D.—consists of personal and place names and a few glosses. Androtion, the Atthido-grapher, even declared that no one in Thrace knew how to write, and, indeed, that all the barbarian peoples of Europe regarded the use of writing as something disgraceful.

Music, dancing and poetry seem, however, to have flourished in Thrace. The worship of the Muses which had its earliest seat in Pieria on Olympus seems to have been of Thracian origin; and the names of the mythical Thracian bards, Orpheus, Musaeus and Thamyris, are well known. But it is possible that this relatively high musical art was derived from the earlier pre-Indo-European population of Thrace, which was connected with that of Asia Minor.

Even among the northern tribes the love of music was not unknown. Theopompus mentions the Getic custom of accom-panying embassies of peace with the playing of the zither. The Agathyrsi learnt their laws by heart in the form of songs. Certain musical instruments (e.g. the magadis, and the shepherd's pipe) were held to have been actually of Thracian invention, though whether with justice we do not know. A song is mentioned named the Sitalkas, which was probably sung in honour of King Sitalces; both a song and a dance bore the name of Zalmoxis; a song accompanied by the flute (named τορελλή) was sung over the dead. We hear also of magical chants with which the Thracian physicians healed both body and soul. Women, too, played an important part as sorceresses and soothsayers. Indeed, Menander makes mock of the deep-rooted superstition of the Getic women, who were always celebrating some festival or other and performing sacrifices with magic rites. Popular medicine had a considerable vogue among the Dacians; the names of quite a number of plants which were used as medicines have come down to us.

The statement of Demosthenes (*In Aristocratem*, 169) that the Thracians were forbidden by law to inflict a death sentence on one of their own race is perhaps to be interpreted in the sense that the death penalty was not expressly laid down in any law; but no doubt the authorities could inflict it both upon enemy Thracians and upon foreigners also. Ancient writers have much to say of

[1] Volume of Plates iii, 62, *a*.

Thracian cruelty and treachery. Herodotus, it is true, declares
that the Getae were the bravest and most just of the Thracians,
but he seems here to have idealized them. In view of the cruelties
which were practised by the Greeks themselves in their own civil
and external wars, we have no reason to think that the Thracians
were more cruel than other peoples on the same level of civilization.

Hellenic influence in Thrace was disseminated from the Greek
colonies planted on the shores of the Euxine (Apollonia, Mesembria) and on the Aegean coast (vol. iv, p. 105). Among the latter
Abdera, Maronea and Aenus were the most important, but the
smaller ones, the 'factories' founded by Samothrace between
Doriscus and Maronea, also contributed to the spread of civilization[1]. The Attic tribute-lists show clearly that the Greek colonies
which served as intermediaries in the trade with the interior had
attained a remarkable degree of both material and intellectual
culture. In these towns there were living and working painters
and sculptors who were well acquainted with the conditions of life
in Thrace and who have left important traces in the Greek art
of the fifth and fourth centuries B.C.[2]

To this must be added the influence of Athens, for to Athens
the Thracian coastal region was one of the most important bases
of her commerce and prosperity. From Thrace she drew exports
of cereals, cattle, slaves and metals. These commercial interests
explain the friendly relations which Athens maintained with the
Odrysian kingdom. The Odrysian kings even attempted to
connect the lineage of the ruling house with the famous figures of
Greek legend: King Teres traced his descent to Tereus who
married the daughter of the Attic King Pandion (vol. v, p. 173).
The fact that Thucydides (ii, 29) took the trouble to refute this
genealogical claim, shows that it had met with some acceptance
in Athens also. Seuthes II in his conversation with Xenophon
referred to the kinship and friendship between the Thracians and
the Athenians. Even in later times these friendly relations were
not broken off: Seuthes III in the year 338 B.C.[3] sent his son
Rhebulas to Athens. It is well known that Greeks played an
important part at the Thracian court, and some of them even
took Thracian wives. Nymphodorus of Abdera, for instance, who
had married the sister of Sitalces, brought about the alliance
between Thrace and Athens (vol. v, p. 199). One daughter of
Cotys was married to Iphicrates, another to the mercenary leader

[1] See Volume of Plates iii, 54, *b*.
[2] B. Schröder, *J.D.A.I.* 1912, p. 344.
[3] For the date see Swoboda in *P.W.* *s.v.* Seuthes, col. 2022 *sq.*

Charidemus, who was in the service of Cersobleptes. The latter used Greeks as envoys to Philip II and the Athenians. The mercenary leaders, Athenodorus, Simon and Bianor, were connected by marriage with Cersobleptes' opponents, Berisades and Amadocus.

The coinage of the Thracian kings affords striking testimony to the lively commercial and political relations existing between the Greek colonies and the Thracians[1]. The majority of the coins are of a Greek type, and are stamped with Greek legends. The coins of Sparadocus, the brother of Sitalces, are of Olynthian type, and were probably struck in Olynthus. On the other hand the coins of Seuthes I bear a distinct national Thracian emblem, the figure of a horseman (p. 550 sq.), which also appears on the coins of Cotys I and Seuthes III. The coins of Amadocus I, Amadocus II, and Teres III are modelled upon those of the town of Maronea, where they were struck. Not less popular were the types of Thasos, which are found on the coins of Eminacus (fifth century B.C.), Saratocus (c. 400 B.C.), Bergaeus (? fifth century) and Cetriporis (c. 356 B.C.). Imitations of the coins of Abdera are less frequent, though there are some to be found, e.g. on the coins of the otherwise unknown Spoces (c. 360 B.C.). In the first half of the fourth century Cypsela was the seat of the Thracian mint, and Hebryzelmis, Cotys I, Cersobleptes and (?) Philetas had coins struck there. Orsoaltius, not known in literary sources, in the time of Lysimachus struck coins of Alexandrian type. Seuthes III actually used coins of Philip, Lysimachus, Alexander the Great and Cassander, overstriking them with his own types. After the diadem had been introduced as the symbol of royalty in Macedonia it was probably adopted also by the Thracian kings; but evidence for this is only found later, viz. on the coins of Mostis (c. 200–150 B.C.), Cotys III, Sadalas, etc.

The colonizing activity of Philip in Thrace (vol. VI, p. 251) greatly stimulated the expansion of Hellenic culture. All the cities founded by him (which included Greek settlers) were given constitutions upon the pattern of a Greek *polis*[2]. But the successful efforts of Philip to implant Greek culture on Thracian soil were not followed up by Lysimachus. In fact, the hellenization of Thrace was not taken in hand again until the time of the Roman

[1] The coins mentioned in this section are illustrated in Volume of Plates iii, 18.

[2] Mommsen's view (*Röm. Gesch.* v, p. 279 = *Provinces of the Roman Empire*, I, p. 303 sq.) of the character of Philip's colonies requires modification.

Empire. The spread of the Greek language could not be long delayed. Seuthes II, though he understood Greek, made use in his conversations with Xenophon of the services of an interpreter, but from the *Anabasis* (VII, 4, 15) we learn that even the highlanders of Eastern Thrace could speak Greek.

For further light on the question now before us we have to turn to archaeological evidence. The finds from the Hallstatt period in Thrace, which are still very scanty, show a close affinity with the contemporary culture of Illyria. An interesting find at Bukyovtsi (8 miles south-west of Orechovo in northern Bulgaria), probably dating from the end of the Hallstatt period, included two silver vessels and jewellery consisting of five fibulae (originally probably six) each with a handsome chain[1]. The ornament seems to have been made, in imitation of a Greek prototype, in Thrace itself. A form of silver, bronze, or iron fibula from the early La Tène period is very often met with in Bulgaria, and must be considered as a local variation of the Certosa type[2]. Curiously enough, a similar fibula is represented on an earthenware funerary urn from Pashaköi (neighbourhood of Kizilagach in Thrace) which is adorned with fantastic animal figures[3]. Isolated examples of this form of fibula are found also in Dacia.

A very instructive find was made in a grave in a tumulus near Duvanli (probably the grave of a woman of princely rank who lived in the fifth century B.C.) in which two different groups of objects could be distinguished. In the first group there were objects imported from Ionia: *e.g.* a fine silver two-handled amphora[4], which bore traces of gilding, a golden necklace, eight golden earrings, silver omphalos bowl, two bronze hydriae and other vessels of bronze and earthenware. But in addition there were local objects, also of Ionian type but of a coarser character: *e.g.* a diadem, a torc, two massive arm-rings with serpent-head terminals, a small box ornamented with spirals and rosettes, and two finger-rings, all of gold[5]. Finally, there were three fishes hammered out of gold plate such as are found in the Dnieper region[6].

Scythian influence in Thrace is evidenced chiefly by graves at Panagyurishte, Brezovo, Bednyakovo and the find at Radyuvene of the fourth to third century B.C. In the tumulus grave near Panagyurishte there again appear Greek imported objects, made at Amphipolis, two small gold discs ornamented with embossed

---

[1] See Volume of Plates iii, 58.   [2] *Ib.* 60, *a.*

[3] *Ib.* 60, *b.*   [4] *Ib.* 62, *e.*   [5] *Ib.* 62, *b, c.*

[6] *Ib.* 64, *b.*

heads of Apollo, small quadrilateral silver slabs ornamented with a head of Apollo embossed in high relief, two silver discs with a relief of Hercules fighting with the Nemean lion, small silver jars, a bronze jar with trefoil-shaped mouth and a double-handled bronze bucket[1]. Along with horse-trappings in Scythian style, there were some *phalerae* with representations in a barbarized Ionian style[2]. Especially notable was a small silver plate (an ornament for a horse's forehead) of native work with mythological scenes and figures (such as Hercules and Cerberus(?), Griffins, Siren), though the interpretation is uncertain[3].

Scythian influence is recognizable in some silver horse-trappings from Brezovo[4], where also were found an iron sceptre and a gold finger-ring with figures of religious significance—a horseman wearing an upper garment and breeches to whom a woman in a long robe is handing a drinking-horn. This scene, which is often represented on monuments in Southern Russia, is to be interpreted as the investiture of the king by the goddess, or as a communion in a sacred beverage. This shows that a local ruler was buried here (a Scythian, or the vassal of a Scythian ruler).

The tumulus grave of Bednyakovo contains a similar burial with Scythian horse-trappings of bronze and a drinking-cup of the fourth century with red figures. The find at Radyuvene consists of twelve silver vessels (omphalos bowls and a small jar) and two ornaments[5].

According to Rostovtzeff the explanation of this strong Scythian influence in Thrace is to be found in their political relations. The Odrysian kingdom, which in the fifth century stemmed the tide of Scythian expansion towards the west, fell to pieces in the fourth century, since it was no longer supported by Athens. Consequently the Scythians were able to resume their offensive, and established their supremacy at that time over certain of the Thracian tribes[6] (see below, pp. 572 *sqq.*).

The story of the commercial relations of Thrace with Macedonia and the Greek coast-towns is clearly told by the numismatic evidence. In what is now Bulgaria are found great numbers of bronze, silver and gold coins of Philip II, Alexander the Great and Lysimachus, and silver coins of Abdera and the towns of the

---

[1] Volume of Plates iii, 66, *a, b, c*.   [2] *Ib.* 68, *a*.
[3] *Ib.* 68, *b*.   [4] *Ib.* 70, *a*.
[5] *Ib.* 70, *b*.
[6] M. Rostovtzeff, *Iranians and Greeks*, p. 85; B. Filov, *Bull. de l'Inst. arch. bulgare*, IV (1926–7), p. 27; H. Schmidt, *Prähist. Zeitschr.* XVIII, p. 1.

Thracian Chersonese; most frequent of all are the silver tetradrachms of Thasos, while only a few examples of Athenian
tetradrachms appear. On the other hand imitations of the coins
of Philip II, Alexander and Lysimachus, as well as of Thasian
coins, are found in great numbers. Farther north in Daco-Getic
territory Greek influence was less powerful though the colony of
Istros played a notable part. Tomi did not acquire importance
until the third century B.C., while Callatis was more of an agricultural colony and its trading was chiefly in corn. Istros, on the
other hand, had attained considerable prosperity as early as the
sixth century.

It exported fish, corn, hides, slaves, etc., while in return its
Greek traders passed on to the Dacians wine, oil, pottery and
other goods from Athens or the towns of the Pontic coast, as well
as other products of Greek craftsmanship. On the banks of the
Danube, especially between Călăraşĭ and Turnu Măgurele there
arose Graeco-Getic trading-stations which served as points of
departure for traders who penetrated farther into the valleys of
the Danube basin, Seret, Yalomitza, and Argesh. After Philip II
had extended the sphere of Macedonian power as far as the
Danube, the Getae also began to strike a coinage in which they
imitated the coins of Philip, Alexander, Lysimachus and those of
Thasos. The coins of the Greek towns on the Pontic coast are
less often found, which proves that in Hellenistic times trade was
chiefly in the hands of wholesale traders from Greece proper and
Macedonia. Later (between the third and first century B.C.), both
Rhodian and Italian traders began to appear on the banks of the
Danube and many fragments of Thasian, Rhodian and Cnidian
amphorae have been unearthed in Moldavia and Wallachia. In
the hinterland of the Greek colonies in the Dobrudsha Thracians
and Greeks intermarried and there thus arose the *Mixhellenes*, who
could speak both languages.

The appearance of the Celts in the region of the lower Danube,
and in Southern Thrace where they founded the kingdom of
Tylis (vol. VII, p. 107), threw racial relations into confusion.
Although the economic connections of the Greek colonies with
the interior were not broken off they fell into great distress, for
there was no longer any dominant power in Thrace, and so these
towns were exposed to incursions from the neighbouring tribes,
which plundered their territory and exacted an annual tribute
from them.

Celtic influence in Dacia, especially in the second and first
centuries B.C., left deep traces behind it. Alongside the native

hand-made pottery, which preserves the older forms (of the neolithic and bronze ages), there can be found importations or imitations of Celtic pottery as well as various iron tools of Celtic form (ploughshares, scythes, sickles, etc.). The iron weapons, on the other hand, are of Dacian form (p. 546), though the *fibulae* whether iron, bronze or silver are of Celtic type. Among ornaments, arm-rings and neck-rings with serpent-heads of geometrical pattern are characteristic of Dacia. In Thrace, alongside of the native curved sabres, long swords and lances of Celtic type, fibulae, bridles, spurs, and so on, are found[1]. The collection of ornaments found in a tumulus grave near Kran (southern Bulgaria) deserves notice: a silver ornament in the form of an S, two gold earrings, a silver arm-ring, a necklace of silver pearls and a silver fibula[2].

Finally we may mention a find of the second or first century which shows evidence of Sarmatian influence on Thrace. In the neighbourhood of Galiče (Orechovo district in northern Bulgaria) there were found fourteen gilded silver *phalerae*, which doubtless formed part of a horse's trappings. On one of these *phalerae* there is a representation, in high relief, of a richly-ornamented woman's bust (a goddess)[3]; as a counterpart to this there is a *phalera* with the representation of a horseman whose right hand is raised in a gesture of adoration. Obviously we have here the same religious scene, of Scythian (Iranian) origin, which was noted at an earlier point (p. 558). The remaining *phalerae* are adorned with rosettes and leaf ornaments. They belong to a series of *phalerae* from Southern Russia, which are characteristic of Sarmatian burials.

In what precedes various cultural elements which the Greeks borrowed from the Thracians have been pointed out; it is also, as we have seen, possible to produce evidence of numerous points of contact between the two peoples, especially in the realm of cultus and myth. There can be no doubt that, with the progress of the archaeological exploration of Thrace, their mutual influence will become still more clearly manifest.

---

[1] Volume of Plates iii, 72.   [2] *Ib.* 74.   [3] *Ib.* 76.

CHAPTER XVIII

THE BOSPORAN KINGDOM

I. BOSPORUS IN THE FIFTH CENTURY B.C.

THE peculiar form which the Greek city-state constitution, Greek life and Greek religion assumed on the shores of the Black Sea and especially in the Bosporan kingdom merits special treatment in a general survey of Greek history. Despite some peculiarities the development of the Bosporan kingdom is typical for the general trend of Greek history, and in many respects anticipated the Hellenistic monarchy, especially that aspect of it which is represented by Syracuse in Sicily and Pergamum in Asia Minor. In the field of civilization and art Bosporus exemplifies that marvellous adaptability of Greek creative genius to new conditions and new surroundings which again must be recognized as one of the main features of the Hellenistic age.

The history of Greek colonization on the shores of the Black Sea has already been dealt with (vol. III, pp. 660 *sqq.*). It will, however, be convenient here to emphasize some important facts which have a direct bearing on the development of the Bosporan kingdom. The Greek colonies in the Black Sea region are to be divided into five distinct groups. The earliest is the group on the south coast along the route to the rich mining districts of northern Asia Minor and to the gold-fields of the Caucasus. Next comes the line of Milesian colonies which gradually occupied the western and northern shores as far as the mouths of the Bug and of the Dnieper. In founding these colonies the Milesians were looking for an abundant and accessible supply of food-stuffs, especially of fish and grain. They were created with the consent and blessing of the masters of the steppes of South Russia—the Scythians[1]. This group might be called, therefore, so far as South Russia is concerned, the Graeco-Scythian or the Olbian group.

The Scythians had pushed the former rulers of South Russia—the Cimmerians—southwards or westwards or locked them up in the Taman peninsula and the adjacent regions and in the hills of the southern part of the Crimea, but they were never able to conquer these parts of the former Cimmerian empire. Our

[1] On the Scythians and their neighbours in this early period see vol. III, chap. IX.

tradition is full of half-legendary stories of their prolonged struggle with the Sindians, the inhabitants of the Taman peninsula, and we never hear of the Taurians, the residents of South Crimea, as subjects of the Scythians.

Like the Scythians the Sindians were not hostile to the Greeks. They had long been wont to receive their metals from the south coast of the Black Sea, in all probability through the Carians, and as soon as the Greeks established themselves near the mining regions, they opened their shores to them. Thus a third group—Graeco-Sindian—of colonies was created in this region: Teïan Phanagoreia, Mitylenaean Hermonassa, and fishing stations of the Clazomenians.

Meanwhile the Milesians began to colonize the Crimea, probably from their colonies of Sinope and Amisus. They knew, no doubt, how rich the Crimea and Taman were in fish and corn. The excellent harbours of the later Chersonesus and Theodosia were occupied and, finally, Panticapaeum was founded at a spot which commanded the straits of Azov, and had been, no doubt, an ancient Cimmerian stronghold. There is no reason to doubt the statement of Stephanus of Byzantium that the Milesians sent their colony to Panticapaeum with the permission of the Scythians, who were used to the Milesians and preferred to deal with them rather than to depend on the Greek colonies of the Sindian coast.

Perhaps as early as the fifth century, or even earlier, the city of Chersonesus was taken from the Milesians by Dorian Heraclea Pontica[1], and became the nucleus of a group of Greek cities along the south and west shores of the Crimea which dealt chiefly with the Taurians and may be called therefore the Graeco-Taurian group. Panticapaeum, however, remained Milesian and soon began to grow and to extend its tentacles both along the straits to the Sea of Azov and to the mouth of the Don (where Tanais was founded) and along the Sindian shore of the straits. Thus arose a strong Panticapaean or Bosporan group of Greek cities in close connection both with the Scythians and the Sindians.

The early history of this Bosporan group is almost a blank. A group of coins shows that three of these cities began to strike money using the Aeginetan standard (like Olbia) and, in the main, Samian types[2]. One of these cities was Phanagoreia, another Panticapaeum, the third with the name apparently of Apollonia is a puzzle: a city of this name never appears again in our tradition.

[1] The early presence of the Milesians on the site of Chersonesus is attested by the pottery found there.

[2] See Volume of Plates iii, 20, *a, b, c*.

The uniformity of this early coinage points either to an agreement between the three cities or to the supremacy of one of them, presumably Panticapaeum. Unfortunately these coins cannot be dated exactly; some of them no doubt were struck in the fifth century and the earliest of them may go back to the sixth. More than that we cannot say.

It is by way of Athens that we are first able to approach the history of Panticapaeum. After 480 B.C. the names and dates of some of its rulers appear in what is probably Attic historical tradition, represented by excerpts from Diodorus Siculus. After the correction of some characteristic errors by Diodorus or his chronographical source and the checking of his chronology by reference to Bosporan affairs in the speeches and inscriptions of the fourth and third centuries, we are in the possession of a trustworthy tradition.

The first rulers of Panticapaeum are, according to Diodorus, who calls them 'kings,' the Archaeanactids, reigning from 480/79 B.C. to 438/7 B.C. His statement may be accepted, for no reason can be detected for the invention of so shortlived a dynasty either by local or Athenian historical tradition. Tyrannies were common in the Greek East of the time, and it is reasonable to suppose that in the Archaeanactids we have either a tyranny created by the Scythian overlords of Panticapaeum, like the tyrannies in Asia Minor which served the purposes of Persia, or rulers set up by the Greeks of the city in order to assert more effectively their rights against these same overlords. The name Archaeanax itself is a good Greek name, and is found in the early historical tradition of Mitylene.

During the fifth century the Black Sea region was well known to Greek merchants for its corn and fish, as is attested by Herodotus, whose statements are confirmed by the abundance of Greek pottery, first Ionian and then a little later Corinthian and Attic, found in the Greek cities and in Scythian and Sindian graves[1]. Trade was free, and produce went to anyone in Greece who was able to buy it. After the Persian Wars and the conversion of the Delian

---

[1] The same conclusions may be drawn from the study of the archaic bronzes. Some of them are undoubtedly Ionian (perhaps Samian, see W. Malmberg and S. Zhebelev, *Mat. for the Arch. of S. Russia*, XXXII; B. Pharmakovsky, *ib.* XXXIV, p. 33; E. H. Minns, *Scythians and Greeks*, pp. 374 *sqq.*; F. Studniczka, *J.D.A.I.* 1919, pp. 2 *sqq.*; G. Borovka, *Izvestija of the Acad. of Mat. Cult.* II, 1922, pp. 193 *sqq.*), some Corinthian (see Miss W. Lamb in paper read to the Hellenic Society, Feb. 4, 1930), some Attic (see Minns, *op. cit.* p. 380). See Volume of Plates iii, 92, *a, d, e.*

confederacy into an Athenian empire Athens turned her attention
to the Black Sea. She had failed to seize the corn market of Egypt
and to establish her hegemony over Phoenicia, Cyprus, and south-
west Asia Minor. She had now to find either in the West or in the
North-East a secured and ample supply both of food-stuffs and
shipbuilding material. In the West Athens had a formidable rival
in Syracuse and, as has been described above (vol. v, pp. 173 *sqq.*),
she made the North-East the principal sphere of her activity.
Probably between 437 and 435 Pericles himself led an expedition to the Black Sea which paraded the power of Athens before
'the barbarian peoples and their kings and dynasts' in that region.
The Greek cities gained in security by this display, and in return
were brought under Athenian influence. Sinope, Astacus, and
Amisus received Athenian colonists; Heraclea, which threatened
to dominate the Milesian colonies in the Crimea, was weakened,
and Athens formed a friendship with a new dynasty which in
438/7 had begun to rule at Panticapaeum.

The new dynasty was that of the Spartocids. Its founder,
Spartocus, is not mentioned in Athenian sources, but his successors are, and from the time of Leucon I, the third ruler of the
dynasty, we have local inscriptions containing the names of almost
all the rulers after Spartocus' son Satyrus. Among these names
Spartocus is found at least three times, and we need not doubt
Diodorus' statement that a Spartocus was the founder of the
dynasty. There are three facts which are significant. Not only
have the rulers of Panticapaeum Thracian names, Spartocus and
Paerisades, but these names are also found as dynastic names in the
Odrysian kingdom, which was no less a new friend of Athens
(vol. v, p. 173). Moreover, it is probable that the Spartocids knew
of a mythical genealogy worked out for them, no doubt, by
Athenian scholars which connected them with the Thracian hero
Eumolpus and through his father Poseidon and Heracles with
Athens. The genealogy became fashionable later in the Roman
period of the Bosporan kingdom, when the ruling dynasty was
again half Thracian, but it is presumably of earlier origin. A
parallel with this is the Attic genealogy invented for Teres, the
founder of the Odrysian dynasty, which made him a descendant of
Tereus, the husband of Procne, King Pandion's daughter. In the
third place, at about the same time that Spartocus became the
ruler of Panticapaeum we hear of similar rulers or kings in the
Sindian region. A story which may be dated in the early period
of the Bosporan kingdom—the tale of Tirgatao—related by
Polyaenus (VIII, 55), speaks of an independent Sindian king

Hecataeus who married a Maeotian princess Tirgatao and later became the son-in-law of Satyrus, the ruler of Bosporus, presumably the son of Spartocus I. The story names also a Gorgippus as son of Satyrus. Though the story is a historical novel (one of the earliest of its kind) it reveals a real knowledge of the history of the Bosporan kingdom. Further, the name Hecataeus recurs on early monuments of the region of Gorgippia. At Gorgippia also have been found tiles with the name of Gorgippus, probably a local ruler. Finally, Strabo (XI, 495) speaks of Gorgippia as the capital of the Sindians, and there are some fifth-century coins inscribed with their name (ΣΙΝΔΩΝ)[1]. All this suggests that in the fifth century B.C. the Sindians had their own kings, all of them Greeks. The residence of these kings was a Sindian town renamed probably after the first king of the dynasty Gorgippia.

We may then conjecture that the half-Thracian dynasty at Panticapaeum and the half-Sindian dynasty at Gorgippia came from the same source. This source may have been Athens, anxious to control the two shores of the Cimmerian Bosporus in the same way in which she controlled the Thracian Bosporus. Whether Spartocus was an Odrysian prince who came to Panticapaeum with a retinue at the call of the Archaeanactids, and with the permission of Athens, or an earlier Thracian resident of the city related to the Odrysian dynasty, or a scion of the Cimmerian royal family, if we assume the Cimmerians to be Thracians—we do not know. It is, however, no accident that the establishment of new dynasties at Panticapaeum and probably at Gorgippia was contemporary with the establishment of an Athenian cleruchy at Nymphaeum, a small Ionian city not far from Panticapaeum and perhaps with the creation of a similar stronghold—Stratocleia on the east shore of the Cimmerian Bosporus.

Of the early history of the new dynasties we know little, but the archaeological evidence suggests no very great prosperity during the reign of Spartocus I (438/7–431/0 B.C.), or the early years of Satyrus I (431/0–389/8 B.C.). The graves of this period are sparse and poor, and the coinage is not abundant. The Athenian monopoly, whereby the corn of the North-East was concentrated in Athens, no doubt hampered the trade of the Bosporan kingdom. Thus Athenian policy, acting through the Spartocids, was burdensome, even if Athens exacted no tribute from Bosporan cities[2].

[1] See Volume of Plates iii, 20, d.
[2] It is doubtful whether the cities mentioned in I.G.[2] 1, 63, frag. Z′′′′′ (ll. 195–211) belong to Pontus rather than to Thrace. The same doubt applies to frag. Z′′′′ (l. 190), which is generally taken to refer to Nymphaeum.

It is significant that Olbia appears to be outside the orbit of Athenian interests. In Herodotus, who draws on Ionian sources, much is said about Olbia, nothing about Panticapaeum, whereas in the Athenian tradition after the middle of the fifth century the converse is true. A reason for this Athenian neglect of the northern route by Olbia in contrast to her intensive cultivation of the southern route is hard to see, unless the internal conditions of Olbia either reduced its export of corn or prevented an effective Athenian control of it. Archaeological data give no explanation. While fifth-century remains do not show any great prosperity, they show no catastrophic decline, and Athenian influence, so far as it is suggested by the spread of Attic pottery, is felt at Olbia no less than at Panticapaeum.

II. THE BOSPORAN KINGDOM IN THE FOURTH CENTURY

The downfall of the Athenian domination in the Black Sea during and after the Peloponnesian War freed the corn-trade of Bosporus and so led to a new period in the life of this region. Even the allies of Athens, not to speak of cities outside her empire, had not been able to import Bosporan corn without special permission[1], and this fact, of course, kept prices down, but presently we find Mitylene on the eve of her revolt dealing directly with the Pontus and, later, with Leucon I, the son of Satyrus[2]. The effective beginning of this period is marked by the betrayal of Nymphaeum and its garrison by Gylon, the grandfather of Demosthenes, who entered the Bosporan service and married a Scythian, receiving as a reward for his treachery the town of Cepi[3]. This presumably happened at the end of Satyrus' reign, so that Leucon I inherited the blessings of an unrestricted corn-trade.

None the less, the official relations between Athens and the Bosporus remained close. Except for a short period Athens was the strongest naval power in Greece, and the commercial importance of the Piraeus was very little affected by political misfortunes. To Athens the Bosporus continued to be the one safe source of overseas food, which she needed in ever-increasing quantities (see below, p. 574 sq.), while the Bosporan kingdom found in Athens its richest and steadiest customer, with a stable

[1] [Xen.] de Rep. Ath. ii, 12; I.G.² i, 57 (Methone); Ib. 58 (Aphytis).
[2] Thucydides iii, 2; Ditt.³ 212.
[3] Aeschines in Ctes. 171–2; Zosimus, Vita Dem. (Dem. ed. Dindorf, viii, 18) and Anon. Vita Dem. (ib. viii, 23).

currency and a navy strong enough to convoy the corn-fleets past the hungry cities that lay between the Crimea and the Piraeus.

The first 'treaty' between Satyrus and Athens, indeed, appears to follow on the recovery of Athenian naval power after the battle of Cnidus in 394. That it was not earlier is suggested by the speaker of Isocrates' *Trapeziticus*, the son of Sopaeus, Satyrus' general, who is made, in that year, to refer to the Athenians being allowed to buy corn before other merchants as though this was not a right secured by agreement but a favour granted from time to time (*Trap.* 57). But with the rebuilding of the Long Walls at Athens and the gradual partial restoration of an Athenian maritime confederacy the bonds between the two powers became closer. There is extant an Attic decree (*Ditt.*[3] 206) whereby honours were granted to the sons of Leucon, and these are connected with privileges secured to Athens. It is explicitly stated that grants or benefactions (δωρεαί) given to Athens by Leucon's sons are identical with those given to her by Satyrus and Leucon (l. 26) and so are the honours given by Athens (l. 46). This implies that the first agreement between Bosporus and Athens was formally made during the reign of Satyrus, and was afterwards renewed under his successor. After the death of Spartocus, the elder son of Leucon, in 342, the compact was once more renewed by Paerisades, who, after reigning jointly with his brother, now became sole ruler of the Bosporan state.

These compacts between the democracy of Athens and the dynasts of Bosporus take a peculiar form. On the side of Athens they are decrees bestowing on the Spartocids as 'guest-friends and benefactors (ξένοι καὶ εὐεργέται)' certain privileges: Athenian citizenship, *ateleia*, crowns and statues. They in return make benefactions: 'exemption from customs duties to those merchants who import corn to Athens, and a proclamation that those merchants who sailed to Athens had the right of loading their ships first[1].' This right of pre-emption secured to the importers to Athens a full cargo, regardless of variations in the visible supply of corn at Panticapaeum or Theodosia. The benefactions are not based on any formal decision of the Council and People of Panticapaeum—for indeed such constitutional organs did not exist— but they are made effective by the 'proclamation' of the rulers to the customs and harbour-officials and the population at large. Thus the benefactions remain the acts of the individual rulers, who are officially to the Athenians private persons. Athens has,

---

[1] Demosthenes *c. Lept.* 29, cf. *Ditt.*[3] 206, l. 15.

therefore, no responsibility for the constitutional position of the Spartocidae, to whom in extant Attic inscriptions their official title of *Archon* is never applied. Demosthenes, it is true, uses the title, but it was apparently unknown to the Athenian chancery[1].

The position of the Bosporan dynasty was consolidated with the growing prosperity that followed the freedom of the trade in corn. As we have no inscriptions of Spartocus I or Satyrus I, we cannot tell what were their formal relations to the Bosporan state. But Leucon was called the *Archon* of Bosporus and after the annexation of Theodosia, to be described later, he was also *Archon* of Theodosia. To this republican title was added (we do not know when) that of 'king of the Sindians, Toretians, Dandarians and Psessians.' Thus to the Greek dwellers in the Bosporan cities the Spartocids were simply *Archons*, and Panticapaeum was still nominally a free city, as is shown by the fact that its beautiful gold and silver coins are all minted in the name of the city without any mention of the *Archon*. To foreign states, if we may judge from Athens, they were officially no more than private citizens. Even Arcadian mercenaries in the service of Leucon describe him as 'Leucon, son of Satyrus, citizen of Panticapaeum (Παντικαπαΐταν).' At this point the inscription breaks off, but the above phrase is republican enough. But this constitutional masquerade does not obscure the essential fact that Panticapaeum had lost its civic liberties. We never hear of a Council or Assembly, foreigners are honoured not by the state but by its rulers, and no magistrates appear on its inscriptions or coins. The Spartocids' rule was in fact a thinly disguised military and hereditary monarchy or tyranny. Their power had no doubt meant some violence, and the exile and confiscation of their opponents. From time to time we hear of exiles at Athens or Theodosia, and of plots and revolts against tyrants[2]. But the dynasty remained unmoved, and no doubt many citizens in the realm welcomed its stability.

Their main support was no doubt the army and navy. Whether the earlier Spartocids employed the citizen militia we do not

[1] With the Athenian restrictions imposed on corn-trade and the 'benefactions' of the Spartocids to Athens as regards corn-export from Panticapaeum may be compared the recently discovered fragments of laws by which the city of Thasos regulated the wine-trade in Thasos and its Peraea, G. Daux, *B.C.H.* L, 1926, pp. 213 *sqq.*, nos. 1–2; Ch. Picard, *ib.* XLV, 1921, p. 146 *sq.*; *L'Acropole*, I, pp. 335 *sqq.*; E. Ziebarth, *Beiträge zur Geschichte des Seeraubs*, p. 75. These laws must be dated in the second half of the fifth century B.C.

[2] Isocrates, *Trap.* 5; Anon., *Periplus Ponti Euxini*, LXXVII (51), cf. Polyaenus VI, 9, 2.

know, but there may be a reference to it in a passage of Polyaenus
(VI, 9, 4) in which Leucon, probably Leucon I, employs his
Scythian archers to make retreat dangerous for his hoplites. But
we may assume that the bulk of the army and navy[1] consisted of
mercenaries, and of 'allies,' that is detachments of Scythians who
were probably no more than mercenaries themselves. The navy was
commanded by trierarchs, some of whom at least were Bosporan
citizens. The rulers themselves were surrounded by nobles who
gave faithful service. Such was Sopaeus who commanded Satyrus'
army and was connected with him by marriage. He had wide
lands from which he exported corn and was no doubt a feudal
grandee as was Gylon, the betrayer of Nymphaeum. Other
courtiers whom we can trace are Sosis and Theodosius, who came
to Athens as ambassadors, and Stratocles, the friend of Sopaeus'
son. A further support for the dynasty were the foreign merchants, who were numerous enough to be of service to Leucon at a
critical moment[2]. Finally, the dynasty was immensely rich, as is
shown by the finds in some of the royal graves at Panticapaeum,
finds which are a mere remnant of the original contents. Their
wealth was derived from their extensive traffic in corn and fish,
as is reflected in the symbols found on the Bosporan coins[3]. The
corn came partly from their own domains, partly from the contributions of their subjects and vassals, partly by purchase from neighbouring tribes in the Crimea and in the Kuban and Don deltas.
No doubt they also owned rich fisheries in the straits, in the Sea
of Azov and on the Don. How great were the resources of the
realm is shown by the abundance and excellence of its currency.

Besides the consolidation of their position in Panticapaeum
and the efficient regulation of their overseas trade by adroit
diplomacy, the Spartocids were chiefly concerned to extend their
territory and with it their exportable supplies of corn and fish.
Their first aim was to secure for themselves the corn of the Crimea
and the Taman peninsula. The natural harbour for the Crimean
corn was, and still is, Theodosia. In the early fifth century
Theodosia was a free city, and in the time of her domination Athens
prevented Heraclea from taking an important part in the corn-
trade of the Black Sea by controlling Theodosia, but when the
power of Athens was broken, Heraclea tried again to compete with
Panticapaeum, and looked to Theodosia as her natural ally. But
Satyrus was determined to secure the city for himself, and in con-

[1] See *Ditt.*[3] 206, ll. 60 *sqq.*, in which the men referred to are undoubtedly
connected with the fleet.
[2] Polyaenus VI, 9, 2.			[3] Volume of Plates iii, 20, *e, f, g.*

sequence there was a prolonged war with Heraclea, which was brought to a successful conclusion by Leucon I, and probably had as result the setting up of a tyranny at Heraclea in 364 B.C. Theodosia was now annexed to the Bosporan kingdom and with its annexation the corn-export controlled by the Spartocids was doubled.

Satyrus probably sought to effect a union of the country of the Sindians with Panticapaeum. Traces of this process may be detected in the romance of Tirgatao which has been already described. In the end, the Sindian rulers acknowledged the suzerainty of the Bosporan dynasty which added to its title of 'Archons of Bosporus and Theodosia' that of 'Kings of the Sindians[1]'. Whether Satyrus or Leucon was first to assume this title we do not know, but doubtless Leucon reaped where his predecessor had sown. But Bosporan suzerainty did not mean that the Sindian dynasty disappeared. The two ruling houses probably coalesced, but the Sindian country retained its own dynasts as vassals of Panticapaeum. It is noteworthy that Athens took no official cognisance of the new state of things: Athenian decrees make no mention of the new title of the Bosporan rulers and statues were set up not only of Paerisades I and his son, but also of Gorgippus who was probably Paerisades' father-in-law and dynast of the Sindians[2]. Whether Phanagoreia was part of the Sindian 'kingdom' cannot be determined until it is systematically excavated. The city is never mentioned as a constituent part of the Bosporan state, and the same is true of Hermonassa. Yet it is hard to believe that Phanagoreia remained independent, the more so as dedications dated by Leucon I have been found upon its site.

Once masters of the Sindian region, the Bosporan rulers, especially Leucon I, extended their power far to the north and the east. In two inscriptions[3] Leucon is described as king not only of the Sindians, but of the Toretians, Dandarians and Psessians, tribes to the east and north of the Taman peninsula. We know nothing of a similar advance in the Crimea, though something could be discovered by the investigation and dating of the earth

[1] Presumably the Sindians had regarded their rulers as kings. A surprising exception to the regular titulature is revealed by an inscription o. Panticapaeum (*Bull. Arch. Comm.* LXIII, 1917, p. 109), if rightly restored by Shkorpil as [ἄρ]χοντος Λεύκωνος [Βοσπόρου καὶ Θεο]δοσίης κ[αὶ Σινδῶν κ]αὶ βασιλεύοντος [Τορετέων, Δανδ]αρίων, Ψησσῶν. If the title is not due to confusion, it suggests that there were political considerations, connected with the Greek cities or the Sindians, which led Leucon for a time to style himself not king but *Archon* of the Sindians.

[2] Dinarchus *c. Dem.* 43; *Ditt.*[3] 216.

[3] *Insc. Antiquae orae Septentrionalis Ponti Euxini* (*Ios. P.E.*) II, 6 and 7; *Ditt.*[3] 211.

walls which surround the territory of Panticapaeum and Theodosia. Nor have we direct evidence of the relations of the Bosporan
rulers with the Scythians, though we may assume that they were
friendly on the whole. Finally, as regards Panticapaeum itself
we do not know the date of its Acropolis, and while the extant
remains of the city walls cannot be earlier than the fourth century,
we cannot tell whether or not these remains belong to the oldest
system of fortification.

The influence and growth of the Bosporan state is illustrated
not only by its coinage (p. 586), but even more conclusively by
the fact that in the fourth century Olbia was gradually losing
ground in her commercial relations with the Scythian empire, and
her primacy was passing to Bosporus. For the Scythians, as for
the Greek cities of the Pontus, the late fifth century B.C. was a
time of comparative decline in prosperity. While the Scythian
graves of the sixth and the early fifth centuries are exceedingly
rich and full of imported gold and silver objects, we have but
few rich Scythian graves of the later fifth century. It was not
until the fourth century that the marvellous series of the richest
Scythian royal graves begins, only comparable in wealth and
artistic value of the objects with certain graves of the sixth or
early fifth century (see vol. III, p. 202 sq.).

Most of the best objects in the Scythian graves of the sixth
century are imported, partly from Persia, partly from the Ionian and
Aeolian cities of Asia Minor[1]. Alongside these appear in increasing
numbers objects in native style and of native workmanship[2],
and imitations of them made no doubt at Olbia and perhaps at
Panticapaeum both in precious metals and in bronze[3]. The general
aspect of the Scythian graves remains more or less the same in the
next century. Some of the objects found in them might have been
made in Athens, but most are either Ionian and Graeco-Persian,
or Olbian or Panticapaean imitations of Ionian, Persian and native
originals[4]. The fourth-century graves present striking contrasts.
They become richer and richer and at the same time the Olbian
products in them gradually vanish. Imported objects are equally
rare. The bulk of the gold and silver plate, of the gold-plated arms
and weapons, of the gold and silver horse trappings show all of
them a new style, a kind of neo-Ionian of a peculiar type[5]. No
doubt this originated in Panticapaeum, and the fact that objects
of this style appear both on the Bug and the Dnieper and on the

[1] Vol. of Plates iii, 78, 80, a.　[2] E.g. the objects ib. 84, c, 86, 88, 112, b, c.
[3] Ib. 80, b, 84, a, b. Cf. Vol. of Plates i, 256, b, c.
[4] Ib. 90, 92, 112 a.
[5] Ib. 102, 104, 106. Cf. Vol. of Plates i, 252, 254, 262, 264.

Don and the Kuban shows that it was Bosporus which now controlled Scythian commerce. The evidence of these graves makes it certain that relations were on the whole friendly. Trade not war was their policy and commercial gain not tribute was the aim of Bosporus and Scythians alike.

III. BOSPORUS AND THE SCYTHIANS

The time of Satyrus and Leucon I in Bosporus was a period of expansion and consolidation. The new form of government was recognized both by the Greek dwellers of the Bosporan state and by the foreign powers, both 'barbarian' and Greek. The rulers of Bosporus became immensely rich themselves and enriched some of their subjects. They became indispensable both for the Scythians, who understood the great advantages of a commerce with the Greek world undisturbed by wars, and for the Greek customers of the Bosporan state, for whom it was a great privilege to be sure of a safe and constantly growing supply of the staple food of the masses of the Greek city-dwellers—corn and fish. While Athens policed and controlled the sea route from the Thracian Bosporus westwards, the Bosporan rulers, masters of a strong navy, succeeded in keeping well in hand the dangerous pirates of the Black Sea— the Caucasian and Taurian professional sea-robbers[1].

The main concern of the Bosporan dynasts was to increase and stabilize their corn-trade. For this was needed on the one hand a careful management of their internal affairs and their relations to the Scythians, and on the other a close watch on political conditions in the Aegean Sea and a readiness to adapt themselves to the various aspects of political life in Greece. We cannot, therefore, understand the fortunes of the Bosporan state without keeping in mind political developments both on the steppes of South Russia and in the Aegean.

The earlier history of the Scythian empire has been dealt with in a previous volume (vol. III, chap. IX). But certain leading features in its history during the fourth and third centuries deserve special notice in this connection. In the fourth century B.C. the Scythians became enormously rich: their dominion extended from the Kuban and the Don to the Danube, and was felt far into Central Russia, as far as the middle Dnieper in the West and the middle Don in the East. Recent excavations have shown that even the region of the lower Volga and of the Ural river was culturally Scythian in its main features. The Hungarian plain

[1] Diodorus XX, 25 (for the time of Eumelus); Strabo XI, 495.

and large parts of Transylvania had been Scythian since the seventh century, and probably belonged, at least at the beginning, to the great Scythian empire[1]. In the fourth century expansion to the west, temporarily arrested by the expedition of Darius and the growth of the Odrysian Thracian empire, began again. Many Thracian dynasts on the right bank of the Danube became at that time Scythian vassals, and Scythian civilization spread far and wide into modern Bulgaria and to the regions of the lower Danube[2]. The western expansion of the Scythians was, however, soon arrested, and Scythian domination in the west was broken by the pressure of Celtic tribes and Illyrians driven before them (vol. VII, p. 64 sq.). Equally dangerous for the Scythians were the Macedonians when they became united and their state was reorganized by the genius of Philip. Slowly the western part of the Scythian empire split up into political chaos[3]. This slow disintegration of the Scythian empire in the west accounts, as we have seen, for the gradual elimination of Olbia as one of the two important outlets for Scythian commerce. Olbia was no longer a safe place for the corn-trade. Very often she suffered herself from severe famines, and the corn-supply from the Dnieper region became intermittent if it did not cease entirely[4].

The Scythians gradually retreated eastwards and concentrated in the steppes between the Dnieper and the Don. Some of them found a safe refuge in the Dobrudsha at the mouth of the Danube. Further retreat in this direction was, however, impossible. In the third century the steppes east of the Don were becoming occupied by tribes of Iranian origin whom the Greeks called Sauromatae—they probably wrongly identified the newcomers with a branch of Maeotians who bore this name—and the Romans Sarmatians. Of the Sarmatians we know very little in the fourth and third centuries B.C. Archaeological evidence abounds but is difficult to interpret, especially as the steppes between the Don and the Volga and between the Volga and the Ural river are so little excavated. Nevertheless, we may safely assume that the third century was a time of fierce struggle between the Scythians and the Sarmatians, whose movement westwards the Scythians were not able to arrest. They gave up the valley of the Kuban first and

[1] See Volume of Plates iii, 112, b, c.   [2] Ib. 66, c, 70, a, d.
[3] This is well illustrated by the Protogenes inscription at Olbia (Ios. P.E. I², 32, cf. Ditt.³ 495), which must be placed in the early part of the third century.
[4] For the early period the Protogenes inscription quoted above. For the later Polybius IV, 38, 5, who is speaking no doubt of the western Pontus.

gradually—probably very slowly—lost the control even of the steppes between the Don and the Dnieper. Their last refuge and their stronghold was the Crimea. Indeed, the Sarmatians never dislodged them from the lowlands of the Crimea where they established their capital, probably about the end of the third century.

These events were of the utmost importance for the Bosporan state. The more the Scythians were occupied in fighting the Thracians, the Celts and the Macedonians in the West, and the Sarmatians in the East, the less they pressed on the Maeotian tribes and on the Bosporan state. Their withdrawal from the Kuban valley gave to the Bosporan rulers for a while a free hand to expand their territory up the river and along the shores of the Sea of Azov. The decline of Olbia secured for the Bosporans the Scythian trade and made the corn which they exported ever more valuable to their Western customers.

It was some time before the Sarmatians in their turn began to press on the eastern frontier of the Bosporan state. We have no evidence of such a pressure before the late Hellenistic period. More dangerous was the situation in the Crimea. The strong and well-organized Scythians, gradually driven out from the richest parts of their empire, became dangerous neighbours of the Greek cities of the Crimea, and were inclined no doubt to insist on their old and antiquated rights of sovereignty. We know how exorbitant were their demands of tribute from Olbia. The same may be supposed as regards the Bosporan kingdom and the Greek colonies of the Taurian group. Here then great skill and energy was needed if the princes who ruled at Panticapaeum were to keep intact their political independence and to maintain their corn-trade—their main resource—at its old level.

IV. THE CORN-TRADE AND THE SPARTOCIDS IN HELLENISTIC TIMES

The demand for corn in the West was not declining, it was rather increasing. But the conditions in which it was carried out were gradually changing. It was no easy task for Athens, during the political anarchy of the second half of the fourth century, to guarantee for herself the largest share in the corn-export from the Bosporan state and to protect from seizure year after year the corn-fleets that sailed to Athens. We hear repeatedly of such seizures between 362 and 338, whether by Byzantium, Chalcedon, Cyzicus, Chios, Cos, Rhodes or Philip of Macedon. Through waters so threatened safe convoy became ever more difficult.

It is no wonder that Athens tried to make sure of her corn-supply by restrictive measures: she demanded from all her corn merchants that they should import grain exclusively to Athens and reserve for her two-thirds of the cargo. All these efforts were in vain: she first lost control of Thrace and then later of the Bosporus. In 330/29 B.C., for example, Dionysius, the tyrant of Heraclea, dared to use violence towards a corn merchant of Salamis in Cyprus who was sailing to Athens with corn (*Ditt.*³ 304). The famine which raged at Athens for some years after 330 (vol. VI, p. 448 *sq.*) cannot be accounted for, were it not for the loss of control over the Bosporan trade. In these difficult years the Athenians were at the mercy of private corn-dealers, as is shown by her decrees in honour of members of this class[1]. With this famine at Athens we are entering into a new period in the history of the corn-trade. After Alexander it became free, once and for all. The demand for corn increased rapidly. It is true that new corn lands were now opened up. Egypt under the first Ptolemies rapidly increased her production of corn, which became their main source of income (vol. VII, p. 131). Cyprus and Phoenicia exported some corn, as did Asia Minor. On the other hand, Thrace, except for a short period under Lysimachus, was in a state of anarchy; Sicily and Italy could hardly export any large amount of corn to the East; and, as we have seen, the region of Olbia was no more to be relied upon.

The ancient world never knew any period of over-production of foodstuffs. There was no competition between the producers: that was reserved for the consumers. And so it was in the third and second centuries B.C. Whatever ideas we may have on the degree of industrialization of the ancient world in the Hellenistic period, there is no doubt that the population of Greece increased rapidly in the third century in spite of a large emigration to the Orient, and that many places in Asia Minor did not begin their city life till this period. The Greek cities, with their ever-increasing production of wine and olive-oil and ever-decreasing production of cereals, were more than ever before in need of imported corn and fish. Witness the frequent famines in the Greek cities[2] and

---

[1] Among these decrees two are especially significant: *I.G.*² II, 409—for a merchant from Sinope, and II, 408—for two merchants from Heraclea.

[2] A widely spread famine is attested by the recently discovered inscription at Cyrene. See S. Ferri in *Abh. Berl. Ak.* 1925, Nr. 5, pp. 24 *sqq.*; G. Oliverio in *Riv. di Fil.* N.S. VI, 1928, pp. 232 *sqq.*; S. Zhebelev, *The fertility of Cyrene*, C.R. de l'Acad. des Sciences de l'U.S.S.R. 1929, pp. 97 *sqq.*, who fixes the date between 331 and 328 B.C.

the measures—sometimes desperate—which were taken by various cities to guarantee a sufficient food-supply for their population; pressure on rich citizens; honours to corn merchants; ever increasing importance of the magistrates concerned with it (*sitonai, agoranomoi,* etc.). Thus everyone who was able to export large quantities of corn might count on becoming not only rich but also politically influential.

Thus in Hellenistic times the corn-trade became all important. There was, however, at no time during this period any one single power which was in control of the Mediterranean corn-supply. Trade was free, and the only obstacle to its peaceful development were the constant wars in the Aegean and the corresponding growth of piracy, the pirates being indeed freely used by the combatants as allies and auxiliaries. The burden of policing the seas fell heavily on those powers which succeeded in creating the strongest navies: from Athens it passed to Philip and Alexander the Great, from Antigonus and Demetrius to the Ptolemies, who relied beside their own navy upon the combined naval forces of the Islanders, from the Ptolemies to the Rhodians, now the presidents of the Island League, and finally, after a period of prolonged anarchy, to the Romans.

The changes in the Aegean world which have been described help to explain the vicissitudes of the Bosporan state in the late fourth century and the next two hundred years.

On the death of Leucon I in 349/8 B.C. power was shared for five years by two of his sons, Spartocus II and Paerisades I, who may have ruled with him for the later part of his reign. In 344/3 their joint rule ended with the death of Spartocus, and Paerisades reigned alone till 310/9. He extended Bosporan territory far to the east, including in his title the tribes of the Thateans and Doschians, while in place of the several Maeotian tribes enumerated in his father's title, there sometimes appears the proud formula—'and of all the Maeotians.' This territorial expansion is no doubt explained by the withdrawal of the Scythians from the Kuban region. He also was engaged in war with the Scythians, probably, though this is not recorded, to defend his dominions from their migration into the Crimea under the pressure of Celts and Sarmatians. We may assume that he was successful, for during many years we hear of no more wars between Bosporus and the Scythians, who indeed appear as allies of Paerisades' son Satyrus II at the very time that they are pressing hard on the neighbouring city of Chersonesus. An elegiac inscription (*Ios. P.E.* II, 9), which describes the kingdom as including all the land between the

Caucasus and Taurian mountains, even suggests that, for a time at least, the Scythians of the Crimea acknowledged Paerisades' suzerainty. This would explain their military help to his son and the fact that exactly at that time Scythian dynasts built near Panticapaeum the splendid tomb of Kul-Oba and a similar tomb in the so-called *tumulus Patinioti*.

During this period the corn-trade kept to the paths marked out by Satyrus and Leucon. The 'treaties' with Athens were renewed, and the commercial relations of Bosporus were extended, as is shown by many inscriptions of Panticapaeum, Gorgippia and Phanagoreia, all of the fourth century. These testify to trade with the Crimean Chersonesus, with Heraclea, Amisus, Chalcedon, Colophon, Cromne, Chios and Syracuse, and the evidence for these commercial relations continues throughout the third century. Despite the warlike preoccupations of Paerisades, which once at least hindered the export of corn, Bosporus continued to hold its place as the chief centre of corn-export for many Greek cities, especially Athens. In Bosporus itself Strabo (VII, 310) records an official cult of Paerisades as a god. If this was established in his lifetime, it was an anticipation of the policy of the Diadochi. His wife Komosarye was a daughter of Gorgippus, presumably lord of the Sindians (p. 570), a fact which suggests that the subordinate dynasty continued to exist under the shadow of the Bosporan state. Finally, like other Greek tyrants, and like his father Leucon[1], Paerisades was a patron of the arts: at least he welcomed at his court the wandering musician Stratonicus, and his over-exigent hospitality provoked the sharp tongue of that Greek Voltaire[2].

For the period after his death we have more evidence in a detailed excursus in Diodorus (xx, 22–6), which is no doubt ultimately derived from a local historical source favourable to the dynasty. There was a short civil war between the three sons of Paerisades, Satyrus, Eumelus and Prytanis, which ended in the victory of Eumelus. What is of importance is that the Scythians supported Satyrus and Prytanis and made up their army except for 4000 Greek and Thracian mercenaries, while the forces of Eumelus were wholly composed of Sirakians, in whom we may recognize the first Sarmatians who appeared to the north of the Kuban region and gradually pushed on west and south[3]. There is

[1] Polyaenus v, 44, 1.   [2] Athenaeus VIII, 349 D.
[3] The MSS of Diodorus give Thracians, which Boeckh emended to Thateans, but it would be strange if that tribe was so powerful, and it seems better to adopt the suggestion of Bonnell and read Sirakians.

no mention of any Bosporan citizen army and it may be conjectured that Paerisades and his heirs relied wholly on mercenaries
and had suppressed the citizen militia. Eumelus set himself to
conciliate the goodwill of the Greek population of Bosporus, and
announced the restoration of the 'ancestral constitution.' This
proclamation suggests that Paerisades at least had made changes
in the traditional policy of the dynasty, especially in the imposition
of heavy taxes and war contributions, and Eumelus now abolished
these burdens and perhaps restored the Greek citizen militia.

His aim in doing so was to strengthen the Greek element in
his kingdom and with its help to carry out an ambitious project,
similar to that of his contemporary Lysimachus and later of
Mithridates the Great, namely to unite all the Greek cities of the
Pontus under his rule and to transform the Black Sea into a
Bosporan lake. Consequently he helped Byzantium and Sinope—
no doubt in their struggle for independence against Lysimachus—
and tried to save Callatis from subjection. In this he failed, but
he used the opportunity to attract a thousand Callatians to his
land and to strengthen the Greek element in Bosporus by founding
a new Greek city, Psoa, and by planting there a group of Greek
military settlers. His panegyrist has no doubt that he would have
succeeded in his plan had he not met an untimely end after a reign
of five years. He was succeeded by his son Spartocus III (304/3–
284/3).

Spartocus III inherited a strong and well-organized kingdom,
for after Eumelus the Bosporan state may fairly be so described.
Whether, in fact, it was Eumelus who first called himself *basileus*
both at home and abroad, we do not know. Diodorus' use of the
title is not decisive, since for Diodorus all the Bosporan rulers
are kings and we have no inscriptions which mention his name
and his title. His son, however, appears as *basileus* both in his
kingdom and in foreign lands. In Bosporus the usage varies: in
inscriptions dated by his rule he is sometimes styled *archon*
(*Ios. P.E.* ii, 13), sometimes *basileuon* (*ib.* 14), sometimes both titles
are used together (*ib.* 348, 349). In his foreign relations he was
more consistent. There is an interesting Athenian decree of
289/8 B.C. (*Ditt.*[3] 370). The Athenians had just recovered their
liberty (see vol. vii, pp. 86 *sqq.*) and were anxious to renew their
relations both with the Paeonians and with the powerful ruler of
the Bosporus. An Athenian embassy was sent under the pretext
of announcing the happy event to Spartocus III, who negotiated
with the embassy. The result was the decree. It is interesting
to compare this decree with that voted for Spartocus II and

Paerisades I (p. 567). While the former, like those which had preceded it, was a disguised commercial treaty, the decree of 289–8 B.C. is a formal alliance. While the predecessors of Spartocus were treated by Athens as private citizens, Spartocus III is given the title of *basileus*. While in the former treaties trade privileges to the Athenians were specially mentioned and formed the core of the document, in this decree the 'grants' are mentioned as a matter of the past. Beside a modest gift of corn Spartocus gives no definite privileges to Athens, but only promises to do his best for her. Whether any definite privileges were secured, we do not know. The question was probably settled by the ambassadors who were sent to Bosporus to carry with them the decree. And last, but not least, the king was granted a statue not only in the agora like his predecessors, but also on the Acropolis.

The Bosporan kingdom continued to flourish throughout Spartocus' reign and that of his successor Paerisades II, who succeeded to the throne in 284/3 and ruled until after the middle of the century. For this Paerisades we have no literary evidence, and the inscriptions of Bosporus merely show him as inconstant in his titles as his predecessor. But we have interesting information from abroad which throws light on his foreign policy. Whereas no mention of him has survived at Athens, we find the trade which is his policy connecting him with Rhodes, Egypt and Delos. It is probable that close commercial relations with Rhodes began much earlier than this time and they continued into the first century B.C.[1] As regards Egypt we find Apollonius, the minister of Ptolemy Philadelphus, instructing his agent Zeno to make all due preparations for a visit from Paerisades' ambassadors in 254 or 253 B.C.[2] Whether or not the Battle of Cos had been fought, Egypt was at that moment the chief naval power in the Aegean, and the hostility of Egypt would be a fatal handicap to Paerisades' trade. Equally many Egyptian manufactured goods found their way to the Black Sea and there was regular commerce,

---

[1] The lasting connections of Rhodes with the Pontus are emphasized by Dio Chrysostom in his Rhodian Speech (xxxi), 103, which is supported by *Ios. P.E.* ii, 35 and 1², 340, and 30. Their duration into the first century is attested by *I.G.* xii, 1, 11; 46, 1 and A. Maiuri, *Nuova Silloge di Rodi e Cos*, no. 166; cf. a Borysthenite married woman at Rhodes (*ib.* no. 95) and Sarmatian, Scythian and Maeotian slaves (*I.G.* xii, 1, 514, 525–7, Maiuri, *op. cit.* nos. 229, 233 and 421). See further below, p. 629.

[2] H. I. Bell, *Symbolae Osloenses*, v, 1927, 36–37; cf. the present writer in *J.E.A.* xiv, 1928, p. 13, and W. Otto, *Abh. d. Bay. Akad.* xxxiv, 1928, 1, p. 43.

for example, between Alexandria and Sinope[1]. Thus we need not be surprised to find these two crowned merchants seeking to be on good terms with each other. About the same time two Bosporans appear together with four Rhodians and some other Greeks in an Alexandrian inscription[2]. Whether they were merchants or soldiers we cannot say, but their presence is significant. Equally significant is the appearance of two Bosporans and many citizens of Chersonesus at Delos, and the dedication of a bowl by Paerisades in 250 B.C.[3] It is characteristic of Bosporan policy that in this year Paerisades appears at Delos with Antigonus Gonatas and Stratonice. The star of Philadelphus is setting; the star of Antigonus is in the ascendant.

With Paerisades II ended, in all probability, the great age of the Bosporan kingdom. The close of the fourth century and the first half of the third are distinguished by the richest finds both in Panticapaeum, Phanagoreia and Gorgippia and in the steppes of Southern Russia, so that the archaeology of this whole region bears eloquent testimony to the able policy of the Spartocid rulers from the First to the Second Paerisades. At some time within this period begins also the new royal gold coinage of Bosporus in imitation of that of Lysimachus, bearing the name of Paerisades instead of the name of the city and a portrait head in place of the gods and badges of Panticapaeum. That Paerisades II was the first to issue these gold staters is, however, not probable, for the style is poor and hardly consistent with his date.

For more than a century after the death of Paerisades, some time after 250 B.C., the dynasty continued to reign in Bosporus, but little is known of the several rulers[4]. There was a Fourth Spartocus and a Second Leucon, with whom it is tempting to connect a grim story mentioned in Ovid's *Ibis*. The scholia tell how a Bosporan King Leucon killed his brother Spartocus, who had seduced his wife Alcathoe, and was then himself killed by her in revenge. In the judgment of Ovid, the queen bore the

[1] Athenodorus, *F.H.G.* III, 487; Polybius IV, 38.
[2] Preisigke, *Sammelbuch*, III, 6831. One of the Bosporans, Molpagoras, may be identical with a man of the same name in *Ios. P.E.* II, 14 of the time of Spartocus III.
[3] *I.G.* XI, 4, 609, cf. 1143 and *Ios. P.E.* II, 11; *I.G.* XI, 2, 287 B, 124 *sqq.*; F. Durrbach, *Insc. de Délos, Comptes des Hiéropes*, 298, 95–6 with note. How important the corn trade with Bosporus was in the times of Spartocus II and Paerisades II is shown by the fluctuation of prices in Delos in 282 B.C. according as the passage through the Thracian Bosporus was closed or reopened by Lysimachus; see A. Jardé, *Les céréales dans l'antiquité grecque*, I, p. 168 *sq.*   [4] See the genealogical table at the end of the volume.

surname of Eusebes and belied it. With these murders began a period of anarchy, made worse by the vigorous advance of the Sarmatians, which in turn caused the Scythians of the Crimea to exert pressure probably both on Bosporus and Chersonesus. Panticapaeum, it is true, remained so strong that Chersonesus appealed to her for help[1] in the evil plight which is well illustrated (for a later period) by the romantic story of the Sarmatian Queen Amage who at last saved Chersonesus from the Scythians[2]. But the dynasty was, no doubt, weakened by its dissensions, and by the end of the third century there is evidence for the rise of usurpers. There is one Hygiaenon who appears in coins and inscriptions. He has the title of *Archon*, which suggests that he stood for an attempt by the Greeks to regain their civic liberty. Another usurper, Akes—known from a single coin—looks like a Scythian or Sarmatian.

At some time in the first half of the second century there was peace once more in Bosporus. A Paerisades appears as a contemporary of Prusias II of Bithynia, that is between 168 and 149 B.C., and there were two other kings of the same name and at least one other Spartocus. Bosporus itself enjoyed a revival of prosperity which is probably to be connected with the consolidation of the Scythian dynasty in the Crimea and the final settlement of the Sarmatians in the Kuban valley. The Bosporan kings were now able to reach a lasting understanding with these powers and to resume regular trade relations with the outer world. It is possible that this revival of trade began quite early in the second century and that the period of anarchy was of short duration. As early as 195/4 B.C. citizens of Bosporus and Chersonesus are mentioned in a list of *proxenoi* at Delphi (*Ditt.*[3] 585, ll. 20–24) and some two years later the same privilege is awarded to envoys from Chersonesus (*Ditt.*[3] 604). We may assume that both cities were regaining their position in the society of Greek cities[3].

We know little indeed of life in the Bosporus during this period, but some information may be gathered from an unusual source. Romantic tales of the Bosporan kingdom began to circulate in Greece probably as early as the fourth and third centuries B.C. There is first the story of Tirgatao and later that of Amage, and in the late Hellenistic period these are followed by full-dress Scytho-Bosporan novels. A fragment of one of these has recently

---

[1] *Ios. P.E.* I[2], 343.   [2] Polyaenus VIII, 56.
[3] Cp. *Ditt.*[3] 1126, a dedication at Delos (*c.* 100 B.C.) of a merchant of Nymphaeum for himself, his son and οἱ πλοϊζόμενοι πάντες to Zeus Ourios and the Egyptian gods.

been discovered in Egypt (*P.S.I.* VIII, 981) and similar novels are probably the main source of one episode—that of Macentas, Lonchatas and Arsacomas—in Lucian's *Toxaris*. Valueless as they are for the political history of Bosporus, these later novels may well give a fairly accurate picture of life in South Russia at the time of their composition. Bosporan kings are engaged in constant warfare with Scythians and Sarmatians, sometimes fighting each with the help of the other. At court, even in time of peace, Scythians and Sarmatians are familiar figures, and Bosporan princes marry Iranian ladies and *vice versa*. Archaeological evidence partly confirms and partly refutes this strange picture. The graves of this period are still Greek, and Sarmatian influence does not become dominant till later. The Bosporans cannot be called poor: in many graves in Panticapaeum or the Sindian country there is still evidence of wealth. But the general standard has declined and the Hellenic character of the graves is in no way as pure as in the fourth and third centuries.

V. CIVILIZATION AND ART

The constitution of the Bosporan state, which according to the Greek ideas was a military tyranny, grew up out of a compromise between the Greek colonists and the native population. To the natives the Spartocids were always kings; to the Greeks the rule of these hellenized barbarians, accepted because of bitter necessity, was a tyranny thinly disguised under the constitutional title of *archon*. The Bosporan tyranny is the more interesting for an historian of the ancient world, since it was not a passing incident in the life of a Greek city, like most of the earlier and later Greek tyrannies—even the tyrannies of Heraclea and of Syracuse—but a settled government which existed for centuries and was gradually transformed into a typical Hellenistic monarchy comparable with monarchies of Asia Minor: Pergamum, Bithynia, Cappadocia, Pontus, Armenia and Commagene, with their more or less hellenized native kings and a population which consisted both of Greeks (in the cities) and of natives (in the country).

The social structure of the Bosporan kingdom differed little from the social structure of the Hellenistic kingdoms named above. The population of the Greek cities was probably engaged mainly in trade and industry. Some of the Greek residents of the cities may have been tillers of the soil like the citizens of Chersonesus, where the small territory of the city (the Heracleotic peninsula) was divided into *kleroi* which were owned and tilled by the Chersonesites. Such tillers of the soil, small landowners (*klerouchoi*), were the Callatians whom Eumelus settled in Psoa. These Greek farmers, however, played a relatively subordinate rôle in the economic and social life of the Bosporan cities. The prosperity of Bosporus was based not on them but on an agricultural native population both in the Crimea and the Sindian region. This native population was probably tied to the soil. We may draw this conclusion from an interesting inscription of A.D. 151 (*Ios. P.E.* II, 353) found in the Sindike. A certain Letodorus (probably long before) had dedicated to 'the goddess' certain lands and serfs who tilled them (πελάται), as was stated in a special document which he had drawn up and published. These possessions of the goddess, which had diminished by lapse of time, King Rhoemetalces now declares that he had collected and restored to her. The inscription shows that in this region both in Roman and in pre-Roman times private landowners and temples owned land to which native serfs were attached, a state of affairs similar to that which prevailed all over Asia Minor in the Hellenistic period.

While there were some private landowners in the territory of the Spartocid kingdom, the largest landowner and the largest producer of grain and master of native serfs was the ruler of the Bosporan state. He probably claimed ownership over all the land which was not held by the Greek citizens of the larger cities. The grant, for instance, of the small city of Cepi by Satyrus I to the Athenian Gylon, or the status of Sopaeus, the friend and prime minister of that king, shows that the ruler claimed the right of disposing of all the land of the Bosporus and of giving up this right temporarily or for ever in favour of friends and officers, who in this way became real feudal lords. There is nothing strange in this, since we know that similar conditions prevailed in all the monarchies of the ancient world, especially in the Graeco-Iranian states.

Being the largest landowners in the state, the Bosporan rulers owned enormous quantities of corn, cattle and fish. As war lords they had from time to time large masses of slaves to dispose of. All these goods were sold and exported abroad. There is no evidence that the kings owned a commercial fleet, nor can we suppose that ships were normally owned by other landowners—the visit of Sopaeus' son to Athens on ships which belonged to his father and were loaded with corn from his estates was probably an exception. Trade with the cities of the Aegean was as a rule carried on by regular Greek merchants, a motley crowd from various cities, some of them Bosporans. Some of these merchants may have had their permanent residence at Panticapaeum, but the majority came and went like birds of passage. Along with the landowners and merchants there also existed in the cities of the Bosporan state, as in any Greek city, a large population of artisans and shop-keepers, of workmen and sailors and slaves.

The most interesting feature of the social and economic as well as of the cultural life of the Bosporus is the mixture in it of often heterogeneous elements. The state was like a double-faced statue of Janus or a triple-headed pillar of Hecate. The two strongest elements in this mixture were the Greek, especially the Ionian element, and the various native elements, especially Thracian (if we consider the Cimmerians to be Thracians), Sindian and Maeo-tian (if these are to be regarded as the pre-Cimmerian population) and Iranian. None of these native elements deserves the name of barbarian, for all of them could look back upon a long evolution of civilized life.

This dualism of Greek and non-Greek is noticeable in every department of Bosporan life. At first sight the cults of Panti-capaeum or Phanagoreia reveal no important peculiarities if com-pared with those of other Ionian cities; we notice a set of Greek cults with that of Apollo predominant. But if we look a little deeper, we shall see that, along with the Greek cults, the native slightly hellenized cults take an ever more leading part in the religious life of the Bosporus. All over the Sindian region were scattered rich and revered sanctuaries of the native Great Mother, the Asiatic 'Lady of the beasts' (Πότνια θηρῶν). In the temple at Phanagoreia the goddess was worshipped under the name of Aphrodite, in another temple on the shore of the lake Tsukur the same goddess is styled Artemis Agrotera. In a dedicatory inscription found on the Taman peninsula it may be the same goddess who passes under the name of the Ephesian Artemis. And there were at least two more of her temples: one near Her-monassa and another near Gorgippia. We have thus in Bosporus the same phenomenon which is so familiar all over Asia Minor[1].

There is the same dualism in the material life of the population, especially of the ruling class. We are well informed about the city cemeteries of most of the Bosporan cities, and the picture is the same everywhere. The tombs of the urban middle class, sometimes rich and well constructed, show a surprisingly pure Greek char-acter: Ionian in Bosporus and at Olbia, Dorian at Chersonesus. In Bosporus we have the same mixture of cremation and inhumation as in other Ionian cities. The funeral rites of these graves are purely Greek, as is the funeral furniture; athletic objects prevail,

[1] For two pole-ends of funeral standards from a third-century Scythian grave, see Volume of Plates iii, 108, *e, f.*

weapons are rare. In the tombs of the sixth to the second centuries many, if not most, of the objects are imported from Greece, especially bronze and silver plate, jewellery, pottery[1], rich textiles and glass. Whether there existed local pottery factories in Bosporus, which imitated first Ionian and afterwards Attic ware, we do not know. Style is not always decisive; we need extensive chemical analysis of the clay[2].

While the tombs of the middle-class population of the cities are purely Greek, we cannot say the same of the monumental tombs of the rulers and of the aristocracy—stone chambers hidden in high earth or stone tumuli. Scores of such tumuli are still to be seen on the summits of the two ranges of hills in the neighbourhood of Panticapaeum, many lie along the road which leads from the city into the steppes and many others are to be found on most of the hill-tops in the Taman peninsula and the Crimea, mostly near the ruins of the other Bosporan cities.

The stone chambers inside the tumuli were very carefully constructed and were gorgeously adorned with paintings and hangings of costly stuffs, often sewn with gold plaques. The chambers and the corridors leading into the chambers were usually vaulted[3]: the vault is often of the corbelled type, round or square, with one course of stones projecting beyond the next, though true barrel vaults are occasionally found. In the middle of the chamber was placed a coffin, usually of wood, rarely of marble, carved, inlaid and painted. Round the coffin were Greek vases of the finest ware[4]. The bodies laid in the coffins wore festal dress; the men had their weapons, the women jewels. Some of the graves, which were discovered intact or only half plundered, have yielded superb collections of ancient jewellery and metal-work: engraved stones signed by celebrated artists, necklaces, bracelets, earrings of the best workmanship, bronze and silver vessels[5]. The funeral rites are not the same in all the graves. The graves in the Taman preserve features which recall the native Cimmerian and Scythian burial-rites as, for example, the interment of horses and of funeral chariots. The graves in the territory of Panticapaeum have none of these foreign elements. And yet they are not purely Greek. The Greeks of this period did not bury their dead under barrows, in stone chambers with 'Egyptian' vaults, in sumptuous coffins, nor did they any longer deposit whole fortunes in their tombs. They had no blood sacrifices and no magnificent funeral feasts. If not Greek and not Scythian, what type do these graves repre-

---

[1] See Volume of Plates iii, 96, 98, 100, *b*.   [2] *Ib.* 100, *a*.
[3] *Ib.* 94.   [4] *Ib.* 96, 98.   [5] *Ib.* 82.

sent? True analogies with the funerary ritual and the sepulchral structures of Panticapaeum and the other Greek cities of the Bosporus are to be found partly in heroic Greece (*e.g.* blood sacrifices and funeral feasts), partly in those lands which reveal a great similarity with heroic Greece—in Thrace and in Macedonia—, and there is a striking similarity between the tumuli cemeteries of the Bosporan cities and those of Amisus and Sinope and in Etruria, especially the recently excavated groups of tumuli near Caere. Everything suggests that the great tombs of the Bosporan kingdom were built for members of the ruling class, which was not of pure Greek origin, but of mixed stock: half-Thracian, half-Greek, with some Scythian and Sindian blood.

Some of the objects found in these tomb-chambers were imported from Greece or from the Orient (especially from Persia), but side by side with these there are others which are unquestionably local work, and it is these which concern us more nearly.

There is no doubt that the coins of Panticapaeum were struck in the city itself. In the sixth and fifth centuries they differ very little from the coins of the Ionian cities in Asia Minor. But in the fourth century—the exact date of the new series of coins is unknown—the coinage suddenly changes. Gold staters were now struck, and the types of these staters and of the corresponding silver coinage are quite new[1]. These types are not imitated from the contemporary coinage of other Greek cities. They are original creations of Bosporan artists, and they are generally recognized as masterpeices of original and forcible art. The chief types of the coins—heads of bearded Silens and beardless Satyrs—are still a puzzle. They cannot be etymological allusions to the name of Panticapaeum, for they do not represent the god Pan. Nor are they faithful reproductions of the established types of Silens and Satyrs. Possibly they are heads of Thracian gods akin to the Thracian Dionysus. The types on the reverse of the Bosporan coins are also of local origin. The arms of Panticapaeum are not Greek: the lion-griffin or eagle-griffin treading upon an ear of corn or a fish and holding in its mouth a spear came no doubt to the Bosporus from Persia, either directly or through Asia Minor. Of the same origin is the group of a lion and a deer and the other types.

The style of the coins is notably similar to that of those peculiar products of Greek metal-work which spread in the late fourth and in the early third centuries B.C. all over the Scythian steppes: gold and silver vessels, gold and silver mounts of Scythian arms and weapons, gold plaques sewn on Scythian garments and rugs,

[1] See Volume of Plates iii, 20, *e–j.*

and gold and silver parts of Scythian horse-trappings. These objects in the seventh to fifth centuries show either a purely Ionian style or are a mixture of various Oriental styles with the peculiar Scythian or Pontic animal style predominant[1]. It is possible that both the first and the second class were produced by Ionian artists, resident in the Greek cities of the southern and northern shores of the Black Sea, the artists to whom are probably due the so-called Graeco-Persian gems[2] and some rare Graeco-Persian and Graeco-Anatolian sculptures.

With the fourth century B.C. there begins a change. Alongside commonplace subjects of a purely ornamental character[3], the artists who worked for the Scythians began to reproduce in a conventional late Ionian or late Attic style subjects which bore on Scythian life and Scythian religion. Scythian gods, Scythian religious rites, scenes of the investiture of kings by the gods, and, last but not least, scenes of war, are now the main topics treated by the Greek artists[4]. The most famous and the richest graves in the steppes of South Russia are full of such subjects. Kul Oba and the Patinioti tumulus near Panticapaeum, Chertomlyk and Solokha on both banks of the lower Dnieper, Karagodeuashkh in the Kuban valley, not far from the Black Sea coast, Chastye Kurgany on the middle Don, may serve as instances of this numerous class. The date of this group of Scythian royal burials is disputed, but the present writer has no doubt that they all belong to the time of the zenith of the Bosporan kingdom. The manner of treatment of all the subjects mentioned above testifies to an intimate knowledge of Scythian life. The artists who treated the subjects had not only heard of and seen the Scythians, but had lived with them and breathed the air of the Russian steppes. They idealized them slightly but they are exact in reproducing their dress and weapons, their horses and dogs, their religious and military life. Such a choice of subjects and such a treatment are novelties in the Greek art of this period. The Greeks of the late fourth century B.C. did not care for the barbarians. If they reproduced figures of barbarians, even of those whom they knew very well, they gave highly conventionalized pictures of them. They took the barbarians from the Greek point of view and showed but little interest in them. The only monuments of art which may be compared with the objects found in the Scythian tombs are the so-called Graeco-Persian gems mentioned above. These considerations compel the conclusion that the objects from the

---

[1] See Volume of Plates iii, 80, *b*, 84, *a, b, c*, 86, 88, 90, 92, *b, c*, 112, *a* cf. Vol. of Plates i, 256.   [2] *Ib.* 90, *f.*   [3] *Ib.* 84, *d*, 104, *a*, 106, *f, i, k, m*, 108, *a–d.*   [4] *Ib.* 102, 104, 106, *a–d*; cf. Vol. of Plates i, 252, 254, 262, 264.

Scythian graves were not produced either in Greece proper or in Asia Minor. They are local.

The similarity of the style of these objects with the style of the Panticapaeum coins of the fourth century is striking. The heads of the Silens and Satyrs of the coins look exactly like some heads of Scythians on the best objects of the Scythian graves. This fact, and the fact that the area over which the graves in question are spread radiates around the Bosporan kingdom, make it certain that in the fourth and third centuries there was at Panticapaeum and in the other cities of the Bosporus a school of artists who made it their special task to furnish their Scythian, Sindian and Maeotian neighbours with pieces of their equipment which suited their taste and represented their life. If so, there is no praise too high for what some of these artists have achieved. Never were these scenes of Scythian life surpassed in the history of ancient art: neither in the Hellenistic nor in the Roman period. They can easily bear comparison with the admirable figures of the Gauls created by Pergamene art (pp. 679 *sqq.*).

After the end of Scythian supremacy in the South Russian steppes, when new customers replaced the old ones both in the north and in the east, and the requirements of these customers appeared to be quite different compared to those of the Scythians, the Bosporan artists adapted themselves at once to the new conditions. The trend of the time was for polychromy. Jewellery with inset stones was what the new fashion and the new patrons liked most, and the Bosporans began to work in this new style, adapting it to or combining it with the new forms of objects used by their new customers, mostly Sarmatians[1]. The graves of the Taman and of the Kuban valley and some graves in the Dnieper region from the late third century onwards show all the stages of this development. The achievements of the Bosporan school in polychrome jewellery and metal-work were lasting, more lasting than those of their predecessors, and have survived by many centuries those who were responsible for them.

We have almost no material to illustrate the intellectual life of the Bosporan kingdom. We hear of no great Bosporans who made a lasting contribution to the development of Greek civilization. The only name which might be quoted in this connection is that of Sphaerus, the philosopher, who lived in Egypt in the time of Ptolemy Philadelphus and of his successors[2]. There is,

---

[1] See Vol. of Plates iii, 110, *a, b*; gold *phalerae* in a peculiar style which recalls monuments of the Hellenistic period made in and for Northern India.

[2] F. Hiller von Gaertringen, *I. G.* iv, 1², p. 83, suggests that the poet Isyllus was a native of Bosporus.

as we have seen, some little evidence for a Bosporan trade in music and for the visits of famous musicians to the Bosporus (p. 577). Yet neither at Panticapaeum nor in any other city of the Bosporus is there the slightest indication of ruins of theatres or other similar buildings. This may be due to the scarcity of good building material, or possibly the theatres were wooden buildings. Of one thing we may be sure, the Bosporus produced some historians of its own. We cannot account for the surveys of Bosporan history, or for some details which have been preserved, unless we postulate the existence of a school of local historians, most of them in the service of the rulers. And it is also not unreasonable to suppose that the origin of the Bosporan and Scythian novels goes back to the vivid imagination of Bosporan writers. And finally, some fine verse is to be found among the votive and funeral inscriptions which time has spared.

The Bosporan state, therefore, was not by any means an insignificant little group of Greek towns lost on the shores of the Cimmerian Bosporus. It developed an interesting and original form of life. It had the sagacity to invent a semi-Greek constitution which held the state together for centuries. It contrived to make this form of government popular in Greece and to gain for Bosporan tyrants such as Leucon I a place in the great gallery of famous statesmen whose names were familiar to Greek readers and even to Greek schoolboys. It succeeded in spreading Greek civilization among the Scythians its neighbours and the Sindians and Maeotians its subjects. For many centuries it guaranteed the Greek world a cheap and abundant supply of foodstuffs. It transformed wide tracts of steppes into cultivated fields. It kept the Black Sea free of pirates. It connected the Greek world with Central Asia. And last but not least, it created a vigorous art which achieved brilliant triumphs.

In a word, the Bosporus of the Classical and of the Hellenistic periods played no unimportant part in the life of the ancient world. The time is past when, in the imagination of cultivated persons, the Greek world is bound by the shores of Attica and of the Peloponnese. The Greek genius succeeded not only in creating lasting values for the Greeks, it showed at the same time an incomparable universality and flexibility, a power of adapting itself to unfamiliar conditions, and of constructing, in foreign surroundings, new centres of civilization, in which whatsoever was strong and fertile in the native life was combined with the eternal creations of Greek intelligence. Bosporus is one of the earliest examples of this wonderfully stimulating power of Greece.

CHAPTER XIX

PERGAMUM

I. THE EVOLUTION OF THE PERGAMENE KINGDOM

THE Kingdom of Pergamum was a peculiar product of the troubled and creative third century. From time immemorial Asia Minor was a land of small half-independent states, whether tribal states with their chieftains, or temple-states under king-priests, or city-states which later became half-Greek, and were ruled by local tyrants. So it was in the times of the Hittite domination, and so it remained later, under the Persian kings, Alexander the Great and his early successors. In Persian times Pergamum was one of these small city-states ruled by half-Greek tyrants, descendants of a certain Gongylus. It was therefore nothing new both for the land and for its overlords when in 282 B.C. a half-Greek from Tius, Philetaerus son of Attalus, to whom Lysimachus had entrusted the fortress of Pergamum containing part of his treasure amounting to 9000 talents, betrayed his master and went over to Seleucus (vol. VII, p. 197). In return he was, no doubt, recognized as the 'dynast' of Pergamum and of the adjacent country, a title which left to the ruler rather more independence than that of *epistates*, or even that of the *strategos* of a satrapy (*ib.* p. 166).

We do not know how large a territory Philetaerus acquired by his own skill and by the acquiescence of his suzerain, to whom he proved a faithful servant, setting on his coinage along with his own name the portrait of Seleucus[1]. We must not underestimate its size. To the geographer Strabo it may have appeared insignificant, for the standard of Strabo was very high, but in comparison with most of the cities of Asia Minor, which were not very rich in land, it certainly possessed a large and fertile territory, even if it was confined to the valley of the Caïcus. Philetaerus adopted at once the policy which became that of his successors. He set himself to win over his Greek neighbours, as Pitane and Cyzicus, by loans and other services, and to secure fame and recognition by gifts and dedications in such important centres of Hellenic life as Delos and Thespiae (p. 604). He began to build up a strong army, by whose help he extended his sway over Mysia and protected the Greek cities of Mysia, the Aeolis and the Troad against the attacks of the semi-barbarous tribes of the mountains.

[1] See Volume of Plates iii, 4, *c*.

Finally, he was diligent to discover and exploit the abundant resources of the neighbouring country. All this shows that his territory was not small and that he knew how to develop it by the skilful investment of the 9000 talents which he had stolen from Lysimachus. The ambition of Philetaerus and of his immediate successors was probably to control what had been the Mysian satrapy of the Persian Orontes, a world in itself, rich and self-supporting, closely connected with the Greek cities of Aeolis and of the Troad.

Philetaerus was succeeded by his nephew and adopted son Eumenes I[1], under whom Pergamum remained as before—a *dynasteia*, or a tyranny closely connected with one city. The only novelty was that Eumenes allied himself with Egypt, broke with the Seleucids and, after defeating Antiochus I near Sardes in 262 B.C. proclaimed his independence (vol. VII, p. 709 *sq.*). How far he extended his territory is unknown. We hear of two colonies with the names of Philetaereia and Attaleia which guarded his northern and southern borders and were held by his mercenaries, probably at the very beginning of his rule. Whether, however, it was he who established these fortresses or whether he had inherited them from his predecessor, we do not know. In any event, his efforts and aims were the same as those of Philetaerus: to rule quietly over as large a part of Mysia as possible, to control as many neighbouring Greek cities as he conveniently could, and patiently to lay the foundations for a larger expansion.

This policy was replaced by the more ambitious programme of Attalus I, who assumed the title of king after defeating the Galatians, the scourge of their Greek neighbours (vol. VII, p. 721). Pergamum was no longer to be merely a modest prosperous *dynasteia*; it was now one of the great Hellenistic monarchies, whose rulers steadily sought to dominate Asia Minor. But Attalus was soon driven by his wars against the Seleucids and by the protracted struggle against Philip V of Macedon to recognize that the new kingdom of Pergamum could not, even by the most adroit use of treaties and alliances, secure lasting predominance, unless the power both of Macedon and Syria was undermined, if not wholly destroyed, by some stronger state. The one state in the world at the time strong enough for this was Rome. Whether the kings of Pergamum realized that support of Rome, while it brought them a certain increase of territory, was destined to mean for them vassalage and ultimate subjection it is idle to speculate. They

---

[1] It is convenient to describe this Eumenes as Eumenes I, although he did not rank as king (see vol. VII, p. 709).

made their choice, and the reason for it was their boundless ambition. In this they were not alone, and they share the responsibility for Roman domination over Greek lands with many other political leaders of an age which was so poor in national aspirations and so rich in short-sighted political ambitions.

The immediate reward of Pergamene policy was ample enough. The settlement which followed Magnesia gave to the Attalids the greater part of Asia Minor. A few Greek cities remained free. Lycia and a large part of Caria were assigned to Rhodes, and the kings of Bithynia, Pontus, and Cappadocia were left independent, as was Galatia under pledge to respect her neighbours' borders. Elsewhere, Pergamum was the ruling power (pp. 230 *sqq.*). This sudden increase of sovereignty and territory was bound to mean a profound change in the constitution, administration, social and economic structure, religious and cultural policy of the Attalid kingdom.

For the internal history of Pergamum our evidence is scanty, and it bears mostly on the later period, the 55 years between 188 and 133 B.C. Most of what we know is to be gleaned from casual references in the literary sources, especially Polybius, and from many inscriptions found both at Pergamum by the German excavators and in the other cities of Asia Minor. Knowledge from this last source is increasing rapidly and the picture which is to be drawn here may become out of date in a few years. It should further be remembered that most of what is here said about the *kingdom* of Pergamum does not apply to the *dynasteia* which preceded it. Even if we are not always able to discriminate between what is evidence for each of these periods, it is clear that between the two there were many points of difference. On essential features, indeed, of the *dynasteia* it is not probable that we shall ever possess full and precise information.

II. THE KING. THE COURT. THE ARMY

The little we know of Pergamum before the kingdom shows that its dynasts or tyrants were not exactly similar to the typical tyrants of the Greek cities of the later period. Their strength, like that of the tyrants, lay in their armed forces, but their relations to the city constitution were not so close, since the Pergamene dynasts were not originally citizens of Pergamum, though they insisted on being styled *Pergameis*. In this their tyranny is very similar to those of Bosporus and of Pontic Heraclea (see pp. 568 *sqq.*). How early the Pergamene dynasts re-arranged the constitution of the city to suit themselves we do not know. It is certain, however, that the concentration of

executive power in city affairs in their own hands was one of
their first achievements, as is shown by the fact that at the time
of Eumenes I the five *strategoi*, who were the real presidents of
the Pergamene commonwealth, were no longer elected by the
city but appointed by the ruler himself. There is little evidence
about the relations between the early dynasts of Pergamum and
their military colonies in the 'country' (χώρα as against the
polis, which is Pergamum), and between them and the few Greek
cities which formed in a certain sense a part of the Pergamene
'country,' especially Elaea, the harbour of Pergamum. Towards
the natives who lived in the scattered villages they behaved as
absolute masters, as also towards those Greek settlers who were
not citizens of Pergamum or of one of the Greek cities in Pergamene territory.

As soon as the dynasts became kings in Asia Minor they introduced into Pergamum all the familiar forms and setting of the
Hellenistic *basileia* (see vol. VII, pp. 11, 114, 161 *sqq.*). The rulers
were linked with the gods by a twofold fictitious divine genealogy,
one which made them the descendants of Heracles, another—or a
modification of the first—which connected them with Dionysus.
This genealogy appears fully established in the time of Eumenes II
(not only in Pergamum but also in such a neutral place as Delos),
but it is, no doubt, of earlier origin. It is interesting to note that
the Pergamene genealogy is far nearer to that of the Ptolemies
than to the divine genealogy of the Seleucids. A cult both of the
ancestors of the kings and of the living rulers was established in
Pergamum and in the Greek cities inside and outside the kingdom,
apparently without any pressure from the rulers. Some beginnings
of this dynastic cult may date from the time of the first Eumenes,
certainly from that of Attalus I. Princesses of the royal house had
their share in it, especially Apollonis, wife of Attalus I, the famous
mother of four exemplary sons, and Stratonice, wife of Eumenes II.
The forms were true to type: sacred precincts (Attaleia and
Eumeneia are known), altars, statues in the temples of the gods,
sacrifices, priests and priestesses, celebrations and games on
certain dates (as the birthday of a ruler or a memorable date in his
reign), dynastic names for months and days, and the like. Whether
there were any attempts to introduce the cult into the villages and
the temples of native gods we do not know. The royal cult was, no
doubt, closely connected with mystic cults protected by the kings,
first and foremost with that of Dionysus, but also with those of
Sabazius, the Cabiri and perhaps the Magna Mater (p. 616 *sq.*);
but we cannot say how far these fairly hellenized mystic cults
were accepted by the natives.

Like the other great kings the Attalids had their own court and their own bureaucracy. The family of the king, his *syntrophoi*, his *somatophylakes* and his *philoi*, formed the group of his nearest (the *anankaioi*), and some of them were summoned from time to time to discuss the great problems of the kingdom. Two vivid pictures of such meetings of a royal council survive, one in Polybius (v, 41, 6), under the Syrian monarchy, another in a letter addressed by Attalus II to the archpriest of the Magna Mater at Pessinus (*O.G.I.S.* 315, vi)[1]. A recently found inscription (*S.E.G.* 1, 374) attests the existence of a keeper of the royal seal at the court of Attalus II. We hear of a kind of prime minister (ὁ ἐπὶ τῶν πραγμάτων), of royal treasurers (one called *rhiskophylax*, another perhaps *gazophylax*[2]), of a special treasurer in charge of the sacred revenues, of royal judges and of police agents scattered all over the country, but of their numbers, duties and importance we are ignorant.

The main problem of the kingdom was, of course, the organization of a strong and efficient army. The impression produced by the scattered evidence in our literary sources and in inscriptions, would suggest that the army was never very large and consisted exclusively of mercenary corps. But such an impression is probably misleading. If, as appears from the historians, the kings did not send very large auxiliary corps to help the Romans, that does not mean that they did not use larger armies for fighting their own enemies on their own account—the Galatians and the Seleucids in the reign of Attalus I, the Galatians again and the kings of Bithynia and Pontus under Eumenes II and Attalus II. If the troops sent to help Rome consisted exclusively of foreign mercenaries, this does not prove that the Attalids had no detachments of soldiers levied in the country, and no military formations resembling the Macedonian phalanx.

We are able to reconstruct a general picture of the constitution of the army under Attalus I and his successors. Valuable assistance for this reconstruction has quite recently come to hand from a group of inscriptions discovered at Delphi[3]. The inscriptions were set up by the city of Lilaea in Phocis in honour of the

[1] For abbreviations in the references see the list at the end of the volume.
[2] *Rhiskophylax* is mentioned in the decree in honour of Timarchus, W. Buckler, *Sardis*, IV, no. 4, pp. 10 *sqq.* The same title or that of *gazophylax* should perhaps be restored in *O.G.I.S.* 290. There may be a reference to the *gaza* in the inscription, *Ath. Mitt.* XXXIII, 1908, p. 382, no. 3, l. 9.
[3] One of these inscriptions has been recently published by F. Courby from his own and Bourguet's copy in *Fouilles de Delphes*, II, 2, *Topographie et Architecture* (*La terrasse du Temple*, par M. F. Courby), 1921, p. 224 *sq.*

officers and soldiers whom Attalus I, in accordance with his compact with the Aetolians, sent to defend it from the attacks of Philip V, most probably in 209–8 B.C. (see above, p. 126). There are four decrees for six detachments of soldiers (two of mercenaries from various places, three of Mysians and one exclusively of Pergamene citizens). If we combine their evidence with that already known (especially *O.G.I.S.* 266 of the reign of Eumenes) we may conclude that the infantry of the Pergamene army was organized in small detachments (*hegemoniai*) under the command of a chief officer or *hegemon* and his subordinates, who were also styled *hegemones*. In each detachment there was a *xenagos*, who played an important part in its affairs and was sometimes himself the chief *hegemon*. There were also detachments of cavalry under hipparchs. That the navy was strong and well organized is certain, but we do not know how it was financed or manned. Special garrison troops (*phrouroi*) were posted in the fortified cities of the kingdom (*O.G.I.S.* 266)[1], and royal gendarmerie (*paraphylakitai*) patrolled the country. In Pergamum itself there was a permanent garrison besides the king's body-guard. In the famous 'testament' of Attalus III these are called 'those registered in the citadel and in the ancient city[2].' The great efficiency of the Attalids in everything connected with the military technique of the time, war-engines, weapons, and the like, suggests that they gave permanent employment to skilled specialists.

In time of peace the Pergamene army was stationed partly in the city itself and the fortresses, partly settled throughout the 'country' of Pergamum and later throughout the provinces in city-like towns, villages and farms. Most of these military settlers were of non-Greek origin: Macedonians, Mysians, Mazdyenes and Myso-macedonians. The Mysians, however (and also the Mazdyenes), were completely hellenized, if we may judge from the many examples of their names which appear both in the lists of soldiers and the lists of ephebes. The conditions on which these soldiers were settled on the land are unknown.

The present writer owes the copies of the other three to the kindness of M. M. Holleaux, who first drew his attention to these documents of very great importance for the history of Pergamum, and has allowed him the use of his own notes collected for their publication.

[1] In Aegina a garrison was maintained under the command of two *epistatai* or *strategoi*, and officered by *hegemones*. See Ἀρχ. ἐφ. 1913, p. 90, no. 3.

[2] *O.G.I.S.* 338, l. 16. The recent German excavations in the acropolis of Pergamum have laid bare what is almost certainly the headquarters of this royal body-guard, the great arsenal of the Citadel and the quarters of the soldiers stationed in the Citadel near the arsenal.

Fragments of a charter given to a group of these soldiers before settlement (*Inschr. v. Perg.* 158) show that there existed various types of such *katoikoi*. The difference between them may have consisted in the different quality of the land assigned to them; in the conditions of allotment[1], and in the obligations attached to the assignment. It is interesting to note that the soldiers might not only receive an allotment from the king but also buy land from the crown in addition.

In time of war a field-army was formed, which included detachments composed entirely of soldiers levied in the city of Pergamum, all of them Pergamene citizens. Many other detachments were levied in the territory of the Pergamene kingdom among the Mysian tribes; and an important part of the army was made up of similar formations recruited among the Mazdyenes and Trallians. Some units (but not the majority) were composed of mercenary soldiers from various countries. Most of them came from the most warlike parts of Greece—Thrace, Thessaly, Macedonia, Crete—but they included inhabitants of the most peaceful cities of Greece and Asia Minor and even Italians, Sicilians, Africans from Cyrene and Massiliotes from Gaul. No doubt all these received pay for their services and were 'with pay' (ἔμμισθοι), as they are called for example in the inscription of Eumenes I (*O.G.I.S.* 266). The same inscription, however, mentions other soldiers who were 'without pay' (ἄμισθοι). Who these soldiers 'without pay' were, we do not know; they can hardly have been the citizen-soldiers of Pergamum. Some troops were no doubt supplied by the cities subject to the Attalids, not to mention the contingents of their allies. Andros, for example, sent some soldiers to Pergamum to take part probably in one of the wars of the second century in Asia Minor[2].

The system of recruiting a large part of the army among the citizens of Pergamum and the hellenized natives of the country induced the Attalids to take careful measures to train suitable recruits for the army in the kingdom itself. The great attention which they paid to the military training of boys, ephebes and young men in the gymnasia both of Pergamum itself and of the subject cities, the lavish subsidies which they gave to these gymnasia, the diligence which they showed in fostering a loyal spirit among the younger generation associated with them, prove that the gymnasia of the kingdom were the schools of the army both for officers and

[1] We hear occasionally of a tithe, which was paid from the uncultivated land assigned to one group of military settlers.
[2] Th. Sauciuc, *Andros*, no. 3.

common soldiers, in this similar to the *collegia iuvenum* of Rome and Italy in the time of Augustus[1]. Lists of ephebes described below show how comprehensive was the use of the Gymnasium at Pergamum for this purpose.

Some information, but only on points of detail, about the conditions of the soldiers' service, is found in the contract and oath of Eumenes I by which a mutiny in his army was brought to an end (*O.G.I.S.* 266). Thus we hear of the price of grain and wine, probably a tariff for the deliveries in kind to the soldiers; of the duration of the fiscal or military year, which consisted of ten months; of payments in full of arrears due to those soldiers whose contract expired (not pensions); of the regulation of succession of orphans; of the general dispensation for taxes (*ateleia*) granted to the soldiers during the time of service; of a special dispensation granted to those who were about to leave the service and the country; of full payment for the time of the mutiny, and of special privileges for those who won a particular military decoration. The regulations, and especially the oaths, are interesting as showing the strong *esprit de corps* of the soldiers and the mutual distrust which existed between them and their employers. They give us very little evidence, however, about the general conditions which prevailed in the regular army. The fact that after successful expeditions the soldiers and sailors would put up a statue or a votive offering to their commanders, the Pergamene kings, does not testify to more cordial relations between the Attalids and their soldiers than in other Hellenistic monarchies[2].

III. THE ORGANIZATION OF THE KINGDOM

In the official language of the time[3] the Pergamene state consisted, probably from the very beginning, of the *polis* and the 'country' (p. 593). It is almost the same terminology as is found

[1] On the gymnasium of Pergamum and on that of Sestos, see *O.G.I.S.* 764 and 339, and the numerous other inscriptions found in the Pergamene gymnasium. For lists of ephebes: W. Kolbe, *Ath. Mitt.* xxxii, 1907, pp. 415 *sqq.*; P. Jacobsthal, *ibid.* xxxiii, 1908, pp. 384 *sqq.*, and H. Hepding, *ibid.* xxxv, 1910, pp. 426 *sqq.*

[2] Interesting information on the quartering of royal soldiers, especially those of the train (ἔξω τάξεων), in private houses to the discomfort of the citizens is to be found in an inscription of Soli in Cilicia (R. Heberdey and A. Wilhelm in *Denk. d. Wien. Akad.* xliv, 1896, vi, p. 43, no. 101), a letter of a king to one of his officers in reply to a complaint from the citizens. The present writer is inclined to adopt the view advanced by C. B. Welles on stylistic grounds that the king is an Attalid (probably Eumenes II), not a Seleucid.

[3] *O.G.I.S.* 338, cp. *Ath. Mitt.* xxxiii, 1908, p. 407, no. 36, l. 4.

in Egypt. By *polis* is meant, no doubt, the city of Pergamum. What is the meaning of 'country' as coupled with or opposed to *polis*? Was it the territory of the city of Pergamum which was managed by the magistrates, the council and the popular assembly of the city, and was opposed to the lands which were administered directly by the king? Or was the territory of the kingdom legally identical with the territory of the city? In the opinion of the present writer the city of Pergamum had no territory of its own in the former sense, until it received it when Attalus III made the city free by his last will and testament. Before this liberation the 'country' legally or theoretically coincided with the early territory of the kingdom, except for those parts of it which were in law the territories of allied or subject Greek cities, and those cities or lands which were purchased by the kings. Earlier, before Eumenes II, the expansion of the 'country' of the city of Pergamum coincided with that of the kingdom. The lands of smaller cities were absorbed by Pergamum, those of larger Greek cities which preserved a certain amount of autonomy were in a certain sense appended to the territory of Pergamum. This is shown by the fact that in lists found in the Pergamene gymnasium the ephebes of the city of Pergamum are divided into three classes: citizens of Pergamum belonging to particular tribes, those who came from the *topoi*, and those who were in law foreigners (ξένοι). The *topoi* are no doubt subdivisions of the territory of Pergamum—cities which had lost their autonomy, villages, estates (ἀγροί), settlements of soldiers (Mysians and Mazdyenes). The 'foreigners' came from autonomous cities, and are probably to be identified with boys from Pitane, Myrina and Cyzicus who are mentioned in some lists in which the names are not divided into groups. Thus the territory of the kingdom and of the city alike contained citizens of Pergamum itself, *paroikoi*, *i.e.* inhabitants of the *topoi*, soldier-settlers who lived partly in scattered farms, partly in military colonies, and citizens of other cities than the city of Pergamum, legally foreigners. It is almost exactly the same subdivision as appears in the above-mentioned testament of Attalus III.

The legal classification of the inhabitants of the Pergamene kingdom (excluding dwellers on the estates of the ruler or of the native temples, and the members of native tribes, about whom more will be said later), which is closely connected with the legal characterization of the territory of the Pergamene state, was the creation of the earlier rulers and applied first and foremost to the ancient *dynasteia*. When under Eumenes II large new territories were granted by the Romans personally to the king, not to the city of Pergamum, these were administered by the kings as what they were—their personal possessions, whereas the original domain continued to be legally the territory of the city of Pergamum. The new territories were managed by the king's agents, governors of what may be called the royal provinces. It is indeed exactly the same evolution as that which has been observed in Ptolemaic Egypt (vol. VII, chap. IV). Some of these provincial governors had both military and civil powers. We know of such governors (*strategoi*) for the province of Hellespontine Phrygia (*S.E.G.* II, 663) and for the province of the Chersonese and the adjacent Thracian *topoi* (*O.G.I.S.* 339, cf. 330 and 301). Others might have had exclusively civil powers and were regarded merely as collectors of revenues[1].

If the territory of the Attalid kingdom was really subdivided into the various areas enumerated above, we must deal with all these subdivisions separately, viz. on one hand, (1) the city of Pergamum; (2) the 'country' of Pergamum or the *topoi*; (3) the Greek cities dependent on the city of Pergamum, *i.e.* the Greek cities which belonged to the early *dynasteia* of Pergamum; (4) the Greek cities allied with the early *dynasteia*; and, on the other hand, (5) the new acquisitions of the Attalids after 188 B.C., *i.e.* (a) the new allied Greek cities, (b) the tributary Greek cities, (c) the cities and territories granted to the kings, and (d) the cities and lands purchased by the kings with the permission of the Romans.

The city of Pergamum existed before the Attalids made it the centre of their kingdom, but of its constitution in the time of the Gongylids and later nothing is known, nor have any important remains of this early city been discovered in the course of excavation. What has been discovered are the ruins of the Attalid citadel and acropolis, and of some parts of the Hellenistic city outside the citadel and the acropolis on the steep slope of the hill. The city, as excavated, is a beautiful creation of the Attalids, very little changed later by the Romans, so far as the acropolis is concerned. We know, as it were, the head and feet of the city; the body is still a problem. Nor can we yet trace its gradual growth, but we know that it was Attalus I who gave it its fortifications, Eumenes II who made the city one of the most beautiful in the Greek world, and Attalus II who found a city of trachyte and *marmoream reliquit*. By the efforts of Eumenes II the citadel and the acropolis became a sequence of beautiful religious and public buildings. The same king enclosed within walls an area which went far beyond the eyrie

[1] οἱ ἐπὶ τῶν προσόδων. These occur at Eriza in an inscription (*O.G.I.S.* 238) which belongs probably to the time of the Pergamene domination over Phrygia, the organization being presumably inherited from the Seleucids.

of Philetaerus and the fortified city of Attalus, and built the main public buildings which lie in the intervening space. We know two of these buildings: the magnificent Gymnasium on three terraces recently excavated by the Germans and the fine second agora of the city. Of the temples connected with the Gymnasium and the agora, that of Demeter and Kore is one of the oldest buildings of Pergamum, first dedicated by Philetaerus and Eumenes I. It existed long before the Gymnasium was built. The other temples are contemporary with the Gymnasium and the agora.

As regards the top of the hill, the fortifications of the citadel and the military constructions connected with the royal palace, the Arsenal and the barracks for the soldiers, as well as the core of the palace itself, are much earlier than Eumenes II, and so is, no doubt, the early temple of Athena, the early agora and the early theatre. There was, however, hardly one earlier building which was not remodelled by him, and the Hellenistic city as revealed by excavation is Eumenian and Attalian in its very essence: the palace with its gardens, the Arsenal and an altar of Zeus on the summit, the theatre and the temple of Athena with the famous library in the middle, the great altar with the famous sculptures, the terrace of the theatre with the temple, perhaps of Dionysus Kathegemon, and an Attaleion where the Dionysiac artists met, and the upper market-place (agora) with a temple of Dionysus at the bottom. It was the first great city which was built by Greek architects on the slopes of a hill, on terraces according to a definite plan, and even in its ruins it still produces the impression of an architectural composition in which the useful and practical have been fused with the beautiful and artistic[1]. What is more especially significant for this chapter is the fact that the city of Pergamum as excavated is a royal capital and not a Greek autonomous city. All the buildings bear the seal of the kings, and the name of the council and assembly of the city appears as no more than ornaments.

These names were equally ornamental in the political life of the Pergamene state. In law the *dynasteia* and later the central part of the kingdom were the territory of the city of Pergamum. In fact, however, it is almost certain that the city itself played very little part in their administration and that most if not all of the income derived from the territory of Pergamum went directly into the royal treasury. The city appears, indeed, to have enjoyed very little freedom even in managing its own municipal affairs. It is true that it presented the form of a city-state. The citizens were divided

---

[1] On the art, architecture and town-planning of Pergamum see further below, pp. 679 *sqq.*, and Volume of Plates iii, 184, 186.

into *phylai* and *demoi*; there was a city council and a popular
assembly; a chief magistrate and priest of the city—the *prytanis*
—probably elected by the assembly, as was the secretary of the
people. The real power, however, was not concentrated in the
hands of these magistrates or in the hands of the council and
people. The masters of the city, presidents of the assembly and
of the council, managers of the income and expenditure of the
city were the *strategoi* (probably five), and these were appointed
by the king. The city lived, not according to the laws voted by the
popular assembly but according to royal orders incorporated in
the city-laws or royal rescripts announced to the city. If, besides
this, laws or decrees were voted by the council and the assembly,
it was done on the initiative or with the permission of the *strategoi*.
Guardians of the laws, *nomophylakes*, were regarded as occupying
a high position, probably because they enjoyed the confidence of
the king and were practically his agents. Even such minor things
as police regulations regarding the streets and houses of the city,
their proper management and cleanliness, were regulated by a
royal law and carried out by minor municipal magistrates, the
astynomoi and *amphodarchai*, under the strict supervision of the
strategoi and, in some respects, of a special governor of the city
(ὁ ἐπὶ τῆς πόλεως) appointed by the king. If by chance the city
was called upon to appoint judges for arbitration, those judges,
while acting *de jure* in the name of the people, *de facto* made their
decisions according to the pleasure of the king. Nor had the city
very much freedom in the management of its income. The citizens
paid various types of taxes (among them some municipal taxes), but,
if compared with the taxes paid to the king, they were of very little
importance. In one of its decrees the city plaintively describes the
ateleia granted to a certain Asclepiades as: 'freedom from all the
taxes of which the city is in control' (*Ditt.*[3] 1007, l. 20). The
financial executive officers, the treasurers of the city, were entirely
dependent on the *strategoi*. And last but not least the city had only
a nominal right of coinage confined to copper alone.

The temples were a serious problem for the kings. They were
no doubt very rich, especially such shrines as the temple of Athena
Nikephoros[1], the counterpart to the shrine of Apollo at Daphne,
near Antioch, or that of Dionysus Kathegemon, or that of Asclepius, a centre of medical studies. According to Greek tradition
the wealth of temples was vested in the city, though it formed
a special department in its financial administration. The Attalids
solved the problem in their own way: they left the income of the

[1] The goddess is the regular reverse type on the royal coinage (Volume
of Plates iii, 4, *c*, *d*).

temples in the hands of the city, but they appointed a special supervisor of this department of the city administration (ὁ ἐπὶ τῶν ἱερῶν προσόδων). Further, the chief priests and probably the *neokoroi* of the richest temples were appointed by the kings, and were often members of the royal family or former officers of the crown. They managed the large Gymnasium in the same way, the centre of the military and intellectual education of the youth, and the main support of their loyalty. Since the Gymnasium or the Gymnasia (there were three sections in the Gymnasium—the boys, the ephebes and the young men) lived largely on royal endowment (like the temples), there is no doubt that it was the king who in practice appointed the gymnasiarchs and the *paidonomoi*. Finally, it was the king who maintained order in his capital; the chief of police, ὁ πρὸς τῇ παραφυλακῇ, was probably a royal officer.

The part which the kings played in the life of the city of Pergamum is best illustrated by the stamps on the tiles found in the ruins of the city. Almost all are royal stamps; city stamps are exceptional. They may be divided into those which were used for the private buildings of the kings, especially their palace, those which were used especially for the fortifications, those which were made for building temples and for the use of the priests, and finally those which bear the stamp δωρεῶν, *i.e.* were used by the kings for buildings which were given as gifts probably to the city, or were granted as building material to the city or to some private friends of the king.

Very little is known of the relations between the kings and the Greek cities of the early *dynasteia,* and of the first extension of the *symmachia* of Pergamum in the time of Attalus I. One passage in a letter of that king to Magnesia on the Maeander (*O.G.I.S.* 282) shows the king speaking for the cities which are subject to him without consulting them. It proves that, at least from the time of Attalus I, very little autonomy was enjoyed by the Greek cities of the Pergamene kingdom. The most probable assumption (supported by some, though not conclusive, evidence) is that the early subject cities of the Attalids were organized more or less on the same lines as Pergamum itself.

However, the cities were but exceptions in the early Pergamene kingdom. Their territories were small and the kings regarded themselves as free to carry out synoecisms of various cities or to deprive decayed cities of their city-rights. This is shown by the arbitrary acts of the kings towards Priapus and Dardanus, Gergis in the Troad, Miletopolis and Gargara. The suppression of Gergis, at least, can be dated definitely in the time of Attalus I. The larger part of the Pergamene 'country' was not divided into city

territories. Our information about this rural part of the Pergamene land is scanty indeed. It appears in the possession of temples
of native gods, of native peasants living in villages, or as owned by
private persons. Such at least is the impression produced by the
names which are given to the various *topoi* in the list of ephebes
mentioned above. Some of them have geographical names
(Lycetta, Dascylium, Timni) and were probably villages (*komai*)
of natives, one has the significant name Abbukome, another is
called 'the estate of Apasion.' It seems, however, that the ultimate
owner of all the land which did not belong to city territories was
the king, as is shown by his assignments of land to new settlers,
both military and civil, by sales of land, by his building of fortresses,
and by the fact that he exercised his right of taxation even as
regards the native temples[1]. It is difficult to assume that he acted
in this way exclusively on lands which he owned privately in the
way of purchase or which he had inherited from the former lords
of the country, with whom in fact Philetaerus and his successors
were not connected either directly or indirectly.

How much of this land the kings distributed, by grant or sale,
to soldiers and civil settlers, both Greeks and barbarians, to the
grandees of their court, and to the temples and various institutions
of their capital, we do not know. We hear of few military colonies
in the earlier period, and those only in the original domain of
Pergamum; Philetaereia, Attaleia, Apollonis, the first two early
creations of Philetaerus or Eumenes I, the last founded in 190-
186 B.C. But we must not underestimate the numbers of military
settlers who lived not in colonies but scattered all over the open
country. The Mysians and Mazdyenes are often mentioned in
the lists of the ephebes of Pergamum. The settlement of the
Mazdyenes is probably of late date, but there is no doubt that
their settlements were not the first in the country.

Our information about the new acquisitions of the Pergamene
kings after the battle of Magnesia is slightly fuller. The Romans
in dealing with the land taken from Antiochus III in Asia Minor
discriminated sharply between the 'country' (specified as *castella,
vici, agri, silvae,* and *oppida non libera*) and the Greek cities. The
country and some of the Greek cities (Tralles, Ephesus, Telmessus)
were given by Rome to Eumenes II as 'gifts' (δωρεαί). The same
term is applied to the land granted to the Rhodians in Lycia and
Caria (p. 230). A little later Eumenes II was very eager to receive
on the same conditions the cities of Aenus and Maronea in Thrace,
beside Lysimacheia and its territory (p. 249). Those Greek cities
which were not given as gifts to Eumenes II were divided into

[1] *Ath. Mitt.* XXIV, 1899, p. 213.

two classes: the cities which did not pay tribute to Attalus I before the war and did not help Antiochus III were declared *liberae et immunes*, *i.e.* non-tributary to Eumenes II; those who did pay tribute to Attalus I before the war and those which helped Antiochus III were now to pay tribute to Eumenes II, i.e. were made subject to him (see above, p. 231).

With the cities that remained free the Attalids sought to maintain the best relations. They made gifts to the city of Miletus and the Ionian League, loans to Pitane and Chios. Both before and after Magnesia they gave privileges to Cyzicus and they appear in close relations with Colophon and Iasus[1]. It was indeed the same policy as that which they followed towards the cities of Greece and the islands, Athens, Delphi, Delos, Calauria, Thespiae and the rest[2]—a policy of benevolence or bribery on a large scale.

The subject cities[3] were dealt with in an entirely different way. Doubtless there were some general principles which were applied to all the cities, and certainly there was a strict control of finance as in the city of Pergamum. In this the policy of the Attalids resembles that of the Ptolemies. But this policy admitted of variation in practice. Thus we know that the city of Amblada paid to the king a lump sum of two talents as tribute (*O.G.I.S.* 751), while we have every reason to suppose that most of the subject cities paid a variety of taxes into the king's treasury.

How far the Attalids changed the constitutions of the cities we cannot say. There is some evidence which points to an attempt at introducing the magistracy of the *strategoi* into many of the cities subject to the Attalids and at giving to these magistrates a leading position in the life of the cities. There is, however, no strict proof that this policy was applied to all or to the majority of the Greek cities. It is known that the orders of the kings were regarded as laws by the cities of the kingdom, and that some of these orders were incorporated into the city-laws by a special order of the king; and this privilege of the crown must, in varying degrees,

[1] Miletus, *Milet. Erg.* 1, 9, 1928, nos. 306 and 307; Pitane, *O.G.I.S.* 335; Chios, *S.G.D.I.* iv, 4, pp. 894 *sqq.*; Colophon and Iasus, *B.C.H.* 1906, p. 349; *C.R. Ac. Inscr.* 1927, p. 137; *Rev. Arch.* xxix, 1929, pp. 107 *sqq.*

[2] Athens, *O.G.I.S.* 318; Delphi, *Ditt.*[3] 523, 628–30, 670–72; Delos, Durrbach, *Choix*, 52; Calauria, *O.G.I.S.* 297; Thespiae, *O.G.I.S.* 749–50.

[3] Under subject cities are included both tributary cities and cities received as a gift from the Romans. It is probable that there were differences in details as regards the treatment of these two classes by the kings, but evidence is lacking.

have replaced the right of the cities to legislate for their domestic affairs. It is equally natural that the kings appeared as arbiters in territorial disputes between neighbouring cities and sent their own surveyors to settle the disputes in a more or less decisive way[1]. But the chief anxiety of the kings was to keep the finances of the cities in good order. The inhabitants of most of them paid various and probably quite heavy royal taxes. This can be gathered from some recently discovered documents. Of these the most important are an inscription (*S.E.G.* II, 663) set up by an unknown city in honour of Corragus, the governor of Hellespontine Phrygia probably during the reign of Eumenes II, and an inscription of Teos (*ib.* 580) of about the same time dealing with a purchase of a piece of land for the association of Dionysiac artists. In the former the city has been just taken over by the Pergamene governor after a ruinous war, probably that between Pergamum and Antiochus III. In this war the city had forfeited all her privileges—liberty, autonomy and the rest—and was at the mercy of her new master. He takes no advantage of this situation and restores its former privileges: but the city is not *immunis*; the citizens pay taxes (πρόσοδοι) to the king. Since, however, they are in financial straits they receive a remission of taxation for three years, increased by the governor to five, and it is possible that a like remission was granted by Eumenes II to all the cities of which he now became the overlord.

Along with these royal taxes the cities no doubt paid municipal taxes as well, as is true, for instance, of Teos. It is possible that most of the taxes paid to the king were the usual taxes formerly paid by the citizens of Greek cities into the treasury of their own cities, as specified, for instance, in a late fourth-century inscription of Teos (*S.E.G.* II, 579). The difference was that the kings introduced some new taxes and that the assessment and the collection of the old ones were now carried out by or under the control of the officers of the king. It is, however, curious that while taxing heavily the population of the subject cities with one hand, the kings paid with the other hand both to the cities and to the temples, and to the associations of the young men (probably to the Gymnasia) certain subsidies in specie and in kind. In the inscription for Corragus this payment was described as made 'for the management (or administration)' (εἰς διοίκησιν) of the city. Since such a payment recurs twice more in inscriptions concerning Teos (*S.E.G.* II, 580) and Temnos (*Inschr. v. Perg.* 157) the practice seems to have been common. Thus the kings satisfied their desire to control the

[1] Keil-Premerstein, *II Reise*, p. 13, no. 18.

finances of the cities and to appear as benefactors of the community, which, heavily taxed by the kings as it was, was not able to increase municipal taxation and thus to cover the expense of civic administration and the maintenance of temples and gymnasia.

Similar to that of the subject cities or of the cities granted to the Pergamene kings was the situation of Aegina which Attalus I acquired by purchase from the Aetolians. Though the city kept her constitution and her magistrates (we know of the existence of *strategoi*) there was a royal governor, and the life of the citizens was regulated exclusively by the laws and orders of the king. The governor was supreme judge in all disputes between the citizens[1]. The island of Andros may have been similarly treated though we have no precise evidence on the point[2].

It is difficult to say how much the Attalids contributed to the urbanization of their kingdom. Very little was done in this respect in the original territory of the kingdom: all that is recorded is the establishment of two fortresses (p. 591), which probably never developed into real cities. In the new territory the Attalids inherited about a score of Macedonian colonies created by the Seleucids. How many new military colonies they themselves created is uncertain. One (Apollonis) is beyond doubt, others are probable (*e.g.* a Eumeneia in Caria, another in Phrygia, Dionysopolis in Phrygia, Stratoniceia in the Hyrcanian valley, Philadelpheia in Lydia, and Attaleia in Pamphylia), others are quite problematic. In Apollonis the Attalids no doubt intended to create a new city, and this was done by means of a synoecism, and the new community is definitely called a *polis*[3]. In some other colonies there are traces of city life both under the Seleucids and under the Attalids. Most of them, however, did not develop into regular cities until the period of Roman domination. Of the military colonies which did not attain to the status and constitution of a city, some, as Philetaereia, were administered by military governors and probably had no elected magistrates; others, as probably Nacrasa, had their own magistrates, probably appointed by the king. The inhabitants formed various associations, and as such took common decisions. Most of them probably paid taxes to the king in addition to the service of their inhabitants in the royal army and perhaps in the navy.

Next to the cities and to military colonies come the large and rich temples, some of them attached to a city, some centres of a rural

[1] *O.G.I.S.* 329, cf. 281; *Ditt.*[3] 642.
[2] Th. Sauciuc, *Andros,* pp. 85 *sqq.*
[3] Keil-Premerstein, *II Reise,* p. 53, no. 113.

district. The former were administered by their several cities, as at
Ephesus and Sardes. Since some of them were very rich and played
an important part in the economic life of the country as centres of
banking and industry, the Attalids had every reason for claiming
a kind of control over their finances and the right to dispose of
their income and landed property. This right of control they carried
out by appointing financial managers of the temples (*neokoroi*),
as for the temple of Sardes; the claim to rights over some of the
temple income was emphasized when one of the Attalids confiscated the income derived by the temple of Ephesus from fisheries.
Probably the relations between the Attalids and those temples
which were not attached to any city were not very different. Like
the subject cities they paid taxes on their property, and nothing
prevented the king from appointing a manager of their finances
or from seizing some of their sources of income or some of their
land. At Aezani in Phrygia the kings, both Seleucid and Attalid,
made use of this right of partial confiscation (*O.G.I.S.* 502).
Some temples, like some Greek cities, were more on terms of
alliance or vassalage than of subjection to the Attalids. This was
true of the important temple of Pessinus with its hereditary king-
priests. A series of letters of Eumenes II and of Attalus II to these
priests gives us a vivid idea of their mutual relations (*O.G.I.S.*
315). We must not forget, however, that Galatia was never a
regular Pergamene province and that Pessinus succeeded in
keeping its semi-independence even towards Galatian rulers.
Further, it is to be remembered that, from the time of Attalus I,
the priests of Pessinus had kept up cordial relations with
Pergamum.

In the new territory, beside cities, colonies and temples there
were villages and fortified refuges of the natives and large stretches
of forests, mines and lakes. It seems beyond doubt that all the
land occupied by the native population and all the natural resources of the land above and below the surface of the earth were
regarded as private property of the kings. Of this land which was
regarded as belonging to the royal treasury, important tracts were
given to court grandees, some parcels to citizens of Greek subject
cities (perhaps new settlers) and large allotments to soldiers of the
territorial army. Corragus, for instance, is able to present to the
city from his own estates cattle for sacrifices, and the king assigns
from the royal property parcels of land to the citizens of the city
who had none. Probably these landless citizens were not poor
proletarians but new colonists to whom land was not yet assigned.
For the military colonies interesting evidence is supplied by an

inscription of Pergamum quoted above (p. 596), the inscriptions dealing with the synoecism of Apollonis, and the inscriptions of Aezani.

IV. ECONOMIC POLICY

If the kings of Pergamum were able patiently to build up a rich and flourishing kingdom, to make this kingdom famous in Greece, to protect it against the attacks of their neighbours, both Greeks and barbarians, and to appear as patrons of learning and art, they owed it to their own skill, to their own sound economic policy and unceasing efforts to develop the natural resources of their territory, which remained very small for the first century of the kingdom's existence. When Eumenes II became master of almost the whole of Asia Minor the wealth of the kingdom increased in proportion to its territory, but the economic and social policy of Eumenes II and of his two successors remained, so far as we can see, exactly as it had been during the long period of expansion and consolidation.

Asia Minor was endowed with the greatest possible resources for developing a sound and prosperous economic life. The original Pergamene kingdom, rich in good arable land, in pasture, in excellent wine and garden land, in forests, in mines, in quarries, is typical of the resources of Asia Minor as a whole. The kings of Pergamum knew their land well and missed no opportunity for developing its natural resources. They could dispose of great quantities of grain, which was constantly sent as gifts or as subsidies to their allies both Roman and Greek, and to cities of their own kingdom. Though direct evidence is lacking, we must assume that the kings also carried on an extensive commerce in this commodity. Part of it they certainly received as payments for one or another form of land-tax. These payments formed the chief income of the king. We have no exact information about the assessment and collection of these taxes, but their existence cannot be doubted, and in general the Hellenistic monarchies favoured payment of land-taxes in kind. The amount paid by the various landowners varied. Appian (*Bell. civ.* v, 4) records a speech by Antony at Ephesus which implies that the Attalids exacted taxes in accordance with an assessment of property ($\pi\rho\dot{o}s$ $\tau\dot{a}$ $\tau\iota\mu\dot{\eta}\mu\alpha\tau\alpha$).

Besides the kings there were many landowners in the kingdom, both small and large. The temples certainly had great estates though the kings probably claimed the right of ownership over the land tilled by the temple-serfs. Nor were the temples alone in this. In the 'testament' of Attalus III mention is made of large estates confiscated by that king. We hear of rich men such as Craton, the famous flautist and president of the association of Dionysiac artists at Teos, later resident at Pergamum; Menas, a citizen of Sestos; Corragus, the general of Eumenes II; Diodorus Pasparus, the nabob of Pergamum just after the death of Attalus III. Menas and Corragus, we know, had large estates. How they came by them and what was their title we do not know, but it is probable that these favourites of the kings received tracts of land from the crown as gifts or purchases for a nominal sum. To the class of small or medium landowners belonged the majority of landowners in the territories of the Greek cities of the kingdom. Very often the kings also owned some land in city territories as in Pitane and Priene. To the same class of small or medium landowners we must assign the soldier-settlers, though we do not know exactly what the conditions were on which they received or purchased their *kleroi*. Some of them no doubt paid a tithe. And finally there were many landowners in the 'country' of Pergamum in the various *topoi*—former cities, villages, and rural areas.

Along with these large and small landowners whose titles to the land no doubt varied but who probably all paid one land-tax or another into the treasury of the king, the king himself exploited land in the territory of the kingdom and in the territories of the allied and subject cities (*e.g. Inschr. v. Priene*, 111, col. xvi, l. 112). As we have already seen (p. 603), there is evidence which suggests that the Attalids adopted the theory which prevailed in the Seleucid and Ptolemaic monarchies and claimed a right of property over all land which did not belong to the territory of cities. The existence of such a claim may indeed be deduced from survivals in the terminology of Roman times[1]. It may, however, be conjectured that this theory did not obtain until the reign of Attalus I or Eumenes II.

However that may be, the kings of Pergamum, like the Seleucids before them, not only collected one or another form of land-tax from the landholders of the kingdom but had estates of their own from which they derived a large income. We have no direct evidence for it, no such vivid pictures of the life on the royal estates as those which we possess for the period of the Seleucid domination: yet the fact may be regarded as beyond doubt. The Attalids certainly had

---

[1] *E.g.* Keil-Premerstein, *I Reise*, p. 64, no. 134: ὅρος βασιλεικῶ(ν) Σωσάνδρ[ων, cf. Rostowzew, *Studien*, p. 287. It is, of course, possible that the βασιλικός in this inscription is not a survival but a new term of Roman times used as Greek equivalent to the Latin 'Caesaris.'

inherited many a large estate from the Seleucids in various parts
of Asia Minor. And they kept most of these. At least we have no
evidence of any efforts to transform this royal land into private or
city land as was a common practice with the Seleucids. We may
believe, therefore, that this land remained in the same condition
under which it had been when they first took possession of it, being
inhabited and tilled by groups of 'royal peasants,' half-serfs, half-
tenants. It is very probable that these domains of the Attalids
survived as separate economic units until the time of the Roman
emperors, when we again have some information on their legal
and economic status. Needless to say, the legal overlords of these
estates changed with the times: the Roman people represented by
the *publicani*, Roman grandees, leaders in the civil wars.

Thrifty and efficient husbandmen as they were, the Attalids
showed a real interest for agriculture. In all fields of activity they
were great admirers of Greek science and learning. No wonder,
therefore, if they paid much attention to systematic scientific agriculture. A text-book on agriculture was compiled by Attalus III,
no doubt an attempt to adapt the theories of Greek scientists
(such as Theophrastus) to the actual conditions of agriculture as
they existed in Asia Minor, and the same ruler spent his last years
in his gardens experimenting on plants and herbs. A further piece
of evidence comes from Rome. In his treatise on agriculture Varro
(and after him Columella and Pliny) gave a long list of writers on
agriculture, most of them of the Hellenistic period, and of these
writers the majority were natives of Asia Minor, the larger
Greek islands and some places of the Thracian coast, all connected
in one way or another with the kingdom of Pergamum, while writers
from other parts of the civilized world are rare. It is fair to suppose
that such a profusion of scientific works was not unconnected
with the interest of the Attalids in the progress of agriculture.

The same keen interest in new devices and in improvements
was shown by the Attalids in the field of cattle raising. Asia Minor
was famous for its sheep and goats, pigs and horses. We have no
evidence which shows any special interest of the kings of Pergamum
in sheep and goats. But we know that the royal Pergamene horses
were prominent at Olympia and at the other great racing centres
of Greece, and we hear incidentally that Eumenes II bought some
famous white boars at Assus, no doubt in order to improve the
breed of pigs on his own estates. Another incidental piece of evidence tells us that rare pheasants were bred in the royal palace of
   mum (Athenaeus xiv, 654c).
 less active were the Pergamene kings in developing industry

in the cities of their kingdom, especially in Pergamum. Asia Minor was always famous as one of the greatest centres of woollen manufactures. Sardes, Phrygia in general and especially Laodicea and Pessinus, Miletus and scores of other Greek and native cities are often mentioned in this connection. We hear, for instance, that Palaiscepsis, Percote and Gambreum in Aeolis and the Troad were famous for their cloths and carpets. In an inscription of the third century B.C. (*Mnemosyne*, XLVII, 1919, p. 69) Aegae is named as an important centre of production of coloured cloths. Another inscription (*S.E.G.* II, 579) shows that Teos was busy manufacturing woollens at the end of the previous century. And we may fairly assume that the woollen industry of Hierapolis in Phrygia which flourished later was introduced into this city by its probable founder, Eumenes II.

Pergamum itself became a great centre of this industry under the Attalids. It became especially famous for its curtains (*aulaea*) and its cloths woven with gold (*vestes Attalicae*) which in former times had been a speciality of Lydia, especially of Sardes. Besides these articles *de luxe* Pergamum and the royal factories produced plain woollen garments which in a much later period still bore the name of *Attaliana* (*P. Giessen*, 21, 5–6). It is very probable that the Pergamene kings, here as elsewhere, profited by the progress of contemporary technique as applied especially to the dyeing of stuffs. It is about this time that the mining of two dyes was begun, of *rubrica Sinopensis* in Sinope and of *sandarake* near what was later Pompeiopolis. Once established, the woollen industry continued to flourish at Pergamum in the Roman period.

Pergamum also cultivated with fair success other branches of industrial production. Most famous of all was the parchment of Pergamum. We now know that parchment was used in Mesopotamia from very early times, and that writing on parchment was as popular in Assyria as writing on clay tablets. Papyrus and parchment were both used in Doura in the Hellenistic and Roman periods. And yet the fact that the European world knows leather-paper under the name of 'parchment' shows that it was Pergamum which made it popular with the Greeks and later with the Romans. It is not irrelevant to observe that from time immemorial the leather industry of Asia Minor had competed with that of Egypt.

In the manufacture of perfumes also Pergamum was a rival of Alexandria. The splendid and varied flora of Asia Minor was busily transmuted into scents (*aromata*), and Stratonice, queen of Eumenes II, popularized a special brand of unguent produced at Adramyttium, while at Pergamum an unknown perfumer invented another brand (Athenaeus xv, 689 a–b). In the Gymnasium of Pergamum, indeed, scented oil was served out to the youths.

Pergamene territory was very rich in silver, and the Attalids were able to produce a currency which, though without artistic distinction, became very popular in the Hellenistic world[1]. They also promoted the circulation of a special type of municipal coin, the *cistophorus*, for use in the cities of the kingdom, and these coins had a great vogue in Roman times. Otherwise the cities of the Pergamene kingdom were reduced to a local coinage exclusively in copper. It is noteworthy that the *cistophori* started at Ephesus[2] and that this, among other things, shows that the later Attalids were inclined to make Ephesus, the greatest harbour of Asia Minor, the second capital of their kingdom. Silver, however, was not used only for the coinage. The more archaeologists study the silver plate of the Hellenistic period, the more it becomes evident that Alexandria did not completely dominate the market in the third and second centuries. Tarentine dishes were still famous at this time, Campanian silversmiths were about to start their own production, and Pergamene engravers made efforts to export their own ware especially to the regions of the Black Sea.

Nor is there any reason to suppose that the kingdom was not active in ceramics. Some brands of red-glazed pottery not unlike Samian ware are probably products of Pergamene factories. Excavations have shown also that a flourishing production of tiles and bricks was developing at Pergamum through both royal and private enterprise.

Thus much of the income of the Pergamene kings was derived from industry. Of the setting up of royal monopolies there is no evidence, and the kings seem to have competed with private business men on an equal footing, yet the royal workshops played a great part in the industrial life of the city, as is attested by the large number of male and female slaves recorded in our scanty sources employed by the Attalids. The 'testament' of Attalus III expressly mentions female slaves, of whom a number were bought under the two last kings, and also a class of royal slaves (*basilikoi*), similar to the *Caesaris servi* later in Rome, and freedmen, not all of them liberated by the will of the king. If we add the public and temple slaves, we shall realize how large was the servile population of Pergamum and the kingdom. In the city many of these were used in the royal household, but the majority no doubt were royal workmen and artizans. Skilled craftsmen were needed for the building

[1] See Volume of Plates iii, 4, *d*.   [2] *Ib.* 14, *f, h*.

activity of the kings and for their various workshops[1]. The technique revealed in the ruins of various buildings built by Pergamene rulers in various cities of Greece and Asia Minor prove that the workmen who built them were educated and trained at Pergamum. There is very little doubt that slaves were also employed by the kings outside the city, as, for instance, in the mines, and in the royal gardens and farms.

We know hardly anything about the extent of Pergamene overseas commerce. The fact that the kings steadily maintained a strong and efficient navy, and that they tried to defend the freedom of the seas, in alliance with Rhodes, against Philip and his allies the Cretan pirates, shows that they had important commercial interests in the Aegean (p. 627). Their policy of maintaining excellent relations with Rhodes, Athens and Delos, the greatest commercial cities of the third and second centuries B.C., makes it more probable that ships of the mercantile fleet of the Pergamene kingdom often visited the great international harbours of the eastern Mediterranean.

V. THE LEADING IDEAS AND THE MAIN ACHIEVEMENTS OF THE PERGAMENE KINGS

The Attalids were of course most concerned with the safety and the expansion of their kingdom and the increase and consolidation of their own power, transmitted from one member to another of the family of the first Attalus, father of Philetaerus. Though they fought the Galatians with all their energy and all the resources of their kingdom, it was first and foremost for the safety of their own territory, not for the more or less abstract aim of saving Greek civilization from the wave of barbarism. Indeed, when they considered it necessary, they did not shrink from hiring these same enemies of civilization to crush their own enemies of Greek origin. True, they posed as protectors and promoters of Hellenic culture in general and as great helpers of the Greeks wherever the Greeks were in difficulties. For example, their interest in the education of children at Rhodes and Delphi (*Ditt.*[3] 672) evokes our sympathy. And yet they were not very liberal masters to the Greek cities, their tributaries and subjects, and they never thought seriously of granting even a modest amount of liberty to the venerable city of Aegina.

[1] Skilled labour, both slaves and free men (painters), were sent by Eumenes II and Attalus II to Delphi (*Ditt.*[3] 671, B, 12, and 682, cf. 523), and Attalus I endowed the temple of Asclepius at Pergamum with the revenue of some workshops (*ib.* 1018).

Nevertheless there is no doubt that they really were fervent admirers of Hellenism and of the great achievements of Greek genius. Their creation of the second greatest library in the world, their lively interest in Greek plastic arts and painting[1], which they showed both as collectors of the greatest works of art and as employers of great contemporary artists, their keen attention to the progress of Greek science and learning which they tried to use for their own profit, have been described elsewhere (vol. VII, p. 251; below, p. 617 *sq.*), but a new illustration has recently been afforded by the excavations of 1927. The great storehouses built on the top of the citadel show so strict a conformity to the theoretical science of fortification in this period that there is no doubt that Attalus I, the builder of the arsenal, was in close touch with the achievements of this branch of science and that both he and his successors promoted this field of knowledge as far as they could. It has been pointed out[2] that some of the military engineers and scholars of the Hellenistic period appear in our tradition as connected with Attalus I: Biton, the author of a work on the construction of instruments of war, and perhaps Athenaeus, the writer on siege-engines.

The kingdom of Attalus I was the smallest of the Hellenistic kingdoms of its day, and even that of Eumenes II and of his successors embraced only one portion of the great Seleucid Empire, and that not the richest. And yet in our history of Greek civilization the insignificant Attalids loom larger than the greatest of the Seleucids. This must be ascribed not only to policy, to propaganda, and endeavours to maintain their collaboration with Rome, but also to a sincere enthusiasm for Greek civilization. Themselves half-Greek only, they showed more understanding for Greek art, literature and science than many true Hellenes. And this the Greeks, especially in the times when they began to feel how great was the danger which threatened Greek liberty and Hellenism from the West, understood very well indeed. There is a sincere note in the praise of Eumenes II by the League of the Ionians, when they passed a decree in his honour after the king had been so deeply humiliated by the Roman Senate (p. 287). 'Inasmuch,' it begins, 'as the king, having chosen from the very beginning to do the best things, and having shown himself bene-factor of the Greeks, underwent many and great struggles against the barbarians, doing his best to allow the residents of the Greek

---

[1] See below, pp. 679 *sqq.*; also Volume of Plates iii, 114.

[2] By Th. Wiegand, *Bericht über die Ausgrabungen zu Pergamon* 1927, Abh. der Berl. Ak. 1928, no. 3.

cities to live in peace and under the best possible conditions[1].'
The same note is sounded in the decree of the Amphictyones of
Delphi (*Ditt.*[3] 630). No doubt there were many Greeks who
bitterly resented the enslavement of the Greek cities of Asia
Minor, with the help of the Romans, and were always ready to
tell the Pergamene tyrants that they were not liberators of the
Greeks but enslavers of them, half-barbarians and natural masters
of barbarians[2] as they were, but the note of philhellenism and
praise rings clearer, at least in the tradition as we have it. We must
not forget, however, that the documents which we have are all
official documents and that Polybius' account is written by a great
admirer of the Romans.

As regards hellenization in the sense of building Greek cities
or promoting Greek city life, we have seen that the Attalids
achieved comparatively little (p. 606). In their own territory,
indeed, the original kingdom of the Attalids, they acted more like
the Ptolemies of Egypt than like the Seleucids in Syria and Asia
Minor. We have every reason to suppose that they deprived some
ancient places of their city organization, and not the slightest
evidence that they promoted a village or a temple territory to the
rank of a city. They may have done so in the provinces after
Eumenes II, though there is no strict proof of it, but not in the
original territory of their kingdom.

In the Ptolemaic kingdom of Egypt we have seen how the
Ptolemies tried to create in the cult of Sarapis a common ground
for the Greeks and the natives in the religious field (vol. VII, p. 114
sq.). Can we detect anything similar in the religious policy of the
Attalids; did they try to hellenize the native cults of their kingdom
or to create some common cults for Greeks and natives alike? The
religious policy of the Attalids is well known. The most important
cults of the capital were Greek: the cult of Zeus Soter and of
Athena Polias and Athena Nikephoros, the cult of Dionysus
Kathegemon and of Demeter and Kore, the cult of Asclepius
(which is so closely connected with the protection and promotion
of medical science by the Attalids), and the cult of Hera, and lastly
the cult of the gods of the Gymnasium and the Palaestra, of
Heracles and of Hermes. Some, if not all, of these cults have
political significance. Many are connected with the cult of the
kings, like that of Dionysus, which was linked with the powerful
organization of Dionysiac actors and took the artists half-way

---

[1] Milet, *Ergebnisse der Ausgrabungen*, I, 9, no. 306.
[2] See the distich of Daphitas, so cruelly punished for it, in Strabo XIV,
p. 647. Daphitas appears also in *O.G.I.S.* 316.

towards the cult of the king. But one thing true of them all is that they were purely Hellenic, first and foremost the great cult of Athena Nikephoros in her splendid suburban sanctuary surrounded by parks and gardens, a rival of the Seleucid shrine of Apollo at Daphne.

If, however, we take a closer view of the religious policy of the Attalids, we notice one phenomenon. One of the oldest royal sanctuaries of Pergamum was the shrine of Demeter and Kore built for their mother Boa by Philetaerus and Eumenes[1]. Boa was a Paphlagonian, no doubt a devotee of the Anatolian Great Mother, and it is possible that the creation of the sanctuary was an attempt to introduce into Pergamum an Anatolian mystic cult in Eleusinian disguise. We must not forget that an Eumolpid Timotheus, the companion of Manetho in Egypt, was a student of the mysteries of Magna Mater, and that the sanctuary of Pergamum had an unmistakably mystic character, having been built on the pattern of the Eleusinian sanctuary, as witness the theatre. It can hardly be a pure coincidence that the same Philetaerus built near Pergamum (at Mamurt Kaleh) a sanctuary of the Magna Mater of this place. Finally we must explain the early relations of Pessinus to Pergamum and the well-known story of the black stone which Attalus I had sent to Rome from Pessinus (p. 115). It is hardly believable that Attalus I tricked the Romans and sent them the black stone of a minor goddess of his own kingdom.

Half-Anatolian by origin, the Attalids had always a predilection for mystic religions and mystic cults of half-Anatolian character. Dionysus of course was a Greek god in the third century. Yet the mystic form which the cult assumes in Pergamum is very interesting, with all the primitive ideas and rites embodied in it: the Bacchi, the Bucoli, the Sileni, the Cistophori and the rest, and the originally wild rite of the Criobolia and Taurobolia are possibly to be connected with this cult. It is a fact that the Attalids endeavoured to make this mystic cult the official religion of their kingdom and to connect it as closely as possible with the royal cult. One of the minor measures of the Attalids for spreading the cult of Dionysus was the protection which they gave to the use of the royal-municipal coins, the so-called *cistophori* with the symbol of Dionysiac mysteries (the *cista mystica*), as their main type. The success of the Attalids in making the cult of Dionysus popular is shown by the number of inscriptions and objects of art connected

---

[1] See H. Hepding in *Ath. Mitt.* xxxv, 1910, pp. 437 *sqq.*, and A. Ippel, *ib.* xxxvii, 1912, pp. 285 *sqq.* on the inscriptions, and W. Dörpfeld, *ib.* xxxv, 1910, pp. 355 *sqq.* on the buildings.

with the Bacchic mysteries which are found all over Asia Minor and belong mostly to the Hellenistic and Roman periods—an interesting parallel to what was going on in Egypt in the time of Ptolemy Philopator.   Dionysus was not the only mystic god who received the worship of the Attalids.   Another great mystic god who migrated to Pergamum with a royal lady—Stratonice, the wife of Eumenes II—was Sabazios, the Cappadocian, whose *epiphanies* and whose help were so strongly emphasized by the queen. We may suspect that Zeus Tropaios, who vied with Sabazios in revealing himself in critical times, was not a pure Greek[1].   Finally there were the Thracian Cabiri who came to Pergamum, not from Boeotia or Samothrace, but probably from the Thracian provinces of Eumenes II.

When all is told, there are good reasons for suggesting that the Attalids were conscious of being not pure Greek but Graeco-Anatolian kings, that they were themselves inclined towards mystery religions, and that they endeavoured by favouring the mystic cults and by connecting them with the royal cult to unite in one religion the Anatolians and the Greeks. In their own religious aspirations Dionysus and Demeter were probably nearer to their souls than Athena and Zeus. Whether they were successful or not in their endeavour to create an understanding between the natives and the Greeks on religious grounds we are unable to say. Dionysus and Demeter no doubt became very popular among the Anatolian Greeks of the Roman Imperial period. How popular they were with the real Anatolians we do not know. Did they not contribute, however, to the creation of that typical race of men whom we may call Anatolian Greeks or Hellenized Anatolians?

One question remains. The Attalids were very fond of philosophy and had a special predilection for the members of the Platonic Academy. We still have the base of a statue which Attalus II set up at Athens to the philosopher Carneades (*Ditt.*[3] 666). Can we form an idea of what kind of principles they followed in exercising their rule, especially over the Greeks? The Aeginetan decree (*O.G.I.S.* 329) in honour of the governor Cleon who remained *epistates* of the island for sixteen years seems to contain a good deal of what we may call the philosophy of

---

[1] On Zeus Tropaios see L. Robert, *B.C.H.* LII, 1928, pp. 438 *sqq.* The present writer would restore the inscription of Bizye in Thrace referred by Robert to the victory of Attalus II over Diegylis in the following way : [ο]ί περὶ τ[ὴ]ν α[ὐλὴν νεανίσκοι] | [Δ]ιὶ Τροπαίω[ι καὶ τοῖς θεοῖς τοῖς συν | α]ὐξουσιν τὴ[ν τοῦ βασιλέως 'Αττάλου | ἀρχ]ὴν χαριστήριον.

government of the Attalids. For self-government and democracy they had small regard. The king and his laws and orders
were paramount. However, the ruler must not be harsh and
selfish. His endeavour must be to act as peacemaker. And in
doing so his chief task is to secure justice for everybody 'in
order that equal justice be for the weakest against the strongest
and for the poorest against the richest.' It is a philosophy which
has always been the philosophy of enlightened autocracy from
the time of Peisistratus to the twentieth century.

To sum up. The monarchy of the Attalids with all its draw-
backs and weak points was a blessing for Asia Minor. At a very
critical time the Attalids succeeded in protecting the Greek cities
of the peninsula against the Galatians. This is their greatest claim
to glory. Not only did they fight the Galatians themselves but
they soon realized that without the Romans they could not reduce
them to impotence. Their submission to the Romans cannot of
course be explained by the fear of the Galatians. In siding with
the Romans they wished to secure for themselves a leading position in Asia Minor. But after the victory of the Romans at
Magnesia they persuaded Manlius Vulso to humble the Galatians, as nobody but the Romans was able to do (p. 228 *sq.*).

By reducing the Galatians to insignificance the Attalids secured
for Asia Minor years of peace and prosperity. The first to profit by
it were the kings themselves. They were too shrewd ever to be
poor, and, rich as they were, they were never mean. Their great
passion was to make their own city not only one of the most
beautiful cities in the world but also one of the greatest centres
of Greek civilization. And they spent their money lavishly
in achieving this noble aim. Their efforts were crowned with
success. Pergamum became one of the capitals of Hellenistic
civilization. Not the capital *par excellence*, for there never was in
the Hellenistic world any city which had such a claim. When the
time came, and the last Attalid realized that there was no longer
any useful activity for a king in Asia Minor, he did not struggle
against the inevitable. By his own act he handed over the great
creation of his predecessors—the city of Pergamum—their great
preoccupation—the development of Hellenism in Asia Minor—
to what he conceived to be the loving care of the Romans. And
in this he was not mistaken. Asia Minor paid heavily for the
privilege of becoming a Roman province, but Hellenism was
saved, and it was protected and spread by the Romans perhaps
even more efficiently than by the Attalids.

CHAPTER XX

RHODES, DELOS AND HELLENISTIC COMMERCE

I. THE UNIFICATION OF RHODES.
RHODIAN COMMERCE

IT is not an easy task to give an adequate picture of the life of the Greek islands of the Aegean Sea in the Hellenistic period. The literary evidence is scanty and the archaeological material, especially inscriptions, most unevenly distributed. Very few of the Greek cities of the islands of the Aegean sea have been carefully and systematically excavated. Good, almost exhaustive, work has been done for Delos, Cos and Thera; partial excavations of a scientific character have been, and still are being carried out on Samos, Thasos, Aegina, Tenos, Crete, Cyprus and Rhodes; but most of the Greek islands have been never even touched by the spade. All that has been done is careful surface investigation. This is the reason why for some of the islands and island cities we have abundant epigraphical material, of which in some instances only part is published—this is true of Cos, of Lindus in Rhodes, and to a certain extent of Delos—whereas for others evidence of this kind is almost lacking.

It is not, however, possible by merely combining such evidence as we have to give a satisfactory *general* picture of the Greek islands. Each had its own development, its own cultural and political conditions, its own preoccupations. As in the Greek cities of the mainland of Greece, of Asia Minor and of the other parts of the Mediterranean world, life on the Greek islands was highly individualized. It was, indeed, perhaps more individualized than in the cities of the mainland. A real history of the islands will only be possible when we have good monographs based on abundant material for each. This was fully understood by the ancients as is shown by the notable development of local historical production, for example the chronicle of Lindus compiled with the help of numerous local and general works by a Lindian citizen Timachidas (vol. vii, p. 259 *sq.*). This historical material, however, has almost wholly perished, leaving very slight traces in the extant tradition, and a modern substitute for this lost wealth of knowledge is still to seek.

Finally, among the many islands of the Aegean there were but
few that had any real importance in the history of the period.
Most of the islands were little provincial communities living in
the shadow of one of their more progressive continental or insular
neighbours, and their life, however interesting it might be in itself,
is, for the historian of Greek civilization, no more than a variant
and often an imitation of the type of life which prevailed among
their more powerful neighbours. We cannot yet tell for certain
which of the islands were among the leaders of politics and
culture in Hellenistic times. Lesbos and Samos had, no doubt,
lost the importance which they possessed at the dawn of Greek
history, and the same is true of Aegina and Euboea. Crete has
some effectiveness—but it is in the ways of destruction rather
than of progress—and the tiny island of Cos looms large in the
literary history of the early Hellenistic period. But all our evidence
suggests that in the third and second centuries two islands alone
—Rhodes and Delos—played a really important part in the
historical developments of the time.

Of the two, far the more important was Rhodes. The marvellous
advance of this little island struck the imagination of those who
witnessed the zenith of its greatness and elicited from them enthusiastic eulogies which were later repeated by writers of the
Roman period. If there was unanimous agreement among the
ancients on any subject, it was in high praise of the achievements
of Rhodes in politics, war and civilization. Among historians
Polybius and the writer followed by Diodorus come first; then
follows Strabo or his source, and after him Dio Chrysostom and
the rhetorician Aristides, to name only the more important. 'The
city of the Rhodians,' says Diodorus (xx, 81), 'strong in her navy
and enjoying the best government among the Greeks, was ever
a subject of competition between dynasts and kings, as each
sought to win her to their friendship.' Strabo (xiv, 652) is still
more explicit: 'The city of the Rhodians,' he says, '...with her
harbours, streets, walls and other public works (κατασκευῇ) so
greatly surpasses all other cities that there is none which is her
match much less her superior. Equally admirable are her constitution and laws (εὐνομία) and the care which she lavishes upon
her institutions, especially upon all that concerns her navy.'

From the dawn to the evening of her history Rhodes was first
and foremost a commercial community. An island so limited in
size and natural resources cannot maintain a very large population
or aspire to play any important rôle unless it has an extensive
commerce, especially a carrying-trade not confined to her own

products. And so it was with Rhodes from the earliest period of her existence. Above all else it was her situation between Egypt, Cyprus, the Syrian and Phoenician coast and the world of the Greek cities, which made Rhodes, from the Mycenean age at least, an important intermediary between Greece and the Orient. This fact was as obvious to ancient observers, like Polybius (v, 90, 3), as it is to us. Thus the first task of the historian is to trace her commercial development.

We are not concerned here with the earlier development of Rhodes. Archaeology shows beyond doubt that from time immemorial Rhodes turned her face to the East, and that her civilization had in early times a semi-oriental aspect. Our task begins with the great reform in the constitution of Rhodes, the synoecism in 407 B.C. of the three ancient communities, Camirus, Ialysus and Lindus, into one, the new city and state of Rhodes. Ancient and modern historians agree in tracing the brilliant commercial development of Rhodes back to this fateful decision of some political genius who lived at that time in the island. It is true that even before that time, in the period after the Persian Wars when Rhodes became a member of the Delian Confederacy and subsequently a subject of the great commercial city of Athens, she had a considerable trade and commercial resources. The Athenians had no intention of destroying Rhodian commerce with Egypt and Syria, especially after the failure of their own oriental enterprises. There are, indeed, two inscriptions which show how close even in the late fifth century were the commercial relations between Rhodes and Naucratis[1]. But the hostility between Persia and Greece and the state of war which prevailed most of the time in the southern waters of the Aegean naturally prevented the exchange of goods between the Orient and Greece from being very large, quite apart from any jealousy which may have existed between Athens and Rhodes.

However that may be, it is certain that, once the synoecism was complete, Rhodian commerce advanced by leaps and bounds, despite the fact that in the closing years of the fifth and in the fourth century Rhodes was in turn dependent politically on Athens, on Sparta, again on Athens, and finally on the dynasts of Halicarnassus. We know it from such statements as that of the orator Lycurgus[2], who describes the Rhodians as 'men who sail for trade all over the inhabited earth,' from the fact that Cleomenes, the powerful governor of Egypt in the time of Alexander

---

[1] Ditt.³ 110; Schwyzer, Dial. gr. ex. ep. 278-9.
[2] In Leocratem, c. 15 (330 B.C.).

the Great, chose Rhodes and not Athens as his agent in his well-known commercial operations (vol. VI, p. 448 *sq.*) and, above all, from the story of the first great attempt of Rhodes in 305 B.C. to free herself from external political control by her struggle against Antigonus (vol. VI, p. 499 *sq.*). Unless we assume the existence of enormous resources in men and money accumulated in the city of Rhodes, and of far extended commercial relations which made the existence and prosperity of Rhodes a vital question for many of her clients and partners[1], we cannot account for the success with which the little city withstood the overwhelming forces and consummate siege-craft of Demetrius.

It is evident that during the fourth century B.C. Rhodes succeeded in concentrating a large volume of trade in her harbour and a large population in her towns. This trade cannot have been in oriental luxuries alone, though they were far from unimportant; it must have included a commodity which was vital for everybody in Greece. This commodity was no doubt the corn of Egypt and of Cyprus, second to which came metals from Cyprus and linen and dyed woollens from Egypt and Syria. Without the concentration of the corn-trade of Egypt in the hands of the Rhodians we cannot account for the marvellous growth of the city. And as we have seen elsewhere (p. 574 *sq.*), the fourth century was a time when regular corn-import became more vital for Greece than ever. This concentration of a part of the corn-trade in the hands of Rhodes Athens was unable to prevent. She was content to enjoy for a while a prior claim on Pontic corn and to have a fair share in corn that came from the West.

Freed from the danger of political subjection to one of the great powers, Rhodes sedulously guarded her independence. She understood that however great the privileges which she might derive from siding with one or other of the kings, it would be foolish to forfeit her liberty for a temporary material gain. For some decades after the great siege she remained, as was natural, in close commercial and political relations with Egypt and the first two Ptolemies, especially Soter. Rhodes, indeed, was probably the first to establish a real cult in honour of that monarch. But so soon as the successor of Soter, Ptolemy Philadelphus, sought to maintain a true hegemony in the Aegean, to treat the Island League, created by Antigonus and reorganized on new lines by Soter, as a subject, and probably to use Rhodes as he used the

[1] Cf. the proclamation of Antigonus at the beginning of the war promising safety on the seas to Rhodian sailors and traders in Syria, Phoenicia, Cilicia and Pamphylia, provided they do not put in at Rhodes. Polyaenus IV, 6, 16.

other islands and to promote Delos to her detriment, Rhodes became recalcitrant, joined Antigonus Gonatas, and defeated an Egyptian fleet off Ephesus (vol. VII, p. 713).

This spirited action by Rhodes did not spoil for long her relations with Egypt and the Ptolemies. Since they were not able to force Rhodes into subjection, it was in their own interests to maintain friendly relations with her. And this they did. We hear of no conflict between the two navies after the battle of Ephesus. Indeed, almost the only monuments erected to kings at Rhodes were those made for the Ptolemies[1]. Apart from these the Rhodians showed extreme moderation in granting honours and statues to monarchs, in this respect so unlike Delians and so like Romans.

The years of the *entente cordiale* with the Ptolemies were years of great prosperity for the island. Even our scanty evidence reveals Rhodes in the early third century as the home of powerful merchants and influential bankers. With her money and by means of her diplomacy Rhodes endeavoured not only to promote her own interests but also to help the Greek cities to secure and maintain independence and constitutional government. Thus in 300 B.C. the Rhodians lent money to the citizens of Priene to assist them to assert their liberty against a tyrant (*Inschr. v. Priene*, 37, ll. 65 *sqq.*; *Ditt.*[3] 363 and n. 4). Another act of the same kind is the loan, without interest, of 100 talents to Argos for the improvement of their fortifications and of their cavalry (Vollgraff, *Mnem.* XLIV, 1916, pp. 219 *sqq.*). These two loans were clearly political, and this explains why they were given by the city and not by private Rhodian bankers. The state, it appears, had important sums of money stored in her treasury or kept on deposit in private or public banks in or outside the city of Rhodes. It was indeed more usual for similar loans, even political in purpose, to be made not by the city but by private citizens, rich merchants and bankers. Thus Ephesus, a city which maintained most cordial relations with Rhodes and largely depended on her for its food-supply and no doubt its commerce, as appears from the reform of the Ephesian coinage about this time on Rhodian patterns, was helped in critical times by a rich Rhodian who sold her a considerable amount of grain at less than the very high ruling price[2].

With the naval battle of Ephesus which was presently followed

[1] Besides the inscriptions and literary texts, see the sculpture published by M. P. Nilsson, *Timbres Amphoriques de Lindos*, p. 169, fig. 2.
[2] *Ditt.*[3] 354 (c. 300 B.C.); cf. *I.G.* XII, 7, 9; cf. 8; *O.G.I.S.* 10, and Heberdey, *Forsch. in Eph.* II, 104, no. 453.

by the two defeats of the Ptolemies by the Antigonids—the battles of Cos and Andros—the situation in the Aegean changed completely. Macedonia now became theoretically the mistress of the sea and the suzerain of many islands, among them Delos. The Island League displayed no signs of activity, and Egypt retained very few of her possessions in the Aegean area. Rhodes gained everywhere. There was no question of dependence on Macedonia, which, at least in the time of Antigonus Gonatas, made no effort to attract Rhodes into her political orbit. On the contrary, it seems as if the Macedonian kings, after their great victories over Egypt, neglected their navy and tacitly allowed the Rhodians to be masters of the sea with all the consequences which this fact implied, first and foremost the duty of curbing piracy, a task which had been previously performed by the Ptolemies and the fleet of the Island League. In the Aegean Rhodes stood for the 'freedom of the sea,' which meant no privileges for anyone like those enjoyed by Athens in the fifth and fourth centuries, the greatest possible security afloat, a minimum of taxes and duties, and the recognition of some general legal principles as applied to the maritime commerce. Those principles Rhodes tried to carry out by means of a common understanding on the part of all the cities which took an active share in overseas commerce, and she soon acquired the reputation of being the 'protector of those who use the sea[1].'

The new rôle which Rhodes began to play implied of necessity the maintenance of a strong permanent navy in Aegean waters. The cost of such an achievement was very high—according to the treaty between Rhodes and Hierapytna (*Ditt.*[3] 581) the maintenance of one trireme cost the Rhodians 10,000 drachmae a month—but it was more than covered by the extension of Rhodian commerce. From the third century onwards her trade spread from the South to the North-East and to the West. The abundant finds of Rhodian jars and sherds show how Rhodes, in extending her commercial relations in general, took the opportunity to sell her own goods, especially wine, in the newly acquired markets, for example in Asia Minor, in the Black Sea, Southern Italy and Northern Africa. The coin-standard which Rhodes introduced soon after the synoecism was adopted, not only by most of the islands of the Aegean and many towns of Asia Minor, but also by cities on the Hellespont and the Propontis and in Thrace. Besides this sign of the extension of Rhodian trade, we find the spread of alliances especially among the islands,

[1] προεστάναι τῶν κατὰ θάλατταν, Polybius iv, 47, 1.

e.g. with Ios (*I.G.* XII, 5, 8 = 1009), and vigorous action against piracy in the Aegean, as Demetrius of Pharos and the Cretans found to their cost[1]. Most remarkable of all is the constant endeavour of Rhodes to take her share along with Athens and her successor Delos in the Black Sea trade. When Byzantium imposed *c.* 220 B.C. a ruinous tax on those who passed through the Bosporus, it was not Athens but Rhodes to whom the merchants appealed to force Byzantium to abandon it, and Rhodes promptly and willingly carried out the commission. A little later (219 B.C.), when hard pressed by Mithridates II of Pontus, Sinope appealed to Rhodes and received from her substantial help in form of war-machines and food. All this shows how influential Rhodes was in the North and how rapid was the decline of Athenian prestige (pp. 575, 579 n. 1).

Rhodes presently began to be too strong for the Macedonian kings who had so quickly succeeded in getting rid of the Ptolemaic domination in the Aegean Sea. However, in the reigns of Demetrius II and Antigonus Doson relations between Rhodes and Macedonia remained friendly. There may have been a short interruption during the problematic expedition of Antigonus Doson to Caria and at the time of his short-lived attempt to establish a real domination in the Aegean Sea[2]. But, on the whole, Rhodes and Macedonia even in the first years of Philip V appear as friends and allies. This explains the offers of the Rhodians (together with other Greek commercial powers) to mediate between Philip and the Aetolians in 218 (vol. VII, p. 767 *sq.*), in 217 and again in 207, another proof how seriously Rhodes regarded her mission of safeguarding peace in the Aegean waters.

And yet there are some signs that Macedonia from the very beginning of the Rhodian ascendancy regarded it with suspicion. It is interesting to see how Antigonus Gonatas and his successors, soon after their great victories over the Ptolemies, established their suzerainty over the sacred island of Delos and began to use this island, with its splendid situation, as a rival to their old enemy Athens and the new commercial power Rhodes. There are inscriptions which show that the Antigonids made Delos their own clearing-house and attracted to it especially the northern corn-trade and traffic in the chief products of the Macedonian

---

[1] Polybius IV, 19, 8; Diodorus XXVII, 3. The Rhodians never compromised with the pirates, unlike the Antigonids, who from Demetrius onwards were always inclined to use them as political allies.

[2] See vol. VII, p. 722 and J. Delamarre in *Revue de Phil.* XXVI, 1902, pp. 301 *sqq.*

kingdom, such as timber, pitch, and tar. Thus Demetrius II through his agent[1], and about the same time a *sitones* of Histiaea, a subject city of Macedonia, buy corn at Delos[2], which is full of inscriptions testifying to honours granted to Macedonians[3]. All this together with the fact that the Bosporan kings ceased to court Egypt and began to cultivate the friendship of Delos (see p. 580) shows that the Antigonids did their best to promote Delian trade with the North, which began its natural development as early as the beginning of the third century B.C.[4]

It cannot, however, be said that the Antigonids succeeded in destroying the friendship of the two islands. From very early times Delos maintained cordial relations with Rhodes[5], and it seems as if Rhodes intended to make the sacred island a kind of a branch institution of her own clearing-house. It is true that after the collapse of the Ptolemaic hegemony in the Aegean and down to the early second century the relations between Rhodes and Delos begin to cool. But their business ties were too strong to be wholly broken. Thus in the inscription which speaks of the Histiaeans buying corn at Delos it is a Rhodian banker, probably established at Delos, who advances him the money without interest. In the light of this evidence it is easy to understand why Philip V, in his endeavour to extend his own power at the expense of Egypt, looked upon Rhodes as the main hindrance of his plans rather than the Seleucids, the legal overlords of Asia Minor, or Attalus I, the new aspirant to this same suzerainty (p. 591). Philip had, however, no good justification for an open attack on Rhodes, the champion of liberty and the guardian of the seas, the great republic which had earned the enthusiastic assistance of states from Asia Minor to Syracuse when, in 227/6 B.C., a terrible earthquake almost destroyed the city. Meanwhile Rhodes grew stronger every day. Philip decided not to attack Rhodes at once, but first to weaken her by undermining her commercial prosperity. His natural though unavowed associates were those who made piracy their profession, especially the Cretans, bitter enemies of the Rhodians—not without cause, for it was the Rhodians who had supplanted them in commerce and left them piracy as

---

[1] *I.G.* XI, 4, 666; Durrbach, *Choix*, 48.
[2] *I.G.* XI, 4, 1055, cf. 1025; *Ditt.*[3] 493; Durrbach, *Choix*, 50.
[3] *I.G.* XI, 4, 679–680; Durrbach, *Choix*, 47; cf. *I.G.* XI, 4, 661–5, cf. 1053; Durrbach, *Choix*, 49.
[4] *I.G.* XI, 4, 622; Durrbach, *Choix*, 46.
[5] Durrbach, *Choix*, 39 for the time of the Ptolemaic control of the Aegean, cp. *I.G.* XI, 4, 751–5, 683.

their one resource. The Cretans were assisted by the malignant activities of the agents of Philip, Dicaearchus and Heracleides, until Rhodes realized her danger and viewed Philip with justified suspicion (p. 145). There were constant hostilities against Crete, followed by a declaration of war against Philip himself (p. 152). Only the fact that Rhodes foresaw that any delay was fraught with danger for her prosperity could have driven her peace-loving citizens to challenge the power of Macedon. More than this, it led them to ally themselves with Attalus and invoke the intervention of Rome which led to the utter defeat of Philip. It is in their fear of Philip and his imperialistic ambitions that we must seek the explanation of the Rhodians' alliance with Rome. They sincerely expected that Rome would pursue a policy of *laissez-aller* towards the Greeks, which meant the continuation of Rhodian prosperity and security, whereas it was evident that Philip's victory meant for Rhodes at the very least subjection.

The humiliation of Philip brought Rhodes a notable increase in wealth and power. She was not only now the chief power in the Aegean Sea, the recognized president of the Island League which she now revived, but also the sovereign of considerable possessions on the mainland of Asia Minor. Antiochus III had already ceded to her Stratoniceia in Caria and she had purchased Caunus from the Ptolemies. Finally, in return for the active and efficient aid which she had given to the Romans in their struggle against Antiochus, she received Caria south of the Maeander and all Lycia except Telmessus (pp. 230 *sqq.*). For about twenty years after the Peace of Apamea Rhodes became one of the most important factors in the balance of power which the Romans temporarily set up in the East.

For these palmy days of Rhodes we have ample and trustworthy information. We see the Rhodians fighting the pirates with all their strength. Many of her citizens fell in these conflicts and were honoured by their countrymen[1]. The number of her allies steadily increased. Even certain influential cities of Crete became allies of Rhodes and pledged themselves to combat the pirates hand in hand with the Rhodians, as is shown by the treaty with Hierapytna[2]. Rhodian admirals and captains were everywhere. They appear in time of war as commanders of strong squadrons of Rhodian and allied ships[3]. They firmly resisted such attempts at blockading the trade in the Hellespont, as that of King

---

[1] *Ditt.*[3] p. 1225.   [2] *Ib.* 581.
[3] *Ib.* 582–3; Durrbach, *Choix*, 63.

Eumenes II *c.* 183/2[1]. If need arose they sent their governors (*epistatai*) to the cities of the Island League in order to defend them from enemies or to settle their internal and external affairs[2]. Most interesting, as showing the relations they had with the cities of the League, is a group of inscriptions from Tenos, which at that time was the headquarters both of the Island League and of the Rhodian and allied navy[3]. This fact made it the administrative and the financial centre of the League. Financially, however, Tenos was entirely dependent on the great bankers of Delos and behind them probably on those of Rhodes. This appears from a group of inscriptions relating to a banker, Timon of Syracuse, who resided at Delos and had business relations with Delos herself and with other islands[4]. Tenos, too, at that time adopted the Rhodian currency and imitated her political institutions. Not very different were the relations of Rhodes to the other members of the League, such as Ceos[5] and Amorgos[6]. Outside the Cyclades Rhodes was satisfied with making new allies. We hear, for example, of alliances with Eresus in Lesbos[7] and with Miletus[8]. Rhodian influence stretches as far as Cyzicus[9], Sinope[10], Olbia, the Scythians of the Crimea and the Bosporan kingdom[11].

This great increase in power and prestige meant for Rhodes a corresponding increase in wealth. This is attested by the Rhodian currency which is dominant in the Aegean market and far beyond it and, *faute de mieux*, by the Rhodian stamps on the handles of their jars. The export of wine was but a trifling part of Rhodian trade, but its spread testifies to the extended voyages of the Rhodian ships which imposed their mediocre wine on customers with whom they were in constant relations and for

[1] Polybius XXVII, 7, 5.
[2] To Syros, *I.G.* XII, 5, 652; to Tenos, *Ditt.*[3] 658.
[3] *B.C.H.* XXVII, 1903, pp. 233 *sqq.*; *Musée Belge*, XIV, 1910, p. 19, No. 2; *Ditt.*[3] 658.
[4] *I.G.* XII, 5, 816–7; Durrbach, *Choix*, 66, cf. *Comptes des hiéropes de Délos*, B.C.H. XXVI, 1902, p. 400.
[5] Michel, *Recueil*, 399; *Musée Belge*, XXV, 1921, p. 108.
[6] *I.G.* XII, 7, 31, cf. 1, 842.
[7] *Rev. des Études grecques*, XXVII, 1914, p. 459; cf. F. Bechtel, *Aeolica*, 1909, p. 33, No. 38.
[8] *Milet*, I, no. 150, 35; *Ditt.*[3] 633; note that in this treaty between Miletus and Heraclea the two cities agree not to do anything which was not acceptable to Rhodes.
[9] *S.G.D.I.* 3752.
[10] Sinope was an ally of Rhodes *c.* 219 B.C. (p. 625).
[11] *Ios. P.E.* I[2], 340 and 30.

whom Rhodian merchants with their money and influence were always welcome guests. The collection and examination of Rhodian stamps found outside and inside the island show that most of the Rhodian amphorae were produced between 225 and 150 B.C., especially in the early second century. Rhodian stamps are found in great numbers in Alexandria and in Egypt in general, in Syria, in Palestine, in Asia Minor (especially in Pergamum), even as far as Susa in Persia, and, in the West, in Sicily and southern Italy and at Carthage. Rhodes failed, however, to conquer the whole of the northern market for her wine, a fact which suggests that she never succeeded in becoming dominant in the north Aegean. Of the jar stamps found at Delos 70 per cent. are Cnidian, and only 25 per cent. Rhodian[1]. The same is true for the Aegean in general. On the other hand in South Russia of 1500 stamps found in the excavations at Olbia some scores only belong to Thasos, Cnidos and elsewhere, while the remainder are Rhodian[2]. During the second century Rhodes reached the Crimea by way of Olbia and her trade dominated the capital of the Scythian kings Scilurus and Palacus. In the Bosporan kingdom Rhodes is less prominent and shares her commercial influence almost equally with Thasos and Sinope. Apparently the dynasts of the Bosporus refused to submit entirely to the Rhodian maritime hegemony.

Finally, just as many foreign merchants resided at Rhodes (see below, p. 640), so Rhodians are found at this time at all the great commercial centres of the Greek world. This is abundantly proved, although all the available evidence has not yet been put together except for Alexandria, where, in the early Ptolemaic period, Rhodians play an important part. We need not be surprised to find Rhodian merchants all-powerful in many of the smaller Greek islands[3].

It is not easy to say wherein lay the main business of Rhodes. The little we know shows that Rhodes, like Athens in the fifth century and London in modern times, was a great clearing-house for international commerce and exchange, especially between Greece and the Orient. Greece was at that time the main market,

---

[1] J. Paris in P. Roussel, *Délos, colonie Athénienne*, p. 29 n. 4.

[2] According to the calculations of B. N. Grakov, *The ancient Greek pottery stamps with the names of the Astynomoi*, p. 32 *sq.* (in Russian). E. Pridik in *Berl. S.B.* xxiv, 1928, pp. 342 *sqq.* reckons that 5100 Rhodian stamps have been found in South Russia as against 6800 stamps (mainly of Sinope) bearing the names of the *Astynomoi*.

[3] See, for example, *I.G.* xii, 5, 2, 1010 (Ios).

the western market gradually gaining in importance. The staple article of trade was corn. All our evidence converges to suggest that except for a large part of the Black Sea trade, which never left Delos, Rhodes had become the greatest corn-market of the world. To Egypt and Cyprus Rhodes added the western market, especially Sicily and Southern Italy, and it was Rhodes that opened up Numidia to the products of Greek industry and attracted Numidian corn to the Aegean world[1]. Rhodian bankers, as we have seen, were actively concerned in the corn-trade of Delos, and their influence is further attested by the part played by a Rhodian merchant in the corn supply of the little island of Ios and by the relations between Rhodes and Tenos which have been mentioned already. Trade in slaves also played an important rôle in the business life of Rhodes. The island itself possessed a great number of slaves (see below, p. 641), and it was from the slave-market of Rhodes that Mysta, after being taken prisoner and enslaved by the Galatians, was restored with all due ceremony to her royal lover, Seleucus III[2].

We must not underestimate, however, another side of Rhodian business. The Rhodians were not only merchants, but more than merchants, they were bankers. Capital migrated largely from Athens to Rhodes and to Delos, which was a still safer place even than Rhodes for people who wished their money to be deposited out of the reach of pirates and the admirals of rival monarchies. To the instances already cited of Rhodian banking operations (p. 628) may be added a modest document, characteristic in its modesty. Epitaphs of Rhodians rarely reveal what professions or trades they had followed. One of the rare exceptions is that of a respectable Rhodian, whose profession is thus described: 'for three decades he kept on deposit gold for foreigners and citizens alike with purest honesty[3].'

But the heyday of Rhodes' prosperity was soon past. After the Third Macedonian War, Rome decided to punish her for having behaved as though she was free and independent, and chose her

[1] Ditt.[3] 652; Durrbach, Choix, 68–69: a gift of grain to Delos made by Masinissa through the good services of a Rhodian ambassador.

[2] Athenaeus XIII, 593 E.

[3] Maiuri, Nuova Silloge (N.S.), 19, c. 200 B.C. With this inscription may be compared Theocritus, Epigram 14 (Anth. Pal. IX, 435), as explained by Wilamowitz (Textgeschichte der griech. Bukoliker, p. 119), W. Leaf (in G. M. Calhoun, The business life of ancient Athens, p. 105 sq.) and E. Ziebarth (Beiträge zur Gesch. des Seeraubs, etc., p. 87 and Anhang, II, no. 74): the banker Caecus boasts of giving the same interest both to natives and foreigners and of keeping his bank open even at night.

most vulnerable point—her commerce. To undermine Rhodian prosperity, the source of her pride and self-confidence, it was not necessary for Rome to declare war against her or to send her legions to Rhodes. That would be a scandal in the Greek world, and scandals Rome avoided as much as she could. A simpler and less drastic measure sufficed. It was suggested by the policy of the Antigonids. Delos was played off against Rhodes. By an apparently benevolent gesture towards the merchants of the Greek world Delos was made a free harbour. And inevitably a large volume of commerce, especially in slaves, at once migrated to Delos. This did not, however, mean ruin. Rhodes was still the great centre of banking, and of course not all the merchants moved to Delos. We do not know how Rhodes answered the declaration of Delos as a free port. A few years later the Rhodians complained to the Senate that as a result of its action, the customs-dues of the State fell from 1,000,000 Rhodian drachmae to 150,000. This may have been because commerce migrated to Delos or because the Rhodians were forced to match the attractions of Delos by reducing the rate of their own duties. But the loss fell on the revenues of the State and had only an indirect and lessened effect on the commerce and banking of the Rhodian merchants. Another great blow to the State treasury was the loss of Rhodian possessions on the mainland, particularly of Stratoniceia and Caunus, which had brought in a revenue of 120 talents. But, as Rhodes had grown rich and powerful without foreign possessions apart from the Peraea, so the forfeiture of these territories did not mean utter ruin to Rhodian merchants and to the business community as a whole (p. 643 *sq.*).

In fact, the loss experienced after Pydna was great but not irreparable. What was more serious was that the Romans made it very difficult for the Rhodians to police the sea. From now onwards piracy grew steadily, despite all that Rhodes could do, and developed at the end of the century into a plague which made commerce in the Aegean almost impossible. Rome made spasmodic efforts to take the lead in fighting piracy with the help of Rhodes as one of her agents. This is shown by the operations of M. Antonius in Cilicia (102 B.C.) and the law against piracy of about 100 B.C. found at Delphi. But she failed ignominiously. It was hard on the one hand to patronize the trade in slaves and on the other to strike at the main source of the supply. Along with the growth of piracy went a general impoverishment of Greece. The cosmopolitan foreign colony of Delos and, through it, some Athenians, grew rich, but the rest of Greece became ever poorer. The Greek commerce which had once enriched Rhodes was now of little importance. And Italy and the West were able to deal with Egypt and Syria without the help of Rhodes.

The convulsions of the East in Mithridates' times and the subsequent civil wars aggravated the situation. Not that Rhodes was even yet wholly ruined and powerless. The brilliant part which her navy played in the Mithridatic war of Sulla, the dramatic story of the last battles of Rhodes for liberty, the many monuments which belong to this time and the renown of the city in the eyes of the Romans, a renown based on the great achievements of Rhodes in the field of civilization, show that Rhodes was still the city *par excellence* among the other Greek communities. It was reserved for Cassius in 42 B.C. to reduce Rhodes to real poverty and temporary desolation. But even Cassius was not able finally to undermine the resources of the city. As soon as the Orient recovered its shattered prosperity under the Roman Empire and Greece became a little richer, Rhodes once more became a wealthy and famous city which earned the enthusiastic panegyrics of Dio Chrysostom and Aristides.

II. THE CITY OF RHODES. RHODIAN CONSTITUTION. ARMY AND NAVY. SOCIAL AND ECONOMIC CONDITIONS

It was the common opinion of the Greeks that Rhodes was the most beautiful city of the Greek world. We have not the means to judge how far Greek opinion was right. The city of Rhodes itself has not been excavated, and the excavations of the much ruined acropolis of Lindus and of some buildings (for instance, a beautiful public fountain) of Ialysus are a poor substitute. The best descriptions of Rhodes are those of Strabo (xiv, 652 *sqq.*), of Diodorus (xix, 45, and xx, 85) and of Dio Chrysostom (*Or.* xxxi, 162). They show us the three harbours of Rhodes, all the work of man, the city descending to the harbours from the hills, fan-like or theatre-like, the city walls surrounding the city even on the sea side, the famous *deigma*, where the wares of all nations were displayed, the squares around it, the shrine of Dionysus and the gymnasium near it, and, last but not least, the pride of the Rhodians, the famous docks. We hear also of the acropolis with its open spaces and groves, of the temple of Helios, of that of Apollo Pythias and of Zeus Atabyrios, but we are not able to determine their sites. No doubt the story about the famous Hippodamus of Miletus being the builder of Rhodes is an invention. It is significant, however, of the great reputation of the city that her building should be attributed to the greatest town-planner of the ancient world.

We are also ill-informed about the adornment of the city by statues and pictures. Most of the famous sculptures of the Rhodian school found homes in later times away from Rhodes and we do not know what part they played in the beauty of the city. Even the famous colossus of Rhodes is a mystery to us. We believe that we know its face from the coins[1], but we are still ignorant what the figure of the Rhodian harbour-Apollo as sun-god was like. The statues which have been found at Rhodes are few and, in general, disappointing; strangely enough, none of them show the peculiarities of what is called the Rhodian school of sculpture (pp. 672 *sqq.*).

Better known than the external aspect of the city is the peculiar constitution of the island after the synoecism. The constitution and the legal system—the *eunomia*—of Rhodes were famous. Of the latter we know very little, a little more about her political institutions. The constitution in the main was democratic, but Rhodes was notable for having found a middle way between democracy and aristocracy: 'The Rhodians,' says Strabo (XIV, 652, probably following Panaetius and Posidonius), 'care for the *demos*, though they are not ruled by it, but they intend to exercise control over the masses of the poor. The people are rationed with corn and the well-to-do support with provisions those in need according to ancestral practice (and there are also liturgies). Thus the poor have the means to live, and at the same time the city has its needs amply supplied especially as regards its shipping.'

Such was the spirit of the Rhodian constitution. Like the Roman it was an aristocracy disguised as a democracy. The forms of constitutional life were as follows. The citizens were divided into three *phylai*, representing the ancient cities of Lindus, Camirus and Ialysus, and these again into *damoi*, the same *damoi* as existed before the synoecism, the constituent parts of the three ancient cities. A similar division into *damoi* is also found in Rhodian territory outside the island, that of the mainland (the Peraea) and of the subject islands. There existed a complicated system, little known to us, of relations between those *damoi* and the three cities of Rhodes. Outside the *damoi* stood the provinces or subject cities of the Rhodian possessions in Caria and Lycia, which were administered in the same way as the subject cities of the other Hellenistic powers. The system of taxation in the provinces is unknown to us, but, as we have seen, the revenues from Stratoniceia and Caunus amounted to 120 talents.

[1] See Volume of Plates iii, 14, *g.*

The government was in the hands, not so much of the popular assembly, as of the Council and of its presidents, the five *prytaneis*. Both the Council and the chief magistrates were elected for six months, during which period one of the *prytaneis* acted as president of the republic. He and the council were assisted by a secretary and an under-secretary. In time of war there were commanders-in-chief of the naval and land forces, the *navarch* and the chief General (στρατηγὸς ἐκ πάντων). The *navarch* was assisted by a group of advisers, mostly former presidents of the republic or *prytaneis*. In his hands lay diplomatic relations with foreign countries, and in this capacity he might represent Rhodes abroad, as Foreign Secretaries do now on great occasions.

Beside the *prytaneis* there were of course other magistrates and public officers. The most important were the ten or twelve *strategoi* and the seven treasurers. Characteristic of Rhodes are the curators of the merchant harbour and the guardians of the corn with a special *prytanis* (known from a later inscription[1]) at their head. A special curator was appointed for dealing with the affairs of the foreigners. A group of *epistatai* took charge of public education, the cost of which was borne by liturgies. We know from a recently discovered inscription the minute care that was taken, for example, of the public libraries[2]. The gymnasia and the provision of games were the care of the *agonothetai* and *choregoi*. Order was maintained by special *astynomoi*, and the public cults had their appointed priests.

We would gladly know in greater detail than Strabo gives how the State took care of the poor and thus avoided revolutions. It was not, in fact, very difficult for a city that controlled a large part of the world corn-trade to provide an abundant food-supply for its population. At the same time the Rhodians, even more than the Athenians, relied upon imported corn. The large export of wine alone shows that the island itself produced but little corn. Some, indeed, may have been supplied by the other islands of the Dodecanese and by the Peraea. But it appears probable that these parts of the Rhodian State availed themselves of the chance of selling their wine along with that of the island and devoted themselves chiefly to its production. In any event, whether the task was difficult or not, intelligent organization was needed, and Strabo is witness that the Rhodians found a fair scheme for

[1] Maiuri, *Ann. d. Scuola Ital.* II, 1916, p. 146, No. 18.
[2] Maiuri, *N.S.* 4; F. Hiller von Gaertringen, *Gnomon*, II, 195; G. de Sanctis, *Riv. di Fil.* LIV, 167 *sqq.*; C. Wendel, *Spuren einer alten Bibliothek auf Rhodos*, Zentralblatt für Bibliothekswesen, XLVI, 1929; A. Vogliano, *Il πίναξ di una Biblioteca rodia*, Riv. indo-greco-italica, X, pp. 96 *sqq.*

satisfying the needs of the population and for preventing hunger riots. It is probably not an accident that we have no evidence at Rhodes of gifts of corn for feeding the populace. The present of corn made by Eumenes II was a substitute for money and was destined to pay for the education of children, and the permission to import corn from Sicily granted to Rhodes by the Senate in 169 B.C. was a war measure (p. 288).

The most important reasons, however, for the peaceful life of the Rhodian community are to be found not so much in the organization of the corn-supply as in its steadily growing prosperity and the resulting social and economic progress of the Rhodians. The prosperity of Rhodes depended very largely on its foreign policy, and this in its turn on the great care which the Rhodians devoted to the maintenance of their naval pre-eminence over other Greek states. As yet little is known of the technical progress achieved by the Rhodians in shipbuilding. The ancients admired their achievements immensely. We know from Strabo (xiv, 653) that the Rhodians themselves kept some of their docks strictly closed and that no stranger was admitted into them. It was not only because of the danger of damage which might be done to the ships by agents of some foreign power like Philip's emissary Heracleides (p. 145), but also because the Rhodians had secret devices which they sought to keep for themselves. The Rhodians showed their engineering skill in countering the attacks of Demetrius and it is evident that they improved their technique after the siege[1]; as we have seen, Rhodian war-engines were sent to help the citizens of Sinope. But they also enjoyed a like reputation as shipbuilders, and it is not impossible that a careful study of the ship monuments of Rhodes (see below, p. 637 sq.) may reveal some of the novelties invented by the Rhodians in this field. Inscriptions supply evidence of the care which the Rhodians took of their dockyards. In some Rhodian inscriptions set up to commemorate war services we find not only names of those who served in the navy as soldiers and officers but also of men connected with the docks. In one inscription (S.G.D.I. 4335; Maiuri, N.S. 5) we have at the end of the list the name of a shipbuilder and of the workmen. It is interesting to observe that all the workmen (six names are preserved) are Rhodian citizens, from which we may conclude that slaves and foreigners were not admitted to the docks even in that capacity. In another similar inscription (M. Chaviaras, Ἀρχ. ἐφ. 1915, p. 128, no. 1) are found the names of a chief ship-guard

---

[1] H. Diels, Laterculi Alexandrini, Abh. d. Berl. Akad. 1904, Col. 8.

(ἀρχιναυφύλαξ) and of a guard (φύλαξ), very probably belonging to the police force of the docks.

The navy of Rhodes was highly organized and consisted of all kinds of craft from quinqueremes downwards, with a hierarchy of officers and skilled seamen and marines. The fighting men on board were Rhodian citizens, as we know from lists of soldiers and officers[1], and the same may be true of the sailors and rowers[2]. Whether naval service was compulsory or voluntary we do not know, nor how long it lasted or how often a Rhodian might be called upon. Most of the ships were built by rich citizens, the trierarchs, who in time of war provided pay for the crews, but on the understanding that the State would reimburse them[3]. The emulation of the trierarchs was kept up by competitions between the ships, and a victory in such an *agon* was counted a very high distinction[4]. The Rhodian sailors, whether in the navy or the merchant fleet, enjoyed a great reputation for bravery and skill among all the Greeks. One piece of their sea-lore time has spared in a Rhodian sailor's song recently found in Egypt (*P. Oxy.* 1383; A. Körte, *Arch. Pap.* VII, 1924, p. 141).

The most lasting of Rhodian achievements in nautical matters was probably the famous Rhodian Law. It is characteristic of the state of our information that our only evidence on the Rhodian Law consists of a fragment of the Roman jurist Paulus (*Dig.* 14, 2, 1, cf. *Sent.* 2, 7, 1) who mentions the *lex Rhodia de iactu*. Appended to this fragment (l. 9) is a statement of Volusius Maecianus who speaks of a *decretum* of an emperor Antoninus (Antoninus Pius or M. Aurelius) in which the emperor directs that in naval suits the 'law of the Rhodians' should be taken into consideration so far as it does not contradict the Roman law. From these references is derived the description of the law in Isidore of Seville (*Orig.* 5, 17). The quasi-historical evidence which is contained in the title of and the introduction to the so-called *lex Rhodia* of the Byzantine period has no value, the title and the introduction being compiled in the twelfth century. Meagre as our evidence is, it shows that the current sea-law of the Mediterranean, the rules which were known to every seaman and of which

---

[1] *Explor. arch. de Rhodes*, Bull. de l'ac. de Danemark, 1905, pp. 48 *sqq.*; cf. *Ditt.*³ 455.

[2] If the καθήμενοι or παρακαθήμενοι of two inscriptions (M. Chaviaras, ᾽Αρχ. ἐφ. 1915, p. 128, n. 1; Hiller von Gaertringen, *Ath. Mitt.* xx, 1895, pp. 222 *sqq.*; *Ditt.*³ 1225) are oarsmen.

[3] Aristotle, *Pol.* VIII (v), 5, 1304 *b*.

[4] On this and the Rhodian trierarchy in general see Maiuri, *N.S.* 18, cf. 21.

the Roman administration and the Roman jurists had to take account in building up their own sea-law, was commonly called in the Mediterranean the law of the Rhodians. This implies that the Rhodians, in the period of their rule, enforced on the seas a set of rules which probably sought to sum up and perhaps to codify[1] all that the Greeks had previously achieved in this field, a law which thus was acceptable to all who used the sea.

About the Rhodian army less is known than about the navy. The general belief of modern scholars is that the army consisted exclusively of mercenaries. This belief is founded on the provision for the raising of mercenaries in Crete in the treaty between Rhodes and Hierapytna (*Ditt.*[3] 581, l. 40–5). We may however deduce from a statement of Livy (xxxiii, 18, 3) that along with detachments of allies most of the soldiers of the Rhodian land army were recruited in the Peraea of Rhodes[2]. These soldiers probably served for money and so far may be called mercenaries[3], but it is to be remembered that the inhabitants of the Peraea were incorporated in the Rhodian *damoi* (p. 633). It is, however, worthy of note that service in the land army was apparently regarded as inferior to service in the navy. While highborn Rhodians never fail to mention in their *cursus honorum* that they began their public life by serving in the navy as marines, they never mention service of the same type in the army. It was probably taken for granted that service in the army, except as an officer or general, was no occupation for a respectable Rhodian. The Rhodian army stood under the command of *strategoi* and *hegemones* and was divided between the island and the Peraea. In time of war a generalissimo was sometimes appointed. It is not probable that the Rhodians maintained a standing army, though during the short period in which they had considerable overseas possessions they may have kept permanent garrisons in some cities. The high regard in which service in war was held is attested by the beautiful monuments built in honour or to the memory of heroes on sea or land in the form of a ship's stern or of a panoply or trophy[4]. Some of these monuments are very fine, especially the

---

[1] The existence of a written code of sea-laws compiled by the Rhodians is not attested in our evidence.

[2] M. Holleaux, *B.C.H.* xvii, 1893, p. 60 and E. Meyer, *Die Grenzen der hell. Staaten*, p. 54, have shown that the Pisuetae, Nisuetae, Tamiani and probably the Arei mentioned in the passage are all of them tribes of the Peraea (the Livian *ex Africa* is corrupt).

[3] See the fragmentary inscription, Maiuri, *Ann. d. Scuola Ital.* iv–v, 482 *sqq.*

[4] Maiuri, *N.S.* 22; H. v. Gaertringen, *Gnomon*, ii, p. 197. See Volume of Plates iii, 116, *a*.

ship's stern cut in the rock near the entrance into the Acropolis of Lindus[1], and it is natural to compare them with the Nike of Samothrace (p. 675).

It is striking, indeed, how high was the spirit of comradeship. Such a spirit is indeed characteristic of all Hellenistic armies. It is a common feature of the military dedications all over the Hellenistic world that officers and men appear together in the inscription, and that in the appended lists of dedicants no distinction is made between officers and privates. But in Rhodes alone do we find associations of men who served on the same ship. The ties of comradeship formed during service were made permanent, and officers and men alike belonged to the same associations of ex-service men (οἱ στρατευσάμενοι), which, beyond doubt, did much to keep alive in many a Rhodian citizen the spirit of military valour, of patriotism and of comradeship.

The normal career of Rhodians of good birth may be reconstructed from the inscriptions. Though the highest offices, both civil and military, and the more eminent priesthoods were, in practice at least, the monopoly of an aristocracy of birth, wealth and state service, even the noblest Rhodians began their career as private soldiers in the fleet. After that their advancement begins[2]. As an example may be given the *cursus honorum* of one Polycles, son of Sosus, as attested by an inscription set up by his grandchildren. After serving as a private in the fleet, he became a *hegemon* in the army without salary, then commanded first light vessels and then a squadron of quinqueremes and finally held a high command either on the island itself or on the mainland. The climax of his military career was that he was *navarch*[3], and after that was three times appointed general of the land forces in the Peraea. At this point begins the list of his civil distinctions. He was *prytanis* during the First Mithridatic War and at the same time adviser to the *navarch*, Demagoras, and took part in the funeral ceremonial for fallen citizens. During this war and later he supported exceptionally burdensome liturgies, being probably a very rich man. He twice built a quadrireme and was active in his support of the gymnasia and the games and in providing choruses. He received honours from his fellow-soldiers, from citizen associations, from allied communities and foreign cities.

[1] See Volume of Plates iii, 116, *b*.
[2] Maiuri, *N.S.* 18. The career of Polycles falls in the period of the First Mithridatic War, but it may be regarded as typical.
[3] The present writer would read ναυαρ]χήσαντα instead of ναυμα] χήσαντα as Maiuri.

No doubt he added to his military positions the practice of diplomacy. Such was the career of a Rhodian even in the time when Rome overshadowed the free Greek states.

We do not know how large was the population of the cities of Rhodes and of the State as a whole. No ancient statistics are available, and modern conditions are misleading, for Rhodes is nowadays an agricultural not a commercial community. Nor do we know what was the proportion of citizens, slaves and foreigners. If, however, we analyse the population of Rhodes according to its political rights and social standing we find it highly differentiated. The full citizens are those who belong to one of the old cities of Rhodes. They append to their names the name of their fathers and the name of the *damos* to which they belong. Next to the full citizens stood those who had the right of naming their father but did not belong to a *damos*. As will be seen later, there were great numbers of foreigners in Rhodes, and it is no wonder that many of them tried to become in one way or another Rhodian citizens. It was not easy. Foreigners first received the right of residence, the *epidamia*, and later might be advanced to the standing of a 'Rhodian,' a kind of minor franchise. But no examples are known of a foreigner who became a full citizen. On the contrary those born of one Rhodian parent became a kind of political mongrel with the name of *matroxenos*, *i.e.* born of a foreign mother. The constitution of such a mixed family is well illustrated by an inscription of about 200 B.C. (Maiuri, *N.S.* 19). In a well-to-do Rhodian family of prosperous bankers the grandfather was a regular Rhodian citizen. He married a foreign woman, and his son was therefore a Rhodian, but only a *matroxenos*. Finally his grandson, perhaps in turn born of a foreign mother, was not reckoned as a citizen but as a foreigner, a Samian with the right of residence.

A special class was that of *paroikoi* and *katoikoi*. Their standing is a riddle. We have two references to a special group of residents in the city of Lindus, 'resident and holding land'[1] ($\kappa\alpha\tau\omicron\iota\kappa\epsilon\hat{\upsilon}\nu\tau\epsilon\varsigma$ $\kappa\alpha\grave{\iota}$ $\gamma\epsilon\omega\rho\gamma\epsilon\hat{\upsilon}\nu\tau\epsilon\varsigma$). In the first of the two they are called aliens ($\xi\acute{\epsilon}\nu\omicron\iota$), and yet they were permanent residents and land-owners and apparently well-to-do people, since the city of Lindus decrees they should take part in the provision of choruses. Parallels from Asia Minor suggest that these *katoikoi* were natives of Rhodes, but belonged to the pre-Hellenic population of the island. It is possible that this class was also widely spread in the Peraea and formed there the population of the 'country.'

[1] *I.G.* XII, 1, 762, and *Arch.-Ep. Mitth.* XVIII, 1895, p. 123, no. 4.

Our scanty evidence produces the impression of a strict exclusiveness if not of the Rhodian citizens in general at least of the
group of aristocratic families. They have their own associations
of an archaic character, based on a mixture of religious and family
ties. No foreigners were admitted to these associations and on
the other hand no good Rhodian would take an active part in the
associations reserved for the foreigners. Families were kept alive
by adoption, a habit as widely spread at Rhodes as at Rome.
Lastly, the Rhodians educated their children and took their
exercise in gymnasia which were strictly reserved for Rhodian
citizens[1]. We have seen in the inscription about Polycles that those
who granted honours to him were his former colleagues as magistrate, his fellow-soldiers, members of eight associations of the
type described above, and, finally, allies and foreign cities. Not
one of the associations of foreigners at Rhodes presumes to vote
any honour to him—a striking contrast to the practice which
prevailed in Rome. If we take into account how much the
citizens of Rhodes were supposed to do for the State in the naval
service, in the docks, as public officers and members of the
council, we need not wonder that the economic life of Rhodes
was based, not on the work of Rhodian citizens, but on that of
foreigners and of slaves.

Among the foreigners also we may distinguish different classes.
The right of residence seems to have been a kind of distinction carrying with it the right to the description *metoikos*[2] and
differentiating its possessors from 'aliens.' It is possible that
some *metoikoi* were freedmen[3]. Foreigners and freedmen formed
the most active and the most numerous body of the free residents
of Rhodes. In their epitaphs and in the inscriptions bearing on
their associations—the only evidence which we have of them—
they almost never tell us of their occupation. Many of them,
however, were very rich. They take part in the liturgies of the
state, they make liberal benefactions to the associations to which
they belong. It is evident that they become rich by productive
work—no doubt, commerce, banking, industry. Their proven-
ance supports this suggestion. Most of them come from regions
which had brisk commercial relations with Rhodes. The majority
are natives of Asia Minor, the Greek islands, Syria and Phoenicia
and Egypt. Very few Greeks from Southern Italy and Sicily are

---

[1] *I.G.* xii, 1, 46.   [2] *I.G.* xii, 1, 382.

[3] In *I.G.* xii, 1, 383, a former public slave becomes *metoikos* and also is
granted by the Council the rights of an 'alien,' which permits him to take
part in the provision of choruses.

found among them and not very many from Greece itself and from the Black Sea region. It is striking not to find Romans and romanized Italians. They were, perhaps, too proud to settle on an island where they would have such restricted rights.

Excluded from public life and from the aristocratic associations of the citizens, the foreigners developed a life of their own in the scores of associations which they formed all over the island. All these associations are religious; some, if not all of them, provide for a burial for their members[1]. None of them are strictly national or vocational. In all of them we find a mixture of men of various origin and probably men of different professions. Thus in the inscription cited below (*S.E.G.* ɪɪɪ, 674) the great benefactor of the association is a man from Selge. In the same document are mentioned three other foreigners, one from Phaselis, another a Galatian, and the third an Arab. Some associations admit slaves. Otherwise slaves, especially public slaves, have their own associations[2].

The slave population seems to have been very large. The public slaves form the upper class and intermarry with foreigners. Next come the class of slaves born in Rhodes, which corresponds to the home-bred slaves of other cities, and finally a mass of those who were bought in the slave-market and who are designated in their short epitaphs by the name of their country of origin. Most of them came from Asia: Lydians, Phrygians, Cilicians, Cappadocians, Galatians, Syrians, Armenians, Medians. There are very few from Thrace, some from South Russia—Scythians, Sarmatians, and Maeotians.

To sum up, Rhodes enjoyed a long and glorious life. By her energy and skill she created for a while conditions which made commerce possible and profitable, and that not for herself alone. She did her best to keep peace among the Greeks, to safeguard liberty for the Greek cities and to combat destructive forces in Greek life. Submission to a monarch seemed to her more dangerous than an alliance with a city-state in Italy. She could not foresee that this sister Republic would become a greater menace than any Hellenistic monarch. And, last but not least, from the beginning to the end, Rhodes was a home of Greek civilization, Greek learning and Greek art. A glance at the long list of names of the sculptors active at Rhodes[3] or even the reading of the Lindian Chronicle will show how active a part Rhodes took in the building up and the spread of Greek civilization. Her greatest

---

[1] See especially Maiuri, *Ann. d. Scuola Ital.* ɪv–v, 223 *sqq.*; *S.E.G.* ɪɪɪ, 674.   [2] *I.G.* xɪɪ, 1, 31.

[3] See F. Hiller von Gaertringen in *P.W. s.v.* Rhodos, Anhang, ɪɪ.

sons, indeed, one a Rhodian by birth, the other by adoption, Panaetius and Posidonius, had a widespread influence on the hellenization of Rome (pp. 459 *sqq.*), possessing as they did instincts and intellects which may even be called Roman rather than Greek.

III. DELOS. ITS COMMERCE, CONSTITUTION, SOCIAL AND ECONOMIC CONDITIONS

As has been said, close relations existed between Rhodes and Delos, especially in the third century B.C. It was natural for Delos, the age-old sacred island of Apollo, the seat of an ancient religious federation, to become a trading and banking centre of importance. The *panegyris* of Delos attracted large masses of pilgrims and the sanctity of the place guaranteed safety for deposits which were under the care of Apollo and of his attendants.

So long, however, as the island was a subject or subject ally of Athens, she could not look for commercial development of any importance. The situation changed when in 315/4 B.C. Delos recovered complete independence (vol. VI, p. 485). She soon became the centre of the Ptolemaic Island League and therefore no negligible factor in the political and economic life of the Aegean. We hear occasionally of Delos lending money to the islands (probably for paying the contribution to Demetrius) and trying to collect it in 280 B.C., not without difficulties, with the help of Philocles, king of the Sidonians and admiral of Ptolemy (Durrbach, *Choix*, 18; Ditt.[3] 391). After the collapse of the League Delos enjoyed the protection and patronage of the Antigonids, who sought to find in her a substitute for their enemy—Athens. The corn-trade and some commerce in other products of the North concentrated gradually at Delos. It is no wonder that the banking operations of the island assumed at this period ever growing proportions. This is true, not so much of the banking of the temple, which was strictly limited in its operations and gave loans on very precise conditions, as of the business of many private bankers, most of them foreigners, who took an active part in the corn-trade and were no doubt connected with the banking houses of Rhodes. Corn attracted to Delos both sellers and buyers, and both brought with them in exchange other goods. Relations with Egypt and with the cities in the North—Cyzicus, Lampsacus, Abydos, Byzantium, Chalcedon, Olbia and Panticapaeum—were firmly established and lasting[1]. This fact accounts for the gradual growth

[1] Durrbach, note to *Choix*, 46.

of the foreign colony at Delos, composed partly of residents in the city, partly of visitors. The earliest mention (about 178 B.C.?) of an important group of such foreign traders is the honorary inscription for Heliodorus, the prime minister of King Seleucus IV of Syria, set up by a group of shipowners and storehouse-owners of Berytus, who probably had important trade relations with Delos of a permanent, not merely casual, character. These were not, of course, the first oriental merchants of whom this can be said (Durrbach, *Choix*, no. 72). Meanwhile, the Syrian kings came to rely more and more in the development of their trade on their Phoenician cities and the Greek and Italian markets (see vol. VII, p. 191). For example, from the fourth century B.C. onward we have abundant evidence of Tyrian merchants at Delos (the earliest is in *C.I.S.* I, 114), and about the same time many important business men came to reside in Delos from the neighbouring islands, such as Eutychus of Chios (Durrbach, *Choix*, 43 and note). The first Italians arrived a little later.

A new era began for Delian commerce in 167 or 166 when the Romans declared Delos 'free of taxes,' which is commonly interpreted as the proclamation of Delos as a free port. This measure of the Senate cannot be explained by a desire to promote the interests of the few Italian merchants and bankers who had at that time business in the Aegean Sea. Their influence with the Senate was negligible, and the Senate had not the knowledge of economics needed to foresee how its decision would influence the commercial life of the Aegean Sea. It was as we have seen a strictly political measure, intended to inflict on Rhodes an exemplary punishment, and at the same time to promote the interests of Rome's faithful ally, the rival of Rhodes—Athens. The sufferers were not only the Rhodians but also and no less the native Delians themselves. Whether these latter had carried on trade and banking before 167 B.C. or not we do not know. What our ancient sources suggest about them points rather to the fact that they lived from the revenue derived from pilgrims and merchants. For them the decree of Rome meant ruin. The administration of the temple was handed over to the Athenians, and all duties from foreigners were abolished.

It is hard to say whether the gift of the Romans was of great material value to the Athenians or not. The few Athenians who engaged in profitable business at Delos were of little concern to the State of Athens, and the free port of Delos did as much injury to what was left of the commerce of the Piraeus as it did to Rhodes. The new status of Delos merely meant a bonus for speculators and profiteers—that class of cosmopolitan merchants and bankers in whose hands was concentrated the international commerce of those days.

A sequence of further acts of political vengeance contributed to the increasing prosperity of this class. The constant watch over Rhodes and the endeavour to prevent her from building up her navy again gave an opportunity to the pirates to carry on their business on a large scale (p. 292). The free port of Delos, left completely in the hands of bankers, merchants and traders, was the best possible place for them to sell their plunder, especially their prisoners, who were sold *en masse* to Italy as agricultural, industrial and domestic slaves[1]. The destruction of Carthage and Corinth as cities ruined large communities of prosperous and energetic merchants and forced those of them who survived and had something of their capital left to look for another home where they could carry on their hereditary business. Finally, the conditions which prevailed in the East—the growing disintegration of the various political units and their gradual impoverishment—turned the attention of traders in Asia Minor, Syria and Egypt to Italy, which gradually became the richest market in the world.

The residents of Southern Italy and Sicily were for a long time in close connection with the Greek world first through Athens, then through Rhodes and Delos. Allies of the Romans, Romans themselves in the eyes of the Orient, protected by Roman magistrates and the Roman-Italian armies, the Greeks and hellenized Italians of Southern Italy could not miss the great opportunity which the growing importance of the Italian market, the increased production of Italy, especially in olive-oil and wine[2], and the opening of the harbour of Delos presented them. With the money which they acquired during the great wars of Rome in the West and in the East they began gradually to settle down in Delos and to get into immediate touch with the producers of Italy, the slave-traders of Greece and the merchants of Asia Minor, Phoenicia and Egypt. The proud island of Rhodes, celebrated for her laws and honesty, was not exactly the place of residence which the Italian dealers would choose. At Délos they had a free hand and complete security.

---

[1] Trade in slaves began of course earlier than the time of the free port. See the interesting inscription published by R. Vallois, Ἀραί, in *B.C.H.* XXXVIII (1914), pp. 250 *sqq.* Piracy was endemic in the Aegean.

[2] See the inscriptions of the Italian *olearii* and *oinopolai* found at Delos (Durrbach, *Choix*, 141–2), and the abundance of fragments of jars of Italian origin and with Italian stamps (*ib.* p. 230).

After 167 B.C. Delos was nominally a cleruchy of Athens. This meant that Athenian magistrates carried out the administration of the temple and of the city, while the Athenian residents of the island had the semblance of forming a community, which in fact depended wholly on Athens. The new Athenian settlers began at once a bitter feud with the Delians, a struggle for existence. The Delians succumbed, and were evacuated to Achaea in Greece (p. 294). The Athenians and the motley crowd of international merchants were left alone.

No doubt some of the Athenians had their share in the brisk business which was developing on Delos. But they were few in comparison with the masses of foreign traders—Italians and Orientals. The more numerous these last became, the less interesting Delos was for Athens. Finally by a natural and slow process the Athenians were practically absorbed by the foreigners. After about 130 B.C. decrees of the Athenians, even the honorary decrees, are no longer found, but are replaced by decrees of a composite body: the Athenians, both residents of Delos and visitors, the Romans, that is Italians, and the rest of the Greeks— the slightly hellenized oriental merchants; the formula varies, but in all the versions it is expressly mentioned that these men are merchants and shipowners.

This composite body kept no doubt a close grasp upon the island. The Athenian governors (the *epimeletai*) and the other Athenian magistrates of the island represented the ruling power, but had probably very little to say as regards the vital questions which concerned the community. The foreign bodies were not loose aggregations of individuals. They were organized into associations (κοινά). In describing the activity of these associations we cannot use the word companies, in the sense of large business concerns. They were religious and social groups with a national character and with common interests—merchants, shipowners and storehouse-owners. The combination of the last two features was new in the history of the Greek associations. Of these there were many all over the Greek world, scores of them for example in Rhodes. None, however, were both national and professional. Their peculiar evolution in Delos may be regarded, perhaps, as due to the combination of a natural process with oriental traditions.

The Italians grouped themselves around the cult of Mercury and Maia, so popular in Southern Italy (*e.g.* at Pompeii), and around the cults of Apollo and Poseidon, again typical cults for Campania and the rest of Southern Italy. Soon—about the end of the second century B.C.—they built a large religious and social centre of their common life near the temple of Apollo, the meeting-hall of the Italians (*Italike Pastas*). Each group had its own magistrates, called according to the Italian traditions 'magistri,' whose duty it was to provide for the cult. In later times the three leading Italian associations sometimes took common action. In these cases they were represented by twelve presidents (*magistri*) who acted on behalf of their respective societies. A separate group of *Kompetaliastai* (worshippers of the *Lares compitales*) was formed by slaves and freedmen of the rich Italians.

Among the foreign groups of the population of Delos the Italians no doubt were the best organized. The *Italike Pastas* is unique, and is far more impressive than the sanctuary and club-house of the Berytians or the cosmopolitan sanctuaries of the Syrians and Alexandrians. On the other hand the few documents which speak of the activity of the three leading Italian associations do not justify us in assuming, with some eminent modern scholars, the existence at Delos in the late second century B.C. of a regular *conventus civium Romanorum* or of a kind of precursor of such a *conventus*, a permanent body of Italian residents which was recognized as such both by Athens and the Roman government. We must not forget that in the second century B.C. most of the Italians were not Roman citizens, and that the regular *conventus civium Romanorum* appeared in the Orient at a much later date, not earlier than the beginning of the Roman Empire.

How exclusive the Italians at Delos were it is not easy to say. They spoke both Latin and Greek, they intermarried freely with the Greeks and the Orientals and educated their children according to the Greek fashion in the Greek gymnasia. On the other hand they seem to have kept strictly to the religious traditions of Italy. The numerous frescoes which adorn some of the street altars of Delos and the adjoining house walls have been ingeniously interpreted[1] to show that the Italians of Delos worshipped in their houses and at the street corners the Genius, the Lares and the Penates of the Italian domestic religion in exactly the same fashion as was done at Rome and in the cities of Latium and Campania at the same time or a little later. But it must be said that this interpretation cannot be regarded as established beyond doubt. Most of the 'Romans' of Delos came from South Italy, and we do not know whether the Samnites and the Oscans had the same household religion as the Latins whose representa-

[1] By M. Bulard, *Explor. Arch. de Délos*, IX, and *La religion domestique dans la colonie italienne de Délos*, 1926.

tives at Delos were but few. Moreover, very little is known of Greek domestic religion and we are therefore not able to recognize and isolate the Greek elements in the ceremonies of Delian domestic and street worship.

Alongside the Italians stood the oriental merchants—Alexandrians in great numbers, Syrians, Phoenicians, men from various parts of Asia Minor. Many of them were permanent residents of Delos. Like the Italians, some of them were organized in rich and powerful associations, such as the *Herakleistai* of Tyre, the *Poseidoneistai* of Berytus, and the representatives of a professional merchant association of Alexandria. Syrians no doubt predominated. A recently found and still unpublished list of ephebes of 119/8 B.C. enumerates almost exclusively boys of Syrian origin. Hundreds of other foreigners came to Delos for a shorter or longer stay, among them the picturesque figures of Gerrhaeans from the Persian Gulf, of Nabataeans from Petra, of Minaeans from Southern Arabia and of Arabs. And sovereigns of the surviving Hellenistic states, the last Ptolemies and Seleucids, the Bithynian, Cappadocian and Pontic kings, vied in securing for themselves the good services of the Delian merchant community.

The artificial prosperity of Delos did not last for very long. There were no natural reasons why Delos should be a great trading centre. It was not the two catastrophes of 88 and 69, the repeated looting of the city by Mithridates and the pirates, which undermined her prosperity. The reason for Delos' decay lay deeper. So soon as normal and stable conditions were created in the East, the pirates exterminated and the safety of trade restored, there was no reason for commerce to concentrate at Delos. Puteoli and Ostia were better centres for the Egyptian and Syrian trade with Italy and Rhodes for the same trade with Greece. And it seems very probable that this fact was recognized by the Romans, and that at some time the Roman government did away with the free port privilege and the immunity of the Delians. Otherwise it is not possible to account for the passing of the Lex Gabinia Calpurnia of 58 B.C. (Durrbach, *Choix*, 163), by which immunity was given to the island from *vectigalia*, which were probably paid to Rome, among them of a special tax for the custody of public corn. If immunity was given to Delos by this law, it implies that the immunity of 167/6 no longer existed.

In the hundred years of her prosperity Delos was a unique phenomenon in the history of the ancient world. A barren and arid little island, with rather poor vegetation, with very bad harbours, with the temple towering over the humble houses of the servants of the gods, developed in a very short period into a large and prosperous community. While in the early days of Delos the city was an annex to the temple, now the temple became a kind of appendix to the community, which, in form a city, was really a loose aggregation of merchants, shipowners and bankers with the corresponding amount of labour, mostly servile. It was a new phenomenon among the city-states of Greece. The motley population of Delos had not the slightest inclination to become a city. They were perfectly happy to live the peculiar life of a free merchant community with no civic duties to fulfil and no liturgies to bear.

In earlier times it was probably the temple which dominated the place. The resources of the temple, gifts and foundations which were lavished on it by rich benefactors, made it an economic and financial force in Greece. From the second half of the third century onwards the centre of gravity shifted gradually from the temple to the city. We have good information about the finances of the temple in the accounts of the Athenian Amphictiones for the early period[1], in those of the *Hieropes* for the period of independence[2] and in those of the Athenian *epimeletai* for the times of the cleruchy[3]. The sources of income and the expenditure remained the same in the various periods. The regular income of the temple consisted of the money in which the rent for the use of farms and gardens on Delos, Rheneia and Myconos and of houses in the city was paid, of the interest on sums lent out to private people and cities at a comparatively low rate, and of small gifts in the temple collection-boxes ($\theta\eta\sigma\alpha\nu\rho\omega\iota$). The farms and houses were rented, the first for ten, the second for five years to private people. In the later Athenian period a model contract ($\iota\epsilon\rho\grave{\alpha}$ $\sigma\nu\gamma\gamma\rho\alpha\phi\acute{\eta}$) was drawn up regulating the renting of real estate. The money for the loans came mostly from gifts and foundations bestowed on the temple by many crowned and uncrowned donors for sacrifices, games and the like. A reserve capital in specie was gradually formed and kept in jars, amounting in the later period to about 120,000 drachmae. Another reserve consisted of the votive offerings in precious metals. The income of the temple and capital owned by it were never very large. The whole of the property of the temple, including the sacred buildings, which of course involved outlay and did not yield any direct income, has been estimated at about 5½ million drachmae[4]. Of

---

[1] *Ditt.*[3] 153.　　　　　[2] Durrbach, *Comptes des hiéropes.*
[3] P. Roussel, *Délos colonie athénienne*, pp. 383 *sqq.*
[4] By Homolle. The calculation is admittedly in part hypothetical.

all this capital the part which yielded income was not larger than 200,000 drachmae, and the part of it which was available at any given time and could be exploited directly never amounted to more than 50,000 drachmae. In the times when the richest residents lived in modest houses rented from the temple and richer and better houses were rare in the city of Delos, the capital and the income of the temple meant a good deal, but it became relatively a trifle once Delos became the centre of international commerce, banking and speculation with large capital sums invested in business.

There is little evidence to show the size of the fortunes owned by the rich residents of Delos in the later period of its existence. However, a comparison with other parts of the ancient world at the same period, conclusions drawn from large benefactions given by private citizens to their own and to foreign cities and other scattered evidence show that there was in the second century b.c. a large accumulation of capital in the hands of a few private persons. The importance of Delos in the business life of the period makes it probable that the merchants and bankers of the island were not poorer than their contemporaries in Asia Minor, Syria and the commercial cities of the North.

There is also scattered information which confirms this statement. Thus an epigram dedicated to a rich Cypriote, Simalus by name, one of the most influential men at Delos, by an Athenian grandee, Stolus, probably himself a business man, describes the beauty of Simalus' palace and the lavishness of his hospitality. Like Stolus himself, Simalus was a friend of Egyptian kings and of Roman consuls. Wealth and influence were hereditary in his family, which was widely scattered, one branch residing in Tarentum. The young boys of both the Cypro-Delian and the Tarentine branches of the family received their education in the famous gymnasia of Delos and of Athens[1]. Another interesting instance is Philostratus of Ascalon, a rich Delian banker who became a citizen of Naples and thus a member of the Italian colony of Delos. His rich house at Delos near Mt Cythnus[2] has been discovered. Simalus and Philostratus, both of whom were Orientals, were rivalled by opulent Italian families. Two examples will suffice—the banker Maraeus Gerillanus and the famous family of the Orbii[3].

[1] Durrbach, *Choix*, 127–8 and the texts quoted in his notes.   [2] *Ib.* 132.
[3] Evidence on the influential Italians has been collected in full by Hatzfeld (see bibliography), Durrbach, *Choix*, 138 and 146 with notes. It is interesting to note that while the grandees of the second century were

A great part of the income of these rich men was invested by them in improving and building up the steadily growing city. Delos was never a very beautiful place. The temple square early became overcrowded and the buildings round it were not planned out systematically. Some of these, of the early Hellenistic period, were handsome, some ugly, others neither one nor the other. Still lower was the artistic standard of the Athenian period. No public building of this period can claim to be called beautiful. The various smaller public monuments—chapels, exedrae, honorary monuments—are strikingly poor, and so are the statues. Not very much better were the private and the semi-private buildings— the *Italike Pastas*, the Berytian club-house, the private sanctuaries and the hundreds of private residential houses, some of them with fine wall-paintings or exquisite mosaics. None of them, however, can vie with the contemporary similar buildings of the larger Italian cities such as Pompeii. Moreover, the few finer private residential houses were lost in the mass of commercial buildings, some of them belonging to the temple—blocks of flats, inns and restaurants, shops, docks and warehouses. Every little space in the crowded and doubtless dirty centre of the city was taken up by a shop or a little factory. It is evident that the residents of Delos were not very much interested either in the temple or in the city. Delos was for them not their home but their business residence. What they cared for most was not the city or the temple but the harbours, the famous sacred harbour, and especially the three adjoining so-called basins with their large and spacious storehouses. It is striking that while these storehouses are open to the sea there is almost no access to them from the city. This shows that very few of the goods stored in them ever went as far as even the market-places of the city. Most of them came to the harbour, spent some time in the storehouses and moved on, leaving considerable sums in the hands of the Delian brokers. In fact in the Athenian period the city of Delos was but an appendix to the harbour. So soon as the activity of the harbour stopped, the city became a heap of ruins and it was again the temple which towered over these ruins in splendid isolation.

most of them foreigners, the rich men of the third century are Delians. See, for example, the inscription of Mnesalcus, the *proxenos* of a foreign city which he helps in her purchase of corn (*I.G.* xi, 4, 1049; M. Holleaux, *B.C.H.* xxxi, 1907, p. 375). In the second century most of the Greeks at Delos were Athenians (Durrbach, *op. cit.* p. 210; note to no. 130).

IV. THE SPREAD OF HELLENISTIC COMMERCE

The two merchant cities of Rhodes and Delos, with their peculiar development and life, are true representatives of the highly complicated and peculiar Hellenistic period. Their history, when examined in connection with a general study of the economic life and especially of the commerce of the last three centuries B.C., refutes easy generalizations, which some eminent scholars, both economists and historians, have recently revived, about the ancient world living in conditions of primitive house-economy. It is, therefore, not out of place to survey in brief what is known of the development of commerce in the Hellenistic period in general, for commerce was the most important factor in ancient economic life in all periods of ancient history.

It is no easy task to give such a survey. Our information is scanty and scattered. The literary sources are almost silent. Nothing comparable with the Athenian orators and other writers, especially Xenophon and Aristotle, who throw such a vivid light on the economic life of Athens in the fourth century B.C., is available for Hellenistic times. In comparison the stories in the pseudo-Aristotelian *Oeconomica* and references in Polybius (pp. 11 *sqq.*), together with anecdotes of the period collected by Athenaeus, and material derived from the poets are a very meagre harvest indeed. Far more important are inscriptions and papyri. Among the former the place of honour is occupied by the Delian inscriptions, among the latter by the correspondence of Zeno. Neither of these sources has yet been published in full or completely investigated from the economic point of view. Finally, the archaeological material—the ruins of the cities and especially the so-called small finds, first and foremost the coins—have been but little used for the reconstruction of Hellenistic economic development. Thus a satisfactory description of the commercial evolution of the ancient world in this period, so long as the main sources of our information are not collected and studied, remains a *pium desiderium*. What is offered here is merely a sketch pointing out problems rather than suggesting solutions.

Alexander's conquests made intercourse between the Orient and Greece much easier than it had been during the existence of the Persian Empire. In the West there was rapid development: Rome broke the power of Carthage to the advantage of the Greeks and herself secured an ascendancy which opened up important and increasing new areas in Western Europe to the economic and especially the commercial activity of the Greeks and hellenized Italians. Thus for the first time in the history of the ancient world a well-organized international commerce became possible, and towards its achievement much progress was made in the Hellenistic period.

All the forms of commerce which were inherited from the past gained ground during the three centuries after Alexander. Of this commerce there were three main branches. These are first the commercial relations of the Greek and hellenized world with the countries which had little or no share in Greek civilization and which were not governed by Greeks—the Iranian lands (from the middle of the third century), India, Central Asia and China in the East, Arabia and Central Africa in the South, and Western, Central, Northern and Eastern Europe and West Africa in the West. Second comes commercial intercourse between the various states, large and small, within the Hellenistic system. Finally there is trade inside the boundaries of the various Greek and hellenized communities. Of the trade that existed within the frontiers of the un-hellenized countries we know little. All this commerce may be subdivided into four main types. There is first, the caravan trade which connected the Greek world with Asia; second, river trade which was of great importance in Mesopotamia and Egypt, in Gaul, Germany, the Danube lands and South Russia; third, maritime trade which connected India with Arabia and Egypt, the shores of the Mediterranean with each other, the Mediterranean with the Black Sea and with the Northern Ocean and the Baltic Sea; and finally, local trade carried on with the help of all the three above-mentioned means of communications —land-routes, sea and rivers.

It is beyond doubt that commercial relations between the Greek world and Asia become more regular in the Hellenistic period than ever before, so far as the trade of the Asiatic lands with Syria and Egypt on the one hand and with the Bosporan kingdom on the other is concerned. It is important not to underestimate the commerce of the Persian Empire with India and the Far East in the pre-Hellenistic period. On this we have little direct information, but the fact that Persian art had so deep an influence both on Indian and on Chinese art shows how close these trading relations were[1]. In comparison the direct influence of Greek art on India, Central Asia and China in the Hellenistic period was but small. However,

[1] See the present writer's *Statuette d'un cavalier de la coll. de M*me *John D. Rockefeller*, Mon. et Mém. Piot, xxviii, 1927; cf. *Seminarium Kondako-vianum*, i, 1927, pp. 141 *sqq.* and *Artibus Asiae*, iv, 1927, p. 297.

it is very probable that the general impulse given to art which is notable at that time both in India and in China must in part be ascribed to the Greek influence[1]. We have, moreover, positive proofs of the existence of a lively intercourse between the Far East and Greek lands. It will be enough to adduce the deep influence of Greek art and industry on Parthia, the long existence of Greek states in Bactria and North India with their almost purely Greek coinage, the half-Greek character of the Kushan coins and of the material civilization of that empire[2], the finds of Greek textiles (probably of Syrian workmanship) in Mongolia[3] and a recent discovery on the trade route between South Russia and China in Zungaria (between the Altaï and Tien-shan) of a hoard of Panticapaean coins[4]. The Seleucids made great efforts to develop commerce with the Far East and diligently protected the trade routes in Mesopotamia and Iranian lands (vol. VII, pp. 173 sqq.). Their efforts were not without success, and the flourishing prosperity of Seleuceia on the Tigris testifies to the development both of the caravan trade and of the sea traffic in the Persian Gulf. In competition with the Seleucids the Ptolemies were active in building up commerce with Nubia and Central Africa and with Arabia and India. Their main endeavour was to establish direct relations between these lands and Alexandria, to the detriment of the Petraean commerce and especially of the caravan route which from Petra reached the Palestinian and Phoenician harbours through the cities of Transjordania.

Less known since less studied are the relations between the Greek and the Italian part of the Hellenistic world especially in the third century B.C. It is a well-established fact that Pompeii in its early Oscan period was deeply influenced by Alexandria and to a lesser extent by the cities of Asia Minor and Syria. Whether, however, the general aspect of life in this part of Italy in the third and second centuries B.C. is due to direct importation of products of Hellenistic art and industry or to a natural development of Graeco-Italian art and industry on Hellenistic lines it is very difficult to say, so long as the material is not carefully investigated. Better known are the relations between Italy and the Hellenistic

[1] See the present writer's *Inlaid Bronzes of the Han Dynasty*, 1927 (with bibliography).

[2] *Cambridge History of India*, I, chaps. XVII, XXII, XXIII, XXVI, cf. W. W. Tarn, *Notes on Hellenism in Bactria and India*, J.H.S. XXII, 1902, pp. 268 sqq.

[3] See the present writer, *The Animal Style in South Russia and China*, Princeton, 1929, pp. 84 sqq.

[4] E. Diehl, *Blätter für Münzfreunde*, 1923, no. 10–11.

lands in the second and first centuries, when Italians became prominent in the commerce and business life of the Aegean in general and began to lay the foundations of their commercial expansion in the West.

Commerce with Africa, India and the Far East no doubt contributed a great deal to the prosperity of many famous commercial cities of the Hellenistic world, such as Seleuceia on the Tigris and Alexandria. To these we may add, especially in the second century, the Phoenician cities, above all Tyre, whose currency became so prominent in the Near East and whose commerce was probably more important than that of Seleuceia in Pieria and Laodicea, the harbours of Antioch. Not less prominent was Berytus. Asiatic commerce probably helped to enrich Panticapaeum, and it may likewise be responsible to a certain extent for the revival of the cities of Asia Minor, especially Miletus, Smyrna and Ephesus. It is interesting to observe how the great Hellenistic monarchs sought to maintain and stabilize their influence, for example, in Miletus. It is significant that the gifts of the Seleucids to Miletus consist of great quantities of various aromatic gums, resins and the like from Arabia[1], while those of the Ptolemies are scores of elephant tusks[2].

It is an interesting fact—a precursor of what happened to Palmyra in the time of the Roman Empire—that in the later Hellenistic period the caravan lands of Arabia, especially the Petraeans, the Minaeans, the Sabaeans and the Gerrhaeans, began to emancipate themselves from the Greek cities of the Near East and sought to establish direct relations with the great markets of the West, especially Rhodes and Delos (pp. 640 *sqq.*). As we have seen, it was through the good offices of the merchants of these cities that a large part of the products which the caravans brought to Syria and the ships to Egypt reached customers in the West.

More important than foreign commerce was the trade between the members of the Hellenistic system in which gradually Italy was included. A glance at the references to the supplying of fish collected by Athenaeus (vi, 227 b–228 c) from Hellenistic writers shows how difficult was the problem of providing food for the population of most of the Greek cities, both for those which were, and those which were not, great centres of trade and industry. These cities never raised grain in sufficient quantities, especially after they began to vie with each other in producing wine and olive-oil; moreover Greek lands often experienced rainless springs and

[1] *O.G.I.S.* 214.
[2] *O.G.I.S.* 193; B. Haussoullier, *Rev. Phil.* xlv, 1921, pp. 45 *sqq.*; Plutarch, *Aratus*, 15.

summers which caused failures of crops. Nor was there abundance of fish, another staple food of the Greeks, or of olive-oil. Thus even in normal times most of the Greek cities were not able to live on the produce of their own territory. The situation became acute in times of bad harvests, of devastation by war or of plundering by pirates, more acute for the inland than for the maritime cities since land transport was slow and very expensive. Moreover the constant wars which raged all over the Mediterranean required large quantities of food for the comparatively large armies mostly of mercenaries. But it was not all supplied by requisitions and pillage. To buy food often appeared a better policy than to requisition it.

All this explains why commerce in food-stuffs and especially in corn assumed, as has been shown above, very large proportions in the Hellenistic world and required so much attention from all the states, both consumers and producers. The inscriptions which speak of measures taken by the cities for buying corn and for distributing it among their own population are excellent testimony for this[1]. The same is true for wine, olive-oil, fish and salt[2]. How large was the importation of food-stuffs of various kinds to the larger cities is shown by many documents in the correspondence of Zeno, which speaks of food-stuffs imported into Alexandria from Syria, Asia Minor and Greece[3]. It must not be forgotten that life in Hellenistic times became ever more refined, and that it was not only food for the poorer part of the population which was imported in large quantities, but such luxuries as are attested by the many Hellenistic anecdotes about food for which Athenaeus had so marked a predilection.

Besides food-stuffs the Hellenistic monarchies and the Greek cities required large quantities of raw materials the production of which was mostly concentrated in few and restricted areas,—metals, timber, pitch and tar, hemp and flax, etc.[4] Labour, too,

---

[1] These inscriptions have not yet been collected in full. On the well-known Samian inscriptions bearing on it see E. Ziebarth, *Zum samischen Finanz- und Getreidewesen*, Zeit. f. Num. xxxiv, 1924, pp. 356 *sqq.* See further, the Bibliography.

[2] For wine and olive-oil see E. Ziebarth, *Beiträge zur Geschichte des Seeraubs*, pp. 73 *sqq.*; for salt, Anon. περὶ αἰσχροκερδείας 73: ἁλῶν δὲ φόρτος ἔνθεν ἦλθεν ἔνθ' ἦλθεν; in G. A. Gerhard, *Phoinix von Kolophon*, 1909: cf. A. D. Knox in *Herodes, Cercidas*, etc., Loeb, 1929, pp. 229 *sqq.*

[3] *P. Cairo Zen.* 59012–14; *P.S.I.* iv, 428; H. Schaal, *Flussschiffahrt und Flusshandel im Altertum*, Festschrift…des Alten Gymnasiums zu Bremen, 1928, pp. 399 *sqq.*

[4] No full collection of material exists. A model investigation bearing on lumber, pitch and tar will be found in G. Glotz, *L'histoire de Délos d'après les prix d'une denrée*, Rev. E.G. xxix, 1916, pp. 281 *sqq.*

was largely imported, sometimes from far distant places. Slaves from foreign countries are a common phenomenon both in the Greek city-states and the monarchies. How considerable was the actual import and export of manufactured goods it is difficult to say. It may be regarded as certain that special products such as papyrus and parchment[1], perfumes and other cosmetics, various glass articles, especially beads, some special brands of textiles, rugs, finer articles of art and artistic industry[2], war-machines and some special types of arms and weapons were objects of import and export. The same, however, was hardly true of most of the everyday articles of use—domestic tools, agricultural implements, kitchen-ware of metal and pottery, ordinary clothes, shoes, slippers and the like. Some of these articles, especially clothes, were made at home, but most of them were, no doubt, produced by local artisans of the Greek cities, who were at the same time dealers in their own products. A good picture of such a dealer-artisan is given in the seventh mime of Herodas, which describes Cerdon, a typical city shoemaker. He is selling various shoes of fine quality which are produced in his own shop with the help of thirteen men in his employ. It reflects exactly the same conditions as we find in Pompeii at a much later period. Some artisans in order to avoid payment of taxes worked in the houses of their customers. Such a house-artisan is another Cerdon, whose activity is also described by Herodas[3]. The dyeing of shoes is carried out by a specialist—a *byrsodepses*. Another typical instance of small 'factories' or rather larger workshops are the shops which produced the large jars in which wine, olive-oil and the like were exported from such places as Rhodes, Thasos, Cnidus, Paros, Crete, the Pontic Heraclea, Sinope, and Chersonesus in the Crimea. The stamps of these jars show hundreds of names of potters (*kerameis*) and sometimes of masters of workshops (*ergasteriarchai*). Many of these names are those of resident aliens and even of slaves. A large number of names and the character of the factory-depôt found at Villanova in Rhodes show that we have to do with small and not very rich concerns.

For supplying the hundreds and thousands of markets, the numerous city-states of the Greek and hellenized world, the country population of the Hellenistic monarchies and the tribes

---

[1] See below p. 665 and G. Glotz, *Le prix du papyrus dans l'antiquité grecque*, Annales d'hist. écon. et soc. I, 1929.

[2] *E.g.* terracottas, Volume of Plates iii, 190, 192.

[3]   κατ' οἰκίην δ' ἐργάζετ' ἐμπολέων λάθρη,
          τοὺς γὰρ τελώνας πᾶσα νῦν θύρη φρίσσει.
                                                        VI, 63–4.

of Western, Central and North Europe and of the Near East with all the products which they needed[1] an army of merchants was required, both merchants *en gros* (*emporoi*), importers and exporters, and retail traders (*kapeloi*). Equally large was that of the shipowners (*naukleroi*) and caravan leaders (*synodiarchai*) and of storehouse-owners (*ekdocheis*). All these men and a large amount of labour which they employed concentrated in the great and smaller commercial cities, many of which grew large and rich through commerce in the Hellenistic period. It is true that most of them were not creations of that period, but for many of them it was the time of their most flourishing prosperity. It is worth while to enumerate some instances. Panticapaeum, Olbia, Tyras and Chersonesus on the north shore of the Black Sea were first and foremost wholesale exporters of corn, fish, hides, hemp and slaves from Russia. Most of the cities of the west shore of the Black Sea as Tomi, Istros, and Callatia, of the Thracian Bosporus as Byzantium and Chalcedon, of the Sea of Marmara, as Perinthus and especially Cyzicus (the last as important as Rhodes in the eyes of Strabo), of the Hellespont as Lampsacus and Abydos, and of the Thracian and Macedonian coasts, especially Abdera and Thessalonica, owed their prosperity to trade in the same products including metals which came from the mines of the southern Caucasus and northern Asia Minor through the cities of the south shore of the Black Sea (Trapezus, Sinope[2], Amisus, Heraclea) and from those of Thrace and Paeonia. Such ancient centres of commerce in Greece and Asia Minor as Corinth, Athens[3], Patrae, Gytheum in Greece, Halicarnassus, Xanthus and Tarsus in Asia Minor, not to speak of Miletus, Ephesus and Smyrna, remained great trading communities. To them we may add such creations of the Hellenistic period as Elaea, the harbour of Pergamum, Attaleia in Pamphylia and Seleuceia in Cilicia. As has been seen, there were prosperous Syrian, Phoenician and Palestinian commercial cities. In the West many ancient Greek cities still enjoyed a flourishing trade, such as Tarentum, Dicaearchia, Neapolis, Syracuse, Panormus, Massilia and Emporium.

[1] It is a fact familiar to all excavators that imported products become more frequent in the graves and ruins of the non-Greek population of the ancient world in Hellenistic times than they used to be in the earlier period.

[2] On the trade of Sinope see B. Grakov, *Ancient Greek pottery stamps with the names of the Astynomoi*, Moscow, 1929 (in Russian).

[3] On the revival of Athenian trade in the second century B.C. see S. Zhebelev, *On the history of Athens* (229–31 B.C.), St Petersburg, 1898, pp. 198 *sqq.* (in Russian), and W. S. Ferguson, *Hellenistic Athens*, pp. 278 *sqq.*, 297 *sqq.*

We know, chiefly from inscriptions, the names of some of those merchants who lived scattered all over the Hellenistic world and concentrated in larger groups in the most flourishing commercial cities. We have seen them at work in Alexandria, Panticapaeum, Rhodes and Delos, and have become acquainted with their associations. It is very probable that what is true of them is roughly true also of the merchants in other cities of the Hellenistic world. A notable feature of these groups was their international character. This is characteristic of Panticapaeum, Rhodes and Delos, and not less of Alexandria. A recently deciphered papyrus of the second century B.C.—a sea-loan granted to a group of merchants who dealt with the Somali coast—shows us a motley group of diverse origin engaged in trade probably in Alexandria: one of the merchants is a Lacedaemonian, another comes from Massilia, the banker through whom they act is an Italian, of their sureties two are citizens of Massilia, one of Carthage, one of Thessalonica and one of Elaea[1].

Another interesting feature of the time is the great part which rich merchants play in their respective cities, especially in the smaller ones. Their influence and activity is well attested by voluminous honorary decrees. Of such prominent merchants may be cited Aristagoras of Istros (*Ditt.*³ 708), Protogenes and Niceratus of Olbia (*Ditt.*³ 495 and 730), Posideos of the same city (*Ios. P.E.* I², 672, cf. 325), Acornion of Dionysopolis (*Ditt.*³ 762), Python of Abdera, who was able to mobilize a small private army of two hundred of his own slaves and freedmen (Diodorus, xxx, 6, Livy, XLIV, 12), and certain Romans, Vallius and the Apustii, of Abdera (*B.C.H.* XXXVII, 1913, p. 117, cf. XXXVIII, 1914, p. 63).

V. THE ORGANIZATION OF COMMERCE; CURRENCY; BANKING

Though we know many names of merchants and are able to realize their importance in the life of the Hellenistic period we know little of the organization of commerce. A good deal was done for commerce by the rival kings of the Hellenistic balance of power as they sought to attract trade to the cities of their own kingdoms. The Ptolemies endeavoured to get Indian trade concentrated in Egypt, whereas the Seleucids made the greatest efforts to divert it to the Persian Gulf and to Seleuceia on the

---

[1] U. Wilcken, *Punt-Fahrten in der Ptolemäerzeit*, Zeit. f. Aeg. Sprache, LX, 1925, pp. 86 *sqq.*; P. Meyer, *Zeit. d. Sav. Stiftung* (*Rom. Abt.*), XLVI, 1926, p. 330.

Tigris. Egypt and Macedonia strove to secure for themselves the mastery of the Aegean Sea. Minor Hellenistic kings played their part, as may, for instance, be seen by an inscription of Ziaelas of Bithynia (*Ditt.*[3] 456), in which the king promises safety to the merchants of Cos in the harbours which were under his control and fair treatment to those who suffered shipwreck near his coast. We have here a good parallel to the efforts of the Seleucids and of the Ptolemies, and later of the Parthians, to make the caravan roads which ran through their lands safe for merchants, and to the creation by the Ptolemies of a set of fortified harbours on the Red Sea coast. To the same class of acts belong the efforts of the Ptolemies and later of the Rhodians to combat piracy.

The history of the shifting of trade from one centre to another and of the competition between the various lands is well illustrated by the coinage of the Hellenistic kings. The whole of the material which bears on this question has still to be collected and collated. It would be fascinating to study the gradual decline of the Attic currency in competition first with the coinage of Philip and afterwards with that of Alexander. For a while the currency of Lysimachus conquered the Western markets and competed successfully with the coinage of the Bosporan kings and with those of Cyzicus and Lampsacus[1]. Meanwhile the coinage of the Ptolemies gained ever more ground and was for a time dominant in the Aegean, until a little later it was supplanted by that of Rhodes, whereas the Pergamene coinage never became a world currency and remained confined to Asia Minor. In the Near East the coinages of the Seleucids reigned supreme for a while. Soon, however, it was replaced in the Far East by the Bactrian coinage and later by that of Parthia and Kushan. In the west of their huge empire the Seleucids were forced to recognize the coinage of many Phoenician cities. However that may be, the efforts of all the Hellenistic kings were directed towards adapting their coinage to the needs of their trade and towards facilitating trade by making the coins both abundant and handy[2]. No one of them, however, succeeded in making his own currency a real world currency, comparable with the Athenian currency of the fifth century and with the Roman currency of the Empire.

This competition of kings and cities rendered a great service to business and especially commerce, inasmuch as enormous quantities

[1] Two finds of gold coins of Lysimachus at Anadol in Bessarabia and at Tuapse in the Caucasus (Bauer, *Zeit. f. Num.* xxxv, 1925, p. 276) are typical.

[2] W. Schubart, *Zeit. f. Num.* xxxiii, 1923, pp. 68 *sqq.*

of currency were thus put into circulation. We have no statistics, but it is evident that it sufficed to place almost all transactions on a money basis and to eliminate natural economy and barter almost completely, except for some departments of taxation in Egypt. The thousands of business documents of the Hellenistic period found in Egypt and the increasing numbers of them found in Mesopotamia and Iranian lands testify to a rapid spread of money economy even on the borders of the Hellenistic world. The parchments of Avroman and those of Doura bear an eloquent testimony to it. It is evident that the spread of money economy and of the habit of transacting business on a money basis was largely responsible for the creation of local currencies by the border-states of the Hellenistic world both in the East and in the West, by Parthia, Bactria and the Greek states of North India and the Kushan Empire in the East, and by Italy and Gaul in the West. It was not until towards the end of the fourth century B.C. that Rome began to mint her own money and a real Roman silver currency did not exist earlier than the first half of the third century (vol. VII, pp. 662 *sqq.*). About the same time Celtic coinage begins. It is evident that this change in the economic life of both Italy and Gaul depended not only on the political conditions of the time but also and more effectively on the rapid development of commercial relations between the Hellenistic East and the Italo-Celtic West.

Money economy and rapid development of commerce gave a strong impulse to the rapid growth of banking. Banking is a very ancient institution in world history. The first banks and bankers were the temples, and their first operation was the keeping of money on deposit (vol. I, p. 534). Under the protection of the gods the depositors regarded their deposits as safe. The brisk development of commerce in Mesopotamia soon transformed the money deposits in the temples into real banking concerns. Private banks were not slow to appear, and both temples and private banks began to undertake various operations, especially loans. In Persian times there is the well-attested activity of the Babylonian bank of the Murashu Brothers. We have no information of any parallel development in Egypt. It may however be regarded as certain that banking was not unknown to those states and cities in the Near East which took an active part in the development of commerce and were dependent in their cultural development on Babylonia. Phoenicia and Lydia carried on no doubt a regular banking business. It is fair to suppose that from here banking migrated to the Greek cities of the west coast of Asia Minor where the earliest pioneers were the numerous oriental temples connected with them. Indeed such temples as that of Jerusalem or those of Sardes and Ephesus acted as regular banking concerns even in Hellenistic and Roman times.

The money-changer was from early times a well-known figure in the world of Greek city-states. Where each city had its own currency, no commercial operations were possible without the help of a specialist who sat near his table (*trapeza*) in the market-place or in the street and practised the profession of a *trapezites*, accepting foreign currency and exchanging it for local money or *vice versa*. These money-changers in Asia Minor probably got very early into touch with the great deposit banks of the temples and soon began to transact various business familiar to the temple banks, either in the name of the temples as their agents or in imitation of them. A tremendous impulse was given to the development of private banking business by the growth of inter-state and international commerce. It is therefore no wonder that the best-organized private banks in Greek history were met with in the leading commercial city of the Greek world in the fifth and fourth centuries b.c.—Athens. But it was not the Athenian bankers who invented the business routine of their banks; rather they inherited it from their Ionian predecessors in Asia Minor and those last from their Lydian and Phoenician business friends, who in their turn were pupils of the Babylonian bankers.

With the Hellenistic period and closely connected with its commercial development came the great age of Greek banking. Individual bankers, private and city banks and associations of bankers are now comparatively often mentioned, especially in inscriptions and papyri[1]. Bankers and banks appeared scattered all over Hellenistic lands. Larger groups appear in the leading commercial cities. Everywhere banking appears closely connected with commerce, for money-changing was as necessary and perhaps even more necessary than ever before. Without a *trapezites* no merchant could transact his business in a foreign city. Still more important became deposit and loan business. Accumulations of capital in the hands of private people and corporations was one of the leading features of Hellenistic economic life. To all capitalists the question of where to keep their money and how to invest it was a vital one. On the other hand, commerce badly needed

---

[1] See E. Ziebarth, *Hellenistische Banken*, Zeit. f. Num. xxxiv, 1923, pp. 36 *sqq.* and in *Beiträge zur Geschichte des Seeraubs*, pp. 85 *sqq.* R. Herzog, *Aus der Geschichte des Bankwesens im Altertum*, Tesserae nummulariae 1919.

credit, without which it could not exist. To a lesser extent credit was needed also by landowners and artisans. Thus banks became not only the keepers of deposits but also loan and investment institutions[1]. There were loans of money to cities which became ever more frequent, loans granted to landowners and farmers on mortgage, commercial and especially sea loans. Not many of this last type of loan are mentioned, but the references to them show that such transactions were familiar and common. In an inscription of Miletus (*c.* 160/59 B.C.) the city bank has large sums of money invested in 'export loans[2].' About a century later in an inscription of the time of Mithridates sea loans stand at the head of a long list of transactions of the kind (*Ditt.*[3] 742).

Egypt in Ptolemaic times went over to money economy and banking assumed a peculiar form. Large commerce was concentrated in Alexandria, and retail and interstate commerce, though to a large extent stabilized by the government, flourished in the country. In spite of the thorough stabilization of economic life capital accumulated in the hands of private persons and credit was badly needed even by those who transacted business with the state and as concessionnaires of the state. In short, economic life, peculiarly organized as it was, became nevertheless more and more complicated. In such an atmosphere banks were bound to appear and to develop by leaps and bounds. Whether it was from the very beginning or after the banks arose spontaneously that the government monopolized banking business we do not know. We are equally ignorant whether all the banks in Egypt (including those in Alexandria) were state monopolies or not. It is however certain that banking, although a state monopoly, was nevertheless carried out by private business men, who paid the state for the right of doing so, and not by government officers. We know but little of the activity of these banks in Egypt, and what we know refers to the small country towns and villages, not to Alexandria or to the larger towns. This, together with the special part which the banks played in Egypt, prevents us from applying the little that we know of the banks in Egypt to the activity of the banks in the rest of the Hellenistic world. For example, the prominence of operations connected with taxation was probably peculiar to the Egyptian banks. Equally peculiar to Egypt were the limited possibilities for investment. If, however, we deduct all that may be

[1] A typical instance which has apparently escaped notice is that of Aegias of Sicyon, the banker of Aratus, Plutarch, *Aratus* 18–20.

[2] ἐμπορικὰ δάνεια, Th. Wiegand, *Milet*, VII Bericht, pp. 27 *sqq.* and above, p. 658.

regarded as special to Egypt there remain many operations with which we may credit banks in general. Chief among these is the business routine of payments from and to the banks, of transfers of money, of cheques, of the handling of deposits and so on.

A characteristic feature in the development of banking outside Egypt was the tendency of the cities to concentrate it into their own hands, to create state banks and to reserve for these state banks the monopoly of the various operations. In early Hellenistic times the cities had recourse for their own operations to private bankers. Later the city endeavoured to eliminate the private bankers or at least to make them her own concessionnaires. There is no need to suppose that for this development the example of Ptolemaic Egypt was responsible, for a tendency towards monopolies may be noticed in Greek city-life from its early beginnings.

VI. ROADS, SHIPPING, EXPLORATION, LANGUAGE, LAW

Sea trade and caravan trade were the leading forms of Hellenistic commerce. It is natural therefore to expect that the development of both these types of trade would lead to a marked improvement in the technical devices which may make trade safer, speedier and cheaper. It must, however, be confessed that our knowledge of it is slight. We are ignorant first and foremost of how much was done for the improvement of roads. The later activity of the Romans obscured the achievements of Hellenistic kings and cities in this field. However, the fact that we hear of royal roads in Asia Minor (*O.G.I.S.* 225) as opposed probably to the private and city roads implies a certain activity of kings, cities and private landowners in this matter. It is also worthy of note that both Ptolemies and Seleucids kept and developed the state post organization which they inherited from the Persians. But the posting service was reserved for government use, and had no direct influence on the development of trade.

Little is known of the development of ship-building. What we know refers mostly to ships of war, and even here modern research has not yet succeeded in explaining the progress made in the Hellenistic period. On the advance in commercial ship-building the evidence is still more meagre. And yet we may be certain that the Hellenistic kings who vied with each other in inventing new forms of warships extended this competition to commercial ships as well. Thus Antigonus Gonatas after building his famous big ship the *triarmenos* built immediately a corresponding commercial ship of the same name[1]. In the reign of Hiero II technical skill had so far advanced as to construct his enormous cargo-boat, the Syrakosia or Alexandreia, and Ptolemy Philopator astonished the civilized world by his huge pleasure-ship for trips on the Nile. Much, however, remains to be done before the scattered hints of our literary tradition can be explained with the help of all available material, especially the pictures of ships in sculpture and painting[2].

The advance in ship-building was matched by the gradual improvement of the harbours, of which the best examples are those of Alexandria and of Delos; in close connection went the systematic construction of lighthouses, the most famous of which, one of the seven wonders of the world, was the Pharos of Alexandria. The discovery among the objects belonging to the famous sunken ship of Anticythera of an astronomical instrument probably used by the ship's crew for finding the position of the ship at a given moment, an instrument never mentioned in our literary tradition, reveals rather than assists our ignorance of the progress of ancient seafaring technique.

A great help to the merchants was the remarkable development of geographical knowledge in the Hellenistic period. Hand in hand with the progress made by both mathematical and descriptive geography went the adaptation of this progress to the practical needs of merchants and travellers. We still possess many *periploi* or *stadiasmoi* belonging to the Hellenistic period—descriptions of the shores of the Mediterranean or part of it, and of the Black Sea, the Red Sea and the Persian Gulf. The purpose of most of these was practical—to serve as guide books to the merchants and travellers of the time. It was reserved for the Roman period to work out a corresponding set of *itineraria* for the roads. But the well-known itinerary of Isidorus of Charax for the Parthian empire shows that long before the Roman *itineraria* the caravan trade had had its own perfectly reliable handbooks based on the study of the land-routes begun by Persian officers and carried on by the bematists of Alexander the Great.

Foreign and interstate trade was greatly assisted by the gradual spread of a knowledge of the Greek language and the corre-

---

[1] See W. W. Tarn, *The dedicated ship of Antigonus Gonatas*, J.H.S. xxx, 1910, pp. 209 *sqq.*, cf. A. Köster, *Das antike Seewesen*, p. 163 *sq.*

[2] A useful summary of our knowledge will be found in A. Köster, *op. cit.* More detail will be found in his larger work of which one part has been recently published, *Schiffahrt und Handelsverkehr des östlichen Mittelmeeres im 3. u. 2. Jahrtausend v. Chr.*, 1924.

sponding creation of a sort of juridical *koine* which was familiar to everybody in the Hellenistic world. This does not mean that there was ever anything like one code of civil laws by which everybody in all the lands in which the Greeks ruled would abide. But it remains true that in spite of local differences in laws and legal practice, there was a large stock of common principles which were familiar to everybody, and which were gradually incorporated into the local laws which regulated business. Little as we know about the law-making of the Hellenistic period, we have many business documents found in Egypt and a little group of similar documents from the Euphrates and from Iranian lands in the Hellenistic and Parthian periods.

It is natural that Macedonians on the Euphrates should use the Greek language for their business transactions and act according to Greek laws. It is not surprising that Greek speech and law gradually gained ground in the business life of Hellenistic Egypt. It is astonishing, however, how rapidly parchment and papyrus replaced clay tablets in Mesopotamia, and how, parallel to it, the Babylonian language retreated before the Greek and, to a certain extent, the Aramaic and Iranian languages[1]. It is still more surprising that the Parthians and Arabs, Kurds and Iranians in Mesopotamia and the Iranian lands use in their transactions the Greek language and Greek legal formulae, probably also to a certain extent Greek laws and regulations. To all appearance Greek law, formulae and language took hold of the population of the Mesopotamian and Iranian lands in the short period of Macedonian domination and were never given up by the Parthians. It would not be surprising if excavation in Bactria and North India yielded business documents in Greek. The true explanation of this adoption of Greek law and language in Mesopotamia and Parthia is probably not so much the superiority of Greek law or the compulsion of the Hellenistic monarch as the fact that there was an increasing number of Greek business men in these places and that trade relations with them were vital for the natives. It must, however, not be forgotten that the State was represented in

---

[1] On the early use of parchment and papyrus in Mesopotamia see R. Dougherty, *Writing upon parchment and papyrus among the Babylonians and Assyrians*, J. Amer. Or. Soc. xlviii, 1928, pp. 109 *sqq.* The number of documents on parchment and papyrus in such places as Uruk, Nippur and Seleuceia on the Tigris is illustrated by the finds of clay *bullae* with official and private seals in which the documents were kept in the archives. The present writer is preparing a study of these *bullae*, most of which belong to the second century B.C.

these lands by men of Greek training and education even in Parthian times and this fact contributed a good deal to the recognition of Greek as the official business language.

For the development of Greek commerce the triumph of Greek law, language and legal formulae meant a good deal. It was easy for Apollonius and Zeno to deal with the population of Transjordania, provided that they were sure of being understood if they used Greek. And that it was so is shown by the excellent Greek (even if it be that of his secretary) which Tobias, the emir of Transjordania, uses in his correspondence with Ptolemy Philadelphus and with Apollonius, and by the fact that we still have documents which show that Zeno transacted his business in Palestine and beyond the Jordan in Greek and according to Greek law[1].

The short sketch given above shows how little justification there is for the theory that house-economy prevailed all through ancient times. However, we must not exaggerate. Commerce in Hellenistic times developed, no doubt, by leaps and bounds and assumed gradually ever more modern forms. And yet its sound development was greatly handicapped, chiefly by the uncertainties of the times. War was raging all over the Hellenistic world almost without interruption. The methods of warfare were primitive and brutal in spite of efforts to make them more civilized. The devastation of flourishing fields and gardens, the sack and pillage of rich cities, the enslavement of thousands of men, women and children were the order of the day especially in the second century B.C. The efforts of some states such as Egypt and Rhodes to check piracy and to exterminate robbery on land were mostly short-lived and in vain. Rival states were only too ready to use the methods of robbery by sea and land and welcomed an alliance with organized pirates. Even in peace time rival states did not hesitate to seize corn ships and to take them to their own harbours. Thus commerce was and remained a risky operation and consequently never completely lost its speculative character.

Moreover, in many Greek cities the accumulation of capital had its dangers. As soon as the cities were freed from strict control by royal officers they indulged freely in internal revolution, in confiscations of property, in re-distributions of land and abolition of debts. Social and political revolution became endemic in Greece. The atmosphere was not exactly well suited for a sound

1 G. McLean Harper, Jr., *Commercial relations between Egypt and Syria*, A. J. Ph. XLIX, 1928, pp. 1 *sqq.*

development of economic activity, of a quiet wholesale and retail commerce. It prevented equally the volume of commerce from increasing, since it never allowed industry to assume capitalistic forms and to work for mass production with the help of adequate machinery. Capital in the cities was mostly in hiding. Even the large stocks of capital found in the Hellenistic monarchies were not an exception. Instead of the city mob there was a king who was happy to confiscate the fortune of a man who became too rich to be safe. No sound development of capitalism was possible in that land of stabilization which was Egypt. Perhaps still more important was the fact that commerce of various types affected mostly the upper classes of the population and the cities, the masters and not the subjects, whose buying capacity was small and whose requirements were not satisfied by objects made by city-Greeks for Greek and hellenized dwellers of the cities. Since we have every reason to think that the prosperity of the lower classes of the population in all the Hellenistic monarchies was not increasing as rapidly as was that of the upper classes, we can understand why the production of goods in the Hellenistic workshops never assumed the character of true mass production and why commerce never permanently attracted into its orbit the millions of the country population. Thus while it is true that the Hellenistic world had advanced far beyond a strict natural economy, it is also true that it stopped far short of capitalism in the modern sense of the word.

CHAPTER XXI

HELLENISTIC ART

I. INTRODUCTION

THE authority on whom Pliny drew for the chapters on art in his *Natural History* ended his account of sculpture in Greece with the pupils of Lysippus. Pliny therefore tells us that art died in the beginning of the third century, and did not come to life again for a hundred and fifty years. When we remember that this period covers the activities of the Pergamene school amongst others, we may wonder whether he is saying exactly what he means. But we do know that his statement is intended to refer to the break-up of the mainland schools at that time, and however untrue in particular it may be to declare the succeeding century and a half a void, much of the time old Greece was silent. Her artists, widening a movement which had begun in the fourth century, followed the flow of wealth and power eastwards, and were to be found as single masters or in small groups executing commissions for the new kings, for the new cities which now sprang up, or for those among the old cities which now throve luxuriantly. This dispersal makes the task of the historian of art difficult. From time to time new schools were formed, made up of various elements, yet producing works of one style: but more often a single sculptor would carve or cast a statue in a city of which he was not a native, and, leaving it, would leave us nothing but a name, or a nameless copy of his work. Knowledge, too, was now more accessible than before, and one is likely to find, instead of a consistent development, reminiscence of several styles, which renders it impossible, in the absence of a signature or other external evidence, to say to what school the sculptor of such an eclectic work belongs. Stylistic comparison, one of the most trustworthy guides to the classification of works of art, thus begins to fail at the same time as literary evidence; and the virtual stereotyping of alphabetical forms robs inscriptions of much of their chronographical value.

These difficulties, and the consequent absence of a reasonably certain chronological arrangement and classification, may have contributed to the neglect with which Hellenistic art has until lately been treated. To-day it is hardly necessary to insist on the importance of studying it, not only for itself but also in its bearings on that which succeeded. For the art of Rome is the direct heir, not of the fifth century nor even of the fourth (though there were fashions for works of these centuries among her connoisseurs and classical revivals besides that of Hadrian); but of the living tradition of Hellenistic art, modified in its new surroundings and embodying strong native elements, yet still a continuous development. One cannot determine the precise artistic importance of Roman monuments without knowing the Hellenistic age, although one may derive aesthetic pleasure from them, just as one cannot fully understand, although one can enjoy, Virgil without knowing Homer; and not only Homer, but Theocritus.

Hellenistic art has often been called decadent. If by decadence is meant a falling-off in technique, a loss of vitality, or a tendency to shirk difficulties, then, to speak generally, the charge does not hold. If it means imitating old fashions without improving on them, examples of it can be found then, as at almost any other time. The real difficulty in which sculptors most of all, architects to some degree, and painters far less, now found themselves, was this:—the past centuries had been too comprehensive in their success, and had exhausted most of the subjects available, while the new political and material conditions had not created corresponding demands for new kinds of dedications calling for new art-forms, nor supplied new subjects. Sculpture suffers particularly because it is comparatively limited in its repertory; and when technique has been perfected, a style worked out to its climax, and the range of subjects genuinely exhausted, some kind of revolution must occur before significant works of art are again produced in any number.

One thing at least the fifth and fourth centuries had bequeathed to sculptors, a superb technical skill, not forgotten for many a generation. There is naturally a change in the spirit which animates it: in these three centuries before Christ works by Pheidias are not to be expected, just as one does not expect another Aeschylus or another Socrates. The only questions one is entitled to ask are 'How far are these works original?' and 'Are they good, in their kind?' We are not primarily concerned with the comparative value of various kinds.

II. ATHENIAN SCULPTORS IN THE EARLY HELLENISTIC AGE; ALEXANDRIA

Let us look first at Athens, which, one is inclined to think, with no rich patron to stimulate her, will have fallen into the second rank. But when the evidence is examined, it will be found that even if there were not many commissions in Athens itself, and although some executed there are of no high quality, yet Athenians, with their great technical skill, were still playing a large part elsewhere in the Greek world, and the best of her home-keeping sculptors could produce splendid work when occasion demanded, at least until the middle of the third century. There is, it is true, a tendency towards an academic style, at its best among gentle or even romantic emotions, and somewhat out of place in vast scenes of tragedy. But it would be surprising not to find some such reaction after the brilliance of the fourth century, and even if the general failure of ambitious ideal sculpture seems to show that ideals had become the business of philosophers, the Athenian sculptor set to make a portrait—if we do not hold portraiture to be a separate art—acquits himself well and is not dominated by the past. Attainment is uneven, but how can it fail to be so at any period, when we judge it not only by its great masters, but by anything we may happen to have left to us, no matter from how mean a workshop it proceeded?

Of the sculpture found in Athens itself the most important is a colossal head of Ariadne[1] from the south slope of the Acropolis, which may be dated about the end of the fourth century: a diluted blend of Scopas and Praxiteles, like the imperfectly animated Niobid group by the same artist, the authorship of which puzzled ancient critics. Such a style is more at home in a statue representing Selene as she sinks towards Latmus[2], the soft vertical lines of her dress imitating her subdued radiance, a kind of rendering rarely found, or at least rarely found so obvious. The statue of Dionysus seated[3], from the monument of Thrasyllus, probably of 271 B.C., is a conscientious piece of work and sufficiently monumental, but it lacks first-hand feeling, its grandeur being derived from a tradition which has overwhelmed the tenuous spirit of the sculptor. In the Themis by Chaerestratus[4], of some years before, emptiness of expression stands for impartiality, stiffness for uprightness. The unintelligent repetition of stock formulae for drapery, hair and features, is the sculptor's substitute for fresh observation of the material means by which the goddess might have been embodied. A sapless stick—and the unexpected incidents in the drapery, which are intended to give life, hang on it like abortive leaves. Chaerestratus would not have been a great sculptor even in a great period: here he puts forth crude borrowings from masters of the last generation.

[1] Volume of Plates iii, 118, *a*.   [2] *Ib.* 118, *d*.
[3] *Ib.* 120, *a*.   [4] *Ib.* 118, *c*.

The genuine tradition of Praxiteles seems to have been kept alive by his sons Cephisodotus and Timarchus, to one of whom may be due a pleasing head (known in a copy at Taranto[1]) which possesses a girlish freshness and a distinct personality rather in the sense of the earlier head from Chios[2]. The two sons collaborated in a portrait of Menander set up in the theatre at Athens about 290: and its head is thought to have been identified in many copies[3]. One other portrait, of a decade later, may be mentioned—a masterpiece—the statue of Demosthenes by Polyeuctus[4]. It shows a power of characterization, not only in the head but in body, limbs, and drapery (the much worn, much washed, much fingered himation, whether invented or historical, is as subtle as the rest), which will bear comparison with anything which had preceded it.

A statue which, though commissioned for Alexandria, may have been the work of a sculptor from Greece proper and perhaps from Athens, is the colossal Nile, of which there is a copy (much restored in details) in the Vatican[5]. Nile, with rippling hair and beard, lies against the Sphinx, displaying a broad smooth body at the same time fluent and monumental, and looks back towards the hills, yearning, like all water-beings, for intercourse with the constant earth. The sixteen cubits of his yearly rise lie in the swirling folds of his cloak, lap his feet, caressing the animals he shelters, climb, and pause, and scale at last his full height, to crown him and sit proudly among his and their yield of corn and fruits. A pretty enough allegory, and, even if rather obvious, worked out with humour.

In Alexandria the cult of Sarapis was promoted by Ptolemy Philadelphus, who commissioned one Bryaxis to execute the colossal cult-statue. Copies of this on a small scale—and varying in detail, because the size of the image prevented the making of casts—are numerous, having been used no doubt in private shrines: one at Alexandria itself seems to give a fair general notion of the original, and Clement of Alexandria has left an account of the great richness of the statue, and of the various metals and precious stones employed. Its colouring was gloomy: its jewelled eyes mysterious. Cerberus, his make-up more monstrous than ever, is to the fore, louring. In Egypt the more awful aspects of the cult will not have been neglected.

Both Nile and Sarapis were probably the work of recent immigrants. There must have been many such, where there was

---

[1] Volume of Plates iii, 122, *a*.   [2] *Ib.* ii, 86, *c*.
[3] *Ib.* iii, 118, *b*.   [4] *Ib.* 120, *b*.   [5] *Ib.* 120, *c*.

constant demand for sculpture, but we have no evidence that, either by themselves or in combination with those already established, they evolved a distinctive homogeneous style, that they maintained a general standard high enough to serve as a hotbed for occasional masterpieces, or that they contributed much to art save some excellent grotesques, mostly small bronzes, and from time to time one or two good portraits.

III. THE PUPILS OF LYSIPPUS AND THE RHODIAN SCHOOL

We now turn to the school of Lysippus, some of whose many pupils were still engaged at Sicyon in the production of the kind of works for which there was always a steady demand—victorious athletes, charioteers with their teams, and other votive statues— in a watered version of his style, by the aid of the technical processes, including plaster casts, which he and his brother Lysistratus had brought to perfection; while others were carrying his manner and methods to various parts of the Greek world. Chares, of Lindus, made for the city of Rhodes, after its repulse of Demetrius Poliorcetes in 305 and from the sale of his abandoned siege-train, that bronze colossus of the sun-god, a hundred feet high, which became one of the seven wonders of the ancient world. It stood for fifty-six years, was then overthrown by an earthquake, destroying many houses in its fall; remained, fallen, to stir men's wonder for another thirteen hundred years, and finally passed out of history, sold for its metal to a Jew, on a caravan of nine hundred and eighty camels.

It has left few traces save in literature and, in faint reflections, on coins, but a short account which we possess of its erection bears witness to a high degree of technical skill, and its example evoked many more colossi in Rhodes, which now became a great centre for bronze-founding, and the home of a flourishing school of statuary. Unfortunately we know little of it except names, and are obliged to argue back from its later productions. Some of the works soon to be mentioned as of Lysippic descent may well have been made there, but the increasing mobility of sculptors and ideas renders it increasingly difficult to fix a style down to a particular place. A rich city anywhere acts as a magnet for various sculptors. They are bound at this time less than ever before by the tradition of one school: knowledge of other styles than that of their own teacher is widespread, and inspiration may be drawn at second-hand from many sources.

One or two convenient fixed points we have.

Starting with the Apoxyomenos[1], which may be dated approximately by the resemblance of the head to some of the coin-portraits of Demetrius Poliorcetes, we come next to a statue closely resembling it, a boy praying, now in Berlin, which may be a copy of the *adorans* by Boedas, a pupil of Lysippus[2]. It testifies to careful study of a model, though it is far from being so free from convention as Lysippus himself seems to have claimed: nevertheless there certainly is here a more direct attempt to imitate soft young flesh, and less dependence on the traditional divisions of musculature, than we have yet seen. Another fixed point is the group made by Eutychides, pupil of Lysippus, for the city of Antioch on the Orontes, presumably soon after its foundation in 300, of the Tyche of the city crowned by Seleucus and Antiochus. Eutychides is described by ancient writers as a Sicyonian: most of his recorded works were dedicated in Greece itself, and he certainly remained at Sicyon long enough to instruct a pupil; whence it is dangerous to assume that his commission in Antioch led to the establishment there of a school with Lysippic traditions. For a full understanding of the group itself (or rather of the figure of Antioch, for trustworthy copies of that alone remain) a few words are needed on the stage of development which it helps to date and illustrate. Lysippus had been making statues of women which differ from the Praxitelean in having the clothes stretched rather than draped upon them. Patterns are thus produced to which the body serves as a background, and, in addition, sometimes a series of external patterns, complementary to those on the body, is formed by stretching loose ends of drapery across the figure in a more forward plane or letting them hang, such schemes being facilitated by the use of bronze, a material of high tensile strength. The idea is, as we shall see, then carried farther, and statues are produced which, in their sacrificing of probability to the desire for particular shapes, are comparable to those of the Italian baroque.

To speak generally, the dress of the archaic *korai* was abstracted pattern, showing a tendency to neglect fresh study of the real garment: the statues of the fifth century were women, their clothes worn naturally, the artist making a discreet selection and adjustment of normal incidents; those of the fourth century mannequins, pinned into the fashion of the day; while those of the progressive Hellenistic schools are lay-figures, their draperies here looped, there stretched on their inelastic limbs. If they are still, one

---

[1] Volume of Plates ii, 94, *a*.   [2] *Ib.* iii, 132, *b.*

shrinks from anticipating their movement: if they are represented moving, one cannot picture them still. For to the basis of the lay-figure the sculptor is apt to add from his imagination or his memory flying pieces of drapery which would embarrass the runner were she to stop, and seated figures have loose ends lying about them the fall of which, if they were to stand, could not be foretold. Again there is a searching for pattern, but more conscious than in archaic days. Yet there are many Hellenistic statues which do not conform to these generalizations: the age was one both of experiment and of reaction, and we are constantly being surprised by fresh study of nature, and by dry memories of the past.

The Antioch of Eutychides, then, forms a convenient index to the problems with which many sculptors were at this time occupied. The best copies of the figure[1] show us a sleek girl seated broadly on a rock, in an attitude the contortion of which only reveals itself on close study. At her foot a youth, the river Orontes, plunges impetuously along: of another river-god by Eutychides, the Eurotas, ancient epigrams exclaim that it is more liquid than water, thus betokening a mimetic tendency such as we have already seen in the statue of Selene: but our copies of Orontes tell us little. The drapery of the demigoddess, in which the different materials are faithfully rendered, is stretched and looped elaborately across the figure and over the rock, so that we are presented not only with the interest of lines running in a number of different directions, and not only with the contrast between smooth and crinkly, but also with that between taut and loose, straight and curved, dry and full; to which confection the rendering of laundry-creases is intended to give additional piquancy. Now at last there is a full, conscious attempt to work out the composition for many points of view, one of the first pre-occupations of the modern, which had not before been forced upon sculptors because most statues were made to be set up with sides and back away from the spectator. Even in the fourth century there are many works in which lateral and even three-quarter views have been little considered, and many which, like the Hermes of Praxiteles, compose well from one point, the frontal, well enough from a second, third, or fourth, and poorly from the others.

The Apoxyomenos, we may recall, is for us the link between old and new. It carried on the tradition of the standing athletic statue, but broke away from it with the bold projection of its

right arm into the third dimension, just as the Lansdowne
Hermes[1], which also has the new proportions, small head and
wiry limbs, translated an old motive from two dimensions into
three. But not all Hellenistic sculptors who set about making
statues to be viewed from every aspect always succeeded in doing
so. The copy of another, younger Tyche[2] (Tyche is popular
in an age of changing fortunes), perhaps also by Eutychides,
illustrates a partial failure; charming though she is, the line
of the back when seen from her left sags in a curiously frog-like
way. One of the most successful compositions of this time
and school is the boy taking a thorn from his foot, not the famous
bronze of the Capitol, which gives only the body, and owes its
head of inconsistent style to Roman taste, but the marble copy
(the original was of bronze) in London, where the urchin has his
own head[3]. The seated Hermes from Herculaneum[4], which resembles it in many ways, fails in one view, that from his left,
whence the back looks excessively heavy, and has legs (partly
restored) which would appear too long if he stood up, an interesting contrast in this particular to the old two-dimensional
type of seated figure, which usually has thighs too short for
nature in order to make a frontal view tolerable. The statue of
Hermes is on the whole a successful personification of supple
lightness and speed: and the Lysippic school, with its tradition
of athletic statues, is naturally happy in its representation of the
naked male figure. The heads generally show little evidence of
mental life: these and the dry, highly-trained bodies we may
suppose characteristic of the athletes of the day.

The Victory found at Samothrace[5] and now in the Louvre is
one of the great monuments of this age, and a faithful reflex
through one of its facets. The divergence of centuries between
the dates proposed for it shows how weak internal evidence can
be for dating and classifying in a period when more than a few
lines of development are being followed and when old fashions
can be adopted at will. It is treated here because of the fragment
of an inscription—...Σ ΡΟΔΙΟΣ—found with it, though since lost,
which can hardly have been anything but the signature of the
sculptor, since there was no other building near to which it could
belong. It was formerly thought that this monument, like the
coins issued by Demetrius Poliorcetes, which also bear the device
of Victory on a prow, commemorated the naval victory of 306 B.C.
off Salamis in Cyprus. But Samothrace was in enemy hands then

[1] Volume of Plates ii, 98, *a*.   [2] *Ib.* iii, 124.
[3] *Ib.* 132, *c*.   [4] *Ib.* 132, *a*.   [5] *Ib.* 126.

and for years after. Nor do any of the coin-dies show evidence
of having been actually copied from the statue: not only will the
position of the arms have been different, but the drapery on the
coins is that of an ordinary running figure conceived and worked
out in the manner of the fourth century, with no hint of the
alighting movement of the statue. In face of these arguments,
another occasion for the dedication has been sought, and Studniczka has proposed the decisive event of the Second Syrian War,
the battle of Cos (c. 258 B.C.), in which the triple alliance of
Antigonus, Antiochus II and Rhodes was victorious over Ptolemy
II. This explains the general resemblance to the coins, for the
statue thus becomes a dedication of filial piety by Antigonus; it
explains, as is pointed out above (vol. VII, p. 714 n. 2), the erection
on Samothrace, otherwise inexplicable in the third century and
with difficulty explicable in the second. For Samothrace was
Arsinoe's island, captured in this Second Syrian War by Antiochus. At Cos Antigonus was taking revenge for the Chremonidean
War, and Antiochus for his father's losses in the First Syrian
War, in both of which Arsinoe's influence had been dominant.
And it justifies the commissioning of a Rhodian artist; while the
date seems more suitable for the style than any yet proposed.

It may be urged that the date is unimportant for the appreciation of it as a work of art. But even if it gains no more aesthetic
significance from being dated, it gains interest as the work of a
member of the Rhodian school of this time, and for the comparison it affords with the work which Pergamene sculptors were
soon to produce. It has been shown that the coins of Demetrius
represent Victory on a despoiled prize[1], a parallel to the common
representation, especially common at this time, of Victory setting
up a trophy of captured armour. But the Samothracian monument, like Antigonus' dedication of his flagship, instead of hulks,
on Delos, refines this motive. Cos was fought during the Isthmia,
and here Victory brings to the *Isthmia*, the victorious flagship,
the Isthmian victor's crown. No longer the calm messenger of
Olympus, but the stormy partisan, her feet now touch deck,
and poised, with wings still beating, she is carried on with
the onward surge of the vessel, the breeze driving the cloak
against and across her tense forward leg and eddying in the light
folds of her dress. The figure is strongly built; the powerful
wings suggest more successfully than ever before organic articu-
lation with the body, and are ably balanced by the deep breasts
and massive chest. An extremely clever study of body and

[1] By E. T. Newell, *The Coinages of Demetrius Poliorcetes*, p. 35.

drapery combined in movement: solid and bright on the one side; fluttering, shadowy, almost feathery on the other; finical perhaps in some details, but still without detriment to the main conception, which, with its bold transverse bars of shadow and great upward wrench from the waist, as of one flung hither and thither by the currents of battle and then torn by main force from the enemy, is highly sensational, because violent emotion was to be expressed.

A further development in drapery which may have culminated in the Rhodian school about 200 B.C., is that of making the folds of the under-garment show through the upper, a subtle inversion of flavour from the old heavy cloak fully masking or fully revealing the chiton. Matron and maiden from Herculaneum[1] show the first traces of the new fashion. A figure in relief from the altar of the temple of Athena Polias at Priene[2], though not necessarily later, is in a more advanced stage, and proves that the tendency goes back at least to the beginning of the third century, if not to the end of the fourth; while the climax is reached in a statue from Magnesia now in Constantinople[3]. But at Pergamum, in the early second century, on the great frieze transparent over-drapery does not occur: on the smaller frieze it is used discreetly. We must therefore assume either that it was falling out of fashion or that it was not yet perfected when they were carved. And when we remember that it was never an exclusive style, others everywhere appearing beside it, and that it was not Pergamene in origin; that extreme renderings like the statue from Magnesia were probably abnormalities without wide vogue, and that our evidence points to the beginnings of the fashion a century before—then we may be persuaded that it was reaching its full development during the third century, and shall probably not be far wrong in assigning a statue of Polyhymnia[4], in other ways related to the two Tychai by Eutychides, but with transparent over-drapery, to the end of that century.

The origins of the groups of Muses of which we have copies are extremely uncertain, and although the head of another Muse is illustrated here[5] for its sweet but not cloying beauty, no direct connection with that of Polyhymnia is implied. Brother of Polyhymnia is a satyr boy[6] (several copies of a lost original furnish his various parts) who, having just discovered the existence of his tail (tail-consciousness doubtless being one of the concomitants of satyric pubescence), twists himself round in order to gain a glimpse

---

[1] Volume of Plates iii, 130, *a, b*.   [2] *Ib.* 130, *c*.   [3] *Ib.* 130, *d*.
[4] *Ib.* 142, *c*; 122, *c*.   [5] *Ib.* 122, *b*.   [6] *Ib.* 142, *b*.

of it, and smiles whimsically at the perverse fate which will never grant full success to his efforts. The motive may seem trivial, but shows genuine feeling, and the movements of the lithe young body are carefully studied and expressed. The warmth of the modelling and the elasticity both of the taut abdomen and of the folds on the back are equally admirable. Here (with a spiral composition) the silhouettes are not especially satisfying: more noticeably than, for example, in the Hermes resting, the beauty of the various aspects depends on a steady consciousness of the third dimension, into which eye and mind are continually being led.

No account, however short, of the activities of the Rhodian school can close without reference to two famous works of art connected with Rhodes.

The punishment of Dirce, a group made at the end of the second century B.C. by Apollonius and Tauriscus of Tralles (adopted sons of one of the sculptors of the great Pergamene frieze) for the city of Rhodes, has survived in a much restored and altered copy of the third century A.D.[1] It is an attempt to represent plastically a group of persons, a bull, and a portion of the surrounding country. Its success is with difficulty estimated owing to the fragmentary condition of the piece. All we can say is that though the views from all points have been considered by the sculptor, and an approximately pyramidal composition attained by poising some of the figures ingeniously on rocks (as in another group of the time which has been discovered at Pergamum), one main aspect is intended.

On the other hand the group of Laocoon and his sons[2], by Agesander, Athenodorus and Polydorus of Rhodes, is designed like a relief and intended to be set against a wall. The proportions of the limbs are adjusted for this purpose in such a way that the exaggeration is not obvious in a frontal view, though some uneasiness may be felt about the size of the torso. Of the aesthetic significance of the group, which Pliny has not been alone in ranking unhesitatingly as the greatest work of art in the world, it is difficult to speak, so detached do we now feel from its horror. Its spirit seems most like that of the second Attalid dedication at the end of the first Pergamene school, though it has something in common with the great frieze of the altar: actually it is at least a hundred years later than either. In judging it we must discount patching and retouching, which have spoilt both the compactness and the swing of the composition

[1] Volume of Plates iii 128, *b*.   [2] *Ib.* 128, *a*.

by raising Laocoon's right arm too high, and have intruded several discordant details. But the main conception we are able to estimate with reasonable accuracy: and the contrast between the mighty straining of the grown man, tried to the utmost, and the tense elasticity of the elder son which acts as a foil to it and to the crumpled body of the younger, will not fail of their effect. Nor can we disregard the unsurpassed technical skill, even when we are asking ourselves what there is besides.

IV. THE FIRST PERGAMENE SCHOOL

The struggle between the Pergamene kingdom, under Attalus I, and the Gauls, was not the first occasion in Greek history when a desperate war had been accompanied by a blossoming of great and austere sculpture. In Greece proper the end of the Persian Wars of the early fifth century witnessed such a phenomenon; and there can be little doubt that in Pergamum the cathartic effects of a period of trial followed by the call for commemorative monuments, together with the provision of new subjects, gave the needed stimulus to an art which, efficient enough technically, tended to lack a supply of significant material and a high and serious purpose.

The name First Pergamene school has been given to a group of sculptors who produced, between 240 and 225 B.C., the great thanksgiving dedications for the victories of Attalus I over Antiochus and the Gauls (vol. VII, p. 721 *sq*.). Fragmentary inscriptions from the bases of these have been found at Pergamum, which, when brought into relation with a statement of Pliny (*N.H.* xxxiv, 84), seem to show that Isigonus was one of the sculptors, and perhaps Antigonus another, for these two names are among the four given by him for the dedications of Attalus and Eumenes, and the endings -gonus of two signatures have been preserved.

The groups themselves, scenes of battle, are best known to us from the dying Gaul of the Capitol, the statue (from the Ludovisi collection, now in the Museo delle Terme) of a Gaul who, at bay, turns the sword against himself after having killed his wife[1], the head of a dead man in Asiatic headdress[2], a torso at Dresden, a head at Cairo, as well as many other fragments. They may have been made soon after the originals themselves, and though they vary in excellence and cannot reproduce fully the original freshness of touch, yet, as copies, they reach a high level.

---

[1] Volume of Plates iii, 134, *b*.   [2] *Ib.* 134, *a*.

The original statues evidently embodied close studies of racial types and of muscular action, rest and motion being carefully differentiated. There is, generally, a spareness in the modelling, and the planes tend to be large and flat with dry hollows; as though representing a skin like hide, stretched over a frame meagrely padded, far different from the thin skin which comes of a genial climate, and covers the rippling evenly-developed musculature of the Greek in the convention of the fourth-century sculptors. In proportions the figures are somewhat less slender than the Lysippic, though the heads would seem small were it not for their long wild hair. The conceptions (and it should be noticed that even from the copies some differences in the personalities of the sculptors may be deduced) show a tendency to the ostentatious mitigated by the soberness and sympathy with which emotion is delineated in the faces. There are no traces of any attempt to belittle the enemy. In the compositions the use of bronze has encouraged considerable freedom: there is no hesitation in representing great strides, unsupported limbs, or hanging drapery; and bold projections and recessions are not avoided. Altogether a series in which high technical ability, invention, and fresh anatomical study supplementing a traditional scheme are still the means of expressing aesthetic emotion.

A dedication of about the same date as the first Pergamene symbolizes through an old Phrygian myth the victory of culture over barbarism, whence we may suppose that it was set up somewhere in the Pergamene kingdom and refers to the Attalid repulse of the Gauls. This myth had been treated before in Greek art, but never in such a way as to suggest its horror. Myron's bronze group, made about the middle of the fifth century, showed the first incident, where Athena flings away the disfiguring pipes: from a design of Praxiteles, or, as some will have it, by his grandson, the second, that of the contest between Apollo and Marsyas, was modelled in relief; Apollo waiting, Marsyas piping madly: and now the third, the penalty, is represented by a group of three figures, the god seated, the Silen bound by hands and feet to a tree[1], and the flayer crouching to whet his knife[2]. The statue of Apollo is preserved only in a torso and a sketch on a marble disk: he sits almost languidly, his arm over his head: Marsyas, half-animal resigned to an unintelligible fate, yet belongs to a higher type than the barbarous Scythian, who looks up with dull wonder and a hint of pity. Even here, though there is a pathos lacking in the earlier representations of the

[1] Volume of Plates iii, 136, a.   [2] Ib. 136, b.

subject, the physical horror is inherent, not explicit. It remained for the next generation to make Marsyas fully human and fully conscious of the coming torture, to simulate the straining body with red-streaked marble, to elaborate swollen veins and sweat-drenched hair, and so to transform the drama from tragedy into Grand Guignol.

This later phase of the first Pergamene school we are helped to define by another great dedication of Attalus I, a series of bronze statues, under life-size, set up on the parapet of the Acropolis at Athens at the end of the century. Greeks, Gauls, Amazons, Persians, Giants and Gods were the subjects, and if the copies we have are typical[1], they were represented in every conceivable attitude of violent attack, defence, pain, death and terror. Epigonus may be the sculptor responsible for that extreme of pity where her child seeks its milk at the breast of a dead Amazon. Throughout, no device to stir the spectator is neglected. Yet he is left, in the main, cold and detached.

The grouping, now lost, no doubt helped the effect. The figures are copies and have suffered in the copying and in the translation from bronze to marble. Restorations and working-over have marred or misrepresented actions and details. The small scale makes them remote from reality. All this is true. But even so, are there not fundamental causes for their failure? The sculptors of the first dedication will by now have been passing. These are pupils or imitators, and they are overcome by their inheritance. No thought can be perfectly expressed more than once. How originate new feelings or new formulae when the same subjects have been rendered in a masterly way not many years before?

To disguise deficiency of feeling the sculptors have expressed all they knew, keeping nothing in reserve and leaving nothing to the imagination. And they have repeated the formulae twice as loud, in the hope that they will be, if not twice, at least more than half, as effective. The result is that the figures, with some exceptions, being occupied not only with the fight but with the onlooker, attitudinize, and instead of feeling genuine emotion, exhibit a conventional substitute for it.

But the torso of a warrior, a Gaul whose helmet lies by his side, at Athens[2], from Delos, an original contemporary with the second Pergamene dedication, is an astonishing piece of work which gives us fuller understanding of both first and second dedications. It is not in the taste of the fifth century nor yet of

[1] Volume of Plates iii, 138, b.   [2] Ib. 138, a.

the fourth, but of its kind it is excellent, and for sheer technical ability it is unsurpassed. It helps us also to an appreciation of the group of Menelaus and the dead Patroclus[1], and of the pendant, lately reconstructed, Achilles and Penthesilea[2], which resembles in general construction the group of the Ludovisi Gaul. The originals of these will have been made in the last quarter of the third century. Both, known to us from copies only, depend for their effect on the physiological contrast between tension and relaxation, and on the pathetic contrast between the vibrant living body and the poor limp corpse; to which is added, especially in the second group, a strong sentimental interest.

Statues of this date have been criticized on the ground that they show too much of what lies beneath the surface, as though they had been flayed, or that the modelling is too emphatic. But it is not exactly that the skin appears to have been removed or that convexes have been unduly inflated and hollows made unduly concave, though some exaggeration of the contours may be detected: it is rather that certain features have been brought further forward from the main mass than is reasonable. The effect is not so much of normal strain, however great, as of a kind of morbid protrusion.

The need of new subjects has already been mentioned. The satyr, much favoured in the archaic age, fallen somewhat into neglect in the classical, and perhaps over-humanized in the fourth century, lives again now as an organic creature and becomes a vehicle of new ideas. A satyr-world with its own life again springs up, more credible than the world of gods, more interesting to the artist than yesterday's fight with the Gauls, which, even when Gauls were a new subject, closely resembled for the most part those other fights so often and so well depicted for centuries. Thus a large proportion of the tolerable Hellenistic statues represent satyrs. One, which seems to be Pergamene of the later third century, is reproduced by the dancing satyr from Pompeii[3]: a masterpiece of rhythmic movement, to which details like the snapping fingers, curling tail (more nervous no doubt in the original) and tossing flamy beard all contribute. Its composition exemplifies one of the schemes which tend to afford satisfactory views from every point, that of the spiral: the plane of the legs swings into that of the abdomen, and this in turn, retarded, slides into that of the chest and arms; the spiral is checked and split by the two planes of the neck, one of which accelerates while the

[1] Volume of Plates iii, 138, c.   [2] *Bollettino d' Arte*, vi (1926), p. 193.
[3] Volume of Plates iii, 142, a.

other gently reverses it, and is capped by the head, a well-poised
finial. A similar plan is followed at the back with the planes of
legs, buttocks and shoulders. But the statuette is naturally
susceptible of many analyses, for a thousand thoughts have
gone to its making; and this sketch of one of the main schemes
serves only as partial explanation of its resiliency.

Then, too, as a kind of variation on the main theme of the
conflict between Greeks and barbarians, or Gods and giants, come
conflicts on a smaller scale, yet no less serious, of the satyrs of
Dionysus[1] with giants (possibly though not probably belonging
to the smaller Attalid dedication), and the more intimate struggles
between old satyr and hermaphrodite, young satyr and nymph.
Although the small satyrs who fight and die in the coils of
their snake-footed opponents reflect the heroic postures of the
Attalid dedications, the heads are close and clever studies of low
types of boy. But their agony is genuine enough. The other two
groups are playful, one might almost say innocent. The young
satyr is an animal who takes his repulse in good part[2]. The
hermaphrodite[3] is simply a country girl, untroubled by moral
misgivings, though glad to escape from the inconvenient attentions of the old satyr.

It is noteworthy that the scale and subject of many of these
pieces fit them for the decoration of a private house or garden.
In this individualistic and commercial age the call for purely
religious dedications loses strength; memorials of victory, of
civic or royal pride, are in demand, and precious pieces for the
cabinets and shrines of princes or wealthy private citizens.

V. THE SECOND AND FIRST CENTURIES

The first half of the second century is not marked by any
falling-off of creative activity. New subjects, or subjects regarded
with new eyes, are now exploited: youth and age, complexes
like the hermaphrodite, 'sweet marble monster of both sexes,'
or the older Pan, satyr, triton, centaur, are submitted to psychological as well as physiological study, and are invested with a
subtlety of meaning they have not hitherto borne. Groups suggesting complex emotions are invented; introspection thrives.

The Pergamene kingdom and other flourishing cities, especially those of Asia Minor, no doubt continued during this
period to attract numbers of artists from abroad. Inscriptions
and literary records furnish the names of sculptors of other
schools than that which was flourishing at Pergamum, and some

---

[1] Volume of Plates iii, 140, *a, c.*   [2] *Ib.* 140, *b.*   [3] *Ib.* 140, *d.*

of their works we can identify with probability: while we can also from time to time detect other styles than the Pergamene in statues to which no name or nationality can, on external evidence, be attached. One Polycles, of Athens, made in bronze an hermaphrodite which met with the approval, passed on to us by Pliny, of some ancient critic. The hermaphrodite apparently most often copied is a delicately modelled figure, like a slender long-limbed woman, with something of the monstrous in the tapering skull, who lies stretched prone, stirring in an uneasy sleep. A copy in the Museo delle Terme in Rome[1] seems to preserve the touches which made the original bronze effective. The complicated hair has a twisted band and a gem braided into it, its roots on the temples are wiry, and it will have been executed with minute crisp chasing; the forehead, brows, nose and mouth are worked out in flattish planes which pass into one another at sharp angles, and the drapery is stretched in order to produce, for the most part, flat or tubular folds of simple section, and narrow, sharp hollows.

We may perhaps recognize here a copy of the bronze of Polycles made about 200 b.c. (though there is little to tie the style to Athens), and we can give to the same sculptor an Eros[2], superficially alike but subtly differentiated, supine, easy, carefree; a saucy boy, his mischief sleep-surprised, like his ranging hands. It is interesting to compare with this rendering of childhood the boy[3] made by Boëthus of Chalcedon not many years later. There is about the same degree of naturalism in the body, but the head of Eros, who seems the elder of the two, is less dependent on tradition and shows more evidently the careful study of a model. Boëthus' boy struggles with a goose, a common domestic pet in a country where dogs were outcast, and the scene, like much of the modelling, will have been taken direct from life. But it is by no means devoid of monumental feeling, being broad and restrained, though at the same time not uninteresting. Boëthus was famous as a worker in metal, and a bronze fragment signed by him, the support of a statue, has survived: from its nature a piece of conventional archaism, it tells little of his own style but only of an excellent technique.

We have called the hermaphrodite woman-like, but the feminine ideal of the time was rather the statue of which the Capitoline Aphrodite is a copy, too succulent, or the bathing Aphrodite[4] of Doedalsas of Bithynia, too fleshy for modern taste.

[1] Volume of Plates iii, 146, c, d.   [2] Ib. 146, a, b.
[3] Ib. 144, c.   [4] Ib. 144, a.

The motive of the first is that of the Cnidian Aphrodite of
Praxiteles, coarsened to vulgarity by a century and a half of
currency; that of the second is borrowed from the women's
bath, whatever its ritual application: in attitude it resembles the
slave in the Marsyas group, and the one surviving head among
the copies which shows any appreciable style indicates that we
are well on in the third century if not already in the second.

Parallel to the study of children is the study of old men and
women; and often these, too, are presented humorously. Myron
of Thebes has left an inscription at Pergamum which may have
belonged to one of the Attalid dedications. But other traces of
his work there are lost, and he is known to us only by the copies
of a statue, in bronze, of a drunken old woman[1], set up at
Smyrna. In the fable, the old woman sees the jar as an image of
herself:

> O suavis anima! quale in te dicam bonum
> Antehac fuisse, tales cum sint reliquiae?
> Hoc quo pertineat, dicet, qui me noverit.

In the statue, the two are one. The composition is something
between pyramid and cone; the drapery cascades down the sides
into an agitated pool, so that the body appears to be floating,
while the head swims. The results of age have been studied, but
there has been strict selection and emphasis of details for the
purpose of conveying certain effects, and nothing like exact
reproduction has been attempted.

From the groups we choose two music lessons, Pan instructing
Olympus and Chiron Achilles. Of the first, the copy in Naples[2]
is most complete, but, being of the second century A.D. it does
not afford trustworthy evidence for the technique of the original.
This is a new conception of Pan, no longer a human being with
accidental animal traits, but an entity terrifyingly harmonious.
Ingenious, even in the copies, are the contrasts between full
virility and tender boyishness, between rough shag, or lank
hircine beard, and rippling curls, between hoarse urgency and
tremulous doubt. Adroit, the relief of erotic strife cut, scholias-
tically, on the pipes.

No less ingenious must have been the contrasts in the companion group of the centaur Chiron teaching young Achilles to
play the lyre, now lost but for paintings and a good copy in
marble of the head of Chiron[3]. See how, even in the head alone,
his nature and something of his history are sculptured: how the
horse is suggested in the sensitive ears and dilated nostrils (the

---

[1] Volume of Plates iii, 144, *b*.   [2] *Ib.* 152, *c*.   [3] *Ib.* 152, *a, b*.

clownish tip of the nose shown in the photograph was modern and is now removed), in the loose strands on the back of the neck, and in those below the right ear, which, mane-like, are tossed round with the movement of the head: how the hair is thinning on the crown; how the tutor of old heroes turns sharply, almost incredulous, with a wry look of mingled anger and pain, at the discordant note struck by this young generation. We must notice the technical freedom of the sculptor, and the facility with which he now handles his masses in three dimensions. They are abstracted from nature and treated, in the spirit of the baroque, as so much material for producing effects. The right eyebrow sheers away in a spiral; the beard is pulled not only from side to side, but backwards and forwards; the forehead is drawn this way and that and corrugated arbitrarily.

The Pan and Chiron groups, judged on internal evidence, were by the same sculptor: what external evidence there is tells against their having been made by one Heliodorus, a Rhodian of the second century, who, according to Pliny, made a group of Pan and Olympus; for the two pendants are also mentioned by Pliny separately as being of unknown authorship. However that may be, those we have been studying were made in the first half of the second century and probably in the second quarter, and they seem to be the product of a second Pergamene school with whose most pretentious monument we now have to deal.

The medium admirably employed in the two musical groups by a vigorous and interested mind in order to express a living idea, proves spiritless in the hands of those set to represent an old-fashioned subject which has, for them, no reality. Such is the Great Frieze[1]. The pageant creaks by entertainingly enough, animated by the self-confidence of its highly-skilled manipulators. Each actor wears the correct clothes, is furnished with the correct attributes, and goes through the appropriate motions with the correct weapons. It is a triumph of virtuosity, and as empty and humourless as only virtuosi could make it. There is no decay of technique: indeed the handling of the marble is as skilful as it has ever been, and more daring. The sense of design is strong. But the basic idea is not believed, and therefore is not made believable. 'The first boar that is well made in marble should be preserved as a wonder. When men arrive at a facility of making boars well then the workmanship is not of such value.' The devices which help to conceal the fundamental deficiency of inspiration need no detailed analysis—the splendid wings

[1] Volume of Plates iii, 148.

deployed, the tumid muscles, the curly snakes with jaws that snap, the woolly dogs, the pantomime lions. Nevertheless the school of sculptors which produced the great frieze of the altar, reached, in those statues found at Pergamum which may reasonably be attributed to it, among some affectations and eccentricities, a living and consistent style, which displays itself even in their copies of older works. If its statues are not grand, most are grandiose[1]. The bodies are full, strong and erect. The main arrangements of drapery may be unduly artificial or merely conventional, but there is often a rhythmic swirl in the smaller folds which, with the crisp carving, saves them from dullness. Women's heads are massive and sensuous[2], with deep swimming eyes, and yearning mouths in which one sees the emotional intake of breath. The sculptors have studied Scopas, but have combined with his manner an impressionism carried further than by Praxiteles.

The great external frieze of the altar may commemorate the battle of Magnesia, which greatly augmented the power of Eumenes II, and may thus have been made soon after 190: other possible dates for it are something under ten and something over twenty years later, to commemorate victories over the Gauls. It may be that the external frieze celebrates Magnesia, and the frieze within the columned hall of the altar one of these later series of victories. Certainly the smaller frieze[3], with its circumstantial account of the life of Telephus, the mythical founder of Pergamum, is the innovator, and shows a narrative method which argues some previous development. We must pause to examine what traces of this there may be. The evidence is remarkably scanty, for most Hellenistic reliefs that have survived are difficult to date, and many belong to old types which tell us nothing. Nor is this the place to discuss the question of what influence predominates in the various reliefs (mostly copies) which we do possess, in marble, in stucco, and on the now popular vessels of precious metal. Sufficient to say that, although a rough classification is not impossible, no completely satisfactory localization has yet been carried out. There is a class of rural scenes into which various landscape and architectural elements have been introduced: some of these can be grouped as having the same origin; and there are also smaller groups; but, generally speaking, each relief must be analysed carefully by itself before being rigidly attached to one class.

We shall therefore confine ourselves to a few remarks on the

[1] Volume of Plates iii, 156, a.   [2] *Ib.* 140, e; 154, a.   [3] *Ib.* 150, a.

new factors which are now apparent, and in order to make these clear we must look back for a moment to the fifth century, where almost any relief will serve as an example. There the scene was worked in from a front plane to a background which actually varied in depth according to the sculptor's eye, but ideally was infinite. In the next stage, that of certain reliefs in the fourth century, the figures seem to be built up on a given flat background. This, in theory, was still unlimited in depth, was free air in which the figures stood; but when working in this method it was difficult for the sculptor to fight free of the background and suggest roundness where it did not actually exist.

The next stage is that which was reached during the Hellenistic age. It may owe its origin to the increasing fondness for groups, since the difficulty of working out the composition of a group of two or more detached figures for many points of view seems to lead back to the provision of a background and the re-limitation to one aspect. It was undoubtedly helped by painting. Relief thus might appear to be at the same stage as in the fifth century, and the free figures to be paralleled by those in a pediment. But in pediments the heavy cornices provided an ideal background of shadow, and the need for relating it to the figures did not arise. Now, the types created for free sculpture are offered a background: which background also, if one may so express it, being in the round, must be treated as part of the scene. And here are difficulties which have been sometimes skilfully evaded but never completely overcome in marble, in spite of the great assistance received from the discoveries made by painters. The problem will be clearer if we take an example, a relief from Corinth[1] probably of the third century. The traditional frame of columns surmounted by entablature and roof-tiles, taken over complete from reliefs of the late fifth century onwards: inside it a scene of sacrifice. A god and goddess are seen against a curtain. To their altar comes a family of worshippers.

Notice first the difficulties of scale. The goddess is smaller than the god, not merely because she is younger, but in order to suggest greater distance from the spectator; next come the man and wife, represented, in accordance with tradition, on a smaller scale, together with children and acolyte of appropriate sizes; and finally, against the tree which bounds the composition on the left are seen two figures, of onlookers or intending worshippers, on a smaller scale still, to suggest that they are not yet approaching the altar. The two images on a distant column need not concern

---

[1] Volume of Plates iii, 150, b.

us, since they are not brought into close enough relation with any of the living figures for their size to be a matter of importance. But the other discrepancies will be found disturbing. The mind can compass the divine and human scales (it naturally makes its standard the human) and can tolerate the difference between the god and his daughter. But what of the relation of the various figures to the old and knotted plane-tree? A few more points call for notice. The deities are sculptural types transferred direct to the relief. The little distant onlookers are like terracotta statuettes taken bodily and placed in the corner. Curtain and tree conveniently mask a landscape which would need a number of pictorial devices to collate it with the main scene; and it will constantly be found, from now onwards, that the sculptor uses wall or curtain to block his background and bring his relief virtually into two main planes again.

In the great frieze of the Pergamene altar the designer has made his figures almost in the round, but has obscured his background with bodies, wings and serpent coils. And the small frieze accepts the condition of a landscape background only in part. As in many other Hellenistic reliefs, some of its peculiarities and many of its faults arise from a mistaken attempt to imitate painting. To this are due the frontal, three-quarter, and profile heads not in the front plane, which lack rotundity and appear to have been sliced off and mounted on a slab: and it shows itself clearly in the perspective, in the different sizes of the figures and the different levels at which they are set, and in the attempt to render figures or objects in a farther plane, an attempt which will always fail because the sculptor has not at his command those devices of light and shade which assist the painter to represent distance, but is confined to a marble block which cannot be cut back indefinitely, and cannot be given such a surface as will suggest objects less clear because more distant. The position of this relief in the columned hall even shows that it is, in a sense, the substitute for a painting, and explains why the outer frieze departs less from sculptural tradition. We do not find, and hardly expect to find, such innovations in external friezes of the order, which merely follow the conventions and grouping of the fourth century, though the figures are usually in rather higher relief. The frieze of the temple of Artemis at Magnesia, to take but one example, is nothing but so many yards of a stock wall-covering.

About the middle of the second century, in the Peloponnese, a new sculptor, Damophon of Messene, came into prominence. He had not full measure of either the exuberant self-confidence or the skill of the Pergamene sculptors, and he is therefore more dependent than they were on older models. His name stands out more than it should because of its isolation and because some of the cities on the mainland could now again afford to give commissions for imposing cult-statues. One of his groups, Demeter and Kore enthroned and flanked by standing figures of Artemis and a local giant, Anytus, has been excavated at Lycosura, and by the aid of these fragments a colossal head in the Capitoline Museum at Rome[1] has also been identified as his. We thus possess ample material for passing a judgment on his style, which, without imitating the Pergamene, is not yet entirely independent of it. It also draws elements from masterpieces of the fourth and fifth centuries. In the head of the Capitoline the broad oval face recalls Pheidias, the eyes are short, wide-open, and more overhung by the brows than would have been possible with him. The mouth is short, in the manner of the fifth century, but more fleshy and set more seductively: the hair recalls older fashions, yet could not belong to any time before its own. One wonders whether the sculptor was trying to remember or trying to forget what his predecessors had done.

The general conceptions imitate those of the cult-statues of the fifth century, in colossal scale, in corresponding simplification of modelling, and probably in some attempt to reproduce the effect of gold and ivory by giving a high polish to the surface of the flesh. At Lycosura some of the drapery, cleverly worked in marble, copies richly embroidered stuff: yet not directly: the sculptor seems to have in mind the embossed and inlaid golden drapery of such statues as the Parthenos and the Zeus of Pheidias. The rest of the drapery is feebly conceived and executed in a niggling way: the limbs are structureless. Evidently the carving of these large masses of marble was left to assistants, who no longer maintained a high standard.

The adjective eclectic has been applied to this kind of sculpture. If we use it we must be aware of its meaning. Granted that there has been a selection of features from older sculpture, we must still try to determine how far they are stolen bodily, how far they are understood and fused into an organic whole; how far the new style lives. In the work of Damophon the elements chosen were incongruous, and therefore the results are inharmonious and not satisfying: but the effort to digest them was far more conscientious than in the baser form of eclecticism which we shall encounter in the first century B.C. Thus the label eclectic must be attached

[1] Volume of Plates iii, 154, c.

with the consciousness that it may cover varying degrees of crudity.

The work of Damophon is to some extent symptomatic of a new movement widespread if not universal, sedulous study of the past. The forms in which this study manifests itself may be said to be two, which however graduate into one another—the borrowing of older elements which are worked up into a more or less homogeneous but somewhat nerveless academic style, and the borrowing of older types which are modified and worked out in detail in the style of the day, which itself is inevitably though less consciously influenced by the past, and so has more claim to be considered an evolutionary growth, and generally shows greater vitality. To judge from what remains the one form was prevalent on the mainland, the other outside it. There is hardly a better example of this taking of an old type and modifying it than the Aphrodite from Melos. The original was a statue at Corinth, of the late fourth century: it is reproduced on coins, and the Venus from Capua[1] in the museum at Naples is a tolerably accurate Roman copy. It represented Aphrodite naked to the waist, the shield of Ares propped on her thigh so as to hold her drapery, admiring her beauty in its burnished surface. Before her stood Eros. It will at once be noticed, even if the line of the plinth of the Capuan copy and the coins did not indicate it, that this group was intended by the original sculptor to be seen, ordinarily, from one view, that with the head of Aphrodite almost in profile towards the right. The sculptor of the Melian statue[2] (one ...sandros, Agesandros or Alexandros, son of Menides of Antioch on the Maeander) in the mid-second century borrows the old type, obliterates Eros and the shield, lowers the right arm to hold up the drapery, and the left to rest on a tall column (with the hand holding an apple, the canting device of Melos), broadens the hips and the modelling generally, poises the head differently, modernizes the drapery and the composition, changes the point of view. The hair[3] follows an old fashion when compared, for example, with the Pergamene head we have illustrated or with those of the great frieze, but the shapes of eyes and mouth have not been able to escape the new, though its principles are not fully mastered, as we may see by the only partially successful rendering of the half-open mouth. Each sculptor adds what he knows to the old types. One from Ephesus, Agasias, made the statue of a warrior now in the Louvre[4]. It is Lysippic in

---

[1] Volume of Plates iii, 156, *b*.   [2] *Ib.* 156, *c*.
[3] *Ib.* 154, *b*.   [4] *Ib.* 158, *a*.

inspiration, but is worked out with an extraordinary display of anatomical knowledge.

At Athens, sculptors of less merit give evidence of a similar study of the past, resulting in statues less interesting even than those of Damophon. The head of Athena[1], from a large monument by Eubulides of the second half of the second century, comes near being an exact copy of an earlier statue, while the body of Victory from the same monument shows some attempt at original work; but it lacks any force in the main design, and the details resolve themselves into the meaningless repetition of a few commonplaces.

No promising growth was cut short by the sack of Corinth in 146, which flooded Rome with masterpieces and helped to create that demand for Greek art among Roman connoisseurs which, by keeping alive schools of competent craftsmen both in Rome and in Greece itself, was partially responsible for the production of a few not unpleasing pieces and of a host of mediocrities and worse. Athens now became the home of factories whose object was to supply the Roman market. Their products were not of one class only. Straight copies of various statues, chiefly those old masterpieces still remaining in Greece, were in demand; fancy versions were also made. A specialty was the so-called neo-Attic relief, a large class varying in both quality and subject. One of its series includes Dionysiac processions, usually maenads and satyrs, sometimes Pans and Silens, or nymphs with fluttering draperies, carved in a frankly decorative manner. Earlier votive reliefs usually furnished the models for these; sometimes even architectural sculptures. Another series (which was to grow excessively in the early years of the Roman Empire) was the archaistic. Something like it had been known as far back as the fifth century B.C. (and after the archaic age the tendency is seldom absent everywhere), but it now sprang up again with great vigour. At its lowest it consists in the use of a number of supposed archaic formulae, polished to excess—affected gestures, swallow-tail drapery, tip-toe gait, exaggerated slenderness—applied again and again to series of figures (identifiable only by their attributes) ranged in meaningless procession[2]. At its best it gives some simple scene—a god standing in his sanctuary, for instance[3]— executed in a somewhat archaic manner, although the attitudes may be far from archaic. The marble furniture on which these reliefs are often found borrows motives from many centuries. Statues in archaistic style, though less common, are not rare.

---

[1] Volume of Plates iii, 154, d.   [2] Ib. 160, a.   [3] Ib. 160, b.

Probably at this time another group of Athenians (and there are parallels from other centres of art) were turning out statues like the torso Belvedere (signed by Apollonius, son of Nestor), and the bronze boxer of the Terme[1] on whose glove the signature of the same artist has lately been found. The idiom employed here is not entirely original and not spontaneous enough to beget full harmonies. But they are genuine attempts at new creations, and we cannot deny them a restrained and suggestive modelling, brightened by vivid touches of fresh observation which the sculptor's double sympathy, for past and present, has enabled him to graft on to the older stock.

Other sculptors meanwhile were fulfilling local commissions at or near Athens itself, such as the large but uninspired relief at Eleusis dedicated by Lacrateides about 100, wholly dependent on the past, with no evidence of the study of nature, and burking the problem of depth in relief by its arbitrary arrangement of figures at different levels without regard for perspective; and the Caryatids (one now in the Fitzwilliam Museum at Cambridge) from the propylaea at Eleusis, of some fifty years later, which are crisply carved in a dry, rather similar style. At Rome, too, factories for sculpture were being formed. Pasiteles, writer on art, sculptor and metal-worker, realized the artistic possibilities of clay-modelling, his followers, perhaps he as well, the commercial. Arcesilaus, his contemporary, made clay models and sold them for wholesale reproduction. The work of Pasiteles himself is not known to us, but only that of Stephanus[2] his pupil and of the pupil of Stephanus, Menelaus. We have had occasion to speak of the half-unconscious imitation of older models, and of the frank employment of pseudo-archaic conventions in the commonplace pieces of the neo-Attic school. This is a baser kind of eclecticism. These are not copies of earlier works, though all the elements are old. To judge by what we have of him, it was early classical statues which Stephanus chiefly selected for misuse: a little adjustment of the limbs in the direction of greater elegance and of the features in that of so-called refinement, a little tampering with proportions, a little sugaring over, and the thing could be passed off as a new creation. Sometimes it is combined with its fellows in groups of a vapid sentimentality. Compared with the bronze boxer this kind of statue is dead and meaningless. It results from a classical revival, accompanied by the usual mistaken belief that it is possible to

[1] Volume of Plates iii, 158, *b*.   [2] *Ib.* 160, *c*.

imitate form without understanding it, and followed by the customary confusion between the classical and the academic.

Better in some ways than the boy of Stephanus, or at least with more claim to originality, is the big group by Menelaus in the Terme[1], with its reminiscences of various periods. But stolen goods are difficult to handle, and there is ludicrous discord in the scale: either Orestes is undergrown or Electra a giantess.

We may conclude this survey with a word on portraits. Throughout these three centuries portraiture (if we except that of women) never failed to reach a high level. The selection of coins in the Volume of Plates (164) may serve to give some idea of its widespread excellence; the two or three heads in the round[2] are taken from many of almost equal merit, and the last, the head of Pompey[3], for its characterization, for interest without excessive detail, and for generalization without dullness, is worthy to stand beside any of its predecessors.

We have already mentioned the statue of Demosthenes, and the interrelation of its parts[4]. Whenever the bodies of these Hellenistic portrait statues are preserved, it will be found that they not only harmonize with the main conception of the character of the subject, but enrich and elucidate it.

VI. PAINTING

Painting, at the beginning of the Hellenistic age, is in a very different situation from sculpture. Sculpture had gone far towards exhausting its always limited repertory: painting had not explored half its sphere. Sculpture had had at its disposal since its first few years every important medium; at the end of the fourth century it had mastered almost every technical device: painting had been limiting itself to a few methods, and a few colours, and had not grasped the full possibilities of tonality. Since sculpture had taken three centuries or more to realize fully the third dimension, although its medium was tridimensional, it is no surprise that painting had not long achieved the rendering of the human figure in space and was only half way towards one of the solutions of spatial as against two-dimensional composition. Thus with new possibilities and new problems to interest him, the Hellenistic painter is not driven, like the sculptor, to the elaboration of old technique or to the search for new subjects.

Painting had been in constant touch with sculpture and it still

---

[1] Volume of Plates iii, 160, *d*.　　　　[2] *Ib.* 162, *a, b.*
[3] *Ib.* 162, *c, d.*　　　　　　　　　　　[4] *Ib.* 120, *b.*

derives some of its types thence. But to speak generally, we are in a painter's world, and though the old sculptural monumentality and the old expressive contours are not forgotten, the grouping of figures, their relations in space, and their colouring are now the dominant interests. On the other hand, landscape, as we think of it, is not yet conceived.

Our information is mainly derived from wall-paintings of Roman period, chiefly at Pompeii and Herculaneum, which many times clearly misrepresent the Greek originals which they copy; and we are therefore limited to the consideration of comparatively few, namely those which we have reason to believe are accurate reproductions of masterpieces. More or less worthless versions of great pictures, and worthless versions of what seem mediocre pictures abound. These we are obliged to leave aside.

Of the masterpieces we select first one of the third century, that of Achilles in Scyros, known to us best from a Pompeian reproduction[1], how accurate we cannot altogether tell. The story is that of how Achilles' mother Thetis hid him among the daughters of Lycomedes, how Odysseus and Diomedes, disguised as merchants, made their way into the palace, and displayed the divine armour made for him by Hephaestus, how at a sign the trumpeter blows the alarm; Achilles, forgetful of his part, leaps instinctively to arms and is seized by his comrades, while Deidameia starts back in alarm and Lycomedes looks up to heaven. This, the very climax of the action, is the moment chosen by the painter. We cannot do more than point out some of the means by which he has been able to represent it successfully. The scene takes place against an architectural background, columns, curtains, open doors—night outside—with a guard, he too part of the architecture, before each of the two central columns. The centre (part of the picture is missing on the left) of this upper and further stage (for the scene is arranged in two principal planes) is held by Lycomedes; and his sceptre and the staff of Odysseus, with which it is parallel, serve to relate the two and to make a diagonal division in space which encloses the two main actors and counteracts a certain centrifugal tendency in the subject.

We may notice a few other points: the patterns and expressions of arms and legs, the use of shields, behind as a repeating geometrical motive, in front as a focalizing and compacting shape. One thing it is most important to notice; the exceedingly skilful colour-scheme, conceived almost as a modern painter might conceive it, with a limited scale, wonderful harmony of tones, and

[1] Volume of Plates iii, 166.

accented rather in the way that he might accent it. The bodies of Odysseus and Diomedes are of a warm brown, the shield—the device on which, Achilles' training in manhood at the hands of the noble centaur Chiron, sums up the underlying theme of the whole picture—a brown warmer still, verging on red: Achilles' body is much lighter, almost pink, and gives back less metallic reflections, as through soft living and too much shade: his head and shoulders are thrown up against the pale green of his own dress and the light pinkish brown of Lycomedes' cloak. Deidameia's body is framed in a mantle of palest lilac and white shadowed with green. This is the whole range: white, olive green, pale green, pale lilac, pink, chestnut red, and several shades down to a dark brown. How much of this harmony is due to the original painter, how much to the Pompeian copyist? We do not know.

In a villa at Boscoreale is a great wall-painting[1], not a simple panel-picture, but a full decoration, in a painted architectural setting which, with the conventional scarlet background, serves to detach the figures from real life. Its meaning is not clear, but some of the figures seem to be portraits of members of the Macedonian court in the second half of the third century. The copyist, working perhaps not much more than a hundred years after the original painter, has preserved much of his spirit. There is no action, yet there is no lack of interest. The main forms and the attitudes are broad and heroic, the details are throbbing with life; over all there breathes a rarefied, almost an Olympian air. This is Hellenistic painting at its best: complete master of its medium, yet entirely without ostentation.

We pass on some years, but are perhaps still in the third century with a great picture of the enslavement of Heracles by Omphale[2], painted by an artist of Asia Minor, copied for a Pompeian house some two or three hundred years later.

There is no background here; figures fill, almost crowd, the field; less than a quarter above is filled by a plain light greenish blue which finds echoes throughout the draperies, and passes through yellow to brown and red. The centre is held by the gigantic figure of Heracles, out-topping the rest by a head, his body almost bare, a rich, light bronze, his head turned aside, vine-crowned, but in anguish, with the shaded side thrown up against a bright cymbal, which tortures the ear with its senseless din, like the shrill tuneless piping of the insectile Eros on the other side. His arm rests round the shoulders of a sly, sensual

olding, Priapus; else he would reel: a swinish satyr brings up
the rear of this rout, which is only four strong with three Erotes,
and yet so disposed as to seem a noisy throng. Foil to this is the
group on the right, again four; three heads and one full-length
figure arranged so as to recede into the depth of the picture: the
snake-like satisfaction of Omphale bedizened with the lion's
spoils and holding the mighty club, a dark attendant whose
gaze follows hers staringly and emphasizes it, a girl looking up at
Heracles, and another, with sensitive mouth and eyes cast down,
troubled, not liking to see so great a man in such company, as
when one blushes to see a good actor in a bad part.

We come now to the copy[1] (from Herculaneum) of a great
picture of the Pergamene school, identified as such by both subject
and style; one would say of the second century and therefore
nearly contemporary with the Great Altar, but superior to it in
feeling. On a rocky ledge, and like carved rock herself, is seated
a goddess, vast and grand, whose eyes look into the distance.
Mountainous, for the clear coldness of the drapery is like a
mountain-peak, though flower-crowned and fruitful, she sits
there for ever. She takes no part in the action, but is herself the
scene. If any help in identifying her were needed, the satyr's
head and crook are the symbols of Arcadia on its coins. Beneath
her, and as it were to her side of the picture, sits the infant Telephus, marvellously suckled by a hind, miraculously guarded by an
eagle. Heracles, his father, has been divinely led to the spot and
dimly feels the wonder and the portent. The theme is the
glorification of the Attalid house, and the story of Telephus
occurs not only on the small frieze of the Great Altar but on
Pergamene coins. We shall not stop to analyse the composition
in detail: sufficient, to point out the two pairs of heads, the two
diagonals sloping away from the two lower corners into space in
the upper: to remark that Arcadia resembles some of the sculptural types of the mid-second century and that Heracles is of the
old Lysippic type: but whereas her body has more grandeur than
they and the head is free of the sensuousness we saw in them, the
head of Heracles is astonishingly debased, has feeble nose, coarse
unintelligent mouth, and is over-naturalistic throughout: conceive another head on that body and the picture would gain
infinitely in harmony.

We pass to a painting, that in the Villa Item[2], different in many
ways from the last. That was the copy, probably fairly accurate,

---

[1] Volume of Plates iii, 172.   [2] *Ib.* 174.

of a single self-contained picture: this has been adapted to three walls of a room, and though its present composition satisfies, we cannot tell that it has not been adjusted in the copying.

The figures there were realistically conceived in space; these stand against a conventional scarlet background. There the subject was clear and we were able to date it with an approach to certainty: this has been variously explained and is difficult to date. Lately its subject has been interpreted convincingly as the initiation of a bride[1]. Dionysus, in the lap of Ariadne, perfect type of wedded blessedness, is the dominating figure at the performance of his ritual. The bride-to-be is seen to pass through its successive stages—the reading of sacred formulae, a ritual repast and ablution, divination by water of the marriage-fate, and the unveiling of the *liknon*, basket-cradle of the god containing his sacred emblems. The culminating rite is that of flagellation, fertility-inducing magic: here Nike, goddess of success, plies the purging whip: and clashing cymbals drown the cries of the victim, which, being of ill-omen, might break the charm. Finally, the bride is seen decking herself for her wedding, and in the last panel is left seated on the marriage-couch. In style the paintings show a tendency to the academic, to lose touch with nature and to take refuge in a simplicity which is false because it deliberately adopts formulae which should have been outgrown. These are the characteristics which we find in some though not all schools of sculpture in the second century, and it may be that we ought to ascribe to that century the original from which these paintings are derived.

We come now to the work of Timomachus of Byzantium, of the first half of the first century B.C., who stands out as the last great Greek painter in the true line of succession. Two of his pictures have probably come down to us in copies: one the Medea[2] which he did not live to finish, focussed as one would expect on one personality, the mother, goaded by jealousy, meditating the murder of her children. A type recalling earlier statues has been chosen for this figure, but it is given a new meaning: the tenseness of feeling is reflected in the upper drapery, twisted and tightly drawn, and in the interlacing hands with thumbs pressed hard together, conflicting like the rage and love in her agonized mind. All is at full strain but in equilibrium.

[1] J. Toynbee in *J.R.S.* xix, 1929, pp. 67 *sqq.* See also M. Bieber in *J.D.A.I.* xliii, 1929, pp. 298 *sqq.*
[2] Volume of Plates iii, 176, *a.*

The other picture by Timomachus (if indeed it be his, for
the evidence shows probability but no certainty) is best seen in
a copy from Pompeii[1]. It represents Pylades and Orestes, bound,
before King Thoas, and Iphigenia issuing from the temple:
another tense and pregnant moment, pregnant with a whole
complex of action and emotion rather than, as in the simple conflict of the last, with the sudden crumbling of resistance followed
by flashing murder. The connection between the two groups is
hinted appropriately by the ready altar. Above them—the apex
of the triangle of which they are the base-angles—isolated,
stands Iphigenia, on whom the interest of all is centred. The
irony of the situation has a Greek relish. Noteworthy, otherwise,
the diagonal movement into space given by the placing of the steps,
and, once more, the grouped heads.

Also to the second century belonged two pictures reproduced
in the first century by a worker in mosaic, Dioscurides of Samos,
one of which we illustrate[2]. It is a scene from comedy: the
participants sit on the *podium* of the stage and wear masks. Two
ladies have come to consult a wise woman: on the table before
her lie a laurel branch, an incense-burner and an incense- or
charm-box: in her right hand she holds a long-stemmed cup, and
compresses the finger-tips of her left as she strains at prophecy,
and squints, we may imagine more than usually, with the effort.
The others hang on her pronouncement; one, in the centre,
relieving her impatience by chattering volubly, the other swelling
with anxiety. We do not recognize the scene, but the main idea
is clear, and the humour and characterization admirable. The
masks accentuate the types and yet allow the artist to put into
them much individual feeling.

We reach last two branches of painting, the development of
which is characteristic of the Hellenistic age, still-life and landscape. Still-life is the product of a painter's mind, who does not
need to go to epic or myth for his subjects, but finds ready to his
hand in the commonest of things numberless problems of his
art and an infinity of beauty and interest. Closely connected
with it, though inspired often rather by the interest of the subject
in its relation with life than primarily by interest in the artistic
problem, is the picture of manners; and even quite early in the
Hellenistic age there were painters (and writers as well) who
concentrated on something between the two—drinking-scenes,
shops, the life of peasants and their animals. Pictures of still-life
and manners are made in a time when the demand for purely

[1] Volume of Plates iii, 176, *b*.   [2] *Ib.* 178, *a*.

religious dedications is flagging, and the artist, no longer commissioned for a memorial of victory, or of divine help, or of death, looks round him and chooses at will. His pictures will often, though not always, be panel pictures, set up in houses as curiosities or rarities, rather than as integral parts of the decoration. At the highest they are of extraordinary skill, solid and full of light. We show one[1]—peaches, a peach-branch and a glass jar of water—which is of great beauty in design, in rendering of form, and in colouring. Animals seem to have been a favourite element in this kind of composition, and one of the most famous was the mosaic of doves by Sosus, a Pergamene of the third century, which has reached us in several versions. His 'Unswept Floor,' the offal of a banquet worked out, not meanly, to the meanest detail, is partially preserved in a copy in the Lateran Museum at Rome.

Landscape so far has always occurred, when it occurred at all, which is rarely, as an adjunct necessary to the full understanding of a picture, and inserted for that reason, typified usually by the smallest extract possible. And even now pure landscape is not found: it is still only the setting for life, whether human or mythical—the converse of Turner's method, where a mythological or biblical subject serves as a pretext for some grand landscape painted for its own sake. There is a series of scenes from the Odyssey, preserved in the Vatican, which will serve for an example[2]. The old scheme was, whenever possible, to show the figures only; the human, the only important element. Here figures and setting are both shown, and the balance between them is even. But there is no trace of landscape painting in the modern sense. The painter needs woods and rocks and sea, because the story mentions them. But he does not paint a study of wild rocky scenery or wooded country or seascape. He understands abstract form, and puts down abstractions. His wood is a grove, his sea clear moodless water, his rocks fantastic like Patinir's but without half their naturalistic detail. Everything is subservient to his artistic purpose, and that is not objective but subjective, not only not interpretational but not even imitative. Even in other landscapes where the figures are definitely subordinate, this is always the aim, to depict man's world, not nature's.

[1] Volume of Plates iii, 178, b.   [2] Ib. 180.

VII. ARCHITECTURE AND TOWN-PLANNING

The achievements of Hellenistic architecture, so far as they are known to us, may most conveniently be summarized by treating of the several kinds of buildings, and indicating briefly the trend of the development of each.

Of temples, the Didymaeum at Miletus, a vast shell containing as its kernel the tiny Ionic shrine of the archaic image carried off by Xerxes and now restored by Seleucus, has already been described (vol. vi, p. 555). Externally it was a normal Ionic dipteros; but its great columns, five deep at the entrance, must have seemed a forest. The temple of Zeus Olympios at Athens, continued in 174 B.C. by Antiochus Epiphanes (with Cossutius as architect) on Peisistratid foundations, was dipteral, with three rows of columns at front and back. The scale, the grouping, and the proportions of the columns give to the sixteen which still survive from its hundred and four a place among the most impressive remains of antiquity. About the beginning of the second century the architect Hermogenes, in his temple of Artemis Leucophryene at Magnesia on the Maeander, built an Ionic pseudodipteros, by eliminating the inner row of columns in a dipteral plan; so leaving an unusually wide space within the peristyle and effecting an immense economy of material[1]. Hermogenes has been credited with the invention of this plan, but there are far earlier temples that approach very close to it. Probably, then, being writer as well as architect, he systematized it as an evolved form, distinct from the more or less accidental approximations of earlier times. It is strange to reflect that the dipteros itself had originally been introduced to enable the slender Ionic column to hold its own against the sturdiness of the Doric.

Many temples were built during these centuries—many large, and of small more than before, these last for the growing number of small religious groups. There are numerous variations on orthodox plans which had now reached the limit of normal evolution: and these variations, based on arbitrary taste, and, rarely, on the study of foreign models, seem to be designed either to avoid the commonplace or to meet the requirements of some abnormality in the cult: some, especially those devoted to the celebration of mysteries, deviate widely from tradition[2]. In temple-architecture generally, the Doric order is supplanted by

[1] No. 1 (on Sheet of Plans ii, facing p. 708), and Volume of Plates iii, 182, a.

[2] Sheet of Plans ii, no. 3.

the Ionic (later, too, by the Corinthian), and even where admitted is Ionicized. The stereotyped form of both Ionic and Corinthian capitals is now reached, and though a good deal of variety is found, none of the modifications which either underwent remained popular, save the convenient four-sided Ionic, which seems to have led to the Composite in the first century A.D. There are some curious experiments, as in the Didymaeum, where a bust, sculptured in the manner of the Pergamene Great Altar (though held by some to be of Roman date), projects from each volute of an Ionic capital; and inventions based on eastern models, such as the bull-capitals of Delos, in a late fourth-century building apparently designed to accommodate a votive ship[1]. But the unpleasing Ionic capital reconstructed by Puchstein, and widely accepted as embodying the formula of Vitruvius, results from a misunderstanding: Vitruvius was describing the capital of the living Hellenistic tradition of his day, familiar to us from surviving examples[2].

There is now a fondness for leaving the lower part of columns, both Doric, Ionic, and Corinthian, unfluted, a proceeding natural enough when the flutes would have been in a position to be chipped by crowds, by porters' baskets, or by the hazards of domestic life. Columns entirely unfluted were also used, but not, as later, for a new aesthetic purpose.

In buildings other than temples, new forms were demanded by new purposes. The ship of Hiero II, a kind of houseboat, with exceedingly rich decoration and a luxuriant garden; the still more elaborate floating palace of Ptolemy IV; the lighthouse built by Sostratus for Ptolemy on the island of Pharos at Alexandria, a three-storey building nearly four hundred feet high with a beacon on the third storey, which earned its designer wide fame and served as a model for many others; the time-and-weather-indicator ('Tower of the Winds') of Andronicus Cyrrhestes at Athens[3], about 50 B.C.—these are but examples of the varied tasks on which architects were now employed. Some palaces were built, but most, if we judge from the description of Vitruvius and the scanty remains, were enlarged Greek houses rather than palaces in the Oriental sense.

Traditional plans underwent improvement and modification, generally in the sense of greater specialization. Gymnasia were more formal, and the parts more clearly differentiated, the gymnasium proper being separated from the enclosed palaestra

[1] Plans II, no. 6, and Volume of Plates iii, 182, b.
[2] See Carpenter in Amer. Journ. Archaeology, xxx, 1926, p. 259.
[3] Volume of Plates iii, 188, b, c.

where wrestling and boxing took place, and the bath again from these: some of their developments may have contributed, through the hypertrophy of that part devoted to the baths, to the plan of the Roman thermae. Theatres now began to approach the modern plan, by the truncation of the circular orchestra, and the aggrandizement of the raised stage.

The form usually associated with the ancient theatre—and its acoustic properties—also commended itself to architects as suitable for debating halls. It contrasts not unfavourably with the commonest modern type (not unknown in antiquity) where a speaker faces only half his audience, and members have to turn their heads to see the president. At Priene, the *ecclesiasterion* resembles a quadrate theatre, and is thus in essentials like a petrification of the Thersilion[1]. At Miletus, the *bouleuterion* erected by Antiochus Epiphanes in the second quarter of the second century B.C. is simply a theatre roofed in and adapted to a rectangular plan[2]. The use of an ordinary gable roof, which, even with the help of four internal columns, could only span the building by having its ridge run down the long axis at right angles to the axis of the theatre, was a timid expedient which brought difficulties into the design of the elevation, and led the architect into an unhappy reminiscence of a pseudo-dipteral temple on a podium, with engaged columns, and four somewhat insignificant entrances on the short axis[3].

The agora, the focus of daily life, was normally surrounded on three sides, internally by colonnades, externally by a wall[4]. Its smells and cries were thus cut off from the rest of the city, yet it was centrally placed and easily accessible. Here was freedom from draughts, and from the accompaniment of draughts, dust-eddies. Here, under the columns, sheltered sunny places, and shady places. Everywhere, save for the obstruction offered by haphazard dedications, ample space for circulation. So little changed are the circumstances of this primary human activity, that even in our own more rigorous climate the designer of a modern market might do worse than adopt such a general scheme.

The colonnade remained one of the chief elements of design. Medieval philosophy was to find shelter in the cloister: its southern prototype cradled one of the great philosophical systems of antiquity. The colonnaded street, a protection against sun and rain, common in Roman times, was perhaps first introduced at Antioch in the first century B.C.; while it was Sostratus, the maker of the lighthouse on Pharos, who built at Cnidus, in the

[1] Cf. vol. vi, p. 557.
[2] Plans ii, no. 5.
[3] Volume of Plates iii, 182, c.
[4] Plan iii.

third, a series of superimposed colonnades with ambulatories in the upper storeys.

The mention of the agora calls to mind the science and the art of town-planning, which may be said to have been now first systematically studied; for although streets had been laid out at right angles to each other by Hippodamus of Miletus in the fifth century B.C. (an arrangement preserved by the modern streets in the Piraeus) the practice had not become usual. The circumstances were indeed such as to stimulate the growth of this study, for with the opening up of new and vast territories, especially in the East, hundreds of new towns were being built, often on virgin sites. It is difficult to make statements which will hold good of even a majority of these, for we have examples of several —no doubt there were many others—where abnormal natural conditions or older buildings created special problems demanding special solutions just as they do to-day. Rhodes and Halicarnassus, for example, using natural contours, gave expression to the importance of their maritime life by laying out their streets as if they were the seat-rows and gangways of a great theatre, the orchestra of which was the harbour basin. But so far as one can generalize from the few towns fully excavated (and even these have accretions of later date), the usual plan was to build an encircling wall of fortifications, now highly efficient, along the contours which best suited it; and within this area, which naturally was often irregular, to lay out the town with streets regularly spaced cutting each other at right angles. The blocks thus formed would ordinarily be occupied by houses of one storey, though on cramped sites the buildings might run up to several; private gardens were rare. Towards the centre of the city would be the agora, with a main street sometimes bounding one side.

Priene is often taken as an example of Hellenistic town-planning, because its evidence is clear and full, but we cannot be certain that it was typical (in some ways we know that it was not), and, having been laid out as early as the end of the fourth century, it will represent a comparatively rudimentary stage. Many cities may have been more formal—indeed Strabo implies that a common plan was to divide the city into four quarters by two main streets connecting the four main gates—many cities were certainly less formal in plan: and the expedients for solving local problems were numerous.

Priene stands on the lower southern slope of a hill which as it rises becomes too precipitous for ordinary habitation[1].

[1] Plan III.

This precipitous side and the summit were therefore enclosed within the fortifications, but not used for building. The occupied slope was divided by fifteen streets running north and south, intersected at right angles by six, of which the largest, that leading to the West Gate, ran through the agora near its north side. The slope of the hill relieved any monotony which might arise from the regular rectangular crossings, for the streets running north and south sloped, and were stepped at intervals. The agora itself and the civic buildings were not far from the centre of the city, and actually adjoined one of the temples, that of Asclepius, though this faced away from the agora. The chief temple, of Athena Polias, which lay near, was not disregarded by the plan, but yet was not intimately correlated with the other main buildings.

Theatres usually took advantage of natural slopes, and that at Priene was no exception, being built against the steepening slope on the north of the city, while on the south, where the ground was more nearly level, were placed the gymnasia and stadium. Another arrangement, and a more spectacular use of the natural features of a site, was at Pergamum, where all the sacred buildings, including the Great Altar, were grouped, together with the agora, to crown the skyline of the Acropolis, the theatre stretched below them down the slope, and beneath it was cut a magnificent terrace to serve as basis for the whole design[1]. The planning of the less important parts of Pergamum seems however to have been somewhat neglected. And indeed we find, in general, that architects had a quicker eye for natural features and the use which might be made of them, than for the possibilities of artificial grouping and approach. Thus the absence of squares and gardens usually prevented impressive views of buildings or groups of buildings, though many temples had forecourts and even propylaea. Too rigid an adherence to the chessboard plan brought with it the usual defects. The parallel rather than the axis dominated[2]. It is rare to find a street centred on the axis of a building: instead, it runs past, parallel to the façade, or down one side, not leading up to it. You turned aside to go in. St Peter's in a side-street. At Priene the widest street touches twenty-four feet: the main streets of Pergamum were fixed by law at not less than thirty. In Hellenistic cities generally they were not paved, for Smyrna boasted that she was the first to pave them. One of the greatest problems of to-day, that of traffic, hardly existed. Sewers were now sometimes closed; and the importance of pure and abundant

[1] Volume of Plates iii, 184, 186.   [2] Plan iii.

water-supply (brought in under pressure where necessary, otherwise by gravitation) was realized, though public fountains were not in general superseded by supplies to private houses. A fragmentary inscription at Pergamum describes arrangements made for scavenging, for dealing with dangerous structures, for the repair of roads, and for the prevention of damp in houses set one below the other on a slope.

For domestic architecture, the main sources of information are Priene again, and Delos[1], which happen to be the cities most fully known and published. Vitruvius also gives an account of the Greek house[2]; but this is somewhat difficult to reconcile in all points with the actual remains. The excavations have made one point clear, namely that the Mycenaean plan persisted into Hellenistic times, and therefore must have been used (though sparingly, for the house of the ordinary citizen was always box-like) in the previous centuries for which we have not so much information. At Priene the normal plan of the third and second centuries is for the houses to be entered by a narrow covered passage varying in length, leading to an open rectangular court-yard, on the north of which (facing south) is a portico with two columns *in antis*, opening on to the main room. This is the survival of the Mycenaean *megaron*, which in essentials survives also in any ordinary Doric temple of the fifth century. It is a plan designed to give the maximum of sun in winter and of shade in summer, for the portico admitted the winter sun, but was shaded in the hottest months, because the sun is then higher in the sky; while shelter from excessive heat or cold could always be had in the main room. Sometimes both porch and main room connected with other rooms beside them, and one or more of the remaining sides of the courtyard were taken up by store-rooms, bedrooms or the like. All rooms were normally lighted from the courtyard. The house ordinarily presented a blank wall to the street, with an unpretentious entrance door, often set back to form a small porch. At Delos, in those houses (of the second century) which have been excavated, the *megaron* plan cannot be distinguished, but most have one room opening on to the pillared court. Some of these Delian houses were lighted by windows on the street, and there are evidences of an upper storey (presumably of bedrooms, the natural corollary of external lighting) although the wooden staircases have disappeared. The description by Vitruvius (substantiated in some measure by a house at Priene) refers to luxurious houses having a normal Greek plan, though

---

[1] Plans II, nos. 2, 4.　　　　　　　　[2] VI, 7 (10).

much elaborated: and this is the form that royal residences would generally take. It mentions two or more courts, the first being the old nucleus of main room facing south, used normally by the mistress of the house, and bedrooms; with the dining-room and rooms for slaves round the other sides of the courts. The second, reserved for the use of the men, has colonnades on all sides, that facing south sometimes being more lofty (a fashion called Rhodian) with large banqueting and gaming rooms behind: such colonnades have been found at Pompeii and Palmyra, and, facing east instead of south, at Delos. The side facing north contained a picture-gallery (or a special dining-room called Cyzicene, perhaps for hot weather); that facing east a library, that west *exedrae*—open-air resting-places; while separate rows of guest-rooms were annexed on two sides, presumably east and west. At Pompeii the houses are of the Italic plan, which bears only a superficial resemblance to the Greek. It is sometimes used by itself, sometimes in combination with the Greek peristyle. This combination appears as a building with two courts, the first the Roman *atrium*, with *tablinum* and *alae*, the second, the Greek, now beside, now behind it, serving as a kind of pleasure-court or garden.

Greek interiors were decorated by marble panelling, or by painted imitations of it, by stucco painted and gilded, by inlay of rich woods, and by paintings. These were sometimes architectural perspectives (of which the most famous and fantastic was in the *ecclesiasterion* of Tralles): or they consisted of simple architectural ornament, sometimes with small devices added, sometimes forming the frame for more ambitious wall-pictures. Ceilings were coloured and inlaid, floors variegated with marbles or mosaics. But the internal decoration of the dwelling-house is best studied in Graeco-Roman buildings on Italian soil: otherwise we depend on casual references by ancient writers.

For exteriors, polygonal masonry never went quite out of fashion. The effect of rectangular masonry was enhanced by drafting the edges and bossing the surface of the blocks, as well as by varying the height of the courses. The arch, rarely found in temples, less rarely in tombs, continued to be used with fine effect in large wall-surfaces, especially for the gates of city or fortification walls.

If it were possible to sum up in a few words the achievements of architects during so long a period and over so wide and diverse an area, it might be said that they were content, when building a traditional building, with a traditional plan, modifying, elaborating, sometimes improving it; but that they tended to be timid in departing from a comparatively narrow orbit of plans, methods and materials: nor had economic pressure yet forced them to demand of those materials the maximum load or the maximum strain. On the other hand, examples are not wanting of those who, when faced with exceptional tasks, were bold enough to ignore traditional forms, and instead of attempting to adapt to a new purpose the plan or elevation of another kind of building, allowed function to dominate, and so produced designs which may fairly be called original.

NOTES

1. THE TICINUS AND TREBIA

This and the two following notes are intended only to indicate the main reasons for adopting the view taken in the text of chapter II. It is not possible here to present the statement of the rival arguments, for which the reader is referred to the works cited in the Bibliography under the several sections.

The topographical reconstruction of the campaign is substantially that of Kromayer, *Antike Schlachtfelder*, III, 1, pp. 47 *sqq.*, and *Schlachten-Atlas*, Röm. Abt. 1, 1, which the writer considers, after visiting the ground, to be the most reasonable solution. (For rival theories and full bibliography see the above-mentioned works.) The position of the battle of Ticinus presents few difficulties except for the mention by Livy (XXI, 45) of Victimulae—'quinque milia passuum a Victimulis consedit—ibi Hannibal castra habebat.' Either this is a mistake of Livy's annalist sources, since Victimulae lay 'in Vercellensi agro' (Pliny, *N.H.* XXXIII, 78), or the reference is to another village of the same name (see De Sanctis, *Storia dei Romani*, III, pp. 90 *sqq.*). The narrative of the events which lead up to the battle of Trebia, on the other hand, bristles with difficulties owing to the conflict between the accounts of Livy (XXI, 47–56) and Polybius (III, 66–74). Livy's account is based upon inferior sources and produces a reversed positioning of the battle on the right bank of the river which seems very improbable (see the criticisms of Kromayer and De Sanctis). Polybius' account can be followed in general, if Livy is wholly rejected, though Scipio's second camp after the retreat from Ticinus seems more likely to have been at the strategic point of the Stradella than actually on the left bank of the river (Polybius' περὶ πόλιν Πλακεντίαν, III, 66, 9). It must be admitted, however, that certain difficulties are presented by the retreat of his army from the Stradella to the right bank of the Trebia after the desertion of the Gauls in the face of Hannibal's superiority in cavalry. Further, it must be assumed that the 10,000 troops who cut through Hannibal's army after the battle were able to get to Placentia by crossing a bridge over the Trebia close to the city, as Mommsen suggested.

Prof. Tenney Frank (*J.R.S.* IX, 1919, p. 205) proposes to avoid these difficulties and to reconcile Livy and Polybius, by assuming that the position of Placentia at this time, before it was refounded, was at the Stradella. This ingenious suggestion is unsupported hitherto by archaeological evidence or by any hint in the ancient sources. A supply depôt at Clastidium is also surprising, if the city was at the Stradella. Further, it is difficult to see, in that case, why Scipio should have retreated from his position περὶ πόλιν Πλακεντίαν at the Stradella to the far side of the Trebia after the desertion of the Gauls. Geographical inexactitude in Polybius and untrustworthiness in Livy seem to the present writer more probable than this hypothesis.

2. TRASIMENE

For a full bibliography see Kromayer, *Antike Schlachtfelder*, III, 1, pp. 148 *sqq.*, and *Schlachten-Atlas*, Röm. Abt. 1, 1, and De Sanctis, *op. cit.* III, 2, p. 110. See also map 3, facing p. 45.

That the battle took place on the north side of Lake Trasimene none can deny. The dispute concerns the exact site of the battle. The view taken in the text is that the battlefield was the broad open plain between the pass of Borghetto and Montigeto. This is the most natural identification of the αὐλῶν ἐπίπεδος of Polybius, III, 83, 1, whose whole description is that of a person looking at the battlefield from a boat in the lake. This view (that of Fuchs and Pareti) is adopted by De Sanctis, *op. cit.* III, 2, pp. 109 *sqq.*, who gives a detailed criticism of the elaborate theory of Kromayer, *Antike Schlachtfelder*. The kernel of Kromayer's argument for placing the Roman army along the shore between Passignano and Monte Colognola is a calculation of the amount of space required by a Roman army of 25,000 men marching in column; for this, in his opinion, the plain Borghetto to Montigeto is too small. But no such calculation can be made with precision. Sadée, Grundy and Reuss interpret αὐλῶν ἐπίπεδος as the valley of the Sanguineto, which runs up from the lake. This is inconsistent with Polybius (III, 83, 1), διελθὼν τὸν αὐλῶνα παρὰ τὴν λίμνην.

3. CANNAE

The complicated arguments for the two possible views of the site of the battle are summed up by Kromayer, *op. cit.* pp. 278 *sqq.* and *Schlachten-Atlas* and De Sanctis, *op. cit.* pp. 137 *sqq.* In the text the battle is placed on the left bank of the Aufidus. Kromayer, who argues for the right bank, supposes a Roman army of eight legions, which, in his opinion, could only be fed from the sea. If the Roman army was smaller (see above, p. 52), much of the force of this argument vanishes (see for further criticism of Kromayer, De Sanctis, *op. cit.* pp. 141 *sq.*). Polybius and Livy agree that the Roman right wing rested on the river. If the battle happened on the left bank the Romans thus faced north-east. But Polybius (III, 114) says that the Romans faced south, and Livy (XXI, 43) that they had the 'Volturnus wind' in their faces. It appears, however, probable that both statements arise from a faulty orientation in a common source, and they cannot outweigh the improbability that the Romans, despite the threat of Hannibal's cavalry, moved down into the open plain so far as to fight with their backs to the sea.

4. THE BOOKS OF MACCABEES

For the Jewish nationalist struggle which ended in the establishment of an independent Jewish kingdom under High Priests of the house of Hashmon our chief authorities are the two 'Books of Maccabees.' These are two wholly separate documents, the 'First Book of Maccabees' being a translation from a lost Hebrew or Aramaic original, written probably about 100 B.C. or soon after, and covering the period till the accession of John Hyrcanus (134/3 B.C.), the 'Second Book of Maccabees' being the epitome of a work in five books written in Greek, probably before the end of the second century B.C., by an otherwise unknown Hellenistic Jew, Jason of Cyrene; this epitome contains an account of the events of the struggle parallel to that of the 'First Book,' though stopping short at the battle of Adasa (160 B.C.).

Opinion is divided on the value of these two accounts. Much, for instance, depends on whether what profess to be copies of original documents—letters, treaties, rescripts—given in the First or the Second Maccabees, are genuine or forgeries: the view that they are all genuine, the view that they are all forgeries, the view that some are genuine and some forgeries, each has its supporters amongst scholars.

Those in 2 Macc., which are important historical documents, if genuine, have been generally pronounced by historians in modern times to be falsifications. But Niese in that essay of his, published in 1900, which did so much to reverse current opinion, asserted their authenticity. He was followed in this by Laqueur (1904) and Wellhausen (1905) with modifications, inasmuch as Laqueur supposed that, though mainly genuine, they had been in some respects garbled, and Wellhausen was disposed to regard one of the documents as a forgery. They have recently found a magisterial champion in Eduard Meyer (*Ursprung und Anfänge des Christentums*, vol. II, pp. 454–462, 1921), though Meyer, too, allows some garbling. On the other hand Willrich re-asserts the view that they are all forgeries (*Urkundenfälschung*, pp. 30–36, 1924), and we have a careful study by the papyrologist, W. Schubart, of the form of hellenistic state documents (*Archiv für Papyrusforschung*, VI, 1920, pp. 324 *sqq.*) which is not unfavourable to the documents in 2 Macc. xi, though unfavourable to the letter of Antiochus in chap. ix, whilst W. Kolbe in his no less careful study of the chronology of the period (*Beiträge zur syrischen und jüdischen Geschichte*, 1926) pronounces all to be fabrications on the ground of their conflict with ascertained facts.

It will be seen that there are grave considerations against their genuineness, which have perhaps never been met by any of their champions. Yet it may be equally true that those who impugn their genuineness do not always seem to realize the difficulty of supposing them fabrications. If they are forgeries they are not at all what we should have expected forgeries to be like. The letter of Antiochus IV to the Jews (2 Macc. ix, 19–27) has no hint of recognition that his policy has been a bad one, no hint of humiliation under the hand of God; it is a plain business letter, in substance just what Antiochus might have written to the hellenizing citizens of Jerusalem-Antioch. The letter of Antiochus V (xi, 27–33) makes Menelaus the negotiator with the Seleucid goverment—Menelaus, the person most obnoxious to all the faithful—very odd for a forger in the nationalist interest! Glorification of the Jews, acknowledgment of the power of the God of Israel—things which one would have thought almost certainly a forger would have put in—they are quite absent in these documents. Perhaps the documents will always be a problem. It is those apparently who test them by the minutiae of chronology and language, like Schubart and Kolbe, who are led to an unfavourable conclusion, and those who judge, on broad familiarity with the material of history, what bears the stamp of authenticity and what does not, like Eduard Meyer, who are disposed to accept the documents as genuine.

With regard to the supposed royal letters in 1 Macc. and the text of the treaty between Rome and the Jews in chap. viii, Willrich brings arguments to show that the letters are all fabrications incompatible in substance with the real historical situation; the original text of the treaty on the other hand he believes to have been genuine, but to be misdated, the treaty having really been made under John Hyrcanus, not in the time of Judas. Eduard Meyer again contends that the doubts as to the genuineness of these documents are 'quite groundless.' He even accepts the letter of Demetrius I in chap. x, which so sober a critic as Schürer gave up as an impossible fabrication. Meyer does not, of course, claim that the documents, as we are given them, are the originals. What we have is a re-translation into Biblical Greek from a Hebrew translation of the original documents which were written in the official Greek of the time.

When there is no consensus amongst scholars, no writer can do more than follow his individual judgment, though where he is not supported by a consensus, readers should be plainly warned of the state of the case. To the writer of this chapter, as at present advised, probability seems on the whole against the genuineness of the documents in question. The chronological difficulties which Kolbe has set forth against those of 2 Macc. xi seem to weigh more than inferences drawn from what forgers are likely to do: in the mentality of forgers there is no doubt a certain incalculable play of caprice and complexity of motive. The construction of the history therefore here presented will be one which leaves these documents aside.

In regard to the relative worth of the two books of Maccabees generally we have now something much more like agreement: the extreme exaltation of 2 Macc. and depreciation of 1 Macc. which marked Niese's swing-round against current opinion in 1900 has been abandoned. Wellhausen's phrase 'eclectic procedure' is accepted by Kolbe as giving the true line. Both books are put on a level and are held to embody a record written close in time to the events. The general course of events is given better in 1 Macc.; the writer of 2 Macc. is vague as to military operations and is more interested in prayers and portents, yet he often furnishes richer details than the First Book regarding the status and policy of the persons who act on behalf of the Seleucid government.

Kolbe seems to the present writer to have constructed his chronological scheme on sound evidence, and this chapter will generally follow his admirable little monograph. In two respects however the present writer would question Kolbe's conclusions. One is in regard to the expeditions of Lysias against Jerusalem. Both books of Maccabees describe two expeditions, in the first of which Lysias goes without the young Antiochus V, in the second of which he is accompanied by the boy-king. Since it is impossible to square the chronology of the second expedition as given in the First Book with the chronology of it given in the Second Book, Kugler makes *three* expeditions. Kolbe on the other hand makes only *one* expedition, that which in our Books of Maccabees is the second, and cuts out the first expedition in both books as purely mythical. But it is surely improbable that two independent accounts of the struggle, based on contemporary memories, should have agreed in mentioning two expeditions when there had in fact been only one. The second point in which Kolbe seems unconvincing is his argument that the two books must have behind them a common source. Kolbe argues this from the resemblance of the two accounts; it does not seem to have occurred to him that this might be due to one set of real events being behind both. If two people to-day wrote independently an account of the World War from their memories the two accounts would probably show a good deal of resemblance. If indeed the two books showed verbal resemblances beyond what could be accounted for by the common theme, we should have evidence for a common source, but such verbal resemblance Kolbe does not show.

The account of Josephus of the Maccabaean revolt up to the accession of Simon, and perhaps up to that of John Hyrcanus, is derived from 1 Macc. and has no independent value. For the period between the accession of Seleucus IV to the Syrian throne and the outbreak of the revolt, Josephus is very brief and confused: his account in the *Wars* differs from that in the *Antiquities*. Hölscher, approved by Eduard Meyer, has conjectured that in the former Josephus was drawing on Nicolaus of Damascus. Josephus shows no knowledge of 2 Macc.

5. THE SON OF SELEUCUS IV

No ancient authority tells us expressly that Antiochus IV maintained his brother's son till 169 as joint-king, or that the name of this boy was Antiochus. The view here put forward is based on circumstantial evidence. (1) Coins exist with the head of a child seemingly about five years old and strongly resembling Seleucus IV with the legend ΒΑΣΙΛΕΩΣ ΑΝΤΙΟΧΟΥ which in Sir George Macdonald's opinion were 'undoubtedly struck early in the reign of Antiochus IV.'[1] 'The issue,' Sir George says, in a letter to the writer of this chapter, 'though large, was not spread over a long period— a year at the outside.' (2) The cuneiform documents prove that from the years 138 to 143 of the Seleucid Era (174/3 B.C. to 169/8 B.C.) two kings Antiochus were officially reigning together. (3) We know from Diodorus xxx, 7, 2, that the son of Seleucus IV was killed by Andronicus, and from 2 Macc. that the wave of popular indignation against Andronicus, which caused Antiochus IV to execute him, occurred in the early months of 169; and although 2 Macc. says that the murder of Onias was the cause, it is now generally believed that the cause was really the murder of the son of Seleucus (p. 504). It seems probable therefore that the murder did not take place till the winter of 170–169 when Antiochus IV was in Cilicia. (4) We have the analogy in Macedonia of Antigonus Doson taking the place of king-regent during his kinsman's minority. The coins of Antiochus IV which have the simple legend ΒΑΣΙΛΕΩΣ ΑΝΤΙΟΧΟΥ without ΘΕΟΥ ΕΠΙΦΑΝΟΥΣ[2] are held to have been issued before 169 (E. T. Newell, *The Seleucid Mint of Antioch*, American Journal of Numismatics, LI, 1917, pp. 16 *sqq.*). If this is so, and if the theory just stated about the infant Antiochus is true, we have to suppose that in the early years of the reign coins were issued with the head sometimes of one of the kings, sometimes of the other, though with an identical legend. Sir George Macdonald, in the letter already referred to, tells the writer that he thinks there is nothing impossible about this; though he considers that the issue with the child's head, limited as it is to a comparatively brief period, requires some special conjunction of circum-

[1] See Vol. of Plates iii, 12, *f*.　　[2] *Ib.* 12, *g*.

stances to account for it. The fact that there is no mention of such a joint
kingship in our literary texts does not in this case give ground for any
argumentum ex silentio, since all that survives of the ancient historical literature dealing with the reign of Antiochus IV is a few miserable fragments.
It may be noted that the objection raised by Mr Newell (*op. cit.* p. 20)
against the attribution of coins with the child's head to the son of Seleucus IV
—that there are too many of them to have been issued 'during the few weeks
of turmoil and uncertainty that intervened between the death of Seleucus IV
and the arrival of Antiochus IV'—falls to the ground, if over five years
elapsed between the death of Seleucus and the boy's murder, and if Sir
George Macdonald is right in holding that all these coins must have been
issued within one year. Of course, if the view taken here is right, we ought
to call the baby-king Antiochus IV and Antiochus the uncle Antiochus V,
as indeed Otto does in *P.W. s.v.* Heliodorus (6), but the other numeration
is now so established that it would lead to confusion to try to alter it.

Two cuneiform inscriptions of the year 143 of the Seleucid Era (spring 169
to spring 168) still show a dating by two kings Antiochus: we may suppose
that some Babylonian scribes did not realize the new state of things immediately after the boy-king's murder, so as to change the formula hitherto
usual. After the year 169/8 B.C. the cuneiform inscriptions, to the end of
the reign of Antiochus Epiphanes, show one Antiochus only as sole king.
(Kugler's supposition that two kings Antiochus appear again in 165/4, *i.e.*
Antiochus Epiphanes and his infant son Antiochus Eupator, is shown by
Kolbe, *op. cit.* p. 48, to be baseless. On the documentary evidence Antiochus
Eupator was not left as joint-king when his father went on his eastern
expedition, as has been ordinarily supposed.)

LIST OF ABBREVIATIONS[1]

Abh.	Abhandlungen.
Abh. Arch.-epig.	Abhandlungen d. archäol.-epigraph. Seminars d. Univ. Wien.
Acad. Roum. Bull.	Bulletin de l'Académie roumaine (Section historique).
A.J.A.	American Journal of Archaeology.
A.J.Num.	American Journal of Numismatics.
A.J.Ph.	American Journal of Philology.
Ann. Serv.	Annales du Service des antiquités de l'Égypte.
Arch. Anz.	Archäologischer Anzeiger (in J.D.A.I.).
Ἀρχ. Ἐφ.	Ἀρχαιολογικὴ Ἐφημερίς.
Arch. Pap.	Archiv für Papyrusforschung.
Arch. Relig.	Archiv für Religionswissenschaft.
Ath. Mitt.	Mitteilungen des deutschen arch. Inst. (Athenische Abteilung).
Atti Acc. Torino	Atti della r. Accademia di scienze di Torino.
Bay. Abh.	Abhandlungen d. bayerischen Akad. d. Wissenschaften.
Bay. S.B.	Sitzungsberichte d. bayerischen Akad. d. Wissenschaften.
B.C.H.	Bulletin de Correspondance hellénique.
Berl. Abh.	Abhandlungen d. preuss. Akad. d. Wissenschaften zu Berlin.
Berl. S.B.	Sitzungsberichte d. preuss. Akad. d. Wissenschaften zu Berlin.
B.M.I.	Greek Inscriptions in the British Museum.
Boll. Fil. Class.	Bollettino della Filologia Classica.
B.P.W.	Berliner Philologische Wochenschrift.
B.S.A.	Annual of the British School at Athens.
B.S.R.	Papers of the British School at Rome.
Bursian	Bursian's Jahresbericht.
C.I.E.	Corpus Inscriptionum Etruscarum.
C.I.G.	Corpus Inscriptionum Graecarum.
C.I.L.	Corpus Inscriptionum Latinarum.
C.I.S.	Corpus Inscriptionum Semiticarum.
C.J.	Classical Journal.
C.P.	Classical Philology.
C.Q.	Classical Quarterly.
C.R.	Classical Review.
C.R. Ac. Inscr.	Comptes rendus de l'Académie des Inscriptions et Belles-Lettres.
Ditt.³	Dittenberger, Sylloge Inscriptionum Graecarum. Ed. 3.
D.S.	Daremberg et Saglio, Dictionnaire des antiquités grecques et romaines.
E.Brit.	Encyclopaedia Britannica. Ed. 11.
F.G.H.	F. Jacoby's *Fragmente der griechischen Historiker.*
F.H.G.	C. Müller's *Fragmenta Historicorum Graecorum.*
G.G.A.	Göttingische Gelehrte Anzeigen.
Gött. Nach.	Nachrichten von der königlichen Gesellschaft der Wissenschaften zu Göttingen. Phil.-hist. Klasse.
Harv. St.	Harvard Studies in Classical Philology.
Head H.N.²	Head's Historia Numorum. Ed. 2.
H.Z.	Historische Zeitschrift.
I.G.	Inscriptiones Graecae.

[1] For Abbreviations for names of collections of Papyri see the Bibliography to volume VII, chapter IV, pp. 889 *sqq.*

I.G.[2]	Inscriptiones Graecae. Editio minor.
Jahreshefte	Jahreshefte d. österr. archäol. Instituts in Wien.
J.A.O.S.	Journal of American Oriental Society.
J.D.A.I.	Jahrbuch des deutschen archäologischen Instituts.
J.d.Sav.	Journal des Savants.
J.E.A.	Journal of Egyptian Archaeology.
J.H.S.	Journal of Hellenic Studies.
J.I. d'A.N.	Journal International d'Archéologie Numismatique.
J.P.	Journal of Philology.
J.R.A.S.	Journal of the Royal Asiatic Society.
J.R.S.	Journal of Roman Studies.
Klio	Klio (Beiträge zur alten Geschichte).
Liv. A.A.	Liverpool Annals of Archaeology.
Mém. Ac. Inscr.	Mémoires de l'Académie des Inscriptions et des Belles-Lettres.
Mem. Acc. Lincei	Memorie della r. Accademia nazionale dei Lincei.
Mem. Acc. Torino	Memorie della r. Accademia di scienze di Torino.
Mnem.	Mnemosyne.
Mon. d. I.	Monumenti Antichi dell' Instituto.
Mon. Linc.	Monumenti Antichi pubblicati per cura della r. Accademia dei Lincei.
Mus. B.	Musée belge.
N. J. f. Wiss.	Neue Jahrbücher für Wissenschaft und Jugendbildung.
N.J. Kl. Alt.	Neue Jahrbücher für das klassische Altertum.
N.J.P.	Neue Jahrbücher für Philologie.
N.S.A.	Notizie degli Scavi di Antichità.
Num. Chr.	Numismatic Chronicle.
Num. Z.	Numismatische Zeitschrift.
O.G.I.S.	Orientis Graeci Inscriptiones Selectae.
O.L.Z.	Orientalistische Literaturzeitung.
Phil.	Philologus.
Phil. Woch.	Philologische Wochenschrift.
P.W.	Pauly-Wissowa-Kroll's Real-Encyclopädie der classischen Altertumswissenschaft.
P.Z.	Prähistorische Zeitschrift.
Rend. Linc.	Rendiconti della r. Accademia dei Lincei.
Rev. Arch.	Revue archéologique.
Rev. Belge	Revue Belge de philologie et d'histoire.
Rev. Bib.	Rev. biblique internationale.
Rev. Celt.	Revue des études celtiques.
Rev. E. A:	Revue des études anciennes.
Rev. E.G.	Revue des études grecques.
Rev. Eg.	Revue de l'Égypte ancienne (from 1925 incorporating Revue Égyptologique).
Rev. E.J.	Revue des études juives.
Rev. E.L.	Revue des études latines.
Rev. H.	Revue historique.
Rev. N.	Revue numismatique.
Rev. Phil.	Revue de philologie, de littérature et d'histoire anciennes.
Rh. Mus.	Rheinisches Museum für Philologie.
Riv. Fil.	Rivista di filologia.
Riv. stor. ant.	Rivista di storia antica.
Röm. Mitt.	Mitteilungen des deutschen arch. Inst. Römische Abteilung.
S.B.	Sitzungsberichte.

S.E.G.	Supplementum epigraphicum Graecum.
S.G.D.I.	Sammlung der griechischen Dialektinschriften.
St. Fil.	Studi italiani di filologia classica.
Wien Anz.	Anzeiger d. Akad. d. Wissenschaften in Wien.
Wien S.B.	Sitzungsberichte d. Akad. d. Wissenschaften in Wien.
Wien. St.	Wiener Studien.
Z. Aeg.	Zeitschrift für aegyptische Sprache und Altertumskunde.
Z. d. Sav.-Stift.	Zeitschrift d. Savigny-Stiftung f. Rechtsgeschichte.
Z.N.	Zeitschrift für Numismatik.

BIBLIOGRAPHIES

These bibliographies do not aim at completeness. They include modern and standard works and, in particular, books utilized in the writings of the chapters. Some technical monographs, especially in journals, are omitted, but the works that are registered below will put the reader on their track.

The works given in the General Bibliography for Greek and Roman History are, as a rule, not repeated in the bibliographies to the separate chapters. The first page only of articles in journals is given if the whole article is cited.

GENERAL BIBLIOGRAPHY

I. General Histories and Treatises

Beloch, K. J. *Griechische Geschichte seit Alexander.* (In Gercke-Norden, Einleitung in die Altertumswissenschaft, III, Ed. 2.) Leipzig-Berlin, 1914.
—— *Griechische Geschichte.* Vol. IV. Ed. 2. Berlin-Leipzig, 1925.
Bevan, E. R. *The House of Seleucus.* London, 1902.
—— *A History of Egypt under the Ptolemaic Dynasty.* London, 1927.
Bloch, G.–Carcopino, J. *Histoire romaine.* Vol. II, Fasc. 1. (In Glotz, Histoire Générale), Paris, 1929.
Bouché-Leclercq, A. *Histoire des Lagides.* Paris, 1903.
—— *Histoire des Séleucides.* Paris, 1913.
Cardinali, G. *Il Regno di Pergamo.* Rome, 1906.
Cavaignac, E. *Histoire de l'Antiquité.* Vol. III. Paris, 1914.
Colin, G. *Rome et la Grèce de 200 à 146 avant J.-C.* Paris, 1908.
De Sanctis, G. *Storia dei Romani.* Turin. III, 2, 1917; IV, 1, 1923.
Droysen, J. G. *Geschichte des Hellenismus.* Ed. 2. Gotha, 1876–   .
Ferguson, W. S. *Hellenistic Athens.* London, 1911.
Frank, T. *Roman Imperialism.* New York, 1914.
—— *A History of Rome.* New York [n.d.].
—— *An Economic History of Rome.* Ed. 2. Baltimore, 1927.
Freeman, E. A. *History of Federal Government in Greece and Italy.* Ed. J. B. Bury. London, 1893.
Hartmann, L. M. and Kromayer, J. *Römische Geschichte* (in Hartmann's Weltgeschichte). Ed. 2. Gotha, 1921.
Heitland, W. E. *The Roman Republic.* Ed. 2. Cambridge, 1923.
Holleaux, M. *Rome, la Grèce et les monarchies hellénistiques au IIIe siècle avant J.-C. (273–205).* Paris, 1921.
Homo, L. *L'Italie primitive et les débuts de l'impérialisme romain.* Paris, 1925. (English Translation, London, 1927.)
—— *Les Institutions politiques romaines de la Cité à l'Etat.* Paris, 1927. (English Translation, London, 1929.)
Ihne, W. *Römische Geschichte.* Ed. 2. Vol. II. Leipzig, 1896.
Jouguet, P. *L'Impérialisme macédonien et l'Hellénisation de l'Orient.* Paris, 1926.
Kaerst, J. *Geschichte des Hellenismus.* Ed. 2. Leipzig, 1917–26.
Kahrstedt, U. *Geschichte der Karthager von 218–146.* Berlin, 1913.
Kromayer, J. *Antike Schlachtfelder.* Berlin, 1903–   .

Meyer, Ernst. *Die Grenzen der hellenistischen Staaten in Kleinasien.* Zürich-Leipzig, 1925.
Mommsen, Th. *Römische Geschichte.* Ed. 7. Berlin, 1881. (English Translation, London, 1901.)
Niese, B. *Geschichte der griechischen und makedonischen Staaten seit der Schlacht bei Chaeronea.* Gotha, 1893–1903.
—— *Grundriss der römischen Geschichte.* Ed. 5 (by E. Hohl). Munich, 1923.
Pais, E.–Bayet, J. *Histoire romaine.* Vol. i. (In Glotz, Histoire Générale), Paris, 1926.
Piganiol, A. *La conquête romaine.* Paris, 1927.
Rostovtzeff, M. *A History of the Ancient World.* Vol. ii. Rome. Oxford, 1927.
Roussel, P. *La Grèce et l'Orient des guerres médiques à la conquête romaine.* Paris, 1928.
Tarn, W. W. *Hellenistic Civilisation.* Ed. 2. London, 1930.
Täubler, E. *Imperium Romanum.* Vol. i. Leipzig-Berlin, 1913.

II. Works of Reference, Dictionaries, etc.

Daremberg et Saglio. *Dictionnaire des antiquités grecques et romaines.* 1877–1919. (D.S.)
De Ruggiero, G. *Dizionario Epigrafico di Antichità romane.* Rome, 1895– .
Encyclopaedia Britannica. Ed. 11 and 12. Articles on Greek and Roman History.
Gercke, A. and Norden, E. *Einleitung in die Altertumswissenschaft.* Ed. 2. Leipzig and Berlin, 1914. Ed. 3: part appeared.
Lübkers Reallexikon des klassischen Altertums. Ed. 8. Berlin, 1914.
Mommsen, Th. and Marquardt, J. *Handbuch der römischen Altertümer.* Ed. 2. Leipzig, 1876–88.
Müller, Iwan. *Handbuch der klassischen Altertumswissenschaft.* Munich, various dates. (Handbuch.)
Pauly-Wissowa-Kroll. *Real-Encyclopädie der classischen Altertumswissenschaft.* Stuttgart, 1893– . (P.W.)
Roscher, W. *Ausführliches Lexikon der griechischen und römischen Mythologie.* Leipzig, 1884– . (Roscher.)
Sandys, Sir J. E. *A Companion to Latin Studies.* Ed. 2. Cambridge, 1913.
Stuart Jones, H. *A Companion to Roman History.* Oxford, 1912.
Whibley, L. *A Companion to Greek Studies.* Ed. 3. Cambridge, 1916.

CHAPTER I

POLYBIUS

I. Ancient Sources

The main source for this chapter is Polybius' own history, and the text followed is the Teubner edition by Th. Büttner-Wobst, Leipzig, 1882 onwards: a second edition of vols. I and II has appeared, 1922 and 1924. Occasional notices are found in such writers as Appian, Dionysius of Halicarnassus, Livy, Pausanias, Pliny, Strabo, etc., etc.

B. Modern Works

Notices of Polybius will be found in all the standard histories of Classical Greek Literature such as Christ-Schmid, Croiset, Susemihl, etc.

The following list is a select one of books which may be found useful:

Breska, L. *Untersuchungen über die Quellen des Polybius.* Berlin, 1880.

Bury, J. B. *Ancient Greek Historians.* Cambridge, 1919. (Chap. VI.)

Büttner-Wobst, Th. *Beiträge zu Polybius.* Jahresberichte der Kreuzschule zu Dresden, 1901.

Cuntz, O. *Polybius und sein Werk.* Leipzig, 1902.

De Sanctis, G. *Storia dei Romani.* III, 1, pp. 200 *sqq.* (Composizione ed economia delle Storie di Polibio). Turin, 1916.

Goetzler, L. *De Polybii elocutione.* Würzburg, 1887.

Hartstein, L. *Über die Abfassungszeit der Geschichte des Polybius.* Phil. XLV, 1886, p. 715.

Laqueur, R. *Polybius.* Leipzig, 1913.

—— Review of W. Siegfried (see below) in Phil. Woch. Aug. 1929.

La-Roche, P. *Charakteristik des Polybius.* Leipzig, 1857.

Meinecke, F. *Die Idee der Staatsräson.* Munich, 1924. pp. 40 *sqq.*

Neumann, K. J. *Polybiana.* Hermes, XXXI, 1896. p. 519.

Nissen, H. *Die Oekonomie der Geschichte des Polybius.* Rh. Mus. XXVI, 1871, p. 241.

Reitzenstein, R. *Die hellenistischen Mysterienreligionen.* Ed. 2. Leipzig, 1920. pp. 4 *sqq.*

von Scala, R. *Die Studien des Polybius.* I. Stuttgart, 1890.

Schmidt, M. *De Polybii geographia.* Berlin, 1875.

Schulte, A. *De ratione quae intercedit inter Polybium et tabulas publicas.* Halle, 1909.

Seipt, O. *De Polybii olympiadum ratione et de bello Punico primo quaestiones chronologicae.* Leipzig, 1887.

Siegfried, W. *Studien zur geschichtlichen Anschauung des Polybios.* Berlin, 1928.

Steigemann, H. *De Polybii olympiadum ratione et oeconomia.* Breslau, 1885.

Strachan-Davidson, J. L. Chapter on *Polybius* in *Hellenica*, Oxford. 1880.

Swoboda, H. *Die Abfassungszeit des Geschichtwerkes des Polybios.* Phil. LXXII, 1913, pp. 465 *sqq.*

Taeger, F. *Die Archäologie des Polybios.* Stuttgart, 1922.

Täubler, E. *Tyche.* Leipzig, 1926. pp. 75 *sqq.*

Thommen, R. *Über die Abfassungszeit der Geschichten des Polybius.* Hermes, XX, 1885, p. 196.

Valeton, P. *De Polybii fontibus.* Paris, 1879.

Werner, H. M. *De Polybii vita et itineribus quaestiones selectae.* Leipzig, 1877.

Wunderer, C. *Polybius-Forschungen.* Leipzig, 1898–1909.

—— *Polybios.* Leipzig, 1927.

—— *Die psychologischen Anschauungen des Historikers Polybios.* Erlanger Gymnasialprogramm, 1905.

CHAPTERS II–IV

HANNIBAL'S INVASION OF ITALY; THE ROMAN DEFENSIVE; SCIPIO AND VICTORY

A. Ancient Sources

(*a*) *Epigraphical*

C.I.L. I, 530, 1503; VI, 284, 1283; x, pp. 365 *sqq.*; XI, 1828. Dessau, 11, 12, 56.
Fasti Capitolini. See G. Costa, *I Fasti consolari romani dalle origini alla morte di C. Giulio Cesare*, Milan, 1910.

(*b*) *Literary*

Appian, *Hann., Iber.* 4–38, *Lib.* 6–67, *Sicel.* 3–5.
Asconius, *in Pisonem.* p. 3. Clark.
Auctor *de viris illustribus*, 42, 43, 45, 48, 49, 50, 51.
Cato, frags. 86, 87, Peter.
Cicero, *de nat. deorum*, II, 3, 8; III, 32, 80; *de div.* I, 24, 49; 35, 77; II, 33, 71; *Tusc.* I, 37, 89; *in Verr.* III, 6, 13; v, 22, 56; 51, 133.
Claudius Quadrigarius, frags. 53–60, Peter.
Coelius Antipater, frags. 10–43, Peter.
Cornelius Nepos, *Hannibal*, 1–6.
Dio Cassius, ed. Boissevain. Frags. of Bks. XIII–XVII.
Diodorus, XXV, XXVI.
Ennius, ed. Vahlen², Frags. of Bks. VIII, IX, 265 *sqq.*, 274, 286, 312. (Cf. E. Norden, *Ennius und Virgilius*, Leipzig, 1915, pp. 57 *sqq.*, 87 *sqq.*, 117, 127, 135 *sqq.*)
Eutropius, III, 7–23.
Festus, ed. Lindsay, pp. 254, 468, 502.
Florus, I, 22.
Frontinus, *Strategemata*, passim.
Horace, *Odes*, I, 12, 38; IV, 4, 36 *sqq.*
Justin, XXIX; XLIV, 5.
Livy, XXI–XXX, ed. Weissenborn; ed. Conway.
Macrobius, I, xi, 26, 31; xvi, 26.
Orosius, IV, 14–19.
Ovid, *Fasti*, I, 593; II, 241; III, 147; IV, 247, 292, 347, 619; VI, 65, 241, 765 *sqq.*
Pliny, *N. H.* II, 200; III, 9, 123; VII, 92; XXIII, 38, 44, 47, 96, 97; XXXIV, 40.
Plutarch, *Q. Fabius Maximus, M. Claudius Marcellus; Apophthegmata regum et imperatorum* (Fabii, Scipionis).
Polyaenus, VI, 38–41; VII, 48, 50; VIII, 11, 14, 16.
Polybius, III, and the relevant parts of VII–XI, XIV–XV (Büttner-Wobst).
Ps.-Quintilian, *Declam.* IX, 17.
Sallust, *Hist.* II, 98, 4. Maurenbrecher.
Seneca, *Quaest. Nat.* III, praefatio; V, 16, 4. *Epist.* 51, 5, 7; 86.
Servius, ap. *Aen.* X, 13.
Silius Italicus, *Punicorum* Libri XVII.
Sosylus and Silenus, Bilabel, *Die kleineren Historikerfragmente auf Papyrus*, no. 10.
Strabo, III, 147, 158 *sq.*; v, 209, 216 *sq.*, 218, 226, 245, 249, 250; VI, 254, 273, 278, 281, 283, 285.
Valerius Maximus, *passim.*
Zonaras, VIII, 21–IX, 14.

B. Modern Works on Ancient Authorities

On Polybius see also Bibliography to Chapter I.

Arnold, T. *The Second Punic War*: being chapters of his History of Rome. Ed. by W. T. Arnold. London, 1886. pp. 351–422.

Baumgartner, A. *Ueber die Quellen des Cassius Dio für die ältere römische Geschichte.* Tübingen Diss., 1880.

Beloch, K. J. *Polybius' Quellen im dritten Buche.* Hermes, L, 1915, p. 357.

—— In A. Gercke and E. Norden, *Einleitung in die Altertumswissenschaft*, vol. III², pp. 144 (Polybius), 191 (Livy), 193–4 (Appianus), 194 (Cassius Dio).

Böttcher, C. *Kritische Untersuchungen über die Quellen des Livius.* Jahrbücher für klassische Philologie, Supplementband V, 1869, p. 363.

Breska, L. *Untersuchungen über die Quellen des Polybius im dritten Buch.* Berlin Diss., 1880.

Brewitz, W. *Scipio Africanus Maior in Spanien, 210–206 B.C.* Tübingen, 1914. pp. 1–32.

Bruns, I. *Die Persönlichkeit in der Geschichtsschreibung der Alten.* Berlin, 1898. pp. 1 *sqq.*, 41 (Polybius and Livy).

Buchholz, M. *Quibus fontibus Plutarchus in vitis Fabii Maximi et Marcelli usus sit.* Greifswald Diss., 1865.

Bury, J. B. *The Ancient Greek Historians.* Cambridge, 1919. Chapter VI (Polybius).

Cichorius, E. *Römische Studien.* Die Fragmente historischen Inhalts aus Naevius' Bellum Punicum. Berlin, 1922. pp. 24–51

De Sanctis, G. *Storia dei Romani*, III, i. Turin, 1916. pp. 201 *sqq.* (on Polybius); III, 2, pp. 166 *sqq.*, 355 *sqq.*, 638 *sqq.*

Dessau, H. *Ueber die Quellen unseres Wissens vom zweiten punischen Kriege.* Hermes, LI, 1916, p. 355.

Egelhaaf, G. *Polybios und Livius über den italischen Krieg der Jahre 218/7.* Jahrbuch für classische Philologie, Supplementband X, 1879, p. 471.

Feliciani, N. *Le fonti per la seconda guerra Punica nella Spagna.* Boletin de la Acad. de Hist. XLVII, 1907.

Frank, Tenney. *Roman Historiography before Caesar.* Amer. Hist. Rev. XXXII, 1926/7, p. 232.

Haenel, G. *Die Quellen des Cornelius Nepos in Leben Hannibals.* Jena Diss. Greifswald, 1888.

Hesselbarth, H. *Historische-Kritische Untersuchungen zur dritten Dekade des Livius.* Halle, 1889.

Heyer, F. *Die Quellen des Plutarch im Leben des Marcellus.* Bartenstein, 1871.

Hirschfeld, O. *Hat Livius im 21 und 22 Buche den Polybius benutzt?* Zeitschrift für die österreichischen Gymnasien, XXVIII, 1877, p. 801.

Kahrstedt, U. Meltzer's *Geschichte der Karthager.* Vol. III. Berlin, 1913. pp. 143–362.

Keller, L. *Zu der Quellen des Hannibalischen Krieges.* Rh. Mus. XXIX, 1874, p. 88.

—— *Der zweite punische Krieg und seine Quellen.* Marburg, 1875.

Luterbacher, F. *De fontibus libri XXI et XXII T. Livi.* Strassburg, 1875.

Michael, G. *De ratione qua Livius in tertia decade opere Polybiano usus sit.* Bonn Diss., 1867.

Nissen, H. *Italische Landeskunde.* Berlin, 1883. Vol. I, pp. 12–14. (On Polybius as a geographer.)

Pais, E. *Storia di Roma durante le guerre puniche.* Rome, 1927. Vol. I, pp. 371 *sqq.*

Peter, H. *Die Quellen Plutarchs in den Biographieen der Römer.* Halle Diss., 1865.

Peter, K. *Zur Kritik der Quellen der älteren römischen Geschichte.* Halle, 1879.

Posner, M. *Quibus auctoribus in bello Hannibalico enarrando usus sit Cassius Dio.* Bonn Diss., 1874.

Rosenberg, A. *Einleitung und Quellenkunde zur römischen Geschichte.* Berlin, 1921. pp. 144 *sqq.* (Livy), 188 *sqq.* (Polybius), 203 *sqq.* (Appian), 260 (Dio).

Sanders, H. A. *Die Quellencontamination im 21 und 22 Buche des Livius.* Berlin, 1898.

Scullard, H. H. *Scipio Africanus in the Second Punic War.* Cambridge, 1930. pp. 1–31.

Seeck, O. *Der Bericht des Livius über den Winter* 218/17. Hermes, VIII, 1873, p. 152.

Sihler, E. G. *Polybius of Megalopolis.* A.J. Ph. XLVIII, 1927, pp. 38–81.

Soltau, G. *De fontibus Plutarchi in secundo bello Punico enarrando.* Bonn Diss., 1870.

Soltau, W. *Livius' Quellen in der dritten Dekade.* Berlin, 1894.

—— *Die Quellen des Livius im 21 und 22 Buche.* Zabern, 1894.

—— *Livius' Geschichtswerk, seine Komposition und seine Quellen.* Leipzig, 1897.

Svoboda, K. *Die Abfassungszeit des Geschichtswerkes des Polybios* Phil. LXXII, 1913, p. 465.

Wilcken, U. *Ein Sosylos-Fragment.* Hermes, XLI, 1906, p. 103; XLII, 1907, p. 510.

Witte, K. *Ueber die Form der Darstellung in Livius' Geschichtswerk.* Rh. Mus. LXV, 1910, p. 276.

Woelfflin, E. *Antiochos von Syrakus und Coelius Antipater.* Winterthur Diss., 1872.

Wolf, A. *Die Quellen von Livius* XXII. 138. Giessen Diss., 1918.

Articles in P.W.: *Appianus* (Schwartz), *Cassius Dio* (Schwartz), *Coelius* (Gensel), *Claudius Quadrigarius* (Niese), *Livius* (Klotz).

Also the following general works: Christ, W. von, Schmid, W. and Stählin, O., *Geschichte der griechischen Litteratur,* II, i, ed. 6 (Handbuch,VII, ii, 1), München, 1920, pp. 384 *sqq.* (Polybius), 517 *sqq.* (Plutarch); II, ii, ed. 6 (Handbuch, VII, ii, 2), München, 1924, pp. 751 (Appian), 795 *sqq.* (Dio). Schanz, M. and Hosius, C., *Geschichte der römischen Litteratur,* vol. I, ed. 4 (Handbuch, VIII, 1), München, 1927, pp. 173, 196, 317 (the annalists used by Livy); II, i, ed. 3, ib. VIII, ii, 1, 1911, pp. 429 *sqq.* (Livy); 448 *sqq.* (Pompeius Trogus; Justin). Susemihl, F., *Geschichte der griechischen Litteratur in der Alexandrinerzeit,* vol. II, Leipzig, 1892, pp. 80 *sqq.* (Polybius).

C. General Works

See the works on Roman history cited in the General Bibliography. Also:

Arnold, T. *The Second Punic War.* London, 1886.

Clerc, M. *Massalia: histoire de Marseille dans l'antiquité des origines à la fin de l'empire romain d'occident.* Vol. I. Marseille, 1927.

Delbrück, H. *Geschichte der Kriegskunst.* Ed. 3. Berlin, 1920. Vol. I.

Dodge, T. A. *Hannibal.* 2 vols. Boston, U.S.A., 1891.

Egelhaaf, G. *Analekten zur Geschichte des zweiten punischen Krieges.* H.Z. LIII, 1885, p. 430.

—— *Analekten zur Geschichte.* Stuttgart, 1886.

—— *Hannibal.* Ein Charakterbild. Stuttgart, 1922.

Ehrenberg, V. *Karthago.* Leipzig, 1927.

Gelzer, M. *Die Nobilität der römischen Republik.* Leipzig, 1912.

Gilbert, O. *Rom und Karthago in ihren gegenseitigen Beziehungen,* 241–218 *v. Chr* Leipzig, 1876.

Groag, E. *Hannibal als Politiker.* Vienna, 1929.

Gsell, S. *Histoire Ancienne de l'Afrique du Nord.* Vols. I to IV. Paris, 1913–20.

Hart, B. H. Liddell. *A Greater than Napoleon; Scipio Africanus.* Edinburgh and London, 1926.

Hennebert, E. *Histoire d'Annibal.* Paris, 1870–91.

Holm, A. *Geschichte Siciliens im Alterthum.* Leipzig, 1870–98. Vol. III.

Huvelin, P. *Une guerre d'usure, La Deuxième Guerre Punique.* Paris, 1917.

Jullian, C. *Histoire de la Gaule.* Vol. I. Paris, 1908.

Kahrstedt, U. In Meltzer's *Geschichte der Karthager,* vol. III, Berlin, 1913.

Kromayer, J. *Hannibal als Staatsmann.* H.Z. CIII, 1909, pp. 237–73.

—— *Rom's Kampf um die Weltherrschaft.* Leipzig, 1912.

Kromayer, J. and Hartmann, L. M. *Römische Geschichte.* Gotha, 1921.

Kromayer, J. and Veith, G. *Antike Schlachtfelder.* III, 1, 2. Berlin, 1912.

—— —— *Schlachten-Atlas zur antiken Kriegsgeschichte.* Röm. Abt. 1–2. Leipzig, 1922– .

—— —— *Heerwesen und Kriegführung der Griechen und Römer.* Munich, 1928.

Meyer, Ed. *Hannibal und Scipio.* (Meister der Politik, vol. I, ed. 2.) Stuttgart-Berlin, 1923.

Montanari, T. *Annibale.* Rovigo, 1900.

Morris, W. O'C. *Hannibal.* New York, 1897. (Heroes of the Nations.)

Münzer, F. *Römische Adelsparteien und Adelsfamilien.* Stuttgart, 1920.

Neumann, C. *Das Zeitalter der punischen Kriege.* Breslau, 1883.

Pais, E. *Storia di Roma durante le guerre Puniche.* I, II. Rome, 1927.

—— *Storia della Sardegna e della Corsica durante il dominio Romano.* Rome, 1923.

Pareti, L. *Contributi per la storia della guerra Annibalica.* Riv. Fil. 1912, pp. 37, 246, 385, 543.

Reid, J. S. *Problems of the Second Punic War.* J.R.S. III, 1913, p. 175.

Schur, W. *Scipio Africanus und die Begründung der römischen Weltherrschaft.* Leipzig, 1927.

Scullard, H. H. *Scipio Africanus in the Second Punic War.* Cambridge, 1930.

Smith, R. Bosworth. *Carthage and the Carthaginians.* Ed. 2. London, 1879.

Varese, P. *Ricerche di storia militare dell' Antichità.* I. Palermo, 1914.

de Vaudoncourt, G. *Histoire des campagnes d'Annibal.* Paris, 1812. (The first scholar to study the military topography of the war.)

See also the following articles in P.W., *s.vv. Q. Fabius Maximus* (Münzer), *C. Flaminius* (Münzer), *Hannibal* (Lenschau), *Hasdrubal* (Münzer), *Hasdrubal Gisgo* (Münzer), *Karthago* (Oehler and Lenschau), *Lokroi* (Oldfather), *M. Claudius Marcellus* (Münzer).

D. Special Works

(a) The Causes of the War

See especially the works of De Sanctis, Groag, Gsell, Kahrstedt and Kromayer. Also:

Cary, M. *The origin of the Punic Wars.* History, VII, 1922, p. 109.

Drachmann, A. B. *Sagunt und die Ebro-Grenze in der Verhandlungen zwischen Rom und Karthago,* 220–218. Kgl. Danske Videnskab. Selskab. Hist. fil. Meddelelser, III, 3, 1920.

Frank, T. *Rome, Marseilles and Carthage.* In The Military Historian, 1916, p. 394.

Fuchs, J. *Der zweite punische Krieg und seine Quellen. Die Jahre* 219 *und* 218. Wiener-Neustadt, 1894. pp. 24 *sqq.*

Laqueur, R. *Scipio Africanus und die Eroberung von Neukarthago.* Hermes, LVI, 1921, p. 138.

Meyer, Ed. *Der Ursprung des Kriegs und der Händel mit Sagunt* u.s.w. Kleine Schriften. Halle, 1924, Bd. II, pp. 333–400.

Reid, J. S. In *J.R.S.* III, 1913, p. 175.
Schnabel, P. *Zur Vorgeschichte des zweiten punischen Krieges.* Klio, xx, 1926, p. 110.
Täubler, E. *Die Vorgeschichte des zweiten punischen Kriegs.* Berlin, 1921.

(b) Military History. Hannibal's Army

See De Sanctis, *op. cit.* III, ii, pp. 83, 84. Kahrstedt, *op. cit.* p. 373 n. 1. Also:
Beloch, K. J. *Bevölkerung....* pp. 468 *sqq.*
Hirschfeld, O. *Kleine Schriften*, pp. 759 *sqq.*
Niese, B. In *G.G.A.*, CLXIII, 1901, p. 620. (Review of Delbrück's *Geschichte der Kriegskunst.*)
Von Stern, E. *Das hannibalische Truppenverzeichnis bei Livius*, xxi, c. 22. Berliner Studien, xxi, 1891.

(c) The Roman Legions in the Second Punic War

See De Sanctis, *op. cit.* III, ii, pp. 87 *sqq.*, 116 *sqq.*, 131 *sqq.*, 220 *sqq.*, 249 *sqq.*, 256 *sqq.*, 287 *sqq.*, 300, 456, 469, 481, 506, 509, 538, 545, 631 and the Tables on pp. 632–7. Kahrstedt, *op. cit. passim.* Meyer, *Kleine Schriften*, II, p. 415. Also:
Beversdorff, G. *Die Streitkräfte der Karthager und Römer im zweiten punischen Kriege.* Berlin, 1910.
Cantalupi, P. *Le legioni romane nella guerra d'Annibale.* Studi di Storia antica, I, 1891, pp. 1 *sqq.*
Luterbacher, F. *Die römischen Legionen und Kriegschiffe während des zweiten punischen Krieges.* Burgdorf, 1895.
Schemann, L. *De legionum per alterum bellum Punicum historia.* Bonn, 1875.
Steinwender, Th. *Die legiones urbanae.* Phil. xxxix, 1880, p. 527.

(d) The Crossing of the Alps

See the bibliographies of Azan, P., *Annibal dans les Alpes*, Paris, 1902. Jullian, C., *Histoire de la Gaule*, I, pp. 451 *sqq.*, Paris, 1908. De Sanctis, *op. cit.* III, ii, pp. 66 *sqq.* W. Osiander's *Hannibalweg*, Berlin, 1900. Also the following more recent publications:
Bonus, A. R. *Where Hannibal passed.* London, 1925.
Cary, M. and Warmington, E. H. *The Ancient Explorers.* London, 1929. p. 122 n. 83.
Constans, L. A. *La route d'Hannibal.* Rev. des Études hist. CXLVII, 1924, p. 22.
Forstner, M. *Hannibals und Hasdrubals Alpenübergang bei Silius Italicus.* Hermes, LVII, 1917, p. 293.
Freshfield, D. *Hannibal once more.* London, 1914.
Klotz, A. *Zu Hannibal's Alpenübergang.* Erlangen, 1925.
Lehmann-Haupt, C. F. *Zu Hannibals Alpenübergang.* Klio, xx, 1925, p. 118.
Meyer, Ed. *Kleine Schriften*, II, pp. 409–15.
Sontheimer, W. *Der Exkurs über Gallien bei Ammianus Marcellinus mit besonderer Berücksichtigung des Berichtes über Hannibals Alpenübergang.* Klio, xx, 1925, p. 19.
Terrell, G. *Hannibal's pass over the Alps.* C.J. XVIII, 1922.
Torr, C. *Hannibal crosses the Alps.* Cambridge, 1924.
Viedebantt, O. *Hannibal's Alpenübergang.* Hermes, LIV, 1919, p. 337.
Wilkinson, H. Spenser. *Hannibal's march through the Alps* Oxford, 1911.
Wolf, A. *Die Quellen von Livius* xxi. 1–38. Giessen Diss., 1918.

(e) Ticinus-Trebia Campaign

For full bibliography up to 1908 see Kromayer, *Antike Schlachtfelder*, III, p. 47 *sq.*; of the works there cited see especially

Fuchs, J. *op. cit.* (Left bank.) Grundy, G. B. *J.P.* XXIV, 1896, p. 83; *C.R.* X, 6, 1896, p. 284. (Right bank.) Hennebert, E. *op. cit.* II, p. 490. (Right bank.) How and Leigh. In *C.R.* 1896, p. 399. Kromayer, J. *op. cit.* (Left bank.) Mommsen, Th. *op. cit.* (Left bank.) Neumann, C. *op. cit.* p. 305. (Left bank.) Pittaluga, V. E. In *Riv. militare ital.* LII, 1908, fasc. 6, p. 1190. (Left bank.)

See also:

Beloch, K. J. *Die Schlacht an d. Trebia.* H.Z. CXIV, pp. 1–16. (Right bank.)
Frank, T. *Placentia and the battle of the Trebia.* J.R.S. 1919, p. 202. (New placing of Placentia at the Stradella.)
Fuchs, J. *Die Schlacht an d. Trebia.* Vienna, 1914.
Lehmann, K. *Das Trebia-Schlachtfeld.* H.Z. CXVI, 1916, p. 101.
Pareti, L. *Contributi per la storia della guerra Annibalica* (218–217 av. Cr.). Riv. Fil. XL, 1912, p. 40. (Left bank.)
Woelfflin, E. In *Hermes*, XXIII, 1888, pp. 307, 479.

(f) The Crossing of the Apennines and the Military Topography of Italy

For full bibliography up to 1909 see Kromayer, *op. cit.* p. 104 *sq.*; of the works there cited see especially:

Faltin, G. In *Hermes*, XX, 1885, p. 71. Fuchs, J. In *Wien. St.* XXVI, 1904, p. 118. Jung, J. In *Wien. St.* XXIV, 1902, pp. 152, 313. Neumann, C. *op. cit.* p. 330 *sqq.* Nissen, H. *Italische Landeskunde*, I, II; and in *Rh. Mus.* XXII, 1867, p. 573. Pittaluga, V. *op. cit.* p. 1209. Reuss, F. In *Klio*, VI, 1906, p. 226. Sadée, E. In *Klio*, IX, 1909, p. 48. Seeck, O. In *Hermes*, VIII, 1872, p. 152. de Vaudoncourt. *op. cit.* I, pp. 156 *sqq.* See also:

Toscanelli, N. *La marcia di Annibale della Trebia al Trasimeno.* Pisa, 1926.

(g) Trasimene

For full bibliography up to 1911 see Kromayer, *op. cit.* pp. 148 *sqq.*; of the works there cited see especially:

Arnold, T. *op. cit.* pp. 41 *sqq.*, 384 *sqq.*: Ashby, T. in *J.P.* XXXI, 1908, p. 117: Caspari, M. in *Eng. Hist. Review*, 1910, p. 417: Faltin, G. in *Rh. Mus.* XXXIX, p. 260: Fuchs, J. in *Wien. St.* XXVI, 1904, p. 134: Groebe, P. in *Zeitschrift für die öesterreich. Gymnasien*, LXII, 1911, p. 590: Grundy, G. B. in *J.P.* XXIV, 1896, p. 83 (and also XXV, 1897, p. 273): Henderson, B. W. in *J.P.* XXV, 1897, p. 112 (and also XXVI, 1899, p. 203): Kromayer, J. in *N.J. Kl. Alt.* XXV, 1910, p. 185: Nissen, H. in *Rh. Mus.* XXII, 1867, p. 566: Sadée, E. in *Klio*, IX, 1909, p. 48: Stürenburg, H. *De Romanorum cladibus Trasumenna et Cannensi.* Leipzig Diss., 1883, and *Zu den Schlachtfeldern am Trasimenischen See und in den Caudinischen Pässen.* Leipzig Diss., 1889: and Tilley, A. A. in *C.R.* VII, 1893, p. 300.

See also:

Bellini, A. *La battaglia romana-punica al Ticino.* Turin, 1922.
Neumann, C. *op. cit.* pp. 332 *sqq.*
Pareti, L. *op. cit.* p. 37, p. 385, and p. 543.

(h) Cannae and the Tactics of the Roman and Carthaginian Armies

For full bibliography up to 1909 see Kromayer *op. cit.* pp. 278 *sqq.*; of the works there cited see especially:

Arnold, T. *op. cit.* pp. 66 *sqq.*: Delbrück, H. in *Hermes*, XXI, 1886, p. 83, and in *H.Z.* (N.F.) XV, 1883, p. 239; CIX, 1912, p. 481: Fry, E. in *Eng. Hist. Review*, xii, 1897, p. 748: Hesselbarth, H. *De pugna Cannensi*. Göttingen Diss., 1874: Strachan-Davidson, J. L. *Selections from Polybius*. Oxford, 1888, p. 34: and Stürenburg, H. *op. cit.*

See also the following:

Delbrück, H. *Theologische Philologie*. Preuss. Jahrb. cxvi, p. 211; cxxi, p. 164.

Judeich, W. *Cannae*. H.Z. cxxxvi, 1927, p. 1.

Kähler, B. *Die Schlacht von Cannae, ihr Verlauf und ihre Quellen*. Berlin Diss., 1912.

Kromayer, J. *Wahre und falsche Sachkritik*. H.Z. xcv, p. 1.

—— *Vergleichende Studien zur Geschichte des griechischen und römischen Heereswesens*. Hermes, xxxv, 1900, p. 243.

Lammert, E. *Polybius und die römische Taktik*. Leipzig Progr., 1889.

Lehmann, K. *Das Schlachtfeld von Cannä*. Klio, xv, 1918, p. 172.

Nissen, H. *op. cit.* Vol. ii, pp. 852 *sqq.*

Piganiol, A. *Hannibal chez les Péligniens*. Rev. E. A. xxii, 1930, p. 22.

Steinwender, Th. *Die römische Taktik zur Zeit der Manipularstellung*. Danzig, 1913.

Viedebantt, O. *Hannibal und die römische Heeresleitung bei Cannae*. N. J. Kl. Alt. xxxvii, 1915, p. 321.

(i) The War in Italy after Cannae

For the alliance between Philip V and Carthage see bibliography to chapters v–vii, D,1.

Beloch, K. J. *Der Italische Bund*. Leipzig. 1880. pp. 154 *sqq.*

Bossi, E. *La guerra Annibalica in Italia da Canne al Metauro*. (Studi e documenti di Storia e Diritto). xii, 1891, pp. 73 *sqq.*

Friedrich, T. *Biographie des Barkiden Mago*. (Untersuchungen aus der alten Geschichte.) Vienna, 1880.

Haupt, H. *La marche d'Hannibal contre Rome en 211*. (Mélanges Graux.) Paris, 1884.

Lauterbach, A. *Untersuchungen zur Geschichte der Unterwerfung von Oberitalien durch die Römer*. Breslau Diss., 1905.

Lehmann, K. *Die Angriffe der drei Barkiden auf Italien*. Leipzig, 1905.

Streit, W. *Zur Geschichte des II punischen Krieges in Italien nach der Schlacht von Cannae*. Berliner Studien, vi, 1887, p. 10.

(j) Metaurus

For full bibliography up to 1911 see Kromayer, *op. cit.* pp. 424 *sqq.*; of these works see especially:

Henderson, B. W. in *C.R.* 1898, p. 11, and in *Eng. Hist. Review*, xiii, 1898, p. 417 and p. 625: Kromayer, J. in *G.G.A.* 1907, p. 458: Oehler, R. in *Berliner Studien* (N.F.) ii, 1897, p. 1: and Pittaluga, V. E. in *Riv. milit. italiana*, 1894.

See also the following:

Kromayer, J. Review of Kahrstedt, *op. cit.* in *G.G.A.* 1917, p. 463.

Vulić, N. *Hasdrubals Marschziel im Metaurusfeldzuge*. In Klio, xi, 1911, p. 382.

(k) The War in Spain

Brewitz, W. *Scipio Africanus Maior im Spanien, 210–206*. Tübingen, 1914.

Droysen, H. *Der polybianische Beschreibung der zweiten Schlacht bei Baecula*. Rh. Mus. xxx, 1875, p. 281.

Feliciani, N. *La Seconda Guerra Punica nella Spagna, 211–208 B.C.* Studi e Documenti di Storia e Diritto, 1904, p. 205.

Feliciani, N. *L'Espagne à la fin du IIIme Siècle avant J.-C.* Boletin de la Acad. de Hist. XLVI, May 1905.

—— *La rivolta di Sucrone.* Boletin de la Acad. de Hist. XLVI, Nov. 1905: XLVII, Feb., May, Aug. 1907.

Frantz, J. *Die Kriege der Scipionen in Spanien.* Munich Diss., 1883.

Genzken, H. *De rebus a P. et Cn. Corneliis Scipionibus in Hispania gestis.* Göttingen Diss., 1879.

Gotzfried, K. *Annalen der römischen Provinzen beider Spanien*, 218–154. Erlangen Diss., 1907.

Jumpertz, M. *Der römisch-karthagische Krieg in Spanien* 211–206 B.C. Berlin Diss., 1892.

Kahrstedt, U. *Zwei Spanische Topographien.* Arch. Anz. 1912, p. 217.

Laqueur, R. *Scipio Africanus und die Eroberung von Neukarthago.* Hermes, LVI, 1921, p. 131.

Mommsen, Th. *Römische Forschungen.* Vol. I. Berlin. 1864, pp. 98 *sqq.*

Schulten, A. *Eine unbekannte Topographie von Emporion.* Hermes, LX, 1925, p. 66.

—— *Fontes Hispaniae Antiquae.* Vol. II. Barcelona, 1925.

—— *Iliturgi.* Hermes, LXIII, 1928, p. 288.

—— Review of A. V. y Escudero's *La moneda Hispanica* in Phil. Woch. 1927, p. 1582.

Wilsdorf, D. *Fasti Hispaniarum provinciarum.* Leipzig, 1878.

See also the articles in P.W. *s.vv. Carthago nova* (Hübner), *Cessetani* (Hübner), *Dertosa* (Hübner), *Gades* (Hübner), *Hispania* (Schulten).

(l) The War in Sicily and the Re-formation of the Roman Province

Arendt, A. *Syrakus im II punischen Kriege.* Königsberg Diss., 1899.

Beloch, K. J. *Bevölkerung....* pp. 324 *sqq.*

—— *La pop. antica della Sicilia.* Archivio storico Siciliano, XIV, 1889, p. 78.

Carcopino, J. *La Loi d'Hiéron et les Romains.* Paris, 1919.

—— *Les cités de Sicile devant l'impôt romain.* (Mélanges d'arch. et d'hist.) XXV, 1905, p. 4.

De Sanctis, G. *op. cit.* Vol. III. ii, p. 347 and bibliography.

Lupus, B. *Die Stadt Syrakus in Altertum.* Strassburg, 1887.

Marquardt, J. *Römische Staatsverwaltung*, Vol. II².

Pais, E. *Alcune osservazioni.* Arch. storia Siciliana, XIII, 1888, p. 170.

Rostovtzeff, M. *Geschichte der Staatspacht in der römischen Kaiserzeit.* Phil. Supplementband IX, 1902, p. 424.

—— *Studien zur Gesch. des röm. Kolonates.* Arch. Pap. Beiheft I. Leipzig, 1910, p. 234.

(m) The War in Africa and Zama

For full Bibliography up to 1911 see Kromayer-Veith, *op. cit.* pp. 575 *sqq.*; of the works there cited see especially:

K. Lehmann, in *Jahrb. f. kl. Phil.* Supplementband XXI, 1894, p. 525: Th. Mommsen, in *Hermes*, XX, 1885, p. 144: J. Schmidt, in *Rh. Mus.* XLIV, 1889, p. 397: F. von. Wettinghausen, in *Wien. St.* XIX, 1897, p. 295: and Th. Zielinski, *Die letzten Jahre des zweiten punischen Krieges.* Leipzig, 1880.

See also the following:

C.I.L. VIII, p. 1240.

Cavaignac, E. *La chronologie romaine de* 215 *à* 168. Klio, XIV, 1914, p. 37.

Friedrich, T. *op. cit.* (see section *i*).

Lehmann, H. *Hannibal's letzte Kriegsentwurf.* Delbrück-Festschrift. Leipzig, 1908.
Meyer, E. *op. cit.* p. 408 *sq.*
Müller, L. *Numismatique de l'ancienne Afrique,* Vol. III, and Supplément, Paris, 1875.
Neumann, C. *op. cit.* (see Section *c*).
Pareti, L. *Zama.* Atti Acc. Torino, XLVI, 1911, p. 302.
Sann, G. *Untersuchungen zu Scipio's Feldzug in Afrika.* Leipzig, 1914.
Saumagne, C. περὶ τὰ Μεγάλα Πεδία, and *Zama.* Rend. Linc. 1925.

(*n*) The Peace after Zama

Nissen, H. *De pace anno 201 a Chr. Carthaginiensibus data.* Marburg Diss., 1870.
Täubler, E. *Imperium Romanum.* Vol. I. Leipzig-Berlin, 1913. pp. 190–202.

(*o*) Chronology and the Roman Calendar

Beloch, K. J. *Der römische Kalender von 218–18.* Klio, XV, 1918, p. 382.
—— *Die Sonnenfinsternis des Ennius und der vorjulianische Kalender.* Hermes, LVII, 1922, p. 119.
Boissier, G. *Calendrier romain.* Rev. Phil. VIII, 1884, p. 55.
Cavaignac, E. *La chronologie romaine de 215 à 168.* Klio, XIV, 1914–15, p. 37.
Ginzel, F. K. *Handbuch der math. und techn. Chronologie,* I. Leipzig, 1906. pp. 520 *sqq.*
—— *Spezieller Kanon der Sonnen- und Mondfinsternisse.* Berlin, 1899.
Holleaux, M. *Rome, la Grèce et les monarchies hellénistiques.* Paris, 1921. pp. 68 *sqq.*, 137, 181, etc.
Holzapfel, L. *Römische Chronologie.* Leipzig, 1885.
Kubitschek, W. *Grundriss der antiken Zeitrechnung.* Munich, 1927.
Matzat, H. *Die römische Zeitrechnung für die Jahre 219 bis 1 v. Chr.* Berlin, 1889.
Mommsen, Th. *Die Römische Chronologie*[2]. Ed. 2. Berlin, 1859.
Niese, B. *Geschichte d. griech. und maked. Staaten.* Gotha, 1893–1903. Vol. II, p. 543.
Nissen, H. *Metrologie....* pp. 889 *sqq.*
Oppolzer, Th. von. *Die Sonnenfinsterniss des J. 202 v. Chr.* Hermes, XX, 1885, p. 318.
Pareti, M. *Intorno al περὶ γῆς di Apollodoro.* Atti Acc. Torino, XLIV, 1910, p. 299.
Soltau, W. *Römische Chronologie.* Freiburg, 1889. pp. 196 *sqq.*
—— *Die Kalenderverwirrung zur Zeit des zweiten punischen Krieges.* Phil. XLVI, 1888, p. 670.
Staude, G. *Untersuchungen zum II pun. Kriege.* Halle Diss., 1911.
Stein, E. *Die Ennianische Sonnenfinsternis.* Hermes, LII, 1917, p. 558.
Tuzzi, G. *Ricerche cronologiche sulla seconda guerra punica in Sicilia.* Studi di storia antica, I, 1891, p. 815.
Unger, G. F. *Zeitrechnung der Griechen und Römer.* Ed. 2. (Müller's Handbuch.) Munich, 1892.
Varese, P. *Cronologia Romana.* Vol. I. Rome, 1908. pp. 299 *sqq.*

(*p*) Finance and Coinage

De Sanctis, G. *op. cit.* III, ii, pp. 623 *sqq.*
Giesecke, W. *Italia numismatica.* Leipzig, 1928. pp. 156–70.
—— *Sicilia numismatica.* Leipzig, 1923. pp. 147 *sqq.*
Mattingly, H. *Roman Coins.* London, 1928.
—— *The First Age of Roman Coinage.* J.R.S. XIX, 1929, p. 19.
Mommsen, Th. *Römische Münzwesen,* pp. 402 *sqq.*

CHAPTERS V–VII

ROME AND MACEDON: PHILIP AGAINST THE ROMANS; ROME AND MACEDON: THE ROMANS AGAINST PHILIP; ROME AND ANTIOCHUS

I. Ancient Sources

A. Documentary

Inscriptions

(*a*) *Greek.* Chap. v

I.G. iv², i, 622.

—— vii, 3166.

O.G.I.S. 79, 80–1, 119, 281, 286–7.

Ditt.³ 543, iv–vi, 547, 551–2, 555–6 (better G. Colin, *Fouilles de Delphes*, vol. iii, *Épigraphie*, iv, Paris, 1922, pp. 19–21, nos. 21–4), 685, ll. 40 *sqq.*, 97, 107, 120–1.

See also the following: Courby, F., *Fouilles de Delphes*, vol. ii, *Topographie et Architecture*, ii, Paris, 1921, p. 224 (provisional and incomplete). Holleaux, M., *Inscription de Thespies*, Rev. E.G. x, 1897, p. 26; *Note sur une inscription de Colophon Nova*, B.C.H. xxx, 1906, p. 349 (cf. *Rev. E.A.* xxv, 1923, p. 334 n. 5). Reinach, A. J., *Inscriptions d'Itanos*, Rev. E.G. xxiv, 1911, pp. 400 *sqq.* Wilhelm, A. in *G.G.A.* 1898, pp. 217–8.

Chap. vi

B.M.I. iv, 2, 1035 (better A. Wilhelm, *Ein Brief Antiochos III*, Wien Anz. 57, 1920, xvii–xxvii, p. 40), 1065 ('Rosetta Stone,' see below).

I.G. ii², 991.

—— ii², 885–6, 891.

—— iv², i, 621 (cf. A. Wilhelm, *Beiträge zur griechischen Inschriftenkunde*, Sonderschr. des österr. archaeol. Instituts in Wien, vol. vii, 1909, pp. 110–2, no. 95 (facsimile); *Wien Anz.* 58, 1921, xviii, p. 1, 1).

—— v, i, 885 a–d.

—— xi, iv, 1117.

—— xii, iii, *Supplementum*, 1291, 1296.

—— xii, v, 8, cf. p. 303, 1009 facsimile (better A. Wilhelm, *Neue Beiträge zur griech. Inschriftenkunde*. ii. Wien S.B. 166 (3), 1912, p. 26).

—— xii, ix, 233 (?).

O G.I.S. 59 (cf. F. Hiller von Gärtringen, *Festschrift zu O. Hirschfelds 60ten Geburtstage*, Berlin, 1903, pp. 92–7; *Klio*, xvii, 1921, p. 94), 75 (cf. M. Schede, *Ath. Mitt.* xliv, 1919, p. 24, no. 11; A. Wilhelm, *Wien Anz.* 57, 1920, p. 53; 61, 1924, p. 111, no. 9), 90, 91–3, 102 and 110 (cf. F. Hiller von Gärtringen, *Festschrift....* pp. 93 *sqq.*; M. Holleaux, *Arch. Pap.* vi, 1920, p. 20; F. Hiller von Gärtringen, *Klio*, xvii, 1921, p. 94; Ἀρχ. Ἐφ. 1925–6, [1928], p. 69 *sq.*; U. Wilcken, *U.P.Z.* i, p. 496), 112, 217 (cf. A. Wilhelm, *Wien Anz.* 57, 1920, pp. 40–2, 51), 230–7, 239 (better *I.G.* xi, iv, 1111), 240, 245–6, 270 (?), 283–4, 288.

S.E.G. ii, 536 (?).

S.G.D.I. iii, 2, 3590, 3624, 5167, 5169–71, 5176–80.

Ditt.³ 561, 567–8 (cf. M. Holleaux, *Rev. E.A.* xxv, 1923, pp. 341 n. 6, 342), 569–70, 572 (cf. M. Holleaux, *Rev. E.G.* xxx, 1917, p. 102), 573 (cf. R. Vallois,

Le Portique de Philippe, Exploration archéologique de Délos, vol. VII, i, Paris, 1923, p. 156 facsimile), 574–5 (cf. R. Vallois, *ib.* pp. 5–6, 19 facsimile, 155 facsimile), 576, 579 B, 580–1, 583–4 (586 belongs to a later period, according to the author), 587 (?), 591 (better M. Holleaux, *Rev. E.A.* XVIII, 1916, p. 1; cf. M. Clerc, *Massalia*, vol. I, Marseille, 1927, p. 296, fig. 75 facsimile), 592–3 (cf. A. S. Arvanitopoullos, Ἀρχ. Ἐφ. 1913, p. 145 facsimile), 594–5 A–B, 673 (cf. M. Holleaux, *Rev. E.G.* XXX, 1917, pp. 95, 103; *Rev. E.A.* XXV, 1923, p. 345), 674, 1028 (better R. Herzog, *Berl. Abh.* 1928 (6), pp. 25–7, no. 9). *Tituli Asiae Minoris*, II, i, 263 (= *O.G.I.S.* 91), 266 (c) (= *O.G.I.S.* 746).

See also the following: Arvanitopoullos, A. S., Θεσσαλικαὶ ἐπιγραφαί, Ἀρχ. Ἐφ. 1910, col. 344, no. 3; 1912, p. 66, no. 92. Blinkenberg, C., *Die Lindische Chronik*, Bonn, 1915, p. 34, C. xlii (better A. Wilhelm, *Wien Anz.* 59, 1922, xv–xxviii, pp. 70–2). Clerc, M. and Zakas, A. J. Περὶ τῶν τῆς πόλεως Θυατειρῶν, Athens, 1900, p. 17 (= *B.C.H.* XI, 1887, p. 104; cf. W. H. Buckler, *Lydian records*, J.H.S. XXVII, 1917, p. 110, no. 23 facsimile). Cousin, G. and Holleaux, M., *Inscriptions du sanctuaire de Zeus Panamaros*, B.C.H. XXVIII, 1904, pp. 345, 353, nos. 1–3 (cf. H. Oppermann, *Zeus Panamaros*, Religionsgeschichtliche Versuche und Vorarbeiten, vol. XIX, 3, Giessen, 1924, pp. 18–22, nos. 1–3). Hiller von Gärtringen, F., Letter of Antiochus III to the Nysaeans in W. von Diest, *Nysa ad Maeandrum*, J.D.A.I. Ergänzungsheft X, 1913, p. 64 (better A. Wilhelm, *Jahreshefte*, XXIV, 1928, p. 195, no. x); *Historische griechische Epigramme*, Bonn, 1926, pp. 45, no. 105, 47, no. 108 *a–b* (= Plutarch, *Titus*, 12); Ἐπιγραφαὶ ἐκ τοῦ Ἱεροῦ τῆς Ἐπιδαύρου, Ἀρχ. Ἐφ. [1925–6], 1928, pp. 71 *sqq.*, no. viii. Holleaux, M., *Trois décrets de Rhodes*, Rev. E.G. XII, 1899, p. 20 (better *Rev. E.A.* V, 1903, p. 224). Klaffenbach, G., *Samische Inschriften*, Ath. Mitt. LI, 1926, p. 28, no. 2. Kougeas, S. B., Ἐπιγραφικαὶ ἐκ Γυθείου συμβολαί..., Ἑλληνικά, I, 1928, pp. 17–18, 24–5 (cf. E. Kornemann, *Neue Dokumente zum lakonischen Kaiserkult*, Abh. der Schlesischen Gesellschaft für vaterländische Cultur, I, Breslau, 1929, p. 8, no. 3; H. Seyrig, *Inscriptions de Gythion*, Rev. Arch. XXIX, 1929, p. 85, no. 1). Mezger, F., *Inscriptio Milesiaca de pace cum Magnetibus facta*, Diss. München, 1913. Oikonomos, G. P., Ἐπιγραφαὶ τῆς Μακεδονίας, I, Athens, 1915, p. 2, no. 1. Papageorgiou, P. N., Ῥόδος καὶ Λέσβος κατὰ ψήφισμα τοῦ γʹ αἰῶνος νεοφανὲς ἐν Ἐρέσωι, Athens, 1913 (better P. Roussel, *Rev. E.G.* XXVII, 1914, p. 459, and L. Robert, *Lesbiaca*, Rev. E.G. XXXVIII, 1925, p. 42 *sq.*; cf. E. Ziebarth, Bursian, vol. 213, 1927, p. 18). Perdrizet, P. and Lefebvre, G., *Les graffites grecs du Memnonion d'Abydos*, Nancy-Paris-Strasbourg, 1919, p. 7, no. 32 *bis* (= F. Preisigke, *Sammelbuch griech. Urkunden aus Aegypten*, I, Strassburg, 1915, no. 3776). Pomtow, H., *Delphica*, II, B.P.W. XXIX, 1909, col. 287 (cf. G. De Sanctis, *Mon. Linc.* XI, 1901, cols. 527–8). Roussel, P., *Les épimélètes aitoliens à Delphes*, B.C.H. L, 1926, p. 124, nos. 1–4. Sauciuc, Th., *Andros*, Sonderschr. des österr. archaeol. Institutes in Wien, vol. VIII, 1914, pp. 130–1, 134, nos. 3–4. Wilhelm, A., *Zu den Inschriften von Priene*, Wien. St. XXIX, 1907, pp. 11–12 (*Inschr. von Priene*, no. 82) (cf. *Wien Anz.* 57, 1920, xvii–xxvii, p. 51 *sq.*); *Eine Inschrift des Königs Nikomedes*, Jahreshefte, XI, 1908, p. 75; *Ein Brief Antiochos III*, Wien Anz. 57, 1920, p. 40.

Chap. VII

I.G. IV², i, 244.

—— XI, iv, 713, 756.

S.E.G. I, 144–5 (?), 147.

Ditt.² 588, ll. 85–6, 90–1, 94–5, 100–4, 178 (cf. F. Durrbach, *Inscriptions de Délos; comptes des hiéropes* (II), Paris, 1929, no. 422 B, and pp. 165–8; *B.C.H.* XL, 1916, pp. 324 *sqq.*; M. Holleaux, Στρατηγὸς ὕπατος, Paris, 1918, pp. 150 *sqq.*).

Ditt.³ 582, 585 (see notes 13–15, 18, 26–7, 32–6, 46–8; cf. p. 102), 600–1, 605 A–B, 606–7, 609–10 (cf. 826 E, col. iii *s.f.*; 827 C, col. ii; D, col. iii; E, col. iv; F, col. v), 611–12 (better M. Holleaux, Στρατηγὸς ὕπατος, pp. 159 *sqq.*, 147 *sqq.*), 613, 616–17 (cf. F. Durrbach, *op. cit.*, commentary to no. 442, p. 167), 618 (better G. De Sanctis, *Atti Acc. Torino*, LVII, 1921–2, p. 242; cf. *Riv. Fil.* LVII, 1929, p. 294; M. Holleaux, *Riv. Fil.* LII, 1924, pp. 39 *sqq.*; cf. *Rev. E.A.* XIX, 1917, p. 237), 619–20, 633, 636, 688.

See also the following: Arvanitopoullos, A. S., Πρακτικὰ τῆς ἐν Ἀθήναις Ἀρχαιολογικῆς Ἑταιρείας, 1912, p. 185. Guarducci, M., *Gli Scipioni in una nuova iscrizione cretese e in altri monumenti dell' epigrafia greca*, Riv. Fil. LVII, 1929, p. 60. Holleaux, M., *Inscription trouvée à Brousse*, B.C.H. XLVIII, 1924, p. 1 (cf. G. De Sanctis, *Riv. Fil.* LIII, 1925, p. 68). Picard, C., *Éphèse et Claros*, Paris, 1922, p. 145 n. 5 (better M. Holleaux, *Riv. Fil.* LII, 1924, pp. 31 *sqq.*). Sauciuc-Saveanu, Th., *Le décret en l'honneur du Macédonien Corrhagos*, Rev. E.G. XXXVI, 1923, p. 197.

(b) Latin

C.I.L. I (ed. 2), part I (1893). *Fasti consulares*, pp. 140, 142; cf. p. 25 (*Fasti consulares Capitolini*). Add: N.S.A. ser. VI, i, 1925, pp. (379), 381–2 (tav. XXIII). *Acta triumphorum*, pp. 174–5; cf. pp. 48 (*Acta triumphorum Capitolina*), 75 (*Tabula triumphorum Tolentinas*). See also: Pais, E., *Fasti triumphales populi Romani*, voll. I–II, Rome, 1920. Add: A. M. Colini, *Bull. della Comm. arch. comunale di Roma*, LV, 1927, p. 269 (tavola). *Elogia*, XIV (p. 194), XXXVII (p. 201=*C.I.L.* IX, 4854).
— part II, i (1918). *Scipionum elogia*, 12 (=*C.I.L.* VI, 1290; Dessau, 5), 13 (=*C.I.L.* VI, 1291; D. 8). *Tituli consulares*, 613 (=*C.I.L.* XIV, 2935; D. 14), 615 (=*C.I.L.* VI, 1307; D. 16), 616 (=*C.I.L.* XIV, 2601; D. 17).

(c) Egyptian

Most of the inscriptions after 217 B.C. will be found mentioned, with full bibliography, in:

Gauthier, H., *Le Livre des Rois d'Égypte*. Vol. IV, 2. Mémoires publiés par les Membres de l'Institut français d'archéologie orientale du Caire, vol. XX. Le Caire, 1916. pp. 264–88, 423–9 (Appendice: *Les Rois de Nubie contemporains des Ptolémées*). See also Otto, W., *Ägyptische Priestersynoden in hellenistischer Zeit*, Bay. S.B. 1926 (2), pp. 21 *sqq.*

The most important inscriptions are:

1. Priestly decree from Memphis ('Rosetta Stone').

A full publication, giving the hieroglyphic, demotic (transliteration) and Greek texts, with a facsimile, and copious bibliography, will be found in *The Decrees of Memphis and Canopus*, by Sir E. A. Wallis Budge, voll. I–II, London, 1904. Greek text is also to be found in *B.M.I.* IV, 2, 1065 and *O.G.I.S.* 90.

See also:

Sethe, K. In G. Steindorff, Urkunden des aegyptischen Altertums. II, 3. *Hieroglyphische Urkunden der griechisch-römischen Zeit*. III. *Historisch-biographische Urkunden aus den Zeiten der Könige Ptolemaeus Soter und Ptolemaeus V. Epiphanes*. Leipzig, 1916. No. 36 (full tri-lingual text), pp. 166 *sqq.*
— *Zur Geschichte und Erklärung der Rosettana*. Gött. Nach. 1916, p. 275.
Spiegelberg, W. *Das Verhältnis der griechischen und ägyptischen Texte in den zweisprachigen Dekreten von Rosette und Kanopus*. Berlin-Leipzig, 1922.

Cf. W. Otto, *op. cit.* Bay. S.B. 1926 (2), p. 21.

On a copy discovered at Elephantine, see H. Sottas in *Mém. Ac. Inscr.* XIII, 2, 1927, p. 485.

2. Priestly decree from Alexandria (in hieroglyphic and demotic). ('IInd Philae Decree.')

Sethe, K. *Hieroglyphische Urkunden*....III. No. 38, pp. 214 *sqq.* See also: Sethe, K., *Die historische Bedeutung des 2. Philä-dekretes aus der Zeit des Ptolemaios Epiphanes*, Z. Aeg. LIII, 1917, p. 35. Otto, W., *op. cit.* Bay. S.B. 1926 (2), p. 21 (no. 6).

3. Hieroglyphic inscription on the western outer wall of the temple of Horus at Edfu. (H. Gauthier, *op. cit.* vol. IV, 2, pp. 265, 267, 279, nos. x, xvi, xviii.)

Dümichen, J. *Bauurkunde der Tempelanlagen von Edfu.* Z. Aeg. VIII, 1870, pp. 1, 7–9 (pl. I, ll. 21–2; II, ll. 23–5). See also: Brugsch, H., *Historische Notiz*, Z. Aeg. XVI, 1878, p. 43. Mahaffy, J. P., *The Empire of the Ptolemies*, London, 1895, pp. 239 *sqq.* (Appendix II): English translation of part of the inscription.

4. Hieroglyphic inscription of Ergamenes in the temple of Arsnuphis at Philae. (H. Gauthier, *op. cit.* vol. IV, 2, p. 425 and n. 2, no. ii.)

Weigall, A. E. P. *A Report on the Antiquities of Lower Nubia.* Oxford, 1907. Pl. XVI, no. i, and p. 42. Bevan, E., *A history of Egypt under the Ptolemaic Dynasty.* London, [1927]. p. 247, fig. 44 facsimile.

(d) Cuneiform

Most of the cuneiform inscriptions relating to the reign of Antiochus III are to be found in:

Clay, A. T. *Legal documents from Erech dated in the Seleucid era* (312–65 B.C.). Babylonian Records in the Library of J. Pierpont Morgan. Vol. II. New York, 1913. pp. 13–14 (cf. p. 85, nos. 29–34).

Kugler, F. X. *Von Moses bis Paulus. Forschungen zur Geschichte Israels.* Münster in Westf. 1922. pp. 321–5.

Beloch, K. J. *Griechische Geschichte.* Ed. 2. Vol. IV, 2. Berlin-Leipzig, 1927. p. 192.

See also: Contenau, G., *Contrats néo-babyloniens.* II. *Achéménides et Séleucides*, Musée du Louvre, Textes cunéiformes, vol. XIII, Paris, 1929, nos. 241–3. Schröder, O., *Kontrakte der Seleukidenzeit aus Warka*, Vorderasiatische Schriftdenkmäler der königl. Museen zu Berlin, vol. XV, Leipzig, 1916, nos. 34, 50, 41, 48, 25, 18–19, 32, 47, 44, 14, 38, 52. Speelers, L., *Recueil des inscriptions de l'Asie antérieure des Musées Royaux du Cinquantenaire à Bruxelles*, Bruxelles, 1925, nos. 293–4. Thureau-Dangin, F., *Tablettes d'Uruk à l'usage des prêtres du temple d'Anu au temps des Séleucides*, Musée du Louvre, Textes cunéiformes, vol. VI, Paris, 1922, nos. 23, 27–8.

Papyri

For the abbreviations here used see vol. VII, pp. 889 *sqq.*

(a) Greek

P. Columbia no. 480 (Westermann, W. L., *Upon Slavery in Ptolemaic Egypt.* New York, 1929).

P. Tebt. I, pp. 66–9, no. 8, Pl. IV (=Mitteis, L. and Wilcken, U., *Grundzüge und Chrestomathie der Papyruskunde*, vol. I, ii, Leipzig-Berlin, 1912, p. 7, no 2). [It is doubtful whether this belongs to the fourth year of Ptolemy IV or Ptolemy V: the earlier date appears more probable; cf. K. J. Beloch, *Griechische Geschichte*[2], IV, 2, p. 345 n. 1.]

P. Gur. pp. 27–8, no. xii.
P. Tur. I, p. 34, i, col. 5, ll. 27–9; cf. p. 141.

(b) Demotic

The papyri mentioning King Harmachis are enumerated by H. Gauthier, *op. cit.* vol. IV, 2, pp. 426–7, nos. i–v.

Add: Spiegelberg, W., *Ein Schuldschein aus der Zeit des Gegenkönigs Harmachis.* Z. Aeg. LIV, 1918, p. 114.

For papyri mentioning King Anchmachis see also H. Gauthier, *op. cit.* vol. IV, 2, p. 428, nos. i–iii.

Coins

See generally: Head, H. N.[2] pp. 232, 235, 300, 304, 311, 334, 357, 416, 435, 761, 853, 855.

Greece. (1) Greek Confederations

Caspari, M. O. B. *A survey of Greek federal coinage.* J.H.S. XXXVII, 1917, pp. 169 (Achaea), 170 (Aetolia), 174 (Euboea), 175 (Magnetes), 176 (Perrhaebi), 177 (Thessaly).

Gardner, P. Brit. Mus. Catalogue. *Peloponnesus.* London, 1887. pp. xxiii *sqq.*, 2 *sqq.* (Achaea).

Hill, G. F. *Greek coins acquired by the British Museum in 1920.* Num. Chr. 1921, p. 172 (coin of Psophis).

Poole, R. S. Brit. Mus. Catalogue. *Thessaly to Aetolia.* London, 1883. pp. xxx *sqq.*, 1–3 (Thessaly), 34 (Magnetes), lvii–viii, 194–200 (Aetolia).

(2) Sparta (Nabis)

Lambros, J. P. Ἀνέκδοτον τετράδραχμον Νάβιος, τυράννου τῆς Σπάρτης. B.C.H. xv, 1891, p. 415.

—— Ἀναγραφὴ τῶν νομισμάτων τῆς κυρίως Ἑλλάδος. Πελοπόννησος. Athens, 1891. p. 89.

Perdrizet, P. *Sur un tétradrachme de Nabis.* Num. Chr. 1898, p. 1.

Wace, A. J. B. *Excavations at Sparta 1908. A hoard of Hellenistic coins.* B.S.A. xiv, 1907–8, pp. 153, 156–7.

Wroth, W. *Greek coins acquired by the British Museum in 1896. Lacedaemon.* Num. Chr. 1897, pp. 107–11, no. 25.

(3) Stater struck in honour of Flamininus

Babelon, E. *Description historique et chronologique des Monnaies de la République romaine.* Vol. II. Paris, 1886. pp. 389–91, no. 1.

Giesecke, W. *Italia numismatica.* Leipzig, 1928. p. 326 (cf. p. 299).

Hill, G. F. *Historical Greek coins.* London, 1906. pp. 136–7, no. 81.

Kubitschek, W. *Studien zu Münzen der römischen Republik.* Wien S.B. 1911, 167 (6), pp. 1–2, 16 and *passim* (with bibliography).

Voigt, W. *Der Goldstater des T. Quinctius.* J.I. d'A.N. XII, 1910, p. 319 (with bibliography).

Macedonia. Philip V

Gäbler, H. *Die antiken Münzen Nord-Griechenlands.* Vol. III. *Makedonia und Paionia.* I. Berlin, 1906. pp. 1 *sqq.*, 26 *sqq.*

—— *Zur Münzkunde Makedoniens.* I. Z.N. XX, 1897, p. 169.

Grose, S. W. *Catalogue of Greek coins in the Fitzwilliam Museum.* Vol. II. Cambridge, 1926. pp. 73 *sqq.*

Hill, G. F. *Historical Greek coins.* pp. 132–4, nos. 78–9 (Philip V and the Cretans), 134–6, no. 80 (Athens and Crete in the League against Philip V).

Kubitschek, W. *Studien*.... Wien S.B. 1911, 167 (6), pp. 20, 23, 32–3, 75, etc.
Regling, K. *Ein Goldstater Philipps V.* Amtliche Berichte aus den königl. Kunstsammlungen, xxxii, 1910–1, cols. 150–4.
—— *Zur griechischen Münzkunde.* v. *Lychnidos.* Z.N. xxxv, 1925, pp. 255 *sqq.*, 263–4.
Reinach, A. J. *La base aux trophées de Délos.* J.I. d'A.N. xv, 1913, pp. 119 *sqq.*
Wroth, W. Brit. Mus. Catalogue. *Crete and the Aegean Islands.* London, 1886. pp. xvii–ix, 68, no. 18.

Syria. Antiochus III

Babelon, E. Catalogue des monnaies grecques de la Bibliothèque Nationale. *Les rois de Syrie, d'Arménie et de Commagène.* Paris, 1890. pp. lxxvii–xxxvi, 45–60, cxciv–vii, 212 (Xerxes, king of Armenia).

    See also: Allotte de la Fuye, Colonel, *Monnaie inédite de Xerxès roi d'Arsamosate,* Rev. N. xxx, 1927, p. 144, especially pp. 152–3. Gardner, P., Brit. Mus. Catalogue, *The Seleucid Kings of Syria,* London, 1878, pp. xxiii–vi, 25–9; *Macedonian and Greek coins of the Seleucidae,* Num. Chr. 1878, pp. 95–102 (Antiochus in Greece).
Hill, G. F. Brit. Mus. Catalogue *Phoenicia.* London, 1910. Introduction, *passim.*
—— Brit. Mus. Catalogue. *Palestine.* London, 1914. Introduction, *passim.*
—— *Greek coins acquired by the British Museum in* 1914–16. Num. Chr. 1917, pp. 5–6 (bronze of Lysimacheia).
Macdonald, Sir G. *Seltene und inedierte Seleukidenmünzen.* Z.N. xxix, 1912, pp. 94–5.
Newell, E. T. *The Seleucid mint of Antioch.* A.J. Num. li, 1917, pp. 5–13.
—— *The first Seleucid coinage of Tyre.* Numismatic notes and monographs. 10. New York, 1921. pp. 4–17.
Poole, R. S. Brit. Mus. Catalogue. *Thessaly to Aetolia.* p. liii (Antiochus in Acarnania).
Rogers, E. *Some new Seleucid copper types.* Num. Chr. 1912, pp. 245–8.
Voigt, W. *Die Seleukidenmünzen des kaiserlichen Eremitage zu St Petersburg.* J.I. d'A.N. xiii, 1911, pp. 145–9.

Egypt. Ptolemy IV and V, Arsinoe III

Hill, G. F. Brit. Mus. Catalogue. *Palestine.* Introduction, *passim.*
Kahrstedt, U. *Frauen auf antiken Münzen.* Klio, x, 1910, pp. 272–3 (Arsinoe III).
Koch, W. *Die ersten Ptolemäerinnen nach ihren Münzen.* Z.N. xxxiv, 1924, pp. 88–9.
Poole, R. S. Brit. Mus. Catalogue. *The Ptolemies Kings of Egypt.* London, 1883. pp. xlix–lviii, 62–77.
Robinson, E. S. G. Brit. Mus. Catalogue. *Cyrenaica.* London, 1927. Introduction, *passim,* pp. 82–3.
Svoronos, J. N. Τὰ νομίσματα τοῦ Κράτους τῶν Πτολεμαίων. Athens, 1904–8. Vol. i, cols. σοη΄–τξγ΄; vol. ii, pp. 178–222; vol. iv, cols. 201–78.
—— Μεθάνα ἢ Ἀρσινόη τῆς Πελοποννήσου. J.I. d'A.N. vii, 1904, pp. 398–400.
Ptolemy of Telmessus. (See the Genealogical Table at the end of the volume.)
Hill, G. F. *Some coins of Southern Asia minor. Ptolemy, son of Lysimachus, prince of Telmessus.* Anatolian Studies presented to Sir W. M. Ramsay. Manchester, 1923. pp. 211–12. See also: Durrbach, F., *Inscriptions de Délos; comptes des hiéropes* (ii), pp. 166–7. Wilamowitz-Moellendorff, U. von, *Hellenistische Dichtung,* vol. ii, Berlin, 1924, p 316.

Rome. (1) M. Aemilius Lepidus; denarius commemorating his mission in Egypt

Babelon, E. *Description historique et chronologique....* Vol. I. Paris, 1885. p. 128, nos. 23–4.

Grueber, H. A. *Coins of the Roman Republic in the British Museum.* Vol. I. London, 1910. pp. 447 n. 1, 449, nos. 3648–9.

Hill, G. F. *Historical Roman coins.* London, 1909. pp. 51–6, no. 29.

Svoronos, J. N. Τὰ νομίσματα...τῶν Πτολεμαίων. Vol. IV, cols. 260–3.

(2) T. Quinctius Flamininus; denarius commemorating his victories

Babelon, E. *Description historique et chronologique....* Vol. II, pp. 391–3, nos. 2–5.

Giesecke, W. *Italia numismatica.* pp. 267–8.

Grueber, H. A. *Coins of the Roman Republic....* Vol. I, pp. 154–5, nos. 1038 *sqq.*

Hill, G. F. *Historical Roman coins.* pp. 65–6, no. 34.

Kubitschek, W. *Studien....* Wien S.B. 1911, 167 (6), p. 30.

(3) Q. Fabius Labeo; denarius commemorating his naval operations

Babelon, E. *Description historique et chronologique....* Vol. I, pp. 480–1, nos. 1–4.

Grueber, H. A. *Coins of the Roman Republic....* Vol. II, pp. 264–5, nos. 494 *sqq.*

B. Literary

Appian, frags. of *Macedonica*, I–IX, 5; *Syriaca*, I (cf. A. Wilhelm in *Hermes*, LXI, 1926, p. 465)–XLIV; *Mithradatica*, LXII.

Dio Cassius, frags. 57, 57–59, 76–77; 58, 1–4; 60; 62; 62, 1a–2 (Boissevain).

Diodorus Siculus, III, 6, 3; frags. of books XXVII, 1; 3; XXVIII, 1–8, 1; 9–13; 15; XXIX, 1–13.

Jerome, *Comm. in Danielem*, XI, 13–19, pp. 708–10 Vallarsi (=Migne, *Patrologia Latina*, vol. XXV, cols. 562–4). See also F. Jacoby, *F.G.H.* II B, no. 260, pp. 1224–5; II D, p. 880 *sq.* for Jerome's borrowings from Porphyrius.

Justin, XXIX, 3, 6–8; 4; XXX–XXXII, 1, 1–3; XLI, 5, 7.

Livy, the relevant portions of books XXIII–XXXVIII.

Plutarch, *Vitae: Aratus*, 49–54; *Cleomenes*, 33; *Philopoemen*, 7–17; *Titus* (Flamininus), 2–17; *Philopoemenis et Titi comparatio*; *Cato* (Major), 12–14.

—— *Moralia: Regum et imperatorum apophthegmata*, pp. 183 F; 196 E–F; 197 A–D; 197 D–E; *de mulierum virtutibus*, iii, p. 245 B–C; xxii, p. 258 D–F; *de Pythiae oraculis*, 11, p. 399 C–D; *amatorius*, 9, p. 753 D; 16, p. 760 A–B.

Polybius, the relevant portions of books III, V, VII–XI, XIII–XVI, XVIII, XX–XXI (Büttner-Wobst).

Zonaras, IX, 4, 2–4; 6, 12; 9, 4; 11, 4 and 7; 15, 1–6; 16, 1–5 and 9–12; 18–21, 4.

These nine are the most important; for other references see:

Agatharchides Cnidius, *de rebus Europaeis*, frag. 11 (F.H.G. vol. III, p. 194 = F.G.H. II A, no. 86, p. 210, frag. 16; cf. Ed. Meyer, *Geschichte des Königreichs Pontos*, Leipzig, 1879, p. 53 n. 1); *de mari Erythraeo*, I, frag. 20 (Geogr. Gr. min. vol. I, p. 119).

Alcaeus Messenius, *Anth. Pal.* VII, 247 (cf. Plutarch, *Titus*, 9); IX, 518–19 (cf. 520 and Plutarch, *ib.*); XI, 12; append. XVI, 5.

Ampelius, XXIV.

Auctor *de viris illustribus*, 47, 3; 49, 16; 51–3, 1; 54–5.

Aulus Gellius, V, 6, 24–6; VI, 2, 5–7.

Caesius Bassus, *de metris*, 8 (in *Grammatici Latini*, vol. VI, p. 265, Keil).

Cicero, *Philipp.* XI, 7, 17; *pro Archia*, XI, 27; *pro Mur.* XIV, 31; *de prov. cons.* VIII, 18; *pro rege Deiot.* XIII, 36; *de orat.* II, 18, 75; *Tusc.* I, 3; *de fin.* V, 22, 64.

Ennius, *Annales* in J. Vahlen, *Ennianae poeseos reliquiae*[2], Leipzig, 1903, vss. 326–30, 332–7, 381–3, 397–409.

Eratosthenes of Cyrene, frag. of *Arsinoe* in Athenaeus, VII, 2, p. 276 A–C (=*F.G.H.* II B, no. 241, pp. 1016–17, frag. 16; cf. F. Jacoby, *ib.* II D, p. 713).

Eutropius, IV, 1–5.

Festus, p. 196 Lindsay.

Florus, I, 23, 4–15; 24–25; 27.

Frontinus, I, 8, 7; II, 4, 4; 7, 14; 8, 1; IV, 7, 30.

Hermippus Callimachius, frag. 72 (*F.H.G.* vol. III, p. 51).

Johannes Antiochenus, frags. 53–4 (*F.H.G.* vol. IV, pp. 557–8).

Josephus, *Antiq. Jud.* XII, 129–55, 158–85.

Macrobius, I, 10, 10.

Memnon, frag. XXVI, 1–3 (*F.H.G.* vol. III, p. 539).

Nepos, *Hannibal*, II; VII–VIII; XIII.

Orosius, IV, 20, 1–3, 5–6, 12–13, 18–19, 20–2, 25.

Pausanias, I, 36, 5–6; II, 9, 4; IV, 29, 10; VII, 7, 5–9; 8, 1–5; 7–8; 17, 5; VIII, 49–51, 4; X, 33, 3; 34, 3–4.

Phlegon Trallianus, frag. 32 from Antisthenes Peripateticus (*F.H.G.* vol. III, pp. 615–18=*F.G.H.* II B, no. 257, pp. 1174–8, frag. 36 (iii); cf. F. Jacoby, *ib.* II D, pp. 845–6).

Pliny, *N.H.* XXXIII, 148; XXXIV, 14; XXXV, 66; XXXVII, 12.

Polyaenus, IV, 18; V, 17, 2; VI, 17.

Porphyrius Tyrius. See above, Jerome, and below, Eusebius.

Ptolemaeus Megalopolitanus, frag. 2 (*F.H.G.* vol. III, p. 67=*F.G.H.* II B, no. 161, p. 888, frag. 2; cf. F. Jacoby, *ib.* II D, pp. 592–3).

Rufius Festus, 11–12.

Schol. Aristophanis *Thesmophor.* v. 1059.

Strabo, VIII, 6, 23, p. 381; IX, 5, 20, p. 441; XII, 4, 3, p. 563; XVII, 1, 11, p. 795; VI, 4, 2, p. 287; XI, 14, 5, p. 528; 15, p. 531; XII, 2, 11, p. 540; 3, 41, p. 562; 4, 3, p. 563; XIII, 1, 27, p. 594; 4, 2, p. 624; XIV, 3, 4, p. 665.

Tacitus, *Annales*, II, 63, 67; III, 62.

Trogus, *Prol.* XXX–XXXII.

Valerius Maximus, II, 5, 1; III, 5, 1; IV, 8, 4–5; V, 2, 6; 5, 1; VI, 1 *extr.* 2; 6, 1; VII, 3, 4; VIII, 1 *damn.* 1.

Chronographers

Claudius Ptolemaeus. Κανὼν βασιλέων (or βασιλειῶν) in F. K. Ginzel, *Handbuch der mathematischen und technischen Chronologie*, vol. I, Leipzig, 1906, § 28, p. 139.

Eusebius. *Chronicorum libri duo*, Ed. A. Schoene. Vol. I. *Chronicorum liber prior.* Berlin, 1875. (From the Armenian version, in Latin, with parallel Greek extracts.) Cols. 127, 161–2, 169–70, 237, 241, 243, 245, 247, 253, 263–4. Append. i A, cols. 14–16; ii B, cols. 27–9; iii, p. 56; iv, cols. 91–2; vi (*Excerpta latina Barbari*), pp. 221–3. Vol. II. *Chronicorum Canonum quae supersunt.* Berlin, 1866. (Greek and Armenian versions parallel with Jerome's Latin version.) p. 124.

—— *Die Chronik aus dem armenischen übersetzt mit textkritischem Commentar....* Ed. J. Karst. Die griechischen christlichen Schriftsteller der ersten drei Jahrhunderte...Vol. 20. Eusebius, vol. V. Leipzig, 1911. pp. 60, 75, 79, 112–16, 119, 124, 151, 153, 202–3. See also F. Jacoby, *F.G.H.* II B, no. 260, pp. 1198 *sqq.*, 1213 *sqq.*; cf. *ib.* II D, pp. 854 *sqq.*, *passim* (Eusebius' borrowings from Porphyrius).

Hieronymus (Jerome). Latin version of Eusebius' Chronici Canones. Schoene, A., *op. cit.* vol. II, pp. 123, 125.

—— *Eusebii Pamphili Chronici Canones latine vertit...S. Eusebius Hieronymus.* Ed. J. K. Fotheringham. London, 1923. pp. 216–19. See also *Die Chronik des Hieronymos (Hieronymi Chronicon)....* Ed. R. Helm, part II. Die griechischen christlichen Schriftsteller...Vol. 34. Eusebius, vol. VII, 2. Leipzig, 1926. pp. 401–10.

Chronicon Paschale. Ed. L. Dindorf. Vol. I. Bonn, 1832. p. 334.

II. MODERN LITERATURE

A. *General*

See the general works of Bevan, Bouché-Leclercq, Cardinali, Colin, De Sanctis, Ferguson, Frank, Heitland, Holleaux, Homo, Ihne, Jouguet, Kahrstedt, Meyer, Mommsen, Neumann, Niese, Pais, Piganiol, Rostovtzeff, Roussel, Tarn, and Täubler cited in the General Bibliography. Also:

Beloch, K. J. *Griechische Geschichte seit Alexander.* (A. Gercke and E. Norden, Einleitung in die Altertumswissenschaft, vol. III, ed. 2, Leipzig-Berlin, 1914, pp. 134 *sqq.*)

Brandstäter, F. A. *Die Geschichten des aetolischen Landes, Volkes und Bundes.* Berlin, 1844. pp. 385 *sqq.*

Degen, E. *Kritische Ausführungen zur Geschichte Antiochus des Grossen.* Diss. Zürich. Basel, 1918.

Ferrabino, A. *La dissoluzione della libertà nella Grecia antica.* Padova, 1929. pp. 87 *sqq.*

Flathe, L. *Geschichte Macedoniens und der Reiche, welche von macedonischen Königen beherrscht wurden.* Vol. II. Leipzig, 1834. pp. 270 *sqq.*, 311 *sqq.*

Frank, T. *Mercantilism and Rome's foreign policy.* Amer. Historic. Rev. XVIII, 1912–13, p. 233.

Freeman, E. A. *History of Federal Government in Greece and Italy.* Ed. 2, by J. B. Bury. London, 1893. pp. 438 *sqq.*, 472 *sqq.*

Fustel de Coulanges (N.). *Polybe ou la Grèce conquise par les Romains.* In Questions historiques, Paris, 1893, pp. 121 *sqq.*

Gelder, H. van. *Geschichte der alten Rhodier.* Haag, 1900. pp. 119 *sqq.*

Heinze, R. *Von den Ursachen von der Grösse Roms.* Leipzig-Berlin, 1925. pp. 16 *sqq.*

Hertzberg, G. F. *Geschichte Griechenlands unter der Herrschaft der Römer.* Vol. I (French trans.). Paris, 1886. pp. 23 *sqq.*

Heyden, E. A. *Res ab Antiocho III. Magno Syriae rege praeclare gestae ad regnum Syriae reficiendum donec in Graeciam exercitum traiecit;* 223–192. Diss. Göttingen. Münster, 1877.

—— *Beiträge zur Geschichte Antiochus des Grossen, Königs von Syrien.* Emmerich, 1873.

Holleaux, M. *Recherches sur l'histoire des négociations d'Antiochos III avec les Romains.* Rev. E. A. XV, 1913, p. 1.

—— *La politique romaine en Grèce et dans l'Orient hellénistique au IIIᵉ siècle.* Rev. Phil. L, 1926, pp. 207 *sqq.*

Kahrstedt, U. *Syrische Territorien in hellenistischer Zeit.* Abh. Göttingen, XIX (2), 1926, *passim.*

Kromayer, J. *Antike Schlachtfelder in Griechenland.* Vol. II. Berlin, 1907. pp. 3–115, 127–227.

—— *Roms Kampf um die Weltherrschaft.* Leipzig, 1912. pp. 10 *sqq.*, 64 *sqq.*

Kromayer, J. and Hartmann, L. M. *Römische Geschichte.* (L. M. Hartmann, Weltgeschichte in gemeinverständlicher Darstellung, vol. III, ed. 2). Gotha, 1921. pp. 71 *sqq.*

Lenschau, T. *Bericht über griechische Geschichte*, 1903–6, 1907–14, 1915–25. Bursian, 1907, pp. 206 *sqq.*; 1919, pp. 237 *sqq.*; 1928, pp. 141 *sqq.*

Mahaffy, J. P. *The Empire of the Ptolemies.* London, 1895. pp. 263 *sqq.*

—— *A history of Egypt under the Ptolemaic dynasty.* London, 1899. pp. 135 *sqq.*

—— *Greek Life and Thought.* Ed. 2. London, 1896. pp. 451 *sqq.*, 466 *sqq.*

Meyer, Ed. *Der Gang der alten Geschichte: Hellas und Rom.* Kleine Schriften (1), Halle, 1910, pp. 271 *sqq.*

—— *Die Entwicklung der römischen Weltherrschaft.* Weltgeschichte und Weltkrieg, Stuttgart-Berlin, 1916, pp. 66 *sqq.*

—— *Hannibal und Scipio.* (E. Marcks and K. A. von Müller, Meister der Politik, vol. 1, ed. 2, Stuttgart-Berlin, 1923, pp. 138 *sqq.*)

Münzer, F. *Römische Adelsparteien und Adelsfamilien.* Stuttgart, 1920. *passim.*

—— *Die politische Vernichtung des Griechentums.* Das Erbe der Alten, 11, 9. Leipzig, 1925. pp. 26 *sq.*, 30 *sqq.*

Neumann, K. J. *Die hellenistischen Staaten und die römischen Republik.* (J. von Pflugk-Harttung, Weltgeschichte: Geschichte des Altertums, Berlin, [1909], pp. 428 *sqq.*)

Niccolini, G. *Le relazioni fra Roma e la Lega Achea.* E. Pais, Studi storici per l'antichità classica, 11, Pisa, 1909, pp. 249 *sqq.*

—— *La Confederazione Achea.* Pavia, 1914. pp. 86 *sqq.*

Peter, C. *Studien zur Römischen Geschichte. Ein Beitrag zur Kritik von Th. Mommsen's Römischer Geschichte.* 111. *Die macchiavellistische Politik der Römer in der Zeit vom Ende des zweiten punischen Kriegs bis zu den Gracchen.* Halle, 1863. pp. 115 *sqq.*

Pöhlmann, R. von. *Grundriss der griechischen Geschichte.* (I. von Müller, Handbuch der Altertumswissenschaft, 111, 4, ed. 4.) München, 1909. pp. 312 *sqq.*

Rosenberg, A. Reviewing T. Frank's *Roman Imperialism*, *B.P.W.* 1916, cols. 1104–5.

Salvetti, C. *Ricerche storiche intorno alla Lega etolica.* G. Beloch, Studi di storia antica, 11, Rome, 1893, pp. 119 *sqq.*

Schorn, W. *Geschichte Griechenlands von der Entstehung des ätolischen und achäischen Bundes bis auf die Zerstörung Korinths.* Bonn, 1833. pp. 173 *sqq.*, 215 *sqq.*

Schur, W. *Scipio Africanus und die Begründung der römischen Weltherrschaft.* Das Erbe der Alten, 11, 13. Leipzig, 1927. pp. 48, 69 *sqq.* See: Th. Lenschau in *Phil. Woch.* 1928, cols. 1193–4. W. Kolbe in *H.Z.* 139, 1928, p. 337. T. Frank in *A.J.Ph.* XLIX, 1928, p. 211.

Shebelew, S. *History of Athens from 229 to 31 B.C.* (In Russian.) St Petersburg, 1898. pp. 73 *sqq.*

Tetzlaff, J. *De Antiochi III. Magni rebus gestis ad regnum Syriae reficiendum usque ad illa tempora quibus cum Romanis congressus est.* Diss. Münster, 1874.

Theiler, W. *Die politische Lage in den beiden makedonischen Kriegen.* Diss. Halle, 1914.

Walek, T. *Dzieje upadku monarchji macedońskiej.* (*History of the fall of the Macedonian monarchy.*) Cracow, 1924.

—— *La politique romaine en Grèce et dans l'Orient hellénistique au III⁰ siècle.* Rev. Phil. XLIX, 1925, pp. 45 *sqq.*

Wilamowitz-Moellendorff, U. von. *Staat und Gesellschaft der Griechen.* (P. Hinneberg, Die Kultur der Gegenwart, 11, 4, i, ed. 2, Leipzig-Berlin, 1923) pp. 149 *sqq.*

Wilcken, U. *Griechische Geschichte im Rahmen der Altertumsgeschichte.* Ed. 2. München-Berlin, 1926. pp. 203 *sqq.*

See also the following articles in P.W.: *Achaia* (1), cols. 174 *sqq.* (J. Toepffer); *Aitolia*, cols. 1124 *sqq.*; *Antiochos* (25) 111, cols. 2461 *sqq.*; *Attalos* (9) 1, cols. 2163 *sqq.* (U. Wilcken); *L. Cornelius* (337) *Scipio*, cols. 1472 *sqq.*; *P. Cornelius* (336) *Scipio*, cols. 1468 *sqq.* (F. Münzer); *Eumenes* (6) 11, cols. 1091 *sqq.* (U.

Wilcken); *Hannibal* (8), cols. 2348 *sqq.* (Th. Lenschau); *Makedonia*, cols. 747 *sqq.*
(F. Geyer); *Rhodos*, (F. Hiller von Gärtringen); *Sparta*, cols. 1436 *sqq.* (V.
Ehrenberg).

B. *On the Ancient Sources*
I. General

Beloch, K. J. In A. Gercke and E. Norden, Einleitung in die Altertumswissenschaft,
    III², pp. 144 (Polybius), 191 (Livy), 193 (Appian), 194 (Dio Cassius).
Bruns, I. *Die Persönlichkeit in der Geschichtsschreibung der Alten.* Berlin, 1898.
    pp. 1 *sqq.*, 41 (Polybius and Livy).
Cavaignac, E. *Quelques remarques sur l'historicité de Tite-Live.* Rev. Phil. XXXIX,
    1915, pp. 1 *sqq.*, 21 *sqq.*
—— *Sur l'économie de l'histoire de Polybe d'après Tite-Live.* ib. L, 1926, p. 103.
De Sanctis, G. *Storia dei Romani.* Vol. III, i. Turin, 1916. pp. 201 *sqq.* (on Polybius).
Gutschmid, A. von. *Trogus und Timagenes.* Kleine Schriften, vol. v. Berlin, 1894.
    p. 218.
Rosenberg, A. *Einleitung und Quellenkunde zur römischen Geschichte.* Berlin, 1921.
    pp. 144 *sqq.* (Livy), 188 *sqq.* (Polybius), 203 *sqq.* (Appian), 260 (Dio Cassius).
Soltau, W. *Livius' Geschichtswerk, seine Komposition und seine Quellen.* Leipzig,
    1897.
Witte, K. *Ueber die Form der Darstellung in Livius' Geschichtswerk.* Rh. Mus.
    LXV, 1910, pp. 276–8, 281–7, 296–300, 304–5, 377–93, 394 n. 1.
    Articles in P.W.: *Antisthenes* (9); *Appianos* (2), cols. 219–22; *Cassius* (40) *Dio
Cocceianus*, cols. 1695–7; *Diodoros* (38), cols. 689–90 (E. Schwartz); *M. Junianius
Justinus* (W. Kroll); *T. Livius* (9), cols. 840–3 (A. Klotz).
    Also the following general works: Christ, W. von, Schmid, W. and Stählin, O.,
Geschichte der griechischen Litteratur, vol. II, i, ed. 6 (I. von Müller and W. Otto, Hand-
buch der klassischen Altertumswissenschaft, VII, ii, 1), München, 1920, pp. 384 *sqq.*
(Polybius), 517 *sqq.* (Plutarch); II, ii, ed. 6 (ib. VII, ii, 2), München, 1924, pp. 751
sqq. (Appian), 795 *sqq.* (Dio). Schanz, M. and Hosius, C. *Geschichte der römischen
Litteratur*, vol. I, ed. 4 (Handbuch, VIII, i), München, 1927, pp. 195 *sq.*, 316 *sqq.*
(the annalists used by Livy); II, i, ed. 3 (ib. VIII, ii, 1), München, 1911, pp. 429 *sqq.*
(Livy); 448 *sqq.* (Pompeius Trogus; Justin). Susemihl, F., *Geschichte der griechischen Litteratur in der Alexandrinerzeit*, vol. II, Leipzig, 1892, pp. 80 *sqq.* (Polybius).

II. Special
a. (*Chap.* v.)

Groag, E. *Hannibal als Politiker.* Wien, 1929. pp. 81 *sqq.* (on Polybius VII, 9 and
    Livius XXIII, 33, 10–12).
Hesselbarth, H. *Historisch-kritische Untersuchungen zur dritten Dekade des Livius.*
    Halle, 1889. pp. 468 *sqq.*, 511 *sqq.*, 555 *sqq.*, 564 *sq.*
Kahrstedt, U. *Geschichte der Karthager von* 218–146 (O. Meltzer's *Geschichte der
    Karthager*, vol. III). Berlin, 1913. pp. 251–2, 283–5, 306, 313–5, 331, 360–2.
Soltau, W. *Livius' Quellen in der dritten Dekade.* Berlin, 1894.
—— *Livius' Geschichtswerk.* pp. 79 *sqq.* and *passim.*
Täubler, E. *Imperium Romanum.* Vol. I. Leipzig-Berlin, 1913. pp. 210 *sqq.*, 214
    sqq.

b. (*Chaps.* VI, VII.)

Kahrstedt, U. *Die Annalistik von Livius* (B. XXXI–XLV). Berlin, 1913. See
    A. Klotz, in *B.P.W.* 1915, cols. 10–16.
Klotz, A. *Zu den Quellen der vierten und fünften Dekade des Livius.* Hermes, L,
    1915, p. 481.

Kümpel, E. *Die Quellen zur Geschichte des Krieges der Römer gegen Antiochus III.* Progr. Hamburg, 1893.

Meyer, Ed. *Die Quellen unserer Überlieferung über Antiochos' des Grossen Römer-krieg.* Rh. Mus. xxxvi, 1881, p. 120.

Mommsen, Th. *Der Friede mit Antiochos und die Kriegszüge des Cn. Manlius Volso.* Römische Forschungen. Vol. ii. Berlin, 1879. p. 511.

Nissen, H. *Kritische Untersuchungen über die Quellen der vierten und fünften Dekade des Livius.* Berlin, 1863. pp. 1–210; 280 *sqq.* (Plutarch and Pausanias), 305 *sq.* (Justin), 308 *sqq.* (Dio Cassius). (Standard work.)

Peter, H. *Die Quellen Plutarchs in den Biographieen der Römer.* Halle, 1865. pp. 80 *sqq.* (Flamininus), 89 *sqq.* (Cato).

Rühl, F. *Der letzte Kampf der Achäer gegen Nabis.* Jahrb. für class. Philologie, cxxvii, 1883, pp. 39 *sqq.* (Polybius as a source for Pausanias).

Soltau, W. *Livius' Geschichtswerk.* pp. 21 *sqq.*

Täubler, E. *Imperium Romanum.* Vol. i, pp. 228 *sqq.*, 373 *sqq.* and *passim.*

Ullmann, R. *La technique des discours dans Salluste, Tite Live et Tacite.* Skrifter utgitt av Det Norske Videnskaps-Akademi i Oslo, ii, Hist.-Filos. Klasse, 1927, no. 2. Oslo, 1927. pp. 133 *sqq.*, 143 *sqq.*

Ullrich, H. *De Polybii fontibus Rhodiis.* Diss. Leipzig, 1898. pp. 5 *sqq.*, 29 *sqq.*

Unger, G. F. *Die römischen Quellen des Livius in der vierten und fünften Dekade.* Phil. Supplementband iii, 2, 1878, p. 3.

C. Chronology
I. General
a. Greece (Achaea)

Aymard, A. *Les stratèges de la Confédération achéenne de 202 à 172 av. J.-C.* Rev. E. A. xxx, 1928, p. 1 (with bibliography).

De Sanctis, G. *Storia dei Romani.* Vol. iv, i. Turin, 1923. pp. 402 *sqq.* (*Appendice cronologica*).

Niccolini, G. *Gli strateghi della Lega Achea.* Studi storici, i, 1908, p. 224.

—— *La Confederazione Achea.* pp. 284 *sqq.*

(Aetolia)

De Sanctis, G. *Storia.....* Vol. iv, i, pp. 400 *sqq.*

Gillischewski, H. *De Aetolorum praetoribus inter annos 221 et 168 a. Chr. n. munere functis.* Diss. Berlin, 1896.

Levi, M. A. *La cronologia degli strateghi Etolici degli anni 221–168 a. C.* Atti Acc. Torino, lvii, 1921–22, p. 179.

Plassart, A. *Remarques sur divers décrets de la Ligue étolienne...* B.C.H. xxxix, 1915, p. 127.

Pomtow, H. Art. *Delphoi* in P.W. cols. 2677–8

—— in Ditt.[3] 546 *A*, n. 1; cf. 554, n. 1.

Sotiriadis, G. Ἐπιγραφαὶ Θέρμου. Ἀρχ. Δελτίον, i, 1915, p. 45.

(Delphi)

Bergk, Th. *Die Liste der delphischen Gastfreunde.* Phil. xlii, 1884, p. 228.

Mommsen, A. *Delphische Archonten nach der Zeit geordnet* [199–168 B.C.]. Phil. xxiv, 1866, p. 1.

Pomtow, H. *Zur delphischen Archontentafel des III. Jahrhunderts.* Klio, xiv, 1914–15, p. 305 (col. 4, group ix). See also E. Rüsch and H. Pomtow reviewing T. Walek, G. G. A. 1913, p. 145 (col. 4, F).

Walek, T. *Die delphische Amphictyonie in der Zeit der aitolischen Herrschaft.* Diss. Berlin, 1911. pp. 143 *sqq.*, 186 *sq.*

(Thessaly)

Kern, O. In *IG.* ix, ii, p. xxiv.

Kroog, W. *De foederis Thessalorum praetoribus.* Diss. Halle, 1908. pp. 1 *sqq.*, 59.

(Boeotia)

Holleaux, M. *Recherches sur la chronologie de quelques archontes béotiens.* Rev. E. G. viii, 1895, p. 183; xiii, 1900, p. 187.

Schönfelder, W. *Die städtischen und Bundesbeamten des griechischen Festlandes...* Diss. Leipzig, 1917. pp. 25 *sqq.*

(Athens)

Johnson, A. C. *The creation of the tribe Ptolemais at Athens.* A.J.Ph. xxxiv, 1913, pp. 381, 416 (Archon lists).

Kirchner, J. In *IG.* ii², iv, 1 (1918), pp. 16 *sqq.* (*Archontum tabulae*).

Kolbe, W. *Die attischen Archonten von 293/2–31/0 v. Chr.* Abh. königl. Gesellschaft zu Göttingen, x (4), 1908, pp. 67 *sqq.*

b. Egypt

Beloch, K. J. *Zur Chronologie der ersten Ptolemäer.* Arch. Pap. vii, 1924, pp. 171 *sqq.*; viii, 1927, pp. 5 *sqq.*

—— *Griechische Geschichte.* Ed. 2. Vol. iv, 2. Berlin-Leipzig, 1927. pp. 172 *sqq.*

Meyer, Ernst. *Untersuchungen zur Chronologie der ersten Ptolemäer auf Grund der Papyri.* ii. Beiheft zum Arch. Pap. 1925, pp. 33–45, 85 *sq.* See: K. J. Beloch in *Arch. Pap.* viii, p. 1; C. E. Edgar, *Zenon Papyri,* i, 1925, p. vii; W. Ensslin in *Phil. Woch.* 1927, cols. 876–8; W. W. Tarn in *C.R.* xl, 1926, p. 86.

Strack, M. L. *Die Dynastie der Ptolemäer.* Berlin, 1897. Especially pp. 182 *sq.*, 194 *sqq.*

c. Syria

Beloch, K. J. *Griechische Geschichte*². Vol. iv, 2, pp. 190 *sqq.*

Kolbe, W. *Beiträge zur syrischen und jüdischen Geschichte.* Beiträge zur Wissenschaft vom Alten Testament, 10. Berlin-Stuttgart-Leipzig, 1926. *passim.*

Kugler, F. X. *Von Moses bis Paulus.* pp. 321 *sqq.*

—— *Sternkunde und Sterndienst in Babel.* ii, ii, 2. Münster-i.-W. 1924. pp. 440 *sq.*

Leuze, O. *Die Feldzüge Antiochos' des Grossen nach Kleinasien und Thrakien.* Hermes, lviii, 1923, pp. 187, 241.

d. Rome

Beloch, K. J. *Der römische Kalender von* 218–168. Klio, xv, 1918, p. 382.

—— *Die Sonnenfinsternis des Ennius und der vorjulianische Kalender.* Hermes, lvii, 1922, p. 119. See W. Soltau in *Rh. Mus.* lxxii, 1917–18, p. 526 n. 1.

—— *Der römische Kalender Varr.* 565 *und* 566 (189 v. Chr.). Klio, xxii, 1929, p. 464.

Cavaignac, E. *La chronologie romaine de* 215 *à* 168. Klio, xiv, 1914–15, p. 37.

De Sanctis, G. *Storia....* Vol. iv, i, pp. 368 *sqq.* (*Appendice cronologica*).

Holzapfel, L. *Römische Chronologie.* Leipzig, 1885. pp. 302 *sqq.*

Kahrstedt, U. *Geschichte der Karthager.* p. 370, n. 2.

Matzat, H. *Die römische Zeitrechnung für die Jahre* 219 *bis* 1 *v. Chr.* Berlin, 1889. pp. 127 *sqq.*

Maxis, E. *Die Prätoren Roms von* 367–167 *v. Chr.* Diss. Breslau, 1911. pp. 22 *sqq.*

Nissen, H. *Kritische Untersuchungen....* p. 68 n.

Soltau, W. *Römische Chronologie.* Freiburg-i.-B., 1889. *passim.*

Stella Maranca, F. *Fasti praetorii.* i. Mem. Acc. Lincei, serie vi, ii, 4, 1927, pp. 296 *sqq.*

Unger, G. F. *Der Gang des altrömischen Kalenders.* Bay. Abh. xviii (2), 1890, pp. 342 *sqq.*

—— *Zeitrechnung der Griechen und Römer.* (Handbuch der klassischen Altertumswissenschaft, vol. i, ed. 2, München, 1892, pp. 803 *sqq.*)

Varese, P. *Cronologia romana.* Vol. i. *Il calendario Flaviano.* Rome, 1908. pp. 216 *sqq.*, 320 *sq.*

e. Chronology of Polybius

See the works of Nissen, Seipt, and Steigemann cited in the Bibliography to chapter i. Also:

De Sanctis, G. *Storia*. . . .Vol. iii, i, pp. 219 *sqq.* (*Cronologia polibiana*).

Nissen, H. *Kritische Untersuchungen*. . . .pp. 68 n.

—— *Ueber Tempel-Orientierung.* iv, ii. *Olympia.* Rh. Mus. xl, 1885, p. 355 *sq.*

Unger, G. F. *Der Strategenjahr der Achaier.* Bay. S.B. 1879, ii, p. 118.

—— *Der Olympienmonat.* Phil. xxxiii, 1874, pp. 234 *sqq.*

II. Special

a. (*Chap.* v.) *First Macedonian War*

Boethius, A. *Der argivische Kalender.* Uppsala Universitets Årsskrift, 1922, p. 42 *sq.* (the Nemean Games of 209 and 207).

Clementi, G. *La guerra annibalica in Oriente.* Studi di storia antica, i, 1891, p. 51.

Costanzi, V. *Sulla cronologia della prima guerra macedonica.* Studi storici, i, 1908, pp. 31 *sqq.*; ii, 1909, pp. 214 *sqq.*

De Sanctis, G. *Storia*. . . .Vol. iii, ii, pp. 440 *sqq.* (*Cronologia della prima guerra macedonica*).

Kahrstedt, U. *Geschichte der Karthager.* p. 283 *sq.*

Niccolini, G. *Quando cominciò la prima guerra macedonica.* Studi storici, v, 1912, p. 108.

Niese, B. *Geschichte der Griechischen und Makedonischen Staaten seit der Schlacht bei Chaeronea.* Vol. ii. Gotha, 1899. p. 476 n. 4.

Oldfather, W. A. Art. *Lokris* (1) in P.W. cols. 1225 *sqq.*

Varese, P. *Cronologia romana.* Vol. i, pp. 216 *sqq.*, 320.

Walek-Czernecki, T. *La chronologie de la première guerre de Macédoine.* Rev. Phil. liv, 1928, p. 5.

b. (*Chap.* vi.) *Birth and joint kingship of Ptolemy V. Death of Ptolemy IV. Accession of Ptolemy V*

Bouché-Leclercq, A. *Histoire des Lagides.* Vol. i. Paris, 1903. pp. 321 n. 1, 335 *sqq.*; ii. Paris, 1904. p. 391.

De Sanctis, G. *Storia*. . . .Vol. iv, i, pp. 1 n. 2, 4 n. 10, 126 n. 37, 128 n. 41.

Holleaux, M. In *Rev. E. G.* xiii, 1900, p. 190 n. 2; *B.C.H.* xxx, 1906, p. 473 n. 2; *Klio*, viii, 1908, p. 268 n. 6; *Rev. E. A.* xv, 1913, p. 9 n. 3; *Rev. Phil.* l, 1926, p. 215.

Meyer, Ernst. *Untersuchungen*. . .pp. 39 *sqq.*, 69.

Niese, B. *Geschichte*. . . .Vol. ii, pp. 572 *sq.*, 573 n. 2.

Sethe, K. *Zur Geschichte und Erklärung der Rosettana.* Gött. Nach. 1916, pp. 275, 299.

Smyly, J. G. *Greek papyri from Gurob*. . . .p. 27 *sq.*, no. xii. See also U. Wilcken in *Arch. Pap.* vii, 1924, p. 71.

Stark, K. B. *Gaza und die philistäische Küste.* Jena, 1852. pp. 397 *sqq.*

Strack, M. L. *Die Dynastie der Ptolemäer.* pp. 182 *sq.*, 195 *sq.*

Wilcken, U. *Urkunden der Ptolemäerzeit*. Vol. I. Berlin, 1927. p. 503 (commentary to no. 112).

Wilhelm, A. *Ein Brief Antiochos III*. Wien Anz. 57, 1920, xvii–xxvii, p. 55 *sq.*

 c. (Chap. VI.) *Antiochus III*, 216–204 B.C. *Philip V and Antiochus III*, 204–200 B.C.

Holleaux, M. *L'expédition de Dikaiarchos dans les Cyclades et sur l'Hellespont.* Rev. E. G. XXXIII, 1920, p. 223.

——— *L'expédition de Philippe V en Asie en* 201 *av. J.-C.; précisions chronologiques.* Rev. E. A. XXV, 1923, p. 350.

——— *La chronologie de la Cinquième guerre de Syrie.* Klio, VIII, 1908, p. 267.

——— *Remarques sur les décrets des villes de Crète relatifs à l'ἀσυλία de Téos.* Klio, XIII, 1913, p. 137.

Kugler, F. X. *Von Moses bis Paulus.* p. 324.

——— *Sternkunde* .... II, ii, 2, p. 440.

Wilhelm, A. *Ein Brief Antiochos III*. Wien Anz. 57, 1920, xvii–xxvii, pp. 51 *sqq.*, 56 *sq.*

 d. (Chap. VI.) *Second Macedonian War*

Beloch, K. J. *Der römische Kalender* .... Klio, XV, 1918, pp. 384, 407.

Cavaignac, E. *Le calendrier romain vers* 198. Rev. E. G. XXXVII, 1924, p. 164.

De Sanctis, G. *Storia* .... Vol. IV, i, pp. 383 *sqq.*

Holleaux, M. *L'année de la bataille de Kynoskephalai.* Rev. E. A. XVII, 1915, p. 165.

Kromayer, J. *Antike Schlachtfelder.* Vol. II, pp. 106 *sqq.*

Leuze, O. *Die Feldzüge* .... Hermes, LVIII, 1923, pp. 195 *sqq.*

Varese, P. *Cronologia romana.* Vol. I, pp. 55 *sqq.*

 e. (Chaps. VI, VII.) *Coronation and marriage of Ptolemy V*

Bouché-Leclercq, A. *Histoire des Lagides.* Vol. I, pp. 368 *sq.*, 384 n. 1; II, p. 392.

De Sanctis, G. *Storia* .... Vol. IV, i, p. 126 n. 37, 128 n. 41.

Leuze, O. *Die Feldzüge* .... IV. Hermes, LVIII, 1923, pp. 221 *sqq.*

Meyer, Ed. *Ursprung und Anfänge des Christentums.* Vol. II. Stuttgart-Berlin, 1921. p. 124 n. 6.

Meyer, Ernst. *Untersuchungen* .... p. 39 *sq.*

Nock, A. D. *Notes on Ruler-Cult.* III. J.H.S. XLVIII, 1928, p. 38.

Otto, W. *Priester und Tempel im hellenistischen Aegypten.* Vol. II. Leipzig-Berlin, 1908. p. 292 n. 3.

——— *Ägyptische Priestersynoden in hellenistischer Zeit.* Bay. S.B. 1926 (2), pp. 21, 29 n. 2.

 f. (Chap. VII.) *Antiochus III*, 200–192 B.C.; *Antiochus' war; Aetolian war*

Beloch, K. J. *Der römische Kalender* .... Klio, XV, 1918, pp. 386 *sqq.*

——— *Der römische Kalender Varr.* 565 *und* 566 (189 *v. Chr.*). ib. XXII, 1929, p. 464.

Cavaignac, E. *La mort du fils d'Antiochus le Grand* (192). Rev. d'Assyriol. XIX, 1922, p. 161.

De Sanctis, G. *Storia* .... Vol. IV, i, pp. 388 *sqq.*

Holleaux, M. *Recherches* .... Rev. E. A. XV, 1913, p. 1.

Kromayer, J. *Antike Schlachtfelder.* Vol. II, pp. 220 *sqq.*

Kugler, F. X. *Von Moses bis Paulus.* p. 325.

——— *Sternkunde* .... II, ii, 2, p. 440 *sq.*

Leuze, O. *Die Feldzüge* .... II–VI. Hermes, LVIII, 1923, pp. 190, 241.

Varese, P. *Cronologia romana.* Vol. I, pp. 62 *sqq.*

D. Special topics

1. Alliance between Philip V and Carthage

Beloch, J. *Die 'Herren Karthager.'* Klio, I, 1901, p. 283 *sq.*

De Sanctis, G. *Storia....* Vol. III, ii, pp. 407 *sqq.*

Egelhaaf, G. *Analekten zur Geschichte des zweiten punischen Kriegs.* 2. *Der Vertrag Hannibals mit Philippos V.* H.Z. LIII, 1885, p. 456.

—— *Hannibal; ein Charakterbild.* Stuttgart, 1922. pp. 13 *sqq.*

Frank, T. *Roman Imperialism.* New York, 1914 pp. 142 *sq.*

Groag, E. *Hannibal....* pp. 81 *sqq.*, 97.

Gsell, S. *Histoire ancienne de l'Afrique du Nord.* Vol. IV. Ed. 3. Paris, 1929. p. 222 *sq.*

Holleaux, M. *Rome, la Grèce et les monarchies hellénistiques au IIIe siècle avant J.-C.* Paris, 1921. pp. 179 *sqq.*

Kahrstedt, U. *Geschichte der Karthager.* pp. 237, 449 *sqq.*

—— *Zwei Urkunden aus Polybios.* II. *Die 'Herren Karthager.'* Gött. Nach. 1923, p. 99.

Kromayer, J. *Hannibal als Staatsmann.* H.Z. CIII, 1909, pp. 244 *sqq.*

Scott, F. A. *Macedonien und Rom während des Hannibalischen Krieges.* I. Diss. Leipzig, 1873. pp. 45 *sqq.*

Articles in P.W.: *Mago* (8); *Magonos* (V. Ehrenberg).

2. Messenian affairs. Philip V and Aratus

Beloch, G. *La madre di Perseo.* Riv. Stor. ant. VI, 1901, p. 3.

—— K. J. *Griechische Geschichte*². Vol. IV, 2, p. 140.

Ferrabino, A. *Il problema della unità nazionale nella Grecia.* I. *Arato di Sicione e l'idea federale.* (G. De Sanctis and L. Pareti, Contributi alla Scienza dell' Antichità, vol. IV.) Firenze, 1921. pp. 227 *sqq.*

Freeman, E. A. *History of Federal Government.* pp. 444 *sqq.*

Holleaux, M. *Rome....* pp. 197 *sq.*, 202 *sq.*

Nicolaus, M. *Zwei Beiträge zur Geschichte König Philipps V. von Makedonien.* I. *Philippos und Aratos.* Diss. Berlin, 1909. pp. 59 *sqq.*

Seeliger, K. *Messenien und der achäische Bund.* Progr. Zittau, 1897. pp. 12 *sqq.*

Articles in P.W.: *Aratos* (2), cols. 388–9; (3) (B. Niese); *Demetrios* (44a) *von Pharos,* Supplementband I, col. 344 (Th. Büttner-Wobst).

3. Antiochus III against Achaeus

Cardinali, G. *Il regno di Pergamo.* Studi di storia antica, V, 1906, pp. 48, 81 *sqq.*

Holleaux, M. *Les auxiliaires aitoliens d'Achaios.* Rev. E. A. XVIII, 1916, p. 223.

Leuze, O. *Die Feldzüge....* I. Hermes, LVIII, 1923, pp. 188 *sqq.*

Meyer, Ernst. *Die Grenzen der hellenistischen Staaten in Kleinasien.* Zürich-Leipzig, 1925. pp. 103 *sq.*, 140.

Articles in P.W.: *Achaios* (4); *Bolis* (U. Wilcken); *Laodike* (17) (F. Stähelin); *Lydia* (1), col. 2184 (J. Keil).

4. Alliance of Rome and Aetolia. Philip V in Illyria

Boguth, W. *M. Valerius Laevinus. Ein Beitrag zur Geschichte des zweiten punischen Krieges.* Progr. Krems, 1892. pp. 3 *sqq.*

De Sanctis, G. *Storia....* Vol. III, ii, pp. 414 *sqq.*

Holleaux, M. *Rome....* pp. 208 *sqq.*

Horn, H. *Foederati.* Diss. Frankfurt, 1930. pp. 22 *sqq.*

Kahrstedt, U. *Geschichte der Karthager.* p. 485.

Kromayer, J. and Veith, G. *Schlachten-Atlas zur antiken Kriegsgeschichte.* II. *Römische Abteilung,* II. Leipzig, 1922. Bl. 10, no. 6, with explanatory text (cols. 51–2) and bibliography.

Münzer, F. *Römische Adelsparteien.* p. 209 *sq.* (M. Valerius Laevinus).
Scott, F. A. *Macedonien und Rom.* pp. 64 *sqq.*
Täubler, E. *Imperium Romanum.* Vol. I, pp. 210 *sqq.*
Articles in P.W.: *Dorimachos* (G. Wissowa); *Lissos* (2), col. 735 (Fluss).

5. *First Macedonian War*, 211–208 B.C. *Intervention of neutrals. Rome and Egypt*

Bandelin, E. *De rebus inter Aegyptios et Romanos intercedentibus usque ad bellum Alexandrinum a Caesare gestum.* Diss. Halle, 1893. p. 11 *sq.*
Ciaceri, E. *Le relazioni politiche fra Roma e l' Egitto.* In *Processi politici e Relazioni internazionali.* (E. Pais and F. Stella Maranca, Ricerche sulla storia e sul diritto romano, vol. II.) Rome, 1918. pp. 33 *sqq.*
Ferguson, W. S. *Hellenistic Athens.* London, 1911. pp. 254 *sqq.*
Gelder, H. van. *Geschichte der alten Rhodier.* pp. 119 *sqq.*
Holleaux, M. *Rome....*pp. 35 *sqq.*, 66 *sqq.*, 73 *sqq.*
Meyer, Ed. *Kleine Schriften.* II. Halle, 1924. p. 420 n. 6 (Roman embassy to Ptolemy IV).
Roussel, P. *Les épimélètes aitoliens à Delphes.* B.C.H. L, 1926, p. 124.
Stählin, F. *Das hellenische Thessalien.* Stuttgart, 1924. pp. 55 (Tisaeum), 180 *sq.* (Pteleon), 182 *sq.* (Larisa Cremaste), 186 (Echinus), 217 (Phalara).
Täubler, E. *Imperium Romanum.* Vol. I, pp. 202 *sq.*, 204, 216.
Wilhelm, A. In *G.G.A.* 1898, p. 217 (Amynander).
Articles in P.W.: *Amynandros* (2) (U. Wilcken); *Echinos* (2) (A. Philippson); *Elis*, cols. 2413–14 (H. Swoboda); *Euboia*, Supplementband IV, col. 445 (F. Geyer); *Lamia* (8), col. 555; Λάρισα (2) Κρεμαστή, col. 841 (F. Stählin); *Lokris* (1), cols. 1225–7 (W. A. Oldfather); *Machanidas* (V. Ehrenberg).

6. *Philopoemen. Battle of Mantinea*

Delbrück, H. *Geschichte der Kriegskunst.* Ed. 3. Vol. I. Berlin, 1920. pp. 252 *sqq.*
Fougères, G. *Mantinée et l'Arcadie orientale.* Paris, 1898. pp. 591 *sqq.*
Freeman, E. A. *History of Federal Government*, pp. 453 *sqq.*, 461 *sqq.*
Kromayer, J. *Antike Schlachtfelder.* Vol. I. Berlin, 1903. pp. 281 *sqq.*
Kromayer, J. and Veith, G. *Heerwesen und Kriegführung der Griechen und Römer.* (Handbuch der Altertumswissenschaft, IV, 3, 2.) München, 1928. pp. 136, 219.
Loring, W. *Some ancient routes in the Peloponnese.* VII (*battle of [Mantinea]* 207 B.C.). J.H.S. XV, 1895, p. 88.
Roloff, G. *Probleme aus der griechischen Kriegsgeschichte.* Historische Studien, XXXIX, 1903, p. 116.
Articles in P.W.: *Geschütze*, col. 1307 (R. Schneider); *Kriegskunst*, col. 1847 (E. Lammert and F. Lammert); *Machanidas*; *Mantinea*, col. 1330 (F. Bölte).

7. *Peace of 206 B.C. between Philip V and Aetolia. Peace of Phoenice*

Bauer, E. *Untersuchungen zur Geographie und Geschichte der nordwestlichen Landschaften Griechenlands nach den delphischen Inschriften.* Diss. Halle, 1907. pp. 72 *sqq.*
Beloch, K. J. *Griechische Geschichte*[2]. Vol. IV, 2, pp. 414 *sqq.*
Busolt, G. and Swoboda, H. *Griechische Staatskunde.* Vol. II. (Handbuch der klassischen Altertumswissenschaft, IV, 1, i.) München, 1926. pp. 1450 n. 1, 1490 *sq.*, 1517.
Costanzi, V. *Le relazioni degli Etoli coi Romani dopo la pace di Fenice.* Studi storici, I, 1908, p. 420.
De Sanctis, G. *Storia....*Vol. III, ii, pp. 431 *sqq.*
Ferguson, W. S. *Hellenistic Athens.* p. 256 n. 2.
Holleaux, M. *Notes d'épigraphie béotienne.* B.C.H. XVI, 1892, pp. 466 *sqq.*
—— *Rome....*pp. 254 *sq.*, 258 *sqq.*

Klaffenbach, G. *Zur Geschichte der Ost-Lokris.* Klio, xx, 1925, pp. 82 *sqq.*
—— In *Gnomon*, I, 1925, p. 88.
Niese, B. *Geschichte....* Vol. II, pp. 501 *sqq.*
Pomtow, H. *Fasti Delphici.* II. 2. Jahrbücher für classische Philologie, CLV, 1897, pp. 785 *sqq.*
Salvetti, C. *Ricerche storiche....* Studi di storia antica, II, 1893, pp. 119 *sqq.*
Schober, F. *Phokis.* Diss. Jena, 1924. p. 80.
Stählin, F. *Pharsalica.* II: *Die Phthiotis und der Friede zwischen Philippos V. und den Aetolern.* Phil. LXXVII, 1921, p. 199.
Swoboda, H. *Staatsaltertümer.* (K. F. Hermann, Lehrbuch der griechischen Antiquitäten, I, 3, ed. 6.) Tübingen, 1913. pp. 237, 321, 342 *sq.*
—— *Studien zu den griechischen Bünden.* I. *Zur Urkunde I(nschriften) v(on) M(agnesia)* 28. Klio, XI, 1911, p. 450.
—— *Zwei Kapitel aus dem griechischen Bundesrecht.* II. *Die Sympolitien von Keos und Ost-Lokris.* Wien S.B. 199 (2), 1924, pp. 59 *sqq.*
Täubler, E. *Imperium Romanum.* Vol. I, pp. 214 *sqq.*
Walek, T. *Die delphische Amphictyonie....* pp. 161 *sqq.*
Zippel, G. *Die römische Herrschaft in Illyrien.* Leipzig, 1877. p. 72 *sq.*
   Articles in P.W.: *Kypaira* (F. Stählin); *C. Laetorius* (2) (F. Münzer); Λάρισα (2) Κρεμαστή, col. 841; *Lokris* (1), col. 1227; *P. Sempronius* (96) (F. Münzer).

8. *Antiochus III, 212–204 B.C.*

Beloch, K. J. *Griechische Geschichte*[2]. Vol. IV, 2, p. 361 (Armenia).
Bevan, E. R. *Antiochus III and his title 'Great King.'* J.H.S. XXII, 1902, p. 241.
Gutschmid, A. von. *Geschichte Irans.* Tübingen, 1888. pp. 36 *sqq.*
Holleaux, M. Ἀντίοχος Μέγας. B.C.H. XXXII, 1908, p. 266.
Kromayer, J. *Hannibal und Antiochos der Grosse.* N.J. Kl. Alt. XIX, 1907, pp. 687 *sqq.*
Kugler, F. X. *Von Moses bis Paulus.* p. 324.
Macdonald, G. *Cambridge History of India.* Vol. I. Cambridge, 1922. pp. 440 *sqq.*; see also p. 512.
Marquart, J. *Untersuchung zur Geschichte von Eran.* II. Phil. Supplement-Band X, 1907, pp. 60 *sqq.*
Meyer, Ed. *Blüte und Niedergang des Hellenismus in Asien.* Berlin, 1925. pp. 49 *sqq.*
Rawlinson, H. G. *Bactria.* London, 1912. pp. 65 *sqq.*
Smith, V. A. *The early history of India.* Ed. 2. Oxford, 1908. pp. 209 *sq.*, 226. Ed. 3. 1914. pp. 222 *sq.*, 239, 241.
Tarn, W. W. *Ptolemy II and Arabia.* J.E.A. XV, 1929, pp. 11, 22 (on Antioch in Persis and the Gerrhaeans).
—— *Seleucid-Parthian Studies.* Proc. Brit. Acad. XVI, [1930], p. 23 *sq.*
Willrich, H. *Juden und Griechen vor der makkabäischen Erhebung.* Göttingen, 1895. pp. 39 *sqq.*
   Articles in P.W.: *Antiochos* (26) (U. Wilcken); *Armenia*, col. 1183 (A. Baumgartner); *Arsakes* (8), col. 1270 (Ed. Meyer); *Baktrianoi*, col. 2809 (W. Tomaschek); *Euthydemos* (9) (H. Willrich); *Guriane*; *Hekatompylos* (1), cols. 2791, 2793, 2795; *Hyrkania*, cols. 493, 501–2, 506, 515 (M. Kiessling); *Sophagasenos* (F. Geyer).

9. *Egypt under Ptolemy IV. Native risings. Ergamenes.* (For the birth and joint kingship of Ptolemy V see above C. II. *b*.)

Bevan, E. *A history of Egypt under the Ptolemaic dynasty.* London, [1927]. pp. 236 *sqq.*
Gauthier, H. *Le livre des Rois.* Vol. IV, 2, pp. 424–5 (Ergamenes), 426–7 (Harmakhis), 428 (Ankhmakhis), 429 (Azakheramon).
Griffith, F. Ll. *Meroitic Inscriptions.* Vol. II. Archaeological survey of Egypt, 20th Memoir. London, 1912. pp. 20 *sqq.*, 32 *sq.*

Griffith, F. Ll. *Oxford excavations in Nubia.* Liv. A.A. xi, 3–4, 1924, p. 116.
Jouguet, P. *Les Lagides et les indigènes égyptiens.* Rev. Belge, iii, 1923, p. 419.
Krall, J. *Studien zur Geschichte des alten Aegypten.* ii. *Aus demotischen Urkunden.* Wien S.B. 105, 1884, pp. 368 *sqq.*
Mahaffy, J. P. *The Empire of the Ptolemies.* pp. 264 *sqq.*, 272 *sqq.*
—— *A history of Egypt under the Ptolemaic dynasty.* pp. 135 *sqq.*
Perdrizet, P. and Lefebvre, G. *Les graffites grecs du Memnonion d'Abydos.* p. xiii *sq.*
Reisner, G. A. *The Meroitic Kingdom of Ethiopia.* J.E.A. ix, 1923, p. 77.
Révillout, E. *Les décrets de Rosette et Canope.* Rev. Arch. xxxiv, 1877, pp. 332 *sqq.* (=*Chrestomathie démotique.* Paris, 1880. pp. xci *sqq.*).
—— *Le roi Harmachis.* Z. Aeg. xvii, 1879, p. 131.
—— *Le roi (Anchmachis) et le roi (Harmachis).* Rev. Eg. ii, 1881–2, p. 145.
—— *Supplément sur le décret de Philée....* ib. xiii, 1910–11, p. 111 *sq.*
Roeder, G. *Die Kapellen zweier nubischer Fürsten in Debod und Dakke.* Z. Aeg. lxiii, 1928, pp. 126 *sqq.*, especially pp. 139–40.
Sethe, K. *Die historische Bedeutung des 2. Philä-dekretes....* ib. liii, 1917, pp. 35 *sqq.*
Sottas, H. *Notes complémentaires sur le décret en l'honneur de Ptolémée IV.* Rev. de l'Égypte ancienne, i, 1927, p. 237.
Spiegelberg, W. *Beiträge zur Erklärung des neuen dreisprachigen Priesterdekretes zu Ehren des Ptolemaios Philopator.* Bay. S.B. 1925 (4), p. 22. But see W. Otto, *Beiträge zur Seleukidengeschichte des 3. Jahrhunderts v. Chr.* iv. Bay. Abh. xxxiv (1), 1928, p. 82 n. 5.
—— *Weitere Beiträge zur Erklärung des Priesterdekretes zu Ehren des Ptolemaios Philopator.* Bay. S.B. 1928 (2), pp. 6 *sqq.*
Weigall, A. E. P. *A Report on the Antiquities of Lower Nubia.* pp. 20 *sq.*, 39, 42, 85 *sqq.*

Articles in P.W.: *Agathokleia* (2); *Agathokles* (19); *Arsinoe* (27) III (U. Wilcken); *Ergamenes* (1) (G. Steindorff); *Harmachis* (2), cf. vol. viii, col. 2625: Nachtrag zu Art. *Harmachis* (W. Otto).

10. *The Aegean at the close of the Third Century*
Beloch, K. J. *Griechische Geschichte*[2]. Vol. iv, 2, pp. 336 *sqq.*, 344 *sqq.*, 513.
Costanzi, V. *Il dominio egiziano nelle Cicladi sotto Tolomeo Filopatore.* Klio, xi, 1911, p. 277. See W. W. Tarn, *Antigonos Gonatas.* Oxford, 1913. p. 461 n. 1.
Durrbach, F. *Choix d'inscriptions de Délos.* Vol. i. Paris, 1921. pp. 42 *sq.*, 73, 277 *sqq.*
—— *Inscriptions de Délos; comptes des hiéropes* (1). Paris, 1926. p. 170 (commentary to no. 366).
Fritze, M. L. *Die ersten Ptolemäer und Griechenland.* Diss. Halle, 1917. pp. 128 *sqq.*
Glotz, G. *L'histoire de Délos d'après le prix d'une denrée.* Rev. E. G. xxix, 1916, pp. 318 *sqq.*
Hiller von Gärtringen, F. *Thera.* Vol. i. Berlin, 1899. pp. 167 *sqq.*
Holleaux, M. *Dédicace d'un monument commémoratif de la bataille de Sellasia.* B.C.H. xxxi, 1907, pp. 97, 105 n. 1, 107.
Kolbe, W. Reviewing W. W. Tarn, *Antigonos Gonatas,* G.G.A. 1916, pp. 463 *sqq.*
—— *The neutrality of Delos.* J.H.S. l, 1930, p. 20.
König, W. *Der Bund der Nesioten.* Diss. Halle, 1910. pp. 34 *sqq.*
Ormerod, H. A. *Piracy in the Ancient World.* Liverpool-London, 1924. pp. 132 *sqq.*
Pozzi, E. *Le battaglie di Cos e di Andro....* Mem. Acc. Torino, lxiii, 1911–12, p. 386 n. 3.
Roussel, P. *Les inscriptions de Délos.* J. d. Sav. 1924, pp. 113 *sqq.*
—— Reviewing F. Durrbach, *Choix* (see above), Rev. E. A. xxv, 1923, p. 78.
Swoboda, H. *Staatsaltertümer.* pp. 419 *sqq.*

Swoboda, H. *Zwei Kapitel aus dem griechischen Bundesrecht.* II. *Die Sympolitien von Keos und Ost-Lokris.* Wien S.B. 199 (2), 1924, p. 40 *sq.*
Tarn, W. W. *Antigonos Gonatas.* Appendix XIII: *The Macedonian protectorate of the Cyclades,* p. 466.
—— *The political standing of Delos.* J.H.S. XLIV, 1924, p. 141.
—— *Note on the neutrality of Delos.* J.H.S. L, 1930, p. 30.
Vallois, R. *Le Portique de Philippe.* Exploration archéologique de Délos. Vol. VII, i. Paris, 1923. pp. 154 *sqq.*
Ziebarth, E. *Beiträge zur Geschichte des Seeraubs und Seehandels im alten Griechenland.* Abh. aus dem Gebiet der Auslandskunde, 30. Hamburg, 1929. pp. 25 *sqq.*

11. *The 'Cretan War.' Philip and Rhodes. Philip and Egypt. Antiochus III in Asia Minor*

Cardinali, G. *Creta nel tramonto dell' Ellenismo.* Riv. Fil. XXXV, 1907, pp. 5 *sqq.*
Gelder, H. van. *Geschichte der alten Rhodier.* p. 120 *sq.*
Guarducci, M. *Demiurgi in Creta.* Riv. Fil. LVIII, 1930, p. 67 (the 'Cretan War').
Herzog, R. Κρητικὸς πόλεμος. Klio, II, 1902, p. 316.
Holleaux, M. *Remarques sur les décrets des villes de Crète....*Klio, XIII, 1913, pp. 145 *sqq.*
—— *Sur la 'Guerre crétoise'* (Κρητικὸς πόλεμος). Rev. E. G. XXX, 1917, p. 88.
—— *L'expédition de Dikaiarchos....*ib. XXXIII, 1920, p. 223.
Müttelsee, M. *Zur Verfassungsgeschichte Kretas im Zeitalter des Hellenismus.* Diss. Hamburg. Glückstadt, 1925. p. 51 *sq.*
Westermann, W. L. *Upon Slavery in Ptolemaic Egypt.* New York, 1929. pp. 22 *sqq.* (Dicaearchus). See also G. De Sanctis in *Riv. Fil.* LVIII, 1930, p. 118.
Wilhelm, A. *Ein Brief Antiochos III.* Wien Anz. 57. 1920, XVII–XXVII, p. 51.
Articles in P.W.: *Delos,* col. 2483 (F. Hiller von Gärtringen) *Herakleides* (63) (E. Fabricius).

12. *Nabis*

Busolt, G. and Swoboda, H. *Griechische Staatskunde.* Vol. II, p. 731 *sq.*
Homolle, T. *Le roi Nabis.* B.C.H. XX, 1896, p. 502.
Mundt, J. *Nabis, König von Sparta.* Diss. Münster-i.-W. 1903.
Pareti, L. *Per la storia di alcune dinastie greche nell' Asia Minore.* Atti Acc. Torino, XLVI, 1910–11, p. 625.
Poehlmann, R. von. *Geschichte der sozialen Frage und des Sozialismus in der antiken Welt.* Ed. 3, by F. Oertel. Vol. I. München, 1925. p. 391 *sq.*
Tarn, W. W. *Hellenistic Civilisation.* Ed. 2. London, 1930. pp. 23, 114.
—— *The social question in the third century.* The Hellenistic age. Cambridge, 1923. p. 139 *sq.*
Wilhelm, A. *Hellenistisches.* Wien Anz. 58, 1921, XVIII, p. 1.
Wolters, P. *König Nabis.* Ath. Mitt. XXII, 1897, p. 139.

13. *Expeditions of Philip V and Antiochus III,* 202–1 B.C.

Beloch, J. *Die Bevölkerung der griechisch-römischen Welt.* Leipzig, 1886. p. 10 (on the battle of Chios).
—— K. J. *Griechische Geschichte²*. Vol. IV, 2, pp. 550 *sqq.*
Busolt, G. and Swoboda, H. *Griechische Staatskunde.* Vol. II, p. 1511 n. 3.
Cousin, G. and Holleaux, M. *Inscriptions du sanctuaire de Zeus Panamaros.* B.C.H. XXVIII, 1904, pp. 345, 353 (nos. 1–3).
Degen, E. *Kritische Ausführungen zur Geschichte Antiochos des Grossen.* pp. 1 *sqq.*
De Sanctis, G. *Storia....*Vol. IV, i, pp. 4 *sqq.*, 117 *sqq.*

De Sanctis, G. *La date d'une dédicace du roi Philippe V à Délos.* Compte-rendu du Ve Congrès international des sciences historiques, Bruxelles, 1923, p. 464.

Gelder, H. van. *Geschichte der alten Rhodier.* pp. 121 *sqq.*, 129 n. 1.

Haussoullier, B. *Études sur l'histoire de Milet et du Didymeion.* Paris, 1902. pp. 139 *sqq.*, 148 *sq.*

Herzog, R. Κρητικὸς πόλεμος. Klio, II, 1902, pp. 327 *sqq.*

Hiller von Gärtringen, F. *Nikagoras, ein rhodischer Stratege.* Abh. Arch.-epig. XVI, 1893, pp. 102, 247.

Holleaux, M. *Trois décrets de Rhodes.* Rev. E. G. XII, 1899, pp. 20 *sqq.* See also Rev. E. A. V, 1903, pp. 223 *sqq.*

—— *La chronologie.*...Klio, VIII, 1908, p. 267.

—— *Remarques sur les décrets des villes de Crète....* Klio, XIII, 1913, pp. 142 *sqq.*

—— *L'expédition de Philippe V en Asie.* Rev. E. A. XXII, 1920, p. 237; XXIII, 1921, p. 181; XXV, 1923, p. 330.

Klaffenbach, G. *Samische Inschriften.* Ath. Mitt. LI, 1926, pp. 29 *sqq.*

Meyer, Ed. *Ursprung und Anfänge....* p. 121 *sq.*

Meyer, Ernst. *Die Grenzen....* pp. 54–6, 60–2, 65–73, 77–8, 80, 105, 124–5.

Meyer, M. A. *History of the city of Gaza.* Columbia University. Oriental Studies. V. New York, 1907. p. 48.

Momigliano, A. *Note su fonti ellenistiche. III. Un errore di Giuseppe Flavio e un passo di Daniele*; *Jos. A.J.* XII, 3, 3. Boll. Fil. Class. XXXV, 1928, p. 261.

Nicolaus, M. *Zwei Beiträge zur Geschichte König Philipps V. II. Die Beziehungen Philipps zu Karien.* pp. 71 *sqq.*

Niese, B. *Geschichte....* Vol. II, pp. 577 *sqq.*

Rehm, A. *Das Delphinion in Milet.* Th. Wiegand, Milet, I, iii. Berlin, 1914. pp. 200–2 (commentary to nos. 36–38), 345 (commentary to no. 148).

Salvetti, C. *Ricerche storiche....* Studi di storia antica, II, 1893, p. 114.

Serre, Contre-amiral. *Les marines de guerre de l'Antiquité et du Moyen-âge* (I). Paris, 1885. pp. 119 *sqq.* (the battle of Chios).

Tarn, W. W. *The Greek warship.* J.H.S. XXV, 1905, pp. 141 and n. 13, 147 and n. 37, 152 and n. 59, 155, 208 and n. 94 (id.).

—— *Antigonos Gonatas.* Appendix X, p. 458 (id.).

Ullrich, H. *De Polybii fontibus Rhodiis.* pp. 36 *sqq.*

Wilhelm, A. *Eine Inschrift des Königs Nikomedes Epiphanes.* Jahreshefte, XI, 1908, pp. 78 *sqq.*

—— *Neue Beiträge zur griechischen Inschriftenkunde. I. Kleinasiatische Dynasten.* Wien S.B. 166 (1), 1911, p. 54.

Articles in P.W.: *Agathokleia* (2); *Agathokles* (19); *Arsinoe* (27) III; *Hierakome* (L. Bürchner); *Kios*, col. 487 (W. Ruge); *Lydia*, col. 2185; *Lysimacheia* (4), col. 2555 (J. Weiss); *Sosibios* (3), col. 1151; *Sosibios* (4) (F. Geyer).

14. Attalus I and Rhodes appeal to Rome, 201 B.C. Roman intervention in the East, 200 B.C. Nabis and the Achaeans

Bandelin, E. *De rebus....* pp. 12 *sqq.*

Cichorius, C. *Römische Studien.* Leipzig-Berlin, 1922. p. 23.

Culmann, P. *Die römische Orientgesandtschaft vom Jahre* 201–0. Diss. Giessen, 1922.

De Sanctis, G. *Storia....* Vol. IV, 1, pp. 18 *sqq.*, especially p. 22 n. 56, p. 32 n. 65.

Ferguson, W. S. *Hellenistic Athens.* pp. 267 *sqq.*

Frank, T. *Roman Imperialism.* pp. 144 *sqq.*

Holleaux, M. *Rome....* pp. 269 *sqq.*, 306 *sqq.*

—— *Recherches....* Rev. E. A. XV, 1913, p. 4 n. 1, 2.

—— *Le prétendu recours des Athéniens aux Romains en* 201–0. ib. XXII, 1920, p. 77.

Horn, H. *Foederati.* pp. 65 *sqq.*

Kolbe, W. *Die attischen Archonten....* Abh. Göttingen, x (4), 1908, pp. 49 *sqq.*

Loring, W. *Some ancient routes in the Peloponnese.* E, II. *The ambush laid by Philopoemen in* 200 B.C. J.H.S. xv, 1895, p. 63.

Münzer, F. *Römische Adelsparteien.* p. 170 *sq.* (M. Aemilius Lepidus).

Niese, B. *Geschichte....* Vol. II, pp. 588 *sqq.*, 637 (and n. 2)–8.

—— *Grundriss der römischen Geschichte.* Ed. 5, by E. Hohl (Handbuch der Altertumswissenschaft, III, 5). München, 1923. p. 131 n. 1, 2.

Nissen, H. *Kritische Untersuchungen....* p. 306 (M. Aemilius as 'guardian' of Ptolemy V).

Täubler, E. *Imperium Romanum.* Vol. I, pp. 204, 215 *sqq.*

Walek-Czernecki, T. *Les origines de la Seconde Guerre de Macédoine.* Eos, xxxi, 1928, p. 369.

Wilamowitz-Moellendorff, U. von. *Reden und Vorträge.* Vol. II. Ed. 4. Berlin, 1926. p. 193 n. 1.

Articles in P.W.: *M. Aemilius* (68) *Lepidus* (E. Klebs); *C. Claudius* (246) *Nero*, col. 2776 (F. Münzer); *Kephisodoros* (3) (Mittelhaus).

15. *The Second Macedonian War,* 200–197 B.C.

Béquignon, Y. *La retraite de Philippe V en* 198 *et l'incursion étolienne en Thessalie.* B.C.H. LII, 1928, p. 444.

Delbrück, H. *Geschichte der Kriegskunst*[3]. Vol. I, p. 424 *sq.*

De Sanctis, G. *Storia....* Vol. IV, i, pp. 44 *sqq.*

Ferguson, W. S. *Hellenistic Athens.* pp. 273 *sqq.*

Holleaux, M. *Les conférences de Lokride et la politique de T. Quinctius Flamininus.* Rev.E.G. xxxvi, 1923, p. 115.

Homo, L. *Les conférences de Nicée et la diplomatie romaine en Grèce.* Mélanges Cagnat. Paris, 1912. p. 31.

—— *Flamininus et la politique romaine en Grèce* (198–194 *av. J.-C.*). Rev. H. cxxi, 1916, p. 241; cxxii, 1916, p. 1.

Kromayer, J. *Antike Schlachtfelder.* Vol. II, pp. 3–115 (maps 1–4).

Kromayer, J. and Veith, G. *Schlachten-Atlas zur antiken Kriegsgeschichte.* II. *Römische Abteilung,* II. Leipzig, 1922. Bl. 9, nos. 1–4 with explanatory text (cols. 39–42).

Münzer, F. *Römische Adelsparteien.* pp. 117 *sqq.* (Flamininus).

Niccolini, G. *Aristeno o Aristeneto.* Studi storici, vi, 1913, p. 194.

Stählin, F. *Das hellenische Thessalien.* pp. 101 *sqq.* (Atrax), 108 (Cynoscephalae), 125 *sq.* (Gomphi), 132 *sq.* and *passim.*

Tarn, W. W. *Antigonos Gonatas.* Append. III, p. 424 *sq.*

Täubler, E. *Imperium Romanum.* Vol. I, pp. 210 *sqq.*

Veith, G. *Der Feldzug von Dyrrhachium zwischen Caesar und Pompejus.* Wien, 1920. pp. 61 *sqq.*

Articles in P.W.: *Alexandros* (32) Ἴσιος (U. Wilcken); *Amynandros* (2); *L. Apustius* (2) (E. Klebs); *Aristainos* (2) (U. Wilcken); Γόμφοι (F. Stählin); *Euboia*, Supplementband IV, col. 445; Κυνὸς κεφαλαί (F. Stählin); Λάρισα (2) Κρεμαστή, col. 841; Λάρισα (3) Πελασγίς, col. 856.

16. *Antiochus III,* 200–197 B.C.

Benndorf, O. *Historische Inschriften vom Stadtthor zu Xanthos.* Festschrift für O. Hirschfeld. Leipzig, 1903. p. 75.

Cardinali, G. *Il regno di Pergamo.* Studi di storia antica, v, 1906, pp. 53 n. 4, 58 *sqq.*

Corradi, G. *Studi Ellenistici.* Turin, [1930]. pp. 217 *sqq.*

Degen, E. *Kritische Ausführungen....* pp. 27 *sqq.*

Frank, T. *Roman Imperialism.* pp. 163 *sqq.*
Gelder, H. van. *Geschichte der alten Rhodier.* pp. 130 *sqq.*
Holleaux, M. *Notes sur l'épigraphie et l'histoire de Rhodes.* B.C.H. XVII, 1893, pp. 61 *sqq.*
—— *La chronologie.*...Klio, VIII, 1908, pp. 270 *sqq.*
—— *Ardys et Mithridates.* Hermes, XLVII, 1912, p. 481.
—— *Recherches.*...Rev. E. A. XV, 1913, p. 1.
—— *Lampsaque et les Galates.* ib. XVIII, 1916, p. 1.
Kahrstedt, U. *Syrische Territorien.*...Abh. Göttingen, XIX (2), 1926, pp. 42, 90.
Klaffenbach, G. *Samische Inschriften.* Ath. Mitt. LI, 1926, p. 32 n. 3.
Meyer, Ed. *Ursprung und Anfänge.*...Vol. II, p. 123 *sq.*
—— *Geschichte des Königreichs Pontos.* Leipzig, 1879. p. 53 n. 1.
Meyer, Ernst. *Die Grenzen.*...pp. 45, 48, 60–1, 105–6, 137–8, 140 *sqq.*
Mezger, F. *Inscriptio Milesiaca de pace cum Magnetibus facta.* Diss. München, 1913.
Niese, B. *Geschichte.*...Vol. II, pp. 578 (and n. 6) *sqq.*
Preuner, E. *Griechische Siegerlisten.* Ath. Mitt. XXVIII, 1903, p. 361 *sq.*
Rehm, A. *Das Delphinion in Milet.* pp. 344 *sqq.* (commentary to no. 148), 373 (commentary to no. 152).
Treuber, O. *Geschichte der Lykier.* Stuttgart, 1887. pp. 151 *sqq.*
Wellhausen, J. *Israelitische und Jüdische Geschichte.* Ed. 7. Berlin, 1914. pp. 218, 228.

Articles in P.W.: *Lydia,* col. 2185; *Lykia,* col. 2274 (W. Ruge); *Lysimacheia* (4), col. 2555.

17. *Peace between Rome and Philip V. The Isthmian Games. Reorganization of Greece. Roman protectorate*

Busolt, G. and Swoboda, H. *Griechische Staatskunde.* Vol. II, pp. 1450, 1458, 1467, 1491 *sq.,* 1494 *sq.,* 1517 *sq.,* 1543.
Frank, T. *Roman Imperialism.* pp. 155 *sqq.*
Holleaux, M. Στρατηγὸς ὕπατος. Paris, 1918. pp. 86 *sqq.*
—— *L'alliance de Rome et de l'Achaïe.* Rev. E. G. XXXIV, 1921, p. 400.
Kip, G. *Thessalische Studien.* Diss. Halle, 1910. pp. 61 *sq.,* 87 *sqq.,* 112, 129 *sqq.*
Klaffenbach, G. *Zur Geschichte der Ost-Lokris.* Klio, XX, 1926, p. 83.
Rosenberg, A. *Amyntas, der Vater Philipps II.* Hermes, LI, 1916, p. 503 (the Perrhaebi).
Salvetti, C. *Ricerche storiche.*...Studi di storia antica, II, 1893, pp. 123 *sqq.*
Schober, F. *Phokis.* p. 81.
Stählin, F. *Das hellenische Thessalien.* pp. 37, 46, 126, 154 and *passim.*
Swoboda, H. *Staatsaltertümer.* pp. 238 *sqq.,* 303, 321, 348, 378, 429 *sqq.,* 442.
Täubler, E. *Imperium Romanum.* Vol. I, pp. 220 *sqq.,* 228 *sqq.,* 432 *sqq.*

Articles in P.W.: *Euboia,* Supplementband IV, cols. 445–6; *Koinon,* ib. cols. 920–1 (E. Kornemann); Λάρισα (3) Πελασγίς, col. 857; *Lokris* (1), col. 1229; *Lychnidus* (1), cols. 2112–3 (Fluss); *Magnesia* (1), col. 465 (F. Stählin).

18. *First clash between Rome and Antiochus. Peace between Antiochus and Ptolemy V*

Degen, E. *Kritische Ausführungen.*...pp. 50 *sqq.*
Frank, T. *Roman Imperialism.* pp. 167 *sqq.*
Holleaux, M. *Recherches.*...Rev. E. A. XV, 1913, pp. 5 *sqq.*
Leuze, O. *Die Feldzüge.*...III. Hermes, LVIII, 1923, pp. 202 *sqq.*
Meischcke, K. *Symbolae ad Eumenis II. Pergamenorum regis historiam.* Diss. Leipzig, 1892. p. 71 *sq.*
—— *Zur Geschichte des Königs Eumenes II. von Pergamon.* Progr. Pirna, 1905. p. 8 *sq.*

Articles in P.W.: *Aristomenes* (2) (B. Niese); *Cn. Cornelius* (176) *Lentulus*; *L. Cornelius* (188) *Lentulus* (F. Münzer); *Laodike* (18) (F. Stähelin).

19. *Coronation of Ptolemy V.* (See above, C. ii. *e.*)

20. *War with Nabis. Evacuation of Greece*

Busolt, G. and Swoboda, H. *Griechische Staatskunde.* Vol. ii, pp. 732 *sq.*, 1543.
De Sanctis, G. *Storia....* Vol. iv, i, pp. 104 *sqq.*
Foucart, P. In Ph. Le Bas and W. H. Waddington, *Voyage archéologique....* *Explication des inscriptions.* Vol. ii. Paris (n.d.). p. 110 *sq.*
Freeman, E. A. *History of Federal Government.* p. 484 *sq.*
Hatzfeld, J. *Esclaves italiens en Grèce.* Mélanges Holleaux. Paris, 1913. p. 93.
Kornemann, E. *Neue Dokumente zum lakonischen Kaiserkult.* Abh. der Schlesischen Gesellschaft für vaterländische Cultur. 1. Breslau, 1929. pp. 11, 21, 25.
Kougeas, S. B. Ἐπιγραφικαὶ ἐκ Γυθείου συμβολαί. Ἑλληνικά, i, 1928, p. 24 *sq.*
Loring, W. *Some ancient routes in the Peloponnese.* E, iii. *The expedition of T. Quinctius against Nabis in* 195 B.C. J.H.S. xv, 1895, p. 64.
Meischcke, K. *Symbolae....* pp. 46 *sqq.*
Niccolini, G. *La Confederazione Achea.* pp. 125 *sqq.*, 131 and n. 1.
Swoboda, H. *Staatsaltertümer.* p. 378 *sq.*
—— *Studien zu den griechischen Bünden.* 3. *Die Städte im achäischen Bunde.* Klio, xii, 1912, p. 21.
Täubler, E. *Imperium Romanum.* Vol. i, p. 440 *sq.*
Article in P.W.: *Sparta*, col. 1356 (F. Bölte).

21. *Hannibal at the court of Antiochus*

Degen, E. *Kritische Ausführungen....* pp. 88 *sqq.*
De Sanctis, G. *Storia....* Vol. iv, i, p. 115 and n. 3.
Groag, E. *Hannibal....* pp. 114 n. 4, 124 *sqq.*
Gsell, S. *Histoire ancienne de l'Afrique du Nord.* Vol. ii. Ed. 2. Paris, 1921. pp. 275 *sqq.*
Holleaux, M. *La rencontre d'Hannibal et d'Antiochos le Grand à Éphèse.* Hermes, xliii, 1908, p. 296.
Kahrstedt, U. *Geschichte der Karthager.* p. 584 n. 1.
Leuze, O. *Die Feldzüge....* iii. Hermes, lviii, 1923, pp. 204 n. 2, 205 n. 2, 3.
Niese, B. *Grundriss⁵....* p. 136 n. 1.
Schur, W. *Scipio Africanus.* pp. 74 *sq.*, 140.

22. *Breach between Antiochus and Rome. Hannibal and Antiochus*

Degen, E. *Kritische Ausführungen....* pp. 59 *sqq.*, 88 *sqq.*
Egelhaaf, G. *Hannibal; ein Charakterbild.* pp. 22 *sqq.*
Frank, T. *Roman Imperialism.* pp. 170 *sqq.*
Groag, E. *Hannibal.....* pp. 129 *sqq.*
Holleaux, M. *Recherches....* Rev. E. A. xv, 1913, pp. 8 *sqq.*
—— *L'entretien de Scipion l'Africain et d'Hannibal.* Hermes, xlviii, 1913, p. 75.
See also M. Guarducci in *Riv. Fil.* lvii, 1929, p. 74 *sq.*
Kromayer, J. *Hannibal und Antiochos der Grosse.* N.J. Kl. Alt. xix, 1907, p. 681.
—— *Antike Schlachtfelder.* Vol. ii, pp. 130 *sqq.*
Lehmann, K. *Hannibals letzter Kriegsentwurf.* Delbrück-Festschrift. Berlin, 1908. p. 67.
Leuze, O. *Die Feldzüge....* iv–v. Hermes, lviii, 1923, pp. 205 *sqq.*, 241 *sqq.*
Articles in P.W.: *Antiochos* (26); *Ariarathes* (4) IV (B. Niese); *Hegesianax* (1), cols. 2602–3.

23. Marriage of Ptolemy V and Cleopatra. Question of Coele-Syria

Bouché-Leclercq, A. *Histoire des Lagides*. Vol. I, pp. 381 *sqq.*

—— *Histoire des Séleucides* (II). pp. 572 *sqq.*

Cuq, E. *La condition juridique de la Coelé-Syrie au temps de Ptolémée V Épiphane.* Syria, VIII, 1927, p. 143. See M. San Nicolò, *O.L.Z.* XXXII, 1929, cols. 168–9.

De Sanctis, G. *Storia*....Vol. IV, i, p. 127 n. 39.

Holleaux, M. *Sur un passage de Flavius Josèphe*. Rev. E. J. XXXIX, 1899, p. 161.

Meyer, Ed. *Ursprung und Anfänge*....Vol. II, pp. 124 *sq.* and notes, 129 n. 1.

Stark, K. B. *Gaza*....pp. 425 *sqq.*

Willrich, H. Reviewing M. Holleaux (see above), *B.P.W.* XX, 1900, cols. 1318–19.

—— *Urkundenfälschung in der hellenisch-jüdischen Literatur.* (R. Bultmann, H. Gunkel and others, Forschungen zur Religion und Literatur des Alten und Neuen Testaments.) Göttingen, 1924. p. 76.

Article in P.W.: *Kleopatra* (14) I, cols. 738–9 (F. Stähelin).

24. The Aetolian movement

Costanzi, V. *La catastrofe di Nabide*. Riv. stor. ant. XII, 1908, p. 53.

Holleaux, M. *Sur les assemblées ordinaires de la Confédération aitolienne*. B.C.H. XXIX, 1905, p. 368 *sq.*

Leuze, O. *Die Feldzüge*....v. Hermes, LVIII, 1923, pp. 244 *sqq.*

Loring, W. *Some ancient routes in the Peloponnese*. E, IV. *The march of Philopoemen against Nabis in 192 B.C.* J.H.S. XV, 1895, p. 64.

Meischke, K. *Symbolae*....pp. 48 *sqq.*, 79 *sqq.*

Pomtow, H. In Ditt.³ 563 n. 2.

Rühl, F. *Der letzte Kampf der Achäer gegen Nabis.* Jahrbücher für classische Philologie, CXXVII, 1883, p. 33.

Swoboda, H. *Staatsaltertümer.* p. 356 n. 7.

Articles in P.W.: *A. Atilius* (60) *Serranus* (E. Klebs); *Magnesia* (1), cols. 465–6.

25. Antiochus in Greece. Thermopylae. Aetolian War, 191 B.C. Corycus

De Sanctis, G. *Storia*....Vol. IV, i, pp. 147 *sqq.*

Ferguson, W. S. *Hellenistic Athens*. pp. 282 *sqq.*

Heyden, E. A. *Beiträge*....*Die Hochzeit zu Chalcis*. pp. 29 *sqq.*

Kromayer, J. *Antike Schlachtfelder*. Vol. II, pp. 134 *sqq.*, 154 *sqq.* (map 5).

Kromayer, J. and Veith, G. *Schlachten-Atlas.* II. Römische Abteilung, II. Bl. 9, nos 5–6 with explanatory text (cols. 42–3).

Leuze, O. *Die Feldzüge*....VI. Hermes, LVIII, 1923, pp. 268 *sqq.*

Meyer, Ernst. *Die Grenzen*....p. 143.

Münzer, F. *Römische Adelsparteien*. pp. 91 (M'. Acilius Glabrio), 232 *sq.* (C. Livius Salinator).

Stählin, F. *Das hellenische Thessalien*. pp. 69, 72, 88, 204 *sq.* (Thermopylae), 206 *sqq.* (Heraclea), 215 *sqq.* (Lamia).

Tarn, W. W. *Queen Ptolemais and Apama.* C.Q. XXIII, 1929, p. 140 *sq.* (Alexander of Megalopolis).

Articles in P.W.: *M. Acilius* (35) *Glabrio* (E. Klebs); *Amynandros* (2); *M. Baebius* (44) *Tamphilus* (E. Klebs); Ἡράκλεια (4) ἡ ἐν Τραχῖνι, col. 427 (F. Stählin); *Korykos* (1) (L. Bürchner); Κυρετίαι (F. Stählin); *Lamia* (8), col. 556; Λάρισα (3) Πελασγίς, cols. 858–9; *C. Livius* (29) *Salinator* (F. Münzer); *Magnesia* (1), col. 466; *Mal(l)oia* (F. Stählin).

26. *Side. Myonnesus. Magnesia*

Bürchner, L. *Hafen Panormos und Vorgebirg Palinuros auf der Insel Samos.* Phil. XIX, 1906, p. 481.

Costanzi, V. *L' eco probabile d' una tradizione rodia presso Livio.* Riv. Fil. XXXVI, 1908, p. 392.

Delbrück, H. *Geschichte der Kriegskunst*[3]. Vol. I, pp. 426 *sqq.*

De Sanctis, G. *Storia....* Vol. IV, i, pp. 182 *sqq.*

—— *Una lettera dei Scipioni.* Atti Acc. Torino, LVII, 1921–22, p. 242.

Holleaux, M. Ἀντίπατρος ἀδελφιδοῦς. Rev. E. A. XVIII, 1916, p. 166. See also F. Stähelin in P.W. art. *Laodike* (13), col. 702.

—— *La lettera degli Scipioni agli abitanti di Colofone a mare.* Riv. Fil. LII, 1924, p. 29.

Kromayer, J. *Antike Schlachtfelder.* Vol. II, pp. 158 *sqq.* (map 6).

Kromayer, J. and Veith, G. *Schlachten-Atlas.* II. Römische Abteilung, II. Bl. 9, nos. 7, 8 with explanatory text (cols. 43–6).

Leuze, O. *Die Feldzüge....* VI. Hermes, LVIII, 1923, pp. 281 *sqq.*

Meyer, Ernst. *Die Grenzen....* p. 143 *sq.*

Picard, C. *Éphèse et Claros.* Paris, 1922. pp. 142 *sqq.*

Schur, W. *Scipio Africanus.* pp. 79 *sqq.*

Articles in P.W.: *M. Aemilius* (127) *Regillus* (E. Klebs); *P. Cornelius* (325) *Scipio*; *Cn. Domitius* (18) *Ahenobarbus* (F. Münzer); *Hyrkanion Pedion* (L. Bürchner); *C. Laelius* (2), cols. 403–4 (F. Münzer); *C. Livius* (29) *Salinator*; *Lydia*, cols. 2185–6; *Lysimacheia* (4), col. 2556; *Seleukos* (6) IV, col. 1242 (F. Stähelin); *Side* (3) (W. Ruge).

27. *End of the Aetolian War. Peace between Rome and Aetolia*

Beloch, K. J. ΑΙΤΩΛΙΚΑ. Hermes, XXXII, 1897, p. 667.

—— *Der römische Kalender....* Klio, XXII, 1929, p. 464.

Biedermann, G. *Die Insel Kephallenia im Altertum.* Diss. Würzburg. München, 1887. pp. 36 *sqq.*, 55 *sqq.*

Busolt, G. and Swoboda, H. *Griechische Staatskunde.* Vol. II, pp. 1513 *sqq.*, 1518.

De Sanctis, G. *Storia....* Vol. IV, i, pp. 209 *sqq.*, 231 *sqq.*

Dittenberger, W. *Die delphische Amphictionie im Jahre* 178 *vor Christus.* Hermes, XXXII, 1897, p. 161. See also *Hermes*, XXXIII, 1898, p. 324.

Horn, H. *Foederati.* pp. 28 *sqq.*

Klaffenbach, G. *Zur Geschichte der Ost-Lokris.* Klio, XX, 1925, p. 82.

Münzer, F. *Römische Adelsparteien.* p. 209 *sq.* and n. I (M. Fulvius Nobilior and C. Valerius Laevinus).

Oberhummer, E. *Akarnanien, Ambrakia, Amphilochien, Leukas im Altertum.* München, 1887. pp. 181 *sqq.*

Partsch, J. *Kephallenia und Ithake.* Petermanns Mitteilungen, Ergänzungsband XXI (98). Gotha, 1890. (Taf. 2: plan of old Same.)

Pomtow, H. *Die Befreiung Delphis durch die Römer.* Klio, XVI, 1920, pp. 119 *sqq.* See also Ditt.[3] commentary to 611, 613, 636.

Salvetti, C. *Ricerche storiche....* Studi di storia antica, II, 1893, pp. 126 *sqq.*

Swoboda, H. *Staatsaltertümer.* pp. 334 *sqq.*

Täubler, E. *Imperium Romanum.* Vol. I, pp. 62 *sqq.*, 69 *sqq.*, 99 *sqq.*, 321 *sq.*

Vollgraff, W. *Note sur la fin et les conséquences de la guerre étolienne.* Rev. Phil. XXVII, 1903, p. 236.

Articles in P.W.: *Amynandros* (2); *M. Fulvius* (91) *Nobilior* (F. Münzer); *Kephallenia*, cols. 205–6, 214 (L. Bürchner); *Lamia* (8), col. 556; *Lokris* (1), cols. 1230–1; *Malier*, col. 903 (F. Stählin).

28. *Cn. Manlius Volso and the Galatae. Q. Fabius Labeo in Crete*

Anderson, J. G. C. *Exploration in Gallia cis Halyn.* II, § 7. *The march of Manlius.* J.H.S. XIX, 1899, p. 311 *sq.*

Cardinali, G. *Creta....* Riv. Fil. XXXV, 1907, p. 15.

De Sanctis, G. *Storia....* Vol. IV, i, pp. 218 *sqq.*

Frank, T. *Roman Imperialism.* pp. 176 *sqq.*

Groag, E. *Hannibal....* pp. 144 *sqq.*

Körte, A. *Gordion und der Zug des Manlius gegen die Galater.* Ath. Mitt. XXII, 1897, p. 1.

Körte, G. and A. *Gordion.* J.D.A.I. Ergänzungsheft V, Berlin, 1904, pp. 30, 218.

Meyer, Ernst. *Die Grenzen....* pp. 132 *sqq.*

Mommsen, Th. *Der Friede mit Antiochos und die Kriegszüge des Cn. Manlius Volso.* Römische Forschungen. Vol. II, p. 538.

Ramsay, (Sir) W. M. *The historical geography of Asia Minor.* Royal Geographical Society, Supplementary Papers, IV, London, 1890, pp. 45 *sq.*, 134 *sqq.*, 169, 225, 231, 405, 408, 421 *sqq.* and *passim.*

—— *Res Anatolicae.* Klio, XXII, 1928, p. 376.

Reinach, A. Reviewing F. Stähelin (see below), *Rev. Celt.* XXX, 1909, p. 47.

—— *L'origine du Marsyas du Forum.* Klio, XIV, 1914–15, p. 323.

Stähelin, F. *Geschichte der kleinasiatischen Galater.* Ed. 2. Leipzig, 1907. pp. 39 *sqq.* (Standard work: full bibliography.)

Wilhelm, A. *Neue Beiträge....* II. *Ein Vertrag aus Termessos.* Wien S.B. 166 (3), 1912, pp. 5 *sqq.* (Moagetes).

Articles in P.W.: *Athenaios* (12); *Attalos* (10) II, col. 2169 (U. Wilcken); *Q. Fabius* (91) *Labeo* (F. Münzer); *Galatia* (1–2), cols. 527–8 (L. Bürchner), 542–4 (C. G. Brandis); *Kibyra* (1), col. 375; *Magaba* (W. Ruge); *Cn. Manlius* (91) *Vulso*, cols. 1217–20 (F. Münzer).

29. *Peace between Rome and Antiochus. Treaty of Apamea. Settlement of Asiatic affairs*

Cardinali, G. *Regno di Pergamo.* Studi di storia antica, V, 1906, pp. 73 *sqq.*, 96 *sqq.*

—— *Ancora per i confini della pace d' Antioco.* Klio, X, 1910, p. 249.

De Sanctis, G. *Storia....* Vol. IV, i, pp. 205 *sqq.*, 224 *sqq.*

—— *Eumene II e le città greche d' Asia.* Riv. Fil. LIII, 1925, p. 68.

Ghione, P. *I Comuni del regno di Pergamo.* Mem. Acc. Torino, LV, 1905, p. 67.

Kahrstedt, U. *Zwei Urkunden aus Polybios.* I. *Die Westgrenze des Seleukidenreichs seit 188.* Gött. Nach. 1923, p. 93.

Kiepert, R. *Formae orbis antiqui*, tab. VII with explanatory text.

Mago, U. *Appunti di cronologia ellenistica: Anno dell' arrivo a Roma di Antioco, figlio di Antioco III.* Riv. Fil. XXXV, 1907, p. 576.

Meyer, Ed. *Die Quellen....* Rh. Mus. XXXVI, 1881, p. 125 *sq.*

Meyer, Ernst. *Die Grenzen....* pp. 145 *sqq.*, 163 (Nachtrag). See also W. Ruge reviewing Ernst Meyer, *Phil. Woch.* XLVIII, 1928, cols. 1373–4.

Mommsen, Th. *Der Friede mit Antiochos....* Römische Forschungen. Vol. II, pp. 511 *sqq.*

Niese, B. *Geschichte....* Vol. III. Gotha, 1903. pp. 61 *sqq.*

Täubler, E. *Imperium Romanum.* Vol. I, pp. 75 *sqq.*, 81 n. 2, 86, 88 *sqq.*, 101 *sqq.*, 320, 442 *sqq.* and *passim.*

Viereck, P. *Die Festsetzung der Grenze im Frieden des Antiochos.* Klio, IX, 1909, p. 371.

Articles in P.W.: *Ariarathes* (4) IV; *Cn. Manlius* (91) *Vulso*, cols. 1220–1; *Lykia*, cols. 2274–5.

30. *Philip after the Aetolian War. Achaea and Sparta*

Busolt, G. and Swoboda, H. *Staatskunde.* Vol. II, p. 1544.
Freeman, E. A. *History of Federal Government.* pp. 500 *sqq.*
Niccolini, G. *La Confederazione achea.* pp. 144 *sqq.*
Swoboda, H. *Studien zu den griechischen Bünden.* 3. *Die Städte im achäischen Bunde.* Klio, XII, 1912, p. 37.
Täubler, E. *Imperium Romanum.* Vol. I, pp. 222 *sqq.*

Articles in P.W.: *Elis*, col. 2415; *Lykortas*, col. 2386 (F. Stähelin); *Magnesia* (1), col. 466.

CHAPTERS VIII AND IX

FALL OF THE MACEDONIAN MONARCHY; ROME AND THE HELLENISTIC STATES

I. ANCIENT SOURCES

Appian, *Illyrica*, 9–11; *Macedonica*, 9–19; *Mithradatica*, 62; *Syriaca*, 44–7, 66–8.
Diodorus, XXIX–XXXII.
Eutropius, IV, 6–8, 13–15.
Florus, I, 28–32.
Justin, XXXI–XXXV.
Livy, XXXVIII–XLV. *Epit.* XLVI–LIII. Pap. Oxy. IV, no. 668.
Orosius, IV, 20; V, 3.
Pausanias, VII, 7–17.
Plutarch, *Aemilius Paullus, Cato maior, Flamininus, Philopoemen.*
Polybius, XXII–XL Büttner-Wobst. [Most of these fragments are connected with the subjects of these chapters, the only important exceptions being those which concern Carthage, the still smaller number referring to the Ligurians, and much of the geographical material in XXXIV.]
Zonaras, IX, 21–31.
There are many other scattered allusions, e.g. in the fragments of Cato, the works of Cicero, Frontinus, II, 3, 20 (Pydna), and the minor works of Plutarch.
All the important inscriptions are contained in Ditt.³, 607–75 (vol. II, pp. 139–259). Other inscriptions are cited in the text of these chapters or in notes to them: Dessau, 20, 21 (Mummius), *I. G.* IV, 894 (the Epidaurians who fell at the Isthmus).

II. MODERN LITERATURE

Most of the works cited in the preceding bibliography II, *A* and *D*, 20–30 deal with one or more of the subjects of chapters VIII and IX also.

A. On the Ancient Sources

Nearly all the valuable part of what has reached us through the secondary sources comes ultimately from Polybius. The main questions about the ancient sources are accordingly two:
(1) The value of the narrative given by Polybius (see the bibliography to chapter 1).
(2) The possibility of tracing a passage in a later writer back to Polybius and of allowing for alterations from the narrative of Polybius which have occurred in the course of transmission (see the bibliography to chapters V–VII II, *B.*)
Plutarch's life of *Aemilius Paullus*, which is of special interest, is examined by Schwarze, *Quibus fontibus Plutarchus in vita L. Aem. Paulli usus sit*, Leipzig, 1891, as well as by several of the writers referred to in the above bibliography II, *B.*

B. General

The following works, in addition to those cited in the above-mentioned bibliography, are connected with the subjects of these chapters:

Casson, S. *Macedonia, Thrace, and Illyria.* Oxford, 1926.
Curtius, E. *Die Stadtgeschichte von Athen.* Berlin, 1891.
Homo, L. *Primitive Italy and the Beginnings of Roman Imperialism.* London, 1927.
Mahaffy, J. P. *The Greek World under Roman Sway.* London, 1890.

Thirlwall, C. *History of Greece*. London, 1845–52. Chapters 65 and 66.
Zinkeisen, G. *Geschichte Griechenlands*. Leipzig, 1832. (Vorlesungen, 9, 10.)

C. *Chronology—General*

See the works cited in the bibliography to chapters v–vii, II, *C*, 1.

D. *Special Topics*

Works dealing with the history of Bithynia, Cappadocia, Delos, Egypt, Galatia, Pergamum, Pontus, Rhodes, and Syria, are given in the bibliographies to chapters v–vii, xvi, xviii–xx.

The following deal with questions mentioned in these chapters:

Clinton, H. F. *Fasti Hellenici*. Oxford, 1851.
Ferguson, W. S. *Legalized absolutism en route from Greece to Rome*. American Historical Review, xviii, p. 29.
Frank, T. *The Diplomacy of L. Marcius Philippus in* 169 B.C. C.P. v, p. 358.
—— *Representative Government in the Macedonian Republics. ib.* ix, p. 49.
Hammond, B. E. *The Political Institutions of the Ancient Greeks*. London, 1895.
Homo, L. *Flamininus et la politique romaine en Grèce*. Rev. Hist. cxxi, p. 241; cxxii, p. 1.
Kromayer, J. *Antike Schlachtfelder in Griechenland*. Berlin, 1907. Vol. ii, pp. 231–348.
Kromayer, J. and Veith, G. *Schlachten-atlas zur antiken Kriegsgeschichte*. Leipzig, 1922. Röm. Abt. ii, Blatt 10.
Matthaei, L. E. *On the Classification of Roman Allies*. C.Q. i, p. 182.
—— *The Place of Arbitration and Mediation in Ancient Systems of International Ethics. ib.* ii, p. 241.
Meyer, E. *Die Schlacht bei Pydna*. Kleine Schriften, ii, p. 463, Halle, 1924.
Reinach, Ad.-J. *Delphes et les Bastarnes*. B.C.H. xxxiv, 1910, p. 249.
—— *La frise du monument de Paul-Émile à Delphes. ib.* 1910, p. 433.
Roberts, W. R. *The Ancient Boeotians*. Cambridge, 1895.
Roussel, P. *Le Sénatus-Consulte de Délos*. B.C.H. xxxvii, 1913, p. 310.
Tod, M. N. *International Arbitration among the Greeks*. Oxford, 1913.

See also the following articles in P.W., besides many of those cited in the bibliography to chapters v–vii: L. *Aemilius* (114) *Paullus* (E. Klebs), *Andriskos* (4) (U. Wilcken), *Anicius* (15) (E. Klebs), Q. *Caecilius* (94) *Metellus, Cassius* (55), P. *Cornelius* (202) *Lentulus,* Ser. *Cornelius* (208 a, b) *Lentulus,* P. *Cornelius* (353) *Scipio Nasica,* Q. *Fabius* (91) *Labeo* (F. Münzer), *Genthios* (F. Stähelin), *Gortyn* (L. Bürchner), *Herennius* (1), *Hortensius* (4), *Hostilius* (16) (F. Münzer), *Ismenias* (3) (H. Swoboda), P. *Iuventius* (30) *Thalna, Iuventius* (31) *Thalna* (F. Münzer), *Knosos, Kydonia* (1) (L. Bürchner), *Licinius* (60), *Lucretius* (23), *Marcius* (61) *Figulus, Marcius* (79) *Philippus* (F. Münzer), and the article by Cless on *Perseus* in the earlier edition of Pauly.

CHAPTER X

THE ROMANS IN SPAIN

A. Ancient Sources.

Appian, *Iberica*, 39–99.

Cato, Fragments in Peter, *Hist. Rom. Fragm.*, especially 92, 93 and in Aulus Gellius, xvi, 1.

Dio Cassius, xv–xviii (Boissevain) *passim*.

Florus, 1, 33–9.

Justin, xliv.

Livy, xxxi–xlii. (For the period after 168 b.c. Livy is preserved only in the *Periochae*.)

Polybius, xxxv, 1–5, frs. 95, 96.

Valerius Maximus, *passim*.

NOTE. For the Celtiberian and Lusitanian Wars (from 154 onwards), the lost books of Polybius contained matter of first-class importance, e.g. the events of 153–151 in book xxxv, the monograph upon the Numantine War (143–133), and the excursuses on the geography and ethnology of Spain in book xxxiv. Fortunately we still possess fragments and in part (as for instance in the Siege of Numantia) detailed extracts in Appian, *Iberica*, 44 *sqq.* (See Schulten, *Numantia, eine topographische-historische Untersuchung.* Gött. Abh. Phil.-Hist. Klass. N.F. viii. 4. 1905, p. 77, also *Numantia*, i, p. 281 and iii, pp. 7 *sqq.*) In addition there are fragments from Posidonius in Diodorus xxxi *sqq.* and the annalistic tradition in Livy (*Periochae*) which are valuable for chronology.

A collection of the Sources will be found in Schulten, *Fontes Hispaniae Antiquae*, vol. iii, Barcelona, to be published in 1931.

B. Modern Literature

(*a*) General:

De Sanctis, G. *Storia dei Romani.* Vol. iv, i. Turin, 1923. pp. 442 *sqq.* (Down to 153 b.c. only.)

Del Moro, I. *Le guerre dei Romani nella Spagna dalla fine della seconda Punica alla metà del II secolo a. Cr.* Atti della Univ. di Genova, xx, 1913.

Del Pozzo, A. *Il console M. Porcio Catone in Spagna nel 195 av. Cr.* Venice, 1921.

Fraccaro, P. *Le fonti per il consolato di M. Porcio Catone.* Stud. storic. per l' ant. class. iii, 1910, pp. 130 *sqq.*

Götzfried, K. *Annalen der römischen Provinzen beider Spanien*, 218–154. Erlangen Diss., 1907.

Kornemann, E. *Die neue Livius-epitome.* Klio, zweiter Beiheft, 1904.

Pais, E. *Fasti triumphales populi Romani.* Rome, 1923.

Schulten, A. *Numantia.* i (Die Keltiberer und ihre Kriege mit Rom). Munich, 1914.

—— *Viriatus.* N. J. Kl. Alt. xxxix, 1917, p. 209.

Wilsdorf, D. *Fasti Hispaniarum provinciarum.* Diss. Leipzig, 1878.

(*b*) Division of the provinces.

Albertini, E. *Les divisions administratives de l'Espagne romaine.* Paris, 1923.

Braun, O. *Die Entwicklung der spanischen Provinzialgrenzen.* Berlin, 1909.

(*c*) Roman camps.

Schulten, A. *Numantia.* iii and iv. (Numerous maps and plans.) Munich, 1927 and 1929.

On the coins with Iberian legends, see Vives, A., *Moneda Hispanica*, vol. ii, Madrid, 1926; for a description of conditions in Spain, *c.* 200 b.c., see Feliciani, N., *L'Espagne à la fin du troisième siècle avant J.-C.*, Boletin de la Acad. de Hist. xlvi, 1905.

See also articles *Hispania* in P.W. and in Ruggiero, *Dizionario Epigrafico*.

CHAPTERS XI and XII

ITALY AND ROME

A. Ancient Sources

Appian, *Bell. Civ.* i, 1–11; *Libyca* 67–94, 112.

Dio Cassius, frags. of bks. xviii–xxiii (Boissevain).

Cato, *De Agri cultura*; historical frags. in *Hist. Rom. Frag.* ed. H. Peter, pp. 40 *sqq.*; frags. from Orations, in *Orat. Rom. Frag.* ed. H. Meyer, pp. 119 *sqq.*

Cicero, *De Re publica*, and important incidental references, *passim.*

C.I.L. i², 581 (*S.C. De Bacchanalibus*).

Diodorus Siculus, frags. of bks. xxviii–xxxv.

Historicorum Romanorum Fragmenta, ed. H. Peter. Leipzig, 1883. (Cato, p. 40; Cornelia's letters, p. 222.)

Livy xxxi–xlv, *Epit.*, xlvi–lviii, and Pap. Oxy. iv, no. 668. (Cf. *Klio*, Beiheft ii.)

Oratorum Romanorum Fragmenta, ed. H. Meyer, Ed. 2. Zürich, 1842.

Orosius, iv–v.

Plautus, Comedies (generally portray Greek manners).

Plutarch, *Aemilius Paulus, M. Cato, Titus Flamininus, Ti.* and *C. Gracchus.*

Polybius, vi and xvi–xxxix.

Terence, Comedies (translations from the Greek).

Zonaras, *Epitome*, ix.

 Incidental references in Cornelius Nepos, Festus, Gellius, Pliny, Strabo, Valerius Maximus, Velleius Paterculus.

B. Modern Authorities

Abbott, F. F. and Johnson, A. C. *Municipal Administration.* Princeton, 1926.

Beloch, K. J. *Der Italische Bund unter Roms Hegemonie.* Leipzig, 1880.

Botsford, G. W. *The Roman Assemblies.* New York, 1909.

Cavaignac, E. *Population et Capital.* Paris, 1923. p. 95.

De Sanctis, G. *Una lettera degli Scipioni.* Atti Acc. Torino, 1922, p. 242.

Ensslin, W. *Die Demokratie und Rom.* Phil. lxxxii, 1923, p. 313.

Fraccaro, P. In *Studi Storici.* Vol. iii, 1910, p. 129, and iv, 1911, p. 217.

—— In *Atti e mem. dell' Acc. Virg. di Mantova*, 1910.

Frank, T. *Roman Buildings of the Republic.* Rome, 1924.

Gelzer, M. *Die Nobilität der römischen Republik.* Leipzig, 1912.

Greenidge, A. H. J. *A History of Rome.* Vol. i. London, 1909.

Gummerus, H. *Der römische Gutsbetrieb.* Klio, Beiheft v, 1906.

Hardy, E. G. *Some Problems of Roman History.* Oxford, 1924 (chap. i).

Hatzfeld. *Les trafiquants italiens dans l'Orient hellénique.* Paris, 1919.

Heitland, W. E. *Agricola.* Cambridge, 1921.

Holleaux, M. *Rome, la Grèce et les monarchies hellénistiques.* Paris, 1921.

Kornemann, E. *Die neue Livius-Epitome.* Klio, Beiheft ii, 1904.

—— Arts. *Colonia* and *Conventus* in P.W.

Lauterbach, A. *Untersuchungen zur Geschichte der Unterwerfung von Oberitalien.* Breslau, 1905.

Marsh, F. B. *The Founding of the Roman Empire.* Ed. 2. Oxford, 1927.

Matthaei, L. E. *The Classification of Roman Allies.* C.Q. 1907, p. 182.

Mau, A. and Ippel, A. *Führer durch Pompeii.* Ed. 6. Leipzig, 1928.

Meyer, E. *Kleine Schriften*, i. Ed. 2. Halle, 1924. p. 366.

Mommsen, Th. *Die Scipionenprozesse.* Röm. Forsch. ii, 417.

Münzer, F. *Römische Adelsparteien und Adelsfamilien*. Stuttgart, 1920.
—— Art. *Cornelius* in P.W.
Niese, B. and Hohl, E. *Grundriss der römischen Geschichte*. Ed. 5. Munich, 1923.
Pais, E. *Ricerche sulla Storia e sul Diritto pubblico di Roma*. Serie II. Rome, 1916.
—— *Dalle Guerra Puniche a Cesare Augusto*. Vol. II. Rome, 1918.
Park, M. *The Plebs in Cicero's Day*. Bryn Mawr Diss., 1918.
Platner, S. B. *Ancient Rome*. Ed. 2. New York, 1911.
Pöhlmann, R. von. *Geschichte der sozialen Frage*. Ed. 3. By Oertel. Munich, 1925.
Schur, W. *Scipio Africanus*. Leipzig, 1927.
Stella Maranca, F. *Fasti Praetorii*. Mem. Acc. dei Lincei, 1927, p. 280.
Willems, G. *Le sénat de la république romaine*. Ed. 2. Paris, 1885.

CHAPTER XIII

THE BEGINNINGS OF LATIN LITERATURE

I. Ancient Sources for Early Latin Literature

The larger histories of Roman literature give references to the main classical passages from which information is derived. For sources of the fragmentary texts of poets and dramatists, see Baehrens, Diehl, Morel (*F.P.L.*), Ribbeck under III, 'Collections'; for sources of oratory, H. Meyer's *Oratorum Romanorum Fragmenta* and for history, H. Peter's *Historicorum Romanorum Reliquiae.*

Accius. Scanty fragments of his *Didascalica*, a history (in verse with prose prefaces to different books) of Greek and Roman poetry, especially drama. G. L. Hendrickson, *A.J.Ph.* xix, 1898, reconstructs its contents. Cicero, *Brutus*, xviii, 72, corrects his blunder about date of Andronicus.

Acro, Helenius. Commentary on Terence (lost). See Porphyrio.

Asconius Pedianus, Q. *Orationum Ciceronis quinque enarratio*, ed. A. C. Clark, Oxford, 1907. (References to writers on Second Punic War and to Tuditanus: Accius quoted.)

Caesius Bassus. In H. Keil, *Grammatici Latini*, Leipzig, 1857–80, vi, pp. 265–6 (Saturnian verse).

Charisius. Quotations from dramatists and others in vol. i of Keil, *Gramm. Lat.*

Cicero. *Brutus* (notices of nearly 200 Roman orators); *De Oratore* (views of Crassus and Antonius on oratory); *De Optimo Genere Oratorum*, vi, 18 (Latin adaptations from Greek drama). Cicero makes frequent citations in his rhetorical and philosophical works from ancient Latin poets.

Diomedes. Quotations from texts in vol. i of Keil, *Gramm. Lat.*: *satura* defined, p. 485.

Donatus, Aelius. In Keil, *Gramm. Lat.* vol. iv. Donatus prefixed Suetonius' *Vita Terenti* to his Commentary on Terence, which however contains portions by a Pseudo-Donatus.

Euanthius. *Donati Commentum de comoedia*, ed. Reifferscheid, Breslau, 1874; also in *Donati Commentum Terenti*, ed. Wessner, Leipzig, 1902.

Festus, Sextus Pompeius. (Epitome of Verrius Flaccus.) *De verborum significatione quae supersunt, cum Pauli epitome*, K. O. Mueller, Leipzig, 1880; ed. W. M. Lindsay, I. Leipzig, 1913.

Fronto, M. Cornelius. Represents archaism of second century A.D. His favourites include Naevius, Ennius, Pacuvius, Plautus, Accius, C. Gracchus: in Fronto's eyes Cato was greatest of orators and generals.

Gellius, Aulus. *Noctes Atticae*, text and translation by J. C. Rolfe, 3 vols., London and New York, 1927. (Many extracts from early authors are preserved by Gellius alone. Among his sources was Varro's lost *De Poetis*.)

Glossaria Latina, vol. i, Paris, 1926.

Hieronymus. See Jerome.

Horace. Besides a good deal in *Epistles* and *Ars Poetica*, the following may be specified: *Odes*, iv, xv, 25–32 (ancient lays); *Sat.* i, iv, 6–12, 57; x, 1–5, 20–4, 48–71; ii, i, 17, 29–34, 62–75 (on Lucilius); *Epist.* i, xix, 7 (Ennius; cf. ii, i, 50–2, and for heavy verses of Accius and Ennius, *A.P.* 255–64); *Epist.* ii, i bears on the older poetry, including dramatists (55–62), Livius Andronicus (69–78), Atta (79–82), Carmen Saliare (86–8), Greek genius contrasted with Roman (90–107; cf. *A.P.* 323–32), Hellenic influence (108–17; cf. 156–7, 161–7), Fescennine licence (139–55), Saturnian verse (157–60), comedy and Plautus (168–81; cf. *A.P.* 270–4), historical pageant-plays (189–207, cf. *A.P.* 285–91 on *praetextae* and *togatae*).

Isidori Etymologiae, ed. W. M. Lindsay, 2 vols. Oxford 1910. Quotations from authors: for *satura*, xx, ii, 8.

Jerome. *Eusebii Chronicorum libri* ii, ed. A. Schoene, Berlin, 1866–75.

Livy. On drama and satura, vii, 2. Citations from early historians. (See H. Peter, *Hist. Rom. Reliq.*, Leipzig, 1914.)

Macrobius, Ambrosius Theodosius. *Saturnalia*, ed. F. Eyssenhardt, Leipzig, 1868.

Metrical Writers (Velius Longus, Terentius Scaurus and others) in Keil, *Gramm. Lat.* vol. vi and vii.

Nepos, Cornelius. Ed. Nipperdey, Berlin, 1881. Like Suetonius after him, Nepos wrote a *De Viris Illustribus*: it included *De Poetis* (lost), *De Grammaticis* (lost), *De historicis latinis* (surviving in the brief *Cato* and scraps of letters ascribed to Cornelia). Nepos was used by Suetonius, e.g. *De Rhetoribus*, iii, and *Vita Terenti*.

Nonius Marcellus. *De Conpendiosa Doctrina*, libros xx ed. W. M. Lindsay, 3 vols. Leipzig, 1903.

Pauli Diaconi Excerpta (with Festus), ed. K. O. Müller, 1839; new ed., 1880.

Pliny the Elder. *Naturalis Historia* (quoted as *N.H.*), ed. D. Detlefsen, Berlin, 1866–71; Jan Mayhoff, Leipzig, 1892–1909. Scattered references to earlier history and learning.

Pliny the Younger. *Epist.* i, xvi, 6 (Plautus and Terence as criteria of style in letters: cf. vi, xxi, 4); v, iii, 6 (on light verses by Ennius and Accius).

Plutarch. *Elder Cato, Gracchi.*

Porcius Licinus. In *F.P.L.* ed. Morel, 1927.

Porphyrio, Pomponius. Ed. W. Meyer, Leipzig, 1874. His commentary on Horace includes matter drawn from Acro and Suetonius. He cites Ennius, Plautus, Terence, Lucilius and others.

Priscian. In Keil, *Gramm. Lat.* vols. ii–iii.

Probus, Valerius. In Keil, *Gramm. Lat.* vol. iv.

Quintilian. *Institutionis Oratoriae Libri XII* (esp. parts of X), ed. with translation, by H. E. Butler, 4 vols., London and New York, 1920–22.

Servius Maurus Honoratus. *In Vergilii carmina commentarii*, ed. G. Thilo et H. Hagen, 4 vols. Leipzig, 1881–1902 (esp. for Naevius and Ennius).

Spartianus. *Hadrian*, xvi, of the emperor's archaistic taste for Ennius, Cato and Coelius in preference to Virgil, Cicero and Sallust.

Suetonius. *De Grammaticis* (esp. i, ii, iv for Greek influence: viii for a book of criticisms on Ennius). His *De Viris Illustribus*, esp. sections *De Poetis* and *De Oratoribus*, provided facts respecting Roman literature for Jerome's Latin edition of Eusebius' *Chronicle*. The *Vita Terenti* is preserved by Donatus.

Tacitus. *Dialogus de Oratoribus*, xvii–xviii (the old oratory), xx. 6 and xxi, 13 (old-fashioned style of Pacuvius and Accius); xxiii, 2 (archaizers who preferred Lucilius to Horace).

Varro. *De Lingua Latina* (Books v–x are extant). Later scholarship drew from Varro's lost works such as *De Poetis, De Actis Scenicis, Quaestiones Plautinae* and *Hebdomades* or *Imaginum libri*. Information from Varro is transmitted through Suetonius, Gellius and Nonius.

Velleius Paterculus. Esp. i, vii [quotes Cato (*Origines*)]; i, x, xii and xiii, 3; i, xiii, 4; i, xvii; ii, ix. Ed. R. Ellis, Oxford, 1898; ed. 2, 1928.

Verrius Flaccus. *De Verborum Significatu*. Of his lost encyclopaedia, written under Augustus, abridgments were made by Festus and in the eighth century by Paulus Diaconus (an inferior one). Verrius borrowed from Aelius Stilo, from Santra and from contemporaries like Valgius Rufus, Sinnius Capito, Ateius Capito and Antistius Labeo. Remnants of Verrius are imbedded in Pliny the Elder, Quintilian, Gellius, Nonius, Placidus and others.

Victorinus, Marius. In Keil, l.l., vol. vi.

Virgil. *Georg.* II, 385–97, Augustan view of rustic poetry, mumming and hymns.
Volcacius Sedigitus. *Liber de Poetis* (in Morel, *F.P.L.*) containing his 'canon' on
the comic poets.

II. LANGUAGE

(The following is a selection)

A. *Comparative Philology bearing on Latin*

Brugmann, K. and Delbrück, B. *Grundriss der vergleichenden Grammatik der indo-
germanischen Sprachen.* (Grammar and syntax.) 8 vols. Ed. 2. Strassburg,
1897–1916 *sqq.* Partly accessible in English as *Elements of the Comparative
Grammar of the Indo-Germanic Languages,* translated by J. Wright, 4 vols.
London, 1888–95.
Giles, P. *A Short Manual of Comparative Philology.* London, 1895. Ed. 2. 1901.

B. *The Latin Language and Grammar*

The older grammars by J. N. Madvig and C. G. Zumpt, of which several English
editions appeared, are in some respects superseded by modern inquiry. The following
list covers various aspects of the field:

Conway, R. S. *The Making of Latin.* London, 1923.
Dräger, A. *Historische Syntax der lateinischen Sprache,* 2 vols. Ed. 2. Leipzig,
1878, 1881.
Lindsay, W. M. *The Latin Language.* Oxford, 1894.
—— *A Short Historical Latin Grammar.* Oxford, 1895. Ed. 2. 1915.
—— *Handbook of Latin Inscriptions.* (Illustrating the history of the language.)
London and Boston, 1897.
Riemann, O. *Syntaxe latine.* Ed. 7, revised by A. Ernout. Paris. 1927.
Roby, H. J. *A Grammar of the Latin Language from Plautus to Suetonius.* 2 vols.
London, 1872, 1892, 1896, etc.
Skutsch, F. *Die lateinische Sprache* in Die Kultur der Gegenwart, ed. 2, 1, viii,
Leipzig, 1907; ed. 3, 1922.
Sommer, F. *Handbuch der lateinischen Laut- und Formenlehre.* Ed. 2. Heidelberg.
1915.
Stolz, F. and Schmalz, J. H. *Lateinische Grammatik* in Iw. Müller's Handbuch,
vol. II, 2, ed. 5, revised by M. Leumann and J. B. Hofmann, Munich, 1926–8.
Weise, O. *Language and Character of the Roman People.* Eng. translation from
German. London, 1909.

C. *Kindred Languages and Dialects*

Buck, C. D. *A Grammar of Oscan and Umbrian.* Boston, 1904; ed. 2, 1928.
Conway, R. S. *Italic Dialects.* 2 vols. Cambridge, 1897.
Gröber, G. *Grundriss der romanischen Philologie.* Strassburg, 1888–1905. (Chap-
ters by Meyer-Lübke, Windisch and Deecke.)

D. *Spoken Latin*

Baehrens, W. *Skizze der lateinischen Volkssprache* in Neue Wege zur Antike. II.
Leipzig, 1926.
De Groot, W. *Idées d'hier et d'aujourd'hui sur l'histoire de la langue latine* in Rev.
E. L., I, 1923, p. 110.
Grandgent, C. H. *An Introduction to Vulgar Latin.* Boston, 1908.
Mohl, F. G. *Introduction à la chronologie du Latin vulgaire.* Paris, 1899.

III. Collections illustrative of Archaic and Early Republican Latin

Baehrens, E. *Fragmenta Poetarum Romanorum*. Leipzig, 1886. (See Morel *infra*.)
Buecheler, F. and Riese, A. *Anthologia Latina sive Poesis Latinae Supplementum*. II, i (Carmina Epigraphica). Leipzig, 1921.
Cortese, J. *Oratorum Romanorum reliquiae*. Turin, 1892.
Diehl, E. *Poetarum Romanorum Veterum Reliquiae*. (Kleine Texte.) Bonn, 1911.
Ernout, A. *Recueil de textes latins archaïques*. Paris, 1916.
Girard, P. F. *Textes de droit romain*. Ed. 4. Paris, 1913. (Esp. for XII Tables.)
Maurenbrecher, B. *Carminum Saliarium Reliquiae*. Fleckeisen Jahrb. Supplementband XXI, 1894.
Merry, W. W. *Selected Fragments of Roman Poetry*. Oxford, 1891.
Meyer, H. *Oratorum Romanorum Fragmenta*. Zürich, 1832. Ed. 2. 1842.
Morel, W. *Fragmenta Poetarum Latinorum epicorum et lyricorum praeter Ennium et Lucilium* (post Aem. Baehrens iterum edidit W. Morel). (*F.P.L.*) Leipzig, 1927.
Peter, H. *Historicorum Romanorum Fragmenta*. Leipzig, 1883.
—— *Historicorum Romanorum Reliquiae* (with Prolegomena). Ed. 2. Leipzig, 1914.
Reichardt, A. *Die Lieder der Salier und das Lied der Arvalbrüder*. Leipzig, 1916.
Ribbeck, O. *Scaenicae Romanorum Poesis Fragmenta*. 2 vols. Ed. 3. Leipzig, 1897–8.
Vollmer, F. *Laudationum funebrium Romanorum historia et reliquiarum editio*, Jahrb. f. class. Phil., Suppl. XVIII, 1892, pp. 445–528: cf. P.W. *s.v. Laudatio*, cols. 992–4.
Wordsworth, J. *Fragments and Specimens of Early Latin*. Oxford, 1874.
Zander, C. *Carminis Saliaris Reliquiae*. Lund, 1888.

IV. General Works which include a Treatment of the Earlier Roman Authors

(For XII Tables, etc., see vol. VII)

Amatucci, A. G. *Storia della letteratura romana*. I. *Dalle origini all' età ciceroniana*. Naples, 1912.
Bailey, C. *The Mind of Rome*. (By various contributors.) Oxford, 1926.
Berger, A. and Cucheval, V. *Histoire de l'éloquence latine, depuis les origines de Rome jusqu'à Cicéron*. Ed. 3. Paris, 1892.
Cichorius, C. *Römische Studien*. Leipzig, 1922.
Cocchia, E. *Introduzione storica allo studio della letteratura latina*. Bari, 1915.
Dimsdale, M. S. *A History of Latin Literature*. London, 1915.
Duff, J. Wight. *A Literary History of Rome from the Origins to the Close of the Golden Age*. London, 1909. Ed. 7. 1927.
Enk, P. J. *Handboek der Latijnsche letterkunde*. I. Zutphen, 1928. (Gives good bibliographies.)
Grenier, A. *Le Génie Romain dans la religion, la pensée et l'art*. Paris, 1923. (Eng. trans. London, 1926.)
Kroll, W. *Studien zum Verständnis der römischen Literatur*. Stuttgart, 1924.
Lejay, P. *Histoire de la littérature latine*. (Posthumous and unfinished.) Paris, 1923.
Leo, F. *Geschichte der römischen Literatur*. Vol. 1. Berlin, 1913.
—— *Die römische Literatur des Altertums* in Die Kultur der Gegenwart, I, viii, ed. 3. Berlin, Leipzig, 1922.
Mackail, J. W. *Latin Literature*. New ed. 1906.
Norden, E. *Die antike Kunstprosa*. Ed. 2. Leipzig, 1909.
Pichon, R. *Histoire de la littérature latine*. Ed. 5. Paris, 1912.

Plessis, F. *La poésie latine de Livius Andronicus à Rutilius Namatianus.* Paris, 1909.
Ribbeck, O. *Geschichte der römischen Dichtung.* Ed. 2. Stuttgart, 1894.
Schanz, M. *Geschichte der römischen Literatur.* Erste Teil, *Von den Anfängen.* Ed. 4, by C. Hosius. 1927.
Sellar, W. Y. *The Roman Poets of the Republic.* Ed. 3. Oxford, 1889.
Teuffel, W. S. *Geschichte der römischen Literatur.* Ed. 6. Kroll and Skutsch, Leipzig and Berlin, 1916. (Eng. trans. from ed. 5. London, 1900.)

V. Special Subjects connected with Early Latin Literature

A. *Annales Maximi and similar records*

(See Vol. vii, p. 910 *sq.*)

B. *Ballad theory (Niebuhr's) and its Bearing on Early History and Poetry*

Duff, J. Wight. *A Literary History of Rome.* London, 1909. pp. 72–3.
Fowler, W. Warde. *Roman Essays and Interpretations.* Oxford, 1920. pp. 171–3, 238–40.
Niebuhr, B. G. *The History of Rome.* Eng. trans. 2 vols. London, 1855. Esp. Vol. i, pp. 254–61; vol. ii, Introd. p. 6.
—— *Lectures on the History of Rome.* Ed. Schmitz. London, 1849. Vol. ii, p. 12 *sq.*
Schwegler, A. *Römische Geschichte.* 4 vols. Tübingen, 1856–73. Vol. i, pp. 58–63.

C. *Drama and Theatre*

Allen, J. T. *Stage Antiquities of the Greeks and Romans and their Influence.* New York and London, 1927.
Bethe, E. (and collaborators). *Das Theater der Griechen und Römer.* (Handbuch d. Altertums.) In preparation.
Burckhardt, G. *Die Akteinteilung in der neuen griechischen und in der römischen Komödie.* Basel Diss., 1927.
Courbaud, E. *De Comoedia Togata.* Paris, 1899.
Fescennini Versus. Hoffmann, E. *Die Fescenninen,* Rh. Mus. li, 1896, pp. 320 *sqq.* (Cf. Wissowa, G. in P.W. *s.v.*)
Lejay, P. 'Les Origines du théâtre latin,' in *Histoire de la littérature latine,* pp. 171–82. Paris, 1923.
Leo, F. *De Tragoedia Romana.* Göttingen, 1910.
Mantzius, K. *A History of theatrical art in ancient and modern times.* Introd. by W. Archer: trans. by L. von Cossel. London, 1903. Vol. i, pp. 209–38.
Marx, F. Art. *Fabulae Atellanae* in P.W.
Michaut, G. *Sur les tréteaux latins.* Paris, 1912.
Munk, E. *De fabulis Atellanis.* Breslau, 1840.
Oehmichen, G. *Das Bühnenwesen der Griechen und Römer.* (Handb. der klass. Altertums.) Munich, 1890.
Palliatae (except Plautus and Terence). O. Ribbeck, *Comicorum romanorum fragmenta,* ed. 2. Leipzig, 1873.
Praetextae. For remains, O. Ribbeck's *Tragicorum latinorum reliquiae,* ed. 2, Leipzig, 1871: Schöne, A., *Das historische Nationaldrama der Römer.* Kiel, 1893.
Reich, H. *Der Mimus: ein litterar-entwickelungsgeschichtlicher Versuch.* Berlin, 1903.
Ribbeck, O. *Die römische Tragödie der Republik.* Leipzig, 1875. (See also Ribbeck under 'Collections' and 'General Works.')

Robert, C. *Die Masken der neueren attischen Komödie*. (Illust.) Halle, 1911.
Saunders, C. *Costume in Roman Comedy*. (Columbia Univ. Press.) New York 1909.
Skutsch, F. Art. *Exodium* in P.W.
Spengel, A. *Ueber die lateinische Komödie*. Munich, 1878.
Togatae. Remains collected in O. Ribbeck's *Comicorum romanorum fragmenta*. See Courbaud cited above.

D. *Hellenic Influences*

The subject enters into all histories of Roman literature.
Colin, G. *Rome et la Grèce de 200 à 146 avant J.-C.* Paris, 1905. (Esp. pp. 97–165, 343–72, 569–94).
Conway, R. S. *How Greek Culture came to Rome* in Harmsworth's Universal History of the World, pt. 16, pp. 1755–63, London, 1928.
Duff, J. Wight. *The Invasion of Hellenism* in A Lit. Hist. of Rome, pp. 92–117. London, 1909.
Farrington, B. *Primum Graius Homo* (Anthology of Latin translations from Greek from Ennius to Livy). Cambridge, 1927.
Hendrickson, G. L. In *A.J.Ph.* xv, 1894, pp. 1–30. (Claims that many descriptions and incidents in Latin historical prose are modelled on Greek writers.)
Kroll, W. *Römer und Griechen* in Studien zum Verständnis der römischen Literatur pp. 1–23, Stuttgart, 1924.
Pascal, C. *Graecia Capta: saggi sopra alcune fonti greche di scrittori latini*. Florence, 1905.
Zarncke, E. *Der Einfluss der griechischen Literatur auf die Entwickelung der römischen Prosa* in Commentationes...quibus...Ribbeckio congratulantur discipuli, pp. 269–325. Leipzig, 1888.

E. *Metre and Prosody*

For a full list of books on metre and prosody see W. M. Lindsay, *Early Latin verse*, App. E. See also Reports on Plautine Literature in Bursian.
Christ, W. *Metrik der Griechen und Römer*. Ed. 2. Leipzig, 1879.
Evans, W. J. *Alliteration in Latin Verse*. London, 1921.
Hardie, W. R. *Res Metrica*. Oxford, 1920.
Klotz, R. *Grundzüge altrömischer Metrik*. Leipzig, 1890.
Leo, F. *Plautinische Forschungen*. Ed. 2. Berlin, 1912.
—— *Die Plautinischen Cantica und die hellenistische Lyrik*. Berlin, 1897. (Abhandl. Gesellschaft zu Göttingen, neue Folge 1.)
Lindsay, W. M. *Early Latin Verse*. Oxford, 1922.
Müller, L. *De Re Metrica poetarum Latinorum praeter Plautum et Terentium*. Ed. 2. Leipzig, 1894.
Skutsch, F. *Iambenkürzung und Synizese*. Breslau, 1896.
—— *De Lucilii Prosodia*. Rh. Mus. xlviii, 1893, p. 303.
Sonnenschein, E. A. *Accent and Quantity in Latin Verse*. C.R. xx, 1906, p. 156.
—— *The Law of Breves Breviantes in the light of Phonetics* in C.P. vi, 1911, pp. 1–11.

F. *Originality of Roman Literature*

Castiglioni, L. *Il problema della originalità romana*. Turin, 1928.
Duff, J. Wight. *A Lit. Hist. of Rome*. London, 1909. (Preface and *passim* for the typically Roman note.)
Fowler, W. Warde. *The Imagination of the Romans* in Proceedings of Class. Association. London, 1920.

Guillemin, A. *L'Imitation...dans la littérature latine* in Rev. E. L. ii, 1924, p. 35.
Jachmann, G. *Die Originalität der römischen Literatur*. Leipzig, 1926.
Leo, F. *Die Originalität der römischen Literatur*. Göttingen, 1904.
Ussani, V. *Originalità e caratteri della letteratura latina*. Venice, 1921.

G. *Satura—Was it dramatic?*

[Dieterich, Knapp and Webb are among the defenders of the traditional account.]
Casaubon, I. *De Satyrica Graecorum Poesi et Romanorum Satira*. Paris, 1605. (Ed. Rambach, Halle, 1774; Italian translation by A. M. Salvini, Florence, 1728.)
Dieterich, A. *Pulcinella*. Leipzig, 1897, pp. 75–8.
Fairclough, H. R. In *A. J. Ph.* xxxiv, 1913, p. 183.
Fiske, G. C. *Lucilius and Horace*. University of Wisconsin, 1920.
Hendrickson, G. L. In *A. J. Ph.* xv, 1894, pp. 1 *sqq.*; xix, 1898, pp. 306 *sqq.* *C.P.* vi, 1911, pp. 129 *sqq.* and 334 *sqq.*
Jahn, O. In *Hermes*, ii, 1867, p. 225.
Knapp, C. *The Sceptical Assault on the Roman Tradition concerning the Dramatic Satura*. A. J. Ph. xxxiii, 1912, p. 125.
Kroll, W. Art. *Satura* (summary of modern theories) in P.W.
Leo, F. In *Hermes*, xxiv, 1889, pp. 67 *sqq.*; xxxix, 1904, pp. 63 *sqq.*
Mendell, C. W. In *C.P.* xv, 1920 (on source and nature of satire—its cynic strain).
Nettleship, H. *The Roman Satura: its original form*. Oxford, 1878.
Tiddy, R. J. E. *Satura and Satire* in English Literature and the Classics. Oxford, 1912.
Ullmann, B. L. In *C.P.* viii, 1913, pp. 172 *sqq.*
Webb, R. H. In *C.P.* vii, 1912, pp. 177 *sqq.*
Weinreich, O. *Zur römischen Satire—Die Quellenfrage von Livius*, vii, ii. Hermes, li, 1916, Berlin, p. 386.

H. *Saturnian Verse—Was it quantitative or accentual?*

For literary specimens see "Collections" (Baehrens, Merry, Morel, Wordsworth); for Saturnian inscriptions, Buecheler, F. (*Anthologia latina*, ii, 1) *Carmina latina epigraphica*, Leipzig, 1921.
Bartsch, K. *Der Saturnische Vers und die altdeutsche Langzeile*. Leipzig, 1867.
Fitzhugh, T. *Prolegomena to the History of Italico-Romanic Rhythm*. University of Virginia, 1908.
—— *The Literary Saturnian*. University of Virginia, 1910.
Garrod, H. W. *Oxford Book of Latin Verse*. Oxford, 1912, pp 505 *sqq.* (Concise account of theories regarding Saturnian.)
Havet, L. *De saturnio latinorum versu*. Paris, 1880.
Keller, O. *Der saturnische Vers als rythmisch erwiesen*. Leipzig-Prag, 1882.
Leo, F. *Der saturnische Vers*. Berlin, 1905.
Lindsay, W. M. *The Saturnian Metre*. A. J. Ph. xiv, 1893, pp. 139, 305
—— *Early Latin Verse*. Oxford, 1922, pp. 1 *sqq.*
Müller, L. *Der saturnische Vers und seine Denkmäler*. Leipzig, 1885.
Thulin, C. *Italische sacrale Poesie und Prosa*. Berlin, 1906.
Thurneysen, R. *Der Saturnier und sein Verhältnis zum späteren römischen Volksverse*. Halle, 1885.
Westphal, R. *Allgemeine Metrik*. Berlin, 1893, p. 228.
Zander, C. *Versus Saturnii*. Lund, 1918.

VI. The Chief Early Authors represented by Separate Editions

For fragments of poets and dramatists see above, III, 'Collections,' under Baehrens, Diehl, Merry, Morel, Ribbeck, Wordsworth; of historians under Peter and Wordsworth; of orators under Meyer and Wordsworth. Fuller bibliographies will be found in Bursian, in Schanz, *Röm. Literaturgesch.* 1927, and Teuffel, *Geschichte der röm. Lit.* 1916. For editions and relative literature between 1700 and 1878 see W. Engelmann, *Bibliotheca Scriptorum Classicorum*, ed. 8, E. Preuss, zweite Abtheilung, *Scriptores Latini*, Leipzig, 1882.

Accius

Marx, F. Art. in P.W. *s.v.* Accius.
Müller, L. *De Accii Fabulis Disputatio.* Berlin, 1890.
—— Edition of *Lucilius*, Leipzig, 1872, contains Accius' non-dramatic fragments, pp. 303 *sqq.*
Ribbeck, O. *Trag. Rom. Frag.* Leipzig, 1897.

Andronicus, Livius

Kunz, F. *Die älteste römische Epik in ihrem Verhältnis zu Homer.* Unter-Meidling, 1890.
Müller, L. *Der Saturnische Vers und seine Denkmäler.* Leipzig, 1885.
—— *L. Andronici et Cn. Naevii Fabularum Reliquiae.* Berlin, 1885.
Tolkiehn, J. *Homer und die römische Poesie.* Leipzig, 1900.

Cato

For fragments of *Origines* and of Speeches, see above, III. 'Collections,' under Peter and Meyer.

Goetz, G. *De Agricultura.* Leipzig, 1922.
Jordan, H. *M. Catonis praeter librum De Re Rustica quae extant.* Leipzig, 1860.
Keil, H. *Rerum rusticarum libri.* (Including Varro.) Leipzig, 1884–1902.

Ennius

Müller, L. *Q. Enni Carminum Reliquiae: accedunt Cn. Naevi Belli Poenici quae supersunt.* St Petersburg, 1884.
—— *Fragmenta Annalium et Saturarum* in Postgate's C.P.L. vol. 1, London, 1894.
—— *Q. Ennius: eine Einleitung in das Studium der römischen Poesie.* St Petersburg, 1884.
Skutsch, F. Art. *Ennius* in P.W.
Steuart, E. M. *The Annals of Q. Ennius.* Cambridge, 1925.
Vahlen, J. *Ennianae Poesis Reliquiae*, 1854. Ed. 2. Leipzig, 1903.

Lucilius

Cichorius, C. *Untersuchungen zu Lucilius.* Berlin, 1908.
Fiske, G. C. *Lucilius and Horace.* (Univ. of Wisconsin Studies in Language and Literature, 7.) Madison, 1920.
Kappelmacher, A. Art. in P.W. *s.v.* Lucilius.
Marx, F. *C. Lucilii Carminum Reliquiae.* 2 vols. Leipzig, 1904–5. [With Prolegomena on life, chronology of works, metre, and previous editions of Lucilius.]
Müller, L. *C. Lucili Saturarum Reliquiae: accedunt Acci praeter scenica...reliquiae.* Leipzig, 1872.
Stewart, H. *The Date of Lucilius' Birth*, reprint from Proceedings of Leeds Philosophical Society, vol. 1, pt. vi, pp. 285–91, Leeds, 1928. [A review of the debated problem and some of the main arguments.]

Naevius

See above III. 'Collections' under Baehrens, Diehl, Merry, Morel, Ribbeck, Wordsworth.

Müller, L. *Enni Carminum Reliquiae: accedunt Cn. Naevi Belli Poenici quae supersunt.* St Petersburg, 1884.
—— *L. Andronici et Cn. Naevi Fabularum Reliquiae.* Berlin, 1885.
Vahlen, J. *Cn. Naevi De Bello Punico Reliquiae.* Leipzig, 1854.

Pacuvius

Müller, L. *De Pacuvii fabulis Disputatio.* Berlin, 1889.

Plautus

A. Text.

J. L. Ussing, Copenhagen, 5 vols., 1875–86; F. Ritschl, G. Götz, G. Löwe, F. Schöll, Leipzig, 1871–94; F. Leo, Berlin, 1895–96; G. Götz and F. Schöll, Leipzig, ed. 2, 1904 *sqq.*; W. M. Lindsay, 2 vols., Oxford, 1904–5; ed. 2, 1910.

B. Separate Editions of Plays. (Some older editions, which have been superseded, are omitted.)

Amphitruo, A. Palmer, London, 1890. *Asinaria*, J. H. Gray, Cambridge, 1896; L. Havet and A. Freté, Paris, 1925 (treating the play as by a pseudo-Plautus). *Aulularia*, E. J. Thomas, Oxford, 1913. *Bacchides*, J. McCosh, London, 1896. *Captivi*, A. R. S. Hallidie, London, 1891; E. A. Sonnenschein, London, 1899; J. Brix, ed. 6 by M. Niemeyer, Leipzig, 1910; W. M. Lindsay, ed. 2, London, 1924 (with study of Plautine prosody). *Epidicus*, J. H. Gray, London, 1893. *Menaechmi*, J. Brix, (1866) ed. 5 by M. Niemeyer, Leipzig, 1912; P. T. Jones, Oxford, 1918; C. M. Knight, Cambridge, 1919. *Miles Gloriosus*, R. Y. Tyrrell, ed. 3, London, 1889; J. Brix and O. Koehler, ed. 4, Leipzig, 1916. *Mostellaria*, E. A. Sonnenschein, Oxford, 1907. *Persa*, G. Ammendola, Lanciano, 1922. *Pseudolus*, A. Lorenz (with study on Plautus' language), Berlin, 1876; H. W. Auden, Cambridge, 1896. *Rudens*, E. A. Sonnenschein, Oxford, 1902. *Stichus*, C. A. M. Fennell, Cambridge, 1893. *Trinummus*, J. H. Gray, Cambridge, 1897; H. C. Nutting, Boston, 1904. *Truculentus*, A. Spengel, Göttingen, 1868.

C. English Translations.

Prose: H. T. Riley, 2 vols. London, 1881; P. Nixon, 5 vols. (Loeb), London and New York, 1916 *sqq.* (in progress); Five plays translated in the original metres, E. H. Sugden (*Amph., Asin., Aul., Bacch., Capt.*), London, 1893.

D. Works on Plautus. (See also above, V, E, 'Metre.')

Denecke, A. *Zur Würdigung des Plautus.* Dresden, 1911.
Engelbrecht, A. *Ueber den Sprachgebrauch der lateinischen Komiker.* Wien, 1884.
Fränkel, E. *Plautinisches im Plautus.* Philologische Untersuchungen herausgegeben von Kiessling und Wilamowitz, Heft 28. Berlin, 1922.
Hueffner, F. *De Plauti comoediarum exemplis Atticis quaestiones.* Göttingen, 1894.
Knapp, C. *References to Painting and Literature in Plautus and Terence.* C.P. XII, 1917, p. 143.
Langen, P. *Beiträge zur Kritik und Erklärung des Plautus.* Leipzig, 1880.
—— *Plautinische Studien.* Berlin, 1886.
Lejay, P. *Plaute.* Paris, *n.d.* (Posthumous.)
Leo, F. *Plautinische Forschungen zur Kritik und Geschichte der Komoedie.* Berlin, 1895. Ed. 2. 1912.

Lindsay, W. M. *Syntax of Plautus.* Oxford, 1907.
Michaut, G. *Histoire de la Comédie Romaine: Plaute.* Paris, 1920.
Prescott, H. W. *Some Phases in the Relation of Thought to Verse in Plautus.* Berkeley, California, 1907.
—— *The interpretation of Roman Comedy.* C.P. xi, 1916, p. 125.
Ritschl, F. W. *Neue Plautinische Excurse.* Leipzig, 1869.
Sedgwick, W. B. *Parody in Plautus.* C.Q. xxi, 1927, pp. 88–9.
Westaway, K. M. *The Original Element in Plautus.* Cambridge, 1917.

Terence

A. Text.

W. Wagner, Cambridge, 1869, ed. 3, 1892; K. Dziatzko, Leipzig, 1884; A. Fleckeisen, ed. 2, Leipzig, 1898; R. Y. Tyrrell, Oxford, 1902; S. G. Ashmore, Oxford, 1908; R. Kauer and W. M. Lindsay, Oxford, 1926.

B. Separate editions of plays.

Adelphi, F. Plessis, Paris, 1884; W. L. Cowles, Boston, 1896; K. Dziatzko and R. Kauer, ed. 2, Leipzig, 1903; A. Gustarelli, Milan, 1909. *Andria*, A. Spengel, ed. 2, Berlin, 1888; H. R. Fairclough, Boston, 1905; E. H. Sturtevant, New York, 1914; U. Moricca, Florence, 1921. *Eunuchus*, P. Fabia, Paris, 1895; G. B. Bonino, Rome, 1910. *H(e)auton Timorumenos*, J. H. Gray, Cambridge, 1895; F. G. Ballentine, Boston, 1910. *Hecyra*, P. Thomas, Paris, 1887. *Phormio*, K. Dziatzko and E. Hauler, ed. 4, Leipzig, 1913; J. Sargeaunt, Cambridge, U.S.A., 1914; F. Guglielmino, Florence, 1922; P. Giardelli, Turin, 1923.

C. English Translations.

PROSE: J. Sargeaunt (facing Latin), London and New York, 2 vols. 1912.
VERSE: Blank, G. Colman, London, 1765; translated into parallel English metres, W. Ritchie, London, 1927.

D. Works on Terence.

Baese, W. *De canticis Terentianis.* Halle, 1903.
Bartel, E. *De vulgari Terentii sermone.* Karlsbad, 1910.
Craig, J. D. *Archaism in Terence.* C.Q. xxi, 1927, pp. 90–4.
Donatus. *Aeli Donati quod fertur commentum Terenti.* Ed. Wessner, Leipzig, 1902.
Fabia, P. *Les prologues de Térence.* Paris, 1888.
Norwood, G. *The Art of Terence.* Oxford, 1923.

CHAPTER XIV

ROMAN RELIGION AND THE ADVENT OF PHILOSOPHY

A. ROMAN RELIGION

I. Ancient Sources

Corpus Inscriptionum Latinarum, especially Vol. i. Berlin, 1863.
Conway, R. S. *The Italic Dialects*. 2 vols. Cambridge, 1897.
Sancti Aurelii Augustini *De Civitate Dei*. Rec. B. Dombart. Leipzig, 1877.
M. Porcii Catonis *De Agri cultura Liber*. Rec. G. Goetz. Leipzig, 1912.
M. Tullii Ciceronis *De Natura Deorum*. Ed. J. B. Mayor. Cambridge, 1891.
Dionysii Halicarnassensis *Antiquitates Romanae*. Rec. F. Jacoby. Leipzig, 1885–99.
Festi *De Verborum Significatione*. Rec. W. M. Lindsay. Leipzig, 1913.
P. Ovidii Nasonis *Fasti*. Ed. Sir J. G. Frazer. London, 1929.
Plutarchi *Quaestiones Romanae*. Rec. G. N. Bernardakis. Leipzig, 1889. (Translation and Commentary by H. J. Rose. Oxford, 1924.)
M. Terentii Varronis *De Lingua Latina*. Rec. G. Goetz et F. Schoell. Leipzig, 1910.
  Also references in other authors, particularly in Plautus, Horace, Virgil, Livy, Pliny the Elder, Macrobius and Aulus Gellius.

II. Modern Works

1. *General*

Aust, E. *Die Religion der Römer*. Münster-i.-W. 1899.
Bailey, C. *The Religion of Ancient Rome*. London, 1907.
—— Articles in *Encyclopaedia Britannica*, 1910, and *The Legacy of Rome*, Oxford, 1923.
Boissier, G. *La Religion romaine*. Paris, 1906.
Deubner, L. *Die Römer* in Lehrbuch der Religionsgeschichte, ed. 4, Tübingen, 1925.
—— *Die ältesten Priestertümer der Römer*. Riga, 1913.
Fowler, W. Warde. *The Religious Experience of the Roman People*. London, 1911.
—— *The Roman Festivals*. London, 1899.
—— *Roman Essays and Interpretations*. Oxford, 1920.
Halliday, W. R. *History of Roman Religion*. Liverpool, 1922.
Marquardt, J. *Römische Staatsverwaltung. Das Sacralwesen*. (Marquardt and Mommsen, Handbuch der Römischen Alterthümer, vol. iii, Leipzig, 1885.)
Roscher, W. H. *Ausführliches Lexicon der griechischen und römischen Mythologie*. Leipzig, 1884–1924.
Wissowa, G. *Religion und Kultus der Römer*. Ed. 2. 1912.
—— *Gesammelte Abhandlungen*. Munich, 1904.
  See also articles on special deities and festivals in P.W., and in particular the articles *Aberglaube* (Riess); *Augures* and *Auspicium* (Wissowa); *Etrusca Disciplina* (Thulin); *Fasti* (Schön); *Indigitamenta* (Richter); and *Lustratio* (Boehm).

2. *Special*

Bréal, M. *Les Tables Eugubines*. Paris, 1875.
Buecheler, F. *Umbrica*. Bonn, 1883.
De Marchi, A. *Il Culto Privato di Roma Antica*. Milan, 1896.
Ducati, P. *Etruria Antica*. 2 vols. Turin, 1925.

Fell, R. A. L. *Etruria and Rome*. Cambridge, 1924.
Huschke, E. *Die Iguvischen Tafeln*. Leipzig, 1859.
Müller, K. O. *Die Etrusker*. Neuarbeitet von W. Deecke. 2 vols. Stuttgart, 1877.
Randall-MacIver, D. *The Etruscans*. Oxford, 1927.
—— *Italy before the Romans*. Oxford, 1928.
Rose, H. J. *Primitive Culture in Italy*. London, 1926.
—— *The Roman Questions of Plutarch*. Oxford, 1924.
Taylor, L. Ross. *Local Cults in Etruria*. Rome, 1923.

B. THE ADVENT OF PHILOSOPHY

I. Ancient Sources

M. Tullii Ciceronis *De Divinatione*. Rec. C. F. W. Müller. Leipzig, 1915. Ed.
    A.S. Pease. Illinois, 1920–3.
—— *De Finibus Bonorum et Malorum*. Rec. Schiche. Leipzig, 1915.
—— *De Legibus*. Rec. C. F. W. Müller. Leipzig, 1912.
—— *De Natura Deorum*. Rec. Plasberg. Leipzig, 1917. Ed. J. B. Mayor.
    Cambridge, 1891.
—— *De Officiis*. Rec. Atzert. Leipzig, 1923. Ed. H. A. Holden, Cambridge,
    1899.
—— *De Re publica*. Rec. Ziegler. Leipzig, 1929.
—— *Disputationes Tusculanae*. Rec. Pohlenz. Leipzig, 1918.
—— *Paradoxa Stoicorum*. Rec. Plasberg. Leipzig, 1908.
Diogenis Laertii *Vitae Philosophorum*. Lib. vii. Ed. and trans. R. D. Hicks (Loeb
    Library). London, 1925.
Epicurus. The extant remains. Ed. C. Bailey. Oxford, 1926.
Metrodori Epicurei Fragmenta. Rec. A. Koerte. Leipzig, 1890.
Panaetii et Hecatonis librorum fragmenta. Rec. H. N. Fowler. Bonn, 1885.
Polybius, book vi. Rec. Th. Büttner-Wobst. Leipzig, 1924.
Sexti Empirici *Adversus Mathematicos*, vii. Rec. H. Mutschmann Leipzig, 1914.
—— Πυρρωνείων Ὑποτυπώσεων. Rec. H. Mutschmann. Leipzig, 1912.
Usener, H. *Epicurea*. Leipzig, 1887.
von Arnim, H. *Stoicorum Veterum Fragmenta*. 3 vols. Leipzig, 1903–24.

II. Modern Works

Arnold, E. V. *Roman Stoicism*. Cambridge, 1911.
Bailey, C. *The Greek Atomists and Epicurus*. Oxford, 1928.
Bevan, E. R. *Stoics and Sceptics*. Oxford, 1913.
Brochard, V. *Les Sceptiques Grecs*. Paris, 1923.
Crönert, W. *Kolotes und Menedemos*. Leipzig, 1906.
Heinemann, S. *Posidonios Metaphysische Schrift*. Berlin, 1921.
Hicks, R. D. *Stoic and Epicurean*. London, 1910.
More, P. E. *Hellenistic Philosophies*. Princeton, 1929.
Reinhardt, K. *Posidonios*. Munich, 1921.
Schmekel, A. *Die Philosophie der mittleren Stoa*. Berlin, 1892.
Zeller, E. *The Stoics, Epicureans and Sceptics*. Trans. O. J. Reichel. London, 1870.

CHAPTER XV

THE FALL OF CARTHAGE

A. Ancient Sources

I. *Inscriptions*

C.I.L. viii, Supplement 1275; ix, 6348 = *Dessau*, 67.
I.G. xiv. 315 = Ditt.[3] 677. See also the Masinissa Inscription from Thugga, *Catalogue du Musée Alaoui*, 1910, pp. 106 *sqq.*, 122, 1127: and cf. Lidzbarski, M., *Eine punische-altberberische Bilinguis aus einem Tempel des Massinissa.* Berl. S.B. 1913, p. 296.

II. *Literary*

Appian, *Bell. Civ.* i, 24. *Libyca*, 67–136. *Syriaca*, 4.
Auctor *de viris illustribus*, 49, 12; 58, 4.
Cicero, *de leg. agr.* ii, 51. *Verr.* i, 11; ii, 3, 85 *sqq.*, 38, 2. *de off.* i, 79; ii, 76. *Cato Major*, 18. *Tusc.* iii, 51.
Cornelius Nepos, *Hannibal*, 7–12.
Dio Cassius, ed. Boissevain, xxi, frag. 70.
Diodorus, xxxii; xxxiv, 33.
Justin, xxxi, 1, 7–9.
Livy xxxii, 2; xxxiii, 45. 6–49, 7; xxxiv, 49, 62; xxxvii, 5; xli, 22; xlii, 23; xliii, 3, 5, 6, 11. *Epit.* xlviii, xlix, l, li (and Pap. Oxy. iv, no. 668).
Lucan, *Pharsalia*, iv, 585.
Macrobius, *Sat.* iii, ix, 10.
Orosius, iv, 22–3.
Pliny, *N.H.* v, 17, 22, 25 *sqq.*; xviii, 22; xxii, 13; xxxv, 23.
Plutarch, *Cato Maior*, 26, 27; *Apophthegmata regum et imperatorum*: Scipionis Minoris, 3, 5, 6, 7.
Polybius, xxxvii, 1, 3; xxxviii, 1–3; xxxix, 3–5.
Sallust, *Jugurtha*, 19, 7.
Silius Italicus, xvi.
Strabo, xvii, 833.
Valerius Maximus, *passim.*
Velleius Paterculus, i, 12; ii, 4.
Zonaras, ix, 26–30.

B. Modern Literature

See the general works of Gsell, Kahrstedt, Pais, and Piganiol cited in the Bibliography to Chapters ii–iv, and also the following:

(a) *Hannibal's Reforms*

De Sanctis, G. *Storia dei Romani*, iv, i. Turin, 1923. p. 119 *sq.*
Egelhaaf, G. *Hannibal: ein Charakterbild.* Stuttgart, 1922.
Groag, E. *Hannibal als Politiker.* Vienna, 1929.
Holleaux, M. *Recherches sur l'histoire des négociations d'Antiochos III avec les Romains.* Rev. E.A. xv, 1913. p. 1.
Kromayer, J. *Hannibal als Staatsmann.* H.Z. ciii, 1909, p. 244.
Meyer, Ed. *Hannibal und Scipio.* (Meister der Politik, vol. i, ed. 2.) Stuttgart-Berlin, 1923.

(b) Masinissa and Carthage

Babelon, E., Cagnat, R. and Reinach, S. *Atlas archéologique de la Tunisie.* Paris, 1893.
Barthel, W. *Römische Limitation in der Provinz Africa.* Bonner Jahrbücher, cxx, 1911, p. 104.
Cagnat, R. *Fossa Regia.* In C.R. Ac. Inscr. 1894, p. 43.
Carton, L. *Carthage punique.* Rev. Arch. xvii, 1923, p. 329.
Contenau, G. *La Civilisation phénicienne.* Paris, 1926.
Gsell, S. *Atlas archéologique de l'Algérie.* Algiers, 1902–11.
—— *Etendue de la domination Carthaginoise en Afrique.* Orientalisten-Kongress. Algiers, 1905.
Thieling, W. *Der Hellenismus in Klein-Africa.* Leipzig-Berlin. 1911.
Tissot, Ch. *Géographie comparée de la province romaine d'Afrique.* Paris, 1884–8.
   See also the articles in P.W. *s.v. Karthago* (Oehler and Lenschau) and *Massinissa* (Schur).

(c) The Walls of Carthage and the Topography of the Siege. (See also in Section *(b)*.)

Audollent, A. *Carthage Romaine,* 146 avant *J.-C.*–698 après *J.-C.* Paris, 1901.
Gardthausen, V. *Die Mauern von Carthago.* Klio, xvii, 1917, p. 122.
Gauckler, P. *Les Nécropoles puniques de Carthage.* Paris, 1915.
Graux, Ch. In *Bibl. de l'Ecole des Hautes Etudes,* xxxv, 1878, p. 175.
Groh, H. K. *Die Belagerung von Karthago im dritten punischen Kriege.* Leipzig Diss., 1921.
Kromayer, J. and Veith, G. *Schlachten-Atlas,* ii (Leipzig, 1922), pp. 51 *sqq.*
Oehler, R. *Die Häfen von Karthago.* Arch. Anz. 1898, p. 171; 1899, pp. 7 and 93.
—— Review of P. Aucler's *Carthage* (Les Villes Antiques) in *Phil. Woch.* 1899, p. 1583.
—— *Die Mauer des "schwachen Winkels" von Karthago* (*Appian, Pun.* 95 *a,* E; 98) *und ihr Wasserschutz.* Klio, xxvii, 1927, p. 385.
Schulten, A. *Archäologische Neuigkeiten aus Nordafrika.* Arch. Anz. 1898, p. 112; 1899, p. 66; 1905, p. 73.
Torr, C. *Les Ports de Carthage,* and *Encore les Ports de Carthage.* Rev. Arch. 1894, pp. 34 and 294.

(d) The Destruction of Carthage and the Formation of the Roman Province

Barthel, W. *Zur Geschichte der römischen Städte in Africa.* Bonner Jahrbücher, cxx, 1911, p. 82.
Cagnat, R. *Notes sur les limites de la province romaine d'Afrique en* 146 avant *J.-C.* C.R. Ac. Inscr. 1894, p. 51.
Lincke, E. *P. Cornelius Scipio Aemilianus.* Dresden Progr. 1898.
Schulten, A. *L'Arpentage romain en Tunisie.* Bull. Arch. du Comité des Travaux. 1902, p. 128 (esp. pp. 140 *sqq.*).

(e) Epilogue

Apart from the notices preserved in Greek and Roman writers the only other means available for reconstructing Carthaginian history and civilization are the Punic inscriptions and the results of archaeological research. The inscriptions will be found in the *Corpus Inscriptionum Semiticarum* (C.I.S.), Paris, 1881. See also: Lidzbarski, *Handbuch der nordsemitischen Epigraphik,* Weimar, 1898, and G. A. Cooke, *Textbook of North Semitic Inscriptions,* Oxford, 1903. New finds are usually published in the French periodicals (see below) and in the *Ephemeris für semitischen Epigraphie* (Giessen, 1902–   ). For the archaeological material consult the articles and publications of MM. Albertini, Audollent, Boissier, Carcopino, Chabot, Delattre, Gauckler, Gsell, Merlin and Poinssot: new finds are usually published in the *Comptes-Rendus de l'Académie des Inscriptions et Belles-Lettres* (C.R. Ac. Inscr.) or the *Revue Archéologique* (Rev. Arch.), or in such special local publications as the *Bulletin Archéologique du Comité des Travaux Historiques*, the *Revue Africaine*, or the *Revue Tunisienne*. See also: S. Gsell, *Les Monuments Antiques de l'Algérie*, Paris, 1901 and R. Cagnat and P. Gauckler, *Les Monuments Historiques de la Tunisie*, Paris, 1898. On religion see P. Lagrange, *Études sur les religions sémitiques*, Paris, 1905.

Two modern and authoritative histories are O. Meltzer, *Geschichte der Karthager*, Berlin, vol. I, 1879; II, 1896; III (by U. Kahrstedt), 1913, and S. Gsell, *Histoire ancienne de l'Afrique du Nord*, Paris, vols. I–IV, 1913–1920: this last contains an immense collection of material, and notes practically everything discovered down to 1920. See also the article *Karthago* in P.W., by Oehler and Lenschau.

CHAPTER XVI

SYRIA AND THE JEWS

I   Ancient Authorities

1. *Contemporary*

(*a*) Jewish

The Book of Daniel.
* The Book of Enoch, vi–xxxvi, lxxii–lxxxii, lxxxiii–xc, xci. 12–17, xciii. 1–10.
* The Book of Jubilees.
* The Testaments of the Twelve Patriarchs.
* The Book of the 'New Covenant' [called 'Fragments of a Zadokite Work' in
      Charles, *Pseudepigrapha*, pp. 785 *sqq.*: there is a German translation with
      commentary by Eduard Meyer, *Die Gemeinde des neuen Bundes im Lande
      Damaskus.* Berl. Abh. 1919].
1 Maccabees.
Jason of Cyrene (of whose work in 5 books 2 Maccabees is an epitome).
   [The date of all the documents marked above with an asterisk is a matter of very
doubtful conjecture, and possibly some of them are really later than the time covered
by this chapter. In the case of Enoch, Jubilees, and the Testaments, the date intended
is of course that of the lost Hebrew or Aramaic original, not that of the translations
which we still possess.]

   Translations and commentaries:
Bevan, A. A. *A Short Commentary on the Book of Daniel.* Cambridge, 1892.
Charles, R. H. *The Apocrypha and Pseudepigrapha of the Old Testament in English,
      with Introductions and Critical and Explanatory Notes*, 2 vols. Oxford, 1913.
—— *A Critical and Exegetical Commentary on the Book of Daniel.* Oxford, 1929.
Fritzsche, O. F. and Grimm, C. L. W. *Kurzgefasstes exegetisches Handbuch zu den
      Apokryphen des Alten Testaments*, 3 vols. Leipzig, 1851–9.
Kautzsch, E. *Apokryphen und Pseudepigraphen des Alten Testaments.* 2 vols.
      Tübingen, 1900.
Montgomery, J. *A Critical and Exegetical Commentary on the Book of Daniel.*
      London, 1927.

(*b*) Greek

Polybius, xxii–xl.

2. *Later, but embodying earlier material*

(*a*) Jewish

2 Maccabees.
4 Maccabees (otherwise called Περὶ αὐτοκράτορος λογισμοῦ, and wrongly attributed
      by Church Fathers to Josephus), based either on Jason of Cyrene himself or
      on 2 Maccabees.
Josephus, *Ant.* xii, 223–xiii, 300; *Wars*, i, 31–69; *Contra Apion.* ii, 80.
Passages in Rabbinical literature (scanty and confused) referring to the Maccabaean
      period are given in J. Dérenbourg, *Essai sur l'histoire et la géographie de la
      Palestine*, Paris, 1867.

(*b*) Greek and Latin

Posidonius (his lost history in 52 books covered the period from 145/4 B.C., where
      Polybius stopped, to 96 B.C.), named quotations in Jacoby, *F.G.H.* ii,

pp. 222–317; much of the material has passed, unnamed, into Diodorus, Strabo, etc.

Diodorus Siculus, XXIX–XXXIV.

Strabo, XVI, 2 (also some fragments of lost books, quoted by Josephus; see T. Reinach, *Textes d'Auteurs Grecs et Romains, relatifs au Judaïsme*, Paris, 1895, pp. 89 *sqq.*).

Appian, *Syriaca.*

Livy, XXXIX–LXII.

Justin, Epitome of the *Historiae Philippicae* of Trogus Pompeius, XXXII–XXXIX.

Granius Licinianus (ed. Flemisch, Teubner, 1904).

Porphyry, *Chronica* (lost, but used by Eusebius and Syncellus, see Jacoby, *F.G.H.* II, pp. 1197–1229).

Porphyry, *Contra Christianos*, Book XII. (This book, now lost, expounded the Book of Daniel in relation to the history of the time, as to which Porphyry drew on Polybius, Posidonius and later historians: St Jerome in turn drew on Porphyry.)

Eusebius, *Chronica* (?): the work in the original is lost, but it survives in an Armenian version, a Syriac version, and a Latin version by St Jerome. There is a translation of the Armenian into Latin by Schoene (1866–75): the title of the work in the original Greek is uncertain.

St Jerome, *Commentary on the Book of Daniel.*

Sulpicius Severus, *Sacrae Historiae.*

3. Coins

Babelon, E. *Les Rois de Syrie, d'Arménie et de Commagène.* Paris, 1890.

Hill, G. F. *Catalogue of the Greek Coins in the British Museum.* London. *The Greek Coins of Phoenicia* (1910), *The Greek Coins of Palestine* (1914).

Macdonald, Sir George. *Catalogue of Greek Coins in the Hunterian Collection.* Vol. III. Edinburgh, 1905.

Newell, E. T. *The Seleucid Mint of Antioch.* A. J. Num. LI, 1907, p. 13.

Reinach, T. (translated by Mrs Hill). *Jewish Coins.* London, 1903.

4. Inscriptions

O.G.I.S. 245–60.

(For the cuneiform inscriptions see the work of Kugler mentioned below, and references there given.)

II. Modern Works

General Histories

For those earlier than 1900, reference may be made to the bibliography in Schürer, vol. 1 (4th ed.), pp. 4–31: here only the two most important may be noted:

Grätz, H. *Geschichte der Juden von den ältesten Zeiten bis auf die Gegenwart.* Ed. 4. Leipzig. Vol. II, 1876; vol. III, 1888. Eng. trans. *History of the Jews.* London, 1891, 1892.

Renan, E. *Histoire du Peuple d'Israël.* Vols. IV and V. Paris, 1893.

Later than 1900:

Beloch, K. J. *Griechische Geschichte* (Ed. 1), vol. III, 1904.

Bevan, E. *The House of Seleucus.* London, 1902.

Bouché-Leclercq, A. *Histoire des Séleucides.* Paris, 1913, 1914.

Meyer, Eduard. *Ursprung und Anfänge des Christentums.* Vol. II. Stuttgart and Berlin, 1921.

Niese, B. *Geschichte der griechischen und makedonischen Staaten.* Vol. III. Gotha, 1903.

Schlatter, A. *Geschichte Israels von Alexander dem Grossen bis Hadrian*. Ed. 3. Stuttgart, 1925.

Schürer, E. *Geschichte des jüdischen Volkes im Zeitalter Jesu Christi*. Leipzig. Vol. i, Ed. 4, 1901; vols. ii and iii, Ed. 3, 1898. Eng. trans. (from Ed. 2), *A History of the Jewish People in the Time of Jesus Christ*. London, 1880, etc.

Wellhausen, J. *Israelitische und jüdische Geschichte*. Ed. 4. Berlin, 1901.

Monographs on Special Points

Abel, F. M. *Topographie des campagnes machabéennes*. Rev. Bib. xxxii, 1923, p. 495, and following years.

Abrahams, I. *Campaigns in Palestine from Alexander the Great*. Schweich Lectures, 1922. London, 1927.

Dhorme, P. Articles in *Rev. Bib.* 1923–6.

Ginsburg, M. S. *Rome et la Judée*. Paris, 1928.

Haefeli, L. *Geschichte der Landschaft Samaria*. Münster, 1923.

Hölscher, G. *Palästina in der persischen und hellenistischen Zeit*. Berlin, 1902.

—— *Die Quellen des Josephus*. Leipzig, 1904.

Hunkin, J. W. *From the Fall of Nineveh to Titus*. Schweich Lectures, 1926. London, 1929.

Kahrstedt, U. *Syrische Territorien in hellenistischer Zeit*. Abh. Göttingen, xix (2), 1926.

Kolbe, W. *Beiträge zur syrischen und jüdischen Geschichte*. Stuttgart, 1926.

—— *Die Seleukidenära des i Makkabäerbuches*. Hermes, lxii, 1927, p. 225.

Kugler, F. X. *Von Moses bis Paulus*. Münster, 1922. (Important for the cuneiform data.)

Laqueur, R. *Kritische Untersuchungen zum zweiten Makkabäerbuch*. Strassburg, 1904.

Mago, U. *Antioco Epifane, Re di Siria*. Sassari, 1907.

Maisler, B. *Untersuchungen zur alten Geschichte und Ethnographie Syriens und Palästinas*. Giessen, 1929.

Niese, B. *Kritik der beiden Makkabäerbücher*. Hermes, xxxv, 1900, pp. 268, 453.

Smith, G. A. *Jerusalem*. 2 vols. London, 1908.

Täubler, E. *Imperium Romanum*. Leipzig, 1913. pp. 240–54. (For the treaty between Rome and the Jews.)

Volkmann, I. H. *Demetrius I und Alexander Balas*. Klio, xix, 1925, pp. 373 *sqq.*

Wellhausen, J. *Über den geschichtlichen Wert des zweiten Makkabäerbuches im Verhältnis zum ersten*. Gött. Nach. 1905, pp. 117 *sqq.*

Willrich, H. *Urkundenfälschung in der hellenistischen-jüdischen Literatur*. Göttingen, 1924.

Also articles in *P.W. s.vv. Demetrius I* (40), and *Demetrius II* (41) (H. Willrich); *Heliodoros* (6) and *Hyrkanos* (3) (W. Otto); *Jason von Kyrene* (F. Jacoby); *Jerusalem, Juda und Israel*, and *Judaea* (Beer); *Judas Makkabaios* (Wolff); *Kleopatra Thea* (24), *Seleucus IV* (6), and *Seleucus V* (7) (F. Stähelin).

CHAPTER XVII

THRACE

I. Ancient Literary Sources

Appian, *Bell. Civ.* IV, 102, 105.
Arrian, *Anab.* I, 1 *sqq. Perip. Pont. Eux.* in *Geog. Graec. Min.* I, pp. 397 *sqq.*
Ephorus, fragments in *F.G.H.* II, A, pp. 50 *sqq.*
Hecataeus (of Miletus), fragments in *F.G.H.* I, pp. 26 *sqq.*
Herodotus, IV, 93–7; V, 1–16; VII–VIII; IX, 119.
Pindar, *Paean for the Abderites.* Pap. Oxy. V, pp. 27 *sqq.*, no. 841.
Pliny, *N.H.* IV, 34–44.
Pomponius Mela, *Chorographia*, II.
Ps. Scylax, *Periplus* in *Geog. Graec. Min.* I, pp. 54 *sqq.*
Ps. Scymnus, *Periegesis* in *Geog. Graec. Min.* I, pp. 220 *sqq.*
Stephanus of Byzantium, περὶ πόλεων.
Strabo, VII; IX, 2, 4 and 25; X, 3, 16–18; XI, 14, 14; XII, 3, 3; XIII, 1, 21; XIV, 5, 28.
Theophrastus, *Hist. plant.* IV, 5, 5; 9, 1; *De odor.* II, 4; *De caus. plant.* III, 23, 4; IV, 11, 5.
Theopompus, *Philippica.* (Ed. Grenfell-Hunt.)
Thucydides, II, 95–101; IV, 101–2, 107; V, 6, 101–2; VII, 27.
Xenophon, *Anab.* VI, 1; VII.
On lost works see Casson, *Macedonia, Thrace and Illyria*, pp. 275 *sqq.*

II. Modern Works

Avezou, Ch. et Picard, Ch. *Inscriptions de Macédoine et de Thrace.* B.C.H. XXXVI, 1913, p. 82.
Bulanda, E. *Les thraces sur une oenochoé à figures noires.* Eos, XXXI, 1918, p. 297.
Casson, S. *Macedonia, Thrace and Illyria.* Oxford, 1926. (With full bibliography.)
—— *Thracian tribes in Scythia Minor.* J.R.S. XVII, 1927, p. 97.
Chapot, V. *L'Hellénisation du monde antique.* Paris, 1914. p. 161.
Cichorius, C. *Dakische Kriegsmaschinen.* Rh. Mus. LXXVI, p. 329.
Clemen, C. *Religionsgeschichte Europas*, I, Heidelberg, 1926. pp. 191, 306.
Detschew, D. *Bedy als makedonischer Gott.* Glotta, XVI, 1928, p. 280.
—— *Die thrakische Inschrift auf dem Goldring von Ezerovo.* Glotta, VII, 1916, p. 81.
—— *Die dakischen Pflanzennamen.* Ann. Univ. de Sofia, fac. hist.-phil. XXIV, 1928, p. 1.
Diakovitsch, B. *Hallstattzeitliche und Latènefibeln aus Bulgarien.* Bull. Inst. Arch. Bulg. I, 1921, p. 31.
—— *Grabfund von Duvanli.* ib. III, 1925, p. 111.
Dölger, Fr. J. IXΘΥΣ, II, Münster-i.-W., 1922. p. 420.
Dottin, G. *Les anciens peuples de l'Europe.* Paris, 1916. p. 156.
Dumont, A.-Homolle, Th. *Mélanges d'archéologie.* Paris, 1892. p. 200.
Filow, B. *Denkmäler der thrakischen Kunst.* Röm. Mitt. XXXII, 1917, p. 21.
—— *Neue Funde aus dem Hügelgrab bei Duvanli.* Bull. Inst. Arch. Bulg. IV, 1926–7, p. 27.
—— *Goldener Ring mit thrakischer Inschrift.* Bull. Soc. Arch. Bulg. III, 1912–13, p. 202.
—— *Zwei Tumulusgräber im Balkan.* ib. I, 1910, p. 155.
—— *L'art antique en Bulgarie.* Sofia, 1925.
—— *Bibliographie de l'archéologie en Bulgarie.* Ann. du musée nation. à Sofia, 1922–5, p. 613.
—— *Die archäische Nekropole von Trebenischte.* Berlin and Leipzig, 1927. p. vii.

Frazer, Sir J. G. *The Golden Bough.* London, 1912–13. Part v, vol. ii, p. 1.

Furtwängler, A. *Antike Gemmen,* vol. iii, p. 262. Leipzig, 1900.

Hasluck, F. W. *A Tholos-tomb at Kirk-Kilisse.* B.S.A. xvii, 1910–11, p. 76.

Head, B. *Historia Numorum.* Ed. 2. Oxford, 1911.

Heuzey, L. *Notes sur quelques manteaux grecs: L'éphaptide et la zeira.* Rev. E. G. xl, 1927, p. 5.

Hoeck, A. *Das Odrysenreich in Thrakien.* Hermes, xxvi, 1891, p. 76.

Hünerwadel, W. *Forschungen zur Geschichte des Königs Lysimachos von Thrakien.* Zürich Diss., 1900.

Jokl, N. *Reallexikon der Vorgeschichte,* vol. xiii, p. 278.

Kalinka, E. *Antike Denkmäler in Bulgarien.* Wien, 1906.

Kazarow, G. *Deloptes.* Arch. Relig. xi, 1908, p. 409.

—— *Grabfund bei Mesembria.* Ath. Mitt. xxxvi, 1911, p. 308.

—— *Zalmoxis.* Klio, xii, 1912, p. 355.

—— *Beiträge zur Kulturgeschichte der Thraker.* Sarajevo, 1916.

—— Article *Heros* (thrakischer Reiter) in P.W. Suppl. iii.

—— *Zur Archäologie Thrakiens.* Arch. Anz. 1918, p. 2.

—— *Vorgeschichtliches aus Bulgarien.* Wiener Prähist. Zeitschrift, x, 1923, p. 109.

—— *Zur Geschichte Alexanders des Grossen.* Phil. Woch. xlvii, 1927, p. 1310.

—— Article Μέγας θεὸς Ὀδρησιτῶν in P.W.

Kern, O. *Die Religion der Griechen.* Vol. i. Berlin, 1926. p. 226.

Kretschmer, P. *Einleitung in die Geschichte der griechischen Sprache.* Göttingen, 1896. p. 171.

—— *Zur Deutung der thrakischen Ringsinschrift.* Glotta, vii, 1916, p. 86.

—— *Die erste thrakische Inschrift.* Glotta, vi, 1915, p. 74.

Lehmann-Haupt, C. F. *Der thrakische Gott Zbelsurdos.* Klio, xvii, 1921, p. 283.

Malkina, K. *Zu dem skythischen Pferdegeschirrschmuck aus Craiova.* P.Z. xix, 1928, p. 177.

Mauss, M. *Une forme ancienne de contrat chez les Thraces.* Rev. E. G. xxxiv, 1921, p. 388.

Minns, E. H. *Scythians and Greeks.* Cambridge, 1913.

Mouschmov, N. *Les monnaies des rois thraces.* Recueil Diakovitsch, Plovdiv, 1927, p. 195.

—— *Münzfunde aus Bulgarien.* Num. Z. li, 1918, p. 52.

Müllenhoff, K. *Deutsche Altertumskunde,* iii, 1892, p. 125.

Münzer, Fr. und Strack, M. *Die antiken Münzen von Thrakien,* i, 1. Berlin, 1912.

Nilsson, M. P. In Chantepie de la Saussaye, *Lehrbuch der Religionsgesch.*[4] ii, pp. 320, 366.

—— *The Minoan-Mycenaean Religion.* Lund, 1927. p. 492.

Oberhummer, E. *Die Balkanvölker.* Wien, 1917.

Pârvan, V. *La pénétration hellénique et hellénistique dans la vallée du Danube.* Acad. Roum. Bull. sect. hist. x.

—— *Dacia.* Cambridge, 1928.

—— *Getica.* Bucarest, 1926.

—— *La Dacie à l'époque celtique.* C. R. Ac. Inscr. 1926, p. 86.

—— *Considérations sur les sépultures celtiques de Gruia.* Dacia, i, 1924, p. 51.

—— *Une nouvelle inscription de Tomi.* ib. p. 273.

Patsch, C. *Die Völkerschaft der Agathyrsen.* Wien Anz. 1925, p. 69.

Perdrizet, P. *Cultes et mythes du Pangée.* Paris, 1910.

—— *Skaptésylé.* Klio, x, 1910, p. 1.

—— *Études Amphipolitaines.* B.C.H. xlvi, 1922, p. 36.

—— *Géta, Roi des Édones.* B.C.H. xxxv, 1911, p. 108.

Picard, Ch. *Les dieux de la colonie de Philippes.* Rev. Hist. Rel. lxxxvi, 1922, p. 117.

—— *Zeus, "dieu du ciel sombre."* ib. xciii, 1926, p. 65.

Pick, B. *Thrakische Münzbilder.* J.D.A.I. xiii, 1899, p. 134.

Popow, R. *Materialien zur Erforschung der Hallstatt- und Latènezeitkultur in Bulgarien und Makedonien.* Ann. du musée nat. à Sofia, 1921, p. 152.

—— *Monuments inédits de l'âge du fer en Bulgarie.* Bull. Inst. Arch. Bulg. v, 1928–9, p. 213.

—— *Der Silberschatz von Bukjovtzi.* Ann. du musée nat. à Sofia, 1922–5. p. 1.

—— *Vorgeschichtliche Forschungen im Gebiete von Vratza.* Bull. Inst. Arch. Bulg. ii, 1923–4, p. 99.

—— *Die Nekropole beim Dorf Bailovo. ib.* i, 1921–2, p. 68.

—— *Hallstattzeitliche und Latènefibeln aus Bulgarien.* Zeitschr. der Bulg. Akad. der Wiss. vi, 1913, p. 141.

Reinach, A. J. *L'origine du thyrse.* Rev. Hist. Rel. lxvi, 1912, p. 1.

Rohde, E. *Psyche.* Ed. 8. Freiburg, 1921. Band ii, p. 1.

Rose, H. J. *Thrace,* in *Hastings' Encyclopaedia of Religion and Ethics.* Vol. xii, pp. 324–331.

Rostovtzeff, M. *Iranians and Greeks in South Russia.* Oxford, 1922.

—— *Les antiquités sarmates et les antiquités indo-scythes.* Recueil N. P. Kondakov, Prag, 1926, p. 239.

—— *Le dieu équestre dans la Russie méridionale, en Indo-Scythie et en Chine.* Seminarium Kondakovianum, i, 1927, p. 141.

—— *Une tablette votive thraco-mithriaque.* Mém. Ac. Inscr. xiii, 2, p. 385.

—— *Ancient Decorative Painting in the South of Russia* (in Russian). Petrograd, 1914.

—— *The animal style in South Russia and China.* Princeton, 1929. pp. 21, 37, 42, 44, 48.

Schmidt, H. *Skythischer Pferdegeschirrschmuck.* P.Z. xviii, 1927, p. 1.

Schrader, O.-Nehring, A. *Reallexikon der indogermanischen Altertumskunde,* ii², 523.

Schröder, B. *Thrakische Helme.* J.D.A.I. xxvii, 1912, p. 317.

Schweitzer, B. *Heracles.* Tübingen, 1922. p. 42.

Seltman, C. T. *Athens, its history and coinage.* Cambridge, 1924. pp. 55 *sqq.,* 142.

Seure, G. *Inscriptions de Thrace.* B.C.H. xxiv, 1900, p. 147.

—— *Voyage en Thrace.* B.C.H. xxv, 1901, p. 156.

—— *Archéologie thrace.* Rev. Arch. 1911–25.

—— *Études sur quelques types curieux du cavalier thrace.* Rev. E. A. xiv, 1912, p. 137; xxv–xxvi, 1923–4, p. 305; Rev. Phil. liv, 1928, p. 1.

—— *Connaîtrions-nous, enfin, un texte en langue thrace?* Rev. E. A. xxii, 1920, p. 1.

—— *Les images thraces de Zeus Kéraunos.* Rev. E. G. xxvi, 1913, p. 225.

Seyrig, H. *Quatre cultes de Thasos.* B.C.H. li, 1927, p. 178.

Solari, A. *Sui dinasti degli Odrisi.* Pisa, 1912.

Strazzula, V. Θραική. Bessarione, vi, 1901–2, fasc. 63–6.

Tafrali, O. *La cité pontique de Dionysopolis.* Paris, 1927.

Tomaschek, W. *Die alten Thraker.* Wien S.B. cxxviii, 4. Abh. cxxx, 2. Abh. cxxxi, 1. Abh. 1893–4.

Velkow, Iv. *Neue Grabhügelfunde in Bulgarien.* Bull. Instit. Arch. Bulg. v, 1928–9, p. 13.

Von Gaertringen, H. *De Graecorum fabulis ad Thraces pertinentibus.* Berlin, 1886.

Vulpe, R. et E. *Les fouilles de Tinosul.* Dacia, i, 1924, p. 166.

Weinreich, O. *Zum dreiköpfigen thrakischen Reiter und zum lykischen Trikasbos.* Arch. Anz. 1927, p. 19.

—— *Heros Propylaios und Apollon Propylaios.* Ath. Mitt. xxxviii, 1913, p. 62.

Weiss, J. *Die Dobrudscha im Altertum.* Sarajevo, 1911.

Wilamowitz-Moellendorff, U. von. *Kronos und die Titanen.* Berl. S.B. 1929, i–v, p. 51.

Wilcke, G. *Reallexikon der Vorgeschichte,* vol. ii, p. 204.

CHAPTER XVIII

THE BOSPORAN KINGDOM

A. Ancient Sources

1. *Literary*

The Greek and Latin texts will be found in the excellent collection published by
V. V. Latyshev, *Scythica et Caucasica**, St Petersburg: 1, *Scriptores Graeci*, 1890;
ii, *Scriptores Latini*, 1904. They may be divided into three classes:

(*a*) Contemporary notices in Athenian orators, Lysias, Isocrates, Demosthenes.
Aeschines, and Dinarchus.

(*b*) Historical: as in Diodorus Siculus, xiii, xiv, xvi, xx (which incorporates
earlier material, chronological and historical), and in Justin, *Prol.* 1, xxxvii.

(*c*) Scattered notices in various authors, such as Aeneas Tacticus, Chrysippus,
Strabo, Athenaeus, ps.-Aristotle, *Oeconomica*, and especially Polyaenus. These are
probably derived from some earlier local historical works, of which the earliest traceable may be dated to the time of Paerisades I. Some evidence can also be extracted
from the Scytho-Bosporan novels (P.S.I. viii, 981) and Lucian, *Toxaris*.

2. *Epigraphic*

(*a*) Inscriptions found in the Greek cities of the Black Sea.

A full collection will be found in V. V. Latyshev, *Inscriptiones Antiquae orae
Septentrionalis Ponti Euxini Graecae et Latinae* (quoted as *IosPE*), St Petersburg,
1 (Tyras, Olbia, Chersonesus Taurica), ed. 2, 1916; ii (Regnum Bosporanum), 1890;
a second edition of vol. ii is nearly ready; iv (containing inscriptions found 1885–
1900), 1901. The third volume, edited by E. Pridik (Instrumentum Domesticum),
is ready for printing (cp. E. Pridik, *Catalogue of inscriptions on the amphora handles of
the Hermitage**, Petrograd, 1917). New inscriptions will be found in the *Bulletin
of the Imperial Archaeological Commission** (1898–1918) and in the *Bulletin of the
Academy of the History of Material Civilization** (vols. i–v). See also E. Pridik,
Die Astynomennamen auf Amphoren- und Ziegelstempeln. Berl. S. B. xxvii. 1928.
pp. 342 *sqq.*

(*b*) Inscriptions found outside the Greek cities.

These have never been collected in full. The most important are quoted in the
text (cp. E. H. Minns, *Scythians and Greeks*, Cambridge, 1913, p. 639).

3. *Coins*

The fullest catalogue is still P. O. Burachkov, *General catalogue of coins belonging
to the Greek colonies on the North coast of the Euxine**, Odessa, 1884 (cf. corrections
published by Berthier de la Garde at Moscow in 1907). A Corpus of Bosporan coins
is in preparation.

A selection of the most important coins, with an excellent bibliography, will be
found in E. H. Minns, *op. cit.* p. 661, Plates v and vi, and p. 637.

An attempt at a historical treatment of all the sources (including the archaeological
evidence) will be found in M. Rostovtzeff, *Scythia and the Bosporus** (a German
translation is forthcoming).

* An asterisk denotes that the book is written in Russian.

B. Modern Literature[1]

1. General histories

Boeckh, G. *C.I.G.* Vol. ii, pp. 90–107.

Brandis, C. G. In P.W. *s.v.* Bosporos.

Ebert, M. *Südrussland im Altertum.* Leipzig, 1921.

Latyshev, V. V. Introduction to *IosPE.* Vol. ii, p. ix, 1890 (in Latin), and Ποντικά*, St Petersburg, 1909, p. 60.

Minns, E. H. *Scythians and Greeks.* Cambridge, 1913. p. 563.

Neumann, K. *Die Hellenen im Skythenlande.* Berlin, 1855. p. 469.

Ortmann, K. *De Regno Bosporano Spartocidarum.* Halle, 1894.

Rostovtzeff, M. *Iranians and Greeks in South Russia.* Oxford, 1922. Chapter iv, p. 61.

von Stern, E. *Die politische und sociale Struktur der Griechenkolonien am Nordufer des Schwarzmeergebietes.* Hermes, l, 1915, p. 161.

2. Corn production, corn trade and corn policy of the Greek cities

Andreades, A. M. Ἱστορία τῆς Ἑλληνικῆς δημοσίας οἰκονομίας. I. Athens. 1928.

Bonner, S. *Commercial policy of Imperial Athens,* C.P. xviii, 1923, p. 196.

Calhoun, G. M. *The Business Life of Ancient Athens.* University of Chicago Press. 1926.

Francotte, H. *Le pain à bon marché et le pain gratuit dans les cités grecques.* Mélanges Nicole, Geneva, 1905, p. 135. (Cf. *Mélanges de Droit Public Grec,* Paris, 1910, p. 291.)

Gernet, L. *L'approvisionnement d'Athènes en blé au Vme et IVme siècles.* Bibl. de la Fac. des Lettres de Paris, xxv, 1909, p. 269.

Glotz, G. *Les prix des denrées à Délos.* J. d. Sav., 1913, p. 16.

—— *L'Histoire de Délos d'après les prix d'une denrée.* Rev. E.G. xxix, 1916, p. 1.

Grundy, G. B. *Thucydides and the History of his age.* London, 1911. p. 74 and p. 159.

Hasebroek, J. *Staat und Handel im alten Griechenland.* Tübingen, 1928.

Jardé, A., *Les céréales dans l'antiquité grecque.* I. La production. Paris, 1925.

Katzevalov, A. *Corn trade of the Greek colonies of the Northern shore of the Black Sea*.* Nauchnye Zapiski (Scientific Bulletin), 1928, p. 33.

Knorringa, H. *Emporos.* Amsterdam, 1926.

Laqueur, R. *Epigraphische Untersuchungen zu griechischen Volksbeschlüssen.* Leipzig, 1927.

Mishchenko, Th. G. *Trade Relations of the Athenian Republic with the Bosporan Kingdom*.* Bulletin of the University of Kiev, vii, 1878, p. 477.

Ormerod, H. A. *Piracy in the Ancient World.* London, 1924. Chap. iv, p. 108.

Perrot, G. *Le commerce des Céréales en Attique au IVme siècle avant notre ère.* Rev. H. iv, 1877, p. 1.

Ramsay, Sir W. *Asianic Elements in Greek Civilization.* London, 1927. Chap. xi: The varying movement of ancient trade in wheat, p. 118.

Roussel, P. *Délos colonie Athénienne.* Paris, 1916.

—— *Délos.* Paris, 1925. p. 11.

Sauciuc-Saveanu, T. *Cultura cerealelor in Grecia antica şi politica cerealista a Atenienilor.* Bucureşti, 1923.

—— *Ath. Mitt.* xxxvi, 1911, p. 1.

—— *Andros.* Vienna, 1914. p. 77.

---

[1] A full bibliography up to 1913 will be found in E. H. Minns, *op. cit.* p. 635. The more important earlier works only and those which have been published since 1913 are here given.

Schaefer, A. *Demosthenes und seine Zeit.* Ed. 2. Leipzig, 1885–87.
—— *Athenischer Volksbeschluss von J.* 346. Rh. Mus. XXXIII, 1878, p. 418.
—— *Die Regierungszeit des Königs Paerisades von Bosporus.* Rh. Mus. XXXVIII, 1883, p. 310.
Schede, M. *Aus dem Heraion von Samos.* Ath. Mitt. XLIV, 1919, p. 1.
von Wilamowitz-Moellendorf, U. *Ein Gesetz von Samos über die Beschaffung von Brotkorn aus öffentlichen Mitteln.* Berl. S.B. 1904, p. 917. (Cf. *Ditt.*³ 976.) (The Samian corn law.)
Ziebarth, E. *Zum Samischen Finanz- und Getreidewesen.* Z.N. XXXIV, 1924, p. 356.
—— *Beiträge zur Geschichte des Seeraubs und Seehandels im alten Griechenland.* Abh. d. Hamburg. Univ. XXX, 1929.
Zimmern, A. *The Greek Commonwealth.* Ed. 4. Oxford, 1924. Chap. XIII, p. 344.

C. VARIA

Bell, H. I. *Greek sightseers in the Fayum in the Third Century B.C.* Symb. Osl. V, 1927, p. 1.
Gernet, L. *Note sur les parents de Démosthène.* Rev. E.G. XXXI, 1918, p. 185.
Grakov, B. N. *Ancient Greek pottery stamps with the names of the Astynomi*.* Moscow, 1929.
Klym, P. *Die milesischen Kolonien im Skythenland bis zum III. Jahrh.* Progr. Czernowitz, 1914.
Latyshev, V. V. Ποντικά*. St Petersburg, 1909. pp. 171, 174, 293 and 376.
Mateescu, G. C. *Nomi Traci nel territorio scito-sarmatico.* Ephem. Dacoromana, II, 1924, p. 223.
Otto, W. *Beiträge zur Seleukidengeschichte des III. Jahrh. v. Chr.* Bay. Abh. XXXIV, 1, 1928, p. 43 (on the Zeno Papyrus).
Rostovtzeff, M. *Ancient decorative wall-painting in South Russia*.* Text and Atlas. St Petersburg, 1913.
—— *The idea of kingly power in Scythia and in the Bosporus*.* Bull. Arch. Comm. XLIX, 1913, p. 1.
—— *Amage and Tirgatao*.* Memoirs of the Odessa Society of History and Antiquities, XXXII, 1913.
—— *Strabo as a source for the history of the Bosporus*.* Volume in honour of V. Buzeskul. Kharkov, 1914.
—— *Syriscus, the historian of the Tauric Chersonesus*.* Journ. of the Min. of Publ. Educ. 1915, April, p. 151.
—— *Ancient decorative wall-painting.* J.H.S. XXXIX, 1919, p. 144.
—— Ἐπιφάνειαι. Klio, XVI, 1920, p. 203.
—— *Le Culte de la Grande Déesse dans la Russie Méridionale.* Rev. E.G. XXXII, 1919 (publ. 1921), p. 462.
—— *Greek sightseers in Egypt.* J.E.A. XIV, 1928, p. 13.
—— *A Scythian Novel.* Seminarium Kondakovianum, Prague, II, 1928, p. 135.
Schmitz, H. *Ein Gesetz der Stadt Olbia.* Freiburg, 1925.
Tolstoi, I. I. jr. *The cult of Apollo in the Bosporus and at Olbia*.* Journ. of the Min. of Publ. Educ. 1904, January.
—— *The White Island and the Tauris of the Euxine Pontus*.* St Petersburg, 1918. (Cf. the author's review in Bull. Arch. Comm. LXV, 1918, p. 177.)
Zhebelev, S. A. *The Bosporan Archaeanaktids*.* Journ. of the Min. of Publ. Educ. 1902, March, p. 130.
See also the articles in P.W. *s.vv.*
Eumelos (II) (Willrich), *Gorgippia* (Kiessling), *Gylon* (Kirchner), *Hermonassa* (Kiessling), *Kepoi, Leukon* (3, 4) (Geyer), *Satyros* (4, 5) (Fluss), *Sindoi* (1) (Kretschmer).

CHAPTER XIX

PERGAMUM

A. Ancient Sources

1. *Literary texts*

For the literary sources for the period of the existence of the kingdom of Pergamum see the Bibliography to vol. VII, chapters III, VI, XXII and XXIII, and this volume, chapters V–VII, IX. The best and most reliable information will be found in Polybius and the corresponding books of Livy.

2. *Inscriptions*

The inscriptions have been published in:

Fränkel, M. *Die Inschriften von Pergamon* in *Altertümer von Pergamon*, VIII, 1 and 2 (1890–1895) (quoted I. v. Perg.), and, for the period after 1900, in the reports on the excavations published in the *Athenische Mittheilungen* (see next section).

An excellent selection of inscriptions will be found in *O.G.I.S.*, I, nos. 264–339, and II, no. 483 (cf. Appendix, nos. 748–751 and 763), and in Ditt.[3] (Index s.v. Πέργαμον). Cf. Fouilles de Delphes III, 1, Epigraphie (1929), no. 732 and II, Topographie et Architecture. La Terrasse du Temple (1927), p. 222.

3. *Coins*

von Fritze, H. *Die Münzen von Pergamon*. Berl. Abh. 1910, p. 15.
—— *Die antiken Münzen Mysiens*, I. Berlin, 1913.

See also the corresponding volumes of the Catalogue of coins of the British Museum.

4. *Archaeological sources*

On the excavations at Pergamum and in the neighbourhood see for the first period, before 1900: *Staatliche Museen zu Berlin. Altertümer von Pergamon*, vols. I–VIII (the publication is complete but for vol. V, 1, which will contain the palaces).

The reports on the second period of excavations (1900–1914) will be found in *Ath. Mitt.* for 1902, 1904, 1907, 1908, 1910 and 1912. The inscriptions are published as separate chapters of these reports.

On the third period of excavations which started in 1927 see Wiegand, Th. *Bericht über die Ausgrabungen in Pergamon*, 1927. Berl. Abh. 1928, Phil.-hist. Kl. no. 3.

On the excavations in various other cities of Asia Minor which belonged at one time or another to the kingdom see the bibliography in vol. VII, p. 899. Cf. also:

Bohn, R. and Schuchhardt, C. *Altertümer von Aegae*. J.D.A.I. Erg. II, 1889.
Conze, A. and Schazmann, P. *Mamurt-Kaleh. Ib*. Erg. IX, 1911.
Schuchhardt, C. *Altertümer von Pergamon*, I, 1, *Stadt und Landschaft*. Historische Topographie der Landschaft, Berlin, 1912.

B. Modern Literature

1. *General works*

Separate chapters or occasional sections are devoted to the kingdom of Pergamum in most of the general histories of the Hellenistic period; see the General Bibliography, and vol. VII, p. 881.

Special works on the general history of Pergamum are as follows:

Cardinali, G. *Il regno di Pergamo*. Turin, 1906.

Collignon, M. and Pontremoli, E. *Pergame*, etc. Paris, 1900.

Collignon, M. *Führer durch die Ruinen von Pergamon*. Ed. 5. Berlin, 1911.

Ghione, P. *I comuni del regno di Pergamo*. Mem. Acc. Torino, LV, 1905, p. 67.

Meyer, Ernst. *Die Grenzen der hellenistischen Staaten in Kleinasien*. Leipzig, 1925.

Pedroli, U. *Il regno di Pergamo*. Turin, 1896.

Stähelin, F. *Geschichte der kleinasiatischen Galater*. Ed. 2. Leipzig, 1907.

Thraemer, Ed. *Pergamos*. Leipzig, 1888.

Ussing, J. L. *Pergamos*. Berlin, 1899.

2. *Special contributions*

Cardinali, G. *La Morte di Attalo III e la rivolta d'Aristonico*. Saggi di Storia Antica e di Archeologia offerti a Giulio Beloch, Roma, 1910, p. 269.

—— *La genealogia dei Attalidi*. Mem. Acc. Bologna, 1913, p. 8.

—— *Ancora sull' albero genealogico degli Attalidi*. Rendic. Acc. Bologna, VII (1913–14), p. 37.

—— *La Amministrazione Finanziaria del comune di Pergamo*. Mem. Acc. Bologna, 1915–16, p. 1.

Corradi, G. *Gli strateghi di Pergamo*. Atti Acc. Torino, XLVIII, 1912–13, p. 719.

—— *Sugli astinomi Pergameni*. Boll. Fil. Class. XXVIII, 1921, p. 112.

—— Gli ἀμφοδάρχαι *a Pergamo*. ib. XXIX, 1922, p. 65.

Cumont, F. *Les religions orientales dans le paganisme romain*. Ed. 3. Paris, 1928. p. 195. (Mystères de Bacchus.)

Dougherty, R. P. *Writing upon parchment and papyrus among the Babylonians and the Assyrians*. J.A.O.S. XLVIII, 1928, p. 109.

Foucart, P. *De collegiis scenicorum artificum apud Graecos*. Paris, 1873.

Grote, K. *Das griechische Söldnerwesen der hellenistischen Zeit*. Jena Diss., 1913.

Holleaux, M. *Notes sur une inscription de Colophon Nova*. B.C.H. XXX, 1906, p. 349.

—— *Un nouveau document relatif aux premiers Attalides*. Rev. E.A. 1918, p. 83.

—— *Sur la lettre d'Attale aux* Ἀμλαδεῖς. ib. p. 91.

—— *Le décret de Bargylia en l'honneur de Poseidonios*. ib. p. 94.

—— *L'expédition de Philippe V en Asie*. ib. 1920, p. 133; 1921, p. 157; 1923, p. 190.

—— *Sur la guerre Crétoise*. Rev. E.G. XXX, 1917, p. 1.

—— *L'expédition de Dikaiarchos dans les Cyclades et sur l'Hellespont*. ib. XXXIII, 1920, p. 223.

—— *Inscription trouvée à Broussa*. B.C.H. XLVIII, 1924, p. 1.

—— *Le décret des Ioniens en l'honneur d'Eumenes II*. Rev. E.G. XXXVII, 1924, p. 305.

—— C.R. Ac. Inscr. 1927, p. 137 (on the inscription of Iasus).

Klaffenbach, G. *Symbolae ad historiam collegiorum artificum Bacchiorum*. Berlin, 1914.

Lambrino, S. *Lettre du roi Eumenes II et le decret de Iasos relatif aux Nicephoria de Pergame*. Rev. Arch. XXIX, 1929, p. 107.

Laqueur, R. *Epigraphische Untersuchungen zu den griechischen Volksbeschlüssen*. Leipzig, 1927.

Lueders, O. *Die Dionysischen Künstler*. Berlin, 1873.

Meyer, Ed. *Die makedonischen Militärkolonien*. Hermes, XXXIII, 1898, p. 643.

Meyer, Ernst. *Zum Stammbaum der Attaliden*. Klio, XIX, 1923–25, p. 462.

Oertel, F. In P.W. *s.v.* Κάτοικοι.

Poland, F. *De collegiis artificum Dionysiacorum*. Dresden, 1895.

—— *Geschichte des Griechischen Vereinswesen*. Leipzig, 1909, p. 138.

von Prott, H. *Dionysos Kathegemon.* Ath. Mitt. xxvii, 1902, p. 161.

Quandt, G. *De Baccho ab Alexandri aetate in Asia Minore culto.* Halle, 1912.

Radet, G. *De coloniis a Macedonibus in Asiam cis Taurum deductis.* Paris, 1897.

—— *Eumenia.* Anatolian Studies presented to Sir William Ramsay. Manchester, 1923. p. 1.

Rehm, A. and Schramm, E. *Biton's Bau von Belagerungs-maschinen und Geschützen.* Bay. Abh. ii, 1929.

Reinach, A. J. *Les Mercenaires et les colonies militaires de Pergame.* Rev. Arch. xii, 1908, p. 174, p. 364; xiii, 1909, p. 102, p. 363. (The article remained unfinished.)

Robert, L. *Décret de Delphes.* Rev. E.G. xlii, 1929, p. 430.

Rostovtzeff, M. *Notes on the economic policy of the Pergamene kings.* Anatol. Studies, etc. p. 359.

de Sanctis, G. *Eumene II e le città greche d'Asia.* Riv. Fil. liii, 1925, p. 68.

Sauciuc-Saveanu, Th. *Le décret en l'honneur du Macédonien Corrhagos.* Rev. E.G. xxxvi, 1923, p. 197.

—— *Andros.* Vienna, 1914.

Schulten, A. *Die makedonischen Militärkolonien.* Hermes, xxxii, 1897, p. 523.

Swoboda, H. *Staatsaltertümer.* Vol. i, 3 (ed. 6), 1913, p. 169 and p. 199.

Tscherikover, V. *Die hellenistischen Städtegründungen von Alexander bis auf die Römerzeit.* Phil. Suppl. xix, Leipzig, 1927.

Wilhelm, A. *Pergamena.* Ath. Mitt. xxxix, 1914, p. 148.

—— *Zum griechischen Wortschatz.* Glotta, xiv, 1925. p. 74. (On ζημίαι and πρόστιμον in the law of the astynomes.)

—— *Zu griechischen Ehrenbeschlüssen und Briefen.* Jahreshefte, xxiv, 1929, p. 162 and p. 174.

CHAPTER XX

RHODES, DELOS, AND HELLENISTIC COMMERCE

I. Rhodes

1. *Literary Texts*

For the literary sources (those which give a description of Rhodes are quoted in the text) for the general history of the Greek world during the period covered by this volume see the bibliographies to chapters v–vii, viii–ix, xix.

2. *Archaeological evidence*

(a) *Inscriptions*

I.G. xii, 1 (1895), F. Hiller von Gaertringen (an Editio Minor of this volume with the inscriptions of the Rhodian islands and of the Peraea is in preparation), cf. *I.G.* xii, 3 (1908).

Collitz-Bechtel, *S.G.D.I.* iii, 1, nos. 3749–4351 (H. van Gelder, *Die rhodischen Inschriften*); including the jar-stamps, the inscriptions on the coins, the inscriptions of the Rhodian colonies and of the Rhodian dominions.

Schwyzer, E., *Dialectorum Graecorum Exempla epigraphica potiora*, 1923, nos. 272–294 (selection of the more important texts); cf. also *Ditt.*[3] and the Appendix epigraphica to H. van Gelder, *Geschichte der alten Rhodier*. Hague, 1900.

Blinkenberg, Ch. and Kinch, K. F., *Exploration archéologique de Rhodes*, Fondation Carlsberg, i, 1903; ii, 1904; iii, 1905; iv, 1907; vi, 1912. The last contains Ch. Blinkenberg, *La chronique du temple Lindien*. This important inscription has been republished in Lietzmann's *Kleine Texte*, no. 131, 1915.

Holleaux, M. *B.C.H.* xvii, 1893, p. 52; xviii, 1894, p. 390.

Picard, Ch. *Annales de l' Université de Grenoble*, 1925, p. 136.

Maiuri, Porro, Oliverio, Pernier and others are publishing the new inscriptions of Rhodes, the Peraea and Caria in *Annuario della Scuola archeologica di Atene*, vols. i–v (1914–24).

Maiuri, A., *Nuova Silloge epigrafica di Rodi e Cos*, 1925; cf. A. Wilhelm, *Ath. Mitt.* li, 1926, p. 2; G. de Sanctis, *Riv. Fil.* liv, 1926, p. 57; F. Hiller von Gaertringen, *Gnomon*, ii, 1926, pp. 193, 365.

Scrinzi, A. *Iscrizioni inedite di Rodi*. Atti d. R. Ist. Veneto, lvii, 1899, pp. 251 *sqq.* (46 hitherto unpublished texts).

(b) *Stamps on Rhodian jars*

Bleckmann, F. *De inscriptionibus quae leguntur in vasculis Rhodiis*, 1907. Cf. *Klio*, xii, 1912, p. 249.

Nilsson, M. P. *Timbres amphoriques de Lindos publiés avec une étude sur les timbres amphoriques rhodiens*. 1909. (Bulletin Royal Acad. of Denmark, with excellent up-to-date bibliography.)

Gelder, H. van, *Over Rhodische Kruikstempels en hun belang voor onze kennis van den Rhodischen Handel*. Verslagen en Mededeelingen der K. Ak. van Wetenschappen, Amsterdam, v Reeks, i, 1914, p. 186.

Gaertringen, F. Hiller von, *Die rhodischen Heliospriester*. Klio, xiv, 1914, p. 388.

On the finds of Rhodian jars in Rhodes and outside see the bibliography in Nilsson, to which may be added the following references to recent publications.

Rhodes. A. Maiuri, *Una fabbrica di anfore Rodie*, Ann. d. Sc. arch. ad Atene, iv–v, 1924, p. 249; cf. G. G. Porro, *ib.* ii, 1916, p. 103; P. Paris, *Timbres amphoriques de Rhodes*, B.C.H. xxxviii, 1914, p. 300.

S. Russia. E. H. Minns, *Scythians and Greeks in S. Russia,* 1913, p. 358, note 8 (bibliography); E. Pridik, *Inventory catalogue of the inscriptions on the amphora handles, etc., of the Hermitage,* 1917 (in Russian); cf. *Klio,* xx, 1926, p. 303 and *Berl. S. B.* 1930. A full bibliography of the publications of amphora-stamps found in S. Russia in B. N. Grakov, *Englyphic stamps on the necks of some Hellenistic amphorae,* in Trudy Rossijskago, Istoričeskago Muzeja (Works of the Russian Historical Museum in Moscow), I, 1928, p. 165 (in Russian) and *id., Ancient Greek pottery stamps with the names of Astynomi,* Moscow, 1929 (in Russian).

Alexandria in Egypt. Preisigke-Bilabel, *Sammelbuch, etc.* III, 1, 1926, nos. 6320–524.

Syria (frontier of Egypt and Syria). Ch. Picard, *Notes sur les timbres amphoriques rhodiens trouvés à Cheick-Zouède dans le Sahel.* B.C.H. XL, 1916, p. 357.

Palestine. R. Wuensch in Bliss, Macalister, Wuensch, *Excavations in Palestine during the years* 1898–1900, p. 178 (Palest. Explor. Fund, 1902).

Persia. F. Cumont. *C.R. Ac. Inscr.* 1926, p. 236 and *Syria,* VII, 1927, p. 49.

(c) Coins

Head, B. V. *Brit. Mus. Catalogue of the Greek coins of Caria, Cos, Rhodes, etc.* 1897.
—— *H.N.*² p. 637.
Babelon, E. *Traité des Monnaies grecques et romaines.* Paris, vol. II, 1910, p. 1013.

3. Modern books

Blinkenberg, Ch. *Lindiaka,* I, 1912, II–IV, 1926, V, 1926, in Bulletin Royal Acad. of Denmark, vols. I, XI, XIII. Preliminary reports on the excavations, by Ch. Blinkenberg and F. Kinch, are quoted above, Section II, Inscriptions.
Francotte, H. *L'organisation des cités à Rhodes et en Carie.* Mus. B. x, 1906, p. 127.
Gaertringen, F. Hiller von. The forthcoming article on *Rhodos* in *P.W.* Suppl. The present writer owes the privilege of using this masterly summary of what we know of Rhodes to the kindness of the author. In the four 'Anhänge' the author gives: I. Quellen und Literatur (a survey of the sources on the history of Rhodes and of the contributions of Rhodes to Greek literature). II. Die in und um Rhodos tätigen Künstler (list of the names of sculptors who have worked for Rhodes and are known from inscriptions). III. Vereine (list of the Rhodian associations known from inscriptions). IV. Die eponymen Priester des Helios (list of the Helios priests as they appear on the stamps of the Rhodian jars).
Gelder, H. van. *Geschichte der alten Rhodier.* Hague, 1900. (Standard work with excellent bibliography.)
Kinch, R. F. *Vroulia.* 1914.
Kreller, H. *Lex Rhodia.* Zeitschr. für d. ges. Handelsrecht u. Konkursrecht, LXXXV, 1921, p. 257.
Maiuri, A. and Jacopich, A. *Clara Rhodos, Studi e materiali pubblicati a cura dell'Istituto storico-archeologico di Rodi.* I. Rapporto generale sul servizio archeologico a Rodi e nelle isole dependenti dall' anno 1912, all' anno 1927. Rhodes, 1928. (With full bibliography of Italian contributions to the history, archaeology and topography of Rhodes.)
Robert, L. *Trois inscriptions de l'Archipel.* Rev.E.G. XLII, 1929, p. 1.
Schneiderwirth, J. H. *Geschichte der Insel Rhodos nach den Quellen bearbeitet.* 1868.
Selivanov, S. *Outlines of the ancient topography of the island Rhodes.* Kazan, 1892. (In Russian.)
Torr, C. *Rhodes in ancient times.* Cambridge, 1885.
Vogliano, A. *Il πίναξ di una Biblioteca rodia.* Riv. indo-greco-italica, x, 1926, p. 96.

This short list of modern books and articles gives the titles of those contributions only which contain general surveys of the history of Rhodes. An excellent bibliography of Rhodes will be found in van Gelder, *op. cit.* and (for the recent contributions) in F. Hiller von Gaertringen.

II. DELOS

1. *Literary Texts*

For the literary sources for the general history of the Greek world during the period covered by this volume see the bibliographies to chapters v–vii, viii–ix, xix.

2. *Archaeological Evidence*

(*a*) *Inscriptions*

The inscriptions of Delos, mostly found during the French excavations of the temple and the city, are not yet published in full. A copious selection of the more important texts from the general historical point of view is given in F. Durrbach, *Choix d'inscriptions de Délos*. I. Textes historiques, 1921–22, and in *Ditt.*³, cf. Michel's *Recueil*. The volume (xi) of the *I.G.* devoted to Delos is not yet complete. After the war the French Academy started a special publication of the inscriptions of Delos: F. Durrbach, *Inscriptions de Délos*, Comptes de hiéropes, parts i–ii, 1927–9. A selection of important inscriptions bearing on the history of Delos in the period after 167/6 will be found in P. Roussel, *Délos Colonie Athénienne*, Paris, 1916, p. 341. The new inscriptions found at Delos are published in the *B.C.H.*

(*b*) *Excavations*

The results of the excavations are embodied in the volumes of the *Exploration archéologique de Délos* published under the direction of Th. Homolle, M. Holleaux, G. Fougères, Ch. Picard and P. Roussel from 1909 on. The following volumes have been printed:

A. Introduction (cartography, geology, geography). Three fascicules published, three more in preparation.
B. Descriptions des monuments.
   II and II bis, La Salle hypostyle (C. Leroux, R. Vallois, G. Poulsen).
   V, Le Portique d'Antigone (F. Courby).
   VI, L'Établissement des Poseidoniastes de Bérytos (Ch. Picard).
   VII, Les portiques au Sud du Hiéron (R. Vallois).
   VIII, 1. 2. Le quartier du théâtre (I. Chammonard).
   VIII, Le quartier du théâtre (Planches).
   IX, Description des Revêtements peints à sujets religieux (M. Bulard).

4. *Modern Books and Articles*

Bulard, M. *La Religion domestique dans la colonie Italienne de Délos*. Bibl. des Éc. fr. d'Athènes et de Rome, cxxxi (1926).
Durrbach, F. La Ἱερὰ Συγγραφή à *Délos*. Rev.E.G. xxxii, 1919, p. 167.
Ferguson, W. S. *The Delian Gymnasiarchs*. C.P. viii, 1913, p. 220.
——— *Researches in Athenian and Delian documents*. I. Klio, vii, 1907, p. 236; ii, *ib.* viii, 1908, p. 338.
——— *Hellenistic Athens*. London, 1911, p. 346.
Glotz, G. *Le prix des denrées à Délos*. J. d. Sav. 1913, p. 16.
——— *Les salaires à Délos*. ib. pp. 206, 251.
——— *L'Histoire de Délos d'après les prix d'une denrée*. Rev.E.G. xxix, 1916, p. 281.
——— *Un transport de marbre pour le théâtre de Délos*. ib. xxxii, 1929, p. 240; cf. ib. xxxi, 1918, p. 207.
——— *Les prix du papyrus dans l'antiquité grecque*. Annales d'Histoire Économique et Sociale, i, 1929, p. 3.

Hatzfeld, J. *Les Italiens résidant à Delos, etc.* B.C.H. xxxvi, 1912, p. 5.

—— *Les trafiquants italiens dans l'Orient hellénique.* Paris, 1919.

Heichelheim, F. *Wirtschaftliche Schwankungen der Zeit von Alexander bis Augustus.* Jena, 1930. (Published too late to be used in this chapter. See the author's review in the *Zeitschrift für die ges. Staatswissenschaft.*)

Herzog, R. *Aus dem Asklepieion von Kos.* Arch. Relig. x, 1902, p. 201.

Holleaux, M. *Inscriptions de Délos.* B.C.H. xxxi, 1907, p. 374.

Homolle, Th. *Les Romains à Délos.* ib. viii, 1884, p. 75.

—— *Les Archives de l'intendance sacrée à Délos.* Bibl. des Éc. fr. d'Athènes et de Rome, xlix (1887).

—— Articles on the current excavations at Delos in *B.C.H.*

Jardé, A. *Note sur une inscription de Délos.* B.C.H. xlvii, 1923, p. 301.

Kampter, H. O. *Die Römer auf Delos.* Münster Diss., 1913.

Kornemann, E. *De civibus Romanis in provinciis imperii consistentibus.* Berlin, 1892.

Krasheninnikoff, M. *The Augustales and the Sacralmagisterium.* St Petersburg, 1895. (In Russian.) (Memoirs of the Faculty of History and Philology of the Univ. of St Petersburg, vol. 37.)

Lacroix, M. *Les architectes et entrepreneurs à Délos de* 314 *à* 240. Rev.Phil. xxxviii, 1914, p. 304.

—— *Une famille à Délos.* Rev.E.G. xxix, 1916, p. 188.

Lebègue, A. *Recherches sur Délos.* Paris, 1876.

Lehmann, K. Hartleben. *Die antiken Hafenanlagen.* Klio, Beiheft 14, Leipzig, 1923.

Maroi, F. *La proprietà sacra nel diritto ellenico e l' origine della locazione di case.* Riv. Ital. di Sociologia, xix, 1915, p. 401.

Molinier, S. *Les "Maisons sacrées" de Délos au temps de l'indépendance de l'île* 315–166/5 *av. J.-C.* Paris, 1914. Univ. de Paris, Bibl. de la Fac. d. Lettres, no. 31.

Paris, J. *Contributions à l'étude des ports antiques du monde grec.* II. Les établissements maritimes de Délos. B.C.H. xl, 1916, p. 5.

Philippart, H. *Délos, notes bibliographiques.* Rev. Belge de Phil. i, 1922, p. 784.

Picard, Ch. *Observations sur la Société des Poseidoniastes de Bérytos et sur son histoire.* B.C.H. xliv, 1920, p. 263.

Roussel, P. *Délos.* 1925.

—— *Délos Colonie Athénienne.* 1916.

—— *Les cultes égyptiens à Délos.* 1916.

Schoch, P. *Kultur- und Wirtschaftsgeschichtliches aus dem hellenistischen Delos.* Stuttgart, 1923. (Cf. Neue Jahrbücher, li, 1923, p. 77.)

Schoeffer, von. *De Deli insulae rebus.* Berl. Stud. f. Kl. Phil. u. Arch. ix, 1889.

—— Art. *Delos* in P.W. cols. 2459 sqq.

Schulten, A. *De conventibus civium Romanorum.* Berlin, 1892.

Weiss, E. Ἱερὰ Συγγραφή, Ἐπιτύμβιον H. Swoboda dargebracht, Reichenberg, 1925, p. 325.

Westermann, W. L. *Upon Slavery in Ptolemaic Egypt.* New York, 1930. (See the author's review in the *Econ. Hist. Review*, 1930.)

Ziebarth, E. *Delische Stiftungen.* Hermes, lii, 1917, p. 435.

—— *Beiträge zum griechischen Recht.* Zeitschr. f. Vergl. Rechtswiss. xix, 1906, p. 291. (On inns in Greek Sanctuaries.)

—— *Die* Ἱερὰ Συγγραφή *von Delos.* Hermes, lxi, 1926, p. 87.

—— *Hellenistische Banken.* Z.N. xxxiv, 1924, p. 36.

—— *Beiträge zur Geschichte des Seeraubs und Seehandels im alten Griechenland.* Hamburg, 1929.

For Hellenistic Commerce in general see also the works cited in the footnotes of the chapter, pp. 651–667.

CHAPTER XXI

HELLENISTIC ART

Sculpture

Dickins, G. *Hellenistic Sculpture*. Oxford, 1920.
Klein, W. *Vom antiken Rokoko*. Vienna, 1921.
Krahmer, G. *Stilphasen der hellenistischen Plastik*. Röm. Mitt. xxxviii–ix (1923–4), p. 138.
Lawrence, A. W. *Later Greek Sculpture*. London, 1927; *q.v.* for fuller bibliography and appendix of references.
Schmidt, E. *Archaistische Kunst in Griechenland und Rom*. Munich, 1922.
Schuchhardt, W. H. *Die Meister des grossen Frieses von Pergamon*. Berlin-Leipzig, 1925.
Watzinger, C. *Die griechisch-ägyptische Sammlung Ernst von Sieglin*. (Malerei und Plastik: Zweiter Teil, B.) Leipzig, 1927.
Winter, F. *Kunstgeschichte in Bildern*, parts 11–12. Leipzig (in progress); a convenient collection of illustrations.

Painting

Pfuhl, E. *Malerei und Zeichnung der Griechen*. Munich, 1923; with full references.
Pfuhl, E., tr. Beazley, J. D. *Masterpieces of Greek Drawing and Painting*. London, 1926. (A translation of the smaller book: an excellent general account.)

Architecture and Town-planning

Anderson, W. J. and Spiers, R. P. *The Architecture of Ancient Greece*. Revised and re-written by Dinsmoor, W. B. London, 1927.
Caspari, F. *Das Nilschiff Ptolemaios IV*. J.D.A.I. xxxi, 1916, p. 1.
Durm, J. *Die Baukunst der Griechen*. Ed. 3. Leipzig, 1910.
von Gerkan, A. *Griechische Städteanlage*. Berlin-Leipzig, 1924.
Kohte, J. and Watzinger, C. *Magnesia am Maeander*. Berlin, 1904.
Noack, F. *Die Baukunst des Altertums*. Berlin, n.d.
Pontremoli, E. and Haussoullier, B. *Didymes*. Paris, 1903.
Rider, B. C. *The Greek House: its history and development from the Neolithic period to the Hellenistic Age*. Cambridge, 1916.
Robertson, D. S. *Greek and Roman Architecture*. Cambridge, 1928.
Wiegand, Th. *Milet*. Berlin (in progress).
Wiegand, Th. and Schrader, H. *Priene*. Berlin, 1904.

For the excavations at Delos see the *Exploration archéologique de Délos*, in course of publication since 1902 under the general editorship of Th. Homolle at Paris; for Pergamum see the Bibliography to chapter xix, A. 4.

GENERAL INDEX

Romans are entered under their gentile names, and, for purposes of identification, the
year of their first or most significant tenure of office, usually the consulship (cos.), is inserted.
Table I refers to the table of legions and commanders facing p. 104.

Abbukome, 603
Abdera in Thrace, 264, 543, 555, 657;
  coinage, 558, imitation of, 556
Abrupolis, 255 sq.
Abydos, 180, 181 n., 184, 657; besieged
  by Philip, 164 sq.; seized by Antiochus
  III, 179
Acanthus, 168
Acarnania, 127, 173, 176, 194; Aetolians
  and, 125; and Philip, 161; Antiochus
  III in, 213
Accius, L., tragic poet, 391, 394, 400, 416
Acerrae, 56, 75
Achaea, Achaean League, 1, 4, 7, 13, 20 sq.,
  162 sq., 166 sqq., 170, 178, 194, 205, 260,
  266, 296 sqq.; and Antiochus III, 209; and
  Antiochus IV, 506; and Argos, 171 sq.,
  191; and Corinth, 184; and Elis, 128,
  135, 235; exiles in Rome, 9, 302, 398 sq.;
  after Magnesia, 243; at Mantinea, 133;
  and Messene, 128, 135, 298 sqq.; as a military power, 132; and Nabis, 204; and
  Peloponnese, 168, 217, 235, 243; and
  Perseus, 257; and Philip V, 120 sq., 129,
  131, 146, 167; and Rome, 170 sq., 296 sq.,
  363; and Sparta, 147, 189, 195, 207, 235,
  297; League dissolved, 304
— Phthiotic, 127, 135, 170, 173 sq., 183 n.,
  184, 195, 214
Achaeus, Syrian usurper, 117, 124, 139
Achilles in Scyros, painting, 695
— and Penthesilea, group, 682
Acholla, 478
Acilius (Aculius), C., historian, 419 sq.
— M'. Glabrio (cos. 191), 213 sq., 216,
  219, 227, 235, 245, 247; and Scipio,
  365 sq., 368 sq.; and Cato, 370
Acornion of Dionysopolis, merchant, 658
Acrillae, 66
Acrocorinth, 172, 182, 184, 192
Adana (Antioch), 499 n.
Adasa, 520
Adida, 526
Adora, 532
Adramyttium, 611
Adranodorus, regent of Sicily, 63 sq.
Aebutius, T. Parus (praetor 180), 331
Aecae, 49, 55, 77
Aegae, 611
Aegean, Philip V and, 143 sqq.; Rhodes
  and piracy in, 143 sq., 625; Antiochus

III and Greek towns on, 178, after
  Magnesia, 230; and Egypt and Mace-
  donia, 659
Aegias of Sicyon, banker, 662 n.
Aegimurus, island, 480
Aegina, 128 and n., 161, 197, 620; and
  Rome, 128; Attalids and, 606; decree to
  Cleon, Attalid governor, 617
Aegium, 129, 131, 209
Aelii, 368
Aelius, L., Stilo, critic and orator, 406
— P., Paetus (praetor 203), Table I
— P., Tubero (praetor 201), Table I
Aemilia, wife of Scipio, Polybius on, 381
Aemilii, 365; coin of, 166
Aemilius, L., Paullus (cos. 219, 216), 40,
  52 sq., 55, Table I
— L., Paullus (cos. 182, 168), 6, 8, 267;
  in Spain, 313; in Liguria, 329, 331; at
  Pydna, 270 sq.; and Epirus, 272; and
  settlement of Macedonia, 273 sq.; travels
  in Greece, 273; and library of Perseus,
  398; oratory of, 421
— L., Regillus (praetor 190), 220
— M., Lepidus (praetor 218, ? = praetor
  213), 40, Table I
— M., Lepidus (cos. 187, 175), 330, 333,
  352, 369; envoy to Greece and East,
  162 sqq.; to Philip V, 164; basilica of, 385
Aenis, 227
Aenus, 150, 163, 181 n., 186 n., 199, 232
  247, 249 sq., 542, 555, 603
Aeolis, 591, 611
Aesculapius, 452
Aeson (Pelicas), 269
Aetolia, Aetolian League, 117, 119 sqq.,
  123 sqq., 168, 172, 192, 196, 202, 215;
  Polybius on, 20; and Achaea, 210; and
  Antiochus III, 203, 206 sq.; at Cynoscephalae, 175 and n.; and Elis, 127, 131 n.;
  war with Macedon, 226; after Magnesia,
  242 sqq.; and Magnetes, 205; and Messene,
  122 sq., 127; and Nabis, 191, 203; and
  Philip, 127 sq., 135, 146, 151, 162, 203;
  and Rome, 127, 132, 135, 152, 216; Roman
  alliance with, 72, 80 sq., 122 sqq., 144, 361,
  etc.; discontent with Roman policy, 176
  sq., 182 sq., 185 sq., 193 sq.; war with Rome,
  216 sqq., settlement with, 226 sqq.; and
  Scopas, 147, 187; and Sparta, 127
Aezani, 607 sq.

INDEX TO MAPS

Maps containing more than a few names have each their own index and reference is made here only to the number of the map. The alphabetical arrangement ignores the usual prefixes (lake, etc.).

Abdera, 7, 9, 12
Abydos, 8
Acanthus, 9
Acarnania, 7, 9
Acerrae, 4
Achaea Phthiotis, 7, 9
Achaean League, 7, 9
Acholla, 6
Acrae, 5
Acrillae, 5
Acroceraunia Pr., 7
Acrolissus, 9
Adasa, 8
Adida, 8
Adora, 8
Adramyttium, 8
Adriatic Sea, 7
Aecae, 4
Aegates, Is., 5
Aegean Sea, 7, 9
Aegimurus I., 6
Aegina, 9
Aegium, 7, 9
Aenus, 8, 12
Aesernia, 4
Aetna, Mt, 5
Aetolian League, 7, 9
Aezani, 8
Agrigentum, 5
Agyrium, 5
Alabanda, 8
Alba (Fucens), 4
Alexandria Troas, 8
Alipheira, 7, 9
Allifae, 4
Almanzora, R., 11

Alope, 9
Ambracia, 7, 9
Ambracia, Gulf of, 7
Amphilochia, 9
Amphipolis, 7, 9, 12
Amphissa, 9
Ampsaga, R., 6
Amyzon, 8
Anagnia, 4
Anapus, R., 5
Anas, R., 1, 11
Ancyra, 8
Andros, 7, 8, 9
Antibes, 2
Anticyra, 7, 9
Antigoneia, 7, 9
Antigoneia, 7
Antigoneia, 7, 9
Antioch, 8
Antioch-Adana, 8
Antipatreia, 7, 9
Antium, 4
Antron, 9
Anxur, 4
Aoüs, R., 7, 9
Apamea (Celaenae), 8
Apennines, 2
Aperantia, 7, 9
Apollonia, 7, 9, 12
Apollonis, 8
Appia, Via, 4
Apsus, R., 7, 9
Apuani, 2
Apulia, 4
Aquileia, 2
Ardea, 4

Arevaci, 11
Argesh, R., 12
Argos, 7, 9
Ariminum, 2
Arno, R., 2
Arpi, 4
Arpinum, 4
Arretium, 2, 4
Arsinoe (Patara), 8
Ascalon, 8
Ashdod, 8
Aspendus, 8
Assisi, 2
Astapa, 1, 11
Atella, 4
Aternus, R., 4
Athamania, 7, 9
Athenaeum, 9
Athens, 7, 9
Atintania, 7, 9
Atrax, 7, 9
Attaleia, 8
Attaleia, 8
Attica, 9
Aufidus, R., 4
Aulon, 7
Aulon, Bay of, 7
Axius, R., 7, 9, 12
Azov, Sea of, 13

Babylon, 8
Babylonia, 8
Baecula, 1
Baetis, R., 1, 11
Baeturia, 11
Bagradas, R., 6

Bailovo, 12
Baleares Is., 1, 11
Banitza pass, 9
Barbanna, *R.*, 7
Barbosthenes, Mons, 9
Bargylia, 8
Baria, 11
Bednyakovo, 12
Belbina, 9
Belli, 11
Beneventum, 4
Beroea, 7, 9
Berytus, 8
Beth-horon, 8
Beth-sur, 8
Beth-zachariah, 8
Bisaltica, 9
Bisanthe, 8
Bithynia, 8
Bizerta, 6
Bizye, 12
Black Sea, 13
Boeotian League, 7, 9
Boii, 2
Bologna, 2
Bora Mons, 9
Borghetto, 3
Borghetto, Passo di, 3
Bosporus, 13
Bradanus, *R.*, 4
Brezovo, 12
Brundisium, 5, 7
Bruttium, 5
Bug, *R.*, 13
Bukyovtsi, 12
Bylazora, 7, 9
Byzantium, 8, 12

Caere, 4
Caiatia, 4
Caïcus, *R.*, 8
Calarasi, 12
Calatia, 4
Cales, 4
Callaici, 11
Callatis, 12
Camarina, 5
Camerinum, 4
Campania, 4
Campi Magni, 6
Cannae, 4
Canusium, 4
Capanne, Pgio, 3
Capena, 4
Caphyae, 7
Cappadocia, 8
Capua, 4
Caria, 8
Carmo, 11
Carpetani, 1, 11
Carsioli, 4

Carteia, 11
Carthage, New (Nova Carthago), 1, 11
Carthaginian Frontier in 150 B.C., 6
Carthago, 6
Carystus, 7, 9
Casilinum, 4
Casinum, 4
Cassandreia, 7, 9
Castellonchio, 3
Castelluccio, M., 3
Castelnuovo, M., 3
Castiglione, M., 3
Castra Cornelia, 6
Castulo, 1, 11
Catana, 5
Cauca, 11
Caudini, 4
Caulonia, 5
Caunus, 8
Celaenae, 8
Celetrum, 9
Celtiberi, 1, 11
Cenchreae, 7, 9
Cenomani, 2
Centuripa, 5
Ceos, 9
Cephallenia, 7, 9
Cephaloedium, 5
Cercinitis, 13
Chaeronea, 7
Chalcedon, 8
Chalcidice, 9
Chalcis, 7, 9
Chersonesus, 13
Chios, 8
Chylemat, *R.*, 6
Chyretiae, 9
Cibyra, 8
Cierium, 7, 9
Cilicia, 8
Cimmerian Bosporus, 13
Circeii, 4
Cirta, 6
Cissa, 1
Clastidium, 2
Clazomenae, 8
Clupea, 6
Clusium, 4
Cnidus, 8
Coele-Syria, 8
Collina, Pass of, 2
Colognola, Monte, 3
Colophon, 8
Compsa, 4
Conii, 11
Consentia, 5
Contrebia, 11
Corcyra, 7, 9
Corduba, 1, 11

Corinth, 7, 9
Coronea, 9
Cortona, 2, 4
Cos, 8
Costesti, 12
Crannon, 7, 9
Cremona, 2
Crete, 8
Crimea, 13
Croton, 5
Cumae, 4
Cyme, 8
Cynaetha, 7
Cynoscephalae, 7, 9
Cyprus, 8
Cypsela, 8, 12
Cythnos, 9
Cyzicus, 8

Dandarians, 13
Danube, *R.*, 12
Dardania, 7, 9
Dardanus, 8
Dauni, 4
Delium, 9
Delos, 7, 8, 9
Delphi, 7, 9
Demetrias, 7, 9
Dertosa, 1
Dionysopolis, 8, 12
Dium, 7, 9
Dnieper, *R.*, 13
Dniester, *R.*, 13
Dodona, 7, 9
Dolopia, 7, 9
Don, *R.*, 13
Doriscus, 12
Doschians, 13
Douro, *R.*, 1, 11
Drepana, 5
Drilo, *R.*, 7, 9
Drinus, *R.*, 9
Druentia, *R.*, 2
Drymaea, 9
Duvanli, 12
Dyme, 7, 9
Dyrrhachium, 7, 9, 12
Dysorus, M., 12

Ebro, *R.*, 1, 11
Ebusus, 11
Echinus, 7, 9
Ecnomus, C., 5
Edessa, 7, 9
Edetani, 1
Egypt, 8
Elaea, 8
Elatea, 7, 9
Eleusis, 7, 9
Elimiotis, 7, 9
Elis, 7, 9

[1] Table I refers to the Table of legions and commanders facing p. 104.

HELLENISTIC DYNASTIES

I. The Ptolemies

	B.C.
Ptol. I Soter	–283
Ptol. II Philadelphus	285–246
Ptol. III Euergetes I	246–221
Ptol. IV Philopator	221–203
Ptol. V Epiphanes	203–181/0
Ptol. VI Philometor	181/0–145
Ptol. VII Euergetes II (Physcon)	145–116
Ptol. VIII Soter II (Lathyrus)	116–108/7
	88–80
Ptol. IX Alexander I	108/7–88
Ptol. X Alexander II	80
Ptol. XI Auletes	80–51
⎰Ptol. XII	51–48
⎱Cleopatra VII	
⎰Ptol. XIII	
⎱Cleopatra VII	47–44
⎰Cleopatra VII	
⎱Ptol. XIV Caesar (Caesarion)	? 44–30

II. The Seleucids

	B.C.
Seleucus I Nicator	–280
Antiochus I Soter	280–262/1
Antiochus II Theos	261–247
Seleucus II Callinicus	247–226
Seleucus III Soter	226–223
Antiochus III (the Great)	223–187
Seleucus IV Philopator	187–175
Antiochus IV Epiphanes	175–163
Antiochus V Eupator	163–162
Demetrius I Soter	162–150
Alexander Balas	150–145
Demetrius II Nicator	145–139/8
Antiochus VI Epiphanes	145–142/1
Antiochus VII (Sidetes)	139/8–129
Demetrius II Nicator	129–125
⎰Cleopatra Thea	125–121
⎱Antiochus VIII (Grypus)	125–121
Antiochus VIII (Grypus)	121–96
Antiochus IX (Cyzicenus)	115–95

III. The Antigonids

	B.C.
Antigonus I	–301
Demetrius I (Poliorcetes)	307–283
Antigonus II (Gonatas)	283–239
Demetrius II	239–229
Antigonus III (Doson)	229–221
Philip V	221–179
Perseus	179–168

IV. The Attalids

	B.C.
Attalus I Soter	241–197
Eumenes II Soter	197–160/59
Attalus II	160/59–139/8
Attalus III	139/8–133

THE SPARTOCID DYNASTY

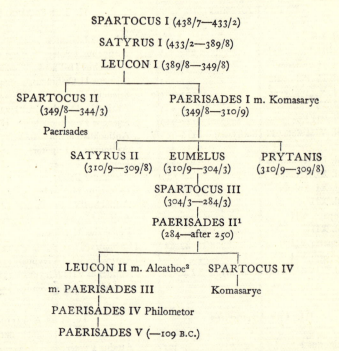

SPARTOCUS I (438/7—433/2)

SATYRUS I (433/2—389/8)

LEUCON I (389/8—349/8)

SPARTOCUS II (349/8—344/3)
Paerisades

PAERISADES I m. Komasarye (349/8—310/9)

SATYRUS II (310/9—309/8)　EUMELUS (310/9—304/3)　PRYTANIS (310/9—309/8)

SPARTOCUS III (304/3—284/3)

PAERISADES II[1] (284—after 250)

LEUCON II m. Alcathoe[2]　SPARTOCUS IV

m. PAERISADES III　Komasarye

PAERISADES IV Philometor

PAERISADES V (—109 B.C.)

[1] The *Stemma* after Paerisades II becomes highly conjectural, and the dates for the reigns of the later Spartocids are not known. That Spartocus IV and Leucon II were brothers is probable from *Ios. P.E.* II 15 and 18 and the scholia to Ovid, *Ibis* 309 *sq.* Komasarye was daughter of a Spartocus, wife and mother of a Paerisades (*Ios. P.E.* II, 19, *Ditt.*³ 439). If her father was Spartocus IV, the conjectures may be hazarded that her husband was Paerisades III and that he was the son of Leucon II, and that her marriage with him ended a feud in the royal house due to the murders of Spartocus and Leucon (p. 580). Her son Paerisades IV appears to have been for some time a minor in the care of the Queen-mother Komasarye and her second husband Argotes (*Ios. P.E.* II, 19). He therefore probably had a long reign and may be the Paerisades mentioned with Komasarye in a list at Didyma (Haussoullier, *Études sur l'histoire de Milet*, p. 206 *sq.*, no. 2855; cf. p. 212) in which the name of Prusias II of Bithynia (168–149 B.C.) also appears. The last king was a Paerisades and was killed *c.* 109 B.C. and he may well be the son of Paerisades IV. It is, however, possible that, *e.g.*, there was a Spartocus V son of Leucon II and father of Komasarye. A recently discovered inscription of Panticapaeum (*Bull. Arch. Com.* LVIII, 1915, p. 18) mentions a Paerisades son of Paerisades, who may be the Fourth or Fifth of that name.

[2] In the period following the death of Leucon may be set the usurpers, Hygiaenon and Akes (p. 581).

THE ATTALIDS

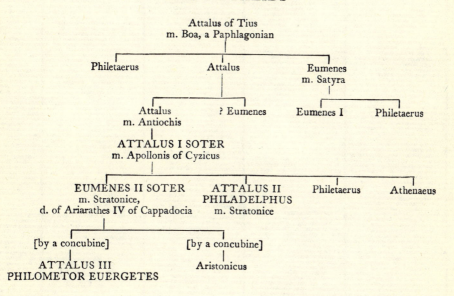

Attalus of Tius
m. Boa, a Paphlagonian

Philetaerus   Attalus   Eumenes
m. Satyra

Attalus   ? Eumenes   Eumenes I   Philetaerus
m. Antiochis

ATTALUS I SOTER
m. Apollonis of Cyzicus

EUMENES II SOTER   **ATTALUS II**   Philetaerus   Athenaeus
m. Stratonice,   **PHILADELPHUS**
d. of Ariarathes IV of Cappadocia   m. Stratonice

[by a concubine]   [by a concubine]

ATTALUS III   Aristonicus
PHILOMETOR EUERGETES